Provided As a Reference For The "Viewing Society in Global Perspective" Maps That Appear Throughout the Text

W9-CUH-652

www.wadsworth.com

wadsworth.com is the World Wide Web site for
Wadsworth Publishing Company and is your direct source
to dozens of online resources.

At **wadsworth.com** you can find out about supplements, demonstration software, and student resources. You
can also send e-mail to many of our authors and preview
new publications and exciting new technologies.

wadsworth.com
Changing the way the world learns®

THIRD EDITION

Sociology

The Essentials

Margaret L. Andersen
University of Delaware

Howard F. Taylor
Princeton University

THOMSON

WADSWORTH

Australia • Canada • Mexico • Singapore • Spain
United Kingdom • United States

THOMSON
WADSWORTH

Sociology Editor: *Robert Jucha*
Development Editor: *Julie Sakaue*
Assistant Editor: *Stephanie Monzon*
Editorial Assistant: *Melissa Walter*
Technology Project Manager: *Dee Dee Zobian*
Marketing Manager: *Matthew Wright*
Marketing Assistant: *Tara Pierson*
Advertising Project Manager: *Linda Yip*
Project Manager, Editorial Production: *Cheri Palmer*
Print/Media Buyer: *Karen Hunt*
Permissions Editor: *Sarah Harkrader*
Production Service: *Dustine Friedman, The Book Company*
Text and Cover Designer: *Carolyn Deacy*
Photo Researcher: *Myrna Engler*
Copy Editor: *Cathy Baehler*
Illustrator: *Impact Publications*
Compositor: *Thompson Type*

The cover and title painting (Feast of Mirrors) and the details of paintings used in the interior are from the work of Hessam Abrishami, whose colorful art reflects the diversity of society. Hessam's passion for art began in his homeland of Iran when he was in the eighth grade. Later, as a teenager, he won two drawing contests, which encouraged him to pursue his passion and to obtain a master's degree in fine arts. His work is exhibited in Asia, Europe, and the United States.

For more information about our products, contact us at:
Thomson Learning Academic Resource Center
1-800-423-0563
For permission to use material from this text or product,
submit a request online at:
http://www.thomsonrights.com
Any additional questions about permissions can be submitted by email to:
thomsonrights@thomson.com

Library of Congress Control Number: 2003111915

Student Edition: ISBN 0-534-62697-1

Instructor's Edition: ISBN 0-534-62698-X

Thomson Wadsworth
10 Davis Drive
Belmont, CA 94002-3098
USA

Asia
Thomson Learning
5 Shenton Way #01-01
UIC Building
Singapore 068808

Australia/New Zealand
Thomson Learning
102 Dodds Street
Southbank, Victoria 3006
Australia

Canada
Nelson
1120 Birchmount Road
Toronto, Ontario M1K 5G4
Canada

Europe/Middle East/Africa
Thomson Learning
High Holborn House
50/51 Bedford Row
London WC1R 4LR
United Kingdom

Dedication

To Richard and Pat, with love

Brief Contents

Contents

PART FIVE
Social Change

Boxes

Maps

Preface

Sociology: The Essentials introduces students to the basic concepts and theories of sociology. It is the condensed, paperback version of our hardcover text, *Sociology: Understanding a Diverse Society* (2004). We have been pleased by the success of the earlier editions and have made revisions we think strengthen the book. One of the strongest features of this book has been its close attention to the most current and detailed research in sociology. Our experience in teaching introductory students shows us that students can appreciate the revelations of sociological research and theory if presented in a way that engages them and connects to their lives. We have kept this in mind throughout this revision and have focused on material that students can understand and apply to their own social worlds.

▪ *Major Themes*

DIVERSITY The study of diversity is central to our book. Our own scholarship is known for its analysis of diversity and we have made this part of the structure of our book. Unlike other introductory texts that add diversity to a preexisting approach to sociology, we see diversity as part of the texture of society. Diversity is central to how society is organized, how inequality shapes the experiences of different groups, and how diversity is shaping (and is shaped by) contemporary social changes. Our attention to diversity pervades the book and is reflected in some of the book's special features (see especially the box feature "Understanding Diversity" in every chapter).

We define diversity to include the differences in experience created by social factors including race, ethnicity, class, gender, age, religion, sexual orientation, and region of residence. But we also see diversity as contributing to the rich texture of society through the diverse cultures and identities of different groups in society. We stress the positive aspects of a diverse society, as well as its prob-

lems. We do not think of diversity as just the study of victims, although systems of disadvantage are clearly part of society. But diversity is also reflected in the social and cultural values and contributions of various groups and we think this is just as important for students to recognize and understand. We are pleased that our thorough integration of diversity has led reviewers to comment that our book provides the most comprehensive coverage of diversity of any book on the market.

CURRENT THEORY AND RESEARCH According to readers and reviewers of this book, our presentation of current theory and research is one of its strongest features. We use the most current research throughout the book to show students the value of a sociological education. The new edition continues this strength, with new areas of research also included.

New to this edition is the integration of research exercises that are easy for students to do by using **MicroCase Online,** a statistical data analysis program on our companion Web site as well as the Web site for the Virtual Society, the Wadsworth Sociology Resource Center. Each chapter includes an exercise that students can do utilizing this user-friendly research tool. For example, in Chapter 7 students can look at the question from the General Social Survey on whether support for spending on social welfare varies by social class. The simple cross-tabulation students do lets them examine differences by social class in support of welfare spending. In other chapters, students can do research with other items from the General Social Survey; or they can map data from the 2000 U.S. Census; or they can look at international data that ranks nations on various items. The MicroCase feature is integrated into the chapter content through the exercises we have specifically developed to accompany each chapter. We also provide questions with each MicroCase exercise that encourage students to think further about what the data show them. This is an excellent—and easy to do—way to introduce students to actually doing sociological research. Students can also explore further projects on their own or instructor's can guide them through the MicroCase feature on Wadsworth's Web site.

We want students to understand not just the concepts and procedures of research methods, but also how sociologists do their work and how the questions they ask are linked to the methods of inquiry that they use. Thus the box feature, "Doing Sociological Research," showcases different research studies. Each begins by identifying the question asked by the researcher, then it describes the method of research, presents the findings and conclusions, and briefly discusses the implications. These boxes also show students the diverse ways that sociologists conduct research and thus feature the rich and varied content of the discipline.

We also want students to understand the contributions that different theoretical traditions offer. Thus, we present various theoretical perspectives in a balanced way. All chapters explore how alternative theoretical frameworks reveal different aspects of the particular subjects in research studies. We help students see this by including tables in every chapter that concisely compare different theoretical viewpoints, showing how each illuminates certain questions and principles. We think this comparison of theories helps students understand an important point: Starting from a different set of assumptions can change how you interpret different social phenomena.

DEBUNKING AND CRITICAL THINKING

We use the theme of *debunking* in the way first developed by Peter Berger—to look behind the facades of everyday life, challenging the ready-made assumptions that permeate commonsense thinking. We think debunking is one significant way for students to develop their critical thinking through the study of sociology, and we use the debunking theme to help students understand how society is constructed and sustained. This theme is highlighted in the "Debunking Society's Myths" feature found throughout every chapter.

We also think that *critical thinking* is a term widely used, but often vaguely defined. We use it to define the process by which students learn to apply sociological concepts to observable events in society. Throughout the book, we ask students to use sociological concepts to analyze and interpret the world they inhabit. This is reflected in the "Thinking Sociologically" feature that is also present in every chapter.

In this edition, we have added a new feature to Chapter 1 to help students use critical thinking to interpret the many research studies they hear or see reported in the media. This box feature, "Developing a Critical Eye:

Research and the Media," provides questions that can help students spot flawed studies, learn to interpret research in the media, and become better informed critical consumers of the vast amount of information to which they are exposed. In addition, we have added "Questions to Consider" to the box feature "Doing Sociological Research" that probe students to think more about the research being presented.

Because the current generation of students is so strongly influenced by the media, we have introduced the box feature "A Sociological Eye on the Media." This box feature, found in several chapters, examines how sociological research challenges some of the ideas and images portrayed in the media. This not only improves students' critical thinking skills, but also shows them how research can debunk these ideas and images.

SOCIAL ACTION/SOCIAL POLICY   There is a focus on social policy throughout the book because we want students to see the utility of a sociological perspective. We broadly define social policy to include the various ways that sociological research and theory can be applied to addressing social issues. Social policy can include specific formal policies (such as federal and state legislation), but also can include practices such as the development of sociological research centers or local community groups that address specific needs. The box feature "Sociology in Practice" shows students how sociologists have used their knowledge in concrete, applied ways. We also include a box feature in each chapter, "Taking on Social Issues." In this box feature, students are asked to analyze a contemporary policy issue (such as decriminalizing drugs (Chapter 6), encouraging marriage to reduce poverty (Chapter 7), or federal support for faith-based initiatives (Chapter 12). These boxes include a Web-based exercise ("Taking Action") that allows students to link to the Web site of an organization working on a particular policy issue. On the companion Web site for the book we provide critical thinking questions that ask students to interpret different sociological features of various action groups. This feature serves several purposes: It helps students identify various groups that are organized around different policy and social change issues; it enriches critical thinking by asking students to analyze the structure, goals, strategies, and constituents of different action groups; and, it connects sociological research to the activities of organized groups, thus allowing students to see how sociological knowledge can be applied. This feature has the added benefit of directing students to organizations where they can potentially pursue internships, service learning projects, or, possibly careers. It can show students the different ways that sociological research and theory can be applied in "real" life.

SOCIAL CHANGE The sociological perspective helps students see society as characterized both by constant change and social stability. We use the change theme in every chapter by examining social change at the conclusion of each chapter. In addition, the "Forces of Social Change" box feature allows students to reflect on how certain social realities have evolved by including a historical dimension that is often shown in photographs. By bringing a historical perspective to bear on sociological thinking, students can better see some of the social forces that operate in the present. The social change theme is especially significant in light of the events of September 11, 2001. What effect have these events had on society? This is a question we address in several places throughout the book, including discussion of al Qaeda as a transnational social movement (see Chapter 16); new attention to racial and ethnic profiling (see Chapters 6 and 9); and the use of Durkheim's theory to understand suicide bombers (Chapter 6).

GLOBAL PERSPECTIVE Diversity includes the increasingly global character of society. The United States is increasingly being changed by globalization. We use a global perspective to examine how global changes are affecting all parts of life within the United States, as well as other parts of the world. This means more than including cross-cultural examples. It means, for example, examining phenomena such as migration and immigration, the formation of world cities, the increasingly cultural diversity found within the United States, and the impact of an international division of labor on work within the United States. This global perspective is found in the research and examples cited throughout the book, as well as in various chapters that directly focus on the influence of globalization on particular topics, such as work, culture, and crime. The map program "Viewing Society in Global Perspective" found in virtually every chapter also brings a global perspective to the subject matter of each chapter.

■ *New to the Third Edition: Organization and Chapter-by-Chapter Revisions*

We have made many changes to the third edition to make it stronger and more effective. We added new research plus made a few large changes to the organization

of the text. Together, these changes should make the third edition easier for instructors to teach, and more accessible and interesting for students.

Sociology: The Essentials is organized into five major parts: "Introducing the Sociological Imagination" (Chapter 1); "Society, Individuals, and Social Structure" (Chapters 2 through 6); "Social Inequality" (Chapters 7 through 11); "Social Institutions" (Chapters 12 through 14); and "Social Change" (Chapters 15 and 16).

Within these five parts, we reorganized a few of the chapters. One major change is the addition of a new chapter on sexuality, which was previously combined with aging. This chapter brings added attention to the rapidly expanding sociological study of sexuality. By adding this chapter, we have integrated the material on aging into several chapters where it is relevant, including **Socialization and the Life Course (Chapter 3)**, the section on families in **Families and Religion (Chapter 12)**, and the section on social change in **Social Change and Social Movements (Chapter 16)**. We further strengthened the text by listening to feedback from reviewers who indicated that it made more sense to pair education and health care in one chapter (**Chapter 13**) and politics and the economy in another (**Chapter 14**). (In the second edition, education and work were covered in one chapter, and government and health care were covered in another.) We agreed with the reviewers and thus modified the organization. Other than the reorganization of the chapters, there are many detailed revisions, some of which are highlighted here.

Part I, Introducing the Sociological Imagination introduces students to the unique perspective of sociology, differentiating it from other ways of studying society, particularly the individualistic framework students tend to assume. Within this section, **Chapter 1, Sociological Perspectives and Sociological Research,** introduces students to the sociological perspective and the basics of sociological research methods. This chapter briefly reviews the development of sociology as a discipline, with a focus on the classical frameworks of sociological theory, and a new section on postmodernism as a theoretical perspective. The chapter also incorporates the contributions of early theorists sometimes excluded from the history of sociological thought, such as W.E.B. Du Bois and Jane Addams. A new box feature, "Developing a Critical Eye: Research and the Media," is included to help students interpret publicly disseminated research studies.

In **Part II, Society, Individuals, and Social Structure,** students learn some of the core concepts of sociology. It begins with the study of culture (**Chapter 2**) and includes more research on the influence of popular culture and the media. This chapter presents new research on tattooing and body art. We have also added material on the influence of the fast food industry on U.S. culture—a topic that we think students will find fascinating. **Chapter 3, Socialization and the Life Course,** now includes more material on aging and the life course since we have combined it with the chapter on socialization. We have strengthened our discussion of identity formation, added new material on resocialization in light of current world events and terrorism, and included more material on the influence of media violence—all topics that we think will capture student interest. **Chapter 4, Society and Social Interaction** differentiates microanalysis and macroanalysis in sociology by introducing students to the nuances in the study of social interaction and moving onto the complex structure of society and social institutions. New to this chapter is an expanded section on cyberspace interaction. In **Chapter 5** we study social groups and formal organizations, using sociology to understand the complex processes of group influence, organizational dynamics, and the bureaucratization of society. Added are new findings on social networks, risky shift, and the breakup of the space shuttle *Columbia* on February 1, 2003. Finally, **Chapter 6** on deviance includes a look at the sociological theories of deviance with more attention to labeling theory, corporate crime and deviance, and the effects of race, class, and gender on arrest rates.

In **Part III, Social Inequality,** each chapter explores a particular dimension of stratification in society. Beginning with the significance of class, **Chapter 7, Social Class and Social Stratification,** provides an overview of basic concepts central to the study of social stratification, as well as current sociological perspectives on class inequality, poverty, and welfare. There is new material on the effects of welfare reform, growing debt among the middle class, updated data on increasing social inequality, and more on the effects of economic restructuring on different class groups. **Chapter 8** follows with a particular emphasis on understanding the significance of global stratification, which is the inequality that has developed among, as well as within, various nations. Throughout this text, we see globalization as a process that is transforming many societies, including the United States. Here we examine global events and processes, including corporate globalization, and explore their consequences worldwide. We have added material on global epidemics, global domestic workers, and the effects of war on children. **Chapter 9, Race and Ethnicity** is a comprehensive review of the significance of race and ethnicity in society. Although these concepts are integrated throughout the book because of our focus on diversity, they also require particular focus on how race and ethnicity differentiate the experiences of diverse groups in society. In-

cluded are new topics such as multiracial census classification and new information on the affirmative action debate and court cases. Likewise, although the study of gender is integrated throughout this text, **Chapter 10** focuses on gender as a central concept in sociology closely linked to systems of stratification in society. In this edition, we have devoted an entire chapter to sexuality (**Chapter 11**) because of the increased attention in sociological research to sexuality as a component of social stratification. This chapter includes the discussion of concepts central to the study of sexuality, as well as high-interest box features on topics of teen sex, birth control, and sex and cyberspace. Our expanded coverage of sexuality allows us to explore sociological theory and sexuality in greater detail than in prior editions.

Part IV, Social Institutions, includes three chapters, each focusing on basic institutions within society. Beginning with **Chapter 12** on families and religion, these chapters explore the basic structure of social institutions and examine how different theoretical perspectives within sociology help us interpret different dimensions of people's experiences within social institutions. Interracial dating is discussed, as are topics such as gay and lesbian households, religious cults, and diversity and religion. New to this edition is a box on "hooking up"—a new form of social interaction among many students. There is also increased attention to fatherhood, gender roles within families, and family violence. **Chapter 13** is on the institutions of education and health care, and overviews education in the United States, including recent developments in education and inequality, plus a look at health and sickness seen globally. It includes theoretical perspectives on health care and the health care crisis in America. New to this chapter is recent research on inequality in education, tracking, and gender, as well as coverage of new health care topics such as global aspects of sickness, fraud and abuse in medicine, and alternative medicine. **Chapter 14,** on politics and the economy analyzes the state, power, and authority, and bureaucratic government. It also contains a detailed discussion of theories of power, in addition to coverage of the economy seen globally and characteristics of the labor force. New to this chapter are updated discussions on the power elite in America, women and minorities in government, and sexual harassment in the workplace.

Chapter 15 is on population, urbanization and the environment, and covers demographic processes and urbanization, as well as pollution and depletion of the physical environment. New data are included on population growth and change, the new suburbanites, and new policies on saving the physical environment. The last chapter, **Chapter 16,** addresses social change and social movements, with a detailed coverage of theories of social change, the causes of social change, and the nature and types of social movements. New updates include information on war and terrorism as causes of social change, environmental racism and classism, cultural diffusion as a source of social change, and the cyberspace revolution.

■ *Features and Pedagogical Aids*

The special features of this book flow from its major themes: diversity, current theory and research, debunking and critical thinking, social action and social policy, social change, and global perspective. The features are also designed to help students develop critical thinking skills so that they can apply abstract concepts to observed experiences in their everyday life, and learn how to interpret different theoretical paradigms and approaches to sociological research questions. The following features accomplish these goals in various ways.

Critical Thinking Features

The feature "**Thinking Sociologically**" takes concepts from each chapter and asks students to think about these concepts in relationship to something they can easily observe in an exercise or class discussion. The feature "**Debunking Society's Myths**" takes certain common assumptions and shows students how the sociological perspective would inform such assumptions and beliefs. In addition to these two features, many other box features—such as "**Sociology in Practice**"—include questions designed to foster critical thinking skills.

Unparalleled Integration of Web-Based Resources

Instructors will find that several technology-based teaching enhancements are integrated throughout the book, making this book the best conceived in using Internet tools for teaching and learning introductory sociology. Many graphs in the chapters are based on **Web sites,** and at the end of each chapter is a list of stable Web-based resources that students and faculty can use to explore data and information pertinent to the chapter topic. We have deliberately selected sites we know are stable and provide the latest information or resources on a given subject.

The new MicroCase feature developed in this edition will be especially valuable for faculty who want to expose students to actual sociological research. Following the

Key Terms at the end of each chapter, we have developed a **MicroCase Online** exercise that explores some dimensions of the chapter's subject. These research exercises are simple to do and we think will help students discover the excitement of doing sociological research.

Each chapter includes a box feature, "**Taking on Social Issues**," which is designed to help students explore current public issues and show students how the sociological perspective can provide different viewpoints about social issues. This feature integrates Web-based instruction by giving instructors and students the option of using the **Web links** that we have added to link to the Web site of an organization that works on the topic of the box feature. The critical thinking questions about each organization allow students to use sociological analysis to think about the structure and goals of each organization. This feature also shows students how sociology can be used to make a difference in the world, and has the added benefit of pointing them toward organizations where they might even pursue careers.

We have eliminated the InfoTrac exercises that applied in earlier editions. Instead, the **InfoTrac College Edition** feature is integrated into the "**Doing Sociological Research**" box features to allow students to further explore research on those topics.

An Extensive and Content-Rich Map Program

Also in our book, each chapter includes a map feature (usually two maps): One map feature is "**Mapping America's Diversity**" and the other is "**Viewing Society in Global Perspective.**" These maps have multiple uses for instructional value, beyond instructing students about world and national geography. The maps have been designed primarily to show the differentiation by country and/or by state on certain key social facts. For example, in Chapter 3 we show the dispersion of the population under five years of age, both nationally and worldwide. Students can use this information to ask questions about how the age distribution of the population might be related to immigration, poverty, or global stratification. In other cases, maps are drawn to show the penetration of U.S.-based culture throughout the world, such as the map in Chapter 2, "Technological Penetration," which shows how much technological innovation (in the case of cell phones) has infiltrated the world.

We have added a critical thinking component to the maps to integrate them more effectively with the chapter material. Thus, each map includes **critical thinking questions** that ask students to interpret the map data within the context of concepts and ideas from the chapter.

High-Interest Theme Boxes

We use six high-interest themes for box features that embellish our focus on diversity and sociological research throughout the text. "**Understanding Diversity**" further explores the approach to diversity taken throughout the book. In most cases, these box features provide personal narratives or other information designed to teach students about the experiences of different groups in society. Because many are written as first-person narratives, they can invoke student empathy toward groups other than those to which they belong—something we think is critical to teaching about diversity. We hope to show students the connections between race, class, and other social groups that they otherwise find difficult to grasp.

The box feature "**Doing Sociological Research**" is intended to show students the diversity of research questions that form the basis of sociological knowledge, and, equally important, how the question a researcher asks influences the method used to investigate the question. We see this as an important part of sociological research—that how one investigates a question is determined as much by the nature of the question as by allegiance to a particular research method. Some questions require a more qualitative approach, others, a more quantitative approach. In developing these box features, we ask, "What is the central question sociologists are asking?" "How did they explore this question using sociological research methods?" "What did they find?" and "What are the implications of this research?" We deliberately selected questions that show the full and diverse range of sociological theories and research methods, as well as the diversity of sociologists. In the third edition, we have also added "**Questions to Consider**" at the end of this box feature to encourage students to think further about the implications and applications of the research.

A new feature we have added is the box feature "**A Sociological Eye on the Media**." This feature, found in several chapters, examines some aspect of how the media influence public understanding of some of the subjects in this book. We think this is important because sociological research often debunks taken-for-granted points of view presented in the media and we want students to be able to look at the media with a more critical eye. Because of the enormous influence of the media, we think this is increasingly important in educating students about sociology.

Our box feature "**Sociology in Practice**" is designed to show the application of the sociological perspective in various contexts. Thus we show examples where sociologists have testified before Congress, advised presidents, changed an organization, or elucidated a cultural phenomenon, such as the "Dead Heads" (Chapter 2).

Finally, the box feature "**Forces of Social Change**" highlights some of the major changes currently affecting society, such as the growth of the fast food industry and its impact on society (Chapter 2), the growth of women's sports (Chapter 3), and changes in college dating patterns, such as "hooking up" (Chapter 12). We think students will find all these features readable, interesting, and a strong supplement to the textual material.

In-Text Learning Aids

In addition to the features just described, there is an entire set of learning aids within each chapter that promote student mastery of the sociological concepts.

Chapter Outlines. A concise chapter outline at the beginning of each chapter provides students with an overview of the major topics to be covered.

Key Terms. Key terms and major concepts are in bold when first introduced in the chapter. A list of the key terms is found at the end of the chapter, which makes study more effective. Definitions for the key terms may be found in the glossary.

Theory Tables. Each chapter includes a table that summarizes different theoretical perspectives by comparing and contrasting how these theories illuminate different aspects of different subjects.

Chapter Summary. Questions highlight the major points in each chapter, and provide a quick review of major concepts and themes covered in the chapter.

Suggested Readings and Web Resources. An annotated list of suggested readings and related Web sites is found at the end of each chapter to encourage further study.

A **Glossary** and complete **Bibliography** for the whole text is found at the back of the book.

■ *Supplements*

Supplements for the Instructor

INSTRUCTOR'S EDITION OF *SOCIOLOGY: THE ESSENTIALS* An Instructor's Edition (IE) of this text containing several useful features for instructors is available. Found in the IE is the Resources Integration Guide, a 16-page chart that correlates the key instructor's and student supplements by chapter. The IE also contains the Visual Preface, a walk-through of the several themes and many features of *Sociology: The Essentials,* plus a complete listing of available bundles for this text. To obtain a copy of the Instructor's Edition contact your Thomson Sales Representative.

INSTRUCTOR'S RESOURCE MANUAL (WITH THE MULTIMEDIA MANAGER CD-ROM)

This manual offers instructors chapter-specific learning objectives, lecture outlines, lecture suggestions to facilitate in-class discussion, student activities, worksheets that instructors can copy and use as handouts, suggestions for further reading and other relevant print, video, and online resources. Ideas for *WebTutor* online threaded discussion groups are integrated throughout the manual, and concise user guides for both *InfoTrac* and *WebTutor* and the table of contents for the *CNN Today* Sociology Video Series are also included. A new Multimedia Manager CD-ROM is now located in the print Instructor's Resource Manual. A noteworthy part of the CD are Teaching Tips—ten 4–6 minute videos of Margaret Andersen and Howard Taylor sharing their insights and tips on teaching introductory sociology. The CD also includes book-specific Power-Point lecture slides, graphics from the book itself, the Instructor's Resource Manual and Test Bank provided as Word documents, CNN video clips, and links to many of Wadsworth's important sociology resources.

TEST BANK

The test items for each chapter consist of 75–100 multiple-choice questions and 20–30 true/false questions, all with answers and page references to the text. Also included are 10–15 short-answer questions and 5–10 essay questions for each chapter. This test bank is also available electronically on the *ExamView Computerized Testing CD-ROM* as well as on the *Multimedia Manager CD-ROM* that comes packaged in the *Instructor's Resource Manual.*

EXAMVIEW COMPUTERIZED TESTING

Create, deliver, and customize tests and study guides (both print and online) in minutes with this easy-to-use assessment and tutorial system. *ExamView* offers both a Quick Test Wizard and an Online Test Wizard that guide you step-by-step through the process of creating tests. The test appears on screen exactly as it will print or display online. Using *ExamView*'s complete word processing capabilities, you can enter an unlimited number of new questions or edit existing questions included with *ExamView.*

WADSWORTH'S INTRODUCTION TO SOCIOLOGY 2005 TRANSPARENCY ACETATES

A set of four-color acetates consisting of tables and figures from Wadsworth's introductory sociology texts is available to help prepare lecture presentations. Free to qualified adopters.

VIDEOS

Adopters of *Sociology: the Essentials* have several different video options available with the text.

WADSWORTH'S LECTURE LAUNCHERS FOR INTRODUCTORY SOCIOLOGY

An exclusive offer jointly created by Wadsworth/Thomson Learning and DALLAS TeleLearning, this video contains a collection of video highlights taken from the *Exploring Society: An Introduction to Sociology* telecourse (formerly the *Sociological Imagination*). Each 3–6 minute long video segment has been especially chosen to enhance and enliven class lectures and discussions of 20 key topics covered in any introductory sociology text. Accompanying the video is a brief written description of each clip, along with suggested discussion questions to help effectively incorporate the material into the classroom.

SOCIOLOGY: CORE CONCEPTS

An exclusive offer also jointly created by Wadsworth/Thomson Learning and DALLAS TeleLearning, this video contains a collection of video highlights taken from the *Exploring Society: An Introduction to Sociology* telecourse (formerly the *Sociological Imagination*). Each 15–20 minute video segment will enhance student learning of the essential concepts in the introductory course and can be used to initiate class lectures, discussion, and review. The video covers topics such as the sociological imagination, stratification, race and ethnic relations, social change, and more.

CNN® TODAY SOCIOLOGY VIDEO SERIES, VOLUMES I–VII

Illustrate the relevance of sociology to everyday life with this exclusive series of videos for the introduction to sociology course. Jointly created by Wadsworth and CNN, each video consists of approximately 45 minutes of footage originally broadcast on CNN and was specifically selected to illustrate important sociological concepts. The videos are broken into short 2- to 7-minute segments, perfect for use as lecture launchers or as illustrations of key sociological concepts. Each video includes an annotated table of contents, descriptions of the segments, and suggestions on their use within the course.

WADSWORTH SOCIOLOGY VIDEO LIBRARY

Bring sociological concepts to life with videos from Wadsworth's Sociology Video Library, which includes thought provoking offerings from Films for Humanities, as well as other excellent educational video sources. This extensive collection illustrates important sociological concepts covered in many sociology courses. Certain adoption conditions apply.

Supplements for the Student

STUDY GUIDE

Designed to aid student learning of chapter concepts, this guide includes both brief and detailed chapter outlines, a list of key terms and key people with page references, questions to guide student reading, Internet and InfoTrac exercises, and practice tests consisting of 20–25 multiple-choice questions, 10–15 true-false questions, 3–5 fill-in-the-blank questions, and 3–5 essay questions. All multiple-choice and true-false items include answer explanations and page references to the text.

PRACTICE TESTS Designed to help students test their knowledge of chapter concepts, this booklet contains 30–40 multiple-choice questions, 10–15 true-false questions, and 4–6 short-answer questions for each chapter of the text. All answers for the multiple-choice and true-false questions include explanations and page references to the main text.

WADSWORTH'S SOCIOLOGY ONLINE RESOURCES AND WRITING COMPANION, FIRST EDITION This valuable guide shows students how they can use Wadsworth's exclusive online resources— *InfoTrac College Edition,* the *Opposing Viewpoints Resource Center (OVRC),* and *MicroCase Online*—to assist them in their study of sociology and to build essential research and writing skills. Part One provides informative user guides that introduce each powerful research tool. Part Two contains directed exercises designed to develop research and critical thinking proficiency for each core topic in sociology. Part Three provides an overview of some of the research and writing tools available online, such as *InfoWrite* and the *OVRC Research Guide,* and shows students how to effectively integrate their research findings into class assignments.

SOCCOACH CD-ROM FOR ANDERSEN/ TAYLOR'S *SOCIOLOGY: THE ESSENTIALS,* 3rd Edition The new, interactive SocCoach CD-ROM is packaged with each new copy of the text and can be found inside the back cover. This CD-ROM tutorial is firmly grounded in sociology. It enables students to review chapter content, conduct online research, think critically about sociology statistics, watch well-known sociologists discussing important concepts, and complete book-specific quizzes, all on one easy to use CD-ROM! The new Study Plan feature prompts students to take a diagnostic chapter quiz, then generates a personalized Study Plan that shows students exactly what they need to review further. Students can then access study material for each concept, including material from the book, illustrative graphs, videos, and statistics that help students to better understand each concept.

READERS Among the several excellent introductory sociology readers Wadsworth publishes (see the Instructor's Edition) the authors of *Sociology: The Essentials* have written a reader especially matched to this text.

UNDERSTANDING SOCIETY: AN INTRODUCTORY READER, **2nd Edition** Edited by Margaret Andersen, University of Delaware, Kim Logio, St. Joseph's University, and Howard Taylor, Princeton University, this reader complements the *Sociology: The Essentials,* 3rd edition text. It includes articles with a variety of styles and perspectives, with a balance of the classic and contemporary. The editors selected readings that students will find accessible yet intriguing, and maximize the instructional value by prefacing each with an introduction and following each with discussion questions. The articles center on the following five themes: classical sociological theory, contemporary research, diversity, globalization, and the application of the sociological perspective.

Online Resources

WADSWORTH'S VIRTUAL SOCIETY: THE WADSWORTH SOCIOLOGY RESOURCE CENTER
http://www.wadsworth.com/sociology

Here you will find a wealth of sociology resources such as Census 2000: A Student Guide for Sociology, Breaking News in Sociology, a Guide to Researching Sociology on the Internet, Sociology in Action, and much more. Contained on the home page is the text specific site for *Sociology: The Essentials,* 3rd Edition.

ANDERSEN/TAYLOR, *SOCIOLOGY: THE ESSENTIALS* COMPANION WEB SITE
http://sociology.wadsworth.com/andersen_taylor/ essen3e

Access useful learning resources for each chapter of the book. Some of these resources include:

- Tutorial Practice Quizzes that can be scored and emailed to the instructor
- Internet exercises and Web links
- Video exercises
- Periodical exercises via InfoTrac College Edition
- Flashcards of the text's glossary
- Crossword puzzles
- Essay questions
- Learning objectives
- MicroCase Online data exercises
- Virtual explorations

And much more!

WEBTUTOR™ ADVANTAGE ON WEBCT AND BLACKBOARD This Web-based software for students and instructors takes a course beyond the classroom to an anywhere, anytime environment. Students gain access to a full array of study tools, including chapter outlines, chapter-specific quizzing material, interactive games and maps, and videos. With WebTutor Advantage, instructors can provide virtual office hours, post syllabi, track student progress with the quizzing material, and even customize the content to suit their needs. Instructors can also use the communication tools to do such things as set up threaded discussions and conduct real-time chats, as well as bring the latest developments from the field into the classroom using *NewsEdge,* an authoritative news source that delivers customized news feeds daily. Out of the box or customized, WebTutor Advantage provides powerful tools for instructors and students alike.

INFOTRAC® COLLEGE EDITION With each purchase of a new copy of the text comes a free four-month passcode to *InfoTrac College Edition,* the online library, that gives students anytime, anywhere access to reliable resources. This fully searchable database offers 20 years' worth of full-text articles from almost 5000 diverse sources, such as academic journals, newsletters, and up-to-the-minute periodicals including *Time, Newsweek, Science, Forbes,* and *USA Today.* This incredible depth and breadth of material—available 24 hours a day from any computer with Internet access—makes conducting research so easy, your students will want to use it to enhance their work in every course! Through InfoTrac's InfoWrite, students now also have instant access to tools for critical thinking and writing papers. Both adopters and their students receive unlimited access for four months.

OPPOSING VIEWPOINTS RESOURCE CENTER (OVRC) Newly available from Wadsworth, this online center presents varying perspectives on today's most compelling issues. OVRC draws on Greenhaven Press's acclaimed Social Issues Series, as well as core reference content from other Gale and Macmillan Reference USA sources. The result is a dynamic online library of current event topics—the facts as well as the arguments of each topic's proponents and detractors. Special sections focus on critical thinking that walks students through the steps involved in critically evaluating point-counterpoint arguments, and focus on researching and writing papers. OVRC is also available through Wadsworth's Sociology Online Resources and Writing Companion.

■ *Acknowledgments*

We relied on the comments of many reviewers to improve the book and we thank them for the time they gave in developing very thoughtful commentaries on the different chapters. Thanks to:

E.M. Beck, *University of Georgia*

Susan Crafts, *Niagara Community College*

Lorna Forster, *Clinton Community College*

Bethany Gizzi, *Monroe Community College*

Jennifer Hamer, *Wayne State University*

Katherine Johnson, *Niagara Community College*

Brian Moss, *Oakland Community College–Waterford Campus (MI)*

Timothy Owens, *Purdue University*

Ralph Pyle, *Michigan State University*

Lesley Williams Reid, *Georgia State University*

We would also like to extend our thanks to those who reviewed the first and second editions of *Sociology: The Essentials.* We would like to thank the following individuals for reviewing the second edition: Brenda N. Bauch, Jefferson College; James E. Coverdill, University of Georgia; Jean E. Daniels, California State University, Northridge; Lois Easterday, Onondaga Community College; Cynthia K. Epperson, St. Louis Community College at Meramec; Lynda Ann Ewen, Marshall University; James Fillman, Bucks County Community College; Patricia Gibbs, Foothill College; Carol A. Jenkins, Glendale Community College; Elizabeth D. Leonard, Vanguard University; Martha O. Loustaunau, New Mexico State University; Susan A. Mann, University of New Orleans; Tara Perrello, Fordham University; Melvin Thomas, North Carolina State University; Stephani Williams, Arizona State University; Sheryline A. Zebroski, St. Louis Community College, Florissant; Carl W. Zeigler, Elgin Community College.

Our gratitude also goes to the following individuals for reviewing the first edition: Alessandro Bonanno, Sam Houston State University; G. M. Britten, Lenoir Community College (North Carolina); Ione Y. DeOllos, Ball State University; Marlese Durr, Wright State University; Grant Farr, Portland State University; Irene Fiala, Kent State University–Ashtabula; James R. Hunter, Indiana University–Purdue University Indianapolis; Jon Iannitti, SUNY College of Agriculture and Technology at Morrisville; Diane E. Johnson, Kutztown University of Pennsylvania; Alice Abel Kemp, University of New Orleans; Keith Kirkpatrick, Victoria College (Texas); James Lindberg, Montgomery College, Rockville Campus, Maryland; Martha O. Loustaunau,

New Mexico State University; Brad Lyman, Baltimore City Community College; Leland C. McCormick, Minnesota State University–Mankato; David L. Phillips, Arkansas State University; Billie Joyce Pool, Homes Community College; David Redburn, Furman University; Lisa Riley, Creighton University; Michael C. Smith, Milwaukee Area Technical College; Tracey Steele, Wright State University; Judith Warner, Texas A&M International University.

We also thank the following people, each of whom provided critical support in different, but important ways: Blanche Anderson, Vicky Baynes, Alison Bianchi, Cindy Gibson, Linda Keen, and Judy Watson. We particularly thank Keeley McGill for her research on the maps and figures throughout the book.

We are fortunate to be working with a publishing team with great enthusiasm for this project. We thank all of the people at Wadsworth who have worked with us on this and other projects, but especially we thank Bob Jucha, Julie Sakaue, Dee Dee Zobian, and Cheri Palmer for their efforts on behalf of our book and the guidance and advice, not to mention the hard work, they have given to this project. We especially thank Dusty Friedman of The Book Company for her extraordinary attention to detail; we appreciate enormously her talent and perseverance. We thank Cathy Baehler for her very careful copyediting of the manuscript. Finally, our special thanks also go to Richard Morris Rosenfeld and Patricia Epps Taylor for their ongoing support of this project.

About the Authors

Margaret L. Andersen, raised in Oakland, California, Rome, Georgia, and Boston, is Professor of Sociology and Women's Studies at the University of Delaware. She received her Ph.D. from the University of Massachusetts, Amherst, and her B.A. from Georgia State University. She is the author of *Thinking About Women: Sociological Perspectives on Sex and Gender* (Allyn and Bacon) and the best-selling Wadsworth text, *Race, Class, and Gender: An Anthology* (with Patricia Hill Collins). In 2003, she was awarded the SWS Feminist Lecturer Award, given annually by SWS (Sociologists for Women in Society) to a social scientist whose work has contributed to improving the status of women in society. She currently serves as Chair of the National Advisory Board of the Center for Comparative Studies in Race and Ethnicity at Stanford University. She has served as the Interim Dean of the College of Arts and Science and Vice Provost for Academic Affairs at the University of Delaware, where she has also won the university's Excellence in Teaching Award. She lives on the Elk River in Maryland with her husband Richard Rosenfeld.

Howard F. Taylor was raised in Cleveland, Ohio. He graduated Phi Beta Kappa from Hiram College and has a Ph.D. in sociology from Yale University. He has taught at the Illinois Institute of Technology, Syracuse University, and Princeton University, where he is presently Professor of Sociology, and former Director of the African American Studies Program. He has published over forty articles in sociology, education, social psychology, and race relations. His books include *The IQ Game* (Rutgers University Press), a critique of hereditarian accounts of intelligence; *Balance in Small Groups* (Van Nostrand Reinhold); and the forthcoming *Race, Class, and the Bell Curve in America.* He has appeared widely before college, radio, and TV audiences, including ABC's *Nightline.* He is past president of the Eastern Sociological Society; a member of the American Sociological Association, and the Sociological Research Association, an honorary society for distinguished research. He is a winner of the DuBois-Johnson-Frazier Award, given by the American Sociological Association for distinguished research in race and ethnic relations and the Presidents Award for Distinguished Teaching at Princeton University. He lives in Pennington, New Jersey, with his wife, a corporate lawyer.

Sociology

CHAPTER ONE

Sociological Perspectives and Sociological Research

*i*magine that you had been switched with another infant at birth and raised in very different conditions. How different would your life have been? What if your accidental family was very poor . . . or very rich? How might this have affected the schools you attended, the health care you received, the possibilities for your future career? What if you had been raised in a different religion—how would this have affected your beliefs, values, and attitudes? Taking a greater leap, what if you had been born another sex or a different race? What would you be like now?

We are talking about changing the basic facts of your life—your family, social class, education, religion, sex, and race. Each has major consequences for who you are and how you will fare in life. These factors play a major part in writing your life script. They are important because they put you in a specific social location—that is, a place in society that nestles individual lives in a social context.

Consider this:

- Men who father children before marriage leave school earlier, have lower earnings, and are more likely to live in poverty than men who do not have children before marriage (Nock 1998).

- Black Americans who kill Whites are much more likely to face the death penalty than Blacks who kill other Black people (Paternoster 2003).

- Men who work in jobs traditionally defined as "women's work" behave in ways that emphasize their masculinity; doing so brings rewards because they tend to be promoted faster than similarly qualified women in the same occupations (Williams 1995).

- The physical transformations that female impersonators must make to deliver a convincing performance are more easily mastered than the behavioral changes they have to make (Tewksbury 1994).

These conclusions, drawn from current sociological research, describe some consequences of particular social locations in society. Although we may take our place in society for granted, our social location has a profound effect on our chances in life. The power of sociology is that it teaches us to see how society influences our lives and the lives of others, and it helps us explain the consequences of different social arrangements.

▪ *What Is Sociology?*

Sociology is the study of human behavior in society. Sociologists are interested in the study of people and have learned a fundamental lesson: All human behavior occurs in a societal context. That context—the institutions and culture that surround us—shapes what people do and think. In this book, we will examine the dimensions of society and analyze the elements of social context that influence human behavior.

Sociology is a scientific way of thinking about society and its influence on human groups. Observation, reasoning, and logical analysis are the tools of the sociologist, coupled with knowledge of the large body of theoretical and analytical work done by previous sociologists and others. Sociology is inspired by the fascination people have for the thoughts and actions of other people, but it goes far beyond casual observations. It attempts to build on observations that are objective and accurate to create analyses that are reliable and that can be validated by others.

Every day, the media in their various forms (television, film, video, and print) bombard us with social commentary. Whether it is Oprah Winfrey or Jerry Springer,

© Bob Daemmrich/The Image Works

Sociology is the study of human groups. As such, sociologists analyze the significance of diversity in society.

media commentators provide endless opinion about the various and sometimes bizarre forms of behavior in our society. Sociology is different. Sociologists may study the same subjects that the media examine—such as domestic violence, religious cults, and interracial dating. Many sociologists make appearances on the media, but sociologists use specific research techniques and well-tested theories to explain social issues. Indeed, sociology can provide the tools for testing whether the things we hear about society are actually true. Much of what one hears in the media and elsewhere about society, delivered as it may be with perfect earnestness and sincerity, is misstated and sometimes completely wrong.

The subject matter of sociology is everywhere. Social behavior and social change—these are the topics of sociological study. Psychologists, anthropologists, political scientists, economists, social workers, and others also study social behavior and social change. Along with sociologists, these disciplines make up what are called the social sciences.

Psychology analyzes individual behavior. Sociologists share the interest of psychologists in individuals, but the unit of analysis for psychology is the individual, whereas for sociologists, it is the whole of society.

Anthropology is the study of human cultures. Anthropology sees culture as the basis for society and tries to see how different human societies have evolved and changed. Sociologists also see culture as a piece of a complex configuration of other social systems that together compose society. Generally, anthropologists tend to study cultures other than their own, whereas sociologists are more likely to study a society of which they are a part.

Political science and economics are the other pillars of the social sciences. *Political science* is the study of politics, including political behavior, political philosophy, and the organization of government and political parties. *Economics* studies the production, distribution, and consumption of goods and services.

Social work and sociology are closely allied, but they are not the same. Social work is an applied field that makes use of the lessons of all the social sciences to serve people in need. Studying sociology is a good way to prepare for a career in social work because it delivers a perspective that will help the social worker better understand the plight of various individuals and how they are influenced by society.

The Sociological Perspective

Think back to the opening of this chapter where you were asked to imagine yourself having grown up under completely different circumstances. Our goal in that passage was to make you feel the stirring of the *sociological perspective*—the ability to see the societal patterns that influence individual and group life. The beginnings of the sociological perspective can be as simple as the pleasures of watching people or wondering how society influences people's lives. Indeed, many students begin their study of sociology because "they are interested in people." Sociologists

convert this curiosity into the systematic study of how society influences different people's experience within it.

C. Wright Mills (1916–1962) was one of the first to write about the sociological perspective in his classic book, *The Sociological Imagination* (1959). He wrote that the task of sociology was to understand the relationship between individuals and the society in which they lived. He defined the **sociological imagination** as the ability to see the societal patterns that influence the individual as well as groups of individuals. Sociology should be used, Mills argued, to reveal how the context of society shapes our lives; Mills thought that to understand the experience of a given person or group of people, one had to have knowledge of the social and historical context in which people lived.

Think, for example, about the time and effort that many people put into their appearance. Although, on the one hand, you can think about this merely as personal grooming or an individual attempt to "look good," there are significant social origins of this behavior. An individual may stand in front of the mirror, seemingly just one person not particularly thinking about how society is present in that reflection. But we likely look in the mirror to see how others see us; therefore, this is a very social act. Furthermore, if by looking, we are trying to achieve a particular look, that look has likely been established by the social forces that tell us to achieve a particular ideal—ideals that are produced by industries that profit enormously from the products and services that people buy. Some industries suggest that you should be thinner or curvier, your pants should be baggy or straight, your breasts should be minimized or maximized—either way you need more products. Maybe you should have a complete makeover! Many people then go to great lengths—sometimes extreme lengths that are hazardous to physical and mental health—to try to achieve a constantly changing beauty ideal, one that is probably not even attainable (i.e., flawless skin, hair never out of place, perfectly proportioned body parts).

The point is that the alleged standard is produced by social factors that extend far beyond the individual's immediate concerns with personal appearance. The ideals are produced in particular social and historical contexts. People may come up with all kinds of personal strategies for achieving a presumed ideal—they may buy more products, try to lose more weight, get a Botox treatment, or even become extremely depressed and anxious if they perceive their efforts as failing. These personal behaviors may seem to be only individual issues, but they have a basic social cause. That is, the origins of these behaviors originate beyond personal lives. The sociological imagination, which permits us to see that something as seemingly personal as how you look—and what you do to create that look—arises from a social context, not just individual behavior. Sociologists are

UNDERSTANDING DIVERSITY

Becoming a Sociologist

ndividual biographies often have a great influence on the subjects sociologists choose to study. The authors of this book are no exception. Margaret Andersen, a White woman, now studies the sociology of race and women's studies. Howard Taylor, an African American man, studies race, social psychology, and especially, race and intelligence testing. Here, each of them writes about the influence of their early experiences on becoming a sociologist.

Margaret Andersen ▪ As I was growing up in the 1950s and 1960s, my family moved from California to Georgia, then to Massachusetts, and then back to Georgia. Moving as we did from urban to small-town environments and in and out of regions of the country that were very different in their racial character, I probably could not help becoming fascinated by the sociology of race. Oakland, California, where I was born, was highly diverse; my neighborhood was mostly White and Asian American. When I moved to a small town in Georgia in the 1950s, I was ten years old, but I was shocked by the racial norms I encountered. I had always loved riding in the back of the bus—our major mode of transportation in Oakland—and could not understand why this was no longer allowed. Labeled by my peers an outsider, because I was not southern, I painfully learned what it meant to feel excluded just because of "where you are from."

When I moved again to suburban Boston in the 1960s, I was defined by Bostonians as a southerner and ridiculed. Nicknamed "Dixie," I was teased for how I talked. Unlike in the south, where, despite strict racial segregation, Black people were part of White people's daily lives, Black people in Boston were even less visible. In my high school of 2500 or so students, Black students were rare. To me, the

school seemed not much different from the strictly segregated schools I had attended in Georgia. My family soon returned to Georgia, where I was an outsider again; when I later returned to Massachusetts for graduate school in the 1970s, I worried about how a southerner would be accepted in this "Yankee" environment. Because I had acquired a southern accent, I think many of my teachers stereotyped me and thought I was not as smart as the students from other places.

These early lessons, which I may have been unaware of at the time, must have kindled my interest in the sociology of race relations. As I explored sociology, I wondered how the concepts and theories of race relations applied to women's lives. So much of what I had experienced growing up as a woman in this society was completely unexamined in what I studied in school. As the women's movement developed in the 1970s, I found sociology to be the framework that helped me understand the significance of gender and race in people's lives. To this day, I write and teach about race and gender, using sociology to help students understand their significance in society.

Howard Taylor ▪ I grew up in Cleveland, Ohio, the son of African American professional parents. My mother, Murtis Taylor, was a social worker and the founder and then president of a social work agency, called the Murtis H. Taylor Center, in Cleveland, Ohio. She is well known for her contributions to the city of Cleveland and was an early "superwoman," working days and nights, cooking, caring for her two sons, and being active in many professional and civic activities. I think this gave me an early appreciation for the roles of women and the place of gender in society though I surely would

not have articulated it as such at the time.

My father was a businessman in a then all-Black life insurance company. He was also a "closet scientist," always doing experiments and talking about scientific studies. He encouraged my brother and me to engage in science, so we were always experimenting with scientific studies in the basement of our house. In the summers, I worked for my mother in the social service agency where she worked—as a camp counselor and other jobs. Early on, I contemplated becoming a social worker, but I was also excited by science. As a young child, I acquired my father's love of science and my mother's interest in society. In college, the one field that would gratify both sides of me, science and social work, was sociology. I wanted to study human interaction, but I also wanted to be a scientist, so the appeal of sociology was clear.

At the same time, growing up African American meant that I faced the consequences of race everyday. It was always there, and like other young African American children, I spent much of my childhood confronting racism and prejudice. When I discovered sociology, in addition to bridging the scientific and humanistic parts of my interests, I found a field that provided a framework for studying race and ethnic relations. The merging of two ways of thinking, coupled with the analysis of race that sociology has long provided, made sociology fascinating to me.

Today, my research on race and intelligence testing and Black leadership networks seems rooted in these early experiences. I do quantitative research in sociology and see sociology as a science that reveals the workings of race, class, and gender in society.

certainly concerned about individuals, but they direct their attention to the social and historical context that shapes the experiences of individuals and groups.

A fundamental distinction within the sociological imagination is that between troubles and issues. **Troubles** are privately felt problems that spring from events or feelings in one individual's life. **Issues** affect large numbers of people and have their origins in the institutional arrangements and history of a society (Mills 1959). This distinction is the crux of the difference between individual experience and **social structure,** which is defined as the organized pattern of social relationships and social institutions that together constitute society. Issues shape the context within which troubles arise. Sociologists employ the sociological perspective to understand how issues are shaped by social structures.

Mills used the example of unemployment to explain the meaning of troubles versus issues. When a person becomes unemployed, he or she has a personal trouble. In addition to financial problems, the person may feel a loss of identity, may become depressed, may lose touch with former work associates, or may have to uproot a family and move. The problem of unemployment, however, is deeper than the experience of one person. Unemployment is rooted in the structure of society; this is what interests sociologists. What societal forces cause unemployment? Who is most likely to become unemployed at different times? How does unemployment affect an entire community (for instance, when a large plant shuts down) or an entire nationwide group (such as the corpo-

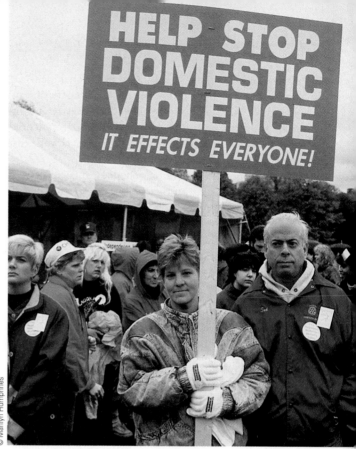

© Marilyn Humphries

Personal troubles are felt by individuals who are experiencing problems; social issues arise when large numbers of people experience problems that are rooted in the social structure of society. Violence against women is an example.

rate downsizing of older workers)? Sociologists know that unemployment causes personal troubles, but understanding unemployment is more than understanding one person's experience. It requires understanding the social structural conditions that influence people's lives.

The specific task of sociology, according to Mills, is to comprehend the whole of human society—its personal and public dimensions—historical and contemporary—and its influence on the lives of human beings. Mills had an important insight: People often feel that the situation they are in is larger than their experience alone because they feel the influence of society in their lives, even though the specific social forces shaping people's experiences may not be readily apparent to them. Consider this: Most likely you remember what you were doing on September 11, 2001, when you first heard that terrorists had flown planes into the World Trade Center in New York City. Obviously, this affected people's personal lives, but its impact—and its causes—go beyond the personal troubles it produced. Events like this influence our lives in profound ways, even though we may not know how at the time. Now we can use the sociological perspective to explain many dimensions of this event and its aftermath, including, for example, the significance of cultural symbols, how people respond to unexpected

TAKING ON SOCIAL ISSUES

Sexual Abuse

Sexual abuse provides a good example of the distinction C. Wright Mills makes between personal troubles and social issues. To the person experiencing the abuse, this is a personal trouble. Sociologists would add that it is a social issue. It is more common than commonly believed and is rooted in some of the social structures of society (such as the power of men over women, family conflict, the abuse of children used as sexual objects, and others). What different ways of explaining this social issue can you identify? Which are the more sociological explanations?

Taking Action

Go to the Taking Action Exercise on the companion Web site at **sociology.wadsworth.com /andersen_taylor/essen3e** to learn more about an organization that addresses this topic.

events, and how religious, ethnic, and national identities are created in society. Of course, the social forces that influence people's lives are not always so drastic and include the ordinary events of everyday life. One contribution sociology makes is revealing the forces at work that shape society and people within it.

An important part of the sociological perspective is that sociology is an **empirical** discipline; this distinguishes sociology from ordinary common sense. The empirical approach to knowledge requires that conclusions be based on careful and systematic observations—not on previous assumptions, but on what one observes. For empirical observations to be useful to other observers, they must be gathered and recorded rigorously. Sociologists are also obliged to reexamine their assumptions and conclusions constantly. Only careful, unprejudiced observations add to the fund of sociological knowledge. Although the specific methods that sociologists use to examine different problems vary, as we will see, the empirical basis of sociology is what distinguishes it from mere opinion or other forms of social commentary.

Discovering Unsettling Facts

In studying sociology, it is crucial to examine the most controversial topics and to do so with an open mind, even when you see the most disquieting facts. Revealing troubling facts about society is the price of seeing society for what it is. Consider the following:

- Despite the idea that Asian Americans are a "model minority," poverty among Asian American families is higher than that among White American families and has increased in recent years; among certain Asian American groups, namely Laotians and Cambodians, poverty strikes two-thirds of all families (Proctor and Dalaker 2002; Lee 1994).

- Women's income (on average) has generally risen, while men's has generally fallen. Still, women with a college degree earn less on average than men with only some college experience (DeNavas-Walt and Cleveland 2002; Mishel et al. 2003).

- The United States has the highest rate of imprisonment of all nations in the world (Mauer 1999).

- Infant mortality in the United States, especially among African Americans and Hispanics, exceeds that of many impoverished nations (U.S. Census Bureau 2002).

These facts provide unsettling evidence of persistent problems in the United States, *problems that are embedded in society,* not just in individual behavior. Sociologists try to

DOING SOCIOLOGICAL RESEARCH

Debunking the Myths of Black Teenage Motherhood

The common view of teen pregnancy is that many of the social and economic problems of today's poor result from female-headed households, households where "babies are having babies" and where a cycle of poverty is generated because of the high rate of teen pregnancy.

Sociologist Elaine Bell Kaplan wanted to know: What truth is there to this image? Kaplan knew that there was a stereotypical view of Black teen mothers—that they had grown up in fatherless households where their mothers had no moral values and no control over their children. The myth of Black teenage motherhood also depicts teen mothers as unable to control their sexuality, as having children to collect welfare checks, and as having families who condone their behavior.

Kaplan did extensive research in two communities in the San Francisco Bay Area—East Oakland and Richmond, both communities with a large African American population and typical of many inner-city, poor neighborhoods. Once thriving Black communities, East Oakland and Richmond are now characterized by high rates of unemployment, poverty, inadequate schools, crime and drug-related violence, and high numbers of single-parent households. Having grown up herself in Harlem, Kaplan knew that communities like those she studied have not always had these problems, nor have they condoned teen pregnancy. She spent several months in the community, working as a volunteer in a community teen center that provided educational programs, day care, and counseling to teen parents, and

"hanging out" with a core group of teen mothers. She did extensive interviews with thirty-two teen mothers, supplementing them when she could with interviews with their mothers and, sometimes, the fathers of their children.

She found that these teen mothers adopt strategies for survival that help them cope with their environment even though these same strategies do not help them overcome the problems they face. Unlike what the popular stereotype suggests, she did not find that the Black community condones teen pregnancy; quite the contrary, the teens felt embarrassed and stigmatized by being pregnant and experienced tension and conflict with their mothers who saw their pregnancy as disrupting the hopes they had for their daughters' success. When the women had to go on welreveal the social factors that shape society and determine the chances of success for different groups. The sociological perspective reveals that there are currents underlying ordinary life that carry people along paths not always of their own choosing. Some never get the chance to go to college; others are likely never to go to jail. These divisions persist because of people's placement within society.

Sociologists do not study only the disquieting side of society. Sociologists may study questions that affect everyday life, such as how families adapt to changing societal conditions (Lempert and DeVault 2000), how street people live (Duneier 1999), how children of immigrants fare (Portes and Rumbaut 2001), or how racism has changed in recent years (Zuberi 2001; Bonilla-Silva 2001). There are also many insightful and intriguing studies of unusual groups, including dog owners (Sanders 1999), cyberspace users (Turkle 1995; Kendall 2002), and tattoo collectors (Irwin 2001). The subject matter of sociology is vast. Some work illuminates odd corners of society; other work addresses urgent problems of society that may affect the lives and futures of millions.

Debunking in Sociology

The power of sociological thinking is that it helps us see everyday life in new ways. Sociologists question actions and ideas that are usually taken for granted. Peter Berger (1963) calls this process debunking. **Debunking** refers to looking behind the facades of everyday life—what Berger called the "unmasking tendency" of sociology (1963: 38). In other words, sociologists look at the behind-the-scenes patterns and processes that shape the behavior they observe in the social world.

Take schooling, for example: We can see how the sociological perspective debunks taken-for-granted assumptions about education. Most think that education is primarily a way to learn and get ahead. Although this is true, a sociological perspective on education reveals something more. Sociologists have concluded that more than learning takes place in schools; other social processes are at work. Social cliques are formed where some students are "insiders" and others are excluded "outsiders." Young school children acquire not just formal knowledge, but also the expectations of society and people's place within it. Race and class conflicts are often played out in schools. Relative to boys, girls are often shortchanged by the school system—receiving less attention and encouragement, less interaction with teachers, less instruction in the sciences, and many other deficits disproportionately forced upon them (American Association of University Women 1998; Sadker and Sadker 1994). Poor children seldom have the same resources in schools

fare, they also felt embarrassed, often developing strategies to hide the fact that they were dependent on welfare to make ends meet. These conclusions are directly counter to the public image that such women do not value success and live in a culture that promotes welfare dependency.

Instead of simply stereotyping them as young and tough, she sees them as struggling to develop their own gender and sexual identity. Like other teens, they are highly vulnerable, searching for love and aspiring to create a meaningful and positive identity for themselves. But failed by the educational system and locked out of the job market, the young women's struggle to develop an identity is compounded by the disruptive social and economic conditions in which they live.

Kaplan's research is a fine example of how sociologists debunk some of the commonly shared myths that surround contemporary issues. Carefully placing her analysis in the context of the social structural changes that affect these young women's lives, Kaplan provides an excellent example of how sociological research can shed new light on some of our most pressing social problems.

Questions to Consider

1. Suppose that Kaplan had studied middle-class teen mothers. What similarities and differences would you predict in the experiences of middle-class and poor teen mothers? Does race matter? In what ways does your answer *debunk* myths about teen pregnancy?

Keywords: *poverty and adolescence; Black motherhood*

2. Make a list of the challenges you would face were you to be a teen parent. Having done so, indicate those that would be considered personal troubles and those that are social issues. How are the two related?
Keywords: *teen mothers; teen pregnancy*

We have included InfoTrac College Edition keywords at the end of each question to make it easier for you to find more to read on these topics. Go to **www.infotrac-college.com,** an online library, to begin your search.

Source: Kaplan, Elaine Bell. 1996. *Not Our Kind of Girl: Unraveling the Myths of Black Teenage Motherhood.* Berkeley: University of California Press.

as middle-class or elite children, and they are often assumed to be incapable of doing schoolwork and are treated accordingly. The somber reality is that schools may actually stifle the opportunities of some children rather than launch all children toward success.

THINKING SOCIOLOGICALLY

School violence is now widely presented in the public media. How is school violence generally depicted in common-sense explanations? What questions might sociologists ask to *debunk* these everyday explanations of school violence?

Debunking is sometimes easier to do when looking at a culture or society different from one's own. Consider how behaviors that are unquestioned in one society may seem positively bizarre to an outsider. For a thousand years in China, it was usual for the elite classes to bind the feet of young girls to keep the feet from growing bigger—a practice allegedly derived from one mistress of the emperor. Bound feet were a sign of delicacy and vulnerability. A woman with large feet (defined as more than 4 inches long!) was thought to bring shame to her husband's household. The practice was supported by the belief that men were highly aroused by small feet even though men never actually saw the naked foot. If they had, they might have been repulsed, because a woman's

---

SOCIOLOGY IN PRACTICE

Careers in Sociology

Estimating how many sociologists are in the United States is difficult because people often hold degrees in sociology and work with sociological skills but call themselves something different. The American Sociological Association, the national professional organization, has more than 13,000 members. About 80 percent of the members are employed as teachers in colleges and universities; 20 percent are employed in government positions, private organizations, and public agencies. Sociologists have an important role in education, in community and public services, and in the development of public policy.

Most students see sociologists in their roles as educators—an important part of the work that sociologists do. An education in sociology can help you think logically and analytically about society and its problems. Many students who take sociology courses do not become professional sociologists, but the skills acquired prepare them for a variety of careers.

In addition to their work as teachers, sociologists have become more active in the formation of public policy. Their research and theory are often the basis for changes in public policy. Sociologists are frequently

called upon as experts for the U.S. Congress, by the media, by state and federal agencies, and by private organizations to consult on a variety of subjects. For example, when the Family and Medical Leave Act of 1993 was passed, sociologists gave briefings to congressional staff members on the sociological research on family–work connections and sociologists from the American Sociological Association provided briefings for the press on the implications of the bill. Sociological research documenting the gender and race bias in a widely used test of job aptitudes (called the General Aptitude Test Battery, or GATB) resulted in the Department of Labor and Department of Health and Human Services stopping use of the test in thirty-three states until it was revised to ensure more fairness.

Other examples of the impact of sociological research on social policy are numerous. Sociologists use their sociological imaginations to affect change in a variety of areas. As an example, feminist scholars, Latino sociologists, African American sociologists, and Asian American sociologists have been leaders in the movement to make education more multicultural. Some sociologists hold positions of political office. Sociologists also work

in the offices of U.S. representatives and senators doing background research on the various issues being addressed in the political process. Several sociologists have been direct advisors to U.S. presidents. Other sociologists have worked in their communities to deliver more effective social services. Some are employed in business organizations and social services where they use their sociological training to address issues such as poverty, crime and delinquency, population studies, substance abuse, violence against women, family social services, immigration policy, and any number of other important issues.

Critical Thinking Exercise

1. Read a national newspaper over a period of one week and identify any experts who use a sociological perspective in their commentary. What does this suggest to you as a possible career in sociology? What are some of the different subjects about which sociologists provide expert information?

2. Identify some of the students from your college who have finished degrees in sociology. What different ways have they used their sociological knowledge?

Cultural practices that seem bizarre to outsiders may be taken for granted or defined as appropriate by insiders.

actual foot was U-shaped and often rotten and covered with dead skin (Blake 1994).

Outside the social, cultural, and historical context in which it was practiced, footbinding seems bizarre, even dangerous. Feminists have pointed out that Chinese women were crippled by this practice, making them unable to move about freely and making them more dependent on men (Chang 1991). This is an example of outsiders debunking a practice that was taken for granted by those within the culture.

Debunking can also call into question practices in one's own culture that may normally go unexamined. Strange as the practice of Chinese footbinding may seem to you, how might someone from another culture view the implantation of silicone in women's breasts to enhance their size? Or wearing shoes with heels that make it difficult to walk? Or wearing a completely useless cloth necktie snugly around one's neck? These practices of contemporary U.S. culture are taken for granted by many, just as was Chinese footbinding. Until these cultural processes are debunked, seen as if for the first time, they might seem normal. One can step away from cultural familiarity to glimpse the social structures behind them, revealing these practices in their sociological context.

In debunking the taken-for-granted world, sociologists find their subject matter all around them. They carefully observe social behavior and reveal different lev-els of meaning that are ordinarily hidden from consciousness in everyday life. Simply put, sociology is appealing to those who find human beings fascinating.

DEBUNKING
Society's Myths

Myth: Violence is at an all-time high.

Sociological research: Although rates of violence are high in the United States, at least twice before—1930 and 1980—the murder rate was at a comparable level. It is also true, however, that rates of violence in the United States are higher than in any other industrialized nation (Levine and Rosich 1996; Best 1999).

Key Sociological Concepts

As you build your sociological perspective, you must learn certain key concepts to begin understanding how sociologists view human behavior. *Social structure, social institutions, social change,* and *social interaction* are not the only sociological concepts, but they are fundamental to grasping the sociological perspective.

SOCIAL STRUCTURE. Earlier, we defined social structure as the organized pattern of social relationships and social institutions that together constitute society. Social structure is not a "thing," but refers to the fact that social forces, not always visible to the human eye, guide and shape human behavior. It is as if there were a network of forces embracing people and moving them in one direction or another. Acknowledging that social structure exists does not mean that humans have no choice in how they behave, only that those choices are largely conditioned by one's location in society.

SOCIAL INSTITUTIONS.   In this book, you will also learn about the significance of **social institutions,** defined as established and organized systems of social behavior with a particular and recognized purpose. The family, religion, marriage, government, and the economy are examples of major social institutions. Social institutions confront individuals at birth and they transcend individual experience—but still influence individual behavior. Understanding the character of social institutions is one product of the sociological imagination.

SOCIAL CHANGE.   As you can tell, sociologists are also interested in the process of **social change**—the alteration of society over time. As much as sociologists see society as producing certain outcomes, they do not see society as fixed or immutable, nor do they see human be-

Understanding diversity is important in a society comprising so many different groups, each with unique, but interconnected, experiences.

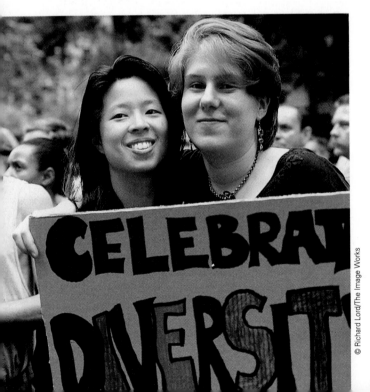

ings as passive recipients of social expectations. In other words, sociologists do not take a determinist approach to human behavior—as if all is fixed and without any possibility for change, or even surprise. Instead, sociologists view society as both stable, but constantly changing.

SOCIAL INTERACTION.   Sociologists see **social interaction** as behavior between two or more people that is given meaning. Through social interaction, people react and change, depending on the actions and reactions of others. Society results from social interaction; thus, people are active agents in what society becomes. Since society changes as new forms of human behavior emerge, change is always in the works. As you read this book, you will see that these key concepts—social structure, social institutions, social change, and social interaction—are central to the sociological imagination.

▪ *The Significance of Diversity*

The analysis of diversity is one central theme of sociology. Differences among groups, especially differences in the treatment of groups, are significant in any society, but they are particularly compelling in a society as diverse as the United States.

Defining Diversity

Today, the United States includes people from all nations and races. In 1900, one in eight Americans was not White; today, racial and ethnic minority groups, including African Americans, Latinos, American Indians, and Asian Americans, are one-quarter of Americans and that proportion is growing (see Figure 1.1; U.S. Census Bureau 2002). These broad categories themselves are internally diverse, including, for example, those with long-term roots in the United States, as well as Cuban Americans, Salvadorans, Cape Verdeans, Filipinos, and many others.

Perhaps the most basic lesson of sociology is that people are shaped by the social context around them. In the United States, with so much cultural diversity, people will share some experiences, but not all. Experiences not held in common can include some of the most important influences on social development, such as language, religion, and the traditions of family and community. Understanding diversity means recognizing this diversity and making it central to sociological analyses.

In this book, we use the term *diversity* to refer to the variety of group experiences that result from the social

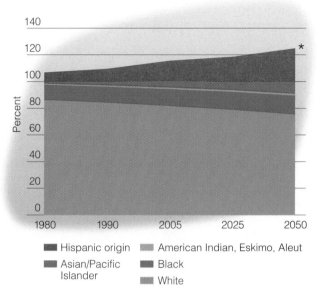

FIGURE 1.1 Diversity in U.S. Population

*Hispanics may be included in any race; thus, the total exceeds 100 percent.

SOURCE: U.S. Census Bureau. 2002. *Statistical Abstract of the United States: 2002*. Washington, DC: U.S. Department of Commerce, p. 13.

structure of society. **Diversity** is a broad concept that includes studying group differences in society's opportunities, the shaping of social institutions by different social factors, the formation of group and individual identity, and the process of social change. Diversity includes the study of different cultural orientations, although diversity is not exclusively about culture.

Understanding diversity is crucial to understanding society because the population is increasingly diverse and because fundamental patterns of social change and social structure are increasingly patterned by diverse group experiences. Race, class, and gender are fundamental to understanding diversity because they have been so central in shaping social institutions in the United States. They are not, however, the only sources of diversity. Age, nationality, sexual orientation, and region of residence, among other social factors, also differentiate the experience of diverse groups in the United States. And, as the world is increasingly interconnected through global communication and a global economy, the study of diversity also encompasses a global perspective—that is, an understanding of the international connections existing across national borders and the impact of such connections on life throughout the world.

Society in Global Perspective

No society can be understood apart from the global context that now influences the development of all societies. The social and economic system of any one society is increasingly intertwined with those of other nations. Cou-

pled with the increasing ease of travel and telecommunication, this means that a global perspective is necessary to understand change both in the United States and in other parts of the world.

To understand globalization, you must look beyond the boundaries of your own society to see how patterns in any given society are increasingly being shaped by the connections between societies. Sociologists and other social scientists typically have used a cross-cultural or comparative perspective to study different societies. Comparing and contrasting societies across different cultures is valuable. It helps you see patterns in your own society that you might otherwise take for granted, and it enriches your appreciation of the diverse patterns of culture that mark human society and human history. A global perspective, however, goes beyond just comparing different cultures; it also helps you see how events in one society or community are linked to events that may be on the other side of the globe.

For example, return to the example of unemployment that C. Wright Mills used to distinguish troubles and issues. One man may lose his job in Peoria, Illinois, and a woman in Los Angeles may employ a Latina domestic worker to take care of her child while she pursues a career. On the one hand, these are individual experiences—for all three people—but they are linked in a pattern of globalization that shapes the lives of all three. The Latina domestic may have a family whom she has left in a different nation so that she can afford to support them. The corporation for which the Los Angeles woman works may have invested in a new plant overseas that employs cheap labor, resulting in the unemployment of the man in Peoria. The man in Peoria may have seen immigrant workers moving into his community, and one of his children may have made a friend at school who speaks a language other than English. Such processes are increasingly shaping many of the subjects examined in this book—work, family, education, politics, just to name a few. Without a global perspective, you would not be able to fully understand the experience of any one of the people just mentioned—much less how society is being shaped by these processes of change and global context.

In this book, we introduce a global perspective particularly to understand those aspects of U.S. society that are most influenced by worldwide developments. Something as seemingly simple as what toys children play with can be fully understood only by analyzing the international economic system in which these toys are produced and distributed. Throughout this book, we will use a global perspective to understand some of the developments shaping contemporary life in the United States.

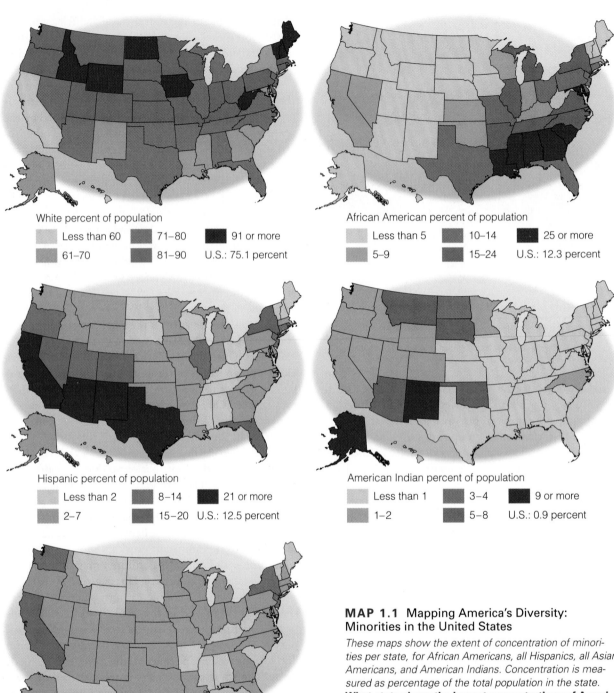

White percent of population

Less than 60	71–80	91 or more
61–70	81–90	U.S.: 75.1 percent

African American percent of population

Less than 5	10–14	25 or more
5–9	15–24	U.S.: 12.3 percent

Hispanic percent of population

Less than 2	8–14	21 or more
2–7	15–20	U.S.: 12.5 percent

American Indian percent of population

Less than 1	3–4	9 or more
1–2	5–8	U.S.: 0.9 percent

Asian American, Native Hawaiian, and other
Pacific Islander percent of population

Less than 1	5–8	51%
1–4	9–12	U.S.: 3.7 percent

MAP 1.1 Mapping America's Diversity:
Minorities in the United States

These maps show the extent of concentration of minorities per state, for African Americans, all Hispanics, all Asian Americans, and American Indians. Concentration is measured as percentage of the total population in the state.
What states have the largest concentrations of American Indians? What states have the largest concentrations of the other ethnic minority groups? What are the minority group concentrations for your own home state?

DATA: From the U.S. Census Bureau. 2002. *Statistical Abstract of the United States, 2002.* Washington, D.C.: U.S. Government Printing Office, p. 27.

"Actually, Lou, I think it was more than just my being in the right place at the right time. I think it was my being the right race, the right religion, the right sex, the right socioeconomic group, having the right accent, the right clothes, going to the right schools..."

■ *The Development of Sociological Theory*

Like the subjects it studies, sociology is itself a social product. It is an intellectual framework deeply influenced by the social and historical conditions in which it is produced. Sociology first emerged in western Europe during the eighteenth and nineteenth centuries. In this period, the political and economic systems of Europe were rapidly changing. Monarchy, the rule of society by kings and queens, was disappearing in western Europe. These changes generated new ways of thinking. Religion as the system of authority and law was giving way to scientific authority. At the same time, capitalism grew. Contact between different societies increased, and worldwide economic markets developed. The conservative, traditional ways of the past were giving way to a new social order. The time was ripe for a new understanding.

The Influence of the Enlightenment

The **Enlightenment** in eighteenth- and nineteenth-century Europe had an enormous influence on the development of modern sociology. Also known as the Age of Reason, the Enlightenment was characterized by faith in the ability of human reason to solve society's problems. Intellectuals believed that there were natural laws and processes in society to be discovered and used for the

general good. Modern science was gradually supplanting traditional and religious explanations for natural phenomena with theories confirmed by experiments.

The earliest sociologists promoted a vision of sociology grounded in careful observation. **Auguste Comte** (1798–1857), a French philosopher who coined the term *sociology,* believed that just as science had discovered the laws of nature, sociology could discover the laws of human social behavior and thus help solve society's problems. Sociology, according to Comte, was the most highly evolved of the sciences since it involved the study of a complex and changing system—society. This approach is called **positivism,** a system of thought, still prominent today, in which scientific observation and description is considered the highest form of knowledge, as opposed to, say, religious dogma or poetic inspiration. The modern scientific method, which guides sociological research, grew out of positivism.

Alexis de Tocqueville (1805–1859), a French citizen, traveled to the United States as an observer beginning in 1831. The book that followed from his experience, *Democracy in America,* is an insightful analysis of U.S. democratic culture and society. Tocqueville thought that democratic and egalitarian values in the United States influenced American social institutions for the better and transformed personal relationships. Less admiringly, he felt that in the United States the tyranny of kings had been replaced by the "tyranny of the majority." He was

Globalization brings diverse cultures together, but it is also a process by which Western markets have penetrated much of the world.

As one of the earliest observers of American culture, Harriet Martineau used the powers of social observation to record and analyze the social structure of American society. Long ignored for her contributions to sociology, she is now seen as one of the founders of early sociological thought.

© Culver Pictures

Emile Durkheim established the significance of society as something larger than the sum of its parts. Social facts stem from society and have profound influence on the lives of people within society.

© Bettmann/CORBIS

referring to the ability of a majority to impose its will on everyone else in a democracy. Tocqueville also felt that despite the emphasis on individualism in American culture, Americans had little independence of mind and that individualism made people self-centered and anxious about their social-class position (Collins and Makowsky 1972).

Another early sociologist is **Harriet Martineau** (1802–1876). Like Tocqueville, Martineau, a British citizen, embarked on a long tour of the United States in 1834. She was fascinated by the newly emerging culture in America. Her book, *Society in America* (1837), is an analysis of the social customs that she observed. This important work was overlooked for many years, probably because the author was a woman. It is now recognized as a classic. Martineau also wrote the first sociological methods book, *How to Observe Manners and Morals* (1838), in which she discussed how to observe behavior when one is a participant in the situation being studied. Martineau was also the original English translator of Comte's book *Positive Philosophy*.

Classical Sociological Theory

Of all the contributors to the development of sociology, the giants of the European tradition were Emile Durkheim, Karl Marx, and Max Weber. They are classical thinkers because the analyses they offered more than one hundred years ago continue to enlighten our understanding of society—not just in sociology, but in other fields as well (such as political science and history).

EMILE DURKHEIM. During the early academic career of the Frenchman **Emile Durkheim** (1858–1917), France was in the throes of great political and religious upheaval. Anti-Semitism (hatred of Jews) was being expressed, along with ill feeling among other religions, as well. Durkheim, himself Jewish, was fascinated by how the public degradation of Jews by non-Jews seemed to calm and unify a large segment of the divided French pub-

lic. Durkheim later wrote that public rituals have a special purpose in society, creating social solidarity, referring to the bonds that link the members of a group. Some of Durkheim's most significant works explore the question of what forces hold society together and make it stable.

According to Durkheim, people in society are glued together by belief systems (Durkheim 1912/1947). The rituals of religion and other institutions symbolize and reinforce the sense of belonging that insiders in a society or group feel. Public ceremonies create a bond between people in a social unit. Drawing on this insight, Durkheim made a creative leap that helps explain social deviance. Durkheim argued that deviance has a purpose in society—that by labeling some people as deviant, the society confirms a sense of normalcy and strengthens social solidarity. Identifying some behaviors as deviant gives definition to nondeviant or "normal" behaviors. Durkheim thought that deviance, like public rituals, sustains moral cohesion in society. In this sense, society actually *creates* deviance—a type of behavior that it claims to want to eliminate.

Durkheim viewed society as an entity larger than the sum of its parts. He described this as society *sui generis* ("thing in itself"), meaning that society is a subject to be studied separate from the sum of the individuals who compose it. Society is external to individuals, yet its existence is internalized in people's minds—that is, people come to believe what society expects them to believe. Durkheim conceived of society as an integrated whole—each part contributing to the overall stability of the system. His work is the basis for *functionalism,* an important theoretical perspective that we will return to later in this chapter.

One contribution from Durkheim was his conceptualization of the *social.* Durkheim conceptualized **social facts** as those social patterns that are *external* to individuals. Things such as customs and social values exist outside individuals, whereas psychological drives and motivation exist inside people. Social facts, therefore, are not to be explained by biology or psychology, but are the proper subject of sociology; they are its reason for being. A striking illustration of this principle was Durkheim's study of suicide (Durkheim 1897/1951). He analyzed rates of suicide in a society, as opposed to looking at individual (psychological) causes of suicide. He showed that suicide rates varied according to how clear the norms and customs of the society were, whether the norms and customs were consistent with each other and noncontradictory. Where norms were either grossly unclear or contradictory, a condition that he called *anomie* ("normlessness") existed, and the suicide rates were higher in such societies or such parts of a society. It is important to note that this condition was "external," thus outside of each individual taken singly. In this sense such a condition is truly societal.

Durkheim held that social facts, though they exist outside individuals, nonetheless pose constraints on individual behavior. Durkheim's major contribution was the discovery of the social basis of human behavior. He proposed that a social system could be known through the discovery and analysis of social facts and that adding to the fund of reliable social facts was the central task of the sociologist (Bellah 1973; Coser 1977; Durkheim 1938/1950).

KARL MARX. It is hard to imagine another scholar who has had as much influence on intellectual history as **Karl Marx** (1818–1883). Along with his collaborator, Friedrich Engels, Marx not only changed intellectual history, but world history, too.

Marx's work was devoted to explaining how capitalism shaped society. He argued that capitalism is an economic system based on the pursuit of profit and the sanctity of private property. Marx used a class analysis to explain capitalism, describing capitalism as a system of relationships among different classes—including capitalists (also known as the bourgeois class), the proletariat (or working class), the petty bourgeoisie (small business owners and managers), and the *lumpenproletariat* (those "discarded" by the capitalist system, such as the homeless). In Marx's view, profit, the goal of capitalist endeavors, is produced through the exploitation of the working class. Workers sell their labor in exchange for wages, and capitalists make certain that wages are worth less than the goods the workers produce. The difference in value is the profit of the capitalist. In the Marxist view, the capitalist class system is inherently unfair because the entire system rests on workers getting less than they give.

Marx thought that the economic organization of society was the most important influence on what humans think and how they behave. He found that the beliefs of the common people tended to support the interests of the capitalist system, not the interests of the workers themselves. Why? Because the capitalist class controls not

Karl Marx analyzed capitalism as an economic system with enormous implications for how society is organized, in particular how inequality between groups stems from the economic organization of society.

only the production of goods but also the production of ideas. It owns the publishing companies, endows the universities where knowledge is produced, and controls information industries.

Marx considered all of society to be shaped by economic forces. Laws, family structures, schools, and other institutions all develop, according to Marx, to suit economic needs under capitalism. Like other early sociologists, Marx took social structure as his subject rather than the actions of individuals. It was the *system* of capitalism that dictated people's behavior. Marx saw social change as arising from tensions inherent in a capitalist system—the conflict between the capitalist and working classes.

Marx's ideas are often misperceived by U.S. students because communist revolutionaries throughout the world have claimed Marx as their guiding spirit. It would be naive to reject his ideas solely on political grounds. Much that Marx predicted has not occurred—for instance, he claimed that the "laws" of history made a worldwide revolution of workers inevitable, and this has not happened. Still, he left us an important body of sociological thought springing from his insight that society is systematic and structural and that class is a fundamental dimension of society that shapes social behavior.

MAX WEBER. **Max Weber** (1864–1920; pronounced "Vay-ber") was greatly influenced by Marx's work and built upon it. But, whereas Marx saw economics as the basic organizing element of society, Weber theorized that society had three basic dimensions: political, economic, and cultural. According to Weber, a complete sociological analysis must recognize the interplay between economic, political, and cultural institutions (Parsons 1947). Weber is credited with developing a *multidimensional* analysis of society that goes beyond Marx's more one-dimensional focus on economics.

Weber also theorized extensively about the relationship of sociology to social and political values. He did not believe there could be a value-free sociology because

Max Weber used a multidimensional approach to analyzing society, interpreting the economic, cultural, and political organization of society as together shaping social institutions and social change.

© AKG/London

values would always influence what sociologists considered worthy of study. Weber thought sociologists should acknowledge the influence of values so that ingrained beliefs might not interfere with objectivity. Weber professed that the task of sociologists is to teach students the uncomfortable truth about the world. Faculty should not use their positions to promote their political opinions, he felt; rather, they have a responsibility to examine all opinions, including unpopular ones, and use the tools of rigorous sociological inquiry to understand why people believe and behave as they do.

An important concept in Weber's sociology is *verstehen* (pronounced, "ver-shtay-en"). **Verstehen,** a German word, refers to understanding social behavior from the point of view of those engaged in it. Weber believed that to understand social behavior one had to understand the meaning that a behavior had for social actors. He did not believe sociologists had to be born into a group to understand it (in other words, he didn't believe "it takes one to know one"), but he did think sociologists had to develop some subjective understanding of how other people experience their world. One major contribution from Weber was the definition of *social action* as a behavior to which people give meaning (Gerth and Mills 1946; Parsons 1951b; Weber 1962). In other words, social behavior is more than just action; people do things in a context and use their interpretive abilities to understand and give meaning to their action. Weber's work emphasized this subjective dimension of social life. Like Durkheim and Marx, Weber continues to have a profound impact on sociology.

Sociology in America

American sociology was built on the earlier work of Europeans, but unique features of U.S. culture contribute to its distinctive flavor. *Pragmatism* (the belief in practicality) influenced sociologists in the United States to value social planning. Less theoretical and more practi-

cal than their European counterparts, American sociologists believed that if they exposed the causes of social problems, they could alleviate some of the consequences, which are measured in human suffering.

Early sociologists in both Europe and the United States conceived of society as an organism, a system of interrelated functions and parts that work together to create the whole. This perspective is called the **organic metaphor.** Sociologists saw society as constantly evolving, like an organism. The question many early sociologists asked was to what extent humans could shape the evolution of society.

Many were influenced in this question by the work of British scholar **Charles Darwin** (1809–1882), who had revolutionized biology when he identified the process called *evolution,* a process by which new species are created. **Social Darwinism** was the application of Darwinian thought to society. According to the social Darwinists, the "survival of the fittest" is the driving force of social evolution. They conceived of society as an organism that evolved from simple to complex in a process of adaptation to the environment. They theorized that society was best left alone to follow its natural evolutionary course. Because they believed that evolution always took a course toward perfection, he advocated a *laissez-faire* (that is, hands-off) approach to social change. Social Darwinism was thus a conservative mode of thought; it assumed that the current arrangements in society were natural and inevitable (Hofstadter 1944).

Most other early sociologists in the United States took a more reform-based approach. **Lester Frank Ward** (1831–1914) thought sociology could be used to engineer social change. He called this *social telesis*—the idea that human intervention in the natural evolution of society would advance the interests of society. Ward and the reform-minded sociologists of the early twentieth century were optimistic about the ability of sociology to address society's problems. They saw industrialization and urbanization as the cause of society's problems and wanted to use sociology to create change. This activist tradition has left an important legacy for contemporary sociologists. **Applied sociology** is the use of sociological research and theory in solving real human problems.

Nowhere was the emphasis on application more evident than at the University of Chicago, where a style of sociological thinking known as the Chicago School developed. The Chicago School is characterized by thinkers who were interested in how society shaped the mind and identity of people. They thought of society as a human laboratory where they could observe and understand human behavior to be better able to address human needs.

Charles Horton Cooley (1864–1929) was one of the foremost theorists of the Chicago School. Cooley theorized that individual identity developed through people's understanding of how they are perceived by others. This was further elaborated in the work of **George Herbert Mead** (1863–1931), who, like Cooley, was interested in specifying the processes that linked the individual to society. Cooley and Mead saw the individual and society as interdependent. Individuals developed through the relationships they established with others, and society existed because it was perceived in the minds of people. We return to the work of Cooley and Mead in Chapter 3 when we discuss socialization, the process by which individuals are shaped to fit within society.

Sociologists at the University of Chicago worked close to home using the city in which they lived as a living laboratory. Race riots, immigrant ghettoes, poverty, and delinquency were all features of "modern" life in pre-war Chicago, seeding the work of the Chicago theorists. The five-volume study of Polish immigrants in Chicago produced by **W. I. Thomas** (1863–1947) and his colleague **Florian Znaniecki** (1882–1958; pronounced "Znan-yetski") remains a classic study of ethnicity, immigration, neighborhood segregation, and urban life (Thomas 1918 [1919/1958]).

W. I. Thomas promoted the use of personal documents to reveal how people interpreted their experiences. There are legends of Thomas sifting through the garbage of Polish immigrants to retrieve personal letters, which he used to study their social relationships and to learn how they felt about their lives in the New World. Thomas also thought that the influence of society was so strong that people would behave according to what they thought was true—even if confronted with evidence to the contrary. Thomas's famous dictum (developed in collaboration with Dorothy Swaine Thomas, his wife) was: *If people define situations as real, they are real in their consequences* (Thomas and Thomas 1928). Also called the principle of "definition of the situation," Thomas's dictum is regarded as one of the most profound of sociological principles.

Robert Park (1864–1944) was another founder of sociology from the University of Chicago. Originally a journalist who worked in several Midwestern cities, Park was interested in urban problems and how different racial groups interacted with each other. He was also fascinated by the sociological design of cities, noting that cities were typically sets of concentric circles. The very rich and the very poor lived in the middle, ringed by slums and low-income neighborhoods. Progressing to the outer rings, the residents became increasingly affluent (Collins and Makowsky 1972; Coser 1977; Park and Burgess 1921). Although this particular geometric shape to cities has changed, with increased suburbanization and the concentration of poverty in inner cities, Park

Jane Addams, the only sociologist to win the Nobel Peace Prize, used her sociological skills to try to improve people's lives. The settlement house movement provided social services to groups in need, while also providing a social laboratory in which to observe the sociological dimensions of problems such as poverty.

AP/Wide World Photos

would still be intrigued by sociological research showing how boundaries are defined and maintained in urban neighborhoods. You might notice this yourself. A single street crossing might delineate a Vietnamese neighborhood from an Italian one, a White affluent neighborhood from a barrio. This social design of cities continues to be a subject of sociological research.

Many early sociologists of the Chicago School were women whose work is only now being rediscovered. **Jane Addams** (1860–1935), close friend of and collaborator with W. E. B. Du Bois, was one of the most renowned sociologists of her day. She was a leader in the settlement house movement, which provided community services and did systematic research designed to improve the lives of slum dwellers, immigrants, and other dispossessed groups. Addams, the only practicing sociologist ever to win a Nobel Peace Prize (in 1931), never had a regular teaching job. Instead, she used her skills as a research sociologist to develop community projects that assisted people in need (Deegan 1988).

African American thinkers, like many women thinkers whose work has not been properly recognized, are now finally being credited for their contribution to the history and evolution of the discipline. They made their contributions despite formidable obstacles to their success, including exclusion from White universities where they would have been more likely to have the resources for teaching and research that facilitate professional success.

W. E. B. Du Bois (1868–1963; pronounced "due boys"), though not a part of the Chicago School, took an applied focus. Du Bois was a prominent Black scholar, a cofounder in 1909 of the NAACP (National Association for the Advancement of Colored People), a prolific writer, and one of America's best minds. He also studied for a time in Germany, hearing several lectures by Max Weber. His Ph.D. was the first awarded by Harvard to a Black person in any field. Du Bois's vision of sociology differed

Courtesy of University of Massachusetts at Amherst

An insightful observer of race and culture, W. E. B. Du Bois was one of the first sociologists to use community studies as the basis for sociological work. His work, long excluded from the "great works" of sociological theory, is now seen as a brilliant and lasting analysis of the significance of race in the United States.

in some ways from that of the White European–American mainstream. He was deeply troubled by the racial divisiveness in society, writing in a classic essay published in 1901 that "the problem of the twentieth century is the problem of the color line" (Du Bois 1901: 354). Like many of his women colleagues, he envisioned a community-based, activist profession committed to social justice (Deegan 1988). At the same time, like Weber, he believed in the importance of a scientific approach to sociological questions. W. E. B. Du Bois thought sociology should be used to study the pressing issues of the time. He believed that convictions always directed one's studies. He also thought sociology should use the most rigorous tools of sociological research to ensure accuracy and fairness.

Theoretical Frameworks: Functionalism, Conflict Theory, and Symbolic Interaction

The founders of sociology have established theoretical traditions that ask basic questions about society and inform sociological research. For many students, the idea of theory seems dry because it connotes something that is only hypothetical and divorced from "real life." To the contrary, sociological theory is one of the tools that sociologists use to interpret real life. Sociologists use theory to organize their empirical observations, to produce logically related statements about observed behavior, and to relate observed social facts to the broad questions sociologists ask: How are individuals related to society? How is social order maintained? Why is there inequality in society? How does social change occur?

Within sociology, there is not one single overriding theoretical perspective. Different theoretical frameworks within sociology make different assumptions about the nature of society. In the realm of *macrosociology* are theories that strive to understand society as a whole. Durkheim, Marx, and Weber were macrosociological theorists. Theoretical frameworks that center on face-to-face social interaction are

known as *microsociology.* Some of the work derived from the Chicago School—research that studies individuals and group processes in society—is microsociological. Although sociologists draw from diverse theoretical perspectives to understand society, three broad traditions form the major theoretical perspectives that they use: functionalism, conflict theory, and symbolic interaction.

FUNCTIONALISM. Functionalism has its origins in the work of Durkheim, who, you will recall, was especially interested in how social order is possible, or how society remains relatively stable. **Functionalism** interprets each part of society in terms of how it contributes to the stability of the whole. As Durkheim suggested, functionalism conceptualizes society as more than the sum of its component parts. Each part is "functional" for society—that is, contributes to the stability of the whole. The different parts are primarily the institutions of society, each of which is organized to fill different needs, and each of which has particular consequences for the form and shape of society. The parts are each then dependent on one another.

The family as an institution, for example, serves multiple functions. At its most basic level, the family has a reproductive role. Within the family, infants receive protection and sustenance. As they grow older, they are exposed to the patterns and expectations of their culture. Across generations, the family supplies a broad unit of support and enriches individual experience with a sense of continuity with the past and future. All these aspects of family can be assessed by how they contribute to the stability and prosperity of society. The same is true for other institutions. The economy (an institution) supplies a framework for the production and distribution of goods and services. Religion (also an institution) advocates a set of beliefs, which has proved to be one of the greatest sources of stability within societies. Together, these institutions compose society.

The functionalist framework emphasizes the consensus and order that exist in society, focusing on social stability and shared public values. From a functionalist perspective, disorganization in the system, such as deviant behavior and so forth, leads to change because societal components must adjust to achieve stability. This is a key part of functionalist theory—that when one part of society is not working (or it is *dysfunctional,* as they would say), it affects all the other parts and creates social problems. Change may be for better or worse; changes for the worse stem from instability in the social system, such as a breakdown in shared values or a social institution no longer meeting people's needs (Collins 1994; Eitzen and Baca Zinn 2004; Turner 1974).

Functionalism was a dominant theoretical perspective in sociology for many years, and one of its major theorists was **Talcott Parsons** (1902–1979). In Parsons's view, all parts of a social system are interrelated. Different parts of society have different functions, the basic ones of which are: (1) adaptation to the environment (a function served by the economic institution), (2) goal attainment (served by the political institution), (3) integrating members into harmonious units (done by the family), and (4) maintaining basic cultural patterns (done by the church).

Functionalism was further developed by **Robert Merton** (1910–2003). Merton elaborated an important point in functionalist theory: Social practices have consequences for society that are not always immediately apparent, nor are they necessarily the same as the stated purpose of a given practice. Merton suggested that human behavior has both manifest and latent functions. *Manifest functions* are the stated and intended goals of social behavior. *Latent functions* are the unintended consequences of behavior (Merton 1968), which still serve as functions. For example, reforming social welfare programs may have the manifest function of reducing federal budget expenditures, but the policy may also have the latent function of increasing crime (because people have to support themselves through illegitimate means) or increasing homelessness and street violence.

THINKING SOCIOLOGICALLY

What are the *manifest functions* of grades in college? What are the *latent functions*?

Critics of functionalism argue that its emphasis on social stability is inherently conservative and that it understates the roles of power and conflict in society. Critics also disagree with the explanation of inequality offered by functionalism—that it persists because social inequality creates a system for the fair and equitable distribution of societal resources. Functionalists would, for example, argue that it is fair and equitable that the higher social classes earn more money since they—so it is argued—are more important (functional) to society. Critics of functionalism argue that functionalism is too accepting of the status quo. Functionalists would counter this argument by saying that, regardless of the injustices that inequality produces, inequality serves a purpose in society: It provides an incentive system for people to work and promotes solidarity among groups linked by common social standing.

CONFLICT THEORY. **Conflict theory** emphasizes the role of coercion and power, a person's or group's ability to exercise influence and control over others, in producing social order. Whereas functionalism emphasizes cohesion within society, conflict theory emphasizes strife and friction. Derived from the work of Karl Marx, conflict theory pictures society as fragmented into groups that compete for social and economic resources. Social order is maintained not by consensus, but by domination, with power in the hands of those with the greatest political, economic, and social resources. When consensus exists, according to conflict theorists, it is attributable to people being united around common interests, often in opposition to other groups (Dahrendorf 1959; Mills 1956).

According to conflict theory, inequality exists because those in control of a disproportionate share of society's resources actively defend their advantages. The masses are not bound to society by their shared values, but by coercion at the hands of the powerful. In conflict theory, the emphasis is on social control, not consensus and conformity. Groups and individuals advance their own interests, struggling over control of societal resources. Those with the most resources exercise power over others; inequality and power struggles are the result. Conflict theory gives great attention to class, race, and gender in society because these are seen as the grounds of the most pertinent and enduring struggles in society.

Whereas functionalists find some benefit to society in the unequal distribution of resources, conflict theorists see inequality as inherently unfair, persisting only because groups who are economically advantaged use their social position to their own betterment. Their dominance even extends to the point of shaping the beliefs of other members of the society, by controlling public information and having major influence over institutions such as education and religion. From the conflict perspective, power struggles between conflicting groups are the source of social change. Typically, those with the greatest power are able to maintain their advantage at the expense of other groups.

Conflict theory has been criticized for neglecting the importance of shared values and public consensus in society while overemphasizing inequality. Like functionalist theory, conflict theory finds the origins of social behavior in the structure of society, but it differs from functionalism in emphasizing the importance of power.

SYMBOLIC INTERACTION. The third major framework of sociological theory is **symbolic interaction theory.** Instead of thinking of society in terms of abstract institutions, symbolic interactionists consider immediate social interaction to be the place where "society" exists. Because of the human capacity for reflection, people give meaning to their behavior, and this is how they interpret the different behaviors, events, or things that are significant for sociological study. Because of this, symbolic interaction, as its name implies, relies extensively on the symbolic meaning that people develop and rely upon in the process of social interaction. Symbolic interaction theory emphasizes face-to-face interaction and thus is a form of microsociology, whereas functionalism and conflict theory are more macrosociological.

Derived from the work of the Chicago School, symbolic interaction theory analyzes society by addressing the subjective meanings that people impose on objects, events, and behaviors. Subjective meanings are given primacy because, according to symbolic interactionists—and according to Thomas's dictum mentioned earlier—people behave based on what they *believe,* not just on what is objectively true. Thus, society is considered to be socially constructed through human interpretation (Berger and Luckmann 1967; Blumer 1969; Shibutani 1961). Symbolic interactionists see meaning as constantly modified through social interaction. People interpret one another's behavior, and it is these interpretations that form the social bond. These interpretations are called the "definition of the situation."

To illustrate a symbolic interactionist interpretation of human behavior, let us consider a recent study of African American mothers and sickle cell anemia. Sickle cell anemia is the result of a defective gene whose gene product, a curved or "sickle-shaped" red blood cell, causes impaired circulation of the blood. The disease is painful, debilitating, and can result in early death. Many African American mothers who are told they carry the sickle cell trait (making their offspring susceptible to full-blown sickle cell anemia should they be fathered by someone also carrying the sickle cell trait) nevertheless decide to have children. The sociologist Shirley Hill studied this issue and found that the mothers construct two important definitions of the situation. First, the women have acquired a mistrust of the medical system, so they choose to define the warnings they are given about sickle cell anemia as unreliable. Second, many times (though not always) motherhood confers high status among African Americans, and many women are unwilling to forgo motherhood even if they carry the sickle cell gene. This is particularly true among low-income women who have few other routes to elevated status (Hill 1994). In the end, the mothers' definition of the situation is more influential in determining their behavior than the objective presence of a potentially dangerous condition.

Symbolic interactionists see social order as constantly negotiated and created through the interpretations people give to their behavior. To interpret society, symbolic interactionists seek not simply facts but "social constructions," the meanings attached to things, whether those are concrete symbols (like a certain way of dress or a tattoo) or nonverbal behaviors. To a symbolic interactionist, society is highly subjective—existing in the minds of people, even though its effects are very real.

Functionalism, conflict theory, and symbolic interaction theory are by no means the only theoretical frameworks in sociology. For some time, however, they have provided the most prominent general explanations of society. Each has a unique view of the social realm. None is a perfect explanation of society, yet each has something to contribute. Functionalism gives special weight to the order and cohesion that usually characterizes society.

Conflict theory emphasizes the inequalities and power imbalances in society. Symbolic interaction emphasizes the meanings that humans give to their behavior. Together, these frameworks provide a rich, comprehensive perspective on society, individuals within society, and social change (see Table 1.1).

Diverse Theoretical Perspectives

Sociological theory is in transition. In addition to the three frameworks just discussed previously, other theories are also used within sociology. Contemporary sociological theory has been greatly influenced by the development of **feminist theory,** which analyzes the status of women and men in society with the purpose of using that knowledge to better women's lives. Feminist theory has created vital new knowledge about women and transformed what is understood about men. Feminist scholarship in sociology, by focusing on the experiences of women, provides new ways of seeing the world and contributes to a more complete view of society. We examine feminist theory throughout this book in the context of particular topics, such as family (see Chapter 12) and politics (see Chapter 14).

Exchange theory argues that the behavior of individuals is determined by the rewards or punishments they receive as they interact with others (Homans 1961; Homans 1974). Exchange theory has been especially useful in analyzing as social networks. **Rational choice theory** is a relatively recent development used by political scientists and economists as well as sociologists. Rational choice theory posits that the choices human beings make are guided by reason. Society is seen as the sum of these individual decisions and actions (Smelser 1992b).

Many contemporary theorists are increasingly influenced by postmodernism—a strand of thinking now influencing many disciplines. **Postmodernism** is based on the idea that society is not an objective thing. Instead, it is found in the words and images—or *discourses*—that people use to represent behavior and ideas. Postmodernist theory challenges the idea that anything, including society, is objectively real. Postmodernists think that images and texts reveal the underlying ways that people think and act. Postmodernist studies typically involve detailed analyses of images, words, film, music, and other forms of popular culture. In a civilization such as that in the United States, saturated by the imagery of the mass media, postmodernist analysis illuminates much about society. Postmodernist thinkers see contemporary life as involving multiple experiences and interpretations, but they avoid categorizing human experience into broad and abstract concepts such as institutions or society (Rosenau 1992).

Whatever theoretical framework one uses, theory is evaluated in terms of its ability to explain observed so-

TABLE 1.1 Three Sociological Frameworks

	Functionalism	Conflict Theory	Symbolic Interaction
View of Society			
	Objective; stable; cohesive	Objective; hierarchical; fragmented	Subjective; perceived in the minds of people
Basic Questions			
Relationship of Individual to Society	Individuals occupy fixed social roles	Individuals subordinated to society	Individual and society are interdependent
View of Inequality	Inevitable; functional for society	Result of struggle over scarce resources	Inequality demonstrated through meaning of status symbols
Basis of Social Order	Consensus among public on common values	Power; coercion	Collective meaning systems; society created through social interaction
Source of Social Change	Social disorganization and adjustment to achieve equilibrium; change is gradual	Struggle; competition	Ever-changing web of interpersonal relationships and changing meaning of things
Major Criticisms			
	A conservative view of society that underplays power differences among and between groups	Understates the degree of cohesion and stability in society	Has a weak analysis of inequality and tends to ignore material differences between groups in society; overstates the subjective basis of society

cial facts. The sociological imagination is not a single-minded way of looking at the world. It is the ability to observe social behavior and interpret that behavior in light of societal influences.

■ *Doing Sociological Research*

Sociological research is the tool sociologists use to answer questions. There are various methods that sociologists use to do research, all of which involve rigorous observation and careful analysis. The method you use depends on the kind of question you ask.

Suppose you wanted to know if gang violence had increased in recent years. You might turn to official police records and measure the number of arrests made for gang-related crimes. If you wanted to take your question further and ask if gang violence was related to the unemployment rate for youth in inner cities or the rate at which young people drop out of school, you might collect additional **data** (that is, the systematic information used to investigate research questions) and then analyze the relationships among the crime data, unemployment rates, and school dropout rates in given cities. These

questions and their answers would require both a sociological imagination and some research tools, including the ability to gather and interpret data.

Suppose, on the other hand, that you were interested not so much in the extent of gang violence or its relationship to unemployment and education, but instead wanted to know more about the dynamics of gang behavior—what encourages people to join and what gangs mean to the women and men who join them. These research questions would require an approach different from the one described earlier—one that would introduce you to gang members (and perhaps others in the community where they exist). You would need to get more of an insider's view of gang members, as Mártin Sánchez Jankowski (1991) did when he studied gangs in several major U.S. cities. Being careful not to put yourself in danger, you might hang out with gangs for a time, interviewing members and observing their behavior.

These different approaches to studying gangs reflect various research methods sociologists use to answer the questions they ask. Some questions require more direct involvement with those whom one is studying and involve a qualitative research approach. Other methods involve more quantitative skills. Either way, the chosen research method must be appropriate to the sociological question being asked. In the "Doing Sociological Research" boxes

The research process involves several operations that can be performed on the computer, such as entering data in numerical form and writing the research report.

later); others use more open-ended methods. Science is *empirical,* meaning it is based on careful and systematic observation, not just on conjecture. Although some sociological studies are highly quantitative and statistically sophisticated, others are qualitatively based—that is, based on more interpretive observations, not statistical analysis. Both quantitative and qualitative studies are empirical. Sociological studies may be based on surveys, observations, and many other forms of analysis, but they always depend on an empirical underpinning.

Science generally relies on prediction and explanation. When we study social behavior, can we ever predict what humans will think or say or do under specified conditions, or are human beings too unique to conform to scientific predictability? The answer to both questions is, roughly, yes. Human social, behavioral, and attitudinal characteristics can be measured and, within a margin of error, can be predicted. Humans are not, however, mechanical beings, and there is a special quality to the predictions we make about people.

Some sociological studies analyze, explain, and predict human social behavior in terms of probabilities. A **probability** is the likelihood that a specific behavior or event will occur. We cannot predict that a specific individual will die within the next five years, yet we can predict how *likely* it is that a person will die in the next five years knowing only his or her age, and we can predict how many people in a large population will die in the next five years to within a rather fine margin of error. Some sociological conclusions are stated in terms of probability. For example, if you are a divorced woman with children, there is a 39 percent chance that you live in poverty (Kurz 1995).

The Research Process

When sociologists do research, they engage in a process of discovery. Like scientists who do research in a laboratory, sociologists organize their research questions and procedures systematically. Their laboratory is the social world. Through research, they organize their observations and interpret them.

DEVELOPING A RESEARCH QUESTION. Sociological research is an organized practice that can be described in a series of steps (see Figure 1.2). The first step in sociological research is to develop a research question. One source of questions is past research. For any number of reasons, the sociologist might disagree with a research finding and decide to carry out further research or develop a detailed criticism of previous research. The work of someone else may suggest an idea, seem incomplete, or appear to be seriously in error. The best research frequently inspires other sociologists to study a question further.

in this book, we explore different research projects that sociologists have done, showing what question they started with, how they did their research, and what they found.

Research is an engaging and demanding process. It requires skill, careful observation, and the ability to think logically about the things that spark your sociological curiosity. But sociologists also ask many different kinds of questions, and their techniques for answering questions are limited only by the horizon of the sociological imagination.

Sociology and the Scientific Method

Sociological research derives from the scientific method, originally defined and elaborated by the British philosopher Sir Francis Bacon (1561–1626). The **scientific method** involves several steps in a research process, including observation, hypothesis testing, analysis of data, and generalization. The crux of the scientific method is observation and the testing of theory. For more than a hundred years, a lively debate has been ongoing about whether sociology is a "true" science. Sociology aspires to be both scientific and humanistic, and sociological research differs in how strictly it adheres to the scientific method. Some sociologists test hypotheses (discussed

© Deborah Davis/PhotoEdit

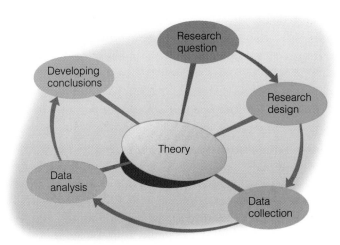

FIGURE 1.2 The Research Process

Developing a sociological research question typically involves reviewing the existing literature on the subject, such as past studies and research reports. Digital technology has vastly simplified the task of reviewing the literature. Researchers who once had to burrow through paper indexes and card catalogs to find material relevant to their studies can now scan much larger swaths of literature in far less time, using online databases. The catalogs of most major libraries in the world are accessible on the Internet, as are specialized indexes, discussion groups, and other research tools developed to assist sociological researchers. Increasingly, many journals that report new sociological research are now available online and can often be electronically read in full text, by means of the JSTOR (journal storage) procedure, a computer routine that allows such viewing on-screen. Although some books are now available online, most research is still done with paper books.

Sometimes a review of past research may prompt you to wonder if the same result would be found again if the study were repeated, perhaps examining a different group. Research that is repeated exactly, but on a different group of people or in a different time or place, is called a **replication study.** As an example, suppose earlier research found that women managers have fewer opportunities for promotion than men. You might want to know if this still holds several years later. You would then replicate the original study, probably using a different group of women and men managers, but asking the same questions that were asked earlier. A replication study can tell you what changes have occurred since the original study was conducted and may also refine the results of the earlier work. Research findings should be reproducible; if research is sound, other researchers who repeat a study should get the same results, unless, of course, change has occurred in the interim.

CREATING A RESEARCH DESIGN. A research design is the overall logic and strategy underlying a research project. Sociologists engaged in research may distribute questionnaires, interview people, or make direct observations in a social setting or laboratory. They might analyze cultural artifacts, such as magazines, newspapers, television shows, or other media. Some do research using historical records. Others base their work on the analysis of social policy. All these are forms of sociological observation. Research design consists of choosing the observational technique best suited to a particular research question.

THINKING SOCIOLOGICALLY

If you wanted to conduct research that would examine the relationship between student alcohol use and family background, what *measures* would you use to get at these two variables: alcohol use and family background? How might you *design* your study?

Suppose you wanted to study the career goals of student athletes. In reviewing past studies, perhaps you found research that discussed how athletics is related to academic achievement (Schacht 1996). You may also have read an article in your student newspaper reporting that the rate of graduation for women college athletes is much higher than the rate for men athletes and wondered if women athletes are better students than men athletes. In other words, are athletic participation, academic achievement, and gender interrelated and, if so, how?

Your research design lays out a plan for investigating these questions. Which athletes will you focus on? How will you study them? To begin, you will need to get sound data on the graduation rates of the groups you are studying to verify that your assumption of better graduation rates among women athletes is actually true. Perhaps, you think, the differences between men and women are not so great when the men and women play the same sports, or perhaps the differences depend on other factors, such as how the students were recruited, what kind of financial support they get, or whether coaches encourage academic success. To observe the influence of coaches you might observe interactions between coaches and student athletes, recording what coaches say about class work. As you proceed, you would probably refine your research design, and even your research question. Do coaches encourage different traits in men and women athletes? To answer this question, you have to build into your research design a comparison of coaches interacting with men and with women. Perhaps you even want to compare female and male coaches and how they interact with women and men. *The details of your research design flow from the specific questions you ask.*

The research design often involves deciding whether the research will, for the most part, be qualitative or quantitative, or perhaps some combination of both. *Quantitative research* is research that uses numerical analysis. *Qualitative research* is somewhat less structured than quantitative research, yet still focused on a central research question. Qualitative research allows for more interpretation and nuance in what people say and do and thus can provide a very in-depth look at a particular social behavior. Both forms of research are useful, and both are used extensively in sociology. The form used depends in large part on what research question is being asked. Thus, quantitative studies provide data from which one can calculate average incomes, the percentage employed, marriage statistics, and so forth. Thus, if you wanted to study the measurable factors that produce differences in group earnings, you would likely use a quantitative approach. But, if you were more interested in how employees perceive their work environment, you would likely use a more qualitative research design. Both approaches yield data, but qualitative data usually not reduced to numbers (Babbie 2004).

Some research designs involve the testing of hypotheses. A **hypothesis** (pronounced "hy-POTH-i-sis") is a prediction, or a hunch, a tentative assumption that one intends to test. If you have a research design that calls for the investigation of a very specific hunch, you might formulate a hypothesis. Hypotheses are often formulated as if–then statements. For example,

> **hypothesis:** *If a person's parents are racially prejudiced, that person will, on average, be more prejudiced than a person whose parents are free of prejudice.*

This is merely a hypothesis or expectation, not a demonstration of fact. Having phrased a hypothesis, the sociologist must then determine if it is true or false. To test the preceding example, one might take a large sample of people and determine their prejudice level by interviews or some other mechanism. One would then determine the prejudice level of their parents. According to the hypothesis, one would expect to find a preponderance of prejudiced children among prejudiced parents and a preponderance of nonprejudiced children among nonprejudiced parents. If such a preponderance or association is found, the hypothesis is supported. If it is not found, then the hypothesis would be rejected.

Not all sociological research follows the model of hypothesis testing. What is called *exploratory research* is more broad and open-ended, as we will see. Any research design includes a plan for how data will be gathered. (Note that "data" is the plural form; one says, "data are used . . . ," not "data is used. . . .") Quantitative data are numeric and can be analyzed using statistical techniques. Qualitative data are not numeric, although they can be logically interpreted and analyzed. The point is, data can be qualitative or quantitative; either way, they are still data. Sociol-

FIGURE 1.3 The Analysis of Variables
Sociological research seeks to find out whether some independent variable (X) affects an intervening variable (Z), which in turn affects a dependent variable (Y).

ogists often try to convert their observations into a quantitative form (see "Doing Sociological Research: Statistics in Sociology"). Quantifying the responses to questionnaires or interviews, for example, helps categorize the data, makes it possible to analyze qualitative responses statistically, and removes an element of subjectivity from the interpretation of research results. Research data are the heart of sociological research; the research design specifies what kinds of data an investigator plans to use.

Sociologists frequently design research to test the influence of one variable on another. **A variable** can have more than one value or score. A variable can be relatively straightforward, such as age or income, or a variable may be more abstract, such as social class or degree of prejudice. In much sociological research, variables are analyzed to understand how they influence each other. With proper measurement techniques and a good research design, the relationships between different variables can be discerned.

An **independent variable** is the one that the researcher wants to test as the presumed cause of something else. The **dependent variable** is the one on which there is a presumed effect. That is, if X is the independent variable, then X leads to Y, the dependent variable. In the previous example of the hypothesis, the amount of prejudice of the parent is the independent variable, and the amount of prejudice of the child (offspring) is the dependent variable. In some sociological research, *intervening variables* are also studied: variables that fall between the independent and dependent variables (see Figure 1.3). Sociological variables are often sensitive to a variety of influences, and trying to control for the influence of factors other than the one being studied is a challenge to the creativity of the researcher.

Variables are sometimes used to show more abstract concepts that cannot be directly measured, such as the concept of social class. In such cases the variables are **indicators**—something that points to or reflects an abstract concept. An example is shown in Map 1.2 on the United Nations' human development index. Here, the human development index is an *indicator* used to show different levels of well-being around the world. The index involves several variables, including life expectancy and educational attainment, combined to show levels of well-being.

The **validity** of a measurement is the degree to which it accurately measures or reflects a concept. To en-

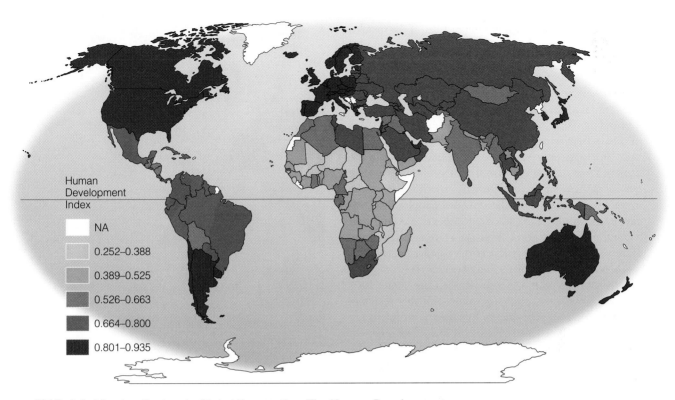

MAP 1.2 Viewing Society in Global Perspective: The Human Development Index

The human development index uses several measures, including life expectancy, educational attainment, and standard of living. **Are these reasonable indicators of well-being? What else might you use?**

DATA: United Nations 2000. *Human Development Report 2000.* **www.undp.org**

sure the validity of their findings, researchers usually use more than one measure for a particular concept. If two or more chosen measures of a concept give similar results, it is likely that the measurements are giving an accurate—that is, valid—depiction of the concept.

Sociologists also must be concerned with the **reliability** of their research results. A measurement is reliable if repeating the measurement gives the same result. If a person is given a test daily, and every day the test gives different results, then the reliability of the test is poor. One way to ensure that sociological measurements are reliable is to use measures that have proved sound in past studies. Another technique is to have a variety of people gather the data, to make certain the results are not skewed by the tester's appearance, personality, and so forth. The researcher must be sensitive to all factors that affect the reliability of a study.

GATHERING DATA. After research design comes data collection. During this stage, the researcher interviews people, observes behaviors, or collects facts that throw light on the research question. When sociologists gather original material, the product is known as *primary data.* Examples include the answers to questionnaires or notes made while ob-

serving group behavior. Sociologists often rely on *secondary data,* namely data that have already been gathered and organized by some other party. A large collection of data is known as a *data set* or *database* and can include national opinion polls, census data, national crime statistics, or data from an earlier study made available by the original researcher. Secondary data may also come from official sources, such as university records, city or county records, national health statistics, or historical records. Historical archives are a source of secondary data that can give insight into social change or give historical perspective on contemporary issues.

When gathering data, often the groups that sociologists want to study are so large or so dispersed that research on the whole group is impossible. To construct a picture of the entire group, they take data from a subset of the group and extrapolate to get a picture of the whole. A **sample** is any subset of a population. A **population** is a relatively large collection of people (or other units) that a researcher studies and about which generalizations are made. Suppose a sociologist wants to study the students at your school. All the students together constitute the population being studied. A survey could be done that reached every student, but conducting a detailed interview with every student would be highly impractical. If the sociologist wants the sort of information that can be gathered only during a personal interview, she would study only a portion, or sample, of all the students at your school.

How is it possible to draw accurate conclusions about a population by studying only part of it? The secret lies in making sure that the sample is representative of the population as a whole. The sample should have the same mix of people as the larger population and in the same proportions. If the sample is representative, then the researcher can generalize what she finds from the sample to the entire population. For example, if she interviews a sample of one hundred students and finds that 10 percent of them are in favor of a tuition increase, and if the sample is representative of the population, then she can conclude that about 10 percent of *all* the students at your school are in favor of a tuition increase. Note that a sample of five or six students would probably result in generalizations of poor quality because the sample is not large enough to be representative. A *biased* (nonrepresentative) sample can lead to grossly inaccurate conclusions.

The best way to ensure a representative sample is to make certain that the sample population is selected randomly. A scientific **random sample** gives everyone in the population an equal chance of being selected. Quite often, striking and controversial research findings prove to be distorted by inadequate sampling. The man-on-the-street survey, much favored by radio and TV news reports, is the least scientific type of sample, and the least representative.

ANALYZING THE DATA. After the data have been collected, whether primary or secondary data, they must be analyzed. **Data analysis** is the process by which sociologists organize collected data to discover the patterns and uniformities that the data reveal. The analysis may be statistical or qualitative. Survey data require statistical treatment, whereas a study based on an analysis of rap music lyrics, for example, would likely have a large qualitative component. When the data analysis is completed, conclusions and generalizations can be made.

Data analysis is labor intensive, but it is also an exciting phase of research. Here is where research discoveries are made. Computers have greatly facilitated the process of analyzing data. Computational operations that were once done by hand, perhaps over weeks, can now be performed by computer in seconds. Especially valuable is the ability to perform complex operations on large data sets, those containing many thousands or even millions of data points. Government data are now instantly accessible on the Internet, and increasingly, researchers are creating public electronic archives for their own data and that of colleagues working in similar areas.

Taking the census involves people completing what is called a survey. Here, a woman completes the Census Bureau form.

REACHING CONCLUSIONS AND REPORTING RESULTS. The final stage in research is developing conclusions, relating findings to sociological theory and past research, and reporting the findings.

An important question researchers will ask at this stage is whether their findings can be generalized. **Generalization** is the ability to draw conclusions from specific data and be able to apply them to a broader population. One asks, do my results apply only to those people who were studied, or do they also apply to the world beyond? Assuming that the results have wide application, one can then ask if the findings refine or refute existing theories and whether the research has direct application to social issues. Using the earlier example of the relationship between parent and offspring prejudice, if you found that racially prejudiced people did tend to have racially prejudiced parents (thus supporting your hypothesis), then you might report these results in a paper or research report. You might also ask, what kinds of programs for reducing prejudice do the results of your study suggest?

▪ *The Tools of Sociological Research*

There are several tools or techniques sociologists use to gather data. Among the most widely used are survey research, participant observation, controlled experiments, content analysis, historical research, and evaluation research.

The Survey: Polls, Questionnaires, and Interviews

Whether in the form of a questionnaire, interview, or telephone poll, surveys are among the most commonly used tools of sociological research. Typically, a survey questionnaire will solicit data about the respondent, such as income, occupation, educational level, age, race, and gender, coupled to questions that throw light on a particular research subject. In a *closed-ended questionnaire,* people must reply from a list of possible answers, such as a multiple-choice test; *open-ended questionnaires* allow the respondents to elaborate on their answer.

Questionnaires are typically distributed to large groups of people. The *return rate* is the percentage of questionnaires returned out of all those distributed. A low return rate introduces possible bias because the small number of responses may not be representative of the whole group.

Like questionnaires, interviews provide a structured way to ask people questions. They may be conducted face-to-face, by phone, even by electronic mail. Interview questions may be open-ended or closed-ended, though the open-ended form is particularly accommodating if respondents wish to elaborate.

As a research tool, surveys make it possible to ask specific questions about a large number of topics and then to perform sophisticated analyses to find patterns and relationships among variables. The disadvantages of surveys arise from their rigidity. Responses may not accurately capture the opinions of the respondent or fail to capture nuances in people's behavior and attitudes. Also, what people say and what they do are not always the same. Respondents may disguise their true opinion if it is not the most socially acceptable answer. Survey researchers must be persistent to get answers that are truthful, one reason for allowing respondents to be anonymous.

Participant Observation

A unique and interesting way for sociologists to collect data and study society is to actually become part of the group they are studying. This is the method of **participant observation.** Two roles are played at the same time: subjective participant and objective observer. Usually, the group is aware that the sociologist is studying them, but not always. The group being studied might be a youth gang, a religious cult, or people hanging out in the corner bar. Participant observation is sometimes called *field research,* a term from the field of anthropology.

Participant observation combines subjective knowledge gained through personal involvement and objective knowledge acquired by disciplined recording of what one

The men in this bar, much like Jelly's Bar on Chicago's South Side as studied by sociologist Elijah Anderson, reveal status differences among themselves such as "regulars" versus "winos."

has seen. The subjective component supplies a dimension of information that is lacking in survey data.

The power of participant observation studies has been dramatically shown in a study by a Black woman sociologist, Judith Rollins (1985), who examined the relationships between Black domestic workers and their White employers. Rollins posed as a maid and hired herself out to employers in the Boston, Massachusetts, area. She discovered that Black female domestic workers were treated by their employers as virtually invisible and as inferior. White employers, women as well as men, often openly discussed the domestics with other Whites as if the Black woman herself were not even present. One woman employer turned down the heat in the house when she left even though Rollins was expected to stay there. Through participant observation, Rollins was able to observe directly how social class status combines with race and gender to shape the world of Black domestic workers.

DEBUNKING
Society's Myths

Myth: People who are just hanging out together and relaxing don't care much about social differences between them.

Sociological research: Even casual groups have organized social hierarchies. That is, they make distinctions within the group that give some people higher status than others (Anderson 1976, 1990; Whyte 1943).

There are a few built-in weaknesses to participant observation as a research technique. We already mentioned that it is very time-consuming. Participant observers have to cull data from vast amounts of notes. Such studies usually focus on fairly small groups, posing problems of generalization. Observers may also lose their objectivity by

Developing a Critical Eye:

On any given day, if you watch the news, read a newspaper, or search the Web, you are likely to learn about various new research studies purporting some new finding. How do you know if the research results reported in the media are accurate?

Most people are not likely to check the details of the study or have the research skills to verify the study's claims. But, one benefit of learning the basic concepts and tools of sociological research is to be able to critically assess the research frequently reported in the media. The following questions will help:

1. What are the major variables in the study? Are the researchers claiming a causal connection between two or more variables? For example, recent media reports claim that researchers have found a causal connection between teen sex and parental smoking. The press reported that one way parents can reduce the chances of their children becoming sexually active at an early age is to quit smoking (O'Neil 2002). The researcher who conducted this study actually claimed there was no direct link between parental smoking and teen sex, although she did find a correlation between parents' risky behaviors—smoking, heavy drinking, and not using seat belts—and children's sexual activity. She argued that parents who engage in unsafe activities provide a model for their children's own risky behavior (Wilder and Watt 2002).

Correlation is not cause. Seeing parental behavior as a model for what children do is hardly the same thing as

seeing parents' smoking as the cause of early sexual activity!

2. How have researchers defined the major topics of their study? How were the variables in the study measured? For example, if someone claims that 10 percent of all people are gay, how is "being gay" defined? Does it mean having had one such experience over one's entire lifetime or does it mean actually having a gay identity? The difference matters because one definition will likely inflate the number reported. Sometimes you must look up the original study to learn how things are defined or how they are measured, yet if you read press reports carefully, you can often see this without further work. And, with the widespread availability of electronic information, you can often find the full text of original articles online. Ask yourself if the same conclusions would be reached had the researchers used different definitions and measurements.

3. What is the sample of people on which the research was based? Is it scientifically generated? Is it a random sample or is it biased? You might have to go to the original source of the study to learn this, but often the sample will be reported in the press (even if in nonscientific language). For example, a study widely reported in the media in 2002 had headlines exclaiming: "Study Links Working Mothers to Slower Learning" (Lewin 2002). But, if you read even the news report closely, you will learn that this study included only white, non-Hispanic families. Black and Hispanic children were dropped from some of the published results because there were too few cases in the sample to make meaningful statistical comparisons (Brooks-Gunn,

Han, and Waldfogel 2002). A later study by the same research team found that there were no significant effects of mother's employment on children's intellectual development among African American or Hispanic children (Waldfogel, Han, and Brooks-Gunn 2002). The point is not that the study is invalid, but that its results have more limited implications than the headlines suggest.

4. Is there false generalization in the media report? Often a study has more limited claims in the scientific version than what is reported in the media. Using the example just given about the connection between maternal employment and children's learning, it would be a big mistake to generalize from the study's results to all children and families. Remember that some groups were not included. Even within the study, the researchers found less effect of mother's employment in female-headed households than among married couples. You cannot generalize the findings reported in the media to all families.

5. If a study uses numerical data to support its claims, what do the numbers mean and how were they generated? Numbers can also be misleading. How were the numbers or statistics in the reports you see generated? When people do statistical research, they make choices about how to record and analyze

Research and the Media

data. These choices may be poorly decided, depending on the skill of the researcher. Are the numbers reported reasonable? Sometimes people can use statistics to exaggerate—or downplay—a given issue. Numerical information is no more accurate than the procedures used to produce the numbers (Best 2001).

6. Can the study be replicated? Unless there is full disclosure of the research methodology (that is, how the study was conducted), this will not be possible. But, you can ask yourself how the study was con-

ducted, whether the procedures used were reasonable and logical and whether the researchers made good decisions in constructing their research question and research design. Although you will likely have to read the original study to know this, you can always ask yourself how you would proceed to investigate the conclusions reached in a given research report.

7. Who sponsored the study and do they have a vested interest in the study's results? Find out if a group or organization with a particular interest in the outcome sponsors the research. If so, did they use objective methods of research or did they bias the research results by developing the study in a way that would produce a desired outcome? Research sponsored by interested parties does not necessarily negate research findings, but it can raise questions about the researchers' objectivity and the standards of inquiry they used. For example, would you give as much validity to a

study of environmental pollution that was funded and secretly conducted by a chemical company as compared with a study on the same topic conducted by independent scientists who openly report their research methods and results?

8. Who benefits from the study's conclusions? Although this question does not necessarily challenge the study's findings, it can help you think about whom the findings are likely to help. This, in turn, can help you think through some of the assumptions made by the researcher and the logic of what the researchers have concluded.

9. What assumptions did the researchers have to make to ask the question they did? For example, if you started from the assumption that poverty is not the individual's fault, but is the result of how society is structured, would you study the values of the poor or perhaps the values of policy makers? Especially when research studies explore matters where social values influence people's opinions, it is important to identify the assumptions made by certain questions.

10. What are the implications of the study's claims? Thinking through the policy implications of a given result can often help you see things in a new light, particularly given how the media tend to sensationalize much of what is reported. Consider the study of maternal employment and children's intellectual development examined in Question 3. If you take the media headlines at face value, you might leap to the conclusion that working mothers hurt their children's intellectual develop-

ment, and you might then think it would be best if mothers quit their jobs and stayed at home. But is this a reasonable implication of this study? Does the study not have just as many implications for day-care policies as it does for encouraging stay-at-home mothers? Especially when reported research studies involve politically charged topics (such as issues of "family values"), it is important to ask questions that explore various implications of social policies.

Do these questions mean you should never believe anything you hear in the media? Of course not. Thinking critically about research does not mean being negative or cynical about everything you hear or read. Being overly cynical will make you just as ignorant as if you never read or thought about anything at all. The point is not to reject all media claims as out of hand, but instead to be able to evaluate good versus bad research. All research has limitations. Knowing the limitations of a given study can teach you just as much about the subject of study as do the particular conclusions that are reached. The point is to know how to interpret what you read and to do so with a critical eye. Just asking the questions discussed here will make you a better informed citizen. Learning the basic tools of research, even if you never conduct research yourself or pursue a career where you would use such skills, can make you a better informed citizen and prevent you from being duped by claims that are neither scientifically nor sociologically valid.

becoming too much a part of what they study. These limitations aside, participant observation has been the source of some of the most arresting and valuable studies in sociology.

Controlled Experiments

Controlled experiments are highly focused ways of collecting data and are especially useful for determining a pattern of cause and effect. To conduct a controlled experiment, two groups are created, an *experimental group,* which is exposed to the factor one is examining, and the *control group,* which is not. In a controlled experiment, external influences are either eliminated or equalized, that is, held constant. This is necessary in order to establish cause and effect.

Suppose you wanted to study whether violent television programming causes aggressive behavior in children. You could conduct a controlled experiment to investigate this question. The behavior of children would be the dependent variable; the independent variable is exposure to violent programming. To investigate your question, you would expose an experimental group of children (under monitored conditions) to a movie containing lots of violence (martial arts, for example, or gunfighting). The control group would watch a movie that is free of violence. Aggressiveness in the children would be measured twice: a pretest measurement made before the movies are shown, and a posttest measurement made afterward. You would take pre- and post-test measures on both the control and the experimental groups. Studies of this sort actually find that the children who watched the violent movie are indeed more violent and aggressive afterward than those who watched a movie containing no violence (Worchel et al. 2000; Goldstein 1994).

Among its advantages, a controlled experiment can establish causation, and it can zero in on a single independent variable. On the downside, controlled experiments can be artificial. They are for the most part done in a contrived laboratory setting (unless it is a field experiment), and they tend to eliminate many real-life effects. Analysis of controlled experiments includes making judgments about how much the artificial setting has affected the results.

Content Analysis

Researchers can learn a vast amount about a society by analyzing cultural artifacts such as newspapers, magazines, TV programs, or popular music. **Content analysis** is a way of measuring by the cultural artifacts of what people write, say, see, and hear. The researcher studies not people but the communications the people produce as a way of creating a picture of their society.

Content analysis is frequently used to measure cultural change and to study different aspects of culture (La-

mont 1992). Sociologists also use content analysis as an indirect way to determine how social groups are perceived—they might examine, for example, how Asian Americans are depicted in television dramas or how women are depicted in advertisements.

Content analysis has the advantage of being *unobtrusive.* The research has no effect on the person being studied, because the cultural artifact has already been produced. Content analysis is limited in what it can study, however, because it is based only on mass communication—either visual, oral, or written. It cannot tell us what people really think about these images or whether they affect people's behavior. Other methods of research, such as interviewing or participant observation, would be used to answer these questions.

Historical Research

Historical research examines sociological themes over time. It is commonly done in historical archives, such as official records, church records, town archives, private diaries, or oral histories. The sources of this sort of material are critical to its quality and applicability. Oral histories have been especially illuminating, most dramatically in revealing the unknown histories of groups that have been ignored or misrepresented in other historical accounts. For example, when developing an account of the spirituality of Native Americans, one would be misguided to rely solely on the records left by Christian missionaries or U.S. Army officials. These records would give a useful picture of how Whites perceived Native American religion, but they would be a very poor source for discovering how Native Americans understood their own spirituality. In a similar vein, the writings of a slave owner can deliver fascinating insights into slavery, but a slave owner's diary will certainly present a different picture of slavery as a social institution than will the written or oral histories of former slaves themselves.

Handled properly, comparative and historical research is rich with the ability to capture long-term social changes and is the perfect tool for sociologists who want to ground their studies in historical or comparative perspectives.

Evaluation Research

Evaluation research assesses the effect of policies and programs on people in society. If the research is intended to produce policy recommendations, then it is called *policy research.*

Suppose you want to know if an educational program is actually improving student performance. You could design a study that measured the academic performance of two groups of students, one that participates in the program and one that does not. If the academic performance

Statistics in Sociology

Certain basic statistical concepts are basic to sociological research. Although not all sociologists do quantitative research, basic statistics are important to interpreting sociological studies.

A **percentage** is the same as parts per hundred. To say that 22 percent of U.S. children are poor tells you that for every one hundred children randomly selected from the whole population, approximately twenty-two will be poor. A **rate** is the same as parts per some number, such as per 10,000 or 100,000. The homicide rate in 2000 was 5.5, meaning that for every 100,000 in the population, approximately 5.5 were murdered (Federal Bureau of Investigation 2000). A rate is meaningless without knowing the numeric base on which it is based—it is always the number per some other number.

A **mean** is the same as an average. Adding a list of fifteen numbers and dividing by 15 gives the mean. The median is often confused with the mean but is actually quite different. The **median** is the midpoint in a series of values arranged in numeric order. In a list of fifteen numbers arrayed in numeric order, the eighth number (the middle number) is the median. In some cases, the median is a better measure than the mean because the mean can be skewed by extremes at either end. Another often-used measure is the **mode,** which is simply the value (or score) that appears most frequently in a set of data.

Let's illustrate the difference between mean and median using national income distribution as an example. Suppose that you have a group of ten people. Two make $10,000 per year, seven make $40,000 per year, and one makes $1 million per year. If you calculate the mean, it comes to $130,000. The median, on the other hand, is $40,000—a figure that more accurately suggests the income profile of the group. That single million-a-year earner dramatically distorts, or skews, the picture of the group's income. If we want information about how the group in general lives, we are wiser to use the median income figure as a rough guide, not the mean. Note also that in this example the mode is the same as the median: $40,000.

Sociologists frequently choose to relate different variables to each other. **Correlation** is a widely used technique for analyzing the patterns of association, or correlation, between pairs of variables such as income and education. We might begin with a questionnaire that asked for annual earnings (Y) and level of education (X). Correlation analysis delivers two dimensions of information: It tells us the "direction" of the relationship between X and Y and the strength of that relationship. The direction of a relationship is positive (that is, a positive correlation exists) if X is low when Y is low *and* if X is high when Y is high. But there is also a correlation if Y is low when X is high (or vice versa); this is a negative, or inverse, correlation. The strength of a correlation is simply how closely or tightly the variables are associated, regardless of the direction of correlation.

A correlation does not necessarily imply cause and effect. A correlation is simply an association, one whose cause must be explained by means other than simple correlation analysis. A *spurious correlation* exists when there is no meaningful causal connection between apparently associated effects.

Statistical information is notoriously easy to misinterpret, willfully or accidentally. Examples of some statistical mistakes include the following:

- **Citing a correlation as a cause.** A correlation reveals an association between things, nothing more. Correlations do not necessarily indicate that one thing causes the other.

- **Overgeneralizing.** Statistical findings are limited by the extent to which the sample group actually reflects or represents the population from which the sample was obtained. Generalizing beyond the population is a misuse of statistics. Studying only men, and then generalizing conclusions to both men and women, would be an example of overgeneralizing.

- **Building in bias.** In a famous advertising campaign, public taste tests were offered between two soft drinks. A wily journalist verified that in at least one site, the brand sold by the sponsor of the test was a few degrees colder than its competitor when it was given to testers, which biased the results. Bias can also be built into studies by careless wording on questionnaires.

- **Faking data.** Perhaps one of the worse misuses of statistics is actually making up, or faking, data. A famous instance of this occurred in a study of separated identical twins (Burt 1966). The researcher wished to show that despite their separation, the twins remained similar in certain traits such as measured intelligence (IQ), thus suggesting that their (identical) genes caused their striking similarity in intelligence. It was later shown that the data were fabricated (Kamin 1974; Hearnshaw 1979; Taylor 1980, 2001; Mackintosh 1995).

- **Using data selectively.** Sometimes a survey includes many questions, but the researcher reports on only a few of the answers. Doing so makes it quite easy to misstate the findings. Researchers often do not report findings that show no association between variables, but these can be just as telling as associations that do exist. For example, researchers on gender differences typically report the differences they find between men and women, but seldom publish their findings when the results for men and women are identical. This tends to exaggerate the differences between women and men and falsely confirms certain social stereotypes about gender differences.

TABLE 1.2 A Comparison of Six Research Techniques

Technique (Tool)	Advantages	Disadvantages
The survey (polls, questionnaires, interviews)	Permits the study of a large number of variables; results can be generalized to a larger population if sampling is accurate.	Difficult to focus in great depth on a few variables; difficult to measure subtle nuances in people's attitudes.
Participant observation	Studies actual behavior in its home setting; affords great depth of inquiry.	Is very time-consuming; it is difficult to generalize beyond the research setting.
Controlled experiment	Focuses on only two to three variables; able to study cause and effect.	Difficult or impossible to measure large number of variables; may have an artificial quality.
Content analysis	A way of measuring culture; is "unobtrusive."	Limited by studying only cultural products or artifacts (music, TV programs, stories, other), rather than people's actual attitudes.
Historical research	Saves time and expense in data collection; takes into account differences over time.	Data often reflect biases of the original researcher and reflect cultural norms that were in effect when the data were collected.
Evaluation research	Evaluates the actual outcomes of a program or strategy; often has direct policy application.	Limited in the number of variables that can be measured; maintaining objectivity is problematic if research is done or commissioned by administrators of the program being evaluated.

of students in the program is better, and if the groups are alike in other ways (they are often matched to accomplish this), you would conclude that the program was effective. If you use this research to recommend social policy, you would be doing policy research.

Somewhat closely allied with evaluation research is *market research.* In market research, the aim is to evaluate the sales potential of some product or service. For example, a company may want to estimate how many people in a population are likely to purchase a new toothpaste the company produces. The company might then hire a researcher who would survey a sample of people to find out how they rate various types of toothpaste (see Table 1.2).

■ *Research Ethics: Is Sociology Value-Free?*

The topics dealt with by sociology are often controversial. People have strong opinions about social questions, and, in some cases, the settings for sociological work are highly politicized. Imagine spending time in an urban precinct house to do research on police brutality, or doing research on acquired immune deficiency syndrome (AIDS) and sex education in a conservative public school system. Under these conditions, can sociology be scientifically objective? How do researchers balance their own political and moral commitments against the need to be objective and open-minded? Sociological knowledge has an intimate connection to political values and social views. Often, the very purpose of sociological research is

to gather data as a step in creating social policy. Can sociology be value-free? Should it be?

This is an important question without a simple answer. Most sociologists do not claim to be value-free, but they do try to produce objective research. It must be acknowledged that researchers make choices throughout their research that can influence their results. The problems sociologists choose to study, the people they decide to observe, the research design they select, and the outlets through which they choose to disseminate their results can all be influenced by the values of the researcher; thus, it is appropriate to ask, do politics poison research?

THINKING SOCIOLOGICALLY

Based on your knowledge of Judith Rollins's research, would you say it is *value-free*? Drawing on the concept of *verstehen* from Max Weber, would you say a person has to be Black to understand Rollins's observations of Black domestic workers and their employers?

Sociological research often raises ethical questions. In fact, ethical considerations of one sort or another exist with any type of research. In a survey, the person being questioned is often not told the purpose of the survey or who is funding the study. Is it ethical to conceal this type of information? In controlled experiments, deception is often employed: Many experiments depend on respondents giving natural, spontaneous responses to staged situations. Researchers often reveal the true purpose of an experiment only after it is completed. The deception is therefore temporary. Does that lessen the potential ethical violation?

Participant observation research, if done without the knowledge of the people being studied, is a form of deception. When Judith Rollins did her research on Black women domestic workers, she posed as a maid and did not tell her employers that she was a Ph.D. student writing her dissertation. Had she done so, her study would have been ruined, because surely the subjects would have acted differently toward her. Was this unethical? Most sociologists would say no, as long as no harm came to her subjects. The definition of harm, however, can be debated. The professional code of ethics is clear, though, that if a research subject is at risk of physical, mental, or legal harm, then the subject must be informed of the rights and responsibilities of both researcher and subject. Sociologists also take measures not to identify their subjects through the use of pseudonyms or without the use of names at all.

This chapter has covered the basics of doing sociological research and introduced you to the general contours of a sociological perspective. The remaining chapters of the book explore different dimensions of human society and the different conclusions that sociologists have drawn from the study of society. As you read, you should begin to see the fascination with which sociologists view the social world and how social change and social stability influence the people who constitute society.

■ *Chapter Summary*

■ **What is sociology?**

Sociology is the study of human behavior in society. The *sociological imagination* is the ability to see societal patterns that influence individuals. Sociology is an *empirical* discipline, relying on careful observations as the basis for its knowledge.

■ **What is debunking?**

Debunking in sociology refers to the ability to look behind taken-for-granted things, looking instead to the origins of social behavior.

■ **Why is diversity central to the study of sociology?**

One of the central insights of sociology is its analysis of social diversity and inequality. Understanding *diversity* is critical to sociology because it is necessary to analyze *social institutions* and because diversity shapes most of our social and cultural institutions.

■ **When and how did sociology emerge as a field of study?**

Sociology emerged in western Europe during the *Enlightenment* and was influenced by the values of critical reason, humanitarianism, and positivism. *Auguste Comte,* one of the earliest sociologists, emphasized sociology as a positivist discipline. *Alexis de Tocqueville* and *Harriet Martineau* developed early and insightful analyses of American culture.

■ **What are some of the basic insights of classical sociological theory?**

Emile Durkheim is credited with conceptualizing society as a social system and with identifying *social facts* as patterns of behavior that are external to the individual. *Karl Marx* showed how capitalism shaped the development of society. *Max Weber* sought to explain society through cultural, political, and economic factors.

■ **What are the major theoretical frameworks in sociology?**

Functionalism emphasizes the stability and integration in society. *Conflict theory* sees society as organized around the unequal distribution of resources, held together through power and coercion. *Symbolic interaction* theory emphasizes the role of individuals in giving meaning to social behavior, thereby creating society. Other theories include: *feminist theory* (analyses of women and men in society intended to improve women's lives); *exchange theory* (a theory arguing that behavior is determined by the rewards or punishments people receive as they interact with others); and, *rational choice theory* (a theory positing that choices human beings make are guided by reason). *Postmodernism* argues that constructed cultural products are the realities of our postindustrial, postmodern society.

■ **Is sociology scientific?**

Sociological research is derived from the *scientific method,* meaning that it relies on *empirical* observation and, sometimes, the testing of *hypotheses.* The research process involves several steps: developing a research question, designing the research, collecting data, analyzing data, and developing conclusions. Different designs are appropriate to different questions, but sociologists have to be concerned about the *validity, reliability,* and *generalization* of their studies.

■ **What different tools of research do sociologists use?**

The most common tools of sociological research are surveys and interviews, participant observation, controlled experiments, content analysis, comparative and historical research, and evaluation research. Each has its own strengths and weaknesses. Surveys, for example, tend to be more generalizable than participant observation, but they are unable to capture the subtle nuances in social behavior and its meaning that participant observation can.

- *Can sociology be value-free?*

   Although no research in any field can always be value-free, sociological research nonetheless strives for objectivity while recognizing that the values of the research may have some influence on the work. There are ethical considerations in doing sociological research, such as whether one should collect data without letting research subjects (people) know they are being observed.

■ *Key Terms*

applied sociology 16	population 25
conflict theory 19	positivism 13
content analysis 30	postmodernism 20
controlled experiment 30	probability 22
correlation 31	random sample 26
data 21	rate 31
data analysis 26	rational choice theory 20
debunking 7	reliability 25
dependent variable 24	replication study 23
diversity 11	sample 25
empirical 6	scientific method 22
Enlightenment 13	social change 10
evaluation research 30	social Darwinism 16
exchange theory 20	social facts 14
feminist theory 20	social institution 10
functionalism 18	social interaction 10
generalization 26	social structure 5
hypothesis 24	sociological
independent variable 24	imagination 3
indicator 24	sociology 2
issues 5	symbolic interaction
mean 31	theory 19
median 31	troubles 5
mode 31	validity 24
organic metaphor 16	variable 24
participant observation 27	verstehen 16
percentage 31	

■ *Researching Society with MicroCase Online*

You can see the results of actual research by using the Wadsworth MicroCase® Online feature available to you.

This feature allows you to look at some of the results from national surveys, census data, and other data sources. You can explore this easy-to-use feature on your own, but try this example. Suppose you want to know some social facts, such as:

How do different states compare in the percentage of births to mothers under age 20?

To answer this question, go to **sociology.wadsworth. com/andersen_taylor/essen3e**, select MicroCase Online from the left navigation bar, and follow the directions there to analyze the following data.

Data file: STATES

Task: Mapping

Variable 1: MA <AGE20-PERCENTAGE OF BIRTHS TO MOTHERS UNDER 20 YEARS OLD

View: Map

Questions

Once you have your results, answer the following questions:

Which region of the country has the *highest* rate of births to mothers under age 20?

Now select the Back button, and select the Rank Table view.

1. Which state has the highest rate of births to mothers under age 20?

2. What is the percentage for this state?

3. Which state has the lowest rate of births to mothers under age 20?

4. What is the percentage for this state?

5. What is the ranking for your state?

■ *The Companion Web Site for Sociology: The Essentials, Third Edition*

sociology.wadsworth.com/andersen_taylor/essen3e

Supplement your review of this chapter by going to the companion Web site to take one of the Tutorial Quizzes, use the flash cards to master key terms, and check out the many other study aids you'll find there. You'll also find special features such as GSS Data and Census 2000 information, data and resources at your fingertips to help you with that special project or do some research on your own.

■ *Suggested Readings and Web Resources*

Babbie, Earl. 2004. *The Practice of Social Research,* 10th ed. Belmont, CA: Wadsworth.
One of the most widely used texts on research methods and techniques, this book is both comprehensive and readable.

Becker, Howard. 1986. *Writing for Social Scientists.* Chicago: University of Chicago Press.
This engaging book is not only an excellent discussion of how to improve one's writing, it is also a good guide to sociological thinking. Premised on the idea that poor writing produces errors in thinking, Becker's book will help students at all levels improve their sociological perspective and their ability to communicate it.

Duneier, Mitchell. 1999. *Sidewalk.* New York: Farrar, Strauss, and Giroux.
Based on participant observation, this book is a study of homeless men in New York who support themselves as Greenwich Village street vendors. It is a classic and engaging example of this kind of research.

Johnson, Allan G. 1997. *The Forest and the Trees: Sociology as Life, Practice, Promise.* Philadelphia: Temple University Press.
This brief introduction to sociology provides an excellent overview of the basic concepts of the field and the application of sociology to interpreting contemporary social issues. The book also grounds its discussion in an awareness of the diversity among different groups in the United States.

Mills, C. Wright. 1959. *The Sociological Imagination.* New York: Oxford University Press.
This book is a classic statement of the meaning and significance of the sociological perspective.

American Sociological Association Home Page
www.asanet.org
The American Sociological Association (ASA) is a national organization of sociologists. The home page provides information on careers in sociology, resources for sociological research, special reports on current initiatives in social policy, and information on how students can get involved in this sociological organization, including the Minority Fellowship Program.

Society for the Study of Social Problems
www.sssp1.org
This national professional group sponsors an annual meeting and publishes one of the major journals in sociology, Social Problems.

Culture

In one contemporary society known for its advanced culture, many women would not consider going to work in the morning without encasing their legs in nylon sleeves. The nylon covers them from waist to toe and is believed to make their legs more attractive. If, as often happens, the delicate nylon filaments tear, the women are embarrassed. Many women put on their leg sleeves during a morning ritual that includes smearing oily pigments on their faces to achieve striking, unnatural hues, and dusting their faces with powder to eliminate the skin's natural shininess. The hair on the scalp is slathered with gels and liquids and then modeled into decorative forms. The hair may be augmented with knots; strips of cloth; and small items of hardware made of plastic, wood, or metal. Beads, metals, and glittering objects are often inserted into holes punched into the women's earlobes. Plastic may be glued onto the fingernails and then adorned with bright colors, paint, and sparkles. All this effort is expended in the belief that it makes women more attractive to others.

Most men in this culture begin their day by scraping their faces with sharp-bladed tools to remove all traces of facial hair. The scraping tools of the wealthiest men may be embellished with silver and brass, but most men use plain metal or plastic tools sold in local markets. After removing the hair from their faces, the men douse their skin with healing spirits that are usually scented with fragrances thought to be sexually provocative.

Some men modify this ritual by arranging their facial hair in elaborate designs, even packing the hair above their lips with wax and modeling it into dramatic shapes. Men usually slather the hair on their scalps with substances similar to those used by women, but they generally do not augment their hair designs with the ornamental objects commonly used by women. Individuals incur social penalties if they do not engage in these rituals. Men who appear in public without removing the day's growth of facial hair may be considered unkempt.

Women who do not wear nylon sleeves on their legs may be considered ugly or unfeminine, and they may jeopardize their chances of being appointed to the highest-paying and most prestigious jobs. Reflecting the importance of these cultural adornments, elaborate markets have developed to sell these products. People in this culture exchange millions of the tokens they are paid for work to pay for these bodily decorations.

From outside the culture, these practices seem strange, yet few within the culture think the rituals are anything but perfectly ordinary. They sometimes wish they did not have to go through the elaborate morning ritual, and many forgo the elaborate grooming and costuming on weekends. Most of the time, people neither analyze these rituals nor spend time thinking about their meaning. You have surely guessed that the practices described here are taken from U.S. culture.

When viewed from the outside, cultural habits that seem perfectly normal take on a strange aspect. The Tchikrin people—a remote culture of the central Brazilian rain forest—paint their bodies in elaborate designs. Painted bodies communicate to others about the relationship of the person to his or her body, society, and the spiritual world. The designs and colors symbolize the balance the Tchikrin think exists between biological powers and the integration of people into the social group. The Tchikrin associate hair with sexual powers, and lovers get a special thrill from using their teeth to pluck an eyebrow or eyelash from their partner's face (Turner 1969). To the Tchikrin people, these practices are no more exotic than the morning rituals we adhere to in the United States.

To study culture, to analyze it and measure its significance in society, we must separate ourselves from judgments such as "strange" or "normal." We must see a culture as it is seen by insiders, but we cannot be completely taken in by that view. One might say we should know the culture as insiders and understand it as outsiders.

These illustrations are inspired by a classic article on the "Nacirema"—"American," backwards—by Horace Miner 1956.

■ *Defining Culture*

Culture is the complex system of meaning and behavior that defines the way of life for a given group or society. It includes beliefs, values, knowledge, art, morals, laws, customs, habits, language, and dress, among other things. Culture includes ways of thinking as well as patterns of behavior. Observing culture involves studying what people think, how they interact, and the objects they make and use. As stated by two sociologists, "Culture appears to be 'built into' all social relations, constituting the underlying assumptions and expectations on which social interaction depends" (Wuthnow and Witten 1988: 50).

In any society, culture defines what is perceived as beautiful and ugly, right and wrong, good and bad. Culture helps hold society together. It gives people a sense of belonging, instructs them in how to behave, and tells them what to think in particular situations. Culture gives meaning to society.

Cultural traditions represent the different values and beliefs of diverse groups. Here, Hanukkah, Christmas, Ramadan, and Kwanza are celebrations of diverse cultures.

Culture is both material and nonmaterial. *Material culture* consists of the objects created in a given society—its buildings, art, tools, toys, print and broadcast media, and other tangible objects. In the popular mind, material artifacts constitute culture because they can be collected in museums or archives and analyzed for what they represent. These objects are significant because of the meaning they are given. A temple, for example, is not merely a building, nor is it only a place of worship. Its form and presentation signify the religious meaning system of the faithful.

Nonmaterial culture includes the norms, laws, customs, ideas, values, and beliefs of a group of people. Nonmaterial culture is less tangible than material culture, but it has a strong influence on social behavior. The significance of nonmaterial culture can be seen by the fact that people will go to great lengths, even war or, perhaps, suicide, to defend beliefs and ideals (that is, nonmaterial culture) that they hold dear. You can, for example, interpret the conflict between the highly traditional culture of religious extrem-

ists and the modern, capitalist culture of the United States as a conflict over nonmaterial culture. When terrorists attacked the United States, they attacked the material symbols of this culture (that is, the World Trade Center and the Pentagon), but this conflict is rooted in the differences associated with nonmaterial culture—that is, the values and beliefs of Western culture versus the traditional values of some extremist groups (Barber 1995). Note here, as well, the link between nonmaterial and material culture: Material culture can be the manifestation of nonmaterial culture; at the same time, nonmaterial culture can be shaped by material culture (such as when widespread marketing fosters a culture of consumerism).

Characteristics of Culture

Across societies, certain features of culture are noted by sociologists. These different characteristics of culture are examined here.

Symbols can be powerful expressions of human emotion, such as in the many shrines that were created to commemorate those killed in the terrorist attacks on the United States on September 11, 2001.

1. Culture is shared. Culture would have no significance if people did not hold it in common. Culture is not idiosyncratic; rather, it is collectively experienced and collectively agreed upon. The shared nature of culture makes human society possible. The shared basis of culture may be difficult to see in complex societies where groups have different traditions, perspectives, and ways of thinking and behaving. In the United States, for example, different racial and ethnic groups have unique histories, languages, and beliefs—that is, different cultures. Even within these groups, there are diverse cultural traditions. Latinos, for example, comprise many groups with distinct origins and cultures. Still, there are features of Latino culture, such as the Spanish language and some values and traditions, that are shared. The different groups constituting Latino culture also share a culture that is shaped by their common experiences as minorities in the United States. Similarly, African Americans have created a rich and distinct culture that is the result of their unique experience within the United States. What identifies African American culture are the practices and traditions that have evolved from both the U.S. experience and African and Caribbean traditions. Placed in another country, such as an African nation, African Americans would likely recognize elements of their culture, but they would also feel culturally distinct as Americans.

Within the United States, culture varies by age, race, region, gender, ethnicity, religion, class, and other social factors. A person growing up in the South is likely to develop different tastes, modes of speech, and cultural interests than a person raised in the West. Despite these differences, there is a common cultural basis to life in the United States. Certain symbols, language patterns, belief systems, and ways of thinking are distinctively American and form a common culture even though great cultural diversity exists.

2. Culture is learned. Cultural beliefs and practices are usually so well learned that they seem perfectly natural, but they are learned nonetheless. How do people come to prefer some foods to others? How is musical taste acquired? Sometimes, culture is taught through direct instruction. A parent teaching a child to use silverware is one example of direct instruction; children learning songs, myths, and traditions in school is another. Much of culture is learned indirectly through observation and imitation. Think of how we learn what it means to be a man or a woman. Although we may never be taught explicitly the "proper" roles for men and women, we learn what is expected from observing others. These expectations change over time and vary with different contexts, as we will see when we explore gender more thoroughly in Chapter 10.

A person becomes a member of a culture through transmission of culture, both formal (for example, schooling) and informal (such as peer pressure). Until the culture is learned, the person will feel like an outsider. The process of learning culture is referred to by sociologists as socialization, a subject we will return to in Chapter 3.

3. Culture is taken for granted. Because culture is learned, members of a given society seldom question the culture of which they are a part, unless for some reason they become outsiders or establish some critical distance from the usual cultural expectations. People engage unthinkingly in hundreds of specifically cultural practices every day; culture makes these practices seem "normal." If you suddenly stopped participating in your culture and questioned each belief and every behavior, you would soon find yourself feeling detached and perhaps a little disoriented; you would also become increasingly ineffective at functioning within your group. Little wonder that tourists stand out so much in a foreign culture. They rarely have much knowledge of the culture they are visiting and, even when they are well informed, typically approach the society from their own cultural orientation.

Think, for example, of how you might feel if you were a Native American student in a predominantly White classroom. Many, though not all, Native American people are raised to be quiet and not outspoken. If students in a classroom are expected to assert themselves and state what is on their minds, a Native American student may feel awkward, as will others for who these expectations are contrary to their cultural upbringing. If the professor is not aware of these cultural differences, he or she may penalize students who are quiet, resulting perhaps in a lower grade for the student from a different cultural background. Culture binds us together, but lack of communication across cultures can have negative consequences, as this example shows.

4. **Culture is symbolic.** The significance of culture lies in the meaning it holds for people. **Symbols** are things or behaviors to which people give meaning; the meaning is not inherent in a symbol but is bestowed by the meaning people give it. The U.S. flag, for example, is literally a decorated piece of cloth. Its cultural significance derives not from the cloth of which it is made, but from its meaning as a symbol of freedom and democracy, as was witnessed by the widespread flying of the flag after the terrorist attacks on the United States on September 11, 2001.

That something has symbolic meaning does not make it any less important or influential than objective facts. In fact, symbols are powerful expressions of human life. Protests over the flying of the Confederate flag provide a good example. Those who object to the flag being displayed on public buildings see the Confederate flag as a symbol of racism and the legacy of slavery. Those who defend the flying of the flag see it as representing Southern heritage, a symbol of group pride and regional loyalty. Similarly, the use of Native American mascots to name and represent sports teams is symbolic of the exploitation of Native Americans. (Think of the Washington Redskins, the Cleveland Indians, the Atlanta Braves "tomahawk chop," and various college mascots). Native American activists and their supporters see these mascots as derogatory and extremely insulting, representing gross caricatures of Native American traditions. The protests that have developed over controversial symbols are indicative of the enormous influence of cultural symbols.

UNDERSTANDING DIVERSITY

The Social Meaning of Language

Language reflects the assumptions of a culture. This can be seen and exemplified in several ways:

- *Language affects people's perception of reality.*

Example: Researchers have found that men tend to think that women are not included when terms such as *man* are used to refer to all people. Studies find that when college students look at job descriptions written in masculine pronouns, they assume that women are not qualified for the job (Hyde 1984; Switzer 1990).

- *Language reflects the social and political status of different groups in society.*

Example: A term such as *woman doctor* suggests that the gender of the doctor is something exceptional and noteworthy. The term *working woman* (used to refer to women who are employed) also suggests that women who do not work for wages are not working. Ask yourself what the term *working*

man connotes and how this differs from *working woman*.

- *Groups may advocate changing language referring to them as a way of asserting a positive group identity.*

Example: Some advocates for the disabled challenge the term *handicapped*, arguing that it stigmatizes people who may have many abilities, even if they are physically distinctive. Also, though someone may have one disabling condition, they may otherwise be perfectly able.

- *The implications of language emerge from specific historical and cultural contexts.*

Example: The naming of so-called "races" comes from the social and historical processes that define different groups as inferior or superior. Racial labels do not come just from physical, national, or cultural differences. The term *Caucasian,* for example, was coined in the seventeenth century

when racist thinkers developed alleged scientific classification systems to rank different societal groups. Alfred Blumenbach used the label *Caucasian* to refer to people from the Caucuses of Russia whom he thought were more beautiful and intelligent than any group in the world.

- *Language can distort actual group experience.*

Example: Terms used to describe different racial and ethnic groups homogenize experiences that may be unique. Thus, the terms *Hispanic* and *Latino* lump together Mexican Americans, island Puerto Ricans, U.S.-born Puerto Ricans, as well as people from Honduras, Panama, El Salvador, and other Central and South American countries. *Hispanic* and *Latino* point to the shared experience of those from Latin cultures, but like the terms *Native American* and *American Indian,* they obscure the experiences of unique groups, such as the Sioux, Nanticoke, Cherokee, Yavapai, or Navajo.

Symbols mean different things in different contexts. The U.S. flag, for example, is to Shiite extremists in Iraq and Iran a despised symbol of U.S. imperialism. A flag tattooed on someone's arm has a meaning different from a flag insignia stitched on a military uniform. Similarly, a cross on a church altar has a meaning different from a cross burning in someone's front yard.

One interesting thing about culture is the extent to which symbolic attachments guide human behavior. For example, people stand when the national anthem is sung, and they may be emotionally moved by displays of the cross or the Star of David. Under some conditions, people organize mass movements to protest what they see as the defamation of important symbols, such as the burning of a flag or the burning of a cross. The significance of the symbolic value of culture can hardly be overestimated. Learning a culture means not just engaging in particular behaviors but learning their symbolic meanings within the culture.

5. Culture varies across time and place. Culture develops as humans adapt to the physical and social environment around them. Since this environment varies from one society to another, and since human beings use their creative imagination to develop cultural solutions to the challenges they face, culture is not fixed from one place to another. In the United States, for example, there is a strong cultural belief in scientific solutions to human problems; consequently, many think that problems of food supply and environmental deterioration can be addressed by scientific breakthroughs, such as genetic engineering to create high-yield tomatoes or bacteria that eat oil spills. In another cultural setting, other solutions may seem preferable. Indeed, a religious culture might think that genetic engineering trespasses on divine territory, and in many cultures science may be seen as creating more problems than it solves (Harding 1998).

Because culture varies from one setting to another, the meanings that develop within a culture must be

■ ***Language shapes people's perceptions of groups and events in society.***

Example: Native American victories during the nineteenth century are typically described as "massacres"; comparable victories by White settlers are described in heroic terms. The statement that Columbus "discovered" America implies that Native American societies did not exist before Columbus "found" the Americas. Indians are frequently referred to as "savages," whereas White colonists are called "settlers" (Moore 1992). Likewise, the word *tribe* to describe nations of African or Native American people suggests primitive, backward societies. Even the term American is problematic. It is used synonymously with *United States* when the Americas include Canada, Mexico, Central America, and South America. To say that the culture of the United States is American culture suggests that the United States encompasses the other Americas or

that the other cultures of the Americas are not worth notice.

■ ***Terms used to define different groups change over time and can originate in movements to assert a positive identity.***

Example: In the 1960s, *Black American* replaced the term *Negro* because the civil rights and Black Power movements inspired Black pride and the importance of self-naming (Smith 1992). Earlier, *Negro* and *colored* were used to define African Americans. Currently, it is popular to refer to all so-called racial groups as "people of color." This phrase was derived from the phrase "women of color," created by feminist African American, Latina,[1] Asian American, and Native American women to emphasize their common experiences. Some people find the use of "color" in this label offensive since it harkens back to the phrase "colored people," a phrase generally seen as paternalistic and racist because it was a label used by dominant groups to refer to African Ameri-

cans prior to the civil rights movement. The phrase "women of color" now has a more positive meaning than the earlier term *colored women* because it is meant to recognize common experiences, not just label people because of their presumed skin color.

In this book, we have tried to be sensitive to the language used to describe different groups. We recognize that the language we use is fraught with cultural and political assumptions and that what seems acceptable now may be offensive later. Perhaps the best way to solve this problem is for different groups to learn as much as they can about one another, becoming more aware of the meaning and nuances of naming and language and more conscious of the racial assumptions embedded in the language. Greater sensitivity to the language used in describing different group experiences is an important step in promoting better intergroup relationships.

[1]Latina is the feminine form in Spanish and refers to women; Latino, to men.

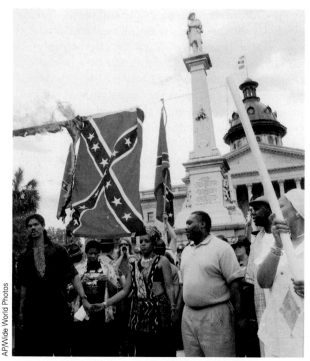

AP/Wide World Photos

Cultural values can clash when groups have strongly held, but differing, value systems. A good example is the conflict over the flying of the Confederate flag.

seen in their cultural context. **Cultural relativism** is the idea that something can be understood and judged only in relationship to the cultural context in which it appears. This does not make every cultural practice morally acceptable, but it suggests that without knowing the cultural context, it is impossible to understand why people behave as they do. For example, in the United States, burying or cremating the dead is the cultural practice. It may be difficult for someone from this culture to understand that in Tibet, with a ruggedly cold climate and the inability to dig the soil, the dead are cut into pieces and left for vultures to eat. Although this would be repulsive (and illegal) in the United States, within Tibetan culture, this practice is understandable.

Not only does culture vary from place to place, it also varies over time. As people encounter new situations, the culture that emerges is a mix of the past and present. Second-generation immigrants to the United States are raised in the traditions of their culture of origin, and children of immigrants typically grow up with both the traditional cultural expectations of their parents' homeland and the cultural expectations of a new society. Adapting to the new society can create conflict between generations, especially if the older

generation is intent on passing along their cultural traditions. The children may be more influenced by their peers and may choose to dress, speak, and behave in ways that are characteristic of their new society but unacceptable to their parents.

To sum up: Culture is concrete because we can observe the cultural objects and practices that define human experience. Culture is abstract because it is a way of thinking, feeling, believing, and behaving. Culture links the past and the present because it is the knowledge that makes us part of human groups. Culture gives shape to human experience.

Biology and Human Culture

It is cultural patterns that make humans so interesting. Recent studies have also found that some animal species also develop culture. Chimpanzees, for example, learn behavior through observing and imitating others—a point proven by observing the different eating practices among chimpanzees in the same species, but raised in different groups (Whiten et al. 1999). Others have observed elephants picking up the dead bones of other elephants and fondling them, perhaps evidence of grieving behavior (Meredith 2003). Many animal species have also developed systems of communication used for various purposes, including attracting mates and alerting others to danger. Dolphins, for example, are now known to have a complex auditory language.

Apparently, humans are not unique in their ability to develop systems of communication. But, scientists generally conclude that animals lack the intelligence required to develop elaborate symbol-based cultures common in human societies. But, it would seem, as Charles Darwin has written, "The difference in mind between man [sic] and the higher animals, great as it is, certainly is one of degree and not of kind" (Darwin, cited in Gould 1999).

Studying animal groups reminds us of the interplay between biology and culture. Human biology sets limits and provides certain capacities for human life and the development of culture. Similarly, the environment in which humans live establishes the possibilities and limitations for human society. Nutrition, for instance, is greatly influenced by environment, thereby affecting human body height and weight. Not everyone can drive a golf ball like Tiger Woods, leap like Shaquille O'Neal, or play baseball like Sammy Sosa, but with training and conditioning, people can enhance their physical abilities. Biological limits exist, but cultural factors have an enormous influence on the development of human life.

■ *The Elements of Culture*

As we have seen, culture consists of both material objects and abstract thoughts and behavior. In sociological work, several elements of culture are of particular interest: language, norms, beliefs, and values (see Table 2.1).

Language

Language is a set of symbols and rules that, put together in a meaningful way, provides a complex communication system. The formation of culture among humans is made possible by language. Learning the language of a culture is essential to becoming part of a society, and it is one of the first things children learn. Indeed, until children acquire at least a rudimentary command of language, they seem unable to acquire other social skills. Language is so important to human interaction that it is difficult to think of life without it; indeed, as one commentator on language has said, "Life is lived as a series of conversations" (Tannen 1990: 13).

Think about the experience of becoming part of a social group. When you enter a new society or a different social group, you have to learn its language to become a member of the group. This includes any special terms of reference used by the group. Lawyers, for example, have their own vocabulary and their own way of constructing sentences. The intricate prose rendered by lawyers is called (not always kindly) "legalese"; anyone who is not adept in the language of the law is likely at a disadvantage in any legal proceeding. Likewise, becoming a sociologist requires learning the words and concepts that sociologists use to communicate their ideas. Becoming a part of any social group—a friendship circle, fraternity or sorority, professional organization, or any other group—involves learning the language the group uses. Those who do not share the language of a group cannot participate fully in its culture.

Language is fluid and dynamic and evolves in response to social change. Think, for example, of how the introduction of computers and other electronic systems of communication has affected the English language. People now talk about needing "downtime" and providing "input." Only a few years ago, had you said you were going to "fax" someone or "click on" something, people would have thought you were speaking in some private code. Even now, those without exposure to advanced electronic technologies might not understand what you mean by some of these terms.

TABLE 2.1 Elements of Culture		
	Definition	**Examples**
Language	A set of symbols and rules that, put together in a meaningful way, provides a complex communication system	English; Spanish; hieroglyphics
Norms	The specific cultural expectations for how to behave in a given situation	Behavior involving use of personal space; manners
Folkways	General standards of behavior adhered to by a group	Cultural forms of dress; food habits
Mores	Strict norms that control moral and ethical behavior	Religious doctrines; formal law
Values	Abstract standards in a society or group that define ideal principles	Liberty, freedom
Beliefs	Shared ideas held collectively by people within a given culture	Belief in a higher being

DOES LANGUAGE SHAPE CULTURE? Language is clearly a big part of culture. Edward Sapir (writing in the 1920s) and his student, Benjamin Whorf (writing in the 1950s), thought that language was central in determining social thought. Their theory, the **Sapir–Whorf hypothesis,** was that language determines other aspects of culture since language provides the categories through which social reality is defined and constructed. In other words, Sapir and Whorf thought that language determines what people think and perceive because language forces people to perceive the world in certain terms (Sapir 1921; Whorf 1956). It is not that you think or perceive something first and then think of how to express it, but that language itself determines what you think or perceive.

If the Sapir–Whorf hypothesis is correct, then speakers of different languages have different perceptions of reality. Whorf used the example of the social meaning of time to illustrate cultural differences in how language shapes perceptions of reality. He noted that the Hopi Indians conceptualize time as a slowly turning cylinder, whereas English-speaking people conceive of time as running forward in one direction at a uniform pace. Linguistic constructions of time shape how the two different cultures think about it and therefore how they think about reality. In Hopi culture, events are located not in specific moments of time, but in "categories of being"—as if everything is in a state of becoming, not fixed in a particular time and place (Carroll 1956). To the Hopi, a house "houses"; a stone "stones." In contrast, the way English sentences are constructed locates things in a definite time and place. For example, European languages place great importance on verb tense—things are located precisely in the past, present, or future.

Recent critics do not think that language is as deterministic as Sapir and Whorf proposed—language does not single-handedly dictate the perception of reality—but there is no disagreement that language has a strong influence on culture. Most scholars now see two-way causality between language and culture. Asking whether language determines culture or vice versa is like asking which came first, the chicken or the egg. Language and culture are inextricable. Each shapes the other, and to understand either, we must know something of both.

Consider again the example of time. Contemporary Americans think of the week as divided into two parts: weekdays and weekends. The words *weekday* and *weekend* reflect the way we think about time. When does a week end? Having language that defines the weekend encourages us to think about the weekend in specific ways. It is a time for rest, play, chores, and family. In this sense, language shapes the way we think about the passage of time—we look forward to the weekend, we prepare ourselves for the work week—but the language itself (the very concept of the weekend) stems from patterns in the culture—specifically, the work patterns of advanced capitalism. Language and culture shape each other.

Concepts of time in American society are tied to the work ethic. The rhythm of life in the United States is the rhythm of the workplace. "9 to 5" is the name for an entire lifestyle, as is the new expression "24/7," defined as working 24 hours a day, seven days a week. The capitalist work ethic makes it morally offensive to merely "pass the time"; instead, time is to be managed. Concepts of time in preindustrial, agricultural societies follow a different rhythm. In agricultural societies, time and calendars are based on agricultural and seasonal patterns; the year proceeds according to this rhythm, not arbitrary units of time like weeks and months. In preindustrial societies, the line between work and private life is less clear than in industrialized societies, where clock time replaces seasonal time and productivity is measured in the units of labor, that is, "man-hours" and the "hourly wage" (Genovese 1972). As patterns of employment are changing, people are working longer hours, and some work is again done at home, language will likely evolve to reflect—and then shape—changing cultural patterns.

SOCIAL INEQUALITY IN LANGUAGE. The
significance of language in culture is particularly apparent in how patterns of race, gender, and class inequality are reflected in language. The language of any culture reflects and reinforces attitudes that are characteristic of the culture. Language can also reproduce these inequalities through the stereotypes and assumptions that may be built into what people say (Moore 1992). As shown in the box "Understanding Diversity: The Social Meaning of Language," names for different groups of people reflect assumptions about those groups. *Mexican American* (hyphenated or not), *Latino/Latina, Hispanic,* and *Chicano/Chicana* all have different meanings and may be interpreted differently by different groups. What someone is called can be significant because it imposes an identity on that person. This is why the names for various racial and ethnic groups have been so heavily debated. Thus, for years, many Native Americans objected to being called "Indian," because it was a term created about them by White conquerors. To emphasize their native roots in the Americas, the term *Native American* was adopted. Now, though many prefer to be called by their actual origin, Native American and American Indian are used interchangeably.

Even conventions like whether to capitalize the word *Black* in Black American can reflect assumptions about the status of different groups. You may have noticed that in this book, the authors capitalize *Black* whenever the label is used as a proper noun. Likewise, the word *White* is capitalized when used to refer to the specific group of White Americans. This convention is relatively new and still debated: Do you treat the color designator as an adjective (as if only color marks the group's experience); or do you recognize that these labels describe particular group experiences and, therefore, treat the name like a proper noun (as you would *American Indian, Latino,* and *Jewish American*)? The standard reference book for writing style, *The Chicago Manual of Style,* now includes capitalization of *Black* and *White* as an acceptable style, illustrating that even the formal rules of language can change and are affected by social and political debate.

Language reflects the social value placed on different groups, which is why it is so demeaning when derogatory terms are used to describe a group or a group member. Throughout the period of Jim Crow segregation in the American South, Black men, regardless of their age, were routinely referred to as "boy" by Whites. Calling a grown man "boy" is an insult; it diminishes his status by defining him as childlike. Referring to a woman as a "girl" has the same effect. If girls become young women when they reach puberty, why are young women—even well into their twenties—routinely referred to as "girls"? Like calling a man, "boy," this diminishes women's status. Who are you likely to consider a serious intellectual or leader, a girl or a woman? Many women, and not just feminists, believe that being called a "girl" is belittling.

Note, however, that terms like *girl* and *boy* are pejorative only in the context of dominant and subordinate group relationships. Whereas African American men would be insulted if called "boy" by a White man, the term is not necessarily insulting when African American men refer to each other that way. Similarly, African American women often refer to each other as "girl" in informal conversation. The term *girl,* used between those of similar status, is not seen as derogatory. When used by someone in a position of dominance, as when a man calls his secretary a "girl," it is demeaning. Likewise, terms like *dyke, fag,* and *queer* are terms lesbians and gay men sometimes use without offense in referring to each other even though the same terms are offensive to lesbians and gays when used about them by others. By reclaiming these terms as positive within their own culture, lesbians and gays build cohesiveness and solidarity (Due 1995). These examples show that power relationships between groups supply the social context for the connotations of language.

The perceived social status of groups is also found in the offensive terms sometimes used to describe different groups. For example, derogatory terms such as *redneck, white trash,* and *trailer park trash* stigmatize people based on regional identity and social class. Such derogatory terms are commonly used to refer to groups of supposed low social status. Even if unintentional, language can insult social groups by making them seem irrelevant or unimportant. An example is the offense some take in Canada, Mexico, and Central and South America when the term *American* is used to refer to people in the United States. To say that the culture of the United States is "American" culture suggests that the United States encompasses the other Americas or that the other cultures of the Americas are not worth notice.

In sum, language can reproduce the inequalities that exist in society. At the same time, changing the language that people use can, to some extent, alter social stereotypes and thereby change the way people think.

Norms

Social norms are another component of culture. **Norms** are the specific cultural expectations for how to behave in a given situation. Society without norms would be chaos;

with norms in place, people know how to act, and social interactions are consistent, predictable, and learnable. There are norms governing every situation. Sometimes they are implicit; that is, they need not be spelled out for people to understand them. For example, when entering a line, there is an implicit norm that you should stand behind the last person, not barge in front of those ahead of you. Implicit norms may not be formal rules, but violation of these norms may nonetheless produce a harsh response. Implicit norms may be learned through specific instruction or by observation of the culture; they are part of a society's or group's customs. Norms are explicit when the rules governing behavior are written down or formally communicated. Typically, specific sanctions are imposed for violating explicit norms.

In the early years of sociology, William Graham Sumner (1906), whose work we described in Chapter 1, identified two types of norms: folkways and mores. **Folkways** are the general standards of behavior adhered to by a group. You might think of folkways as the ordinary customs of different group cultures. Men's wearing pants and not skirts is an example of a cultural folkway. Other examples are the ways that people greet each other, decorate their homes, and prepare their food. Folkways may be loosely defined and loosely adhered to, but they nevertheless structure group customs and implicitly govern much social behavior.

Mores (pronounced "more-ays") are strict norms that control moral and ethical behavior. Mores provide strict codes of behavior, such as the injunctions, legal and religious, against killing others and committing adultery. The mores are often upheld through rules or **laws,** the written set of guidelines that define right and wrong in society. Basically, laws are formalized mores. Violating mores can bring serious repercussions.

When any social norm is violated, sanctions are typically meted out against the violator. **Social sanctions** are mechanisms of social control that enforce norms. The seriousness of a sanction depends on how strictly the norm is held. Violations of folkways carry lighter sanctions than violations of mores. Dressing in an unusual way (that is, violating the cultural folkways of dress) may bring ridicule but is usually not seriously punished. In some cultures, however, the rules of dress are strictly held. For example, Islamic law as interpreted by fundamentalists requires that women appearing in public have their bodies cloaked and their faces veiled. The sanctions for violating mores can be severe—whipping, branding, banishment, even death.

Sanctions include both rewards and punishments. When children learn social norms, for example, correct behavior may elicit positive sanctions—the behavior is reinforced through praise, approval, or an explicit reward. Early on, for example, parents might praise children for learning to put on their own clothes; later, children might get an allowance if they keep their rooms clean. Bad behavior earns negative sanctions, such as getting spanked or grounded. In society, negative sanctions may be mild or severe, ranging from subtle mechanisms of control, such as ridicule, to overt forms of punishment, such as imprisonment, physical coercion, and even death.

One way to study social norms is to observe what happens when they are violated. Once you become aware of how social situations are controlled by norms, you can see how easy it is to disrupt situations where adherence to the norms produces social order. **Ethnomethodology** is a theoretical approach in sociology based on the idea you can discover the normal social order through disrupting it. As a technique of study, ethnomethodologists often deliberately disrupt social norms to see how people respond and to try to reinstate social order (Garfinkel 1967).

In a famous series of ethnomethodological experiments, college students were asked to pretend they were boarders in their own homes for a period of fifteen minutes to one hour. They did not tell their families what they were doing. The students were instructed to be polite, circumspect, and impersonal; to use terms of formal address; and to speak only when spoken to. After the experiment, two of the participating students reported that their families treated the experiment as a joke; another's family thought the daughter was being extra nice because she wanted something. One family believed that the student was hiding some serious problem. In all the other cases, parents reacted with shock, bewilderment, and anger. Students were accused of being mean, nasty, impolite, and inconsiderate; the parents demanded explanations for their son's and daughter's behavior (Garfinkel 1967). Through this experiment, the student researchers were able to see that even the informal norms governing behavior in one's home are carefully structured. By violating the norms of the household, the norms were revealed.

Ethnomethodological research teaches us that society proceeds on an "as if" basis. That is, society exists because people behave as if there were no other way to do so. Usually people go along with what is expected of them. Culture is actually "enforced" through the social sanctions applied to those who violate social norms. Usually, specific sanctions are unnecessary because people have learned the normative expectations. When the norms are violated, their existence becomes apparent (see also Chapter 4).

Beliefs

As important as social norms are the beliefs of people in society. **Beliefs** are shared ideas held collectively by people within a given culture. Shared beliefs are part of what binds people together in society. Beliefs are also the basis for many norms and values of a given culture. In the United States beliefs that are widely held and cherished are the belief in God and the belief in democracy.

Some beliefs are so strongly held that people find it difficult to cope with ideas or experiences that contradict them. Someone who devoutly believes in God may find atheism intolerable; those who believe in reincarnation may seem irrational to those who think life ends at death. Similarly, those who believe in magic may seem merely superstitious to those with a more scientific and rational view of the world.

Whatever beliefs people hold, they orient us to the world. They provide answers to otherwise imponderable questions about the meaning of life. Beliefs provide a meaning system around which culture is organized. Whether belief stems from religion, myth, folklore, or science, it shapes what people take to be possible and true. Although a given belief may be unprovable or even logically impossible, it nonetheless guides people through their lives.

Sociologists study belief in a variety of ways, depending on their theoretical orientation. Functionalists, for example, see beliefs as a necessary component of society in that they integrate people into social groups. Conflict theorists, on the other hand, interpret beliefs as potentially competing worldviews; those with more power are able to impose their beliefs on others. Symbolic interaction theorists are interested in how beliefs are constructed and maintained through the social interaction between people. Each theoretical orientation provides different insights into the significance of beliefs for human culture and society.

Values

Deeply intertwined with beliefs are the values of a culture. **Values** are the abstract standards in a society or group that define ideal principles. Values define what is desirable and morally correct; thus, values determine what is considered right and wrong, beautiful and ugly, good and bad. Although values are abstract, they provide a general outline for behavior. Freedom, for example, is a value held to be important in U.S. culture, as is equality. Values are ideals, forming the abstract standards for group behavior, but they are also ideals that may not be realized in every situation.

Values can be a basis for cultural cohesion, but they can also be the source of conflict. For example, the political conflict over abortion is a conflict over values. Pro-choice groups value reproductive freedom and women's right to control their bodies. Those opposed to abortion value the life of the fetus over the woman's right to choose to terminate a pregnancy. Abortion law has attempted to strike a balance among the values behind competing rights: the right to privacy, the right of the state to protect maternal health, and the right of the state to protect developing life. The abortion issue puts the values of different groups into direct conflict with each other. You can see this value conflict played out in the language the different groups use to describe themselves. By adopting the label "pro-life," those

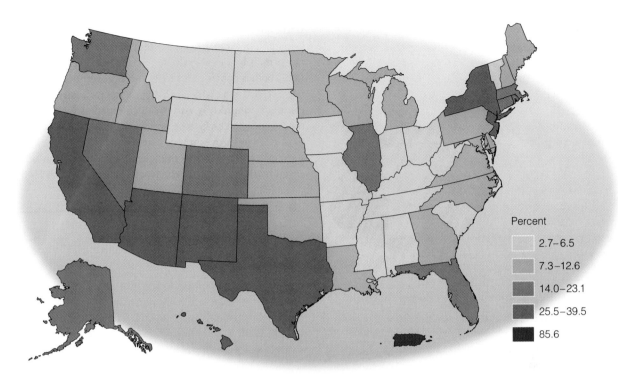

MAP 2.1 Mapping America's Diversity: Percentage Speaking Language Other Than English at Home
With increased immigration and greater diversity in the U.S. population, evidence of cultural diversity can be seen in many areas—language being one of them. **What visible sources of such cultural diversity can you identify?**

SOURCE: U.S. Census Bureau. 2002. *American Fact Finder.* **www.census.gov**

Percent
- 2.7–6.5
- 7.3–12.6
- 14.0–23.1
- 25.5–39.5
- 85.6

opposed to abortion lay claim to moral high ground by suggesting that those who are pro-choice are somehow "anti-life." The political slogans on both sides of this conflict use language that subtly promotes their value position, exploiting the fact that language has the power to define how groups are perceived by themselves and by others.

Values guide the behavior of people in society. Norms are the reflection of underlying values. For example, faithfulness within marriage is a value expressed in a variety of cultural norms, such as the prohibition against dancing too intimately with another's spouse. An example of the impact that values can have on people's behavior comes from an American Indian society known as the Kwakiutl (pronounced "kwa-kee-YOO-ta-l"), a group from the coastal region of southern Alaska, Washington state, and British Columbia. The Kwakiutl developed a practice known as *potlatch,* in which wealthy chiefs would periodically pile up their possessions and give them away to their followers and rivals (Benedict 1934; Harris 1974; Wolcott 1996). The object of potlatch was to give away or destroy more of one's goods than did one's rivals. The potlatch reflected Kwakiutl values of reciprocity, the full use of food and goods, and the social status of the wealthiest chiefs in Kwakiutl society. (By the way, chiefs did not lose their status by giving away their goods because the goods were

eventually returned in the course of other potlatches. They would even burn large piles of goods, knowing that others would soon replace their wealth through other potlatches.)

Compare this practice with the patterns of consumption in the United States. Imagine the CEOs of major corporations regularly gathering up their wealth and giving it away to their workers and rival CEOs! In the contemporary United States, *conspicuous consumption* (consuming for the sake of displaying one's wealth) celebrates values similar to those of the potlatch: High-status people demonstrate their position by accumulating more material possessions than those around them (Veblen, 1899). Indeed, conspicuous consumption encourages consumerism throughout the society—people feel as though they have to "keep up with the Joneses." Values and norms together guide the behavior of people in society. It is necessary to understand the values and norms operating in a situation to understand why people behave as they do.

▪ *Cultural Diversity*

It is rare for a society to be culturally uniform. As societies develop and become more complex, different cultural traditions appear. The more complex the society,

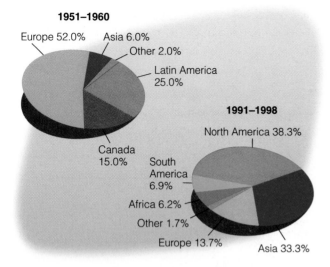

FIGURE 2.1 U.S. Immigrants by Region of Origin

SOURCE: U.S. Census Bureau. 2002. *Statistical Abstract of the United States 2002*. Washington, DC: U.S. Department of Commerce, p. 11.

the more likely its culture will be internally varied and diverse. The United States, for example, hosts enormous cultural diversity stemming from religious, ethnic, and racial differences, as well as regional, age, gender, and class differences. Currently, more than 11 percent of people in the United States are foreign born. In a single year, immigrants from more than 100 countries come to the United States (U.S. Census Bureau 2002). As Figure 2.1 shows, whereas earlier immigrants were predominantly from Europe, now Latin America and Asia are the greatest sources of new immigrants. One result is a large increase in the number of U.S. residents for whom English is the second language, as shown in "Mapping America's Diversity." Cultural diversity is clearly a characteristic of contemporary American society.

The richness of American culture stems from the many traditions that different groups have brought with them to this society, as well as from the cultural forms that have emerged through their experience within the United States. Jazz, for example, is one of the few musical forms indigenous to the United States. An indigenous art form refers to something that originated in a particular region or culture. However, jazz also has roots in the musical traditions of the slave community and African cultures. Since the birth of jazz, cultural greats such as Ella Fitzgerald, Count Basie, Duke Ellington, Billie Holiday, and numerous others have not only enriched the jazz tradition, but have also influenced other forms of music, including rock and roll.

Native American cultures have likewise enriched the culture of our society. One example is the influence of the Iroquois on our style of government. As early as the late

sixteenth century, the Iroquois of northern New York and Canada had established a system of governance based on the principles of self-rule, federation, and representation. Local bodies contributed to a central governing body that protected them. Although the democratic form of government adopted by American colonists is based on the models of ancient Greece and Rome, the particular form of our federal government—its division into executive, judicial, and legislative branches—may have been influenced by the example of the Iroquois nation (Allen 1986).

DEBUNKING
Society's Myths

Myth: Americans share a single culture that is derived from western European traditions.

Sociological perspective: The United States is an increasingly diverse society, and many of its dominant cultural traditions have been derived from African Americans, Latinos, and other groups whose experience is often neglected.

With such great variety, how can the United States be called one culture? The culture of the United States, including its language, arts, food customs, religious practices, and dress, can be seen as the sum of the diverse cultures that constitute this society. Altogether, these behaviors and beliefs constitute "American" (U.S.) culture, but cultural diversity is characteristic of this culture as a whole.

Dominant Culture

Two concepts from sociology help us understand the complexity of culture in a given society: dominant culture and subculture. The **dominant culture** is the culture of the most powerful group in society. It is the cultural form that receives the most support from major institutions and that constitutes the major belief system. Although the dominant culture is not the only culture in a society, it is commonly believed to be "the" culture of a society despite the other cultures present. Social institutions in the society perpetuate the dominant culture and give it a degree of legitimacy that is not shared by other cultures. Quite often, the dominant culture is the standard by which other cultures in the society are judged.

A dominant culture need not be the culture of the majority of people; rather, it is simply the culture of the group in society that has enough power to define the cultural framework. As an example, think of a college or university that has a strong system of fraternities and sororities. On campus, the number of students belonging to fraternities and sororities is probably a numerical minority of the total student body, but the cultural system established by the Greeks may dominate campus life nonetheless. In a society as complex as the United States, it is hard to isolate a single dominant culture, although there is a widely acknowledged "American" culture that constitutes the dominant culture. Stemming from middle-class values, habits, and economic resources, this culture is strongly influenced by instruments of culture such as television, the fashion industry, and Anglo-European traditions, and includes diverse elements such as fast food, Christmas shopping, and professional sports. It is also a culture that emphasizes achievement and

individual effort—a cultural tradition that will we later see has a tremendous impact of how many in the United States view inequality (see Chapter 7).

Subcultures

Subcultures are the cultures of groups whose values and norms of behavior differ from those of the dominant culture. Members of subcultures tend to interact frequently with one another and share a common worldview. They may be identifiable by their appearance (style of clothing

DOING SOCIOLOGICAL RESEARCH

Tattoos: Status Risk or Status Symbol?

Not so long ago tattoos were considered a mark of social outcasts. They were associated with gang members, sailors, and juvenile delinquents. But now tattoos are in vogue—a symbol of who's trendy and hip. How did this happen—that a once stigmatized activity associated with the working class became a statement of middle-class fashion?

This is what sociologist Katherine Irwin wanted to know when she first noticed the increase in tattooing among the middle class. Irwin first encountered the culture of tattooing when she accompanied a friend getting a tattoo in a shop she calls Blue Mosque. She started hanging out in the shop, eventually married the shop's owner, and began a four-year study using participant observation in the shop along with interviews of people getting their first tattoos. At one point, Irwin also interviewed some of the parents of tattooees and potential tattooees.

She found that middle-class tattoo patrons were initially fearful that their desire for a tattoo would associate them with low status groups, but they reconciled this by adopting attitudes that associated tattooing with middle-class values and norms. Thus, they defined tattooing as symbolic of independence, liberation, and freedom from social constraints. Many of the women defined tattooing as symbolizing toughness and

strength—values they thought rejected more conventional ideals of femininity. Some saw tattoos as a way of increasing their attachment to alternative social groups or to gain entrée into "fringe" social worlds. Although tattoos held different cultural meanings to different groups, people getting tattooed used various techniques (what Irwin calls "legitimation techniques") to counter the negative stereotypes associated with tattooing. Irwin concludes that people try to align their behavior with legitimate cultural values and norms— even when that behavior seemingly falls outside of prevailing standards.

Questions to Consider

1. Do you think of tattoos as fashionable or deviant? What do you think influences your judgment about this and how might your judgment be different were you in a different culture, age group, or historical moment?
Keywords: *body art; tattoo artist; tattoo collecting*

2. Are there fashion adornments that you associate with different social classes? What are they and what kinds of judgment (positive and negative) do people make about them? Where do these judgments come from and why are they associated with social class?
Keywords: *fads; fashion; status symbols*

Cultural norms establish what people think of as desirable and beautiful. Tattooing, once associated with the working class, is now a form of "collecting" for many.

We have included InfoTrac College Edition keywords at the end of each question to make it easier for you to find more to read on these topics. Go to **www.infotrac-college.com,** an online library, to begin your search.

Based On: Katherine Irwin. 2001. "Legitimating the First Tattoo: Moral Passage through Informal Interaction." *Symbolic Interaction* 24 (March): 49–73.

or adornments) or perhaps by language, dialect, or other cultural markers. You can view subcultures along a continuum of how well they are integrated into the dominant culture. Subcultures typically share some elements of the dominant culture and coexist within it, though some subcultures may be quite separated from the dominant culture—because they are either unwilling or unable to assimilate into the dominant culture—that is, share its values, norms, and beliefs (Dowd and Dowd 2003).

THINKING SOCIOLOGICALLY

Identify a group on your campus that you would call a *subculture*. What are the distinctive *norms* of this group? Based on your observations of this group, how would you describe its relationship to the dominant *culture* on campus?

Some subcultures actually retreat from the dominant culture, as do the Amish, some religious cults, and some communal groups. In these cases, the subculture is actually a separate community that lives as independently from the dominant culture as possible. Other subcultures may coexist with the dominant society, and members of the subculture may participate in both the subculture and the dominant culture. Rap and hip-hop, for example, formed as subcultures among African American inner-city youth, specifically as a challenge to the dominant culture. Now, rap and hip-hop and their

TAKING ON SOCIAL ISSUES

The English Only Movement

Culture may seem like a relatively neutral concept, but in recent years it has become the basis for numerous social conflicts and policy debates. The movement to make English the official language of the United States and related debates about bilingual education signify the significance of culture in the creation of social policy. What are the arguments on each side of the English only movement? From a sociological point of view, what factors do you think have influenced the emergence of this movement?

Taking Action

Go to the Taking Action Exercise on the companion Web site at **sociology.wadsworth.com /andersen_taylor/essen3e** to learn more about an organization that addresses this topic.

accompanying style of dress are actually part of the dominant culture, because they have been mass-marketed by the music and fashion industry. Likely, another subculture will emerge in their place. For another example see the box, "Sociology in Practice: Touring with the Grateful Dead."

Subcultures also develop when new groups enter a society. Such is the case with the numerous and diverse immigrant cultures characteristic of the United States, both now and in the past. Puerto Rican immigration to the U.S. mainland, for example, has generated distinct Puerto Rican subcultures within many urban areas. Although Puerto Ricans also partake in the dominant culture, their unique heritage is part of their subcultural experience. Parts of this culture are now entering the dominant culture. Salsa music, now heard on mainstream radio stations, was created in the late 1960s by Puerto Rican musicians who were expressing the contours of their working class culture (Sanchez 1999; Boggs 1992). The themes in salsa reflect the experience of barrio people and mix the musical traditions of other Latin music including rumba, mambo, and cha-cha. As with other subcultures, the boundaries between the dominant culture and the subculture are permeable, resulting in cultural change as new groups enter society.

Countercultures

Countercultures are subcultures created as a reaction against the values of the dominant culture. Members of the counterculture reject the dominant cultural values, often for political or moral reasons, and develop cultural practices that explicitly defy the norms and values of the dominant group. Nonconformity to the dominant culture is often the hallmark of a counterculture.

Women's communities are examples of countercultures that have been created to resist the dominant culture. Women's communities are based on woman-centered and feminist social networks, relationships, and cultural activities. Although they typically are not geographically separate from the mainstream society, specific places such as feminist bookstores, community activist groups, and women's shelters promote a feeling of belonging that some women may find absent in the dominant culture. For those within women's communities, this solidarity is a relief from the male domination and harassment that they find in the dominant society (Taylor and Rupp 1993).

Some countercultures directly challenge the dominant political system. The contemporary militia movement is an example. Not only have militia members withdrawn from society into isolated compounds that they have created in rural areas, but they have also armed themselves for what they perceive as a countercultural revolution against the authority of the U.S. government. Like other countercultures, militia groups have unique modes of dress, a commonly shared worldview, and a distinctive lifestyle (Ferber 1998; Stern 1996).

Countercultures may also develop in situations where there is political repression and some groups are forced "underground." Under a dictatorship, for example, some groups may be forbidden to practice their religion or speak their own language. In Spain under the dictator Francisco Franco people were forbidden to speak Catalan—the language of the region around Barcelona.

When Franco died in 1975 and Spain became more democratic, the Catalan language flourished—both in public speaking and in the press.

Ethnocentrism

Ethnocentrism is the habit of seeing things only from the point of view of one's own group. To judge one culture by the standards of another culture is ethnocentric. A White American who sees Latino culture as deficient because it is different from Anglo culture is engaging in

---

SOCIOLOGY IN PRACTICE

Touring with the Grateful Dead

One attraction of being a sociologist is the vast scope for creativity in applying the sociological imagination. Consider the work of sociologist Rebecca Adams, a trained survey researcher whose areas of study are gerontology (the study of aging) and friendship. A member of the faculty at the University of North Carolina at Greensboro, Adams once attended a Grateful Dead concert, by invitation of her husband's boss. At the time, Adams was not a Deadhead herself, but had heard the Dead as a college student. At the concert, she saw some of her students, many of whom were probably surprised to see her. After the run of shows, a group of students asked her to supervise their independent research project surveying Deadheads. This was the beginning of a new dimension to Adams's career.

She subsequently toured with the Dead and extensively analyzed the Deadhead subculture, becoming a Deadhead herself along the way. She has been interviewed by numerous rock music and mainstream publications, has appeared on the television program *Entertainment Tonight,* and has participated in the production of a syndicated PBS video on the Grateful Dead. She has now published a book, based on student research, about Deadhead culture. Over the years, she has received thousands of email messages from Deadheads, many of whom have

ended up helping her with her project in one way or another.

When Jerry Garcia (guitarist for the Grateful Dead) died in 1995, Adams was consulted by senior members of the subculture to write about grieving. This drew on her expertise in the sociology of aging, where she knew the research on mourning; her sociological knowledge also helped her understand her own grief about Garcia's passing though it did not ease her sadness. Elders in the subculture also talked with her about the future of the subculture, wondering how it would be sustained in the absence of the group leader.

Adams notes that people in the Deadhead subculture came disproportionately from middle- and upper middle-class families; thus, they are reasonably well educated. Deadheads make good sociologists, Adams says, because they tend to take a critical perspective on society and are analytical about their own experience. Adams writes that Deadheads actually have the perspective of symbolic interaction, though they would not call it by that name. Symbolic interactionists see that we all create the world we live in as we interact with each other through gestures, language, symbols, and other cultural habits. She sees this reflected in Jerry Garcia's comments about Deadheads. He said, "We didn't invent them, and we didn't invent our origi-

nal audience. In a way, this whole process has kind of invented us" (cited in Adams 1995: 17). Adams interprets this to mean that Garcia understood the sociological notion that people create multiple realities in their minds. Deadheads understand that the world is socially constructed, and they actively question it, challenge it, and thus change it.

Adams describes the research process she uses in studying Deadheads as not that different from the experience of attending a Grateful Dead show. She writes, "Just as Deadheads take mental journeys during improvisational jams and then returned to the reassuring structure of familiar songs, I took conceptual journeys and then return to the comfort of my research design" (1995: 18). Adams's work as a practicing sociologist is surely one of the most intriguing applications of the sociological imagination and an illustration of the diverse ways that sociologists do their work.

Critical Thinking Exercise

1. Identify a music group with which you are familiar. Is there a subculture surrounding the group? If so, how would you describe the subcultural norms and values of the group?

FURTHER RESOURCES: Adams, Rebecca G., and Robert Sardiello, eds. 2000. *Deadhead Social Science: "You Ain't Gonna Learn What You Don't Want to Know."* Walnut Creek, CA: AltaMira Press.

ethnocentric thinking. An ethnocentric perspective prevents you from understanding the world as it is experienced by others, and it can lead to narrow-minded conclusions about the worth of diverse cultures. Any group can be ethnocentric, including members of racial minority groups if they believe their way of living is superior to others. Any group that sees the world only from its own point of view is engaging in ethnocentrism. You might contrast ethnocentrism with *cultural relativism,* which we examined earlier as the idea that things can be understood in their cultural context.

Ethnocentrism can build group solidarity, but it also discourages intercultural or intergroup understanding. A good example is seen in the problems of *nationalism,* the sense of identity that arises when a group exalts its own culture over all others and organizes politically and socially around this principle. Nationalist groups tend to be highly exclusionary, rejecting those who do not share their cultural experience and judging all other cultures to be inferior. Nationalist movements tend to use extreme ethnocentrism as the basis for nation–building. Taken to its limits, ethnocentrism can lead to overt political conflict, war, terrorism, even *genocide,* which is the mass killing of people based on their membership in a particular group. You might wonder how someone could believe in the righteousness of their religious faith so much that they would murder people to express that commitment. Understanding ethnocentrism does not excuse such behavior, but it can help you understand how it can occur. Think of Al Qaeda and the extremist belief that terrorism is justified as a religious *jihad* (defined as a religious struggle to defend Islamic faith). Nationalism and the deep ethnic conflicts associated with it have produced many of the wars of contemporary world affairs.

Ethnocentrism can be extreme, as described in the previous examples, but it can also be subtle—as in the example of social groups who think their way of life is better than any other group. Is there such a ranking among groups in your community? Fraternities and sororities often build group rituals around such claims; youth groups see their way of life as superior to adults; urbanites may think their cultural habits are more sophisticated than those labeled "country hicks." Ethnocentrism is a powerful force since it combines a strong sense of group solidarity with the idea of group superiority.

The Globalization of Culture

The infusion of Western culture throughout the world seems to be accelerating, as the commercialized culture of the United States is marketed worldwide. One can go to quite distant places in the world and see familiar elements of U.S. culture, whether it is McDonald's in Hong Kong, Coca Cola in South Africa, or Disney products in western Europe. From films to fast food, the United States dominates international mass culture—largely through the influence of capitalist markets, as conflict theorists would argue. The diffusion of a single culture throughout the world is referred to as **global culture.** Despite the enormous diversity of cultures worldwide, fashions, foods, entertainment, and other cultural values are increasingly dominated by U.S. markets, thereby creating a more homogenous world culture. Global culture is also increasingly marked by capitalist interests, squeezing out the more diverse folk cultures that have been common throughout the world (Rieff 1993). Some sociologists have argued that the feeling of belonging to a community vanishes, as global cultural diffusion occurs (Albrow et al. 1994).

The increasing grip of global culture nonetheless has produced a more commercially based culture. Some argue that some conflicts in modern history stem from a cultural struggle between the values of a consumer-based, capitalist Western culture and the traditional values of local communities. Benjamin Barber (1995) expresses this as the struggle between "McWorld" and "Jihad"—a struggle he interprets as the tension between global commerce and parochial ethnic or tribal values. As some people resist the influence of market-driven values, movements to reclaim or maintain ethnic and cultural identity can intensify. Thus, you can witness a proliferation of identity-based movements among various racial and ethnic groups both in the United States and worldwide.

▪ *Popular Culture*

Some aspects of culture pervade the whole society, such as common language, general patterns of dress, and dominant value systems. **Popular culture** includes the beliefs, practices, and objects that are part of everyday traditions. This includes mass-produced culture, such as popular music and films, mass-marketed books and magazines, large-circulation newspapers, and other parts of the culture that are shared by the general populace (Gans 1999). Popular culture is distinct from elite culture, that which is shared by only a select few, but highly valued. Unlike elite culture (sometimes referred to as "high culture"), popular culture is mass-produced and mass-consumed. Popular culture has enormous significance in the formation of public attitudes and values and plays a significant role in shaping the patterns of consumption in contemporary society.

The distinction between elite and popular culture is relatively new. The industrialization of modern life in late nineteenth-century America fragmented public life, creating greater cultural divisions between people and establishing a more distinct hierarchy within cultural institutions. Even simple things such as having hierarchical seating arrangements in theaters or the development of separate theaters for the "truly refined" reflect changes in the socioeconomic arrangements of society. During the early twentieth century, as a larger middle and upper middle class emerged, the distinction between elite and mass culture widened. Whereas in the early nineteenth century, Shakespeare and other classic writers were read by a wide spectrum of the reading public, now they are considered more refined (Levine 1984).

This trend has continued although there is some blurring of the distinction. Although elites may derive their culture from expensive theater shows, opera performances, or private libraries, millions of "ordinary" citizens get their primary cultural experience from Harlequin romances, mass-produced magazines, and popular television shows. In common discourse, the very word *cultured* is associated with elite cultural taste.

Different groups partake of popular and elite culture in different ways. These patterns lead sociologists to conclude that cultural taste and participation in the arts are socially structured. First, participation in the elite forms of culture is expensive and, therefore, shaped by the class status of different groups. Second, familiarity with different cultural forms stems from patterns of historical exclusion, as well as integration into networks that provide information about the arts. Black Americans are much more likely than White Americans to attend jazz concerts and listen to soul, blues, rhythm-and-blues music, and other historically African American music (DiMaggio and Ostrower 1990). Participating in elite forms of culture is more likely when one gets an upper-class education in the arts and music. Far more popular is mass culture, especially radio and television.

The Influence of the Mass Media

Popular culture is characterized by mass distribution. **Mass media** are the channels of communication available to wide segments of the population—the print, film, and electronic media (radio and television), and increasingly, the Internet. The mass media have extraordinary power to shape information and public perceptions in an era when complex issues are reduced to "sound bites" and "photo opportunities."

THINKING SOCIOLOGICALLY

Watch a particular kind of television show (situation comedy, sports broadcast, children's cartoon, or news program, for example) and make careful written notes on the depiction of different groups in this show. How often are women and men, boys and girls shown? How are they depicted? You could also observe the portrayal of Asian Americans, Native Americans, African Americans, or Latinos. What do your observations tell you about the cultural ideals that are communicated through *popular culture*?

Television, for example, is a powerful force for transmitting cultural values. For most Americans, leisure time is dominated by television. Over 98 percent of all homes in the United States have at least one television—more than have telephone service. The average person consumes some form of media 72 hours per week—more time than they likely spend in school or at work; thirty-two of these hours are spent watching television (U.S. Census Bureau 2002: 698–699). Watching television is also the most popular leisure activity of Americans; 26 percent say it is their favorite way to spend an evening, compared to 9 percent who would rather read and 1 percent whose favorite evening activity is listening to music (Saad 2002).

Television is a powerful transmitter of culture, but it also portrays a very homogeneous view of culture, because, in seeking the widest possible audience, networks and sponsors find the most common ground and take few risks. Television and other forms of mass media have enormous power to shape public opinion and behavior. If you doubt this, observe how familiar certain characters from television sitcoms and dramas are in everyday life. People at work may talk about last night's episode of a particular show or laugh about the antics of their favorite sitcom character. The media is also ubiquitous—present in airports, elevators, classrooms, bars and restaurants, hospital waiting rooms. You may even be born to the sounds and images of television, since they are turned on in many hospital delivery rooms. Television is now so ever-present in our lives that 42 percent of all U.S. households are now called "constant television household"—that is, those where television is on most of the time. Black children are more likely than White or Hispanic children to live in such households (Gitlin 2001). For many families, TV is the "babysitter."

The mass media (and television, in particular) play a huge role in shaping people's perception and awareness of social issues. For example, even though crime has actually decreased, the amount of time spent reporting crime in the media has actually increased. Sociologists have found that people's fear of crime is directly related to the time they spend watching television or listening to the radio (Angotti 1997; Chiricos et al. 1997). Similarly, given the media attention to school violence, you would think that such violence is increasing. In fact, throughout the 1990s, there was an actual decline in school violence with fewer students carrying guns and other weapons. Although the number of events with multiple-victim homicides in schools has increased, school-associated violent deaths have decreased (U.S. Department of Education and U.S. Department of Justice 2000; Brener et al. 1999).

Although people tend to think of the news as authentic and true, news is actually manufactured in a complex social process. From a sociological perspective, it is

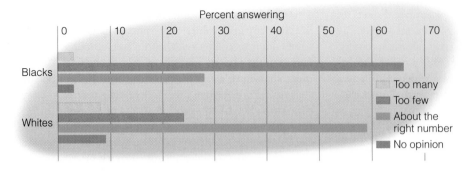

Percent answering

FIGURE 2.2 The Racial Gap: Images in the Media
The question asked: "Thinking about black actors and actresses on prime television shows, would you say there are too many, too few, or about the right number?"

SOURCE: Gallup Organization. 1999. *The Gallup Poll*. Princeton, NJ: Gallup Organization. **www.gallup.com.** Used with permission.

not objective reality that determines what news is presented and how it is portrayed, but commercial interests, the values of news producers, and perceptions of what matters to the public. The media shape our definition of social problems by determining the range of opinion or information that is defined as legitimate and by deciding which experts will be called on to elaborate an issue (Gans 1979; Gitlin 2001).

Race, Gender, and Class in the Media

Many sociologists have argued that the mass media promote narrow definitions of who people are and what they can be. What is considered beauty, for example, is not universal; ideals of beauty change as cultures change and depend upon what certain cultural institutions promote as beautiful. Aging is not beautiful, youth is; light skin is promoted as more beautiful than dark skin (regardless of one's race), although being tan is seen as more beautiful than being pale. In African American women's magazines, the models typified as most beautiful are generally those with clearly Anglo features—light skin, blue eyes, and straight or wavy hair. These depictions have fluctuated over time; in the early 1970s, for example, there was a more Afrocentric ideal of beauty—darker skin, Afro hairdos, and African clothing. European facial features are also pervasive in the images of Asian and Latino women appearing in U.S. magazines. The media communicate that only certain forms of beauty are culturally valued. These ideals are not somehow "natural"; they are constructed by those who control cultural and economic institutions.

Images of women and racial and ethnic minorities in the media are similarly limiting. Content analyses of television reveal that during prime time men are a large majority of the characters shown. There has been an increase in the extent to which women are depicted in professional

SOCIOLOGICAL EYE ON THE MEDIA

Crime and Gender

Reality TV has become more popular in television programming. Reality crime shows (like *Cops*, *Survivor*, and other such programs) have increasingly dominated primetime television. Cheap to produce, they claim to represent actual people and situations—but how true are they? A group of sociologists examined this by studying how women are depicted as crime victims in one crime show: *America's Most Wanted*. By systematically analyzing the content of this show, the researchers hoped to find how reality crime shows portrayed women as victims of crime. To do the

research, the team videotaped all episodes of *America's Most Wanted* during the 1989 and 1996 seasons, then randomly selected twenty-four episodes from which they analyzed ninety-six vignettes of crime stories.

Among other things, they found that men tend to provide the narratives for the shows; women's voices were more silent. Moreover, the programs emphasized women's vulnerability to violence from brutal strangers. Men were portrayed as having technical expertise and authority that would protect women. Images of family were also stressed for women.

The researchers concluded that the portrayals of women in these reality shows actually heighten women's fear of crime and also present unrealistic portrayals of the actual victimization of women. In addition, because reality shows blur fact and fiction, they are, in the words of the researchers, even more insidious. Such analyses of the content of the media show how influential the media are in constructing our concepts of gender, crime, and violence, among other things.

SOURCE: Cavendar, Gray, Lisa Bond-Maupin, and Nancy C. Jurik. 1999. "The Construction of Gender in Reality Crime TV." *Gender & Society* 13 (October): 643–663.

jobs, but such images usually depict professional women as young, suggesting that career success comes early, especially to thin and beautiful women (Signorielli and Bacue 1999). On soap operas, women are cast either as evil or good, but also naive. In music videos, women characters appear less frequently, but typically wear sexy and skimpy clothing, and are more often the object of another's gaze than their male counterparts (Signorielli et al. 1994).

Even though African Americans and Hispanics watch more television than Whites do, they are a small proportion of TV characters, generally confined to a narrow variety of character types, depicted in stereotypical ways. Latinos are often stereotyped as criminals or passionate lovers. African American men are most typically seen as athletes and sports commentators, criminals, or entertainers; African American women, in domestic or sexual roles or as sex objects. It is difficult to find a single show where Asians are the principal characters—usually they are depicted in silent roles as domestics or behind-the-scenes characters. Native Americans make occasional appearances where they usually are depicted as mystics or warriors. Jewish women are generally invisible on popular TV programming, except when they are ridiculed in stereotypical roles (Kray 1993).

Class stereotypes abound as well, with working-class men typically portrayed as being ineffectual, even buffoonish (Butsch 1992; Dines and Humez 1995). A recent study of TV talk shows also shows how such shows exploit working class people. The researcher, Laura Grindstaff, spent six months working on two popular talk shows, carefully doing participant observation and interviewing staff and guests. She found that guests had to enact stereotypes of their groups to get air time. She argues that, although these shows give ordinary people a place to air their problems and be heard, they exploit the working class—making it seem that others care about them when they do not and making a spectacle of their troubles (Grindstaff 2002; Press 2002).

Television is not the only form of popular culture that influences public consciousness, class, gender, and race. Music, film, books, and other industries play a significant role in molding public consciousness. What images are produced by these cultural forms? You can look for yourself. Try to buy a birthday card that contains neither an age or gender stereotype, or watch rock videos and see how different gender and race groups are portrayed. You will likely find that women are depicted as trying to get the attention of men; African Americans are more likely than Whites to be seen singing and dancing.

Do these images matter? Studies find that exposure to traditional sexual imagery in music videos has an effect on college students' attitudes about adversarial sexual relationships (Kalof 1999). Other studies find that even when viewers see media images as unrealistic, they think that others find the images important and will evaluate them accordingly; this has been found especially true for young White girls who think boys will judge them by how well they match the media ideal (Milkie 1999). Although people do not just passively internalize media images and do distinguish between fantasy and reality (Currie 1997), such images form cultural ideals that have a huge impact on people's behavior, values, and self-image.

■ Theoretical Perspectives on Culture

Sociologists study culture in a variety of ways, asking a variety of questions about the relationship of culture to other social institutions and the role of culture in modern life (see Table 2.2). One important question for sociologists studying the mass media is whether these images have any effect on those who see them. Do the media create popular values or reflect them? The **reflection hypothesis** contends that the mass media reflect the values of the general population (Tuchman 1979). The media try to appeal to the most broad-based audience, so they aim for the middle ground in depicting images and ideas. Maximizing popular appeal is central to television program development; media organizations spend huge amounts on market research to uncover what people think and believe and what they will like. Characters are then created with whom people will identify. Interestingly, the images in the media with which we identify are distorted versions of reality. Real people seldom live like the characters on television, although part of the appeal of these shows is how they build upon and then mythologize the actual experiences of people.

The reflection hypothesis assumes that images and values portrayed in the media reflect the values existing in the public, but the reverse can also be true—that is, the ideals portrayed in the media also influence the values of those who see them. As an example, social scientists have studied the stereotyped images commonly found in children's programming. Among their findings, they have shown that the children who watch the most TV hold the most stereotypic gender attitudes (Signorielli 1991). Although there is not a simple and direct relationship between the content of mass media images and what people think of themselves, clearly these mass-produced images have a significant impact on who we are and what we think.

Culture and Group Solidarity

Many sociologists have studied particular forms of culture and have provided detailed analyses of the content

TABLE 2.2 Theoretical Perspectives on Culture

According to:

Functionalism	Conflict Theory	Symbolic Interaction	New Cultural Studies
Culture . . .			
Integrates people into groups	Serves the interests of powerful groups	Creates group identity from diverse cultural meanings	Is ephemeral, unpredictable, and constantly changing
Provides coherence and stability in society	Can be a source of political resistance	Changes as people produce new cultural meanings	Is a material manifestation of a consumer-oriented society
Creates norms and values that integrate people in society	Is increasingly connected by economic monopolies	Is socially constructed through the activities of social groups	Is best understood by analyzing its artifacts—books, films, television images

of cultural artifacts, such as images in certain television programs or genres of popular music. Other sociologists take a broader view by analyzing the relationship of culture to other forms of social organization. Beginning with some of the classical sociological theorists (see Chapter 1), sociologists have studied the relationship of culture to other social institutions. Max Weber looked at the impact of culture on the formation of social and economic institutions. In his classic analysis of the Protestant work ethic and capitalism, Weber argued that the Protestant faith rested on cultural beliefs that were highly compatible with the development of modern capitalism. By promoting a strong work ethic and a need to display material success as a sign of religious salvation, the Protestant ethic indirectly but effectively promoted the interests of an emerging capitalist economy. (We revisit this issue in Chapter 12.) In other words, culture influences other social institutions.

Many sociologists have also examined how culture integrates members into society and social groups. Functionalist theorists, for example, believe that norms and values create social bonds that attach people to society. Culture therefore provides coherence and stability in society. Robert Putnam examines this idea in his book *Bowling Alone* (2000) in which he argues that there has been a decline in civic engagement, defined as participation in voluntary organizations, religious activities, and other forms of public life in recent years. As people become less engaged in such activities, there is a decline in the shared values and norms of the society so that social disorder results. Sociologists are debating the extent to which there has been such a decline in public life, but, from a functionalist perspective, the point is that participation in a common culture is an important social bond—one that unites society (Etzioni, et al. 2001).

Classical theoretical analyses of culture have placed special emphasis on nonmaterial culture—the values,

norms, and belief systems of society. Sociologists who use this perspective emphasize the integrative function of culture, that is, its ability to give people a sense of belonging in an otherwise complex social system (Smelser 1992a). In the broadest sense, they see culture as a major integrative force in society, providing societies with a sense of collective identity and commonly shared worldviews.

Culture, Power, and Social Conflict

Whereas the emphasis on shared values and group solidarity drives one sociological analysis of culture, conflicting values drives another. Conflict theorists (see Chapter 1) have analyzed culture as a source of power in society. From a conflict-oriented perspective, culture is dominated by economic interests. A few powerful groups are the major producers and distributors of culture. With more corporate mergers, a single corporation can control a huge share of television, radio, newspapers, music, publishing, film, and the Internet, as shown in Figure 2.3 As the production of popular culture becomes concentrated in the hands of just a few, there may be less diversity in the content.

Conflict theorists see contemporary culture as produced within institutions that are based on inequality and capitalist principles. As a result, the cultural values and products that are produced and sold promote the economic and political interests of the few—those who own or benefit from these cultural industries. This is especially evident in the study of popular culture, which is marketed to the masses by entities with a vast economic stake in the dissemination of their products. Conflict theorists conclude that the cultural products most likely to be produced are consistent with the values, needs, and interests of the most powerful groups in society. The evening news, for example, typically is sponsored by major financial institutions, oil companies, and automobile makers. Conflict theorists then ask how this com-

THEME PARKS
Warner Bros. Movie World
Theme Park and hotel in Australia
(w/AT&T and Village Roadshow)

MAGAZINES
More than 64, including the 3 bestselling:
Time, Life and *People; MAD Magazine,* DC
Comics (87.5% w/12.5% AT&T); IPC, leading
consumer magazine publisher in Britain

TIME WARNER

INTERNET
America Online, CompuServe,
Netscape, ICQ and AOL Instant
Messenger; websites include MusicNet
(20% w/20% Bertelsmann, 20% EMI and
RealNetworks), digitalcity, moviefone,
mapquest and music sites Spinner.com,
Winamp and SHOUTcast; stakes in
Amazon.com (2%), Dr. Koop (10%),
RoadRunner cable modems (majority
stake w/AT&T and Advance-Newhouse)

MOVIES
Warner Bros., New Line and Fine Line
Features (75% w/25% AT&T); library of
MGM, RKO and pre-1950 Warner Bros. films;
Warner Home Video (75% w/25% AT&T);
theaters: UCI (50% w/50% Viacom); WF
Cinema Holdings (50% w/50% Viacom)

TELEVISION

Networks
WB (50% w/17% AT&T, 22% Tribune Co. and
11% WB officers), HBO and Cinemax, (75%
w/25% AT&T), Comedy Central (37.5% w/12.5%
AT&T and 50% Viacom), Court TV (37.5%
w/12.5% AT&T and 50% Liberty), E! and Style
(7.5% w/AT&T, Liberty, Disney and Comcast),
TBS, TNT, Cartoon Network, Turner Classic
Movies, CNN, Headline News, CNNfn and
CNN/Sports Illustrated; TVKO (75% w/25%
AT&T); Music Choice (w/Sony, EMI, AT&T and
others); wholly and partially owned channels in
Europe, Asia and South America

Cable
Second-largest provider with 12.8 million
customers in wholly and partially owned systems
(most with AT&T)

Production/Programming
Warner Bros., Warner Bros. Animation, Tele-
pictures, Castle Rock; library of 6,500 movies,
32,000 TV shows and 13,500 cartoons (all 75%
w/25% AT&T) Other: TiVo (18% w/GE, Liberty,
News Corp. and others) digital video recording

MUSIC
More than 40 labels, including
Warner Bros., Atlantic, Elektra,
London-Sire and Rhino Records;
manufactures, packages and distributes the
company's CDs, tapes and DVDs, majority
interest in Alternative Distribution Alliance;
Quincy Jones Entertainment Co. (37.5%
w/12.5% AT&T and 50% Quincy Jones),
Columbia House (50% w/50% Sony); Music
publisher Warner/Chappell

SPORTS
Atlanta Braves, Atlanta Hawks,
Atlanta Thrashers, Goodwill
Games, Phillips Arena

OTHER
Time Warner Telecom (37%), Warner
Bros. Studio Stores (75% w/25% AT&T),
licenses rights to DC Comics, Hanna-
Barbera characters, other WB properties
(75% w/25% AT&T); stake in Sportsline
Radio

BOOKS
Warner Books; Little, Brown; Time-Life
Books; Book-of-the-Month Club (50%
w/50% Bertelsmann)

FIGURE 2.3 The Corporate Control of Culture

DATA: *The Nation,* July 7–14, 2002, pp. 27–30.

mercial sponsorship influences the content of the news. If the news were sponsored by labor unions, would conflicts between management and workers always be defined as "labor troubles," or might newscasters refer instead to "capitalist troubles"?

Conflict theorists see culture as increasingly controlled by economic monopolies. Whether it is books, music, films, news, or other cultural forms, monopolies in the communications industry (where culture is increasingly located) have a strong interest in protecting the status quo. As media conglomerates swallow up smaller companies and drive out smaller, less efficient competitors, the control that economic monopolies have over the production and distribution of culture becomes enormous. Mega-communications companies then influence everything—from the movies and television shows you see to the books you read in school.

Sociologists refer to the concentration of cultural power as **cultural hegemony** (pronounced "heh-JEM-o-nee"), defined as the pervasive and excessive influence of one cul-

ture throughout society. Cultural hegemony creates a homogeneous mass culture. It is a means through which powerful groups gain the assent of those they rule. The concept of cultural hegemony implies that culture is highly politicized, even if it does not appear so. Through cultural hegemony, those who control cultural institutions can also control people's political awareness because they create cultural beliefs that make the rule of those in power seem inevitable and right. As a result, political resistance to the dominant culture is blunted (Gramsci 1971).

Conflict theorists point out, however, that culture can also be a source of political resistance and social change. Reclaiming an indigenous culture that had been denied or repressed, as in the case of people who have been colonized by other nations, is one way that groups mobilize to assert their independence. An example from within the United States is the *repatriation movement* among American Indians who have argued for the return of both cultural artifacts and human remains that are held in museum collections. Many American Indians believe that, despite the public good that is derived from studying such remains and objects, cultural autonomy and spiritual respect outweigh such scientific arguments (Thornton 2001). Other social movements, such as the gay and lesbian movement, have also used cultural performance as a means of political and social protest. Cross-dressing, drag shows, and other forms of "gender play" can be seen as cultural performances that challenge homophobia and traditional sexual and gender roles (Rupp and Taylor 2003).

A final point of focus for sociologists studying culture from a conflict perspective lies in the concept of **cultural capital** (also known as **social capital**), which refers to the cultural resources that are socially designated as being worthy (such as knowledge of elite culture) and that give advantages to groups possessing such capital. This idea has been most developed by the French sociologist Pierre Bourdieu (1984), who sees the appropriation of culture as one way that groups maintain their social status.

THINKING SOCIOLOGICALLY

Sociologists argue that those with *cultural capital* have more educational advantage than others. As you have gone through school, have you seen evidence of this? What effect does it have on different groups?

Bourdieu argues that members of the dominant class have distinctive lifestyles that mark their status in society; their ability to display this cultural lifestyle signals their importance to others; that is, they possess cultural capital. From this point of view, culture has a role in reproducing inequality between groups. Those with cultural capital use it to improve their social and economic position in society; sociologists have found a significant relationship, for example, between cultural capital and grades in schools—that is, those from the more well-to-do classes (those with more cultural capital) are able to parlay their knowledge into higher grades, thereby reproducing their social position by being more competitive in school admissions and, eventually, in the labor market (Hill 2001; Treiman 2001).

New Cultural Studies

Especially productive when applied to the study of culture has been symbolic interaction theory—a perspective that analyzes behavior in terms of the meaning people give it. The concept of culture is central to this orientation in that symbolic interaction emphasizes the interpretive basis of social behavior, and culture provides the interpretive framework through which behavior is understood.

Symbolic interaction also emphasizes that culture, like all other forms of social behavior, is socially con-

structed. That is, culture is produced through social relationships and in social groups, such as the media organizations through which culture is disseminated. People do not just passively submit to cultural norms; rather, they are active, skillful makers of culture. Culture is not one-dimensional; it contains diverse elements and provides people with a wide range of choices from which to select how they will behave (Swidler 1986). Culture, in fact, represents the creative dimension of human life.

In recent years, a new interdisciplinary field known as *cultural studies* has emerged that builds on the insights of the symbolic interaction perspective in sociology. Sociologists who work in cultural studies are often critical of classical sociological approaches to culture, arguing that the classical approach has overemphasized nonmaterial culture—that is, ideas, beliefs, values, and norms. The new scholars of cultural studies find that material culture has increasing importance in modern society (Crane 1994; Walters 1999). This includes cultural forms that are recorded through print, film, artifacts, or the electronic media. Postmodernist theory has greatly influenced new cultural studies (see Chapter 1). *Postmodernism* is based on the idea that society is not an objective thing; rather, it is found in the words and images that people use to represent behavior and ideas. Given this orientation, postmodernism often analyzes common images and cultural products found in everyday life.

Classical theorists have tended to study the unifying features of culture; cultural studies researchers tend to see culture as more fragmented and unpredictable. To them, culture is a series of images—images that can be interpreted in multiple ways depending on the viewpoint of the observer. From the perspective of new cultural studies theorists, the ephemeral and rapidly changing quality of contemporary cultural forms is reflective of the highly technological and consumer-based culture on which the modern economy rests. Their fascination is in part with the illusions that such a dynamic and rapidly changing culture produces.

■ *Cultural Change*

In one sense, culture is a conservative force in society; it tends to be based on tradition and is passed on through generations, conserving and regenerating the values and beliefs of society. Culture is also increasingly based on institutions that have an economic interest in maintaining the status quo. People are also often resistant to cultural change because familiar ways and established patterns of doing things are hard to give up; nevertheless, cultures do change. Culture is dynamic, not static, and it develops as people respond to changes in their physical and social environment.

Culture Lag

Culture lag refers to the delay in cultural adjustments to changing social conditions (Ogburn 1922). Some parts of culture may change more rapidly than others; thus, one aspect of culture may "lag" behind another. Rapid technological change is often attended by culture lag since some elements of the culture do not keep pace with technological innovation. In today's world, we have the technological ability to develop efficient, less-polluting rapid transit, but changing people's transportation habits is difficult.

When culture changes rapidly, or someone is suddenly thrust into a new cultural situation, the result can be **culture shock,** the feeling of disorientation when one encounters a new or rapidly changed cultural situation.

Even moving from one cultural environment to another within one's own society can make a person feel out of place and alienated. The greater the difference between cultural settings, the greater the culture shock.

Sources of Cultural Change

There are several causes of cultural change, including (1) a change in the societal conditions, (2) cultural diffusion, (3) innovation, and (4) the imposition of cultural change by an outside agency. Let us examine each.

Cultures change in response to changed conditions in the society. Economic changes, population changes, and other social transformations all influence the development of culture. A change in the makeup of a society's population

---

FORCES OF SOCIAL CHANGE

Fast Food and the Transformation of American Culture

Can you imagine the United States without fast food? Probably not. Fast food is so ubiquitous in contemporary culture that it is hard to imagine life without it. Consider this (Schlossser 2001):

- The average person in the United States consumes three hamburgers and four orders of french fries per week.

- Americans spend more money on fast food than on movies, books, magazines, newspapers, videos, music, computers, and higher education combined.

- One in eight workers has at some point been employed by McDonald's.

- McDonald's is the largest private operator of playgrounds in the United States and the single largest purchaser of beef, pork, and potatoes.

- 96 percent of American schoolchildren can identify Ronald McDonald—only exceeded by the number who can identify Santa Claus.

Eric Schlosser, who has written about the permeation of society by fast food culture, has written that "a nation's diet can be more revealing than its art or literature" (2001: 3). He relates the growth of the fast food industry to fundamental changes in American society, including the vast entry of women into the paid labor market, the development of an automobile culture, the increased reliance on low-wage service jobs, the decline of family farming and the growth of agribusiness. One result is a cultural emphasis on uniformity, not to mention increased fat and calories in people's diets.

You can think about the influence of fast food on contemporary culture by making a list of the values associated with fast food. How has the fast food industry changed cultural practices in the United States? What impact does this have in your community?

© John Philips/Time/Getty Images

© Kathy McLaughlin/The Image Works

FURTHER RESOURCES: Schlosser, Eric. 2001. *Fast Food Nation: The Dark Side of the All-American Meal.* New York: Houghton Mifflin.

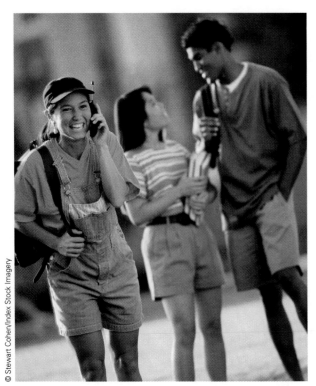

Technology now infiltrates virtually every aspect of modern culture.

may be enough by itself to cause a cultural transformation. The high rate of immigration in recent years has brought many cultural changes to the United States. Some cities, such as Miami and Los Angeles, have a Latin feel because of the large Hispanic population. But even outside urban areas, cultural change from immigration is apparent. Markets selling Asian, Mexican, and Middle Eastern foods are increasingly common; school districts include students who speak a huge variety of languages; popular music bears the imprint of different world cultures. This is not the first time U.S. culture has changed because of immigration. Many national traditions stem from the patterns of immigration that marked the earlier part of the twentieth century—think of St. Patrick's Day parades, Italian markets, and Chinatowns.

Cultures change through cultural diffusion. **Cultural diffusion** is the transmission of cultural elements from one society or cultural group to another. In our world of instantaneous communication, cultural diffusion is swift and widespread. This is evident in the degree to which worldwide cultures have been Westernized. Cultural diffusion also occurs when subcultural influences enter the dominant group. Dominant cultures are regularly enriched by minority cultures. An example is the influence of Black and Latino music on other musical forms. Rap music, for example, emerged within inner-city African American neighborhoods, describing and analyzing in its own form

the economic and political conditions of the urban ghetto. Now, rap music is listened to by White as well as Black audiences and is part of White youth culture. Cultural diffusion is one thing that drives cultural evolution, especially in a society such as ours that is lush with diversity.

Cultures change as the result of innovation, including inventions and technological developments. Cultural innovations can create dramatic changes in society. Think, for example, of how the invention of trolleys, subways, and automobiles changed the character of cities. People no longer walked to work; instead, cities expanded outward to include suburbs. Further, the invention of the elevator let cities expand not just out, but up.

Now the development of computer technology infiltrates every dimension of life. It is hard to overestimate the effect of innovation on contemporary cultural change. Technological innovation is so rapid and dynamic that one generation can barely maintain competence with the hardware of the next. The smallest laptop or handheld computer today weighs hardly more than a few ounces, and its capabilities rival that of computers that filled entire buildings only twenty years ago. Answering machines, cellular phones, and fax machines were glamorous devices just a few years ago; now their use is common. What are some of the social changes that come from, for example, the use of cell phones? (See Map 2.2.) People can now work and be miles—even nations—away from their place of employment. Families can communicate from multiple sites; children can be paged; grandparents sent live photos of a family event; criminals tracked via cellular technology. Conveniences multiply with the growth of such technology, but so do the invasions of privacy and, perhaps, identity theft. In such a rapidly changing technological world, it is hard to imagine what will be common in just a few years.

Cultural change can be imposed. Change can occur when a powerful group takes over a society and imposes a new culture. The dominating group may arise internally, as in a political revolution, or it may appear from outside, perhaps as an invasion. When an external group takes over the society of a "native," or indigenous, group, as White settlers did with Native American societies, they typically impose their own culture while prohibiting the indigenous group from expressing its original cultural ways. Manipulating the culture of a group is a way of exerting social control. Many have argued that public education in the United States, which developed during a period of mass immigration, was designed to force White, northern European, middle-class values onto a diverse immigrant population that was perceived to be potentially unruly and politically disruptive; likewise, the schools run by the Bureau of Indian Affairs have been used to impose dominant group values on Native American children (Snipp 1996).

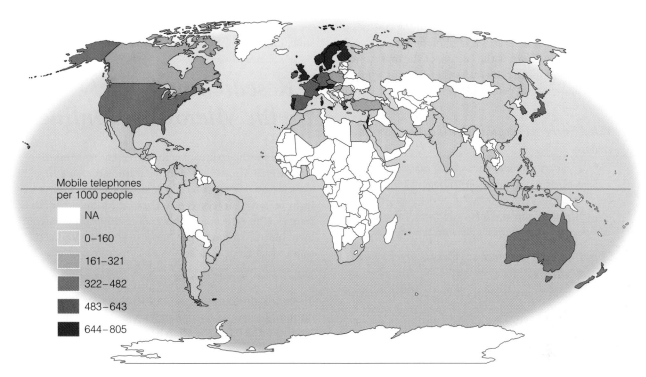

MAP 2.2 Viewing Society in Global Perspective: Technological Penetration

Technological development is a major source of cultural change in any society. Cell phones, for example, are now commonplace in the United States and other nations. **What social changes can you think of that result from the increased use of cell phones?**

SOURCE: U.S. Census Bureau. 2002. *Statistical Abstract of the United States 2002.* Washington, DC: U.S. Government Printing Office, p. 852.

Resistance to political oppression often takes the form of a cultural movement that asserts or revives the culture of an oppressed group; thus, cultural expression can be a form of political protest. *Nationalist movements*—those that identify a common culture as the basis for group solidarity—are an example. Black nationalism in the United States is the idea that African Americans should be united by their African heritage and that this should be the basis for cultural identity and political mobilization. This is not an entirely new phenomenon. Black nationalism was a strong theme in Black protest movements in the 1920s and surfaced again in the 1970s as the Black Power movement emphasized that "Black is beautiful," encouraging African Americans to celebrate their African heritage with Afro hairstyles, African dress, and African awareness. Cultural nationalism has also inspired a similar movement among Latinos—La Raza Unida (meaning, "the race, or the people, united"), which promoted solidarity among Chicanos. As people acquire new means of cultural expression, they can come to question the existing value systems and challenge dominant cultural forms. Cultural change can promote social change, just as social change can transform culture.

■ *Chapter Summary*

■ *What is culture?*

Culture is the complex and elaborate system of meaning and behavior that defines the way of life for a group or society. It is shared, learned, taken for granted, symbolic, and emergent and varies from one society to another.

■ *How do sociologists define norms, beliefs, and values?*

Norms are rules of social behavior that guide every situation and may be formal or informal. When norms are violated, *social sanctions* are applied. *Beliefs* are strongly shared ideas about the nature of social reality. *Values* are the abstract concepts in a society that define the worth of different things and ideas.

■ *What is the significance of diversity in human cultures?*

As societies develop and become more complex, cultural diversity can appear. The United States is highly diverse culturally, with many of its traditions influenced by immigrant cultures and the cultures of African Americans, Latinos, and Native Americans. The *dominant culture* is the culture of the most powerful group in society. *Subcultures* are groups whose *values* and cultural patterns depart significantly from the dominant culture.

■ **What is the sociological significance of popular culture?**

Popular culture includes the beliefs, practices, and objects of everyday traditions. Elements of popular culture, such as the *mass media,* have an enormous influence on group's beliefs and values, including images associated with racism and sexism.

■ **What do different sociological theories reveal about culture?**

Sociological theory provides different perspectives on the significance of culture. *Functionalist theory* emphasizes the influence of values, norms, and beliefs on the whole society. *Conflict theorists* see culture as influenced by economic interests and power relations in society. *Symbolic interactionists* emphasize that culture is socially constructed. This has influenced new *cultural studies,* which interpret culture as a series of images that can be analyzed from the viewpoint of different observers.

■ **How do cultures change?**

There are several sources of cultural change, including change in societal conditions, *cultural diffusion,* innovation, and the imposition of change by dominant groups. As cultures change, *culture lag* can result, meaning that sometimes cultural adjustments are out of synchrony with each other. Persons who experience new cultural situations may experience *culture shock.*

■ *Key Terms*

beliefs 46	folkways 45
counterculture 50	global culture 52
cultural capital 58	language 42
cultural diffusion 60	laws 45
cultural hegemony 57	mass media 53
cultural relativism 42	mores 45
culture 37	norms 45
culture lag 59	popular culture 52
culture shock 59	reflection hypothesis 55
dominant culture 48	Sapir–Whorf
ethnocentrism 51	hypothesis 42
ethnomethodology 46	social capital 58

social sanctions 45	symbols 40
subculture 49	values 46

■ *Researching Society with MicroCase Online*

You can see the results of actual research by using the Wadsworth MicroCase® Online feature available to you. This feature allows you to look at some of the results from national surveys, census data, and some other data sources. You can explore this easy-to-use feature on your own, but try this example. Suppose you want to know some social facts, such as:

Who is most likely to have seen a movie in the last year?

To answer this question, go to **sociology.wadsworth. com/andersen_taylor/essen3e,** select MicroCase Online from the left navigation bar, and follow the directions there to analyze the data described below.

Data file: GSS

Task: Auto-Analyzer

Primary Variable: X-MOVIE? Have you seen an X-rated movie in the last year?

Questions

Once you have your results, answer the following questions

1. Fill in the table below, noting which category (or group) was most likely and least likely to have watched an X-rated movie in the last year.

Socio-Demographic Variable	Category Most Likely	Category Least Likely
Religion		
Party		
Education		

2. Are people thirty and older less likely to have watched an X-rated movie than those under thirty?

3. Are Conservative Protestants the least likely to have watched an X-rated movie?

4. Is there a statistically significant difference in the likelihood of having watched an X-rated movie across different educational levels?

5. Do either race or gender influence the likelihood of one's seeing an X-rated movie?

The Companion Web Site for Sociology: The Essentials, *Third Edition*

sociology.wadsworth.com/andersen_taylor/essen3e

Supplement your review of this chapter by going to the companion Web site to take one of the Tutorial Quizzes, use the flash cards to master key terms, and check out the many other study aids you'll find there. You'll also find special features such as GSS Data and Census 2000 information, data and resources at your fingertips to help you with that special project or do some research on your own.

Suggested Readings and Web Resources

Cerulo, Karen. 1998. *Deciphering Violence.* New York: Routledge.
Using cultural depictions of violence as the reference point, Cerulo's book is a good introduction to the sociology of culture.

Gamson, Joshua. 1998. *Freaks Talk Back: Tabloid Talk Shows and Sexual Nonconformity.* Chicago: University of Chicago Press.
Through extensive interviewing and content analysis, Gamson examines how the increased presence of gays, lesbians, and sexual nonconformists has increased tolerance for sexual diversity. His research also shows the power of the mass media to transform public opinion.

Gans, Herbert J. 1999. *Popular Culture and High Culture: An Analysis and Evaluation of Taste.* New York: Basic Books.
This classic work examines class differences in cultural taste and the role of popular and high culture in American society.

Gitlin, Todd. 2001. *Media Unlimited: How the Torrent of Images and Sounds Overwhelms Our Lives.* New York: Metropolitan Books.
Gitlin is nationally known for his sociological commentaries on the influence of the media. In this book, he describes how the media have created a constant stream of sensation and image, while blunting public imagination.

Media Watch
www.mediawatch.com
An organization dedicated to challenging racism and sexism in the media; the Web site includes archives on the organization's work, as well as lists of the educational videos distributed by the organization.

National Coalition of Television Violence
www.nctvv.org
This Web site provides news and information about violence on television, including recent media stories about television violence.

Popular Culture Association
www2.h-net.msu.edu/~pcaaca
This organization encourages scholarly analysis of popular culture. The Web site includes discussion groups and reviews of recent studies of popular culture.

Socialization and the Life Course

*d*uring the summer of 2000, scientists working on the human genome project announced that they had deciphered the human genetic code. By mapping the complex structure of DNA (deoxyribonucleic acid) on high-speed computers, scientists identified the 3.12 billion chemical base pairs in human DNA and put them in proper sequence, unlocking what they called the genetic code of human life. Scientists likened this to assembling "the book of life"—that is, having the knowledge to make human beings. The stated purpose of the human genome project is to see how genetics influences the development of disease, but it raises numerous ethical questions about the possibility of being able to create human life in the laboratory.

Is our genetic constitution what makes us human? Suppose you created a human being in the laboratory, but left that creature without social contact. Would the "person" seem human?

Rare cases of *feral children*—those who have been raised in the absence of human contact—provide some clues as to what happens during human development when there is little or no social contact. One such case involved a young girl given the pseudonym of Genie. Genie's case was discovered in 1970 when her blind mother appeared in the Los Angeles County welfare office seeking assistance for herself. At first, caseworkers thought the girl was six years old. In fact, she was thirteen, although she weighed only 59 pounds and was 4 feet 6 inches tall. She was small and withered, unable to stand up straight, incontinent, and severely malnourished. Her eyes did not focus, she had two nearly complete sets of teeth, and there was a strange ring of calluses around her buttocks. She could not talk.

As the case unfolded, it was discovered that the girl had been kept in nearly total isolation for most of her life. The first scientific report written about Genie states:

> In the house Genie was confined to a small bedroom, harnessed to an infant's potty seat. Genie's father sewed the harness himself; unclad except for the harness, Genie was left to sit on that chair. Unable to move anything except her fingers and hands, feet and toes, Genie was left to sit, tied-up, hour after hour, often into the night, day after day, month after month, year after year (Curtiss 1977: 5).

At night, she was put in another restraining device—a handmade sleeping bag that held her arms stationary—and was placed in a crib. If she made a sound, her father beat her. She was given no toys and was allowed to play only with two old raincoats and her father's censored version of *TV Guide*. (He had deleted everything "suggestive," such as pictures of women in bathing suits.) Genie's mother, timid and blind, was also victimized by her husband. Shortly after the mother sought help, after years of abuse, the father committed suicide.

Genie was studied intensively by scientists interested in language acquisition and the psychological effects of extreme confinement. They hoped that her development would throw some light on the question of nature versus nurture—that is, are we the product of our genes or our social training? After intense language instruction and psychological treatment, Genie developed some verbal ability and, after a year, showed progress in her mental and physical development; yet, the years of isolation and severe abuse took their toll. Genie now lives in a home for retarded adults (Rymer 1993).

Such a rare case of a feral child sheds some light on the consequences of life without social contact. Knowing the sequence of the human genome may raise the specter of making human beings in the laboratory, but without society, what would we be like? Genes may confer skin and bone and brain, but only by learning the values, norms, and roles that culture bestows on us do we become the social beings that define us in the eyes of others and to ourselves. Sociologists refer to this process as socialization—the subject of this chapter.

■ *The Socialization Process*

Socialization is the process through which people learn the expectations of society. **Roles** are the expected behavior associated with a given status in society. When you occupy a given social role, you tend to take on the expectations of others. For example, when you enter a new group of friends, you probably observe their behavior, their language, their dress—perhaps even their opinions of others—and often modify your own behavior accordingly. Before you know it, you are a member of the group, perhaps socializing others into the same set of expectations. We explore roles further in Chapter 4, but it is important to know here that roles are learned through the socialization process.

Through socialization, people absorb their culture—customs, habits, laws, practices, and means of expression. Socialization is the basis for identity—how one defines oneself. Identity is both personal and social. To a great

Formal and informal learning are part of the socialization process. Here deaf children are learning sign language.

extent, it is bestowed by others, because we come to see ourselves as others see us. Socialization also establishes personality, defined as the relatively consistent pattern of behavior, feelings, and beliefs in a given person.

The socialization experience differs for individuals depending on factors such as race, gender, and class, as well as more subtle factors such as attractiveness and personality. Women and men encounter different socialization patterns as they grow up, because each gender brings with it different social expectations (see Chapter 10). Likewise, growing up Jewish, Asian, Latino, or African American involves different socialization experiences, as "Understanding Diversity: My Childhood (Bong Hwan Kim)" shows. In this example, a Korean American man reflects on the cultural habits he learned growing up in two cultures, Korean and American. His comments reveal the strain when socialization involves competing expectations, a strain that can be particularly acute when a person grows up within different, even if overlapping, cultures. Children of immigrants and biracial people are often caught between these two sets of cultural expectations. As one such student, a second-generation Korean immigrant much like Bong Hwan Kim, has said, "I'm a 1.5 person. Not American enough to be considered an American; not Korean enough to be considered Korean, but Korean American" (Chon 2001; see also Portes and Rumbaut 2001; Rumbaut and Portes 2001).

Through socialization, people internalize cultural expectations and in turn pass these expectations on to others. *Internalization* occurs when behaviors and assumptions are learned so thoroughly that people no longer question them, but simply accept them as correct. The lessons that are internalized can have a powerful influence on attitudes and behavior. For example, someone socialized to believe that homosexuality is morally repugnant is unlikely to be tolerant of gays and lesbians. If such a person, let's say a man, experiences erotic feelings about someone of the same sex, he is likely to have deep inner conflicts about his identity. Similarly, someone socialized to believe that racism is morally repugnant is likely to be more accepting of diverse groups. Of course, people can change the cultural expectations they learn. New experiences can undermine narrow cultural expectations. Attending college, to give one example, often has a liberalizing effect, supplanting old expectations with new ones generated by exposure to the diversity of college life.

Examining the socialization process helps us see the degree to which our lives are socially constructed, meaning that the organization of society and the life outcomes of people within it are the result of social definitions and processes. For example, values and social attitudes are not inborn, but emerge through the interactions we have with others. This is what is meant by the expression that human beings are born as a *tabula rasa,* a "blank slate." From a sociological perspective, it is clear that what a person becomes is more owing to his or her social experiences than his or her innate (inborn or natural) traits, although innate traits are to some extent part of the picture. For example, a person may be born with a great capacity for knowledge, but if not provided with a good education, that person is unlikely to achieve his or her full potential and may not be recognized as intellectually gifted.

Socialization as Social Control

Sociologist Peter Berger pointed out that not only do people live in society, but society also lives in people (Berger 1963). Socialization is, therefore, a mode of social control. **Social control** is the process by which groups and individuals within those groups are brought into conformity with dominant social expectations. Because socialized people conform to cultural expectations, socialization gives society a certain degree of predictability. Patterns are established that become the basis for social order. Although few people match the cultural ideal exactly, most of us fit comfortably within society's expectations.

DEBUNKING

Society's Myths

Myth: We are all individuals, free to be whoever and whatever we want.

Sociological perspective: Although there is an emphasis on individualism in U.S. culture, what we become is largely influenced by the socialization process.

To understand how socialization is a form of social control, imagine the individual in society as surrounded by a series of concentric circles (see the drawing on page 68). Each circle is a layer of social controls, ranging from the most subtle, such as the expectations of others, to the most overt, such as physical coercion and violence. Coercion and violence are usually not necessary to extract conformity, because learned beliefs and the expectations of others are enough to keep people in line. These socializing forces can be subtle, because even when a person disagrees with others, he or she can feel pressure to conform and may experience stress and discomfort in choosing not to conform (Asch 1955). People learn through a lifetime of experience that deviating from the expectations of others invites peer pressure, ridicule, and other social judgments that remind one of what is expected.

UNDERSTANDING DIVERSITY

My Childhood (Bong Hwan Kim)

Childhood is a time when children learn their gender, as well as their racial and ethnic identity. This excerpt from an interview with Bong Hwan Kim, a Korean American man, is a reflection on growing up and learning both Korean and American culture.

I came to the United States in 1962, when I was three or four years old. My father had come before us to get a Ph.D. in chemistry. He had planned to return to Korea afterward, but it was hard for him to support three children in Korea while he was studying in the United States, and he wasn't happy alone, so he brought the family over. . .

The Bergenfield, New Jersey, community where I grew up was a blue-collar town of about 40,000 people, mostly Irish and Italian Americans. I lived a schizophrenic existence. I had one life in the family, where I felt warmth, closeness, love, and protection, and another life outside—school, friends, television, the feeling that I was on my own. I accepted that my parents would not be able to help me much.

I can remember clearly my first childhood memory about difference. I had been in this country for maybe a year. It was the first day of kindergarten, and I was very excited about having lunch at school. All morning, I could think only of the lunch that was waiting for me in my desk. My mother had made *kimpahp* [rice balls rolled up in dried seaweed] and wrapped it all up in aluminum foil. I was eagerly looking forward to that special treat. I could hardly wait. When lunch bell rang, I happily took out my foil-wrapped kim-pahp. But all the other kids pointed and gawked. "What is that? How could you eat that?" they shrieked. I don't remember whether I ate my lunch or not, but I told my mother I would only bring tuna or peanut butter sandwiches for lunch after that.

I have always liked Korean food, but I had to like it secretly, at home. There are things you don't show to your non-Korean friends. At various times when I was growing up, I felt ashamed of the food in the refrigerator, but only when friends would come over and wonder what it was. They'd see a jar of garlic and say, "You don't eat that stuff, do you?" I would say, "I don't eat it, but my parents do; they do a lot of weird stuff like that."

. . . As a child you are sensitive; you don't want to be different. You want to be like the other kids. They made fun of my face. They called me "flat face." When I got older, they called me "Chink" or "Jap" or said "remember Pearl Harbor." In all cases, it made me feel terrible. I would get angry and get into fights. Even in high school, even the guys I hung around with on a regular basis, would say, "You're just a Chink" when they got angry. Later, they would say they didn't mean it, but that was not much consolation. When you are angry, your true perceptions and emotions come out. The rest is a façade.

They used to say, "We consider you to be just like us. You don't seem Korean." That would give rise to such mixed feelings in me. I wanted to believe that I was no different from my white classmates. It was painful to be reminded that I was different, which people did when they wanted to put me in my place, as if I should be grateful to them for allowing me to be their friend.

I wanted to be as American as possible—playing football, dating cheerleaders. I drank a lot and tried to be cool. I had convinced myself that I was "American," whatever that meant, all the while knowing underneath that I'd have to reconcile myself, to try to figure out where I would fit in a society that never sanctioned that identity as a public possibility. Part of growing up in America meant denying my cultural and ethnic identity . . . When I got to college, I experienced an identity crisis. . . . I decided to go to Korea, hoping to find something to make me feel more whole. Being in Korea somehow gave me a sense of freedom I had never really felt in America. It also made me love my parents even more. I could imagine where they came from and what they experienced. I began to understand and appreciate their sacrifice and love and what parental support means. Visiting Korea didn't provide answers about the meaning of life, but it gave me a sense of comfort and belonging, the feeling that there was somewhere in this world that validated that part of me that I knew was real but few others outside my immediate family ever recognized.

SOURCE: Edited by Karin Aguilar–San Juan. Copyright © 1994. *The State of Asian America.* Boston: South End Press. Reprinted with permission of South End Press.

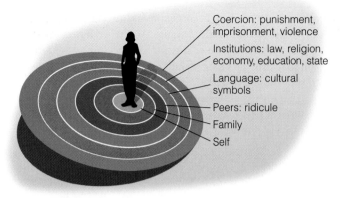

Coercion: punishment, imprisonment, violence

Institutions: law, religion, economy, education, state

Language: cultural symbols

Peers: ridicule

Family

Self

Socialization as Social Control
Though we are all individuals, the process of socialization also keeps us in line with society's expectations. This may occur subtly through peer pressure or, in some circumstances, through coercion and/or violence.

Socialization is thus a subtle form of social control. More coercive means of control can include violence, imprisonment, even death in extreme circumstances. As an example, think of how women were restricted under the rule of the Taliban in Afghanistan, as they were not allowed to leave their homes unless they were accompanied by a male relative; even then, they had to be fully covered in a *burqa*.

Conformity and Individuality

Saying that people conform to social expectations does not eliminate individuality. We are all unique to some degree. Our uniqueness arises from different experiences, different patterns of socialization, the choices we make, and the imperfect ways we learn our roles; furthermore, people resist some of the expectations society has of them. Sociologists warn against seeing human beings as totally passive creatures, because people interact with their environment in creative ways (Wrong 1961). Yet, most people conform, although to differing degrees. Socialization is profoundly significant, but this does not mean that people are robots; instead, socialization emphasizes the adaptations people make as they learn to live in society.

Some people conform too much, for which they pay a price. Socialization into men's roles can encourage aggression and a zeal for risk-taking. Men have a lower life expectancy and higher rate of accidental death than women, probably because of the risky behaviors associated with men's roles (National Center for Health Statistics 2001; Kimmel and Messner 2000). Women's gender roles carry their own risks. Striving excessively to meet the beauty ideals of the dominant culture can result in feelings of low self-worth, and may encourage harmful behaviors, such as smoking or eating less to keep one's weight down. It is not that being a man or women is inherently bad for your health, but conforming to gender roles to an extreme can compromise your physical and mental health.

The Consequences of Socialization

Socialization is a lifelong process with consequences that affect how we behave toward others and what we think of ourselves. First, socialization *establishes self-concepts.* How we think of ourselves—our **identity**—is the result of the socialization experiences we have over a lifetime. Our self-esteem and identity are established through the socialization we experience.

Second, *socialization creates the capacity for role-taking* or, put another way, for seeing ourselves as others see us. Socialization is fundamentally reflective; that is, it involves self-conscious human beings seeing and reacting to the expectations of others. The capacity for reflection and the development of identity are ongoing. As we encounter new situations in life, we are able to see what is expected and to adapt to the situation accordingly. Of course, not all people do so successfully. This can become the basis for social deviance (explored in Chapter 6) or for many common problems in social and psychological adjustment.

Third, *socialization creates the tendency for people to act in socially acceptable ways.* Through socialization, people learn the normative expectations attached to social situations and the expectations of society in general. As a result, socialization creates some predictability in human behavior and brings some order to what might otherwise be social chaos.

Finally, *socialization makes people bearers of culture.* Socialization is the process by which people learn and internalize the attitudes, beliefs, and behaviors of their culture. At the same time, socialization is a two-way process—that is, a person not only is the recipient of culture, but also is the creator of culture who passes cultural expectations on to others. The main product of socialization, then, is society itself. By molding individuals, socializing forces perpetuate the society into which individuals are born. Beginning with the newborn infant, socialization contributes to the formation of a self; the self learns roles and rules, and thus outfitted, the self becomes a bearer of culture, passing on all that it has acquired.

▪ *Theories of Socialization*

Knowing that people become socialized does not explain how it happens. Different theoretical perspectives explain socialization, including psychoanalytic theory, object relations theory, social learning theory, and symbolic interaction theory. Each perspective carries a unique set of assumptions about socialization and its effect on the development of the self (see Table 3.1).

		Object Relations Theory	Social Learning Theory	Functionalism	Conflict Theory	Symbolic Interaction Theory
Table 3–1 Theories of Socialization	Psychoanalytic Theory					
How each theory views:						
Individual learning process	Unconscious mind shapes behavior	Infants identify with the same-sex parent	People respond to social stimuli in their environment	People internalize the role expectations that are present in society	Individual and group aspirations that are part of identity are shaped by the opportunities available to different groups	Children learn through taking the role of significant others
Formation of self	Self (ego) emerges from tension between the id and the superego	Self emerges through separating oneself from the primary caretaker	Identity is created through the interaction of mental and social worlds	Internalizing the values of society reinforces social consensus	Group consciousness is formed in the context of a system of inequality and power relations and can involve both resistance and compliance	Identity emerges as the creative self interacts with the social expectations of others
Influence of society	Societal expectations are represented by the superego	Division of labor in the family shapes identity formation	Young children learn the principles that shape the external world	Society relies upon conformity to maintain stability and social equilibrium	Social control agents exert pressure to conform	Expectations of others form the social context for learning social roles

Psychoanalytic Theory

Psychoanalytic theory originates in the work of **Sigmund Freud** (1856–1939). Among Freud's greatest contributions was the idea that the unconscious mind shapes human behavior. Freud developed the technique of psychoanalysis to help discover the causes of psychological problems in the recesses of troubled patients' minds.

Psychoanalytic theory depicts the human psyche in three parts: the id, the superego, and the ego. The **id** consists of deep drives and impulses. Freud was particularly absorbed by the sexual component of the id, which he considered an especially forceful denizen of the unconscious mind. The **superego** is the dimension of the self that represents the standards of society. The superego incorporates or internalizes acquired values and norms—in short, society's collective expectations. According to Freud, an ordered society requires that people repress the wild impulses generated by the id; thus the id is in permanent conflict with the superego. The superego represents what Freud saw as the inherent repressiveness of society. People cope with the ten-

sion between social expectations (the superego) and their impulses (the id) by developing defense mechanisms, typically repression, avoidance, or denial (Freud 1923/1960, 1930/1961, 1901/1965). Suppose someone has a great desire for the wrong person or for another person's property. This person might refuse to admit this (repression); or, acknowledging the impulse, might avoid the opportunity for temptation (avoidance); or might indulge in misconduct, believing it was not misconduct (denial).

One way that people cope with the tension between the superego and the id is through development of the ego, the third component of the self in Freud's theory. The **ego** is the seat of reason and common sense. The ego plays a balancing act between the id and the superego, adapting the desires of the id to the social expectations of the superego. In psychoanalytic theory, the conflict between the id and the superego occurs in the subconscious mind; yet it shapes human behavior. We get a glimpse of the unconscious mind in dreams and in occasional slips of the tongue—the famous "Freudian slip" that is believed to reveal an underlying state of mind. For example, someone might intend to say, "There were six people at the party," but instead says, "There were sex people at the party," revealing that either the memory of the party or the person he or she is speaking with is causing sexual thoughts to lurk in the unconscious mind. Subconscious desires are forever present and vying for preeminence. Psychoanalytic theory locates the forces that shape the self in the unconscious mind (Freud 1901/1965).

By understanding the self, we can understand the self in society, according to the psychoanalytic school. The id demands gratification for biological desires, the superego forces constant awareness of how society perceives one's actions, and the ego negotiates an uneasy peace between the two parties. As the stabilized three-part self interacts with others, the rules of socialization emerge, with the ego bridging the gap between the primal id and the socialized superego.

Freud's work has never been free from controversy, and among contemporary psychoanalysts, numerous schools of thought provide different interpretations of Freud and rival therapies for assisting patients. Some sociologists have criticized Freud's work for not being generalizable because he worked with only a small and unrepresentative group of clients. Still, psychoanalytic theory is an influential and popular analysis of human personality. We often speak of what motivates people, as if motives were internal, unconscious states of mind that direct human behavior. People also typically think that understanding someone's true self requires knowing about his or her childhood experience—a reflection of Freud's contention that personality is fixed at a relatively early age.

To sum up, the psychoanalytic perspective interprets human identity as relatively fixed at an early age, in a process greatly influenced by one's family. It sees the development of social identity as an unconscious process, developed from dynamic tensions between strong instinctual impulses and the social standards of society. Most important, psychoanalysis sees human behavior as directed and motivated by underlying psychic forces that are largely hidden from ordinary view.

Object Relations Theory

Psychoanalytic theory has been modified by a school of thought known as **object relations theory**. Placing less emphasis on biological drives, object relations theorists contend that the social relationships experienced by children determine the development of the adult personality. Key concepts in object relations theory are *attachment* and *individuation*, the unconscious making and breaking of the bond with parents. Infants may be strongly attached to the parent who is their primary caregiver. As they grow older, they learn to separate themselves from their parents, or individuate, both physically and emo-

tionally. They become a freestanding individual, but early attachments to the primary caregivers persist.

Within sociology, one of the most widely known applications of object relations theory is provided by Nancy Chodorow, a feminist sociologist and practicing psychoanalyst who has used object relations theory to explain how gender shapes personalities. Chodorow asked, "Why do women learn to mother and men, generally speaking, do not?" The modern family, Chodorow argues, has an asymmetrical division of labor—generally, women "mother," and men do not, and women's work as mothers is devalued by society (Chodorow 1978, 1994).

Chodorow agrees with the basic premises of psychoanalytic theory that personality is shaped by early, unconscious forces, adding that children identify with their same-sex parent, meaning that boys and girls separate themselves from their parents differently. Boys identify with the father; the asymmetrical division of labor separates the father from the home and full-time nurturing; boys therefore form personalities that are emotionally detached, independent, less oriented toward other people. Girls, in contrast, identify with the mother; the mother's role is one of close attachment to members of the household; girls therefore develop personalities based on attachment and an orientation toward others.

Chodorow argues that men and women carry these patterns of separation and attachment into their adult lives. The unconscious processes associated with individuation and attachment create the gendered personalities that we think of as "masculine" and "feminine." Indeed, much research has shown that women are more likely to be oriented toward others and to seek and sustain affiliations; men are more likely to repress their attachments to others and to be more individualistic in their orientation toward the world (Chodorow 1978).

One could predict, based on Chodorow's theory, that the greater valuing of motherhood coupled with greater involvement of men in early child care will produce less gender-stereotyped personalities. In other words, her work has interesting practical implications, namely, that if men were to acquire more mothering skills and participate more in the daily tending of the family, the result would be a society where men and women have less gender-stereotyped personalities.

Social Learning Theory

Whereas psychoanalytic theory places great importance on the unconscious processes of the human mind, **social learning theory** considers the formation of identity to be a learned response to social stimuli (Bandura and Walters 1963). Social learning theory emphasizes the societal context of socialization. Identity is regarded not as the product of the unconscious, but as the result of modeling oneself in response to the expectations of others. According to social learning theory, behaviors and attitudes develop in response to reinforcement and encouragement from those around them. Social learning theorists acknowledge the importance of early childhood experience, but they think that the identity people acquire is based more on the behaviors and attitudes of others than on the interior landscape of the individual.

Early models of social learning theory regarded learning rather simplistically in terms of stimulus and response. People were seen as passive creatures who merely responded to stimuli in their environment. This mechanistic view of social learning was transformed by the work of the Swiss psychologist **Jean Piaget** (1896–1980), who believed that learning was crucial to socialization, but that imagination also had a critical role. He argued that the human mind organizes experience into mental categories he called *schema,* which are modified and developed as social experiences accumulate. Schema might be compared to a person's understanding of the rules of a game. Humans do not simply respond to stimulus, but actively absorb experience and figure out what they are seeing to construct a picture of the world.

Piaget proposed that children go through distinct stages of cognitive development as they learn the basic rules of reasoning. They must master the skills at each level before they go on to the next (Piaget 1926). In the initial *sensorimotor* stage, children experience the world only through their senses—touch, taste, sight, smell, and sound. Next comes the *preoperational* stage, in which children begin to use language and other symbols. Children in the preoperational stage cannot think in abstract terms, but they do gain an appreciation of meanings that go beyond their immediate senses. They also begin to see things as others might see them. Third, the *concrete operational stage* is when children learn logical principles regarding the concrete world. This stage prepares for more abstract forms of reasoning. In the *formal operational stage,* children are able to think abstractly and imagine alternatives to the reality in which they live.

Piaget's work stresses the significance of conscious mental processes in social learning. He envisioned the human mind as highly creative and adaptive. Socialization in this framework is a process of developing new ways of thinking about and imagining the world. Most important, Piaget conceptualized humans as actively creating their mental and social worlds. The emphasis in social learning theory is on the influence of the environment in socializing people. The mind mediates the influence of the environment. Just as children learn appropriate behavior when they are rewarded or punished, social learning theory holds that behavior can be changed by altering the social environment (Bandura and Walters 1963).

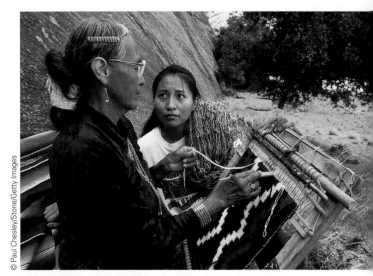

Social learning theory emphasizes how people model their behaviors and attitudes on that of others.

Building on Piaget's model of stages of development, psychologist Lawrence Kohlberg (1969) developed a theory of moral development. Kohlberg interpreted the process of developing moral reasoning as occurring in several stages that were grouped into three levels: *preconventional stage,* the *conventional stage,* and the *postconventional stage.* In the first, young children judge right and wrong in simple terms of obedience and punishment, based on their own needs and feelings. In adolescence (the conventional stage), Kohlberg argued, young people develop moral judgment in terms of cultural norms, particularly social acceptance and following authority. In the final stage of moral development, the postconventional stage, people are able to consider abstract ethical questions, thereby showing maturity in their moral reasoning. In Kohlberg's original research, men, he argued, reached a higher level of moral development than women because women remained more concerned with feelings and social opinions (a lower phase), whereas men were concerned with authority.

Kohlberg's work was later criticized by psychologist Carol Gilligan. Gilligan (1982) found that women conceptualize morality in different terms than men. Instead of judging women by a standard set by men's experience, Gilligan showed that women's moral judgments were more contextual than those of men. In other words, when faced with a moral dilemma, women were more likely to consider the different relationships that would be affected by any decision, instead of making moral judgments according to abstract principles. Gilligan's research made an important point—not just about the importance of including women in studies of human development, but also about being careful not to assume that social learning follows a universal course for all groups.

Functionalism and Conflict Theory

Sociologists use a variety of theoretical perspectives to understand the socialization process, including those above. They can also draw from the major theoretical frameworks we have introduced to understand socialization. From the vantage point of functionalist theory, socialization integrates people into society because it is the mechanism through which they internalize social roles and the values of society. This reinforces social consensus because it encourages at least some degree of conformity. Thus, socialization is one way that society maintains its stability.

Conflict theorists would see this differently. Because of the emphasis in conflict theory on the role of power and coercion in society, in thinking about socialization, conflict theorists would be most interested in how group identity is shaped by patterns of inequality in society. A person's or group's identity always emerges in a context and, if that context is one marked by different opportunities for different groups, then one's identity will be shaped by that fact. This may help you understand why, for example, women are more likely to choose college majors in areas of study that have traditionally been associated with women's work opportunities (that is, in the so-called helping professions and in the arts and humanities, but less frequently in math and sciences). Furthermore, though social control agents pressure people to conform, people also resist oppression. Thus, the identities of people oppressed in society often include some form of resistance to oppression. This can help you understand why members of racial groups who identity with their own group, not the dominant white group, tend to have higher self-esteem (i.e., a stronger valuing of self). In other words, resisting the expectations of a dominant group (such as to be subservient or to internalize a feeling of inferiority) can actually heighten one's perceived self-worth.

Symbolic Interaction Theory

Recall that symbolic interaction theory centers on the idea that human actions are based on the meanings people attribute to behavior; these meanings emerge through social interaction (Blumer 1969). Symbolic interaction has been especially important in developing an understanding of socialization. People learn identities and values through the socialization process as they learn the social meanings that different behaviors imply. Learning to become a good student, then, means taking on the characteristics associated with that role. Because roles are socially defined, they are not real, like objects or things, but are real because of the meanings people give them. As did Piaget, symbolic interactionists see the human capacity for reflection and interpretation as having an important role in the socialization process.

For symbolic interactionists, meaning is constantly reconstructed as people act within their social environments. The self is what we imagine we are; it is not an interior bundle of drives, instincts, and motives. Because of the importance attributed to reflection in symbolic interaction theory, symbolic interactionists use the term *self,* rather than the term *personality,* to refer to a person's identity. Symbolic interaction theory emphasizes that human beings make conscious and meaningful adaptations to their social environment; from a symbolic interactionist perspective, identity is not something that is unconscious and hidden from view, but is socially bestowed and socially sustained (Berger 1963).

Symbolic interactionists think people become who they are through their interactions with others. Socialization from this perspective is a fluid and dynamic process, dependent on experiences with others. Although symbolic interactionists see childhood as a very influential period in the human life cycle, they see the self as evolving over the life span. In other words, socialization is an ongoing process, not something fixed at an early age, as psychoanalysts contend.

Two theorists have greatly influenced the development of symbolic interactionist theory in sociology. **Charles Horton Cooley** (1864–1929) and **George Herbert Mead** (1863–1931) were both sociologists at the University of Chicago in the early 1900s (see Chapter 1). Cooley and Mead saw the self developing in response to the expectations and judgments of others in their social environment.

Charles Horton Cooley postulated the **looking glass self** to explain how a person's conception of self arises through reflection about relationships to others (Cooley 1902, 1967/1909). The development of the looking glass self emerges from (1) how we think we appear to others; (2) how we think others judge us; and (3) how the first two make us feel—proud, embarrassed, or other feelings. The looking glass self involves perception and effect; the perception of how others see us and the effect of others' judgment on us.

How others see us is fundamental to the idea of the looking glass self. In seeing ourselves as others do, we respond to the expectations others have of us. This means that the formation of the self is fundamentally a social process—one based in the interaction people have with each other, as well as the human capacity for self-reflection. One unique feature of human life is the ability to see ourselves through others' eyes. People can imagine themselves in relationship to others and develop a definition of themselves, accordingly. From a symbolic interactionist perspective, the reflective process is key to the development of the self. If you grow up with others thinking you are smart and sharp-witted, chances are you will develop this definition of yourself. If others see you as dull-witted and withdrawn, chances are good that you will see yourself this way.

The Looking Glass Self

The looking glass self refers to the process by which we see ourselves as others see us.

George Herbert Mead agreed with Cooley that children are socialized by responding to other's attitudes toward them. According to Mead, social roles are the basis of all social interaction. Roles, as we have seen, are sets of expectations that govern a person's relationship with people and society (see Chapter 4). When people occupy roles, they are expected to fulfill the expectations associated with those roles. Roles can be thought of as the intersection between the individual and society. By occupying different roles, a person acquires the expectations associated with each role.

Taking the role of the other is the process of imagining oneself from the point of view of another. To Mead, role-taking is a source of self-awareness. As people take on new roles, their awareness of self changes. According to Mead, identity emerges from the roles one plays. He explained this process in detail by examining childhood socialization, which he saw as occurring in three stages: the imitation stage, the play stage, and the game stage (Mead 1934). In each phase of development, the child becomes more proficient at taking the role of the other. In the first stage, the **imitation stage,** children merely copy the behavior of those around them. Role-taking in this phase is nonexistent because the child simply mimics the behavior of those in the surrounding environment without much understanding of the social meaning of the behavior. Although the child in the imitation stage has little understanding of the behavior being copied, he or she is learning to become a social being. For example, think of young children who simply mimic the behavior of people around them (such as pretending to read a book, but doing so with the book upside down). In Mead's analysis, this behavior is one way that children begin to learn the expectations of others.

In the second stage, the **play stage,** children begin to take on the roles of significant people in their environment, not just imitating but incorporating their relationship to the other. Instead of just mimicking others' behavior, the child has learned to understand more about context and the nuances of meaning that different behaviors represent. Especially meaningful is when children take on the role of **significant others,** those with whom they have a close affiliation. A child pretending to be his mother may talk to himself as the mother would. The child begins to develop self-awareness, seeing himself or herself as others do.

In the third stage of socialization, the **game stage,** the child becomes capable of taking on a multitude of roles at the same time. These roles are organized in a complex system that gives the child a more general or comprehensive view of the self. In this stage, the child begins to comprehend the system of social relationships in which he or she is located. The child not only sees himself or herself from the perspective of a significant other, but also understands how people are related to each other and how others are related to him or her. This is the phase where children internalize (incorporate into the self) an abstract understanding of how society sees them.

Mead compared the lessons of the game stage to a baseball game. In baseball, all roles together make the game. The pitcher does not just throw the ball past the batter as if they were the only two people on the field; rather, each player has a specific role, and each role intersects with the others. The network of social roles and the division of labor in the baseball game is a social system, like the social systems children must learn as they develop a concept of themselves in society.

In the game stage, children learn more than just the roles of significant others in their environment. They also acquire a concept of the **generalized other**—the abstract composite of social roles and social expectations. In the generalized other, they have an example of community values and general social expectations that adds to their understanding of self; however, children do not all learn the same generalized other. Depending on one's social position (that is, race, class, gender, region, or religion), one learns a particular set of social and cultural expectations.

If the self is socially constructed through the expectations of others, how do people become individuals? Mead answered this by saying that the self has two dimensions: the "I" and the "me." The I is the unique part of individual personality, the active, creative, self-defining part. The me is the passive, conforming self, the part that reacts to others. In each person, there is a balance between the I and the me, similar to the tension Freud proposed between the id and the superego. Mead differed from Freud, however, in his judgment about when identity is formed. Freud felt that identity was fixed in childhood and henceforth driven by internal, not external, forces. In Mead's version, social identity is always in flux, constantly emerging (or "becoming") and dependent on social situations. Over time, identity stabilizes as one learns to respond consistently to common situations.

Expectations associated with given roles change as people redefine situations and as social and historical conditions change; thus, the social expectations learned through the socialization process are not permanently fixed. For example, as more women enter the paid labor force and as men take on additional responsibilities in the home, the expectations associated with motherhood and fatherhood are changing. Men now experience some of the role conflicts that women have faced in balancing work and family. As the roles of mother and father are redefined, children are learning new socialization patterns; however, traditional gender expectations maintain a remarkable grip. Despite many changes in family life and organization, young girls are still socialized for motherhood, and young boys are still socialized for greater independence and autonomy.

▪ *Agents of Socialization*

Socialization agents are those who pass on social expectations. Everyone is a socializing agent, because social expectations are communicated in countless ways and in every interaction people have, whether intentionally or not. When people are simply doing what they consider "normal," they are communicating social expectations to others. When you dress a particular way, you may not feel you are telling others they must dress that way, yet when everyone in the same environment dresses similarly, some expectation about appropriate dress is clearly being conveyed. People feel pressure to become what society expects of them even though the pressure may be subtle and unrecognized.

THINKING SOCIOLOGICALLY

Think about the first week that you were attending college. What expectations were communicated to you and by whom? Who were the most significant *socialization agents* during this period? Which expectations were communicated formally and which informally? If you were analyzing this experience sociologically, what would some of the most important concepts be to help you understand how one "becomes a college student"?

Socialization does not occur simply between individuals; it occurs in the context of social institutions. Recall from Chapter 1 that institutions are established patterns of social behavior that persist over time. Institutions are a level of society above individuals. Many social institutions shape the process of socialization, including, as we will see, the family, the media, peers, religion, sports, and schools. Each institution passes on expectations about appropriate social behavior. If you are religious, for example, you will learn a particular way of thinking about yourself and the world you live in. Similarly, participation in sports can pass on certain values that become part of your identity and worldview.

The Family

For most people, the family is the first source of socialization; through families, children are introduced to the expectations of society. As symbolic interaction theory suggests, children learn to see themselves through the eyes of parents or primary caretakers; thus, how they define and treat a child is crucial to the child's developing sense of self.

An interesting example of the subtlety in familial socialization comes from a study comparing how U.S. and Japanese mothers talk to their children (Fernald and Morikawa 1993). Observers watched mothers from both cultures speak to their infant children, aged six, twelve, and nineteen months. Both Japanese and U.S. mothers simplified and repeated words for their children, but strong cultural differences were evident in what they said. U.S. mothers focused on naming objects for their babies: "Is that a car?" "Kiss the doggy." Japanese mothers were more likely to use their verbal interactions with children as an opportunity to practice social routines (such as "give me" and "thank you"). The behavior of the Japanese mothers implied that the name of the object was less important than the polite exchange. Japanese mothers were also more likely to use sounds to represent the objects, such as "oink-oink" for a pig or "vroom-vroom" for a vehicle. U.S. mothers were more likely to use the actual names for objects. A U.S. mother might say, "See the car? Nice color!" whereas a Japanese mother might say, "Here! It's a vroom-vroom! I give it to you. Now you give this to me. Give me. Yes! Thank you." The researchers saw these interactions as reflecting the beliefs and practices of each culture. Japanese mothers used objects as part of a ritual of social exchange, emphasizing polite routines, whereas U.S. mothers focused on labeling things. In each case, the child receives a message about what is most significant in the culture.

What children learn in families is, of course, not uniform—even though families pass on the expectations of a given culture. Within a given culture, however, families may be highly diverse, as we will see in Chapter 12. Some families may emphasize educational achievement more than others; some may be more permissive, whereas others emphasize strict obedience and discipline. Even within families, children may experience different expectations, based on factors such as gender or birth order (being born first, second, or third). As one illustration, sociologists have found that both fathers' and mothers' support for gender equity increases when they have only daughters (Warner and Steel 1999). Living in a family experiencing the strain of social problems (such as alcoholism, unemployment, domestic violence, or teen pregnancy) also affects how children are socialized. The specific effects of different family structures and processes are the basis for ongoing and extensive sociological research.

As important as the family is in socializing the young, it is not the only socialization agent. As children grow up, they encounter other socializing influences that join the family in molding the child, sometimes in ways that might even contradict family expectations. Parents who, for example, want to socialize their children in less gender-stereotyped ways might be frustrated by the influence of the media, which promotes highly gender-typed toys and activities to boys and girls. These multiple influences on the socialization process create a reflection of society in us.

The Mass Media

Increasingly, the mass media are important agents of socialization. Television alone has a huge impact on what we are socialized to believe and become. Add to that the print messages received in books, comics, newspapers, and now the Internet, plus images from film, music, video games, and radio, and you begin to see the enormous influence the media have on the values we form, our images of society, our desires for ourselves, and our relationships with others. These images are powerful throughout our lifetimes (as we have seen in the chapter on culture), but many worry that their effect during childhood may be particularly deleterious.

Take the issue of violence. When two young boys shot and killed twelve students at Columbine High School in Littleton, Colorado, in 1999, the public wondered whether their behavior originated in violent programming on television. The high degree of violence in the media has led to the development of a rating system for televised programming. No doubt, violence is extensive in the media. Analysts estimate that by age eighteen, the average child will have witnessed at least 18,000 simulated murders on television. The extent of violence during prime time is high enough—about sixteen violent acts, including two murders, in each evening's prime-time programming—but observers estimate that programs targeted to children actually contain more violence than other programming (Wilson et al. 2002). Moreover, violence in children's programming is frequently shown as humorous with no serious consequences (National Television Violence Study 1997).

Violence is pervasive on television, but does it have any effect? This is what researchers debate. There is strong evidence of the unhealthy effects of violence, especially on children. There is evidence that violence in the media encourages both antisocial behavior and fear among children. Media violence also tends to desensitize people to the effects of violence, including less sympathy for victims of violence (Cantor 2000). Children also tend to imitate the aggressive behavior they see in the media. Violence in the media is not solely to blame for violent behavior in society, however. Children, for example, do not watch television in a vacuum—they live in families where they learn different values and attitudes about violent behavior and they observe the society around them, not just the images they see in fictional representations. Most likely, children are not influenced only by the images of televised and filmed violence, but also by the broader social context in which children live. The images of violence in the media in some ways only reflect the violence in society.

The media expose us to numerous images that shape our definitions of ourselves and the world around us. What we think of as beautiful, sexy, politically acceptable, and materially necessary is strongly influenced by the media. If every week, as you read a weekly newsmagazine, someone shows you the new car that will give you status and distinction, or if every weekend, as we watch televised sports, someone tells us that to really have fun we should drink the right beer, it is little wonder that we begin to think that our self-worth can be measured by the car we drive and that parties are perceived as better when everyone is drunk. The values represented in the media, whether they are about violence, racist and sexist stereotypes, or any number of other social images, have a great effect on what we think and who we come to be.

Peers

Peers are those with whom you interact on equal terms, such as friends, fellow students, and coworkers. Among peers, there are no formally defined superior and subordinate roles although status distinctions commonly arise in peer group interactions. Without peer approval, most people find it hard to feel socially accepted.

Peers are enormously important in the socialization process. Peer cultures for young people often take the form of cliques—friendship circles where members identify with each other and hold a sense of common identity. You probably had cliques in your high school and may even be able to name them. Did your school have "jocks," "preps," "druggies," and so forth? Sociologists studying cliques have found that they are formed based on a sense of exclusive membership, like the in-groups and out-groups we will examine in Chapter 6. Cliques are cohesive, but also have an internal hierarchy with certain

AP/Wide World Photos

Support from peers and family is an important source of strong self-esteem. Organized peer groups like the Special Olympics can also foster a desire for achievement and enhance one's sense of self worth.

group leaders having more power and status than other members. Interaction techniques, like making fun of people, produce group boundaries, defining who's in and who's out (Adler and Adler 1998). The influence of peers is strong in childhood and adolescence, but persists in adulthood.

As agents of socialization, peers are important sources of social approval, disapproval, and support. This is one reason groups without peers of similar status are often at a disadvantage in various settings, such as women in male-dominated professions or minority students on predominantly White campuses. Being a "token" or an "only," as it has come to be called, places unique stresses on those in settings with relatively few peers from whom to draw support. This is one reason those who are minorities in a dominant group context often form same-sex or same-race groups for support, social activities, and the sharing of information about how to succeed in this environment.

Religion

Religion is another powerful agent of socialization, and religious instruction contributes greatly to the identities children construct for themselves. Children tend to develop the same religious beliefs as their parents; switching to a religious faith different from the one in which a person is raised is rare (Hadaway and Marler 1993). Even those who renounce the religion of their youth are deeply affected by the attitudes, self-images, and beliefs instilled by early religious training. Very often those who disavow religion return to their original faith at some

TAKING ON SOCIAL ISSUES

Media Violence

Concerns about the influence of *media violence* on young people have led many to advocate more restrictions on the contents of the media, including films, television programs, and music. Some want more censorship; others want a stronger system of warning labels, such as the television chip (V chip) that allows parents to make certain programs and channels unavailable to their children. Others argue that violence in the media does not cause violence in society because the media only reflect violence that already exists. Based on the understanding of socialization you have acquired from this chapter, what do you think is the effect of violent images in the media on the socialization experiences of young children? What social policies would you suggest regarding the content of the media?

Taking Action

Go to the Taking Action exercise on the companion Web site at **sociology.wadsworth.com/ andersen_taylor/essen3e** to learn more about an organization that addresses this topic.

Through religious rituals, such as the traditional Jewish Seder at Passover, children learn the religious values of their families.

point in their life, especially if they have strong ties to their family of origin and after they form families of their own (Wilson 1994).

Religious socialization shapes the beliefs that people develop. An example comes from studies of people who believe in creationism. Typically, they have been taught to believe in creationism over a long period—that is, they have been specifically socialized to believe in the creationist view of the world's origin and to reject scientific explanations. Sociological research further finds that socialization into creationist beliefs is more likely to be effective among people who grow up in small-town environments where they are less exposed to other influences. Those who believe in creationism are also likely to have mothers who have filled the traditional homemaker's role (Eckberg 1992). This shows the influence that social context has on the religious socialization people experience.

Religious socialization influences a large number of beliefs that guide adults in how they organize their lives, including beliefs about moral development and behavior, the roles of men and women, and sexuality, to name a few. One's religious beliefs strongly influence belief about gender roles within the family, including men's engagement in housework and the odds that wives will be employed outside the home (Ellison and Bartkowski 2002; Becker and Hofmeister 2001; Scott 2000). Religious socialization also influences beliefs about sexuality, including the likelihood of tolerance for gay and lesbian sexuality (Reynolds 2003; Sherkat 2002). Religion can even influence child-rearing practices. Thus, sociologists have found that conservative Protestants are more likely to use strict discipline in raising children, but they are also more likely to hug

and praise their children than are parents with less conservative theological views (Wilcox 1998).

Sports

Most people perhaps think of sports as something that is just for fun—or perhaps to provide opportunities for college scholarships and athletic careers—but sports are also an agent of socialization. Through sports, men and women learn concepts of self that stay with them in their later lives. Sports are also where many ideas about gender differences are formed and reinforced (Dworkin and Messner 1999; Messner 2002). For men, success or failure as an athlete can be a major part of a man's identity; even for men who have not been athletes, knowing about and participating in sports is an important source of men's gender socialization. Men learn that being competitive in sports is considered a part of manhood. Indeed, the attitude that "sports builds character" runs deep in the culture. Sports are supposed to pass on values such as competitiveness, the work ethic, fair play, and a winning attitude. Along with the military and fraternities, sports are considered to be where one learns to be a man.

DEBUNKING
Society's Myths

Myth: Sports are basically played just for the fun of it.

Sociological perspective: Although sports are a form of entertainment, playing sports is also a source for socialization into gender roles.

Michael Messner's research on men and sports reveals the extent to which sports shape masculine identity. Messner interviewed thirty former athletes: Latino, Black, and White men from poor, working-class, and middle-class backgrounds. All of them spoke of the extraordinary influence of sports on them as they grew up. Not only are sports a major source of gender socialization, but working-class, African American, and Latino men often see sports as their only possibility for a good career even though the number of men who succeed in athletic careers is a minuscule percentage of those who hold such hopes.

Messner's research shows that, for most men, playing or watching sports is often the context for developing relationships with fathers, even when the father is absent or emotionally distant in other areas of life. Older brothers and other male relatives also socialize young men into sports. For many of the men in Messner's study, the athletic accomplishments of other family members created uncomfortable pressure to perform and compete, although on the whole they recalled their early sporting years with positive emotions. It was through sports relationships with male peers, more than anyone else, however, that the men's identity was shaped. As boys, the men could form "safe" bonds with other men; still, through sports activity, men learned homophobic attitudes (that is, fear and hatred of homosexuals) and rarely developed intimate, emotional relationships with each other (Messner 1992, 2002).

Sports historically have been less significant in the formation of women's identity, although this is changing, largely as the result of Title IX, which opened more opportunities in athletics to girls and women (see "Forces of Social Change"). Athletic prowess, highly esteemed in men, is not tied to cultural images of womanliness. Quite the contrary, women who excel at sports are often stereotyped as lesbians and may be ridiculed for not being womanly enough. These stereotypes reinforce traditional gender roles for women, as do media images of women athletes that emphasize family images and the personality of women athletes (Blinde and Taub 1992a, 1992b; Cavalier 2003). With athleticism and fitness on the rise as com-

---

FORCES OF SOCIAL CHANGE

Women's Athletics and Title IX

Title IX of the Education Amendments of 1972 to the 1964 Civil Rights Act states, "No person in the United States shall on the basis of sex, be excluded from participation in, be denied the benefits of, or be subject to discrimination under any educational program or activity receiving Federal financial assistance." As you can see from Figure 3.1 the impact of Title IX on women's athletic participation has been enormous. In 1972, when Title IX was passed, there were under 30,000 women total in college athletic programs, compared to 170,000 men! Now, in some schools, women's basketball is just as popular (and profitable) as men's, although in many the enthusiasm and financial support for men's sports still far surpasses that for women's athletics.

How has Title IX changed the face of college sports? Some argue that the legal requirements of Title IX hurt

© Matt Suess/Getty Images

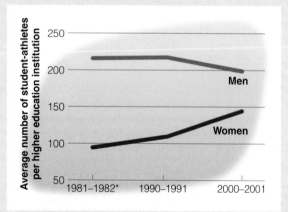

FIGURE 3.1 Student-Athletes: The Impact of Title IX

*Data not available prior to 1981.

SOURCE: National Collegiate Athletic Association. 2002. *NCAA Year-by-Year Sports Participation 1982–2001.* Indianapolis, IN: NCAA. **www.ncaa.org**

men's sports, since some schools have canceled certain men's teams to comply with Title IX. Some supporters of Title IX contend that the huge budgets devoted to men's football and basketball should be reduced to create more gender equity in sports. Data from the National Collegiate Athletic Association show that the share of budgets for women's athletics has increased in recent years, as required by Title IX, and the number of women's sports teams at colleges and universities now exceeds the number of teams for men. But, men's sports still command 65 percent of the $2.7 billion dollars expended on college athletics (National Collegiate Athletic Association, 2002; Suggs 2002).

At the heart of these debates are questions about the role of sports in education. Title IX is based on the premise that schools must not discriminate in offering educational opportunities to women. You might ask yourself, "Is athletic participation about educational opportunity or is it a business?" What changes do you think have taken place as the result of Title IX and how do these affect the socialization of women and men in college environments?

ponents of female beauty, however, the sociological impact of women's participation in sports will likely change.

Current research finds that women in sports develop a strong sense of bodily competence—something typically denied to them by the prevailing, unattainable cultural images of women's bodies. Sports also give women a strong sense of self-confidence and encourage them to seek challenges, take risks, and set goals (Blinde et al. 1993). In addition, women report that sports are frequently the background for forming bonds with other women. Women competing together develop a sense of group power; women athletes also say that playing sports heightens their awareness of gender inequalities off the playing field, although sports participation has not been shown to correlate with activism on women's issues (Blinde et al. 1994).

Research in the sociology of sports shows how activities as ordinary as shooting baskets on a city lot, playing on the soccer team for one's high school, or playing touch football on a Saturday afternoon can convey powerful cultural messages about our identity and our place in the world. Sports are a good example of the power of socialization in our everyday lives.

Schools

Once young people enter kindergarten (or, even earlier, day care), another process of socialization begins. At home, parents are the overwhelmingly dominant source of socialization cues. In school, teachers and other students are the source of expectations that encourage children to think and behave in particular ways. The expectations encountered in schools vary for different groups of students. These differences are shaped by a number of factors, including teachers' expectations for different groups and the resources that different parents can bring to bear on the educational process. The parents of children attending elite, private schools, for example, often have more influence on school policies and classroom activities than do parents in low-income communities. In any context, studying socialization in the schools is an excellent way to see the influence of gender, class, and race in shaping the socialization process.

For example, research finds that teachers respond differently to boys and girls in school. Boys receive more attention than girls from teachers. Even when teachers respond negatively to boys who are misbehaving, they are calling more attention to the boys (American Association of University Women 1992, 1998; Sadker and Sadker 1994). Social class stereotypes also affect teachers' interactions with students. Teachers are likely to perceive working-class children and poor children as less bright and less motivated than middle-class children; teachers are also more likely to define working-class students as troublemakers (Bowditch 1993). These negative ap-

praisals are self-fulfilling prophecies, meaning that the expectations they create often become the basis for actual behavior; thus, they affect the odds of success for children.

DEBUNKING
Society's Myths

Myth: Schools are primarily places where young people learn skills and other knowledge.

Sociological perspective: There is a hidden curriculum in schools where students learn expectations associated with race, class, and gender relations in society influenced by the socialization process.

Boys also receive more attention in the curriculum than girls. The characters in texts are more frequently boys; the accomplishments of boys are more likely portrayed in classroom materials; and boys and men are more typically depicted as active players in history, society, and culture (American Association of University Women 1992, 1998; Sadker and Sadker 1994). This is called the *hidden curriculum* in the schools—the informal and often subtle messages about social roles that are conveyed through classroom interaction and classroom materials— roles that are clearly linked to gender, race, and class.

In schools, boys and girls are quite often segregated into different groups, with significant sociological consequences. Differences between boys and girls become exaggerated when they are separated into groups based on gender and when they are defined as distinct groups (Thorne 1993). Seating children in separate gender groups or sorting them into play groups based on gender heightens gender differences and greatly increases the significance of gender in the children's interactions with each other. Equally important is that gender becomes less relevant in the interactions between boys and girls when they are grouped together in common working groups, although gender does not disappear altogether as an influence. Barrie Thorne, who has observed gender interaction in schools, concludes from her observations that gender has a "fluid" character and that gender relations between boys and girls can be improved through conscious changes that discourage gender separation. (See "Sociology in Practice: Boys and Girls in School.")

THINKING SOCIOLOGICALLY

Visit a local day-care center, preschool, or elementary school and observe children at play. Record the activities they are involved in, and note what both girls and boys are doing. Do you observe any differences between boys' and girls' play? What do your observations tell you about *socialization* patterns for boys and girls?

While in school, young people acquire identities and learn patterns of behavior that are congruent with the needs of other social institutions. Sociologists using conflict theory to understand schools would say that U.S. schools reflect the needs of a capitalist society. School is typically the place where children are first exposed to a hierarchical, bureaucratic environment. Not only does school teach them the skills of reading, writing, and other subject areas, but it is also where children are trained to respect authority, be punctual, and follow rules—thereby preparing them for their future lives as workers in organizations that value these traits. Schools emphasize conformity to societal needs, although not everyone internalizes these lessons to the same degree (Bowles and Gintis 1976; Lever 1978). Research has found, for example, that working-class schoolchildren form subcultures in school that resist the dominant culture. Rejecting the mental labor associated with school values, working-class children are inadvertently learning the expectations associated with working-class jobs. As a result, the subculture of the school fits the needs of the class system (MacLeod 1995; Willis 1977).

■ Growing Up in a Diverse Society

Understanding the institutional context of socialization is important for understanding how socialization affects different groups in society. Socialization makes us members of our society. It instills in us the values of the culture and brings society into our self-definition, our perceptions of others, and our understanding of the world around us. Socialization is not, however, a uniform process, as the different examples developed in this chapter show. In a society as complex and diverse as the United States, no two people will have exactly the same experiences. We can find similarities between us, often across vast social and cultural differences, but variation in social contexts creates vastly different socialization experiences. Furthermore, current transformations in the U.S. population are creating new multiracial and multicultural environments where young people grow up. Schools, as an example, are in many places being trans-

SOCIOLOGY IN PRACTICE

Boys and Girls in School

Barrie Thorne's research on children's interaction in school found that children establish boundaries between themselves that reflect the race and gender divisions in society. Based on her research findings and her observations of teachers' practices, she offers the following suggestions for improving cross-gender and cross-race relationships among children.

1. When grouping students, use criteria other than gender or race. Thorne notes that, when left to themselves, children will separate by gender and, often, race. Although teachers should not devalue same-gender and same-race relationships, she suggests that teachers should promote more intergroup interaction.

2. Affirm and reinforce the values of cooperation among all children, regardless of social categories. Promoting a sense that the class works together as a group creates more inclusive relationships between different groups.

3. Whenever possible, organize students into small, heterogeneous, and cooperative work groups. Small group instruction tends to promote more cooperative interaction among students. When groups focus on shared goals, they are also more likely to value each other.

4. Facilitate children's access to all activities. Thorne suggests that teachers need to make a point of teaching the same skills to everyone rather than letting children segregate into activities that promote one skill for one group and another skill for another group. Without this intervention, children tend to engage in gender-typed activities.

5. Actively intervene to challenge the dynamics of stereotyping and power. Even when groups are integrated, they may interact based on tensions and inequality. If teachers pretend that race makes no difference, these tensions will simply be reproduced. Instead, teachers should help students learn to interact with each other across these differences and to explore the nature and meaning of cultural and racial differences and the dynamics of racism.

Critical Thinking Exercise

1. Using the guidelines Thorne suggests, identify a group or organization on your campus you belong to and make a list of suggestions for facilitating positive cross-race and/or cross-gender relationships within the group.

2. Observe a classroom where young children are interacting. If you were the teacher, how might you implement the suggestions that Thorne gives for children's interracial interactions?

SOURCE: Adapted from Barrie Thorne. 1993. *Gender Play: Girls and Boys in School.* New Brunswick, NJ: Rutgers University Press.

formed by the large number of immigrant groups enter-ing the school system. In such places, children come into contact with other children from a variety of different groups. This creates a new context where children form their social values and learn their social identities.

One task of the sociological imagination is to exam-ine the influence of different contexts on socialization. Where you grow up; how your family is structured; what resources you have at your disposal; your racial–ethnic identity, gender, and nationality—all these shape the so-cialization experience. Growing up White, female, and middle class, for example, is quite different from grow-ing up Latino, male, and working class. Even within a given group, there are great differences in socialization patterns. Growing up as an African American, middle-class woman will produce results quite different from growing up African American and poor. Socialization ex-periences for all groups are shaped by many factors that intermingle to form the context for socialization.

The socialization process is clearly patterned by fac-tors such as class, race, gender, religion, regional back-ground, sexual preference, age, and ethnicity, to name a

---

DOING SOCIOLOGICAL RESEARCH

Children's Understandings of Race

In a racially stratified society, people learn concepts about race that shape their interaction with others. So-ciologists Debra van Ausdale and Joe Feagin wanted to know how children understand racial and ethnic concepts and how this influences their interaction with other children. Prior to their study, most knowledge about children's under-standings of race came from experi-mental studies in a laboratory or from psychological tests and interviews with children. Van Ausdale and Feagin wanted to study children in a natural setting so they observed children in school, systematically observing chil-dren's interactions with one another.

They observed three-, four-, and five-year-olds in an urban preschool. Twenty-four of the children were White; nineteen, Asian; four, Black; three, biracial; three, Middle Eastern; two, Latino; and three classified as "other." The children's racial designa-tions were provided by their parents. The researchers observed in the school five days a week for eleven months and saw one to three episodes involv-ing significant racial or ethnic matters every day.

The researchers concluded that young children use racial and ethnic concepts to exclude other children from play. Sometimes language is the ethnic marker; other times, skin color. The children showed an awareness of negative racial attitudes, even though

Through the socialization process, young children learn the values of their culture. These values shape their relationships with other people.

© Caroline Penn/CORBIS

they were attending a school that prided itself on limiting children's expo-sure to prejudice and discrimination and used a multicultural curriculum to teach students to value racial and ethnic diversity. At times, the children also used racial-ethnic understandings to include others—teaching other students about racial–ethnic identities. Race and ethnicity were also the basis for children's concepts of themselves and others. As an example, one four-year-old White child insisted that her classmate was Indian because she wore her long, dark hair in a braid. When the classmate explained that she was not Indian, the young girl remarked that maybe her mother was Indian.

Throughout the research, the chil-dren showed how significant racial–ethnic concepts were in their interac-tions with others. Race and ethnicity are powerful identifiers of self and others. Despite the importance of race in the children's interactions, Van Aus-dale and Feagin also noted a strong tendency for the adults they observed to deny that race and ethnicity were significant to the children.

Questions to Consider

1. When did you first learn about race and what did you learn? What role did *socialization agents* play in what you learned?
Keywords: racial socialization, learning racism, children and prejudice

2. What practices might teachers use to teach students about race in a way that values all groups? Relate your an-swer to the theories of socialization that are presented in this chapter.
Keywords: teachers and race preju-dice, reducing racism

We have included InfoTrac College Edition keywords at the end of each question to make it easier for you to find more to read on these topics. Go to **www.infotrac-college.com,** an online library, to begin your search.

SOURCE: Van Ausdale, Deborah and Joe R. Feagin. 2000. *The First R: How Children Learn Race and Racism.* Lanham, MD: Rowman and Littlefield.

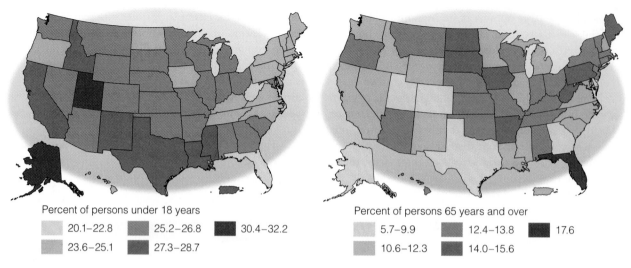

Percent of persons under 18 years

▪ 20.1–22.8	▪ 25.2–26.8	▪ 30.4–32.2
▪ 23.6–25.1	▪ 27.3–28.7	

Percent of persons 65 years and over

▪ 5.7–9.9	▪ 12.4–13.8	▪ 17.6
▪ 10.6–12.3	▪ 14.0–15.6	

MAP 3.1 Mapping America's Diversity: Persons Young and Old: Where They Live
The population distribution of old and young varies by state. **Is your state high or low in the proportion of children and young people? What factors do you think influence this? What impact does the percentage of old and young have on society's needs in your state?**

SOURCE: U.S. Census Bureau. 2002. *American Fact Finder.* Web site: **www.census.gov**

few, but none of these characteristics singly can define the socialization experience. Certainly, some may be more salient at given times than others. A Latina may, for example, be particularly cognizant of her racial identity as she is growing up, but she does not experience it as separate from her gender identity. Race and gender together are integral to her identity, as they are for all people. She may be more conscious of one or the other at different points in her life, but she is never completely unaffected by either.

The point is that you cannot think in narrow terms when thinking like a sociologist. Those with sociological imaginations have to recognize the diversity in human experience, both within and across different cultures, and must understand how these diverse experiences shape the values and identities of the great variety of people who inhabit the world.

▪ Aging and the Life Course

Socialization begins the moment a person is born. As soon as the sex of a child is known (which now can be even before birth), parents, grandparents, brothers, and sisters greet the infant with different expectations, depending on whether it is a boy or a girl. Socialization

does not come to an end as we reach adulthood; rather, it continues through our lifetime. As we enter new situations, and even as we interact in familiar ones, we learn new roles and undergo changes in identity.

Sociologists use the term **life course** to describe and analyze the connection between people's personal attributes, the roles they occupy, the life events they experience, and the social and historical aspects of these events (Stoller and Gibson 2000). The life course perspective underscores the point made by C. Wright Mills that personal biographies are linked to specific social–historical periods. Thus, different generations are strongly influenced by large-scale events (such as a war, immigration, economic prosperity, or depression, for example), at the same time that the immediate expectations of those around us are part of our socialization as we grow older. The phases of the life course are familiar to us: childhood, youth and adolescence, adulthood, and old age. These phases of the life course bind different generations and define some of life's most significant events, such as birth, marriage, retirement, and death.

Childhood

During childhood, socialization establishes one's initial identity and values. In this period, the family is an extremely influential source of socialization, but as we have seen, experiences in school, peer relationships, sports, religion, and the media also have a profound effect. Chil-

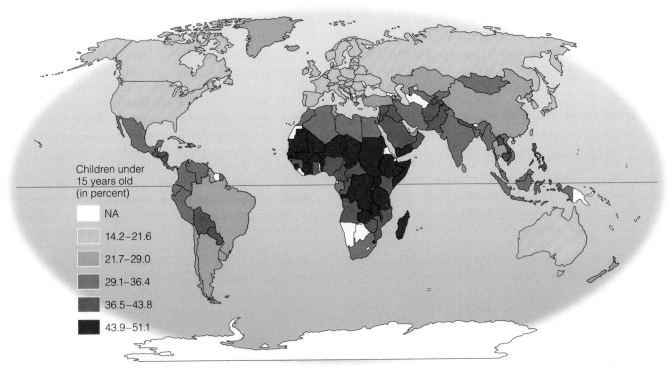

MAP 3.2 Viewing Society in Global Perspective: The World's Children
Throughout the world, the proportion of children as a percentage of the population of a given country tends to be higher in those countries that are most economically disadvantaged and most overpopulated. **What are the consequences of being disadvantaged for children in diverse parts of the world?**

DATA: From the U.S. Census Bureau. 2002. *Statistical Abstract of the United States 2002.* Washington, DC: U.S. Government Printing Office, p. 827.

dren acquire knowledge of their culture through countless subtle cues that provide them with an understanding of what it means to live in society.

Socializing cues begin as early as infancy, when parents and others begin to describe their children according to their perceptions of them. These perceptions are frequently derived from the cultural expectations parents have for children, and they typically vary depending on whether the child is a boy or a girl. In one classic study, parents were asked just twenty-four hours after the birth of their first child to describe the baby. Although the researchers controlled for the physical size of the infant to ensure that there were no objective differences between the boys and the girls, parents of girls described their babies as "softer" and smaller than did parents of boys. Boy infants were described as strong, alert, and well-coordinated (Rubin et al. 1974). Researchers have recently repeated this study with a new twist by comparing how both parents and children describe newborn infants; interestingly, they found that children describe infants in even more gender-stereotyped ways than the adults (Stern and Karraker 1989).

Much socialization in early childhood takes place through play and games. Games that encourage competition help instill the value of competitiveness throughout someone's life; likewise, play with other children and games that are challenging give children important intellectual, social, and interpersonal skills. Extensive research has been done on how children's play and games influence their identities as boys and girls. Generally, the research finds that boys' play tends to be rougher, more aggressive, and involves more specific rules; boys are also more likely to be involved in group play. Girls, in contrast, engage in more conversational play (Moller et al. 1992; Campenni 1999; Raaj and Rackliff 1998). Sociologists have concluded that the games children play significantly influence their development into adults.

Another enormous influence on childhood socialization is what children observe of the adult world. Children are keen observers of their surroundings, and what they perceive will influence their self-concept and how they relate to others. This is vividly illustrated by research revealing how many adult child abusers were themselves victims of child abuse (Fattah 1994). Children become socialized by observing the roles of those around them and internalizing the values, beliefs, and expectations of their culture.

The United States has typically been defined as a child-centered society. Many news commentators, historians, educators, and sociologists have noted that the United States is "youth oriented." The high valuation on youth in U.S. culture is especially evident in the mass media. The young are depicted in television commercials more often, and in a more positive light, than any other age group. Today's youth are generally shown as energetic, smart, and attractive. To be young is revered—aged, reviled; youth is regarded as the prime of life, whereas middle age and old age are regarded as the long decline at the end of life. American culture defines children as economically useless but emotionally "priceless" (Zelizer 1985).

Still, the image of *childhood* as a carefree time is not matched by reality for many children. Violence takes a heavy toll on urban African American and Latino children. More than one-fourth of those living in shelters for the homeless are children (National Coalition for the Homeless 2002). A huge number of children, particularly African American and Hispanic children, live in poverty. While childhood for some may be an idyllic time, for others it is marked by danger.

Adolescence

Only recently has adolescence been thought of as a separate phase in the life cycle. Until the early twentieth century, children moved directly from childhood roles to adult roles. It was only when formal education was extended to all classes that adolescence emerged as a particular phase in life—the phase when young people are regarded as no longer children, but not yet adults. There are no clear boundaries to adolescence, although it is generally taken to last from junior high school until the time one takes on adult roles by getting a job, marrying, and so forth.

Erik Erikson (1980), a noted psychologist, stated that the central task of adolescence is forming a consistent identity. Adolescents are trying to become independent of their families, but they have not yet moved into adult roles. Conflict and confusion can arise as the adolescent swings between childhood and adult maturity. Some argue that adolescence is a period of delayed maturity. Although society expects adolescents to behave like adults, they are denied many privileges associated with adult life: They cannot vote, drink alcohol, or marry without permission, and sexual activity is condemned. The tensions of adolescence have been blamed for numerous social problems, such as drug and alcohol abuse, youth violence, and the school dropout rate, to name a few.

The issues that young people face are a good barometer of social change across generations. Today's young people face an uncertain world—one where adult roles are less predictable than in the past. Later marriage, high divorce rates, a volatile labor market, and technological change create a confusing environment for young people (Csikzentmihalyi and Schneider 2000). Studies of adolescents find that, in this context, young people understand the need for flexibility, specialization, and, likely, frequent job change. And, although the popular media stereotype adolescents as slackers, most teens are willing to work hard, do not engage in criminal or violent activity, and have high expectations for an education that will lead to a good job. Many, however, find that their expectations are out of alignment with the opportunities that are actually available, creating a paradox of a generation that is "motivated but directionless" (Schneider and Stevenson 1999).

Patterns of adolescent socialization vary significantly by race and social class. National surveys find some intriguing class and race differences in how young people think about work and play in their lives. In general, the most economically privileged young people see their activities as more like play than youth, whereas those less well off are more likely to define their activities as work. Likewise, White youth (boys especially) are more likely than other groups to see their lives as playful. The sociologists doing this research interpret these findings to mean that being economically privileged allows you to think of your work as like play. Being in a less advantaged position, on the other hand, makes you see the world as more "work-like." This is supported by further findings that young people from less advantaged backgrounds spend more time in activities they define as purposeless (Schneider and Stevenson 1999).

Young people typically try to mark their unique identity through the establishment of *youth subcultures*—relatively distinct habits, customs, norms, and language that define youth in contrast to other generations. Youth subcultures are seen in the particular styles, demeanors, and special vocabularies that young people develop as signs of belonging. Special vocabularies mark the unique identity of youth; older people who try to imitate these styles may be seen by young people as silly. Youth subcultures also change with the times; that which is now described as "hot" (an attractive man or woman, for example) might have been described as "cool" ten or fifteen years ago. Youth subcultures are crosscut by other cultures as well, such as African American, Hispanic, and Asian culture (Brake, 1985). Youth subcultures are also encouraged by the consumer markets that promote them. Some youth subcultures reflect the alienation that young people feel from their families and schools.

Patterns of adolescent socialization show how socialization is dependent on social context. The values one forms as a young person have a decided influence on where young people find themselves later in life, but it is also true that the values formed in youth reflect the life chances young people think are possible.

Adulthood

Socialization does not end when one becomes an adult. Building on the identity formed in childhood and adolescence, adult socialization is the process of learning new roles and expectations in adult life. More so than at earlier stages in life, **adult socialization** involves learning behaviors and attitudes appropriate to specific situations and roles.

Youths entering college, to take an example from young adulthood, are newly independent and have new responsibilities. In college, one acquires not just an education but also a new identity. Those who enter college directly from high school may encounter conflicts with their family over their newfound status. Older students who work and attend college may experience difficulties (defined as role conflict; see Chapter 4) trying to meet dual responsibilities, especially if their family is not supportive. Research on returning adult women students finds that women who lack the support of family and friends have the greatest emotional difficulty adjusting to the multiple roles of student, mother, and wife (Suitor 1988). Meeting the new demands may require the returning student to develop different expectations about how much she can accomplish or different priorities about what she will attempt—in other words, a change in values and attitudes, reflecting a new stage in her socialization.

Adult life is peppered with events that may require the adult to adapt to new roles. Marriage, a new career, starting a family, entering the military, getting a divorce, or dealing with death in the family all transform an individual's previous social identity. Divorce is a good example of a forced transition from one identity to another. Marital status is a significant part of one's overall social role, and getting divorced will bring changes in how a person is treated by others. Social relationships a person had while married may change or disappear completely. It is little surprise that newly divorced people often feel disoriented and out of place. Divorce may also have an impact on others in the family, especially youngsters, who undergo their own ordeal of new socialization (Demo and Acock 1988).

Another part of learning a new role is **anticipatory socialization,** the learning of expectations associated with a role one expects to enter in the future. One might rehearse the expectations associated with being a professor by working as a teaching assistant, taking a class in preparation for becoming a father, or attending a summer program to prepare for entering college. Anticipatory socialization allows a person to foresee the expectations associated with a new role and learn what is expected in that role in advance.

In the transition from an old role to a new one, individuals often vacillate between their old and new identities as they adjust to fresh settings and expectations. An interest-

Table 3. 2 Slowing the Transition to Adulthood		
	1980	**2000**
Percent aged twenty to twenty-one in school	31.0%	44%
Median age at first marriage		
Women	21.8	25.1
Men	23.6	26.8
Fertility rate, women aged fifteen to nineteen (per 1000 women)	53.0%	48.5%
Percent aged sixteen to nineteen in labor force		
Women	52.9%	51.3%
Men	60.5%	53.0%

SOURCE: U.S. Bureau of the Census. 2002. *Statistical Abstract of the United States, 2002.* Washington, DC: U.S. Government Printing Office, pp. 62, 136, 367; Fields, Jason, and Lynne M. Casper. 2001. *America's Families and Living Arrangements.* Washington, DC: U.S. Census Bureau, p. 9.

ing example is *coming out,* the process of identifying oneself as gay or lesbian. This can be either a public coming out or a private acknowledgment of the homoerotic feelings that one has. The process can take years and generally means coming out to a few people, at first selective family or friends who are likely to have the most positive reaction. Coming out is rarely a single event but occurs in stages on the way to developing a new identity—one that is not only a new sexual identity, but also a new sense of self (Due 1995).

Many people experience the transition into adulthood by finishing school, getting a job, marrying, and starting a family. These four activities, in order, used to be the norm. Increasingly, however, social conditions make it difficult for many people to progress to adulthood following this traditional path. Many people do not finish high school, some never marry or raise a family. Many spend much of their time unemployed, and recent changes in both the sequence of these steps and the length of time between them have also changed the nature of transition to adulthood. Becoming an adult is also taking longer than before. People stay in school longer, are marrying later, and postponing childbearing (see Table 3.2). With these social changes, people have to be inventive in the roles they occupy since some of the old expectations no longer apply. Nonetheless, within this changing context, adult socialization takes place as people encounter the expectations—both old and new—of those around them.

Age and Aging

Passage through adulthood involves many transitions. In our society, one of the most difficult transitions is the passage to old age. We are taught to fear aging in this society, and many people spend a lot of time and money trying to

© Mark Allan/Alpha/Globe Photos

Famous singer Tina Turner shows that chronological age need not limit one's physical appearance. She is sixty years old in this photograph.

keep themselves looking young. Unlike many societies, ours does not revere the elderly but instead devalues them, making the aging process even more difficult.

It is easy to think that aging is just a natural fact. Despite desperate attempts to hide gray hair, eliminate wrinkles, and reduce middle-aged bulge, aging is inevitable. The skin creases and sags, the hair thins, metabolism slows, and one's bones become less dense and more brittle by losing bone mass. Although aging is a physical process, the social dimensions of aging are just as important, if not more so, in determining the aging process. Just think about how some people appear to age much more rapidly than others. Some sixty-year-olds look only forty, and some forty-year-olds look much older. These differences result from combinations of biological and social factors, such as eating and exercise habits, stress, smoking habits, pollution in the physical environment, and many other factors. The social dimensions of aging are what interest sociologists.

Although the physiology of aging proceeds according to biological processes, what it *means* to grow older

is a social phenomenon. **Age stereotypes** are preconceived judgments about what different age groups are like. Stereotypes abound of both old and young people. Young people, especially teenagers, are stereotyped as irresponsible, addicted to loud music, lazy, sloppy, and so on; the elderly are stereotyped as forgetful, set in their ways, mentally dim, and unproductive. Though these stereotypes are largely myths, they are widely believed. Age stereotypes also differ for different groups. Older women are stereotyped as having lost their sexual appeal, contrary to the stereotype of older men as handsome or "dashing" and desirable. Gender is, in fact, one of the most significant factors in age stereotypes. Women may even be viewed as becoming old sooner than men because people describe women as old a decade sooner than they describe men as old (Stoller and Gibson 2000).

Age stereotypes are also reinforced through popular culture. Advertisements depict women as needing creams and lotions to hide "the tell-tale signs of aging." Men are admonished to cover the patches of gray hair that appear or to use other products to prevent baldness. Entire industries are constructed on the fear of aging that popular culture promotes. Face-lifts, tummy tucks, and vitamin advertisements all claim to "reverse the process of aging" even though the aging process is a fact of life.

AGE PREJUDICE AND DISCRIMINATION. **Age prejudice** refers to a negative attitude about an age group that is generalized to all people in that group. Prejudice against the elderly is prominent. As an example, people may talk "baby talk" to the elderly. Doing so defines the elderly as childlike and incompetent. Prejudice relegates people to a perceived lower status in society and stems from the stereotypes associated with different age groups.

Age discrimination is the different and unequal treatment of people based solely on their age. While age prejudice is an attitude, age discrimination involves actual behavior. Some forms of age discrimination are illegal. The Age Discrimination Employment Act, first passed in 1967 but amended several times since, protects people from age discrimination in employment. An employer can neither hire nor fire someone based solely on age nor segregate or classify workers based on age. Age discrimination cases have become one of the most frequently filed cases through the Equal Employment Opportunity Commission (EEOC), the federal agency set up to monitor violations of civil rights in employment.

Ageism is a term sociologists use to describe the institutionalized practice of age prejudice and discrimination. More than a single attitude or an explicit act of discrimination, ageism is structured into the institutional fabric of society. Like racism and sexism, ageism encompasses both prejudice and discrimination, but it is also manifested in the structure of institutions. As such, it does not have to be intentional or overt to affect how age groups are treated. Ageism in society means that, regardless of laws that prohibit age discrimination, people's age is a significant predictor of their life chances. Resources are distributed in society in ways that advantage some age groups and disadvantage others; cultural belief systems devalue the elderly; society's systems of care are often inadequate to meet people's needs as they grow old—these are the manifestations of ageism, a persistent and institutionalized feature of society.

AGE STRATIFICATION. Most societies produce age hierarchies—systems in which some age groups have more power and better life chances than others. **Age stratification** refers to the hierarchical ranking of different age groups in society. Age stratification exists because processes in society ensure that people of different ages differ in their access to society's rewards, power, and privileges. As we will see, in the United States and elsewhere age is a major source of inequality.

Age is an *ascribed status;* that is, age is determined by when you were born. Different from other ascribed statuses, which remain relatively constant over the duration of a person's life, age changes steadily throughout your life. Still, you remain part of a particular generation—something sociologists call an **age cohort**—an aggregate group of people born during the same period (Stoller and Gibson 2000). Cohorts are not homogenous. Within a given cohort, there will be considerable diversity on many dimensions: sexual orientation, gender, race, class, nation, ethnicity. How these cohorts are arrayed in a given society at a given time shapes the character of society and the social issues within it.

People in the same age cohort share the same historical experiences—wars, technological developments, economic fluctuations—although they might do so in different ways depending on other life factors. Living through the Great Depression, for example, shaped an entire generation's attitudes and behaviors, as did growing up in the 1960s and as will being a member of the contemporary youth generation. Recall from Chapter 1 that C. Wright Mills saw the task of the sociological imagination as analyzing the relationship between biography and history. Understanding the experiences of different age cohorts is one way you can do this. People who live through the same historic period experience a similar impact of that period in their personal lives. The troubles and triumphs they experience and the societal issues they face are rooted in the commonality established by their age cohort. The shared historical experiences of age cohorts result in discernible generational patterns—in social attitudes and similarity of life chances (Stoller and Gibson 2000).

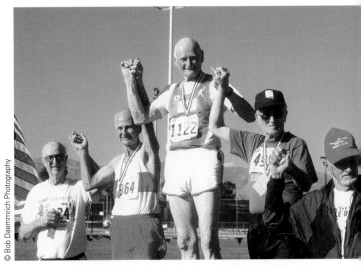

For many, old age is a time for new accomplishments and achievements, such as this marathon runner.

Different generations have to grapple with and respond to different social contexts. Someone born just after World War II would, upon graduation from high school or college, enter a labor market where there was widespread availability of jobs and, for many, expanding opportunities. Now, young people face a labor market where entry-level jobs in secure corporate environments are rare and where many are trapped in low-level jobs with little opportunity for advancement. Many young people worry, as a result, about whether they will be able to achieve even the same degree of economic status as their parents—the first time this has happened in U.S. history. Understanding how society shapes the experiences of different generations is what sociologists mean by saying that age is a structural feature of society.

The age structure of society shapes people's opportunities, is the basis for social expectations, and plays an important part in the development of social change (see Figure 3.2). In many other societies, the elderly also hold very high status. They are esteemed, and their judgment on important matters is sought and respected. In Samoa, as an example, old age is considered to be the best time of life, and the elderly are much revered. In many African nations, social status increases with age, and the elderly are regularly consulted in acknowledgment of their superior wisdom. Chinese children are also required to repay their parents with gratitude for bringing them up (Palmore and Maeda 1985; Cohen and Eames 1985; Kristof 1996).

Why does society stratify people on the basis of age? Once again we find that the three main theoretical perspectives of sociological analysis—functionalism, conflict theory, and symbolic interactionism—offer different explanations (see Table 3.3). Functionalist sociologists ask whether

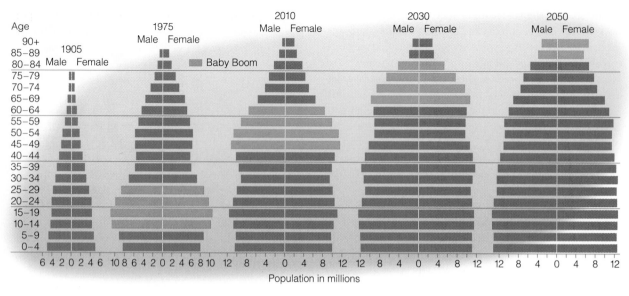

FIGURE 3.2 The Population Pyramid by Age and Sex

SOURCE: Hobbs, Frank B. with Bonnie L. Damos. 1996. *65+ in the United States*. Washington, DC: U.S. Department of Health and Human Services, pp. 5–7.

the grouping of individuals contributes in some way to the common good of society. From this perspective, adulthood is functional to society because adults are seen as the group contributing most fully to society; the elderly are not. Functionalists argue that older people are seen as less useful and are therefore granted lower status in society. Youth are in-between. The constraints and expectations placed on youth—they are prohibited from engaging in a variety of "adult" activities, expected to go to school, not expected to support themselves—are seen to free them from the cares of adulthood and give them time and opportunity to learn an occupation and prepare to contribute to society.

According to the functionalist argument, the elderly voluntarily withdraw from society by retiring and lessening their participation in social activities such as church, civic affairs, and family. **Disengagement theory,** drawn

from functionalism, predicts that as people age, they gradually withdraw from participation in society and are simultaneously relieved of responsibilities. This withdrawal is functional to society because it provides for an orderly transition from one generation to the next. The young presumably infuse the roles they take over from the elderly with youthful energy and stamina. According to the functionalist argument, the diminished usefulness of the elderly justifies their depressed earning power and their relative neglect in social support networks.

Conflict theory focuses on the competition over scarce resources between age groups. Among the most important scarce resources are jobs. Unlike functionalist theory, conflict theory offers an explanation of why both youth and the elderly are assigned lower status in society and are most likely to be poor (see Figure 3.3). Barring

Table 3.3 Sociological Theories of Aging

	Functionalism	**Conflict Theory**	**Symbolic Interaction**
Age differentiation	Contributes to the common good of society because each group has varying levels of utility levels in society	Results from the different economic status and power of age cohorts	Occurs in most societies, but the social value placed on different age groups varies across diverse cultures
Age groups	Are valued according to their usefulness in society	Compete for resources in society, resulting in generational inequities and thus potential conflict	Are stereotyped according to the perceived value of different groups
Age stratification	Results from the functional value of different age cohorts	Intertwines with inequalities of class, race, and gender	Promotes ageism, which is institutionalized prejudice and discrimination against old people

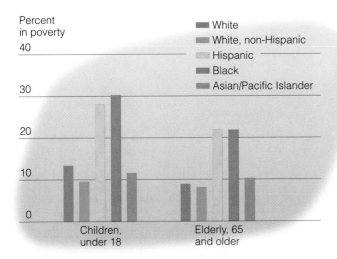

Percent in poverty

- White
- White, non-Hispanic
- Hispanic
- Black
- Asian/Pacific Islander

Children, under 18 / Elderly, 65 and older

FIGURE 3.3 Age, Race, and Poverty

SOURCE: Proctor, Bernadette D., and Joseph Dalaker. 2002. *Poverty in the United States: 2001*. Washington, DC: U.S. Department of Commerce, pp. 27–30.

youth and the elderly from the labor market eliminates these groups from competition, improving the prospects for middle-aged workers. Removed from competition, both the young and the old have very little power, and, like other minorities, they are denied access to the resources they need to change their situation. Conflict theory also helps explain that competition can emerge between age groups, such as whether to limit Social Security payments to save for future generations.

Symbolic interaction theory analyzes the different meanings attributed to social entities. Symbolic interactionists ask what meanings become attached to different age groups and to what extent these meanings explain how society ranks such groups. Definitions of aging are socially constructed, as we will see in discussing age stereotypes. Moreover, in some societies, the elderly may be perceived as having higher status than in other societies. Symbolic interaction considers the role of social perception in understanding the sociology of age. Age clearly takes on significant social meaning—meaning that varies from society to society for a given age group and that varies within a society for different age groups.

Growing old in a society like the United States with such a strong emphasis on youth means encountering social stereotypes about the old, adjusting to diminished social and financial resources, and sometimes living in the absence of social supports, even when facing some of life's most difficult transitions, such as declining health and the loss of loved ones (see Figure 3.4). Still, many people experience old age as a time of great satisfaction and enjoy a sense of accomplishment connected to work, family, and friends. The degree of satisfaction during old

age depends to a great extent on the social support networks established earlier in life—evidence of the continuing influence of socialization.

Rites of Passage

A **rite of passage** is a ceremony or ritual that marks the transition of an individual from one role to another. Rites of passage define and legitimize abrupt role changes that begin or end each stage of life. The ceremonies surrounding rites of passage are often dramatic and infused with awe and solemnity. Examples include graduation ceremonies; weddings; and religious affirmations, such as the Jewish ceremony of the bar mitzvah for boys or the bat mitzvah for girls, confirmation for Catholics, and adult baptism for many Christian denominations.

Formal promotions or entry into some new careers may also include rites of passage. Completing police academy training or being handed one's diploma are examples. Such rites usually include family and friends, who watch the ceremony with pride; people frequently keep mementos of these rites as markers of the transition through life's major stages. Bridal showers and baby showers have been analyzed as rites of passage. At a shower, the person who is being honored is about to assume a new role and identity—from young woman to wife or mother. Rites of passage entail public announcement of the new status, for the benefit of both the individual and those with whom the newly anointed person

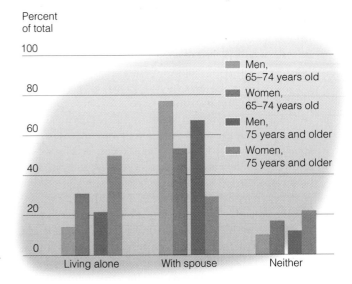

Percent of total

- Men, 65–74 years old
- Women, 65–74 years old
- Men, 75 years and older
- Women, 75 years and older

Living alone / With spouse / Neither

FIGURE 3.4 Living Arrangements of Older Adults

SOURCE: Fields, Jason, and Lynn M. Casper. 2001. *America's Families and Living Arrangements: March 2000*. Current Population Reports, pp. 20–537. Washington, DC: U.S. Census Bureau.

will interact. In the absence of such rituals, the transformation of identity would not be formally recognized, perhaps leaving uncertainty in the rising youngster or the community about the individual's worthiness, preparedness, or community acceptance.

Sociologists have noted that in the United States there is no standard and formalized rite of passage marking the transition from childhood to adulthood. As a consequence, the period of adolescence is attended by ambivalence and uncertainty. As adolescents hover between adult and child status, they may not have the clear sense of identity that a rite of passage can provide. However, although there is no universal ceremony in our culture by which young people are noted as moving from child to adult, some subcultures do mark the occasion. Among the wealthy, the debutante's coming-out celebration is a traditional introduction of a young woman to adult society. Latinos may celebrate the *quinceañera* (fifteenth birthday) of young girls. A tradition of the Catholic Church, this rite recognizes the girl's coming of age, while also keeping faith with an ethnic heritage. Dressed in white, she is introduced by her parents to the larger community. Formerly associated mostly with working-class families in the barrios, the quinceañera has also become popular among affluent Mexican Americans, who may match New York debutante society by spending as much as $30,000 to $50,000 on the event (McLane 1995).

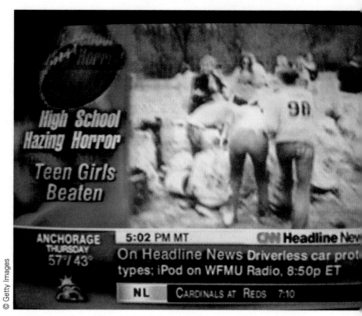
© Getty Images

Hazings are a good example of the rites of passage that often accompany integration into a new group. This hazing incident became national news when an annual hazing ritual at a suburban Chicago high school injured several young women and was broadcast on most major media networks.

■ *Resocialization*

Most transitions people experience in their lifetimes involve continuity with the former self as it undergoes gradual redefinition. Sometimes, however, adults are forced to undergo a radical shift of identity. **Resocialization** is the process by which existing social roles are radically altered or replaced (Fein 1988). Resocialization is especially likely when people enter institutional settings where the institution claims enormous control over the individual. Examples include the military, prisons, monastic orders, and some cults (see also Chapter 5 for a discussion of total institutions). When military recruits enter boot camp, they are stripped of personal belongings, their heads are shaved, and they are issued identical uniforms. Although military recruits do not discard their former identities, the changes brought about by becoming a soldier can be dramatic and are meant to make the military primary, not one's family, friends, or personal history. The military represents an extreme form of resocialization in which individuals are expected to subordinate their identity to that of the group. In such organizations, individuals are interchangeable, and group consensus (meaning, in the military, unanimous, unquestioned subordination to higher ranks) is an essential component of group cohesion and effectiveness. Mili-

tary personnel are expected to act as soldiers, not as individuals. Understanding the importance of resocialization on entry to the military helps us understand such practices as "the rat line" at VMI (Virginia Military Institute) where members of the senior class taunt and harass new recruits.

Resocialization often occurs when people enter hierarchical organizations that require them to respond to authority on principle, not out of individual loyalty. The resocialization process promotes group solidarity and generates a feeling of belonging. Participants in these settings are expected to honor the symbols and objectives of the organization; disloyalty is seen as a threat to the entire group. In a convent, for example, nuns are expected to subordinate their own identity to the calling they have taken on, a calling that requires obedience both to God and to an abbess.

THINKING SOCIOLOGICALLY

Find a group of adults (young or old) who have just entered a new stage of life (getting a new or first job, getting married, becoming a grandparent, retiring, entering a nursing home, and so forth), and ask them to describe this new experience. Ask questions such as what others expect of them in this new role, how these expectations are communicated to them, what changes they see in their own behavior, and what expectations they have of their new situation. What do your observations tell you about *adult socialization*?

Resocialization may involve degrading initiates physically and psychologically with the aim of breaking down or redefining their old identity. They may be given menial and humiliating tasks and be expected to act in a subservient manner. Social control in such a setting may be exerted by peer ridicule or actual punishment. Fraternities and sororities offer an interesting everyday example of this pattern of resocialization. When fraternities and sororities induct new members, the pledges are often given onerous, meaningless chores, and they may be forced to behave in comically degrading, and sometimes life-threatening, ways. Depending on the traditions of the group, resocialization practices range from mildly sadistic mischief to hazardous behavior, such as hazing. Intense resocialization rituals, whether in jailhouses, barracks, convents, or sorority and fraternity houses serve the same purpose: imposing some sort of ordeal to cement the seriousness and permanence of new roles and expectations.

The Process of Conversion

Resocialization also occurs during what people popularly think of as conversion. A conversion is a far-reaching transformation of identity, often related to religious or political beliefs. People usually think of conversion in the context of cults but it happens in other settings as well.

The case of John Walker Lindh—a U.S. citizen who joined the Taliban in Afghanistan and was later charged with conspiring to kill Americans abroad and supporting terrorist organizations—is an example of an extreme conversion. Lindh was raised Catholic in an affluent family, but converted to Islam as a teenager, changing not just his ideas, but also his dress. Neighbors described him as being transformed from "a boy who wore blue jeans and T-shirts to an imposing figure in flowing Muslim garb" (Robertson and Burke 2001: A1). As a young man, he traveled Yemen and Pakistan to study language and the Koran, and was introduced there to the Taliban.

As when people join religious cults, this is a case of extreme conversion, but conversion happens in less extreme situations, too. People may convert to a different religion, thereby undergoing resocialization by changing beliefs and religious practices. Or someone may become strongly influenced by the beliefs of a social movement and abruptly or gradually change their beliefs—even their identity—as a result.

The Brainwashing Debate

Extreme examples of resocialization are seen in the phenomenon popularly called brainwashing. In the popular view of brainwashing, converts have their previous identities totally stripped; the transformation is seen as so complete that only deprogramming can restore the former self.

Potential candidates of brainwashing include people who enter religious cults, prisoners of war, and hostages. Sociologists have examined brainwashing to illustrate the process of resocialization. As the result of their research, sociologists have cautioned against using the word *brainwashing* when referring to this form of conversion. The term implies that humans are mere puppets or passive victims whose free will can be taken away during these conversions (Robbins 1988). In religious cults, however, converts do not necessarily drop their former identity.

Sociological research has found that the people most susceptible to cult influence are the most suggestible, primarily young adults who are socially isolated, drifting, and having difficulty performing in other areas (such as in their jobs or in school). Such people may choose to affiliate with cults voluntarily. Despite the widespread belief that people have to be deprogrammed to be freed from the influence of cults, many people are able to leave on their own (Robbins 1988). *So-called brainwashing is simply a manifestation of the social influence people experience through interaction with others.* Even in cult settings, socialization is an interactive process, not just a transfer of group expectations to passive victims.

Forcible confinement and physical torture can be instruments of extreme resocialization. Under severe captivity and deprivation, a captured person may come to identify with the captor; this is known as the Stockholm Syndrome. In such instances, the captured person has become dependent on the captor. On release, the captive frequently needs debriefing. Prisoners of war and hostages may not lose free will altogether, but they do lose freedom of movement and association, which makes prisoners intensely dependent on their captors and therefore vulnerable to the captor's influence. The Stockholm Syndrome can help explain why some battered women do not leave their abusers. Dependent on their abuser both financially and emotionally, battered women often develop identities that keep them attached to men who abuse them. In these cases, outsiders often think the women should leave instantly, whereas the women themselves may find leaving difficult, even in the most abusive situations.

In sum, resocialization involves establishing a radically new definition of oneself. The new identity may seem dramatically different from the former one, but the process by which it is established is much the same as the ordinary socialization process—a process that, as we have seen, is a critical part of society.

■ *Chapter Summary*

- ■ *What is socialization, and why is it significant for society?*
  Socialization is the process by which human beings learn the social expectations of society. Socialization

is powerful because it creates the expectations that are the basis for people's attitudes and behaviors. Through socialization, people conform to social expectations, although people still express themselves as individuals.

■ *What theoretical perspectives do sociologists use to explain socialization?*

Several theoretical perspectives are used to understand socialization. *Psychoanalytic theory* sees the self as driven by unconscious drives and forces that interact with the expectations of society. *Social learning theory* sees identity as a learned response to social stimuli. *Functionalism* interprets socialization as key to social stability because socialization established shared roles and values. *Conflict theory* interprets socialization in the context of inequality and power relations. *Symbolic interaction theory* sees people as constructing the self as they interact with the environment and give meaning to their experience. Charles Horton Cooley described this process as the *looking glass self.* Another sociologist, George Herbert Mead, described childhood socialization as occurring in three stages: imitation, play, and games.

■ *Who are the agents of socialization?*

Socialization agents are those who pass on social expectations. They include the family, the media, peers, sports, religious institutions, and the schools, among others. The family is usually the first source of socialization. The media also influence people's values and behaviors. Peer groups are an important source of individual identity; without peer approval, most people find it hard to be socially accepted. Schools also pass on expectations that are influenced by gender, race, and other social characteristics of people and groups.

■ *Does socialization mean that everyone grows up the same?*

Socialization is not a uniform process. Growing up in different environments and in such a diverse society means that different people and different groups are exposed to different expectations. Factors such as family structure, social class, regional differences, and many others, influence how one is socialized.

■ *Does socialization end during childhood?*

Socialization continues through the lifetime, although childhood is an especially significant time for the formation of identity. Adolescence is also a period when peer cultures have an enormous influence on the formation of people's self-concepts. *Adult socialization* involves the learning of specific expectations associated with new roles.

■ *What are the social dimensions of the aging process?*

Although aging is a physiological process, its significance stems from social meanings attached to aging. *Age prejudice* and *age discrimination* result in the devaluation of older people. *Age stratification*—referring to the inequality that occurs among different age groups—is the result.

■ *What does resocialization mean?*

Resocialization is the process by which existing social roles are radically altered or replaced. It can take place in an organization that maintains strict social control and demands that the individual conform to the needs of the group or organization.

■ *Key Terms*

adult socialization 85	looking glass self 72
age cohort 87	object relations theory 70
age discrimination 86	peers 76
age prejudice 86	play stage 73
age stereotype 86	psychoanalytic theory 69
age stratification 87	resocialization 90
ageism 86	rite of passage 89
anticipatory socialization 85	role 65
disengagement theory 88	significant others 73
ego 69	social control 66
game stage 73	social learning theory 70
generalized other 74	socialization 65
id 69	socialization agents 74
identity 68	superego 69
imitation stage 73	taking the role of the
life course 82	other 73

■ *Researching Society with MicroCase Online*

You can see the results of actual research by using the Wadsworth MicroCase® Online feature available to you. This feature allows you to look at some of the results from national surveys, census data, and other data sources. You can explore this easy-to-use feature on your own, but try this example. Suppose you want to know some social facts, such as:

Do age groups differ in whether they think women should take care of running their homes and leave running the country up to men?

To answer this question, go to **http://sociology .wadsworth.com/andersen_taylor/essen3e,** select MicroCase Online from the left navigation bar, and follow the directions there to analyze the data described below.

Data file: GSS

Task: Cross-Tabulation

Row Variable: WOMEN HOME

Column Variable: I-AGE

Questions

Once you have your results, answer the following questions:

1. People in which age group are most likely to agree with this statement?

    a. <30

    b. 30–49

    c. 50 and up

2. What percentage of those under the age of 30 agree with this statement?

3. What factors do you think influence this pattern? Could it be that people change over time? Or are the differences due to generational differences? Be sure to use data from the table to support your argument.

■ *The Companion Web Site for Sociology: The Essentials, Third Edition*

sociology.wadsworth.com/andersen_taylor/essen3e

Supplement your review of this chapter by going to the companion Web site to take one of the Tutorial Quizzes, use the flash cards to master key terms, and check out the many other study aids you'll find there. You'll also find special features such as GSS Data and Census 2000 information, data and resources at your fingertips to help you with that special project or do some research on your own.

■ *Suggested Readings and Web Resources*

Scheper-Hughes, Nancy. 1998. *Small Wars: The Cultural Politics of Childhood.* Berkeley: University of California Press.
This collection of essays examines how children around the world are affected by global economic change and the prac- *tices of local cultures. The book is a sobering analysis of the hardships that children face in different societal contexts.*

Stoller, Eleanor Palo, and Rose Campbell Gibson. 2000. *Worlds of Difference: Inequality in the Aging Experience,* 3rd ed. Thousand Oaks, CA: Pine Forge Press.
This anthology explores diverse patterns of aging, particularly given the influence of race, class, and gender on the aging process. Many of the articles are written as personal narratives. Combined with a sociological perspective, they provide students with a compassionate view of diverse norms and social structures that shape the experience of growing old.

Sudnow, David. 1967. *Passing On: The Social Organization of Dying.* Englewood Cliffs, NJ: Prentice-Hall.
A classic study in the sociology of death, this book examines, from a symbolic interaction perspective, how death is routinized in hospitals. The analysis reveals social perceptions of death and dying, as well as institutional practices that reveal the sociology of death.

Van Ausdale, Deborah, and Joe R. Feagin. 2000. *The First R: How Children Learn Race and Racism.* Lanham, MD: Rowman and Littlefield.
Based on observations in elementary school classrooms, Van Ausdale and Feagin analyze how children first learn concepts of race.

Zhou, Min, and Carl L. Bankston, III. 1998. *Growing Up American: How Vietnamese Children Adapt to Life in the United States.* New York: Russell Sage Foundation.
Based on a study of a Vietnamese community in New Orleans, Zhou and Bankston study the children of refugees from Vietnam. Their analysis shows the influence of immigration and resettlement on the socialization experiences of young people.

Annie B. Casey Foundation
www.aecf.org
This is a foundation dedicated to furthering knowledge about and assisting disadvantaged children in the United States. The Web site includes reports, facts, and state-by-state comparisons of various measures of children's well-being.

Children's Defense Fund
www.childrensdefense.org
An organization dedicated to improving children's lives, especially poor and minority children.

National Institute of Aging
www.nih.gov/nia
The home page of the U.S. government agency provides information on the latest research on aging, links to additional sites, and information on funding for research on aging.

Society and Social Interaction

the writer and poet John Donne wrote more than three centuries ago that "No man is an island, entire of itself; every man is a piece of the continent, a part of the main." As humans, we are constantly involved with other humans. Even when we are alone, we think about other people. When we interact with others, we do so in patterned and often predictable ways.

A parent and teenager argue about what the teen should wear to a party. A police officer has a man spread-eagled against an automobile while searching him for drugs. Over lunch, a group of businesswomen confer about a recent sale. A physics professor lectures students on the nature of the universe. A congregation listens to a sermon and then prays together. All these highly diverse actions have something in common: They are regulated, to a greater or lesser degree, by the elements of society—groups, statuses, roles, and social institutions. These elements guide the formation of human society.

Society is much more than the sum of the individuals in it, as we have already learned. Society takes on a life of its own. Society is patterned on humans and their interactions, but it is something that endures in itself and takes on shape and structure. This is one of the basic ideas that guide sociological thinking.

In this chapter, we examine the different pieces of society, beginning with the study of social interaction and proceeding from this close-up level of society to studying the larger forces that hold society together—social institutions and social structures. We will see that human interaction is guided by social forces, at the same time that humans shape the social institutions that characterize different societies. We proceed by discussing the different elements of society—groups, statuses, roles, and the social bonds that people form through social interaction. In the latter part of the chapter, we study the grandest levels of society—social institutions. As you proceed through the chapter, you will begin to see the complexity of diverse societies—how they are arranged and how they are held together.

■ *What Is Society?*

In Chapter 2, we studied culture as one force that holds society together. Culture is the general way of life, including norms, customs, beliefs, and language. Human **society** is a system of social interaction that includes both culture and social organization. Within a society, members have a common culture even though there may also be great diversity within it. Members of a society think of themselves as distinct from other societies, maintain ties of interaction, and have a high degree of interdependence. The interaction they have, whether based on harmony or conflict, is one element of society. That is, **social interaction** is how human beings communicate with each other, and in so doing, they form a social bond.

Sociologists use the term social interaction to mean behavior between two or more people that is given meaning by them. It involves more than simply acting; it involves communication—the conveyance of information to a person, which may be simple (a word, wave, or threatening gesture) or complex (speaking, organizing a social movement, or forming a family).

Social interaction is the foundation of society, but society becomes more than a collection of individual social actions. Emile Durkheim, the classical sociological theorist, described society as *sui generis*—a Latin phrase meaning "a thing in itself, of its own particular kind."

To sociologists, seeing society *sui generis* means that society is more than just the sum of its parts. Durkheim saw society as an organism, something comprised of different parts that work together to create a unique whole. Just as a human body is not just a collection of organs but is alive as a whole organism, society is not only a simple collection of individuals, groups, or institutions, but is a whole entity that consists of all these elements and their interrelationships.

Imagine how a photographer views a landscape. The landscape is not just the sum of its individual parts—mountains, pastures, trees, or clouds—each contributes to the whole. The power and beauty of the landscape is that all its parts *relate* to each other, some in harmony, some in contrast, to create a panoramic view. The photographer who tries to capture this landscape will likely use a wide-angle lens. This method of photography captures the breadth and comprehensive scope of what the photographer sees. Similarly, sociologists try to picture society as a whole, not only by seeing its individual parts, but also recognizing the relatedness of these parts and their vast complexity.

Microanalysis and Macroanalysis

Like photographers, sociologists use different lenses to see the different parts of society. Some views are more microscopic—that is, they focus on the smallest, most immediately visible parts of social life, such as specific people interacting. This is called **microanalysis.** Other views are more "macroscopic," that is, like the wide-angle lens, they try to comprehend the whole of society, how it is organized and how it changes. This is called **macroanalysis.** Each view provides a distinct vision of society, and both reveal different dimensions of society.

Some sociologists study the patterns of social interactions that are relatively small, less complex, and less differentiated—the microlevel of society. Studying a small group, such as your friendship group or your family, is an example. A clique (or subgroup) that forms within your own friendship group is another example. Perhaps you are now a member of one or more cliques, or perhaps you are a leader within your group. All these behaviors would be examples of the microlevel of society. Another example of microanalysis is the study of interpersonal attraction—what attracts people to someone and not to someone else, a topic discussed later in this chapter.

While some sociologists are interested in the microlevels of society, others are interested in the broadest view of society—how it is organized and how it changes. Sociologists who study this macrolevel of society study the large patterns of social interactions that are vast, complex, and highly differentiated by looking at a whole society, or comparing different total societies to each other. The broader framework of social problems in our society, such as poverty, homelessness, and urban crime, are all macrolevel problems.

In this chapter, we continue our study of sociology by starting with the microlevel of social life, continuing through the macrolevel. The idea is to help you see the most immediate ways that social forces influence people's behaviors, proceeding through larger questions of how society is held together and organized.

Social organization is the term sociologists use to describe the order established in social groups at any level. Specifically, it is the order that brings regularity and predictability to human behavior that is present at every level of interaction, from the smallest groups to the whole society.

Groups

At any given moment, each of us is a member of many groups simultaneously, and we are subject to their influence: family, friendship groups, athletic teams, work groups, office staffs, racial and ethnic groups, and so on. Groups impinge on every aspect of our lives and are a major determinant of our attitudes and opinions on everything from child care, politics, and the economy to our view on the death penalty.

To sociologists a **group** is a collection of individuals who:

- interact and communicate with each other;
- share goals and norms;
- have a subjective awareness of themselves as "we," that is, as a distinct social unit.

To be a group, the social unit in question must possess all three of these characteristics. We will examine the nature and behavior of groups in greater detail in Chapter 5.

In sociological terms, not all social units are groups. *Social categories* are people who are lumped together based on one or more shared characteristics. Examples of social categories are teenagers (an age category), truck drivers (an occupational category), and millionaires (an economic category). Some social categories can also form a social stratum or an entire social class, as we shall see in Chapter 7. Ethnic and racial groups may be either categories or groups, depending on the amount of "we" feeling. When "we" feeling is high, racial and ethnic categories are indeed groups.

All people nationwide watching TV programs at 8 o'clock Wednesday evening form another distinct social unit, an *audience.* They are not a group, because they do not interact with one another, nor do they possess an awareness of themselves as "we." If many of the same viewers come together in a TV studio, where they interact and develop a "we" feeling, then they would constitute a group.

Finally, *formal organizations* are highly structured social groupings that form to pursue a set of goals. Bureaucracies, such as business corporations or municipal governments or associations such as the PTA, are examples of formal organizations. A deeper analysis of bureaucracies and formal organizations appears in Chapter 5.

Statuses

Within groups, people occupy different statuses. **Status** is an established position in a social structure that carries with it a degree of prestige (that is, social value), as well as a set of expectations. A status is a rank in society. For example, the position "vice president of the United States" is a status, one that carries very high prestige, as well as a complex set of expectations. "High school teacher" is another status; it carries less prestige than "vice president of the United States," but more prestige than, say, "cab driver." Statuses occur within institutions. "High school teacher" is a status within the education institution. Other statuses in the same institution are "student," "principal," and "school superintendent."

Typically, an individual occupies many statuses simultaneously. The combination of statuses composes the individual's **status set**—the complete set of statuses occupied by a person at a given time (Merton 1968). An individual may occupy different statuses in different institutions. Simultaneously, a person may be a daughter (in the family institution), bank president (in the economic institution), voter (in the political institution), church member (in the religious institution), and treasurer of the PTA (in the education institution). Each status may be associated with a different level of prestige.

Sometimes the multiple statuses of an individual conflict with one another. **Status inconsistency** exists where the statuses occupied by a person bring with them significantly different amounts of prestige, and thus differing expectations. For example, someone trained as a lawyer, but working as a cab driver, experiences status inconsistency. Some recent immigrants from Vietnam and Korea have experienced status inconsistency. Many refugees who had been in high-status occupations in their home country, such as teachers, doctors, and lawyers, could find work in the United States only as grocers and sales clerks—good jobs, to be sure, but jobs of relatively lower status. A relatively large body of research in sociology has demonstrated that status inconsistency (*in addition to* low status) can lead to stress and depression (Taylor et al. 2003; Blalock 1991; Min 1990; Taylor and Hornung 1979; Hornung 1977; Taylor 1973; Jackson and Curtis 1968).

Achieved statuses are those attained by virtue of individual effort. Most occupational statuses—police officer, pharmacist, or boat builder—are achieved statuses. In contrast, **ascribed statuses** are those occupied from the moment a person is born, such as race and your biological sex. Yet, even ascribed statuses are not exempt from the process of social construction. For most individuals, race is fixed at birth although an individual with one light-skinned African American parent and one White parent may appear to be White and may go through life as a White person. This is called "passing," although this term is used less often now than several years ago. Ascribed status may not be clearly defined, as for individuals who are *biracial* or *multiracial.* Finally, ascribed statuses can arise through other means that may be beyond the control of the individual, such as severe disability or chronic illness.

Gender, too, typically thought of as fixed at birth, is a social construct. You can be born female or male, but becoming a woman or a man is the result of social behaviors associated with your ascribed status. In this sense, gender is a social construction. People who cross-dress, have a sex change, or develop some characteristics associated with the other sex are good examples of how gender is achieved. People "do" gender in everyday life—that is, they put on appearances and behaviors that are associated with their presumed gender (West and Zimmerman 1987; West and Fenstermaker 1995; Andersen 2003).

The line between achieved and ascribed status may be hard to draw. Social class, for example, is determined by occupation, education, and annual income—all of which are achieved statuses—yet one's job, education, and income are known to correlate strongly with the social class of one's parents. Hence, one's social class status is at least partly—though not perfectly—determined at birth. It is an achieved status that includes an inseparable component of ascribed status as well.

Although people occupy many statuses at one time, it is usually the case that one status is dominant, called the **master status,** overriding all other features of the person's identity. The master status may be imposed by others, or a person may define his or her own master status. A woman judge, for example, may carry the master status "woman" in the eyes of many. Thus she is seen not just as a judge, but as a woman judge, thus making gender a master status (Webster and Hysom 1998). Being in a wheelchair is another example of a master status. People may see this, at least at first, as the most important, or salient, part of one's identity, ignoring other statuses that define one as a person.

A master status can completely supplant all other statuses in the person's status set. For example, when a person has acquired immune deficiency syndrome (AIDS), that person's health condition becomes their master status. AIDS becomes the defining criterion status and the person is then stigmatized by the master status. Not all master statuses are negative; positive-defining master statuses also exist, such as "hero" or "saint."

THINKING SOCIOLOGICALLY

Make a list of terms that describe who you are. Which of these are *ascribed statuses* and which are *achieved statuses?* What do you think your *master status* is in the eyes of others? Does one's *master status* depend on who is defining you? What does this tell you about the significance of social judgments in determining who you are?

Roles

A **role** is the expected behavior others have for a person associated with a particular status. Statuses are occupied; roles are acted or "played." The status of police officer carries with it many expectations; this is the role of police officer. Police officers are expected to uphold the law,

© Lon C. Diehl/PhotoEdit

In role modeling, a person imitates the behavior of an admired other.

pursue suspected criminals, assist victims of crimes, and so on. When a police officer commits a crime, such as physically brutalizing someone just arrested, he or she has not met the role expectations. Role expectations may vary according to the role of the observer—whether the person observing the police officer is a member of a minority group, for example.

As we saw in Chapter 3, social learning theory predicts that one learns attitudes and behaviors in response to the positive reinforcement and encouragement that one receives from those around them. This is important in the formation of one's own identity in society. "I am Linda, the waitress"; or "I am John, the guitarist." These identities are often obtained through **role modeling,** a process by which we imitate the behavior of another person we admire, and who is in a particular role. A ten-year-old girl or boy who greatly admires the teenage expert skateboarder next door will attempt, through role modeling, to closely imitate the flourishes and "hot dogging" that neighbor performs on the skateboard. As a result, the formation of the ten-year-old's self-identity is significantly influenced.

Just as an individual may occupy several statuses at one time, an individual typically will also occupy many roles. A person's **role set** includes all the roles occupied by the person at a given time. Thus, a person may be not only Linda the waitress, but also Linda the pianist, painter, and comedian as well. Roles may clash with each other, a situation called **role conflict,** wherein two or more roles are associated with contradictory expecta-

tions. Notice that in Figure 4.1, some of the roles diagrammed for this college student may conflict with each other. Can you speculate about which might and which might not?

In U.S. society, some of the most common forms of role conflict arise from the dual responsibilities of job and family. The parent role demands extensive time and commitment; so does the job role. Time given to one role is time taken away from the other. Although the norms pertaining to working women and men are rapidly changing, it is still true that women are more often expected to uphold traditional role expectations and are more likely held responsible for minding the family when job and family conflict. The sociologist Arlie Hochschild captured the predicament of today's women when she described the "second shift": A working mother spends time and energy all day on the job, only to come home to the "second shift" of family and home responsibilities. These are sometimes delegated to the man of the house, who encounters less well-formed role expectations that he will take on those responsibilities and is therefore more likely to leave the jobs undone (Hochschild 1997; Shapiro 1997). Hochschild has further found that the demands of family work, coupled with the demands of jobs, have resulted in a serious time bind for both men and women. She has found that some companies have instituted "family friendly" policies, designed to reduce the conflicts generated by the "second shift." Ironically, however, in her study, she found that few workers take advantage of programs such as more flexible hours, paid maternity leave, and job sharing—except for the on-site child care that actually allowed parents to work more!

Hochschild's studies point to the conflict between two social roles: family roles and work roles. Her research

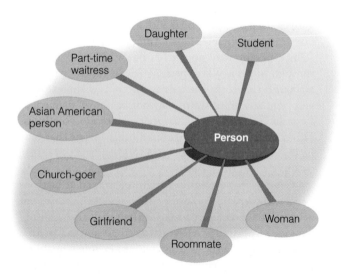

FIGURE 4.1 Examples of Roles in a College Student's Role Set

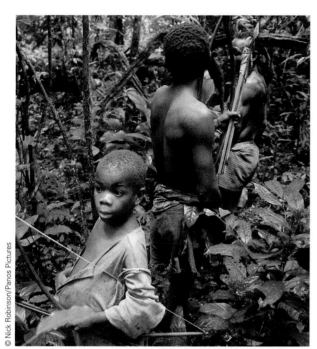

This photograph shows three aspects of society and social interaction: first, men in a foraging society, hunting tools at the ready; second, socialization (the young boy is being trained in hunting techniques); and third, the role of gender in social organization (in this society, men are most likely to do the hunting).

is also illustrative of a different sociological concept: **role strain,** a condition wherein a single role brings conflicting expectations. Different from role conflict, which involves tensions *between* two roles, role strain involves conflicts within a single role. In Hochschild's study, the work role has not only the expectations traditionally associated with work, but also the expectation that one "loves" one's work and be as devoted to it as to one's family. The result is role strain.

The role of student often involves role strain. For example, students are expected to be independent thinkers, yet they feel—quite correctly—that they are often required to simply repeat on an exam what a professor tells them. The tension between the two competing expectations is an example of role strain. This is contrasted with the role conflict some students encounter when they prepare to pursue their education away from home. A common experience of first-generation college students is that their families, though proud of their educational achievement and wishing for their success, have the expectation that the student will remain close to home, fulfilling the role of the dutiful child as it has been filled in the family in the past. If the student chooses a school far from home, he or she is liable to experience resistance from the parents. The result is role conflict, which in a sense is a conflict between success and tradition.

Theories About Analyzing Social Interaction

Groups, statuses, and roles form a web of social interaction. The interaction people have with one another is a basic element of society. Sociologists have developed different ways of understanding social interaction. Functional theory, discussed in Chapter 1, is one such theory. Here we detail five others: the social construction of reality, ethnomethodology, impression management, and social exchange.

The Social Construction of Reality

What holds society together? This is a basic question for sociologists, one that, as we will see at the end of this chapter, has long guided sociological thinking. Sociologists note that society cannot hold together without something that is shared—a shared social reality.

Some sociological theorists have argued convincingly that what is shared is for the most part socially constructed, namely, that there is little actual reality beyond that produced by the process of social interaction itself. This is the principle of *the social construction of reality,* the idea that our perception of what is real is determined by the subjective meaning that we attribute to an experience, a principle central to symbolic interaction theory (Berger and Luckmann 1967; Blumer 1969; Jones and Davis 1965; Lamont 2000). In this way, the process of social interaction and the subjective meanings we give to things arising from it actually determine what we "see" as actual fact. Hence, there is no objective "reality" in itself. Things do not have their own intrinsic meaning; we subjectively impose meaning on things. (The postmodernist view would argue that there is indeed an objective "reality" that exists in the form of communication, culture, text, and other such externalities.)

Children routinely construct reality. Upon seeing a marble roll off a table, the child attributes causation (meaning) to the marble: The marble rolled off the table "because it wanted to." Such perceptions carry into adulthood: The man walking down the street who then accidentally walks smack into a telephone pole at first thought glares at the pole, as though the pole somehow caused the accident! He inadvertently attributes causation and meaning to an inanimate object—the telephone pole (Heider 1958; Taylor et al. 2003).

Considerable evidence exists that people do just that: They force meaning on something when doing so allows them to see or perceive what they want to perceive—even if that perception seems to someone else to be contrary to actual fact. They then come to believe that what they perceived is indeed "fact." A classic and convincing study of this is Hastorf and Cantril's (1954) study of Princeton and Dartmouth students who watched a film of a game of basketball between the two schools. Both sets of students watched the same film. The students were instructed to watch carefully for rule infractions by each team. The results were that the Princeton students reported twice as many rule infractions involving the Dartmouth team than the Dartmouth students saw. The Dartmouth students saw about twice as many rule infractions by Princeton than the Princeton students saw! Remember that they all saw exactly the same game—the same "facts." We see what "facts" we want to see, as a result of the social construction of reality.

As we saw in Chapter 1, our perceptions of reality are determined by what is called the *definition of the situation:* We observe the context in which we find ourselves and then adjust our attitudes and perceptions accordingly. Recall that sociological theorist W. I. Thomas embodies this idea in his well-known dictum *situations defined as real are real in their consequences* (Thomas 1966/1931). The Princeton and Dartmouth students saw different "realities" depending on what college they were attending, and the consequences (the perceived rule infractions) were very real to them.

The definition of the situation is a principle that can also affect a "factual" event such as whether an emergency room patient is perceived to be dead by the doctors. In his research in the emergency room of a hospital, Sudnow (1967) found that patients who arrived at the emergency room with no discernible heartbeat or breathing were treated differently by the attending physician depending on the patient's age. A person in his or her early twenties or younger was not immediately pronounced "dead on arrival" (DOA). Instead, the physicians spent a lot of time listening for and testing for a heartbeat, stimulating the heart, examining the patient's eyes, giving oxygen, and administering other stimulation to revive the patient. If the doctor obtained no lifelike responses, the patient was pronounced dead. Older patients, however, were on the average less likely to receive such extensive procedures. The older person was examined less thoroughly and often was pronounced dead on the spot with only a stethoscopic examination of the heart. In such instances, how the physicians defined the situation—how they socially constructed reality—was indeed real in its consequence for the patient!

Understanding the social construction of reality helps one see many aspects of society in a new light. Race and gender are significant influences on social experience because people believe them to be so. Indeed, society is constructed based on certain assumptions about the significance of race and gender. These assumptions have guided the formation of social institutions, including what work people do, how families are organized, and how power is exercised.

Ethnomethodology

As already discussed in the chapter on culture, our interactions are guided by rules that we follow. These rules are the norms of social interaction. Again, what holds society together? Society cannot hold together without norms, but what rules do we follow? How do we know what these rules or norms are? As we say earlier, an approach in sociology called *ethnomethodology* is a clever technique for finding out.

Ethnomethodology (Garfinkel 1967), after *ethno* for "people," and *methodology* for "mode of study," is a clever technique for studying human interaction by deliberately disrupting social norms and observing how individuals attempt to restore normalcy. The idea is that to study, one must first break those norms, because the subsequent behavior of the people involved will reveal just what the norms were in the first place.

Ethnomethodology is based on the premise that human interaction takes place within a consensus and interaction is not possible without this consensus. The consensus is part of what holds society together. According to Garfinkel, this consensus will be revealed by people's background expectancies, namely, the norms for behavior that they carry with them into situations of interaction (Zimmerman 1992). It is presumed that these expectancies are to a great degree shared, and thus studying norms by deliberately violating them will reveal the norms that most people bring with them into interaction. The ethnomethodologist argues that you cannot simply walk up to someone and ask what norms the person has and uses because most people will not be able to articulate them. We are not wholly conscious of what norms we use even though they are shared.

Ethnomethodologists often use ingenious procedures for uncovering those norms by thinking up clever ways to interrupt "normal" interaction. William Gamson, a sociology professor, had one of his students go into a grocery store where jelly beans, normally priced at that time at 49 cents per pound, were on sale for 35 cents. The student engaged the saleswoman in conversation about the various candies and then asked for a pound of jelly beans. The saleswoman then wrapped them and asked for 35 cents. The rest of the conversation went like this:

Student: Oh, only 35 cents for all those nice jelly beans? There are so many of them. I think I will pay $1 for them.

Saleswoman: Yes, there are a lot, and today they are on sale for only 35 cents.

Student: I know they are on sale, but I want to pay $1 for them. I just love jelly beans, and they are worth a lot to me.

Saleswoman: Well, uh, no, you see, they are selling for 35 cents today, and you wanted a pound, and they are 35 cents a pound.

Student: (voice rising) I am perfectly capable of seeing that they are on sale at 35 cents a pound. That has nothing to do with it. It is just that I personally feel that they are worth more, and I want to pay more for them.

Saleswoman: (becoming quite angry) What is the matter with you? Are you crazy or something? Everything in this store is priced more than what it is worth. Those jelly beans probably cost the store only a nickel. Now do you want them or should I put them back?

At this point the student became quite embarrassed, paid the 35 cents, and hurriedly left (Gamson and Modigliani 1974).

The point here is that the saleswoman approached the situation with a presumed consensus, a consensus that becomes revealed by its deliberate violation by the student. The puzzled saleswoman took measures to attempt to normalize the interaction, to even *force* it to be normal. By so doing, she revealed her expectations, that is, her norms. The ethnomethodological technique used by the student reveals what norms people unconsciously use in everyday interaction and conversation.

Impression Management and Dramaturgy

Another way of analyzing social interaction is to study impression management, a term coined by symbolic interaction theorist Erving Goffman (1959). **Impression management** is a process by which people control how others will perceive them. A student handing in a term paper late may wish to give the instructor the impression that it was not the student's fault, but was because of uncontrollable circumstances ("my computer hard drive crashed," "my dog ate the last hard copy," and so on). The impression that one wishes to "give off" (to use Goffman's phrase) is that "I am usually a very diligent person, but today—just today—I have been betrayed by circumstances."

Impression management can be seen as a type of con *game.* A person willfully attempts to manipulate the other's impression of himself or herself. Goffman regarded everyday interaction as a series of attempts to con the other. In fact, trying in various ways to con the other is, according to Goffman, at the very center of much social interaction and social organization in society. Social interaction is a big con game.

Perhaps this cynical view is not true of all social interaction, but we do present different "selves" to others in different settings. The settings are, in effect, different stages on which we act as we relate to others. For this reason, Goffman's theory is sometimes called the *dramaturgy model* of social interaction, a way of analyzing interaction that assumes the participants are actors on a stage in the drama of

Impression management is a technique we all use to manipulate others' perceptions of us. What impressions is this person "giving off"? As a consequence, what perceptions would you have about this person if the two of you were to meet? What impressions might this person be giving in terms of gender? age? social status? creativity? politics? other?

everyday social life. People present different faces (give off different impressions) on different stages (in different situations or different roles) with different others. To your mother, you may present yourself as the dutiful, obedient daughter, which may not be how you present yourself to a friend. Perhaps you think acting like a diligent student makes you seem a jerk, so you hide from your friends that you are really interested in a class or enjoy your homework. The box "Doing Sociological Research" shows how impression management can be involved in many settings, including the everyday world of the hair salon.

A clever study by Albas and Albas (1988) demonstrates just how pervasive impression management is in social interaction. The Albases studied how students interacted with one another when the instructor returned graded papers during class. Some students got good grades ("aces"), others got poor grades ("bombers"), but both employed a variety of devices (cons) to maintain or give off a favorable impression. For example, the aces wanted to show off their grades, but they did not want to appear to be braggarts, so they casually or "accidentally" let others see their papers. In contrast, the bombers hid or covered their papers to hide their poor grades, said they "didn't care" what they got, or simply lied about their grades.

Analysis of impression management shows how subject to the influence of others we all are. Although we may protest, claiming we are all "individuals," our individuality is shaped by the numerous social forces we encounter in society.

Social Exchange and Game Theory

Another way of analyzing social interaction is through the social exchange model. The *social exchange model* of social interaction holds that our interactions are determined by the rewards or punishments that we receive from others (Thibaut and Kelley 1959; Homans 1974; Blau 1986; Cook et al. 1988; Levine and Moreland 1998; Taylor et al. 2003). An interaction that elicits approval from another (a type of reward) is more likely to be repeated than an interaction that incites disapproval (a type of punishment). According to the exchange principle, one can predict whether a given interaction is likely to be repeated or continued by calculating the degree of reward or punishment inspired by the interaction.

It is often informative to assess the situation in terms of a difference between reward and punishment. If the re-

---

DOING SOCIOLOGICAL RESEARCH

"Doing Hair, Doing Class"

When you begin to study social interaction, you will see that you can study it in many places, including places you would not ordinarily think of as locations for sociological research. Debra Gimlin did this when she began to observe the interaction that takes place in hair salons—interaction that, at least in some salons, she noticed is often marked by differences in the social class status between clients and stylists.

Her research question was: How do women attempt to cultivate the cultural ideals and beauty, and in particular, how is this achieved through the interaction between hair stylists and their clients? She did her research by spending more than 200 hours observing social interaction in a hair salon. She watched the interaction between clients and stylists and conducted interviews with the owner, the staff, and twenty women customers. During the course of her fieldwork, she recorded her observations of the conversations and interaction in the salon, frequently asking questions of patrons and staff. The patrons were mostly middle and upper middle class, the stylists, working class; all the stylists were White, as were most of the clients.

"Beauty work" as Gimlin calls it, involves the stylist bridging the gap between those who seek beauty and those who define it; her (or his) role is to be the expert in beauty culture, bringing the latest fashion and technique to clients. Beauticians are also expected to engage in some "emotion work"—that is, they are expected to nurture clients and be interested in their lives; often put in the position of sacrificing their professional expertise to meet clients' wishes.

According to Gimlin, since stylists typically have lower class status than their clients, this introduces an element into the relationship that stylists negotiate carefully in their routine social interaction. Hairdressers emphasize their special knowledge of beauty and taste as a way of reducing the status differences with their clients. They also try to nullify the existing class hierarchy by conceiving an alternative hierarchy, not one based on education, income, or occupation but only on the ability to style hair competently. Thus, stylists describe clients as perhaps "having a ton of money," but unable to do their hair or know what looks best on them. Stylists become confidantes with clients who often tell them highly personal information about their lives. Appearing to create personal relationships with their clients even though they never see them outside the salon, also reduces status differences. Gimlin concludes that beauty ideals are shaped in this society by an awareness of social location and cultural distinctions. As she says, "Beauty is . . . one tool women use as they make claims to particular social statuses" (1996: 525).

The next time you get your hair cut, you might observe the social interaction around you and ask how class, gender, and race shape interaction in the salon or barbershop that you use. Try to get someone in class to corroborate with you so that you can compare observations in different salon settings. In doing so, you will be studying how gender, race, and class shape social interaction in everyday life.

Questions to Consider

1. Would you expect the same dynamic in a salon where men are the stylists?
Keywords: social interaction, gender interaction

2. Do Gimlin's findings hold in settings where the customers and stylists are not White or where they are all working class?
Keywords: social class, social status

3. In your opinion, would Gimlin's findings hold in an African American *men's* barbershop?
Keywords: racial interaction, barbershop

We have included InfoTrac College Edition keywords at the end of each question to make it easier for you to find more to read on these topics. Go to **www.infotrac-college.com,** an online library, to begin your search.

SOURCE: Gimlin, Debra. 1996 "Pamela's Place: Power and Negotiation in the Hair Salon," *Gender & Society* 10 (October): 505–526.

ward for an interaction exceeds the punishment, then a potential for *social profit* exists and the interaction is likely to occur or continue. If the reward is less than the punishment, then the action will produce a social loss and will be less likely to occur or continue. Exchange theorists analyze human interaction in terms of concepts like reward, punishment, profit, and loss, in addition to the ratio of inputs to outputs. People want to get from an interaction at least as much as they put into it, resulting in an equitable interaction. Calculations of inputs versus outputs constitute a measure of social costs versus rewards. A reward is in effect an approval for conformity; a punishment is a sanction against deviance. Social exchange thus tends to encourage conformity and discourage deviance, and in this way acts as a force toward holding society together in everyday interaction.

Rewards can take many forms. They can include tangible gains such as gifts, recognition, and money, or subtle everyday rewards such as smiles, nods, and pats on the back. Similarly, punishments come in many varieties, from extremes like public humiliation, beating, banishment or execution, to gestures as subtle as a raised eyebrow or a frown. For example, if you ask someone out for a date and the person says yes, you have gained a reward, and you are likely to repeat the interaction. You are likely to ask the person out again, or to ask someone else out. If you ask someone out, and he or she glares at you and says, "No way!" then you have elicited a punishment that will probably cause you to shy away from repeating this type of interaction with that person.

Social exchange theory has grown partly out of *game theory,* a mathematical and economic theory that predicts human interaction has the characteristics of a "game," namely, strategies, winners and losers, rewards and punishments, and profits and costs (Von Neumann and Morgenstern 1944; Nash 1951; Dixit and Sneath 1997; and Kuhn and Nasar 2002). Simply asking someone out for a date indeed has a game-like aspect to it, and you will probably use some kind of strategy to "win" (have the other agree to go out with you) and get "rewarded" (have a pleasant or fun time) at minimal "cost" to you (you don't want to spend a large amount of money on the date; or, you do not want to get into an unpleasant argument on the date). The interesting thing about game theory is that it sees human interaction as just that: a game. Impression management theory also contains a game-like element in its hypothesis that human interaction is a big con game. The mathematician John Nash is one of the inventors of game theory, and was featured in the movie, *A Beautiful Mind.*

Exchange theory has been used to probe the perpetuation of racist and sexist attitudes. Research has shown that anti-woman attitudes and stereotypes among men persist much longer if they are constantly rewarded by one's social group or are reinforced by other aspects of one's social milieu (Taylor et al. 2003; Levine and Moreland 1998; Cook et al. 1988). In contrast, when such attitudes and stereotypes are punished in social exchange, they are unlikely to persist. If a man leaves high school with a few anti-woman attitudes and enters a college that has a strong culture of feminist sophistication, evidence of casual sexism in his interactions is likely to earn quick scorn among disapproving classmates.

■ *Interaction in Cyberspace*

When people interact and communicate with one another by means of personal computers—through email, chat rooms, computer bulletin boards, virtual communities, and other computer-to-computer interactions, they are engaging in **cyberspace interaction** (or virtual interaction). In language that has rapidly become popular only within the last few years, one creates a virtual reality as a result of such activity. Virtual reality is the computer control of human perception. What the individual perceives to be real is what is created by and on the computer (Wadhams 2003; Strate et al. 2003; Gross et al. 2002; Kraut et al. 2002; Holmes 1997; Jones 1997; Turkle 1995).

Cyberspace interaction has characteristics that distinguish it from ordinary face-to-face interaction. First, certain kinds of nonverbal communication are eliminated. Thus, when interacting with someone via a chat room, email, or another computer channel, facial expressions such as smiles, laughter, and the raised eyebrow are eliminated. Also eliminated are hand motions, voice pitch, and other such nonverbal modes of communication. Second, one is free to become a different self. One can literally create a new identity, in fact, several new identities. One can become a cowboy, a cowgirl, a dragon, and even a sex partner in the realm called *cybersex.* A person can even instantly "become" the other gender. Men can interact as (virtual) women, and women as men. While during the 1990s women were significantly less likely to use the Internet for any reason, this gender gap had disappeared by 2000 (Ono and Zavodny 2003). A person with a disability may not feel disabled when interacting on the Internet (Smolan and Erwitt 1996). In creating this new virtual self, interaction becomes anonymous, and one's secrets are hidden from the other, including one's appearance, dress, and personal data such as social security number, city and state address, and other characteristics that would otherwise identify one's actual (as opposed to virtual) self—as long as one takes security precautions not to allow such information to be disclosed.

In this respect, cyberspace interaction is the application of Goffman's principle of *impression management* and *dramaturgy.* The person can put forward a totally different and wholly created self, or identity. One can "give off," in Goffman's terms, any impression one wishes and, at the same time, knows that one's true self is protected by anonymity. This gives the individual quite a large and free range of roles and identities from which to choose and that he or she can become. As predicted by symbolic interaction theory, of which Goffman's is one variety, *the reality of the situation grows out of the interaction process itself.* What one becomes during chat room interaction is a di-

---

FORCES OF SOCIAL CHANGE

Technology and Danger in Cyberspace

Technological change is one major source of social change in society. With the advent of computing technology, many have argued that the emergence of cyberspace is a genuine revolution and will fundamentally change human interaction. In many ways it already has. Phenomena such as email, chat rooms, virtual reality, and other manifestations of the electronic age have already changed how humans interact. At the microlevel, an individual can present or put forward any one of a variety of selves when interacting with another individual. A person can hide certain aspects of the self and present others; children can interact as adults, males as females (and vice versa), the criminal as noncriminal.

A result may be increased deception in human interaction. Another result has been increased invasion of privacy. There has already been extensive and recent concern over security in cyberspace. At the macrolevel of interaction, a single individual can communicate with thousands and millions of people simultaneously and receive responses, thus resulting in increased appearances of "spam" (unwanted solicitations) on one's e-mail. Spam is for cyberspace interaction what "junk mail" is to traditional post-office ("snail") mail.

There is global significance to the cyber revolution: In the near future certain countries may negotiate treaties and bargain for resources via cyberspace, thus rendering security a major potential problem. What social policies can you think of, at either the macrolevel or microlevel that might guide concerns about information privacy and other dimensions of the cyberspace revolution?

In one popular cyberinteraction game called *SIMS,* antisocial behavior has become relatively common and it spills over into the "real" world. While the game currently has over 100,000 subscribers, a small percentage end up being "griefers"—individuals who wish to do at least some measure of harm to other subscribing individuals. Various forms of harassment can occur. In one case, a player sent a small army of players in the real world to urinate on another player's lawn. The interaction may be virtual, but such attacks are not; they are very real. Players have reported online spats that tend to "leak out" of the game, where players have hacked into each others' accounts, posed as acquaintances, and then spread rumors about real people through instant messaging.

Taking Action

Go to the Taking Action Exercise on the companion Web site at: *sociology.wadsworth.com/andersen_taylor/essen3e* to learn more about an organization that addresses this topic.

SOURCE: Nick Waldhams, The Associated Press, July 5, 2003.

The early 1946 electronic computer on the left compares to the contemporary supercomputer and its user, on the right.

"On the Internet, nobody knows you're a dog."

rect outgrowth of the chat room interaction; it is the interaction process that produces the reality. This is a central point of symbolic interaction theory: Interaction creates reality.

Whether cyberspace interaction is ultimately beneficial or harmful to the person has become the subject of much research. Some studies have noted that people can develop extremely close and in-depth relationships as a result of their interaction in cyberspace (McKenna 2002; Jones 1997). Another has noted that individuals who have engaged in virtual interaction sometimes establish some other form of contact, such as communication by telephone or by post office mail, and sometimes they actually meet face to face. Yet such a subsequent face-to-face meeting often prompts an end to the relationship (Strate at al. 2003)! Also, a number of marriages have broken up as a result of cyberspace interaction or cybersex on the part of a spouse (Fernandes-y-Freitas 1996). Finally, while Internet pornography comes in both soft and hard forms, recent research has shown the persistence of violent forms of pornography, such as violent rape of women by male perpetrators. One such investigation showed at least 31 free Internet sites containing instances of violent rape (Gossett and Byrne 2002).

One researcher who specializes in cyberspace interaction (John Suler cited in Wadhams 2003) notes that a cyberspace interaction game, where thousands of people interact electronically, can encourage deviant and antisocial behavior. The anonymity offered by cyberspace allows one to engage in behavior they are too afraid to do in real life. Called "griefers," they can pretend to be Mafia figures and harass others by actually hacking into

their account, stealing information, and spreading unpleasant rumors about real people through instant messaging. In one case, such rumors were actually circulated about a participant, and the participant suffered harm at work as a result. In such instances, the line between cyberspace and the real world becomes blurred, and the consequences can be unpleasant.

Cyberspace interaction has thus resulted in a new subculture (often called *cyberculture,* or *virtual culture*) in our society—in fact, a new social order containing both deviants and conformists (Strate et al. 2003; Turkle 1995). There has been a transition from the use of large mainframe computers to perform mathematical and statistical calculations (what Turkle calls "the culture of calculation" of the 1960s through the early 1980s) to more user-friendly computers (PCs, or personal computers) to perform calculations and provide experiences such as interaction in cyberspace (the "culture of simulation," since the mid-1980s). This new cyberculture is a subculture, as sociologically defined (in Chapter 2). It has certain rules or norms, its own language, a set of beliefs, and practices or rituals—in short, all the elements of culture.

■ *A Study in Diversity: Forms of Nonverbal Communication*

Everyday social interaction involves both verbal and nonverbal communication. *Verbal communication* consists of spoken and written language, and includes a conversation with the person next to you, an exchange of letters, a telephone conversation between you and a friend overseas, or an email exchange. When communication takes place, interaction usually does too, although not always. A television commercial is an example of verbal communication without interaction. The communication is one way, from the advertiser to you, with no communication from you to the advertiser—unless you write or call them, in which case an interaction has occurred.

Nonverbal communication is conveyed by nonverbal means such as touch, tone of voice, and gestures. A punch in the nose is a nonverbal communication; so is a knowing glance. A surprisingly large portion of our everyday communication with others is nonverbal, although we are generally only conscious of a small fraction of the nonverbal "conversations" in which we take part. Consider all the nonverbal signals exchanged in a casual chat: body position, head nods, eye contact, facial expressions, touching, and so on.

Studies of nonverbal communication, like those of verbal communication, show that it is much influenced by social forces, especially culture, including the relationships between diverse groups of people. The meanings of nonverbal communications depend heavily on race, ethnicity, social class, and particularly, gender, as we shall see. In a society as diverse as the United States, understanding how diversity shapes communication is an essential part of understanding human behavior. Sociologists, psychologists, social psychologists, anthropologists, and linguists have classified nonverbal communication into the following four categories: touch, paralinguistic, body language, and use of personal space or "proxemics" (Taylor et al. 2003; Gilbert et al. 1998; Ekman 1982; Argyle 1975).

DEBUNKING
Society's Myths

Myth: What you say is more important than how you say it.

Sociological perspective: Nonverbal forms of communication, such as gazes, gestures, and tone of voice, can communicate meaning even when it is unspoken.

Touch

Touching, also called *tactile communication,* involves any conveyance of meaning through touch. It may involve negative communication (hitting, pushing) as well as positive (shaking hands, embracing, kissing). These actions are defined as positive or negative by the ethnic cultural context. An action that is positive in one culture can be negative in another. For example, shaking the right hand in greeting is a positive tactile act in the United States, but the same action in East India or certain Arab countries would be an insult. A kiss on the lips is a positive act in most cultures, yet if you were kissed on the lips by a stranger, you would probably consider it a negative act, perhaps even repulsive. The vocabulary of tactile communication changes with social and cultural context.

Patterns of tactile communication are strongly influenced by gender. Parents vary their touching behavior depending on whether the child is a boy or a girl. Boys tend to be touched more roughly; girls, more tenderly and protectively. This pattern continues into adulthood, where women touch each other more often in everyday conversation than do men.

Touching appears to have different meanings to women and men. Women are on the average more likely to touch and hug as an expression of emotional support, whereas men touch and hug more often to assert power or to express sexual interest (Worchel et al. 2000; Wood 1994). Clearly, there are also instances where women touch to

express sexual interest and dominance, but the research shows that in general, for women, touch is a supporting activity. For men, touch on average is a dominance-asserting activity, although the touching and hugging that men do in athletic competition is a supporting activity (Worchel et al. 2000; Wood 1994; Tannen 1990).

Professors, male or female, may pat a man or woman student on the back as a gesture of approval; students will rarely do this to a professor. This shows the effect of status differences. Male professors touch students more often than do female professors. This shows the additional effect of gender. Men often approach women from behind and let their hands rest upon the woman's shoulders; women are less likely to do the same to men. Male doctors touch female nurses more often than nurses touch doctors. Because doctors are disproportionately male and nurses disproportionately female in our society (and most others), this illustrates the combined influences of gender and status. Male bosses touch their female secretaries far more often than female secretaries touch their male bosses (Gilbert et al. 1998). As more women are promoted to high-status positions, we may see changes in how often men and women of higher and lower rank touch each other in the workplace. In the context of a power relationship (that is, one where one person by virtue of his or her status has power over another), these learned patterns can constitute sexual harassment, which is discussed further in Chapters 5, 6, and 13.

Paralinguistic Communication

Paralinguistic communication is the component of communication that is conveyed by the pitch and loudness of the speaker's voice, its rhythm, emphasis, and frequency, and the frequency and length of hesitations. In other words, it is not what you say, but how you say it. A baby's cry communicates effectively to its parent: Its pitch, loudness, and frequency convey specific meanings to experienced parents, such as hunger, anger, or discomfort. The baby is communicating paralinguistically.

The exact meaning of paralanguage, like that of tactile communication, varies with the ethnic and cultural context. For some people under some circumstances, a pause may communicate emphasis; for others, it may indicate uncertainty. A high-pitched voice may mean a person is excited—or that the person is lying. During interactions between Japanese businessmen, long periods of silence often occur. Unlike U.S. citizens, who are experts in "small talk," and who try at all costs to avoid periods of silence in conversation, Japanese people do not need to talk all the time and regard periods of silence as desirable opportunities for collecting their thoughts (Worchel et al. 2000; Fukuda 1994). Unprepared U.S. businesspeople in their first meetings with Japanese executives often think, erroneously, that these silent interludes mean the Japanese are responding negatively to a presentation. More traveled Western executives learn to master the art of paralinguistic communication as practiced in Japan. Even though some find the Japanese mode of conversation highly uncomfortable, getting used to it is a key tool in negotiating successfully. The fate of a deal may depend on a glance, an exhalation, or a smile. Americans often consider paralinguistics to be a minor aspect of the conversation, with much greater attention paid to the verbal transaction. The Japanese, conversely, often consider the paralinguistics to be at least as important as the verbal communication as a source of information (Mizutami 1990).

People often reveal their true feelings and emotions by paralinguistic slips. Emotions tend to "leak out" even if a person tries to conceal them, hence the term *nonverbal leakage* (Ekman and Friesen 1974; Ekman 1982; Ekman et al. 1988; Gilbert et al. 1998; Taylor et al. 2003). People who are lying often betray themselves through paralinguistic

expressions of anxiety, tension, and nervousness. Research has shown that when a person is lying, the pitch of his or her voice is higher than when telling the truth. The difference is small and hard to detect simply by listening, but electronic analysis of vocal pitch can reveal lying with considerable, although not perfect, accuracy.

Body Language

Body language, or more technically *kinesic communication*, involves gestures, facial expressions, body position, and the like. American Sign Language (ASL), a mode of communication for the hearing impaired by means of hand signals, uses this principle. Waving hands, crossed arms, and extended legs all transmit meanings. Add hundreds of facial expressions and the infinite nuances of eye contact, and kinesic communication forms a crucial part of nonverbal communication. Facial expressions are gender

UNDERSTANDING DIVERSITY

Interaction on the Street

Sociologist Eli Anderson's book *Streetwise* (Anderson, 1990) notes how people use space to interact with strangers in the street. Even the deceptively simple decision to pass a stranger on the street involves a set of mental calculations. Is it day or night? Are other people around? Is the stranger a child, a woman, a White man, a teenager, or a Black man? Each participant's actions must be matched to the actions and cues of the other. The following field note of Anderson's illustrates how well attuned strangers can be to each other and how capable of subtle gestural communication:

It is about 11:00 on a cold December morning after a snow fall. Outside, the only sound is the scrape of an elderly white woman's snow shovel on the oil-soaked ice of her front walk. Her house is on a corner in the residential heart of the Village, at an intersection that stands deserted between morning and afternoon rush hours. A truck pulls up directly across from the old lady's house. Before long the silence is split by the buzz of two tree surgeons' gasoline-

powered saws. She leans on her shovel, watches for a while, then turns and goes inside. A middle-aged white man in a beige overcoat approaches the site. His collar is turned up against the cold, his chin buried within, and he wears a Russian-style fur-trimmed hat. His hands are sunk in his coat pockets. In his hard-soled shoes he hurries along this east–west street approaching the intersection, slipping a bit, having to watch each step on the icy sidewalk. He crosses the north–south street and continues westward.

A young Black male, dressed in a way many Villagers call "street-ish" (white high-top sneakers with loose laces, tongues flopping out from under creased gabardine slacks, which drag and soak up oily water; navy blue "air force" parka trimmed with matted fake fur, hood up, arms dangling at the sides) is walking up ahead on the same side of the street. He turns around briefly to check who is coming up behind him. The White man keeps his eye on the treacherous sidewalk, brow furrowed, displaying a look of concern

and determination. The young black man moves with a certain aplomb, walking rather slowly.

From the two men's different paces it is obvious to both that either the young Black man must speed up, the older White man must slow down, or they must pass on the otherwise deserted sidewalk.

The young Black man slows up ever so lightly and shifts to the outside edge of the sidewalk. The White man takes the cue and drifts to the right while continuing his forward motion. Thus in five or six steps (and with no obvious lateral motion that might be construed as avoidance), he maximizes the lateral distance between himself and the man he must pass. What a minute ago appeared to be a single-file formation, with the White man ten steps behind, has suddenly become side-by-side, and yet neither participant ever appeared to step sideways at all.

SOURCE: Anderson, Eli. 1990. *Streetwise: Race, Class and Change in an Urban Community.* Chicago: University of Chicago Press, pp. 217–218. A Study in Diversity: Forms of Nonverbal Communication

Researcher Paul Ekman (1982) has demonstrated that these facial expressions of New Guinea tribesmen are almost identical to those given by college students in the United States to the same four situations depicting anger, happiness, sadness, or disgust. This suggests that some emotions are conveyed by facial expressions in the same way across different cultures, rather than in different ways. Can you identify which expression goes with which emotion in these four photographs?

related and reflect dominance patterns in society. For example, White middle-class women have been socialized to smile a lot, and to do so even if they are not happy. Men are taught not to do this and to generally avoid facial expressions that convey emotion.

Meanings conveyed by body language are usually different in different cultures and ethnic subcultures. For example, Mexicans and Mexican Americans may display the right hand held up, palm inward, all fingers extended, as an obscene gesture meaning "screw you many times over." This provocative gesture has no meaning at all in Anglo (White) society, except insofar as Mexican American traditions have been adopted by Anglos—a type of cultural diffusion.

Ignorance of the meanings that gestures have in a society can get you in trouble. Eye contact, a form of kinesic communication, is especially prone to misinterpretation. People who grow up in urban environments learn to avoid eye contact on the streets. Staring at someone for only two or three seconds can be interpreted as a hostile act, if done man to man (Anderson 1999; 1990). If a woman maintains mutual eye contact with a male stranger for more than two or three seconds, she may be assumed by the man to be sexually interested in him. In contrast, during sustained conversation with nonstrangers, women maintain

mutual eye contact longer than do men (Romain 1999; Gilbert et al. 1998; Wood 1994).

Conversely, some gestures retain the same meaning across different cultures, ethnic groups, and societies. The hand gestures for "stop," "come here," "go away," and "good-bye" are the same in the United States across racial, socioeconomic, and other group subcultures, and they are the same in most other societies as well. The obscene gesture of an extended middle finger, palm inward ("giving the finger" or "flipping the bird") is now virtually universal across all ethnic groups, races, social classes, and both genders, inside and outside the United States. The gestures for "OK," "shame on you," and "crazy" are also widespread both inside and outside U.S. society (Gilbert et al. 1998). Certain facial expressions are culturally universal, too. The facial expressions for anger, happiness, sadness, and even disgust appear to be recognized in all cultures, from the tribal peoples of New Guinea to the White middle class of the United States. These expressions appear to be used equally by both men and women in these cultures, which means they are the same across genders for these different cultures (Gilbert et al. 1998; Ekman 1982).

Use of Personal Space

Meaning is conveyed by the amount of space between interacting individuals; this is referred to as **proxemic communication.** As with much nonverbal communication, the persons involved are generally not conscious of the proxemic messages they are sending. Generally, the more friendly people feel toward each other, the closer they will stand. In casual conversation, friends stand closer to each other than strangers. People who are sexually attracted to each other stand especially close, whether the sexual attraction is gay, lesbian, or heterosexual (Taylor et al. 2003).

According to anthropologist E. T. Hall (1966; Hall and Hall 1987), we all carry around us a *proxemic bubble* that represents our personal, three-dimensional space. When people we don't know enter our proxemic bubble, we feel threatened and may take evasive action. Friends stand close; enemies tend to avoid interaction and keep far apart. According to Hall's theory, we attempt to exclude from our private space those we do not know or do not like even though we may not be fully aware that we are doing so.

Proxemic interaction varies strongly by cultural differences and by gender. This can be clearly seen when people in different racial and ethnic groups interact. The proxemic bubbles of different groups have different sizes. Hispanic people tend to stand much closer to each other than White middle-class Americans; their proxemic bubble is, on average, smaller. Similarly, African Americans also tend to stand close to each other while conversing. Interaction distance is quite large between White middle-class British males—their average interaction distances can be as much as several feet.

Proxemic interactions also differ between men and women (Taylor et al. 2003; Romain 1999; Tannen 1990). Women of the same race and culture tend to stand closer to each other in casual conversation than do men of the same race and culture. When a Middle Eastern man (who has a relatively small proxemic bubble) engages in conversation with a White middle-class U.S. man (who has a larger proxemic bubble), the Middle Eastern man tends to move toward the White American, who tends to back away. You can observe the negotiations of proxemic space at cocktail parties or any other setting that involves casual interaction.

THINKING SOCIOLOGICALLY

Try the following experiment. Enter an empty elevator and go to a far (back) corner. Wait for another person to enter the elevator. If proxemic communication theory is correct, and if you do not already know the person, this person will tend to go to a diagonally opposite front corner of the elevator. (This is an illustration of the *proxemic bubble* principle.) Next, instead of staying put in your corner, take a few small steps toward the other back corner. (You will have to get your nerve up a bit to do this!) What does the other person now do? If the theory of proxemics is correct, the person will take some sort of evasive action, such as move toward the opposite front corner or toward the door. If the person does not move at all, then you should move even closer, and observe what the other person does. Repeat the experiment several times, with different people, with people whose gender is different from yours and whose race is different from yours, and see what happens.

■ *Interpersonal Attraction and the Formation of Pairs*

Perhaps the most interesting interactions between humans are pairings, including friendships, romances, and sexual pairings. Pairings constitute one of the most fundamental processes in society and go a long way in answering our central question, "What holds society together?" How do pairs form? Are pairings influenced by social structure, or are they as random as chance encounters? You will not be surprised to learn that formation of pairs has a strong social structural component—that is, it is patterned by social forces and can to a great extent be predicted.

Humans have a powerful desire to be with other human beings; in other words, they have a strong need for affiliation. We tend to spend about 75 percent of our time with other people when doing all sorts of activities—eating, watching television, studying, doing hobbies, working, and so on (Cassidy and Shaver 1999). Overall, women reveal this affiliative tendency somewhat more than men (Basow 1992). People who lack all forms of human contact are very rare in the general population, and their isolation is usually rooted in psychotic or schizophrenic disorders. Extreme social isolation at an early age causes severe disruption of mental, emotional, and language development, as we saw earlier in Chapter 3.

The affiliation tendency has been likened to *imprinting,* a phenomenon seen in newborn or newly hatched animals, who attach themselves to the first living creature they encounter, even if it is of another species (Lorenz 1966). Studies of ducks and squirrels show that once the young animal attaches itself to a human experimenter, the process is irreversible. The young animal prefers the company of the human to the company of its own species. A degree of imprinting may be discernible in human infant attachment, but researchers note that in infants the process is more complex, more changeable, and more influenced by social factors (Brown 1986).

Somewhat similar to affiliation is interpersonal attraction, a nonspecific positive response toward another person. Attraction occurs in ordinary day-to-day interaction and varies from mild attraction (such as thinking your grocer is a nice person) all the way to deep feelings of love. According to one view, attractions fall on a single continuum ranging from hate to strong dislike to mild dislike to mild liking to strong liking to love. Another view is that attraction and love are two different continua, able to exist separately. By this view, you can actually like someone a whole lot, but not be in love. Conversely, it is held that you can feel passionate love for someone that includes strong sexual feelings and intense emotion, yet not really "like" the person. Have you ever been in love with someone you did not particularly like?

Can attraction be scientifically predicted? Can people be identified with whom you are most likely to fall in love? The surprising answer to these questions is a loud, although somewhat qualified, yes. Most of us have been raised to believe that love is impossible to measure and certainly impossible to predict scientifically. We think of love, especially romantic love, as ephemeral, mysterious—a lightning bolt. Countless novels and stories support this view, but extensive research in sociology and social psychology suggests otherwise: In a probabilistic sense, love can be predicted beyond the level of pure chance. Let us take a look at some of these intriguing findings.

Society's Myths

Myth: Love is purely an emotional experience that you cannot predict or control.

Sociological perspective: Whom you fall in love with can be predicted beyond chance by such factors as proximity, how often you see the person, how attractive you perceive the person to be and whether you are similar (not different) to him or her in social class, race–ethnicity, religion, age, educational aspirations, and general attitudes.

Konrad Lorenz, the animal behaviorist, shows that adult ducks that have imprinted *on him the moment they were hatched will follow him anywhere, as though he were their mother duck.*

Proximity

A strong determinant of your attraction toward others is whether you live near them, work next to them, or have frequent contact with them. You are more likely to form friendships with people from your own city than with people from a thousand miles away. As was originally shown in a classic study by Festinger et al. (1950), you are more likely to be attracted to someone on your floor, your residence hall, or your apartment building than to someone even two floors down or two streets over. Such is the effect of proximity in the formation of human friendships.

Segal (1974) demonstrated this effect in a study of recruits at a police academy. Seating assignments for recruits during classes and seminars at the academy was alphabetical. Segal found that when the police officers were listed alphabetically at the end of their training, the list also effectively captured friendship pairings. The major determinant for choosing friends was relative position in the alphabet, by dictating who sat next to whom in class. Proximity had a stronger effect on friendships than all other factors, including race, socioeconomic background, age, religion, and nationality.

Mere Exposure Effect

Our attraction to another person is greatly affected simply by how frequently we see that person or even his or her photograph. Have you ever noticed, when watching a movie, that the central character seems more attractive at the end of the movie than at the beginning? This is particularly true if you already find the person very attractive when the movie begins. Have you ever noticed that the fabulous-looking person sitting next to you in class looks better every day?

You may be experiencing *mere exposure effect*—the more you see someone in person or in a photograph, the more you like him or her. For example, in studies where people are repeatedly shown photographs of the same face, the more often a person sees a particular face, the more he or she likes that person (Moreland and Beach 1992; Zajonc 1968). There are two qualifications to the effect. First, overexposure can result when a photograph is seen too often. The viewer becomes saturated and ceases to like the pictured person more with each exposure. Second, the initial response of the viewer can determine how much liking will increase. If someone starts out liking a particular person, seeing that person frequently will increase the liking for that person; however, if one starts out disliking the pictured person, the amount of dislike tends to remain about the same, regardless of how often one sees the person (Taylor et al. 2003).

Perceived Physical Attractiveness

We hear that "beauty is only skin deep." Apparently that is deep enough. To a surprisingly large degree, the attractions we feel toward people of either gender are based on our perception of their physical attractiveness. A vast amount of research over the years has consistently shown the importance of attractiveness in human interactions: Adults react more leniently to the bad behavior of an attractive child than to the same behavior of an unattractive child (Taylor et al. 2003; Berscheid and Reis 1998; Dion

1972). Teachers evaluate cute children of either gender as "smarter" than unattractive children with identical academic records (Worchel et al. 2000; Clifford and Walster 1973). In studies of mock jury trials, attractive defendants, male or female, receive lighter sentences on average than unattractive defendants convicted of the same crime (Gilbert et al. 1998; Sigall and Ostrove 1975).

As we saw in Chapter 2, standards of attractiveness vary between cultures and between subcultures within the same society. What is highly attractive in one culture may be repulsive in another. In the United States, there is a maxim that you can never be too thin. This cultural belief has been cited as a major cause of eating disorders such as anorexia nervosa and bulimia, especially among White women (Taylor et al. 2003; Wolf 1991), although less so among African American, Hispanic, and Native American women (Thompson 1994). The maxim itself is oppressive for women in U.S. society, yet it is clearly highly culturally relative. In other cultures, plumpness is sexy, as in England and France during the Middle Ages. Among certain African Americans, chubbiness in women is considered attractive. Such women are called healthy and "phatt" (not fat), which means the same as "stacked" or curvaceous. Similar cultural norms often apply in certain U.S. Hispanic populations. The skinny woman is considered ugly, not sexy. Although standards of attractiveness vary from culture to culture, there is considerable agreement *within* a culture about who is attractive and who is not (Crandall et al. 2001; Langlois et al. 2000; Hatfield and Sprecher 1986).

Studies of dating patterns among college students show that the more attractive one is, the more likely one will be asked on a date. This finding is consistent across several studies done over the last thirty-five years (Speed and Gangestad 1997; Walster et al. 1966). However, one very important exception can be added to this finding: Physical attractiveness predicts only the early stages of a relationship. When one measures relationships that last a while, other factors come into play, principally religion, political attitudes, social class background, educational aspirations, and race. Perceived physical attractiveness may predict who is attracted to whom initially, but other variables are better predictors of how long a relationship will last (Berscheid and Reis 1998; Hill et al. 1976).

Similarity

"Opposites attract," you say? Not according to the research. We have all heard that people are attracted to their "opposite" in personality, social status, background, and other characteristics. Many of us grow up believing this to be true. However, if the research tells us one thing about interpersonal attraction, it is that with few excep-

tions we are attracted to people who are similar or even identical to us in socioeconomic status, race, ethnicity, religion, perceived personality traits, and general attitudes and opinions (Taylor et al. 2003; Brehm et al. 2002). "Dominant" people tend to be attracted to other dominant people, not to "submissive" people. Couples tend to have similar opinions about political issues of great importance to them, such as attitudes about abortion, crime, animal rights, and urban violence. Overall, couples tend to exhibit strong cultural or subcultural similarity.

We sometimes fall in love with the exotic—the culturally or socially different. Novels and movies return endlessly to the story of the young, White, preppy woman who falls in love with a Hell's Angel biker, but such a pairing is by far the exception and not the rule. When it comes to long-term relationships, including both friends and lovers (heterosexual, gay, and lesbian), humans vastly prefer a great degree of similarity even though, if asked, they might deny it. In fact, the less similar a heterosexual relationship is with respect to race, social class, age, and educational aspirations (how far in school the person wants to go), the quicker the relationship is likely to break up (Silverthorne and Quinsey 2000; Worchel et al. 2000; Berscheid and Reis 1998; Stover and Hope 1993; Hill et al. 1976).

An especially interesting qualification to all the research on similarity and attraction presents itself, however, in the matter of interracial dating. Although people generally tend to date within their own race, nationality, or ethnicity, many interracial couples today enjoy long-lasting relationships. Similarity research sheds light on these relationships as well. The research tends to show that for interracial couples, similarity in characteristics other than race—social class background, religion, age, political attitudes, and educational aspirations—tends to predict how long the relationship will last. In general, the more similar the couple is in characteristics other than race, the longer, on average, the interracial relationship will last; the less similar the couple, the shorter the relationship (Berscheid and Reis 1998; Stover and Hope 1993; Eagly et al. 1989).

Most young romantic relationships, regrettably, come to an end. On campus, relationships tend to break up most often during gaps in the school calendar, such as Christmas recess and spring vacation. Summers are especially brutal on relationships formed during the academic year. Breakups are seldom mutual. Almost always, only one member of the pair wants to break off the relationship, whereas the other wants to keep it going. The sad truth means that the next time someone tells you that their breakup last week was "mutual," you know they are probably lying or deceiving themselves (Taylor et al. 2003; Hill et al. 1976).

■ *Social Institutions and Social Structure*

So far, we have been studying the microlevels of society. At the macrolevel, sociologists are interested in the role of social institutions in constituting society. Just as sociologists see social forces shaping behavior at the microlevel, so do they see social forces molding society at the macrolevel.

Social Institutions

Societies are identified by their cultural characteristics and the social institutions that compose each society. A **social institution** (or simply an institution) is an established and organized system of social behavior with a recognized purpose. The term refers to the broad systems that organize specific functions in society. Social institutions are a weave of behaviors, norms, and values, and are organized to meet various needs in society. For example, the family is an institution that provides for the care of the young and the transmission of culture. Religion is an institution that organizes the sacred beliefs. Education is the institution through which people learn the skills needed to live.

Unlike group behavior, social institutions cannot be directly observed, but their impact and structure can still be seen. The concept of social institution is relatively abstract, but very useful nonetheless. A social institution is a patterning of social relationships that exist as distinct from individuals or specific groups, with an existence all its own. It impinges on the behavior of people and groups, and persists long after the people and groups are gone. Take the example of the education institution. You and your classmates form a social group whose behavior can be directly observed. This group is part of a broader educational institution which is both a specific school and, at the societal level, the institution called education.

The major institutions in society include the family, education, work and the economy, the political institution (or state), religion, and health care, as well as the mass media, organized sports, and the military. They all represent institutions; they are all complex structures that exist for explicit reasons. Together, institutions meet certain needs that are necessary for society to exist and proceed. Functionalist theorists have identified these needs (functions) as follows (Aberle et al. 1950; Parsons 1951a; Levy 1949):

1. *The socialization of new members of the society.* This is accomplished by the family and other institutions, such as the education institution.

2. *The production and distribution of goods and services.* The economy is generally the institution that performs this set of tasks.

3. *Replacement of the membership.* All societies must have a means of replacing its members who die, move or migrate away, or otherwise leave the society. Child-rearing is one of these means.

4. *The maintenance of stability and existence.* As already noted in Chapter 1, one major assertion of functional theory is that certain institutions within a society (such as the government, the police force, and the military) contribute toward the stability and continuance of the society.

5. *Providing the members with an ultimate sense of purpose.* Societies accomplish this task by having national anthems and patriotism, in addition to providing basic values and moral codes through institutions such as the family, religion, and education.

Functionalists see these societal needs as universal, although societies do not perform them in the same way or by means of the same institutions. This is what makes societies distinct.

In contrast to functional theory, conflict theory further notes that because conflict is inherent in social existence, the social institutions of society do not provide for all its members equally. Some members are provided for better than others, thus demonstrating that institutions affect people by granting more power to some social groups than to others. Racial and ethnic minorities in a society possess considerably less power and less of society's benefits than does the dominant group. In most societies known to anthropologists and sociologists, women occupy lower social status on average than do men. Few exceptions to this exist. Thus, on average, women have less political power, wealth, and prestige in society than do men. Similarly, power is not equally distributed across social class strata; generally, the lower one's social class, the less one's political power, wealth, influence, and prestige. How institutions affect the person, as well as the benefits that accrue to the individual from the institution, depends on the person's race–ethnicity, gender, and social class status, among other factors.

Social Structure

At both the microlevel and macrolevel, we have seen how social behavior is patterned. Sociologists use the term **social structure** to refer to the organized pattern of social relationships and social institutions that together compose society. The social structure of society is observable in the established patterns of social interaction and social institutions. The structures are not immediately visible to the untrained observer; nevertheless, they are present, and they affect all dimensions of human experience in society. Social structural analysis is a way of looking at society in which the sociologist analyzes the patterns in social life that reflect and produce social behavior.

Social class distinctions are an example of a social structure. Class shapes the access that different groups have to the resources of society, and it shapes many interactions people have with each other. People may form cliques with those who share similar class standing, or they may identify with certain values that are associated with a given class. Class then forms a social structure—one that shapes and guides human behavior at all levels, no matter how overtly visible or invisible this structure is to someone at a given time.

The philosopher Marilyn Frye aptly describes the concept of social structure in her writing. Using the metaphor of a birdcage, she writes that if you look closely at only one wire in a cage, you cannot see the other wires. You might then wonder why the bird within does not fly away. Only when you step back and see the whole cage instead of a single wire do you understand why the bird does not escape. Frye writes,

It is perfectly obvious that the bird is surrounded by a network of systematically related barriers, no one of which would be the least hindrance to its flight, but all of which, by their relations to each other, are as confining as the solid walls of a dungeon. It is now possible to grasp one reason why oppression can be hard to see and recognize: one can study the elements of an oppressive structure with great care and some good will without seeing or being able to understand that one is looking at a cage and that there are people there who are caged, whose motion and mobility are restricted, whose lives are shaped and reduced. (Frye 1983: 4–5)

Frye's analysis focuses on oppressive social structures that confine and exploit people. Oppression and social structure are not the same, although many people find existing social structures oppressive. Just as a birdcage is a network of wires, society is a network of social structures, both micro and macro.

THINKING SOCIOLOGICALLY

Using Marilyn Frye's analogy of the birdcage, think of a time when you believed your choices were constrained by *social structure*. When you applied to college, for example, could you go anywhere you wanted? What social structural conditions guided your ultimate selection of schools to attend?

■ *What Holds Society Together?*

What holds societies together? We have been asking this question throughout this chapter. This central question in sociology was first addressed by Emile Durkheim, the French sociologist writing in the late 1800s and early 1900s. He argued that people in society had a **collective consciousness,** defined as the body of beliefs common to a community or society that give people a sense of belonging and a feeling of moral obligation to its demands and values. According to Durkheim, it is collective consciousness that gives groups social solidarity; because members of a group feel they are part of one society.

Where does the collective consciousness come from? Durkheim argued that it stems from people's participation in common activities, such as work, family, education, and religion—in short, society's institutions. Goals, values, and beliefs emanate from the institutions of a society, and individuals aligned with common institutions develop a sense of common purpose, providing solidarity in society.

Mechanical and Organic Solidarity

According to Durkheim, the two types of social solidarity, or holding together, are mechanical and organic, each the basis of a different form of societal solidarity. **Mechanical solidarity** arises when individuals play similar roles within the society; people feel bonded to the group in less complex societies because everyone in the group is so similar. Individuals in societies marked by mechanical solidarity share the same values and hold the same things sacred. This potent source of cohesiveness is weakened when a society becomes differentiated into more complex systems of work behavior. Contemporary examples of mechanical solidarity are rare because most societies of the world have been absorbed in the global trend for greater complexity and interrelatedness. Native American groups before European conquest were bound together by mechanical solidarity; indeed, many Native American groups are now trying to regain the mechanical solidarity on which their cultural heritage rests, but they are finding that the superimposition of White institutions on Native American life interferes with the adoption of traditional ways of thinking and being, which prevents mechanical solidarity from gaining its original strength.

In contrast to societies where individuals play the same roles, we find societies marked by **organic solidarity** (also called *contractual solidarity*) in which individuals play a great variety of roles and unity is based on role differentiation, not similarity. The United States and other industrial societies are built on organic solidarity and each is cohesive *because* of the differentiation within each. Roles are no longer necessarily similar, but they are necessarily interlinked—the performance of multiple roles is necessary for the execution of society's complex and integrated functions.

Durkheim described this state as the **division of labor,** defined as the systematic interrelatedness of different tasks that develop in complex societies. The labor force within the contemporary U.S. economy, for example, is divided according to the kinds of work people do. Within any division of labor, tasks become distinct from one another, but they are still woven into a whole.

The division of labor is a central concept in sociology because it represents how the different pieces of society fit together. The division of labor in most contemporary societies is often marked by age, gender, race, and class. In other words, if you look at who does what in society, you will see that women and men tend to do different things; this is the gender division of labor. Similarly, old and young to some extent do different things; this is a division of labor by age. This is cross-cut by the racial division of labor, the pattern whereby those in different racial–ethnic groups tend to do different work—or are often forced to do different work—in society. At the same time, the division of labor is also marked by class distinctions, with some groups providing work that is highly valued and rewarded and others doing work that is devalued and poorly rewarded. As you will see throughout this book, gender, race, and class intersect and overlap in the division of labor in society.

Durkheim's thinking about the origins of social cohesion can bring light to contemporary discussions over "family values." Some want to promote traditional family values as the moral standards of society. Is such a thing necessarily good, or even possible? The United States is an increasingly diverse society, and family life differs among different groups. It is unlikely that a single set of family values can be the basis for social solidarity; nevertheless, groups in this society are bound together through the division of labor, even when the bond of shared values is not strong. Although contemporary society is enormously diverse, it can still have the cohesion of a unified society because its people are interrelated through social institutions.

DEBUNKING
Society's Myths

Myth: Society is held together because people share common values.

Sociological perspective: Some societies are held together by commonly shared values, such as in mechanical solidarity; other societies, marked by organic solidarity, are held together by the interrelated but different roles that are part of the division of labor.

Gemeinschaft and Gesellschaft

Different societies are held together by different forms of solidarity. Some societies are characterized by what sociologists call **gemeinschaft,** a German word that means "community"; others are characterized as **gesellschaft,** which literally means "society" (Tönnies 1963/1887). Each involves a type of solidarity or cohesiveness. Those societies that are gemeinschafts ("communities") are characterized by a sense of "we" feeling, a moderate division of labor, strong personal ties, strong family relationships, and a sense of personal loyalty. The sense of solidarity between members of the gemeinschaft society arises from personal ties; small, relatively simple social institutions; and a collective sense of loyalty to the whole society. People tend to be well integrated into the whole, and social cohesion comes from deeply shared values and beliefs (often, sacred values). Social control need not be imposed externally, because control comes from the internal sense of belonging that members share. Generally, gemeinschafts tend to be characterized by mechanical solidarity.

In contrast, in societies marked by gesellschaft an increasing importance is placed on the secondary relationships people have—that is, less intimate and more instrumental relationships, such as work roles instead of family or community roles. Gesellschaft is characterized by less prominence of personal ties, a somewhat diminished role of the nuclear family, and a lessened sense of personal loyalty to the total society. The solidarity and cohesion remain and it can be very cohesive, but the cohesion comes from an elaborated division of labor (thus *organic* solidarity), greater flexibility in social roles, and the instrumental ties that people have to one another.

Social solidarity under gesellschaft is weaker than in the gemeinschaft society, however. Gesellschaft societies are marked by an elaborate division of labor; gesellschaft is more likely than gemeinschaft to be torn by class conflict, because class distinctions are less prominent, though still present, in the gemeinschaft. Racial–ethnic conflict is more likely within gesellschaft societies, because the gemeinschaft tends to be ethically and racially very homogeneous; often it is characterized by only one racial or ethnic group. This means that conflict between gemeinschaft societies, such as ethnically based wars, can be very high, because both groups have a strong internal sense of group identity that may be intolerant of others (for example, Palestinians vs. Jews, and Hutus vs. Tutsis in Rwanda).

In sum, complexity and differentiation are what make the gesellschaft cohesive, whereas similarity and unity cohere the gemeinschaft society. In a single society, such as the United States, you can conceptualize the whole society as gesellschaft, with some internal groups marked by gemeinschaft. Our national motto seems to embody this idea: *E pluribus unum,* "Unity within diversity."

■ *Types of Societies: A Global View*

In addition to comparing how different societies are bound together, sociologists are interested in how social organization evolves in different societies. Over time and across different cultures and continents, societies are distinguished by different forms of social organization—forms that evolve from the relationship of a given society to its environment and from the processes that the society develops to meet basic human needs. Simple things such as the size of a society can also shape its social organization, as do the different roles that men and women engage in as they produce goods, care for the old and young, and pass on societal traditions. Societies also differ according to their resource base—whether they are predominantly agricultural or industrial, for example, and whether they are sparsely or densely populated.

Thousands of years ago, societies were small, sparsely populated, and technologically limited. In the competition for scarce resources, larger and more technologically advanced societies dominated smaller ones. Today, we have arrived at a global society with highly evolved degrees of social differentiation and inequality, notably along class, gender, racial, and ethnic lines (Lenski et al. 2001). Sociologists distinguish six types of societies based on the complexity of their social structure, the amount of overall cultural accumulation, and the level of their technology. They are: *foraging, pastoral, horticultural, agricul-*

tural (these four are called *preindustrial* societies), then *industrial,* and *postindustrial* societies (see Table 4.1). Each type of society can still be found on Earth though all but the most isolated societies are rapidly moving toward the industrial and postindustrial stages of development.

These different societies vary in the basis for their organization and the complexity of their division of labor. Some, such as foraging societies, are subsistence economies, where men and women hunt and gather food, but accumulate very little. Others, such as pastoral societies and horticultural societies, develop a more elaborate division of labor as the social roles that are needed for raising livestock and farming become more numerous. With the development of agricultural societies, production becomes more large scale and strong patterns of social differentiation develop, sometimes taking the form of a caste system or even slavery.

The key driving force behind the development of these different societies is the development of technology. All societies use technology to help fill human needs. Technology may be as simple as a rough-hewn shovel or as elaborate as computing technology. Either way, the technology both develops from the society's form and shapes the possibilities for human life.

Preindustrial Societies

A **preindustrial society** is one that directly uses, modifies, and/or tills the land as a major means of survival as a society. There are four kinds of preindustrial societies, listed here by degree of development of their technology:

TABLE 4.1 Types of Societies

	Economic Base	Social Organization	Examples
Foraging Societies	Economic sustenance dependent on hunting and foraging	Gender is important basis for social organization, although division of labor is not rigid; little accumulation of wealth	Pygmies of Central Africa
Pastoral Societies	Nomadic societies, with substantial dependence on domesticated animals for economic production	Complex social system with an elite upper class and greater gender role differentiation than in foraging societies	Bedouins of Africa and Middle East
Horticultural Societies	Society marked by relatively permanent settlement and production of domesticated crops	Accumulation of wealth and elaboration of the division of labor, with different occupational roles (farmers, traders, craftspeople, etc.)	Aztecs of Mexico; Incan empire of Peru
Agricultural Societies	Livelihood dependent on elaborate and large-scale patterns of agriculture and increased use of technology in agricultural production	Caste system develops that differentiates the elite and agricultural laborers; may include system of slavery	American South, pre-Civil War
Industrial Societies	Economic system based on the development of elaborate machinery and a factory system; economy based on cash and wages	Highly differentiated labor force with a complex division of labor and large formal organizations	Nineteenth- and most of twentieth-century United States and Western Europe
Postindustrial Societies	Information-based societies in which technology plays a vital role in social organization	Education increasingly important to the division of labor	Contemporary United States, Japan, and others

foraging (or hunting-gathering) societies; pastoral societies; horticultural societies; and agricultural societies (see Table 4.1).

In *foraging (hunting-gathering) societies,* the technology enables the hunting of animals and gathering of vegetation. The technology does not permit the refrigeration or processing of food, and hence these individuals must search continuously for plants and game. Since hunting and gathering are activities that require large amounts of land, most foraging societies are nomadic, that is, they constantly travel as they deplete the plant supply or follow the migrations of animals. The central institution is the family, which serves as the means of distributing food, training children, and protecting its members. There is usually role differentiation on the basis of gender, although the specific form of the gender division of labor varies in different societies. They occasionally wage war with other clans or similar societies, and spears and bows and arrows are the weapons used. Examples of foraging societies are the Aborigines of Australia and the Pygmies of Central Africa.

In *pastoral societies,* technology is based on the domestication of animals. Such societies tend to develop in desert areas that are too arid to provide rich vegetation. The pastoral society is nomadic, necessitated by the endless search for fresh grazing grounds for the herds of their domesticated animals. The animals are used as sources of hard work that enable the creation of a material surplus. Unlike a foraging society, this surplus frees some individuals from the tasks of hunting and gathering and allows them to create crafts, make pottery, cut hair, build tents, and apply tattoos. The surplus generates a more complex and differentiated social system with an elite or upper class and more role differentiation on the basis of gender. The nomadic Bedouins of Africa and the Middle East are pastoral societies.

In *horticultural societies,* elaborate hand tools are used to cultivate the land, such as the hoe and the digging stick. The individuals in horticultural societies practice ancestor worship and conceive of a deity or deities (God or gods) as a creator. This distinguishes them from foraging societies that generally employ the notion of numerous spirits to explain the unknowable. Horticultural societies recultivate the land each year and tend to establish relatively permanent settlements and villages. Role differentiation is extensive, resulting in different and interdependent occupational roles such as farmer, trader, and craftsperson. The Aztecs of Mexico and the Incas of Peru represent examples of horticultural societies.

The *agricultural society* is exemplified by the pre–Civil War American South. Such societies have a large and complex economic system that is technologically based on large-scale farming using plows harnessed to animals or other sources of energy. Other technological elements such as irrigation, use of the wheel, use of metals, and the ability to write, make such societies considerably advanced technologically. Farms tend to be considerably larger than the cultivated land in horticultural societies. Large and permanent settlements characterize agricultural societies, which also exhibit dramatic social inequalities. A rigid caste system develops, separating the peasants, or slaves, from the controlling elite caste, which is then freed from manual work allowing time for art, literature, and philosophy, activities of which they can then claim the lower castes are incapable.

Industrial Societies

An *industrial society* is one that uses machines and other advanced technologies to produce and distribute goods and services. The Industrial Revolution began only 200 years ago when the steam engine was invented in England, delivering previously unattainable amounts of mechanical power for the performance of work. Steam engines powered locomotives, factories, and dynamos, transforming societies as the Industrial Revolution spread. The growth of science led to advances in farming techniques such as crop rotation, harvesting, and ginning cotton, as well as industrial-scale projects such as dams for generating hydroelectric power. Joining these advances were developments in medicine, new techniques to prolong and improve life, and the emergence of birth control to limit population growth.

Unlike agricultural societies, industrial societies rely on a highly differentiated labor force and the intensive use of capital and technology. Large formal organizations are common. The task of holding society together, falling on institutions such as religion in preindustrial societies, now falls more on the institutions that have a high division of labor, such as the economy and work, government, politics, and large bureaucracies.

Within industrial societies, the forms of gender inequality that we see in contemporary U.S. society tend to develop. With the advent of industrialization, societies move to a cash-based economy, with labor performed in factories and mills paid on a wage basis and household labor remaining unpaid. This introduced what is know as the *family–wage economy,* in which families become dependent on wages to support themselves, but work within the family (housework, child care, and other forms of household work) is unpaid and therefore increasingly devalued (Tilly and Scott 1978). In addition, even though women (and young children) worked in factories and mills from the first inception of industrialization, the family–wage economy is based on the idea that men are the primary breadwinners. A system of inequality in men's and women's wages was introduced—

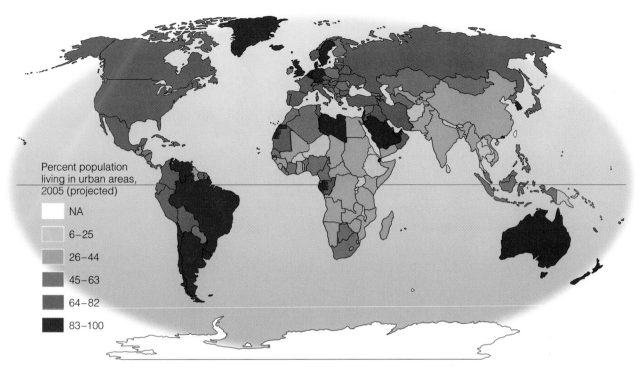

MAP 4.1 Viewing Society in Global Perspective: Global Urbanization
The percentage of the population of a country that is urban is one way of measuring the complexity of a society. Urbanization is one measure of this complexity, but certainly not the only one. **Can you think of other measures of complexity of a society?**

DATA: From the Population Division of the United Nations Secretariat, *World Urbanization Prospects: The 2001 Revision.* New York: United Nations, pp. 26-35.

an economic system that today continues to produce a wage gap between men and women.

Industrial societies tend to be highly productive economically with a large working class of industrial laborers. People become increasingly urbanized as they move from farmlands to urban centers or other areas where factories are located, as we see in Map 4.1 "Viewing Society in Global Perspective: Global Urbanization." Immigration is common in industrial societies, particularly because industries are forming where there is a high demand for more, cheaply paid labor.

Industrialization has brought many benefits to U.S. society—a highly productive and efficient economic system, expansion of international markets, extraordinary availability of consumer products, and for many, a good working wage. Industrialization has, at the same time, however, also produced some of the most serious social problems that our nation faces: industrial pollution, an overdependence on consumer goods, wage inequality and job dislocation for millions, and problems of crime and crowding in urban areas. The portrait of population density depicted in Map 4.2, "Mapping America's Diversity: Population Density in the United States," illustrates where crowding is most extreme. Understanding the

process of industrialization and its accompanying process of urbanization is a major avenue for sociological research and is explored further in Chapter 15.

Postindustrial Societies

In the contemporary era, a new type of society is emerging. Whereas most twentieth-century societies can be characterized in terms of their generation of material goods, *postindustrial society* depends economically on the production and distribution of services, information, and knowledge (Bell 1973). Postindustrial societies are information-based societies in which technology plays a vital role in the social organization. The United States is fast becoming a postindustrial society, and Japan may be even further along. Many of the workers provide services such as administration, education, legal services, scientific research, and banking, or they engage in the development, management, and distribution of information, such as computer use and design. Central to the economy of the postindustrial society are the highly advanced technologies of computers, robotics, genetic engineering, and laser technology. Multinational corporations globally link the economies of postindustrial societies.

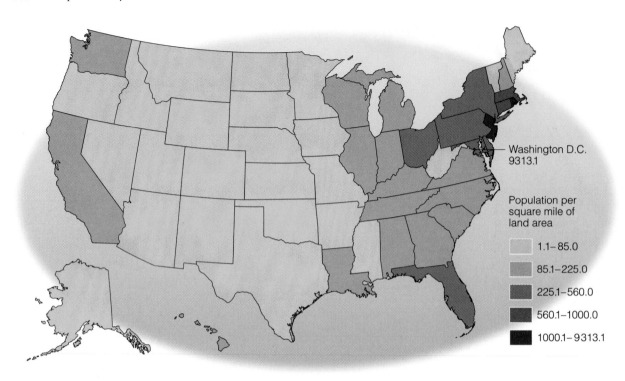

Washington D.C.
9313.1

Population per
square mile of
land area

▢	1.1–85.0
▩	85.1–225.0
▨	225.1–560.0
▧	560.1–1000.0
▉	1000.1–9313.1

MAP 4.2 Mapping America's Diversity: Population Density in the United States

Population density of a state in the United States is measured by the number of people per square mile in that state. Notice which states are densely populated (for example, New York, New Jersey, California) and which are sparsely populated (for example, many states in the Midwest). **How does your home state compare in population density to other states?**

DATA: From the U.S. Census Bureau, 2002. *Statistical Abstract of the United States,* 2002. Washington, DC: U.S. Government Printing Office, p. 23.

© David Young Wolff/PhotoEdit

An information-based technology is the primary characteristic of the postindustrial society, exemplified here by this worker, who is surrounded by computer hardware.

The transition to a postindustrial society has a strong influence on the character of social institutions. Educational institutions acquire paramount importance in the postindustrial society, and science takes an especially prominent place. For some, the transition to a postindustrial society means more discretionary income for leisure activities— tourism, entertainment, and relaxation industries (spas, massage centers, and exercise) become more prominent—at least for people in certain classes. For others, the transition to postindustrialism can mean permanent joblessness or the need to hold down more than one job to simply make ends meet. Workers without highly technical skills may be dispossessed in such a society, and millions may find themselves stuck in low-paid, unskilled work.

The United States is suspended between the industrial and postindustrial phases. Manufacturing jobs are still a major segment of the labor force, although they are in decline because most workers are employed in the service sector of the economy that involves the delivery of services and information, not the actual production of material goods. Postindustrial societies are also increasingly dependent on a global economy because goods tend to be produced in economically dependent areas of the world for consumption in the wealthier nations. As a result, the world, not just individual societies, becomes characterized by poverty and inequality resulting from the social structure that postindustrialism produces.

■ *Chapter Summary*

■ **What are the forms of social interaction in society?**

Society is a system of social interaction that includes both culture and *social organization.* An individual in society is typically a member of several *groups* simultaneously. *Status* is a hierarchical position in a structure; a *role* is the expected behavior associated with a particular status. The individual learns these through *role modeling,* which is imitative behavior. Because the typical individual occupies many statuses as well as the many roles associated with him or her, these can often conflict, thus producing *status inconsistency, role conflict,* or *role strain,* any of which can be stressful and unpleasant.

■ **What theories are there about social interaction?**

Social interaction takes place in society within the context of social structure and social institutions. Social interaction is analyzed in several ways, including the *social construction of reality* (we impose meaning and reality on our interactions with others); *ethnomethodology* (deliberate interruption of interaction to observe how a return to "normal" interaction is accomplished); *impression management* (a person "gives off" a particular impression to "con" the other and achieve certain goals, as in *cyberspace interaction*); and *social exchange* (one engages in game-like reward and punishment interactions to achieve one's goals).

■ **What happens in cyberspace interaction?**

In *cyberspace interaction,* a person can manipulate the impression that one gives off, thus creating a new "virtual" self or new identity. This new identity can then be used to achieve certain goals. Cyberspace interaction has resulted in a new cyberculture, with its own rules and norms.

■ **What is nonverbal communication, and what are its forms?**

Interaction can be verbal or nonverbal. Forms of nonverbal communication are *touch, tone of voice, body language,* and *use of personal space (proxemic).* The study of nonverbal communication reveals much rich information about diverse gender, cultural, and racial–ethnic variations in human interaction.

■ **How do people form attraction pairings?**

People form pairings on the basis of several things, among them proximity, repeated exposure to another; perceived physical attractiveness; and similarity in age, socioeconomic status, race, ethnicity, religion, perceived personality traits, general attitudes and opinions, and educational aspirations. Similarities of such things attract; opposites do not. Such variables also tend to predict how long an interracial relationship will last.

■ **What is a social institution and a social structure?**

A *social institution,* or established organized social behavior, exists for a recognized purpose within a *social structure,* or patterned relationship within a society.

■ **What holds society together?**

According to theorist Emile Durkheim, society with all its complex social organization and culture, is held together, depending on overall type, by *mechanical solidarity* (based on individual similarity) and *organic solidarity* (based on a *division of labor* among dissimilar individuals). Two other forms of social organization also contribute to the cohesion of a society: *gemeinschaft* ("community," characterized by cohesion based on friendships and loyalties) and *gesellschaft* ("society," characterized by cohesion based on complexity and differentiation).

■ **What are the types of societies?**

Societies across the globe vary in type, as determined mainly by the complexity of their social structures, their division of labor, and their technologies. From least to most complex, they are *foraging, pastoral, horticultural, agricultural* (these four constitute *preindustrial* societies), *industrial,* and *postindustrial* societies.

■ *Key Terms*

achieved status 97
ascribed status 97
collective consciousness 113
cyberspace interaction 103
division of labor 114
ethnomethodology 100
gemeinschaft 114
gesellschaft 114
group 96
impression
   management 101
macroanalysis 96
master status 97
mechanical solidarity 113
microanalysis 96
organic solidarity 113

▪ *Researching Society with MicroCase® Online*

You can see the results of actual research by using the Wadsworth MicroCase® Online feature available to you. This feature allows you to look at some of the results from national surveys, census data, and some other data sources. You can explore this easy-to-use feature on your own, but try this example. Suppose you want to know some social facts, such as:

Having a job is a type of role (called occupational role). How much in general do people who work like their jobs? Why do some people like their jobs and some not? You can do the analysis yourself!

To answer this question, go to **sociology.wadsworth.com/andersen_taylor/essen3e,** select MicroCase Online from the left navigation bar, and follow the directions there to analyze the data described below.

Data file: GSS

Task: Cross-Tabulation

Column Variable: I-SEX

Row Variable: LIKE JOB?

Questions

You will get a table that gives the individual's gender (sex) (the columns of the table, which is I-SEX) and also how satisfied that person is with his or her job (the rows of the table, which is LIKE-JOB?). When you get these results (these are actual people), answer the following questions:

1. What are the overall percentages (the total percentages—in the right-hand column) of people who are: Very satisfied with their job? Moderately satisfied? Unsatisfied?

2. What is the total number of women in this study? What is the total number of men?

3. In general (look at the table) which gender (women or men) tends to be "very satisfied" with their job? Which gender tends to be "unsatisfied"?

▪ *The Companion Web Site for Sociology: The Essentials, Third Edition*

sociology.wadsworth.com/andersen_taylor/essen3e

Supplement your review of this chapter by going to the companion Web site to take one of the Tutorial Quizzes, use the flash cards to master key terms, and check out the many other study aids you'll find there. You'll also find special features such as GSS Data and Census 2000 information, data and resources at your fingertips to help you with that special project or do some research on your own.

▪ *Suggested Readings and Web Resources*

Goffman, Erving. 1959. *The Presentation of Self in Everyday Life.* Garden City, NY: Doubleday.
    Goffman's analysis is the classic analysis of impression management and how people negotiate their individual identity, and "con" others about that identity, through social interaction.

Hendrick, S. S., and C. Hendrick. 1992. *Romantic Love.* Newbury Park, CA: Sage.
    The Hendricks still provide the best comprehensive and readable discussion of research on romantic love and the formation of dyads on the basis of love.

Lenski, Gerhard, Jean Lenski, and Patrick Nolan. 2001. *Human Society: An Introduction to Macrosociology,* 9th ed. New York: McGraw-Hill.
    This book offers an expansive account of different types of societies in detail, with clear discussions of Durkheim and other theorists.

Putnam, Robert D. 2000. *Bowling Alone: The Collapse and Revival of American Community.* New York: Simon and Schuster.
    Putnam argues that our society has experienced a decline in participation in voluntary organizations, religious activities, and other forms of public life, and as a result is undergoing a decline of shared values as a part of culture. Hence, our society is in danger of increased social disorder.

Strate, Lance, Ron L. Jacobson, and Stephanie Gibson, eds. 2003. *Communication and Cyberspace.* Cresskill, NJ: Hampton Press.

A collection of readings covering a wide range of cyberspace topics, for example: whom shall control cyberspace; virtual reality and re-definition of self; the role of culture in cyberspace interaction; risk and the Internet; how to construct a virtual organization; how influence works in cyberspace; and other topics.

Turnbull, Colin. 1972. *The Mountain People.* New York: Simon & Schuster.
The Ik were an isolated people living as a separate society in Uganda. This is a powerful account of how the Ugandan government completely destroyed Ik society by moving them onto a government-controlled reservation. Comparisons to the historical treatment of Native Americans are made.

The Psychology of Cyberspace
www.rider.edu/users/suler/psycyber/psycyber.html
This site includes an outline book about social interaction and cyberspace with links to other sites exploring the implications of cyberspace for interpersonal interaction.

Center for Social Informatics
www-slis.lib.indiana.edu/ssi/
The Center for Social Informatics at Indiana University does research on the influence of technology and computerization on society; the Web site includes information on publications, conferences, and other resources.

CHAPTER FIVE

Groups and Organizations

*t*welve citizens sit together in an elevated enclosure, like a choir loft, and silently watch a drama unfold before them, day after day. They are respectfully addressed by highly paid professionals: lawyers, judges, expert witnesses. Their job, ruling on the innocence or guilt of a defendant or the settlement of a legal claim, was once the prerogative only of kings. Their decision may mean freedom or incarceration, fortune or penury, even life or death.

The jurors all hear the same presentations about the evidence. They are given identical instructions by the judge when the time arrives for a decision to be made, yet the jurors' chamber is frequently a battleground, the site of bitter disputes, tears, bullying, flights of reason and unreason. Juries have been the focus of much research, in part because they fill such a vital role in our society and in part because within this curiously artificial, yet intimate, group of random strangers can be found a wealth of interesting sociological phenomena. Jury verdicts and jury deliberations show the same inescapable influences of status, race, and gender that affect the rest of society. Juries are, in some ways, society in miniature.

A vast folklore exists among trial lawyers about jurors and jury performance. During jury selection, in a process called the *voir dire,* lawyers on both sides are entitled to eliminate any potential jurors and no explanation is required. Many lawyers who have great faith in their ability to judge jurors consider jury selection to be the most important part of a trial. By choosing jurors, they are choosing the verdict. Consider some of the folk wisdom clung to by trial lawyers in the past: Farmers believe in strict responsibility, whereas waiters and bartenders are forgiving (Belli 1954); bankers are hard on robbery, but easy on white-collar crime (Campbell 1972); avoid wage

This jury of twelve persons is voting on something, perhaps on whether to acquit a person accused of a serious crime. The social pressures in a jury are extremely strong, making the lone "hold-out" person a very unlikely event.

earners; select married women. A guideline for Dallas prosecutors are advised against selecting "Yankees . . . unless they appear to have common sense" (Guinther 1988: 54).

High-powered legal teams now make room for a new breed of legal specialist—the trial consultant trained in sociological techniques who contributes nothing but juror analysis as part of the jury selection process. Such was the case in the well-publicized trial of actor/football player O. J. Simpson for the alleged murder of his ex-wife. According to some researchers, the jury found Simpson not guilty despite strong evidence of his guilt because the prosecutor ignored social science consultants, especially information regarding the relevance of the racial and gender composition of the jury (Taylor et al. 2003; Toobin 1996). In other trials, simply the size of the jury (six versus twelve members) can make a difference (Saks and Marti 1997).

Juries are groups, and groups behave differently from individuals. Un-derstanding group behavior is critical to predicting the performance of a jury. For instance, it is possible to make an educated prediction about who in a jury will become the most influential. Researchers have found that people with high status in society do the most talking in jury deliberations and other jurors consider them to be the most helpful in reaching a verdict (Taylor et al. 2003; Hans and Martinez 1994; Cohen and Zhou 1991; Berger and Zelditch 1985).

Factions form during jury deliberations, and if jury analysts expect a difficult decision, they can attempt to influence how factionalized juries will resolve their disputes based on sociological and psychological data about small group decision making (Hastie and Pennington 2000; Hastie et al. 1983). For instance, jurors are much less likely to defect from large factions than from small ones. The larger the faction, the less willing a juror will be to defy the weight of group opinion.

What does this say about the state of justice in our legal system, when guilt or innocence depends not only on the legal facts but also on social aspects of the jury? Like society as a whole, and like organizations and bureaucracies, groups are subject to social influences, and understanding these influences can be essential to understanding a process such as the operation of social justice.

This chapter introduces students to the study of groups and the social processes and dynamics that are characteristic of group behavior. Whether a relatively small group, such as a jury, or a large organization, such as a major corporation, groups are influenced by sociological forces.

■ *Types of Groups*

Each of us is a member of many groups simultaneously. We have relationships in groups with family, friends, team members, and professional colleagues. Within these groups are gradations in relationships: We are generally closer to our siblings than our cousins; we are intimate with some friends, merely sociable with others. If we count up all our group associations, ranging from the powerful associations that define our daily lives to the thinnest connections with little feeling (other pet lovers, other company employees), we will uncover connections to literally hundreds of groups.

What is a group? Recall from Chapter 4, a **group** is two or more individuals who interact, share goals and norms, and have a subjective awareness as "we." To be considered a group, a social unit must have all three characteristics. The hazy boundaries of the definition are necessary. Consider three superficially similar examples: The individuals in a line waiting to board a train are unlikely to have a sense of themselves as one group. A line of prisoners chained together and waiting to board a bus to the penitentiary is more likely to have a stronger sense of common feeling. Finally, no doubt the passengers who overpowered the hijacking pilots on American Airlines Flight 92 on September 11, 2001, subsequently crashing the plane into a Pennsylvania farmland, became a group for a few moments.

As you remember from the previous chapter, certain gatherings are not groups in the strict sense, but may be *social categories* (for example, teenagers, truck drivers) or *audiences* (everyone watching a movie). The importance of defining a group is not to perfectly decide if a social unit is a group—an unnecessary endeavor—but to help us understand the behavior of people in society. As we inspect groups, we can identify characteristics that reliably predict trends in the behavior of the group, and even the behavior of individuals in the group.

The study of groups has application at all levels of society, from the attraction between people who fall in love to the characteristics that make some corporations drastically outperform their competitors. The aggregation of individuals into groups has a transforming power, and sociologists understand the social forces that make these transformations possible.

Dyads and Triads: Group Size Effects

Even the smallest groups are of acute sociological interest. A **dyad** is a group consisting of exactly two people. A **triad** consists of three people. This seemingly minor distinction, first scrutinized by the German sociologist **Georg Simmel** (1858–1918), can have critical consequences for group behavior (Simmel 1902). Simmel was interested in discovering the effects of size on groups, and he found that the mere difference between two and three people spawned entirely different group dynamics (the behavior of a group over time).

Imagine two people standing in line for lunch. First one talks, then the other, then the first again. The interaction proceeds in this way for several minutes. Now a third person enters the interaction. The character of the interaction suddenly changes: At any given moment, two

One of the best examples of the primary group is that consisting of parent and child.

people are interacting more with each other than either is with the third. When the third person wins the attention of one of the other two, a new dyad is formed, supplanting the previous pairing. The group, a triad, then consists of a dyad (the pair that is interacting) plus an *isolate.*

Triadic segregation is what Simmel called the tendency for triads to segregate into a pair and an isolate. A triad tends to segregate into a *coalition* of the dyad against the isolate. The isolate then has the option of initiating a coalition with either members of the dyad. This choice is a type of social advantage, leading Simmel to coin the principle of *tertius gaudens,* a Latin term meaning "the third one gains."

Interactions in a triad often end up as two against one. You may have noticed this principle of coalition formation in your own conversations. Perhaps two friends want to go to a movie you do not want to see. You appeal to one of them to go instead to a minor league baseball game. She wavers and comes over to your point of view—now you have formed a coalition of two against one. The friend who wants to go to the movies is now the isolate. He may recover lost social ground by trying to form a new coalition by suggesting a new alternative (going bowling or to a different movie). This flip-flop interaction may continue for some time, demonstrating another observation by Simmel: A triad is an unstable social grouping, whereas dyads are relatively stable. The minor distinction between dyads and triads is one person but has important consequences because it changes the character of the interaction within the group. Simmel is known as the discoverer of **group size effects**—the effects of group number on group behavior. Later in this chapter we will encounter several examples of how something as simple as group size can dramatically change behavior.

Primary and Secondary Groups

Charles Horton Cooley (1864–1929), a famous sociologist of the Chicago School of sociology, introduced the concept of the **primary group** defined as a group consisting of intimate, face-to-face interaction and relatively long-lasting relationships. Cooley had in mind the family and early peer group. In his original formulation, "primary" was used in the sense of "first," the intimate group of the formative years (Cooley 1967/1909). The insight that there was an important distinction between intimate groups and other groups proved extremely fruitful. Cooley's somewhat narrow concept of family and childhood peers has been elaborated upon over the years to include a variety of intimate relations as examples of primary groups.

Primary groups have a powerful influence on an individual's personality or self-identity. The effect of family on an individual can hardly be overstated. The weight of peer pressure on school children is particularly notorious. Street gangs are a primary group, and their influence on the individual is significant. The camaraderie formed among Marine Corps units in boot camp is another classic example of primary group formation.

In contrast to primary groups are **secondary groups,** those that are larger in membership, less intimate, and less long-lasting. Secondary groups tend to be less significant in the emotional lives of people. Secondary groups include all the students at a college or university, all the people in your neighborhood, and all the people in a bureaucracy or corporation. Secondary groups occasionally take on the characteristics of primary groups. The process can be accelerated in situations of high stress or crisis. For example, when a neighborhood meets with catastrophe, such as a flood, people who may be only acquaintances often come to depend on each other and in the process become more intimate. The secondary group of neighbors becomes, for a time, a primary group. This is precisely what happened in the otherwise highly impersonal neighborhoods in New York City near "ground zero" of the September 11, 2001, terrorist attack on the World Trade Center: Thousands of people pitched in to help, and as a result, many primary groups formed. Similar formations of primary groups no doubt took place in many locations in the eastern United States during the power blackout of August 2003.

THINKING SOCIOLOGICALLY

Name a *primary group* and a *secondary group* to which you belong. Compare the two groups in terms of their size, degree of intimacy, and the nature of the interaction you have within them. Are these groups primarily *expressive, instrumental,* or both?

Primary and secondary groups serve different needs. Primary groups give people intimacy, companionship, and emotional support. These human desires are termed **expressive needs** (also called socioemotional needs). Family and friends share and amplify your good fortune, rescue you when you misbehave, and cheer you up when life looks grim. Primary groups are a major influence on social life and an important source of social control. They are also a dominant influence on your likes and dislikes, preferences in clothing, political views, religious attitudes, and other characteristics. Many studies have shown the overwhelming influence of family and friendship groups on religious and political affiliation, as shown in the box "Doing Sociological Research: Sharing the Journey" (Wuthnow 1994).

Secondary groups serve **instrumental needs** (also called task-oriented needs). Athletic teams form to have fun and win games. Political groups form to raise funds and bend the will of the legislature. Corporations form to make profits, and employees join corporations to earn a living. Needless to say, intimacies can develop in the act of fulfilling instrumental needs, and primary groups may also devote themselves to meeting instrumental needs. The true distinction between primary and secondary groups is in how strongly the participants feel about

one another and how dependent they are on the group for sustenance and identity. Both primary and secondary groups are indispensable elements of life in society.

Reference Groups

Primary and secondary groups are groups to which members belong. **Reference groups** are those to which you

---

DOING SOCIOLOGICAL RESEARCH

Sharing the Journey

Modern society is often characterized as remote, alienating, and without much feeling of community or belonging to a group. This image of society has been carefully studied by sociologist Robert Wuthnow, who noticed that in the United States people are increasingly looking to small groups as a place where they can find emotional and spiritual support and where they find meaning and commitment, despite the image of society as an increasingly impersonal force. Wuthnow began his research by noting that, even with the individualistic culture of U.S. society, small groups play a major role in this society. He saw the increasing tendency of people to join recovery groups, reading groups, spiritual groups, and a myriad of other support groups.

Wuthnow began his research by asking some specific questions, including, "What motivates people to join support groups?" "How do these groups function?" and "What do members like most and least about such groups?" His broadest question, however, was to wonder how the wider society is influenced by the proliferation of small support groups. To answer these questions, a large research team of fifteen scholars designed a study that included both a quantitative and a qualitative dimension. They distributed a survey to a representative sample of more than 1000 people in the United States. Supplementing the survey were

interviews with more than 100 support group members, group leaders, and clergy. The researchers chose twelve groups for extensive study; researchers spent six months to three years tracing the history of these groups, meeting with members and attending group sessions.

Based on this research, Wuthnow concludes that the small group movement is fundamentally altering U.S. society. Forty percent of all Americans belong to some kind of small group. As the result of people's participation in these groups, social values of community and spirituality are undergoing major transformation. People say they are seeking community when they join small groups—whether the group be a recovery group, a religious group, a civic association, or some other small group. People turn to these small groups for emotional support more than physical or monetary support.

Wuthnow argues that large-scale participation in small groups has arisen in a social context in which the traditional support structures in U.S. society, such as the family, no longer provide the sense of belonging and social integration that they provided in the past. Geographic mobility, mass society, and the erosion of local ties all contribute to this trend. People still seek a sense of community, but they create it in groups that also allow them to maintain their individuality. In voluntary small groups you are free to leave

the group if the group no longer meets your needs.

Wuthnow also concludes that these groups represent a quest for spirituality in a society when, for many, traditional religious values have declined. As a consequence, support groups are redefining what is sacred. They also replace explicit religious tenets imposed from the outside with internal norms that are implicit and devised by individual groups. At the same time, these groups reflect the pluralism and diversity that characterizes society. In the end, they buffer the trend toward disintegration and isolation that people often feel in mass societies.

Questions to Consider

1. Are you a member of any support groups? If so, which ones?
Keywords: small group, support group

2. Do you think that decline in the traditional church membership is at least partly responsible for an increase in membership in support groups?
Keywords: civic participation, voluntary organizations

We have included InfoTrac College Edition keywords at the end of each question to make it easier for you to find more to read on these topics. Go to **www.infotrac-college.com,** an online library, to begin your search.

SOURCE: Wuthnow, Robert. 1994. *Sharing the Journey: Support Groups and America's New Quest for Community.* New York: Free Press.

may or may not belong, but use as a standard for evaluating your values, attitudes, and behaviors (Merton and Rossi 1950). Reference groups are generalized versions of role models. They are not "groups" in the sense that the individual interacts within (or in) them. Do you pattern your behavior on that of sports stars, musicians, military officers, or business executives? If so, those models are your reference groups for you.

Imitation of reference groups can have both positive and negative effects. Members of a Little League baseball team may revere major league baseball players and attempt to imitate laudable behaviors such as tenacity and sportsmanship. But young baseball fans are also liable to be exposed to tantrums and fights, tobacco chewing and spitting, and scandals of the sort that befall some professionals, such as drug problems and domestic violence.

Research has shown that identification with reference groups can strongly influence self-evaluation and self-esteem. As noted in Chapter 3, in the early days of desegregation, it was thought that all-Black schools contributed to negative self-evaluation among Black students. Desegregation was expected to raise the self-esteem of Black children (Clark and Clark 1947). The original Clark and Clark study suggested that Black children in all-Black schools preferred playing with White dolls over Black dolls. This behavior was presumed to demonstrate a negative self-evaluation and self-rejection on the part of Black children. However, later studies (Powell-Hopson and Hopson 1988; Banks 1976) showed that both Black and White children preferred the Black dolls if first presented by the experimenter in a positive way, such as having the child label the doll as "pretty" and "intelligent."

Current research also shows that the self-esteem of the children is greater when racial or ethnic groups are consistently and methodically presented in a positive way, as in pluralistic and multicultural educational programs designed to increase pride in minority cultures. The same has been found for Latino children enrolled in Latino cultural awareness programs. The representation of racial and ethnic groups in a society can have a striking positive effect on children acquiring their lifetime set of group affiliations (Zhou and Bankston 2000; Baumeister 1998; Steele 1996, 1992).

In-Groups and Out-Groups

When groups have a sense of themselves as "us," there will be a complementary sense of other groups as "them." The distinction is commonly characterized as *in-groups* versus *out-groups*. The concept was originally elaborated by the early sociological theorist W. I. Thomas (Thomas

1931). College fraternities and sororities certainly exemplify "in" versus "out." So do families. The same can be true of the members of your high school class, your sports team, your racial group, your gender, and your social class. Members of the upper classes in the United States occasionally refer to one another as PLUs—"people like us" (Graham 1999; Frazier 1957).

Attribution theory is the principle that we all make inferences about the personalities of others (called *dispositional attributions*), such as concluding what the other is "really like" under certain conditions, such as out-group membership. Thomas F. Pettigrew has summarized the research on attribution theory, showing that individuals commonly generate a significantly distorted perception of the motives and capabilities of other people's acts based on whether that person is an in-group or out-group member (Pettigrew 1992; Gilbert and Malone 1995). Pettigrew describes the misperception as **attribution error,** meaning errors made in attributing causes for people's behavior to their membership in a particular group, such as a racial group. Attribution error has several dimensions, all tending to favor the in-group over the out-group. In a word, we perceive people in our in-group positively and those in our out-groups negatively regardless of their actual personal characteristics.

1. When onlookers observe improper behavior by an out-group member, onlookers are likely to attribute the deviance to the disposition of the wrongdoer. Disposition refers to the perceived "true nature" or "inherent nature" of the person, often considered to be genetically determined. (*Example:* A White person sees a Hispanic person carrying a knife, and without further information, attributes this behavior to the presumed "inherent tendency" for Hispanics to be violent. The same would be true if a Hispanic person, without additional information, assumed that all Whites have an "inherent tendency" to be racist.)

2. When the same behavior is exhibited by an in-group member, the perception is commonly that the act is due to the situation of the wrongdoer, not to the in-group member's inherent disposition. (*Example:* A White person sees another White person carrying a knife and concludes, without further information, that the weapon must be carried for protection in a dangerous area.)

3. If an out-group member is seen to perform in some laudable way, the behavior is often attributed to a variety of special circumstances, and the out-group member is seen as "the exception."

4. An in-group member who performs in the same laudable way is given credit for a worthy personality.

Typical attribution errors include misperceptions between racial groups and between men and women. If a White police officer shoots a Black or Latino, a White individual, given no additional information, is likely to assume that the victim instigated the shooting, whereas a Black person is more likely to assume that the police officer fired unnecessarily, perhaps because the officer is dispositionally assumed to be a racist (Kluegel and Bobo 1993; Bobo and Kluegel 1991).

A related phenomenon has been seen in men's perceptions of women coworkers. Meticulous behavior in a man is perceived positively and is seen by other men as "thorough"; in a woman, the exact same behavior is perceived negatively and is considered "picky." Behavior applauded in a man as "aggressive" is condemned in a woman exhibiting the same behavior as "pushy" or "bitchy" (Uleman et al. 1996; Wood 1994).

TAKING ON SOCIAL ISSUES

Has Racial and Gender Equality Been Achieved in Bureaucracies?

Many organizations have tried to foster a more positive organizational climate for all members by sponsoring diversity workshops and other training efforts designed to make people more aware of racial, ethnic, and gender differences that affect people's interaction in the workplace. Advocates of diversity training say that enhanced awareness and sensitivity toward others makes a more positive environment for all members of the organization. Critics say that, well meaning as such programs are, they do not deal with fundamental problems of equity in the workplace and have done little to advance women and racial–ethnic minorities into senior positions in such firms. Finally, research evidence shows that both minorities and women are still quite a way from complete equality in rank, salary, and promotional opportunities in today's bureaucracies. How would you go about measuring whether equality for minorities and women has been attained? In your opinion, what factors (variables) should one consider?

Taking Action

Go to the Taking Action exercise on the companion Web site at **sociology.wadsworth.com /andersen_taylor/essen3e** to learn more about an organization that addresses this topic.

Social Networks

As already noted, no individual is a member of only one group. Social life is far richer than that. A **social network** is a set of links between individuals or between other social units, such as bureaucratic organizations or even entire nations (Centeno and Hargittai 2003; Mizruchi 1992). One could say that people belong to several networks. Your group of friends, for instance, or all the people on an electronic mail list to which you subscribe, are social networks (Wasserman and Faust 1994).

The network of people you are closest to, rather than those merely linked to you in some impersonal way, is probably most important to you. Numerous research studies indicate that people get jobs via their personal networks more often than through formal job listings, want ads, or placement agencies (Petersen et al. 2000; Granovetter 1995, 1974). This is especially true for high-paying, prestigious jobs. Getting a job is more often a matter of who you know than what you know. Who you know, and who they know in turn, is a social network that may have a marked effect on your life and career.

Networks form with all the spontaneity of other forms of human interaction (Granovetter 1973; Mintz and Schwartz 1985; Wasserman and Faust 1994; Fischer 1981; Knoke 1992). Networks evolve, such as social ties within neighborhoods, professional contacts, and associations formed in fraternal, religious, occupational, and volunteer groups. Neighborhood networks enable individuals to quickly activate their core informal social network ties to assist in recovering from a hurricane (Hurlbert et al. 2000) or any widespread disaster—a process strikingly similar to the neighborhood reactions to the terrorist attack in New York City. Networks to which you are only weakly tied (you may know only one person in your neighborhood) provide you with access to that network; hence, the sociological principle that there is "strength in weak ties" (Petersen et al. 2000; Montgomery 1992; Granovetter 1973).

Networks based on race, class, and gender form with particular readiness. This has been particularly true of job networks. The person who leads you to a job is likely to have a similar social background. Recent research indicates that the "old boy network"—any network of White male corporate executives—is less important than it used to be, although it is certainly not gone. The diminished importance of the old boy network is because of the increasing prominence of women and minorities in business organizations. In fact, among African American and Latino individuals, family can provide network contacts that can lead to jobs and upward mobility (Dominguez and Watkins 2003). Still, as we will see later in this chapter, women and minorities are considerably underrepresented in corporate life, especially in high-status jobs (Green et al. 1999; Collins-Lowry 1997; Reskin and Padavic 1994; Gerson 1993).

Networks can reach around the world, but how big is the world? How many of us, when we discover someone we just met is a friend of a friend, have remarked, "My, it's a small world?" Research into what has come to be known as the *small world problem* has shown that networks make the world a lot smaller than you might think.

Original small-world researchers Travers and Milgram wanted to test whether a document could be routed to a complete stranger more than 1000 miles away using only a chain of acquaintances (Travers and Milgram 1969; Lin 1989; Kochen 1989; Watts and Strogatz 1998; Watts 1999). If so, how many steps would be required? The researchers organized an experiment in which approximately 300 senders were all charged with getting a document to one receiver, a complete stranger. The receiver was a male Boston stockbroker. The senders were one group of Nebraskans and one group of Bostonians chosen completely at random. Every sender in the study was given the receiver's name, address, occupation, alma mater, year of graduation, wife's maiden name, and hometown. They were asked to send the document directly to the stockbroker if they knew him on a first-name basis. Otherwise, they were asked to send the folder to a friend, relative, or acquaintance known on a first-name basis who might be more likely than the sender to know the stockbroker.

How many intermediaries do you think it took, on average, for the document to get through? (Most people estimate from twenty to hundreds.) The answer is that about one-third of the documents arrived at the target. This was quite impressive, considering that the senders did not know the target person. The average number of intermediate contacts was only 6.2! Hence the conclusion that any given person in the country is on average only about "six degrees of separation" from any other person, and in this sense the world is "small."

This original small-world research has recently been criticized on two grounds: First, only one-third of the documents actually arrived at the target person. The 6.2 average intermediaries applied only to the completed chains. Thus two-thirds of the initial documents never reached the target person. For these persons, the world was certainly not "small." Second, the sending chains tended to closely follow occupational, social class, and ethnic lines—just as general network theory would predict (Wasserman and Faust 1994). Thus the world may indeed be "small," but only for people in your social network in the first place (Kleinfeld 2002; Watts 1999).

A recent and on-going study of Black national leaders by Taylor and associates shows that Black leaders form a very closely knit network, one considerably more closely knit than longer-established White leadership networks (Taylor 1992b; Jackson 2000; Jackson et al. 1995, 1994; White leadership networks have been examined by Mills 1956; Domhoff 1988; Kadushin 1974; Moore 1979; and Alba and Moore 1982). The world is indeed quite "small" for America's Black leadership. Included in the study were Black members of Congress, mayors, business executives, military officers (generals and full colonels), religious leaders, civil rights leaders, media personalities, entertainment and sports figures, and others. The study found that when considering only direct personal acquaintances—not indirect links involving intermediaries—one-fifth of the entire national Black leadership network know each other directly, as a friend or close acquaintance. The Black leadership network is considerably more closely connected than White leadership networks. The Black network had greater density. Add only one intermediary, the friend of a friend, and the study estimated that almost three-quarters of the entire Black leadership network are included. Therefore, any given Black leader can generally get in touch with three-quarters of all other Black leaders in the country either by knowing them personally (a "friend") or via only one common acquaintance (a "friend of a friend"). That's pretty amazing when one realizes that the study is considering the population of Black leaders in the entire country.

■ *Social Influence*

The groups in which we participate exert tremendous influence on us. We often fail to appreciate how powerful these influences are. For example, who decides what you should wear? Do you decide for yourself each morning, or is the decision already made for you by fashion designers, role models, and your peers? Consider how closely your hair length, hair styling, and choice of jewelry has been influenced by your peers. Did you invent your baggy pants, your dreadlocks, or your blue blazer? People who label themselves as nonconformists often conform rigidly to the dress code and other norms of their in-group. This was true of the Beatniks in the 1950s, the hippies of the early 1960s and 1970s, the punk rockers of the 1970s and 1980s, and the grunge kids of the 1990s.

After the rebelliousness of youth has faded, the influences of our youth extend to adulthood. The choices of political party among adults (Republican, Democratic, or Independent) correlate strongly with the party of one's parents, again demonstrating the power of the primary group. Seven out of ten people vote with the party of their parents, even though these same people insist that they think for themselves only when voting (Worchel et al. 2000; Taylor et al. 1997; Jennings and Niemi 1974). Furthermore, most people share the religious affiliation of their parents, although they will insist that they chose their own religion, free of any influence by either parent.

We all like to think we stand on our own two feet, immune to a phenomenon as superficial as group pressure. The conviction that one is impervious to social influence results in what social psychologist Philip Zimbardo calls the *Not-Me Syndrome:* When confronted with a description of group behavior that is disappointingly conforming and not individualistic, most individuals counter that some people may conform, "but not me" (Zimbardo et al. 1977). We all think: "*Other* people yield to group pressure, *but not me.*" But sociological experiments often reveal a dramatic gulf between what people think they will do and what they actually do. The conformity study by Solomon Asch discussed in the following section is a case in point.

FIGURE 5.1 Lines from Asch Experiment

SOURCE: Asch, Solomon, 1955. "Opinion and Social Pressure." *Scientific American* 19 (July): 31–35.

the first student gave a wrong answer. The second student gave the same wrong answer. Third, wrong. Fourth, wrong. Then came the fifth student's turn.

In Asch's experiment, fully 33 percent of all students in the fifth position gave the same wrong answer as the confederates at least half the time. Forty percent gave "some" wrong answers. Only about 25 percent consistently gave correct answers in defiance of the invisible pressure to conform.

Line length is not a vague or ambiguous stimulus. It is clear and objective. Wrong answers from one-third of all subjects is a very high percentage. The subjects fidgeted and stammered while doing it, but they did it nonetheless. Those who did not yield to group pressure showed even more stress and discomfort than those who yielded to the (apparent) opinion of the group.

Would you have gone along with the group? Perhaps, perhaps not. Sociological insight grows when we acknowledge the fact that one-third of all participants will yield to the group. The Asch experiment has been repeated many times over the years, with students and nonstudents, old and young, in groups of different sizes, and in different settings (Taylor et al. 2003; Worchel et al. 2000; Cialdini 1993). The results remain essentially the same. One-third to one-half of the participants make a judgment contrary to fact, yet in conformity with the group.

> **THINKING SOCIOLOGICALLY**
>
> Think of a time when you engaged in some risky behavior. What group were you part of, and how did the group influence your behavior? How does this illustrate the concept of *risky shift*? Is there more risky shift with more people in the group? How much prior support do you think is given to suicide bombers who mount terrorist attacks?

The Asch Conformity Experiment

We learned in the previous section that social influences are evidently quite strong. Are they strong enough to make us disbelieve our own senses? In a classic piece of work known as the Asch Conformity Experiment, Solomon Asch showed that even simple objective facts cannot withstand the distorting pressure of group influence (Asch 1951, 1955).

Examine the two figures in Figure 5.1. Which line on the right is equal in length to the line on the left (line S)? Line B, obviously. Could anyone fail to answer correctly?

In fact, Solomon Asch discovered that social pressure of a rather gentle sort was sufficient to cause an astonishing rise in the number of wrong answers. Asch lined up five students at a table and administered the test shown in the figure. Unknown to the fifth student, the first four were confederates—collaborators with the experimenter who only pretended to be participants. For several rounds, the confederates gave correct answers to Asch's tests. The fifth student also answered correctly, suspecting nothing. Then

The Milgram Obedience Studies

What are the limits of social pressure? In terms of moral and psychological issues, judging the length of a line is a small matter. What happens if an authority figure demands obedience—a type of conformity—even if the task

(a)

(b)

(c)

(d)

FIGURE 5.2 Milgram's Setup

These photographs show how intimidating—and authoritative—the Milgram experiment must have been. The first picture (a) shows the formidable-looking shock generator. The second (b) shows the role player, who pretends to be getting the electric shock, being hooked up. The third (c) and fourth (d) show an experimental subject (seated) and the experimenter (standing, in lab coat). The fourth picture (d) shows a subject terminating the experiment prematurely, that is, before giving the highest shock level (voltage). A large majority of subjects did not do this and actually went all the way to the maximum shock level (65 percent did).

SOURCE: Milgram, Stanley. 1974. *Obedience to Authority: An Experimental View.* New York: Harper & Row, p. 25.

is something the test subject (the person) finds morally wrong and reprehensible? A chilling answer emerged from the now-famous Milgram Obedience Studies, done from 1960 through 1974 by Stanley Milgram (Milgram 1974).

In this study, a naive research subject entered a laboratory-like room and was told that an experiment on learning was to be conducted. The subject was to act as a teacher, presenting a series of test questions to another person, the learner. Whenever the learner gave a wrong answer, the teacher would administer an electric shock.

The test was relatively easy. The teacher read pairs of words to the learner, such as:

blue   box
nice   house
wild   duck

The teacher then tested the learner by reading a multiple-choice answer, such as

blue: sky   ink   box   lamp

The learner had to recall which term completed the pair of terms given originally, in this case, blue box.

If the learner answered incorrectly, the teacher was to press a switch on the shock machine, a formidable-looking device that emitted an ominous hum when activated (see Figure 5.2). For each successive wrong answer, the teacher was to increase the intensity of the shock by 15 volts.

The machine bore labels clearly visible to the teacher: Slight Shock, Moderate Shock, Strong Shock, Very Strong Shock, Intense Shock, Extreme Intensity Shock, Danger: Severe Shock, and lastly, XXX at 450 volts. As the voltage rose, the learner responded with squirming, groans, then screams.

The experiment was rigged. The learner was a confederate. No shocks were actually delivered. The true purpose of the experiment was to see if any "teacher" would go all the way to 450 volts. If the subject tried to quit, the experimenter responded with a sequence of prods:

"Please continue."
"The experiment requires that you continue."
"It is absolutely essential that you continue."
"You have no other choice, you *must* go on."

In the first experiment, fully 65 percent of the volunteer subjects ("teachers") went all the way to 450 volts on the shock machine. Milgram himself was astonished. Before carrying out the experiment, he had asked a variety of psychologists, sociologists, psychiatrists, and philosophers to guess how many subjects would actually go all the way to 450 volts. The opinion of these consultants was that one-tenth of 1 percent (one in one thousand) would actually do it.

What would you have done? Remember the Not-Me Syndrome. Think about the experimenter saying, "You have no other choice, you must go on." Most people claim they would refuse to continue as the voltage escalates. The importance of this experiment derives in part from how starkly it highlights the difference between what people *think* they will do and what they *actually* do.

Milgram devised a series of additional experiments in which he varied the conditions to find out what would cause subjects not to go all the way to 450 volts. He moved the experiment from an impressive laboratory to a dingy basement to counteract some of the tendency for people to defer to a scientist conducting a scientific study. One learner was instructed to complain of a heart condition. Still, well over half of the subjects delivered the maximum shock level. Speculating that women might be more humane than men (all prior experiments used only male subjects), Milgram did the experiment again using only women subjects. The results? Exactly the same. Class background made no difference. Racial and ethnic differences had no detectable effect on compliance rate.

At the time that the Milgram experiments were conceived, the world was watching the trial in Jerusalem of World War II Nazi Adolf Eichmann. Millions of Jews, Gypsies, homosexuals, and communists were murdered between 1939 and 1945 by the Nazi party, led by Adolf Hitler. As head of the Gestapo's "Jewish section," Eichmann oversaw the deportation of Jews to concentration camps and the mass executions that followed. Eichmann disappeared after the war, was abducted in Argentina by Israeli agents in 1961, and transported to Israel, where he was tried and ultimately hanged for crimes against humanity.

The world wanted to see what sort of monster could have committed the crimes of the Holocaust, but a jarring picture of Eichmann emerged. He was slight and mild mannered, not the raging ghoul that everyone expected. The psychiatrists who examined him found him to be sane. He insisted that although he had indeed been a chief administrator in an organization whose product was mass murder, he was guilty only of doing what he was told to do by his superiors. He did not hate Jews, he said. In fact, he had a Jewish half-cousin whom he hid and protected. He claimed, "I was just following orders."

How different was Adolph Eichman from the rest of us? The political theorist Hannah Arendt dared to suggest in her book *Eichman in Jerusalem* (1963) that evil on a giant scale is banal. It is not the work of monsters, but an accident of civilization. Arendt argued that to find the villain, we need to look into ourselves.

Other evil figures in history have, of course, existed. For example, Osama bin Laden, the presumed mastermind behind the terrorist attacks on the United States, will no doubt be known in history as an inherently evil despot. Perhaps his followers complied because they were "following orders."

DEBUNKING
Society's Myths

Myth: People are just individuals who make up their own minds about how to behave.

Sociological perspective: The Asch and Milgram experiments conclusively show that people are profoundly influenced by group pressure, often causing them to make up their minds contrary to objective fact.

Groupthink

Wealth, power, and experience are apparently not enough to save us from social influences. **Groupthink,** as described by I. L. Janis, is the tendency for group members to reach a consensus opinion, even if that decision is downright stupid (Janis 1982). Janis reasoned that because major government policies are often the result of group decisions, it would be fruitful to analyze group dynamics that operate at the highest level of government—for instance, in the Office of the President of the United States. The president makes decisions based upon group discussions with his advisers. The president is human and thus susceptible to group influence. To what extent have past presidents and their advisors been influenced by group decision making instead of just the facts?

Janis investigated five ill-fated decisions, all the products of group deliberation:

- The decision of the Naval High Command in 1941 not to prepare for the attack on Pearl Harbor by Japan
- President Harry Truman's decision to send troops to North Korea in 1951
- President John F. Kennedy's attempt to overthrow Cuba by launching the ill-fated invasion at the Bay of Pigs in 1962
- President Lyndon B. Johnson's decision in 1967 to increase the number of U.S. troops in Vietnam
- The fateful decision by President Richard M. Nixon's advisers in 1972 to break into the Democratic Party headquarters at the Watergate apartment complex, launching the famed "Watergate affair."

All were group decisions, and all were absolute fiascoes. For example, the Bay of Pigs invasion was a major humiliation for the United States; a covert outing so ill conceived it is hard to imagine how it survived discussion by a group of foreign policy experts. Fifteen hundred Cuban exiles trained by the CIA to parachute into heavily armed Cuba landed in an impassibly dense 80-mile swamp far from their planned drop zone with inadequate weapons and incorrect maps. A sea landing was demolished by well-prepared, warned defenders. In retrospect, it is impossible to imagine how the plan, even without its tragic foul-ups, could have succeeded in toppling Cuban president Fidel Castro.

The men who advised President Kennedy to undertake the invasion were not stupid. In fact, many considered them the brightest policy team ever assembled—"the best and the brightest" as they were sometimes called. Secretary of State Dean Rusk was a past president of the Rockefeller Foundation. Secretary of Defense Robert Mc-

Namara was a gifted statistician and past president of the Ford Motor Company. McGeorge Bundy, special assistant for national security, had been dean of Arts and Sciences at Harvard University. How could such a smart team perpetrate such a blunder?

Janis discovered a common pattern of misguided thinking in his investigations of presidential decisions. He surmised that outbreaks of groupthink had several things in common:

1. *An illusion of invulnerability.* "With such a brilliant team, and such a nation, how could any plan fail?" thought those in the group.

2. *A falsely negative impression of those who are antagonists to the group's plans.* Fidel Castro was perceived to be clownish, and Cuban troops were supposed to be patsies. In truth, the defenders at the Bay of Pigs were actually highly trained commandoes. Castro has remained in power to this day, several decades after the failed invasion.

3. *Discouragement of dissenting opinion.* As groupthink takes hold, dissent is equated with disloyalty. This can discourage dissenters from voicing their objections.

4. *An illusion of unanimity.* In the aftermath, many victims of groupthink recall their reservations, but at the moment of decision there is a prevailing sense that the entire group is in complete agreement.

Groupthink is not inevitable when a team gathers to make a decision, but it is common and appears in all sorts of groups, from student discussion groups to the highest councils of power (Flowers 1977; McCauley 1989; Aldag and Fuller 1993; Kelley et al. 1999). A striking illustration of the pressure toward consensus is seen in the behavior of juries, especially when jurors must vote by a show of hands or a verbal go-around.

DEBUNKING
Society's Myths

Myth: A group of experts brought together in a small group will solve a problem according to their collective expertise.

Sociological perspective: Groupthink can lead even the most qualified people to make disastrous decisions because people in groups in the United States tend to reach consensus at all costs.

Risky Shift

The term *groupthink* is commonly associated with group decision making whose consequences are not merely un-

© Sutcliffe/Sipa Press

Streaking, or running nude in a public place, is more common as a group activity than as a strictly individual one. This illustrates how the group can provide the persons in it with deindividuation, *or merging of self with group. This allows the individual to feel less responsibility or blame for his or her actions.*

expected but disastrous. Another group phenomenon, **risky shift** (also called polarization shift), may help explain why the products of groupthink are frequently calamities. Have you ever found yourself in a group engaged in a high-risk activity that you would not do alone? When you created mischief as a child, were you not usually part of a group? If so, you were probably in the thrall of risky shift—the tendency for groups to weigh risk differently than individuals do.

Risky shift was first observed by James Stoner (1961). Stoner gave study participants descriptions of a situation involving risk, such as one in which an engineer must choose between job security versus a potentially lucrative but risky advancement. The participants were then asked to decide how much risk the engineer should take. Before performing his study, Stoner believed that individuals in a group would take less risk in a group than individuals alone, but he found that after his groups had engaged in open discussions, they favored greater risk than before discussion. His research stimulated hundreds of studies using males and females, different nationalities, different tasks, and other variables (Pruitt 1971; Johnson et al. 1977; Blaskovitch 1973; Hong 1978; Worchel et al. 2000; Taylor et al. 2003). The results are complex. Most but not all group discussion leads to greater risk-taking. In subcultures that value caution above daring, as in some work groups of Japanese and Chinese firms, group decisions are less risky after discussion than before. The shift can occur in either direction, driven by the influence of group discussion, but there is generally some kind of shift, in one direction or the other, rather than no shift at all (Kerr 1992).

What causes risky shifts? The most convincing explanation is that deindividuation occurs. **Deindividuation** is the sense that one's self has merged with a group. In terms of risk-taking, one feels that responsibility (and possibly blame) is borne not only by oneself but also by the group. The greater the number of people in a group, the greater the tendency toward deindividuation. In other words, deindividuation is a group size effect. As groups get larger, trends in risk-taking are amplified. This may well be the case with so-called "suicide cults," where all (or almost all) members collectively commit suicide, as most likely with David Koresh's Branch Davidian cult of Waco, Texas, in 1993—although the U.S. division of Alcohol, Tobacco, and Firearms (ATF) may, via an assault on the cult, have accelerated the cult's movement toward suicide. Another example was the Heaven's Gate religious cult, where the cult members committed suicide as presumed preparation for a flying saucer that they believed was to come and take them away.

■ *Formal Organizations and Bureaucracies*

Groups, as we have seen, are capable of greatly influencing individuals. The study of groups and their effects on the individual represent an example of microanalysis, to use a concept introduced in Chapter 4. In contrast, the study of formal organizations and bureaucracies, a subject to which we now turn, represents an example of macroanalysis. The focus on groups drew our attention to the relatively small and less complex, whereas the focus on organizations draws our attention to the relatively large and structurally more complex.

A **formal organization** is a large secondary group, highly organized to accomplish a complex task or tasks and to achieve goals efficiently. Many of us belong to various formal organizations: work organizations, schools, and political parties, to name a few. Organizations are formed to accomplish particular tasks and characterized by their relatively large size, compared with a small group such as a family or a friendship circle. Often organizations consist of an array of other organizations. The federal government is a huge organization, comprising numerous other organizations, most of which are also vast. Each organization within the federal government is also designed to accomplish specific tasks, be it collecting your taxes, educating the nation's children, or regulating the nation's transportation system and national parks.

Organizations develop cultures and routinized practices. The culture of an organization may be reflected in certain symbols, values, and rituals. Some organizations develop their own language and styles of dress. The norms can be subtle, such as men being expected to wear long-sleeve shirts and ties, or women being expected to wear stockings, even on hot summer days. It does not take explicit rules to regulate this behavior; comments from coworkers or bosses may be enough to enforce such organizational norms. Some work organizations have recently instituted a practice called "casual day" or "dress down day"—one day per week, usually Friday, when workers can dress less formally.

Organizations tend to be persistent, although they are also responsive to the broader social environment where they are located (DiMaggio and Powell 1991). Organizations are frequently under pressure to respond to changes in the society, by incorporating new practices and beliefs into their structure. Business corporations, as an example, have had to respond to increasing global competition; they do so by expanding into new international markets, developing a globally focused workforce, and trimming costs by downsizing (eliminating workers and various layers of management).

Organizations can be tools for innovation, depending on the organization's values and purpose. Rape crisis centers are examples of organizations that originally emerged from the women's movement because of the perceived need for services for rape victims. Rape crisis centers have, in many cases, changed how police departments and hospital emergency personnel respond to rape victims. By advocating changes in rape law and services for rape victims, rape crisis centers have generated change in other organizations as well (Schmitt and Martin 1999; Fried 1994).

Types of Organizations

Sociologists Blau and Scott (1974) and Etzioni (1975) classify formal organizations into three categories, distinguished by their types of membership affiliation: normative, coercive, and utilitarian.

NORMATIVE ORGANIZATIONS. People join *normative organizations* to pursue goals that they consider worthwhile. They obtain personal satisfaction but no monetary reward for membership in such an organization. In many instances, people join the normative organization for the social prestige that it offers. Many are service and charitable organizations and are often called *voluntary organizations.* They include organizations such as the PTA, Kiwanis clubs, political parties, religious organizations, the National Association for the Advancement of Colored People (NAACP), B'nai B'rith, La Raza, and other similar voluntary organizations that are concerned with specific issues. Civic and charitable organizations such as the League of Women Voters, and political organizations such as the National Women's Political Caucus reflect the fact that for decades women have been excluded from traditionally all-male voluntary organizations and political networks, such as the Kiwanis and Lions clubs. Like other service and charitable organizations, these have been created to meet particular needs, ones that members see as not being served by other organizations.

Gender, class, race, and ethnicity all play a role in who joins what voluntary organizations. Social class is reflected in the fact that many people do not join certain organizations simply because they cannot afford to join. Membership in a professional organization, as one example, can cost hundreds of dollars each year. Those who feel disenfranchised, however, may join grassroots organizations—voluntary organizations that spring from specific local needs that people think are unmet. Tenants may form an organization to protest rent increases or lack of services, or a new political party may emerge from people's sense of alienation from existing party organizations. African Americans, Latinos, and Native Americans have formed many of their own voluntary organizations, in part because of their historical exclusion from traditional White voluntary organizations. African American fraternities and sororities are a classic example (see "Understanding Diversity" on the Delta Sigma Theta sorority).

The NAACP, founded in 1909 by W. E. B. Du Bois (recall him from Chapter 1), and the National Urban League, are two other large national organizations that have historically fought racial oppression on the legal and urban fronts, respectively. La Raza Unida, a Latino organization devoted to civic activities as well as combating racial–ethnic oppression, has a large membership with Latinas holding major offices. In fact, such voluntary organizations dedicated to the causes of people of color have in recent years had more women in leadership positions in the organizations than have many standard White organizations. Similarly, Native American voluntary organizations have boasted increasing numbers of women in leadership positions (Feagin and Feagin 1993; Snipp 1996, 1989).

COERCIVE ORGANIZATIONS. *Coercive organizations* are characterized by membership that is largely involuntary. Prisons are an example of organizations that people are coerced to "join" by virtue of their being punished for a crime. Similarly, mental hospitals are coercive

UNDERSTANDING DIVERSITY

The Deltas—Black Sororities as Organizations

Delta Sigma Theta sorority is one of the largest Black women's organizations in the world, with more than 125,000 members. Its membership has included such significant leaders as Mary Church Terrell, Sadie T. M. Alexander, Patricia Roberts Harris, Barbara Jordan, Leontyne Price, and Dorothy Height. Like other Black women's sororities, the unique history of race and gender discrimination gives this organization an identity very different from that of White sororities. In her history of Delta Sigma Theta, whose members are referred to as "Deltas," Paula Giddings, a contemporary African American scholar, writes that organizations

. . . must be able to adapt to changing environments: in this case, the ever changing exigencies of race relations and the attitudes toward

women. Consequently, Delta has had to alter its purposes and goals throughout the years—and must continue to do so—as well as its internal structure to accommodate change. This makes the Black sorority a particularly dynamic organization.

At the same time, however, changes cannot occur too abruptly or without the consensus of an increasingly diverse constituency. Like other social movement organizations, viability of the sorority is dependent on the growth of its membership, which in turn, is largely determined by the number of its members who feel that the sorority's goals are in harmony with their own.

The challenge of the sorority, one made all the more difficult by the pathos of the Black women's experi-

ence in North America, is to maintain a sense of sisterhood while striving, organizationally, for a more general purpose: aiding the Black community as a whole through social, political, and economic means. This idea can be difficult to realize. But the effort to resolve the tension between the goals of organization, and those of sisterhood, through strengthening social bonds within the context of social action has been an interesting and engaging experiment. It is one that can be seen as a model for Black organizational life, and which adds contour and dimension to the history of Black women in this country.

SOURCE: Giddings, Paula. 1994. *In Search of Sisterhood: Delta Sigma Theta and the Challenge of the Black Sorority Movement.* New York: William Morrow.

organizations: People are placed in them, often involuntarily, for some form of psychiatric treatment. In many respects, prisons and mental hospitals are similar in their treatment of inmates or patients. They both have strong security measures such as guards, locked and barred windows, and high walls (Goffman 1961; Rosenhan 1973). Sexual harassment and sexual victimization are common in both prisons and mental hospitals (Andersen 2003; Chesney-Lind 1992).

The sociologist Erving Goffman has described coercive organizations as total institutions. A **total institution** is an organization cut off from the rest of society in which individuals who reside there are subject to strict social control (Goffman 1961). Total institutions include two populations: the "inmates" and the staff. Within total institutions, the staff exercises complete power over inmates, for example, nurses over mental patients and guards over prisoners. The staff administers all the affairs of everyday life, including basic human functions such as eating and time for sleeping. Rigid routines are characteristic of total institutions, thus explaining the common complaint by those in hospitals that they cannot sleep because nurses repeatedly enter their rooms at night, regardless if the patient needs treatment.

Formal rules of behavior are also typical of total institutions: How you dress, when you eat, even when you use the bathroom are all regulated by the staff. Goffman wrote that individuals placed in total institutions completely surrender their rights to privacy and are frequently subjected to what he called *mortification of the self*—actions taken by the staff to make the inmates surrender their former identity, such as by expecting or requiring them to dress in public, turn over personal possessions, or urinate in bedpans. Also called "degradation ceremonies," Goffman described such actions as intention to support the organizational structure, even if at the cost of human dignity.

UTILITARIAN ORGANIZATIONS. The third type of organization named is *utilitarian.* These are large organizations, either for profit or nonprofit, that individuals join for specific purposes, such as monetary reward. Large business organizations that generate profits (in the case of for-profit organizations) and salaries and wages for their employees (as with either for-profit or nonprofit organizations) are utilitarian organizations. Examples of large for-profit organizations include General Motors, Microsoft, Amazon.com, and Procter & Gamble. Examples of large nonprofit organizations that pay salaries to employees are colleges, universities, and the Educational Testing Service (ETS), the organization that manufactures the Scholastic Assessment Test (SAT).

Some utilitarian organizations may also be coercive organizations. This is especially the case because various organizations have become increasingly privatized. Mental hospitals may be owned by a large for-profit chain, although now run by states or the federal government. Many prisons have now become privatized, and some cities have turned their public schools over to private corporations to see if they can be better managed.

Bureaucracy

As formal organizations develop, many become a **bureaucracy,** a type of formal organization characterized by an authority hierarchy, a clear division of labor, explicit rules, and impersonality. Bureaucracies are notorious for their unwieldy size and complexity, as well as their reputation for being remote and cumbersome organizations that are highly impersonal and machinelike in their operation. The federal government is a good example of a cumbersome bureaucracy that many believe is ineffective because of its sheer size. Numerous other formal organizations have developed into huge bureaucracies: IBM, Disney, and many universities, hospitals, state motor vehicle registration systems, and some law firms. Other formal organizations, such as Enron and WorldCom, quickly developed into a large bureaucracy, then subsequently collapsed under fraudulent accounting procedures.

The early sociological theorist **Max Weber** (1925/1947) analyzed the classic characteristics of the bureaucracy. These characteristics represent what he called the *ideal type bureaucracy*—a model rarely seen in reality but defines the typical characteristics of a social form. The characteristics of bureaucracies are:

1. **High degree of division of labor and specialization.** The notion of the specialist embodies this criterion. Bureaucracies ideally employ specialists in the various positions and occupations, and these specialists are responsible for a specific set of duties. Job titles and job descriptions define the nature of each position. Sociologist Charles Perrow (1994, 1986) notes that many modern bureaucracies have hierarchical authority structures and an elaborate division of labor.

2. **Hierarchy of authority.** In bureaucracies, positions are arranged in a hierarchy so that each position is under the supervision of a higher position. Such hierarchies are often represented in an *organizational chart,* a diagram in the shape of a pyramid that shows relative rank of each position plus the lines of authority between each. These lines of authority are often called the "chain of command," and they show not only who has authority, but also who is responsible to whom and how many positions are responsible to a given position.

3. **Rules and regulations.** All the activities in a bureaucracy are governed by a set of detailed rules and

procedures. These rules are designed, ideally, to cover almost every possible situation and problem that might arise, including hiring, firing, salary scales, rules for sick pay and absences, and the everyday operation of the office.

4. **Impersonal relationships.** Social interaction in the bureaucracy is supposed to be guided by *instrumental* criteria, such as the organization's rules, rather than by *social–emotional* criteria, such as personal attractions or likes and dislikes. The ideal is that the objective application of rules will minimize matters such as personal favoritism—giving someone a promotion simply because you like him or her, or firing someone because you do not personally like him or her. Of course, as we will see, sociologists have pointed out that bureaucracy has another face—the social interaction that keeps the bureaucracy working and often involves interpersonal friendships and social ties, typically among people taken for granted in these organizations, such as the support staff.

5. **Career ladders.** Candidates for the various positions in the bureaucracy are supposed to be selected on the basis of specific criteria, such as education, experience, and standardized examinations. The idea is that advancement through the organization becomes a career for the individual.

6. **Efficiency.** Bureaucracies are designed to coordinate the activities of many people in pursuit of organizational goals. Ideally, all activities have been designed to maximize this efficiency. The whole system is intended to keep social–emotional relations and interactions at a minimum and instrumental interaction at a maximum.

Bureaucracy's Other Face

All the preceding characteristics of Weber's "ideal type" are general defining characteristics. Rarely do actual bureaucracies meet this exact description. A bureaucracy has, in addition to the ideal characteristics of structure, an informal structure—social interactions in bureaucratic settings that ignore, change, or otherwise bypass the formal structure and rules of the organization. Sociologist Charles Page (1946) coined the term *bureaucracy's other face* to describe this condition.

This other face is informal culture. It has evolved over time as a reaction to the formality and impersonality of the bureaucracy. Thus, assistants "bend the rules a bit" when asked to do something more quickly than usual for a boss they like and bend the rules in another direction for a boss they do not like by slowing down or otherwise sabotaging the boss's work. Researchers have noted, for example, that assistants have more authority than their job titles—and salaries—suggest. As a way around the cumbersome formal communication channels within the organization, the informal network or "grapevine" often works better, faster, and sometimes

even more accurately. As with any culture, the informal culture in the bureaucracy has its own norms or rules. One is not supposed to "stab friends in the back," as by "ratting on" them to a boss or spreading a rumor about them that is intended to hurt them, or get them fired. Yet just as with any norms, there is deviation from the norms, and stabbing someone in the back does happen.

Bureaucracy's other face can also be seen in the workplace subcultures that develop, even in the largest bureaucracies. Some sociologists interpret the subcultures that develop within bureaucracies as people's attempts to humanize an otherwise impersonal organization. Keeping photographs of family and loved ones in the office, placing personal decorations on one's desk (if you are allowed), and organizing office parties are some ways people resist the impersonal culture of bureaucracies. Of course, this informal culture can also become exclusionary, increasing the isolation that some workers feel at work. Gay and lesbian workers may feel left out when other workers gossip about people's heterosexual dates; minority workers may be excluded from the casual conversations in the workplace that connect nonminority people to one another. In male-dominated organizations, women may be left out of the informal banter that may intentionally include inappropriate sexual remarks. Sexual harassment occurs when someone in a high status job within the organization makes unwanted sexual overtures, verbal or nonverbal, toward someone with a lower status job. (For further discussion of sexual harassment, see Chapter 10.)

The informal norms that develop within the modern-day bureaucracy often cause worker productivity to go up or down, depending on the norms and how they are informally enforced. The classic Hawthorne Studies, so named because they were carried out at the Western Electric telephone plant in Hawthorne, Illinois, in the 1930s (Roethlisberger and Dickson 1939), discovered that small groups of workers developed their own ideas—their own norms—about how much work they should produce each day. If someone produced too many completed tasks in a day, he would make the rest of the workers "look bad" and run the risk of having the organization raise its expectations of how much work the group might be expected to produce. Because of this, anyone producing too much was informally labeled a "rate buster," and that person was punished by some act, such as punches on the shoulder (called "binging"), or by group ridicule (called "razzing"). By the same token, one could be accused of producing too little, in which case he was labeled a "chiseler" and punished in the same way by either binging or razzing. This informal culture of bureaucracy's other face continues today in a manner similar to the culture initially discovered in the early Hawthorne studies (Perrow 1994, 1986).

© Michael Soforonski/Sipa Press

AP/Wide World Photos

© AP Photo/Tyler Morning Telegraph, Dr. Scott Lieberman

The horror of the explosion of the space shuttle Challenger in 1986 is seen in the face of the observers above. Seven astronauts died. After the Challenger explosion, sociologist Diane Vaughan (1996) attributed the disaster to group interaction phenomena such as risky shift, ritualism, groupthink, and the normalization of deviance. Tragedy struck again in 2003 when the Columbia space shuttle broke up on re-entry, killing seven other astronauts.

Problems of Bureaucracies

Problems have developed in contemporary times that grow out of the nature of the complex bureaucracy. Two problem areas already discussed are the occurrence of risky shift in work groups and the development of groupthink. Additional problems include a tendency to *ritualism* and the potential for *alienation* on the part of those within the organization.

RITUALISM. Rigid adherence to rules can produce a slavish following of them, regardless if it accomplishes the purpose for which the rule was originally designed. The rules become ends in themselves rather than means to an end; this is ritualism.

Two now classic examples of the consequences of *organizational ritualism* have come to haunt us: the explosion of the space shuttle *Challenger* on January 28, 1986; and, to our horror, the recent breakup of yet another space shuttle, the *Columbia,* on February 1, 2003. People in the United States became bound together at the moment of the *Challenger* accident. Many remember where they were and exactly what they were doing when they

heard about the tragedy. The failure of the now-famous O-ring gaskets on the solid fuel booster rockets of the Challenger shuttle caused the catastrophic explosion. It was revealed later that the O-rings became brittle at below-freezing temperatures, as was the temperature at the launch pad the evening before the *Challenger* lifted off.

Why did the managers and engineers at NASA (National Aeronautics and Space Administration) allow the shuttle to lift off given these prior conditions? The managers had all the information about the O-rings before the launch. Furthermore, engineers had warned them against the danger. Sociologist Diane Vaughan (1996), in a detailed analysis of the decision to launch involving extensive interviews with the managers and engineers who were directly involved, uncovered both risky shift and organizational ritualism within the organization. Vaughan documents the incremental descent into poor judgment supported by a culture of high-risk technology. The NASA insiders, confronted with signals of danger, proceeded as if nothing was wrong when they were repeatedly faced with the evidence that something was indeed *very* wrong. They in effect normalized their own behavior, an occurrence of risky shift, so that their actions became acceptable to them, representing nothing out of the ordinary. This is an example of organizational ritualism, as well as what Vaughan calls the "normalization of deviance."

Unfortunately history repeated itself on February 1, 2003, when the space shuttle *Columbia,* upon its return from space, broke up in a fiery descent into the atmosphere above Texas, killing all who were aboard. The most recent evidence shows that a piece of hard insulating foam separated from an external fuel tank during launch and struck the shuttle's left wing, damaging it and dislodging its heat-resistant tiles that are necessary for re-entry. The absence of these tiles caused the burn-up upon re-entry into the atmosphere. With eerie similarity to the earlier 1986 *Challenger* accident, a recent research report concludes that a "flawed institutional culture" and—citing sociologist Diane Vaughan—a normalization of deviance accompanying a gradual erosion of safety margins, were among the causes of the *Columbia* accident (Schwartz and Wald 2003).

No single individual was at fault in either accident. The story is not one of evil but of the ritualism of organizational life in one of the most powerful bureaucracies in the United States. It is a story of rigid group conformity within an organizational setting and of how deviant behavior is redefined, that is, socially constructed, to be perceived as normal. Organizational procedures in this case, or rituals, so dominate that the means toward goals become the goals themselves. A critical decrease in overall safety and dramatic increase in risk are the results. Vaughan's analysis is a powerful warning about the hidden hazards of bureaucracy in a technological age.

ALIENATION. The stresses on rules and procedures within bureaucracies can result in a decrease in the overall cohesion of the organization, resulting in the individual becoming psychologically separated from the organization and its goals. This is a state of *alienation* that results in increased turnover, tardiness, absenteeism, and overall dissatisfaction with the organization.

Alienation can be widespread in organizations where workers have little control over what they do, or where workers themselves are treated like machines—employed on an assembly line, doing the same repetitive action for an entire work shift. Alienation is not restricted to manual labor, however. In organizations where workers are isolated from others, where they are expected only to implement rules, or where they think they have little chance of advancement, alienation can be common (see Chapter 13). As we will see, some organizations have developed new patterns of work to try to minimize worker alienation and thus enhance their productivity.

The McDonaldization of Society

Sometimes the problems and peculiarities of bureaucracy can have effects on the total society. This has been the case with what George Ritzer (2002) has called the *McDonaldization of society,* a term coined from the well-known fast-food chain. In fact, one study (Schlosser 2001) concluded that each month, 90 percent of the children in the United States between ages 3 and 9 visit McDonald's! Ritzer noticed that the principles that characterize fast-food organizations are increasingly dominating more aspects of U.S. society, indeed, of societies around the world. McDonaldization refers to the increasing and ubiquitous presence of the fast-food model in most organizations that shape daily life. Work, travel, leisure, shopping, health care, education, and politics have all become subject to McDonaldization. Each industry is based on a principle of high and efficient productivity, based on a highly rational social organization, with workers employed at low pay, but customers experiencing ease, convenience, and familiarity.

Ritzer argues that McDonald's has been such a successful model of business organization that other industries have adopted the same organizational characteristics, so much so that their nicknames associate them with the McDonald's chain: McPaper for *USA Today,* McChild for child-care chains like Kinder-Care, and McDoctor for the drive-in clinics that deal quickly and efficiently with minor health and dental problems.

Based in part upon Max Weber's concept of the ideal-type bureaucracy mentioned earlier, Ritzer identifies four dimensions of the McDonaldization process: efficiency, calculability, predictability, and control:

1. **Efficiency** means that things move from start to finish in a streamlined path. Steps in the production of a hamburger are regulated so that each hamburger is made exactly the same way—hardly characteristic of a home-cooked meal. Business can be even more efficient if the customer does the work once done by an employee. In fast-food restaurants, the claim that you can "have it your way" really means that you assemble your own sandwich or salad.

2. **Calculability** means there is an emphasis on the quantitative aspects of products sold—size, cost, and the time it takes to get the product. At McDonald's, branch managers must account for the number of cubic inches of ketchup used per day; likewise, ice cream scoopers in chain stores measure out predetermined and exact amounts of ice cream, unless machines do it for them. Workers are monitored for how long it takes them to complete a transaction; every bit of food and drink is closely monitored by computer, and everything has to be accounted for.

3. Predictability is the assurance that products will be exactly the same, no matter when or where they are purchased. Eat an Egg McMuffin in New York, and it will likely taste just the same as an Egg McMuffin in Los Angeles or Paris!

4. Control is the primary organizational principle that lies behind McDonaldization. Behavior of the customers and workers is reduced to a series of machinelike actions. Ultimately, efficient technologies replace much of the work that humans once performed. At one national credit card chain, managers routinely listen in on telephone calls being handled by service workers; in other settings, computers might monitor the speed with which workers handle a particular function. Sensors on drink machines can actually cut off the liquid flow to ensure that each drink is exactly the same size.

McDonaldization clearly brings many benefits. There is a greater availability of goods and services to a wide proportion of the population; instantaneous service and convenience to a public with less free time; predictability and familiarity in the goods bought and sold; and standardization of pricing and uniform quality of goods sold, to name a few benefits. However, this increasingly rational system of goods and services also spawns irrationalities. For example, the majority of workers at McDonald's lack full-time employment, have no worker benefits, have no control over their workplace, and quit on average after only four or five months (Schlosser 2001). Ritzer argues that, as we become more dependent on the familiar and that which is taken for granted, there is the danger of dehumanization. People lose their creativity, and there is little concern with the quality of goods and services, thereby disrupting

FORCES OF SOCIAL CHANGE

Consumerism

According to sociologist George Ritzer, we all live in a society clogged with McDonald's, Toys 'R Us, Disney World, cybermalls, chain stores, discount houses, cruise ships, gated communities, and the Home Shopping Network, to name a few. All these structures have shoved us into hyperconsumption, or, extreme *consumerism.* Drawing partly on early sociological theorists Max Weber and Emile Durkheim, Ritzer argues that these "cathedrals of consumption" have created a spectacular and simulated world that has become capable of luring us again and again into new purchases. They have become cathedrals to which we make "pilgrimages" to practice our consumer religion. These new cathedrals of consumption have enticed us to consume far more than we ever did in the past, in fact consume far beyond our actual needs, giving a picture of the United States envisioned decades ago by the sociologist-economist Thorstein Veblen and his concept of *"conspicuous consumption."* Even universities entice both parents and students to come and stay with "theme" dorms, fast-food restaurants, souvenir shops, and video arcades. Students become "enchanted" with such cathedrals of consumption, and they are thus more compelled to enroll in the university. The result of all this is that consumption pervades our lives, and we have become consumed by consumption.

SOURCE: Ritzer, George. 1999. *Enchanting a Disenchanted World: Revolutionizing the Means of Consumption.* Thousand Oaks, CA: Pine Forge Press.

© PEMCO-Webster & Stevens Collection/CORBIS

© Rick Maiman/CORBIS Sygma

Conspicuous consumption, a term used by sociologist/economist Thorstein Veblen, has become increasingly apparent in a materially based culture, even though its "style" has changed, as shown in comparing these two photographs.

something fundamentally human—the capacity for error, surprise, and imagination. Even with increasing globalization and the opportunities it provides to expose ourselves to diverse ways of life, McDonaldization has come to characterize other societies, too. The tourist can travel to the other side of the world and taste the familiar Chicken McNuggets or Dunkin' Donuts!

Notice, as you go through your daily life, the extraordinary presence of the process Ritzer has observed (see Map 5.1). In what areas of life do you see the process of McDonaldization? How has it influenced the national culture? In a society with as much cultural diversity as the United States, what does it mean that we have developed a system for the production and distribution of goods that relies on such uniformity? These questions will help you see how McDonaldization has permeated U.S. society and will help you think about formal organizations as a sociologist would. You might ask where you see evidence of McDonaldization on your campus and in your community.

New Global Organizational Forms and the Japanese Model

The problem of bureaucratization and increasing rationality in social systems has encouraged some to look beyond Western society bureaucracy for new organizational forms that will potentially avoid some problems of dehumanization in bureaucracies that sociologists have noted (Perrow 1994, 1986). The traditional approach to bureaucracy is that, by nature, people hate their jobs and want to avoid work and responsibility. This theory suggests that people do not care about the needs of the organization, only about their personal needs. As a result, according to this perspective, people will work only when they are rigidly controlled and monitored, as with time clocks, and with a system of promotions and salaries. Behind this organizational model lies, in part, the Max Weber–style classical bureaucracy.

More recent bureaucratic perspectives suggest that people are passive and irresponsible only because of their experience with the organization. Many people do have a desire to work as well as be creative and take on responsibility. This perspective predicts that an organization can operate efficiently and produce if the self-direction of the individual, called *self-actualization,* is permitted expression (Argyris 1990). Management's task, under this theory, is to organize things so people can accomplish their own goals while furthering the organization's goals as well.

In recent years, U.S. competition with Japan has spawned interest in Japanese styles of management.

Evidence of the "McDonaldization of society" can be seen everywhere, perhaps including on your own campus. Shopping malls, food courts, sports stadiums, even cruise ships reflect this trend toward standardization.

Lately, an organizational form used by many Japanese corporations has been adopted by some U.S. companies (Ouchi 1981). This perspective values long-term employment, interpersonal trust, and above all, close personal relationships. In this respect, it advocates the direct opposite of what Western bureaucracy advocates. The Japanese approach places considerable emphasis on primary group relationships, creating a form of work in which small groups of workers meet periodically with managers to discuss ways the organization can work better. By this style of management, managers and their companies are encouraged to take a long-term orientation toward their problems and products. Personal friendships among coworkers are encouraged. Managers are advised to "walk around" to develop closer relationships with their employees.

This style of management emerges from the particular characteristics of Japanese culture, one that emphasizes lifelong employment in the same company, company loyalty, and complete attachment to one's work. Whether it can be successfully transported to the United States and other Western countries, with their unique cultural traditions, is questionable. United States corporate culture still favors individualism—the exact opposite of the Japanese group-oriented, participative-management approach. Sociological research finds some support for the idea that workers are less alienated and experience greater solidarity among themselves in firms that practice more participative management, compared with workers where all power rests with management (Yeats 1991). Participative management does not, however, bring workers the same levels of satisfaction as forms of work where workers make their decisions based on their skills and long-term employment (Hodson 1996).

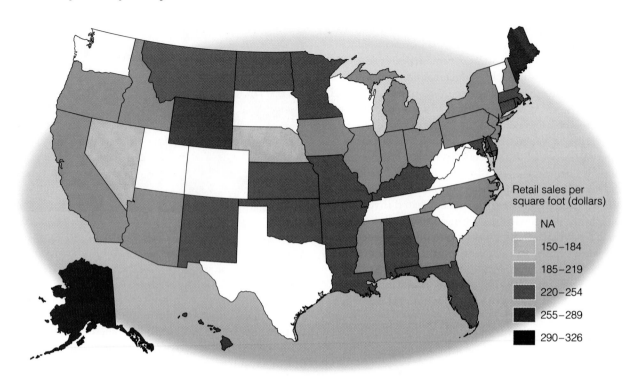

MAP 5.1 Mapping America's Diversity: The McDonaldization of Society
This map shows the retail sales per square foot by state, within the United States. Notice that some states have a high number of retail sales (for example, California, and Florida) and thus a relatively high degree of "McDonaldization"; some states have considerably fewer (for example, Idaho and New Hampshire) and thus a relatively low degree of "McDonaldization." **Relative to other states, where does your state stand in retail sales?**

DATA: From the U.S. Census Bureau, 2002. *Statistical Abstract of the United States 2002.* Washington, DC: U.S. Government Printing Office, p. 650.

▪ Diversity: Race, Gender, and Class in Organizations

The hierarchical structuring of positions within organizations results in the concentration of power and influence with a few individuals at the top. Since organizations tend to reflect patterns within the broader society, this hierarchy, like that of society, is marked by inequality in race, gender, and class relations. Although the concentration of power in organizations is incompatible with the principles of a democratic society (Perrow 1994, 1986), discrimination against women and minorities still occurs. There have been widespread disparities in the promotion rates for White and Black workers, with Whites more likely to be promoted and promoted more quickly—a pattern repeated in many work organizations (Eichenwald 1996; McGuire and Reskin 1993; Collins 1989).

Traditionally, within organizations the most powerful positions are held by White men of upper social class status. Women and minorities, on average, occupy lower positions in the organization. Although very small numbers of minorities and women do get promoted, there is typically a "glass ceiling" effect, meaning that women and minorities may be promoted but only up to a point. The glass ceiling acts as a barrier to the promotion of women and minorities into higher ranks of management, as discussed further in Chapter 10.

Sociological research finds that organizations are sensitive to the climate in which they operate. The more egalitarian the environment in which a firm operates, the more equitable is its treatment of women and minorities. In particular, sociologists have found that industries with the strongest ties to the national government tend to be more favorable in their treatment of women and minorities. Put a little differently, the greater the involvement of the federal government in a given industry, the more favorable jobs and earnings are for Black men and women and White women (Beggs 1995).

Other studies find that patterns of race and gender discrimination persist throughout organizations, even when formal barriers to advancement have been removed. Many minorities are now equal to Whites in education, particularly in organizational jobs that require advanced graduate degrees such as the master of business administration (MBA). Still, White men in organizations are more likely to receive promotions than African American, Hispanic, and Native American workers with the same education (DeWitt 1995; Zwerling and Silver 1992). In such cases, lack of promotion of the minority person cannot then be attributed to a lack of education. The same thing often happens to both White and minority women in organizations: Women are less likely to receive promotions than a White male with the same education, and sometimes even less education. Studies consistently find that women are held to higher promotion standards than men; for men, the longer they are in a position in an organization, the more likely they will be promoted, but the same is not true for women (Smith 1999).

Things work the same way with respect to people being discharged or fired. Studies show quite clearly that Black federal employees (men and women) were more than twice as likely to be dismissed as their White counterparts (DeWitt 1995; Zwerling and Silver 1992). This disparity occurred regardless of education, and regardless of occupational category, pay level, type of federal agency, age, performance rating, seniority, or attendance record. The main reasons cited in the studies for such disparities were lack of network contacts with the old boy network and racial bias within the organization. These studies were particularly well designed because they took into account quite a few factors besides race–ethnicity that are often given as reasons for not promoting minorities. The studies showed quite conclusively that with all factors taken into account, it is still race that is an important reason for the way people are treated in organizations today.

DEBUNKING
Society's Myths

Myth: Programs designed to enhance the number of women and minorities in organizational leadership are no longer needed because discriminatory barriers have been removed.

Sociological perspective: Research continues to find significant differences in the promotion rates for women and minorities in most organizational settings. Even with the removal of formal discriminatory barriers, organizational practices persist that block the mobility of these workers.

The studies strongly suggest that racism still thrives in the bureaucracy.

A classic study by Rosabeth Moss Kanter (1977) shows how the structure of organizations leads to obstacles in the advancement of groups that are tokens in the organizational environment. Kanter demonstrated how the hierarchical structure of the bureaucracy negatively affects both minorities and women who are underrepresented in the organization. In such cases, they represent token minorities or women; they feel put "out front" and under the all-too-watchful eyes of their superiors. As a result, they often suffer severe stress (Jackson 2000; Jackson et al. 1994, 1995; Spangler et al. 1978; Kanter 1977; Yoder 1991). Their coworkers often accuse them of getting the position simply because they are women, minorities, or both. It is a widespread phenomenon in universities and colleges that not only minorities, but women as well, are often accused of being admitted simply because of their gender and/or their race, even in instances when this has clearly not been the case. This is stressful for the person and shows that tokenism can have very negative consequences.

Social class, in addition to race and gender, plays a part in determining people's place within formal organizations. Middle- and upper-class employees in organizations make higher salaries and wages and are more likely to get promoted than are people of less social class status, even for individuals who are of the same race or ethnicity. This even holds for people coming from families of less social class status but who are as well educated as their middle- and upper-class coworkers. Thus, their lower salaries and lack of promotion cannot necessarily be attributed to lack of education on their part. In this respect, their treatment in the bureaucracy only perpetuates rather than lessens the negative effects of the social class system in the United States.

The social class stratification system in the United States produces major differences in the opportunities and life chances of individuals and the bureaucracy simply carries these differences forward. Class stereotypes also influence hiring practices in organizations. Personnel officers look for people with "certain demeanors," a code for those who convey middle-class or upper middle-class standards of dress, language, manners, and so on, which some people may be unable to afford.

Patterns of race, class, and gender inequality in organizations persist at the same time that many organizations have become more aware of the need for a more diverse workforce. Responding to the simple fact of more diversity within the working-age population, organizations have developed human relations experts who work within organizations to enhance sensitivity to diversity. Such diversity training has become commonplace in most large organizations.

TABLE 5.1 Theoretical Perspectives on Organizations

	Functionalist Theory	Conflict Theory	Symbolic Interaction Theory
Central Focus	Positive functions (such as efficiency) contribute to unity and stability of the organization	Hierarchical nature of bureaucracy encourages conflict between superior and subordinate, men and women, and people of different racial or class backgrounds	Stresses the role of self in the bureaucracy and how the self develops and changes
Relationship of individual to the organization	Individuals like parts of a machine, irrelevant for their personal characteristics	Individuals subordinated to systems of power and experience stress and alienation as a result	Interaction between superiors and subordinates forms the structure of the organization
Criticism	Hierarchy can result in dysfunctions such as ritualism and alienation	De-emphasizes the positive ways that organizations work	Tends to downplay overall social organization

▪ *Functional, Conflict, and Symbolic Interaction: Theoretical Perspectives*

All three major sociological perspectives—functional, conflict, and symbolic interaction—are exhibited in the analysis of formal organizations and bureaucracies (see Table 5.1). The functional perspective, based in this case on the early writing of Max Weber, argues that certain functions, called *eufunctions* (that is, positive functions) characterize bureaucracies and contribute to the overall unity of the bureaucracy. The bureaucracy exists to accomplish these eufunctions, such as efficiency, control, impersonal relations, and a chance for the individual to develop a career within the bureaucracy. As we have seen, however, bureaucracies develop the other face (informal interaction and culture, as opposed to formal or bureaucratic interaction and culture) as well as the problems of ritualism and alienation of the person from the organization. These latter problems are called dysfunctions (negative functions), which have the consequence of contributing to the disunity and lack of harmony in the bureaucracy.

The conflict perspective argues that the hierarchical or stratified nature of the bureaucracy in effect encourages rather than inhibits conflict among the individuals within it. These conflicts are between superior and subordinate, as well as between racial and ethnic groups, men and women, and people of different social class backgrounds, hampering the smooth and efficient running of the bureaucracy.

Consider the symbolic interaction perspective as underlying two management theories, those of Argyris and of Ouchi. Symbolic interaction stresses the role of the self in any group, and especially how the self develops as a product of social interaction. Argyris's theory advocates increased involvement of the self within the organization as a way of "actualizing" the self and, as a result, reducing the disconnection between individual and organization as well as other organizational problems and dysfunctions. Ouchi's theory argues that increased interaction between superior and subordinate, based on the Japanese organization model of executives "walking around" and interacting more on a primary group basis, will reduce organizational dysfunctions.

▪ *Chapter Summary*

▪ *What are the types of groups?*

Groups are a fact of human existence and permeate virtually every facet of our lives. Group size is important, as is the otherwise simple distinction between dyads and triads. *Primary groups* form the basic building blocks of social interaction in society. *Reference groups* play a major role in forming our attitudes and life goals, as do our relationships with *in-groups* and *out-groups*. *Social networks* partly determine things such as whom we know and the kinds of jobs we get. Networks based on race–ethnicity, social class, and other social factors are extremely closely connected, or very dense.

▪ *How strong is social influence?*

The social influence groups exert on us is tremendous, as seen by the Asch conformity experiments. The Milgram experiments demonstrated that the interpersonal influence of an authority figure can cause an individual to act against his or her deep convictions.

- **What is the importance of groupthink and risky shift?**

  Groupthink can be so pervasive that it adversely affects group decision making. *Risky shift* similarly often compels individuals to reach decisions that are at odds with their better judgment.

- **What are the types of formal organizations and bureaucracies, and what are some of their problems?**

  Formal organizations are of several types, such as normative, coercive, or utilitarian. Groups occur within organizations, and thus individuals within organizations are subject to group effects, like groupthink and risky shift. Weber typified *bureaucracies* as organizations with an efficient division of labor, an authority hierarchy, rules, impersonal relationships, and career ladders. Bureaucratic rigidities often result in organizational problems such as ritualism and resulting "normalization of deviance" which may have been significantly responsible for the space shuttle *Challenger* explosion in 1986, and the space shuttle *Columbia* breakup in 2003. The "McDonaldization of society" has resulted in greater efficiency, calculability, and control in many industries, probably at the expense of some individual creativity.

- **What is the Japanese model as a new global organizational form?**

  Some new organizational forms have attempted to reduce worker alienation by adopting Japanese styles of management, such as the use of small groups, and participatory management, instead of traditional top-down management styles. Whether such practices can thrive in a different cultural context such as the United States is as yet uncertain.

- **What are the problems of diversity in organizations?**

  Formal organizations perpetuate inequality on the basis of race–ethnicity, gender, and social class. Blacks, Hispanics, and Native Americans are even today less likely to get promoted, and more likely to get fired, than Whites of comparable education and other qualifications. Women experience similar effects of inequality, especially negative effects of tokenism such as stress and lowered self-esteem. Finally, persons of less than middle-class origins make less money and are less likely to get promoted than a middle-class person of comparable education. Diversity training has been introduced into some organizations as an attempt to combat such problems.

- **What do the functional, conflict, and symbolic interaction theories say about organizations?**

  Functional, conflict, and *symbolic interaction* theories highlight and clarify the analysis of organizations by specifying both organizational functions and dysfunctions (functional theory); by analyzing the consequences of hierarchical, gender, race, and social class conflict in organizations (conflict theory); and, finally, by studying the importance of social interaction and integration of the self into the organization (symbolic interaction theory).

▪ Key Terms

attribution error 127	instrumental needs 125
attribution theory 127	primary group 125
bureaucracy 136	reference group 126
deindividuation 134	risky shift 133
dyad 124	secondary group 125
expressive needs 125	social network 128
formal organization 134	total institution 136
group 124	triad 124
group size effect 125	triadic segregation 125
groupthink 132	

▪ Researching Society with MicroCase Online

You can see the results of actual research by using the Wadsworth MicroCase® Online feature available to you. This feature allows you to look at results from national surveys, census data, and some other data sources. You can explore this easy-to-use feature on your own, but try this example. Suppose you want to know some social facts, such as:

Is high communication technology in a country, such as the presence of cell phones, related to some other aspect of communication technology, such as the number of televisions per 1000 people in the country? You can do the analysis yourself!

To answer this question, go to **sociology.wadsworth.com/andersen_taylor/essen3e,** select MicroCase Online from the left navigation bar, and follow the directions there to analyze the data described below:

Data file: NATIONS

Task: SCATTERPLOT

Dependent Variable: CELL PHONE

Independent Variable: TV1000

Questions

You will get a diagram called a scatterplot, where each dot represents a country. One axis of the scatterplot (the X-axis) represents the number of televisions per 1000 persons, and the other axis (the Y-axis) represents the number of cell phone subscribers per 100,000 people. Do you see a pattern among the dots? Answer the following questions:

1. The greater the number of televisions in a country, then is the number of cell phones greater, or less?

2. How closely is the number of cell phones tied to the number of televisions?

3. What does all this tell you about different types of communication technology in a country, that "ism" about how different technologies may be related? What for example might this tell you about the number of computers with Internet capability in a country?

■ *The Companion Web Site for Sociology: The Essentials, Third Edition*

sociology.wadsworth.com/andersen_taylor/essen3e

Supplement your review of this chapter by going to the companion Web site to take one of the Tutorial Quizzes, use the flash cards to master key terms, and check out the many other study aids you'll find there. You'll also find special features such as GSS Data and Census 2000 information, data and resources at your fingertips to help you with that special project or do some research on your own.

■ *Suggested Readings and Web Resources*

Collins-Lowry, Sharon M. 1996. *Black Corporate Executives.* Philadelphia: Temple University Press.
Based on extensive interviewing of successful Black executives, this research examines the experiences of some of the first
Black managers to succeed in major corporations. Collins-Lowry's work shows the continuing significance of race in structuring experiences within corporate organizations.

Homans, George C. 1992/1950. *The Human Group.* New Brunswick, NJ: Transaction.
A classic that combines knowledge about groups with knowledge about formal organizations, this book has been one of the most useful and has served to stimulate research in group interaction over numerous decades.

Kanter, Rosabeth Moss. 1977. *Men and Women of the Corporation.* New York: Basic Books.
This classic study shows the significance of gender in structuring opportunities for women in corporations. Although more than twenty years old, the book's insights continue to be supported by subsequent research on gender dynamics in work organizations.

McDonaldization of Society
www.sociology.net/mcdonald/
This is the home page for George Ritzer's book. It provides additional information about links to discussion and illustration of this concept.

Ritzer, George. 2002. *The McDonaldization of Society: An Investigation into the Changing Character of Contemporary Society and Life,* 2nd edition. Thousand Oaks, CA: Pine Forge Press.
An entertaining and updated account of the fast-food approach to bureaucratic organization. The book highlights the influence of this model of bureaucracy upon many kinds of bureaucracies in American society, even the structure of the community health clinic.

Vaughan, Diane. 1996. *The* Challenger *Launch Decision: Risky Technology, Culture, and Deviance in NASA.* Chicago: The University of Chicago Press.
Vaughan's research explores how ordinary behavior and ritualism within organizations can result in disastrous consequences, such as the Challenger *space shuttle explosion. In many ways, this study foretold the February 1, 2003 breakup upon decent of the space shuttle* Columbia.

Deviance and Crime

*i*n the early 1970s, an airplane carrying forty members of an amateur rugby team crashed in the Andes mountains in South America. The twenty-seven survivors were marooned at 12,000 feet in freezing weather and deep snow. There was no food except for a small amount of chocolate and some wine. A few days after the crash, the group heard on a small transistor radio that the search for them had been called off.

Scattered in the snow were the frozen bodies of dead passengers. Preserved by the freezing weather, these bodies became, after a time, sources of food. At first, the survivors were repulsed by the idea of eating human flesh, but as the days wore on, they agonized over the decision about whether to eat the dead crash victims, eventually concluding that they had to eat if they were to live.

In the beginning, only a few ate the human meat, but soon the others began to eat, too. The group experimented with preparations as they tried different parts of the body. They developed elaborate rules about how, what, and whom they would eat. Some could not bring themselves to cut the meat from the human body, but would slice it once someone else had cut off large chunks. They all refused to eat certain parts—the lungs, skin, head, and genitals; no one was expected to eat an immediate friend or relative. The survivors also developed other uses for the bodies, including making warm, insulated "socks" from human skin (Read 1974; Henslin 1993).

After two months, the group sent out an expedition of three survivors to find help. The group was rescued, and the world learned of their ordeal. Their cannibalism (the eating of other human beings) was generally accepted as something they had to do to survive. Although people might have been repulsed by the story, the survivors' behavior was understood as a necessary adaptation to their life-threatening circumstances. The survivors also maintained a sense of themselves as good people even though what they did profoundly violated ordinary standards of socially acceptable behavior in most cultures in the world.

Was the behavior of the Andes crash survivors socially deviant? Were the people made crazy by their experience, or was this a normal response to extreme circumstances?

Compare the Andes crash to another case of human cannibalism. In 1991, in Milwaukee, Wisconsin, a man named Jeffrey Dahmer pleaded guilty to charges of murder after he killed at least fifteen men in his home, then chopped them up, cooked them, and ate some of their body parts. Dahmer had lured the men, eight of them African American, two White, and one a fourteen-year-old Laotian boy, to his apartment where he murdered and dismembered them. For those he considered most handsome, he boiled the flesh from their heads so that he could save and admire their skulls. Dahmer was seen as a total social deviant, someone who violated every principle of human decency. Even hardened criminals were disgusted by Dahmer. In fact, he was killed in prison by another inmate in 1994.

Why was Dahmer's behavior considered so deviant when that of the Andes survivors was not? The answer can be found by looking at the situation in which these behaviors occurred. The same behavior—eating other human beings—is considered reprehensible in one context and acceptable in another. For the Andes survivors, eating human flesh was essential for survival. Dahmer, in contrast, murdered his victims. From a sociological perspective, the deviance of cannibalism resides *not just in the act itself* but also the social context in which it occurs.

For many, Dahmer was simply a sociopath. Psychological explanations are not without merit, but a sociological perspective reveals more. In Dahmer's case, racism and homophobia contributed to Dahmer's atrocity. Most of his victims were African American and he was White, yet people who knew him described him as a racist. Even more telling is the reaction of the police to a tragic incident that occurred before Dahmer's crimes were discovered. A fourteen-year-old Laotian victim actually escaped from Dahmer and was seen wandering around naked, bleeding, crying, and looking dazed. When a Black woman in the neighborhood notified the police, they returned the boy to Dahmer's custody, interpreting the episode as a homosexual lovers' quarrel. Dahmer then murdered the boy. Many people saw this as police disregard for homosexuals and police dismissal of the complaints of Black residents. Homophobia and racism in this case cost the boy his life (Miller 1991). At the time, Dahmer was on probation for an earlier sexual assault against a teenage boy. His probation officer never visited Dahmer in his apartment because she had a heavy caseload, and Dahmer lived in a high-crime, low-income neighborhood. These sociological factors allowed Dahmer's deviance to continue unnoticed until he committed murder.

Deviant behavior and crime are all around us, or so most of us think. As with deviance, crimes vary in type, seriousness, and victims. The impression that youth as well as adult crime is all around us is complicated by how crime records are collected and kept in our society. Some crimes get reported and become a part of official statistics, and some do not. The keeping of official crime records is subject to sociological influences, as we shall see in this chapter. Whether a person's crime goes on record is to a large extent a matter of sociological forces such as institutional practices, race, ethnicity, social class, and age.

Serious crimes, such as assault and robbery, are more likely to go on record if the person committing them is a person of color, poor or working class, male, and/or young, than if the person committing them is White, middle class, and dressed in a suit and tie. If the crime in question is embezzlement, income tax fraud, or insider trading—so-called elite crimes—then the person committing it is more likely to be White, middle class, and male, and the crime is less likely reported in any official records.

We will see in this chapter not only how strange and unconventional deviant behavior is analyzable in its social context, but also how crime and the criminal justice system in the United States is structured. We will see that crime is not simply a series of random acts, but is patterned and highly predictable. We will see the role of race, social class, and gender, as well as age, in the occurrence of crime and in the recording and dispensation of justice in this society.

■ *Defining Deviance*

Sociologists define **deviance** as *behavior that is recognized as violating expected rules and norms.* Deviance is more than simple nonconformity; it is behavior that departs significantly from social expectations. In the sociological perspective on deviance, there is subtlety that distinguishes it from commonsense understandings of the same behavior:

■ *The sociological definition of deviance stresses social context, not individual behavior.* Sociologists see deviance in terms of group processes, definitions, and judgments, not just as unusual individual acts.

■ *The sociological definition of deviance recognizes that not all behaviors are judged similarly by all groups.* What is deviant to one group may be normative to another. Understanding what society sees as deviant also requires understanding the context that determines who has the power to judge some behaviors as deviant and others not.

■ *The sociological definition of deviance recognizes that established rules and norms are* socially created, *not just morally decreed or individually imposed.* Sociologists emphasize that deviance lies not just in behavior, but in the social responses of groups to behavior by others.

Sociological Perspectives on Deviance

Strange, unconventional or nonconformist behavior is often understandable in its sociological context. Consider suicide. Are people who commit suicide crazy, or might their behavior be explained? Are there conditions under which suicide is acceptable behavior? Should one who commits suicide in the face of a terminal illness be judged differently from a despondent person who jumps from a window? These are the kinds of questions probed by sociologists who study deviance.

Once you have a sociological perspective on deviance, you are likely to see things a little differently when you observe someone behaving in an unusual way. Sociologists sometimes use their understanding of deviance to explain otherwise ordinary events—such as tattooing and body piercing (Irwin 2001; Vail 1999), eating disorders (Sharp et al. 2001; Lovejoy 2001; Thompson 1994), or drug and alcohol use (Inciardi 2001; Humphries 1999; Logio 1998). Sociologists who examine behavior such as mental illness, suicide, delinquent behavior, and substance abuse as examples of deviance, also examine how people respond to social stigmas, such as having a disability, or how people become deviant, such as in prostitution, drug dealing, or crime. Deviant behavior varies in its severity, as well as in how ordinary or unusual the behavior might be.

Sociologists distinguish two types of deviance: formal and informal. *Formal deviance* is behavior that breaks laws or official rules, such as crime. There are formal sanctions against formal deviance, such as imprisonment and fines. *Informal deviance* is behavior that violates customary norms (Schur 1984). Although such deviance may not be specified in law, it is judged to be deviant by those who uphold the society's norms. A good example is the body piercing that is popular among young people. Although there are no laws against such a practice, it violates older norms about dress and appearance, and is judged by many outside of the youth culture to be socially deviant even though it is quite fashionable for others.

The study of deviance can be divided into the study of why people violate laws or norms and the study of how society reacts. This reaction includes the labeling process by which deviance comes to be recognized as such. *Labeling theory* is discussed in detail later, but it is important to point out here that the meaning of deviance is not just in the breaking of norms or rules; it also includes how people react to those behaviors. This societal reaction to deviant behavior suggests that social groups actually *create* deviance "by making the rules whose infraction

RAWA/WorldPicture News

This widely distributed photo of a woman being executed by the Taliban in Afghanistan illustrates the extreme sanctions that can be brought against those defined as deviant by a powerful group. In this case, the photo also mobilized world condemnation of the Taliban regime for its treatment of women.

constitutes deviance, and by applying those rules to particular people and labeling them as outsiders" (Becker 1963: 9).

THE CONTEXT OF DEVIANCE.

Certain situations are more conducive to the formation of deviant behavior. Even the most unconventional behavior can be understood if we know the context in which it occurs. Behavior that is deviant in one circumstance may be normal in another, or behavior may be ruled deviant only when performed by certain people. For example, people who break gender stereotypes may be judged as deviant even though their behavior is considered normal for the other sex. Heterosexual men and women who kiss in public are the image of romance; lesbians and gay men who even dare to hold hands in public are seen as flaunting their sexual orientation.

The definition of deviance can also vary over time. Date rape, for example, was not considered social deviance until recently. Women have been presumed to mean yes when they said no, and men were expected to "seduce" women through aggressive sexual behavior. Even now, women who are raped by someone they know may not think of it as rape. If they do, they may find that prosecuting the offender is difficult because others do not think of it as rape. Studies have found that students

think that date rape is justified if the victim was wearing provocative clothing (Workman and Freeburg 1999; Johnson 1995; Cassidy and Hurrell 1995). People with more traditional attitudes about gender roles are more likely to excuse men's aggression in date rape and to define the situation as something other than rape. These examples show that the definition of deviance derives not only from what one does, but also from who does it, when, and where.

The sociologist Emile Durkheim argued one reason that acts of deviance are publicly punished is that the social order is threatened by deviance. Judging those behaviors as deviant and punishing them confirms general social standards. Therein lies the value of widely publicized trials, public executions, or the historical practice of displaying a wrongdoer in the stocks or pillory. The punishment affirms the collective beliefs of the society, reinforces social order, and inhibits future deviant behavior, especially as defined by those with the power to judge others.

DEBUNKING
Society's Myths

Myth: Deviance is bad for society because it disrupts normal life.

Sociological perspective: Deviance tends to stabilize society. By defining some forms of behavior as deviant, people are affirming the social norms of groups.

Durkheim argued that societies actually *need* deviance to know what presumably normal behavior is. In this sense, Durkheim considered deviance "functional" for society (Durkheim 1897/1951; Erikson 1966). You could observe Durkheim's point in the aftermath of the terrorist attacks of September 11, 2001. Horrified by the sight of hijacked planes flying into the World Trade Center and the Pentagon, and crashing in a Pennsylvania field, U.S. citizens responded through publicly demonstrating strong patriotism. Durkheim would interpret this as deviance (i.e., the terrorist acts) producing strong social solidarity. This was one of Durkheim's most important insights: Deviance produces social solidarity. If societies did not have deviance, they would have no way to integrate and socialize people into social norms.

You may remember the photo of a Taliban man in Afghanistan firing a rifle into the head of a woman in a blue burqa (gown)—an image widely distributed to provide evidence of the Taliban's cruelty to women. During the rule of the Taliban, Afghan women accused of violating Islamic law were herded into trucks and publicly executed in a large stadium. The image of a rifle being put to a woman's head repulsed and infuriated those opposed to the Taliban regime, including the Afghan women's resistance organization, RAWA (the Revolutionary Association of Women of Afghanistan; see **www.rawa.org**). Durkheim would say that this, like other public executions, by condemning alleged deviant behavior, promoted social solidaritry among the Taliban. At the same time, the fear these executions engendered also reinforced Taliban law.

THE INFLUENCE OF SOCIAL MOVEMENTS.

The perception of deviance may also be influenced by social movements, which are networks of groups that organize to support or resist changes in society (see Chapter 16). With a change in the social climate, formerly acceptable behaviors may be newly defined as deviant. Smoking, for instance, was once considered glamorous, sexy, and "cool." Now, smokers are widely scorned as polluters and, despite strong lobbying by the tobacco industry, regulations against smoking have proliferated.

Whereas in 1987 only 17 percent of the public thought that smoking should be banned in restaurants, by 2000 close to half (47 percent) thought so (Gallup Organization 2000b). The increase in public disapproval of smoking results as much from social and political movements as it does from the known health risks. The success of the antismoking movement has come from the mobilization of constituencies able to articulate to the public that smoking is dangerous (Nathanson 1999). Note that the key element here is the ability of people to mobilize—not just the evidence of risk. In other words, there has to be a social response for deviance to be defined as such; only scientific evidence alone of harm is not enough.

Social movements like the gay and lesbian movement can also organize to remove the deviant label from certain behaviors. Whereas gay and lesbian behavior traditionally has been defined as deviant, this movement has encouraged people to see gay and lesbian relationships as legitimate. Organizing to legalize gay marriage or to extend employment benefits to domestic partners, people in this movement have not only advocated new rights for lesbian women and gay men, but have challenged the public label of gays and lesbians as deviant.

THE SOCIAL CONSTRUCTION OF DEVIANCE.

Perhaps because it violates social conventions or because it sometimes involves unusual behavior, deviance captures the public imagination. Commonly, however, the public understands deviance as the result of individualistic or personality factors. Many people see deviants as crazy, threatening, "sick," or in some other ways inferior, but sociologists see deviance as influenced by society—by the same social processes and institutions that shape all social behavior.

Deviance, for example, is not necessarily irrational or "sick," and may be a positive and rational adaptation to

Moral judgments about deviant behavior, such as drug abuse, are often the basis for the development of social movements that then define the behavior as a social problem.

a situation. Think of the Andes survivors in this chapter's opener. Was their action irrational, or was it an inventive and rational response to a dreadful situation? To use another example, are gangs the result of the irrational behavior of maladjusted youth or are they predictable responses to a social situation? Sociological studies of gangs in the United States shed light on this question. The family situations of gang members are often problematic, although girls in gangs tend to be more isolated from their families than are boys in gangs (Fleisher 2000; Esbensen-Finn et al. 1999). Given the class, race, and gender inequality faced by minority youth, many turn to gangs for the social support they lack elsewhere (Walker-Barnes and Mason 2001; Moore and Hagedorn 1996). For example, some young Puerto Rican girls, as well as others, live in relatively confined social environments with little opportunity for educational or occupational advancement. Their community expects them to be "good girls" and to remain close to their families. Joining a gang is one way to reject these restrictive roles (Campbell 1987; Messerschmidt 1997). Are these young women irrational or just doing the best they can to adapt to their situation? Sociologists interpret their behavior as an understandable adaptation to conditions of poverty, racism, and sexism.

Although deviance is a violation of social norms, it is not always behavior of which others disapprove. In some subcultures or situations, deviant behavior is encouraged and praised. Have you ever been egged on by friends to do something that you thought was deviant, or done something you knew was wrong? Many argue that the reason so many college students drink excessively is that the student subculture encourages them—even though students know it is harmful. Similarly, the juvenile delinquent regarded by school authorities as defiant and obnoxious is rewarded and praised by peers for the very behaviors that school authorities loathe. Much deviant behavior occurs, or escalates, because of the social support from the group in which it develops.

Some behavior patterns defined as deviant are also surprisingly similar to so-called normal behavior. Is a heroin addict who buys drugs with whatever money he can find so different from a business executive who spends a large proportion of his discretionary income on alcohol? Each may establish a daily pattern that facilitates drug use; each may select friends based on shared interests in drinking or taking drugs; and each may become so physically, emotionally, and socially dependent on their "fix" that life seems unimaginable without it. Which of the two is more likely to be considered deviant?

Deviance is not just weird, pathological, irrational, off-putting, or unconventional behavior. Sociologists who study deviance understand it in the context of social relationships and society. They define deviance in terms of existing social norms and the social judgments people make about one another. Sometimes behavior that is deviant in one context may be perfectly normal in another (for example, men wearing earrings or women wearing boxer shorts). Indeed, deviant behavior can sometimes be indicative of changes that are taking place in the cultural folkways. Thus, whereas only a few years ago body piercing and tattooing were associated with gangs and disrespectable people, now it is considered fashionable among young, middle-class people—even though to some it is still a mark of deviance (Irwin 2001).

Psychological Explanations of Deviance

Psychologists explain deviance by emphasizing individual personality factors as the underlying cause of deviant behavior. Sociologists have criticized this perspective not because it is wrong but because it is incomplete. By locating causes of deviance within individuals, many psychological explanations tend to overlook the context in which deviance is produced. Individual motivation simply does not explain the social patterns that sociologists observe in studying deviance. Why is deviance more common in some groups than others? Why are some more likely to be labeled deviant than others, even if they engage in the

Deviance can be encouraged in certain peer subcultures, such as the widespread phenomenon of binge drinking among college students.

same behavior? How is deviance related to patterns of inequality in society? To answer these questions requires a sociological explanation. Sociologists do not ignore individual psychology but integrate it into an explanation of deviance that focuses on the social conditions surrounding deviant behavior, going beyond explanations of deviance that root it in the individual personality.

Commonly, people will say that someone who commits a very deviant act, such as a child molester, is "sick" or a sociopath. This common explanation sees the origin of deviance in psychological terms. Sociologists, instead, have introduced the idea of the **medicalization of deviance,** referring to explanations of deviant behavior that interpret deviance as the result of individual pathology or sickness (Conrad and Schneider 1992). Medicalizing deviance attributes deviant behavior to a "sick" state of mind where the solution is to "cure" the deviant through therapy or other psychological treatment.

THINKING SOCIOLOGICALLY

Ask some of your friends to explain why rape occurs. What evidence of the *medicalization of deviance* is there in your friends' answers?

An example is found in alcoholism. There is evidence that there may be a genetic basis to alcoholism, and certainly alcoholism must be understood at least in part in medical terms, but viewing alcoholism *solely* from a medical perspective ignores the social causes that influence the development and persistence of this behavior. Practitioners know that medical treatment alone does not solve the problem. The social relationships, social conditions, and social habits of alcoholics must be altered, or the behavior is likely to recur.

Sociologists criticize the medicalization of deviance for ignoring the effects of social structures on the development of deviant behavior. From a sociological perspective, deviance originates in society, not only in individuals. Changing the incidence of deviant behavior requires changes in society, in addition to changes in individuals. Deviance, to most sociologists, is not a pathological state, but an *adaptation to the social structures* in which people live. Factors such as family background, social class, racial inequality, and the social structure of gender relations in society produce deviance, and these factors must be considered to explain deviance.

▪ *Sociological Theories of Deviance*

Sociologists have drawn on several major theoretical traditions to explain deviant behavior, including functionalism, conflict theory, and symbolic interaction theory.

Functionalist Theories of Deviance

Recall that functionalism is a theoretical perspective that interprets all parts of society, including those that may seem dysfunctional, as contributing to the stability of the whole. At first glance, deviance seems dysfunctional for society. Functionalist theorists argue otherwise (see Table 6.1). They contend that deviance is functional because it creates social cohesion. Branding certain behaviors as deviant provides contrast with behaviors that are considered normal, giving people a heightened sense of social order. According to functionalist theorists, norms are meaningless unless there is deviance from the norms; thus, deviance is necessary to clarify what society's norms are. Group coherence then comes from sharing a common definition of legitimate, as well as deviant, behavior. The collective identity of the group is affirmed when those who are defined as deviant are ridiculed or condemned by group members (Erikson 1966).

To give an example, think about how many people define gay men as deviant. Although lesbians and gay men have rejected this label, labeling homosexuality as deviant is one way of affirming the presumed normality of hetero-

TABLE 6.1 Sociological Theories of Deviance

Functionalism	Symbolic Interaction	Conflict Theory
Deviance creates social cohesion	Deviance is a learned behavior, reinforced through group membership	Dominant classes control the definition of and sanctions attached to deviance
Deviance results from structural strains in society	Deviance results from the process of social labeling, regardless of the actual commission of deviance	Deviance results from inequality in society, including that of class, race, and gender
Deviance occurs when people's attachment to social bonds is diminished	Those with the power to assign deviant labels actually create deviance	Elite deviance goes largely unrecognized and unpunished

sexual behavior. Labeling someone else an outsider is, in other words, a way of affirming one's "insider" identity.

DURKHEIM: THE STUDY OF SUICIDE. The functionalist perspective on deviance stems originally from the work of Emile Durkheim. Recall that one of Durkheim's central concerns was how society maintains its coherence (or social order). Durkheim saw deviance as functional for society because it produces solidarity among society's members. He developed his analysis of deviance in large part through his analysis of suicide. Through this work, he discovered a number of important sociological points. First, he criticized the usual psychological interpretations of why people commit suicide, turning instead to sociological explanations with data to back them up. Second, he emphasized the role of social structure in producing deviance. Third, he pointed to the importance of people's social attachments to society in understanding deviance. Finally, he elaborated the functionalist view that deviance provides the basis for social cohesion. His studies of suicide illustrate these points.

Durkheim was the first to argue that the causes of suicide were to be found in social factors, not individual personalities. Observing that the rate of suicide in a society varied with time and place, Durkheim looked for causes linked to time and place rather than emotional stress. Durkheim argued that suicide rates are affected by the different social contexts in which they emerge. He looked at the degree to which people feel integrated into the structure of society and their social surroundings as social factors producing suicide.

Durkheim analyzed three types of suicide: anomic suicide, altruistic suicide, and egoistic suicide. **Anomie,** as defined by Durkheim, is the condition that exists when social regulations in a society break down; the controlling influences of society are no longer effective, and people exist in a state of relative normlessness. **Anomic suicide** occurs when the disintegrating forces in the society make individuals feel lost or alone. Teenage suicide is often cited as an example of anomic suicide. Studies of college campuses, for example, trace the cause of campus suicides to feelings of depression and hopelessness (Langhinrichsen-Rohling et al. 1998). These feelings are, however, more likely to arise in certain sociological contexts. Thus, suicide is more likely committed by those who have been sexually abused as children or by those whose parents are alcoholics (Thakkar et al. 2000; Yama et al. 1995; Bryant and Range 1995; Peters and Range 1995).

Altruistic suicide occurs when there is excessive regulation of individuals by social forces. An example is someone who commits suicide for the sake of a religious or political cause. For example, after hijackers took control of four airplanes, crashing two into the World Trade Center in New York, one into the Pentagon, and one crashing in Pennsylvania, many wondered how anyone could do such a thing, killing themselves in the process. Although sociology certainly does not excuse such behavior, it can help explain it. Terrorists and suicide bombers are so regulated by their extreme beliefs that they are willing to die while killing as many people as possible to achieve their goals. As Durkheim argued, altruistic suicide results when individuals are excessively dominated by the expectations of their social group.

Egoistic suicide occurs when people feel totally detached from society. This helps explain the high rate of suicide among the elderly in the United States. People over seventy-five years of age have one of the highest rates of suicide, presumably because the elderly lose many of their functional ties to society (National Center for Health Statistics 2003; Cohen and Hewitt 1999). Ordinarily, people are integrated into society by work roles, ties to family and community, and other social bonds. When these bonds are weakened through retirement or loss of family, the likelihood of egoistic suicide increases. Elderly people who lose these ties are the most susceptible to egoistic suicide. Suicide is also more likely to occur among people who are not well integrated into social networks (Berkman et al. 2000; Nisbet 1997). Thus, it should not be surprising that women have lower suicide rates than men (National Center for Health Statistics 2003). Sociologists explain this fact as a result of men being less embedded in social relationships of care and responsibility than women (Watt and Sharp 2001).

Durkheim's major point is that suicide is a social, not just an individual, phenomenon. Recall from Chapter 1 that Durkheim sees sociology as the discovery of the social forces that influence human behavior. As individu-

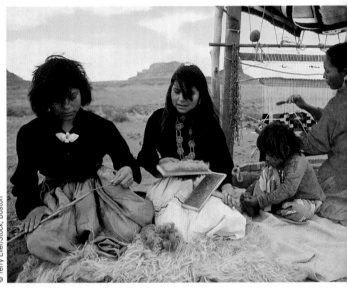

Strong ties among the Navajo produce social integration, resulting in the fact that the Navajo have one of the lowest suicide rates of any group in the United States.

istic as suicide might seem, Durkheim discovered the influence of social structure even here.

DEBUNKING
Society's Myths

Myth: People who commit suicide are crazy or sick.

Sociological perspective: Some people who commit suicide may suffer from psychological problems, but sociologists explain suicide in a social context instead of looking only at factors internal to the individual.

MERTON: STRUCTURAL STRAIN THEORY.

The functionalist perspective on deviance has been further elaborated by the sociologist Robert Merton (1910–2003). Merton's **structural strain theory** traces the origins of deviance to the tensions caused by the gap between cultural goals and the means people have to achieve those goals. Merton noted that societies are characterized by both culture and social structure. Culture establishes goals for people in society; social structure provides, or fails to provide, the means for people to achieve those goals. In a well-integrated society, according to Merton, people use accepted means to achieve the goals society establishes. In other words, the goals and means of the society are in balance. When the means are out of balance with the goals, deviance is likely to occur.

To explain further, a collective goal in U.S. society is the achievement of economic success. The legitimate means to achieve are education and jobs, but not all groups have equal access to those means. The result is

© Terry Eiler/Stock, Boston

structural strain that produces deviance. According to Merton, lower-class individuals are most likely to experience these strains since they internalize the same goals and values of the rest of society but have blocked opportunities for success (Merton 1968). Structural strain theory therefore helps explain the high correlation that exists between unemployment and crime. Rather than blaming poor and unemployed criminals for not having the values of the middle class, structural strain theory explains their deviant behavior as the product of structural obstacles that make illegitimate means the only option for achieving the goals established by cultural values.

To illustrate this theory, consider the case of prostitution. From the perspective of structural strain theory, the prostitute has accepted the cultural values of the dominant society—she (or, in some cases, he) wishes to be economically successful and accepts the commercialization of sexuality that characterizes the dominant culture. If located in a situation with few other options for economic support, she turns to prostitution because of these structural strains, not because of holding values different from the dominant culture.

The theory of structural strain has recently been used to explain the phenomenon of eating disorders, common particularly (though not exclusively) among young women. Cultural norms establish thinness as an ideal for women. These norms (in Merton's terms, are a cultural goal) and are coupled with other life goals. Research among college women finds that structural strain results when women fail to achieve their goals. This leads to a higher probability of developing an eating disorder, such as bulimia—purging oneself after eating (Sharp et al. 2000).

SOCIAL CONTROL THEORY. Taking functionalist theory in another direction, Travis Hirschi has developed social control theory to explain deviance. **Social control theory,** a type of functionalist theory, posits that deviance occurs when a person's (or group's) attachment to social bonds is weakened (Hirschi 1969; Gottfredson and Hirschi 1995, 1990) because most of the time, people follow the rules of behavior. According to this view, people internalize social norms because of their attachments to others. People care what others think of them and therefore conform to social expectations because they accept what people expect. You can see here that social control theory, like the functionalist framework from which it stems, assumes the importance of the socialization process in producing conformity to social rules. When that conformity is broken, deviance occurs.

Social control theory assumes that there is a common value system within society and breaking allegiance to that value system is the source of social deviance. This theory focuses on how deviants are attached (or not) to common value systems and what situations break people's commitment to these values. Social control theory suggests that most people probably feel some impulse toward deviance at some times, but that the attachment to social norms prevents them from actually participating in deviant behavior. When conditions arise that break those attachments, deviance occurs. Sociologists find that juveniles whose parents exercise little control over violent behavior and who learn violence from aggressive peers are most likely to engage in violent crimes (Heimer 1997). This helps you understand how from a sociological explanation two teenaged boys, alienated from the dominant peer culture in their school, could murder twelve high school students and a teacher, plant bombs throughout their school, and kill themselves in Littleton, Colorado.

FUNCTIONALISM: STRENGTHS AND WEAKNESSES. Functionalism emphasizes that social structure, not just individual motivation, produces deviance. Functionalists argue that social conditions exert pressure on individuals to behave in conforming or nonconforming ways. Types of deviance are linked to one's place in the social structure; thus, a poor person blocked from economic opportunities may use armed robbery to achieve economic goals, whereas a stockbroker may use insider trading to achieve the same. Functionalists acknowledge that people choose whether to behave in a deviant manner, but believe that they make their choice from among socially structured options. The emphasis in functionalist theory is on social structure, not individual action.

Functionalists also point out that what appears to be dysfunctional behavior may actually be functional for the society. An example is the fact that most people consider prostitution to be dysfunctional behavior; from the point of view of an individual, that is true—it demeans the women who engage in it, puts them at physical risk, and subjects them to sexual exploitation. From the view of functionalist theory, however, prostitution supports and maintains a social system that links women's gender roles with sexuality, associates sex with commercial activity, and defines women as passive sexual objects and men as sexual aggressors. In other words, what appears to be deviant may actually be functional for society.

Critics of the functionalist perspective argue that it does not explain how norms of deviance are first established. Despite its analysis of the ramifications of deviant behavior for society as a whole, functionalism does little to explain why some behaviors are defined as normative and others as illegitimate. Questions such as who determines social norms, and on whom such judgments are most likely to be imposed, are seldom asked by anyone using a functionalist perspective. Functionalists see deviance as having stabilizing consequences in society, but they tend to overlook the injustices that labeling someone deviant can produce. Others would say that the functionalist perspective too easily assumes that deviance has a positive role in society; thus functionalists rarely consider the differential effects that the administration of justice has on various social groups. The tendency in functionalist theory to assume that the system works for the good of the whole too easily ignores the inequities in society and how these inequities are reflected in patterns of deviance. These issues are left for sociologists who work from the perspectives of conflict theory and symbolic interaction.

Conflict Theories of Deviance

Recall that conflict theory emphasizes the unequal distribution of power and resources in society. It links the study of deviance to social inequality. Based on the work of Karl Marx (1818–1883; see Chapter 1), conflict theory sees a dominant class as controlling the resources of society and using its power to create the institutional rules and belief systems that support its power. Like functionalist theory, conflict theory is a *macrostructural* approach; that is, both theories look at the structure of society as a whole in developing explanations of deviant behavior.

Because some groups of people have access to fewer resources in capitalist society, they are forced into crime to sustain themselves. Conflict theory posits that the economic organization of capitalist societies produces deviance and crime. The high rate of crime among the poorest groups, especially economic crimes such as theft, robbery, prostitution, and drug selling, are a result of the economic status of these groups. Rather than emphasizing values and conformity as a source of deviance, as do functional analyses, conflict theorists see crime in terms of power relationships and economic inequality (Grant and Martínez 1997).

The upper class can also better hide crimes they commit because affluent groups have the resources to mask their deviance and crime. As a result, a working-class man who beats his wife is more likely to be arrested and prosecuted than an upper-class man who engages in the same behavior. In addition, those with greater resources can afford to buy their way out of trouble by paying bail, hiring expensive attorneys, or even resorting to bribes.

Conflict theorists expand our view of crime and deviance, revealing, for example, the significance of *corporate crime*—crime committed within the legitimate context of doing business. They argue that appropriating profit based on exploitation of the poor and working class is built into the fabric of capitalist society. **Elite deviance** refers to the wrongdoing of wealthy and powerful individuals and organizations (D. R. Simon 2001). Elite deviance includes tax evasion, illegal campaign contributions, corporate scandals that endanger or deceive the public but profit the corporation or individuals within it, and government actions that abuse the public

trust. The deceptive accounting practices by the Enron corporation that robbed many workers of their retirement pensions are a good example.

Elite deviance includes what early conflict theorists called *white-collar crime* (Sutherland 1940; Sutherland and Cressey 1978). Examples of white-collar crime are bribery, embezzlement, and antitrust violations—such as the U.S. government's case against the Microsoft Corporation and its founder and CEO Bill Gates, for unfairly sabotaging the competition.

The ruling groups in society develop numerous mechanisms to protect their interests according to conflict theorists who argue that law, for example, is created by elites to protect the interests of the dominant class. Thus, law, supposedly neutral and fair in its form and implementation, works in the interest of the most well-to-do (Weisburd et al. 1991; Spitzer 1975). Another way that conflict theorists see dominant groups as using their power is through the excessive regulation of populations that are a potential threat to affluent interests. The current support among government leaders for new prison construction is an example of this. Periodically sweeping the homeless off city streets, especially when there is a major political event or other elite event occurring, is another example. Conflict theory has also produced analyses of institutions that purportedly "treat" deviants (prisons, mental hospitals, detention homes, for example), but routinely fail those they are intended to help.

Social control is the process by which groups and individuals within those groups are brought into conformity with dominant social expectations. Social control, as we saw in Chapter 3, can take place simply through socialization, but dominant groups can also control the behavior of others through marking them as deviant. An example is the historic persecution of witches during the Middle Ages in Europe and during the early Colonial period in America (Ben-Yehuda 1986; Erikson 1966). Witches often were women who were healers and midwives—those whose views were at odds with the authority of the exclusively patriarchal hierarchy of the church, then the ruling institution. "Witch hunt" is a term still used today to refer to the aggressive pursuit of those who dissent from prevailing political and social norms.

SOCIAL CONTROL AGENTS. One implication of conflict theory, especially when linked with labeling theory, is that the power to define deviance confers an important degree of social control. **Social control agents** are those who regulate and administer the response to deviance, such as the police and mental health workers. Members of powerless groups may be defined as deviant for even the slightest infraction against social norms, whereas others may be free to behave in deviant ways without consequence. Oppressed groups may actually engage in more deviant behavior, but it is also true that they have a greater likelihood of being labeled deviant and incarcerated or institutionalized, whether or not they have actually committed an offense. This is evidence of the power wielded by social control agents.

When powerful groups hold stereotypes about other groups, the less powerful people are frequently assigned deviant labels. As a consequence, the least powerful groups in society are subject most often to social control. You can see this in the patterns of arrest data. Poor people are more likely considered criminals and therefore more likely to be arrested, convicted, and imprisoned than middle- and upper-class people. The same is true of Latinos, Native Americans, and African Americans. Sociologists point out that this does not necessarily mean that these groups are somehow more criminally prone; rather, they take it as evidence of the differential treatment of these groups by the criminal justice system.

Conflict theorists argue that those with the least power are most likely to be labeled criminal by more powerful authorities, which, as we will see shortly, links conflict theory to *labeling theory*—a type of symbolic interaction theory. Although it is the poor and members of racial minority groups who are most likely to appear in the arrest data, conflict theorists would argue that this is because of the relatively greater vulnerability of these groups to police power and injustice in the application of justice.

CONFLICT THEORY: STRENGTHS AND WEAKNESSES. The strength of conflict theory is its insight into the significance of power relationships in the definition, identification, and handling of deviance. It links the commission, perception, and treatment of crime to inequality in society and offers a powerful analysis of how the injustices of society produce crime and result in different systems of justice for disadvantaged and privileged groups. Not without its weaknesses, however, critics point out that laws protect most people, not just the affluent, as conflict theorists argue.

In addition, although conflict theory offers a powerful analysis of the origins of crime, it is less effective in explaining other forms of deviance. For example, how would conflict theorists explain the routine deviance of middle-class adolescents? They might point out that much of the middle-class deviance is driven by consumer marketing. Profits are made from the accoutrements of deviance—rings in pierced eyebrows, "gangsta" rap music, and so on—but economic interests alone cannot explain all the deviance observed in society. As Durkheim argued, deviance is functional for the whole of society, not just those with a major stake in the economic system.

Symbolic Interaction Theories of Deviance

Whereas functionalist and conflict theories are *macrosociological* theories, certain *microsociological* theories of deviance look directly at the interactions people have with one another as the origin of social deviance. Symbolic interaction theory holds that people behave as they do because of the meanings people attribute to situations (see Chapter 1). This perspective emphasizes the meanings surrounding deviance, as well as how people respond to those meanings. Symbolic interaction emphasizes that deviance originates in the interaction between different groups and is defined by society's reaction to certain behaviors. Symbolic interactionist theories of deviance originate in the perspective of the Chicago School of sociology, examined earlier in Chapter 1.

W. I. Thomas (1863–1947), one of the early sociologists from the University of Chicago, was among the first to develop a sociological perspective on social deviance. Thomas explained deviance as *a normal response to the social conditions in which people find themselves.* He called this *situational analysis,* meaning that people's actions and the subjective meanings attributed to these actions, including deviant behavior, must be understood in social, not individualized, frameworks. Much influenced by his women students in the Chicago School (Deegan 1990), Thomas was one of the first to argue that delinquency was caused by the social disorganization brought on by slum life and urban industrialism; he saw it as a problem of social conditions, not individual character.

DIFFERENTIAL ASSOCIATION THEORY. Thomas's work laid the foundation for a classic theory of deviance: differential association theory. **Differential association theory** interprets deviance, including criminal behavior, as behavior one learns through interaction with others (Sutherland 1940; Sutherland and Cressey 1978). Edwin Sutherland argued that becoming a criminal or a juvenile delinquent is a matter of learning criminal ways within the primary groups to which one belongs. To Sutherland, people become criminals when they are more strongly socialized to break the law than to obey it. Differential association theory emphasizes the interaction people have with their peers and others in their environment. Those who "differentially associate" with delinquents, deviants, or criminals learn to value deviance. The greater the frequency, duration, and intensity of their immersion in deviant environments, the more likely it is that they will become deviant.

Consider the career path of con artists and hustlers. Hustlers seldom work alone. Like any skilled worker, they have to learn the "tricks of the trade." A new recruit becomes part of a network of other hustlers who teach the recruit the norms of the deviant culture (Prus and Sharper 1991). Crime also tends to run in families. This does not necessarily mean that crime is passed on in genes from parent to child. It means that youths raised in deviant families are more likely socialized to become deviant themselves (Miller 1986). Differential association theory offers a compelling explanation for how deviance is culturally transmitted—that is, people pass on deviant expectations through the social groups in which they interact, of which the family is but one.

Critics of differential association theory have argued that this perspective tends to blame deviance on the values of particular groups. Differential association has been used, for instance, to explain the higher rate of crime among the poor and working class, arguing that this is because they do not share the values of the middle class. Such an explanation, critics say, is class-biased, because it overlooks the deviance that occurs in the middle-class culture and among elites. Disadvantaged groups may share the values of the middle class, but cannot necessarily achieve them through legitimate means (a point, you will remember, made by Merton's structural strain theory). Still, differential association theory offers a good explanation of why deviant activity may be more common in some groups than others, and it emphasizes the significant role that peers play in encouraging deviant behavior.

LABELING THEORY.   Labeling theory interprets the responses of others as the most significant factor in understanding how deviant behavior is both created and sustained (Becker 1963). Labeling theory stems from the work of W. I. Thomas who wrote, "If men define situations as real, they are real in their consequences" (Thomas and Thomas 1928: 572). A *label* is the assignment or attachment of a deviant identity to a person by others, including by agents of social institutions. Therefore, the peoples' reactions, not the action itself, produce deviance as a result of the labeling process. Once applied, the deviant label is difficult to shed.

Linked with conflict theory, labeling theory shows how those with the power to label an act or a person deviant and to impose sanctions—such as police, court officials, school authorities, experts, teachers, and official agents of social institutions—wield great power in determining societal understandings of deviance. When they apply the "deviant" label, it sticks. Furthermore, because deviants are handled through bureaucratic organizations, bureaucratic workers "process" people according to rules and procedures, seldom questioning the basis for those rules or being willing or able to challenge them (Cicourel 1968; Kitsuse and Cicourel 1963; Margolin 1992; Montada and Lerner 1998).

Once the label is applied, it is difficult for the deviant to recover a nondeviant identity. To give an example, once a social worker or psychiatrist labels a client mentally ill, that person will be treated as mentally ill, regardless of his or her actual mental state. Pleas by the accused that he or she is mentally sound are typically taken as evidence of illness! Likewise, anger and frustration about the label are taken as further support for the diagnosis. Once labeled, a person may have great difficulty changing his or her classification; the label itself has consequences.

A person need not have actually engaged in deviant behavior to be labeled deviant; yet, once applied, the label has social consequences. Labeling theory helps explain why convicts released from prison have such high rates of *recidivism* (return to criminal activities). Convicted criminals are formally and publicly labeled wrongdoers. They are treated with suspicion ever afterward and have great difficulty finding legitimate employment: The label "ex-con" defines their future options.

Labeling theory points to a distinction often made by sociologists between primary, secondary, and tertiary deviance. *Primary deviance* is the actual violation of a norm or law. *Secondary deviance* is the behavior that results from being labeled deviant, regardless if the person has engaged in deviance. A student labeled a "troublemaker," for example, might accept this identity and move from being merely mischievous to engaging in escalating delinquent acts. In that case, the person at least partly accepts the deviant label and acts in accordance with that role. *Tertiary deviance* occurs when the deviant fully accepts the deviant role but rejects the stigma associated with it, as when lesbians and gays proudly display their identity (Lemert 1972; Kitsuse 1980).

Both social class and the role of prisons in society play an important role in the creation of secondary deviance. Jeffrey Reiman (2002) notes that the prison system in the United States is in effect designed to train and socialize prisoners into a career of secondary deviance, and to tell the public that crime is a threat primarily from the poor. He sees the goal of the prison system not as reducing crime, but as impressing upon the public that crime is inevitable and that it originates only from the lower classes. Prisons accomplish this, even if unintentionally, by demeaning prisoners, not training them in marketable skills, and stigmatizing them as different from "decent citizens." As a consequence, the person will never be able to pay his or her debt to society and the prison system has created the very behavior it intended to eliminate.

Labeling theory suggests that deviance refers not just to something one does, but to something one becomes. **Deviant identity** is the definition a person has of himself or herself as a deviant. Most often, deviant identities emerge over time (Lemert 1972). A drug addict, for example, may not think of herself as a junkie until she realizes she no longer has nonusing friends. The formation of a deviant identity, like other identities, involves a process of social transformation in which a new self-image and new public definition of a person emerges. This is a process that involves how people view the deviant and how the deviant views himself or herself. Studies of tattoo "collectors" (i.e., those who are very heavily tattooed) find, for example, that if collectors first learn to interpret tattooing as a desirable thing, they then begin to feel connected to a subculture of other collectors, and eventually come to see their tattoos as part of themselves (Irwin 2001; Vail 1999).

© Mark Peterson/CORBIS Saba

Some deviance develops in deviant communities, such as the Skinheads shown here marching in a Ku Klux Klan rally protesting the Martin Luther King Jr. holiday. Such right-wing extremist groups have become more common in recent years.

DEVIANT CAREERS. In the ordinary context of work, a career is the sequence of movements a person makes through different positions in an occupational system (Becker 1963). A **deviant career** is the sequence of movements people make through a particular subculture of deviance. Deviant careers can be studied sociologically, like any other career. Within deviant careers, people are socialized into new "occupational" roles and encouraged, both materially and psychologically, to engage in deviant behavior. The concept of a deviant career emphasizes that there is a progression through deviance: Deviants are recruited, given or denied rewards, and promoted or demoted. As with legitimate careers, deviant careers involve an evolution in the person's identity, values, and commitment over time. Deviants, like other careerists, may have to demonstrate their commitment to the career to their superiors, perhaps by passing certain tests of their mettle, such as when a gang expects new members to commit a crime, perhaps even shoot someone.

The concept of a deviant career helps explain why being caught and labeled deviant may actually reinforce, rather than deter, one's commitment to a deviant career. For example, hospitalized mental patients are often re-

warded with comfort and attention for "acting sick" but are punished when they act normally—for instance, if they rebel against the boredom and constraints of institutionalization. Acting the sick role will foster their career as "a mentally ill person" (Scheff 1984, 1966).

A first arrest on weapons charges may be seen as a rite of passage that brings increased social status among peers. Whereas those outside the deviant group may think that arrest is a deterrent to crime, it may actually encourage a person to continue along a deviant path. Punishments administered by the authorities may even become badges of honor within a deviant community. Similarly, labeling a teenager "bad" for behavior that others think is immoral may actually encourage the behavior to continue because the juvenile may take this as a sign of success as a deviant.

Like anyone else, deviants may experience career mobility—that is, they may move up or down in rank within the deviant community. Male prostitution, for example, is a career organized around a hierarchy of illicit sexual services. Men or boys are recruited into prostitution at different ranks: as street hustlers, bar hustlers, or escorts. Some may become specialists in sadomasochism, cross-dressing, or catering to pederasts—those who molest children sexually—for example. Newcomers often acquire mentors who educate them in the deviant lifestyle. Someone who "learns the ropes" is more likely to continue in a deviant career (Luckenbill 1986).

DEVIANT COMMUNITIES. The preceding discussion indicates an important sociological point: Deviant behavior is not just the behavior of maladjusted individuals;

it often takes place within a group context and involves group response. Some groups are actually organized around particular forms of social deviance; these are called **deviant communities.**

Like subcultures and countercultures, deviant communities maintain their own values, norms, and rewards for deviant behavior. Joining a deviant community closes one off from conventional society and tends to solidify deviant careers, because the deviant individual receives rewards and status from the in-group. Disapproval from the out-group may only enhance one's status within. Deviant communities also create a worldview that solidifies the deviant identity of their members. They may develop symbolic systems such as emblems, forms of dress, publications, and other symbols that promote their identity as a deviant group. Gangs wear their "colors"; prostitutes have their own vocabulary of *tricks* and *johns;* skinheads have their insignia and music. All are examples of deviant communities. Ironically, subcultural norms and values reinforce the deviant label both inside and outside the deviant group, thereby reinforcing the deviant behavior.

Some deviant communities are organized specifically to provide support to those in presumed deviant categories. Groups such as Alcoholics Anonymous, Weight Watchers, and various twelve-step programs help those identified as deviant overcome their deviant behavior. These groups, which can be quite effective, accomplish their mission by encouraging members to accept their deviant identity as the first step to recovery.

FORCES OF SOCIAL CHANGE

Guns and Violence in America

School violence, shootings in the workplace, drive-by-shootings: these are the images of violence in America. Has violence increased over time?

Despite public concerns about violence, the rate of violent crime has decreased. Still, the United States has one of the highest rates of violence among industrialized nations. Violence is not unusual in the United States. The murder rates in the 1930s and 1980s were comparable to those of the early 1990s and, although no official data are available, violence was common in earlier periods as well.

Sociologists emphasize that violence has a social context. It is higher in some regions than others namely in the south and in urban areas. Violence is also more likely against certain groups, particularly young African American men, for whom homicide is the leading cause of death. Violence is growing more rapidly among youth than any other groups—both as victims and as perpetrators.

What can be done about violence? There is not a single answer to such a question. Some suggest that gun control is key to reducing violence; others attribute the cause of violence to family problems. Poverty and unemployment are also strongly related to violence. Some sociologists suggest that the media sensationalizes violence, exaggerating the true extent of violence and creating a "culture of fear" (Best 1999; Glassner 1999). According

to sociologist Barry Glassner, politicians, corporations, and advocacy groups profit from creating a culture of fear and use the media to convey a sense that the nation is wracked by crime, drug abuse, and disease. These fears, according to Glassner, divert attention and financial resources from other problems such as poverty, education, and housing—problems that could be addressed with increased resources.

THE PROBLEM WITH OFFICIAL STATISTICS. Because labeling theorists see deviance as produced by those with the power to assign labels, they question the value of official statistics as indicators of the true extent of deviance. Reported rates of deviant behavior are themselves the product of socially determined behavior, specifically the behavior of identifying what is deviant. Official rates of deviance are produced by people in the social system who define, classify, and record certain behaviors as deviant and others as legitimate. Labeling theorists are more likely to ask how behavior becomes labeled deviant than they are to ask what motivates people to become deviant (Best 2001; Kitsuse and Cicourel 1963). In the aftermath of terrorist attacks on the World Trade Center, officials debated whether to count the deaths of thousands as murder, or as a separate category of terrorism. The decision would change the official rate of deviance by inflating or deflating the reported crime rate of murder in New York City in that year.

Labeling theorists think that official rates of deviance do not reflect the actual commission of crimes or deviant acts. Instead, the official rates reflect social judgments. Consider the example of suicide. Officially reported suicide rates are based on records typically produced in a coroner's office where someone determines and records the cause of death. Suicide carries a stigma, and staff members in a coroner's office possess stereotypes about who is likely to commit suicide that influence how a death is recorded. As a result, a determination of suicide is less likely for upper-class people. Mentally ill people, especially from the working class, are more likely to be recorded as suicides than people not labeled mentally ill. In deference to the family, a terminally ill middle-class person who takes his or her own life may not be recorded as a suicide. Other factors, such as religious affiliation and nationality, as well as unofficial interference by interested parties, may also influence whether a death is recorded as a suicide. As one sociologist has concluded, "The more socially integrated an individual is, the more his significant others will try to avoid having his death categorized as a suicide" (Douglass 1967: 209).

Likewise, when AIDS (acquired immunodeficiency syndrome) first emerged, it was highly stigmatized because of its perceived association with gay men. Obituaries of AIDS victims seldom noted that the death was a result of AIDS. More typically, obituaries reported only that the person died following a "long illness." Official rape rates are underestimates of the actual extent of rape, largely due to victims' reluctance to report. Also, certain instances of rape are less likely to be "counted" as rape by police, such as if the victim is a prostitute, was drunk at the time of the assault, or had a previous relationship with the assailant. Moreover, rapes resulting in death are classified as homicides and therefore do not appear in the official statistics on rape. There is also enough evidence of discriminatory treatment by the police to know that official statistics showing higher arrest rates for African American men tell us as much about police behavior as about the behavior of African American men (Babbie 2001; DeFleur 1975).

LABELING THEORY: STRENGTHS AND WEAKNESSES. The strength of labeling theory is its recognition that the judgments people make about presumably deviant behavior have powerful social effects. Labeling theory does not, however, explain why deviance occurs in the first place. It may illuminate the consequences of a young man's violent behavior, but it does not explain the actual origins of the behavior. Bluntly, it does not explain why some people become deviant and others do not. Although it gives focus to the behaviors and beliefs of officials in the enforcement system, labeling theory does not explain why those officials define some behaviors as deviant or criminal, but not others. This shortcoming in the analysis of deviance has been carefully scrutinized by conflict theorists who place their analysis of deviance within the power relationships of race, class, and gender.

■ *Forms of Deviance*

Although there are many forms of deviance, the sociology of deviant behavior has focused heavily on subjects such as mental illness, social stigmas, and crime. As we review each, you will also see how the different sociological theories about deviance contribute to understanding each subject. In addition, you will see how the social structural context of race, class, and gender relationships shape these different forms of deviance. Race, class, and gender are not just individual attributes; they are patterns of relationships supported by social institutions and social ideologies. Consequently, they are an important part of the social context in which different forms of deviance emerge and from which people make judgments about who is deviant and who is not.

Mental Illness

Sociological explanations of mental illness look to the social systems in which mental illness is defined, identified, and treated, even though it is typical for many to think of mental illness only in psychological terms. This has several implications for understanding mental illness. Functionalist theory suggests, for example, that by recognizing mental illness, society also upholds normative values about more conforming behavior. Symbolic interaction theory tells us that mentally ill people are not necessarily "sick," but are the victims of societal re-actions to their behavior. Some go so far as to say there is no such thing as mental illness, only people's reactions to unusual behavior. From this point of view, people learn faulty self-images and then are cast into the role of patient when they are treated by therapists. Once some-one becomes a "patient," he or she is in the role, as ex-pected by those who reinforce it (Szasz 1974).

DEBUNKING
Society's Myths

Myth: Mental illness is an abnormality best studied by psychologists and physicians.

Sociological perspective: Mental illness follows pat-terns associated with race, class, and gender relations in society and is subject to a significant labeling effect. Those who study and treat mental illness benefit from combining a sociological perspective with both medical and psychological knowledge.

Labeling theory, combined with conflict theory, sug-gests that those people with the fewest resources are most likely to be labeled mentally ill. Women, racial minori-ties, and the poor all suffer higher rates of reported men-tal illness and more serious disorders than groups of higher social and economic status. Furthermore, research over the years has consistently shown that middle- and upper-class persons are more likely to receive some type of psychotherapy for their illness. Poorer individuals and minorities are more likely to receive only physical reha-bilitation and medication, with no accompanying psy-chotherapy (Hollingshead and Redlich 1958).

Sociologists give two explanations for the correlation between social status and mental illness. On the one hand, the stresses of being in a low-income group, being a racial minority, or being a woman in a sexist society contribute to higher rates of mental illness; the harsher social environment is a threat to mental health. On the other hand, the same behavior that is labeled mentally ill for some groups may be tolerated in others. For exam-ple, behavior considered crazy in a homeless woman (who is likely to be seen as "deranged") may be seen as merely eccentric or charming when exhibited by a rich person. To illustrate this, ask yourself what would have happened to a low-income African American man who exhibited the same violent and threatening behavior that many people reported of John Du Pont—the wealthy heir of the Du Pont fortune who shot and killed Olympic cham-pion wrestler Dave Schultz on his estate in 1996. For years, people observed Du Pont's eccentric and crazy be-havior but did nothing about it (Longman 1996).

Patterns of mental illness also reflect gender relations in society. Women have higher rates of mental illness than men, although men and women differ in the kinds of mental illnesses they experience (Horton 1995). Most so-ciologists conclude that the higher rates of mental illness for women stem from the roles women are forced to play in society. Learned personality traits developed by women are joined by other sources of stress that can lead to men-tal illness (Walters 1993). Poverty, unhappy marriages, physical and sexual abuse, the stress of rearing children, and even a high percentage of time doing household work all contribute to higher rates of mental illness for women (Elliott 2001). Labeling theory also suggests that women are more likely than men to be labeled mentally ill be-cause this label is one way that dominant groups can exert social control over others. The frequency with which physicians label women's complaints to be "psychologi-cally grounded" is evidence of this tendency.

Social Stigmas

A **stigma** is an attribute that is socially devalued and discredited. Some stigmas result in people being labeled deviant. The experiences of people who are disabled, dis-figured, or in some other way stigmatized are studied in much the same way as other forms of social deviance. Like other deviants, people with stigmas are stereotyped and defined only in terms of their presumed deviance.

Think, for example, of how disabled people are treated in society. Their disability can become a **master status** (Chapter 4), a characteristic of a person that over-rides all other features of the person's identity (Goffman 1963b). Physical disability can become a master status when other people see the disability as the defining fea-ture of the person; a person with a disability becomes "that blind woman" or "that disabled guy." People with a particular stigma are often seen to be all alike. This may explain why stigmatized individuals of high visibil-ity are often expected to represent the whole group. When Michael J. Fox was found to have Parkinson's dis-ease, he was quickly accepted as a symbolic leader on be-half of research and education about this affliction. Master statuses can also be oppressive—an ever-present possibility when someone is seen as representing his or her entire group in a world of prejudices.

People who suddenly become disabled often have the alarming experience of their new master status rapidly erasing their former identity. They may be treated and seen differently by people they know. A master status may also prevent people from seeing other parts of a per-son. A person with a disability may be assumed to have no meaningful sex life, even if the disability is unrelated to sexual ability or desire. Sociologists have argued that the negative judgments made about people with stigmas tend to confirm the "usualness" of others (Goffman 1963b: 3). For example, when welfare recipients are stigmatized as lazy and undeserving of social support, others are indirectly promoted as industrious and deserving.

Stigmatized individuals are measured against a presumed norm and may be labeled, stereotyped, and discriminated against. In Goffman's words, people with stigmas are perceived to have a *spoiled identity.* Seen by others as deficient or inferior, they are caught in a role imposed by the stigma. They may respond by trying to hide their stigma or by blaming others. What happens, for example, to those who have a sexually transmitted disease? Particularly since this is associated with sexual immorality, there is typically shame and embarrassment; those with a sexually transmitted disease may initially try to conceal that they have it (Nack 2000).

Sometimes, people with stigmas bond with others, perhaps even strangers. This can involve an acknowledgment of "kinship" or affiliation that can be as subtle as an understanding look, a greeting that makes a connection between two people, or a favor extended to a stranger whom the person sees as sharing the presumed stigma. Public exchanges are common between various groups that share certain forms of disadvantage, such as people with disabilities, lesbians and gays, or members of other minority groups.

Substance Abuse: Drugs and Alcohol

As with mental illness and stigmas, sociologists study the social factors that influence drug and alcohol use. Who uses what and why? How are users defined by others? These questions guide sociological research on substance abuse.

One of the first things to notice when thinking about drugs and alcohol is to ask why using some substance is considered deviant and stigmatizing while using others is not. How do such definitions of deviance change over time? Until recently, cigarette smoking was considered normative—indeed, glamorous and sexy. Now, although smoking is still common, it has become more of a negative stigma. Some might say that this change resulted from the known risks of nicotine addiction. But just knowing the risks of smoking is not enough to define it as deviant behavior. Sociologists study how social groups have mobilized to define smoking as deviant, and analyze how the tobacco industry has navigated through the climate of public opinion to maintain the industry's profits (Kall 2002; Brown 2000).

Like cigarettes, alcohol is also a legal drug. Whether one is labeled an alcoholic depends in larger part on the social context in which one drinks—not solely on the amount of alcohol consumed. For years, the businessman's lunch where executives drank two or three martinis was viewed as normative. Drinking from a bottle in a brown bag on the street corner is considered highly deviant; having martinis in a posh bar is seen as cool.

Sociological understandings challenge views of drug and alcohol use as stemming from individual behaviors that lead to substance abuse. Patterns of use vary by factors such as age, gender, and race. Age is one significant predictor of illegal drug use. Young people are more likely to use marijuana and cocaine and binge drink than are people over age 25. Alcohol is more likely to be used by those aged 18 to 34, although the difference here is less than for other drugs.

■ *Crime and Criminal Justice*

The concept of deviance in sociology is a broad one, encompassing many forms of behavior—both legal and illegal, ordinary and unusual. **Crime** is one form of deviance, specifically, behavior that violates specific criminal laws. Not all deviance is crime. Deviance becomes crime when it is designated by the institutions of society as violating a law or laws. *Deviance* is behavior that is recognized as violating rules and norms of society. Those rules may be formal laws, in which case the deviant behavior would be called crime, or informal customs or habits, in which case the deviant behavior would not be called crime.

Criminology is the study of crime from a scientific perspective. Criminologists include social scientists such as sociologists who stress the societal causes of crime, psychologists who stress the personality causes of crime, and political scientists who view crime as being both caused and regulated by the powerful institutions in society.

All the theoretical perspectives on deviance that we examined earlier contribute to our understanding of crime (see Table 6.2). According to the functionalist perspective, crime may be necessary to hold society together—a profound hypothesis. By singling out criminals as socially deviant, others are defined as good. The nightly reporting of crime on television is a demonstration of this sociological function of crime. Conflict theory suggests that disadvantaged groups are more likely to become criminal; it also sees the well-to-do as better able to hide their crimes and to be less likely to be punished. Symbolic interaction helps us understand how people learn to become criminals or come to be accused of criminality even when they may be innocent. Each perspective traces

TABLE 6.2 Sociological Theories of Crime

Functionalist Theory	Symbolic Interaction Theory	Conflict Theory
Societies require a certain level of crime in order to clarify norms.	Crime is behavior that is learned through social interaction.	The lower the social class, the more the individual is forced into criminality.
Crime results from social structural strains within society.	Labeling criminals tends to reinforce rather than deter crime.	Inequalities in society by race, class, gender, and other forces tends to produce criminal activity.
Crime may be functional to society, thus difficult to eradicate.	Institutions with the power to label, such as prisons, produce rather than lessen crime.	Reducing social inequalities in society will reduce crime.

criminal behavior to social conditions rather than only to the intrinsic tendencies or personalities of individuals.

Measuring Crime: How Much Is There?

Is crime increasing in America? One would certainly think so from watching the media. Images of violent crime abound and give the impression that crime is a constant threat and is on the rise. Data on crime actually show that violent crime peaked in 1990, but decreased through the 1990s and leveled off a bit between 1999 and 2001 (see Figure 6.1). Assault and robbery, in particular, decreased quite significantly through the 1990s. Murder and rape remained more constant, though they too showed some decline in the 1990s.

Data about crime come from the Federal Bureau of Investigation (FBI) based on reports from police departments across the nation. The data are distributed annually in the *Uniform Crime Reports* and are the basis for official reports about the extent of crime and its rise and fall over time. These data show that, while media reporting of crime has remained high and about the same, the officially reported rate of crime has decreased.

A second major source of crime data is the National Crime Victimization Surveys published by the Bureau of Justice Statistics in the U.S. Department of Justice. These data are based on surveys in which national samples of people are periodically asked if they have been the victims of one or more criminal acts. These surveys also show that violent crime, including rape, assault, robbery, and murder, declined by 15 percent over the 1990s.

Another problem arises in the attempt to measure crime by means of official statistics. The FBI's *Uniform Crime Reports* stress what are called **index crimes,** which includes the violent crimes of murder, manslaughter, rape, robbery, and aggravated assault plus property crimes of burglary, larceny-theft, and motor vehicle theft. These crimes are committed mostly by individuals who are disproportionately minority and poor. Statistics based on

these offenses do not reflect the crimes that tend to be committed by middle-class and upper-class persons, such as tax violations, insider trading, embezzlement, and other so-called elite crimes. The official statistics provide a relatively inflated picture for index crimes but an underreported picture of elite crimes, giving a biased picture of crime. A final result is, unfortunately, that the public sees the stereotyped "criminal" as a lower-class person, most likely African American or Latino male, not as a middle- or upper-class White person who has committed tax fraud. The official statistics give biased support to the stereotype. This in turn perpetuates the public belief that the "typical" criminal is lower class and minority instead of upper class and nonminority. Criminals, however, can be either (Zuberi 2001).

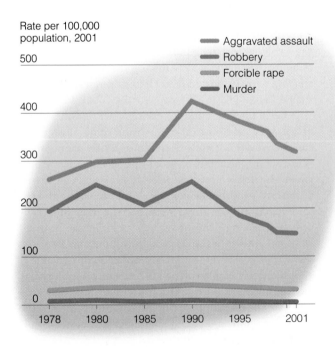

Rate per 100,000 population, 2001

Legend:
- Aggravated assault
- Robbery
- Forcible rape
- Murder

FIGURE 6.1 Violent Crime in the United States

Source: Federal Bureau of Investigation. 2001. *Uniform Crime Reports.* Washington, DC: U.S. Department of Justice.

PERSONAL AND PROPERTY CRIMES. The *Uniform Crime Reports* are subject to the same biases in official statistics mentioned earlier, but they are the major source of information on patterns of crime and arrest, with crimes classified into four categories. *Personal crimes* are violent or nonviolent crimes directed against people. Included in this category are murder, aggravated assault, forcible rape, and robbery. As we see in Figure 6.1, aggravated assault is the most frequently reported personal crime. **Hate crimes** refer to assaults and other malicious acts (including crimes against property) motivated by various forms of social bias, including that based on race, religion, sexual orientation, ethnic/national origin, or disability. This form of crime has been increasing in recent years (U.S. Bureau of Justice Statistics 2002), especially against gays and lesbians. *Property crimes* involve theft of property, without threat of bodily harm. These include burglary (breaking and entering), larceny (the unlawful taking of property, but without unlawful entry), auto theft, and arson. Property crimes are the most frequent criminal infractions. Finally, *victimless crimes* violate laws but are not listed in the FBI's serious crime index. These include illicit activities, such as gambling, illegal drug use, and prostitution, in which there is no complainant. Enforcement of these crimes is typically not as rigorous as the enforcement of crimes against persons or property, although periodic crackdowns occur, such as the current policy of mandatory sentencing for drug violations.

ELITE AND WHITE-COLLAR CRIME. Sociologists use the term *white-collar crime* to refer to criminal activities by people of high social status who commit their crimes in the context of their occupation (Sutherland and Cressey 1978). White-collar crime includes activities such as embezzlement (stealing funds from one's employer), involvement in illegal stock manipulations (insider trading), and a variety of violations of income tax law, including tax evasion. Also included are manipulations of accounting practices to make one's company appear profitable, thus artificially increasing the value of the company's stock.

White-collar crime seldom generates great concern in the public mind—far less than the concern directed at street crime. In terms of total dollars, however, white-collar crime is even more consequential for society. Scandals involving prominent white-collar criminals come to the public eye

© A. Ramey/Photo/Edit

Both "boy" and "girl" gangs use hand signals to demonstrate their uniqueness, membership, and terrories.

occasionally, such as the insider stock sale by media personality Martha Stewart in 2002. Nonetheless, white-collar crime is generally the least investigated and least prosecuted. Some would argue, for example, that tobacco executives are guilty of crimes, given the known causal relationship between smoking and lung disease. From a sociological point of view, one interesting question that stems from studies of deviant behavior is how those who engage in deviance "normalize" their behavior. Most tobacco executives, for example, likely believe they are doing nothing wrong; they are likely to believe they are pursuing good business practices even though that business may have serious consequences for public health and safety. From the perspective of conflict theory, sociologists argue that class bias lies at the heart of what is perceived as criminal behavior.

Organized Crime and Corporate Crime

The structure of crime and criminal activity in the United States often takes on an organized, almost institutional character. This is crime in the form of mob activity and racketeering, and is called *organized crime.* Also, there are crimes committed by bureaucracies, known as *organizational* or *corporate crime.* Both types of crime are so highly organized, complex and sophisticated that they take on the nature of social institutions. In this sense the criminal activity is highly "organized."

ORGANIZED CRIME. Organized crime is crime committed by structured groups typically involving the provision of illegal goods and services to others (A. Block 1991). Organized crime syndicates are typically stereotyped as the Mafia, but it can refer to any group that exercises control over large illegal enterprises, such as the drug trade, illegal gambling, prostitution, weapons smuggling, or money laundering. These organized crime syndicates are often based on racial or ethnic ties, as well as family and kinship ties, with different groups dominating and replacing each other in different criminal "industries."

A key concept in sociological studies of organized crime is that these industries are organized along the same lines as legitimate businesses; indeed, organized crime has taken on a corporate form, such as in the control of the waste industry (Carter 1999). There are likely to be senior partners who control the profits of the business, workers who manage and provide the labor for the business, and clients who buy the services that organized crime provides. In-depth studies of the organized-crime underworld are difficult, owing to its secretive nature and dangers. As organized crime has moved into seemingly legitimate corporate organizations, it is even more difficult to trace, although some sociologists have penetrated underworld networks and provided fascinating accounts of how these crime networks are organized (Block and Scarpitti 1993; Carter 1999). Movies such as *The Godfather* and *Goodfellas,* as well as the popular TV series *The Sopranos,* have tended to glamorize organized crime.

The dons or godfathers that head crime organizations often lead relatively quiet lives in the suburbs and are good family men who attend religious services and spend time with their children. Women have been traditionally excluded from meaningful leadership roles in organized crime, which is distinguished from other kinds of crime by its rigid hierarchy of godfathers, bosses, captains, underlings, hit men, and the like. The financial success of organized crime depends upon monopolistic control of prostitution and drug dealing; infiltration of legitimate business monopolies, such as waste and garbage removal; and dependence upon torture and murder for enforcement. *Racketeering,* the extortion of money from legitimate small and large businesses on a regular basis, is another widespread and well-organized undertaking. *Extortion* is accomplished by forcing business people to buy "protection" for their businesses, or insisting that they purchase products that they do not want or need (Scarpitti et al. 1997; Carter 1999).

CORPORATE CRIME AND DEVIANCE. Corporations and even entire governments may engage in deviance—behavior that can be very costly to society. Sociologists estimate that the costs of corporate crime may be as high as $200 billion every year, dwarfing the take from street crime (roughly $15 billion), which most people imagine is the bulk of criminal activity. Tax cheaters in business alone probably skim $50 billion a year from the IRS, three times the value of street crime. Taken as a whole, the cost of corporate crime is almost 6000 times the amount taken in bank robberies in a given year and eleven times the total amount for all theft in a year (Reiman 2002).

Corporate crime and deviance is wrongdoing that occurs within the context of a formal organization or bureaucracy and is actually sanctioned by the norms and operating principles of the bureaucracy. This can occur within any kind of organization—corporate, educational, governmental, or religious. It exists once deviant behavior becomes institutionalized in the routine procedures of an organization. The recent scandals involving sexual assaults of youths by Catholic priests, and the attempted cover-ups by assigning offending priests to different parishes in different towns or states, constitute examples of corporate, or organizational, crimes. Individuals within the organization may participate in the deviant behavior with little awareness that their behavior is illegitimate. In fact, their actions are likely to be defined as in the best interests of the organization—business as usual. New members who enter the organization learn to comply with the organizational expectations or leave.

In the 1980s, Beech Nut baby foods proudly claimed that their "nutritionists prepare fresh-tasting vegetables, meats, fruits, cereals, and juices without artificial flavoring." Not only was there no artificial flavoring in the company's apple juice, but there were also no apples either. Beech Nut was selling sugar water colored brown to resemble apple juice (Ermann and Lundman 1992). No one ordered plant operations to make fake juice. Instead, the owners insisted that the plant make a stronger return on its investment by cutting corners, and the pursuit of higher profits resulted in corporate crime. Most of the people in the production line probably never knew what was happening.

Sociological studies of corporate deviance show that this form of deviance is embedded in the ongoing and

David F. Meyers, left, former WorldCom controller, and Scott D. Sullivan, its former chief financial officer, being arrested by FBI agents for their role in falsely inflating corporate earnings by means of fraudulent corporate accounting.

routine activities of organizations (Punch 1996; Lee and Ermann 1999). Instead of conceptualizing organizational deviance only as the behavior of bad individuals, sociologists see it as the result of employees following rules and making decisions in more ordinary ways. A recent case in point has been the stock trading and accounting practices of the Enron Corporation of Houston, Texas. These deviant practices led to the downfall of that organization early in 2002. In the summer of 2001, company executives who found company profits and thus their own personal company stock holdings declining in value quickly sold off their own stock and pocketed the resulting money before the stocks declined further in value. At the same time they forbade their own rank-and-file employees from selling their own company stock. The stock held by these unfortunate employees declined to almost nothing over the next several months, thus wiping out the retirement accounts, or "nest eggs," of hundreds of Enron employees. Furthermore, the Enron executives enlisted their own accounting firm, the nationally known firm of Arthur Andersen, to cover up these practices and "cook the books" to conceal illegal stock transactions.

Another recent example of corporate and accounting malfeasance involved the WorldCom Corporation, a telecommunications company of worldwide repute. The company engaged in a multimillion dollar accounting fraud that disguised mounting losses from early in the year 2000 through the summer of 2002. By incorrectly reporting its operating expenses as though they were capital gains—a type of "cooking the books," or illegal ac-

counting—the company was able to inflate the value of its own stock even though its own finances were rapidly deteriorating. Two former executives of WorldCom, chief financial officer Scott D. Sullivan, and controller David F. Myers, were arrested by the FBI. Upon their arrest, the United States Attorney General proclaimed: "Corporate executives who cheat investors, steal earnings, and squander pensions will meet the judgment they fear and the punishment they deserve" (Eichenwald 2002).

Race, Class, Gender, and Crime

Arrest data show a clear pattern of differential arrests along lines of race, gender, and class. To sociologists the central question posed by such data is whether this reflects actual differences in the extent of crime among different groups, or whether this reflects differential treatment by the criminal justice system. The answer is both (D'Alissio and Stolzenberg 2003).

Certain groups are more likely to commit crime than others, because crime is distinctively linked to patterns of inequality in society. Unemployment, for example, is one correlate of crime, as is poverty. In a direct test of the association between inequality and crime, sociologist Ramiro Martinez Jr. (2002, 1996) has explored the connection between rates of violence in Latino communities and the degree of inequality in 111 U.S. cities. His research shows a clear link between the likelihood of lethal violence and the socioeconomic conditions for Latinos in these different cities.

Sociologists use the analysis of socioeconomic conditions to explain the commission of crime, but they also make the important point that prosecution by the criminal justice system is significantly related to patterns of race, gender, and class inequality. We see this in the bias of official arrest statistics, in treatment by the police, in patterns of sentencing, and in studies of imprisonment.

RACE, CLASS, AND CRIME. One of the most important areas of sociological research on crime is the relationship between social class, crime, and race. Arrest statistics show a strong correlation between social class

and crime, the poor being more likely than others to be arrested for crimes. Does this mean that the poor commit more crimes? To some extent, yes. Sociologists have demonstrated a strong relationship between unemployment, poverty, and crime (Scarpitti et al. 1997; Hagan 1993; Britt 1994; M. Smith et al. 1992). The reason is simple: Those who are economically deprived often see no alternative to crime.

Moreover, law enforcement is concentrated in lower-income and minority areas. People who are better off are further removed from police scrutiny and better able to hide their crimes. Although white-collar crime costs so-

---

DOING SOCIOLOGICAL RESEARCH

Bad Boys

How do young African American boys get associated with images of failure and deviance? This is what Ann Ferguson wanted to know when she began her research on young Black boys in an urban school. She became a participant observer in an urban school where for three and one half years she observed how the rules and practices of school discipline "branded" young Black boys as criminally prone.

Ferguson observed children in the 5th and 6th grades. She identified two types of school children whom she calls the *Schoolboys* and the *Troublemakers*. School personnel (teachers, counselors, and staff members) think of the Schoolboys as doing well in school, but see the Troublemakers as always in trouble and "at risk." But, Ferguson argues that the two groups are fundamentally not different: All come from the same neighborhood and from similar family backgrounds. Yet, Ferguson writes, "as African American males, *schoolboys* were always on the brink of being redefined into the *troublemaker* category" (2001: 10).

When children get into trouble, they are sent to a disciplinary room that Ferguson calls "The Punishing Room." For children, the Punishing Room became a place to escape the drudgery of schoolwork, have fun, and actively

challenge school rules. Ironically, it is a place where students proudly acquire a deviant identity—one rooted in their resistance to school authorities. They can make a name for themselves by transgressing school rules. A second room, which students called "The Jailhouse," holds students who are detained after school. The vast majority of students in both "The Punishing Room" and "The Jailhouse" are Black boys. In both places, once labeled as deviant, the boys assert their identities by contesting adult power. As Ferguson writes, "In The Punishing Room, school identities and reputations are constituted, negotiated, challenged and confirmed for African American youth in a process of categorization, reward and punishment, humiliation, and banishment. Children passing through the system are marked and categorized as they encounter state laws, school rules, tests and exams, psychological remedies, screening committees, penalties and punishments, reward and praise. Identities such as worthy, hardworking, devious or dangerous are proffered, assumed, or rejected" (2001: 40–41).

On Ferguson's first day in the school, one school staff member pointed to a young Black boy and said, "That one has a jail-cell with his name on it" (2001: 1). Ferguson's research reveals

the extraordinary power of institutions and the labeling process to create, shape, and regulate deviant identities, particularly for young Black boys.

Questions to Consider

1. Make a list of all the different cliques that were part of your high school. What are their names? What characteristics and behaviors were associated with each? What does this tell you about *labeling theory*?
Keyword: labeling theory

2. When you think about the groups who were considered "bad" in your high school, what was the racial, social class, and gender make-up of the group? How did social stereotypes about either race, class, or gender (or all three) influence what people thought about this group? How might students work to overcome such stereotypes?
Keyword: race and punishment

We have included InfoTrac College Edition keywords at the end of each question to make it easier for you to find more to read on these topics. Go to **www.infotrac-college.com,** an online library, to begin your search.

SOURCE: Ferguson, Ann Arnett. 2001. *Bad Boys: Public Schools in the Making of Black Masculinity.* Ann Arbor: University of Michigan Press.

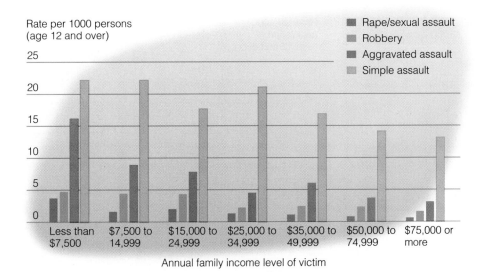

Rate per 1000 persons
(age 12 and over)

- Rape/sexual assault
- Robbery
- Aggravated assault
- Simple assault

Annual family income level of victim

FIGURE 6.2
Victimization by Crime:
A Class Phenomenon

SOURCE: U.S. Bureau of Justice Statistics. 2003. *Personal Crimes, 2001.* Washington, DC: U.S. Department of Justice.

ciety more than street crime, it often goes undetected. When and if white-collar criminals are prosecuted and convicted, they typically receive light sentences—often a fine or community service instead of imprisonment. Middle- and upper-income people may be perceived as less in need of imprisonment, because they likely have a job and high-status people to testify for their good character. White-collar crime is simply perceived as less threatening than crimes by the poor. Class also predicts who will be most likely victimized by crime, with those at the highest ends of the socioeconomic scale least likely to be victims of violent crime (see Figure 6.2).

Paralleling the correlation between class and crime shown by arrest data is a strong relationship between race and crime. Minorities constitute 25 percent of the population in the United States but are more than 33 percent of the people arrested for property crimes and almost 50 percent of the people arrested for violent crimes. African Americans, and Hispanics, are more than twice as likely to be arrested for a crime than are Whites. Native Americans and Asians are exceptions, with both groups having relatively low rates of arrest for crime (see Table 6.3) (Federal Bureau of Investigation 2002).

These data may seem to reinforce racial stereotypes, but sociologists have learned not to take these statistics at face value. Instead, they consider how poor and rich communities are policed and the social origins of crime to explain the differences in criminal behavior among groups. What do they find? Police have wide latitude in deciding when to enforce laws and make arrests. Their discretion is greatest when dealing with minor offenses, such as disorderly conduct. Sociological research has shown that police discretion is strongly influenced by class and race judgments, just as labeling theory would predict (Avakame et al. 1999). In addition, minority

communities are policed much more intensively, which leads to more frequent arrests of the residents.

A research report on juvenile offenders demonstrates that Black and Latino youths with no prior criminal record are treated far more severely in the juvenile justice system than Whites of comparable social class, also with no prior criminal record. Minority youths are more likely to be arrested, held in jail, sent to juvenile or adult court for trial, convicted, and given longer prison terms. The racial disparities in the juvenile court system are magnified with each additional step into the justice system. The report concludes that these racial disparities are not in overt discrimination on the part of prosecutors, judges, and other court personnel, but instead in the stereotypes that these decision makers rely on at each point in the juvenile justice system. Being Black, wearing low-hung baggy pants, and sporting dreadlocks is likely to get a person quickly through the various stages of the juvenile justice system and then quickly into prison (Butterfield 2000).

Bearing in mind the factors that affect the official rates of arrest and conviction—bias of official statistics, influence of powerful individuals, discrimination in patterns of arrest, differential policing—there remains evidence that the actual commission of crime varies by race. Why? Again, sociologists find a compelling explanation in social structural conditions. Racial minority groups are far more likely than Whites to be poor, unemployed, and living in single-parent families. These social facts are all predictors of a higher rate of crime. Note, too, as Figure 6.3 shows, that African Americans are generally more likely to be victimized by crime.

GENDER AND CRIME. Until recently, most sociological research on crime and deviance focused on men. Women's crime was seen as uninteresting or unimportant

TABLE 6.3 Arrests by Race[1,2]

Crime	White	Black	American Indian	Asian/ Pacific Islander
Total arrests	69.7	27.9	1.2	1.2
Murder	48.7	48.8	1.0	1.5
Forcible rape	63.7	34.1	1.1	1.1
Robbery	44.2	53.9	0.6	1.2
Aggravated assault	63.5	34.0	1.1	1.3
Burglary	69.4	28.4	0.9	1.2
Larceny-theft	66.7	30.4	1.3	1.6
Motor vehicle theft	55.4	41.6	1.1	1.9
Arson	76.4	21.7	0.9	1.0
Forgery	68.0	30.0	0.6	1.4
Embezzlement	63.6	34.1	0.4	1.9
Vandalism	75.9	21.6	1.4	1.1
Prostitution	58.0	39.5	0.8	1.7
Sex offenses (not rape or prostitution)	74.4	23.2	1.1	1.3
Driving under influence	88.2	9.6	1.3	0.9
Suspicion	69.0	29.6	0.3	1.2

SOURCE: Federal Bureau of Investigation. 2002. *Uniform Crime Reports.* Washington, DC: U.S. Department of Justice, p. 234.

[1]As percentage of all arrests, 2001.

[2]Hispanics appear in any of these categories.

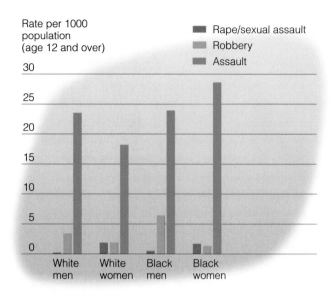

FIGURE 6.3 Crime Victimization (by race and gender)

SOURCE: U.S. Bureau of Justice Statistics. 2003. *Sourcebook of Criminal Justice Statistics.* Washington, DC: U.S. Department of Justice. **www.bjs.gov**

and studied only with the stereotyped vision of women as accomplices to men, or as prostitutes. Newer research focuses on the analysis of crime and deviance among women (Belknap 2001).

Generally, women commit fewer crimes than men. Why? Although the number of women arrested for crime has increased slightly in recent years, the numbers are still small relative to men, except for a few crimes, such as fraud, embezzlement, and prostitution. Some argue that women's lower crime participation reflects their socialization into less risk-taking roles; others say that women commit crimes that are extensions of their gender roles—this would explain why the largest number of arrests of women are for crimes such as shoplifting, credit card fraud, and passing bad checks.

Nonetheless, women's participation in crime has been increasing in recent years. Sociologists relate this to several factors. Women are now more likely to be employed in jobs that present opportunities for crimes, such as property theft, embezzlement, and fraud. Violent crime by women has also increased notably since the early 1980s, possibly because the images that women have of themselves are changing, making new behaviors possi-

ble. Most significantly, crime by women is related to their continuing disadvantaged status in society. Just as crime is linked to socioeconomic status for men, so it is for women (Belknap 2001; Miller 1986).

Despite recent achievements, women remain in disadvantaged low-wage positions in the labor market. At the same time, changes in the social structure of families mean that more women are economically responsible for their children, without the economic support of men. Women often have to turn to illegitimate means of support, a trend that may be exacerbated by reductions in welfare support.

Women are also less likely than men to be victimized by crime, although victimization by crime among women varies significantly by race and age. Black women are much more likely than White women to be victims of violent crime; young Black women are especially vulnerable. Divorced, separated, and single women are more likely than married women to be crime victims. Regardless of their actual rates of victimization, women are more fearful of crime than men. Minority women and widowed, separated, and divorced women are the most fearful. Women's fear of crime increases with age even though the likelihood of victimization decreases with age, a fact that researchers attribute to the elderly's increased sense of vulnerability (Joseph 1997; Gordon and Riger 1989; Weinrath and Gartrell 1996). Women's fear of crime, sociologist Esther Madriz argues, results from an ideology that depicts women as needing protection and identifies public spaces as reserved for men. Women's fear of crime can be seen as a system of social control that keeps women from enjoying the rights of full citizenship (Madriz 1997).

For all women, victimization by rape is probably the greatest fear. Although rape is the most underreported crime, until recently, it has been one of the fastest growing—something criminologists explain as the result of a greater willingness to report *and* an actual increase in the extent of rape (Federal Bureau of Investigation 2002). More than 200,000 rapes (including attempted rapes) are reported to the police annually. Officials estimate that this is probably only about one in four of all rapes committed. Many women are reluctant to report rape because they fear the consequences of having the criminal justice system question them. Rape victims are least likely to report the assault when the assailant is someone known to them, even though a large number of rapes are committed by someone the victim knows.

A disturbingly frequent form of rape is *date rape*—rape committed by an acquaintance or someone the victim has just met. The extent of date rape is difficult to measure. The Bureau of Justice Statistics finds that 3 percent of college women experience rape or attempted rape in a given college year; 13 percent report being stalked (Fisher et al. 2001). A substantial amount of research finds that date rape is linked to men's acceptance of various rape myths (such as believing that a woman's "no" means "yes"), the use of alcohol, and the peer support

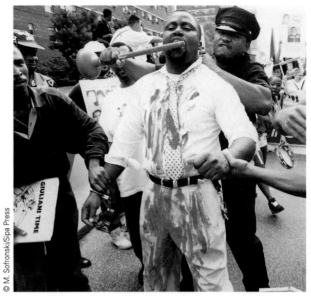

© M. Sofronski/Sipa Press

Social movements can often call public attention to social issues, such as the protests of minority communities against police brutality.

that men receive in some all-male groups and organizations, such as fraternities (Ullman et al. 1999; Boeringer 1999; Belknap, Fisher, and Cullen 1999).

Sociological research on rape shows that it is clearly linked to gender relations in society. Rape is an act of

Images of Violent Crime

The media routinely drive home two points to the consumer: First, that violent crime is always high and may be increasing over time; and second, that there is much *random* violence constantly around us. The media bombard us with stories of "wilding," in which bands of youths kill random victims. Many of us think "road rage" is extensive and completely random. Most of us are now aware of violence in some high schools, where students armed with automatic weapons kill their fellow students. The media vividly and routinely report such occurrences as pointless, at random, and probably increasing.

The evidence shows that violent crime in the United States, while it increased during the 1970s and 1980s,

nonetheless began to decrease in 1990 and continues to decrease nationally through the present. For example, both robbery and physical assaults have declined dramatically since 1990 (see Figure 6.1). Yet according to one source (Best 1999), the media have consistently given a picture that violent crime has increased during this same period, and furthermore, that the violence is completely unpatterned and random.

No doubt there are occasions when victims are indeed picked at random. But the statistical rule of randomness could not possibly explain what has come to be called *random violence*, a vision of patternless chaos that is advanced by the media. If randomness truly ruled, *then each of us would have*

an equal chance of being a victim—and of being a criminal. This is assuredly not the case. As Best notes, the notion of random violence, and the notion that it is increasing, ignores virtually everything that criminologists, psychologists, sociologists, and extensive research studies know about crime: It is highly patterned and significantly predictable, beyond sheer chance, by taking into account the social structure, social class, location, race–ethnicity, gender, labeling, age, and other such variables and forces in society that affect both criminal and victim. The broad picture then is clearly not conveyed constantly in the media: Criminal violence is not increasing, but decreasing; and it is not random, but highly patterned and even predictable.

aggression against women, and as feminists have argued, it stems from learned gender roles that teach men to be sexually aggressive. This is reflected in sociological research on convicted rapists who think they have done nothing wrong and who believe, despite having overpowered their victims, that the women asked for it (Scully 1990). Feminists have argued that the causes of rape lie in women's status in society—that women are treated as sexual objects for men's pleasure. The relationship between women's status and rape is also reflected in data revealing who is most likely to become a rape victim. African American women, Latinas, and poor women have the highest likelihood of being raped, as do women who are single, divorced, or separated. Young women are also more likely to be rape victims than older women (U.S. Bureau of Justice Statistics 2003). Sociologists interpret these patterns to mean that the most powerless women are also most subject to this form of violence.

The Criminal Justice System

Sociological studies consistently find patterns of differential treatment by the institutions that respond to deviance and crime in society. Whether it is in the police

---

TAKING ON SOCIAL ISSUES

Should Drugs Be Decriminalized?

U.S. drug policy has largely focused on prohibition and enforcement, thus laws are in place requiring mandatory sentencing for drug possession. An alternative approach would be legalizing drugs like marijuana, cocaine, and heroin, focusing on treatment, not criminalization. The debate over punishment versus decriminalization engages competing values and strong political differences. What does sociological research contribute to this debate—a debate largely muted because of the political climate of zero tolerance?

Researchers Robert MacCoun and Peter Reuter point out that prohibiting drugs has its own harmful results, including increased crime, corruption, and disease (such as from dirty needles). These harms are disproportionately borne by the poor and by racial minorities. Some argue that drugs should be prohibited because of the dangers they carry. Comparable arguments are seldom made about alcohol and cigarette use—drugs that are equally dangerous and more widely used. Would legalizing drugs increase use? Would people be less likely to seek treatment because use could be more easily concealed if not policed? Would legalization increase workplace intoxication? Would legitimate businesses try to increase their profits by promoting more drug use?

These complex questions show the importance of sound research to guide drug policy. MacCoun and Reuter examined drug policy in the European nations where enforcement is far less aggressive than in the United States, with the purpose of suggesting more effective policies in the United States. Their studies revealed the following:

- There is no research linking strong enforcement and drug prevalence; however, eliminating criminal sanctioning has little or no effect on prevalence of drug use.

- In Holland, where there are no penalties for possessing small amounts of marijuana, use has declined since 1976 when marijuana was decriminalized. There has, however, been increased use by youth in very recent years. This is probably not caused by decriminalization per se; other factors influence increasing usage by young people.

- Eliminating criminal penalties significantly reduces costs in the criminal justice system.

- Allowing legal access to drugs eliminates some forms of harm (mostly those associated with enforcement) and reduces some other harms (such as needle sharing and overdoses), but does not eliminate addictive behavior and its impact.

- Restrictions on other drugs (cigarettes in particular) are compromised by industries that use political contributions to influence policy and that aggressively promote drug use.

MacCoun and Reuter conclude that there is no simple policy to address the complexities of drug use. Yet, based on the research evidence, they support legalizing marijuana when used in small amounts. Given their findings—and the public issues surrounding drug use—what sociological considerations do you think should influence the formation of drug policy?

Taking Action

Go to the Taking Action exercise on the companion Web site at **sociology.wadsworth.com /andersen_taylor/essen3e** to learn more about an organization that addresses this topic.

SOURCE: MacCoun, Robert J., and Peter Reuter. 2001. *Drug War Heresies: Learning from Other Vices, Times, and Place.* New York: Cambridge University Press.

station, the courts, or prison, the factors of race, class, and gender are highly influential in the administration of justice in this society. Those in the most disadvantaged groups are more likely to be defined and identified as deviant, independently of their behavior, and, having encountered these systems of authority, are more likely to be detained and arrested, found guilty, and punished.

THE POLICING OF MINORITIES.

There is little question that minority communities are policed more heavily than White neighborhoods; moreover, policing in minority communities has a different effect from that in White, middle-class communities. To middle-class Whites, the presence of the police is generally reassuring, but for African Americans and Latinos, an encounter with a police officer can be terrifying. Regardless of what

they are doing at the time, minority people, men in particular, are perceived as a threat, especially if they are observed in communities where they "don't belong."

Racial profiling has recently come to the public's attention, although it is a practice that has a long history. Often referred to half in jest as the offense of "DWB," or "driving while Black," **racial profiling** on the part of a police officer is the use of race alone as the criterion for deciding whether to stop and detain someone on suspicion of their having committed a crime. The police argue that racial profiling is justified because a high proportion of Blacks and Hispanics commit crimes. Although the crime rate for Blacks and Hispanics is higher than that of Whites, race is a particularly bad basis for suspicion because the vast majority of Blacks and Hispanics, like the vast majority of Whites, do not commit any crime at all.

SOCIOLOGY IN PRACTICE

Stopping Date Rape

Date rape, also known as acquaintance rape, has been widely acknowledged as a social problem. Sociological research has exposed a number of myths about rape, including the myth that most rapes are committed by strangers. The research done by sociologists and other social scientists on the subject of rape has been used by organizations that provide information to college students about how they can avoid date rape. The Association of American Colleges (AAC), for example, has produced a pamphlet for students intended to educate them about the occurrence of date rape and to give them strategies to avoid it. Their advice has also been informed by sociological research about gender and power. Understand that victims do not "cause" date rape, but the AAC suggests that women can do things to keep themselves out of precarious situations. Many of their recommendations stem from understanding the dynamics of gender relations. Here are some of their suggestions for women:

- Do not do anything you do not want to do just to be popular or pleasant or to avoid a scene.

- Be aware of situations in which you do not feel comfortable or where you may be at risk—for example, large parties where men greatly outnumber women.
- Avoid putting yourself in a vulnerable position. Have your own transportation or money to get home, if needed.
- Examine your attitudes about money and power. If a date pays for you, does that influence your ability to say "no"?
- Avoid falling for lines like, "You would if you loved me." Someone who loves you will respect your feelings and choices. Giving in, even if you do not want to, makes it difficult to argue that a rape was not consensual.
- If things start to get out of hand, protest loudly, leave, and go for help.
- Be aware that alcohol and drugs are often involved in acquaintance rape. They compromise your ability to make responsible decisions. If you choose to drink, do not rely on others to take care of you.
- Understand that it is never OK for someone to force himself on you,

even if you are drunk or have had sex with the person before. If you do not consent, it is rape.

Critical Thinking Exercises

1. Surveys find that men and women differ significantly in their acceptance of rape myths. Men are more likely than women to think that women's behavior increases their risk of rape. How would you explain this gender difference in acceptance of rape myths and how does it influence the prosecution of date rape?

2. What do you think tend to be social characteristics, if any (in terms of social class, race–ethnicity, education, religion, age, others) of men who are most likely to engage in date rape? What do some of your friends and associates think? To what extent do women and men differ in their answer to this question?

SOURCE: Adapted from Hughes, Jean O'Gorman, and Bernice R. Sandler. 1987. "'Friends' Raping Friends." Washington, DC: Project on the Education and Status of Women, American Association of Colleges. Also adopted from Greenfield, Laurence A. 1996. *Child Victimizers: Violent Offenders and Their Victims.* Washington, DC: U.S. Bureau of Justice Statistics.

Annually at least 90 percent of all African Americans are *not* arrested. That means on any given day, there is roughly a 90 percent probability that an African American in a car has not committed a crime, which leaves a 10 percent chance that the African American in the car has actually committed a crime. Nonetheless, *eight out of every ten* automobile searches carried out by state troopers on the New Jersey Turnpike over ten years were in vehicles driven by Blacks and Hispanics; the vast majority of these searches turned up no evidence of contraband or crimes of any sort (Kocieniewski and Hanley 2000).

Racial minorities are more likely than the rest of the population to be victims of excessive use of force by the police, also called police brutality. Studies show that most cases of police brutality involve minority citizens and that there is usually no penalty for the officers involved. Moreover, showing a disrespectful attitude is just as likely to generate police brutality as posing a serious bodily threat to the police (Lersch and Feagin 1996). Increasing the number of minority police officers has some effect on how the police treat minorities. Cities where African Americans head the police department show a concurrent decline in police brutality complaints, an increase in minority police and minority recruitment, and in some cases, a decrease in crime. Simply increasing the number of African Americans in police departments does not, however, reduce crime dramatically, because it does not change the material conditions that create crime to begin with (Cashmore 1991).

THINKING SOCIOLOGICALLY

Have you ever been the victim of what you suspected was *racial profiling*? When it happened, were you in a car or on foot? Was it night or day? Think about some of the other circumstances existing at the time, such as the neighborhood you were in or near. What role do you think your own race had, or did not have, in the incident?

RACE AND SENTENCING. What happens once minority citizens are arrested for a crime? On arraignment, bail is set higher for African Americans and Latinos than for Whites, and minorities have less success with plea bargains. Extensive research finds that, once on trial, minority defendants are found guilty more often than White defendants. At sentencing, African Americans and Hispanics are likely to get longer sentences than Whites, even when they are the same as Whites on such things as prior arrests and socioeconomic background. Young African American men as well as Latino men are sentenced more harshly than any other group, and once sentenced, they are less likely to be released on probation (Steffensmeier and Demuth 2000; Mauer 1999; Steffens-

meier et al. 1998; Chambliss and Taylor 1989; Bridges and Crutchfield 1988). Any number of factors influence judgments about sentencing, including race of the judge, severity of the crime, race of the victim, and the gender of the defendant, but throughout these studies, race is shown to consistently matter—and matter a lot.

DEBUNKING
Society's Myths

Myth: The criminal justice system treats all people according to the neutral principles of law.

Sociological perspective: Race, class, and gender continue to have an influential role in the administration of justice. For example, even when convicted of the same crime as Whites, African American and Latino male defendants with the *same* prior arrest record as Whites are more likely to be arrested, sentenced, and to be sentenced for longer terms than White defendants.

Racial discrimination is particularly evident with regard to the death penalty. Currently, of the approximately 3500 prisoners on death row, 42 percent are Black; 98.5 percent are men (U.S. Bureau of Justice Statistics 2002). Research shows that when Whites and minorities commit the same crime against a White victim, minorities are more likely to receive the death penalty. African American men accused of raping White women are the group most likely to receive the death penalty. African Americans who kill Whites are also three times more likely to get the death penalty than those who kill African Americans (Paternoster 2003; Keil and Vito 1995).

PRISONS: DETERRENCE OR REHABILITA-TION? Racial minorities account for more than half of the federal and state male prisoners in the United States. Blacks have the highest rates of imprisonment, followed by Hispanics, then Native Americans and Asians. (Native Americans and Asian Americans together are less than 1 percent of the total prison population.) Hispanics are the fastest growing minority group in prison (U.S. Bureau of Justice Statistics 2002). Native Americans, though a small proportion of the prison population, are still overrepresented in prisons. In theory, the criminal justice system is supposed to be unbiased, able to objectively weigh guilt and innocence. The reality is that the criminal justice system reflects the racial and class stratification and bias in society.

The United States and Russia have the highest rate of incarceration in the world (see Figure 6.4). In the United States, the rate of imprisonment has been rapidly growing (see Figure 6.5). By all signs, the population of state and federal prisons continues to grow, with the popula-

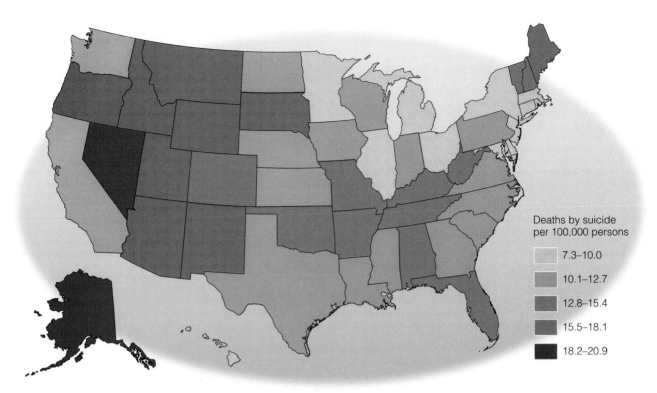

MAP 6.1 Mapping America's Diversity: Suicide Rates by State
Many factors can influence the suicide rate in different contexts. **What are some of the social facts about different regions that might affect the different rates of suicide you see in this map?**

DATA: U.S. Census Bureau. 2001. *Statistical Abstract of the United States, 2001.* Washington, DC: U.S. Government Printing Office, p. 83.

tion in prisons exceeding the capacity of the facilities. The cost to the nation of keeping people behind bars is at least $130 billion (U.S. Bureau of Justice Statistics 2002).

The rate of prison growth in the United States has been so high in recent years that a new trend has emerged: the operation of prisons by private companies. Running corrections systems is now big business, and the "prison market" is expected to more than double in years ahead. For those looking for a business investment, running a prison is a good proposition; as one business publication argued, it's like running a hotel with 100 percent occupancy, booked for years in the future!

The privatization of prisons raises new questions for social policy because, in the interest in running a profit center, prison managers may overcrowd prisons, reduce staffing, and cut back on food, medical care, or staff training. What may be sound business practice can result in less humane treatment of prisoners—locked away from the eyes of the public. Investigators are beginning to see other costs to privatization: The rate of violence in private prisons is higher than in state facilities, and because the private prisons receive money from the state to house

prisoners, there is financial incentive to keep people in prison longer—at the taxpayers' expense (Bates 1998).

Why is there such growth in the prison population when the crime rate has been declining? A major reason for the increasing number of individuals behind bars is the increased enforcement of drug offenses and the mandatory sentencing that has been introduced. Nearly one-quarter of those in state prisons are serving a drug sentence. Sixty percent of federal prisoners are serving drug sentences, more than doubling since 1980. Although the number of drug offenders has grown dramatically, so has the number of violent offenders (U.S. Bureau of Justice Statistics 2002; Mumola and Beck 1997).

The number of women behind bars has also increased at a faster rate than for men, although the numbers of women in prison are small by comparison. Women are only 8 percent of all state and federal prisoners (U.S. Bureau of Justice Statistics 2002). Like men, three-fourths of women in federal prisons are there because of drug offenses; often they have participated in these crimes by going along with the behavior of their boyfriends (Miller 1986). The typical woman in prison is a poor, young minority who

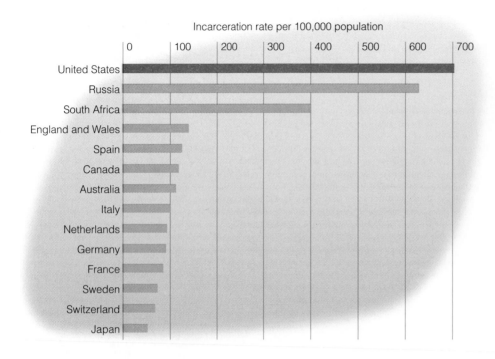

Incarceration rate per 100,000 population

FIGURE 6.4
Incarceration Rates
for Selected Nations

SOURCE: © The Sentencing Project. 2003. Washington, DC:
www.sentencingproject.org
Walmsley, Roy, *World Prison Population List* (2nd ed). United Kingdom Home Office Research, Development and Statistics Directorate, July 2000.

dropped out of high school, is not married, and has two or more children. Of all women prisoners, about two-thirds have been victims of sexual abuse. Women prisoners are also more likely than men to be positive for HIV-infection (Greenfeld and Snell 1999).

The United States is putting offenders in prison at a record pace. Is crime being deterred? Or are prisoners being rehabilitated? If the deterrence argument were correct, we would expect that increasing the risk of imprisonment would lower the rate of crime. For example, we would expect drug use to decline as enforcement of drug laws increases. In the past few years, there has been a marked increase in drug law enforcement, but not the expected decrease in drug use. Although the use of drugs did decline slightly overall, particularly among young people, there has been an increase among Black Americans and inner-city youth—those most likely to feel the crackdown of increased enforcement (Mauer 1999). Using drugs as an example, it appears that the threat of imprisonment does not deter crime.

There is also little evidence that the criminal justice system rehabilitates offenders. Using drugs as the example again, only about 20 percent who are imprisoned for drug offenses ever receive drug treatment. Although the nation is getting "tough on crime," it is doing little to see that offenders do not continue to commit drug crimes once they are released from prison.

In general, prisons seem neither to deter nor rehabilitate offenders. Prisons certainly do nothing to address the societal problems known to promote criminal activity. They concentrate on individual wrongdoers, not on the social structural causes of crime. Although there has been an enormous increase in the number of prisons built and the number of people in prison, it appears that imprisonment is doing little to solve the problem of crime.

If the criminal justice system fails to reduce crime, what does it do? Some radical sociologists contend that the criminal justice system is not meant to reduce crime, but has other functions, namely to reinforce an image of crime as a threat from the poor and from racial groups. The prison experience is a demeaning one, poorly suited to training prisoners in marketable skills or to letting them repay their debt to society. Rather than teaching prisoners self-control and self-direction, prisons deny inmates the least control over their everyday life (Reiman

Prison overcrowding has become common across the United States, putting a strain on public resources and diverting funds from other uses.

Number of
inmates (thousands)

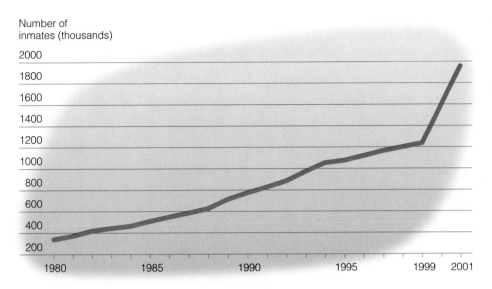

FIGURE 6.5 State
and Federal Prison
Population, 1980–2001

SOURCE: U.S. Bureau of Justice
Statistics. 2002. "Prison Statistics."
**www.ojp.usdoj.gov/bjs/
prisons.htm**

2002). In the end, prisons seem, at least in some cases, to refine criminals rather than rehabilitate them.

▪ *Terrorism as International Crime: A Global Perspective*

Crime now crosses international borders and has become global. Terrorism is an example of the globalization of crime. The morning of Tuesday, September 11, 2001 was not expected to be any different from other early fall mornings. However, at approximately 8:45 A.M., the world stood still with images of a civilian airplane crashing into the north tower of the World Trade Center in New York City. Many at that moment assumed that the incident was nothing more than an accident by a pilot who might have lost consciousness or had a mechanical failure. This was a short-lived assumption. At 9:03 A.M., the second plane crashed into the south tower of the World Trade Center, leaving no doubt that this constituted a terrorist attack on the United States. This was confirmed a short time later by reports that another airplane had crashed into the Pentagon, while still another hijacked plane had crashed in Pennsylvania. Virtually everyone in the United States now remembers where they were and what they were doing during those horrible moments.

The FBI defines **terrorism** as the unlawful use of force or violence against persons or property to intimidate or coerce a government or population in furtherance of political

Threats of terrorism, such as bioterrorism, have resulted in increased security and countermeasures, particularly in urban areas.

AP/World Wide Photos

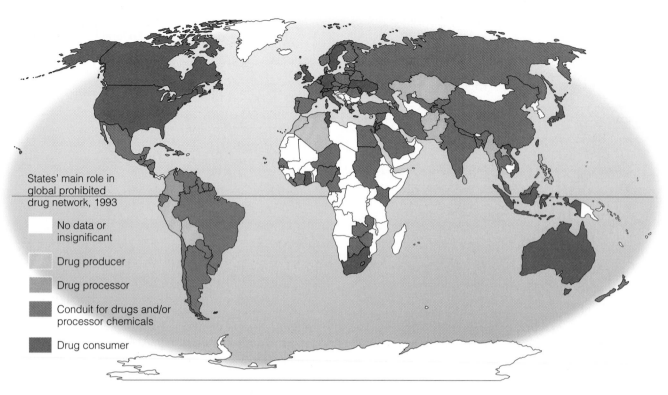

MAP 6.2 Viewing Society in Global Perspective: The Golden Fix
Drug trafficking is an international business, with diverse nations having different roles in what could be described as a global organization. **How does this global perspective change the assumption that drug abuse results from individual deviance?**

SOURCE: "The Golden Fix" from *State of the World Atlas,* 5th ed. by Michael Kidron and Ronald Segal. Copyright © 1995 by Michael Kidron and Ronald Segal, text. Copyright © 1995 by Myriad Editions Limited, maps and graphics. Used by permission of Viking Penguin, a division of Penguin Group (USA) Inc. Putnam Inc.

or social objectives (Jucha 2002). Thus, terrorism is a crime that violates both international and domestic laws. It is a crime that crosses national borders and its understanding requires a global perspective. The origins of modern terrorism are historically traceable from Western European ideology to the Russian Revolution, and then to the incorporation of Russian Revolutionary thought in the nationalist struggle in Ireland. Contrary to what many think, the origins of international terrorism go back further in history than the Israel-Palestine conflict, and farther back than Osama bin Laden's terrorist organization, al-Qaeda.

Terrorism is globally linked to other forms of international crime. A case in point was Osama bin Laden's role in the international opium trade. Afghanistan, where bin Laden's terrorist al-Qaeda organization was headquartered, was the world's largest grower of opium-producing poppies. It is suspected that profits from the international drug trade helped finance the September 11 terrorist attacks. Therefore a global perspective on crime involves recognizing the global basis of some international crime networks that cross national borders (Binns 2003).

Many nations have long experienced terrorism in the form of bombings, hijackings, suicide attacks, and other ter-

rorist crimes. But the attacks of September 11 focused the world's attention on the problem of terrorism in new ways, including increased fears of **bioterrorism**—the form of terrorism involving the dispersion of chemical or biological substances intended to cause widespread disease and death. Fears of bioterrorism were exacerbated in the United States with a threat of the spread of anthrax. This exceptionally deadly poison capable of causing virtually instant death upon inhaling the spores was found in the mail of offices of Congress, the Postal Service, the Supreme Court, and other locations, resulting in the deaths of several persons.

Another form of terrorism and thus cause for international concern is **cyberterrorism,** the use of the computer to commit one or more terrorist acts. Terrorists may use computers in a number of ways. Data-destroying computer viruses may be implanted electronically in an enemy's computer. Another use would be to employ "logic bombs" that lie dormant for years until they are electronically instructed to overwhelm a computer system. The use of the Internet to serve the needs of international terrorists has already become a reality (Jucha 2002).

Without understanding the political, economic, and social relations from which terrorist groups originate, terrorist acts seem like the crazed behavior of violent single individuals. Although sociologists in no way excuse such acts, they look to the social structure of conflicts from which terrorism emerges as the cause of such criminal and deviant behavior. Even then, terrorism is not only the work of international extreme groups, as witnessed by the bombing of the Oklahoma City federal buildings in 1995. For this terrorist act, two White male U.S. citizens were tried and convicted, one of whom was executed. Terrorism, whether domestic or international, is best understood not only as individual insanity, but also as a politically, economically, and socially oriented form of violence.

■ *Chapter Summary*

■ *How do sociologists conceptualize and explain deviance?*

Deviance is behavior that is recognized as violating expected rules and norms and that should be understood in the social context in which it occurs. Psychological explanations of deviance place the cause of deviance primarily within the individual. Sociologists emphasize the total social context in which deviance occurs. Sociologists see deviance as the result of group, not individual, behavior.

■ *What does sociological theory contribute to the study of deviance?*

Functionalist theory sees deviance as functional for the society because it affirms what is acceptable by defining what is not. *Structural strain theory,* a type of functionalist theory, predicts that societal inequalities actually force the individual into deviant behavior. *Conflict theory* explains deviance as a consequence of unequal power relationships and inequality in society. *Symbolic interaction theory* explains deviance as the result of meanings people give to various behaviors. *Differential association theory,* a type of symbolic interaction theory, interprets deviance as behavior learned through social interaction with other deviants. *Labeling theory,* also a type of symbolic interaction theory, argues that societal reactions to behavior produce deviance with some groups having more power than others to assign deviant labels to people.

■ *What are the major forms of deviance?*

Mental illness, stigma, and substance abuse are major forms of deviance studied by sociologists, although deviance is comprised of many different forms of behavior. Sociological explanations of mental illness focus on the social context in which mental illness develops and is treated. Social *stigmas* are attributes that are socially devalued. Substance abuse includes alcohol and drug abuse, but is not limited to these two forms.

■ *What are the connections between inequality, deviance, and crime?*

While *deviance* is violation of norms and rules of society, *crime* is a type of deviance—deviance which violates specific, formal laws of society. Sociological studies of crime analyze the various types of crimes, such as elite crime, organized crime, corporate crime, and personal and property crimes. Many types of crimes are underreported, such as rape, and also certain elite and corporate crimes. Sociologists study the conditions, including race, class, and gender inequality, that produce crime and shape how different groups are treated by the criminal justice system, such as showing group differences in sentencing.

■ *How is globalization affecting the development of deviance and crime?*

International *terrorism* is a crime, and crime is thus global. Other global crimes of significance are *bioterrorism* and *cyberterrorism.* Osama bin Laden's al-Qaeda organization, centered in Afghanistan, is central to the international drug trade.

■ *Key Terms*

altruistic suicide 154
anomic suicide 154
anomie 153
bioterrorism 178
crime 163
criminology 163
cyberterrorism 178
deviance 149
deviant career 159
deviant communities 160
deviant identity 158
differential association theory 157
egoistic suicide 154

elite deviance 156
hate crime 165
index crimes 164
labeling theory 158
master status 162
medicalization of deviance 152
racial profiling 173
social control 156
social control agents 156
social control theory 155
stigma 162
structural strain theory 154
terrorism 178

■ *Researching Society with MicroCase Online*

You can see the results of actual research by using the Wadsworth MicroCase® Online feature available to you. This feature allows you to look at some of the results from national surveys, census data, and some other data sources. You can explore this easy-to-use feature on your own, but try this example. Suppose you want to know some social facts, such as:

Have you ever wondered how many married persons have "strayed" (a type of deviant behavior)—that is, had sexual relations with someone other than his or her spouse? And have you ever wondered what factors (variables) predict this behavior?

To answer this question, go to **sociology.wadsworth .com/andersen_taylor/essen3e,** select MicroCase Online from the left navigation bar, and follow the directions there to analyze the data described below.

Data file: GSS

Task: Auto-Analyzer

Primary Variable: EVER STRAY

Questions

Once you have your results, answer the following questions:

1. For each of the demographic variables listed, indicate whether there is a significant effect. If so, indicate which category is most likely and least likely to have "strayed."

Socio-Demographic Variable	Is the Overall Effect Significant?		Category Most Likely	Category Least Likely
Religion	Yes	No		
Political Party	Yes	No		
Education	Yes	No		
Sex	Yes	No		
Income	Yes	No		

▪ *The Companion Web Site for Sociology: The Essentials, Third Edition*

sociology.wadsworth.com/andersen_taylor/essen3e

Supplement your review of this chapter by going to the companion Web site to take one of the Tutorial Quizzes, use the flash cards to master key terms, and check out the many other study aids you'll find there. You'll also find special features such as GSS Data and Census 2000 information, data and resources at your fingertips to help you with that special project or do some research on your own.

▪ *Suggested Readings and Web Resources*

Adler, Patricia A., and Peter Adler. 2000. *Constructions of Deviance: Social Power, Context, and Interaction,* 3rd ed. Belmont, CA: Wadsworth.

This anthology explores various dimensions of deviant behavior from a labeling theory perspective. Ranging from studies of card sharks and missing children to punks, the book covers a wide range of intriguing sociological analyses of deviant behavior.

Anderson, Elijah. 1999. *Code of the Street: Decency, Violence, and the Moral Life of the Inner City.* New York: W. W. Norton.

Based on his ethnographic studies, Anderson provides a compelling sociological analysis of street life and its relationship to violence and the social construction of morality.

Humphries, Drew. 1999. *Crack Mothers: Pregnancy, Drugs, and the Media.* Columbus, OH: Ohio State University Press.

Humphries shows how the media created a drug scare and moral panic through its exaggerated presentation of cocaine use among low-income women. She argues that poverty and inadequate social services, not moral failings by women, are the basis of these social harms.

Mauer, Marc. 1999. *Race to Incarcerate.* New York: The New Press.

Mauer explores the explosion of growth in the prison industry, including its effects on African Americans and the poor. The book provides a strong analysis of why imprisonment has increased and suggests alternative policies for criminal justice.

Simon, David R, 2003. *Elite Deviance,* 8th edition. Boston: Allyn and Bacon.

By examining the connections between corporate, government, and military institutions, the author explores the causes and consequences of elite deviance and crime, defined as the wrongdoing of wealthy and powerful individuals and organizations.

Federal Bureau of Investigation
http://www.fbi.gov
A federal agency that publishes the Uniform Crime Reports annually, detailing information on crime and arrests.

Bureau of Justice Statistics
http://www.ojp.usdoj.gov/bjs/
A division in the federal government that compiles information on subjects pertinent to the study of crime and deviance.

The Sentencing Project
http://www.sentencingproject.org
The Sentencing Project is a private organization dedicated to promoting alternatives to sentencing and to providing analyses of criminal justice issues for the public and policy makers. Their Web site contains data on various aspects of crime and imprisonment.

Social Class and Social Stratification

One afternoon in a major U.S. city, two women go shopping. They are friends—wealthy, suburban women who shop for leisure. They meet in a gourmet restaurant and eat imported foods while discussing their children's private schools. After lunch, they spend the afternoon in exquisite stores—some of them large, elegant department stores; others, intimate boutiques where the staff knows them by name. When one woman stops to use the bathroom in one store, she enters a beautifully furnished room with an upholstered chair, a marble sink with brass faucets, fresh flowers on a wooden pedestal, shining mirrors, an ample supply of hand towels, and jars of lotion and soaps. The toilet is in a private stall with solid doors; in the stall there is soft toilet paper and another small vase of flowers.

The same day, in a different part of town, another woman goes shopping. She lives on a marginal income earned as a stitcher in a textiles factory. Her daughter badly needs a new pair of shoes, because she has grown out of last year's pair. The woman goes to a nearby discount store where she hopes to find a pair of shoes for under $15, but she dreads the experience. She knows her daughter would like other new things—a bathing suit for the summer, a pair of jeans and a blouse, but this summer the daughter will have to wear hand-me-downs because medical bills over the winter have depleted the little money left after food and rent. For her, shopping is not recreation but a bitter chore because it reminds her of the things she is unable to get for her daughter.

While this woman is shopping, she, too, stops to use the public bathroom. She enters a vast space with sinks and mirrors lined up on one side of the room and several stalls on the other. The tile floor is gritty and gray. The locks on the stall doors are missing or broken. Some of the overhead lights are burned out, so the room has dark shadows. In the stall, the toilet paper is coarse. When the woman washes her hands, she discovers there is no water and no soap in the metal dispensers. The mirror before her is cracked. She exits quickly, feeling as though she is being watched.

Two scenarios, one society. The difference is the mark of a society built on class inequality. The signs are all around you. Think about the clothing you wear. Are some labels worth more than others? Do others in your group see the same marks of distinction and status in clothing labels? Do some people you know never seem to wear the "right" labels? Whether it is clothing, bathrooms, schools, homes, or access to health care, the effect of class inequality is enormous, giving privileges and resources to some and leaving others barely able to get by.

Observing and analyzing class inequality is fundamental to sociological study. Sociologists want to know what features of society cause different groups to have different opportunities.

How does the organization of society lead to an unequal allocation of society's resources, with people's share dependent on class position? Many basic features of life besides wealth are shaped by class, such as where you live, the education you receive, your likely age at first marriage, and the probable cause of your death. Other inequalities intersect with class, such as racial inequality, gender inequality, and age inequality. Why? These are the kinds of questions sociologists pursue in studying social inequality.

As Table 7.1 shows, great inequality divides society; nevertheless, most people think that in the United States equal opportunity exists for all. The tendency is to think that individuals are to blame for their own failures. Instead of understanding inequality as the result of social structural causes, most people think success and failure can be attributed to individual effort, although Whites and those of higher class status are more likely to believe this than are African Americans and Latinos (Hunt 1996; Kluegel and Smith 1986). Many people accuse the poor of being lazy cheaters—a sentiment that has driven national welfare policy. At the same time, those who are rich are admired for their supposed initiative, drive, and motivation. Although sociologists respect distinguished individual achievements, they have found that by far the greatest cause for the disparities in material success is the organization of society.

■ Social Differentiation and Social Stratification

All social groups and societies exhibit social differentiation. **Status,** as we have seen earlier, is a socially defined position in a group or society. **Social differentiation** is the process by which different statuses develop in any group, organization, or society. Think of a sports organization. The players, the owners, the managers, the fans, the cheerleaders, and the sponsors all have a different status within the organization. Together they constitute a whole social system, one that is marked by social differentiation. The fans have a different status from that of the cheerleaders, the owners have a different status from that of the managers, and the sponsors have a different

TABLE 7.1 Inequality in the United States

- Nearly one in six children in the United States live in poverty, including 23 percent of African American children and 21 percent of Hispanic children, and 10 percent of Asian American children (Proctor and Dalaker 2002).

- Fourteen percent of the U.S. population has no health insurance; the average cost of a day's stay in a hospital is $1,149—the equivalent of one and a half week's pay for the average U.S. worker (U.S. Census Bureau 2002).

- When Doris Duke, the tobacco heiress died, she left a $100,000 inheritance to her dog, with the proviso that the dog should only be fed imported baby food (Meng 2001).

- One percent of the U.S. population controls 38 percent of the total wealth in the nation; the bottom 20 percent owe more than they own (Mishel, Bernstein, and Boushey 2003).

- The average CEO of a major company has a salary of $13.1 million dollars per year; workers earning the minimum wage make $10,712 per year, if they work 40 hours a week for 52 weeks and hold only one job (Lavelle 2001; DeNavas-Walt and Cleveland 2002)

- Black family income is 66 percent of White family income—only 6 percent closer than it was in 1970 (DeNavas-Walt and Cleveland 2002).

- Among women heading their own households, one-quarter live below the poverty line (Proctor and Dalaker 2002).

status from that of the players. Altogether, the organization is marked by the social differentiation between these different statuses in the organization.

Status differences can become organized into a hierarchical social system. **Social stratification** is a relatively fixed, hierarchical arrangement in society by which groups have different access to resources, power, and perceived social worth. Social stratification is a system of structured social inequality. To use the sports example, owners control the resources of the teams; players, although they may earn high salaries, do not control the team resources and have less power than the owners and managers. Sponsors (including individuals and corporations) provide the resources on which this system of stratification rests; fans are merely observers who pay to watch the teams play. Sports organizations include a system of stratification because the groups that constitute the organization are arranged in a hierarchy where some have more resources and power than others.

All societies seem to have a system of social stratification, although they vary in the degree to which stratification exists. Socialist societies are supposed to have minimal stratification; however, purely socialist societies are rare. Before the collapse of the Soviet Union in 1991, the Soviet socialist system claimed universal equality,

but in reality was a highly stratified system of privileges and conveniences accessible only to a few. Some societies stratify only along a single dimension, such as age, keeping the stratification system relatively simple. Most contemporary societies are more complex, with many factors interacting to create social strata. In the United States, social stratification is strongly influenced by class, which is in turn influenced by matters such as one's occupation, income, and education, along with race, gender, and other influences such as age, region of residence, ethnicity, and national origin.

Estate, Caste, and Class

Stratification systems can be broadly categorized into three types: estate systems, caste systems, and class systems. In an **estate system** of stratification the ownership of property and the exercise of power is monopolized by an elite who have total control over societal resources. Historically, such societies were feudal systems where classes were differentiated into three basic groups—the nobles, the priesthood, and the commoners. Commoners included peasants (usually the largest class group), small merchants, artisans, domestic workers, and traders. The nobles controlled the land and the resources used to cultivate the land, as well as all the resources resulting from peasant labor.

Estate systems of stratification are most common in agricultural societies. Although such societies have been largely supplanted by industrialization, there are still examples of societies that have a small but powerful landholding class ruling over a population that works mainly in agricultural production. Unlike the feudal societies of the European Middle Ages, however, contemporary estate systems of stratification display the influence of international capitalism. The "noble class" comprises not knights who conquered lands in war, but international capitalists or local elites who control the labor of a vast and impoverished group of people, such as in some South American societies where landholding elites maintain a dictatorship over peasants who labor in agricultural fields.

In a **caste system,** one's place in the stratification system is an ascribed status (see Chapter 4), meaning it is a quality given to an individual by circumstances of birth. The hierarchy of classes is rigid in caste systems and is often preserved through formal law and cultural practices that prevent free association and movement between classes.

The system of *apartheid* in South Africa was a stark example of a caste system. Under apartheid, the travel, employment, associations, and place of residence of Black Africans were severely restricted. Segregation was enforced using a pass system in which Blacks in White

The class status of different groups can be readily seen by looking at the context of different people's everyday lives, as shown in these two shopping areas.

areas were obliged to account for themselves to White authorities. Interracial marriage was illegal, and Black Africans were prohibited from voting. The apartheid system was overthrown by election in 1992. Another example is the traditional caste system of India. Membership in an Indian caste group was determined by birth. Each group was restricted to certain occupations, and the lowest group, "the untouchables," was prohibited from associating with the others. The Brahmans were the highest caste, nobles who were considered spiritually and socially superior to all other groups. The Indian caste system is no longer mandated, but its effects remain. People retain attitudes about the alleged superiority and inferiority of different groups long after formalized distinctions are eradicated, which is one reason social inequalities and prejudices are so tenacious.

In *class systems,* stratification exists, but one's placement in the class system can change according to personal achievements; that is, class depends to some degree on achieved status, defined as status that is earned by the acquisition of resources and power, regardless of one's origins. Class systems are more open than caste systems, since position does not depend strictly on birth, and classes are less rigidly defined than castes, because the divisions are blurred by those who move between one class and the next.

Despite the potential for movement from one class to another, in the class system found in the United States, class placement still depends heavily on one's social background. Although ascription (the designation of ascribed status according to birth) is not the basis for social stratification in the United States, the class a person is born into has major consequences for that person's life. Patterns of inheritance; access to exclusive educational resources; the financial, political, and social influence of one's family;

and similar factors all shape one's likelihood of achievement. Although there is no formal obstacle to movement through the class system, individual achievement is very much shaped by an individual's class of origin.

Defining Class

In common parlance, *class* refers to style or sophistication: "She's got a lot of class!" In sociological use, *class* refers to standing within the stratification system: **Social class** (or **class**) is the social structural position a group holds relative to the economic, social, political, and cultural resources of society. Class determines the different access groups and individuals have to these resources and puts groups in different positions of advantage and disadvantage. Members of a given class have similar opportunities and tend to share a common way of life. Class also includes a cultural component, because class shapes language, dress, mannerisms, taste, and other preferences. Class is not just an attribute of individuals—it is a feature of society. The social structural arrangements of society determine class standing.

The social theorist Max Weber described the consequences of stratification in terms of **life chances,** meaning the opportunities that people have in common by virtue of belonging to a particular class. To Weber, life chances include the opportunity for possessing goods, having an income, and having access to particular jobs. Life chances are the result of social structural arrangements, but the concept of life chances indicates how important these arrangements are for individuals. Put simply, class matters. Class standing determines how well one is served by social institutions. Class influences access to good health care, education, among other things, as well as influencing social and political attitudes. In

THINKING SOCIOLOGICALLY

Take a shopping trip to different stores and observe the appearance of stores serving different economic groups. What kinds of bathrooms are there in stores catering to middle-class clients? The rich? The working class? The poor? Which ones allow the most privacy or provide the nicest amenities? What fixtures are in the display areas? Are they simply utilitarian with minimal ornamentation, or are they opulent displays of consumption? Take detailed notes of your observations, and write an analysis of what this tells you about *social class* in the United States.

general, one's life chances are shaped by one's place in the class system.

Class is a structural phenomenon; it cannot be directly observed. Because sociologists cannot isolate and measure social class directly, they use other indicators to serve as measures of class. A prominent indicator of class is income; other common indicators are education, occupation, and place of residence. These indicators alone do not define class, but they are often accurate measures of the class standing of a person or group. We will see that these indicators tend to be linked. A good income, for example, makes it possible to afford a house in a prestigious neighborhood and an exclusive education for one's children. In the sociological study of class, indicators such as income and education have had enormous value in revealing the outlines and influences of the class system.

■ *Why Is There Inequality?*

Stratification occurs in all societies. Why? This question originates in classical sociology in the works of Karl Marx and Max Weber, theorists whose work continues to inform the analysis of class inequality today.

Karl Marx: Class and Capitalism

Karl Marx (1818–1883) provided a complex and profound analysis of the class system under capitalism—an analysis that, although more than 100 years old, continues to inform sociological analyses and has been the basis for major world change. Marx defined classes in relationship to the *means of production,* defined as the system by which goods are produced and distributed. In Marx's analysis, two primary classes exist under capitalism: the *capitalist class*—those who own the means of production—and the *working class* (or proletariat)—those who sell their labor for wages. There are further divisions

within these two classes: the *petty bourgeoisie*—small business owners, managers (those whom you might think of as middle class) who identify with the interests of the capitalist class, but who do not own the means of production, and the *lumpenproletariat*—those who have become unnecessary as workers and are then discarded. (Today, these would be the underclass, the homeless, and the permanently poor.)

Marx thought that with the development of capitalism, the capitalists and working class would become increasingly antagonistic (something he referred to as class struggle); as class conflicts became more intense, the two classes would become more polarized, with the petty bourgeoisie becoming deprived of their property and dropping into the working class. This analysis is still reflected in contemporary questions about whether the classes are becoming more polarized with the rich getting richer and everyone else worse off—a question further examined later in this chapter.

In addition to the class struggle that Marx thought would characterize the advancement of capitalism, he also thought that capitalism was the basis for other social institutions. Capitalism is the *infrastructure* of society, with other institutions (such as law, education, the family, and so forth) reflecting capitalist interests. Thus, according to Marx, the law supports the interests of capitalists; the family promotes values that socialize people into appropriate work roles; and education reflects the interests of the capitalist class. Over time, capitalism increasingly penetrates society, as we can clearly see with the corporate mergers that characterize modern life and the predominance of capitalist values in society's institutions.

Why do people support such a system? Here is where ideology plays a role. **Ideology** refers to belief systems that support the status quo. According to Marx, the dominant ideas of a society are promoted by the ruling class, as we will explore further in the section on class consciousness. Through their control of the communications industries in modern society the ruling class is able to produce ideas that buttress their interests.

Much of Marx's analysis boils down to the consequences of a system based on the pursuit of profit. If goods were exchanged at the cost of producing them, no profit would be produced. Capitalist owners want to sell commodities for more than their actual value—more than the cost of producing them, including materials and labor. Because workers contribute value to the system and capitalists extract value, Marx saw capitalist profit as the exploitation of labor. Marx believed that as profits became increasingly concentrated in the hands of a few capitalists, the working class would become increasingly dissatisfied. The basically exploitative character of capitalism, according to Marx, would ultimately lead to its destruction as workers organized to overthrow the rule

Class differentiation in the United States results in people having different access to society's resources.

of the capitalist class. *Class conflict* between workers and capitalists, he argued, was inescapable, with revolution being the inevitable result.

At the time Marx was writing, the middle class was small and consisted mostly of small business owners and managers. Marx saw the middle class as dependent on the capitalist class, but exploited by it, because the middle class did not own the means of production. He saw middle-class people as identifying with the interests of the capitalist class because of the similarity in their eco-

nomic interests and their dependence on the capitalist system. Marx believed that the middle class failed to work in its own best interests because it falsely believed that it benefited from capitalist arrangements. Marx thought that in the long run the middle class would pay for their misplaced faith when profits became increasingly concentrated in the hands of a few, and more and more of the middle class dropped into the working class. Because he did not foresee the emergence of the large and highly differentiated middle class we have today, not every part of Marx's theory has proven true. Still, his analysis provides a powerful portrayal of the forces of capitalism and the tendency for wealth to belong to a few, whereas the majority work only to make ends meet. He has also influenced the lives of billions of people under self-proclaimed Marxist systems that were created in an attempt, however unrealized, to overcome the pitfalls of capitalist society.

Max Weber: Class, Status, and Party

Max Weber (1864–1920) agreed with Marx that classes were formed around economic interests, and he agreed that material forces (that is, economic forces) have a powerful effect on people's lives. However, he disagreed with Marx that economic forces are the primary dimension of stratification. Weber saw three dimensions to stratification:

- *class* (the economic dimension)
- *status* (or prestige, the cultural and social dimension)
- *party* (or power, the political dimension).

Weber is thus responsible for a *multidimensional view* of social stratification because he analyzed the connections between economic, cultural, and political systems. Weber pointed out that, although the economic, social, and political dimensions of stratification are usually related, they are not always consistent. A person could be high on one or two dimensions, but low on another. A major drug dealer is an example: high wealth (economic dimension) and power (political dimension), but low prestige (social dimension)—at least in the eyes of the mainstream society, even if not in other circles.

Weber defined *class* as the economic dimension of stratification—how much access to the material goods of society a group or individual has, as measured by income, property, and other financial assets. A family with an income of $100,000 per year clearly has more access to the resources of a society than a family living on an income of $25,000 per year. Weber understood that a class has common economic interests and that economic well-being was the basis for one's life chances. But, in addition, he thought that people were also stratified based on their status and power differences.

Status, to Weber, is the prestige dimension of stratification—the social judgment or recognition given to a person or group. Weber understood that class distinctions are linked to status distinctions—that is, those with the most economic resources tend to have the highest status in society, but not always. In a local community, for example, those with the most status may be those who have lived there the longest, even if newcomers arrive with more money. Physicians are a group who typically earn high incomes and enjoy high social prestige; in this case, status is related to economic standing, but status may be independent of income. Ministers and priests are accorded high social status, but do not typically earn high incomes; drug dealers may earn a lot of money but are not accorded high status by the dominant culture.

Finally, *party* (or what we would now call power) is the political dimension of stratification. It is the capacity to influence groups and individuals even in the face of opposition. Power is also reflected in the ability of a person or group to negotiate their way through social institutions. An unemployed Latino man wrongly accused of a crime, for instance, does not have much power to negotiate his way through the criminal justice system. By comparison, business executives accused of corporate crime can afford expensive lawyers and, thus, frequently go unpunished, or, if they are guilty, serve relatively light sentences in comparatively pleasant facilities. Again, Weber saw power as linked to economic standing, but he did not think that economic standing was always the determining cause of people's power. To the contrary, he wrote that economic standing could be the result of having a strong power base.

Although having power is typically related to also having high economic standing and high social status, this is not always the case. A wealthy crook may have money and power, but be held in low esteem by most of society. The point is that stratification does not rest solely on economics; political power and social judgments are important components of stratification systems. Weber refined the sociological analyses of stratification to account for the subtleties that can be observed when you look beyond the sheer economic dimension to stratification.

Marx and Weber explain different features of stratification. Both understood the importance of the economic basis of stratification, and they knew the significance of class for determining the course of one's life. Marx saw people as acting primarily out of economic interests, but Weber saw people's position in the stratification system as the result of economic, social, and political forces. Together, Marx and Weber provide compelling theoretical grounds for understanding the contemporary class structure.

Functionalism and Conflict Theory: The Continuing Debate

Marx and Weber analyzed what they observed in all societies, and each developed a unique way to understand the development of persistence of inequality. Like more contemporary sociologists, they were trying to understand why differences existed in the resources and power that different groups in society hold. The question persists of why there is inequality and has been further developed by sociologists working from these classical traditions. Two major frameworks in sociological theory—functionalist and conflict theory—take quite different approaches to understanding inequality (see Table 7.2).

THE FUNCTIONALIST PERSPECTIVE ON INEQUALITY. Functionalist theory views society as a system of institutions that are organized to meet society's needs (see Chapter 1). The functionalist perspective emphasizes that the parts of society are in basic harmony with each other; society is characterized by cohesion, consensus, cooperation, stability, and persistence (Parsons 1951a; Merton 1957; Eitzen and Baca Zinn 2000). Different parts of the social system complement one another and are held together through social consensus and cooperation. To explain stratification, functionalists propose that the roles filled by the upper classes—such as governance, economic innovation, investment, and management—are essential for a cohesive and smoothly running society and hence are rewarded in proportion to their contribution to the social order (Davis and Moore 1945).

According to the functionalist perspective, social inequality serves an important purpose in society: It motivates people to fill the different positions in society that are needed for the survival of the whole. This idea is addressed in an argument by sociologists Davis and Moore who argue that some positions in society are more functionally important than others and that inequality is a mechanism to ensure that the most talented people go into the most demanding positions. These positions require the greatest degree of talent or training, thus the higher rewards attached to those positions (such as higher income and prestige) are a way to ensure that people will make the sacrifices needed to acquire the training for functionally important positions (Davis and Moore 1945). **Social mobility** is a person's movement over time from one class to another, and thus comes to those who acquire the necessary talents and tools for success (such as education and job training). In other words,

TABLE 7.2 Functional and Conflict Theories of Stratification

Interprets:	Functionalism	Conflict Theory
Inequality	Inequality serves an important purpose in society by motivating people to fill the different positions in society that are needed for the survival of the whole.	Inequality results from a system of domination and subordination where those resources with the most exploit and control others.
Class structure	Differentiation is essential for a cohesive society.	Different groups struggle over societal resources and compete for social advantage.
Reward system	Rewards are attached to certain positions (such as higher income and prestige) as a way to ensure that people will make the sacrifices needed to acquire the training for functionally important positions in society.	The more stratified a society, the less likely that society will benefit from the talents of all its citizens, since inequality prevents the talents of those at the bottom from being discovered and used.
Classes	Some positions in society are more functionally important than others and are rewarded because they require the greatest degree of talent and training.	Classes exist in conflict with each other as they vie for power and economic, social, and political resources.
Life chances	Those who work hardest and succeed have greater life chances.	The most vital jobs in society—those that sustain life and the quality of life—are usually the least rewarded.
Elites	The most talented are rewarded in proportion to their contribution to the social order.	The most powerful reproduce their advantage by distributing resources and controlling the dominant value system.
Class consciousness/ ideology	Beliefs about success and failure confirm status of those who succeed.	Elites shape societal beliefs to make their unequal privilege appear to be legitimate and fair.
Social mobility	Upward mobility is possible for those who acquire the necessary talents and tools for success (such as education and job training).	There is blocked mobility in the system because the working class and poor are denied the same opportunities as others.
Poverty	Poverty serves economic and social functions in society.	Poverty is inevitable because of the exploitation built into the system.
Social policy	Because the system is basically fair, social policies should only reward merit.	Because the system is basically unfair, social policies should support disadvantaged groups by redirecting society's resources for a more equitable distribution of income and wealth.

functionalist theorists see inequality as an element of a reward system that motivates people to succeed.

THE CONFLICT PERSPECTIVE ON INEQUALITY. Like functionalist theory, conflict theory sees society as a social system; but unlike functionalism, conflict theory emphasizes that the system is held together through conflict and coercion. From a conflict-based perspective, society comprises competing interest groups, some of whom have more power than others. Different groups struggle over societal resources and compete for social advantage. Conflict theorists argue that those who control society's resources also hold power over others. The powerful are also likely to act in ways that reproduce their advantage, and they try to shape societal beliefs in ways that make their unequal privilege appear to be legitimate and fair. In sum, conflict theory emphasizes the friction in society rather than the coherence, and conflict theorists see society as dominated by elites.

From the perspective of conflict theory, derived largely from the work of Karl Marx, social stratification is based on class conflict and blocked opportunity. Conflict theorists see stratification as a system of domination and subordination in which those with the most resources exploit and control others. They also see the different classes as in conflict with each other, with the unequal distribution of rewards reflecting the class interests of the powerful, not the survival needs of the whole society (Eitzen and Baca Zinn 2000). According to the conflict perspective, inequality provides elites with the power to distribute resources, make and enforce laws, and control value systems; elites use these powers in ways that reproduce inequality. Others in the class structure, especially the working class and the poor, experience blocked mobility.

Conflict theorists argue that the consequences of inequality are negative. From a conflict point of view, the more stratified a society, the less likely that society will benefit from the talents of its citizens, because inequality limits the life chances of those at the bottom, preventing their talents from being discovered and used. To the waste of talent is added the restriction of human creativity and productivity.

Implicit in the argument of each perspective is criticism of the other perspective. Functionalism assumes that the most highly rewarded jobs are the most important for society, whereas conflict theorists argue that some of the most vital jobs in society—those that sustain life and the quality of life, such as farmers, mothers, trash collectors, and a wide range of other laborers—are usually the least rewarded. Conflict theorists also criticize functionalist theory for assuming that the most talented get the greatest rewards. They point out that systems of stratification tend to devalue the contributions of those left at the bottom and to underutilize the diverse talents of all people (Tumin 1953). In contrast, functionalist theorists contend that the conflict view of how economic interests shape social organization is too simplistic. Conflict theorists respond by arguing that functionalists hold too conservative a view of society and overstate the degree of consensus and stability that exists.

The debate between functionalist and conflict theorists raises fundamental questions about how people view inequality. Is it inevitable? How is inequality maintained? Do people basically accept it? This debate is not just academic. The assumptions made from each perspective frame public policy debates. Whether the topic is taxation, poverty, or homelessness, if people believe that anyone can get ahead by ability alone, they will tend to see the system of inequality as fair and accept the idea that there should be a differential reward system. Those who tend toward the conflict view of the stratification system are more likely to advocate programs that emphasize public responsibility for the well-being of all groups and to support programs and policies that result in more of the income and wealth of society going toward the needy.

■ *The Class Structure of the United States*

The class structure of the United States is elaborate, arising from the interactions of old wealth, new wealth, intensive immigration, a culture of entrepreneurship and individualism, and in recent times, vigorous globalization. One can conceptualize the class system as a ladder, with different class groups arrayed up and down the rungs, each rung corresponding to a different level in the class system. Conceptualized this way, social class is the common position groups hold in a status hierarchy (Wright 1979; Lucal 1994); class is indicated by factors such as levels of income, occupational standing, and edu-

cational attainment. People are relatively high or low on the ladder depending on the resources they have, whether those are education, income, occupation, or any of the other factors known to influence people's placement (or ranking) in the stratification system. Indeed, an abundance of sociological research has stemmed from the concept of **status attainment,** the process by which people end up in a given position in the stratification system. Status attainment research describes how factors such as class origins, educational level, and occupation produce class location, and it describes the extent to which people are able to move throughout the class system, as we will see in the section on social mobility later in this chapter.

This model of class suggests that in the United States stratification is hierarchical, but somewhat fluid. Although there are different gradients in the stratification system, they are not fixed as they might be in a society where one's placement is completely a matter of the class into which one is born. In a relatively open class system such as the United States, people's achievements do matter, although the extent to which people rise rapidly and dramatically through the stratification system is less than the popular imagination envisions. Some people do begin from modest origins and amass great wealth and influence (celebrities such as Bill Gates, Oprah Winfrey, and millionaire athletes), but these are the exceptions, not the rule. Some people move down in the class system, but as we will see, most people remain relatively close to their class of origin. When people rise or fall in the class system, the distance they travel is usually relatively short, as we will see further in the section on social mobility.

The image of stratification as a laddered system, with different gradients of social standing, emphasizes that one's **socioeconomic status (SES)** is derived from certain factors. Income, occupational prestige, and education are the three measures of socioeconomic status that have been found to be most significant in determining people's placement in the stratification system. **Income** is the amount of money a person receives in a given period; socioeconomic status can be measured in part by income brackets. The **median income** for a society is the midpoint of all household incomes. In other words, half of all households earn more than the median income; half earn less (see Figure 7.1). In the laddered model of class, those bunched around the median income level are considered middle class. Sociologists may argue about which income brackets constitute middle-class standing, but they agree that income is a significant indicator of class, although not the only one.

Occupational prestige is a second important indicator of socioeconomic status. **Prestige** is the value others assign to people and groups. **Occupational prestige** is the subjective evaluation people give to jobs. To determine occupational prestige, sociological researchers typically ask

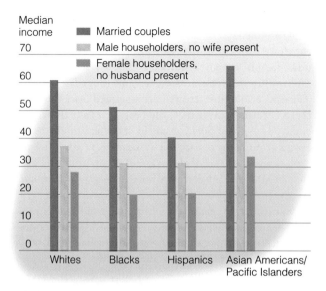

FIGURE 7.1 Median Income by Race and Household Status

SOURCE: U.S. Census Bureau. 20002. *Historical Income Tables, Tables F-7A, 7B, 7C, 7D*. Web site: **www.census.gov**

nationwide samples of adults to rank the general standing of a series of jobs. These subjective ratings provide information about how people perceive the worth of different occupations. People tend to rank U.S. Supreme Court justice as one of the most prestigious occupations, followed by physician, professor, judge, lawyer, and scientist. In the middle ranges are occupations such as electrician, newspaper columnist, insurance agent, and police officer. The occupations typically considered to have the lowest prestige are farm laborer, maid or servant, garbage collector, janitor, and shoe-shiner (Davis and Smith 1984). These rankings do not reflect the worth of people within these positions, but are indicative of the judgments people make about the worth of these jobs and their value to society.

The final major indicator of socioeconomic status is **educational attainment,** typically measured as the total years of formal education. The more years of education attained, the more likely a person will have higher class status. The prestige attached to occupations is strongly tied to the amount of education the job requires—the more education people think is needed for a given occupation, the more occupational prestige people attribute to that job (Blau and Duncan 1967; MacKinnon and Langford 1994; Ollivier 2000).

Layers of Social Class

Taken together, income, occupation, and education are good measures of people's social standing. How then do sociologists understand the array of classes in the United

States? Using a laddered model of stratification, most sociologists describe the class system in the United States as divided into several classes: upper, upper middle, middle, lower middle, and lower class. The different classes are arrayed up and down the ladder with those with the most money, education, and prestige at the top and those with the least at the bottom.

DEBUNKING
Society's Myths

Myth: Unlike other societies where there are distinct social classes, most Americans are middle class and share similar values and life chances.

Sociological perspective: Although middle-class values form the dominant culture in the United States, this assertion overlooks the extent to which class differentiates life chances. Elites control most of the wealth in the United States, and many in the middle class find their class position to be tenuous. Though often ignored in the popular mind, the working class forms a substantial portion of the class structure.

In the United States, the *upper class* owns the major share of corporate and personal wealth; it includes those who have held wealth for generations as well as those who have recently become rich. Only a very small proportion of people actually constitute the upper class, but they control vast amounts of wealth and power in the United States. Those in this class are elites who, in Marxist terms, own the means of production. They exercise enormous control throughout society. Much of their wealth is inherited.

Despite social myths to the contrary, the best predictor of future wealth is the family into which you are born. Each year, the business magazine *Forbes* publishes a list of the 400 wealthiest families and individuals in the country. To be on the list in 2002, your net worth had to be at least $550 million. Bill Gates, the richest person on this list, has an estimated worth of $46 billion. Together, the 400 richest Americans had a net worth of $872 billion—almost as much as the gross national product of China! In the past, almost all of those on the *Forbes' 400* list had inherited their wealth, but in the late 1990s there was a huge increase in the number of people on the list with self-created wealth, largely the result of the soaring stock market and investment in Internet-related businesses. By the time of the 2002 list, much of this wealth had been lost—and many fell off the list—because of the downturn in the stock market. (*Forbes,* September 30, 2002). Because elites control such gigantic amounts of wealth, they wield immense power in society.

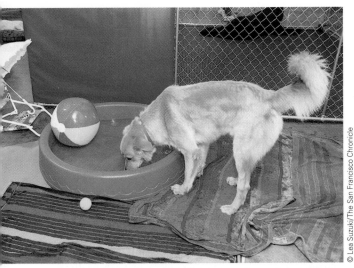

Sociologists have shown that the nouveau riche can be ostentatious in their display of wealth. In this pet care center in San Francisco, even the family pet can engage in conspicuous consumption.

Those in the upper class with newly acquired wealth are known as the *nouveau riche*. A good example are the "dot com millionaires" made rich by investments in Internet start-up companies who ushered in a new age of wealth and glamour. Luxury vehicles, high-priced real estate, and exclusive vacations may mark the lifestyle of the newly rich. However, although they may have vast amounts of money, they are often not accepted into "old rich" circles.

The *upper middle class* includes those with high incomes and high social prestige. They tend to be well-educated professionals or business executives. Their earnings can be quite high indeed—successful business executives can earn millions of dollars a year. It is difficult to estimate exactly how many people fall into this group because of the difficulty of drawing lines between the upper, upper middle, and middle class. Indeed, the upper middle class is often thought of as "middle class" because their lifestyle sets the standard to which many aspire, but this lifestyle is actually unattainable by most. A large home full of top-quality furniture and modern appliances, two or three luxurious cars, vacations every year (perhaps a vacation home), high-quality college education for one's children, and a fashionable wardrobe are simply beyond the means of a majority of people in the United States.

The *middle class* is hard to define; in part because being "middle class" is more than just economic position. A very large portion of Americans identify themselves as middle class even though they vary widely in lifestyle and in resources at their disposal. But the idea that the United States is an open-class system leads many to think that the majority have a middle-class lifestyle; thus, the middle class becomes the ubiquitous norm even

though many who call themselves middle class have a tenuous hold on this class position.

The *lower middle class* includes workers in the skilled trades and low-income bureaucratic workers, many of whom may actually think of themselves as middle class. Also known as the *working class,* this class includes blue-collar workers (those in skilled trades who do manual labor) and many service workers, such as secretaries, hairdressers, waitresses, police, and firefighters. Medium to low income, education, and occupational prestige define the lower middle class relative to the class groups above it. The term lower in this class designation refers to the relative position of the group in the stratification system, but it has a pejorative sound to many people, especially to people who are members of this class, many of whom think of themselves as middle class.

The *lower class* is composed primarily of the displaced and poor. People in this class have little formal education and are often unemployed or working in minimum-wage jobs. People of color and women make up a disproportionate

Working class heroes: The miners who were dramatically rescued from the Quecreek mine in the summer of 2001 signed a deal to tell their story in a made-for-TV movie. This will give them the equivalent of three years' pay each. (They earn about $40,000 per year, counting overtime). That is a pittance compared to the head of the group that owns the mine: He earns about $18 million a year in salary and bonuses—making in five minutes what it would take the miners a year to earn!

part of this class. The poor include the working poor—those who work for wages, but who do not earn enough to work their way out of poverty. The working poor constitute a large portion of those who are poor. Forty percent of the poor work; 10 percent work year-round and full time—a proportion that has generally increased over time.

The concept of the **urban underclass** has been added to the lower class (Wilson 1987). The underclass includes those who have been left behind by contemporary economic developments and who are likely to be unemployed permanently and without much means of economic support. The underclass has little or no opportunity for movement out of the worst poverty. Rejected from the economic system, those in the underclass may become dependent on public assistance or illegal activities.

According to sociologist William Julius Wilson, structural transformations in the economy have left large groups of people, especially urban minorities, in highly vulnerable positions. Without work and unable to sustain themselves in an economy that has discarded them, such groups have formed a growing underclass—a development that has exacerbated the problems of urban poverty and created new challenges for social policy makers (Wilson 1996, 1987).

Class Conflict

Sociologists have also analyzed class according to the perspective of conflict theory, derived from the early work of Karl Marx. This perspective defines classes in terms of their structural relationship to other classes and their relationship to the economic system. Derived from conflict theory in sociology, this analysis emphasizes power relations in society, interpreting inequality as resulting from the unequal distribution of power and resources in society (see Chapter 1). Instead of seeing class simply as a ladder, as suggested earlier, sociologists who work from a conflict perspective see the classes as facing off against each other, with elites exploiting and dominating others. The key idea in this model is that class is not simply a matter of what individuals possess in terms of income and prestige; instead, class is defined by the relationship of the classes to the larger system of economic production (Vanneman and Cannon 1987; Wright 1985).

From a conflict perspective, the position of the middle class in society is unique. The middle class, or the *professional–managerial class,* includes managers, supervisors, and professionals. Members of this group have substantial control over other people, primarily through their authority to direct the work of others, impose and enforce regulations in the workplace, and determine dominant social values. Although, as Marx argued, the middle class is controlled by the ruling class, members of this class tend to identify with the interests of the

elite. The professional–managerial class, however, is caught in a contradictory position between elites and the working class. Like elites, those in this class have some control over others, but like the working class, they have minimal control over the economic system (Wright 1979). As capitalism progresses, according to conflict theory, more and more of those in the middle class drop into the working class as they are pushed out of managerial jobs into working-class jobs or as professional jobs become organized more along the lines of traditional working-class employment.

Has this happened? Not to the extent Marx predicted whereby he thought that ultimately there would be only two classes—the capitalist and the proletariat—but, to some extent, this is occurring. Classes have become more polarized, with the well-off accumulating even more resources and the middle class seeing their income falling, measured in constant dollars (Rose 2000). Levels of debt in the middle class also mean that many have a fragile hold on this class position; the loss of a job, a family emergency (such as the death of a working parent), divorce, disability, or a prolonged illness can quickly leave a family with fewer resources. At the same time, corporate mergers, tax policies that favor the rich, a decline in corporate taxes, and sheer greed are concentrating more wealth in the hands of a few. Perhaps the class revolution that Marx predicted has not occurred, but the dynamics of capitalism that he analyzed are unfolding before us.

Recall that Marx defined the working class as those who sell their labor for wages. This definition, taken from Marx, would include blue-collar workers and many white-collar workers. Members of the working class have little control over their own work lives; instead, they have to take orders from others. This concept of the working class departs from traditional "blue-collar" definitions of working-class jobs because it includes secretaries, salespeople, and nurses—any group that works under the rules imposed by managers or elites. The middle class may exercise some autonomy at work, but the working class has little power to challenge decisions of those who supervise them, except insofar as they can organize collectively, as in union, strikes, or other collective work actions.

Conflict theorists also see the poor as under assault by society in a system of inequality that leaves them especially vulnerable. Poor through no fault of their own, the poor are still blamed for their own poverty, especially because of belief systems about failure propagated by elites and the middle class.

Whether you use a laddered model of class or a class conflict perspective, you can see that the class structure in the United States is hierarchical. Class position gives different people access to jobs, income, education, power, and social status—all of which bestow further opportunities on some and deprive others of success. People sometimes move from one class to another (although this is not the norm), but the class structure is a system with boundaries built into it, generating class conflict. The middle and working classes shoulder much of the tax burden for social programs, producing resentment by these groups toward the poor. At the same time, corporate taxes have declined and tax loopholes for the rich have increased—an indication of the privilege that is perpetuated by the class system. Whatever features of the class system different sociologists study, they see class stratification as a dynamic process—one involving the interplay of access to resources, judgments about different groups, and the exercise of power by a few.

The Distribution of Wealth and Income

There is enormous class inequality in this society, and it is growing. Elites control an enormous share of the wealth in society and exercise tremendous control over others. The gap between the rich and the poor is also increasing, whereas much of the middle class finds its class standing slipping. Consider this: Since the early 1970s, median income (in constant dollars) has actually declined. Since the 1970s, the top 20 percent of the population has received a larger share of the total income (50 percent of all income), whereas the bottom 20 percent has received less (3.5 percent; DeNavas-Walt and Cleveland 2002).

THINKING SOCIOLOGICALLY

Suppose that you wanted to reduce inequality in the United States. Since you know that the transmission of *wealth* is one of the bases of *stratification*, would you be willing to eliminate the right to inherit property to achieve greater equality?

Figure 7.2 shows the increasing gap that has developed between the upper classes and everyone else in recent years. These data show that income growth has been greatest in all racial groups for those at the top end of the population—the upper 20 percent and the upper 5 percent of all income groups. For everyone else, income growth has remained flat. You can also see that, although this pattern holds for Blacks, Hispanics, and Whites, the actual level of income for these groups differs significantly, with the top portions of the Black and Hispanic population not as well off as Whites.

Contributing to the income gap is very high compensation for CEOs of major companies. The average

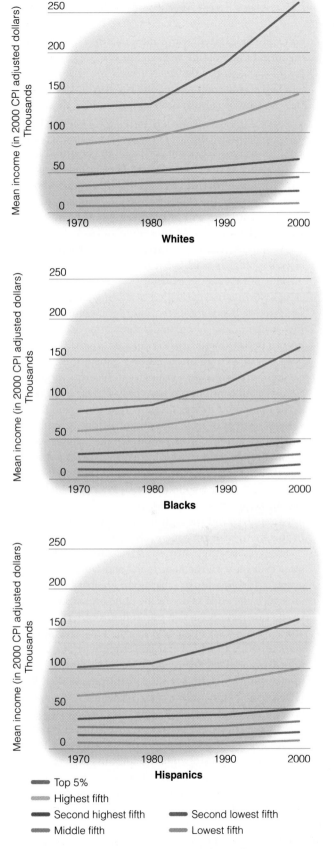

FIGURE 7.2 Income Growth by Income Group, 1970–2000

SOURCE: U.S. Census Bureau. 2002. Historical Income Tables—Households. **www.census.gov/income/hhes/income/histinc/**

CEO in the United States now makes 475 times the earnings of an average worker. Since 1980, the average pay of working people has increased by 74 percent, for CEOs, 1884 percent (Reingold 2000; AFL-CIO 2002). Income gains have also been augmented by tax reforms that have provided breaks for the highest earners. Add to this the enormous differences in wealth for the top compared to everyone else, and you begin to get a full picture of inequality in the United States. These trends verify the popular adage that the rich are getting richer and the poor, poorer. As the classes become more polarized, it is possible that there will be a weakening of the myth that the United States is basically a middle-class society.

When discussing the distribution of resources in society, sociologists make a distinction between wealth and income. **Wealth** is the monetary value of everything one actually owns. It is calculated by adding all financial assets (stocks, bonds, property, insurance, savings value of investments, and so on) and subtracting debts, which gives a dollar amount that is one's *net worth*. Wealth allows you to accumulate assets over generations; thus, it is cumulative—giving advantages to subsequent generations that they might not have had on their own. *Income* is the amount of money brought into a household from various sources (wages, investment income, dividends, and so on) during a given period. Unlike income, wealth is cumulative—that is, its value tends to increase through investment, and it can be passed on to the next generation, giving those who inherit wealth a considerable advantage in accumulating more resources.

To understand the significance of wealth compared to income in determining class location, imagine two college graduates, graduating in the same year, from the same college, with the same major and same grade point average. Imagine further that upon graduation both get jobs with the same salary in the same organization. Yet, in one case parents paid all the student's college expenses and gave her a car upon graduation. The other student worked while in school and graduated with substantial debt from student loans. This student's family has no money with which to help support the new worker. Who is better off? Same salary, same credentials, but wealth (even if modest) matters. It gives one person an advantage—one that will be played out many times over as the young worker buys a home, finances her own children's education, and possibly inherits additional assets.

Where is all the wealth? The wealthiest 1 percent own 38 percent of all net worth; the bottom 80 percent control only 17 percent. The top 1 percent also own almost half of all stock; the bottom 80 percent own only 4 percent of total stock holdings. Moreover, there has been a sharp increase in the concentration of wealth since the 1980s. Moreover, the concentration of wealth is higher in the United States than in any of the other industrialized nations (Mishel et al. 2003). As just one example, John D. Rockefeller is typically heralded as one of the wealthiest men in U.S. history. But comparing Rockefeller with Bill Gates, in the value of today's dollars, Gates has already surpassed Rockefeller's riches (Myerson 1998).

In contrast to the vast amount of wealth and income controlled by elites, a very large proportion of Americans have hardly any financial assets once debt is subtracted. Nearly one-third have net worth of less than $10,000—hardly enough to handle a major emergency. Another 18 percent have zero or negative net worth—usually because their debt exceeds their assets, and levels of debt for U.S. households are now at an all-time high (Sullivan et al. 2000; Mishel et al. 2003). The American dream of owning a home, a new car, taking annual vacations, and sending one's children to good schools—not to mention saving for a comfortable retirement—is increasingly unattainable by many. When you see the amount of income and wealth controlled by a small segment of the population, a sobering picture of class inequality emerges. Wealth allows you to accumulate assets over generations. Thus, it is cumulative—giving advantages to subsequent generations that they might not have had on their own.

Popular legends, however, extol the possibility of anyone becoming rich in the United States. The well-to-do are admired not just for their style of life, but also for their supposed drive and diligence. The admiration for those who rise to the top makes it seem like anyone who is clever enough and works hard can become fabulously rich. Despite the prominence of rags-to-riches stories in American legend, most wealth in this society is inherited. A few individuals make their way into the elite class by virtue of their own success, but this is rare. The upper class is also overwhelmingly White and Protestant. The wealthy also exercise tremendous political power by funding lobbyists, exerting their social and personal influence on other elites, and contributing heavily to political campaigns. Studies of elites also find that they tend to be politically quite conservative (Burris 2000). They travel in exclusive social networks that tend to be open only to those in the upper class. They tend to intermarry, their children are likely to go to expensive schools, and they spend their leisure time in exclusive resorts.

Race also influences the pattern of wealth distribution in the United States; for every dollar of wealth held by White Americans, Black Americans have only 26 cents (Oliver and Shapiro 1995; Conley 1999). At all levels of income, occupation, and education, Black families have lower levels of wealth than similarly situated White families. Being able to draw on assets during times of economic stress means that families with some resources are better able to withstand difficult times than are those without assets. Even small assets, such as home owner-

DOING SOCIOLOGICAL RESEARCH

The Fragile Middle Class

The hallmark of the middle class in the United States is its presumed stability. Home ownership, a college education for children, and other accoutrements of middle class status (nice cars, annual vacations, an array of consumer goods)—these are the symbols of middle class prosperity. But, the rising rate of bankruptcy among the middle class shows that the middle class is not as secure as it is presumed to be. Personal bankruptcy has risen dramatically in recent years—more than one million filings for bankruptcy per year. How can this be happening in such a prosperous society?

This is the question examined by Teresa Sullivan, Elizabeth Warren, and Jay Lawrence Westbrook in their study of bankruptcy and debt among the middle class. They based their study on an analysis of official records of bankruptcy in five states, as well as on detailed questionnaires given to individuals who filed for bankruptcy. Their findings debunk the idea that bankruptcy is most common among poor people. They find that bankruptcy is a middle-class phenomenon representing a cross-section of those in this class

(meaning that those who are bankrupt are matched on the demographic characteristics of race, age, and gender with others in the middle class).

They also debunk the notion that bankruptcy is rising because it is so easy to file. Instead, they find that people in the middle class are so overwhelmed with debt that they cannot possibly pay. The biggest reason people give for filing for bankruptcy is the loss of income from the instability of jobs. But in addition, divorce, medical problems, housing expenses, and credit card debt drive many to bankruptcy court.

Sullivan and her colleagues thus explain the rise of bankruptcy as stemming from structural factors in society that fracture the stability of the middle class. The volatility of jobs under modern capitalism is one of the biggest factors, but add to this that there is a "thin safety net"—no health insurance for many, but rising medical costs. Also, the American dream of owning one's own home means many are "mortgage poor"—extended beyond their ability to keep up.

In addition: The United States is a credit driven society. Credit cards are

routinely mailed to people in the middle class, encouraging them to buy beyond their means. You can now buy virtually anything on credit: cars, clothes, doctor's appointments, entertainment, groceries. You can even use one credit card to pay off other credit cards. Indeed, it is difficult to live in this society without credit cards. Increased debt is the result. Many are simply unable to keep up with compounding interest and penalty payments, and debt takes on a life of its own as consumers cannot keep up even with the interest payments on debt.

Sullivan, Warren, and Westbrook conclude that increases in debt and uncertainty of income combine to produce the fragility of the middle class. Their research shows that "even the most secure family may be only a job loss, a medical problem, or an out-of-control credit card away from financial catastrophe" (2000: 6).

Questions to Consider

1. Have you ever had a credit card? If so, how easy was it to get? Is it possible to get by without a credit card?
Keywords: bankruptcy, credit card debt, student debt

2. What evidence do you see in your community of the fragility or stability of different social class groups?
Keywords: downward mobility, fragile middle class

We have included InfoTrac College Edition keywords at the end of each question to make it easier for you to find more to read on these topics. Go to **www.infotrac-college.com**, an online library, to begin your search.

Bankruptcy cases per million adults

FIGURE 7.3 Cases per million adults

SOURCE: Sullivan, Teresa A., Elizabeth Warren, and Jay Lawrence Westbrook. 2000. *The Fragile Middle Class: Americans in Debt*. New Haven: Yale University Press.

SOURCE: Sullivan, Teresa A., Elizabeth Warren, and Jay Lawrence Westbrook. 2000. *The Fragile Middle Class: Americans in Debt*. New Haven: Yale University Press.

ship or a savings account, provide protection from crises such as increased rent, a health emergency, or unemployment. Because the effects of wealth are intergenerational—that is, they accumulate over time—just providing equality of opportunity in the present does not address the differences in class status that Black and White Americans experience (Oliver and Shapiro 1995).

What explains the disparities in wealth by race? Wealth accumulates over time. Thus, government policies in the past have prevented Black Americans from being able to accumulate wealth. Discriminatory housing policies, bank lending policies, tax codes, and so forth have disadvantaged Black Americans, resulting in the differing assets Whites and Blacks in general hold now. Even though some of these discriminatory policies have ended, many also continue. Either way, their effects persist, resulting in what sociologists Oliver and Shapiro call the *sedimentation of racial inequality.*

Understanding the significance of wealth in shaping life chances for different groups also challenges a monolithic view of Hispanics. Cuban Americans and Spaniards are similar to Whites in their wealth holdings, whereas Mexicans, Puerto Ricans, Dominicans, and other Hispanic groups more closely resemble African Americans on the various indicators of wealth and social class. Likewise, one can better understand differences in class status among Asian American groups by carefully considering the importance not just of income, education, and occupation, but also patterns in the net assets of different groups (Conley 1999). Without significant wealth holdings, families of any race are less able to transmit assets from previous generations to the next generation, one main support of social mobility.

Despite beliefs to the contrary, class divisions in the United States are real, apparently permanent, and becoming more marked. The elite are becoming better off, whereas the positions of the middle class, working class, and poor seem to be worsening. Indeed, many middle-class people feel that their way of life is slipping away. Many factors have contributed to the declining fortunes of the lower and middle classes in the United States, including the profound effects of national and global economic change. Economic restructuring is concentrating wealth increasingly in the hands of a few. Reductions in state and federal spending have eliminated many government jobs—jobs that have traditionally been the route to middle-class standing for many workers. Job layoffs have left many out of work or sent former employees (both middle-class and blue-collar) into jobs with lower pay, less prestige, and perhaps no employee benefits, such as they had come to expect given their levels of education and experience. The government's own research (via the Census Bureau) shows that programs such as Social Security, school lunch programs, Medicaid, and so forth reduce inequality more than do taxes (DeNavas-Walt and Cleveland 2002). Yet, recent changes in tax policy heavily favor the already wealthy, thus amplifying the degree of class polarization.

The new economy has had mixed results for different groups (Andersen 2000). Income levels for women have increased, but, at the same time, they have decreased for men, except for the top 30 percent of earners. Since 1980, women in the bottom 10 percent of wage earners have also seen their wages decline. These are aggregate numbers—they reflect trends in the overall population, but these data show the varying impact of economic restructuring on different groups of people (Kilborn and Clemetson 2002; Mishel, Bernstein, and Boushey 2003). Whether these trends reverse or continue remains to be seen.

The tax structure has also distributed benefits unevenly, leading to some of the resistance to supporting social programs that would be subsidized through federal taxes. Corporations are benefiting the most from the tax structure, as corporate taxes have fallen in recent years (see Figure 7.4). While most Americans are paying more in federal tax than ever before (an increase from 13 to 15 cents per dollar of income earned since 1990), corporate taxes since 1990 have fallen from 26 cents on the dollar to 20 cents, even though corporate profits were up 252 percent in that period (Johnston 2000). Individuals at the upper ends of the class system have also been able to take advantage of numerous tax benefits and loopholes, reducing their tax burden, while that on the middle classes has increased. Understanding the differential impact of changes in the economy is an important part of analyzing the dynamics of social stratification, as well as contemporary politics.

Diverse Sources of Stratification

Class is only one basis for stratification in the United States. Factors like age, ethnicity, and national origin have a tremendous influence on stratification. Race and gender are two primary influences in the stratification system in the United States. In fact, analyzing class without also analyzing race and gender can be misleading. Race, class, and gender, as we are seeing throughout this book, are overlapping systems of stratification that people experience simultaneously. A working-class Latina, for example, does not experience herself as working class at one moment, Hispanic at another moment, and a woman the next. At any given point in time, her position in society is the result of her race, class, *and* gender status.

To explain in another way: Class position is manifested differently, depending on one's race and gender, just as gender is experienced differently depending on

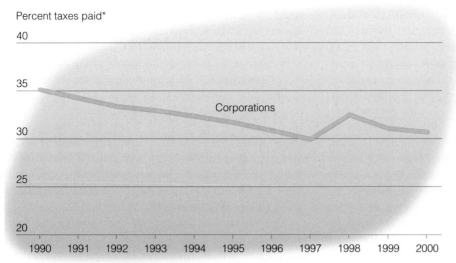

Percent taxes paid*

FIGURE 7.4 The Tax Burden: Declining Corporate Taxes

SOURCE: U.S. Census Bureau. 2002. *Statistical Abstract of the United States 2002.* Washington, DC: U.S. Department of Commerce, p. 495.

*on total income for households; on profits for corporations

one's race and class, and race is experienced differently, depending on one's gender and class. Depending on one's circumstances, race, class, or gender may seem particularly salient at a given moment in a person's life. For example, a Black middle-class man stopped and interrogated by police when driving through a predominantly White middle-class neighborhood may at that moment feel his racial status as his single most outstanding characteristic, but at all times his race, class, and gender influence his life chances. As social categories, race, class, and gender shape all people's experience in this society—not just those who are disadvantaged (Andersen and Collins 2004).

Class also significantly differentiates group experience within given racial and gender groups. Latinos, for example, are broadly defined as those who trace their origins to regions originally colonized by Spain. The ancestors of this group include both White Spanish colonists and the natives who were enslaved on Spanish plantations. Today, some Latinos identify as White, others as Black, and others by their specific national and cultural origins. The very different histories of those categorized as Latino are matched by significant differences in class. Some may have been schooled in the most affluent settings; others may be virtually unschooled. Those of upper-class standing may have had little experience with prejudice or discrimination; others may have been highly segregated into barrios and treated with extraordinary prejudice. Latinos who live near each other geographically in the United States and who are the same age and share similar ancestry, may have substantially different experiences based on their class standing (Massey 1993). Neither class, race, nor gender, taken alone, can be considered an adequate indicator of different group experiences, as shown in the box "Understanding Diversity: Latino Class Experience."

THE RACE–CLASS DEBATE. The relationship between race and class is much debated among sociologists. The Black middle class goes all the way back to the small numbers of free Blacks in the eighteenth and nineteenth centuries (Frazier 1957), expanding in the twentieth century to include those who were able to obtain an education and become established enough in industry, business, or a profession. Although wages for Black middle-class and professional workers never matched those of Whites in the same jobs, within the Black community, the Black middle class has had relatively high prestige. Many sociologists conclude that the class structure among African Americans has existed alongside the White class structure, separate and different.

In recent years, both the African American and Latino middle class have expanded, primarily as the result of increased access to education and middle-class occupations for people of color (Collins 1983; Higginbotham 2001; Pattillo-McCoy 1999). Although middle-class Blacks and Latinos may have economic privileges that others in these groups do not have, their class standing does not make them immune to the negative effects of race. Asian Americans also have a significant middle class, but they have also been stereotyped as the most successful minority group because of their presumed educational achievement, hard work, and thrift. This stereotype is referred to as the *myth of the model minority* and includes the idea that a minority group must adopt alleged dominant group values to succeed. This myth about Asian Americans obscures the significant obstacles to success that Asian Americans encounter, and it ignores the hard work and educational achievements of other racial and ethnic groups. The idea that Asian Americans are the "model minority" also obscures the high rates of poverty among many Asian American groups (Lee 1996).

Despite recent successes, many in the Black middle class also have a tenuous hold on this class status. The Black middle class remains as segregated from Whites as the Black poor, and continuing racial segregation in neighborhoods means that Black middle-class neighborhoods are typically closer to Black poor neighborhoods than the White middle class is to White poor people. This exposes many in the Black middle class to some of the same risks as those in poverty. This is not to say that the Black middle class has the same experience as the poor, but it challenges the view that the Black middle class "has it all" (Pattillo-McCoy 1999). Furthermore, Black Americans are still much more likely to be working class than middle class; they are also more likely to be working class than are Whites (Horton et al. 2000).

THE INFLUENCE OF GENDER AND AGE. The effects of gender further complicate the analysis of class. In the past, women were thought to derive their class position from their husband or father, but sociologists now challenge this assumption. Measured by their own income and occupation, the vast majority of women would likely be considered working class. The median income for women, even among those employed full time, is far below the national median income level. In 2001, when median income for men working year-round and full time was $38,275, the median income of women working year-round, full time was $29,215 (DeNavas-Walt and Cleveland 2002). The vast majority of women work in low-prestige and low-wage occupations, even though women and men have comparable levels of educational attainment. Women's class status is abundantly clear in the aftermath of a divorce, when women's income drops significantly, whereas men's increases (Peterson 1996a 1996b; Weitzman 1996; Weitzman 1985).

Age, too, is a significant source of stratification, as we saw in Chapter 3. Just being born in a particular generation can have a significant influence on one's life chances. The fears of current young, middle-class people that they will be unable to achieve the lifestyles of their parents show the effect that being in a particular generation can have on one's life chances. The effect of one's age on life chances is also not independent of the effect of race or gender. Being a young African American boy, for

UNDERSTANDING DIVERSITY

Latino Class Experience

*L*atinos in the United States are a diverse population of many different groups, each with many different national origins, histories, and cultural backgrounds. This diversity is represented by the fact that Latinos do not agree among themselves on what they should be called; some prefer "Latino," others "Hispanic," and some prefer to be identified by their cultural origins, as in Chicanos, Cuban Americans, or Puerto Riqueños. Some think of themselves as White. Generational differences further add to the diversity among Latinos.

Sociologist Douglas Massey reminds us of this diversity in thinking about the diverse class experiences of Latinos. Massey writes that as a result of different histories, Latinos live in different socioeconomic circumstances:

They may be fifth-generation Americans or new immigrants just stepping off the jetway. Depending on when and how they got to the United States, they may also know a long history of discrimination and repression or they may see the United States as a land of opportunity where origins do not matter. They may be affluent and well educated or poor and unschooled; they may have no personal experience of prejudice or discrimination, or they may harbor stinging resentment at being called a "spic" or being passed over for promotion because of their accent. (1993: 7–8)

Massey also notes that levels of residential segregation and poverty vary across different Latino groups. He notes that as socioeconomic levels rise and as immigrants reach second, third, and later generations within the United States, the degree of segregation for Latinos progressively falls. Puerto Ricans have higher levels of segregation than other Latino groups, as well as some of the highest rates of poverty. The migration route of Latinos into this country also contributes to their class position. Some Latinos are indigenous to the United States—that is, their families owned land in the American Southwest that was colonized by White settlers; others are recent immigrants who enter the economy as low-wage workers with little opportunity for upward mobility.

Diversity among Latinos has many implications for understanding the experience of this population. Some are caught in the economic underclass, others are middle class; a few are among the nation's elites. Massey reminds us that factors such as class, historical origins, residential segregation, race, and migration patterns must be carefully analyzed to understand Latino experiences.

SOURCE: Massey, Douglas S. 1993. "Latino Poverty Research: An Agenda for the 1990s." *Social Science Research Council Newsletter* 47 (March): 7–11.

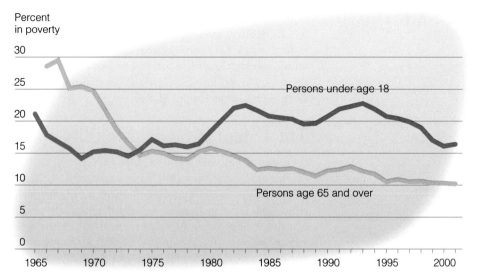

Percent
in poverty

FIGURE 7.5 Poverty among the Old and the Young

SOURCE: Proctor, Bernadette, and Joseph Dalaker. 2002. *Poverty in the United States: 2001.* Washington, DC: U.S. Department of Commerce, p. 4.

example, puts you far more at risk of poverty than being an older, White American man or even a young white boy.

The age group most likely to be poor are children, 16 percent of whom live in poverty in the United States. This represents a change from the recent past when the aged were the most likely to be poor (see Figure 7.5). Although many elderly people are now poor (10 percent of those 65 and over), far fewer in this age category are poor than was the case not many years ago (Proctor and Dalaker 2002). This shift reflects the greater affluence of the older segments of the population—a trend that is likely to continue as the current large cohort of middle-aged, middle-class Baby Boomers grow older.

Class Consciousness

Class consciousness is the perception that a class structure exists and the feeling of shared identification with others in one's class, others with whom one perceives common life chances (Centers 1949). Notice that there are two dimensions to the definition of class consciousness: the idea that a class structure exists and one's class identification.

There has been a long-standing argument that Americans are not very class conscious because of the strong cultural belief that upward mobility is possible. Images of opulence also saturate popular culture, making it seem that such material comforts are available to anyone. Many working-class and middle-class Americans focus on getting ahead individually and have little concern for organizing around class interests. The belief that anyone can succeed interferes with the development of strong class consciousness. The faith that upward mobility is possible ironically perpetuates inequality since, if people believe that everyone has the same chances of success,

then they are likely to think that whatever inequality exists must be fair.

Class inequality in any society is usually buttressed by ideas that support (or actively promote) inequality. Beliefs that people are biologically, culturally, or socially different can be used to justify the higher position of some groups. If people believe these ideas, the ideas provide legitimacy for the system. Karl Marx used the term **false consciousness** to describe the class consciousness of subordinate classes who had internalized the view of the dominant class. Marx argued that the ruling class controls subordinate classes by infiltrating their consciousness with belief systems that are consistent with the interests of the ruling class. If people accept these ideas, which justify inequality, they need not be overtly coerced into accepting the roles designated for them by the ruling class.

Class consciousness in the United States has been higher at some times than others. A significant labor movement in the 1920s and 1930s rested on a high degree of class consciousness. But now the formation of a relatively large middle class and a relatively high standard of living militates against class discontent. Racial and ethnic divisions also make strong alliances within various classes less stable. The recent trends of growing class inequality could result in greater class consciousness. Researchers find that people in the United States do recognize class divisions and believe that classes are organized around opposing interests. Forty-five percent of the public identifies as working class; 46 percent as middle class, 5.4 percent as lower class and 3.6 percent as upper class (National Opinion Research Center 2002; Gorman 2000; Vanneman and Cannon 1987), but this has not developed into a significant class-based movement for change.

▪ *Social Mobility: Myths and Realities*

There is a general belief in the United States that anyone can, by his or her own labor, move relatively freely through the class system. Is class mobility in the United States a fact or a myth? In this section, we will seek an answer to that question.

Defining Social Mobility

Social mobility is a person's movement over time from one class to another. Social mobility can be up or down, although the American dream emphasizes upward movement. Mobility can be either *inter*generational, occurring between generations, as when a daughter rises above the class of her mother or father; or *intra*generational, occurring within a generation, as when a person's class status changes as the result of business success (or disaster).

DEBUNKING
Society's Myths

Myth: The United States is a land of opportunity where anyone who works hard enough can get ahead.

Sociological perspective: Social mobility occurs in the United States, but less often than the myth asserts and over shorter distances from one class to another; most people remain in their class of origin.

Societies differ in the extent to which social mobility is permitted. Some societies are based on *closed class systems,* in which movement from one class to another is virtually impossible. In a caste system, for example, mobility is strictly limited by the circumstances of one's birth. At the other extreme are *open class systems,* in which placement in the class system is based on individual achievement, not ascription. In open class systems, there are relatively loose class boundaries, high rates of class mobility, and weak perceptions of class difference.

The class system in the United States is popularly characterized as an open class system where individual achievement, not birth, is the basis for class placement. Success stories of social mobility do occur, but experiences of mobility over great distances are rare and given far greater prominence in the public imagination than the more usual story: Most people remain in the same class as their parents, and many actually drop. Interestingly, the cultural idols of social mobility are typically men. Women are less frequently depicted as having the entrepreneurial personality or motivational drive alleged

to be a requirement for achieving the American dream. Social mobility in the United States is not impossible. Indeed, many have immigrated to this nation with the knowledge that their life chances are better here than in their countries of origin. How much social mobility actually exists in the United States?

The Extent of Social Mobility

Sociological research has found that social mobility is much more limited than the American dream suggests. What mobility exists is greatly influenced for all groups by education. African Americans, in particular, are traditionally strongly committed to social mobility through education, and increases in educational attainment for African Americans account for a considerable portion of the gains they have made (Smith 1989). In addition, the class status of social contacts (friends, relatives, neighbors) influences class placement for all groups (Hodge and Treiman 1968; Jackman 1983; Vanneman and Cannon 1987); however, education and social contacts are themselves heavily influenced by a person's class of origin.

The social status of an individual is more likely to be influenced by factors that affect the whole society than by individual characteristics. Most people who find themselves moving between classes can ascribe the cause to changes in the occupational system, economic cycles, and demographic factors, such as the number of college graduates in the labor force (Hout 1988; Erikson 1985; Vanneman and Cannon 1987). Most of the time, people remain in the class where they started; the privileges and disadvantages of class reproduce themselves. What mobility exists is typically short in distance (Blau and Duncan 1967; Ganzeboom et al. 1991). In sum, social mobility is much more limited than the American dream of mobility suggests.

Those who are upwardly mobile are often expected to distance themselves from their origins. This may mean creating some distance from their community of origin and can result in many conflicts—with family, with friends, and even within themselves. First-generation college students, for example, often find themselves torn between leaving home to go to school and remaining close to their family and community. Likewise, working-class women who are raised to have greater attachments to family and community may feel pressure from these groups not to move away. White working-class women, for example, are likely to have been socialized to marry, not pursue careers. Even though parents may have encouraged working-class women to become educated and seek a career, when they become successful, their families can be ambivalent about their success if success is seen as taking them away from their family and community origins.

The experience of upward mobility varies significantly by race and gender. African American families, for example, are more likely than White families to prepare their daughters for careers and are less likely to encourage marriage as a primary goal. At the same time, African American working-class parents are likely to steer daughters toward traditionally female occupations. This underscores an important sociological point about mobility: It is not just an individual process but a collective effort that involves kin and sometimes even community (Higginbotham and Weber 1992).

The attention people in the United States give to upward mobility has tended to obscure the experience of *downward mobility*—movement down in the class system. Overall, the rate of upward mobility exceeds the rate downward, but downward mobility is becoming more common (Newman 1988, 1993; Hout 1988). As income distribution is becoming more skewed toward the top, many in the middle class are experiencing a decline—or a very tenuous grip on their current class status.

▪ *Poverty*

Compared with most other nations in the world, the United States is affluent. Despite its relatively high average standard of living, however, poverty afflicts millions of people in the United States. Aside from imposing a grim quality of life on the poor, poverty is also the basis for many of society's problems. Poor health care, inadequate nutrition, failures in the education system, and crime are all related to poverty.

The federal government has established an official definition of poverty used to determine eligibility for government assistance and to measure the extent of poverty in the United States. The **poverty line** is the amount of money needed to support the basic needs of a household, as determined by government; below this line, one is considered officially poor. To determine the poverty line, the Social Security Administration takes a low-cost food budget (based on dietary information provided by the U.S. Department of Agriculture) and multiplies by a factor of three, assuming that a family spends approximately one-third of its budget on food. The resulting figure is the official poverty line, adjusted slightly each year for increases in the cost of living. In 2001, the official poverty line for a family of four was $18,022. Although a cutoff point is necessary to administer antipoverty programs, this definition of poverty can be misleading. A person or family earning $1 above the cutoff point would not be officially categorized as poor.

THINKING SOCIOLOGICALLY

Using the current federal *poverty line* ($18,022) as a guide, develop a monthly budget that does not exceed this income level and that accounts for all of your family's needs. For purposes of this exercise, assume that you head a family of four, the figure on which this poverty threshold is based. Base your budget on the actual costs of such things in your locale (rent, food, transportation, utilities, clothing, and so forth). Don't forget to account for taxes (state, federal, and local), health-care expenses, your children's education, car repairs, and so on. What does this exercise teach you about those who live below the poverty line?

Who Are the Poor?

There are now more than 32.9 million poor people in the United States, representing 11.7 percent of the population. Since the 1950s, poverty has declined in the United States; it increased sharply from about 1978 until the mid-1990s, declined, and has been on the rise again since 2000. Although the majority of the poor are White, disproportionately high rates of poverty are also found among Asian Americans, Native Americans, Black Americans, and Hispanics. One-third of Native Americans, 23 percent of African Americans, 21 percent of Hispanics, 10 percent of Asians and Pacific Islanders, and 8 percent of non-Hispanic Whites are poor (Proctor and Dalaker 2002). Among Hispanics, there are further differences among groups. Puerto Ricans—the Hispanic group with the lowest median income—have been most likely to suffer increased poverty, probably because of their concentration in the poorest segments of the labor market and their high unemployment rates (Tienda and Stier 1996; Hauan, Landale, and Leicht 2000). Asian American poverty has also increased substantially since the 1980s, particularly among the most recent immigrant groups, including Laotians, Cambodians, Vietnamese, Chinese, and Korean immigrants; Filipino and Asian Indian families had lower rates of poverty (Lee 1994).

The vast majority of the poor have always been women and children, but their proportion of the poor has been increasing in recent years. The term **feminization of poverty** refers to the increasing proportion of the poor who are women and children. This trend results from several factors, including the dramatic growth of female-headed households, a decline in the proportion of the poor who are elderly (not matched by a decline in the poverty of women and children), and continuing wage inequality between women and men. The large number of poor women is associated with a commensurate large

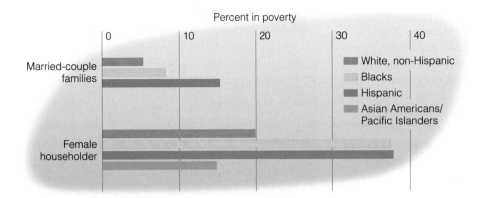

Percent in poverty

FIGURE 7.6 Poverty Status by Family Type and Race

SOURCE: Proctor, Bernadette, and Joseph Dalaker. 2002. *Poverty in the United States: 2001.* Washington, DC: U.S. Department of Commerce, pp. 22–25; U.S. Census Bureau. Detailed Poverty Tables, 2001: Table 1. Age, Sex, Household Relationship, Race, and Hispanic Origin—Poverty Status of People and Families by Selected Characteristics in 2001. Web site: **www.census.gov**

number of poor children. By 2001, 16 percent of all children (those under age eighteen) in the United States were poor, including 9.5 percent of non-Hispanic White children, 30 percent of Black children, 28 percent of Hispanic children, and 11.5 percent of Asian American children (Proctor and Dalaker 2002).

More than one-quarter of all families headed by women are poor (see Figure 7.6). In recent years, wages for young workers have declined; since most unmarried mothers are quite young, there is a strong likelihood their children will be poor. Because of the divorce rate and generally little child support provided by men, women are also increasingly likely to be without the contributing income of a spouse, and for longer periods of their lives. Women are more likely than men to live with children and to be financially responsible for them. However, women without children also suffer a high poverty rate, compounded in recent times by the fact that women now live longer than before and are less likely to be married than in previous periods.

Budget cutbacks in federal support programs and in federal employment have also contributed to the feminization of poverty. Almost two-thirds of the poor receive no food stamps; 80 percent get no housing assistance; less than half receive Medicaid, which is the federal health care system for the poor (U.S. Census Bureau 2002). Government budget reductions also disproportionately affect women because women are more reliant than men on public sector jobs. All told, government support for poor women and their children is quite negligible, despite the fact that the system is reviled as overly generous and producing sloth and dependence.

One marked change in poverty is the growth of poverty in suburban areas to over 8 percent of all poverty. At the same time, 40 percent of the poor live inside central cities. But the focus on urban poverty should not cause you to lose sight of the fact that 20 percent of the poor reside in rural areas.

The poor are not a monolithic group. They are racially diverse, including Whites, Blacks, Hispanics, Asian Americans, and Native Americans. They are di-

verse in age, including not just children and young mothers, but men and women of all ages, and especially a substantial number of the elderly, many of whom live alone. They are also geographically diverse, to be found in areas east and west, south and north, urban and rural, although, as Map 7.1 shows, poverty rates are generally higher in the South and Southwest.

Among the poor are the thousands of homeless. It is difficult to estimate the number of homeless people. Depending on how one defines and measures homelessness, the estimates vary widely. If you count the number of homeless on any given night, there may be about 444,000 to 842,000 homeless people (depending on the month measured), but measuring those experiencing homelessness during one year, the estimates jump to 2.3 to 3.5 million people (Urban Institute 2000; National Coalition for the Homeless 2002).

Despite public stereotypes associating poverty with urban areas, much of the nation's poverty is rural and the majority of poor people are White.

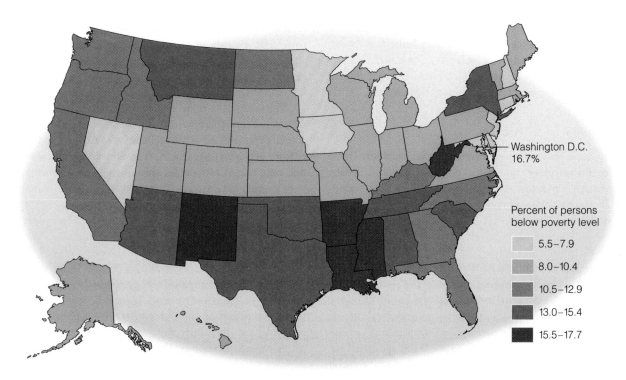

Washington D.C.
16.7%

Percent of persons
below poverty level

5.5–7.9

8.0–10.4

10.5–12.9

13.0–15.4

15.5–17.7

MAP 7.1 Mapping America's Diversity: Poverty in the United States,
2000–2001
*Regional differences in poverty rates reflect various social factors, including regional labor
markets, the degree of urbanization, and population composition, among other factors.*
What do you think are the major causes of poverty in your region?

SOURCE: Proctor, Bernadette D., and Joseph Dalaker. 2002. *Poverty in the United States: 2001.*
Washington, DC: U.S. Census Bureau, p. 10.

Whatever the actual numbers of homeless
people, there has been an increase in homelessness over the past two decades. Families are the
fastest growing segment of the homeless population, now constituting 40 percent of those who
are homeless. The homeless also includes battered women; elderly, poor men; the disabled;
veterans; and AIDS victims. A 2001 survey of
twenty-seven cities found that the homeless population is 50 percent African American, 35 percent White, 12 percent Hispanic, 2 percent Native
American, and 1 percent Asian (U.S. Conference
of Mayors 2001).

There are many reasons for homelessness. The
great majority of the homeless are on the streets
because of unemployment and/or eviction. Reductions in federal support for affordable housing have
left many with no place to live. Coupled with erod-
ing work opportunities (particularly in jobs with
decent benefits), inadequate housing for low-
income people, and reductions in public assistance,
many people have no choice but to live on the street. Add
to that problems of inadequate health care, domestic violence, and addiction and you begin to understand the

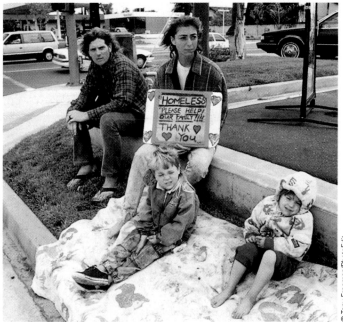

*Families, including women and their children, are the largest
portion of the nation's homeless; they are often left homeless because
of eviction and/or unemployment.*

factors that create homelessness. Some of the homeless (about 20 to 25 percent) are mentally ill; the movement to get mental patients out of institutional settings has left many without mental health resources that might help them (National Coalition for the Homeless 2002).

Causes of Poverty

Most agree that poverty is a serious social problem. There is far less agreement on what to do about it. Public debate about poverty hinges on disagreements about its underlying causes. Two points of view prevail: Some blame the poor for their own condition and some look to social structural causes to explain poverty. The first view, popular with the public and many policymakers, is that poverty is caused by the cultural habits of the poor. According to this point of view, behaviors such as crime, family breakdown, lack of ambition, and educational failure generate and sustain poverty, a syndrome to be treated by forcing the poor to fend for themselves. Sociologists take a more structural view, seeing poverty as rooted in the structure of society, less in the morals and behaviors of individuals.

BLAMING THE VICTIM: THE CULTURE OF POVERTY. Blaming the poor for being poor stems from the myth that success requires only individual motivation and ability. Many in the United States adhere to this view and hence have a harsh opinion of the poor. This attitude is reflected in U.S. public policy concerning poverty, which is rather ungenerous compared with other industrialized nations. Those who blame the poor for their own plight typically argue that poverty is the result of early childbearing, drug and alcohol abuse, refusal to enter the labor market, and crime. Such thinking puts the blame for poverty on individual choices, not on societal problems. In other words, it blames the victim, not the society, for social problems (Ryan 1971).

DEBUNKING
Society's Myths

Myth: If poor people would only get jobs, they could get out of poverty.

Sociological perspective: Forty percent of the poor work; the number of working poor has increased in recent years among those working year-round and full-time (Proctor and Dalaker 2002).

According to the **culture of poverty** argument, the major causes of poverty are welfare dependency, the absence of work values, and the irresponsibility of the poor. In this light, poverty is seen as a way of life that is trans-

ferred, like other cultures, from generation to generation. The culture of poverty argument has now been adapted by many policymakers to argue that the actual causes of poverty are found in the breakdown of major institutions, including the family, schools, and churches.

What truth is there to the culture of poverty argument? To probe this question, first we might ask, is poverty actually transmitted across generations? According to the culture of poverty argument, it is. Researchers, however, find only mixed support for this assumption. Children of poor parents have a 16 to 28 percent probability of being poor adults (Rodgers 1995), but many who are classified as poor remain poor for only one or two years. Their poverty occurs as the result of a household crisis, such as divorce, illness, unemployment, or parental death. More often, poverty occurs as the result of a household crisis, such as divorce, illness, unemployment, or parental death. People also cycle in and out of poverty. The public stereotype that poverty is passed on through generations is not well supported by the facts (Eller 1996; Shea 1995; Stevens 1994).

A second question is, Do the poor want to work? The persistent public stereotype that they do not is central to the culture of poverty thesis. This attitude presumes that poverty is the fault of the poor and that, if they would only change their values and adopt the American work ethic, then poverty would go away. What is the evidence for these claims?

A very large portion of the able-bodied poor do work. Of all poor persons, 41 percent work, but the focus on the jobless poor leads people to overlook the *working poor* (Newman 1999). The federal government has concluded that the proportion of workers who constitute the working poor has increased since 1980 to about 18 percent of the workforce. This means that 18 percent of the full-time work force earn wages at or below the poverty line. If a single mother of three works forty hours per week, fifty-two weeks per year, at minimum wage, her annual income will still fall far below the poverty line.

Current policies that force those on welfare to find employment also tend to overlook how difficult it is for many to retain the jobs they are able to get. The dead-end jobs that poor people get rarely provide a long-term solution to their problems. Prior to the welfare reforms of the 1990s, poor women who went off welfare to take jobs most often found that they soon had to return to welfare because the wages they earned were not enough to support themselves and their families. When people leave welfare for work, they typically lose various benefits, such as health care, that were part of their welfare status, even though their expenses increase (for example, for transportation, child care, clothing, and so forth). Although people want to work, the jobs available often do not lift them out of poverty. Yet, attributing poverty to the values of the poor remains the underlying framework of public policy. If the culture of poverty argument is incorrect, and yet is used to guide public policies, the likely result will be policies that are ineffective, mainly because they do not address the actual societal causes of poverty (Albelda and Tilly 1996; Catanzarite and Ortiz 1996).

STRUCTURAL CAUSES OF POVERTY. From a sociological point of view, the underlying causes of poverty lie in the economic and social transformations taking place in the United States. Careful scholars do not attribute poverty to a single cause. There are many causes. Two of the most important are the *restructuring of the economy,* which has resulted in diminished earning power and increased unemployment, and *the status of women in the family and the labor market,* which has contributed to the overrepresentation of women among the poor. Add to these underlying conditions the federal policies in recent years that have *diminished social support for the poor* in the form of welfare, public housing, and job training. Given these reductions in federal support, it is little wonder that poverty is so widespread.

The restructuring of the economy has caused the disappearance of manufacturing jobs, traditionally an avenue of job security and social mobility for many workers, especially African American and Latino workers (Baca Zinn and Eitzen 2001; Wilson 1996). The working class has been especially vulnerable to these changes (Marks 1991). Economic decline in those sectors of the economy where men have historically received good pay and good benefits has meant that fewer men are the sole support for their families. Most families now need two incomes to achieve a middle-class way of life. The new jobs that are being created fall primarily in occupations that offer low wages and few benefits; they also tend to be filled by women, especially women of color, leaving women poor and men out of work (McCall 2001; Browne 1999; Andreasse 1997). Such jobs offer little chance to get out of poverty. New jobs are also typically located in neighborhoods far away from the poor, creating a mismatch between the employment opportunities and the residential base of the poor.

Declining wage rates caused by transformations taking place within the economy fall particularly hard on young people, women, and African Americans and Latinos, who are the groups most likely to be among the working poor. Nearly 6 percent of people working year-round and full-time fall below the poverty line (Fine and Weis 1998; Proctor and Dalaker 2002).

The high rate of poverty among women is strongly related to women's status in the family and the labor market. Divorce is one cause of poverty, although minority women are more likely than White women to be poor even within marriage (Catanzarite and Ortiz 1996). Women's child-care responsibilities make working outside the home on marginal incomes difficult. Many women with children cannot manage to work outside the home because it leaves them with no one to watch their children. More women now depend on their own earnings to support themselves, their children, and other dependents. Whereas unemployment has always been considered a major cause of poverty among men, for women, wage discrimination has a major role. The median income for all women ($16,614 in 2001) is well below the poverty line (DeNavas-Walt and Cleveland 2002; Proctor and Dalaker 2002). Given these data, no wonder so many women are poor.

The persistence of poverty also increases tensions between different classes and racial groups. William Julius Wilson, one of the most noted analysts of poverty and racial inequality, has written, "The ultimate basis for current racial tension is the deleterious effect of basic structural changes in the modern American economy on Black and White lower-income groups, changes that include uneven economic growth, increasing technology and automation, industry relocation, and labor market segmentation" (1978: 154). This demonstrates the power of sociological thinking by convincingly placing the causes of both poverty and racism in their societal context.

Welfare and Social Policy

A central issue in the public discussion of poverty is welfare, or public assistance to poor individuals and families. Current welfare policy is covered by the 1996 Personal Responsibility and Work Reconciliation Act. Passed in the midst of public support for welfare reform, this federal policy eliminated the long-standing federal welfare program titled Aid to Families with Dependent Children, or AFDC. AFDC had been created in 1935 as part of the Social Security Act. Implemented during the Great Depression, AFDC was meant to assist poor mothers and their children and it acknowledged that some people are victimized by economic circumstances beyond their control and are deserving of public assistance. For much of its lifetime, this law provided support mostly to White mothers and their children; not until the 1960s did welfare come to be identified with Black families.

Current welfare policy eliminated federal welfare support. Instead, the new law gives block grants to states to administer their own welfare programs through what is known as Temporary Assistance for Needy Families (TANF). The new federal policy also stipulates a lifetime limit of five years for people to receive welfare and requires all welfare recipients to find work within two years—a policy known as "workfare." Those who have not found work within two years of receiving welfare can be expected to perform community service jobs for free.

Welfare—Myths and Realities

Current welfare policy mandates that welfare recipients must work if they are to receive benefits. This policy followed years of debate about welfare, much of which was based on fundamental misperceptions about the welfare system and those who receive welfare. Now there are frequent proclamations that welfare reform has reduced the welfare rolls; thus, many politicians laud welfare reform as a success. Is this so? Much of what is commonly understood about welfare has been shown to be wrong, based on sociological research. Sociology contributes to the welfare debate by dispelling many of the myths that cloud a deeply opinionated and political discussion. What do we know about welfare reform from current research?

Myth: The new welfare law passed in 1996 reduced the welfare rolls, indicating the success of welfare reform.

Reality:

- Fewer people are on welfare now than prior to welfare reform, but the implementation of TANF in 1996 occurred when the economy was strong and former welfare recipients could find jobs. When the economy weakened in 2001, welfare caseloads began to rise. Removal of the welfare safety net makes poor people especially vulnerable to economic cycles.

- The number of people on welfare is more a measure of the availability of public assistance than it is an indicator of people's actual well-being.

Myth: Women should be encouraged to marry as a way of reducing welfare dependence.

Reality:

- Forcing women to marry encourages women's dependence on men and punishes women for being independent.

- Large numbers of women receiving welfare have been victims of domestic violence; fear of domestic violence is one reason former welfare recipients give for not wanting to marry.

Myth: Mothers on welfare have more children to increase the size of their welfare checks.

Reality:

- No causal relationship exists between the size of welfare benefits and the number of births by welfare recipients.

- Many states prohibit increasing welfare benefits with the birth of an additional child.

Myth: Once someone goes on welfare, it creates a cycle of dependency and becomes a way of life.

Reality:

- Most people on welfare remain on welfare for a relatively short period, usually following a household crisis (such as health problems, unemployment, disability, domestic violence, or death of a spouse).

- Welfare cycling is the most common pattern; that is, people go on welfare for a relatively short time, exit, but return when jobs cannot sustain them.

Myth: People use their welfare checks to buy things they do not need.

Reality:

- When former welfare recipients find work, their expenses tend to go up. Though they may have increased income, their disposable income remains constant or declines.

- Low-income mothers who buy "treats" for their children (name-brand shoes, a movie, candy, etc.) do so because they want to be good mothers.

Myth: The existence of federal welfare programs encourages people to stay on welfare.

Reality:

- Persistent poverty, especially among children, increases when federal support programs are being cut back.

- Poverty dropped during the period when strong federal support programs were available to assist poor people.

Critical Thinking Exercise:

1. A number of organizations provide research and encourage public policies and programs designed to assist those in need. What current policies on poverty, welfare, and work are being debated? To get more information, use this sampling of organizations and Web sites that will provide both policy information and research on welfare and work:

Coalition for Human Needs:
www.chn.org

Institute for Women's Policy Research:
www.iwpr.oorg

Institute for Poverty Research:
www.northwestern.edu/ipr

Institute for Research on Poverty:
www.ssc.wisc.edu/irp

Joint Center for Poverty Research:
www.jcpr.org

Welfare Information Network:
www.welfareinfo.org

Sources: Butler, Amy C. 1996. "The Effect of Welfare Benefit Levels on Poverty Among Single-Parent Families." *Social Problems* 43 (February): 94–115; Curcio, William Thomas. 1999. "Domestic Abuse, Sexual Trauma, and Welfare Receipt: Prevalence, Effects and Implications for Poverty Theory." Ph. D. Dissertation, Rutgers University; Edin, Kathryn, and Laura Lein. 1997. *Making Ends Meet: How Single Mothers Survive Welfare and Low-Wage Work.* New York: Russell Sage Foundation; Harris, Kathleen Mullan. 1996. "Life after Welfare: Women, Work, and Repeat Dependency." *American Sociological Review* 61 (June): 407–426; Larrison, Christopher R., Larry Nackerud, and Ed Risler. 2001. *Journal of Sociology and Social Welfare* 28 (September): 49–69; Mink, Gwendolyn. 2001. "Violating Women: Rights Abuses in the Welfare Police State." *Annals of the American Academy of Political and Social Science* (September): 79–93; O'Campo, Patricia and Lucia Rojas-Smith. 1998. "Welfare Reform and Women's Health: Review of the Literature and Implications for State Policy." *Journal of Public Health Policy* 19: 420–446. Winship, Scott, and Christopher Jencks. 2002. "The Well-Being of Single Mothers after Welfare Reform, as Measured by Changes in Food Security." Policy Brief, Vol. 4, No. 7. Joint Center for Poverty Research, Northwestern University. Web site: **www.jcpr.org**

In addition, welfare policy denies payments to unmarried teen parents under eighteen years of age unless they stay in school and live with an adult. It also requires unmarried mothers to identify the fathers of their children or risk losing their benefits. The new welfare law also denies a wide range of social support programs to immigrants—both legal and illegal (Mink 1999). These broad guidelines are established at the federal level, but individual states can be more restrictive, as many have been.

At the heart of welfare reform is the idea that poor people do not want to work and that providing public assistance creates dependence that discourages them from seeking jobs. Is welfare reform working? Many studies are finding that low-wage work simply does not lift former welfare recipients out of poverty (McCrate and Smith 1998; Edin and Lein 1997). Critics of the current policy also argue that forcing welfare recipients to work provides a cheap labor force for employers and potentially takes jobs from those already employed. In the first few years of welfare reform, the nation was also in the midst of an economic boom; jobs were thus more plentiful. But in an economic downturn, those who are on aid or in marginal jobs can become even more vulnerable to economic distress, particularly given the time limits now placed on receiving public assistance (Albelda and Withorn 2002).

Research on the effects of the new welfare policy is relatively recent. Politicians brag that welfare rolls have shrunk, but this is a poor measure of the impact of welfare reform because this would be expected if people are cut off from benefits. Because welfare has been decentralized to the state level, studies of the impact of current

law have had to be done on a state-by-state basis. These studies show that those who have entered workfare programs most often earn wages that keep them below the poverty line. Although some states report that family income has increased, earnings are meager. (In Illinois, for example, where one of the most comprehensive studies was done, the family income of former welfare recipients increased from only $7,475 to $11,812 following the implementation of TANF.) Since welfare reform, there has also been an increase in the number of housing evictions because of people falling behind on rent. Families also report an increase in other material hardships—phones and utilities being cut off, for example. In some states the numbers of people neither working nor receiving aid also increased (Lewis, Stevens, and Slack 2002; Acker, Morgen, and Gonzales 2002; Bernstein 2002).

The public debate about welfare rages on, often in the absence of informed knowledge from sociological research and almost always without input from the subjects of the debate, the welfare recipients themselves. Although stigmatized as lazy and not wanting to work, those who have received welfare actually believe that it has negative consequences for them, but they say they have no other viable means of support. Typically, they need welfare when they cannot find work, or have small children and are without childcare. Few leave jobs voluntarily. Welfare recipients also say that the welfare system makes it hard to become self-supporting because the wages one earns while on welfare are deducted from an already minimal subsistence level. Furthermore, there is not enough affordable day care for mothers to leave home and get jobs. Contrary to the popular image of the conniving "welfare queen," the opinions of welfare recipients show that they have respect for family values and that they want to get off welfare, but they think welfare is their only option. Their biggest problem is simple—lack of money (Edin 1991; Popkin 1990).

TAKING ON SOCIAL ISSUES

Is Marriage the Solution to Poverty?

Some, including President George W. Bush, have suggested that the best solution to poverty and welfare spending is for more poor women to be married. Federal legislation has even included funds for programs promoting marriage in the expenditures for social welfare. Certainly having two incomes in a household raises economic well-being, but what other issues should be addressed in considering marriage as a solution to women's poverty?

Taking Action

Go to the Taking Action exercise on the companion Web site at **sociology.wadsworth.com/andersen_taylor/essen3e** to learn more about an organization that addresses this topic.

■ *Chapter Summary*

■ *What different kinds of stratification systems exist?*

Social stratification is a relatively fixed hierarchical arrangement in society by which groups have different access to resources, power, and perceived social worth. All societies have systems of stratification, although they vary in how they are composed and how complex they are. *Estate systems* are those where power and property are held by a single elite class; in *caste systems,* placement in the stratification is by birth, whereas in *class systems,* placement is determined by achievement.

- **How do sociologists define class?**

  Class is the social structural position groups hold relative to the economic, social, political, and cultural resources of society. It is highly significant in determining one's *life chances.*

- **What analyses of social stratification do sociological theorists provide?**

  Karl Marx saw class as primarily stemming from economic forces; Max Weber had a multidimensional view of stratification, involving economic, social, and political dimensions. Two theoretical perspectives are used in sociology to explain inequality—*functionalism* and *conflict theory.* Functionalists argue that social inequality motivates people to fill the different positions in society that are needed for the survival of the whole, claiming that the positions most important for society require the greatest degree of talent or training and are, thus, most rewarded. Conflict theorists see social stratification as based on class conflict and blocked opportunity, pointing out that those at the bottom of the stratification system are least rewarded because they are subordinated by dominant groups.

- **How is the class system structured in the United States?**

  Social class can be seen as a hierarchy, like a ladder, where income, occupation, and education are indicators of class. *Status attainment* is the process by which people end up in a given position in this hierarchy. *Prestige* is the value assigned to people and groups by others within this hierarchy. Classes are also organized around common interests and exist in conflict with one another. Sociological research on the class system shows that the United States is a highly stratified society, with an unequal distribution of wealth and income. Indeed, *wealth* inequality has been increasing. Factors such as gender, race, and age also influence one's location in the class structure.

- **Is this a class-conscious society?**

  Class consciousness is both the perception that a class structure exists and the feeling of shared identification with others in one's class. The United States has not been a particularly class-conscious society because of the belief in upward mobility.

- **Is there social mobility in the United States?**

  Despite the presence of class inequality, the American dream is that people can move up in the class system based on their ability. This myth assumes that the United States has an open class system. *Open class systems* are those in which movement from one class to another is possible. *Social mobility* is the movement between class positions. It is less common than is believed. Education gives some boost to social mobility, but social mobility is limited; most people end up in a class position very close to their class of origin.

- **How do sociologists explain why there is poverty in the United States?**

  The *culture of poverty thesis* is the idea that poverty is the result of the cultural habits of the poor that are transmitted from generation to generation, but sociologists see poverty as caused by social structural conditions, including unemployment, gender inequality in the workplace, and the absence of support for child care for working parents.

- **What current policies address the problem of poverty?**

  Current welfare policy, adopted in 1996, provides support through individual states, but recipients are required to work after two years of support and have a lifetime limit of five years' support.

▪ Key Terms

caste system 183	occupational prestige 189
class consciousness 199	poverty line 201
class 185	prestige 189
culture of poverty 204	social class 185
educational attainment 190	social differentiation 182
estate system 183	social mobility 187
false consciousness 199	social stratification 183
feminization of poverty 201	socioeconomic status 189
ideology 185	status 182
income 189	status attainment 189
life chances 184	urban underclass 192
median income 189	wealth 194

▪ Researching Society with MicroCase Online

You can see the results of actual research by using the Wadsworth MicroCase® Online feature available to you. This feature allows you to look at some of the results from national surveys, census data, and other data sources. You can explore this easy-to-use feature on your own, but try this example. Suppose you want to know some social facts, such as:

Does one's support for spending on social welfare vary according to one's social class?

To answer this question, go to **sociology.wadsworth
.com/andersen_taylor/essen3e**, select MicroCase Online from the left navigation bar, and follow the directions there to analyze the data described below.

Data file: GSS

Task: Cross-Tabulation

Row Variable: WELFARE $

Column Variable: INCOME

Questions

Once you have your results, answer the following
questions.

1. People in which income group are *most* likely to support increased spending on social welfare?

2. What reasons can you find to explain these differences? Be sure to reference data from the table in
   your answer.

Now analyze the following data to answer the rest of the
questions.

Data file: GSS

Task: Auto-Analyzer

Primary Variable: WELFARE $

3. Of the demographic groups (variables) included in
   this analysis, in which groups are there significant
   differences? List the variable names.

4. Does what you found in question 3 change your answer for question 2. Explain how these data do or do
   not support your previous explanation.

▪ *The Companion Web Site for* Sociology: The Essentials, *Third Edition*

sociology.wadsworth.com/andersen_taylor/essen3e

Supplement your review of this chapter by going to the
companion Web site to take one of the Tutorial Quizzes,
use the flash cards to master key terms, and check out the
many other study aids you'll find there. You'll also find
special features such as GSS Data and Census 2000 information, data and resources at your fingertips to help you
with that special project or do some research on your own.

▪ *Suggested Readings and Web Resources*

Albelda, Randy, and Ann Withorn. 2000. *Lost Ground: Welfare Reform, Poverty and Beyond.* Boston: South End Press.
*This collection of essays examines the implications of wel-
fare reform and gives a careful analysis of its effects, particularly on women. The essays cover the effects of reform,
as well as activism to change welfare policy.*

Andersen, Margaret L., and Patricia Hill Collins. 2004.
Race, Class, and Gender: An Anthology, 5th ed. Belmont, CA: Wadsworth.
*This anthology explores the intersections of race, class, and
gender as systems of stratification and how they affect
group experience in a number of social institutions. A
widely used anthology, the book includes personal narratives, as well as analytical accounts of race, class, and gender in the experiences of different groups.*

Ehrenreich, Barbara. 2001. *Nickel and Dimed: On (Not)
Getting By in America.* New York: Metropolitan
Books.
*Ehrenreich, a journalist, spent several months working in
low-wage jobs. Her engaging, first-hand account of the
indignities of this work shows how millions of workers
struggle to make ends meet while performing some of the
most socially devalued labor.*

McCoy, Mary Pattillo. 1999. *Black Picket Fences: Privilege
and Peril among the Black Middle Class.* Chicago: University of Chicago Press.
*McCoy's study debunks the idea that the Black middle
class now has it made. Instead, she shows how tenuous the
hold on middle class status is for many and the continuing
segregation and racism that marks this experience, even in
a context where the middle class is more successful than in
the past.*

Newman, Katherine. 1999. *No Shame in My Game: The
Working Poor in the Inner City.* New York: Russell
Sage Foundation/Vintage.
*Newman's study of Harlem challenges the idea that inner
city communities are only comprised of poor, unemployed
people. By using life histories that provide a close-up view
of the people's lives in Harlem, she documents the experience
of the working poor. It is a compelling and transforming
portrait of not only Harlem, but other working class communities where people strive every day to make ends meet.*

Oliver, Melvin L., and Thomas M. Shapiro. 1995. *Black
Wealth/White Wealth: A New Perspective on Racial In-
equality.* New York: Routledge.
*By focusing their analysis on wealth, not just income,
Oliver and Shapiro provide a compelling analysis of the
source of continuing inequity in the class standing of
African Americans and White Americans.*

U.S. Census Bureau
www.census.gov/
*The U.S. Census Bureau publishes numerous reports that
provide the best national data on income, poverty, and*

other measures that depict the class structure of the United States. In addition, the much-used reference book, Statistical Abstract of the United States, *is available online at this site.*

National Coalition for the Homeless
www.nationalhomeless.org
This site provides information on the extent of homelessness, as well as bibliographies and other information pertinent to the study of homelessness.

The Urban Institute
www.urban.org
The Urban Institute is a nonprofit policy research organization whose goals are to analyze society's problems and the efforts to solve them. This Web site provides analysis and commentary on topics such as the working poor, welfare reform, urban poverty, and other important issues.

CHAPTER EIGHT

Global Stratification

"It takes a village to raise a child," the saying goes. But it also seems to take a world to make a shirt—or so it seems from looking at the global dimensions of the production and distribution of goods. Try this simple experiment: Look at the labels on your clothing. (If you do this in class, try to do so without embarrassing yourself and others!) What do you see? "Made in Indonesia," "Made in Bangladesh," "Made in Malawi"—all indicating the linkage of the U.S. to systems of production around the world. The popular brand Nike, as just one example, has not a single factory in the United States, although its founder and chief executive officer is one of the wealthiest people in the country. Nike products are manufactured mostly in China and Indonesia, nations where human rights abuses of workers are commonly reported. In Vietnam, where one of Nike's manufacturing plants is located, young women provide much of the labor, working sixty-five hours per week for a total of $10 (Sanders and Kaptur 1997).

Taking your experiment further, ask yourself who made your clothing? A young person trying to lift his or her family out of poverty? Might it have been a child? In many areas of the world, one in five children under age 15 work (International Labour Organization 2002). In what countries do the benefits of this system of production most accrue? Answering these questions can reveal much about the interconnection among countries in the *global stratification* system. The status of people in one country is intricately linked to the status of people in others.

Recall from Chapter 1 that C. Wright Mills identified the task of sociology as seeing the social forces that exist beyond the individual. This is particularly important when studying global stratification. The person in the United States (or western Europe or Japan) who thinks he or she is expressing individualism by wearing the latest style is actually located in a global system of inequality whereby the adornments available to that person result from a whole network of forces that produce affluence in some nations and poverty in others.

Dominant in the system of global stratification are the United States and other wealthy nations. Those at the top of the global stratification system have enormous power over the fate of other nations. Although world conflict stems from many sources, including religious differences, cultural conflicts, and struggles over political philosophy, the inequality between rich and poor nations creates much hatred and resentment. One cannot help but wonder if some of the conflicts in the world today might be reduced were there not such huge differences in the wealth of some nations and the poverty of others. In this chapter we examine the dynamics and effects of global stratification.

■ *Global Stratification*

People often call the United States the most powerful nation in the world. That status derives in part from the position of the United States at the top of the global stratification system, a global system of interdependent nations. In the world today, there are not only rich and poor people, but also rich and poor countries. Some countries are well-off, some countries are doing so-so, and a growing number of countries are poor and getting poorer. There is, in other words, a **global stratification** system in which the units are countries, much like a system of stratification within countries in which the units are individuals or families. Just as we can talk about the upper-class or lower-class individuals within a country, we can also talk of the equivalent of upper-class or lower-class countries in this world system. One manifestation of global stratification is the great inequality in life chances that differentiates nations around the world.

Simple measures of well-being, including life expectancy, infant mortality, and access to health services, reveal the consequences of a global system of inequality (see Table 8.1). And, the gap between the rich and poor is sometimes greater in nations where the average person is least well off. No longer can any one of these nations be understood independently from the global system of stratification of which it is a part.

Understanding the global stratification system reminds us that nations cannot be seen independently of economic and sociological processes that link them in a world-based economy. The effects of the global economy on inequality have become increasingly evident, as witnessed by political demonstrations in the United States against world trade policies. A coalition of unions, environmentalists, and other groups has emerged to protest global trade policies that they believe threaten jobs and

TABLE 8.1 Quality of Life: A Comparative Perspective

	Life Expectancy	Infant Mortality (per 1,000 births)	Percentage of Women Enrolled in Elementary School	Child Malnutrition (% under weight)	Percent with Access to Safe Water
Afghanistan	43 yrs.	163	15%	49%	13%
Iran	69	33	74	11	95
Iraq	61	93	74	na	85
Mexico	73	29	100	8	86
United Kingdom	77	7	100	na	100
United States	77	7	95	1	100

SOURCE: World Bank. 2002. *World Bank Atlas 2002*. Washington, DC: The World Bank, pp. 28–29.

workers' rights (in the United States and abroad), contribute to the degradation of the world's natural environment, and encourage further McDonaldization (see Chapter 5). Popular stores such as The Gap, Niketown, and Nordstrom's have often been the target of these protests because they symbolize the expansion of global capitalism. Protestors also see the growth of such stores as representing the decline in local cultural values that comes with economic globalization. Protests over world trade policies have also emerged in a student-based movement against companies that manufacture apparel with college logos. Calling for fair employment practices, students across the nation have protested the treatment of workers in sweatshops at home and abroad (see the box "Sociology in Practice: Symbols, Sportswear, and Sweatshops").

The relative affluence of the United States means that U.S. consumers have access to goods produced around the world. A simple thing, such as a child's toy, can represent this global system. For many young girls in the United States, Barbie™ is the ideal of fashion and romance. Young girls may have not just one Barbie, but several, each with a specific role and costume. Cheaply bought in the United States, but produced overseas, Barbie is manufactured by those probably not much older than the young girls who play with her and who would need all of their monthly pay to buy just one of the dolls that many U.S. girls collect by the dozens. In China, for instance, where more toys are produced than in any other part of the world, workers molding Barbie dolls earn 25 cents per hour, and human rights organizations say violations of basic rights are flagrant (Press 1996: 12).

The manufacturing of toys and clothing are examples of the global stratification that links the United States and other parts of the world. Workers in the United States may lose jobs when companies export jobs. To see this, note that in 1973, more than 56,000 U.S.

workers were employed in toy factories. Now, even though the market has become more glutted with the latest popular items, only 27,000 workers work in toy factories. The companies that make the toys amass profits, but U.S. workers lose jobs and then blame foreign workers for taking them. But who has gained? Indonesian workers making Barbies earn the minimum wage of $2.25 per day. It would take such a worker a full month to earn the money to buy the Calvin Klein Barbie (Press 1996). But the CEO of Mattel (the company that produces Barbie) earns millions both in salary and stock options—exceeding the combined salaries of all the Mattel workers who produce Barbie dolls in China.

Rich and Poor

One dimension of stratification between countries is wealth. Enormous differences exist between the wealth

Many common products marketed in the United States are produced in a global economy, sometimes by child laborers.

of the countries at the top of the global stratification system and the wealth of the countries at the bottom. Although there are different ways to measure the wealth of nations, one of the most common is to use the **per capita gross national income** (per capita GNI). This measures the total output of goods and services produced by residents of a country each year plus the income from nonresident sources, divided by the size of the population. This does not truly reflect what individuals or families receive in wages or pay; it is simply each person's annual share of their country's income, should the proceeds be shared equally.

Per capita GNI is reliable only in countries that are based on a cash economy. It does not measure informal exchanges or bartering in which resources are exchanged without money changing hands. These noncash transactions are not included in the GNP calculation, but they are more common in developing countries. As a result,

measures of wealth based on the GNI, or other statistics that count cash transactions, are less reliable among the poorer countries and may underestimate the wealth of the countries at the lower end of the economic scale.

The per capita GNI of the United States, which is one of the wealthier nations in the world (though not the wealthiest on a per capita basis) was $34,100 in 2000. The per capita GNI in Ethiopia, one of the poorest countries in the world was $100. Using per capita GNI as a measure of wealth, the average person in the United States is 341 times wealthier than an average citizen of Ethiopia. The inequality between the rich and poor nations is also increasing (World Bank 2002).

Which are the wealthiest nations? Figure 8.1 shows data from the World Bank listing the ten richest countries in the world measured by the annual per capita GNI in 2000. Luxembourg, with an annual per capita GNI of

---

SOCIOLOGY IN PRACTICE

Symbols, Sportswear, and Sweatshops

In the late 1990s, as college students became aware that products bearing college logos were being produced in sweatshops, a strong antisweatshop movement emerged on many U.S. campuses. Major companies pay universities royalties in exchange for the right to use the campus logo on shirts, hats, jackets, and other items. Students organized teach-ins, sit-ins, and demonstrations, calling for "sweat-free" campuses. Students at the University of Colorado organized a "Why Shop?" week in November 1999, posting a Web page with information about college logos, sweatshops, and garment workers in the United States and abroad. This large student-led movement was largely organized through electronic mailing lists and Web sites where students posted information about sweatshops and the garment industry worldwide. Noting that business was reaping over $2.5 billion in college merchandise sales, students demanded that workers be paid a living wage and that discrimination against women in this industry end. As a result, some uni-

versities adopted codes of labor rights for those it licenses to sell products with college logos.

The U.S. General Accounting Office defines a *sweatshop* as a workplace where an employer violates more than one law regarding federal or state labor, industrial homework, occupational safety and health, workers' compensation, or industry regulation. The largest number of sweatshop workers in the United States are immigrant women in the garment industry who work sixty to eighty hours a week, often without minimum wage or overtime pay. The garment industry, though high-tech in the design phase, is still very low-tech in production—usually a woman sitting at a sewing machine stitching. Conditions are often dangerous, with blocked exits, unsanitary bathrooms, and poor ventilation. The government estimates that 75 percent of U.S. garment shops violate safety and health laws. Workers are often intimidated from organizing or speaking out for fears of reprisal, such as job loss or deportation. Abroad, conditions are just as bad, if not worse. Compensation is extremely low (see Figure

8.1). Sociologists calculate that workers in places such as Mexico, Indonesia, or Vietnam can earn as little as 12 cents to 50 cents per hour. Labor costs are a tiny fraction of the retail price finally paid by the consumer. Factories are typically unregulated and pose numerous health hazards for workers, including reports of sexual assault of some women workers.

Critical Thinking Exercise

1. Where are the products bearing your college labels manufactured and sold? Who profits from the distribution of these goods? Has there been a movement against this at your school and, if so, what have been the results?

2. Go to two of the stores that are most popular with college students in your region. Make a list of the countries where their clothing products are made. Given the price of the clothing, what can you infer about global stratification?

FOR FURTHER INFORMATION: Applebaum, Richard, and Peter Dreier. 1999. "The Campus Anti-Sweatshop Movement." *The American Prospect* 46 (September–October): 71.

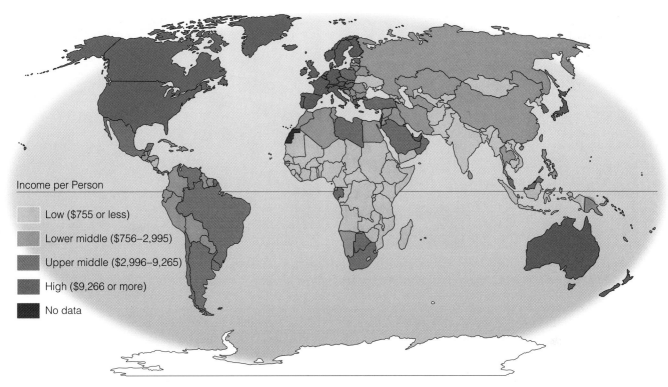

MAP 8.1 Viewing Society in Global Perspective: Rich and Poor Worldwide

Most nations are linked in a world system that produces wealth for some, poverty for others. Identify one of the nations represented here. **Would you say this nation is a core, semiperipheral, or peripheral country in the global economy? Why?**

SOURCE: World Bank. 2002. *World Bank Atlas 2002*. Washington, DC: The World Bank, p. 42. Used by permission of the International Bank for Reconstruction and Development/The World Bank.

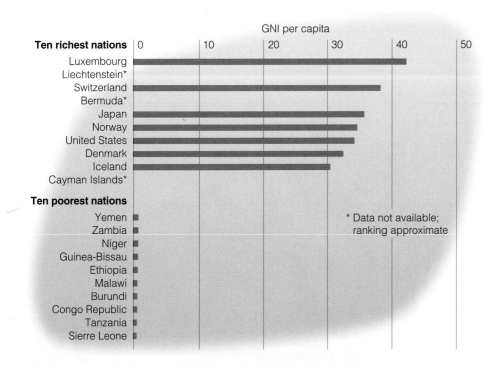

FIGURE 8.1 The Rich and the Poor: A World View

SOURCE: World Bank. 2002. *World Bank Atlas*. New York: The World Bank, pp. 18–19. Used by permission.

The gap between the rich and poor worldwide can be staggering. At the same time that many struggle for mere survival, others enjoy the pleasantries of a gentrified lifestyle.

$42,000 in 2000 in U.S. dollars, is the richest country in the world on a per capita basis. The United States ranks fifth. In terms of total wealth, the United States is the richest country in the world. Most of the wealthy countries are in western Europe, but include the United States and Japan. They are all industrialized countries, mostly urban, and except for the United States and Japan, they have relatively small populations. Among the nations of the world, these countries represent the equivalent of the upper class.

In contrast, let us look at the ten poorest countries in the world, shown in Figure 8.1, again using per capita GNI as the measure of wealth. Several countries are even poorer than these countries, but they are not often listed in official data because they are too poor to report reliable statistics. Note that the world's poorest countries are mostly in eastern or central Africa. These countries have not become industrialized, are largely rural, have high fertility rates, and still depend heavily on subsistence agriculture. Based on the dimension of wealth, these countries rank at the bottom of the global stratification system.

Clearly, many countries in the world are very poor, whereas other countries are rich. This does not mean that all people in rich countries are rich, or that all people in poor countries are poor. But on the average, people in poor countries are much worse off than people in rich countries. In many poor countries, the life of an average citizen is desperate, and starvation is a growing problem. These countries also have the largest populations. In a world with a population of nearly six billion, more than three billion—more than half the world's population—live in the poorest forty-five countries. Often poor nations are rich with natural resources but are exploited for such resources by more powerful nations. We will look more closely at the nature and causes of world poverty later in this chapter.

The Core and Periphery

Global stratification involves nations in a large and integrated network of both economic and political relation-

Global stratification means not only that enormous differences exist in the relative well-being of different countries, but also within nations. Large numbers of people live in poverty such as in this refugee camp at Mazar-i-Sharif in Afghanistan—one of the poorest nations in the world.

ships. Power—meaning the ability of a country to exercise control over other countries or groups of countries—is a significant dimension of global stratification. Countries can exercise several kinds of power over other countries, including military, economic, and political power. The **core countries** have the most power in the world economic system. These countries control and profit the most from the world system, and thus they are the "core" of the world system. These include the powerful nations of Europe, the United States, Australia, and Japan.

Surrounding the core countries, both structurally and geographically, are the **semiperipheral countries** that are semi-industrialized and, to some degree, represent a kind of middle class. They play a middleman role, extracting profits from the poor countries and passing those profits on to the core countries. The semiperipheral countries include such countries as Spain, Turkey, and Mexico.

At the bottom of the world stratification system, in this model, are the **peripheral countries.** These are the poor, largely agricultural countries of the world. Even though they are poor, they often have important natural resources that are exploited by the core countries. This exploitation, in turn, keeps them from developing and perpetuates their poverty. Often these nations are politically

unstable and, though they exercise little world power, political instability can cause a crisis for core nations that depend on their resources. Military intervention by the United States or European nations is often the result.

This categorizing system emphasizes the power of each country in the world economic system. Another way that these countries are sometimes labeled is as first, second, and third world nations. This language grows out of the politics of the Cold War and reflects the political and economic dimensions of global stratification.

First-world countries consist of the industrialized capitalist countries of the world, including the United States, New Zealand, Australia, Japan, and the countries of western Europe. They are industrialized and have a market-based economy and a democratically elected government. The **second-world countries** are socialist countries, which included the former Soviet Union, China, Cuba, North Korea, and, prior to the fall of the Berlin Wall, the eastern European nations. During the Cold War, these countries had a communist-based government and a state-managed economy, as some still do. Although less developed than the first-world countries, the second-world countries tried to provide citizens with services such as free education, health care, and low-cost

DOING SOCIOLOGICAL RESEARCH

Servants of Globalization: Who Does the Domestic Work?

International migration is becoming an increasingly common phenomenon. Women are one of the largest groups to experience migration, often leaving poor nations to become domestic workers in wealthier nations. Rhacel Salazar Parreñas studied two communities of Filipina women—one in Los Angeles and one in Rome, Italy—to learn how these women's experiences were part of the system of global stratification.

She conducted her research through extensive interviewing with Filipina domestics in Rome and Los Angeles, supplementing the interviews with participant observation in church settings, after-work social gatherings, and in employers' homes. The interviews were conducted in English and Tagalog—sometimes a mixture of both.

Among other things Parreñas found that Filipina domestics experienced many status inconsistencies. They

were upwardly mobile in terms of their home country, but were excluded from the middle-class Filipino communities in the communities where they lived. Thus, they experienced feelings of social exclusion, even while they were separated from their own families. Their own families are transnational—that is, they often left family members, including their children, at home as they sought better employment. As part of the process of global restructuring, Filipinas provide some of the labor in more affluent households, even while their own lives are disrupted by new global forces.

Questions to Consider

1. Are there domestic workers in your community who provide child care and other household work for middle and upper-class households? What is the race, ethnicity, nationality, and gender

of these workers? What does this tell you about the division of labor in domestic labor and its relationship to global stratification?
Keywords: domestic work and immigration, global domestic labor, migrant domestics

2. Why do you think domestic labor is so underpaid and undervalued? Are there social changes that might result in a re-evaluation of the value of this work?
Keywords: social policy and care work, value of housework

We have included InfoTrac College Edition keywords at the end of each question to make it easier for you to find more to read on these topics. Go to **www.infotrac-college.com,** an online library, to begin your search.

Source: Parreñas, Rhacel Salazar. 2001. *Servants of Globalization: Women, Migration and Domestic Work.* Stanford, CA: Stanford University Press.

housing, consistent with the principles of socialism, but poverty often prevented them from doing so. Moreover, their governments were not democratically elected. **Third-world countries** in this scheme are the countries that are poor, underdeveloped, largely rural, and with high levels of poverty. The governments of the third-world countries are typically autocratic dictatorships, though there are exceptions. Though these countries are generally poor, wealth is concentrated in the hands of only a few elite.

Because this system of categorization was based on the logic of the Cold War, it has changed. For instance, the oil-rich countries of the Middle East are not part of the first or second world, according to this scheme, but they also do not belong in the same category as the poor countries of Africa and Asia since they have considerably more wealth. The collapse of the Soviet Union and the change in the governments of eastern Europe has led to the transformation of almost all the second-world countries. Although some countries still have a communist-based government, many of them, including China, are moving toward a market economic system. Still, like the terms *core* and *periphery,* the terms *first-, second-,* and *third-world* are useful in denoting the relationship of different countries to the world economy and global stratification.

Race and Global Inequality

In addition to class inequality, there is a racial component to world inequality, just as there is within many nations. Racial inequality in the world system can be seen in several ways. The rich core countries, those that dominate the world system, are largely European, with the addition of the United States and Japan. The populations of these countries, except for Japan, are mostly White. The poor countries of the world are mostly in Africa, Asia, or South America, where the populations are largely people of color. To put it differently, the countries with high standards of living, high levels of education, and the other positive characteristics have populations that are predominantly White. The countries that suffer a poor standard of living have low levels of education, high death rates, and in general, are at the bottom of the world stratification system; they are predominantly populated by people of color.

Exploitation of the human and natural resources of regions populated by people of color has characterized the history of Western capitalism, with people of color being dominated by Western imperialism and colonialism. The inequities that have resulted are enormous. Patterns of malnutrition and hunger show these inequities. More than 1 billion people in the world suffer from malnutrition and hunger. The vast majority of these people are people of color—that is, those not of European descent (Uvin 1998).

How did this racial inequality come about? On the surface, global capitalism is not explicitly racist, as were earlier forms of industrial capitalism. Yet, in fact, it is the rapid expansion of the global capital system that has led to the increase in racial inequality between nations. In the new capitalist system, a **new international division of labor** has emerged that is not tied to place, but can employ cheap labor anywhere. Cheap labor is usually found in non-Western countries. The exploitation of cheap labor has created a poor and dependent workforce that is mostly people of color. The profits accrue to the wealthy owners, who are mostly White, resulting in a racially divided world.

Some have argued further that multinational corporations' exploitation of the poor peripheral nations has forced an exodus of unskilled workers from the impoverished nations to the rich nations. The flood of third-world refugees into the industrialized nations is thereby increasing racial tensions, fostering violence, and destroying worker solidarity (Sirvananadan 1995).

Another way to look at racism around the world is offered in the work of Anthony Marx (1997). Comparing the United States, South Africa, and Brazil, Marx shows how racial groups fare in a country depending on how race is defined, particularly in the early periods of national development. Racial categories are not just based on biology (see Chapter 9), but are constructed by national elites according to each country's history. As a result, countries define racial categories differently, and these definitions can have lasting effects on the ability of various racial groups to organize and fight for equality.

In the cases of South Africa, the United States, and Brazil, each country developed different sets of racial categories. Although all three countries have many people of mixed descent, each defines race differently. In South Africa, the particular history of Dutch and English colonialism led to strongly drawn racial categories that defined people as "White," "coloured," (those of mixed descent) or "native/Bantu" (all black South Africans). However, in the United States, given its history of slavery, the "one drop" rule was used, which defined anyone with any African heritage as Black, thus ruling out any category of mixed race.

Brazil presents yet a different case. The Brazilian elite declared Brazil a racial democracy at the early stages of national development; racial differences were thought not to matter. Yet rather than create an egalitarian society free of racism, this resulted in "Afro-Brazilians" remaining at the bottom of Brazilian society, whereas "Euro-Brazilians" remain at the top. Color continues to matter, but by not creating racial categories, the Brazilian elite robbed Afro-Brazilians of an identity and therefore an opportunity for collective action and group solidarity, as with African Americans in the United

Overpopulation is not restricted to the poorest nations, but these countries do tend to have high birthrates and large populations. India, though not one of the poorest nations, has the second highest population in the world with 843 people per square mile, compared with 76 people per square mile in the United States.

States and Black Africans in South Africa. Ironically, Anthony Marx is suggesting that the creation of arbitrary racial labels in the long run may lead to more racial equality by providing an identity around which political mobilization can take place.

An implication of this research for the United States would be that any attempt to weaken racial categories might weaken the political mobilization of people of color. For instance, in the debate over the racial categories to be used in the U.S. census, many in the Black civil rights establishment have argued strongly for not having new multicultural or mixed-race categories because it could potentially weaken Black solidarity.

■ *Consequences of Global Stratification*

It is clear that some nations are wealthy and powerful and some are poor and powerless. What are the consequences of this world stratification system? Look again at Table 8.1 showing some of the basic indicators of national well-being for selected nations. You can see that there are considerable differences in the quality of life in these different places in the world.

Population

One of the biggest differences in rich and poor nations is population. The poorest countries comprise 3.6 billion people—over half the world's population. To put this into perspective, 25 percent of the people in the world live in countries where the average income is less than $500 per year; 80 percent live where it is less than $10,000 per year (World Bank 2002). In addition, the poorest countries have the highest birthrates and the highest death rates. The total *fertility rate,* defined as how many live births a woman will have over her lifetime at current fertility rates, shows that in the poorest countries women on the average have almost five children over their lifetimes. Because of this high fertility rate, the populations of poor countries are growing faster than the populations of wealthy countries; these countries therefore also have a high proportion of young children. The populations in the poorest countries are mostly rural.

In contrast, the richest countries have a total population of only approximately 825 million—only 15 percent of the world's population. The populations of the richest countries are not growing nearly as fast as the populations of the poorest countries. In the richest countries, women have about two children over their lifetime, and the populations of these countries are growing by only 1.2 percent. Many of the richest countries, including most of the countries of Europe, are actually experiencing population declines. With a low fertility rate, the rich countries have proportionately fewer children, but they also have proportionately more elderly, which can also be a burden on societal resources. Different from the poorest nations, the richest ones are largely urban.

Rapid population growth as a result of high fertility rates can make a large difference in the quality of life of the country. Countries with high birthrates are faced with the challenge of having too many children and not enough adults to provide for the younger generation. Public services, such as schools and hospitals, are strained in high birthrate countries, especially because these countries are poor to start out with. However, very low birthrates, as many rich countries are now experiencing, can also lead to problems. In countries with low birthrates, there are often not enough young people to meet labor force needs, and workers must be imported from other countries. The growing elderly population also puts a strain on retirement programs and retirement funds.

Although the data clearly show that poor countries have large populations and high birthrates and rich countries have smaller populations and low birthrates, does this mean that the large population results in the low level of wealth of the country or that high fertility rates keep countries poor? Scholars are divided on the relationship between the rate of population growth and economic development (Cassen 1994; Demeny 1991). Some theorize that rapid population growth and high birthrates lead to economic stagnation and that too many people keep a country from developing, thus miring the country in poverty (Ehrlich 1990). However, other researchers point out that some countries with very large populations have become developed (Coale 1986). After all, the United States has the third largest population in the world at 281 million people (World Bank 2002), and yet is one of the richest and most developed nations in the world. China and India, the two nations in the world with the largest populations, are also showing significant economic development. Scholars now believe that even though in some situations large population and high birthrates can impede economic development, in general, fertility levels are affected by levels of industrialization, not the other way around. That is, as countries develop, their fertility levels decrease and their population growth levels off (Hirschman 1994; Watkins 1987).

Health and Environment

Significant differences are also evident in the basic health standards of countries, depending on where they are in the global stratification system. The high-income countries have lower childhood death rates, higher life expectancies, and fewer children born underweight. In addition, most of the people in the high-income countries, but not all, have clean water and access to adequate sanitation. People born today in wealthy countries can expect to live about seventy-seven years, and women outlive men by several years. Except for some isolated or poor areas of the rich countries, almost all people have access to clean water and acceptable sewer systems.

In the poorest countries the situation is completely different. Many children die within the first five years of life, people live considerably shorter lives, and fewer people have access to clean water and adequate sanitation. In the low-income countries, the problems of sanitation, clean water, childhood death rates, and life expectancies are all closely related. In many of the poor countries,

drinking water is contaminated from poor or nonexistent sewage treatment. This contaminated water is then used to drink, to clean eating utensils, and to make baby formula. For adults, the water-born illnesses such as cholera and dysentery sometimes cause severe sickness, but seldom result in death. However, children under five, and especially those under the age of one, are highly susceptible to the illnesses carried in contaminated water. A common cause of childhood death in countries with low incomes is dehydration brought on by the diarrhea contracted by drinking contaminated water.

Degradation of the environment is a problem that affects all nations—linked as they are in one vast environmental system. But global stratification also means that some nations suffer at the hands of others. Deforestation is a problem throughout the world as overdevelopment results in the depletion of this natural resource. But it is most severe in South America, Africa, Mexico, and southeast Asia (World Bank 2002). On the other hand, the overproduction of "greenhouse gas"—emission of carbon dioxide from the burning of fossil fuels—is most severe in the United States, Canada, Australia, parts of

TAKING ON SOCIAL ISSUES

Global Epidemics

Although disease is usually understood as primarily a medical problem, global epidemics involve much more than the medical treatment of disease. Epidemics like AIDS (Acquired Immune Deficiency Syndrome) or SARS (Severe Acute Respiratory Syndrome) develop in the context of world poverty, with the poorest nations often being the hardest hit by the epidemic. In addition, cultural norms, technological and scientific resources, the status of women, political institutions, and other sociological factors all influence the ability of the medical community to respond to health crises. Thus, controlling or eliminating disease requires more than medical knowledge. It requires understanding the social and cultural context in which diseases like AIDS or SARS develop. What sociological factors have influenced the spread of AIDS and SARS in different parts of the world and what can health organizations—or other groups—do to respond?

Taking Action

Go to the Taking Action exercise on the companion Web site at **sociology.wadsworth.com/ andersen_taylor/essen3e** to learn more about an organization that addresses this topic.

western Europe and Russia—places that use the most energy. Energy use per capita in the high income nations far exceeds that of other parts of the world. The World Bank uses an indicator of energy efficiency that computes use according to the oil equivalent in kilograms. By this measure, energy use in the United States is over 8000 kilograms (second only to Iceland). By comparison, in Europe and Central Asia, the average is 2628 kilograms; in East Asia and the Pacific, 920; and South Asia, 441 (World Bank 2002). If seen in terms of availability of safe water, many areas of the world have seen a decline in recent years in the percent of the population with access to an improved water source. Clearly global stratification has environmental effects—some of them irreversible— that are felt around the globe.

Education

In the high-income nations of the world, education is almost universal, and the vast majority of people have attended school at least at some level. Literacy and school enrollment are now taken for granted in the high-income nations, although people in these wealthy nations who do not have a good education stand little chance of success. In the middle- and lower-income nations, the picture is quite different. Elementary school enrollment, virtually universal in wealthy nations, is less common in the middle-income nations and even less common in the poorest nations.

How do people survive who are not literate or educated? In much of the world, education takes place outside formal schooling. Just because many people in the poorer countries never go to school, this does not mean that they are ignorant or that they are uneducated. Most of the education in the world takes place in family settings, in religious congregations, or in other settings where elders teach the next generation the skills and knowledge they need to survive. This type of informal education often includes basic literacy and math skills that people in these poorer countries need for their daily lives.

The disadvantage of this informal and traditional education is that, although it prepares people for their traditional lives, it often does not give them the skills and knowledge needed to operate in the modern world. In an increasingly technological world, this can perpetuate the underdeveloped status of some nations.

Gender

The position of a country in the world stratification system also affects gender relations within different countries. Poverty is usually felt more by women than by men. Although gender inequality has not been achieved in the industrialized countries, compared with women in other parts of the world, women in the wealthier countries are much better off.

You can see this in something the United Nations calls the **gender development index,** which is calculated based on gender inequalities in life expectancy, educational attainment, and income for different countries. It provides an indication of the relative well-being or deprivation of women in different nations of the world. In every nation, the gender development index is less than the general human development index; if there were gender equality within a nation the human development index and gender development index would be the same. Many countries have shown improvement in the gender development index in recent years, including industrialized countries such as Denmark, France, and New Zealand, as well as countries in eastern Europe (Estonia, Hungary, and Poland), and developing countries (Jamaica, Sri Lanka, and Thailand). The diversity of these countries shows that gender equality can be achieved at different income levels and in different stages of national development (United Nations 2000b).

▪ *World Poverty*

One sad fact of global inequality is the growing presence and persistence of poverty in many parts of the world. There is poverty in the United States, but very few people in the United States live in the extreme levels of deprivation found in some of the poor countries of the world.

Defining World Poverty

In the United States, the poverty level is determined by the yearly income for a family of four that is considered necessary to maintain a suitable standard of living. As mentioned in Chapter 7, the official poverty line in 2001 (for a family of four) was $18,022. By this definition, 32.9 million Americans, or about 11.7 percent, live in poverty (Proctor and Dalaker 2002). This definition of poverty in the United States identifies **relative poverty:** The households in poverty in the United States are poor compared with other Americans, but when one looks at other parts of the world, an income of $18,022 would make a family very well off.

Absolute poverty is the situation in which human beings do not have enough money for basic survival. On the world level, this can be measured and defined in various ways. The United Nations (UN) has established the *international poverty line* as the situation in which individuals live on less than $365 a year—or $1 a day. The UN

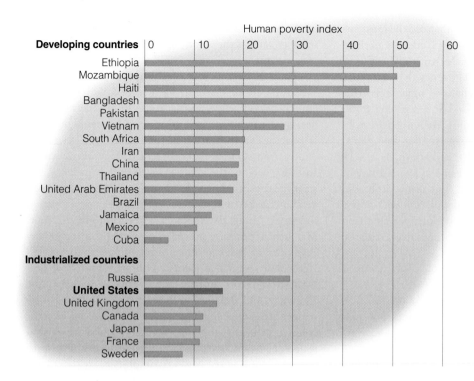

FIGURE 8.2 Human Poverty Index for Selected Countries

Source: United Nations. 2000. *Human Development Index*. New York: United Nations, pp. 169–173.

also identifies a more severe level of poverty, called **extreme poverty,** defined as the situation in which people live on less than $275 a year, that is, on less than 75 cents a day. There are 600 million people who live at or below this extreme poverty level.

However, money does not tell the whole story, because many people in the poor countries do not always deal in cash. In many countries, people survive by raising crops for personal consumption and by bartering or trading services for food or shelter. These activities do not show up in calculations of poverty levels that use amounts of money as the measure. As a result, the United Nations Development Program also defines what it calls the human poverty index.

The **human poverty index** is a multidimensional measure of poverty, meant to indicate the degree of deprivation in four basic dimensions of human life: a long and healthy life, knowledge, economic well-being, and social inclusion. Different specific indicators of these different dimensions are used to measure poverty in the industrialized and developing countries since what constitutes these different dimensions of life can vary substantially in such different environments. In developing countries, the following indicators are used:

- the percentage of people born not expected to live to age 40;
- the adult literacy rate;
- the proportion of people lacking access to health services and safe water;

- and the percentage of children under five who are moderately or severely underweight.

In industrialized countries, the human poverty index is measured by:

- the proportion of people not expected to live to age 60;
- the adult functional illiteracy rate;
- the incidence of income poverty (since income is the largest source of economic provisioning in industrialized countries);
- and long-term unemployment rates.

Figure 8.2 compares the human poverty index in select developing and industrialized nations (United Nations 2000a).

Who Are the World's Poor?

Using the World Bank's definition of international poverty (those whose level of consumption falls below $1 per day), 23 percent of the world's population live in poverty. The proportion of people living in poverty has declined from 29 percent in 1990, with most of the reduction attributable to progress in East Asia, particularly in the People's Republic of China. At the same time, in Africa, Latin America, and South Asia, poverty has increased substantially, as it also has in eastern Europe and Central Asia. Sub-Saharan Africa has the highest incidence of poverty of anywhere in the world, despite the rich natural resources of this region. Almost half—46 percent—of the population in this region lives below

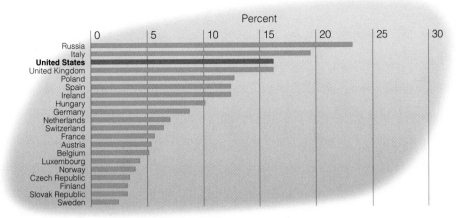

FIGURE 8.3 Child Poverty in the Wealthier Nations

Source: Vieminckx, Koen, and Timothy Smeeding, eds. 2001. *Child-Well-Being, Child Poverty, and Child Policy in Modern Nations.* Tonawanda, NY: University of Toronto Press.

the international poverty line. As a result, as we will see, infant mortality here is high; 151 children per 1000 die before the age of five. Life expectancy is also low and getting lower because of high death rates from AIDS; school enrollment is also low (World Bank 2002).

There are some differences in the nature of poverty in different areas of the globe. In Asia, the pressures of large population growth leave many without sustainable employment. And, as manufacturing has become less labor-intensive with more mechanized production, the need for labor in certain industries has declined. Though new technologies provide new job opportunities, they also create new forms of illiteracy as many people have neither the access nor the skills to use information technology (see the map, "The Digital Divide"). In sub-Saharan Africa, the poor live in marginal areas where poor soil, erosion, and continuous warfare have created extremely harsh conditions. Political instability and low levels of economic productivity contribute to the high rates of poverty. Solutions to world poverty in these different regions require sustainable economic development, as well as an understanding of the diverse regional factors that contribute to high levels of poverty.

Women and Children in Poverty

There is no country in the world in which women are treated as well as men. As with poverty in the United States, women bear a larger share of the burden of world poverty. Some have called this *double deprivation*—in many of the poor countries women suffer because of their gender and because they disproportionately carry the burden of poverty. For instance, in situations of extreme poverty, women have the burden of taking on much of the manual labor because in many cases the men have left to find work or food. The United Nations Commission on the Status of Women estimates that women constitute almost 60 percent of the world's population, perform two-thirds of all working hours, receive only

one-tenth of the world's income, and own less than 1 percent of the world's wealth (United Nations Commission on the Status of Women 1996).

In poor countries, women also suffer greater health risks. Although women outlive men in most countries, the difference in life expectancy is *less* in the countries in poverty. In Bangladesh, men outlive women. Women's health suffers because of several factors. For one, fertility rates are higher in poor countries. Giving birth is a time of high risk to women, and women in poor countries with poor nutrition, poor maternal care, and the lack of trained birth attendants are at higher risk of dying during and after the birth.

High fertility rates are also related to the degree of women's empowerment in society—an often neglected aspect of the discussion between fertility and poverty. Societies where women's voices do not count for much tend to have high fertility rates along with social and economic hardships for women, including lack of education, job opportunities, and information about birth control. Empowering women through providing them employment, education, property and voting rights can have a strong impact on reducing the fertility rate (Sen 2000).

Women also suffer in some poor countries because of traditions and cultural norms. Most (though not all) of the poor countries are patriarchal, meaning that men control the household. As a result, in some situations of poverty, the women eat after the men, and boys are fed before girls. In poverty areas, women have been found to have higher rates of malnutrition than men, which leads to anemia and other diseases (Doyal 1990). In conditions of extreme poverty, baby boys are fed before baby girls because boys have higher status than girls. As a result, female infants have a lower rate of survival than male infants (see Figure 8.3).

Children in poverty do not have the luxury of an education. Schools are usually few or nonexistent in poor areas of the world, and families are so poor that they cannot afford to send their children to school. Children from

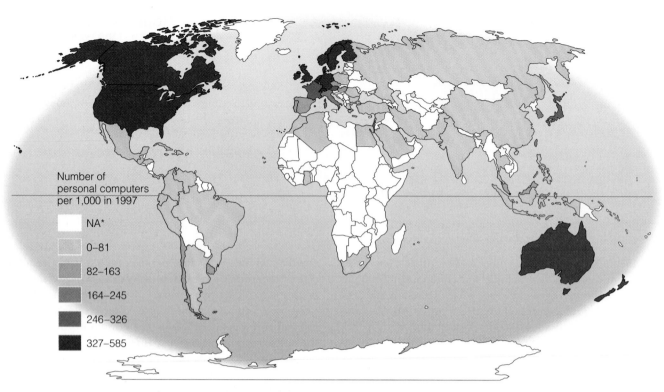

MAP 8.2 Viewing Society in Global Perspective: The Digital Divide

Global stratification is manifested in various ways. Here differences in access to information are depicted by the number of personal computers per 1000 persons in different nations. **What advantages and disadvantages does access to digital technology provide for a country?**

SOURCE: U.S. Census Bureau. 2002. *Statistical Abstract of the United States 2002*. Washington, DC: U.S. Government Printing Office, p. 836.

a very early age are required to help the family survive by working or performing domestic tasks such as fetching water. In extreme situations, children at a young age work as beggars, young boys and girls are sold to work in sweatshops, and young girls are sold into prostitution by their families. This may seem unusually cruel and harsh by Western standards, but it is difficult to imagine the horror of starvation and the desperation that many families in the world must feel that would force them to take such measures to survive. In poor countries, families feel they must have more children for their survival, yet having more children perpetuates the poverty. The United Nations estimates that there are 211 million children between the ages of five and fourteen in the paid labor force throughout the world. Most of the children, 127 million, are in Asia, and 48 million are in sub-Saharan Africa (International Labour Organization 2002). Many of these children work long hours in difficult conditions and enjoy few freedoms, making products (soccer balls, clothing, and toys, for example) for those who are much better off.

Another problem in the very poor areas of the world is homeless children (Mickelson 2000). In many situations, families are so poor that they can no longer care for their children, and the children must go without education out on their own, even at young ages. Many of these homeless children end up in the streets of the major cities of Asia and Latin America. In Latin America, it is estimated that there are 13 million street children, some as young as six years old. Alone, they survive through a combination of begging, selling, prostitution, drugs, and stealing. They sleep in alleys or in makeshift shelters. Their lives are harsh, brutal, and short.

Poverty and Hunger

How can you live on less than $1 a day? The answer is that you cannot, or at least you cannot live very well. Malnutrition and hunger are growing problems since many of the people in poverty cannot find or afford food. An estimated 1.2 billion people in the world are so poor that they are unable to obtain enough food to meet their nutritional needs (Gardner and Halweil 2000).

Hunger results when there is not enough to eat to feed a designated area (such as a region or country). It may be that there is an inadequate supply of food or that households simply cannot afford to purchase enough food to feed themselves. Hunger stifles the mental and physical development of children and leads to disease and death. Malnutrition results when there is a deficiency in the necessary nutrients for healthy living. It is estimated that 5 million children under the age of five die each year in the developing world as the result of malnutrition. Although the food supply is plentiful in the world, and is actually increasing faster than the population, malnutrition is still dangerously high (World Health Organization 2002).

Why are people starving? Is there not enough food to feed all the people in the world? In fact, plenty of food is grown in the world. The world's production of wheat, rice, corn, and other grains is sufficient to adequately feed all the people in the world. Much grain grown in the United States is stored and not used. The problem is that the surplus food does not get to the truly needy. The people who are starving lack what they need for obtaining adequate food, such as arable land or a job that would pay a living wage. In many cases, in the past the people grew food crops and were able to feed themselves, but today much of the best land has been taken over by agribusinesses that grow cash crops, such as tobacco or cotton, and subsistence farmers have been forced onto marginal lands on the flanks of the desert where conditions are difficult and crops often do not grow.

Many areas of the world have seen a marked decrease in hunger. In China, for instance, 46 percent of the population was chronically underfed in 1970. Just twenty years later, only 16 percent of China's population was underfed. The only region of the globe where hunger has increased is sub-Saharan Africa.

Causes of World Poverty

What causes world poverty, and why are so many people so desperately poor and starving? More to the point, why is poverty decreasing in some areas but increasing in others? We do know what does *not* cause poverty. Poverty is not necessarily caused by too rapid population growth, although high fertility rates and poverty are related. In fact, many of the world's most populous countries, India and China, for instance, have large segments of their population that are poor, but these countries have begun to reduce poverty levels, even with very big populations. Poverty is not caused by people being lazy or uninterested in working. People in extreme poverty work tremendously hard just to survive, and they would work hard at a job if they had one. It is not that they are lazy; it is that there are no jobs for them.

Poverty is a result of a mix of causes. For one, the areas where poverty is increasing have a history of unstable governments or, in some cases, virtually no effective government to coordinate national development or plans that might alleviate extreme poverty and starvation. World relief agencies are reluctant to work in or send food to countries where the national governments cannot guarantee the safety of relief workers or the delivery of food and aid to where it should go. Food convoys may be hijacked or roads are blocked by bandits or warlords.

In many countries with high proportions of poverty, the economies have collapsed and the governments have borrowed heavily to remain afloat. As a condition of these international loans, lenders, including the World Bank and the International Monetary Fund, have demanded harsh economic restructuring to increase capital markets and industrial efficiency. These economic reforms may make good sense for some and may lead these countries out of economic ruin over time, but in the short run, these imposed reforms have placed the poor in a precarious position because the reforms also called for drastically reduced government spending on human services.

Poverty is also caused by changes in the world economic system. Although poverty has been a long-term problem and has many causes, increases in poverty and starvation in Africa and Latin America can be attributed in part to the changes in world markets that favored Asia economically but put sub-Saharan Africa and Latin America at a disadvantage. As the price of products declined with more industrialization in places like India, China, Indonesia, South Korea, Malaysia, and Thailand, commodity-producing nations in Africa and Latin America suffered. In Latin America, the poor have flooded to the cities, hoping to find work, whereas in Africa, they did the opposite, fleeing to the countryside hoping to be able to grow subsistence crops. Governments often had to borrow to provide help to their citizens. Many governments collapsed or found themselves in such great debt that they were unable to help their own people. This has created massive amounts of poverty and starvation.

In sum, poverty has many causes. It is now a major global problem that not only affects the billions of people who are living in poverty, it also affects all people on

Earth in one way or another. In some areas, poverty rates are declining as some countries begin to improve their economic situation; however, in other areas of the world, poverty is increasing, and countries are sinking into financial, political, and social chaos.

■ *Theories of Global Stratification*

How did this world inequality occur? Why have so many countries fallen into poverty whereas other countries have developed and become wealthy? How do we understand the geographic distribution of wealth and poverty? Sociological explanations of world stratification generally fall into three camps: modernization theory, dependency theory, and world systems theory, each explained here (see Table 8.2).

Modernization Theory

Modernization theory views the economic development of a country as a worldwide process involving nearly all countries that have been touched by technological change.

According to the theory, a country becomes more "modernized" by increased technological development, and this technological development is dependent on other countries as well. The role of technological and economic development was first proposed by W. W. Rostow, who was an economic advisor to President Kennedy in the 1960s (Rostow 1978). Modernization theory was developed to explain why some countries (such as those in Latin America) had achieved economic development and why some had not; it was also developed to guide the United States in helping unsuccessful countries succeed.

Modernization theory sees economic development as a process by which traditional societies, such as pastoral or agricultural societies, become more complex and it posits the steps by which this happens. For economic development to occur, modernization theory predicts, countries must change their traditional attitudes, values, and institutions. Specifically, economic achievement is thought to derive from attitudes and values that emphasize hard work, saving, efficiency, and enterprise. These values are said by the theory to be found in modern (developed) countries, but lacking in traditional societies. Traditional societies are perceived as fatalistic, not valuing hard work or thrift, and not controlling their fertility. Fatalism is particularly a hindrance to economic development, according to modernization theory, be-

UNDERSTANDING DIVERSITY

War, Childhood, and Poverty

Surgeons were forced to amputate both of Ali Ismaeel Abbas's arms after an errant U.S. bomb slammed into his Baghdad home during the opening phase of the Iraq war. Pictures of the 12-year-old, who lost his parents in the attack, soon appeared on TV screens and in newspapers around the world. Since then, Abbas, who was treated in Kuwait, has come to represent a grim reality: all too often the victims of war are innocent children. (McClelland 2003: 20)

In the past ten years alone, UNICEF estimates that over 2 million children have died in war, with even more injured, disabled, orphaned, or forced into refugee camps (Machel 1996). One estimate is that, of all the victims of war, 90 percent are civilian—half of

those, children (McClelland 2003). Young children are often exploited as combatants or may be used as human shields.

In the aftermath of war children are also highly vulnerable to outbreaks of disease. In Iraq, following the war in 2003, many children died of diseases like anemia and diarrhea—diseases that can be prevented. Children in Iraq were already living under extreme hardship under the regime of Saddam Hussein. Economic sanctions against Iraq during his regime also produced high infant mortality because of food shortages.

The United Nations has passed resolutions prohibiting the use of children under 18 in combat, but also has

Graeme Robertson/Getty Images

linked the threats to children from violence with high rates of poverty around the world. Although reducing poverty would not eliminate the threat of war, it would go a long way toward improving children's lives in war-torn regions.

TABLE 8.2 Theories of Global Stratification

	Modernization Theory	Dependency Theory	World Systems Theory
Economic Development	Arises from relinquishing traditional cultural values and embracing new technologies and market-driven attitudes and values	Exploits the least powerful nations to the benefit of wealthier nations that then control the political and economic systems of the exploited countries	Has resulted in a single economic system stemming from the development of a world market that links core, semiperipheral, and peripheral nations
Poverty	Results from adherence to traditional values and customs that prevent societies from competing in a modern global economy	Results from the dependence of low-income countries on wealthy nations	Is the result of core nations extracting labor and natural resources from peripheral nations
Social Change	Involves increasing complexity, differentiation, and efficiency	Is the result of neocolonialism and the expansion of international capitalism	Leads to an international division of labor that increasingly puts profit in the hands of a few while exploiting those in the poorest and least powerful nations

cause people who are fatalistic accept their condition in life and do not work to change it. If poor people see their plight as the result of fate, they will be less inclined to try to improve their condition.

An outgrowth of functionalist theory, modernization theory, derives much of its thinking from the work of Max Weber. In *The Protestant Ethic and the Spirit of Capitalism* (1904/1958), Weber saw the economic development that occurred in Europe during the Industrial Revolution as a result of the values and attitudes of Protestantism. The Industrial Revolution took place in England and northern Europe, Weber argued, because the people of this area were hard-working Protestants who valued achievement and believed that God helped those who helped themselves.

Modernization theory is similar to the culture of poverty theory, which sees people as poor because they have poor work habits, poor time management, are not willing to defer gratification, and do not save or take advantage of educational opportunities (see Chapter 7). Modernization theory sees the people in poor countries as not saving enough and the governments of the poor countries as not investing in infrastructure development, such as building roads and schools. Countries are poor, in other words, because they have poor attitudes and poor institutions.

Modernization theory has been criticized on several fronts. Although it seems to explain the situation of some countries, it does not account for the development, or lack of development, in others. Critics point out that it blames countries for being poor when in fact other causes may be outside their control.

Another criticism of modernization theory is that it posits that governments should not be involved in making economic decisions or policies that restrict free trade or business activities. Developing countries, modernization theory says, are better off if they let the natural forces of competition determine which companies and individuals become successful and which do not. However, the experience of countries that have made rapid economic gains in the last few decades seems to show that government intervention may spur economic development rather than hinder it. In many newly developed countries, particularly those in East Asia, government policies and actions have played an important role in economic development by working directly with the private sector to enact specific export strategies and by restricting imports to allow indigenous industries to develop.

Dependency Theory

Although market-oriented theories may explain why some countries are successful, they do not explain why some countries remain in poverty or why some countries have not developed. It is necessary to look at issues outside the individual countries and to examine the ties and connections between countries. Drawing on the fact that many of the poorest nations are former colonies of European powers, another theory of world stratification focuses on the processes and results of European colonization and imperialism. This theory, called **dependency theory,** focuses on explaining the persistence of poverty in the world. It holds that the poverty of the low-income countries is a direct result of their political and economic dependence on the wealthy countries. Specifically, dependency theory argues that the poverty of many countries is a result of exploitation by powerful countries. This theory is derived from the work of Karl Marx, who foresaw that a capitalist world economy would create an exploited class of dependent countries, just as capitalism within countries had created an exploited class of workers.

Dependency theory begins by examining the historical development of this system of inequality. As the European countries began to industrialize in the seventeenth century, they needed raw materials for their factories and places to sell their product. To do so, the European nations colonized much of the world, including most of Africa, Asia, and the Americas. Colonization worked best for the industrial countries when the colonies were kept undeveloped so that they would not compete with the home country. For instance, India was a British colony for many years (1757–1947). Britain bought cheap cotton from India, made it into cloth in British mills, and then sold it back to India, making large profits. Although India was able to make cotton into cloth at a much lower cost than the British, and very fine cloth at that, the British nonetheless did not allow India to develop its cotton industry. As long as India was dependent on Britain, Britain became wealthy and India remained poor.

During the period of colonization, powerful developed countries created dependency by the direct political and military control of the poor countries. Most colonial powers were European countries, but in fact other countries, particularly Japan and China, had colonies as well. However, the era of colonization came to an end soon after the Second World War, largely because it became too expensive to maintain large armies and administrative staffs in other lands. As a result, according to dependency theory, the powerful countries turned to other ways to control the poor countries and keep them dependent. Sometimes the powerful countries still intervene directly in the affairs of the dependent nations by sending troops or, more often, by imposing economic or political restrictions and sanctions. But other methods, largely economic, have been developed to control the dependent poor countries, such as price controls, tariffs, and especially, the control of credit.

The rich industrialized nations, according to dependency theory, are able to set prices for raw material produced by the poor countries at very low levels so that the poor countries are unable to accumulate enough profit to industrialize. As a result, the poor dependent countries must borrow from the rich countries. However, debt creates only more dependence. Many poor countries are so deeply indebted to the major industrial countries that they must follow the economic edicts of the rich countries that loaned them the money, thus increasing their dependency. This form of international control has sometimes been called **neocolonialism,** a form of control of the poor countries by the rich countries, but without direct political or military involvement.

Multinational corporations are companies that draw a large share of their profits from overseas investments and that conduct business across national borders. They play a role in keeping the dependent nations poor, dependency theory suggests. Although their executives and stockholders are from the industrialized countries, multinational corporations recognize no national boundaries and pursue business where they can best make a profit. Multinationals buy resources where they can get them cheapest, manufacture their products where production and labor costs are lowest, and sell their products where they can make the largest profits. Many critics fault companies such as Nike for perpetuating global inequality by taking advantage of cheap overseas labor to make large profits for U.S. stockholders. Nike is, in fact, doing what it should be doing in a market system: trying to make a profit. Nonetheless, dependency theory views the multinationals as another way that poverty is maintained in the poor parts of the world.

Dependency theory focuses primarily on the connections between specific countries or groups of countries. It faults the powerful countries for causing poverty in the poor countries by exploiting them and keeping the poor countries dependent, either through colonization, neocolonialism, or the work of multinationals. The theory works well in explaining much of the poverty created in low-income countries in Africa and Latin America in the 1960s and 1970s. Yet the theory does not explain development in other parts of the world (McCord and McCord 1986). One criticism of dependency theory is that many poor countries were never colonies, for example, Ethiopia.

Some former colonies have also done well. Two of the greatest postwar success stories of economic development are Singapore and Hong Kong. Both of these countries were British colonies—Hong Kong until 1997—and clearly dependent on Britain, yet they have had successful economic development precisely because of their dependence on Britain. Other former colonies are also improving economically, including India.

World Systems Theory

Modernization theory examines the factors internal to an individual country, and dependency theory looks to the relationship between countries or groups of countries. Another approach to global stratification is called **world systems theory.** Like dependency theory, this theory begins with the premise that no nation in the world can be seen in isolation. Each country, no matter how remote, is tied in many ways to the other countries in the world. However, unlike dependency theory, world systems theory argues that there is a world economic system that must be understood as a single unit, not in terms of individual countries or groups of countries. This theoretical approach derives to some degree from the work of the dependency theorists and is most closely associated with the work of Immanuel Wallerstein in *The Modern World System* (1974) and *The Modern World System II* (1980). According to this theory, the level of economic development is explained by understanding each country's place and role in the world economic system.

This world system has been developing since the sixteenth century. The countries of the world are tied together in many ways, but of primary importance are the economic connections in the world markets of goods, capital, and labor. All countries sell their products and services on the world market and buy products and services from other countries. However, this is not a market of equal partners. Because of historical and strategic imbalances in this economic system, some countries are able to use their advantage to create and maintain wealth, whereas other countries that are at a disadvantage remain poor. This process has led to a global system of stratification, in which the units are not people, but countries.

World systems theory sees the world divided into three groups of interrelated nations, although Wallerstein originally talked of four groups of countries. We introduced these categories earlier in the chapter. At the center of the world economic system are the rich, powerful industrialized countries that control the system, the *core countries,* including the western European countries (Germany, France), the United States, and Japan. Around these nations are the *semiperipheral countries.* These countries occupy an intermediate position in the world system and include countries such as South Korea, Mexico, and Turkey. The semiperipheral countries, which are at a middle level of income and partly industrialized, extract profits from the peripheral countries and pass the profits on to the core countries. Finally, there are the *peripheral countries.* Mostly in Africa, Asia, and Latin America, these countries are poor, not industrialized, largely agricultural, and manipulated by the core countries that extract resources and profits from them.

THINKING SOCIOLOGICALLY

Look at the labels in your clothes and note where your clothing was made. What does this tell you about the relationship of *core, semiperipheral,* and *peripheral* countries within world systems theory? What further information would reveal the connections between the country where you live and the countries where your clothing is made and distributed?

This world economic system has resulted in a modern world in which some countries have obtained great wealth and other countries have remained poor. The core countries control and limit the economic development in the peripheral countries so as to keep the peripheral countries from developing and competing with the core countries on the world market, thus the core countries can continue to purchase raw materials at a low price.

Although world systems theory was originally developed to explain the historical evolution of the world system, modern scholars now focus on the international division of labor and its consequences. This new international division of labor approach is an attempt to overcome some of the shortcomings in world systems theory by focusing on the specific mechanism by which differential profits are attached to the production of goods and services in the world market. A tennis shoe made by Nike is designed in the United States; uses synthetic rubber made from petroleum from Saudi Arabia; is sewn in Indonesia; is transported on a ship registered in Singapore, which is run by a Korean management firm using Filipino sailors; and is finally marketed in Japan and the United States. At each of these stages, profits are taken, but at very different rates.

THINKING SOCIOLOGICALLY

What are the major industries in your community? Find out in what parts of the world they do business, including where their product is produced. How does the *international division* of labor affect jobs in your region?

World systems theorists call this global production process a **commodity chain,** the network of production and labor processes by which a product becomes a finished commodity (Gereffi and Korzeniewicz 1994). By following a commodity through its production cycle and seeing where the profits go at each link of the chain, one can identify which country is getting rich and which country is being exploited.

World systems theory helps explain the growing phenomenon of international migration. An international division of labor means that the need for cheap labor in some of the industrial and developing nations draws workers from poorer parts of the globe. International migration is also the result of refugees seeking asylum from war-torn parts of the world or from countries where political oppression, often against particular ethnic groups, forces some to leave. The development of a world economy, however, is resulting in large changes in the composition of populations around the globe. **World cities,** that is, those that are closely linked through the system of international commerce, have emerged. Within

© Willitz/Network/CORBIS Saba

The development of a global economy results in much international migration as diverse groups seek opportunities in new parts of the world. One result is the presence of immigrant enclaves in world cities, such as Pakistani immigrants in London.

these cities, families and their surrounding communities often form *transnational communities,* that is, communities that may be geographically distant, but socially and politically close. Linked through various communication and transportation networks, transnational communities share information, resources, and strategies for coping with the problems of international migration.

International migration, sometimes legal, sometimes not, has radically changed the racial and ethnic composition of populations not only in the United States, but also in many European and Asian nations (Rodriquez 1999; Light et al. 1998). Some of those who migrate internationally are professional workers, but many others remain in the lowest segments of the labor force where, although their work is critical to the world economy, they are treated with hostility and suspicion, discriminated against, and stereotyped as undeserving and threatening. In many nations, including the United States, this has led to numerous political tensions over immigration, even while the emergence of migrant groups in world cities is now a major feature of the urban landscape (White 1998).

There are a number of criticisms of world systems theory. Certainly, it is useful to see the world as an interconnected set of economic ties between countries and to understand that these ties often result in the exploitation of poor countries. However, it is not at all clear that the system always works to the advantage of the core countries and to the detriment of the peripheral countries. For one, countries that were once at the center of this world system no longer occupy such a lofty position—England, for example.

In addition, the world economic system does not always work to the detriment of the peripheral countries and the benefit of core countries. Peripheral countries often benefit by housing low-wage factories and the core countries are sometimes hurt when jobs move overseas. Also, low-wage sweatshops are found in all nations, not just the peripheral countries. Nonetheless, world systems theory has provided a powerful tool for understanding global inequality.

■ *Globalization and Social Change*

As we have seen, many countries in the world are well off, but many countries in the world are poor, some very poor. This global stratification system has been created over several centuries, but the conditions of extreme poverty and even starvation that we see in the world system at this time are relatively new. We must ask, is the world getting better or worse, and what will happen in the future?

There is some good news. In some areas of the world, particularly East Asia, but also in Latin America, many countries have shown rapid growth and have emerged as developed countries. These countries are sometimes called the **newly industrializing countries (NICs),** and they include South Korea, Malaysia, Thailand, Taiwan, and Singapore. In these countries, individuals have saved and invested, and the governments have invested in social and economic development. Because some of the NICs have large populations, their success demonstrates that economic development can occur in heavily populated countries. China has embarked on an aggressive policy of industrial growth, and India is also improving economically.

Yet for all the success stories, there are also nations that are not making it. These include nations on all continents. In many cases, governments have collapsed or are functioning only at minimal levels, the economy is bankrupt, the standard of living has plummeted, and people are starving. More disturbing is the situation in many areas of the world where the increase in ethnic hatred has led to mass genocide and forced millions from their homes, creating a huge mass of refugees. These situations have increased poverty and hunger. And these countries, some of which used to be relatively well off, have experienced downward mobility in the global stratification system.

There has been continued growth of capitalism and of capital markets around the world. With the collapse of the Soviet Union and with China moving rapidly in the direction of capitalism, there has developed a world capitalistic system. The opening of new markets, the increasing global trade, the growth of multinational corporations, and the development of world financial markets will bring prosperity and wealth to many nations and to many individuals. The growing world market economy may allow some of the emerging countries that were once poor to move into the ranks of the rich nations and share in the newly created wealth, but whether this wealth will filter down to the people at the lower levels of society is another question.

The new push to further develop the world as one large capital market will also leave some countries behind, and therefore poverty and hunger will continue in many parts of the world. Market economies create opportunities to become wealthy, both for individuals and for nations. For those who can take advantage of these opportunities, the future looks bright, but many nations and individuals do not have this opportunity. Their conditions are so desperate that they do not have a chance to participate in the world market, except at a great disadvantage.

Globalization is a strong force that will continue to shape the future of most nations. Some see globalization simply as the expansion of western markets and culture into all parts of the world. Western civilization brings new values (including democracy and more equality for women) and certainly new products (movies, clothing styles, and other commercial goods) to other nations, but it also can be a form of imperialism—that is, the domination of Western nations. Resistance to Western globalization and imperialism produces some of the international problems now dominating U.S. and world history, as evidenced in the hostility of militant, fundamentalist Islamic groups against the United States.

Globalization has created great progress in the world—including trade, migration, the spread of diverse cultures, the dissemination and sharing of new knowledge, greater freedom for women, travel, and so forth. Moreover, globalization has not simply extended the values and knowledge of Western culture. Many of the things we now take for granted in Western culture originated in non-Western cultures. For example, the decimal system—fundamental to modern math and science—originated in India between the second and sixth centuries, and was soon further developed by Arab mathematicians. Western societies certainly get credit for the development of science and technology, but the credit is not theirs alone (Sen 2002).

It is no doubt true that globalization is contributing to the inequality between nations and to the exploitation of some nations and groups by others. Perhaps the solution is not in resisting globalization, but in working

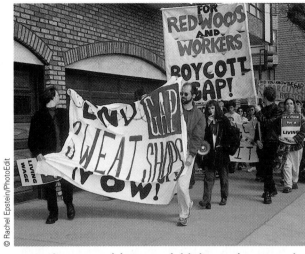

Increased awareness of the impact of globalization has generated a protest movement with an unusual alliance between those concerned about the loss of jobs and those concerned with the impact of globalization on the environment.

so that the benefits of the global economy and global technology and knowledge reach parts of the world in less exploitative ways. As long as great disparities in standards of living, human rights and basic freedoms, environmental quality, and so forth persist, world conflict is likely to be the result.

■ *Chapter Summary*

■ *What is global stratification?*

Global stratification is a system of inequality of the distribution of resources and opportunities between countries. A particular country's position is determined by its relationship to other countries in the world. The countries in the global stratification system can be categorized according to their per capita gross national product, or wealth. The world's countries can also be categorized as *first-, second-,* or *third-world* countries, which describe their political affiliation and their level of development. The global stratification system can also be described according to the economic power countries have.

■ *How do systems of power affect different countries in the world?*

The countries of the world can be divided into three levels based on their power in the world economic system. The *core countries* are the countries that control and profit the most from the world system. *Semi-peripheral countries* are semi-industrialized and play a middleman role, extracting profits from the poor countries and passing those profits on to the core countries. At the bottom of the world stratification system are the *peripheral countries,* which are poor and largely agricultural, but with important resources that are exploited by the core countries. Most of these nations are populated by people of color, perpetuating racism as part of the world system.

■ **What are some of the consequences of global stratification?**

The poorest countries have more than half the world's population and have high birthrates, high mortality rates, poor health and sanitation, low rates of literacy and school attendance, and are largely rural. The richest countries have low birthrates, low mortality rates, better health and sanitation, high literacy rates, high school attendance, and largely urban populations. Although women in the wealthy countries are not completely equal to men, they suffer less inequality than do women in the poor countries.

■ **How do we measure and understand world poverty?**

Relative poverty means being poor in comparison to others. *Absolute poverty* describes the situation where people do not have enough to survive, measured as having the equivalent of $1.00 per day. *Extreme poverty* is defined as the situation in which people live on less than 75 cents a day. The United Nations has developed a *human poverty index*—a multidimensional measure that accounts for life expectancy, knowledge, economic well-being, and social inclusion. Poverty particularly affects women and children. Children in the very poor countries are forced to work at very early ages and do not have the opportunity for schooling. Street children are a growing problem in many cities of the world. Starvation is also a consequence of the global stratification system.

■ **What are the theories of global stratification?**

Modernization theory interprets the economic development of a country in terms of the internal attitudes and values. Modernization theory ignores that the development of a country may be due to its economic relationships with other more powerful countries. *Dependency theory* draws on the fact that many of the poorest nations are former colonies of European powers where colonial powers keep colonies poor and do not allow their industries to develop, thus creating dependency. *World systems theory* argues that no nation can be seen in isolation and that there is a world economic system that must be understood as a single unit.

■ **What is the future of global stratification?**

The future of global stratification is varied and depends on the country's position within the world economic system. Some countries, particularly those in East Asia—commonly referred to as *newly industrializing countries*—have shown rapid growth and emerged as developed countries. Many nations, though, are not making it. Governments collapse, countries suffer economic bankruptcy, the standard of living plummets, and people starve.

■ *Key Terms*

absolute poverty 221	newly industrializing
commodity chain 229	countries (NICs) 230
core countries 217	per capita gross national
dependency theory 227	income (GNI) 214
extreme poverty 222	peripheral countries 217
first-world countries 217	relative poverty 221
gender development	second-world
index 221	countries 217
global stratification 212	semiperipheral
human poverty index 222	countries 217
modernization theory 226	third-world countries 218
multinational	world cities 229
corporation 228	world systems theory 228
neocolonialism 228	
new international division	
of labor 218	

■ *Researching Society with MicroCase Online*

You can see the results of actual research by using the Wadsworth MicroCase® Online feature available to you. This feature allows you to look at some of the results from national surveys, census data, and some other data sources. You can explore this easy-to-use feature on your own, but try this example. Suppose you want to know some social facts, such as:

In what nations is there the greatest gap between rich and poor?

To answer this question, go to **sociology.wadsworth .com/andersen_taylor/essen3e,** select MicroCase Online from the left navigation bar, and follow the directions there to analyze the data described below.

Data file: NATIONS

Task: Mapping

Variable 1: $ Rich 10%

View: Map

Questions

After viewing the map, return to "Rank Table." This table shows what percent of income the richest ten percent of the population in each nation receives.

1. In what five countries do the richest ten percent receive more than half of all national income?

2. What percent of income is received by the richest ten percent of these countries? (You may want to return to the alphabetical list to answer this question.)

United States   _____

Iran   _____

Japan   _____

Mexico   _____

South Africa _____

■ *The Companion Web Site for Sociology: The Essentials, Third Edition*

sociology.wadsworth.com/andersen_taylor/essen3e

Supplement your review of this chapter by going to the companion Web site to take one of the Tutorial Quizzes, use the flash cards to master key terms, and check out the many other study aids you'll find there. You'll also find special features such as GSS Data and Census 2000 information, data and resources at your fingertips to help you with that special project or do some research on your own.

■ *Suggested Readings and Web Resources*

Bonacich, Edna, and Richard Applebaum. 2000. *Behind the Label: Exploitation in the Los Angeles Apparel Industry.* Berkeley: University of California Press.
This book examines the growth of sweatshops in the apparel industry, explaining their presence in terms of the rise in global production. The book examines the experiences of low-wage immigrant workers in Los Angeles, as well as efforts to eradicate sweatshops, including the antisweatshop movement.

Chang, Grace. 2000. *Disposable Domestics: Immigrant Women Works in the Global Economy.* Boston: South End Press.
Chang's book analyzes the patterns of international migration that affect women workers who migrate to different countries, providing the care work for families in better-off nations. She links the provision of domestic work to the development of a global economy and the exploitation of women and their families.

Friedman, Thomas L. 1999. *The Lexus and the Olive Tree.* New York: Farrar Straus & Giroux.
Friedman, an international correspondent for The New York Times, *examines the impact of the global economy on world politics and the character of local cultures. Friedman argues that globalization is the central organizing principle of the post-Cold War world, even though many world conflicts simultaneously evolve through cultures holding on to traditional values.*

The United Nations
www.un.org
The United Nations home page includes a wealth of information about social, economic, and political conditions around the world. Their publications on economic and social development are a good source of data about global stratification.

The United Nations Children's Fund
www.unicef.org
The United Nations Children's Fund (UNICEF) site has information about the well-being of children around the world, including their annual report The State of the World's Children.

The World Bank
www.worldbank.org
The World Bank site includes publications and other information about the global economy and how different nations are faring.

CHAPTER NINE

Race and Ethnicity

You might expect a society based on the values of freedom, equality, and brotherhood, such as ours, to not be deeply afflicted by racial conflict, but think of the following situations:

■ Eight days after the horrific, catastrophic September 11, 2001, terrorist attacks on New York City's now-destroyed World Trade Center and on the Pentagon in Washington, DC, a gunman drove into a Chevron gas station in Mesa, Arizona, and shot to death the owner, a member of the Sikh religious order, who wore a turban on his head. The man who was killed had no known connection whatsoever with suspected Middle Eastern terrorists, but he had dark skin and wore a turban. A few days later, more than 200 Sikhs had reported instances of harassment.

■ Some years ago in Detroit, Vincent Chin, a Chinese American, was clubbed with a baseball bat by a White autoworker and his son, presumably on the grounds that Chin was taking jobs from them. Chin died within minutes of the attack from multiple skull fractures.

■ In 1999, Amadu Diallo, a Black Haitian immigrant, standing in front of his own door, reached for a cell phone in his back pocket. Erroneously thinking that he was reaching for a gun, four White undercover New York police officers fired forty-three separate shots at him in such rapid succession that a witness said it sounded like automatic weapons fire. Nineteen shots hit and killed Diallo instantly.

These ugly incidents, all true, have one thing in common—race. Along with gender and social class, race has fundamental importance in human social interaction, and it is an integral part of social institutions. Of course, the races do not always interact as enemies. Nor is interracial tension always obvious. It can be as subtle as a White person who simply does not initiate interactions with African Americans and Latinos, or an elderly White man who almost imperceptibly leans backward at a cocktail party as a Japanese American man approaches him.

In everyday human interaction, as African American philosopher Cornel West has eloquently noted, race still matters and matters a lot (West 1993). What is race, and what is ethnicity? Why does society treat racial and ethnic groups differently, and why is there social inequality between these groups? How are these divisions and inequalities able to persist so stubbornly, and how extensive are they? These questions fascinate sociologists who do research on racial and ethnic relations and stratification in our society. Just as class stratification differentiates people in society, according to the class privileges and disadvantages that they experience, so does racial and ethnic stratification.

■ Race and Ethnicity

Within sociology, the terms *ethnic, race, minority,* and *dominant group* have very specific meanings, different from the meanings these terms have in common usage. These concepts are important in developing a sociological perspective on racial and ethnic stratification.

Ethnicity

An **ethnic group** is a social category of people who share a common culture—for example, a common language or dialect; a common religion; and common norms, practices, customs, and history. Ethnic groups have a consciousness of their common cultural bond. Italian Americans, Japanese Americans, Arab Americans, Polish Americans, Greek Americans, Mexican Americans, and Irish Americans are examples of ethnic groups in the United States, but ethnic groups are also found in other societies, such as the Pashtuns in Afghanistan, or the Shiites and Sunnis in Iraq whose ethnicity is based on religious differences.

This band, playing for St. Patrick's Day, an Irish holiday, contains people of varied racial-ethnic backgrounds.

© Cameramann/The Image Works

An ethnic group does not exist only because of the common national or cultural origins of a group, however. Ethnic groups develop because of their unique historical and social experiences. These experiences become the basis for the group's *ethnic identity,* meaning the definition the group has of itself as sharing a common cultural bond. Prior to immigration to the United States, Italians, for example, did not necessarily think of themselves as a distinct group with common interests and experiences. Originating from different villages, cities, and regions of Italy, Italian immigrants identified themselves by their family background and community of origin. However, the process of immigration and the experiences Italian Americans faced as a group in the United States, including discrimination, created a new identity for the group (Waters 2002, 1990; Alba 1990).

The social and cultural basis of ethnicity is also proven by ethnic groups that can develop more or less intense ethnic identification at different points in time. Ethnic identification may grow stronger when groups face prejudice or hostility from other groups. Perceived or real threats from other groups and perceived competition from other groups may unite an ethnic group around common political and economic interests. Ethnic unity can develop voluntarily, or it may be involuntarily imposed when ethnic groups are excluded by more powerful groups from certain residential areas, occupations, or social clubs. These exclusionary practices strengthen ethnic identity.

Race

Like ethnicity, race is primarily, though not exclusively, a socially constructed category. A **race** is a group treated as distinct in society based on certain characteristics, some of which are biological, that have been assigned social importance. Because of presumed biologically or culturally inferior characteristics (as defined by powerful groups in society), a race is often singled out for differential and unfair treatment. It is not the biological characteristics per se that define racial groups, but *how groups have been treated historically and socially.*

Society assigns people to racial categories, such as Black, White, and so on, not because of science, logic, or fact, but because of opinion and social experience. In other words, how racial groups are defined is a *social process.* This is what is meant when one says that race is "socially constructed." Although the meaning of race begins from perceived biological differences between groups (such as differences in physical characteristics like skin color, lip form, and hair texture), on closer examination, the assumption that racial differences are purely biological breaks down.

DEBUNKING
Society's Myths

Myth: Racial differences are fixed, biological categories.

Sociological perspective: Race is a social concept, one in which certain physical or cultural characteristics take on social meanings that become the basis for racism and discrimination. The definition of race varies across cultures within a society and across different societies.

The social categories used to presumably divide groups into races are not fixed, and they vary from society to society. Within the United States, laws defining who is Black have historically varied from state to state. North Carolina and Tennessee law historically defined a person as Black if he or she had even one great-grandparent who was Black (thus being one-eighth Black). In other southern states, having any Black ancestry at all defined one as a Black person—the so-called "one drop" (that is, of Black blood) rule (Malcomson 2000).

This is even more complex when we consider the meaning of race in other countries. In Brazil, a light-skinned Black person could well be considered White, especially if the person is of high socioeconomic status, showing that one's race in Brazil is in part actually *defined by* one's social class. Thus, in parts of Brazil, it is often said that "money lightens." In this sense, a category, such as social class, can become racialized (Omi and Winant 1994; Blalock 1982; Sowell 1983).

Racialization is a process whereby some social category, such as a social class or nationality, takes on what are *perceived in the society* to be racial characteristics (Malcomson 2000; Harrison 2000; Omi and Winant 1994). The experiences of Jewish people provide a good example of what it means to say that race is a socially constructed category. Jews are more accurately called an *ethnic group* because of common religious and cultural heritage, but in Nazi Germany, Hitler defined Jews as a "race." An ethnic group had thus become *racialized.* Jews were presumed to be biologically inferior to the group Hitler labeled the Aryans—white-skinned, blonde, tall, blue-eyed people. On the basis of this definition—which was supported through Nazi law, taught in Nazi schools, and enforced by the Nazi military—Jewish people were grossly mistreated: They were segregated, persecuted, and systematically murdered in what has come to be called the Holocaust during the Second World War.

Mixed-race people defy the biological categories that are typically used to define race. Is someone who is the child of an Asian mother and an African American father

Asian or Black? The current practice of using several racial categories to be simultaneously checked by a person in the U.S. census reflects this issue (Wright 1994; Waters 1990), although considerable controversy has arisen over this procedure (Harrison 2000). As Table 9.1 shows, the U.S. census has dramatically changed its racial and ethnic classifications since 1890, reflecting the fact that society's thinking about racial and ethnic categorization has not remained constant through time (Harrison 2000; Lee 1993; Mathews 1996).

The biological characteristics that have been used to define different racial groups vary considerably both within and between groups. Many Asians, for example, are actually lighter skinned than many Europeans and White Americans and, regardless of their skin color, have been defined in racial terms as yellow. Some light-skinned African Americans are actually lighter in skin color than some White Americans. Developing racial categories overlooks the fact that human groups defined as races are biologically much more alike than they are different.

The biological differences that are presumed to define different racial groups are somewhat arbitrary. Why, for example, do we differentiate people based on skin color and not some other characteristic, such as height or hair color? You might ask yourself how a society based on the presumed racial inferiority of red-haired people would compare to other racial inequalities in the United States. The likelihood is that if a powerful group defined another group as inferior because of some biological characteristics and they used their power to create social institutions that treated this group unfairly, a system of racial inequality would result. In fact, *very few biological differences* exist between racial groups. Most of the variability in almost all biological characteristics, such as blood type and various bodily chemicals, is *within* and not between racial groups (Malcomson 2000; Lewontin 1996).

TABLE 9.1 Comparison of U.S. Census Classifications, 1890–2000

Census Date	White	African American	Native American	Asian American	Other Categories
1890	White	Black Mulatto Quadroon Octoroon	Indian	Chinese Japanese	
1900	White	Black	Indian	Chinese Japanese	
1910	White	Black Mulatto	Indian	Chinese Japanese	Other
1920	White	Black Mulatto	Indian	Chinese Japanese	Other
1930	White	Negro	Indian	Chinese Japanese Filipino Hindu Korean	Mexican Other
1940	White	Negro	Indian	Chinese Japanese Filipino Hindu Korean	Other
1950	White	Negro	American Indian	Chinese Japanese Filipino	Hawaiian Other
1960	White	Negro	American Indian Aleut Eskimo	Chinese Japanese Filipino	Hawaiian Other
1970	White	Negro or Black	Indian (American)	Chinese Japanese Filipino Korean	Hawaiian Other
1980	White	Black or Negro	Indian (American) Eskimo Aleut	Chinese Japanese Filipino Korean Vietnamese	Hawaiian Guamanian Samoan Other
1990	White	Black or Negro	Indian (American) Eskimo Aleut	Chinese Japanese Filipino Korean Asian Indian Vietnamese	Hawaiian Guamanian Samoan Asian or Pacific Islander Other
2000[a, b]	White	Black or African American	American Indian Alaskan Native	Chinese Japanese Filipino Korean Asian Indian Vietnamese	Native Hawaiian Other Pacific Islander Other

[a]In 2000, for the first time ever, individuals could select more than one racial category. Only 2% actually did so.
[b]Hispanics are included under "Other."

SOURCE: Lee, Sharon. 1993. "Racial Classification in the U.S. Census: 1890–1990." *Ethnic and Racial Studies* 16(1): 75–94. U.S. Census Bureau. 2003. "Racial and Ethnic Classification Used in Census 2000 and Beyond." Reprinted by permission of Taylor & Francis Ltd. **www.tandf.co.uk.journals/**.

Different groups use different criteria to define racial groups. To American Indians, being classified as an American Indian depends upon proving American Indian ancestry, but this proof varies considerably from tribe to tribe. Among some American Indians, one must be able to demonstrate 75 percent American Indian ancestry to be recognized as American Indian; for other American Indians, demonstrating 50 percent American Indian ancestry is sufficient. It also matters who defines racial group membership. The government makes tribes prove themselves as tribes through a complex set of federal regulations (called the "federal acknowledgment process"); very few are actually given this official status, and the criteria for tribal membership as well as definition as "Indian" or "Native American" have varied considerably throughout American history. Thus, as with African Americans, it has been a state or federal government, and not so much the racial or ethnic group *itself,* that has defined who is a member of the group and who is not!

Official recognition by the government matters, though, because only those groups officially defined as Indian tribes qualify for health, housing, and educational assistance from the Bureau of Indian Affairs (the BIA) or are allowed to manage the natural resources on Indian lands and maintain their own system of governance (Locklear 1999; Brown 1993; Snipp 1989).

This definition of race emphasizes that what is important about race are not only physical and cultural differences per se, but also how definitions of race are created and maintained by the most powerful group (or groups) in society and what these presumed group differences mean in the context of social and historical experience. As a result, who is defined as a race is as much a political question as a biological one. For example, although they probably did not think of themselves as a race, Irish Americans in the early twentieth century were defined by more powerful White groups as a race that was inferior to White people. At that time, Irish people were not considered by many even to be White (Ignatiev 1995)! In fact, a century ago the Irish were called "Negroes turned inside out," while Negroes (Black people) were called "smoked Irish" (Malcomson 2000).

The social construction of race has been elaborated on in a new and insightful perspective in sociology known as racial formation theory (Omi and Winant 1994). **Racial formation** is the process by which a group comes to be defined as a race. This definition is supported through official social institutions such as the law and the schools. This concept emphasizes the importance of social institutions in producing and maintaining the meaning of race; it also connects the process of racial formation to the exploitation of so-called racial groups. A good example comes from African American history. During slavery, an African American was defined as being three-fifths of a person, for purposes of deciding how slaves would be counted for state representation in the new federal government and how they would be defined as property by the government, in order to be taxed as property. The process of defining slaves in

© Allan Fredrickson/Reuters/Getty Images

Tiger Woods, considered among the greatest golfers ever, lines up a putt. He is of Asian American and African American parentage. What race is he?

this way served the purposes of White Americans, not slaves themselves, and it linked the definition of slaves as a race to the political and economic needs of the most powerful group in society (Higginbotham 1978).

The process of racial formation also explains how groups such as Asian Americans, American Indians, and Latinos have been defined as races, despite the different experiences and nationalities of the groups composing these three categories. Race, like ethnicity, lumps groups together that may have very different historical and cultural backgrounds, but once they are so labeled, the groups are perceived as a single entity. This reflects a more general principle in the social sciences called **out-group homogeneity effect** where all members of any out-group are perceived by an individual to be similar or even identical to each other, and differences among them are perceived to be minor or nonexistent (Taylor et al. 2003). This has recently been the case in the United States with Middle Easterners: Lebanese, Iranians, Iraqis, Jordanians, Egyptians, Afghans, and many others are classified as one group and called Middle Easterners or even Arabs.

Minority and Dominant Groups

Minorities are racial or ethnic groups, but not all racial or ethnic groups are always considered minorities. Irish

Americans, for instance, are not now thought of as minorities, although they once were in the early part of the twentieth century. A **minority group** is any distinct group in society that shares common group characteristics and is forced to occupy low status in society because of prejudice and discrimination. A group may be classified as a minority on the basis of ethnicity, race, sexual preference, age, or class status, for example. A minority group is not necessarily a numerical minority but is a group that holds low status in relation to other groups in society, regardless of the size of the group. In South Africa, Blacks outnumber Whites ten to one, but until Nelson Mandela's election as president and the dramatic change of the country's government in 1994, Blacks were an officially oppressed and politically excluded social minority under the infamous *apartheid* (pronounced "apart-hate" or "apart-hite") system of government. The group that assigns a racial or ethnic group to subordinate status in society is called the **dominant group.** In general, a racial or ethnic minority group has the following characteristics (Simpson and Yinger 1985):

1. The minority group possesses characteristics (such as race, ethnicity, sexual preference, age, or religion) that are popularly regarded as different from those of the dominant group.

2. The minority group suffers prejudice and discrimination by the dominant group.

3. Membership in the group is frequently ascribed rather than achieved, although either form of status can be the basis for being identified as a minority.

4. Members of a minority group feel a strong sense of group solidarity. There is a "consciousness of kind" or "we feeling." This bond grows from common cultural heritage and the shared experience of being a recipient of prejudice and discrimination.

DEBUNKING
Society's Myths

Myth: Minority groups are those with the least numerical representation in society.

Sociological perspective: A minority group is any group, regardless of size, that is singled out in society for unfair treatment and that generally occupies lower status in the society.

▪ *Racial Stereotypes*

Racial and ethnic inequality is peculiarly resistant to change. Racial and ethnic inequality in society produces racial stereotypes, and these stereotypes become the lens through which members of different groups perceive one another.

Stereotypes and Salience

In everyday social interaction, people tend to categorize other people. The most common bases for such categorizations are race, gender, and age (Taylor et al. 2003; Worchel et al. 2000). A person *immediately* identifies a stranger as Black, Asian, Hispanic, White, and so on; as a man or woman; and as a child, adult, or elderly person. Quick and ready categorizations help people process the huge amounts of information they receive about people with whom they have come into contact. People quickly assign others to a few categories, saving themselves the task of evaluating and remembering every little discernible detail about a person. People are taught to treat each person as a unique individual, but research over the years clearly shows that they do not. Instead, people routinely categorize others in some way or another. This serves the function that allows thinking about people and processing information about them. Just about everyone tends to do this.

A **stereotype** is an oversimplified set of beliefs about members of a social group or social stratum. It is based on the tendency of humans to categorize a person based on a narrow range of perceived characteristics. Stereotypes are presumed, usually incorrectly, to describe the "typical" member of some social group.

Stereotypes based on race or ethnicity are called *racial–ethnic stereotypes.* Here are some common examples: Asian Americans have been stereotyped as overly ambitious, sneaky, and clannish; African Americans often bear the stereotype of being typically loud, lazy, naturally musical, and so on. Hispanics are stereotyped as lazy, oversexed, and for Hispanic men, macho; Jews have been perceived as materialistic and unethical. Such stereotypes, presumed to describe the "typical" member of a group, are factually inaccurate for the vast majority of members of a group. No group in U.S. history has escaped the process of categorization and stereotyping, even White groups. For example, Italians have been stereotyped as overly emotional and prone to crime, the Irish as heavy drinkers and prone to politics, and so on for virtually any group in U.S. history.

The categorization of people into groups and the subsequent application of stereotypes is based on the **salience principle,** which states that we categorize people on the basis of what appears initially prominent and obvious—that is, salient—about them. Skin color is a salient characteristic; it is one of the first things that we notice about someone. Because skin color is so obvious, it becomes a basis for stereotyping. Gender and age are also salient characteristics of an individual, and thus serve as notable bases for group stereotyping.

THINKING SOCIOLOGICALLY

Observe several people on the street. What are the first things you notice about them (that is, what is *salient*?) Make a short list of these things. Do these lead you to *stereotype* these people? On what are your stereotypes based?

The choice of salient characteristics is culturally determined. In the United States, skin color, hair texture, nose form and size, and lip form and size have become salient characteristics. We use these features to categorize people in our minds on the basis of race. In other cultures, religion may be far more salient than skin color. In the Middle East, whether one is Muslim or Christian is far more important than skin color. Religion in the Middle East is a salient characteristic and takes considerable priority over race.

The Interplay Among Race, Gender, and Class Stereotypes

Alongside racial and ethnic stereotypes, gender and social class are among the most prominent features by which people are categorized. In our society, there is a complex interplay among racial or ethnic, gender, and class stereotypes.

Among *gender stereotypes,* those based on a person's gender, the stereotypes about women are more likely to be negative than those about men. The "typical" woman has been traditionally stereotyped as subservient, overly emotional, and talkative, inept at math and science, and so on. Many of these are *cultural stereotypes.* They are conveyed and supported by the cultural media—music, TV, magazines, art, and literature. Men, too, are painted in crude strokes, although usually not as negatively as women. Men in the media are stereotyped as macho, insensitive, and pigheaded, and are portrayed in situation comedies as inept. Generally, men are depicted as wanting to have sex with as many women as possible in the shortest time available.

Social class stereotypes are based on assumptions about social class status. Upper-class people are stereotyped (by middle- and lower-class people) as snooty, aloof, condescending, and phony. Some of the stereotypes held about the middle class (by both the upper class and the lower class) are that they are overly ambitious, striving, and obsessed with "keeping up with the Joneses." Finally, stereotypes about lower-class people abound: They are perceived by the upper and middle classes as dirty, lazy, unmotivated, violent, and so on.

The principle of **stereotype interchangeability** holds that stereotypes, especially negative ones, are often interchangeable from one social class to another, from one racial

or ethnic group to another, from a racial or ethnic group to a social class, or from a social class to a gender. Stereotype interchangeability is sometimes revealed through humor. Ethnic jokes often interchange different groups as the butt of the humor, stereotyping them as dumb and inept. Take the stereotype of African Americans as inherently lazy. This stereotype has also been applied in recent history to Hispanic, Polish, Irish, and other groups. It has even been applied generally to those people perceived as lower class. In fact, "laziness" is often used to explain *why* someone is lower class or poor. Middle-class people are more likely to attribute the low status of a lower-class person to something *internal,* such as laziness or lack of willpower (Krasnodemski 1996; Worchel et al. 2000). Lower-class people are more likely to attribute their status to discrimination or poor opportunities—that is, to an *external* societal factor (Taylor et al. 2003; Krasnodemski 1996; Kluegel and Bobo 1993; Bobo and Kluegel 1991).

The same kinds of stereotypes have historically been applied to women. Many of the stereotypes applied to women in literature and the media—such as that they are childlike, overly emotional, unreasonable, bad at mathematics, and so on—have also been applied to African Americans, lower-class people, the poor, and earlier in the twentieth century, Chinese Americans. A common theme is apparent: Whatever group occupies the lowest social status in society at a given time (whether racial or ethnic minorities, women, or lower-class people) is negatively stereotyped, and often the same negative stereotypes are used between and among these groups. The stereotype is then used as an "explanation" for the observed behavior of a stereotyped group's member to justify his or her lower status in society. This in turn subjects the stereotyped group to prejudice, discrimination, and racism, which will now be discussed.

■ *Prejudice, Discrimination, and Racism*

Many people use the terms *prejudice, discrimination,* and *racism* loosely, as if they were all the same thing. Typically, in common parlance, people also think of these terms as they apply to individuals, as if the major problems of race were the result of individual people's bad will or biased ideas. Sociologists use more refined concepts to understand race and ethnic relations, distinguishing carefully between prejudice, discrimination, and racism.

Prejudice

Prejudice is the evaluation of a social group and individuals within that group, based on conceptions about the social group, which are held despite facts that disprove them and involve both prejudgment and misjudgment (Allport 1954; Jones 1997). Prejudices are usually defined as negative predispositions or evaluations that are rarely positive. Thinking ill of people only because they are members of group X is prejudice. The negative evaluation arises solely because the person is seen as a member of group X, without regard to countervailing characteristics the person may have.

A negative prejudice against someone not in one's own group is often accompanied by a positive prejudice in favor of someone who *is* in one's own group. Thus, the prejudiced person will have negative attitudes about a member of an *out-group* (any group other than one's own) and positive attitudes about someone simply because he or she is in one's *in-group* (any group a person considers to be one's own).

Most people disavow racial or ethnic prejudice, yet the vast majority of us carry around some prejudices, whether about racial–ethnic groups, men and women, old and young, upper class and lower class, or straight and gay. Virtually no one is free of prejudice. Five decades of research have shown definitively that people who are more prejudiced are also more likely to stereotype and categorize others by race or ethnicity or by gender than those who are less prejudiced (Adorno et al. 1950; Jones 1997; Taylor et al. 2003).

Prejudice based on race or ethnicity is called *racial* or *ethnic prejudice.* If you are a Latino and dislike an Anglo only because he or she is White, then this constitutes prejudice: It is a negative judgment or prejudgment based on race and ethnicity and very little else. If the Latino individual attempts to justify these feelings by arguing that "all Whites have the same bad character," then the Latino is using a stereotype as justification for the prejudice. Note that prejudice can be held by any group against another group.

Prejudice is also revealed in the phenomenon of **ethnocentrism,** which was examined in Chapter 2 on culture. Ethnocentrism is the belief that one's group is superior to all other groups. The ethnocentric person feels that his or her own group is moral, just, and right and that an out-group—and thus any member of that out-group—is immoral, unjust, wrong, distrustful, or criminal. The ethnocentric individual uses his or her own in-group as the standard against which all other groups are compared.

PREJUDICE AND SOCIALIZATION. Where does racial–ethnic prejudice come from? How do moderately or highly prejudiced people end up that way? People are not born with stereotypes and prejudices. Research shows that these attitudes are learned and internalized through the socialization process, including both

primary socialization (family, peers, teachers) as well as *secondary socialization* (such as the media). Children imitate the attitudes of their parents, peers, and teachers. If the parent complains about "Japs taking away jobs from Americans," then the child grows up thinking negatively about the Japanese, including Japanese Americans. Attitudes about race are formed early in childhood, at about age three or four (Allport 1954; Feagin 2000; Van Ausdale and Feagin 1996). There is a very close correlation between the racial and ethnic attitudes of parents and those of their children. The more ethnically or racially prejudiced the parent, the more ethnically or racially prejudiced the child will be.

Major vehicles for the communication of racial–ethnic attitudes to both young and old are the media, especially

TAKING ON SOCIAL ISSUES

The Affirmative Action Debate

Various methods have been suggested for reducing racial inequality in the United States. Some of these remedies are based on color-blind approaches, such as civil rights laws that prohibit employment practices that exclude people because of race. Other suggested remedies are race specific, such as *affirmative action programs* that target racial groups for inclusion in employment or college admissions. Proponents of color-blind strategies base their policies on the argument that all groups should be treated alike, regardless of their historical, social, and cultural differences. Critics of this approach say that it is a racist approach, and cannot address the problems created by past discrimination and the unique experiences of different racial–ethnic groups.

Do you think that race should be used in any way as a criterion for admission to colleges and universities? Do you think that race should be used along with other factors, as long as some form of racial quota is *not* used (as decided by the Supreme Court in June of 2003 in *Grutter v. Bollinger*)? Do you think that a minority candidate for admission to a college or university should get extra "points" for being a minority (the Supreme Court decided against this in *Gratz v. Bollinger* in 2003)?

Taking Action

Go to the Taking Action exercise on the companion Web site at **sociology.wadsworth.com/ andersen_taylor/essen3e** to learn more about an organization that addresses this topic.

television, magazines, newspapers, and books. For many decades, African Americans, Hispanics, Native Americans, and Asians were rarely presented in the media and then only in negatively stereotyped roles. The Chinese were shown in movies, magazines, and early television in the 1950s as bucktoothed buffoons who ran shirt laundries. Japanese Americans were depicted as sneaky and untrustworthy. Hispanics were shown as either ruthless banditos or playful, happy-go-lucky people who took long siestas. American Indians were presented as either villains or subservient characters like the Lone Ranger's famed sidekick, Tonto. Finally, there is the drearily familiar portrayal of the Black person as subservient, lazy, clowning, and bug-eyed, a stereotypical image that persisted from the nineteenth century all the way through the 1950s and early 1960s (Thibodeau 1989).

Discrimination

Discrimination is overt negative and unequal treatment of the members of some social group or stratum solely because of their membership in that group or stratum. Prejudice is an attitude; discrimination is overt behavior. *Racial–ethnic discrimination* is unequal treatment of a person on the basis of race or ethnicity.

Discrimination in housing has been a particular burden on minorities. Many studies have been able to reproduce the situation, showing that when two persons identical in nearly all respects (age, education, gender, social class, and other characteristics) present themselves as potential tenants for the same housing, if one is White and the other is a minority, the minority person will often be refused housing by a White landlord while the otherwise identical White applicant will not. A minority landlord who refuses housing to a White person while granting it to a minority person of similar social characteristics is also discriminating, but reverse discrimination of this sort is far less frequent and far less of a problem in society (Feagin 2000; Feagin and Vera 1995; Feagin and Feagin 1993).

Prejudice is an attitude; discrimination is behavior. The discrimination affecting the nation's minorities takes a number of forms—for example, income discrimination and discrimination in housing. Discrimination in employment and promotion (discussed in Chapter 13) and discrimination in education (also in Chapter 13) are two other forms of discrimination.

Although the median income of Black and Hispanic families has increased somewhat since 1950, the income gap between these two groups and Whites has remained virtually unchanged since 1967, as can be seen from Figure 9.1. Furthermore, per capita income since 1967 has grown at a somewhat faster rate for Whites. Yet even

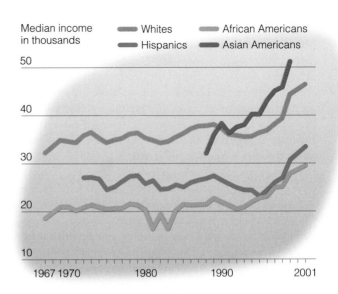

FIGURE 9.1 The Income Gap

SOURCE: U.S. Census Bureau. 2003. *Money Income in the United States: 2001.* Washington, DC: U.S. Department of Commerce.

these median income figures tell only part of the story. Poverty among Blacks decreased from 1960 to 1970, but the poverty level has been somewhat steady since. The current poverty rate (the percent below the poverty level; see Figure 9.2) is highest for African Americans (23 percent) and Hispanics (21 percent), compared to Whites (10 percent). In all these racial groups, children have the highest rate of poverty.

Discrimination in housing is illegal under U.S. law. Nonetheless, banks and mortgage companies often withhold mortgages from minorities based on "redlining," an illegal practice in which an entire minority neighborhood is designated as "no loan." Racial segregation may also be fostered by *gerrymandering,* the calculated redrawing of election districts, school districts, and similar political boundaries in order to maintain racial segregation. As a result, **residential segregation,** the spatial separation of racial and ethnic groups into different residential areas, continues to be a reality in this country—called "American apartheid." (Massey and Denton 1993).

Racism

Racism includes both attitudes and behaviors. A negative attitude taken toward someone simply because he or she belongs to a racial or ethnic group is a prejudice, as has already been discussed. An attitude or prejudice is what you think and feel; a behavior is what you do. **Racism** is the perception and treatment of a racial or ethnic group, or member of that group, as intellectually,

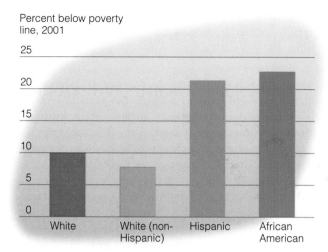

Percent below poverty line, 2001

FIGURE 9.2 Poverty Among Racial Groups

SOURCE: U.S. Census Bureau. 2003. CPS Annual Demographic Survey, March Supplement: 2001.

socially, and culturally inferior to one's own group. It is more than an attitude; it is institutionalized in society. Racism involves negative attitudes that are sometimes linked with negative behavior.

There are different **forms of racism.** Obvious, overt racism, such as physical assaults, from beatings to lynchings, has often been called *old-fashioned racism,* or *traditional racism* (or *Jim Crow racism*), by researchers (for example, Bobo 1999; Sears et al. 1997). This form of racism has declined somewhat in our society since the 1950s, though it certainly has not disappeared (Schumann et al. 1997). Racism can also be subtle, covert, and nonobvious; this is known as *aversive racism,* another form of racism (Jones 1997). Consistently avoiding interaction with someone of another race or ethnicity is an example of aversive racism. This form of racism is quite common and has remained at roughly the same level for more than thirty years, with perhaps a slight increase (Schumann et al. 1997; Kovel 1970; Dovidio and Gaertner 1986; Katz et al. 1986).

After the Second World War and during the 1950s, a shift to *laissez-faire racism* occurred. This type of racism—also called *symbolic racism* by some (Taylor et al. 2003)—involves several elements:

1. The subtle but persistent negative stereotyping of minorities, particularly Black Americans, especially in the media.

2. A tendency to blame Blacks themselves for the gap between Blacks and Whites in socioeconomic standing, occupational achievement, and educational achievement.

3. Clear resistance to meaningful policy efforts (such as affirmative action, discussed later) designed to ameliorate America's racially oppressive social conditions and practices. The last element is rooted in perceptions of threat to maintaining the status quo (Bobo 1999; Bobo and Smith 1998).

A close relative of laissez-faire racism is *color-blind racism*—so named because the individual affected by this type of racism prefers to ignore legitimate racial–ethnic, cultural, and other differences and insists that the race problems in America will go away if only race is ignored all together. Accompanying this belief is the opinion that race differences in America are merely an illusion and that race is not real. Simply refusing to perceive any differences at all between racial groups (thus, being color-blind) is in itself a form of racism. Many of these types of racism do not necessarily involve explicit or purposeful intent on the part of the nonminority individual to harm the minority person.

Institutional racism as a form of racism is negative treatment and oppression of one racial or ethnic group by society's existing institutions based on the presumed inferiority of the oppressed group. It is a form of racism that exists at the level of social structure and is in Durkheim's sense *external* to the individual—thus institutional. Key to understanding institutional racism is seeing that dominant groups have the economic and political power to subjugate the minority group, *even if they do not have the explicit intent* of being prejudiced or discriminating against others. Power, or lack thereof, accrues to groups because of their position in social institutions, not just because of individual attitudes or behavior. The power that resides in society's institutions can be seen in such patterns as persistent economic inequality between racial groups, which is reflected in high unemployment among minorities, lower wages, and different patterns of job placement (Bobo 1999; Bonilla-Silva 1997).

Racial profiling, already discussed in Chapter 6, is an example of institutional racism in the criminal justice system. African American and Hispanic persons are arrested considerably more often than Whites and Asians. In fact, an African American or Hispanic wrongdoer is more likely to be arrested than a White person who commits the *exact same crime,* even when the White person shares the same age, socioeconomic environment, and prior arrest record as the Black or Hispanic.

Institutional racism is also seen in educational institutions, such as when schools assign Blacks and Latinos to the lower cognitive ability tracks than Whites with the *same* ability test scores, as will be seen in Chapter 13. In these instances, racism is a characteristic of the institutions and not necessarily of the individuals within the

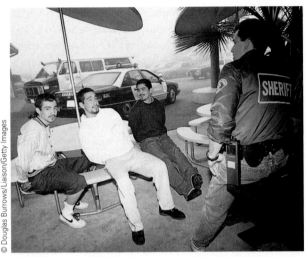

Minorities are more likely to be arrested than Whites for the same offense. Does this reflect institutional racism rather than any individual prejudice of the arresting police officer?

institution. *This is why institutional racism can exist even without prejudice being the cause.*

DEBUNKING
Society's Myths

Myth: The primary cause of racial inequality in the United States is the persistence of prejudice.

Sociological perspective: Prejudice is one dimension of racial problems in the United States, but institutional racism can flourish even while prejudice is on the decline.

Consider this: Even if every White person in the country lost all of his or her personal prejudices and even if he or she stopped engaging in individual acts of discrimination, institutional racism would still persist for some time. Over the years, it has become so much a part of U.S. institutions (hence, the term *institutional racism*) that discrimination can occur even when no single person is deliberately causing it. Existing at the level of social structure instead of at the level of individual attitude *or* behavior, it is external to the individual personality and is thus a *social fact* of the sort about which sociological theorist Emile Durkheim wrote (Chapter 1).

■ *Theories of Prejudice and Racism*

Why do prejudice, discrimination, and racism exist? Two categories of theories have been advanced. The first category consists of psychological theories about prejudice.

The second category consists of sociological theories of racism, including institutional racism, as well as of prejudice and discrimination.

Psychological Theories of Prejudice

Two traditional psychological theories of prejudice are the scapegoat theory and the theory of the authoritarian personality. **Scapegoat theory** argues that, historically, members of the dominant group in the United States have harbored various frustrations in their desire to achieve social and economic success (Feagin and Feagin 1993). As a result of this frustration, they vent their anger in the form of aggression, and this aggression is directed toward some substitute that takes the place of the original perception of the frustration. Members of minority groups become these substitutes, that is, the scapegoats. The psychological principle that aggression often follows frustration (originally from the frustration-aggression hypothesis of Dollard et al. 1939) is central to the scapegoat principle. For example, a White person who perceived that he or she was denied a job because "too many" Mexican immigrants were being permitted to enter the country would be using Mexican Americans as a scapegoat if he or she felt negatively (thus prejudiced) toward a specific Mexican American person, even if that person did not have the job in question and had nothing at all to do with the White person not getting the job.

The second theory, an older one, argues that individuals who possess an authoritarian personality are more likely to be prejudiced against minorities than are nonauthoritarian individuals. The **authoritarian personality** (after Adorno et al. 1950, who coined the term) is characterized by a tendency to rigidly categorize other people, as well as inclinations to submit to authority, strictly conform, be very intolerant of ambiguity, and be inclined toward superstition. The authoritarian person is more likely to stereotype or categorize another and thus readily places members of minority groups into convenient and oversimplified categories or stereotypes. There is some research that links strong authoritarianism with high religious orthodoxy and extreme varieties of political conservatism (Bobo and Kluegel 1991; Altemeyer 1988).

Sociological Theories of Prejudice and Racism

Current sociological theory focuses more on explaining the existence of racism, particularly institutional racism, although speculation about the existence of prejudice is also a component. The three sociological theoretical perspectives considered throughout this text have bearing

© Lawrence Migdale

Cultural diffusion is evident in this Native American school kitchen, as seen by both the decorations and the food preparations.

on the study of racism, discrimination, and prejudice: functionalist theory, symbolic interaction theory, and conflict theory.

FUNCTIONALIST THEORY.

Functionalist theory argues that for race and ethnic relations to be functional and thus contribute to the harmonious conduct and stability of society, racial and ethnic minorities and women must assimilate into that society. **Assimilation** is a process by which a minority becomes socially, economically, and culturally absorbed within the dominant society. The assimilation perspective assumes that to become fully fledged members of society, minority groups must adopt as much of the dominant society's culture as possible, particularly its language, mannerisms, and goals for success.

SYMBOLIC INTERACTION THEORY.

Symbolic interaction theory addresses two issues: first, the role of social interaction in reducing racial and ethnic hostility, and second, how race and ethnicity are socially constructed. Symbolic interactionism asks, What happens when two people of different racial or ethnic origins come into contact with each other, and how can such interracial or interethnic contact reduce hostility and conflict? **Contact theory,** which originated with the psychologist Gordon Allport (Allport 1954; Cook 1988) argues that interaction between Whites and minorities will reduce prejudice within both groups—but only if three conditions are met:

1. The contact must be between individuals of equal status; the parties must interact on equal ground. A

Hispanic cleaning woman and the wealthier White woman who employs her may interact, but their interaction will not reduce prejudice. Instead, their interaction is more likely to perpetuate stereotypes and prejudices on the part of both.

2. The contact between equals must be sustained; short-term contact will not decrease prejudice. Bringing Whites together with Hispanics, Blacks, Native Americans for short weekly meetings will not erase prejudice. Daily contact on the job between individuals of *equal job status* will tend to remove prejudice.

3. Social norms favoring equality must be agreed upon by the participants. Having African Americans and White skinheads interact on a TV talk show, such as the Jerry Springer Show, will probably not decrease prejudice; this interaction might well increase it.

CONFLICT THEORY.

The basic premise of conflict theory is that class-based conflict is an inherent and fundamental part of social interaction. To the extent that racial and ethnic conflict is tied to class conflict, conflict theorists argue that class inequality must be reduced to lessen racial and ethnic conflict in society.

The current "class versus race" controversy in sociology (reviewed in more detail later in this chapter and in chapter 7 concerns the question of whether class (namely, economic differences between races) or race (caste differences between races) is more important in explaining inequality and its consequences or whether they are of equal importance. Those focusing primarily upon class conflict, such as sociologist William Julius Wilson (1978, 1987, 1996), argue that at times class and changes in the economic structure are at times more important than race in shaping the life chances of different groups, although they see both as important. Wilson argues that being disadvantaged in the United States is more a matter of class, although he sees this clearly linked to race. Sociologists focusing primarily on the role of race (Feagin 2000; Bonilla-Silva 1997; Feagin and Feagin 1993; Willie 1979) argue the opposite: They say that race has been and is relatively more important than class—though class is still important—in explaining and accounting for inequality and conflict in society and that directly addressing the question of race forthrightly is the only way to solve the country's race problems (see Table 9.2).

A recent variety of the conflict perspective is the *intersection perspective*. This perspective refers to the interactive or combined effects of racism, classism (elitism), and gender in the oppression of people. An implication of this theory is that the position of women in society should be studied separately within each racial or ethnic

TABLE 9.2 Comparing Sociological Theories of Race and Ethnicity

	Functionalism	Conflict Theory	Symbolic Interaction
The Racial Order	Has social stability when diverse racial and ethnic groups are assimilated into society	Is intricately intertwined with class stratification	Is based on social construction that assigns groups of people to diverse racial and ethnic categories
Minority Groups	Are assimilated into dominant culture as they adopt cultural practices and beliefs of the dominant group	Have life chances that result from the opportunities formed by the intersection of class, race, and gender	Form identity as the result of sociohistorical change
Social Change	Is a slow and gradual process as groups adapt to the social system	Is the result of organized social movements and other forms of resistance to oppression	Is dependent on the different forms of interaction that characterize intergroup relations (such as contact or competition)

group and within each social class group, because the observed differences between women and men are not the same within the different racial or class groups. This perspective notes that not only are the effects of gender and race intertwined, but also both are intertwined with the effects of class. Class conflict is seen as an integral component of gender and race differences in this society, according to the intersection perspective (Andersen and Collins 2004; Collins 1998, 1990).

■ *Diverse Groups, Diverse Histories*

The different racial and ethnic groups in the United States have arrived at their current social condition through histories that are similar in some ways, yet quite different in other respects. Their histories are related because of a common experience of White supremacy, economic exploitation, and political disenfranchisement. Native Americans were here first, yet they have been the victims of territorial expansion, armed conquest, genocide, and the destruction of their cultures. They were deprived of their land, forced to live on segregated reservations, or systematically exterminated. African Americans were forcibly abducted from West Africa—transported to this hemisphere under filthy inhuman conditions while locked in the holds of slave ships and then sold into slavery. Hispanics from both Mexico and Puerto Rico provided cheap labor, as did indigenous Hispanics. The Chinese were imported to provide labor on the Western frontier and were forced to endure a variety of hardships ranging from hunger and slavelike conditions to murder. Arriving Japanese met with high prejudice and discrimination, and some Japanese Americans who had lived in the United States for several generations suffered the violation of having their

property confiscated and their families forcibly moved to concentration camps after the United States entered the Second World War (in the early 1940s) against Germany and Japan.

Even White ethnic groups, many of whom arrived as indentured servants during the colonial period or arrived later expecting religious, political, and social freedom, found prejudice and discrimination. Such has been the story of the Irish, who fled domination by the British in Ireland and, in the 1840s, the devastating effects of a famine in Ireland brought on partly by the potato blight (Diner 1996). Italians, Poles, and Jews have been excluded in varying degrees from full participation in U.S. society; they have been denied rights and privileges and have failed to receive full protection under the law. Assimilation of White ethnic groups from southern, central, and eastern Europe was slower than for groups from western and northern Europe (Nagel 1996; Healey 1995; Lieberson 1980).

Jewish immigrants are questioned at Ellis Island, the point of entry to the United States for many early European immigrants.

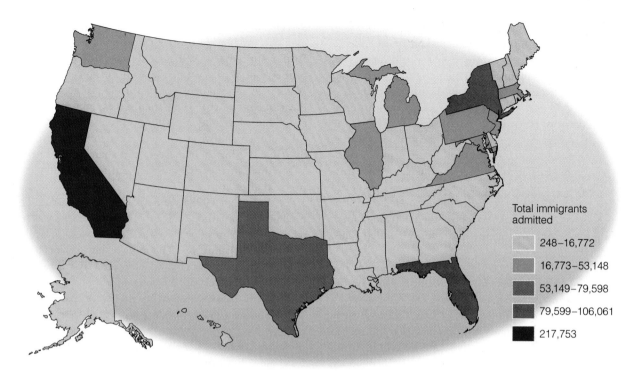

MAP 9.1 Mapping America's Diversity: The New Immigration
This map shows the total number of immigrants per state. Some states have a high num-
ber of immigrants (for example, California, Florida, New York), while other states have
fewer immigrants (for example, Wyoming, South Dakota, and Vermont). **Where does your**
state fall in the number of immigrants to the total population?

Data: U.S. Immigration and Naturalization Service, *Statistical Yearbook,* annual. Printed in the U.S. Census Bureau, *Statistical Abstract of the United States,* 2002, p. 12.

A historical perspective on each group follows, which will aid in understanding how prejudice, discrimination, and racism has operated throughout the history of U.S. society.

Native Americans

The exact size of the indigenous population in North America at the time of the Europeans' arrival with Columbus in 1492 has been estimated at anywhere from one million to ten million people. Native Americans were here tens of thousands of years before they were "discovered" by Europeans. Discovery quickly turned to conquest, and in the course of the next three centuries, the Europeans systematically drove the Native Americans from their lands, destroying their ways of life and crushing various tribal cultures. Native Americans were subjected to an onslaught of European diseases. Lacking immunity to these diseases, Native Americans suffered a population decline, considered by some to have been the steepest and most drastic of any people in the history of the entire world. Native American traditions have sur-

vived in many isolated places, but what is left is only a ghostly echo of the original 500 nations of North America (Nagel 1996; Thornton 1987; Snipp 1989).

From European contacts in the 1640s, there was great linguistic, religious, governmental, and economic heterogeneity among Native American tribes. Most historical accounts have underestimated the degree of cultural and social variety, however. Between the arrival of Columbus in 1492 and the establishment of the first thirteen colonies in the early 1600s, the ravages of disease and the encroachment of Europeans caused a considerable degree of social disorganization. Sketchy accounts of American Indian cultures by early colonists, fur traders, missionaries, and explorers underestimated the great social heterogeneity among the various American Indian tribal groups and the devastating effects of the European arrival on Indian society.

By 1800, the number of Native Americans had been reduced to a mere 600,000, and wars of extermination against the Indians were being conducted in earnest. Fifty years later, the population had fallen by another half. Indians were killed defending their land, or they died of hunger and disease taking refuge in inhospitable country. In 1834, 4000 Cherokee died on a forced march from their homeland in Georgia to reservations in Arkansas and Oklahoma, a trip memorialized as the Trail of Tears. The Sioux were forced off their lands by the discovery of gold and the new push of European immigration. Their reservation was established in 1889 (quite recently in history), and they were designated as wards, subjecting them to capricious and humiliating governmental policies. The following year the U.S. Army mistook Sioux ceremonial dances for war dances and moved in to arrest the leaders. A standoff exploded into violence, during which federal troops killed 200 Sioux men, women, and children at the infamous Wounded Knee massacre.

Today about 55 percent of all Native Americans live on or near a reservation, which is land set aside by the U.S. government for their exclusive use. The other 45 percent live in or near urban areas (U.S. Census Bureau 2002; Snipp 1989). The reservation system has served the Indians poorly. Many Native Americans now live in conditions of abject poverty, deprivation, and alcoholism, and they suffer massive unemployment (more than 50 percent among males—extraordinarily high). They are at the lowest rung of the socioeconomic ladder, with the highest poverty rate. The first here in this land are now last in status, a painful irony of U.S. history.

African Americans

The development of slavery in the Americas is related to the development of world markets for sugar and tobacco. Slaves were imported from Africa to provide the labor for sugar and tobacco production and to enhance the profits of the slaveholders. It is estimated that somewhere between 20 million and 100 million Africans were transported under appalling conditions to the Americas—38 percent went to Brazil; 50 percent to the Caribbean; 6 percent to Dutch, Danish, and Swedish colonies; and 6 percent to the United States (Genovese 1972; Jordan 1969).

Slavery evolved as a *caste system* in which one caste, the slaveholders, profited from the labor of another caste, the slaves. Central to the operation of slavery was the principle that human beings could be *chattel* (or property). As an economic institution, slavery was based on the belief that Whites are superior to other races, coupled with a belief in a patriarchal social order. The social distinctions maintained between Whites and Blacks were castelike, with rigid categorization and prohibitions, rather than merely classlike, which suggests more pliant social demarcations. Vestiges of this caste system still remain in the United States to this day.

The slave system also involved the domination of men over women. In this combination of patriarchy and White supremacy, White males presided over their property of White women as well as their property of Black men and women. This is turn led to gender stratification among the slaves themselves, which reflected the White slaveholder's assumptions about the relative roles of men and women. Black women performed domestic labor for their masters and their own families. White men further exerted their authority in demanding sexual relations with Black women (Blassingame 1973; Raboteau 1978; White 1985; Davis 1981). The predominant attitude of Whites toward Blacks was paternalistic. Whites saw slaves as childlike and incapable of caring for themselves. The more recent stereotypes of African Americans as childlike are directly traceable to the system of slavery.

There is a widespread belief that slaves passively accepted slavery. Scholarship shows this to be false. Instead, the slaves struggled to preserve both their culture and their sense of humanity and to resist, often by open conflict, the dehumanizing effects of a system that defined human beings as mere property (Blassingame 1973; Myers 1998). Slaves revolted against the conditions of enslavement in a variety of ways, from passive means such as work slowdowns and feigned illness to more aggressive means such as destruction of property, escapes, and outright rebellion.

After slavery was presumably ended by the Civil War (1861–1865) and the Emancipation Proclamation (1863), Black Americans continued to be exploited for their labor. In the South, the system of sharecropping emerged, an exploitative system in which Black families tilled the fields for White landowners in exchange for a share of the crop. With the onset of the First World War and the intensified industrialization of society came the Great Migration of Blacks from the South to the urban North. This massive movement, lasting from the late 1800s through the 1920s, significantly affected the status of Blacks in society because there was now a greater potential for collective action (Marks 1989).

In the early part of the century, the formation of Black ghettos had a dual effect. It victimized Black Americans with grim urban conditions and encouraged the development of Black resources, including volunteer organizations, social movements, political action groups, and artistic and cultural achievements. During the 1920s, Harlem in New York City became an important intellectual and artistic oasis for Black America. The Harlem Renaissance gave the nation great literary figures, such as Langston Hughes, Jesse Fausett, Alain Locke, Arna Bontemps, Zora Neale Hurston, Wallace Thurman, and Nella Larson (Bontemps 1972; Ramper-

Novelist and essayist Dorothy West was the oldest living member of the Harlem Renaissance until her death at age 91 in 1998.

sad 1986, 1988; Marks and Edkins 1999). At the same time, many of America's greatest musicians, entertainers, and artists came to the fore, such as musicians Duke Ellington, Billie Holiday, Cab Calloway, and Louis Armstrong, and painter Hale Woodruff. The end of the 1920s and the stock market crash of 1929 brought everyone down a peg or two, Whites as well as Blacks; although in the words of Harlem Renaissance writer Langston Hughes, Black Americans at the time "had but a few pegs to fall" (Hughes 1967).

Latinos

Latino Americans include Chicanos and Chicanas (Mexican Americans), Puerto Ricans, Cubans, and other recent Latin American immigrants to the United States. It also includes Latin Americans who have lived for generations in the United States and are thus not immigrants but very early settlers from Spain and Portugal in the 1400s. The population of Latinos has grown considerably over the past few decades, with the largest increase among Mexican Americans. The terms *Hispanic* and *Latino* or *Latina* mask the great structural and cultural diversity among the various Hispanic groups. The use of such inclusive terms also tends to ignore important differences in their respective entries into U.S. society: Mexican Americans through military conquest of the Mexican War (1846–1848); Puerto Ricans through war with Spain in the Spanish-American War (1898); and Cubans as political refugees fleeing since 1959 from the Communist dictatorship of Fidel Castro, opposed by the U.S. government (Glenn 2002; Bean and Tienda 1987).

MEXICAN AMERICANS. Before the Anglo (White) conquest, Mexican colonists had formed settlements and missions throughout the West and Southwest. In 1834, the U.S. government ordered the dismantling of these missions, bringing them under tight governmental control and creating a period known as the Golden Age of the Ranchos. Land then became concentrated into the hands of a few wealthy Mexican ranchers, who had been given large land grants by the Mexican government. This economy created a class system *within* the Chicano community, consisting of the elite ranchers, mission farmers, and government administrators at the top; *mestizos,* who were small farmers and ranchers as the middle class; a third class of skilled workers; and a bottom class of manual laborers, who were mostly Indians (Mirandé 1985; Maldonado 1997).

With the Mexican-American War of 1846–1848, Chicanos lost claims to huge land areas that ultimately became Texas; New Mexico; and parts of Colorado, Arizona, Nevada, Utah, and California. White cattle ranchers and sheep ranchers enclosed giant tracts of land, thus cutting off many small ranchers, both Mexican and Anglo. It was at this time that Mexicans, as well as early U.S. settlers of Mexican descent, became defined as an inferior race that did not deserve social, educational, or political equality. This is an example of the *racial formation process,* as noted earlier in this chapter (Omi and Winant 1994). Anglos believed that Mexicans were lazy, corrupt, and cowardly, which launched stereotypes that would further oppress Mexicans and were used to justify the lower status of Mexicans and to justify Anglo control of the land that Mexicans were presumed to be incapable of managing (Moore 1976). As has been noted several times in this chapter, stereotyping has been used in this society as a way of explaining and justifying the lower social status of society's minorities.

During the twentieth century, advances in agricultural technology changed the organization of labor in the Southwest and West. Irrigation allowed year-round production of crops and a new need for cheap labor to work in the fields. Migrant workers from Mexico were exploited as a cheap source of labor. Migrant work was characterized by low earnings, poor housing conditions, poor health, and extensive use of child labor. The wide use of Mexican migrant workers as field workers, domestic servants, and other kinds of poorly paid work continues, particularly in the Southwest (Amott and Matthaei 1996).

PUERTO RICANS. The island of Puerto Rico was ceded to the United States by Spain in 1899. In 1917, the Jones Act extended U.S. citizenship to Puerto Ricans, although it was not until 1948 that Puerto Ricans were allowed to elect their own governor. In 1952, the

© Hazel Hankin

Activities such as this Puerto Rican Day Parade in New York City reflect pride in one's group culture and result in greater cohesiveness of the group.

United States established the Commonwealth of Puerto Rico, with its own constitution. Following the Second World War, the first elected governor launched a program known as Operation Bootstrap that was designed to attract large U.S. corporations to the island of Puerto Rico by using tax breaks and other concessions. This program contributed to rapid overall growth in the Puerto Rican economy, although unemployment remained high and wages remained low. Seeking opportunity, unemployed farm workers began migrating to the United States. These migrants were interested in seasonal work, and thus a pattern of temporary migration characterized the Puerto Ricans entrance into the United States (Amott and Matthaei 1996; Rodriguez 1989).

Unemployment in Puerto Rico became so severe that the U.S. government even went so far as to attempt a reduction in the population by some form of population control. Pharmaceutical companies experimented with Puerto Rican women in developing contraceptive pills, and the U.S. government actually encouraged the sterilization of Puerto Rican women. One source notes that by 1974 more than 37 percent of the women of reproductive age in Puerto Rico had been sterilized (Roberts 1997). More than one-third of these women have since indicated that they regret sterilization because they were not made aware at the time that the procedure was irreversible.

CUBANS. Cuban migration to the United States is recent in comparison with the other Hispanic groups. The largest migration has occurred since the revolution led by Castro in 1959; between then and 1980, more than 800,000 Cubans—one-tenth of the entire island population—migrated to the United States. The U.S. government defined this as a political exodus, facilitating the early entrance and acceptance of these migrants. Many of the first migrants had been middle- and upper-class professionals and landowners under the prior dictatorship of Fulgencio Batista, but they had lost their land during the Castro revolution. In exile in the United States, some worked to overthrow Castro, often with the support of the federal government. Yet many other Cuban immigrants were of modest means and, like other immigrant groups, came seeking freedom from political and social persecution and escape from poverty.

The most recent wave of Cuban immigration came in 1980, when the Cuban government, still under Castro, opened the port of Mariel to anyone who wanted to leave Cuba. In the five months following this action, 125,000 Cubans came to the United States—more than the combined total for the preceding eight years. The arrival of people from Mariel has produced debate and tension, particularly in Florida, a major center of Cuban migration. The Cuban government had previously labeled the people fleeing from Mariel as "undesirable;" some had been incarcerated in Cuba before leaving. They were actually not much different from prior refugees such as the "golden exiles," who were professional and high-status refugees (Portes and Rumbaut 1996). Because the refugees escaping from Mariel had been labeled as undesirables, and because they were forced to live in primitive camps for long periods after their arrival, they have been unable to achieve much social and economic mobility in the United Sates. In contrast, the earlier Cuban migrants, who were on average more educated and much more settled, have enjoyed a fair degree of success (Portes and Rumbaut 2001, 1996; Amott and Matthei 1996; Pedraza 1996a).

Asian Americans

Like Hispanic Americans, Asian Americans are from many different countries and diverse cultural backgrounds; they cannot be classified as the single cultural rubric Asians. Asian Americans include migrants from China, Japan, the Philippines, Korea, and Vietnam, as well as more recent immigrants from Cambodia and Laos.

CHINESE. Attracted by the U.S. demand for labor, Chinese Americans began migrating to the United States during the mid-nineteenth century. In the early stages of this migration, the Chinese were tolerated since they provided cheap labor. They were initially seen as good, quiet citizens, but racial stereotypes turned hostile when the Chinese came to be seen as competing with White California gold miners for jobs. Thousands of Chinese laborers worked for the Central Pacific Railroad from 1865 to 1868. They were relegated to the most difficult and dangerous work, worked longer hours than the White laborers, and for a long time were paid considerably less than the White workers.

The Chinese were virtually expelled from railroad work near the turn of the twentieth century (in 1890–1900) and settled in rural areas throughout the western states. As a consequence, anti-Chinese sentiment and prejudice ran high in the West. This ethnic antagonism was largely the result of competition between the White and Chinese laborers for scarce jobs. In 1882, the federal government passed the Chinese Exclusion Act, which banned further immigration of unskilled Chinese laborers. Like African Americans, the Chinese and Chinese Americans were legally excluded from intermarriage (Takaki 1989). The passage of this openly racist act, which was preceded by extensive violence toward the Chinese, drove the Chinese populations from the rural areas into the urban areas of the West. It was during this period that several Chinatowns were established by those who had been forcibly uprooted and who found strength and comfort within enclaves of Chinese people and culture (Nee 1973).

JAPANESE. Japanese immigration to the United States took place mainly between 1890 and 1924, after which passage of the Japanese Immigration Act forbade further immigration. Most of these first-generation immigrants, called *Issei,* were employed in agriculture or in small Japanese businesses. Many Issei were from farming families and wished to acquire their own land, but in 1913, the Alien Land Law of California stipulated that Japanese aliens could lease land for only three years and that lands already owned or leased by them could not be bequeathed to heirs. The second generation of Japanese Americans, or *Nisei,* were born in the United States of Japanese-born parents. They became better educated than their parents, lost their Japanese accents, and in general became more "Americanized," that is, culturally assimilated. The third generation, called *Sansei,* became even better educated and assimilated, yet still met with prejudice and discrimination, particularly where Japanese Americans were present in the highest concentrations, as on the West Coast from Washington to southern California (Glenn 1986).

The Japanese suffered the complete indignity of having their loyalty questioned when the federal government, thinking they would side with Japan after the Japanese attack on Pearl Harbor in December 1941, herded them into concentration camps. By executive order of President Franklin D. Roosevelt, much of the West Coast Japanese American population (many of them loyal second- and third-generation Americans) had

their assets frozen and their real estate confiscated by the government. A media campaign immediately followed, labeling Japanese Americans "traitors" and "enemy aliens." Virtually all Japanese Americans in the United States had been removed from their homes by August of 1942, and some were forced to stay in relocation camps until as late as 1946. Relocation destroyed numerous Japanese families and ruined them financially (Glenn 1986; Kitano 1976; Takaki 1989). In 1986, the U.S. Supreme Court allowed Japanese Americans the right to file suit for monetary reparations. In 1987, legislation was passed, awarding $20,000 to each person who had been relocated and offering an official apology from the U.S. government. One is motivated to contemplate how far this paltry sum and late apology could go in righting what many have argued was the "greatest mistake" the United States made during the Second World War.

FILIPINOS. The Philippine Islands in the Pacific Ocean fell under U.S. rule in 1899 as a result of the Spanish-American War, and for a while, Filipinos could enter the United States freely. By 1934, the islands became a commonwealth of the United States, and immigration quotas were imposed on Filipinos. More than 200,000 Filipinos immigrated to the United States between 1966 and 1980, settling in major urban centers on the West and East Coasts. More than two-thirds of those arriving were professional workers; their high average levels of education and skill have eased their assimilation. By 1985, there were more than one million Filipinos in the United States. Within the next thirty years, demographers project that this population will become the largest group of Asian Americans in the United States, including Chinese Americans and Japanese Americans (Winnick 1990).

KOREANS. Many Koreans entered the United States in the late 1960s after amendments to the immigration laws in 1965 raised the limit on immigration from the Eastern Hemisphere. The largest concentration of Koreans is in Los Angeles. As much as half of the adult Korean American population is college educated, an exceptionally high proportion. Many of the immigrants were successful professionals in Korea; upon arrival in the United States though, they have been forced to take on menial jobs, thus experiencing downward social mobility and status inconsistency. This is especially true of those Koreans who migrated to the East Coast. However, nearly one in eight Koreans in the United States today owns a business; many own small greengrocer businesses. Many of these stores are located in predominantly African American communities and have become one among several sources of ongoing conflict between some African Americans and Koreans. This has fanned negative feeling and prejudice on both sides—among Koreans

An Arab-American community exists in Detroit, illustrating both community as well as residential segregation.

against African Americans and among African Americans against Koreans (Chen 1991).

VIETNAMESE. Among the more recent groups of Asians to enter the United States have been the South Vietnamese, who began arriving following the fall of South Vietnam to the Communist North Vietnamese at the end of the Vietnam War in 1975. These immigrants, many of them refugees who fled for their lives, numbered about 650,000 in the United States in 1975. About one-third of the refugees settled in California. Many faced prejudice and hostility, resulting in part from the same perception that has dogged many immigrant groups before them—that they were in competition for scarce jobs. A second wave of Vietnamese immigrants arrived after China attacked Vietnam in 1978. As many as 725,000 arrived in America, only to face discrimination in a variety of locations. Tensions became especially heated when the Vietnamese became a substantial competitive presence in the fishing and shrimping industries in the Gulf of Mexico on the Texas shore. Many communities have welcomed them, however, and most Vietnamese heads of households have become employed full time (Winnick 1990; Kim 1993).

Middle Easterners

Since the mid-1970s, immigrants from the Middle East have been arriving in the United States. They have come from countries such as Syria, Lebanon, Egypt, and Iran. Contrary to popular belief, the immigrants speak no single language and follow no singular religion, and thus are ethnically diverse. Some are Catholic, some are Coptic Christian, and many are Muslim. Many are from working-class backgrounds, but many were professionals—teachers, engineers, scientists, and other such positions—in their homelands. Some of these immigrants have been able to secure employment in their original occupations, but many have undergone the downward mobility and status inconsistency—often experienced by present-day immigrant professionals—which comes from taking lower-status jobs. Like immigrant populations before them, Middle Easterners have formed their own ethnic enclaves in the cities and suburbs of this country as they pursue the often elusive American dream (Ansari 1991).

After the terrorist attacks on the World Trade Center and the Pentagon on September 11, 2001, many male Middle Easterners of several nationalities became unjustly suspect in this country and were subjected to severe harassment; racially motivated physical attacks; and as already noted, out-and-out racial profiling, if only because they had dark skin and wore a turban on their heads. Most of these individuals, of course, probably had no discernible connection at all with the terrorists.

White Ethnic Groups

The story of White ethnic groups in the United States begins during the colonial period. White Anglo-Saxon Protestants (WASPs), who were originally immigrants from England and to some extent Scotland and Wales, settled in the New World (what is now North America) and were the first ethnic group to come into contact on a large scale with those people already here—namely, Native American Indians. WASPs came to dominate the newly emerging society earlier than any other White ethnic group.

In the late 1700s, the WASPs regarded the later immigrants from Germany and France as foreigners with odd languages, accents, and customs. Tension between the "old stock" and the foreigners continued through the Civil War era until around 1860, when the national origins of U.S. immigrants began to change (Handlin 1951). Of all racial and ethnic groups in the United States during that time and since, only WASPs do not think of themselves as a nationality. The WASPs came to think of themselves as the "original" Americans despite the prior presence of Native American Indians, who in turn the WASPs described and stereotyped as savages. As immigrants from northern, western, eastern, and southern Europe began to arrive, particularly during the mid- to late-nineteenth century, WASPs began to direct prejudice and discrimination against many of these newer groups. Long discriminated against by the male WASP establishment, women began to assert social and political power, challenging the power of male WASPs in the United States. Much of that WASP dominance remains, however, as is evident in their popular use of the terms "race" and "ethnicity" to describe virtually everyone but themselves (Andersen 2003).

There were two waves of migration of White ethnic groups in the mid- and late-nineteenth century. The first stretched from about 1850 through 1880 and included northern and western Europeans: English, Irish, Germans, French, and Scandinavians. The second wave of immigration occurred from 1890 to 1914 and included eastern and southern European populations: Italians, Greeks, Poles, Russians, and other eastern Europeans. The immigration of Jews to the United States extended for well over a century, but the majority of Jewish immigrants came to the United States during the period from 1880 to 1920.

The Irish arrived in large numbers in the mid-nineteenth century as a consequence of food shortages and massive starvation in Ireland. During the latter half of the nineteenth century and in the early twentieth century, the Irish in the United States were abused, attacked, and viciously stereotyped. It is instructive to remember that the Irish, particularly on the East Coast and especially in Boston, underwent a period of ethnic oppression of extraordinary magnitude. A frequently seen sign posted in Boston saloons of the day proclaimed "No dogs or Irish allowed." German immigrants were similarly stereotyped, as were the French and the Scandinavians. It is easy to forget that virtually all immigrant groups go through times of oppression and prejudice, although these periods were considerably longer for some groups than for others. As a rule, where the population density of an ethnic group in a town, city, or region was greatest, so too was the amount of prejudice, negative stereotyping, and discrimination to which that group was subjected.

More than 40 percent of the world's Jewish population lives in the United States, making it the largest community of Jews in the world. Most of the Jews in the United States arrived between 1880 and the First World War, originating from the eastern European countries of Russia, Poland, Lithuania, Hungary, and Romania. Jews from Germany arrived in two phases; the first wave came just prior to the arrival of those from eastern Europe, and the second came as a result of Hitler's ascension to power in Germany during the late 1930s. Because many German Jews were professionals who also spoke English, they assimilated more rapidly than those from the eastern European countries. Jews from both parts of Europe underwent lengthy periods of anti-Jewish prejudice,

anti-Semitism (defined as the hatred of Jewish people), and discrimination, particularly on Manhattan's Lower East Side. Significant anti-Semitism still exists in the United States (Ferber 1999; Simpson and Yinger 1985; Essed 1991).

In 1924, the National Origins Quota Act was passed, one of the most discriminatory legal actions ever taken by the United States in the field of immigration. By this act, the first real establishment of *ethnic quotas* in the United States, immigrants were permitted to enter the United States only in proportion to their numbers already existing in the United States. Thus, ethnic groups who were already here in relatively high proportions (English, Germans, French, Scandinavians, and others, mostly western and northern Europeans) were allowed to immigrate in greater numbers to the country than were those from southern and eastern Europe, such as Italians, Poles, Greeks, and other eastern Europeans. Hence, the act discriminated against southern and eastern Europeans in favor of western and northern Europeans. It has been noted that the European groups who were discriminated against by the National Origins Quota Act tended to be those with darker skins, even though they were White and European.

Immigrants during this period were subject to literacy tests and even IQ tests given in English (Kamin 1974). The act barred anyone who was classified as a convict, lunatic, "idiot," or "imbecile" from immigration. On New York City's Ellis Island, non-English-speaking immigrants, many of them Jews, were given the 1916 version of the Stanford-Binet IQ test in English. Obviously, non-English-speaking persons taking this test were unlikely to score high. On the basis of this grossly biased test, governmental psychologist H. H. Goddard classified fully 83 percent of Jews, 80 percent of Hungarians, and 79 percent of Italians as "feebleminded." It did not dawn on Goddard or the U.S. government that the IQ test, in English, probably did not measure something called intelligence, as intended, but instead simply measured the immigrant's mastery of the English language (Kamin 1994; Gould 1981; Taylor 2002, 1992a, 1980).

■ *Patterns of Racial and Ethnic Relations*

Intergroup contact between racial and ethnic groups in the United States has evolved along a variety of identifiable lines involving specific actions on the part of both the dominant White group and the ethnic or racial minority. The character of the contacts has been both negative and positive, obvious and subtle, tragic and helpful.

The features and forms of racial and ethnic relations that have received the most attention are assimilation, pluralism, colonialism, segregation, and the interaction of class and race.

Assimilation Versus Pluralism

A belief exists among some groups in America that with enough hard work and loyalty to the dominant White culture of the country, any minority can make it. This is the often-heard argument that African Americans, Hispanics, and Native Americans need only to pull themselves up "by their own bootstraps" to become a success.

THINKING SOCIOLOGICALLY

Write down your own racial–ethnic background and list one thing that people from this background have positively contributed to U.S. society or culture. Also list one experience (current or historical) in which people from your group have been victimized by society. Discuss how these two things illustrate the fact that racial–ethnic groups both have been *victimized* and have made *positive contributions* to this society. Share your comments with others: What does this reveal to you about the connections between different groups of people and their experiences as racial–ethnic groups in the United States?

This *assimilation perspective* dominated sociological thinking a generation ago and is still prominent in U.S. thought (Portes and Rumbaut 2001; Glazer 1970). The assimilationist believes that to overcome adversity and oppression, the minority person need only imitate the dominant White culture as much as possible. In this sense, minorities must assimilate "into" White culture and White society. Many Asian American groups have followed this pattern and have thus been called the "model minority," but this label ignores the fact that Asians are still subject to considerable prejudice, discrimination, racism, and poverty (Takaki 1989; Lee 1996; Woo 1998).

There are problems with the assimilation model. First, it fails to consider the time that it takes certain groups to assimilate. Those from rural backgrounds (Native Americans, Hispanics, African Americans, White Appalachians, and some White ethnic immigrants) typically take much longer to assimilate than those from urban backgrounds. Second, the histories of Black and White arrivals are very different, with lasting consequences. Whites came voluntarily; Blacks arrived in chains. Whites sought relatives in the New World; Blacks were sold and separated from relatives. For these

and other reasons, the histories of African American and White experiences as newcomers can hardly be compared, and their assimilation is unlikely to follow the same course. Third, although White ethnic groups did indeed face prejudice and discrimination when they arrived in America, many entered at a time when the economy was growing rapidly and their labor was in high demand. They were thus able to attain education and job skills. In contrast, by the time Blacks migrated to northern industrial areas from the rural South, Whites had already established firm control over labor and used this control to exclude Blacks from better-paying jobs and higher education. Fourth, assimilation is more difficult for people of color because skin color is an especially *salient* characteristic, ascribed and relatively unchangeable. White ethnic group members can change their names, but people of color cannot easily change their skin color.

The assimilation model raises the question of whether it is possible for a society to maintain **cultural pluralism,** which is defined as different groups in society maintaining their distinctive cultures while also coexisting peacefully with the dominant group. Some groups have explicitly practiced cultural pluralism: The Amish people of Lancaster County in Pennsylvania and of north central Ohio—who travel by horse and buggy, use no electricity; and run their own schools, banks, and stores—constitute a good example of a relatively complete degree of cultural pluralism.

Cultural pluralism is the opposite of assimilation. Those groups that have managed to have cultural pluralism are White ethnic groups, many of whom have also assimilated into different aspects of society. Italians in the Little Italys in U.S. cities, for example, maintain some residential segregation. They hold on to cultural traditions and, in some cases, speak their own language, but in other ways, they are highly assimilated in American life. Black Muslims in America also maintain some degree of pluralism, practicing their own culture and trying to maintain some degree of economic self-sufficiency.

Colonialism

In the late 1960s and early 1970s, political activists and scholars advocated a power-based approach to the analysis of race and ethnic relations, replacing concerns with assimilation and pluralism. In his **domestic colonialism** model, sociologist Robert Blauner (1969, 1972) described the condition of U.S. Blacks as an internal colony. He argued that the situation and status of Blacks in the United States is like that of other colonized minorities around the world, except that colonization took the form of forced transport to the country colonizing them. Blauner identified four elements to domestic colonialism. First, there is forced and involuntary entry. Second, the affairs of the colonized group (the minority group) are administered and determined by the colonizers (the dominant group). Blauner argued that in this respect, ghettos were actually devices to achieve social control over minorities; ghettos were thus colonies in themselves. Third, racism and its accompanying stereotypes are used to explain and justify the colonizer's domination over the minority group. Stereotypes are used to explain why the minority group acts or thinks in a particular way. Finally, the colonizers do not allow the minority to express its culture and values. The group history of the minority is rewritten from the colonists' point of view. The minority group is likely to react by developing cultural nationalism—a form of pluralism—and by asserting its own culture, goals, ways of life, music, and identity. Cultural nationalism may lead to revolution. Blauner, who devised his theory in 1968 and 1969, insightfully used his analysis to explain the Black urban riots and revolutionary upheavals of the late 1960s and early 1970s.

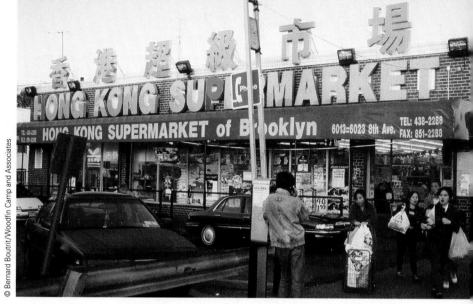

Neighborhoods such as this one in Brooklyn are indicative of residential segregation.

Segregation and the Urban Underclass

Segregation is the spatial and social separation of racial and ethnic groups. Minorities, who are often believed by the dominant group to be inferior, are compelled to live separately under inferior conditions and are given lower-class educations, jobs, and protections under the law. Although desegregation has been mandated by law (thus eliminating *de jure segregation,* or legal segregation), *de facto segregation*—segregation in fact—still exists, particularly in housing and education.

THINKING SOCIOLOGICALLY

Using your community or school as an example, what evidence do you see of *racial segregation*? How might a sociologist explain what you have seen?

Segregation has contributed to the creation of an **urban underclass,** a grouping of people, largely minorities and the poor, who live at the absolute bottom of the socioeconomic ladder in urban areas (Massey and Denton 1993). Currently the rate of segregation of Blacks and Hispanics in U.S. cities is increasing, thus allowing for

less and less interaction between White and Black children and White and Hispanic children (Schmitt 2001; Massey and Denton 1993). Although the proportion of middle-class Blacks has increased in the last two decades, so has the percentage of Blacks, Hispanics, and Native Americans who are in poverty. In 1999, 6 percent of Whites, 20 percent of Hispanics, 22 percent of Blacks, 10 percent of Asians, and fully 35 percent of Native Americans were below the official poverty level. In a seminal study, W. J. Wilson (1987) attributes the causes of the urban underclass to economic and social structural deficits in society, while rejecting the "culture of poverty" explanation, an earlier view that attributes the condition of minorities to their own presumed cultural deficiencies (a view attributed to Lewis 1960, 1966 and Moynihan 1965). The problems of the inner city, such as joblessness, crime, teen pregnancy, welfare dependency, and Acquired Immune Deficiency Syndrome (AIDS) are seen to arise from social class inequalities, that is, inequalities in the structure of society, and these inequalities have dire behavioral consequences at the individual level, in the form of drug abuse, violence, and lack of education (Wilson 1987; Sampson 1987). Wilson argues that the civil rights agendas need to be enlarged and that the major problem of the underclass, joblessness, needs to be addressed by fundamental changes in the economic institution.

The Relative Importance of Class and Race

Which is more important in determining one's chances for overall success: social class or race–ethnicity? This is the "class versus caste (or race)" controversy. The question has been hotly debated in sociology. One view, put forward by Wilson in his controversial book *The Declining Significance of Race* (1978), contends that class has become more important than race in determining Black access to privilege and power. In support of his argument, Wilson cites the simultaneous expansion of the Black middle class and the Black urban underclass. Wilson argues not that race is unimportant, but that the importance of social class is increasing as the importance of race is declining, even though race still remains important. In a more recent work, Wilson (1996) argues that both class and race combine to oppress not only many urban Blacks, but Whites and Hispanics as well. Critics of Wilson's argument (Willie 1979; Farley and Allen 1987; Feagin 1991, 2000; Steffensmeier and Demuth 2000) argue that race is still crucially important, which can be seen when one compares Blacks of a given social class with Whites of the same class.

■ *Attaining Racial and Ethnic Equality: The Challenge*

The variety of racial and ethnic groups in the United States brings much to the society in cultural richness and diverse patterns of group and interpersonal interaction.

But the inequities among these diverse groups also pose challenges for the nation in addressing questions of social justice. Those from other nations often see the United States as a racially divided nation, even though the problems of racial and ethnic conflict are not unique to Americans. Throughout the world, conflicts stemming from racial and ethnic differences are frequently the basis for economic inequalities, cultural conflicts, and war (see Map 9.2 on page 258).

Civil Rights

The history of racial and ethnic relations in the United States shows several strategies to achieve greater equality. Political mobilization, legal reform, and social policy have been the basis for much social change in race relations, but there are continuing questions about how best to achieve a greater degree of racial justice in this society. The major force behind most progressive social change in race relations was the civil rights movement. Marked by the strong moral and political commitment and courage of participants, the civil rights movement is probably the single most important source for change in race relations in the twentieth century. The civil rights movement was based on the passive resistance philosophy of Martin Luther King Jr., learned from the philosophy of *satyagraha* ("soul firmness and force") of the Indian Mahatma (meaning "leader") Mohandas Gandhi. This philosophy encouraged resistance to segregation through nonviolent techniques, such as sit-ins, marches, and appealing to

UNDERSTANDING DIVERSITY

Arab Americans: Confronting Prejudice

Whenever violent confrontations in the Middle East reach one of their periodic surges, Marvin Wingfield braces for the worst: ethnic taunts, stereotypes in the mass media, and violence against Arab Americans. Such occurrences have only increased as a result of the terrorist attacks on the World Trade Center and the Pentagon on September 11, 2001.

"The pattern seems to be that whenever there is a crisis in the Mideast, the incidence of hate crimes against Arab Americans increases," says Wingfield, coordinator of conflict resolution for the American-Arab Anti-Discrimination Committee (ADC) in Washington, D.C.

Wingfield notes that these are a manifestation of centuries-old misperceptions in the West about the nature of Arab culture. Colonial arrogance, he says, fostered stereotypes of Arabs as camel-riding hedonists and devious traders.

Another offshoot is the tendency of many White Americans to view broad segments of the population as *homogeneous*. References to "the Black community," for example, ignore the diversity among African Americans and their interests. Similarly, "the Arab World" is vast and varied. . . .

The ADC has prepared guidelines for community activists to follow in trying to increase the presence and awareness of

Arab culture in school districts. Called "Working With School Systems," it describes various scenarios for involvement, ranging from volunteering at the classroom level to lobbying for districtwide curriculum development.

"Our program is multifaceted," Wingfield says. "It's not a curriculum that can be taken into the schools. Instead, we have many different people doing many different things. We encourage people to take action on their own horizons."

SOURCE: *Teaching Tolerance* (Spring 1997): 49. This article is reprinted by permission of *Teaching Tolerance*, a publication of the Southern Poverty Law Center. Prejudice, Discrimination, and Racism human conscience in calls for brotherhood, justice, and equality.

The major civil rights movement in the United States intensified shortly after the 1954 *Brown v. Board of Education* decision. In 1955, African American seamstress and NAACP secretary Rosa Parks, made news in Montgomery, Alabama. By prior arrangement with the NAACP, Parks bravely refused to relinquish her seat in the "White only" section on a segregated bus when asked to do so by the White bus driver. At the time, the majority of Montgomery's bus riders were African American, and the action of Rosa Parks initiated the now-famous Montgomery bus boycott, led by the young Martin Luther King Jr. The boycott, which took place in many cities beyond Montgomery, was successful in desegregating the buses. It got more African American bus drivers hired and catapulted Martin Luther King Jr. to the forefront of the civil rights movement. Impetus was given to the civil rights movement and the boycott by the brutal murder in 1954 of Emmett Till, a Black teenager from Chicago, who was killed in Mississippi for whistling at a White woman.

The civil rights movement produced many episodes of both tragedy and heroism. In a landmark 1957 decision, President Dwight D. Eisenhower called out the national guard, after initial delay, to assist the entrance of nine Black students into Little Rock Central High School in Little Rock, Arkansas. Sit-ins followed throughout the South in which White and Black students perched at lunch counters until the Black students were served. Organized bus trips from North to South to promote civil rights, "freedom rides," forged on despite the murders of freedom riders Viola Liuzzo, a White Detroit housewife; Andrew Goodman and Michael Schwerner, two White students; and James Chaney, a Black student. The murders of civil rights workers—especially when they were White—galvanized public support for change.

Radical Social Change

While the civil rights movement developed throughout the late 1950s and 1960s, a more radical philosophy of change also developed, as more militant leaders grew increasingly

DOING SOCIOLOGICAL RESEARCH

American Apartheid

The term *apartheid* (pronounced "apart-hate" or "apart-hite") was used to describe the society of South Africa prior to the election of Nelson Mandela in 1994. It refers to the rigid separation of the Black and White races. Sociological researchers Massey and Denton argue that the United States is now under a system of apartheid, and that it is based on a very rigid residential segregation in the country.

Massey and Denton note that the terms "segregation" and "residential segregation" practically disappeared from the American vocabulary in the late 1970s and early 1980s. These terms were spoken little by public officials, journalists, and even civil rights officials. This was because the ills of race relations in America were at the time attributed, though erroneously, to other causes such as a "culture of poverty" among minorities, or inadequate family structure among Blacks, or too much welfare for minority groups. The Fair Housing Act was passed in 1968, and the problem of

segregation and discrimination in housing was declared solved.

Nothing could be farther from the truth, according to researchers Massey and Denton, who amassed a large amount of data demonstrating that residential segregation not only has persisted in American society, but that it has actually increased since the 1960s. Most Americans vaguely realize that urban America is still residentially segregated, but few appreciate the depth of Black and Hispanic segregation or the degree to which it is maintained by ongoing institutional arrangements and contemporary individual actions. They find that most people think of racial segregation as a faded notion from the past, one that is decreasing over time. Today theoretical concepts such as the culture of poverty, institutional racism, and welfare are widely debated, yet rarely is residential segregation considered to be a major contributing cause of urban poverty and the underclass. Massey and Denton argue that their purpose is to redirect the focus of

public debate back to race and racial segregation.

Questions to Consider

1. How racially segregated is the neighborhood you were raised in? **Keyword:** residential segregation

2. Was the neighborhood you raised in racially and/or ethnically homogeneous? **Keywords:** institutional racism, racial segregation

3. For how long has your own neighborhood been racially segregated—or not? **Keywords:** hypersegregation

We have included InfoTrac College Edition keywords at the end of each question to make it easier for you to find more to read on these topics. Go to **www.infotrac-college.com,** an online library, to begin your search.

SOURCE: Massey, Douglas S. and Nancy A. Denton, 1993. *American Apartheid: Segregation and the Making of the Underclass.* Cambridge, MA: Harvard University Press.

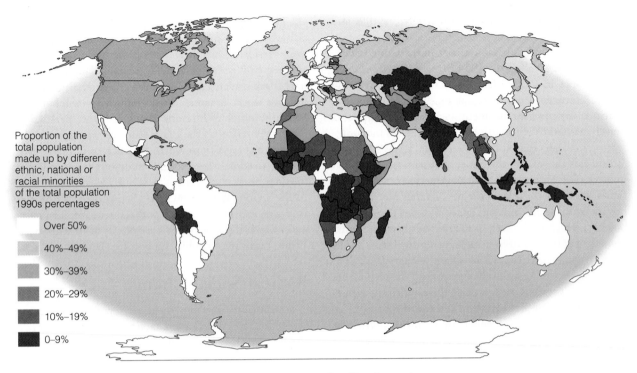

MAP 9.2 Viewing Society in Global Perspective: Ethnic Conflict Around the World

Countries in the world vary greatly in the proportion of their populations that are made up of different ethnic groups. Some countries (for example, Mexico and Brazil) are ethnically very heterogeneous, whereas other countries (for example, India) are more ethnically ho-mogeneous. **To what extent does ethnic heterogeneity of a country contribute to ethnic conflict in that country?**

SOURCE: *The State of War and Peace Atlas* by Dan Smith. Copyright © 1997 by Dan Smith, text. Maps copyright © 1997 by Myriad Editions Ltd. Used by permission of Penguin, a division of Penguin Group (USA) Inc.

disenchanted with the limits of the civil rights agenda, (which was perceived as moving too slowly). The militant Black power movement, taking its name from the book *Black Power* (published in 1967 by political activist Stokely Carmichael, later Kwame Touré, and Columbia University political science professor Charles V. Hamilton), had a more radical critique of race relations in the United States and saw inequality as stemming not just from moral failures, but from the institutional power that Whites had over Black Americans (Carmichael and Hamilton 1967).

Before breaking with the Black Muslims (the Black Nation of Islam in America) and his religious mentor, Elijah Muhammad, and prior to his assassination in 1965, Malcolm X advocated a form of pluralism demanding separate business establishments, banks, churches, and schools for Black Americans. He echoed an earlier effort of the 1920s led by Marcus Garvey's back-to-Africa movement, the Universal Negro Improvement Association (UNIA).

The Black power movement of the late 1960s rejected assimilation and instead demanded pluralism in the form of self-determination and self-regulation of

Black communities. Militant groups such as the Black Panther Party advocated fighting oppression with armed revolution. The U.S. government acted quickly, imprisoning members of the Black Panther Party and members of similar militant revolutionary groups and, in some cases, killing them outright (Brown 1992).

The Black power movement also influenced the development of other groups who were affected by the analysis of institutional racism that the Black power movement developed, as well as by the assertion of strong group identity that this movement encouraged. Groups such as La Raza Unida, a Chicano organization, encouraged "brown power," promoting solidarity and the use of Chicano power to achieve racial justice. Likewise, the American Indian Movement (AIM) used some of the same strategies and tactics that the Black power movement had encouraged, as have Puerto Rican, Asian American, and other racial protest groups. Elements of Black power strategy were also borrowed by the developing women's movement, and Black feminism was developed upon the realization that women, including women of color, shared in the oppressed status fostered by institutions that promoted racism (Collins 1998, 1990). Overall, the Black power movement dramatically altered the nature of political struggle and race and ethnic relations in the United States.

Many of the leaders of the Black power movement were eliminated, either through assassination, imprisonment, or other means, reducing its influence. Its significance, however, remains. Minister Louis Farrakhan, a protege of Malcolm X in the early 1960s, broke from the Black Muslim's Nation of Islam organization to found his own Black Muslim organization. The Black power movement also pushed those in the civil rights movement to a more radical analysis of race relations in the United States. Before his death, even Martin Luther King Jr., the major spokesperson for civil rights, articulated the need for radical economic change to address continuing racial inequality in the United States (Branch 1988). The Black power movement and the movements it spawned changed the nation's consciousness about race and also forced academic scholars to develop a deeper understanding of how racism works in society and how fundamental it is to U.S. institutions. As a result, there were major revisions in sociological theories about race relations, some of which have been reviewed in this chapter.

The civil rights movement, which began in the mid-1950s and continued through the 1980s, resulted in significant social, economic, and political gains for Blacks, although gains have been offset by losses. A major study by the Civil Rights Project at Harvard University shows that schools are now *more segregated* than they were thirty years ago. School desegregation increased from the 1950s through the 1980s, but schools have "resegregated" since. Except in the South and Southwest, White students have little contact with Black and Latino students—hardly representing racial progress (Frankenberg et al. 2003).

Affirmative Action

A continuing question from the dialogue between a civil rights strategy and more radical strategies for change is the debate between race-specific versus color-blind programs

---

SOCIOLOGY IN PRACTICE

Race, the Underclass, and Public Policy

Sociologists use their knowledge in a variety of ways to influence national social policy. One of the most influential to do so is William Julius Wilson, an African American sociologist, currently at the Harvard University School of Government. Wilson's work is so influential that in 1996 he was listed among *Time* magazine's twenty-five most influential Americans.

Wilson's work about the sociology of the underclass—which he defines to include African Americans, Asian Americans, Latinos, Whites, and others who are concentrated in urban poverty—has earned him a place as an advisor to U.S. presidents, as well as to the political campaigns of various presidential candidates. His work came to national prominence with the publication of *The Truly Disadvantaged: The Inner City, the Underclass, and Public Policy* (1987). Wilson argues that deep social and economic transformations have resulted in the formation of an urban underclass, permanently locked in poverty and joblessness. Differing from both liberals and conservatives, Wilson argues that the cause of this persistent poverty is neither overt racial discrimination, as liberals claim, nor the cultural deficiencies of racial groups, as conservatives claim. Rather, Wilson compellingly demonstrates that changes in the global economy have resulted in the concentration of a disenfranchised underclass, permanently jobless, and located primarily in inner cities. Wilson argues that the flight of the more prosperous Black middle class from the inner city contributes, as the flight of traditional heavy industry from the inner city contributes, to the concentration of poverty in the urban core.

In his policy-based work, Wilson argues that addressing the needs of the underclass cannot be based only on race-specific policies. Instead he says, "It's quite clear to me that we're going to have to revise discussion of the need for WPA-style jobs. Only these more structurally based programs, open to all in need, are likely to garner political support among the majority and to address the deep-seated problems that changes in the global economy have wrought" (*Time,* June 17, 1996: 57).

Critical Thinking Exercises

1. In your opinion, which is more important in determining the urban underclass: race, class, or both?

2. In your opinion, will there always be an urban underclass?

3. To what extent do you think sociology actually has an effect on national policy? Should it have more, or less, effect?

SOURCE: Wilson, William Julius. 1996. *When Work Disappears: The World of the New Urban Poor.* Chicago: University of Chicago Press; Wilson, William Julius. 1987. *The Truly Disadvantaged: The Inner City, the Underclass, and Public Policy.* Chicago: University of Chicago Press; and "America's Most Influential People," Time (June 17, 1996): 56–57.

for change. *Color-blind policies* are those advocating that all groups be treated alike, with no barriers to opportunity posed by race, gender, or other group differences. Equal opportunity is the key concept in color-blind policies.

Race-specific policies are those that recognize the unique status of racial groups because of the long history of discrimination and the continuing influence of institutional racism. Those advocating such policies argue that color-blind strategies will not work because Whites and other racial–ethnic groups do not start from the same position. Even given equal opportunities, continuing disadvantage produces unequal results. The tension between these two strategies for change is a major source for many of the political debates surrounding race relations now.

Affirmative action, a heavily contested program for change, is a race-specific policy for reducing job and educational inequality that has also had some success. Affirmative action means two things. First, it means recruiting minorities from a wide base in order to ensure consideration of groups that have been traditionally overlooked, while not using rigid quotas based on race or ethnicity. Second, affirmative action means using admissions slots (in education) or set-aside contracts or jobs (in job hiring) to assure minority representation. The principal objection, heard from both sides of the racial line, is that either interpretation of affirmative action programs is, in effect, use of a quota.

The Legal Defense Fund (LDF), established by the NAACP (National Association for the Advancement of

---

FORCES OF SOCIAL CHANGE

Race Naming

Many have argued for years that people responding to the U.S. census questionnaire should not be limited to checking only one racial category. Instead, they should be allowed to check two or more categories simultaneously—the "multiracial" response. Given this option, the person can self-identify with several racial groups. For the first time ever, the 2000 U.S. Census permitted the individual to select more than one racial category. (Only 2 percent actually did so.) This is useful, for example, if a person has one White parent and one African American parent. That person would then have the option of checking both, thus self-identifying as more than one race instead of, say, "Black," as would have been required on prior censuses. An interesting research problem would then be which kinds of persons—in terms of their gender, social class, religion, and so on—tend to choose one option or the other.

Such policy has the potential for major social change in American society. Should self-naming change over time (for example, more people checking more than one racial category who would have checked only "Black/African American" previously), then the racial composition of the U.S. population itself would change, and could change dramatically, depending upon how many persons elect the multiracial option. Although, as we have already seen, who is of what race is a social construction in society, certain realities do not change, such as who gets state or federal funds that are intended to be allocated on the basis of racial composition of a neighborhood. Arguing that race is a social construction and has no scientific merit only avoids the issue. At least one researcher (Harrison 2000) notes that the 2000 census policy is akin to having Humpty Dumpty fall off of the wall: It has created more problems than it was intended to solve. It is now up to the U.S. Census Bureau to find some way of putting Humpty back together again.

SOURCES: Harrison, Roderick. 2000. "Inadequacies of Multiple Response Race Data in the Federal Statistical System." Manuscript. Joint Center for Political and Economic Studies and Howard University, Department of Sociology, Washington, DC.; and U. S. Census Bureau, 2002.

The man on the right (Allison Davis, a Chicago attorney) is African American, and has so designated himself for his entire life. What would you "name" the person on the left? (She is of Vietnamese and White American parentage.)

Colored People), has argued forcefully and on legal grounds that the push for affirmative action on the basis of race must continue, though not in the form of rigid quotas. It has noted that in the tradition of its founding lawyer and the future member of the Supreme Court, Thurgood Marshall, the affirmative action policies of the LDF have helped to fundamentally change the composition of the nation's formerly segregated universities and colleges, as well as to greatly expand the educational opportunities for African Americans and other minorities. The LDF notes that the last decade has brought an "assault" on affirmative action, and thus the LDF has to expend considerable resources in meeting the legal challenge. It argues that standardized tests (such as the SAT's) are of limited validity but do not adequately predict performance in college and are thus not a legitimate basis on which to judge Black and White candidates against each other, as has been disputed in a number of the legal cases. (The issue of standardized testing is discussed in Chapter 13.) Hence, so it argues, there has been no "discrimination" against the dominant majority, as is often maintained by the (White) plaintiffs in the cases.

Recent data have shown that Blacks admitted to selective colleges and universities under affirmative action programs reveal high rates of social and economic success after graduation. For example, the percentage of Blacks who were admitted to college under affirmative action programs and went on to graduate school and law school was higher than the percentage of Whites from the same schools who did so (Bowen and Bok 1998). This is clearly a benefit of affirmative action in education.

The U.S. Supreme Court decided in 1978 that race could be used as a criterion for admission to undergraduate, professional, and graduate schools or for job recruitment, as long as race is combined with other criteria and as long as rigid racial quotas are not used. Then twenty-five years later, in June of 2003, the U.S. Supreme Court decided two cases that modified its 1978 decision. In *Grutter v. Bollinger,* in a five-to-four decision, the high court decided that, as in the 1978 decision, race could indeed be used as a factor in admissions decisions for the University of Michigan Law school, as long as race was considered along with other factors and the decision to admit or not admit was made on a case-by-case basis—that is, considering many factors, race among them, characterizing any given candidate for admission. In a second case (*Gratz v. Bollinger*), a six-to-three decision, the court threw out as unconstitutional any system of assigning favorable points to minority candidates seeking admission which would increase their chances for admission. This decision thus ruled out the use of any form of minority quotas, interpreting the point system as a type of quota.

■ *Chapter Summary*

■ *How are race and ethnicity defined?*

In virtually every walk of life, race matters. A *race* is a social construction based loosely on physical criteria, whereas an *ethnic group* is a culturally distinct group. A group is *minority* or *dominant* not on the

SOCIOLOGICAL EYE ON THE MEDIA

Racial and Ethnic Stereotyping on TV

The media, particularly prime-time television, have been notorious to researchers over the years for negatively stereotyping various racial and ethnic groups, despite the fact that spokespersons for the media, such as media executives, often deny that this even happens. Gone are the very old stereotypes of Blacks as slow-witted, shuffling wide-eyed minstrels, or of Asians as buck-toothed and subservient, or Mexicans as either happy-go-lucky or criminally prone. So there has been some improvement over the years, between the 1950s and the present.

Yet more *subtle* stereotypes are still put forth in the media—on sitcoms (situation comedies) as well as series TV, and even "reality" shows. For example, even though the long-standing taboo against it has technically been broken, Black-White interracial romance is still very rare, as are other instances of romance across other racial-ethnic lines. Latinos are still disproportionately presented in criminal roles. Native American Indians are rarely seen on prime-time TV—thus being negatively stereotyped by avoidance. As an exercise, devise a scheme for systemati-

cally observing racial presentation on TV: for given episodes, record the number of minorities shown, their occupations, their role in the group, how long they are on-screen, their behaviors, their romances, their ages, and their fates. (This kind of analysis, called *content analysis,* is a useful research technique, and is reviewed in Chapter 1.) What evidence do you find, if any, of negative racial–ethnic stereotyping? Go rent some tapes from fifteen to twenty years ago, and analyze them, then compare what you find to the contemporary programs.

basis of their numbers in a society, but on the basis of which group occupies lower average social status.

- ### What are stereotypes, and how are they important?

  Stereotyping and *stereotype interchangeability* reinforce racial and ethnic prejudices and thus cause them to persist in the maintenance of inequality in society. Racial and gender stereotypes are similar in dynamics in society, and both racial and gender stereotypes receive ongoing support in the media. Stereotypes serve to justify and make legitimate the oppression of groups based on race, ethnicity, and gender. Stereotypes such as "lazy" support attributions made to the minority, which attempt to cast blame on the minority in question, thus, removing some of the blame from the social structure.

- ### What are the differences between prejudice, discrimination, and racism?

  Prejudice is an attitude usually involving negative prejudgment on the basis of race or ethnicity. *Discrimination* is overt behavior involving unequal treatment. *Racism* involves both attitude and behavior. Racism can take on several forms, such as traditional or old-fashioned racism; aversive or subtle racism, laissez-faire racism, color-blind racism; and institutional racism. *Institutional racism* is unequal treatment, carrying with it notions of cultural inferiority of a minority, which has become ingrained into the economic, political, and educational institutions of society.

- ### Do all minority groups have different histories, or are they similar?

  Historical experiences show that different groups have unique histories, although they are bound together by some similarities in the prejudice and discrimination they have experienced. Although each group's experience is unique, they are commonly related by a history of prejudice and discrimination.

- ### What are the general patterns of race–ethnic relations?

  Sociologists analyze different forms of racial and ethnic relations, including *assimilation* versus *pluralism, domestic colonialism, segregation* and the *urban underclass,* and the *relative importance of social class versus race* (or caste).

- ### What are the approaches to racial–ethnic equality?

  The civil rights movement is the basis for social change based on an equal rights philosophy. More rad-

ical activists have developed an analysis of *institutional racism* and the power relationships upon which racism rests. Some programs for change rely on color-blind strategies, whereas others (such as *affirmative action programs*) propose race-specific remedies to address racial inequality. Some argue that only deep-rooted economic change will alleviate persistent racial stratification.

■ Key Terms

affirmative action 260	prejudice 240
anti-Semitism 253	race 236
assimilation 245	racial formation 238
authoritarian personality 244	racialization 236
contact theory 245	racial profiling 243
cultural pluralism 254	racism 242
discrimination 242	residential segregation 242
domestic colonialism 254	salience principle 239
dominant group 239	scapegoat theory 244
ethnic group 235	segregation 255
ethnocentrism 241	stereotype 239
forms of racism 243	stereotype
institutional racism 243	interchangeability 240
minority group 239	urban underclass 255
out-group homogeneity effect 238	

■ Researching Society with MicroCase Online

You can see the results of actual research by using the Wadsworth MicroCase® Online feature available to you. This feature allows you to look at some of the results from national surveys, census data, and some other data sources. You can explore this easy-to-use feature on your own, but try this example. Suppose you want to know some social facts, such as:

Do you ever wonder nowadays whether Blacks and Whites differ in whether they think there should be laws against intermarriage?

To answer this question, go to **sociology.wadsworth .com/andersen_taylor/essen3e**, select MicroCase Online from the left navigation bar, and follow the directions there to analyze the data described below.

Data file: GSS

Task: Cross-Tabulation

Row Variable: INTERMAR

Column Variable: HHRACE

Questions

Once you have your results, answer the following questions.

1. Overall, what percent of the people studied felt that there should be laws against racial intermarriage?

2. How many Whites were in this study? Blacks? Others?

3. Look at the numbers and percentages within the table: Is Race of Household related to how they answered the question about intermarriage? You can tell from these numbers!

■ *The Companion Web Site for Sociology: The Essentials, Third Edition*

sociology.wadsworth.com/andersen_taylor/essen3e

Supplement your review of this chapter by going to the companion Web site to take one of the Tutorial Quizzes, use the flash cards to master key terms, and check out the many other study aids you'll find there. You'll also find special features such as GSS Data and Census 2000 information, data and resources at your fingertips to help you with that special project or do some research on your own.

■ *Suggested Readings and Web Resources*

Malcomson, Scott L. 2000. *The American Misadventure of Race.* New York: Farrar, Straus, and Giroux.
This book is a readable and comprehensive history of the racial formation process and shows how the names and labels for various racial and ethnic groups have changed over time in the United States. An account of the bizarre history of the U.S. census racial classification is given.

Omi, Michael, and Howard Winant. 1994. *Racial Formation in the United States.* 2nd ed. New York: Routledge.
This important work advances racial formation theory, which emphasizes the social constructionist and historical processes by which a group comes to be defined as a "race," and deemphasizes the role of physical or biological traits. The book covers Latinos, American Indians, Asians, African Americans, and other such "racially formed" groups.

Portes, Alejandro, and Ruben G. Rumbaut. 2001. *Legacies: The Story of the Immigrant Second Generation.* Berkeley: University of California Press.
Focusing on the U.S.-born of foreign-born immigrants, this is a detailed account of these legacy persons, and contains rich data on both the similarities and the differences among immigrant groups.

Rodriguez, Clara E. 2000. *Changing Race: Latinos, the Census, and the History of Ethnicity in the United States.* New York: NYU Press.
This is an account of how racial formation has applied to Latinos and other groups and how the concept of race is fluid and changing. The role of self-definition of one's own race is discussed, and how this is affected by the shifting color line.

Snipp, Matthew. 1989. *American Indians: The First of This Land.* New York: Russell Sage Foundation.
This book offers a definitive discussion of how American Indian ancestry is defined and how definitions vary by tribal unit. The role of the U.S. government's Bureau of Indian Affairs (BIA) in this process is discussed.

Yoon, In-Jin. 1997. *On My Own: Korean Businesses and Race Relations in America.* Chicago: University of Chicago Press.
Based on extensive fieldwork among Korean immigrants in Chicago and Los Angeles, this book explores the social problems facing Korean immigrants and examines the tensions between them and African Americans in urban areas.

Racial Legacies and Learning
www.pbs.org/adultlearning/als/race/4.0/index.htm
This site sponsored by the Pubic Broadcasting Service (PBS) and the American Association of Colleges and Universities (AAC&U), is directed at fostering dialogue between college campuses and communities in an effort to improve race relations. It includes important resources on cultivating diversity and numerous educational projects designed to improve race relations.

Center for Research on Women, University of Memphis
www.people.memphis.edu/intprogs/crow/
The research center is dedicated to conducting, disseminating, and promoting research on women of color and southern women in the United States. The Web site includes news and research about education, work, poverty, health, and other issues.

American Indian History and Related Issues
www.csulb.edu/projects/ais
This site features many interesting links to information on Native American history, culture, and sociology.

Gender

*i*magine suddenly becoming a member of the other sex. What would you have to change? First, you would probably change your appearance—clothing, hairstyle, and any adornments you wear. You would most likely change your name because a name often identifies a person's gender. You would also have to change some of your interpersonal behavior. Contrary to popular belief, men talk more than women, are louder, more likely to interrupt, and less likely to recognize others in conversation. Women are more likely to laugh, express hesitance, be polite, and show emotions (Anderson and Leaper 1998; Mast 2001; Crawford 1995; Cameron 1998; Goldshmidt and Weller 2000). Gender differences also appear in nonverbal communication. Women use less personal space, touch less in impersonal settings (but are touched more), and smile more, even when they are not necessarily happy. Generally, women are also more attuned to nonverbal cues than men (Basow 1992), so if you became a woman, you might have to become more attentive. Finally, you might have to change many of your attitudes because men and women differ significantly on many, if not most, social and political issues (see Figure 10.1).

If you are a woman and became a man, perhaps the change would be worth it. You would probably see your income increase (especially if you became a White man). You would have more power in virtually every social setting. You would be far more likely to head a major corporation, run your own business, or be elected to a political office—again, assuming that you are White. Would it be worth it? As a man, you would be far more likely to die a violent death and would probably not live as long (National Center for Health Statistics 2002; U.S. Bureau of Justice Statistics 2002).

If you are a man who becomes a woman, your income would most likely drop significantly. Almost forty years after passage of the Equal Pay Act in 1963, men still earn 24 percent more than women; this is counting only those working year-round and full time (DeNavas-Walt and Cleveland 2002). You would probably become resentful of a number of things because poll data indicate that women are more resentful than men about things such as the amount of money available for them to live on, the amount of help they get from their mates around the house, how they share child care, and how they look. Women also report being more fearful on the streets than men. However, women are more satisfied than men with their roles as parents and with their friendships outside marriage.

For both women and men, there are benefits, costs, and consequences stemming from the social definitions associated with gender. As you imagined this experiment, you may have had difficulty trying to picture the essential change in your *biological* identity—but is this the most significant part of being a man or woman? As we will see in this chapter, nature determines whether you are male or female, but it is society that gives significance to this distinction. Sociologists see *gender* as a social concept. Who we become as men and women is largely shaped by cultural and social expectations.

THINKING SOCIOLOGICALLY

Try an experiment based on the example of changing gender that opens this chapter. For a period of twenty-four hours, note everything you would have to do to change your appearance and behaviors to become a different *gender*. Try to act in accordance with your new identity. How do others respond to you? What does your experiment tell you about "doing gender" (see page 285) and how gender is supported through social interaction?

■ *Defining Sex and Gender*

Sociologists use the terms *sex* and *gender* to distinguish biological sex identity from learned gender roles. **Sex** refers to biological identity, being male or female. For sociologists, the more significant concept is **gender**—the socially learned expectations and behaviors associated with members of each sex. This distinction emphasizes that behavior associated with gender is culturally learned. One is born male or female, but becoming a man or a woman is the result of social and cultural expectations that pattern men's and women's behavior.

From the moment of birth, gender expectations influence how boys and girls are treated. Now that it is possible to identify the sex of a child in the womb, gender expectations may begin before birth. Parents and grandparents might select pink clothes and dolls for baby girls, and sports clothing and brighter colors for boys. They have little choice to do otherwise, because the clothing styles, toys, and baby products are highly gender-typed. Much research shows how parents and others continue to treat children in stereotypical ways throughout their childhood. Girls may be expected to cuddle and be sweet, whereas boys are handled more roughly and given greater independence.

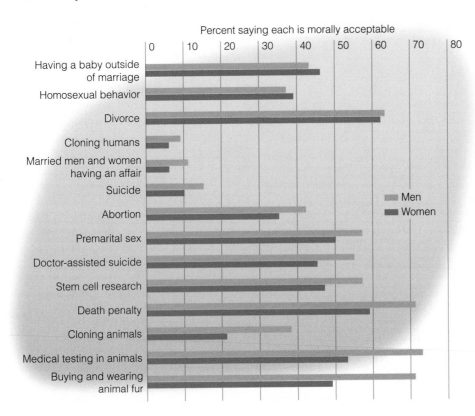

Percent saying each is morally acceptable

FIGURE 10.1 The Gender Gap in Attitudes

DATA: Saad, Lydia. 2003. "Pondering 'Women's Issues, Part II." *The Gallup Poll*. Princeton, NJ: The Gallup Organization. Web site: **www.gallup.com**

Gender: Diversity Across Cultures

The cultural basis of gender is especially apparent when we look at other cultures. Across different cultures, the gender roles associated with masculinity and femininity vary considerably. In Western industrialized societies, people tend to think of masculinity and femininity in dichotomous terms, with men and women decisively different, even defined as opposites. The views from other cultures challenge this assumption. The Navajo, for example, offer interesting examples of alternative gender roles. Historically, the *berdaches* in Navajo society were anatomically normal men who were defined as a third gender considered to fall between male and female. Berdaches married other men, who were not considered berdaches and were defined as ordinary men. Moreover, neither the berdaches nor the men they married were considered homosexuals, as they would be considered in many of today's Western cultures (Nanda 1998; Lorber 1994).

We need not look at striking departures from familiar gender categories to see how differently gender can be constructed in other cultures. For example, in China, the Chinese Marriage Law of 1950 formally defines marriage as a relationship between equal companions who share responsibility for child care and the family. This is in sharp contrast to age-old gender roles in Chinese tradition. The roles did not change overnight in China. As in many societies backed by strong traditions, contemporary roles can coexist with more traditional ones.

There can also be substantial differences in the construction of gender across social classes or subcultures within a single culture. Within the United States, as we will see, there is considerable variation in the experiences of gender among different racial and ethnic groups (Baca Zinn et al. 2000; Baca Zinn and Dill 1996; Andersen and Collins 2004; Chow et al. 1996). In addition, even within a given culture, differences among people of a given gender can be greater than differences across gender (see Figure 10.2). Looking at gender sociologically quickly reveals the social and cultural dimensions of something often popularly defined as biologically fixed.

Sex Differences: Nature or Nurture?

Despite the known power of social expectations, the belief persists that differences between men and women are biologically determined. Biology is, however, only one component in the differences between men and women. The important question in sociology is not whether biology or culture is more important in forming men and women, but how biology and culture interact to produce a person's gender identity. What is the interplay of nature and nurture?

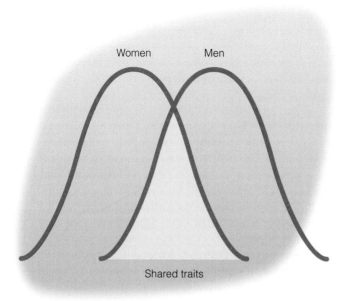

FIGURE 10.2 Within and Between Gender Differences

Notice that within *gender differences on a given trait can be greater than differences* between *genders.*

Biological determinism refers to explanations that attribute complex social phenomena to physical characteristics. The argument that men are more aggressive because of hormonal differences (in particular, the presence of testosterone) is a biological determinist argument. Although people popularly believe that testosterone causes aggressive behavior in men, studies find only a modest correlation between aggressive behavior and testosterone levels. Furthermore, changes in testosterone levels do not predict changes in men's aggression (such as by "chemical castration," the administration of drugs that eliminate the production or circulation of testosterone). What's more, there are minimal differences in the levels of sex hormones between girls and boys during early childhood, yet researchers find considerable differences in the aggression exhibited by boys and girls as children (Fausto-Sterling 1992, 2000).

A person's sex identity is established at the moment of conception when the father's sperm provides either an X or a Y chromosome to the egg at fertilization. The mother contributes an X chromosome to the embryo. The combination of two X chromosomes makes a female, while the combination of an X and a Y makes a male. Under normal conditions, chemical events directed by genes on the sex-linked chromosomes lead to the formation of male or female genitalia.

Hermaphroditism is a condition where irregularities in chromosome formation or fetal differentiation produce persons with mixed biological sex characteristics. In the most common form of hermaphroditism, the infant has either ovaries or testes, but the genitals are physically ambiguous or mixed. An example would be a child born with female chromosomes but an enlarged clitoris, making the child appear to be male. Sometimes, a child may be a chromosomal male, but with an incomplete penis and no urinary canal. In other cases of hermaphroditism, physicians typically advise sex reassignment, including reconstruction of the genitals and hormonal treatment. If biology determines sex identity, why does the medical profession think it must assign those born with mixed sex characteristics to either one sex or the other? One noted biologist has even suggested (partly in jest) that there are not two but five sexes: males, females, herms ("true" hermaphrodites—that is, those with the biological sex characteristics of both males and females); merms (male pseudohermaphrodites—that is, those with mixed sex characteristics, but more male traits than female), and ferms (female pseudohermaphrodites—that is, those with mixed sex characteristics, but more female traits than male). Odd though this may sound, if we really categorized individuals based solely on biology, we would not feel compelled to intervene medically to force those born with mixed sex characteristics to be one sex or the other (Fausto-Sterling 2000).

You can see the strength of gender expectations by thinking about how you and others react when you see someone whose gender you cannot identify.

Case studies of such treatments reveal the extraordinary influence of social factors in shaping a person's identity. Parents of children who are given a sex reassignment are advised not only to allow genital reconstruction, but also to give the child a new name, a different hairstyle, and new clothes—all intended to provide the child with the social signals judged appropriate for the new gender identity. One physician who has worked on such cases gives the directive to parents that they "need to go home and do their job as child rearers with it being very clear whether it's a boy or a girl" (Kessler 1990: 9). Indeed, in cases where adults choose to undergo a sex change operation, they are usually required to live for one year prior to surgery as if they were the sex they are becoming; this is to ensure that they can handle the social expectations associated with being the other gender.

Transgendered people are those who deviate from the binary (that is, male or female) system of gender; they include transsexuals, cross-dressers, and others who do not fit within the normative expectations of gender. Research on transgendered individuals shows that they experience enormous pressure to fit within the ususal expectations. When they were young, for example, they would hide their cross-dressing. Those who change their sex as adults report enormous pressure, particularly during their transition period, because others expect them to be one sex or the other. Most find that whatever their biological sex, they are forced—from fear of rejection and the desire for self-preservation—to manage an identity that would fall into one category or another (Gagné and Tewksbury 1998).

From a sociological perspective, biology alone does not determine gender identity. People must adjust to the expectations of others and the social understanding of what it means to be a man or a woman. A person may remain genetically one sex, while socially being the other—or perhaps something in between. In other words, there is not a fixed relationship between biological and social outcomes (Money 1985). If a person only sees men and women as biologically "natural" states, that person misses some of the fascinating ways that gender is formed in society.

Physical differences between the sexes do, of course, exist from birth. In addition to differences in anatomy, boys tend to be slightly longer and weigh more than girls at birth. As adults, men tend to have a lower resting heart rate, higher blood pressure, higher muscle mass and muscle density, and more efficient recovery from muscular activity (Stockard and Johnson 1992). These physical differences contribute to the tendency for men to be physically stronger than women. However, the public is becoming accustomed to displays of women's athleticism and expects great performances from both men and women in world-class events such as the Olympics.

Women can achieve high degrees of muscle mass and muscle density through bodybuilding and can actually win against men in activities that require endurance, such as the four women who have won the Iditarod—the Alaskan dog sled race considered to be one of the most grueling competitions in the world.

Arguments based on biological determinism assume that differences between women and men are "natural" and, presumably, resistant to change. Like biological explanations of race differences, biological explanations of inequality between women and men tend to flourish during periods of rapid social change. During such times, biological explanations protect the status quo (existing social arrangements) by making it appear that the status of women or people of other races is "natural" and therefore should remain as it is. If social differences between women and men were biologically determined, we would also not find any variation in gender relations across cultures, but the extensive differences are well documented. We could not exist without biology. Without society and culture, we would not be who we are.

In sum, in defining sex and gender, sociologists emphasize the social basis for both sex and gender. Sociologists see people's sex identity and their gender identity as being influenced by society. Culture defines certain sexual behaviors as appropriate (or not) and establishes particular expectations for women and for men. We will explore culture and gender further in the next section.

■ *The Social Construction of Gender*

Socialization is the process by which social expectations are taught and learned. Through **gender socialization**, men and women learn the expectations associated with their sex. The rules of gender extend to all aspects of society and daily life. Gender socialization affects the self-concepts of women and men, their social and political attitudes, their perceptions about other people, and their feelings about relationships with others. Although not everyone is perfectly socialized to conform to gender expectations, socialization is a powerful force directing the behavior of men and women in gender-typical ways. For example, men who believe that the role of women is to act as wife and mother are not likely to share in the housework; women who believe they are incomplete unless they are attached to men are not likely to be very independent.

Even people who set out to challenge traditional expectations often find themselves yielding to the powerful influence of socialization. Women who consciously reject traditional women's roles may still find themselves inclined to act as hostess or secretary in a group setting. Similarly, men may decide to accept equal responsibility for housework yet simply fail to notice when the refrigerator is empty or the child needs a bath—household needs they have been trained to let someone else notice (DeVault 1991). These expectations are so pervasive that it is also difficult to change them on an individual basis. If you doubt this, try buying clothing or toys for a young child without purchasing something that is gender-typed, or talk to parents who have tried to raise their children without conforming to gender stereotypes and see what they report about the influence of such things as children's peers and the media.

Despite cultural changes in gender roles, young girls learn stereotypical ideas for feminine beauty early in life.

> **THINKING SOCIOLOGICALLY**
>
> Visit a local toy store and try to purchase a toy for a young child that is not gender-typed. What could you buy? What could you not buy? What does your experiment teach you about *gender role socialization*? (If you take a child with you, note what toys he or she wants. What does this tell you about how effective gender socialization is?)

The Formation of Gender Identity

One result of gender socialization is the formation of **gender identity,** which is one's definition of oneself as a woman or man. Gender identity is basic to our self-concept and shapes our expectations for ourselves, our abilities and interests, and how we interact with others. Gender identity shapes not only how we think about ourselves and others, but also influences numerous behaviors, including such things as the likelihood of drug and alcohol abuse, violent behavior, depression, or even how aggressive you are in driving (Kulis et al. 2002; Kimmel 2001; Siegel 2002; Sprock and Yoder 1997; Lupton 2002).

One area where gender identity has an especially strong effect is in how people feel about their appearance. Studies find strong effects of gender identity on body image. Concern with body image begins mostly during adolescence. Thus, studies of young children (that is, preschool age) find no gender differences in how boys and girls feel about their bodies (Hendy et al. 2001), but by early adolescence clear differences emerge. At this age, girls report comparing their bodies to others of their sex more often than boys do. By early adolescence, girls report lower self-esteem than boys; they also report more negativity about their body images than do boys. This type of thinking among girls is related to lower *self-esteem*—that is, how well one thinks of oneself (Jones 2001; Polce-Lynch et al. 2001). Among college students, women are also more dissatisfied with their appearances than are men (Hoyt and Kogan 2001). These studies indicate that idealized images of women's bodies in the media, as well as peer pressures, have a huge impact on young girls' and women's gender identity and feelings about their appearances.

Sources of Gender Socialization

As with other forms of socialization, there are different agents of gender socialization: family, play, schooling, religious training, mass media, and popular culture, to name a few. Gender socialization is reinforced whenever gender-linked behaviors receive approval or disapproval from these multiple influences.

Parents are one of the most important sources of gender socialization. Parents may discourage children from playing with toys that are identified with the other sex, especially when boys play with toys meant for girls. Interviews with preschoolers show that young boys in particular report that their fathers think that cross-gender play is bad. As a result, boys are even more likely than girls to choose gender-typed toys to play with (Raaj and Rackliff 1998). Direct observations of fathers and mothers interacting with their young children also show that fathers are less likely to provide basic care, although both parents tend to share responsibility for discipline (LaFlamme et al. 2002).

Parents also tend to give boys and girls different chores around the house. Of course, families improvise widely on these behaviors. For example, researchers have found that gender-linked assignment of chores is less marked in families where mothers are employed outside the home and in families from higher socioeconomic levels (Serbin et al. 1990).

Gender socialization patterns vary within different racial–ethnic families. Latinos, as an example, have generally been thought to be more traditional in their gender roles, although this varies by generation and by the experiences of family members in the labor force. Gender expectations for Mexican and Puerto Rican women are more traditional in the older generations; the orientation of Mexican and Puerto Rican women toward traditional roles is presumably one reason women of the older generations are less likely to participate in the labor force. Younger Mexican and Puerto Rican women are less traditional in their attitudes and are more likely to be employed (Ortiz and Cooney 1984).

From the time they become aware of their surroundings, children are socialized to adopt behaviors and attitudes judged appropriate for members of their sex. Socialization comes not only from parents and other family members, but also from peers. Through play children learn patterns of social interaction, analytical skills, and the values and attitudes of their culture; they also add to their cognitive and physical development. Research shows that girls play more cooperatively when they are in same-sex groups than they do when playing with boys (Neppl and Murray 1997). Boys and girls also organize their play in ways that reinforce not only gender, but also race and age norms (Moore 2001). When they play together, boys exert power over girls and typically establish the conditions of the play activities (Voss 1997).

A variety of other patterns are consistently found in children's play and games. Boys are encouraged to play outside more; girls, inside. Boys' toys are more machine-like and frequently promote the development of militaristic values; they tend to encourage aggression, violence, and the stereotyping of enemies—values rarely associated with girls' toys. Children's books in schools also communicate gender expectations. Even with publishers' guidelines that discourage stereotyping, textbooks still depict men as aggressive, argumentative, and competitive. Men and boys are also more likely to be featured in the titles, pictures, and central roles (Varney 2002; Tepper and Cassidy 1999; Evans and Davies 2000).

The gender norms that children learn seem to be more strictly applied to boys than girls. Thus, boys who engage in behavior that is associated with girls are more negatively regarded than girls who play or act like boys (Sandnabba and Ahlberg 1999). While girls may be called "tomboys," boys who called "sissies" are more harshly judged. Being a tomboy may be acceptable for a girl, but beyond a certain age, the same behavior may result in her being labeled a "dyke." Sociological research shows that girls who become tomboys do so because they recognize the disadvantages of femininity and the privileges of masculinity. They are resisting expected gender roles, even while they also try to conform to existing gender role choices (Carr 1998).

Schools are particularly strong influences on gender socialization because of the amount of time children spend in them. Teachers often have different expectations

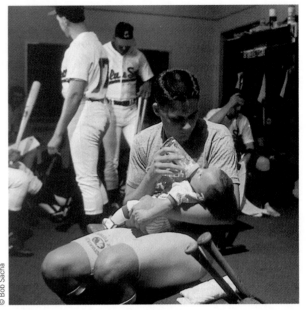

Evidence of changing gender roles for women and men can be seen in many places, such as the involvement of men in child care.

for boys and girls. In school, boys get more attention, even if it is sometimes negative attention. When teachers of either sex respond more to boys, both positively and negatively, they heighten boys' sense of importance (American Association of University Women 1992, 1998; Sadker and Sadker 1994).

Religion is an often overlooked but significant source of gender socialization. The major Judeo-Christian religions in the United States place strong emphasis on gender differences, with explicit affirmation of the authority of men over women. In Orthodox Judaism, men offer a prayer blessing God for not having created them as a woman or a slave. The patriarchal language of most Western religions and, in some faiths, the exclusion of women from positions of religious leadership signifies the lesser status of women in religious institutions. Any religion, interpreted in a fundamentalist way, can be very oppressive to women, as recent events in Islamic societies show. One of the important points to note about any religion and its gender teachings is that religious belief is subject to interpretation and social forces. The most devout believers of any faith tend to hold the most traditional views of women's and men's roles. The influence of religion on gender attitudes cannot be considered separate from other factors. For many, religious faith inspires a belief in egalitarian roles for women and men; both Christian and Islamic women have organized to resist fundamentalist and sexist practices (Gerami and Lehnerer 2001).

The media in their various forms (television, film, magazines, music, and so on) communicate strong—some would even say cartoonish—gender stereotypes.

Despite some changes in recent years, television and films continue to depict highly stereotyped roles for women and men. Men on television heavily outnumber women, and women are underrepresented in the leading roles in film (Eschholz 2002). Men are not only more visible, but also more formidable, stereotyped in strong, independent roles. Women are more likely now than thirty years ago to be portrayed as employed outside of the home and in professional jobs (Signorielli and Bacue 1999), but it is still more usual to see women depicted as sex objects (Lin 1998). Female characters on prime time, regardless of their race, are also shown as being much thinner than actual women, reinforcing cultural ideals of thinness (Fouts and Burggraf 1999).

Gender stereotypes on television also cross with racial stereotypes; White men are shown as being more prominent and exercising more authority than either White women or African American men and women. African American men, however, are shown as aggressive and African American women are shown as inconsequential (Coltrane and Messineo 2000).

Social scientists debate the extent to which people actually believe what they see on television, but research with children shows that they identify with the television characters they see. Children report that they want to be like the television characters when they grow up. Boys tend to identify with characters they see based on their physical strength and activity level; girls relate to perceptions of physical attractiveness (Reeves and Miller 1978; Signorielli 1989; Signorielli et al. 1994). Both boys and girls rate the aggressive toys that they see on television commercials as highly desirable. They also judge them as more appropriate for boys' play, suggesting that something as seemingly innocent as a toy commercial reinforces attitudes about gender and violence (Klinger et al. 2001). Even with adults, researchers find that there is a link between viewing sexist images and having attitudes that support sexual aggression, antifeminism, and more traditional views of women (MacKay and Covell 1997; Garst and Bodenhausen 1997).

Advertisements are another important outlet for the communication of gender images to the public—one that is especially noted for the communication of idealized, sexist, and racist images of women and men (Cortese 1999). Women in advertisements are routinely shown in poses that would shock people if the characters were

SOCIOLOGICAL EYE ON THE MEDIA

Cultural Gatekeepers and the Construction of Femininity

Many have noted the distorted images of women that appear in the media. The common argument is that media images present an unrealistic image of women, which shapes women's self-concepts and limits their sense of possibilities for their appearance, their relationships, their careers, and so forth. Femininity is defined in the media by *cultural gatekeepers*—those who make decisions about what images to project. Cultural gatekeepers also have to respond to audience criticism. How they respond is an important part of the institutional process by which media images are sustained.

One sociologist, Melissa Milkie, wanted to explore how images of femininity are constructed in the media, particularly when producers encounter criticism from their audience. As readers, girls have protested many of the narrow and limiting images in the media, particularly those portraying girl's bodies. Milkie interviewed ten top editors of leading girls' magazines to find out how they, as cultural gatekeepers, responded to the criticism from girls that the images of girls in teen magazines do not reflect what "real girls" are like.

Milkie found that even the top editors think there are institutional limitations on what they can do to respond to girls' criticism. The editors who were very sensitive to the criticisms they received either said there was not much they could do about it or they dismissed the girls' complaints as misguided. They would claim the image was beyond their control, either because of the artistic process, advertisers' needs, or the culture itself. Thus, despite their positions of power, editors believed they could not fully control the images that appear. They pointed to institutional constraints that, in effect, thwarted efforts for change. Some editors simply dismissed the criticisms as girls misreading the intent or meaning of an image.

Either way, Milkie's research shows how the organizational complexity of media institutions limits how much change is possible in how images of femininity are constructed. Market forces, advertisers, the values of producers, and the values of the public all intertwine in shaping the decisions of cultural gatekeepers. Milkie also shows, however, that people are not passive about what they see in the media, suggesting that how people respond to images in the media is an important part of the effect of such images in society.

SOURCE: Milkie, Melissa A. 2002."Contested Images of Femininity: An Analysis of Cultural Gatekeepers' Struggles with the 'Real Girl' Critique." *Gender & Society* 16 (December): 839–859.

male. Consider how often women are displayed in ads dropping their pants, skirts, or bathrobe, or are shown squirming on beds. How often are men shown in such poses? Men are sometimes displayed as sex objects in advertising, but not nearly as often as women. The demeanor of women in advertising—on the ground, in the background, or looking dreamily into space—makes them appear subordinate and available to men.

Popular culture is also a source of stereotypes that contribute to gender socialization. Greeting cards, CD covers, books, songs, films, and comic strips all communicate images representing the presumed cultural ideals of womanhood and manhood. These popular products have an enormous effect on our ideas and self-concepts. To illustrate this, try to buy a friend a birthday card that does not stereotype women or men. Or notice that Father's Day cards imply that all men want to play golf or fish—activities you will rarely, if ever, find on Mother's Day cards! (As you look at greeting cards, you can also see how much gender stereotypes overlap with stereotypes about aging, family roles, and images of beauty.)

The Price of Conformity

A high degree of conformity to stereotypical gender expectations takes its toll on both men and women. The higher rate of early death among men from accidents and violence can be attributed to the stress and injury associated with the cultural definition of masculinity, which includes physical daring and risk taking. The strong undercurrent of violence in today's culture of masculinity encourages men to engage in behaviors that put them at risk in a variety of ways.

Violence associated with gender roles also puts women at risk. Men's power is too frequently manifested in physical and emotional violence against women. Violence against women is endemic in the United States, but is also a worldwide problem, as a recent United Nations (UN) report concluded. According to the UN, violence is a matter of women's human rights—a "manifestation of historically unequal power relations between men and women, which have led to domination over and discrimination against women by men and to the prevention of the full advancement of women" (UNICEF 2000: 1). Violence takes many forms, including sexual abuse, rape, wife beating, genital mutilation, honor killings, and rape. Around the world, the UN is working in various ways to reduce violence against women, including some initiatives to help men examine the cultural assumptions about masculinity that promote violence. As we saw in Chapter 6, rape and sexual assault are all too common in the United States, as well as other cultures. Domestic violence is examined in Chapter 12 on families.

Sociologists are also finding that adhering to gender expectations of thinness for women and strength for men is related to a host of negative health behaviors, including eating disorders, smoking, and for men, steroid abuse. The dominant culture promotes a narrow image of beauty for women—one that leads many women, especially young women, to be disturbed about their body image. Striving to be thin, millions of women engage in constant dieting, fearing they are fat even when they are well within or below healthy weight standards. Many develop eating disorders by purging themselves of food or cycling through various fad diets—behaviors that can have serious health consequences. Many young women develop a distorted image of themselves, thinking they are overweight when they may actually be dangerously thin. And, despite the known risks of smoking, increasing numbers of young women smoke and do so not only because they think it "looks cool," but also because they think it will keep them thin. Eating disorders can be related to a woman having a history of sexual abuse, but

TAKING ON SOCIAL ISSUES

Violence Against Women Act

In May 2000, the United States Supreme Court ruled that victims of rape, domestic violence, and other crimes motivated by gender could not sue their attackers through civil courts. The case came as the result of a suit by a college student against two varsity football players whom she accused of raping her in her residence hall. When the university did not discipline the men, she sued using a civil remedy provision in the Violence Against Women Act, passed by Congress in 1994. The two men then challenged the constitutionality of this act. The Court ruled (5–4) in favor of the men, concluding that the 14th Amendment only forbids states, not individuals, from violating rights (*United States v. Morrison*).

What recourse should victims of gender-based violence have? What is the role of the federal and state government in protecting victims of gender or race-based violence? How would you have ruled were you sitting on the Supreme Court?

Taking Action

Go to the Taking Action exercise on the companion Web site at **sociology.wadsworth.com/ andersen_taylor/essen3e** to learn more about an organization that addresses this topic.

they also come from the promotion of thinness as an ideal beauty standard for women—a standard that can put girls' and women's health in jeopardy (Logio-Rau 1998; Thompson 1994).

DEBUNKING
Society's Myths

Myth: Staying thin is good for your physical and mental health.

Sociological perspective: Dominant gender norms promote a culture of thinness that produces many unhealthy behaviors, including constant dieting, obsession with body image, and poor self-concepts for women. Young, White women who internalize this narrow beauty standard are especially at risk.

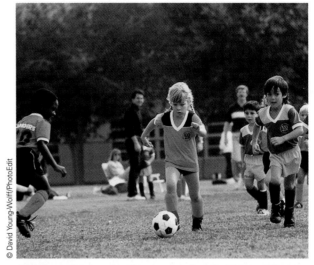

Childhood play is a significant source of gender identity. The increasing participation of young girls and women in team sports is likely to have a significant impact on women's gender identity.

Men may also pay the price of conformity if they too thoroughly internalize gender expectations that say they must be independent, self-reliant, and unemotional. Men's gender socialization discourages intimacy among them, thereby affecting the quality of men's friendships. However, men are more likely now than in the past to say they admire men who show a more sensitive side, and they say they have become better able to express their feelings (Roper Organization 1995). Conformity to traditional gender roles denies women access to power, influence, achievement, and independence in the public world, and it denies men the more nurturing, emotional, and other-oriented worlds that women have customarily inhabited.

Some gender expectations relax with age. Older women describe themselves as more assertive, competent, and effective than do younger women (Sprock and Yoder 1997). Men's attitudes toward women also tend to become more liberal as they age (Baker and Terpstra 1986); both men and women report greater satisfaction with their lives as they get older. Generally, as people collect life experiences,

UNDERSTANDING DIVERSITY

Racializing Gender/Gendering Race

Gender stereotypes go hand-in-hand with racial stereotypes. As discussed in the prior chapter, there is interplay between race and gender stereotypes. You see this interplay by analyzing how gender and race together construct stereotypes of various groups of men and women. African American men are stereotyped as hypermasculine and oversexed; African American women as producing too many babies and being "welfare queens." Asian American women are stereotyped as submissive but dainty sex objects (think of the geisha image); Asian American men as sexless nerds. Jewish Ameri-can women are stereotyped as Jewish American princesses, "JAPS"—rich, spoiled, and materialistic; Jewish men as intellectual, but asexual. Latinos are stereotyped as "macho" and, like African American men, sexually passionate. Latinas are stereotyped as "hot." White women are stereotyped as "madonnas" or "sluts" (This introduces class into the interplay of race and gender, since working-class women are more likely to be seen as "slutty" and upper-class women as frigid and cold.)

These stereotypes also show how racism and sexism shape our views of sexuality and, likewise, how sexuality is used to construct race and gender stereotypes. And, as Ruth Atkin and Adrienne Rich have pointed out (2001), it is probably not accidental that the stereotype of the Jewish American princess—JAP—uses a term that is also associated with anti-Asian racism. Patricia Hill Collins calls these "controlling images"—images that are created by powerful groups and are used to justify race, class, and gender oppression. Whose interests do such stereotypes serve and how do they affect the interactions between different groups?

they gain confidence in themselves and are more likely to challenge dominant cultural norms.

Race, Gender, and Identity

Because the experiences of race and gender socialization affect each other, men and women from different racial groups have different expectations regarding gender roles. The different expectations often are not the ones people would assume based on the gender stereotypes they have absorbed about other groups. For example, when asked to rate desirable characteristics in men and women, White men and women are more likely than Latinos to select different traits for men and women; this runs counter to the idea that Hispanics hold highly polarized views of manhood and womanhood. African Americans are most likely to find value in both sexes displaying traits such as being assertive, athletic, self-reliant, gentle, and eager to soothe hurt feelings (Harris 1994), although African American women tend to be more liberal in this regard than African American men (Hunter and Sellers 1998). Asian American women are more likely than Asian American men to value egalitarian roles for men and women (Chia et al. 1994).

African American women, like White women, are encouraged to become nurturing and other oriented, but African American women are also socialized to become self-sufficient, aspire to an education, want an occupation, and regard work as an expected part of a woman's role. They are also expected to be more independent than White women (Ladner 1995; Slevin and Wingrove 1998). It is more highly probable that African American women will reject the gender stereotyping of the dominant culture than will White women. These attitudes among African American women are probably related to the fact that African American mothers are more likely to have been employed and supporting themselves than has historically been true for White mothers; this encourages more self-sufficient attitudes on the part of daughters (Wharton and Thorne 1997; Collins 1987; Dugger 1988).

Men's gender identity is also affected by race. Latino men, for example, bear the stereotype of *machismo*—exaggerated masculinity. Although machismo is associated with sexist behavior by men, within Latino culture, it is also associated with honor, dignity, and respect (Mirandé 1979; Baca Zinn 1995). Researchers find that Latino families are rather egalitarian, with decision making frequently shared by men and women. To the extent that machismo exists, it is not just a cultural holdover from Latino societies, but can be how men defy their racial oppression.

African American men also define manhood far more complex in ways than simple stereotypes suggest. Self-determination, responsibility, and accountability to family and/or community are attributes African American men most commonly associate with manhood; power over others is rated as one of the least important traits (Hunter and Davis 1992; Harris et al. 1994). Men's roles in society, like women's, are conditioned by the social context of their experience. Gender identity is merged with racial identity for all people. For those in racial minority groups, this means that concepts of womanhood and manhood are shaped by the patterns of domination and exclusion that race *and* gender produce.

Gender Socialization and Homophobia

Homophobia is the fear and hatred of homosexuals. Homophobia plays an important role in gender socialization because it encourages stricter conformity to traditional expectations, especially for men and young boys. Slurs directed against gays encourage boys to act more masculine as a way of affirming for their peers that they are not gay. As a consequence, homophobia also discourages so-called feminine traits in men, such as caring, nurturing, empathy, emotion, and gentleness. Men who endorse the most traditional male roles also tend to be the most homophobic (Burgess 2001; Alden 2001; Basow and Johnson 2000). In this way, homophobia is one of the means by which socialization into expected gender roles takes place. The consequence is not only conformity to gender roles, but a learned hostility toward gays and lesbians.

Homophobia is a learned attitude, as are other forms of negative social judgments about particular groups. Homophobia is also deeply embedded in people's definitions of themselves as men and women. Boys are often raised to be manly by repressing so-called feminine characteristics in themselves. Being called a "fag" or a "sissy" is one of the peer sanctions that socializes a child to conform to particular gender roles. Similarly, pressures on adolescent girls to abandon tomboy behavior are a mechanism by which girls are taught to adopt the behaviors and characteristics associated with womanhood. Being labeled a lesbian may cause those with a strong love of women to repress this emotion and direct love only toward men. We can see, therefore, how homophobic ridicule, though it may be in the context of play and joking, has serious consequences for both heterosexual and homosexual men and women. Homophobia socializes most people into expected gender roles, and it produces numerous myths about gays and lesbians—examined in more detail in the following chapter.

The Institutional Basis of Gender

The process of gender socialization tells us a lot about how gender identities are formed, but gender is not just a matter of identity: Gender is embedded in social institutions. This means that institutions are patterned by gender, resulting in different experiences and opportunities for men and women. Sociologists analyze gender not just as interpersonal expectations, but as characteristic of institutions. This is what is meant by the term *gendered institution.* This concept means that entire institutions are patterned by gender. **Gendered institutions** are the total pattern of gender relations, stereotypical expectations; interpersonal relationships; and the different placement of

DOING SOCIOLOGICAL RESEARCH

Eating Disorders: Gender, Race, and the Body

"A culture of thinness," "the tyranny of slenderness," "the beauty myth": These are terms used to describe the obsession with weight and body image that permeates the dominant culture—especially for girls and women. Just glance at the covers of popular magazines for women and girls and you will very likely find article after article promoting new diet gimmicks, each bundled with a promise that you will lose pounds in a few days if you only have the proper discipline or use the right products. Moreover, the models on the covers of such magazine are likely to be thin, and often dangerously so because being too thin causes serious health problems. How many women that you know have been affected by the culture of thinness?

The learned body image that we develop is deeply tied to our gender identity. Many have documented the range of eating disorders that develop when women—and men—come to believe that their body should match the cultural ideal. Women, especially young women, are most likely to develop serious eating disorders, thinking of themselves as overweight when they are not and sometimes starving themselves to death. But men as well can develop eating disorders, primarily from trying to bulk up through the use of steroids, while women primarily deprive themselves of food.

Meg Lovejoy wanted to know if the drive for thinness is unique to White women and how gendered images of the body might differ for African American and White women in the United States. Her research reviews existing research literature on eating disorders, which has generally concluded that, compared with White women, Black women are less likely to develop eating disorders. Black women are least likely to engage in excessive dieting and are less fearful of fat, although they are more likely to be obese and experience compulsive overeating. White women, on the other hand, tend to be very dissatisfied with their body size and overall appearance, with an increasing number engaging in obsessive dieting. Black and White women also tend to distort their own weight in opposite directions: White women are more likely to overestimate their own weight (that is, saying they are fat when they are not); Black women are more likely to underestimate their weight (saying they are average when they are overweight by medical standards). Why?

Lovejoy argues that the connections between gender, race, social class, and body image are critical to answering this question. She suggests that we cannot understand eating disorders without knowing the different stigmas attached to Black and White women in society. She suggests that Black women develop alternative standards for valuing their appearance as a way of resisting mainstream, Eurocentric standards. Black women who do so are then less susceptible to the controlling and damaging influence of the institutions that promote the ideal of thinness as feminine beauty. On the other hand, the vulnerability that Black women experience in society can foster mental health problems that manifest themselves in overeating. Eating disorders for Black women can also stem from the traumas that result from racism, especially when combined with sexism and other forms of oppression.

Lovejoy, along with others who have examined this issue, concludes that eating disorders must be understood in the context of social structures—gender, race, class, and ethnicity—that affect all women, although in different ways. The cultural meanings associated with bodies differ for different groups in society, but are deeply linked to our concepts of ourselves and the basic behaviors—like eating—that we otherwise think of as "natural."

Questions to Consider:

1. Pay attention to the music and visual images in popular culture and ask yourself what cultural messages are being sent to different race and gender groups? What messages are being conveyed about appropriate appearance? How do they affect people's body image—and their self-esteem?
Keywords: body image and race, gender and body image

2. Lovejoy examines eating disorders in the context of gender, race, class, and ethnicity. What cultural meanings are broadcast with regard to age?
Keywords: age and eating disorders, older women and bodies

3. Is there a "culture of thinness" among your peers? If so, what impact do you think it has on people's self-concept? If not, are there other cultural meanings associated with weight among people in your social groups?
Keywords: culture of thinness; weight, youth, and self-esteem

We have included InfoTrac College Edition keywords at the end of each question to make it easier for you to find more to read on these topics. Go to **www.infotrac-college.com,** an online library, to begin your search.

Source: Lovejoy, Meg. 2001. "Disturbances in the Social Body: Differences in Body Image and Eating Problems among African American and White Women." *Gender & Society* 15 (April): 239–261.

men and women in social, economic, and political hierarchies of institutions. Schools, for example, are not just places where children learn gender roles, but gendered institutions because they are founded on specific gender patterns. Seeing institutions as gendered reveals that gender is not just an attribute of individuals, but is "present in the processes, practices, images and ideologies, and distributions of power in the various sectors of social life" (Acker 1992: 567).

As an example of the concept of gendered institution, think of what it is like to work as a woman in an organization dominated by men. Women in this situation report that men's importance in the organization is communicated in subtle ways, whereas women are made to feel like outsiders. Important career connections may be made in the context of men's informal interactions with each other—both inside and outside the workplace. Women may be treated as tokens or may think that company policies are ineffective in helping them cope with the particular demands in their lives. These institutional patterns of gender affect men, too, particularly if they try to establish more balance between their personal and work lives. To

say that work institutions are gendered institutions means that, taken together, there is a cumulative and systematic effect of gender throughout the institution.

Military academies are a good example of gendered institutions. Although (as shown in the "Sociology in Practice" box), the Virginia Military Institute (VMI) and The Citadel were ordered to admit women as the result of a Supreme Court decision, these institutions have been constructed on a strict gender order in which masculinity was built into the schools—both in their image of themselves, the behaviors expected of cadets, and the opportunities given to (or denied) to women (Kimmel 2000). Other gendered institutions may not be as extreme as this, but nonetheless are structured by gendered hierarchies, differences between what men and women do in the institutions, and ideas about gender-appropriate behaviors and beliefs. You can see this by identifying an institution with which you are familiar and describing what men and women do in this institution, where they are placed relative to each other, what beliefs support this system, and what happens when someone tries to cross presumed gender lines in the institution.

SOCIOLOGY IN PRACTICE

Desegregating Institutions: VMI and The Citadel

In 1996, the U.S. Supreme Court (in *United States v. Virginia*) ruled that the exclusion of women from the Virginia Military Institute (VMI)—a state-supported military academy—was unconstitutional. Writing for the 7–1 majority, Justice Ruth Bader Ginsburg argued that the school's policy of excluding women violated the equal protection clause of the 14th amendment. In a related case, The Citadel, another all-male, state-supported institution in South Carolina, came to national attention after a district court ordered The Citadel to admit Shannon Faulkner, a woman who had gained admission to The Citadel by not identifying that she was a woman on her application. When the institution learned she was a woman, they later rejected her. Prior to the Supreme Court decision, both the VMI and The Citadel cases had been heard by U.S. district courts.

Testifying in the U.S. District Court case involving VMI, sociologist

Michael Kimmel argued that arguments to exclude women from these formerly all-male military academies were based on gender stereotypes. Kimmel is a sociologist well-known for his research on men and gender identity. Analyzing the VMI case, Kimmel argued that the exclusion of women from VMI supported a culture of masculinity, but could not be justified except as based on gender stereotypes. Expert witnesses for the other side, including sociologist David Riesman, argued that the adversarial method of education used at VMI was inappropriate for women, presumably because of their alleged physical weakness and emotionality. Attorneys for VMI argued that women are "not capable of ferocity," are "more emotional," and "cannot take stress." In ruling on behalf of women, the Supreme Court rejected such logic.

This example of a recent case also shows a strong link between research scholarship and social pol-

icy. Without the research evidence about how gender stereotypes develop and how culture shapes men's and women's roles, would arguments to keep women out of all-male institutions succeed?

Critical Thinking Exercise

1. What advantages and disadvantages do you see to single-sex schools? Would you make the same arguments regarding schools for only African American boys or girls? How are your opinions informed by assumptions about government support for public and private education?

2. Using education as the example, do you think that women and men (girls and boys) must be treated the same for there to be greater equality? Can equality and difference coexist?

FURTHER INFORMATION: Kimmel, Michael. 2000. "Saving the Male: The Sociological Implications of the Virginia Military Institute and The Citadel." *Gender & Society* 14 (August): 494–516.

Gender is not just a learned role; it is also part of social structure, just as class and race are structural dimensions of society. Notice that people do not think about the class system or racial inequality in terms of "class roles" or "race roles." It is obvious that race relations and class relations are far more than matters of interpersonal interaction. Race, class, and gender inequalities are experienced within interpersonal relationships, but they extend beyond relationships. Just as it would seem strange to think that race relations in the United States are controlled by race-role socialization, it is also wrong to think that gender relations are the result of gender socialization alone. Like race and class, gender is a system of privilege and inequality in which women are systematically disadvantaged relative to men. There are institutionalized power relations between women and men, and men and women have unequal access to social and economic resources (Lopata and Thorne 1978; Andersen 2000).

■ *Gender Stratification*

Gender stratification refers to the hierarchical distribution of social and economic resources according to gender. Most societies have some form of gender stratification, although the specific form varies from country to country. Comparative research finds that women are more nearly equal in societies characterized by the following traits (Chafetz 1984):

- Women's work is central to the economy.

- Women have access to education.

- Ideological or religious support for gender inequality is not strong.

- Men make direct contributions to household responsibilities, such as housework and child care.

- Work is not highly segregated by sex.

- Women have access to formal power and authority in public decision making.

In Sweden, where there is a relatively high degree of gender equality, the participation of both men and women in the labor force and the household (including child care and housework) is promoted by government policies. Women also have a strong role in the political system, although women still earn less than men in Sweden. In many countries, women and girls have less access to education than men and boys, but that gap is closing. Still, two-thirds of the illiterate people in the world are women (United Nations 2000b).

As the preceding list suggests, gender stratification is multidimensional. In some societies, women may be free in some areas of life but not in others. In Japan, for example, women tend to be well educated and have high labor force participation. Within the family, however, Japanese women have fairly rigid gender roles. Yet the rate of violence against women in Japan (in the form of rape, prostitution, and pornography) is quite low in relation to other nations, even though women are widely employed as "sex workers" in hostess clubs, bars, and sex joints (Allison 1994). Patterns of gender inequality are most reflected in the wage differentials between women and men around the world, as Figure 10.3 shows.

Gender stratification can be extreme, as was the case in Afghanistan under the Taliban regime. The Taliban, an extremist militia group, seized power in Afghanistan in 1996 and stripped women and girls of basic human rights. Women were banished from the labor force, schools were closed to girls, and women who were enrolled in the universities were expelled. In Afghanistan, women were prohibited from leaving their homes unless accompanied by a close male relative. The windows of houses where women lived were painted black to keep women literally invisible to the public. This extreme segregation and exclusion of women from public life has been labeled **gender apartheid**. Gender apartheid is also evident in other nations, although not so extreme as it was under Taliban rule—in Saudi Arabia, women are not allowed to drive and in Kuwait they cannot vote.

Sexism and Patriarchy

Gender stratification tends to be supported by beliefs that treat gender inequality as natural. The term refers to *ideology,* a belief system that tries to explain and justify the status quo. **Sexism** is an ideology that defines women as different from and inferior to men. Like racism, sexism distorts reality, making behaviors seem natural when they are actually rooted in entrenched systems of power and privilege. The idea that men should be paid more than women because they are the primary breadwinners reflects sexist ideology; however, when this concept becomes embedded in the wage structure, people no longer have to explicitly believe in the original idea for the consequences of sexism to be propagated.

Sexism and racism tend to go hand in hand. Both generate social myths that have no basis in fact, but they justify the continuing advantage of dominant groups over subordinates. A case in point is the belief that women of color are being hired more often and promoted more rapidly than others. This belief misrepresents the facts. Women rarely take jobs away from men because most women of color work in gender- and race-segregated jobs. The truth is that women, especially women of color, are burdened by obstacles to job mobility that are not present for men, especially White men (Browne 1999;

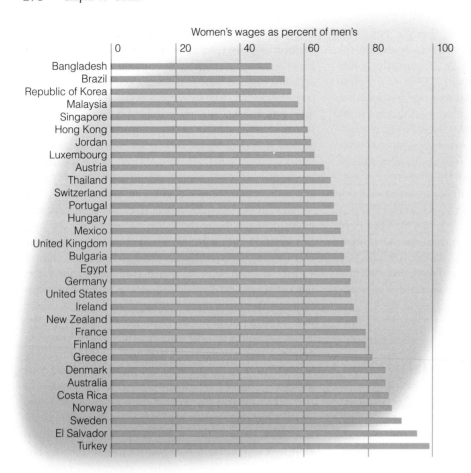

Women's wages as percent of men's

FIGURE 10.3 The Wage Gap: An International Perspective

DATA: From United Nations. 2000. *The World's Women: Trends and Statistics.* Washington, DC: Population Reference Bureau, p. 132. Used by permission of the United Nations.

Padavic and Reskin 2002). The myth that women of color get all the jobs makes White men seem to be the victims of race and gender privilege. Although there may be occasional cases where a woman of color (or a man of color, for that matter) gets a job that a White man also applied for, gender and race privilege favors White men.

DEBUNKING
Society's Myths

Myth: Because of affirmative action, Black women are taking a lot of jobs away from White men.

Sociological perspective: Sociological research finds no evidence of this claim. Quite the contrary, women of color work in gender- and race-segregated jobs and only rarely in occupations where they compete with White men in the labor market.

Patriarchy refers to a society or group in which men have power over women. Patriarchy is common throughout the world. In patriarchal societies, husbands have authority over their wives in the private sphere of their families, and public institutions are also structured around male power. Men hold all or most of the public power positions in patriarchal societies, whether as chief, president, CEO, prime minister, or another leadership position. Forms of patriarchy vary from society to society. In some, it is rigidly upheld in both the public and private spheres, and women may be formally excluded from voting, holding public office, or working outside the home. In societies such as the contemporary United States, patriarchy may be somewhat diminished in the private sphere (at least in some households), but the public sphere continues to be based on patriarchal relations.

Matriarchy has traditionally been defined as a society or group in which women have power over men. Anthropologists have debated the extent to which such societies exist, but new research finds that matriarchies do exist, though not in the form the customary definition implies. Based on her study of the Minangkabau—a matriarchal society in West Sumatra (in Indonesia)—anthropologist Peggy Sanday argues that scholars have used a Western definition of power that does not apply in non-Western societies. The Minangkabau define themselves as a matriarchy, meaning that women hold economic and

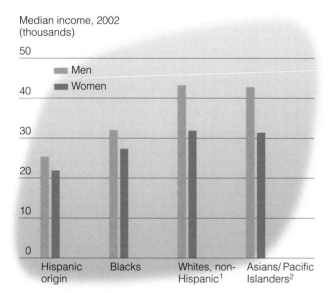

Median income, 2002 (thousands)

FIGURE 10.4 Median Income by Race and Gender
All data include only year-round, full-time workers.

SOURCE: U.S. Census Bureau. 2003. *Historical Income Tables-People*, Tables P36-B, P36-C, P36-D, and P36-E. Washington, DC: U.S. Department of Commerce **www.census.gov**

social power, but this is not rule by women since the people believe that rule should be by consensus, including men. Thus, matriarchy exists but not as a mirror image of patriarchy (Sanday 2002).

In sum, gender stratification is an institutionalized system that rests on specific belief systems supporting the inequality of men and women. Although theoretically one could have a society stratified by gender where women hold power over men that is not how gender stratification has evolved. In the next sections, different manifestations of gender stratification in the United States will be examined, especially as it involves women's economic position in relation to men.

Women's Worth: Still Unequal

Gender stratification is especially obvious in the persistent earnings gap between women and men (see Figure 10.4). Although the gap has closed somewhat since the 1960s when women earned 59 percent of what men earned, women who work year-round and full time still earn, on average, only 76 percent of what men earn. Women with bachelor degrees earn the equivalent of men with associate's degrees (see Figure 10.5). In 2001, the median income for women working full time and year-round was $29,215; for men, it was $38,275 (De-Navas-Walt and Cleveland 2002).

The income gap between women and men persists despite the increased participation of women in the labor

force. The **labor force participation rate** is the percentage of those in a given category who are employed either part time or full time. By 2002, 60 percent of all women were in the paid labor force, compared with 74 percent of men. Since 1960, married women with children have nearly tripled their participation in the labor force. Two-thirds of mothers are now in the labor force, including more than half of mothers with infants. Current projections indicate that women's labor force participation will continue to rise. Men's labor force participation is expected to decline slightly (U.S. Department of Labor 2003).

More women are also in the labor market—a pattern that has long been true for women of color but now also characterizes the experience of White women, as the labor force participation rates of White women and women of color has converged. More women are now also the sole supporters of their dependents, given the changes in family patterns in contemporary society. Why then does the pay gap persist?

Laws prohibiting gender discrimination have now been in place for more than thirty years. The Equal Pay Act of 1963 was the first federal law to require that men and women should receive equal pay for equal work, an idea that is supported by the majority of Americans. Wage discrimination is rarely overt. Employers do not tell women, "You'll be working in the same job as a man, but because you are a woman, I will pay you 70 percent of what he earns." Most employers do not even explicitly set out to pay women less than men. Despite good intentions and legislation, however, differences in men's and women's earnings persist. Why? Research reveals four strong explanations for this: human capital theory, dual labor market theory, gender segregation, and overt discrimination.

HUMAN CAPITAL THEORY. Gender differences in wages are explained by **human capital theory** as the result of differences in the individual characteristics that workers bring to jobs. Human capital theory assumes that the economic system is fair and competitive, and that wage discrepancies reflect differences in the resources (or human capital) that individuals bring to their jobs. Factors such as age, prior experience, number of hours worked, marital status, and education are human capital variables. Human capital theory asserts that the extent to which human beings vary in these characteristics will influence their worth in the labor market. For example, higher job turnover rates or work records interrupted by child-rearing and family responsibilities could negatively influence the earning power of women.

Much evidence supports the human capital explanation for the differences between men's and women's earnings because education, age, and experience do influence

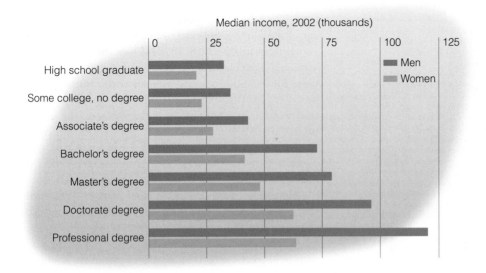

Median income, 2002 (thousands)

■ Men
■ Women

High school graduate
Some college, no degree
Associate's degree
Bachelor's degree
Master's degree
Doctorate degree
Professional degree

FIGURE 10.5 Education, Gender, and Income

DATA: U.S. Census Bureau. 2003. *Historical Income Tables-People,* Table P28. Washington, DC: U.S. Department of Commerce. **www.census.gov**

earnings. When we compare men and women who have the same level of education, previous experience, and number of hours worked per week, women still earn less than men (see Figure 10.5). Intermittent employment is also not as significant in explaining wage differences as human capital theory would lead one to expect (England et al. 1988). Although human capital theory explains some differences between men's and women's earnings, it does not explain it all. Sociologists have looked to other factors to complete the explanation of wage inequality (Browne 1999).

THE DUAL LABOR MARKET. A second explanation of discrepancies in men's and women's earnings is **dual labor market theory,** which contends that women and men earn different amounts because they tend to work in different segments of the labor market. The dual labor market reflects the devaluation of women's work because there generally are low wages in jobs where women are most concentrated. Although it is hard to untangle cause and effect in the relationship between the devaluation of women's work and low wages in certain jobs, once such an earnings structure is established, it is difficult to change. As a result, although equal pay for equal work may hold in principle, it applies to relatively few people, because most men and women are not engaged in equal work.

According to dual labor market theory, the labor market is organized in two different sectors: the *primary market* and the *secondary market.* In the primary labor market, jobs are relatively stable, wages are good, opportunities for advancement exist, fringe benefits are likely, and workers are afforded due process. Working for a major corporation in a management job is an example of this. Jobs in the primary labor market are usually in large organizations where there is general stability, steady profits,

and a rational system of management. In contrast, the secondary labor market is characterized by high job turnover, low wages, short or nonexistent promotion ladders, few benefits, poor working conditions, arbitrary work rules, and capricious supervision. Many of the jobs students take—such as waiting tables, selling fast food, or cooking and serving fast food—fall into this category. For students, however, these jobs are usually short term.

Within the primary labor market, there are two tiers. The first consists of high-status professional and managerial jobs with potential for upward mobility, room for creativity and initiative, and more autonomy. The second tier comprises working-class jobs, which includes clerical work and skilled and semiskilled blue-collar work. Women and minorities in the primary labor market tend to be in the second tier. Although these jobs are secure compared with jobs in the secondary labor market, they are more vulnerable and do not have as much mobility, pay, prestige, or autonomy as jobs in the first tier of the primary labor market.

There is, in addition, an informal sector of the market where there is even greater wage inequality; no benefits; and little, if any, oversight of employment practices. Individuals may hire such workers as private service workers or under-the-table workers who perform a service for a fee (painting, babysitting, car repairs, and any number of services). Although there are no formal data on the informal sector because much of it tends to be in an underground economy, it is likely that women and minorities form a large segment of this market activity. White men are also disadvantaged because of the instability and lack of protection in this sector of work.

GENDER SEGREGATION. Dual labor market theory explains wage inequality as a function of the structure of the labor market, not the individual characteristics of

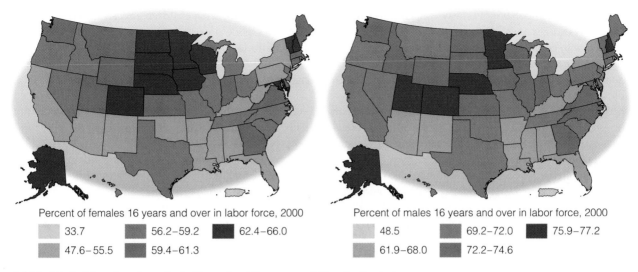

Percent of females 16 years and over in labor force, 2000

| | 33.7 | | 56.2–59.2 | | 62.4–66.0 |
| | 47.6–55.5 | | 59.4–61.3 | | |

Percent of males 16 years and over in labor force, 2000

| | 48.5 | | 69.2–72.0 | | 75.9–77.2 |
| | 61.9–68.0 | | 72.2–74.6 | | |

MAP 10.1 Mapping America's Diversity: Women and Men in the Labor Force
Generally speaking, women's labor force participation has been increasing; men's decreasing. **What might explain this? Using this map, can you think of factors that might explain regional variations in women's and men's likelihood of being in the labor force?**

Source: U.S. Cenus Bureau. 2002. *American FactFinder.* **www.census.gov**

workers, as suggested by human capital theory. Because of the dual labor market, men and women tend to work in different occupations and when working in the same occupation in different jobs. This is referred to as **occupational segregation,** a pattern in which different groups of workers are separated into different occupations. Occupational segregation can be by gender, class, race, and other factors. Wages tend to be linked to occupational segregation—there is a direct association between the number of women in given occupational categories and the wages paid in those jobs. In other words, the greater the proportion of women in a given occupation, the lower the pay (U.S. Department of Labor 2003). **Gender segregation** refers to the distribution of men and women in different jobs in the labor force; it is a specific form of occupational segregation. Despite several decades of legislation prohibiting discrimination against women in the workplace, most women and men still work in gender-segregated occupations (Wootton 1997). That is, the majority of women work in occupations where most of the other workers are women, and the majority of men work mostly with men. Women also tend to be concentrated in a smaller range of occupations than men. To this day, almost two-thirds of all employed women work as clerical workers and sales clerks, or in service occupations such as food service workers, maids, health service workers, hairdressers, and child-care workers. Men are dispersed over a much broader array of occupations. Women make up 75 percent of teachers (not counting college and university teachers), two-thirds of retail sales workers, 99 percent of secretaries, 92 percent

of financial records processors, and 95 percent of private service workers—stark evidence of the persistence of gender segregation in the labor force (U.S. Department of Labor 2003).

OVERT DISCRIMINATION. A fourth explanation of the gender wage gap is discrimination. **Discrimination** refers to practices that single out some groups for different and unequal treatment. Despite the progress of recent years, overt discrimination continues to afflict women in the workplace. It is argued that men (especially White men), by virtue of being the dominant group in society, have an incentive to preserve their advantages in the labor market. They do so by establishing rules that distribute rewards unequally. Women pose a threat to traditional White male privileges, and men may organize to preserve their own power and advantage (Reskin 1988).

Within institutions, dominant groups will use their position of power to perpetuate their advantage (Lieberson 1980). Historically, White men used labor unions to exclude women and racial minorities from well-paying, unionized jobs, usually in the blue-collar trades. A more contemporary example is seen in the efforts of some conservative groups, usually led by men, to dilute legislation that has been developed to assist women and racial–ethnic minorities. These efforts can be seen as an attempt to preserve group power.

Another example of overt discrimination is the harassment that women experience at work, including *sexual harassment* and other means of intimidation. Sociologists see such behaviors as ways for men to protect their advantages in the labor force. No wonder that women who enter traditionally male-dominated professions suffer the most sexual harassment; the reverse seldom occurs for men employed in jobs historically filled by women. Although men can be victims of sexual harassment, this is rare. Sexual harassment is a mechanism for preserving men's advantage in the labor force—a device that also buttresses the belief that women are sexual objects for the pleasure of men.

Each of these explanations—human capital theory, dual labor market theory, gender segregation, and overt discrimination—contributes to an understanding of the continuing differences in pay between women and men. Wage inequality between men and women is clearly the result of multiple factors that together operate to systematically place women at a disadvantage in the workplace.

The Persistence of Gender Segregation

Across the labor force, women tend to be located in those jobs that are the most devalued, causing some to wonder if the fact that the jobs are held by women leads to devaluation of the jobs. Why, for example, is pediatrics considered a less prestigious specialty than cardiology? Why are elementary school teachers (83 percent of whom are women) paid less than airplane mechanics (99 percent of whom are men)? The association of elementary

Jobs that have historically been defined as "women's work" are some of the most devalued in terms of income and prestige, despite their importance for things such as nurturing children.

school teaching with children and its identification as "women's work" lowers its prestige and economic value. Indeed, if measured by the wages attached to an occupation, child care is one of the least prestigious jobs in the nation—paying on average only $252 per week in 2002, which would come out to $13,104 per year if you worked every week of the year (U.S. Department of Labor 2003). This is an annual income far below the official federal poverty line of $18,307!

Only a small proportion of women work in occupations traditionally thought to be men's jobs (such as the skilled trades). The representation of women in skilled blue-collar jobs has increased fourfold since 1940 and from 2 to 8 percent in 2001, but that is still less than one in ten (U.S. Department of Labor 2003). Likewise, very few men work in occupations historically considered to be women's work, such as nursing, elementary school teaching, and clerical work. Interestingly, men who work in occupations customarily thought of as women's work tend to be more upwardly mobile within these jobs than are women who enter fields traditionally reserved for men (Williams 1992; Budig 2002). Gender segregation in the labor market is so prevalent that most jobs can easily be categorized as men's work or women's work. Occupational segregation reinforces the belief that there are significant differences between the sexes. Think of the characteristics of a soldier. Do you imagine someone who is compassionate, gentle, and demure? Similarly, imagine a secretary. Is this someone who is aggressive, independent, and stalwart? The association of each characteristic with a particular gender makes the occupation itself a gendered occupation.

For all women, perceptions of gender-appropriate behavior influence the likelihood of success within institutions. Even something as simple as wearing makeup has been linked to women's success in professional jobs (Dellinger and Williams 1997). When men or women cross the boundaries established by occupational segregation, they are often considered to be gender deviants. They may be stereotyped as homosexual and have their "true gender identity" questioned. Men who are nurses may be stereotyped as effeminate or gay; women Marines may be stereotyped as "butch." Social practices like these serve to reassert traditional gender identities, perhaps softening the challenge to traditionally male-dominated institutions that women's entry challenges (Williams 1989, 1995).

As a result, many men and women in nontraditional occupations feel pressured to assert gender-appropriate behavior. Men in jobs historically defined as women's work may feel impelled to emphasize their masculinity, or if they are gay, they may feel even more pressure to keep their sexual identity secret. Such social disguises can make them seem unfriendly and distant, characteris-

Gender segregation in the labor market intersects with racial segregation, with jobs employing primarily women of color being among the least paid in society.

Although only a small percentage of women work in jobs traditionally defined as for men, a growing number of women are entering such nontraditional fields. Women in such jobs often discover that these are gendered institutions.

tics that can have a negative effect on evaluations of their professional performance. Heterosexual women in male-dominated jobs may feel obliged to squash suspicions that they are lesbians or excessively mannish. Lesbian women may be especially wary about having their sexual identity revealed. Studies have found that lesbian women are more likely to be open about their sexual identity at work when they work predominantly with women and have women as bosses (Schneider 1984).

INTERNAL GENDER SEGREGATION. Gender segregation also occurs within occupations. Women usually work in different jobs from men, but when they work within the same occupation, they are segregated into particular fields or job types. Medical doctors are a good example. Women physicians tend to be concentrated in the least prestigious specialties within medicine—pediatrics, obstetrics/gynecology, and general medicine—and have less representation in the more prestigious specialties, such as neurosurgery, cardiology, and

oncology, where men predominate (American Medical Association 2003). Even in less prestigious jobs, such as sales, women tend to do noncommissioned sales or to sell products that are of less value than those men sell. Among waiters and waitresses, women often work in lower-priced restaurants where they are likely to be tipped less than men (Hall 1993).

EXPLANATIONS OF GENDER SEGREGATION. Why is gender segregation still so prevalent, and why do obstacles to mobility at work persist? One explanation is that women and men are socialized differently, and to some degree, they choose to go into different fields. There is some indication that women who are exposed to masculine tasks in childhood are more likely as adults to enter jobs that use these skills, but many women shy away from traditionally male jobs because they believe that others will disapprove. Gender socialization certainly contributes to why men and women choose the occupations they do, but preference alone does not explain the gender segregation of women and men at work because women move into jobs traditionally defined as men's work when given the opportunity. Although women in such jobs experience sexual harassment, paternalism, and other discouragement from male coworkers and supervisors, and although these behaviors affect women's enjoyment of their work, these factors do not prevent women from being interested in these jobs (Padavic and Reskin 2002).

A second explanation is that structural obstacles discourage women from entering male-dominated jobs and from advancing once they are employed. A well-known obstacle to even the most successful women has been dubbed the *glass ceiling.* This term evokes the subtle yet decisive barrier to advancement that women find in the workplace; they can see the top, they may even get close, but there is an invisible barrier at which they find that advancement stops. Despite three decades of policies meant to address inequality in the labor market, women and minorities are still substantially blocked from senior management positions (Glass Ceiling Commission 1995). Women who have risen to the top attribute their success to social networks, in addition to their abilities, whereas men attribute their success only to their own individual effort (Davies-Netzley 1998).

"I DON'T THINK OF IT AS A GLASS CEILING. I THINK OF IT AS A TRANSPARENT THREAT."

SOURCE: AUTH © 1995. Reprinted with permission of Universal Press Syndicate. All rights reserved.

THINKING SOCIOLOGICALLY

Identify three women working in an occupation where men are the majority. Ask them about what influences the possibilities for promotion within the organization. Do they think a *glass ceiling* exists? Why or why not? Try the same thing by interviewing men who work in occupations traditionally defined as "women's work." Does a glass ceiling exist for them? What stereotypes do they encounter?

The glass ceiling exists at every level where men and women work together but are unequally likely to rise to the next level of authority. Most women can hardly hope to contend for higher positions; instead they hold jobs that are low in status, poorly paid, and offer little opportunity for advancement. Before women can encounter the glass ceiling, in the words of one researcher, they must pull away from the sticky floor (Berheide 1992). Others have added that "glass walls" also prevent women from advancing, meaning that they usually work in parts of organizations where advancement is less likely. Secretaries, for example, may not be able to move to other professional jobs within an organization. Consider your average grocery store: Women are more likely to be found in the deli or bakery, whereas men are usually found in produce and groceries—sections that traditionally have provided a better path to management (Padavic and Reskin 2002).

Despite the difficulties imposed, women continue to move into new areas of work and are advancing to some degree. Change is slow, however, and, as we discuss next, women and men struggle with the competing demands of work and family responsibilities.

Balancing Work and Family

As the participation of women in the labor force has increased, so have the demands of keeping up with work and home life. Although some changes are evident,

women continue to hold primary responsibility for meeting the needs of families, as we will see in more detail in Chapter 13. Many men are now much more involved in housework and child care than has been true in the past, although most of this work still falls to women—a phenomenon that has been labeled "the second shift."

The social speedup that comes from increased hours of employment for both men and women (but especially women), coupled with the demands of maintaining a household, are a source of considerable stress (Hochschild 1989). Women continue to provide most of the labor that keeps households running—cleaning, cooking, running errands, driving children around, and managing household affairs. Although more men are engaged in housework and child care, a huge gender gap remains in the amount of such work done by women and men remains. Women are also much more likely to be providing care not just for children, but also for their older parents. The strains produced by these demands have for many made the home seem more and more like work for many; a large number of women and men report that their days at both work and home are harried and that they find work to be the place where they find emotional gratification and social support. In this contest between home and work, simply finding time can be an enormous challenge (Hochschild 1997). It is not surprising then that women report stress as one of their greatest concerns (Newport 2000).

■ *Theories of Gender*

Why is there gender inequality? The answer to this question is important, not only because it makes us think about the experiences of women and men, but also because it guides attempts to address the persistence of gender injustice. The major theoretical frameworks in sociology provide some answers, but feminist scholars have also found that traditional perspectives in the discipline are inadequate to address the new issues that have emerged from feminist research.

The Frameworks of Sociology

The major frameworks of sociological theory—functionalism, conflict theory, and symbolic interaction—provide some answers to the question of why gender inequality exists, although, as we will see in the next section, feminist scholars have developed new additional theories to address women's lives directly. Functionalists, for example, have been criticized for interpreting gender as a fixed role in society. *Functionalist theory* purported that men fill instrumental roles in society whereas women fill expressive roles and presumed that this arrangement worked to the benefit of society (see Chapter 1). Feminists objected to such a characterization, arguing that this presumed sexist arrangements were functional for society. Limiting women's role to expressive functions and men's to instrumental functions according to feminists is dysfunctional, both for men and women. Although few contemporary functionalist theorists would make such traditionalist arguments, functionalism does emphasize people's socialization into prescribed roles as the major impetus behind gender inequality. Thus, conditions such as wage inequality, a functionalist might argue, are the result of choices women make that may result in their inequality but nonetheless involve functional adaptation to the competing demands of family and work roles.

Conflict theorists, in contrast, see women as disadvantaged by power inequities between women and men that are built into the social structure. This includes economic inequity, as well as women's disadvantages in political and social systems. Conflict theorists, for example, see wage inequality as produced from the power that men have historically had to devalue women's work and to benefit as a group from the services that women's labor provides. At the same time, conflict theorists have been much more attuned to the interactions of race, class, and gender inequality because they fundamentally see all forms of inequality as stemming from the differential access to resources that dominant groups in society have.

From an *ethnomethodological* perspective (see Chapters 2 and 4), feminist scholars have developed what is known as "doing gender"—a theoretical perspective on gender that interprets gender as something that is accomplished through the ongoing social interactions people have with one another (West and Zimmerman 1987; West and Fen-

stermaker 1995). Seen from this framework, people produce gender through the interaction they have with one another and through the interpretations they have of certain actions and appearances. In other words, gender is not something that is an attribute of different people, as functionalists suggest; rather, it is constantly made up and reproduced through social interaction. When you act like a man or act like a woman, you are confirming gender and reproducing the existing social order (Peralta 2002).

From this point of view, gender is relatively easy to change because all it would take for this to occur is for people to behave differently. This is one reason the theory has been criticized by those with a more macrosociological point of view, since they say that it ignores the power differences and economic differences that exist based on gender, race, and class. In other words, it does not explain the structural basis of women's oppression (Collins et al. 1995).

Feminist Theory

Feminism is not a single way of thinking and acting; it fundamentally refers to advocating a more just society for women. **Feminist theory** has emerged from the women's movement and refers to analyses that seek to understand the position of women in society for the explicit purpose of improving their position in society. Four major frameworks have developed in feminist theory: liberal feminism, socialist feminism, radical feminism, and multiracial feminism (see Table 10.1).

Liberal feminism emerged from a long tradition that began among British liberals in the nineteenth century. Liberal feminism argues that inequality for women originates in traditions of the past that pose barriers to women's advancement. It emphasizes individual rights and equal opportunity as the basis for social justice and reform. The framework of liberal feminism has been used to support many of the legal changes required to bring about greater equality for women in the United States. Liberal feminists contend that gender socialization contributes to women's inequality because it is through learned customs that inequality is perpetuated. In the interests of social change, liberal feminism advocates the removal of barriers to women's advancement and the development of policies that promote equal rights for women.

Socialist feminism is a more radical perspective that interprets the origins of women's oppression in the system of capitalism. Because women constitute a cheap supply of labor, they are exploited by capitalism in much the same way that the working class is exploited. In the view of socialist feminists, capitalism interacts with patriarchy to make women less powerful both as women and as laborers. Socialist feminists are critical of liberal

TABLE 10.1 Feminist Theory: Comparing Perspectives

	Liberal Feminism	Socialist Feminism	Radical Feminism	Multiracial Feminism	Gendered Institutions	"Doing Gender"
Gender Identity	Learned through traditional patterns of gender role socialization	Gender division of labor reflects the needs of a capitalist workforce	Women's identification with men gives men power over women	Women and men of color form an oppositional consciousness as a reaction against oppression	Gender is learned in institutional settings that are structured along gender lines	Gender is an accomplished activity created through social interaction
Gender Inequality	Inequality is the result of formal barriers to equal opportunity	Gender inequality stems from class relations	Patriarchy is the basis for women's powerlessness	Race, class, and gender intersect to form a matrix of domination	Organizations reproduce inequity by making gendered activity "business as usual"	People reproduce race and class inequality through assumptions they make about different groups
Social Change	Change accomplished through legal reform and attitudinal change	Transformation of the gender division of labor accompanies change in the class division of labor	Liberation comes as women organize on their own behalf	Women of color become agents of feminist change through alliances with other groups	Comes through policies that redesign the basic structure of institutions	People can alter social relations through changed forms of social interaction

feminism for not addressing the fundamental inequalities built into capitalist and patriarchal systems. To these feminists, equality for women will come only when the economic and political system is changed.

Radical feminism interprets patriarchy as the primary cause of women's oppression. To radical feminists, the origins of women's oppression lies in men's control over women's bodies; thus, they see violence against women—in the form of rape, sexual harassment, wife beating, and sexual abuse—as mechanisms that men use to assert their power in society. Radical feminists think that change cannot come about through the existing system because that system is controlled and dominated by men.

Most recently, **multiracial feminism** has developed new avenues of theory for guiding the study of race, class, and gender (Andersen and Collins 2004; Baca Zinn and Dill 1996; Chow et al. 1996; Collins 1990, 1998). Multiracial feminism evolves from studies pointing out that earlier forms of feminist thinking excluded women of color from analysis, which made it impossible for feminists to deliver theories that informed people about the experiences of all women. Multiracial feminism examines the interactive influence of gender, race, and class, showing how together they shape the experiences of all women and men (Baca Zinn and Dill 1996).

These perspectives provide unique ways of looking at the experiences of women and men in society. These theoretical orientations have been the bedrock on which feminists have built their programs of social and political change.

■ Gender in Global Perspective

Increasingly, the economic condition of women and men in the United States is also linked to the fortunes of people in other parts of the world. The growth of a global economy and the availability of a cheaper industrial labor force outside the United States meant that U.S. workers

Under the rule of the Taliban in Afghanistan, women must be completely veiled. As the Taliban lost control during the war in 2002, many women shed their burqas, showing their faces in public for the first time in years.

AP/Wide World Photos

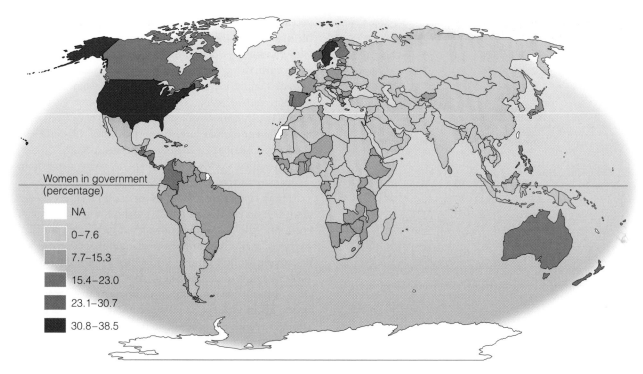

MAP 10.2 Viewing Society in Global Perspective: Women in Government
Being represented in government is an important mark of citizenship. In most parts of the world, although women are politically active, they are highly underrepresented in positions of government leadership. **Why has there never been a woman president of the United States, and what do you think will have to happen before there can be a woman president in the United States? How does this differ from other nations where women have been the major national leader?**

SOURCE: From United Nations. 2002. "Fact Sheet on Women in Government." WomenWatch.
www.un.org/womenwatch

have become part of an international division of labor. U.S.-based multinational corporations looking around the world for less expensive labor often turn to the developing nations and find that the cheapest laborers are women or children. The global division of labor is thus acquiring a gendered component with women workers, usually from the poorest countries, providing a cheap supply of labor for manufacturing products that are distributed in the richer industrial nations.

Worldwide, women work as much or more than men. They receive 30 to 40 percent less pay, and they own only 1 percent of all property. It is difficult to find a single place in the world where the workplace is not segregated by gender. On a worldwide scale, women also do most of the work associated with home, children, and the elderly. While women's paid labor has been increasing, their unpaid labor in virtually every part of the world exceeds that of men (see Table 10.2). Often, unpaid labor is considered to be economically unimportant, even though the value of women's unpaid housework in the developed regions has been estimated to be as much as 30 percent of the gross

national product (United Nations 2000b). Despite their productivity around the world, women are seriously underrepresented in positions of governmental leadership, as the "Women in Government" map shows.

Despite these general trends, women's situations differ significantly from nation to nation. China is unusual in that there is far greater sharing of household responsibilities than in most other nations. In China, both women and men work long hours in paid employment; a typical workweek is six days long or forty-eight hours. In the paid labor force are 82 percent of women and 83 percent of men, and women are encouraged to stay in the labor force when they have children. There are extensive child-care facilities in China and a fifty-six-day paid maternity leave. Many work organizations have extended this paid leave to six months, although women can lose seniority rights when they are on maternity leave (something that is illegal in the United States).

In contrast, Japan has marked inequality in the domestic sphere. Women are far more likely to leave the labor force after marrying or following childbirth, and

TABLE 10.2 Women's Work Around the World

Women spend more time on unpaid work than men, but less on paid work.

	Total Hours:		Paid Work		Unpaid Work	
	Women	Men	Women	Men	Women	Men
Australia	51	49	15	30	35	18
France	46	42	15	26	31	17
Japan	46	42	20	39	26	3
Netherlands	36	37	10	25	26	11
New Zealand	49	49	16	29	33	19
Republic of Korea	40	38	23	36	17	2

SOURCE: United Nations. 2000. *World's Women: Trends and Statistics.* New York: United Nations, p. 125.

Japanese women's identities are more defined by their roles at home, although, for many, this is changing. Compared with China, Japanese women more closely resemble the pattern that exists in Britain and, to some extent, in the United States, although they are less involved in paid employment than in either Britain or the United States. Ironically, when comparing China, Japan, and Britain, researchers have found that Chinese women are the most discontent with what they perceive as gender injustice, whereas Japanese and British women express greater satisfaction with more limited employment. This may seem surprising, given the greater gender equality of Chinese women with Chinese men. Sociologists explain it as the result of the gap Chinese women see between official ideologies of gender equality and their observations of continuing inequalities in promotions and other benefits of work (Xuewen et al. 1992).

Work is not the only measure by which the status of women throughout the world is inferior to that of men. Women are vastly underrepresented in national parliaments (or other forms of government) everywhere; in only sixteen countries of the entire world is women's representation in national parliaments above 25 percent. Only seventeen countries have ever elected a woman president; women have served as prime minister only twenty-two times (United Nations 2000b).

The United Nations has also concluded that violence against women and girls is a global epidemic and one of the most pervasive violations of human rights (UNICEF 2000). Violence against women takes many forms, including rape, domestic violence, infanticide, incest, genital mutilation, and murder (including so-called "honor killings" where women may be killed to uphold the honor of the family if she has been raped or accused of adultery). While violence is

pervasive, some specific groups of women are more vulnerable than others—namely minority groups, refugees, women with disabilities, elderly women, poor and migrant women, and women living in countries where there is armed conflict. Statistics on the extent of violence against women are hard to report with accuracy, both because of the secrecy that surrounds many forms of violence and because of differences in how different nations might report violence. Nonetheless, the United Nations estimates that between 20 and 50 percent of women worldwide have experienced violence from an intimate partner or family member.

Many factors are related to the high rates of violence against women; these include cultural norms, women's economic and social dependence on men, and political practices that either provide inadequate legal protection or provide explicit support for women's subordination (as in the example of the Taliban given above). In recent years, many groups have organized campaigns to educate the public about violence and women and to initiate a global effort to reduce the harm done to women (see The Feminist Majority, http://www.feminist.org; UNICEF 2000).

■ *Gender and Social Change*

Few lives have not been touched by the transformations that have occurred in the wake of the feminist movement (see also Chapter 16). The women's movement has changed how women's issues are perceived in the public consciousness. It has created access to work opportunities, generated laws that protect women's rights, and spawned organizations that lobby for public policies on behalf of women. Many young women and men now take for granted freedoms that their generation is among the first to enjoy. These include access to birth control, equal opportunity legislation, and laws protecting against sexual harassment, as well as an increased presence of women on corporate boards, increased athletic opportunities for women, more presence in political life, and greater access to child care, to name a few. These impressive changes occurred in a relatively short period. How have they affected public consciousness about gender?

Contemporary Attitudes

In recent years, public attitudes toward gender roles have changed noticeably, especially regarding beliefs about the ideal lifestyle. Only a small minority of people disapprove of women being employed while they have young children (16 percent of women and 20 percent of men), and both women and men say it is not fair for men to be the sole decision maker in the household. Half of all women and men surveyed say that the ideal lifestyle is to be in a marriage in which a husband and wife share responsibilities, including work, housekeeping, and child care (Roper Organization 1995). Although the majority of women now want to combine work and family, they believe they will be discriminated against in the labor force if they do so. A majority of women (87 percent) say that making laws to establish equal pay should be a legislative priority (Greenhouse 2000b).

DEBUNKING
Society's Myths

Myth: The men most likely to support equality for women are White, middle-class men with a good education.

Sociological perspective: Although it is true that younger men tend to be more egalitarian than older men, African American men are the most likely to support women's equal rights and the right of women to work outside the home. On most measures of feminist beliefs, African American men tend to be more liberal than White men.

One of the most significant changes is the increased stress that women feel when they combine the demands of family and a job (Greenhouse 2000b). Although most men and women think that society is less critical of women who work while raising children, women and men see both pros and cons to this situation. Both believe that the children of employed mothers learn to be more responsible at an early age and that this provides them with positive role models. Women however, report an increase in stress as the result of combining family and work. Still, there has been a general decline in the numbers of people who think that having mothers work has a negative effect on children (Roper Organization 1995, 1990). This belief is supported by sociological research that finds that mothers' employment does not in itself affect children's well-being. Far more important is having the financial resources available to support one's family. Interestingly enough, public debate seldom revolves around whether fathers' engagement in work has any influence on children's development.

People's beliefs about appropriate gender roles have evolved as women's and men's lives have changed. Less than half of men (47 percent) now believe that it is best for men to hold the provider role, compared with 69 percent who thought so in 1970. Men's support for women's roles in the family and at work, however, varies across different groups.

FORCES OF SOCIAL CHANGE

The Arrival of Women's Sports

During the 1999 Women's World Soccer Cup, 90,000 people filled the Rose Bowl in Pasadena—the largest ever crowd to watch a women's sporting event. Those who watched the event on television saw major companies (such as Nike) present newly designed commercials that encouraged young girls to be strong and self-confident, compete, and develop team spirit. Who could have imagined such change just a few years ago when few women played competitive sports and there were no women sportscasters heard in the major media?

Not many years ago, few women were allowed to play competitive sports in school and, when they did, it was typically in activities judged appropriate for their gender roles. Now women's basketball on many campuses attracts big audiences (although rarely as big as for men's games). Women play in national professional leagues and are increasingly visible in sports broadcasting.

Sociological research shows that girls who play sports are likely to have higher self-esteem, greater self-confidence, lower school dropout rates, and more positive body images than girls who do not play sports (Dworkin and Messner 1999). What long-term effects do you think events like the U.S. women's victory in the World Cup soccer match might have for young women and men? More generally, how will women's increased sports participation affect the gender identities of women in your generation?

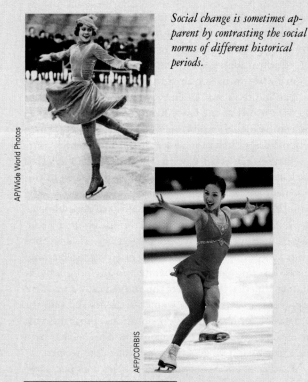

Social change is sometimes apparent by contrasting the social norms of different historical periods.

AP/Wide World Photos

AFP/CORBIS

FURTHER INFORMATION: See Conniff, Ruth. "The Joy of Women's Sports." *The Nation*, August 10–17, 1998, pp. 26–30.

Not surprisingly, women employed full time are most supportive of nontraditional gender roles, and homemakers hold the most traditional views (Cassidy and Warren 1997). Younger men and single men are more egalitarian than older married men. Hispanic men are least likely to support the idea of women earning money. Some of the differences in the attitudes of African American, Hispanic, and White men are the result of differences in their experiences; minority men are more likely to have had employed mothers, and they have different educational and employment backgrounds from White men. Sociologists have concluded that these attitude differences reflect the economic necessity that minority men attribute to women working (Wilkie 1993; Blee and Tickamyer 1995).

Despite these changes, old attitudes do not die easily. Moreover, changed attitudes do not necessarily mean changed behavior. Attitudes change as society changes; thus, it is likely that further adjustments in the attitudes of men and women are on the way because it seems unlikely that the changes in men's and women's roles will reverse in the future. Attitudes, however, are only part of the problem of persistent gender inequality. There is still significant resistance to change in institutionalized gender practices. Social change requires more than adjusting individual attitudes. Supporting more egalitarian gender relations also means changing social institutions.

Legislative Change

Much legislation prohibits, in theory, overt discrimination against women. In addition to the Equal Pay Act of 1963, the Civil Rights Act of 1964, adopted as the result of political pressure from the civil rights movement, banned discrimination in voting and public accommodations and required fair employment practices. Specifically, Title VII of the Civil Rights Act of 1964 forbids discrimination in employment on the basis of race, color, national origin, religion, or sex.

The passage of the Civil Rights Act, and Title VII in particular, opened up new opportunities to women in employment and education. This was further supported by Title IX, adopted as part of the Educational Amendments of 1972, which forbids gender discrimination in any educational institution receiving federal funds. Title IX prohibits colleges and universities from receiving federal funds if they discriminate against women in any program, including athletics. Adoption of this bill radically altered the opportunities available to women students and laid the foundation for many of the coeducational programs that are now an ordinary part of college life. This law has been particularly effective in opening up athletics to women.

Passage of antidiscrimination policies does not, however, guarantee their universal implementation. Has equality been achieved? In college sports, men still outnumber women athletes by more than two to one, and there is still more scholarship support for male athletes than for women. Title IX allows institutions to spend more money on male athletes if they outnumber women athletes, but it also stipulates that the number of male and female athletes should be roughly proportional to their representation in the student body. Studies of student athletes show that although there has been improvement in support for women's athletics since the implementation of Title IX, there is still a long way to go toward equity in women's sports (Lederman 1992; Sigelman and Wahlbeck 1999). Title IX is being challenged by some who argue that it has reduced opportunities for men in sports. Proponents of maintaining strong enforcement of Title IX counter this, however, by noting that budget reductions in higher education, not Title IX per se are responsible for any reduction in athletic opportunities for men. Furthermore, they point out that men still greatly predominate in school sports.

In the workplace, a strong legal framework for gender equity is in place, yet equity has not been achieved. Since most women work in different jobs from men, principles of equal pay for equal work do not address all the inequities women experience in the labor market. **Comparable worth** is the principle of paying women and men equivalent wages for jobs involving similar levels of skill. This policy recognizes that men and women tend to work at different jobs. Comparable worth goes beyond the concept of equal pay for equal work by creating job evaluation systems that assess the degree of similarity between different kinds of jobs. Comparable worth schemes have been introduced in only a few places, but where comparable worth plans have been implemented, women's wages have improved (Blum 1991; Michel et al. 1989; Steinberg 1992; Jacobs and Steinberg 1990).

Many victories in the fight for gender equity are now also at risk. *Affirmative action* is a method for opening opportunities to women and minorities, which specifically redresses past discrimination by taking positive measures to recruit and hire previously disadvantaged groups. Affirmative action has been especially effective in opening new opportunities for women. The national discussion of affirmative action, fueled in part by conservative resistance to these policies, is a good illustration of what many would call the limitations of liberal philosophy. Because affirmative action promotes gender- and race-specific actions to remedy the effects of past discrimination, its opponents have argued that it constitutes reverse discrimination. Those who want social policies that are gender and race blind (a classic liberal position, now articulated by conservatives, as well) find it difficult to support policies that are not gender and race blind. The problem is that gender and race inequalities continue even though these inequities may not always result from conscious discrimination. Proponents of affirmative action argue that as long as the structural conditions of gender and race inequality exist, there is still a need for race- and gender-conscious actions designed to address persistent injustices. This viewpoint was upheld by the U.S. Supreme Court in 2003 in the case *Grutter v. Bollinger* (see prior chapter).

One solution to the problem of gender inequality is to have more women in positions of public power. Is increasing the representation of women in existing institutions enough? Without reforming the sexism in the institutions, change will be limited and may generate benefits only for groups who are already privileged. Feminists advocate restructuring social institutions to meet the needs of all groups, not just those who already have enough power and privilege to make social institutions work for them. The successes of the women's movement demonstrate that change is possible, but change comes only when people are vigilant about their needs.

■ *Chapter Summary*

■ *How do sociologists distinguish sex and gender?*

Sociologists use the term *sex* to refer to biological identity and *gender* to refer to the socially learned expectations associated with members of each sex. *Biological determinism* refers to explanations that attribute complex social phenomena to physical or natural characteristics.

■ *How is gender identity learned?*

Gender socialization is the process by which gender expectations are learned. One result of socialization is the formation of *gender identity*. Overly conforming to gender roles has a number of negative consequences for both women and men, including eating disorders, violence, and poor self-concepts. *Homophobia* plays a role in gender socialization because it encourages strict conformity to gender expectations.

■ *What is a gendered institution?*

Gendered institutions are those where the entire institution is patterned by gender. Sociologists analyze gender both as a learned attribute and as an institutional structure.

■ *What is gender stratification?*

Gender stratification refers to the hierarchical distribution of social and economic resources according to gender. Most societies have some form of gender stratification, although they differ in the degree and kind. Gender stratification in the United States is obvious in the differences between men's and women's wages.

■ *How do sociologists explain the continuing earnings gap between men and women?*

There are multiple ways to explain the pay gap. *Human capital theory* explains wage differences as the result of individual differences between workers. *Dual labor market theory* refers to the tendency for the labor market to be organized in two sectors: the primary and secondary markets. *Gender segregation* persists and results in differential pay and value attached to men's and women's work. *Overt discrimination* against women is another way that men protect their privilege in the labor market.

■ *Are men increasing their efforts in housework and child care?*

Many men are now more engaged in housework and childcare than was true in the past, though women still provide the vast majority of this labor. Balancing work and family has resulted in social speedup, making time a scarce resource for many women and men.

■ *What is feminist theory?*

Different theoretical perspectives help explain the status of women in society. *Feminist theory* links this explanation to the desire for improving women's lives. The major theoretical perspectives in feminism are *liberal feminism, socialist feminism, radical feminism,* and *multiracial feminism*. Each emphasizes different aspects of women's place in society.

■ *When seen in global perspective, what can be observed about gender?*

The economic condition of women and men in the United States is increasingly linked to the fortunes of people in other parts of the world. Women provide much of the cheap labor for products made around the world. Worldwide, women work as much or more than men, though they own little of the world's property and are underrepresented in positions of world leadership.

■ *What are the major social changes that have affected women and men in recent years?*

Public attitudes about gender relations have changed dramatically in recent years. Women and men are now more egalitarian in their attitudes, although women still perceive high degrees of discrimination in the labor force. A legal framework is in place to protect against discrimination, but legal reform is not enough to create gender equity.

▪ *Key Terms*

biological determinism 267	homophobia 274
comparable worth 290	human capital theory 279
discrimination 281	labor force participation
dual labor market	rate 279
theory 280	liberal feminism 285
feminism 285	matriarchy 278
feminist theory 285	multiracial feminism 286
gender 265	occupational
gender apartheid 277	segregation 281
gender identity 269	patriarchy 278
gender segregation 281	radical feminism 286
gender socialization 268	sex 264
gender stratification 277	sexism 277
gendered institution 275	socialist feminism 285
hermaphroditism 267	

▪ *Researching Society with MicroCase Online*

You can see the results of actual research by using the Wadsworth MicroCase® Online feature available to you. This feature allows you to look at some of the results from national surveys, census data, and some other data sources. You can explore this easy-to-use feature on your own, but try this example. Suppose you want to know some social facts, such as:

Do some people still think that men are better suited for politics than women?

To answer this question, go to **sociology.wadsworth .com/andersen_taylor/essen3e**, select MicroCase Online from the left navigation bar, and follow the directions there to analyze the data described below.

Data file: GSS

Task: Auto-Analyzer

Primary Variable: MEN BETTER

Questions:

Once you have your results, answer the following questions.

1. For each of the demographic variables listed in the following table, indicate whether there is a significant effect. If so, indicate which category is most likely and least likely to believe men are better suited emotionally for politics than are women.

Socio-Demographic Variable	Is the Overall Effect Significant?	Category Least Likely	Category Most Likely
Religion	Yes No		
Political Party	Yes No		
Age	Yes No		
Education	Yes No		

2. Using the information you entered in the above table, describe the person who is most likely to believe men are better suited emotionally for politics than are women.

3. Describe the person least likely to believe men are better suited for politics than women.

4. Are men more likely to believe this than women? Does this finding surprise you?

5. Do African Americans and whites have different beliefs regarding women's suitability for politics?

▪ *The Companion Web Site for Sociology: The Essentials, Third Edition*

sociology.wadsworth.com/andersen_taylor/essen3e

Supplement your review of this chapter by going to the companion Web site to take one of the Tutorial Quizzes, use the flash cards to master key terms, and check out the many other study aids you'll find there. You'll also find special features such as GSS Data and Census 2000 information, data and resources at your fingertips to help you with that special project or do some research on your own.

▪ *Suggested Readings and Web Resources*

Andersen, Margaret L. 2003. *Thinking About Women: Sociological Perspectives on Sex and Gender.* 6th ed. Needham Heights, MA: Allyn and Bacon.
  This is a comprehensive review of feminist studies about women. Widely read by undergraduates, it provides an understanding of the sociological analysis of women's lives and a basic introduction to feminist thinking.

Baca Zinn, Maxine, Pierrette Hondagneu-Sotelo, and Michael Messner. 2000. *Through the Prism of Difference.* Needham Heights, MA: Allyn and Bacon.

This anthology includes articles that explore race, class, and sexual diversity among women and men. Together, the essays challenge false generalizations about women and men as uniform groups while revealing the structural forces that shape gender relations in the United States.

Collins, Patricia Hill. 1998. *Fighting Words.* Minneapolis: University of Minnesota Press.

Collins analyzes the experiences of African American women by developing a theory of Black feminism. In this context, she also examines contemporary discussions of Afrocentrism and Black women's lives, the contributions of postmodernist theory, and a global perspective on Black feminism.

Kimmel, Michael S., and Michael A. Messner. 1998. *Men's Lives.* Needham Heights, MA: Allyn and Bacon.

This is an excellent collection of articles on men's experiences. It is notable for its inclusion of diverse groups, including racial minority groups and gay men. The subjects covered include families, work, sexuality, friendships, health, and sports, among others.

The Feminist Majority
www.feminist.org

The Feminist Majority promotes feminist social policies in the United States and abroad. The Web page includes news and information about women's issues, including a site specifically for students with information about feminist action on different college campuses.

Institute for Women's Policy Research
www.iwpr.org/

This is a Washington-based research organization, working to establish public policies for the benefit of women. The Web site includes numerous publications from the Institute, which provide data and research on women's employment, poverty and welfare, work and family, and other matters.

U.S. Department of Labor: Women's Bureau
www.dol.gov/dol/wb

The Women's Bureau is an important source of government data about women's employment. The site includes references to numerous publications and fact sheets.

CHAPTER ELEVEN

Sexuality

visitor from another planet might conclude that people in the United States are obsessed with sex. A glimpse of MTV shows men and women gyrating in sexual movements. A stroll through a shopping mall reveals expensive shops selling delicate, skimpy women's lingerie. Popular magazines are filled with images of women in seductive poses trying to sell every product imaginable; even bumper stickers brag about sexual accomplishments. People dream about sex, form relationships based on sex, fight about sex, and spend money to have sex.

Ample evidence exists of sexual permissiveness in the United States. Young people are now initiating sexual activity at earlier ages. The availability of birth control has separated sex from procreation, allowing people to engage in sex just for the fun of it. Diversity in sexual partnerships is becoming more evident.

Some think that our society is overly promiscuous, that sexuality is rampant when it should be confined to the family. Sex education in schools has been challenged on the grounds that teaching young people about sex will incite them to be more promiscuous. Others say sex education is essential for the prevention of pregnancy and acquired immunodeficiency syndrome (AIDS). Sex is clearly a subject that polarizes political constituencies on various issues, such as abortion, teenage pregnancy, birth control, and gay and lesbian rights.

Others argue that our society is not sexually free enough, and point to repressive attitudes against people of diverse sexual orientations. Gay-bashing runs the gamut from joking and ridicule to extreme violence, even murder, against those believed to be lesbian or gay. Sexual repression affects heterosexuals, as well. Women

who openly engage in multiple sexual relationships may be defined as loose and immoral, whereas men's having multiple partners may be defined as earning a badge of manhood. Some religious faiths have strict mores about open sexual expression. In a sexually repressive culture, some people grow up associating sex with shame or embarrassment.

Is our society repressive or permissive? The answer is both. Neither definition completely characterizes the intricate and sometimes contradictory character of contemporary sexual behavior and attitudes. Sexuality is a complex social phenomenon. This chapter examines the social significance of sexuality and how sexual experience is shaped by society and culture. Using the sociological imagination we can see that human sexuality, like other forms of social behavior, is socially structured.

■ *Sex and Culture*

Sex would seem to be utterly natural. Pleasure and sometimes the desire to reproduce are reasons people have sex, but sexual relationships develop within a social context that establishes what sexual relationships mean, how they are conducted, and what social supports are given (or denied) to particular kinds of sexual relationships. *Sexuality is socially defined and patterned.*

From a sociological point of view, little in human behavior is purely natural, as we have learned in previous chapters. Behavior that appears to be natural is the behavior accepted by cultural customs and sanctioned by social institutions. Sex is a physiological experience, but it is not physiology alone that makes sex pleasurable. Sexuality creates intimacy between people. People engage in sex not just because it feels good, but also because it is an important part of our social identity. Void of a cultural context and the social meanings attributed to sexual behavior, people might not attribute the emotional commitments, psychological interpretations, spiritual meanings, and social significance to sexuality that it has in different human cultures.

DEBUNKING
Society's Myths

Myth: Men and women are naturally attracted to each other.

Sociological perspective: Although there may be some biological ("natural") basis for sexual orientation, sexual identity is learned through social interaction in the context of social norms, values, and institutions.

Sociologists see sexuality as shaped by social influences. We can see the social and cultural basis of sexuality in the following ways:

1. **Human sexual attitudes and behavior vary in different cultural contexts.** If sex were purely natural behavior, sexual behavior would also be uniform among all societies, but it is not. Sexual behaviors considered normal in one society might be seen as peculiar in another. For example, the common practice of French-kissing in the United States is by no means a universal practice; some societies would consider putting your tongue in another's mouth repulsive (Tiefer 1978).

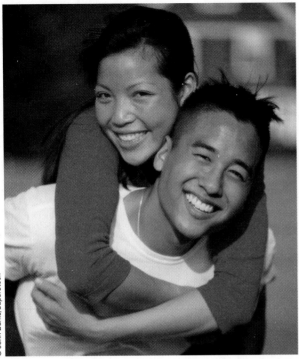

Intimate relationships, though highly personal, are also socially constructed.

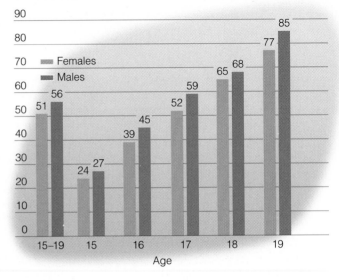

FIGURE 11.1 Sex Among Teenagers

SOURCE: Alan Guttmacher Institute. 1999. *Teen Sex and Pregnancy.* New York: The Alan Guttmacher Institute. Reproduced with the permission of the Alan Guttmacher Institute.

Culture also affects whether we define certain sexual behaviors as normal or deviant. For example, if the culture allowed men to wear dresses, would there be a category of people known as cross-dressers or transvestites?

2. Sexual attitudes and behavior change over time. Fluctuations in sexual attitudes are easy to document. For example, public opinion polls show that young people today are more permissive in their sexual values than were young people in the past, although tolerance of casual sex has decreased somewhat in recent years (Lyons 2002). Behavioral changes are harder to document in the United States because people in this culture generally consider sex to be a private matter and thus do not always talk frankly about what they do. But, we know that young people are having sex at an earlier age (see Figure 11.1). More people also experience sex before marriage than in the past, and people have more sex partners over their lifetimes (Laumann et al. 1994).

DEBUNKING
Society's Myths

Myth: Over time in a society, sexual attitudes become more permissive.

Sociological perspective: All values and attitudes develop in specific social contexts; change is not always in a more permissive direction (Freedman and D'Emilio 1988).

3. Sexual identity is learned. Like other forms of social identity, sexual identity is acquired through socialization and ongoing relationships. Information about sexuality is transmitted culturally and becomes the basis for what we know of ourselves and others. Where did you first learn about sex? For that matter, what did you learn? For some, parents are the source of information about sex and sexual behavior. For many, peers have the strongest influence on sexual attitudes. Long before young people become sexually active, they learn **sexual scripts** that teach us what is appropriate sexual behavior for each gender (Schwartz 1998; Thorne and Luria 1986). Children learn sexual scripts by playing roles—playing doctor as a way of exploring their bodies, or hugging and kissing in a way that can mimic heterosexual relationships. Role-playing teaches children social norms about sexuality. The roles learned in youth profoundly influence our sexual attitudes and behavior throughout life.

THINKING SOCIOLOGICALLY

Observe a popular children's film and describe the *sexual scripts* suggested by the film. What do these sexual scripts tell you about the *social construction of sexual identity*?

4. Social institutions channel and direct human sexuality. Social institutions, such as religion, education, or the family, define some forms of sexual expression as more legitimate than others. For example, being heterosexual is a more privileged status in society than being gay or lesbian. Examples of institutional privileges for heterosexual couples include the right to marry and, as a result, to have mutual employee health care benefits and the option to file joint tax returns.

5. **Sex is influenced by economic forces in society.** Sex sells. In the U.S. capitalist economy, sex appeal is used to hawk everything from cars and personal care products to stocks and bonds. Moreover, sexual acts are bought and sold as some people, particularly poor women, are forced to sell sexual services to earn a living. Sex workers are among some of the most exploited and misunderstood workers. Sometimes the economics of sex and the law intersect as quasi-legal sex trades are regulated in the form of red-light districts, selective enforcement, and even outright state licensing.

6. **Public policies regulate sexual and reproductive behaviors.** Prohibiting federal spending on abortion, for example, eliminates reproductive choices for women who are dependent on state or federal aid. Government decisions about which reproductive technologies to endorse will influence the choices of birth control technology available to men and to women. Government funding, or lack thereof, for sex education can influence how people understand sexual behavior. In many ways, the government intervenes in people's sexual and reproductive decision making. This fact challenges the idea that sexuality is a private matter and shows how social institutions can direct sexual behavior.

To summarize, human sexual behavior occurs within a cultural and social context. The culture defines certain sexual behaviors as appropriate or inappropriate. Like other forms of social identity, sexual identity is learned.

Sexual Politics

Sexual politics refers to the link between sexuality and power, not just within individual relationships. The feminist movement first linked sexuality to the status of women in society, pointing to the possible exploitation of women within sexual relationships. Sexual politics also refers to the high rates of violence against women and sexual minorities, and the privilege and power accorded to those presumed to be heterosexual.

The feminist and gay and lesbian liberation movements have put sexual politics at the center of the public's attention by challenging gender role stereotyping and sexual oppression (D'Emilio 1998). Among other things, this has profoundly changed public knowledge of gay and lesbian sexuality. Gay, lesbian, and feminist scholars have argued, and many now concur, that homo-

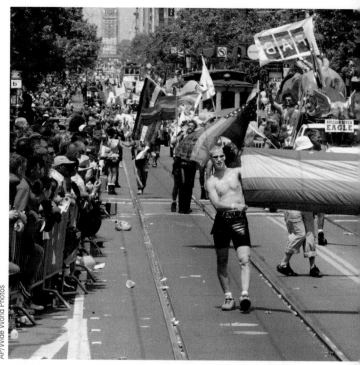

Gays, lesbians, and their allies have mobilized for social change, fostering pride and celebration, as well as a reduction over time in homophobia attitudes.

AP/Wide World Photos

sexuality is not the result of psychological deviance or personal maladjustment but is one of several alternatives for happy and intimate social relationships. The political mobilization of many lesbian women and gay men and the willingness of many to make their sexual identity public have also raised public awareness of the civil and personal rights of gays and lesbians. These changes make other changes in intimate relations possible.

The link between sex and power is well illustrated by the scandals in the Catholic Church involving sexual abuse of young boys by Catholic priests. Without a sociological perspective, you might think of this behavior solely as the result of certain individuals gone astray by violating strong moral values. But from a sociological perspective, and by using the concept of sexual politics, you can interpret sexual abuse within the church in a different light—one that might examine such issues as how the power of priests and the church bureaucracy allowed this to go undetected for so long.

Such an understanding does not excuse such behavior but points to the fact that certain institutional contexts are more prone to sexual violence than others—namely those that are marked by a highly masculine subculture, are exclusive in their membership, organized in a hierarchical fashion, and organized around norms of privacy, secrecy, and silence (Martin and Hummer 1989). The sexual abuse of young boys by priests occurs within such an institutional context. The priesthood within the Catholic Church is highly *patriarchal* (that is, power lies with men). The priest-hood is imbued with a sense of *secrecy* in the private relationship that occurs in the confessional between a parishioner, such as a young boy, and a priest. The Catholic Church is an organization marked by a clear hierarchy of *power,* and it is defined as *sacred;* thus, in some sense, it is immune from the usual forms of social regulation. These institutional characteristics, one could argue, created a climate wherein abuse could occur and be unreported for many years. Understanding the link between sex and power can also help you understand how sexual abuse occurs within other institutional settings that are marked by similar characteristics (such as the military and some families).

The Influence of Race, Class, and Gender

Sexual behavior follows gendered patterns, as well as patterns established by race and class relations (Schwartz and Rutter 1998). Cultural definitions of sexually appropriate sexual behavior differ significantly for women and men. Gender expectations emphasize passivity for women and assertiveness for men in sexual encounters. The "double standard" is the idea that different standards for sexual behavior apply to men than apply to women. Although this idea is weakening somewhat, men are still stereotyped as sexually overactive; women, less so. Women who openly violate this cultural double standard by being openly sexual are then cast in a negative light as "loose," as if the appropriate role for women is the opposite of "loose," say, "secured" or "caged." The double standard forces women into polarized roles as "good" girls or "bad" girls. The belief that women who are raped must have somehow brought it on themselves rests on the images of women as temptresses. Contrary to popular belief, men do not have a stronger sex drive than women. Men are, however, socialized more often to see sex in terms of performance and achievement, whereas women are more likely socialized to associate sex with intimacy and affection.

Sexual politics are also integrally tied to race and class inequality in society. You can see this in the sexual stereotypes that are associated with race and class. Latinas are stereotyped as either "hot" or "virgins"; Latin men are stereotyped as "hot lovers"; African American men are stereotyped as overly virile; Asian American women are stereotyped as compliant and submissive, but passionate. Class relations also produce sexual stereotypes of women and men. Working-class and poor men may be stereotyped as dangerous, whereas working-class women may be disproportionally labeled "sluts."

Class, race, and gender hierarchies historically have been justified based on claims that people of color and

women are sexually promiscuous and uncontrollable (Nagel 2003). During slavery, for example, the sexual abuse of African American women was one way that slaveowners expressed their ownership of African American people. Access to slave women's sexuality was seen as a right of the slaveowner. Under slavery, racist and sexist images of Black men and women were developed to justify the system of slavery. Black men were stereotyped as lustful beasts whose sexuality had to be controlled by the "superior" Whites. Black women were also depicted as sexual animals who were openly available to White men. A Black man falsely accused of having had sex with a White woman could be murdered (that is, lynched) without penalty to his killers (Genovese 1972; Jordan 1968). Sexual abuse was also part of the White conquest of American Indians. Historical accounts show that the rape of Indian women by White conquerors was common (Freedman and D'Emilio 1988; Tuan 1984), as is the rape of women following war and military conquest.

Poor women and women of color are the groups most vulnerable to sexual exploitation. Becoming a prostitute, or otherwise working in the sex industry (as a topless dancer, striptease artist, pornographic actress, or other sex-based occupation), is often the "court of last resort" for women with limited options to support themselves. Women who sell sex are also condemned for their behavior, more so than their male clients—further illustration of how gender stereotypes mix with race and class exploitation. Why, for example, are women, not usually men, arrested for prostitution? A sociological perspective on sexuality helps one see how sexuality is linked to other systems of social stratification.

Sex and Culture: A Global Perspective

Cross-cultural studies of sexuality show that sexual norms, like other social norms, develop differently across cultures. Take sexual jealousy. Perhaps you think that seeing your sexual partner becoming sexually involved with another person would naturally evoke jealousy—no matter where it happened. Researchers have found this not to be true. In a study comparing patterns of sexual jealousy in seven different nations (Hungary, Ireland, Mexico, the Netherlands, the United States, Russia, and the former Yugoslavia), researchers found significant cross-national differences in the degree of jealousy when women and men saw their partners kissing, flirting, or being sexually involved with another person (Buunk and Hupka 1987). Likewise, tolerance for gay and lesbian relationships varies significantly in different societies around the world. Germany has recently legalized gay

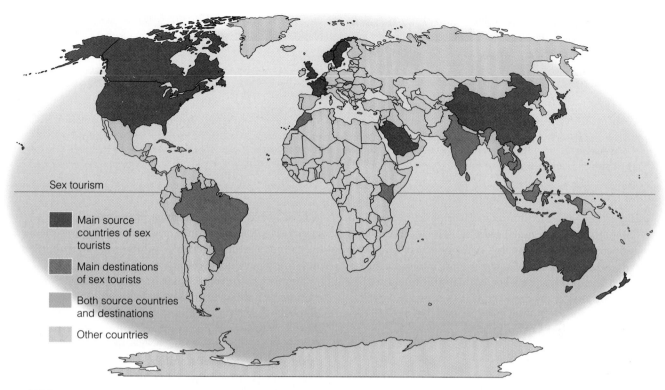

MAP 11.1 Viewing Society in Global Perspective: The International Sex Trade
If you think about sex as an international business, not just as a matter of morality, what sociological questions would you ask? How might you design a study to answer the questions you develop?

SOURCE: Seager, Joni. 1997. *The State of Women in the World Atlas, new edition.* New York: Penguin, pp. 54–55. Copyright © 1997 by Joni Seager, text. © 1997 by Myriad Editions Ltd., maps and graphics. Used by permission of Viking Penguin, a division of Penguin Group (USA) Inc.

and lesbian relationships, allowing them to register same-sex partnerships and have the same inheritance rights as heterosexual couples. The new law does not, however, give them the same tax advantages nor can same-sex couples adopt children. Cross-cultural studies can make someone more sensitive to the varying cultural norms and expectations that apply to sexuality in different contexts. Different cultures simply view sexuality differently. In Islamic culture, for example, women and men are viewed as equally sexual, although women's sexuality is seen as potentially disruptive and needing regulation (Mernissi 1987).

Sex is also big business, and it is deeply tied to the world economic order. As the world has become more globally connected, an international sex trade has flourished—one that is linked to economic development, world poverty, tourism, and the subordinate status of women in many nations. The *international sex trade,* sometimes also referred to as the "traffic in women" (Rubin 1975), refers to the use of women, worldwide, as sex workers in an institutional context where sex itself is a commodity. Sex is marketed in an international marketplace, and women as sex workers are

used to promote tourism, cater to business and military men, and support a huge industry of nightclubs, massage parlors, and teahouses (Enloe 1989).

"Sex capitals" are places where prostitution openly flourishes, such as in Thailand and Amsterdam. Sex is an integral part of the world tourism industry. In Thailand, for example, men as tourists outnumber women by a ratio of three to one. Planeloads of businessmen come to Thailand as tourists, sometimes explicitly to buy sexual companionship. Hostess clubs in Tokyo similarly cater to corporate men. One fascinating study, where the researcher worked as a hostess in a Tokyo club, shows how the men's behavior in these clubs is linked to the expression of their gender identity among other men (Allison 1994). In Amsterdam prostitutes sit in windows in red-light districts to attract customers.

Sociologists see the international sex trade as part of the global economy, contributing to the economic development of many nations and supported by the economic dominance of certain other nations. As with other businesses, the products of the sex industry may be produced in one region and distributed in others. (Think, for example,

TABLE 11.1 Sociological Theories About Sexuality

	Functionalism	Conflict Theory	Symbolic Interaction
Sexual identity	Learned through socialization into roles	Enforced through the power of dominant groups and institutions	Emerges through social relationships
Sexual norms	Support consensus in society	Defined by most powerful groups in society	Defined through symbolic systems, such as the media
Sex and social institutions	Sexual norms contribute to stability of social institutions	Dominant sexual orientations receive more institutional benefits	Change as social beliefs define new possibilities

of the pornographic film industry centered in Southern California, but distributed globally). The sex trade is also associated with world poverty; sociologists have found that the weaker the local economy, the more important the sex trade. The international sex trade is also implicated in problems such as the spread of AIDS worldwide, as well as the exploitation of women where women have limited economic opportunities (Altman 2001).

■ *Sexuality and Sociological Theory*

Is sex something that should be restricted to the family? Should prostitution be legal? Is being gay or lesbian a matter of choice or biological destiny? Any one of these or other questions about sexuality could be the subject of a sociological study. Sociological theory puts an analytical framework around the study of sexuality, examining its connection to social institutions and current social issues. How do the major sociological theories frame an understanding of sexuality?

Sex: Functional or Conflict-Based?

The three major sociological frameworks—functionalist theory, conflict theory, and symbolic interaction—take divergent paths in interpreting the social basis of human sexuality (see Table 11.1).

Functionalist theory with its emphasis on the interrelatedness of different parts of society tends to depict sexuality in terms of its contribution to the stability of social institutions. Norms that restrict sex to marriage encourage the formation of families. Similarly, beliefs that give legitimacy to heterosexual behavior, but not homosexual behavior, maintain a particular form of social organization where gender roles are easily differentiated and the nuclear family is defined as the dominant social norm. From this point of view, regulating sexual behavior is functional for society because it prevents the

instability and conflict that more liberal sexual attitudes supposedly generate. Functionalists would also explain the call for a return to "family values" as producing the uniformity in values necessary for social order.

Conflict theorists see sexuality as part of the power relations and economic inequality in society. Power is the ability of one person or group to influence the behavior of another. Power relations in society influence the power that some sexual groups have over others and influence power within sexual relationships, as discussed earlier in the section on sexual politics. Conflict theorists argue that sexual relations are linked to other forms of stratification, namely, race, class, and gender inequality. According to this perspective, sexual violence such as rape or sexual harassment is the result of power imbalances, specifically between women and men. At the same time, because conflict theorists see economic inequality as a major basis for social conflict, they tie the study of sexuality to economic institutions. They link the international sex trade to poverty, the status of women in society, and the economics of international development and tourism (Enloe 1989). Still, conflict theorists do not see all sexual relations as oppressive. Sexuality is an expression of great social intimacy. In connecting sexuality and inequality, conflict theorists are developing a structural analysis of sexuality, not condemning sexual intimacy.

Because both functionalism and conflict theory are macrosociological theories (that is, they take a broad view of society, seeing sexuality in terms of the overall social organization of society), they do not tell us much about the social construction of sexual identities. This is where the sociological framework of symbolic interaction is valuable.

The Social Construction of Sexual Identity

Symbolic interactionists see sexual identity in any form as created within specific cultural, historical, and social contexts. Symbolic interaction theory uses a **social construction perspective** to interpret sexual identity as learned, not inborn (Connell 1992; Lorber 1994). From

The hijras of India are a sexual minority group; this "man" is considered to be a "third gender"—neither man nor woman. Hijras provide a good illustration of the socially constructed basis of sexuality.

a social construction perspective, one's sexual identity is not innate (that is, inborn). Instead, it develops through social experiences.

Is there a biological basis to sexual identity? This is fiercely debated, especially as it regards gay and lesbian sexuality. Some have searched for a so-called "gay gene." Although the evidence that sexual orientation is biological is inconclusive, biology certainly plays a role in human sexual expression. Hormonal fluctuations, sexual physiology, and perhaps some genetic factors are elements of sexual desire, although the extent to which biology shapes sexual identity is debatable. Sociologists conclude that "the social world tends to mold biology as much as biology shapes humans' sexuality" (Schwartz and Rutter 1998: 5). An example of this comes from anthropological evidence that in some cultures women do not believe that orgasm exists even though, biologically, it does. Cultural dictates about male ejaculation have encouraged men to conserve semen on the presumption that its release will lessen men's intelligence or cause insanity. In the eighteenth century, European and American writers advised men that masturbation robbed them of their physical powers and that instead they should apply their minds to the study of business (Freedman and D'Emilio 1988; Schwartz and Rutter 1998). Although biology cannot be ignored, social and cultural experiences shape and direct our sexual identities. Moreover, sexual identity is constructed over the life course, not just determined at birth.

From a social constructionist perspective, different sexual identities are possible, each learned through the process of socialization. Heterosexuals are sexually attracted to members of the other sex; homosexuals are attracted to the same sex; and bisexuals are attracted to members of both sexes. **Sexual orientation** is how individuals experience sexual arousal and pleasure. The social construction perspective considers no form of sexual identity more natural than another. Instead, this perspective explains all forms of sexual identity as created through the self-definitions that people develop through relationships with others. This point of view sees sexual identity as developing from exposure to different cultural expectations and, in the case of heterosexual identity, adherence to dominant cultural expectations. People who develop heterosexual identities have experiences and receive social supports that reinforce heterosexual identity. This is called **compulsory heterosexuality,** the idea that heterosexual identity is not a choice but an expectation. Institutions define heterosexuality as the only legitimate form of sexual identity and enforce it through social norms and sanctions, including peer pressure, socialization, law, economic policies, and, at the extreme, violence (Rich 1980).

The social construction of sexual identity is also revealed by studies of the "coming out" process. **Coming out** is the process of defining oneself as gay or lesbian in a series of events and redefinitions during which a person comes to see herself or himself as having a gay identity. In coming out, one consciously labels that identity either to oneself or others (or both). Coming out is usually not the result of a single homosexual experience. If it were, there would be far more self-identified homosexuals than there are because researchers find that a substantial portion of both men and women eventually have some form of homosexual experience. Some people experience periods of ambivalence about their identity and may switch back and forth between lesbian, heterosexual, and bisexual identities (Rust 1993). This indicates, as the social construction perspective suggests, that identity is created and not fixed over the course of a life.

People do not necessarily move predictably through certain sequences in developing a sexual identity. Although they may experience certain milestones in their identity development, some people move back and forth over time between lesbian or gay identities and heterosexual identities. Some people may engage in lesbian or gay behavior but not adopt a formal definition of themselves as lesbian or gay. Certainly many gays and lesbians never adopt a public definition of themselves as gay or lesbian, instead remaining "closeted" for long periods of time, if not entire lifetimes.

This shows how sensitive sexual identity is to its social context. Changing social contexts (including dominant group attitudes, laws, and systems of social control), relationships with others, and even changes in the language used to describe different sexual identities all affect people's self-definition. As an example, political movements can encourage people to adopt a sexual identity that they previously had no context to understand. Further, studies of gay and lesbian academics whom are publicly "out" have shown they experience negative consequences in terms of job opportunities, promotions, and inclusion in social networks (Taylor and Raeburn 1995). Such a context can discourage those who are lesbian or gay from publicly acknowledging their identities.

■ *Contemporary Sexual Attitudes and Behavior*

People in the United States today are generally more sexually liberal and have greater tolerance for diverse sexual lifestyles and practices. The U.S. public has also become much more accepting of gays and lesbians. Today 54 percent of the public think that homosexuality is an acceptable lifestyle, compared to 38 percent in 1992; and 50 percent think that homosexual relations between consenting adults should be legal (Gallup Organization 2003; see Figure 11.2). This position was strongly endorsed by the U.S. Supreme Court in 2003 when it ruled that state laws against sodomy were unconstitutional (*Lawrence* v. *Texas*). The decision essentially states that private sexual relations are a constitutional liberty, a conclusion widely interpreted as a major victory for gay rights. Although it will likely be the basis for political, judicial, and legislative action in the years ahead, the Massachusetts Supreme Court ruling in 2003 that allowed gay marriage because of constitutional rights to liberty also reflects a changing social climate on issues of gay and lesbian rights.

> ## THINKING SOCIOLOGICALLY
>
> Using some of the *survey data* that have been discussed in this chapter, select a set of questions that tap contemporary *sexual attitudes* among young people. Ask these questions to a *sample* of men and women on your campus. What do your results reveal about the influence of gender on attitudes about sex? (You should note how you develop your sample; it will not likely be a random or representative sample, so you should interpret your results knowing the limitations of your research method.)

Changing Sexual Values

Public opinion is now a mix of greater liberalism for some along with more conservatism for others on matters involving sexuality. While adults are much less likely now than in the past to think that premarital sex

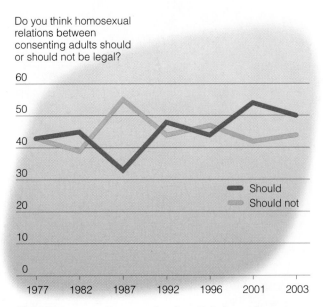

FIGURE 11.2 Support for Gay Relationships

DATA: Gallup Poll. 2003. "Homosexual Relations." Princeton, NJ: The Gallup Organization. **www.gallup.com**

is wrong (38 percent now versus 68 percent in 1969), among teens the number who think premarital sex is morally wrong is now greater than in the late 1970s (see the box, "Doing Sociological Research"). College students, generally quite liberal on sexual matters, have also over time changed their opinions about sexual relationships. Thus, in 1974, 46 percent agreed strongly or somewhat that it was all right for people who really like each other to have sex even if they have known each other only for a very short time. By the 1990s, this had increased to 51 percent, but has now dropped to 42 percent (Higher Education Research Institute 2002).

Attitudes about sex vary significantly, depending on various social characteristics. Significant differences exist between women and men. For example, men are more likely than women—62 percent versus 56 percent—to think that homosexual relations are morally wrong. Significant gender differences are also evident among young people. Figure 11.3 gives an indication of the consequences of the gap in women's and men's descriptions of reasons for their first sexual experience. The gender gap in sexual attitudes may explain some of the personal conflicts that men and women experience about sex.

Sexual attitudes are also shaped by age and education. For example, young people (those under thirty) are more likely than older people (especially those over 65) to think that homosexuality is an acceptable lifestyle. These differences likely reflect not only the influence of age, but also historical influences on different generations. Better educated people are more likely to think that homosexuality is acceptable (Newport 2003). Religion also matters.

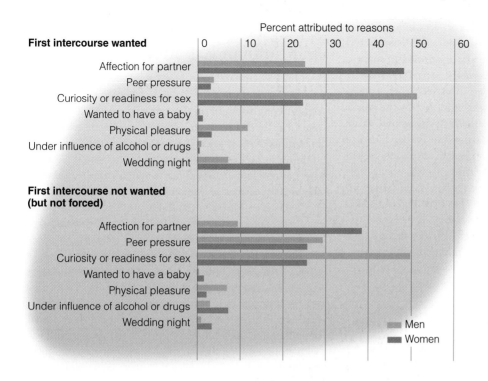

Percent attributed to reasons

FIGURE 11.3 Reasons for First Sexual Intercourse

DATA: From Michael, Robert T., John H. Gagnon, Edward O. Laumann, and Gina Kolata. 1994. *Sex in America: A Definitive Survey.* Boston: Little, Brown, and Company, p. 93.

First intercourse wanted
- Affection for partner
- Peer pressure
- Curiosity or readiness for sex
- Wanted to have a baby
- Physical pleasure
- Under influence of alcohol or drugs
- Wedding night

First intercourse not wanted (but not forced)
- Affection for partner
- Peer pressure
- Curiosity or readiness for sex
- Wanted to have a baby
- Physical pleasure
- Under influence of alcohol or drugs
- Wedding night

Men
Women

DOING SOCIOLOGICAL RESEARCH

Teens and Sex: Are Young People Becoming More Sexually Conservative?

By the late 1990s several national studies reported a decline in sexual activity among teens. The percentage of sexually active teens has dropped from the early 1990s, rates of teen pregnancy have fallen, teens are having fewer abortions, and the rate of sexually transmitted diseases among teens has declined. Does this herald a growth in sexual conservatism among young people and the success of policies encouraging sexual abstinence?

Sociologists Barbara Risman and Pepper Schwartz reviewed the various studies exploring teen sexuality and conclude that the answer to these questions is more complex than typically assumed. Their review of several national studies finds that most of the change in teen sex activity is attributable to changes in behavior of boys, not girls. The number of high school boys who are virgins has increased. Girls' behavior has not changed significantly, except among African American girls whose rates of sexual activity have declined, nearly matching that of White and Hispanic girls. Risman and Schwartz conclude that sexual behavior of boys is then becoming more like girls, the implication being that boys and girls are likely to begin their sexual lives within the context of romantic relationships.

While many declare that the changes in teen sexual behavior mean a decline in the sexual revolution, Risman and Schwartz disagree. Certainly fear of AIDS, education about safe sex, and some growth in conservative values have contributed to changes in teen sexual norms. Risman and Schwartz show that numerous factors influence sexual behavior among teens, just as among adults. They suggest that sexuality is a normal part of adolescent social development and conclude that the sexual revolution—along with the revolution in gender norms—is generating more responsible, not more problematic, sexual behavior among young people.

Questions to Consider:

1. Are people in your age group generally sexually conservative or sexually liberal? What factors influence young people's attitudes about sexuality?
Keywords: sexual conservatism, sexual liberalism

2. Following from the question above, what evidence would you need to find out if young people in your community are more liberal than young people in the past? How would you design a study to investigate this question?
Keywords: sexual attitudes and youth, sexual revolution and age

We have included InfoTrac College Edition keywords at the end of each question to make it easier for you to find more to read on these topics. Go to **www.infotrac-college.com,** an online library, to begin your search.

SOURCE: Risman, Barbara, and Pepper Schwartz. 2002. "After the Sexual Revolution: Gender Politics in Teen Dating." *Contexts* 1 (Spring): 16–24.

Those who attend church regularly are less likely to support homosexuality. Not surprisingly, single people, and those living in urban areas are also more liberal in supporting gay and lesbian lifestyles (Newport 2003).

Public opinion on controversial matters such as teen pregnancy, AIDS, child care, women's place in the workplace, and abortion rights tap underlying sexual value systems, often generating public conflicts that indicate these underlying differences. In general, sexual liberalism is associated with greater education, youth, urban lifestyle, and political liberalism on other social issues. In other words, the meaning that sex has for different groups shapes their support for or resistance to other social issues. The fact that sexual attitudes differ by factors such as gender, age, education, class, religion, and other sociological variables shows that sexual meaning systems are shaped by the social and political systems within society.

Sexual Practices of the U.S. Public

Sexual practices are difficult to document. What we know about sexual behavior is typically drawn from surveys. Most of these surveys ask about sexual attitudes, not actual behavior. What people say they do may differ significantly from what they actually do.

The most comprehensive survey of the sexual practices of the U.S. public was conducted by a team of sociologists in the early 1990s (Laumann et al. 1994; Michael et al. 1994). Researchers surveyed a national random sample of nearly 3500 adults. Although their study has some limitations (for example, they do not analyze gay, lesbian, or bisexual behavior separately from heterosexual behavior), it is the most current study of sexual behavior using careful social science research methods. This study and others tell us several things about the sexual practices of the U.S. public.

- *Young people are becoming sexually active at an earlier age* (Alan Guttmacher Institute 1999b).

- *The proportion of young people who are sexually active has increased,* particularly among young women (Alan Guttmacher Institute 1994).

- *Having only one sex partner in one's lifetime is rare* (Laumann et al. 1994).

- *A significant number of people have extramarital sex* (Laumann et al. 1994).

- *A significant number of people are lesbian or gay* (Laumann et al. 1994; Janus and Janus 1993).

- *For those who are sexually active, sex is relatively frequent.* Almost two-thirds of Americans report having sex a few times per month or two to three times per week (Laumann et al. 1994).

Understanding Gay and Lesbian Experience

Sociological understanding of sexual identity has developed largely through new studies of lesbian and gay experience. Long thought of only in terms of social deviance (see Chapter 6), gays and lesbians have been stereotyped in traditional social science. But the feminist and gay liberation movements have discouraged this approach, arguing that gay and lesbian experience is merely one alternative in the broad spectrum of human sexuality.

There is a growing research literature examining different aspects of gay life. **Queer theory** is a new perspective that interprets various dimensions of sexuality as thoroughly social and constructed through institutional practices. Queer theory underscores the idea that sexual identity evolves and can change over the life course. Instead of seeing heterosexual or homosexual attraction as fixed in biology, queer theory interprets society as forcing these sexual boundaries, or dichotomies, on people. By challenging the "either/or" thinking that one is either gay or straight, queer theory has challenged the idea that only one form of sexuality is normal and all other forms are deviant or wrong. As a result, queer theory has opened up fascinating new studies of gay, straight, bisexual, and transsexual identities and introduced the idea that sexual identity is a continuum of different possibilities for sexual expression and personal identity (Nardi and Schneider 1997; Seidman 1994; Stein and Plummer 1994; Rust 1995).

The institutional context for sexuality within the United States, as well as other societies, is one where homophobia permeates the culture. **Homophobia** is the fear and hatred of homosexuality. It is deeply embedded in people's definitions of themselves as men and women, and manifested in prejudiced attitudes toward gays and lesbians, as well as overt hostility and violence against people suspected of being gay. Homophobia is a learned attitude, as are other forms of negative social judgments about particular groups. Boys are often raised to be manly by repressing so-called feminine characteristics in themselves. Being called a "fag" or a "sissy" is one peer sanction that socializes a child to conform to particular gender roles. Similarly, verbal attacks on lesbians called "butch" are a mechanism of social control because ridicule can be interpreted as encouraging social conformity.

THINKING SOCIOLOGICALLY

Keep a diary for one week and write down as many examples of *homophobia* and *heterosexism* as you observe in routine social behavior. What do your observations tell you about how *compulsory heterosexuality* is enforced?

Homophobia produces many misunderstandings about gay people. One misunderstanding is that gays have a desire to seduce straight people. There is little evidence that this is true. And, if we look at who is most likely to commit sex crimes, we find that heterosexual men are more likely to commit sex crimes than homosexual men. Homosexual men convicted of child molestation are, however, almost seven times more likely to be imprisoned than are heterosexual men who are convicted as child molesters, even when they have the same criminal record (Walsh 1994).

Fears that gay and lesbian parents will have negative effects on their children are also unsubstantiated by research. The ability of parents to form good relationships with their children is far more significant in children's social development than is their parents' sexual orientation (Stacey and Biblarz 2001).

Other myths about gay people are that they are mostly White men with large discretionary incomes who work primarily in artistic areas and personal service jobs (such as hairdressing). This stereotype prevents people from recognizing that gays and lesbians come from all racial–ethnic groups, some of whom are working class or poor and employed in a wide range of occupations (Gluckman and Reed 1997). Some lesbians and gays are also elderly even though the stereotype defines gay people as primarily young or middle aged (Smith 1983). These different misunderstandings reveal just a few of the many unfounded myths about gays and lesbians. Support for these attitudes comes from homophobia, not from empirical truth.

Heterosexism refers to the institutionalization of heterosexuality as the only socially legitimate sexual orientation. Heterosexism is rooted in the belief that heterosexual behavior is the only natural form of sexual expression and that homosexuality is a perversion of "normal" sexual identity. Heterosexism is reinforced through institutional mechanisms that project the idea that only heterosexuality is normal. Institutions also provide different benefits to people presumed to be heterosexual. Businesses and communities, for example, rarely recognize the

UNDERSTANDING DIVERSITY

Gay-Bashing and Gender Betrayal

Carmen Vázquez has related gay-bashing to the phenomenon she labels *gender betrayal*. She explains this by writing:

At the simplest level, looking or behaving like the stereotypical gay man or lesbian is reason enough to provoke a homophobic assault. Beneath the veneer of the effeminate gay male or the butch dyke, however, is a more basic trigger for homophobic violence. I call it gender betrayal.

The clearest expression I have heard of this sense of gender betrayal comes from Doug Barr, who was acquitted of murder in an incident of gay bashing in San Francisco that resulted in the death of John O'Connell, a gay man. Barr is currently serving a prison sentence for related assaults on the same night that O'Connell was killed. . . . When asked what he and his friends thought of gay men, he said, "We hate homosexuals. They degrade

our manhood. We was brought up in a high school where guys are football players, mean and macho. Homosexuals are sissies who wear dresses. I'd rather be seen as a football player."

Doug Barr's perspective is one shared by many young men. I have made about 300 presentations to high school students in San Francisco, to boards of directors and staff of nonprofit organizations, and at conferences and workshops on the topic of homophobia or "being lesbian and gay." Over and over again, I have asked, "Why do gay men and lesbians bother you?" The most popular response to the question is, "Because they act like girls," or "Because they think they're men." I have even been told, quite explicitly, "I don't care what they do in bed, but they shouldn't act like that."

They shouldn't act like that. Women who are not identified by the relationship to a man, who value their female friendship, who like and

are knowledgeable about sports, or work as blue-collar laborers and wear what they wish are very likely to be "lesbian-baited" at some point in their lives. Men who are not pursuing sexual conquests of women at every available opportunity, who disdain sports, who choose to stay at home and be a house-husband, who are employed as hairdressers, designers, or house-cleaners, or who dress in any way remotely resembling traditional female attire (an earring will do) are very likely to experience the taunts and sometimes the brutality of "fag bashing."

The straitjacket of gender roles suffocates many lesbians, gay men, and bisexuals, forcing them into closets without an exit and threatening our very existence when we tear the closet open.

SOURCE: Carmen Vazquez. 1992. "Appearances." Pp. 157–166 in *Homophobia: How We All Pay the Price*, edited by Warren J. Blumenfeld. Boston: Beacon Press.

Douglas McFadd/Getty Images

Although gay marriage is not supported by law in most states, many gays and lesbians define themselves as married and form couples with a long-term commitment to each other.

legal rights of people in homosexual relationships, although this is changing. Within an institution, individual beliefs can reflect heterosexist assumptions. Thus a person may be accepting of gay and lesbian people (that is, not be homophobic) but still benefit from heterosexual privileges. At the behavioral level, heterosexist practices can exclude lesbians and gays, such as when co-workers talk about dating the other sex, assuming that everyone is interested in a heterosexual partner.

In the absence of institutional supports from the dominant culture, lesbians and gays have invented their own institutional support systems. Gay communities and gay rituals, such as gay pride marches, affirm gay and lesbian identities and provide a support system that is counter to the dominant heterosexual culture. Those who remain in the closet deny themselves this support system.

The absence of institutionalized roles for lesbians and gays affects the roles they adopt within relationships. Despite popular stereotypes, gay partners typically do not assume roles as the dominant or submissive sexual partner. They are more likely to adopt roles as equals. Gay couples and lesbian couples are also more likely than heterosexual couples to both be employed, another source of greater equality within the relationship. Re-

searchers have also found that the quality of relationships among gay men is positively correlated with the social support the couple receives from others (Smith and Brown 1997; Metz et al. 1994; Harry 1979).

Lesbians and gays are a minority group in our society, one that has been denied equal rights and is singled out for negative treatment in society. In sociology, the term minority group has a specific meaning. *Minority groups* are not necessarily numerical minorities; they are groups with similar characteristics (or at least perceived similar characteristics) who are treated with prejudice and discrimination (see Chapter 9). As a minority group, gays and lesbians have organized to advocate for their civil rights and to be recognized as socially legitimate citizens. Some organizations and municipalities have enacted civil rights protections on behalf of gays and lesbians, typically prohibiting discrimination in hiring. The Supreme Court ruled in 1996 (*Romer v. Evans*) that gays and lesbians cannot be denied equal protection of the law. This ruling overturned ordinances that had specifically denied civil rights protections to lesbians and gays (Greenhouse 1996a). The case in 2003 that overturned state laws against sodomy also provides new legal protection for gays and lesbians. The implications of this case for domestic partner benefits, child custody and adoption by gay and lesbian parents, and gay marriage are not yet known, but will likely be determined in the courts in the years ahead.

▪ Sex and Social Issues

In studying sexuality, sociologists tap into some highly contested social issues of the time. Birth control, reproductive technology, abortion, teen pregnancy, pornography, and sexual violence are all subjects of public concern and are important in the formation of social policy. Debates about these issues hinge in part on attitudes about sexuality and are shaped by race, class, and gender relations.

Although most people think of sex in terms of interpersonal relationships, sexual norms are deeply intertwined with various social problems. Social issues such as birth control, reproductive technology, pornography, teen pregnancy, and sexual violence can generate personal troubles that have their origins in the structure of society—recall the distinction made by C. Wright Mills between personal troubles and social issues. These issues show us how the structure of society contributes to some of our nation's social problems.

Birth Control

The availability of birth control is now less debated than it was in the not too distant past, but this important reproductive technology has been strongly related to the status of women in society (Gordon 1977). Reproduction has been controlled by men; to this day, men mostly define the laws and make the scientific decisions about what types of birth control will be available. Women are also most likely seen as responsible for reproduction because it is a presumed part of their traditional role. At the same time, changes in birth control technology have also made it possible for women to change their roles in society given that breaking the link between sex and reproduction has freed women from some traditional constraints.

The right to birth control is a recently won freedom. It was not until 1965 that the Supreme Court, in *Griswold v. Connecticut,* defined the use of birth control as a right, not a crime. This ruling originally applied only to married people; unmarried people were not extended the same right until 1972, in the Supreme Court decision, *Eisenstadt v. Baird.* Today, birth control is routinely available over the counter, but there is heated debate about whether access to birth control should be curtailed for the young, while youths are experimenting with sex at younger ages and risking teenage pregnancy and AIDS. Some argue that increasing access to birth control will only encourage more sexual activity among the young.

Class and race relations have also had a role in shaping birth control policy. In the mid-nineteenth century, increased urbanization and industrialization ended the necessity for large families, especially in the middle class, because fewer laborers were needed to support the family. Early feminist activists such as Emma Goldman and Margaret Sanger also saw birth control as a way of freeing women from unwanted pregnancies and allowing them to work outside the home if they chose. As the birthrate fell among White upper- and middle-class families during this period, these classes feared that immigrants, the poor, and racial minorities would soon outnumber them.

The eugenics movement of the early twentieth century grew from the fear of domination by immigrant groups. **Eugenics** sought to apply scientific principles of genetic selection to "improve" the offspring of the human race. It was explicitly racist and class-based, calling for, among other things, the compulsory sterilization of those who eugenicists thought were unfit. Eugenicist arguments appeal to a public that fears the social problems that emerge from race and class inequality; instead of attributing these problems (such as crime) to the structure of society, blame the genetic composition of the least powerful groups in society.

With the rise of new reproductive technologies there is potential for a new eugenics movement. Sophisticated prenatal screenings make it possible to identify fetuses with presumed defects. Might the society then try to weed out those perceived as undesirables—the disabled, certain racial groups, certain sexes? Will parents try to produce "designer children"? If boys and girls are differently valued, one sex may be more frequently aborted, a frequent practice in India and China—two of the most populous nations on earth. Because of population pressures, state

policy in China, for example, encourages families to have only one child. Because girls are less valued than boys, the aborting and selling of girls is common, and has created a U.S. market for the adoption of Chinese baby girls.

New Reproductive Technologies

Developments in the technology of reproduction have ushered in new sexual freedoms, but they have also raised questions for social policy. Practices such as surrogate mothering, in vitro fertilization, and new biotechnologies of gene splicing, cloning, and genetic engineering mean that reproduction is no longer inextricably linked to biological parents (Rifkin 1998). A child may be conceived through means other than sexual relations between one man and one woman. One woman may carry the child of another. Offspring may be planned through genetic engineering. A sheep can be cloned (that is, genetically duplicated). Are humans next? With such developments, those who could not otherwise conceive children (such as infertile couples, single women, or lesbian couples) are now able to do so, thereby raising new questions. To whom are such new technologies available? Which groups are most likely to sell reproductive services, which groups to buy? What are the social implications of such changes?

There are no simple answers to such questions, but sociologists would point first to the class, race, and gender dimensions of these issues (Roberts 1997). Poor women, for example, are far more likely than middle-class or elite women to sell their eggs or offer their bodies as biological incubators. Groups that can afford new, costly methods of reproduction may do so at the expense of women whose economic need places them in the position of selling themselves for economic needs.

Breakthroughs in reproductive technology raise especially difficult questions for makers of social policy. There are no traditions to guide us on questions considered outlandish and remote just a few years ago. Our thinking about sexuality and reproduction will have to evolve. Although the concept of reproductive choice is important to most people, choice is conditioned by the constraints of race, class, and gender inequalities in society. Like other social phenomena, sexuality and reproduction are shaped by their social context.

Abortion

Abortion is one of the most seriously contended political issues. Of the U.S. public, 38 percent support abortion rights at least under most circumstances, and another 42 percent support it in a few circumstances (see Figure 11.4). Despite all the controversy, public support for abortion rights has remained relatively constant over the last twenty years.

The right to abortion was first established in constitutional law by the *Roe v. Wade* decision in 1973. In *Roe v.*

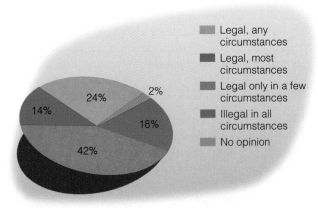

Legend:
- Legal, any circumstances
- Legal, most circumstances
- Legal only in a few circumstances
- Illegal in all circumstances
- No opinion

FIGURE 11.4 Attitudes Toward Abortion

DATA: Saad, Lydia. 2003. "Roe v. Wade Has Positive Public Image."
The Gallup Poll Tuesday Briefing (January 20), Princeton, NJ: The Gallup
Organization. **www.gallup.com**

Wade, the Supreme Court ruled that at different points during a pregnancy, separate but legitimate rights collide—the right to privacy, the right of the state to protect maternal health, and the right of the state to protect developing life. To resolve this conflict of rights, the Supreme Court ruled that pregnancy occurred in trimesters. In the first, women's right to privacy without interference from the state prevails; in the second, the state's right to protect maternal health takes precedence; in the third, the state's right to protect developing life prevails. In the second trimester, the government cannot deny the right to abortion, but it can insist on reasonable standards of medical procedure. In the third, abortion may be performed only to save the life or health of the mother. More recently, the Supreme Court has allowed states to impose restrictions on abortion but it has not, to date, overturned the legal framework of *Roe v. Wade.*

Data on abortion show that it occurs across social groups, although certain patterns do emerge. The abortion rate has declined since 1980 from a rate of 29.3 to 21.3 (per 1000 women aged 15–44). Young women are the most likely to have abortions, although fewer teenagers are having abortions than in prior years. Black and Hispanic women are more likely to have abortions than White women. Poor and low income women account for half of all abortions, and the majority of women having abortions are mothers (Finer and Henshaw 2003; Alan Guttmacher Institute 2003).

The abortion issue provides a good illustration of how sexuality has entered the political realm. Abortion rights activists and antiabortion activists hold very different views about sexuality and the roles of women. Antiabortion activists tend to believe that giving women control over their fertility breaks up the stable relationships in traditional families. They tend to view sex as something that is sacred, and they are disturbed by changes that make sex less restrictive. Abortion rights activists see women's control over reproduction as essential for their independence. They also tend to see sex as an experience that develops intimacy and communication between people who love each other. The abortion debate can thus be interpreted as a struggle over the right to terminate a pregnancy, as well as a battle over differing sexual values, and a referendum on the nature of men's and women's relationships (Luker 1984).

Pornography

Little social consensus has emerged about the acceptability and effects of pornography. Part of this debate is about defining what is obscene. The legal definition of obscenity is one that changes over time and in different political contexts. Public agitation over pornography has divided people into those who think it is solidly protected by the First Amendment, those who want it strictly controlled, those who think it should be banned for moral reasons, and those who think it must be banned because it harms women. Who is right?

Research shows that exposure to violent pornography in a laboratory setting affects sexual attitudes. After exposure to violent pornography, men are more likely to see victims of rape as responsible for their assault, less likely to regard them as injured, and more likely to accept the idea that women enjoy rape. These effects are found, however, only after exposure to pornography that is both sexually explicit and violent (Donnerstein et al. 1987). Little evidence supports the assertion that exposure to pornography in general increases sexual promiscuity or sexual deviance.

Despite public concerns about pornography, a two-thirds majority think pornography should be protected by the constitutional guarantees of free speech and a free press. At the same time, people believe that pornography dehumanizes women. Women tend to be more negative than men about pornography, perhaps because pornography generally portrays women in demeaning ways. The controversy about pornography is not likely to go away because it taps so many different sexual values among the public.

Teen Pregnancy

Each year about one million teenage girls (age 15–19) have babies in the United States; 78 percent of these births are unplanned. The United States has the highest rate of teen pregnancy among developed nations, even though levels of teen sexual activity around the world are roughly comparable. Teens account for almost 12 percent of all births. Teen pregnancy has declined since 1990; most analysts think this is because an increase in the use of birth control and some teens abstaining from sex. Still, one in five teen women who have sex become pregnant in a given year.

Although the rate of pregnancy among teens has dropped, so has the rate of marriage for teens who be-

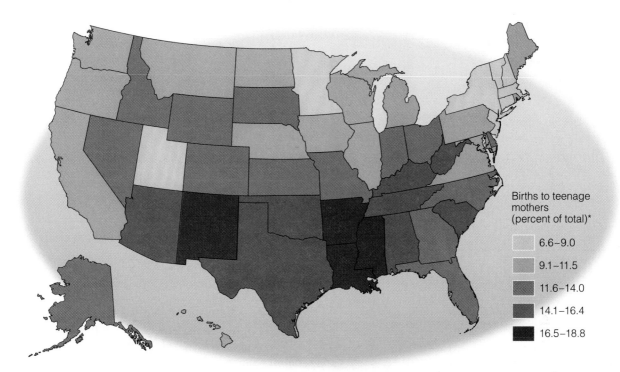

MAP 11.2 Mapping America's Diversity: Births to Teenage Mothers

The rate of teen pregnancy has been declining in the United States, but so has the likeli-hood of marriage for teen mothers who give birth. **What are the consequences of these two phenomena, and what regional differences do you think influence the rate of teen pregnancy in different areas of the country?**

*Represents registered births. Excludes births to nonresidents of the United States. Based on 100 per-cent of births in all states.

DATA: From the U.S. Census Bureau. 2002. *Statistical Abstract of the United States, 2002*. Washington, DC: U.S. Government Printing Office, p. 65.

come pregnant. Thus, most babies born to teens will be raised by single mothers—a departure from the past when teen mothers often got married (U.S. Census Bureau 2002; Alan Guttmacher Institute 2002). What concerns people about teen parents is that teens are more likely to be poor than other mothers, although sociologists have cautioned that this is because teen mothers are more likely poor *before* getting pregnant (Luker 1996). Teen parents are among the most vulnerable of all social groups.

DEBUNKING
Society's Myths

Myth: Providing sex education to teens only encourages them to become sexually active.

Sociological perspective: Comprehensive sex education actually delays the age of first intercourse; abstinence-only education has not been shown to be similarly effective in delaying intercourse (Kirby 1997; Risman and Schwartz 2002).

Teenage pregnancy correlates strongly with poverty, lower educational attainment, joblessness, and health problems. Teen mothers have a greater incidence of problem pregnancies and are most likely to deliver low-birth-weight babies, a condition associated with a myriad of other health problems. Teen parents face chronic unemployment and are less likely to complete high school than those who delay childbearing. Many continue to live with their parents, although this is more likely among Black teens than among Whites. Given the higher rates of poverty among African Americans, the costs of adolescent pregnancy then fall most heavily on those families least able to help, as we saw in the "Doing Sociological Research" box in Chapter 1 (Kaplan 1996).

Although teen mothers feel less pressure to marry now than in the past, if they raise their children alone, they suffer the economic consequences of raising children in female-headed households—the poorest of all income groups. Teen mothers report that they do not marry because they do not think the fathers are ready for marriage. Sometimes their families also counsel them against marrying precipitously. These young women are

Teen pregnancy rates have actually fallen, but still pose challenges for social policies about birth control and support for teen parents.

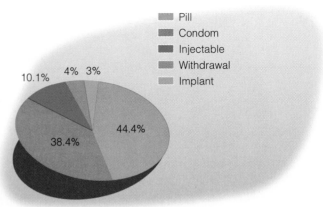

FIGURE 11.5 Contraceptive Use Among Teens

SOURCE: Alan Guttmacher Institute. 1999. *Teen Sex and Pregnancy.* New York: The Alan Guttmacher Institute.

often doubtful about men's ability to support them. They want men to be committed to them and their child, but they do not expect their hopes to be fulfilled (Farber 1990). Research shows that low-income single mothers are distrustful of men, especially after an unplanned pregnancy. They think they will have greater control of their household if they remain unmarried. Many teen mothers also express fear of domestic violence as a reason for not marrying (Edin 2000). Both Black and White teen parents see marriage as an impediment to their career ambitions, although Black teen mothers are more likely than Whites to continue attending school (Farber 1990; Trent and Harlan 1990).

Why do so many teens become pregnant given the widespread availability of birth control? One-third of teenagers use no contraceptive the first time they have sexual intercourse, typically delaying the use of contraceptives until several months after they become sexually active. A sexually active teenager not using contraceptives has a 90 percent chance of becoming pregnant within the first year of sexual intercourse (Alan Guttmacher Institute 1999a). Teens are more likely to use contraceptives if they are in a serious, not just a casual, relationship (Manning et al. 2000). In recent years, the percentage of teens using birth control has increased (especially condom use), al-

though the pill is still the most widely used method (see Figure 11.5; Alan Guttmacher Institute 1999a).

Sociologists have argued that the effective use of birth control requires a person to identify himself or herself as sexually active (Luker 1975). Teen sex, however, tends to be episodic. Teens who have sex on a couple of special occasions may not identify themselves as sexually active and may not feel obliged to take responsibility for birth control. Despite many teens initiating sex at an earlier age, social pressure continues to discourage them from defining themselves openly, or even privately, as sexually active.

Teen pregnancy is integrally linked to the gender expectations of men and women in society. Some teen men consciously avoid birth control, thinking it takes away from their manhood. Teen women often romanticize motherhood, thinking that becoming a mother will give them social value they do not otherwise have. For teens in disadvantaged groups, motherhood confers a legitimate social identity on those otherwise devalued by society (Horowitz 1995). Although their hopes about motherhood are not realistic, they indicate how pessimistic the teenagers feel about their lives that are often marked by poverty, a lack of education, and few good job possibilities (Ladner 1986). For young women to romanticize motherhood is not surprising in a culture where motherhood is defined as a cultural ideal for women, but the ideal can seldom be realized when society gives mothers little institutional or economic support.

Sexual Violence

Before the development of the feminist movement, sexual violence was largely hidden from public view. One great success of the women's movement has been to identify, study, and advocate better social policies to address the problems of rape, sexual harassment, domestic violence, incest, and other forms of sexual coercion. Feminists have argued that sexual coercion is not just a matter of sexuality, but also a form of power relations shaped by the social inequality between women and men. In the thirty years or so that these issues have been identified as serious social problems, volumes of research have been published on these different subjects, and numerous organizations and agencies have been established to serve victims of sexual abuse and to advocate reforms in social policy.

Rape and sexual violence were covered in Chapter 6 on deviance and the criminal justice system, in keeping with the argument that these are forms of deviant and criminal behavior, not expressions of human sexuality. Here we point out that various forms of sexual coercion (rape, domestic violence, and sexual harassment) can best be understood (and therefore changed) by understanding how social institutions shape human behavior and how social interactions are influenced by social factors such as gender, race, age, and class.

Take, for example, the phenomenon now known as *acquaintance rape* (sometimes also called *date rape*). Acquaintance rape is forced and unwanted sexual relations by someone who knows the victim (even if only a brief acquaintance). This kind of rape is common on college campuses, although it is also the most underreported form of rape. Researchers estimate, based on surveys, that 15 to 25 percent of college women will experience some form of acquaintance rape (Rubenzahl and Corcoran 1998).

Studies show that, although rape is an abuse of power, it is related to people's gender attitudes. College men, for example, are more likely than women to see heterosexual relations as adversarial. Men are also more likely to believe in various rape myths (Reilly et al. 1992), such as that women mean yes when they say no or that women's dress is a signal that they want sex or that women precipitate rape by their behavior. Studies find that acquaintance rape is more likely to occur in some organizational contexts than others, especially in organizations set up around a definition of masculinity as competitive, involving alcohol abuse, and where women are defined as sexual prey. This is one explanation given for the high incidence of rape in some college fraternities (Martin and Hummer 1989; Stombler and Padavic 1997).

Research on violence against women also finds that Black, Hispanic, and poor White women are more likely to be victimized by various forms of violence, including rape (U.S. Bureau of Justice Statistics 2002). African American and American Indian women and men report the highest incidence of intimate partner violence; Asian American-Pacific Islanders have the lowest incidence (Tjaden and Thoennes 2000). Studies also find that Black women are more aware of their vulnerability to rape than are White women, and are more likely to organize themselves to resist rape collectively (Stombler and Padavic 1997).

In sum, sociological research on sexual violence shows how strongly sexual coercion is tied to the status of diverse groups of women in society. Rather than explaining sexual coercion as the result of maladjusted men or the behavior of victims, feminists have encouraged a view of sexual coercion that links it to an understanding of dominant beliefs about the sexual dominance of men and the sexual passivity of women. Researchers have shown that those holding the most traditional gender role stereotypes are most tolerant of rapists and least likely to give credibility to victims of rape (Marciniak 1998; Varelas and Foley 1998). Understanding sexual violence requires an understanding of the sociology of sexuality, gender, race, and class in society.

Sex and Social Change

You have seen in this chapter how sexual attitudes and behaviors have changed in society. As with other forms of social behavior, sexual behavior is not static. Sexual norms, beliefs, and practices emerge as society changes. As we will see later, some major changes affecting sexual relations come from changes in gender roles. But technological change, as well as the emphasis on consumerism in the United States, also affects sexuality. As you think about sex and social change, you might try to imagine what other social factors influence human sexual behavior.

The Sexual Revolution

The **sexual revolution** refers to the widespread changes in men's and women's roles and a greater public acceptance of sexuality as a normal part of social development. Many changes associated with the sexual revolution have been changes in women's behaviors. Essentially, the sexual revolution has narrowed the differences in the sexual experiences of men and women. The feminist and the gay and lesbian movements have put the sexual revolution at the center of public attention by challenging gender role stereotyping and sexual oppression, profoundly changing our understanding of gay and lesbian sexuality.

The sexual revolution has meant greater sexual freedom, especially for women, but it has not eliminated the influence of gender in sexual relationships. As we saw in studying sexual politics, sexuality is still nested within a system of power relations—power relations that, despite the sexual revolution, continue to influence how different groups are defined and treated in sexual terms.

Technology, Sex, and Cybersex

Technological change has also brought new possibilities for sexual freedom. One significant change is the widespread availability of the birth control pill. Sex is no longer necessarily linked with reproduction; new sexual norms associate sex with intimacy, emotional ties, and physical pleasure (Freedman and D'Emilio 1988). These sexual freedoms are not equally distributed among all groups, however. For women, sex is still more closely tied to reproduction than it is for men because women are still more likely to take the responsibility for birth control.

Contraceptives are not the only technology influencing sexual values and practices. Now the Internet has introduced new forms of sexual relations as many people seek sexual stimulation from pornographic Web sites or online sexual chat rooms. Cybersex, as sex via the Internet has come to be known, can transform sex from a personal, face-to-face encounter to a seemingly anonymous relationship with mutual online sex. This introduces new risks; for example, two-thirds of those visiting chat rooms are adults masquerading as children (Lamb 1998; Wysocki 1998; Cooper and Scherer 1999). The Internet has introduced new forms of deviance that are difficult to regulate (see the box, "Taking on Social Issues: Sex, Censorship, and Cyberspace").

Commercializing Sex

While the sexual revolution has brought new freedoms and new dangers in expression of sexuality, it has also resulted in more commercialized sex. Sex has been defined as a commodity. Definitions of sexuality in the culture are heavily influenced by the advertising industry, which narrowly defines what is considered "sexy." Thin women, White women, and rich women are all depicted as more sexually appealing in the mainstream media. Images defining "sexy" are also explicitly heterosexual. The commercialization of sex uses women and, increasingly, men in demeaning ways. Poor women are also most likely to have to sell their sexuality for economic survival by working in the sex trade. Thus, although the sexual revolution has removed sexuality from many of its tradi-

---

FORCES OF SOCIAL CHANGE

Technology and the Sexual Revolution

In 1960 the federal Food and Drug Administration gave approval for marketing a new oral contraceptive: the birth-control pill. Initially available only to married women, but now the most widely used form of birth control, the pill is arguably one of the major sources of the sexual revolu-

tion. Initially some expressed fear that the widespread availability of the pill would lead to "sexual excess." By providing an easy and reliable way to have sex without getting pregnant, the pill helped redefine sex as recreation, not reproduction, thereby contributing to changes in public sexual mores.

New forms of contraceptive technology now promise to make birth control even easier, but they do create social controversy. Implants, "the shot" (referring to contraceptive injections), and RU-486 (a pill containing the drug mifepristone that, taken after having sex, induces abortion) all invoke a variety of debates. Some people take the position that the increased ease of birth control leads to promiscuity, especially among young people. In a different view, others note the race and class bias that is reflected in the use of these new technologies because poor women, women of color, and women in poor countries are far more likely to be coerced into using these forms of birth control, often without regard for their long-term effects. RU-486 is widely used in Europe, but has only limited availability in the United States because of controversies over abortion. How do you see technological innovations as influencing sexuality in society, and what social policies are needed to ensure they are used fairly?

Give the Gift of Love & Life
Very Special Egg Donor Needed
Our Donor will have the following qualities:
Caucasian • Under 30 years old
• Athlete for Athletic Family
• Proven college level athletic ability preferred—family waiting
Compensation is $100,000
All expenses will be paid in addition to your compensation
Paid to you and/or the charity of your choice
Please Call Our Family's Representative:
Louisa V. Troemel, Phd, M.F.C.C.
1-800-990-BABY
www.families2000.com, info@families200.com   Your gift will bring boundless joy.

Courtesy www.families2000.com

New reproductive technologies provide new possibilities for those who want to bear children, but also raise new social and ethical issues that can be debated by the public.

FURTHER RESOURCES: Roberts, Dorothy. 1997. *Killing the Black Body: Race, Reproduction and the Meaning of Liberty.* New York: Vintage Books.

tional constraints, the inequalities of race, class, and gender still shape sexual relationships and values.

■ *Chapter Summary*

■ *In what sense is sexuality, seemingly so personal an experience, a part of social structure?*

Sexual relationships develop within a social and cultural context. Sexuality is learned through socialization, is channeled and directed by social institutions, and reflects the race, class, and gender relations in society.

■ *What evidence is there of contemporary sexual attitudes and behavior?*

Contemporary sexual attitudes vary considerably by social factors such as age, gender, race, and religion. Sexual behavior has also changed in recent years. Young people initiate sex at an earlier age. Although the public believes in marital fidelity, many people have extramarital affairs. The number of gays and lesbians in the population, though debated, is significant. Cultural expectations about sexuality are also deeply influenced by gender expectations in the society.

■ *What does sociological theory have to say about sexual behavior?*

Functionalist theory depicts sexuality in terms of its contribution to the stability of social institutions. *Conflict theorists* see sexuality as part of the power relations and economic inequality in society. *Symbolic interaction* focuses on the social construction of sexual identity.

■ *What is meant by the social construction of sexual identity?*

Sociologists see sexual identity, whatever its form, as constructed through socialization experiences. They have moved away from studying gay and lesbian experience as deviant behavior. Debate continues about the underlying origins of homosexuality, although evidence for a biological basis of homosexuality is not as strong as the evidence for social causes. Homophobia is the fear and hatred of homosexuals. Heterosexism is the institutionalization of heterosexuality as the only socially legitimate sexual orientation.

■ *How is sexuality related to contemporary social issues?*

Sexuality is related to some of the most difficult social problems—including birth control, abortion, reproductive technologies, teen pregnancy, pornography, and sexual violence. Such social problems can be understood by analyzing the sexual, gender, class, and racial politics of society.

■ *How is sex related to social change?*

The sexual revolution refers to widespread changes in the roles of men and women, and a greater acceptance of sexuality as a normal part of social development. The sexual revolution has been fueled by social movements, such as the feminist movement and the gay and lesbian rights movement. Technological changes, such as the development of the pill, have also created new sexual freedoms. Now, sexuality is also influenced by the growth of cyberspace and its impact on personal and

TAKING ON SOCIAL ISSUES

Sex, Censorship, and Cyberspace

With widespread access to the Internet, pornography has become more easily available in a seemingly anonymous context. Studies show that one-third of Internet users will visit some site with sexual content. Some worry that this makes pornography easily accessible, particularly to children. This has stimulated debate over how to regulate the Internet. What policies are currently in place regarding pornography and the Internet? What issues arise in balancing concerns about access to pornography with the First Amendment?

Taking Action

Go to the Taking Action exercise on the companion Web site at **sociology.wadsworth.com/ andersen_taylor/essen3e** to learn more about an organization that addresses this topic.

Sexually explicit images are easily available on the Internet, raising new policy questions about balancing the values of First Amendment freedoms of free speech and access to information with questions about censorship.

© Tim Crosby/Liaison/Getty Images

sexual interactions. At the same time, sex is also treated as a commodity in this society—it is bought and sold and used in selling various products.

■ Key Terms

coming out 301	sexual orientation 301
compulsory	sexual politics 297
heterosexuality 301	sexual revolution 311
eugenics 307	sexual scripts 296
heterosexism 305	social construction
homophobia 304	perspective 300
queer theory 304	

■ Researching Society with MicroCase Online

You can see the results of actual research by using the Wadsworth MicroCase® Online feature available to you. This feature allows you to look at some of the results from national surveys, census data, and other data sources. You can explore this easy-to-use feature on your own, but try this example. Suppose you want to know some social facts, such as:

The last time you had sex, was it with someone you were in an on-going relationship with?

To answer this question, go to **sociology.wadsworth .com/andersen_taylor/essen3e,** select MicroCase Online from the left navigation bar, and follow the directions there to analyze the data described below.

Data file: GSS

Task: Auto-Analyzer

Primary Variable: RELATESEX

Questions:

Once you have your results, answer the following questions.

1. People in which age group are most likely to have had sex outside of an ongoing relationship?
    a. <30
    b. 30–49
    c. 50 and up
2. What percentage of those under the age of 30 had their last sexual experience outside of an ongoing relationship?
3. Are the differences larger or smaller than you would have expected? Do you think the differences are due to changes in sexual mores over time or because people's attitudes change as they grow older?

■ The Companion Web Site for Sociology: The Essentials, *Third Edition*

sociology.wadsworth.com/andersen_taylor/essen3e

Supplement your review of this chapter by going to the companion Web site to take one of the Tutorial Quizzes, use the flash cards to master key terms, and check out the many other study aids you'll find there. You'll also find special features such as GSS Data and Census 2000 information, data and resources at your fingertips to help you with that special project or do some research on your own.

■ Suggested Readings and Web Resources

Altman, Dennis. 2001. *Global Sex.* Chicago: University of Chicago Press.
Analyzing sex as big business, Altman discusses the global dimensions of the sex trade. He shows the connection between the growth of the sex trade and national poverty, as well as describing the international networks through which sex is bought and sold.

Gold, Jodi, and Susan Villari, eds. 1999. *Just Sex: Students Rewrite the Rules on Sex, Violence, Equality and Activism.* Lanham, MD: Rowman and Littlefield.
This collection includes the writings of young student activists who have worked on campuses to stop sexual violence. The book includes a review of university policies against gender violence, as well as personal testimonies and scholarly essays on sex, gender, and violence on university campuses.

Irvine, Janice M. 2002. *Talk About Sex: The Battles over Sex Education in the United States.* Berkeley: University of California Press.
Irvine analyzes the politics surrounding debates about sex education. Her book is a sociological analysis of sexual morality and its relationship to liberal and conservative politics.

Schwartz, Pepper, and Virginia Rutter. 1998. *The Gender of Sexuality.* Thousand Oaks, CA: Pine Forge Press.
This review of sociological perspectives on sexuality links the study of sexuality to gender roles in society.

Alan Guttmacher Institute
www.agi-usa.org/
An organization that produces numerous reports on sexual activity and contraceptive practices.

Families and Religion

Suppose you were to ask a large group of people in the United States to describe their families. What would they say? Many would describe divorced families. Some would describe single-parent families, most likely headed by a woman. Some would describe stepfamilies with new siblings and a new parent stemming from remarriage. Others would describe gay or lesbian households in which a single gay parent or a couple of the same sex is raising children. Also included would be adoptive families and families with foster children. Others would describe the so-called traditional family with two parents living as husband and wife in the same residence as their biological children. The variety of descriptions would reflect the enormous diversity in families today. Indeed, families have become so diverse that it is no longer possible to speak of "the family" as if it were a single thing.

The traditional *family ideal*—a father employed as the breadwinner and a mother at home raising children—has long been established as the family to which we should all aspire. The family ideal has been communicated through a variety of sources, including the media, religious doctrine, and socialization within families. Few families now conform to this ideal, and the number of families that ever did is probably fewer than generally imagined (Coontz 1992). Families conforming to this family type will face new challenges, not the least of which may be the difficulty of living on one income. Many families also feel that they are under siege by changes in the society.

Families have an enormous influence on our personal lives and the relationships we form. The emotional climate within families ranges from joyous, loving, and intimate to traumatic, conflict-ridden, and sorrowful. The emotional grounding we acquire in a family is carried with us throughout our lives. Many live in loving families, where the family provides stability and nurturing care for its members. But the popular image of families as loving units that provide refuge from the impersonal, hectic world outside is not shared by everyone. Family affairs are believed to be private, but as an institution, the family is very much part of the public agenda. Many people believe that "family breakdown" is the cause for society's greatest problems. Public policies shape family life directly and indirectly, intentionally and unintentionally, and family life itself shapes the dynamics of behavior in other institutions. Family life is now being openly negotiated in political arenas, corporate boardrooms, and courtrooms, as well as in the bedrooms, kitchens, and "family" rooms of individual households.

Many view the changes taking place in family life as positive. Women have new options and greater independence. Fathers are discovering that there can be great pleasure in domestic and child-care responsibilities. Change, however, also brings difficulties: balancing the demands of family and employment, coping with the interpersonal conflicts caused by changing expectations, and striving to make ends meet in families without sufficient financial resources. These changes bring new questions to the sociological study of families.

Sociologists address the family as a social institution. They are interested in how changes in the society affect the formation and character of families and how families, in turn, affect people's experiences in the society. People commonly believe that families are shaped by the personalities of family members. Sociologists recognize that individual personalities affect relationships with people both inside and outside of families, and they know that personality is heavily influenced by family experience. Sociologists who study families, tend to focus on different issues, such as how families are affected by the economic, political, social, and cultural institutions of the society.

The family is intertwined with other social institutions, such as the law, religion, and education. It is usually within the family that one first learns religious values and customs. Religion in the United States is also integrally tied to beliefs about how families should be organized. When people form families, they most often do so in a religious ceremony; when children are born, they are often given names derived from religious values. People sometimes feel pressure to marry someone of the same religion; indeed, most often, they do. And when someone in a family renounces religion, it can cause family conflict. Differences in religious values affect many family behaviors, including reproduction, marriage, divorce, and sexual behavior.

Even beyond the family, religion has a profound effect on society and human behavior. This is easily observed in everyday life. Church steeples dot the landscape. Invocations to a religious deity occur at the beginning of many public gatherings. The news frequently reports on events generated by religious conflict. Religious beliefs have led to extreme violence as we are witnessing attacks both in the Middle East and in the United States. But religious beliefs have also been the soul of some of the most liberating social movements, including the civil rights movement and other human rights movements around the world. Some of life's sweetest moments are marked by religious celebration, and some of its most bitter conflicts persist because of unshakable religious conviction. This means that it is important to understand religion both as an integrative force in society and as the basis for many of our most deeply rooted social conflicts.

The family and religion are, for most people, the first institutions encountered in life. They have a profound effect on who we are and the values we hold dear. In this chapter we examine both as social institutions.

THINKING SOCIOLOGICALLY

Identify two popular "family" shows on television. Devise a systematic way to conduct a content analysis of the family ideal portrayed by these shows. What do your observations reveal about how the *family ideal* is communicated through the popular media?

▪ *Defining the Family*

As a *social institution,* the family is an established social system that emerges, changes, and persists over time. Studying the family as an institution simply recognizes that families are organized in socially patterned ways. Institutions are "there"; we do not reinvent them every day, although people do make adaptive changes that result in institutions constantly evolving. Institutions shape and direct our action and make it appear that the only options available to us are those deemed acceptable by society. Perhaps you find it hard to imagine living in a family where the husband is expected to have both a wife and a concubine or where children do not live with their parents. The institutional structure of the family in this society does not support such family practices. Institutions shape both the form of families and the expectations that we have for family life.

Like other institutions, families are also shaped by their relationship to systems of inequality in society. Race, class, gender, and age stratification affect how society values certain families, and they influence the resources available to different families. In addition, these systems of stratification influence the power that individual members have within families. Children, for example, have fewer rights than adults and often the very old are relatively powerless within families. Heterosexual privileges also shape the resources available to certain families since our social institutions presume that families will be heterosexual. Those living in gay and lesbian families then have to invent new practices that are not typically supported by the institutional fabric of society.

Given the diversity among families, how do we define the family? The family has traditionally been defined as a social unit of those related through marriage, birth, or adoption who reside together in officially sanctioned relationships and who engage in economic cooperation, socially approved sexual relations, reproduction, and child rearing (Gough 1984). Changes in contemporary family life require some flexibility in this definition since not all families fit these condi-

tions. Following divorce, for example, the family does not typically share a common residence. Or, some working parents leave their children in the care of others as they pursue seasonal or regional employment, sometimes far from their families (including across national borders).

As social scientists have become more aware of the diversity in family life, they have refined their analyses to better show the different realities of family situations. Now, we can define the **family** broadly to refer to a primary group of people—usually related by ancestry, marriage, or adoption—who form a cooperative economic unit to care for any offspring (and each other) and who are committed to maintaining the group over time (adapted from Lamanna and Riedmann 2003: 10).

Comparing Kinship Systems

Families are part of what are more broadly considered to be kinship systems. A **kinship system** is the pattern of relationships that define people's family relationships to one another. Kinship systems vary enormously across cultures and during different times. In some societies, marriage is seen as a union of individuals; in others, marriage is seen as creating alliances between groups. The form families take in different societies varies enormously. In many societies, such as India and China, many still follow traditional practices of arranged marriage, some even involving a broker whose job it is to conduct the financial transactions and arrange the marriage ceremonies (Croll 1995). In still other societies, maintaining multiple marriage partners may be the norm. At the heart of all these diverse family patterns are the social norms and structures associated with kinship systems. Kinship systems can generally be categorized by the following features: how many marriage partners are permitted at one time; who is permitted to marry whom; how descent is determined; how property is passed on; where the family resides; and, how power is distributed.

THINKING SOCIOLOGICALLY

Interview three people from different family backgrounds (for example, a White, a Black, and a Latino student; or people from a stepfamily, a female-headed, and a male-headed household). Ask each about how his or her family is organized. Based on your interviews, how would you describe the *kinship system* of each family? What does each reveal about the *social structure* of families?

Polygamy is the practice of men or women having multiple marriage partners. Polygamy usually involves one man having more than one wife, technically referred to as *polygyny; polyandry* is the practice of a woman having more than one husband, an extremely rare custom. Within the United States, polygamy is commonly associated with Mormons, even though polygamy is practiced now only by a few Mormon fundamentalists (about 2 percent of the state population of Utah) who do so without official church sanction (Bachman and Esplin 1992; Driggs 1990; Brooke 1998).

Monogamy is the practice of a sexually exclusive marriage with one spouse at a time. It is the most common form of marriage in the United States and other Western industrialized nations. In the United States, monogamy is a cultural ideal that is prescribed through law and promoted through religious teachings. Lifelong monogamy is not always realized, however, as evidenced by the high rate of divorce and extramarital affairs. Many sociologists characterize modern marriage as *serial monogamy* in which individuals may, over a lifetime, have more than one marriage, but only one spouse at a time (Lamanna and Riedmann 2003).

Kinship systems determine whom one can marry. In contemporary U.S. society, people are expected to marry outside their own kin group; in other societies, people may be expected to marry within the kinship network. **Exogamy** is the practice of selecting mates from outside one's group; the group may be based on religion, territory, racial identity, and so forth. **Endogamy** is the practice of selecting mates from within one's group. In the United States, neither exogamy nor endogamy is mandated by law, although some religious doctrines condemn marriage outside the faith. Even if certain forms of marriage are not explicitly outlawed, society establishes normative expectations about who is an appropriate marriage partner. In general, people in the United States marry people with very similar social characteristics. For example, there is a clear tendency for people to select mates from similar class, race, religion, and educational backgrounds (Kalmijn 1991). Interracial marriage, although increasing, is still infrequent—only about 2 percent of married couples (U.S. Census Bureau 2002). The increase in interracial marriage contributes to a more multiracial and multicultural society with an increase in those who have a mixed racial identity (Root 1996; Root 2001).

UNDERSTANDING DIVERSITY

Interracial Dating and Marriage

Picture this: A young couple, stars in their eyes, holding hands, intimacy in their demeanor. Newly in love, the couple imagines a long and happy life together. When you visualize this couple, whom do you see? If your imagination reflects the sociological facts, odds are that you did not imagine this to be an interracial couple. Although interracial couples are increasingly common (and have long existed), people are more likely to form relationships with those of their same race—as well as social class, for that matter. What do sociologists know about interracial dating and marriage?

First, patterns of interracial dating are influenced by both race and gender. Black men are those most likely to say they would date a person of another race (81 percent say they would), although, along with White women, they are the least likely to say they would marry someone of another race. White women are least likely to say they would date someone of another race.

Both Blacks and Whites in interracial relationships report negative reactions from their families; the majority of these were not extremely hostile, but strong enough to put pressure on the interracial couple (Majete 1999). And although most Blacks and Whites profess to have a color-blind stance toward interracial marriages, when pressed, they raise numerous qualifications and concerns about such pairings (Bonilla-Silva and Hovespan 2000). Among college students, approval of family and friends is the strongest indicator of one's attitude toward interracial dating. Racial minorities are more accepting of interracial dating than are White students; students in the Greek system on college campuses are less accepting than non-Greeks (Khanna, Harris, and Cullers 1999).

Regardless of these attitudes, interracial marriage is on the rise, although still a small percentage of marriages formed. The most likely marriages are between Black men and White women and between Hispanics and non-Hispanics. National data on Asian American marriage is limited, but studies find that Asian Americans are increasingly likely to marry other Asian Americans, though often someone of a different Asian heritage (Shinagawa and Pang 1996). The data on interracial dating and marriage show how something seemingly "uncontrollable" like love is indeed shaped by many sociological factors.

Sources: Khanna, Nikki D., Cherise Harris, and Rana Cullers. 1999. "Attitudes Toward Interracial Dating." Paper presented at the Annual Meetings of the Society for the Study of Social Problems; Bonilla-Silva, Eduardo, and Mary Hovespan. 2000. "If Two People Are in Love: Deconstructing Whites' Views on Interracial Marriage with Blacks." Paper presented at the annual meetings of the Southern Sociological Society; Majete, Clayton A. 1999. "Family Relationships and the Interracial Marriage." Paper presented at the Annual Meetings of the American Sociological Association; Shinagawa, Larry, and Gin Yong Pang. 1996. "Asian American Panethnicity and Intermarriage." *Amerasia Journal* 22 (Spring): 127–152; *The Washington Post*. 1997.

© Tom Carter/Photo Edit

Despite the high divorce rate, marriage is a cultural ideal, and most people marry at some point in their lives.

Although interracial marriages are not common, historically a tremendous amount of energy has been put into preventing them. **Antimiscegenation laws** have prohibited marriage between various groups, including between Whites and African Americans and between Whites and Chinese, Japanese, Filipinos, Hawaiians, Hindus, and Native Americans (Takaki 1989). Laws against intermarriage have been less rigidly enforced when women of color married White men (Pascoe 1991). Antimiscegenation laws were finally declared unconstitutional in 1967—relatively recently.

Kinship systems shape the distribution of property in society, by proscribing how descent is determined. **Patrilineal kinship** systems trace descent through the father; **matrilineal kinship** systems, through the mother. **Bilateral kinship** (or bilineal) traces descent through both.

Extended and Nuclear Families

Extended families are the whole network of parents, children, and other relatives who form a family unit. Sometimes extended families, or parts thereof, live together, sharing their labor and economic resources. In some contexts, "kin" may refer to those who are not related by blood or marriage, but are intimately involved in the family support system and are considered part of the family (Stack 1974). As an example, among African Americans are women whom sociologists have termed *othermothers*. These are "women who assist bloodmothers by sharing mothering responsibilities" (Collins 1990: 119). Having othermothers is an adaptation to the demands of motherhood and work that characterizes African American women's experience, because they have always been likely to be employed and to have families. This dual responsibility in the family and work has meant that African American women have often created alternative means of providing family care for children— a situation that the majority of all women now face. An othermother may be a grandmother, sister, aunt, cousin, or a member of the local community, but she is someone who provides extensive child care and receives recognition and support from the community around her.

The system of *compadrazgo* among Chicanos is another example of an extended kinship system. In this system, the family is enlarged by the inclusion of godparents, to whom the family feels a connection that is the equivalent of kinship. The result is an extended system of connections between "fictive kin" (those who are not related by birth but are considered part of the family) and actual kin that deeply affects family relationships among Chicanos (Baca Zinn and Eitzen 2002).

In the **nuclear family** a married couple resides together with their children. Like extended families, nuclear families develop in response to economic and social conditions. The origin of the nuclear family in Western society is tied to industrialization. Before industrialization, families were the basic economic unit of society. Large household units produced and distributed goods, whether in small communities or large plantation and feudal systems where slaves and peasants provided most of the labor. Production took place primarily in households, and all family members were seen as economically vital. There was no sharp distinction between economic and domestic life because household and production were one. Women's role in the preindustrial family, although still marked by patriarchal relations, was publicly visible and economically valued. Women performed and supervised much of the household work, engaged in agricultural labor, and produced cloth and food. The work of women, men, and children was also highly interdependent. Although the tasks each performed might differ, together they were a unit of economic production.

With industrialization, paid labor was performed mostly away from the home in factories and public marketplaces. The transition to wages for labor created an economy based on cash rather than domestic production. Families became dependent on the wages that workers brought home. The shift to wage labor was accompanied by a patriarchal assumption that men should earn the "family wage" (that is, be the breadwinner). Thus, men who worked as paid laborers were paid more than women, and women became more economically dependent on men. At the same time, men's status was enhanced by having a wife who could afford to stay at home—a privilege seldom accorded to working-class or poor families. The *family wage system* has persisted and is reflected in the unequal wages of men and women today.

The unique social conditions that racial–ethnic families have experienced also affect the development of family systems. Disruptions posed by the experiences of slavery, migration, and urban poverty affect how families are formed, their ability to stay together, the resources they have, and the problems they face. For example, historically Chinese American laborers were explicitly forbidden to form families by state laws designed to regulate the flow of labor. Only a small number of merchant families were exempt from the law. Under slavery, African American families faced a constant threat of disruption. Marriages among slaves were not officially recognized by law since slaves were not considered to be citizens. Nonetheless, slaves formed families, although the children of slave parents were the legal property of the slaveowners who maintained strict control over slave life and, when it served their needs, would sell or separate family members.

During the westward expansion of the United States, many Mexicans who had settled in the Southwest were displaced. The loss of their land disrupted their families and kinship systems. In the rapidly industrializing United States, many Mexican Americans were able to find work in the mines opening in the new territories or building the railroads spreading from the East toward the Pacific. Employers apparently thought that they had better control over laborers if their families were not there to distract them, so families were typically prohibited from being with the worker. One result was the development of prostitution camps, which followed workers from place to place (Dill 1988).

Now, families continue to be influenced by forces in the social structure. Some families, particularly those with marginal incomes, find it necessary for the entire family to work to meet the economic needs of the household. Migration to a new land and exposure to new customs also disrupts traditional family values. Among Korean immigrants, for example, the majority of Korean wives are employed as full-time workers—a change from traditional Korean values that expect a wife to be totally devoted to her family. As a result, Korean women gain new opportunities and the possibility for expanded social roles. Immigrant women who enter the labor force often change their expectations about their gender role, but they also usually find that they must continue to perform traditional household tasks as well. These examples show how the ability to form and sustain nuclear families is directly linked to the economic, political, and racial organization of society.

■ *Sociological Theory and Families*

The complexity of family patterns makes it impossible to understand families from any single perspective. Is the family a source of stability or change in society? Are families organized around harmonious interests, or are they sources of conflict and differential power? How do new family forms emerge, and how do people negotiate the changes that affect families? These questions and others guide sociological theories of the family. Sociologists who study the family have used four primary perspectives in their analyses—functionalism, conflict theory, feminist theory, and symbolic interaction (see Table 12.1).

Functionalist Theory and Families

According to functionalist theory, all social institutions are organized around the needs of society. Functionalism also emphasizes that institutions are based on the consensual values that members of the society share. Functionalist theorists interpret the family as filling particular societal needs, including socializing the young, regulating sexual activity and procreation, providing physical care for family members, and giving psychological support and emotional security to individuals. According to functionalism, families exist to meet these needs. Marriage, in the functionalist framework, is conceptualized as a mutually beneficial exchange wherein women receive

TABLE 12.1 Theoretical Perspectives on Families			
	Functionalism	**Conflict Theory**	**Feminist Theory**	**Symbolic Interaction**

	Functionalism	**Conflict Theory**	**Feminist Theory**	**Symbolic Interaction**
Families	Meet the needs of society to socialize children and reproduce new members	Reinforce and support power relations in society	Are gendered institutions that reflect the gender hierarchies in society	Emerge as people interact to meet basic needs and develop meaningful relationships
	Teach people the norms and values of society	Inculcate values consistent with the needs of dominant institutions	Are a primary agent of gender socialization	Are where people learn social identities through their interactions with others
	Are organized around a harmony of interests	Are sites for conflict and diverse interests of different family members	Involve a power imbalance between men and women	Are places where people negotiate their roles and relationships with each other
	Experience social disorganization ("breakdown") when society undergoes rapid social changes	Change as the economic organization of society change	Evolve in new forms as the society becomes more or less egalitarian	Change as people develop new understandings of family life

protection, economic support, and status in return for emotional and sexual support, household maintenance, and the production of offspring (Glenn 1987). At the same time, in traditional marriages, men get the services that women provide—housework, nurturing, food service, and sexual partnership. Functionalists also see families as providing care for children, who are taught the values that society and the family purport. In addition, functionalists see the family as regulating reproductive activity, including cultural sanctions about sexuality.

According to functionalist theory, when societies experience disruption and change, institutions such as the family become disorganized, weakening social cohesion. Currently, some analysts interpret the family as "breaking down" under societal strains. Functionalist theory suggests that this breakdown is the result of the disorganizing forces that rapid social change has fostered.

Functionalists also note that, over time, other institutions have begun to take on some functions originally performed solely by the family. For example, as children now attend school earlier in life and stay in school for longer periods of the day, schools (and other caregivers) have taken on some functions of physical care and socialization originally reserved for the family. Functionalists would say that the diminishment of the family's functions produces further social disorganization, because the family no longer carefully integrates its members into society. To functionalists, the family is shaped by the template of society, and such things as the high rate of divorce and the rising numbers of female-headed and single-parent households are the result of social disorganization.

Conflict Theory and Families

Conflict theory makes different assumptions about the family as an institution, interpreting the family as a system of

power relations that reinforces and reflects the inequalities in society. Conflict theorists are interested in how families are affected by class, race, and gender inequality. This perspective sees families as the units through which the advantages, as well as the disadvantages, of race, class, and gender are acquired. Conflict theorists view families as essential to maintaining inequality in society, because they are the vehicles through which property and social status are acquired (Eitzen and Baca Zinn 2003).

The conflict perspective also emphasizes that families in the United States are shaped by capitalism. The family is vital to capitalism because it produces the workers that capitalism requires. Accordingly, within families, personalities are shaped to the needs of a capitalist system; thus families socialize children to become obedient, subordinate to authority, and good consumers. Those who learn these traits become the kinds of workers and consumers that capitalism needs. Families also serve capitalism in other ways, giving a child an allowance is how children learn capitalist habits involving money.

Whereas functionalist theory conceptualizes the family as an integrative institution (meaning it has the function of maintaining social stability), conflict theorists depict the family as an institution subject to the same conflicts and tensions that characterize the rest of society. Families are not isolated from the problems facing society as a whole. The struggles brought on by racism, class inequality, sexism, homophobia, and other social conflicts are played out within family life.

Feminist Theory and Families

Feminist theory has contributed new ways of conceptualizing the family by focusing sociological analyses on women's experiences in the family and by making gender a central concept in analyzing the family as a social institution.

Feminist theories of the family emerged initially as a criticism of functionalist theory. Feminist scholars argued that functionalist theory assumed that the gender division of labor in the household is functional for society. Feminists have also been critical of functional theory for assuming an inevitable gender division of labor within the family. Feminist critics argue that, although functionalists may see the gender division of labor as functional, it is based on stereotypes about men's and women's roles.

Influenced by the assumptions of conflict theory, feminist scholars do not see the family as serving the needs of all members equally. Quite the contrary, feminists have noted that the family is one of the primary institutions producing the gender relations found in society. Feminist theory conceptualizes the family as a system of power relations and social conflict (Thorne and Yalom 1992). In this sense, it emerges from conflict theory, but adds that the family is a gendered institution (see Chapter 10).

Symbolic Interaction Theory and Families

Symbolic interaction emphasizes that meanings people give to their behavior and that of others is the basis of social interaction. Those who study families from this perspective tend to take a more microscopic view of fam-

ilies. A symbolic interactionist might ask how different people define and understand their family experience. Symbolic interactionists also study how people negotiate family relationships, such as deciding who does what housework, how they will arrange child care, and how they will balance the demands of work and family life.

To illustrate, when people get married, they form a new relationship and new identities with specific meanings within society. Some changes may seem very abrupt—a change of name certainly requires adjustment, as does being called a husband or wife. Some changes are more subtle—how one is treated by others and the privileges couples enjoy (such as being a recognized legal unit). Symbolic interactionists see the married relationship as socially constructed; that is, it evolves through the definitions that others in society give it, as well as through the evolving definition of self that married partners make for themselves.

The symbolic interactionist perspective emphasizes the construction of meaning within families. Roles within families are not fixed, but rather evolve as participants define and redefine their behavior toward each other. Symbolic interaction is especially helpful in understanding changes in the family because it supplies a basis for analyzing new meaning systems and the evolution of new family forms over time. Each theoretical perspective used to analyze families illuminates different features of family experiences.

SOCIOLOGICAL EYE ON THE MEDIA

Idealizing Family Life

Cultural norms about motherhood and fatherhood come from many places, but the media is certainly a strong influence on how family ideals—and the ideals for mothers and fathers—are created in society. Media images of the family have certainly changed since the inception of television. In the 1930s, Hollywood Codes—that is, official rules in Hollywood about what could and could not be seen on television—meant that families were always shown with two parents, marriage intact, father working, and mom staying at home. Parents never talked about sex; indeed, it appeared as though they never had it because the Codes forbade any nudity and required that scenes of passion not excite the audience. As a result, if bedroom scenes between married couples were shown, there were typically only twin beds.

Now, family images on television are more diverse. Fathers are shown in parenting roles, and some families are divorced or re-blended following divorce; working mothers are typical, not exceptional, and children may be stepchildren. Not even all families are heterosexual, though most on television are. Still, the media continues to construct an ideal for family life—one that continues to stereotype men and women in family roles. What does research show about these social constructions?

- Most family characters are middle class.

- Men appearing with children are most likely to be shown outside; they are also more likely to be seen with boys, not girls.

- Fathers are infrequently seen with infants.

- Fathers are shown playing with, reading to, talking with, and eating with children, but not preparing meals, cleaning house, changing diapers, and so forth.

- Women are disproportionately shown in family settings in the media.

What gender stereotypes do such images project? How do they influence people's views of ideal family roles? How realistically do they portray the actual gender division of labor in families? What race and class images confound these results?

SOURCES: Kaufman, Gayle. 1999. "The Portrayal of Men's Family Roles in Television Commercials." *Sex Roles* 41 (September): 439–458. Coltrane, Scott, and Melinda Messineo. 2000. "The Perpetuation of Subtle Prejudice: Race and Gender Imagery in 1990s Television Advertising." *Sex Roles* 42 (March): 363–389.

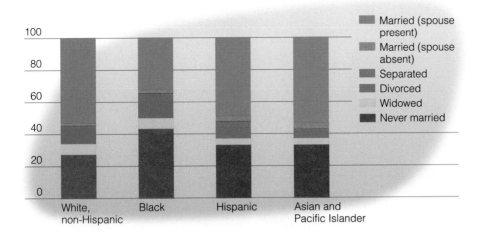

FIGURE 12.1 Marital Status of the U.S. Population

DATA: From Fields, Jason, and Lynne M. Casper. 2001. *America's Families and Living Arrangements: March 2000.* Current Population Reports. Washington, DC: U.S. Census.

▪ *Diversity Among Contemporary American Families*

Today, the family is one of the most rapidly changing of all of society's institutions (Lempert and DeVault 2000). Family forms emerge as adaptations to new societal conditions. Central to sociological analyses of the family is that *families are systems of social relationships that emerge in response to social conditions which in turn, shape the future direction of society.* There is no static or natural form for the family. Change and variation are important to see and understand when examining the sociology of families.

Among other changes in the family, families today are smaller than in the past. There are fewer births, and they are more closely spaced, although these characteristics of families vary by social class, region of residence, race, and other factors. Because of longer life expectancy, childbearing and childrearing now occupy a smaller fraction of the adult life of parents. Death, once the major cause of early family disruption, has been replaced by divorce. During earlier periods, death (often from childbirth) was more likely to claim the mother than the father of small children; thus men in the past would have been more likely than now to raise children on their own after the death of a spouse. That trend is now reversed; it is now women who are more likely to be widowed with children (Rossi and Rossi 1990).

Demographic and structural changes have resulted in great diversity in family forms. Compared to thirty years ago, married couples now make up a smaller proportion of households; single-parent households have increased dramatically, and divorced and never married people make up a larger proportion of the population (Fields and Casper 2001; see Figure 12.1). Overall, married-couple families are three-quarters of household types, but this

varies significantly by race. Single-parent households (typically headed by women), postchildbearing couples, gay and lesbian couples, and those without children are increasingly common. It is now also becoming common for people to spend more years caring for their elderly parents than they did raising their children. Few families actually experience the family ideal often portrayed in popular culture or extolled by politicians as the only desirable family form.

Female-Headed Households

Perhaps one of the greatest changes in family life has been the increase in the number of families headed by women. One-quarter of all children live with one parent. Most single-parent households (88 percent) are headed by women, though the number of households headed by single fathers has also increased. The odds of living in a single-parent household are even greater for African American and Latino children (Fields and Casper 2001).

The two primary causes for the growing number of women heading their own households are the high rate of pregnancy among unmarried teens and the high divorce rate, with death of a spouse also contributing. Although the rate of pregnancy among both White and Black teenagers, married and unmarried, is lower today than in 1960, the proportion of teen births that occur outside marriage has increased. Unlike in the past, teen women who become pregnant are now less likely to marry, thus the number of never-married mothers is higher than in the past (Fields and Casper 2001). Teen mothers, regardless of race, are among the most economically and educationally disadvantaged groups in this society. They find it difficult to get jobs, their schooling is interrupted (if not discontinued), and they are very unlikely to receive child support (Kaplan 1996). Teen fathers, also, are less likely to have completed school, and they have lower earnings (Nock 1998). The likelihood of

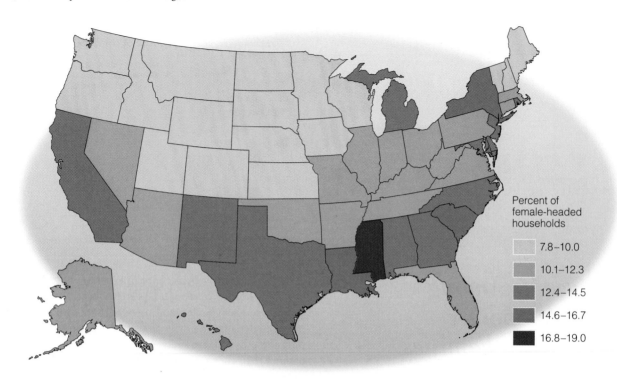

MAP 12.1 Mapping America's Diversity: Female-Headed Households
**What factors might influence the variation you see in female-headed households
in different states?**

Percent of
female-headed
households

7.8–10.0
10.1–12.3
12.4–14.5
14.6–16.7
16.8–19.0

SOURCE: U.S. Census Bureau. 2002. *Statistical Abstract of the United States, 2002.* Washington, DC:
U.S. Department of Commerce, p. 50.

poverty is great for teen parents, many of whom come from families that are already poor.

Divorce, the second reason for the increase in the number of female-headed households, also contributes to the growing rate of poverty among women, as we saw in Chapter 7. Most women see a substantial decline in their income in the year following divorce (Hoffman and Duncan 1988; Peterson 1996a, 1996b; Weitzman 1985). Contrary to popular belief, most men also experience a decline in their standard of living following divorce, mostly because of the loss of wives' income. However, the loss is not as great as it is for women and some men actually benefit economically by having more income available to them (McManus and Diprete 2001). Following divorce, of those supposed to receive child support payments (almost all of whom are mothers), only two-thirds actually receive payments, and only about one-half receive all that is due. The average amount actually paid averages only $3,797 a year (U.S. Census Bureau 2002).

The rise in female-headed households has caused considerable alarm. Many people see this trend as representing a breakdown of the family and a weakening of social values. An alternate view, however, is that the rise of female-headed households reflects the growing independence of women, some of whom are making decisions

to raise children on their own. Not all female-headed households are women who have never married, however; many are divorced and widowed women, whose circumstances may be quite different from those of a younger, never–married woman.

Some claim that female-headed households are linked to problems such as delinquency, the school dropout rate, children's poor self-image, and other social problems. Sometimes the cause of these troubles is attributed explicitly to the absence of men in the family. Sociologists, however, have not found the absence of men as the sole basis for such problems; rather, it is the presence of economic pressure faced by female-headed households, compared with male-headed families, that puts female-headed households under great strain—with the threat of poverty being by far the greatest problem they face. Among households headed by women with children, one-third live below the poverty line—19 percent among Whites (non-Hispanic), 35 percent among Blacks, 37 percent among Hispanics, and 15 percent among Asian Americans (Proctor and Dalaker 2002). Many conclude that it is not the makeup of households headed by women that is a problem, but the fact that they are most likely to be poor (Brewer 1988). This phenomenon is discussed in Chapter 7 as the *feminization of poverty.*

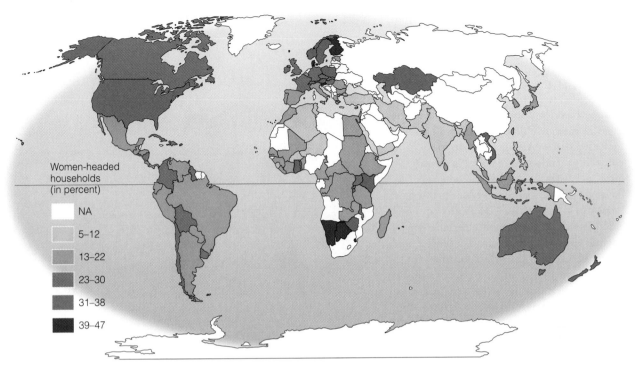

MAP 12.2 Viewing Society in Global Perspective: Female-Headed Households Around the World
What factors might influence the variation you see in female-headed households in different nations? Are these factors similar to or different from those that affect the percentage of female-headed households in different states within the United States?

SOURCE: Population Reference Bureau. 1998. *Women of Our World.* Washington, DC: Population Reference Bureau.

Although the majority of single-parent families are headed by women, families headed by a single father are also increasing. Today, of children living with only one parent, 16 percent were living with their father, compared with 8 percent in 1980 (Fields and Casper 2001). In most of these families the father has gained custody of the children following a divorce or the mother has died.

Male-headed households are, however, less likely than female-headed households to experience severe economic problems. Unlike female-headed households where a man is not present to help with housework and children, single

DEBUNKING
Society's Myths

Myth: Absence of fathers is the cause of numerous social problems; if these fathers would just adopt "family values," families would be stronger and children wouldn't get into so much trouble.

Sociological perspective: Research on never-married, poor, noncustodial African American fathers finds that they want to be able to provide for their children; they may spend a lot of time with their children; and they want to be good "daddies." Understanding what fatherhood means to them requires understanding the context in which they live (Hamer 2001).

© Andrew Ramey/Stock, Boston

Female-headed families are more common among some groups than others. Twenty-three percent of Hispanic families are headed by women.

fathers commonly get domestic help from women—either girlfriends, daughters, or mothers (Popenoe 2001).

Married-Couple Families

Among married-couple families, one of the greatest changes in recent years has been the increased participation of women in the paid labor force. Indeed, as we saw in Chapter 7, families sustain a median income level by having both husband and wife in the paid labor force—a practice historically common among most African American families, many Latino and Asian American families, and many White working-class families. Even though increased labor force participation is most dramatic among White families, most families are experiencing substantial speedup. This is reflected in longer hours worked—especially for women (Mishel et al. 2003).

Women's labor force participation has created other changes in family life. One example is the number of married couples who have *commuter marriages* when work requires one partner in a dual-career couple to reside in a different city, separated by jobs too distant for a daily commute. The common image of a commuter marriage is one consisting of a prosperous professional couple, each holding important jobs, flashing credit cards, and using airplanes like taxis. However, working-class and poor couples do their share of long-distance commuting: agricultural workers follow seasonal work; skilled laborers sometimes have to leave their families to find jobs; many families cross national borders in search of work, often separating one or both parents and children. Although their commute may be less glamorous than that of professional spouses, they are commuting nonetheless. When all types of commuter marriages are included, this form of marriage is more prevalent than is typically imagined.

Stepfamilies

Stepfamilies are becoming more common in the United States, matching the rise in divorce and remarriage. Stepfamilies take numerous forms, including married adults with stepchildren, cohabiting stepparents, and stepparents who do not reside together (Stewart 2001).

About 40 percent of marriages involve stepchildren. These families face a difficult period as they deal with the troubles that arise when two family systems blend, or when new people are introduced into an existing family system. Parents and children discover that they must learn

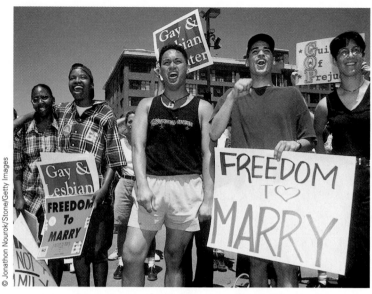

In recent years, there has been increasing mobilization by groups asking for legal recognition of lesbian and gay marriages; many companies have responded by extending employee benefits to domestic partners.

new roles when they become part of a stepfamily. Children accustomed to being the oldest child in the family, or the youngest, may find that their status in the family group is suddenly transformed. New living arrangements may require children to share rooms, toys, and time with people they perceive as strangers.

In stepfamilies, the parenting roles of mothers and fathers suddenly expand to include more children, each with his or her needs. Jealousy, competition, and demands for time and attention can make the relationships within stepfamilies tense. The problems are compounded by the absence of norms and institutional support systems for stepfamilies. Without norms to follow, people have to adapt by creating new language to refer to family members and new relationships. Many develop strong relationships within this new kinship system; others find the adjustment extremely difficult, resulting in a high probability of divorce among remarried couples with children (Baca Zinn and Eitzen 2002).

Gay and Lesbian Households

The increased visibility of gay and lesbian households challenges the traditional understanding of families as only heterosexual and has led to a greater acceptance of gays and lesbians in society. Although they have neither the official blessings nor supports of social institutions, many gay and lesbian couples form long-term, primary relationships that they define as marriage. Like other families, gay and lesbian couples share living arrange-

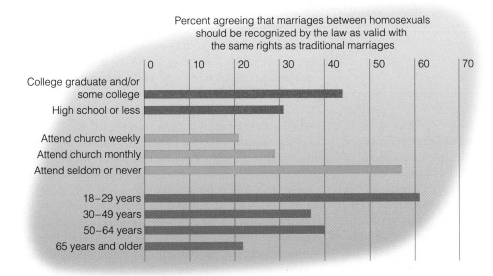

Percent agreeing that marriages between homosexuals
should be recognized by the law as valid with
the same rights as traditional marriages

FIGURE 12.2
Acceptance of Gay
Marriage

SOURCE: Lyons, Lydia. 2003.
"U.S. Next Down the Aisle
Toward Gay Marriage?" Princeton,
NJ: The Gallup Organization.
www.gallup.com

ments and household expenses, make decisions as partners, and in many cases, raise children.

Researchers have found that gay and lesbian couples
tend to be more flexible and less gender-stereotyped in
their household roles than heterosexual couples. Lesbian
households, in particular, are more egalitarian than are
either heterosexual or gay male couples. Unlike heterosexual couples, in lesbian households money has less effect on the balance of power in the relationship or on the
couple's feelings about each other. However, where one
partner is the primary breadwinner and the other the primary caregiver for children, the partner staying at home
becomes economically vulnerable and less able to negotiate her needs, just as in heterosexual relationships (Sullivan 1996).

Gay and lesbian marriages are producing new social
forms and new social debates. Should gay marriage be
recognized in law? Vermont recognizes civil unions between gay and lesbian partners and, in 2003, Massachusetts Supreme Court ruled that restricting marriage to
heterosexuals violated the State constitution. Canada's
courts have also recognized the right to gay marriage. In
the United States, 39 percent of the U.S. public believes
that gay marriages should be recognized as valid and
given the same rights as heterosexual couples; 55 percent disagree. But a larger number (49 percent) believe
that civil unions between gays should be given the same
rights, suggesting that the word *marriage* is imbued with
meaning that many do not want to extend to gay couples
(Lyons 2003). Gay marriage is also far more acceptable in
the eyes of younger people (those aged 18 to 29) than to
older groups, raising the question of whether over time
social support for gay marriages will increase over time or
whether, as young people age, they will shift their values

(see Figure 12.2). In the meantime, in most states and
municipalities, gays and lesbians who form strong and
lasting relationships do so without formal institutional
support and, as a result, have had to be innovative in producing new support systems.

Especially as more lesbian and gay couples choose to
have children, assisted by new reproductive technologies
that let them do so without a heterosexual partner, new
family forms are emerging. Lesbian mothers actively construct new meanings of motherhood and do so in ways
that are collaborative, including elaborate networks of
family and friends (Dunne 2000; Dalton and Bielby
2000). To date, most gay fathers are those who have children from a previous heterosexual marriage, although
the number of those intentionally choosing parenthood
without a heterosexual relationship is increasing.

Public debate about gay marriage often centers on
the implications for children raised in gay and lesbian
families. This discussion is fraught with biases since homophobia is so pervasive. Careful review of the research
on children in gay and lesbian households, however, finds
that for the most part there is little difference in outcomes for children raised in gay and lesbian households
and those raised in heterosexual households. Many of the
differences that are found are the result of other factors—
not only the sexual orientation of parents. The greatest
differences come as the result of the homophobia and discrimination that is directed against children in lesbian
and gay families, who are very likely to be stigmatized
by others. But, such children are also less likely to develop stereotypical gender roles and they are more tolerant and open-minded about sexual matters, although
they are no more likely to become gay themselves (Allen
1997; Stacey and Biblarz 2001). If we lived in a society

more tolerant of diversity, the differences that do emerge might be viewed as strengths, not deficits.

Singles

Single people, including those never married, widowed, or divorced, today constitute 44 percent of the population (over age 15)—an increase from 29 percent in 1970. Some of the increase is a result of the rising number of divorced people, but there has also been an increase in the number of those never married. Men and women are marrying at a later age—25.1 years on average for women, 26.8 for men, compared with 20.8 for women and 23.2 for men in 1970 (Fields and Casper 2001).

Among singles, patterns of establishing intimate relationships have changed significantly. "Hooking up"—a phrase referring to a casual, sexual alliance between two people—has supplanted dating as the pattern by which young people get to know each other (see the box, "Forces of Social Change"). Courtship no longer follows pre-established norms. Still, the path to a committed relationship, possibly marriage, involves increasing phases of commitment and sexual exclusivity. Many people find the same sexual and emotional gratification in single life as they would in marriage. Being single is also no longer the stigma it once was, especially for women. Nonetheless, studies find that married people are generally happier than singles; this changes in different historical periods, however, and depends a lot on other factors, such as financial resources, marital conflict and violence, the extent of other personal ties, and the presence of stressful life problems (Aldous and Ganey 1999; Keith 1997; Lee et al. 1991; Waite 2000).

Cohabitation (living together) has become increasingly common. Some of the increase is the result of better census-taking, but the increase is also real. Cohabitation is more common among the young and the less educated. It is also more common among Black and Native American couples than among Whites (Cohen 1999; Marquis

---

FORCES OF SOCIAL CHANGE

"Hooking Up": Dating and Mating on College Campuses

There was a time when dating on college campuses was a quite formal activity. There were clear social norms about who dated who, how the date was arranged (by the young man), and what was expected—perhaps a first kiss after several dates, then a more formal stage of courtship prior to marriage, and sex only after marriage. Does this sound like the current dating scene on your campus? Not likely!

A national study of a diverse group of women on 11 different campuses, coupled with a nationally representative sample of 1,000 college women interviewed by telephone in 2000–2001, found the following about the current college dating scene:

1. Hooking up—meaning sexual interaction without commitment—is widespread on college campuses and influences the campus culture, although only a minority of students engage in it (about 40 percent of college women).

2. The meaning of dating varies for college women. For some, it means a highly committed relationship, including sex, but rarely going out on dates. For others it just means hanging out. For some, dating and hooking up mean the same thing, but "dating" is not generally used to describe the relationship.

3. Hooking up also carries multiple meanings. For some it means kissing, for others it means sexual-genital play, but not intercourse; for some, it means sexual intercourse. The vagueness of the term contributes to its becoming a shared cultural phenomenon.

4. Hooking up commonly occurs when both participants are drinking or drunk.

5. Two-thirds of women say hooking up made them feel desirable, but also awkward. 40 percent of women say they have experienced a hookup; 10 percent say more than six times. But women are wary of getting a bad reputation from hooking up too often.

6. It is rare for college men to invite college women out on a date; women also report that men do not acknowledge when they have become a couple, although men, not the women, make the decision about when they are committed.

7. Even with the hooking up culture, the majority of college women still want to meet a spouse while at college—a result that is compromised by the sex ratio on campus (79 men for every 100 women).

The sociologists who conducted this study did so for a conservative organization that interpreted the results as interrupting "an important pathway to traditional marriage" (Glenn and Marquist 2001: 7). They recommended more adult involvement in establishing dating norms on college campuses, and recommended that men take more initiative in dating.

What is the hooking up culture on your campus? How do gender relations influence the culture? Given what you see and the results above, do you agree with the recommendations of these authors?

SOURCE: Glenn, Norval, and Elizabeth Marquardt. 2001. "Hooking Up, Hanging Out, and Hoping for Mr. Right." New York: Institute for American Values.

2003). Some of these couples have never been married; others are living together when families are being reformed following divorce. Some cohabit because they are critical of the existing norms surrounding marriage (Elizabeth 2000). Estimates are that one-quarter of all children will at some time during their childhood live in a family headed by a cohabiting couple (Graefe and Lichter 1999), indicating how common cohabitation has become. Cohabitors tend to have more egalitarian attitudes toward gender roles, although they tend to develop a household division of labor similar to that of married heterosexual couples. But, they are more likely to remain together when they establish equality within the relationship (Sanchez et al. 1998; Barber and Axinn 1998; Brines and Joyner 1999).

Finally, a rising number of single people are remaining in their parents' homes for longer periods. Known as the "boomerang generation," these young people in their twenties return home when they would normally be expected to live independently. Today 56 percent of men and 43 percent of women between 18 and 24 years of age live at home with their parents (Fields and Casper 2001). The increased cost of living means that many young people find themselves unable to pay their own way, even after marrying or getting an education. They economize by joining the household of their parents.

▪ *Marriage and Divorce*

Even with the extraordinary diversity of family forms in the United States, the majority of people will still marry at some point in their lives. Indeed, the United States has the highest rate of marriage of any Western industrialized nation, as well as a high divorce rate. People's opinions about their preferred family lifestyle have changed considerably in recent years, however. One-half of all women and nearly one-half of all men (47 percent) now say that the most satisfying lifestyle would be to live in a marriage where the husband and wife share responsibilities for work, housekeeping, and child care, but the public is not unified in this view. Those who still want a traditional marriage with the husband as the sole provider and the woman caring for the home and children include 28 percent of women and 32 percent of men (General Social Survey 1998).

Marriage

The picture of marriage as a consensual unit based on intimacy, economic cooperation, and mutual goals is widely shared, although marital relationships also involve a complex set of social dynamics, including cooperation and conflict, different patterns of resource allocation, and a division of labor. Sociologists must be careful not to romanticize marriage to the point that they miss other significant social patterns within marriage.

Gender roles are a significant reality of family life, shaping power dynamics within marriage, as well as the allocation of work, the degree of marital happiness, the likelihood of marital violence, and even the leisure time that each partner has. Although people do not like to think of marriage as a power relationship, gender shapes the power that men and women have within marriage, as it does in other relationships. For one thing, sociologists have long found that the amount of money a person earns establishes that person's relative power within the marriage, including the ability to influence decisions, the degree of autonomy and independence held by each partner, and the control of expectations about family life. Studies have traditionally shown that greater marital power is exercised by the partner with the highest educational and occupational level, but this is not the case when wives earn more than husbands. Still, wives who contribute more to the family's financial standing than their husbands have greater autonomy within the marriage than wives who contribute less financially (Tichenor 1999; Komter 1989). Thus, gender—not just income and occupational level—influences power within marriage.

DEBUNKING
Society's Myths

Myth: If you find a man with the right attitude, he will be more likely to share the care-giving needed in a family.

Sociological perspective: Men's gender ideology has little effect on how much care work they provide; more significant is the social structure of the family. For example, men with sisters spend less time giving care to elderly family members (Gerstl and Gallagher 2001).

People actively negotiate the power relationships in marriage; how they do so depends on the attitudes and beliefs each partner has about marriage and the resources each brings to the household (Pyke 1994). Thus, a couple's gender expectations strongly influence marital dynamics. For example, couples who disagree about the wife's right to work tend to have the least happy marriages (Pyke 1994).

Within marriage, gender also shapes the division of household labor. Women do far more work in the home and have less leisure time (Baca Zinn and Eitzen 2002). Most employed mothers do two jobs—the so-called *second shift* of housework after working all day in a paid job (Hochschild 1989). With more women in the labor market, wives with children have increased their working hours by nine hours a week since 1979 (counting only employment); fathers, seven hours—an extra day every week (Mishel et al 2003). Little wonder that people are feeling that they have less and less time.

Are men more involved in housework than in the past? Yes and no. Men report that they do more housework, but they devote only slightly more of their time to housework than in the past. Estimates of the amount of housework that men do vary, but studies generally find a large gap between the number of hours women give to housework and child care and the hours men give. Among couples where both partners are employed, only 28 percent equally share the housework. Fathers do more when there is a child in the house under two years of age, but the increase is mostly accounted for by the amount of child care men provide, not the housework they do. The end result is that men have about eleven more hours of leisure per week than women do (Press and Townsley 1998). Interestingly, sociologists have found that the allocation of housework is greatly affected by men's and

women's experience in their own families of origin; those from households with a more egalitarian division of labor are likely to carry this into their own relationships (Cunningham 2001).

Despite a widespread belief that young professional couples are the most egalitarian, studies find that there is little difference across social class in the amount of housework that men do (Wright et al. 1992). Regarding race, African American husbands provide a greater share of housework than do White husbands. Latino households have more diversity in gender roles than stereotypes about machismo would lead us to believe (McLoyd 2000).

The presence of children also influences social dynamics within marriage. The arrival of a first child significantly increases the gender division of labor in households, with women increasing the housework they do and lessening their employment. There is far less effect for men (Sanchez and Thomson 1997). Although children can enrich marriage relationships, the time devoted to caring for children can detract from the quality of the marriage

DOING SOCIOLOGICAL RESEARCH

Men's Caregiving

Much research has documented the fact that women do the majority of the housework and child care within families. Why? Many have explained it as the result of gender socialization—women learn early on to be nurturing and responsible for others, while men are less likely to do so. Yet, things are changing and some men are more involved in the "care work" of family life. What explains whether men will be more engaged in family care work?

This is the question that sociologists Naomi Gerstl and Sally Gallagher examined in their study of 188 married people. They interviewed 94 husbands and 94 wives, married to each other; the sample was 86 percent White and 14 percent African American, but was too small to examine similarities or differences by race. You might expect that men who had attitudes expressing support for men's family responsibilities would be more involved in family care (defined by Gerstl and Gallagher to include elder care, child care, and various household tasks). But, this

is not what Gerstel and Gallagher found.

Gender attitudes did *not* influence men's involvement in caregiving. Rather, the characteristics of the men's families were the most influential determinant of their engagement in housework and child care. Men whose wives spent the most time helping kin and men who had daughters were more likely to help kin. Having sons had no influence. But, in addition, men with more sisters spend less time helping with elder parents than men with fewer sisters. Furthermore, men's employment (neither hours employed, job flexibility, and job stability) did not affect their involvement in care work.

Gerstel and Gallagher conclude that it is the social structure of the family, not gender beliefs, that shape men's involvement in family work. As they put it, "It is primarily the women in men's lives who shape the amount and types of care men provide" (2001: 211). This study shows a most important sociological point: that social structure, not just individual attitudes,

is the most significant determinant of social behavior.

Questions to Consider

1. Who does the work in your family? Is it related to the social organization of your family, as Gerstl and Gallagher find in other families?
Keywords: family division of labor, gender and housework

2. Do you think that men's gender identity changes when they become more involved in care work? What hinders and/or facilitates men's engagement in this kind of work?
Keywords: men and care work, men and nurturing

We have included InfoTrac College Edition keywords at the end of each question to make it easier for you to find more to read on these topics. Go to **www.infotrac-college.com,** an online library, to begin your search.

Source: Gerstel, Naomi, and Sally Gallagher. 2001. "Men's Caregiving: Gender and the Contingent Character of Care." *Gender & Society* 15 (April): 197–217.

relationships. As a result, as reported in one study of over 6700 married couples, people report higher marital quality in the pre- and post-parental stages of the marriage (Benin and Robinson 1997). This does not mean that marriage necessarily suffers because of children, but it points to the time, cost, and stress that raising children involves. This can increase tension within marriage.

Although marriage can be seen as a romantic and intimate relationship, it can also be seen within a sociological context. Marriage relationships are shaped by many social factors, not just the commitment between two people. You see this especially when examining marital conflicts. Life events, such as the birth of a child, job loss, retirement, and other family commitments, such as caring for the elderly or a child with special needs, all influence the degree of marital conflict and stability (Moen et al. 2001; Crowley 1998). As conditions in society change, people make adjustments within their relationships, but how well they can cope within a marriage depends on a large array of sociological—not just individual—factors. Marriage is shaped by systems of social stratification— systems that, although part of the structure of society, have tremendous influence on the social interaction within people's day-to-day lives.

Divorce

The United States leads the world not only in the number of people who marry, but also in the number of people who divorce. More than sixteen million people have divorced but not remarried in the population today; more women are in this group than men since women are less likely to remarry following a divorce. Since 1960, the rate of divorce has more than doubled, although it has declined recently since its all-time high in 1980 (see Figure 12.3).

You will often hear that one in every two marriages ends in divorce, but this is a misleading statistic. The marriage rate is 8.4 marriages per 1000 people and the divorce rate is 4.0 per 1000 people (U.S. Census Bureau 2002). At first glance, it appears there are one-half as many divorces as marriages. But this statistic is for divorces out of *all married couples, not just the marriages formed that year,* so divorce is not as widespread as one in two marriages.

Still, the rate of divorce is high and it has risen since 1950, though fallen again in recent years. The likelihood of divorce is not equally distributed across all social groups, however. Divorce is more likely for couples who marry young while in their teens or early twenties. Second marriages are more likely than first marriages to end in divorce. It also varies by race and class, and is somewhat higher among low-income couples; a fact that re-

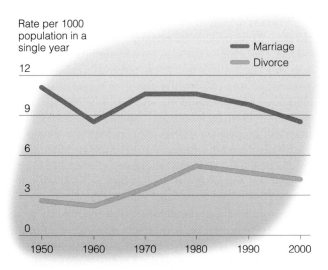

FIGURE 12.3 Marriage and Divorce Rates, 1950–2000

DATA: U.S. Bureau of the Census. 2002. *Statistical Abstract of the United States, 2002.* Washington, DC: U.S. Department of Commerce, p. 59.

flects the strains that financial problems put on marriages. Divorce is also somewhat higher among African Americans than among Whites, partially because African Americans make up a disproportionate part of lower income groups. Hispanics have a lower rate of divorce than either Whites or Blacks, probably the result of religious influence. Recently, the divorce rate among Asian Americans has also risen, interpreted as the possible shedding of cultural taboos (Fields 2003; Armas, 2003). This explanation seems supported by the fact that Asian Americans born in the United States are more likely to be divorced than Asians who immigrated (McLoyd et al. 2000).

A number of factors contribute to the current high rate of divorce in the United States. Demographic changes (shifts in the composition of the population) are part of the explanation. The rise in life expectancy, for example, has an effect on the length of marriages. In earlier eras, people died younger, and thus the average length of marriages was shorter. Some marriages that earlier would have ended with the death of a spouse may be now be dissolved by divorce. Still, cultural factors also contribute to divorce.

In the United States, individualism is a cultural norm, placing a high value on a person's satisfaction within marriage. The cultural orientation toward individualism may predispose people to terminate a marriage in which they are personally unhappy. In other cultural contexts (including years ago in this society), marriage, no matter how difficult, may have been seen as an unbreakable bond, regardless if one was unhappy. As we have seen in the previous data, for racial–ethnic groups in the United States cultural factors can also influence the likelihood of divorce.

Changes in women's roles also are related to the rate of divorce. Women today are now less financially dependent on husbands than in the past, even though they still earn less. As a result, the economic interdependence that bound women and men as a marital unit is no longer as strong. Although most married women would be less well off without access to their husband's income, they could probably still support themselves. This can make it possible for people to end marriages that they find unsatisfactory.

To people in unhappy marriages, divorce, though painful and financially risky, can be a positive option (Kurz 1995). The belief that couples should stay together for the sake of the children is now giving way to a belief, supported by research, that a marriage with protracted conflict is more detrimental to children than divorce. Although there are periodic public outcries about the negative effect of divorce on children, many other factors influence the long-term psychological and social adjustment of children. Few children feel relieved or pleased by divorce; feelings of sadness, fear, loss, and anger are common, along with desires for reconciliation and feelings of conflicting loyalties. But, most children adjust reasonably well after a year or so. Moreover, children's adjustment is influenced most by factors that precede the divorce. The single most important factor influencing children's poor adjustment is marital violence and prolonged discord (Stewart et al. 1997; Arendell 1998; Furstenberg 1998; Cherlin et al. 1998; Amato and Booth 1997). The emotional strain on children is significantly reduced if the couple remain amicable. If both parents remain active in the upbringing of the children, the evidence shows that children do not suffer from divorce; especially important is the ability of the mother to be an effective parent after a divorce. Her ability to be effective can be affected by the resources she has and her ongoing relationship with the father (Buchanan et al. 1996; Simons et al. 1996; Furstenberg and Nord 1985).

In the aftermath of divorce, many fathers become distant from their children. Sociologists have argued that the tradition of defining men in terms of their role as breadwinners minimizes the attachment they feel for their children. If the family is then disrupted, they may feel that their primary responsibility, as financial provider, is lessened, leaving them with a diminished sense of obligation to their children. A man may also distance himself as a way of minimizing or avoiding conflicts with his former wife. Salvaging a sense of masculinity may also play a role. Many fathers report feelings of emasculation when they are displaced from their home, especially if being the head of a household was a primary gender identity. In the absence of this, some men may reassert another aspect of their masculine role—independence (Arendell 1992). One consequence is the limited child support that families receive from fathers after divorce. Only two-thirds of those supposed to receive child support actually receive any; almost one-half of those only receive a partial amount (U.S. Census Bureau 2002).

▪ *Family Violence*

Generally speaking, the family is depicted as a private sphere where members are nurtured and protected, away from the influences of the outside world. Although this is the experience of many, families can also be locales for violence, disruption, and conflict. Family violence is a phenomenon that, hidden for many years, has now been the subject of much sociological research.

Partner Violence

Estimates of the extent of domestic violence are hard to come by and notoriously unreliable, because the majority of cases of domestic violence go unreported. The National Violence Against Women Office estimates that 25 percent of women will be raped, physically assaulted, or stalked by an intimate partner in their lifetime; 22 percent experience physical assault; 7 to 10 percent are raped by intimates; and 5 percent will be stalked by an intimate partner. (The numbers do not total to 25 percent since a given person may experience multiple violent events.) Men also experience partner violence, although far less frequently. Women who experience violence are also twice as likely as men to be injured. Violence also occurs in gay and lesbian relationships, although silence around the issue may be even more pervasive given the marginalized status of gays and lesbians. Men living with male partners are just as likely to be raped, assaulted, or stalked as are women living with men, but the incidence of violence against women by women partners is about half as likely as heterosexual violence. Researchers conclude that this is because most domestic violence is committed by men. Violence is usually accompanied by emotionally abusive and controlling behavior. Jealous and dominating partners are the most likely perpetrators of domestic violence (Tjaden and Thoennes 2000; West 1998; Renzetti 1992).

One of the most common questions asked about domestic violence is why victims stay with their abuser. The answers are complex and stem from sociological, psychological, and economic problems. A victim tends to believe that the batterer will change, but they also find they have few options; they may perceive that leaving will be more dangerous, because violence can escalate when the abuser thinks he (or she) has lost control. Many women are also unable to support their children and meet their living expenses without a husband's income. Mandatory arrest laws in cases of domestic violence can exacerbate this problem, because they may, despite their intentions, discourage a woman from reporting violence for fear her batterer will lose his job (Miller 1997). Despite the belief that battered women do not leave their abusers, however, the majority do leave and seek ways to prevent further victimization (Gelles 1999).

Sociological analyses of violence in the family have led to the conclusion that women's relative powerlessness in the family is at the root of high rates of violence against women. Because most violence in the family is directed against women, the imbalance of power between men and women in the family is the source of most domestic violence. Since women are relatively powerless within the society, they may not have the resources to leave their marriage (Kurz 1989; McCloskey 1996).

Child Abuse

Violence within families also victimizes many children who experience child abuse. Not all forms of child abuse are alike. Some people consider repeated spanking to be abusive; others think of this as legitimate behavior. Child abuse, however, is behavior that puts children at risk and may include physical violence and neglect. As with battering, the exact incidence of child abuse is difficult to know, but annually 1.5 million children receive preventative services (Sedlak and Broadhurst 1996; National Clearinghouse on Child Abuse and Neglect 2003). Whereas men are the most likely perpetrators of violence in other forms of domestic abuse and in sexual abuse, with child abuse, women are as likely to be the perpetrators as men.

Research on child abuse finds a number of factors associated with abuse, including chronic alcohol use by a parent, unemployment, and isolation of the family. Sociologists point to the absence of social supports—in the form of social services, community assistance, and cultural norms about the primacy of motherhood—as related to child abuse, because most abusers are those with weak community ties and little contact with friends and relatives (Gelles and Straus 1988; Eitzen and Baca Zinn 2003).

Incest

Incest is a particular form of child abuse, involving sexual relations between persons who are closely related. A history of incest has been related to a variety of other problems, such as drug and alcohol abuse, runaways, delinquency, and various psychological problems, including the potential for violent partnerships in adult

life. Studies find that fathers and uncles are the most frequent incestuous abusers and that incest is most likely in families where mothers are debilitated (such as by mental illness or alcoholism). In such families, daughters often take on the mothering role, being taught to comply with men's demands to hold the family together. Thus scholars have linked women's powerlessness within families to the dynamics surrounding incest (Herman 1981; Andersen 2003).

Elder Abuse

The National Center on Elder Abuse estimates that between 820,000 and 1,860,000 elders are abused in the United States, but this organization acknowledges the difficulty of gauging the true extent of the problem. Elder abuse tends to be hidden in the privacy of families, and victims are reluctant to talk about their situations, so estimates are only approximations. What is known is that reports of elder abuse have increased since the mid-1980s. Whether elder abuse has increased over time or is simply reported more frequently is open to speculation (Teaster 2000; National Center on Elder Abuse 2003).

Why are the elderly abused? One explanation is that caring for the elderly is very stressful for the caregiver—usually a daughter who may be holding a job as well as caring for the elderly person. Research on elder abuse finds that the abusers are most likely to be middle-aged women, and (sadly) the daughter of the victim—the person most likely to be caring for the older person. Sons, however, are the ones most likely to be engaged in direct physical abuse, accounting for almost half of the known physical abusers. Sometimes the physical abuser is a husband where the abuse is a continuation of abusive behavior in the marriage. The same factors that affect family life in any generation contribute to the problem of elder abuse (Teaster 2000).

■ *Changing Families in a Changing Society*

Like other social institutions, the family is in a constant state of change, particularly as new social conditions arise and as people in families adapt to the changed conditions of their lives. Some changes affect only a given family—the individual changes that come from the birth of a new child, the loss of a partner, divorce, migration, and other life events. These changes are what C. Wright Mills referred to as "troubles" (see Chapter 1). Some may even be happy events; the point is that they are changes that happen at the individual level, as people adjust to the presence of a new child, adjust to a breakup with a long-term partner, or grieve the loss of a spouse.

As Mills would have pointed out, many microsociological things that people experience in families have their origins in the broader *macrosociological* changes affecting society as a whole. Migration, as we will see, is a good example. Certain economic, social, and political conditions may encourage people to move, and how they do so, where they go, what kind of work they seek, and who can go all affect family life. Strains in the society that affect the rate of marriage and divorce; women's changing roles in the workplace; and social policies supporting (or not) child care, battered women, or pregnant teens all affect the sociological situation of families—worldwide.

Global Changes in Family Life

Changes in the institutional structure of families are also being affected by the process of globalization. The increasing global basis of the economy means that people often work long distances from other family members—a phenomenon that occurs at all ends of the social class spectrum, although the experience of such global mobility varies significantly by social class. A corporate executive may accumulate thousands—even millions—of first-class flight miles, criss-crossing the globe to conduct business. A regional sales manager may spend most nights away from a family, likely staying in modestly priced motels, eating in fast-food franchises along the way. Truckers may sleep in the cabs of their tractor-trailers, after logging extraordinary numbers of hours of driving in a given week. Laborers may move from one state to the next, following the pattern of the harvest, living in camps away from families, being paid by the amount they pick.

These patterns of work and migration have created a new family form—the **transnational family,** defined as families where one parent (or both) lives and works in one country while their children remain in the country of origin. A good example is found in Hong Kong, where most domestic labor is performed by Filipina women, who work on multiple-year contracts managed by the government, typically on a live-in basis. They leave their children in the Philippines, usually cared for by another relative, and send money home, because the meager wages they earn in Hong Kong (the equivalent of about $325 per month) far exceed the average income of workers in the Philippines—on average, the equivalent of $1500 per year. This pattern is so common that the average Filipino migrant worker supports five people at home; one in five Filipinos directly depends on migrant workers' earnings (Constable 1997; Parreñas 2001).

One need not go to other nations to see such transnational patterns in family life. In the United States,

Caribbean women and African American women have had a long history of having to leave their children with others while they sought employment in different regions of the country. Central American and Mexican women may come to work in the United States, while their children stay behind. Mothers may return to see them whenever they can, or alternatively, children may spend part of the year with their mothers, part with other relatives.

Mothers in transnational families have to develop new concepts of their maternal role, because their situation means giving up the idea that biological mothers should raise their own children. Many have expanded their definition of motherhood to include breadwinning, traditionally defined as the role of fathers. Transnational women also create a new sense of home, one not limited to the traditional understanding of "home" as a single place where mothers, fathers, and their children reside (Hondagneu-Sotelo 2001; Hondagneu-Sotelo and Avila 1997; Das Gupta 1997; Alicea 1997).

To sociologists, global developments that produce new work patterns, wars that change the mix of women and men in a given region, and gender relations that change with new patterns of societal development are all fascinating processes that affect many dimensions of life, not the least of which is change in the family as a social institution.

Families and Social Policy

Family social policies are the subject of intense national debate. Should gay marriages be recognized by the state? What responsibility does society have to help parents balance the demands of work and family? Many issues on the front lines on national social policy engage intense discussions of families. Some claim the family is breaking down. Others celebrate the increased diversity in families. Many blame the family for the social problems our society faces. Drugs, low educational achievement, crime, and violence are often attributed to a crisis in "family values," as if rectifying these attitudes is all it will take to solve our nation's difficulties. The family is the only social institution that typically takes the blame for all of society's problems. Is it reasonable to expect families to solve social problems? Families are afflicted by most of the structural problems that are generated by racism, poverty, gender inequality, and class inequality. Expecting families to solve the problems that are the basis for their own difficulties is like asking a poor person to save us from the national debt.

BALANCING WORK AND FAMILY. Balancing the multiple demands of work and family is one of the biggest challenges for most families. With more parents employed, it is difficult to have time from one's paid job to care for newborn or newly adopted children, tend to

TABLE 12.2 Maternity Leave Benefits: A Comparative Perspective

Country	Length of Maternity Leave	Percentage of Wages Paid in Covered Period	Provider of Coverage
Zimbabwe	90 days	60–75%	Employer
Cuba	18 weeks	100%	Social Security
Iran	90 days	66.7% for 16 weeks	Social Security
China	90 days	100%	Employer
Saudi Arabia	10 weeks	50 or 100%	Employer
Canada	17–18 weeks	55% for 15 weeks	Unemployment insurance
Germany	14 weeks	100%	Social Security to a ceiling; employer pays difference
France	16–26 weeks	100%	Social Security
Italy	5 months	80%	Social Security
Japan	14 weeks	60%	Social Security or health insurance
Russian Federation	140 days	100%	Social Security
Sweden	14 weeks	450 days, 100% paid	Social Security
United Kingdom	14–18 weeks	90% for 6 weeks; flat rare thereafter	Social Security
United States	**12 weeks**	**0**	**n/a**

SOURCE: United Nations. 2000. *The World's Women 2000: Trends and Statistics.* New York: United Nations, pp.140–143.

sick children, or care for elderly parents or other family members. The **Family and Medical Leave Act (FMLA),** adopted by Congress in 1993, is meant to provide help for these conflicts. It requires employers to grant employees a total of twelve weeks in unpaid leave to care for newborns, adopted children, or other family members with a serious health condition. The Family and Medical Leave Act is the first law to recognize the need of families to care for children and other dependents. A number of conditions, however, limit the effectiveness of the FMLA, not the least of which is that the leave is unpaid, making it impossible for many employed parents. Many workers in firms where there are family friendly policies worry that taking advantage of these policies will harm their prospects for career advancement (Blair-Loy and Wharton 2002). Currently, only 13 percent of workers have child-care benefits available to them from employers (U.S. Bureau of Labor Statistics 2003). Among industrialized nations, the United States provides the least in support for maternity and child-care policies (see Table 12.2).

CHILD CARE. Family leave polices, much as they are needed, also do not address the ongoing needs for child care. Almost one-half of families with children under age thirteen have child care expenses, typically taking 9 percent of their earnings. Single-parent families whose income is likely less need 16 percent of their income (or $258 per month to average) to pay for child care. Moreover, low-income families have to pay 16 percent of their earnings for child care whereas higher earning families pay 6 percent (Giannarelli and Barsimantov 2000).

Many parents struggle to find good and affordable child care for their children, some relying on kin for care; others, on paid providers; and some, a combination of both. In the United States, one-half of three-year-olds and two-thirds of four-year-olds now spend much of their time in child care centers. But the national approach is one of patching together different programs and primarily relying on private initiatives for care. Compare this to France where, although participation is voluntary, almost all parents enroll young children in the *école maternelle* system where a place is guaranteed to every child aged three to six. These child care centers are integrated with the school system and are seen as a form of early education. Moreover, in the United States child care costs match tuition costs at public universities, but in France, child care is seen as a social responsibility and is paid by the government. National norms about whether families are a private or public responsibility clearly shape social policy (Clawson and Gerstel 2002; Folbre 2001).

Care work—work that sustains life, including child care, elder care, housework, and other forms of household labor—is increasingly provided to middle- and upper-class families by women of color and immigrant women. Nannies, cleaners, and personal attendants now do much of the domestic work that was once provided by wives and mothers. These trends raise many new questions for sociologists, such as how work is negotiated outside of the public labor market, how "mothering" is defined when it is provided by multiple people, how domestic workers care for their own families, and what work conditions exist in the lives of domestic laborers (Hondagneu-Sotelo 2001). Clearly, new social policies are needed to address the needs of diverse families.

ELDER CARE. The shrinking size of families means that the proportion of elderly people is growing faster than the number of younger potential caretakers. As life expectancy has increased and people live longer, elder care becomes a greater and greater need. Family members provide 80 to 90 percent of long-term care for the elderly—work that is often taken for granted. Some estimate that for every $120 spent in publicly funded long-term care, families provide $287 of unpaid services (Glazer 1990; Meyer 1994).

Women, who shoulder the work of elder care, can now expect to spend more years as the child of an elderly parent than as the mother of children under eighteen

Most elder care is provided by the family, most typically the elder's daughter. Given the increase in life expectancy, adults can now anticipate spending as many years providing elder care as they have in providing child care.

(Watkins 1987). Indeed, young people now can expect to spend more years caring for an elderly parent than raising their own children. The effects of the burden of care are apparent in the stress that women report from this role. Women also believe they are better at elder care than their husbands and brothers, but with the rapid increase in the older population that lies ahead, these social norms may have to change. As the U.S. population ages, social policies will likely need to respond to this growing need.

Because families are so diverse, different families need different social supports. Family leave policies that give parents time off to care for their children or sick relatives are helpful but of little use to people who cannot afford time off work without pay. Strong enforcement of laws to protect victims of domestic violence can help, but not if removing partners only further reduces the income support for families (Miller 1997). Greater employer support for child care can help men and women meet family needs. Some policies will benefit some groups more than others—one reason why policymakers need to be sensitive to the diversity of family experiences. Social policies cannot solve all the problems that families face, but they can go a long way toward creating the conditions under which diverse family units can thrive.

TAKING ON SOCIAL ISSUES

A Culture of Care?

People in the United States work more than workers in any other industrialized nation. With more mothers in the work force, how do people manage to take care of children, perhaps older parents, and manage the tasks that constitute "care work"? We do not live in a "family friendly" society, so most institutions are organized as if care needs will be met privately—a consequence of the historical assumption that a woman's place is in the home. Care work falls mostly on individuals who have to design their own solutions to the problem of care. What public solutions to these problems are in place and what is still needed? What role should government and employers have in providing such policies, or should individuals develop their own solutions for balancing work and family? Many rely on faith-based organizations to assist with care. Should the government support such initiatives?

To answer these questions, you can find additional resources through your school library or on the Internet. To use the Internet, log onto your computer and open your browser. Select one of your favorite search engines to begin exploring this issue.

Taking Action

Go to the Taking Action exercise on the companion Web site at **sociology.wadsworth.com/ andersen_taylor/essen3e** to learn more about an organization that addresses this topic.

■ *Defining Religion*

Sociologists study religion as both a belief system and a social institution. The belief systems of religion have a powerful hold on what people think and how they see the world. The patterns and practices of religious institutions are among the most important influences on people's lives. Sociologists are interested in several questions about religion: How are religious belief and practice related to other social factors, such as social class, race, age, gender, and level of education? How are religious institutions organized? How does religion influence social change? In using sociology to understand religion, what is important is not what one believes about religion, but one's ability to examine religion objectively in its social and cultural context.

What is religion? Most people think of it as a category of experience separate from the mundane acts of everyday life, perhaps involving communication with a deity or communion with the supernatural (Johnstone 1992). Sociologists define **religion** as an institutionalized system of symbols, beliefs, values, and practices by which a group of people interprets and responds to what they feel is sacred and that provides answers to questions of ultimate meaning (Glock and Stark 1965: 4; Johnstone 1992: 14). The elements of this definition bear closer examination:

1. **Religion is institutionalized.** Religion is more than just beliefs: It is a pattern of social action organized around the beliefs, practices, and symbols that people develop to answer questions about the meaning of existence. As an institution, religion presents itself as larger than any single individual; it persists over time and has an organizational structure into which members are socialized.

2. **Religion is a feature of groups.** Religion is built around a community of people with similar beliefs. It is a cohesive force among believers because it is a basis for group identity, and gives people a sense of belonging to a community or organization. Religious groups can be formally organized, as in the case of bureaucratic churches, or they may be more informally organized, ranging from prayer groups to cults. Some religious communities are extremely close-knit, as in convents; other communities are more diffuse with people who identify themselves as Protestant but attend church only on Easter.

3. **Religions are based on beliefs that are considered sacred.** The **sacred** is that which is set apart from ordinary activity for worship, seen as holy, and protected by special rites and rituals. The sacred is distinguished from the **profane,** which is of the everyday

© Myrleen Cate/Stone/Getty Images

Young people are typically socialized into the religion of their parents. Religious socialization can be a powerful source of social identity and beliefs.

world and specifically not religious (Durkheim 1912/1947; Chalfant et al. 1987). Each religion defines what is to be considered sacred; most religions have sacred objects and sacred symbols. The holy symbols are infused with special religious meaning and inspire awe.

A **totem** is an object or living thing that a religious group regards with special reverence. A statue of Buddha is a totem; so is a crucifix hanging on a wall. Among the Zuni (a Native American group), fetishes are totems; these are small, intrically carved animal objects representing different dimensions of Zuni spirituality. A totem is important not for what it is, but for what it represents. To a Christian taking communion, a piece of bread is defined as the flesh of Jesus; eating the bread unites the communicant mystically with Christ. To a nonbeliever, the bread is simply that—a piece of bread (McGuire 1996). Likewise, Native Americans hold certain ground to be sacred and are deeply offended when the holy ground is disturbed by industrial or commercial developers who see only potential profit.

4. **Religion establishes values and moral proscriptions for behavior.** A proscription is a constraint imposed by external forces. Religion typically establishes proscriptions for the behavior of believers, some of them quite strict. For example, the Catholic Church defines living together as sexual partners outside marriage as a sin; the lifestyle is condemned as immoral "selfishness" and an "unwillingness to make a lifelong commitment" through marriage (National Council of Catholic Bishops 1992). Often religious believers come

Religious spirituality takes many forms, but produces feelings of awe and reverence among believers.

to see such moral proscriptions as simply "right" and behave accordingly. At other times, individuals may consciously reject moral proscriptions, although they may still feel guilty when they engage in a forbidden practice. Of course, what people believe and what they do can be very contradictory, perhaps best exemplified by the various scandals recently reported involving sexual abuse of young boys by Catholic priests.

5. **Religion establishes norms for behavior.** Religious belief systems establish social norms about how the faithful should behave in certain situations. Worshippers may be expected to cover their heads in a temple, mosque, or cathedral, or wear certain clothes. Such behavioral expectations may be quite strong. The next time you are at a gathering where a prayer is said before a meal, note how many people bow their heads, even though some of those present may not believe in the deity being invoked.

6. **Religion provides answers to questions of ultimate meaning.** The ordinary beliefs of daily life are **secular** beliefs and may be institutionalized, but they are specifically not religious. Science, for example, generates secular beliefs based on particular ways of thinking—logic and empirical observation are at the root of scientific beliefs. Religious beliefs, in contrast, often have a supernatural element. They emerge from spiritual needs, and may provide answers to questions

that cannot be probed with the profane tools of science and reason. Think of the difference in how religion and science explain the origins of life. Whereas science explains this as the result of biochemical and physical processes, different religions have other accounts of the origin of life.

■ The Significance of Religion in the United States

The United States is one of the most religious societies in the world, where 95 percent of Americans say they believe in God or a universal spirit (Gallup 2001). Religion is, for millions of people, the strongest component of their individual and group identity. Much of the world's most celebrated art, architecture, and music has its origins in religion, whether in the classical art of western Europe, the Buddhist temples of the East, or the gospel rhythms of contemporary rock.

Religion is also strongly related to a number of social and political attitudes. Religious identification is a good predictor of how traditional a person's beliefs will be. Generally speaking, those with deeper religious involvement have more traditional gender attitudes. Recent studies also find that it is conservative Evangelical Christians who are most likely to believe that the family is in decline (Brooks 2002). There is no simple relationship between religious belief and prejudice, because religious principles are also often the basis for lessening racial prejudice. But, people who belong to religious organizations that encourage intolerance of any form are most likely to be racially prejudiced. Religious conservatives are more critical of Jews and tend to believe that Jews should convert to Christianity (Smith and Woodberry 2001; Smith 1999; Adorno et al. 1950; Allport 1966). *Homophobia* (the fear and hatred of homosexuals) has also been linked to religious belief, although some religious congregations have actively worked to encourage the participation of gays and lesbians.

THINKING SOCIOLOGICALLY

For one week keep a daily log, noting every time you see an explicit or implicit reference to religion. At the end of the week, review your notes and ask yourself how religion is connected to other social institutions. Based on your observations, how do you interpret the relationship between the *sacred* and the *secular* in this society.

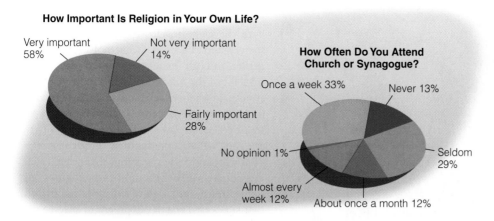

How Important Is Religion in Your Own Life?

Very important 58%

Not very important 14%

Fairly important 28%

How Often Do You Attend Church or Synagogue?

Once a week 33%

Never 13%

No opinion 1%

Seldom 29%

Almost every week 12%

About once a month 12%

FIGURE 12.4
Measuring Religiosity

SOURCE: Gallup Organization. 2003. *The Gallup Poll.* Princeton, NJ: The Gallup Organization. Used with permission.

The Dominance of Christianity

Despite the U.S. Constitution's principle of the separation of church and state, Christian religious beliefs and practices dominate U.S. culture. Indeed, Christianity is often treated as if it were the national religion. It is commonly said that the United States is based on a Judeo-Christian heritage, meaning that our basic cultural beliefs stem from the traditions of the pre-Christian Old Testament of the Bible (the Judaic tradition) and the Gospels of the New Testament. The dominance of Christianity is visible everywhere. State-sponsored colleges and universities typically close for Christmas break, not Yom Kippur. Christmas is a national holiday, but not Ramadan, the most sacred holiday among Muslims. Despite the dominance of Christianity, however, the pattern of religion in the United States is a mosaic one.

Measuring Religious Faith

Religiosity is the intensity and consistency of practice of a person's (or group's) faith. Sociologists measure religiosity both by asking people about their religious beliefs and by measuring membership in religious organizations and attendance at religious services. The majority of people in the United States identify themselves as Protestant (53 percent), Catholic (25 percent), or Jewish (2 percent), Mormon (2 percent), Greek or Russian Orthodox (1), with diverse religions (8 percent) and those with no religious identification (7 percent) or undesignated (2 percent) constituting the balance; 65 percent are members of a church or synagogue, although only 38 percent attend weekly (Gallup Poll 2003).

Religiosity varies significantly among different groups in society. Church membership and attendance is higher among women than men and more prevalent among older than younger people. African Americans are more likely than Whites to belong to and attend church. On the whole, church membership and attendance fluctuate over time; membership has decreased slightly since 1940, but attendance has remained largely the same since (see Figure 12.4). Large national religious organizations, such as the mainline Protestant denominations, have lost many members, whereas smaller, local congregations have increased membership.

These data indicate the extent of religiosity but tell little about how religion influences people's lives. To develop a picture of the day-to-day importance of religion, the sociologist must grapple with measures derived from the answers to subjective questions such as "How important is religion in your life?" In recent years, there has been a decrease in the number of people who think that religion can answer all or almost all of today's problems. There has also been a corresponding increase in people who think religion is largely old-fashioned, and a decrease in the number who say that religion is important in their own lives over time (Moore 2000).

Forms of Religion

Religions can be categorized in different ways according to the specific characteristics of faiths and how religious groups are organized. In different societies and among different religious groups, the form religion takes reflects differing belief systems and reflects and supports other features of the society. Believing in one god or many, worshiping in small or large groups, and associating religious faith with gender roles all contribute to the social organization of religion and its relationship to the rest of society.

One basic way to categorize religions is by the number of gods or goddesses they worship. **Monotheism** is the worship of a single god. Christianity and Judaism are monotheistic in that both Christians and Jews believe in a single god who created the universe. Monotheistic religions typically define god as omnipotent (all-powerful) and omniscient (all-knowing). **Polytheism** is the worship

Young people experience religiosity in a variety of ways such as this group of Billy Graham supporters at the Alamodome in Houston, Texas.

of more than one deity. Hinduism, for example, is extraordinarily complex with millions of gods, demons, sages, and heroes—all overlapping and entangled in religious mythology; within Hinduism, the universe is seen as so vast that it is believed to be beyond the grasp of a single individual, even a powerful god (Grimal 1963).

Religions may also be patriarchal or matriarchal. **Patriarchal religions** are those in which the beliefs and practices of the religion are based on male power and authority. Christianity is a patriarchal religion; the ascendancy of men is emphasized in the role of women in the church, the instruction given on relations between the sexes, and even the language of worship itself. **Matriarchal religions** are based on the centrality of female goddesses, who may be seen as the source of food, nurturance, and love, or who may serve as emblems of the power of women (McGuire 1996). In societies based on matriarchal religions, women are more likely to share power with men in the society at large. Because women and men participate more equally in secular life, it is more possible for them to imagine egalitarian divine beings (Ochshorn 1981). Likewise, in highly sexist, patriarchal societies, religious beliefs are also likely to be patriarchal.

■ *Sociological Theories of Religion*

The sociological study of religion probes how religion is related to the structure of society. Recall that one basic question sociologists ask is, "What holds society to-gether?" Coherence in society comes from both the social institutions that characterize society and the beliefs that hold society together. In both instances, religion plays a key role. From the functionalist perspective of sociological theory, religion is an integrative force in society because it has the power to shape collective beliefs. In a somewhat different vein, the sociologist Max Weber saw religion in terms of how it supported other social institutions. Weber thought that religious belief systems provided a cultural framework that supported the development of specific social institutions in other realms, such as the economy. From yet a third point of view, based in the work of Karl Marx and conflict theory, religion is related to social inequality in society (see Table 12.3).

Emile Durkheim: The Functions of Religion

Emile Durkheim argued that religion is functional for society because it reaffirms the social bonds that people have with each other, creating social cohesion and integration. Durkheim believed that the cohesiveness of society depends on the organization of its belief system. Societies with a unified belief system are highly cohesive; those with a more diffuse or competing belief systems are less cohesive.

Religious **rituals** are symbolic activities that express a group's spiritual convictions. Making a pilgrimage to Mecca, for example, is an expression of religious faith and a reminder of religious belonging. In Durkheim's view, religious rituals are vehicles for the creation, expression, and reinforcement of social cohesion. Groups performing a ritual are expressing their identity as a group. Whether the rituals of a group are highly elaborated or casually informal, they are symbolic behaviors that sustain group awareness of unifying beliefs. Lighting candles, chanting, or receiving a sacrament are behaviors that reunite the faithful and help them identify with the religious group, its goals, and its beliefs (McGuire 1996). Durkheim believed that religion binds individuals to the society in which they live, by establishing what he called a **collective consciousness,** the body of beliefs common to a community or society that give people a sense of belonging. In many societies, religion establishes the collective consciousness and creates in people the feeling that they are part of a common whole.

Durkheim's analysis of religion suggests some of the key ideas in symbolic interaction theory, particularly in the significance he gave to symbols in religious behavior.

TABLE 12.3 Theoretical Perspectives on Religion

	Functionalism	Conflict Theory	Symbolic Interaction
Religion and the social order	Is an integrative force in society	Is the basis for intergroup conflict; inequality in society is reflected in religious organizations, which are stratified by factors such as race, class, or gender	Is socially constructed and emerges with social and historical change
Religious beliefs	Provide cohesion in the social order by promoting a sense of *collective consciousness*	Can provide legitimation for oppressive social conditions	Are socially constructed and subject to interpretations; they can also be learned through religious conversion
Religious practices and rituals	Reinforce a sense of social belonging	Define in-groups and out-groups, thereby defining group boundaries	Are symbolic activities that provide definitions of group and individual identity

Symbolic interaction theory sees religion as a socially constructed belief system, one that emerges in different social conditions. From the perspective of symbolic interaction, religion is a meaning system that gives people a sense of identity, defines one's network of social belonging, and confers one's attachment to particular social groups and ways of thinking.

Max Weber: The Protestant Ethic and the Spirit of Capitalism

Durkheim's views were later elaborated by Max Weber, who saw a fit between the religious principles of society and other institutional needs. In his classic work, *The Protestant Ethic and the Spirit of Capitalism,* Weber argued that the Protestant faith supported the development of capitalism in the Western world. He began by noting a seeming contradiction: How could a religion that supposedly condemns conspicuous consumption coexist in a society with an economic system based on the pursuit of profit and material success?

Weber argued that these ideals were not as contradictory as they seemed. As the Protestant faith developed, it included a belief in predestination—the belief that one's salvation is predetermined, and that it is a gift from God, not something earned. This state of affairs created doubt and anxiety among believers, who searched for clues in the here-and-now about whether they were among the chosen. According to Weber, material success was taken to be one clue that a person was among the chosen and thus favored by God; therefore, early Protestants were driven to relentless work as a means of confirming (and demonstrating) their salvation. As it happens, hard work and self-denial—the key features of the **Protestant ethic**—led not only to salvation but also to the accumulation of capital. The religious ideas supported by the Protestant ethic therefore dovetailed nicely with the needs of capitalism. According to Weber, these austere Protestants stockpiled wealth, had an irresistible motive to earn more (eternal salvation), and were inclined to spend little on themselves, leaving a larger share for investment and driving the growth of capitalism (Weber 1904/1958).

Weber's analysis of the Protestant ethic shows how religious beliefs continue to shape our national culture, even in its secular dimensions. Beliefs that people are poor or on welfare because they do not want to work or the idea that hard work will lead to success are manifestations of the Protestant ethic.

Karl Marx: Religion, Social Conflict, and Oppression

Durkheim and Weber concentrated on how religion contributes to the cohesion of society. Religion can also be the basis for conflict, as we see in the daily headlines of newspapers. Conflict between Protestants and Catholics in Northern Ireland has been the basis for years of social and political warfare. In the Middle East, differences between Muslims and Jews have caused decades of political instability. These conflicts are not solely religious, but religion plays an inextricable part. Certainly religious wars, religious terrorism, and religious genocide have contributed some of the most violent and tragic episodes of world history. The image of religion in history has two incompatible sides: piety and contemplation on the one hand, battle flags on the other. Domestic conflicts over ethical issues such as abortion, assisted suicide, and school prayer evolve from religious values even though they are played out in the secular world of politics and public opinion. Conflict theory illuminates many of the social and political conflicts that engage religious values.

The link between religion and social inequality is also key to the theories of Karl Marx. Marx saw religion

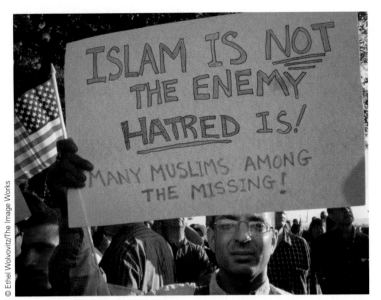

Religion can be interpreted both as producing social conflict and as promoting social justice.

At the same time, religion can be the basis for liberating social change. In the civil rights movement in the United States and in Latin American liberation movements, the words and actions of religious organizations have been central in mobilizing people for change. This does not undermine Marx's main point, however, because there remains ample evidence of the role of religion in generating social conflict and resisting social change.

Symbolic Interaction: Becoming Religious

Symbolic interaction emphasizes the process by which people become religious. This can be slow and gradual, as when someone switches to a new religious faith (such as a Christian person converting to Judaism), or it can be more dramatic, such as when a person joins a cult or some other extreme religious group. In common thought, those who enter extreme religious groups are thought to be brainwashed. This assumes that people are somehow tricked into religious conversion and undergo a radical change in identity. Symbolic interaction theory suggests otherwise.

as a tool for class oppression. According to Marx, oppressed people develop religion, with the urging of the upper classes, to soothe their distress (Marx, 1843/1972). The promise of a better life hereafter makes the present life more bearable, and the belief that "God's will" steers the present life makes it easier for people to accept their lot. To Marx, religion is a form of *false consciousness* (see Chapter 7) because it prevents people from rising up against oppression. He called religion the "opiate of the people" because it encourages passivity and acceptance.

To Marx, religion is an *ideology*—a belief system that legitimates the social order and supports the ideas of the ruling class. When subordinated groups internalize the views of the dominant class, they come to believe in the legitimacy of the social order that oppresses them. Marx thus saw religion as supporting the status quo and being inherently conservative (that is, resisting change and preserving the existing social order). Marx suggested that religion promotes stratification, because it generally supports a hierarchy of people on earth and the subordination of humankind to divine authority.

We can use Marx's argument to see how Christianity supported the system of slavery. When European explorers first encountered African people, they regarded them as godless savages and they justified the slave trade by arguing that slaves were being converted to the Christian way of life. Principles of Christianity thus legitimated the system of slavery in the eyes of the slaveowners and allowed them to see themselves as good people, despite their enslavement of other human beings.

DEBUNKING
Society's Myths

Myth: People who join extreme religious cults are maladjusted and have typically been brainwashed by cult leaders.

Sociological perspective: Conversion to a religious cult is usually a gradual process wherein the convert voluntarily develops new associations with others and through these relationships develops a new worldview.

Symbolic interaction emphasizes that religious conversion is linked to shifting patterns of group association, not simply mind control. People are active participants in their own conversion, not simply passive creatures "programmed" with new ideas. Most conversions to religious cults, for example, do not entail a radical alteration of lifestyle. When people convert, they typically have an experience that leads them to perceive disruption or failure in their previous life; they become open to a serious change in the social environment. How quickly this happens depends on what pressure is exerted by the new religious group with which one affiliates. When joining cults, the new group may manipulate the environment so as to separate new recruits from preexisting ties, intensifying the conditions that promote conversion. Finally, there is a pe-

Percent of
population

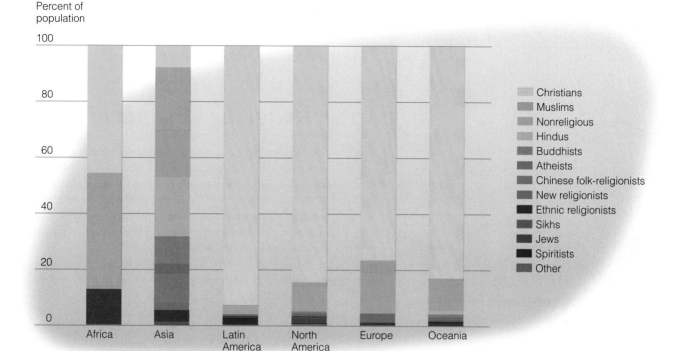

FIGURE 12.5 Viewing Society in Global Perspective: The World's
Religions
*Some religious groups are such a small percentage of the population that they do not
appear in bars on the chart.*

DATA: From the U.S. Census Bureau. 1999. *Statistical Abstract of the United States, 1999.* Washington, DC:
U.S. Government Printing Office, p. 831.

riod of intense interaction with the new group. This can
lead to total conversion. In some religious cults, such as
the Moonies, followers of Sun Myung Moon, or the followers of Heaven's Gate, initiates are also encouraged to
sever ties to their former lifestyles, including abandoning
their material resources (Ayella 1998; Balch 1995, 1980;
Bromley 1979; Long and Hadden 1983; Robbins 1988).

Diversity and
Religious Belief

The world is marked by diverse religious beliefs, often
the basis for world conflict. Christianity has the largest
membership, followed by Islam. But Hindus, Jews, Con-
fucianists, Buddhists, and other folk religions also comprise the world's religions (see Figure 12.5). In the
United States, religious identification varies with a number of social factors, including age, income level, education, and political affiliation (see Figure 12.6). Younger
people, for example, are more likely than older people to
express no religious preference. People over age fifty are

most likely to identify as Protestant, whereas identification as Catholic is most likely among those under thirty.
Those in higher income brackets are more likely to identify as Catholic or Jewish than those in lower income
brackets, who are more likely to identify as Protestant,
although these trends vary among Protestants by denom-
ination. Fundamentalist Protestants, for example, are
most likely to come from lower income groups.

Race is one of the most significant markers when examining patterns of religious orientation. African Americans are more likely to identify as Protestant than are
Whites or Hispanics, although the number of African
American Catholics is increasing (Bezilla 1990). Many
urban African Americans have also become committed
Black Muslims. Religious practice among Black Muslims involves strict regulation of dietary habits and prohibitions of many activities, such as alcohol use, drug
use, gambling, use of cosmetics, and hair straightening.
The emphasis among Black Muslims on self-reliance and
traditional African identity has earned it a fervent following, although the actual number of Black Muslims
in the United States is relatively small.

For many African Americans, religion has been a defense against the damage caused by racism. Churches

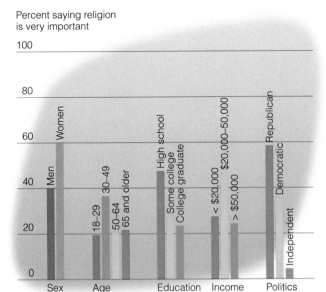

Percent saying religion is very important

FIGURE 12.6 For Whom Is Religion Most Important?

Based on the 35 percent of those who attend services weekly or almost weekly and also consider religion very important.

SOURCE: David W. Moore. 1995. "Most Americans Say Religion Is Important to Them." *The Gallup Poll Monthly* (February), p. 21. Used with permission.

have served as communal centers, political units, and sources of social and community support, making churches among the most important institutions within the African American community (Gilkes 2000; Blackwell 1991).

Religion has also been a strong force in Latino communities; 68 percent of Latinos identify themselves as Catholic. However, there are a significant and growing number of Latino Protestants, both in mainstream Protestant denominations and in fundamentalist groups. Among Latinos, religion helps sustain ties within and between families. Although Catholicism has been seen as particularly oppressive to Latinas, religious practice promotes interaction among women in Latino families and friendship groups.

Asian Americans have a great variety of religious orientations. One reason for this is that the category "Asian American" is constructed from so many different Asian cultures. Hinduism and Buddhism are common among Asians, but many are also Christian as the result of missionary efforts in Asia. As with all groups whose family histories include immigration, religious belief and practice among Asian Americans frequently changes between generations. The youngest generation may not worship as their parents and grandparents did, although some aspects of the inherited faith may be retained. Within families, the discontinuity with a religious past brought on by cultural assimilation can be a source of tension be-

tween grandparents, parents, and children. Within the United States, Asian Americans often mix Christian and traditionally Buddhist, Confucian, or Hindu beliefs, resulting in new religious practices.

▪ *Religious Organizations*

Sociologists have organized their understanding of the various religious organizations into three types: churches, sects, and cults. These are *ideal types* in the sense that Max Weber used the term. That is, the ideal types convey the essential characteristics of some social entity or phenomenon, even though they do not explain every feature of each entity included in the generic category.

Churches are formal organizations that tend to see themselves, and are seen by society, as the primary and legitimate religious institutions. They tend to be integrated into the secular world to a degree that sects and cults are not. They are sometimes closely tied to the state. Churches are organized as complex bureaucracies with division of labor and different roles for groups within. Generally, churches employ professional, full-time clergy who have been formally ordained following a specialized education. Church membership is renewed as the children of existing members are brought up in the church; churches may also actively proselytize. Churches are less exclusive than cults and sects, because they see all of society as potential members of the fold (Johnstone 1992).

Sects are groups that have broken off from an established church. They emerge when a faction within an established religion questions the legitimacy or purity of the group from which they are separating. Leaders of sects sometimes have no formal clerical training, although many sects form as offshoots of existing religious organization. Sects tend to place less emphasis on organization (as in churches) and more emphasis on the purity of members' faith. The Shakers, for example, were formed by departing from the Society of Friends (the Quakers). They retained some Quaker practices, such as simplicity of dress and a belief in pacifism, but departed from Quaker religious philosophy. The Shakers believed that the second coming of Christ was imminent, but that Christ would appear in the form of a woman (Kephart 1993).

Sects typically develop in protest against events or beliefs within the secular world. Different from churches, sects tend to admit only truly committed members, and sectarians typically refuse to compromise their beliefs. Some sects hold emotionally charged worship services, although others, like the Amish, are more stoical. The Shakers, for example, had such emotional services that they shook, shouted, and quivered while "talking with the Lord," earning them their name, from the "Shaking Quakers" (Kephart 1993). The only bodily contact permitted among the Shakers was during the unrestrained religious rituals; they were celibate (did not have sexual relations) and gained new members only through adoption of children or recruitment of newcomers.

Cults, which are like sects in their intensity, are religious groups devoted to a specific cause or charismatic leader. Many cults arise within established religions, and sometimes continue to peaceably reside within the parent religion as simply a fellowship of people with a particular, often mystical, set of dogma. The term *cult* is also used to refer to quasireligious organizations, often dominated by a single charismatic individual. A good example was the Heaven's Gate cult, ninety of whose members committed group suicide in Rancho Santa Fe, California in 1997, believing they were going away on spacecraft that would take them to a new world (Balch 1995).

Many mainstream religions began as cults. As they are developing, it is common for tension to exist between cults and the society around them. Cults tend to exist outside the mainstream of society, arising when believers think that society is not satisfying their spiritual needs, and attract those who feel a longing for meaningful attachments. Internally, cults seldom develop an elaborate organizational structure, but are instead close-knit communities held together by personal attachment and loyalty to the cult leader.

Cults form around leaders with great **charisma,** a quality attributed to individuals believed by their followers to have special powers (Johnstone 1992). Typically, followers are convinced that the charismatic leader has received a unique revelation or possesses supernatural gifts. Although there are exceptions, cult leaders are usually men, probably because men are more likely to be seen as having the aggressive and charismatic characteristics associated with heroic leadership.

■ *Religion and Social Change*

What is the role of religion in social change? Durkheim saw religion as promoting social cohesion; Weber saw it as culturally linked to other social institutions; Marx assessed religion in terms of its contribution to social oppression. Is religion a source of oppression, or is it a source of personal and collective liberation from worldly problems? There is no simple answer to this question.

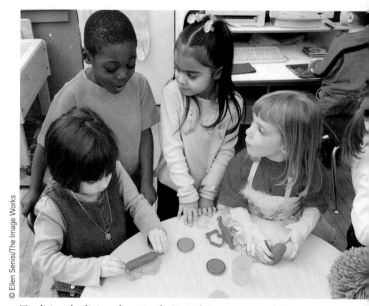

Traditional religious forms in the United States are now being joined by new religious practices, especially as the population is increasingly diverse.

Religion has had a persistent conservative influence on society, but it has also been an important part of movements for social justice and human emancipation.

The role of religious organizations in social change has of late become a question of public policy. Should faith-based organizations receive government support for work they do in helping people, or does this violate the constitutional separation of church and state? The constitutional issues will ultimately be settled by law, but sociological research sheds light on the implications of such organizations. Though liberals fear that faith-based organizations will infuse religion into government too much and conservatives hope that faith-based initiatives will support their political agenda, we know from research that faith-based initiatives enhance the participation of traditionally disadvantaged groups in the democratic process (Wood 2002; Kniss 2003).

The public debate about faith-based initiatives is occurring at a time when evangelical groups have increased membership and influence, and have affiliated with conservative political causes, dramatically increasing the influence of religion on politics. At the same time, there has been a decrease in the importance of religion to many people. As a social institution, religion is in transition. Religion, like other aspects of society, is also becoming more commercialized. A large self-help industry has developed in religious publication; religious music is increasingly successful as a form of enterprise. All sorts of religious products are bought and sold in what sociologists now call a "spiritual marketplace" (Roof 1999; Wuthnow 1998).

Clearly religion influences social change, but it is also influenced by the same changes that affect other social institutions.

At the same time, religion continues to have an important role in liberation movements around the world. Religion has played an important role in the development of social movements for the liberation of Latinos; throughout the world liberation theologians have used the prestige and organizational resources of the Catholic Church to develop a consciousness of oppression among poor peasants and working-class people.

Likewise, in the United States, churches have had a prominent role in the civil rights movement (Marx, 1967/1867; Morris 1984). Churches supplied the infrastructure of the developing Black protest movements of the 1950s and 1960s, and the moral authority of the church was used to reinforce the appeal to Christian values as the basis for racial justice. Now, they continue to be important places for the mobilization of Black politics, and provide an important source of community support—often when other institutions have abandoned the Black community, a point early noted by W. E. B. DuBois in his analyses of religion written early in the twentieth century (Zuckerman 2002).

The role of women is also changing in most religious organizations. Women have long been denied the right to full participation in many faiths. Some religions refuse to ordain women as clergy, and in the past women were denied admission to divinity schools. Women now earn 29 percent of theological degrees (U.S. Census Bureau 2002), and the public generally supports the ordination of women. And, whereas traditional religious images of women have provided the basis for the subordination of women, many of those stereotypes are giving way. In sum, religion is both a force of social change and social stability.

■ *Chapter Summary*

■ *How are different kinship systems defined?*

All societies are organized around a *kinship system,* varying by how many marriage partners are allowed, who can marry whom, how descent is determined, family residence, and power relations within the family. *Extended family* systems develop when there is a need for extensive economic and social cooperation. The *nuclear family* is the result of the rise of Western industrialization that separated production from the home.

■ *What does sociological theory contribute to our understanding of families?*

Functionalism emphasizes that families have the function of integrating members to support society's needs. *Conflict theorists* see the family as a power rela-

tionship, related to other systems of inequality. *Feminist theory* emphasizes the family as a gendered institution and is critical of perspectives that take women's place in the family for granted. *Symbolic interaction* takes a more microscopic look at families, emphasizing how different family members experience and define their family experience.

■ *What changes characterize the diversity in contemporary families?*

One of the greatest changes in families has been the increase in female-headed households, which are most likely to live in poverty. The increase in women's labor force participation has also affected families, resulting in dual roles for women. Stepfamilies face unique problems stemming from the blending of two households. Gay and lesbian households are also more common and challenge traditional heterosexual definitions of the family. Single people make up an increasing portion of the population, due in part to the later age when people marry.

■ *Is marriage declining as the divorce rate increases?*

The United States has both the highest marriage rate and the highest divorce rate of any industrialized nation. The majority of people now prefer a lifestyle in which husband and wife work and share household responsibilities, although many retain more traditional values. The high divorce rate is explained as the result of a cultural orientation toward individualism and personal gratification, as well as structural changes that make women less dependent on men within the family.

■ *Why is family violence such a problem?*

Family violence takes several forms, including partner violence, child abuse, incest, and elder abuse. Power relationships within families, as well as gender differences in the division of labor, help explain domestic violence.

■ *What major changes are affecting contemporary families?*

Changes at the global level are producing new forms of families—*transnational families*—where at least one parent lives and works in a different nation from the children. Social policies designed to assist families should recognize the diversity of family forms and the interdependence of the family with other social conditions and social institutions.

■ *What are the elements of a religion?*

Sociologists are interested in religion because of the strong influence it has in society. *Religion* is an institutionalized system of symbols, beliefs, values, and practices by which a group of people interprets and responds to what they feel is sacred; and that provides answers to questions of ultimate meaning. The *sacred* is that which is set apart from ordinary activity, is seen as holy, and is protected by special rites and *rituals. Totems* are sacred objects that people regard with special awe and reverence.

■ How do sociologists measure the significance of religion for people and what forms does religion take?

The United States is a deeply religious society. Christianity dominates the national culture, even though the U.S. Constitution specifies a separation between church and state. *Religiosity* is the measure of the intensity and practice of religious commitment. Religions may be *polytheistic* or *monotheistic, patriarchal,* or *matriarchal.*

■ How do the different sociological theories analyze religion?

Durkheim understood religions and religious rituals as creating social cohesion. Weber saw a fit between the ideology of the *Protestant ethic* and the needs of a capitalistic economy. Religion is also related to social conflict. Marx saw religion as supporting societal oppression and encouraging people to accept their lot in life. *Symbolic interaction theory* focuses on the process by which people become religious. Religious conversion involves a dramatic transformation of religious identity and involves several phases through which individuals learn to identify with a new group and lose other existing social ties.

■ What diversity exists in religious faith and practice?

The United States is a diverse religious society. Protestants, Catholics, Jews, and increasingly, Muslims, make up the major religious faiths in the United States. Patterns of religious faith and participation vary by age, income level, education, ethnicity, and race.

■ How is a religion organized?

Churches are formal religious organizations. They are distinct from *sects* that are religious groups that have withdrawn from an established religion. *Cults* are groups that have also rejected a dominant religious faith, but they tend to exist outside the mainstream of society.

■ How has religion been affected by social change?

In recent years, there has been an enormous growth in conservative religious groups. Evangelical groups have linked to numerous conservative political causes and have had a great influence on recent national elections. Religion is a conservative influence in society, but religion also has an important part in movements for human liberation, including the civil rights movement and the move to ordain women in the church.

■ Key Terms

antimiscegenation laws 319	monotheism 339
bilateral kinship 319	nuclear family 319
charisma 345	patriarchal religion 340
church 344	patrilineal kinship 319
collective consciousness 340	polygamy 318
cult 345	polytheism 339
endogamy 318	profane 337
exogamy 318	Protestant ethic 341
extended families 319	religion 337
Family and Medical Leave Act (FMLA) 335	religiosity 339
	ritual 340
family 317	sacred 337
kinship system 317	sect 345
matriarchal religion 340	secular 338
matrilineal kinship 319	totem 337
monogamy 318	transnational family 334

■ Researching Society with MicroCase Online

You can see the results of actual research by using the Wadsworth MicroCase® Online feature available to you. This feature allows you to look at some of the results from national surveys, census data, and other data sources. You can explore this easy-to-use feature on your own, but try this example. Suppose you want to know some social facts, such as:

How often do you take part in the activities and organizations of a church or place of worship other than attending services?

To answer this question, go to **sociology.wadsworth .com/andersen_taylor/essen3e**, select MicroCase Online from the left navigation bar, and follow the directions there to analyze the data described below.

Data file: GSS

Task: Auto-Analyzer

Primary Variable: RELG.ACTIV

Questions

Once you have your results, answer the following questions.

1. People reporting to follow which religion are most likely to have taken part in religious activities?

a. Liberal Protestants
b. Conservative Protestants
c. Catholics
d. Jews
e. No religion

2. What percentages of those in each political party shown often take part in religious activities?
_____ % Democrats
_____ % Republicans
_____ % Independents

3. How do African Americans and Whites compare in their participation in religious activities? How might you explain these differences?

4. Is gender a significant factor in predicting people's participation in religious activities? Why do you think this is so?

■ *The Companion Web Site for Sociology: The Essentials, Third Edition*

sociology.wadsworth.com/andersen_taylor/essen3e

Supplement your review of this chapter by going to the companion Web site to take one of the Tutorial Quizzes, use the flash cards to master key terms, and check out the many other study aids you'll find there. You'll also find special features such as GSS Data and Census 2000 information, data and resources at your fingertips to help you with that special project or do some research on your own.

■ *Suggested Readings and Web Resources*

Ammerman, Nancy Tatom. 1997. *Congregation and Community.* New Brunswick, NJ: Rutgers University Press.
Ammerman studies various religious institutions in communities with a highly diverse population. She examines how religious institutions respond to such changes.

Baca Zinn, Maxine, and Stanley D. 2002. *Diversity in Families,* 6th ed. Boston: Allyn and Bacon.

A comprehensive sociological analysis of families that focuses on the different family experiences across race, class, and gender.

Garey, Anita. 1999. *Weaving Work and Motherhood.* Philadelphia: Temple University Press.
Based on an interview study with women hospital employees in various jobs, Garey examines how working mothers construct their identities. Unlike the prevailing idea that women see work and motherhood as "either/or" choices, Garey demonstrates how women see both as a part of who they are, despite the difficulties of managing these two roles.

Gerstl, Naomi, Dan Clawson, and Robert Zussman, eds. 2002. *Families at Work: Expanding the Boundaries.* Nashville, TN: Vanderbilt University Press.
This anthology explores contemporary issues and social policies in the connection between families and work, including such topics as child care and family labor.

Gilkes, Cheryl Townsend. 2000. *"If It Wasn't for the Women . . ." Black Women's Experience and Womanist Culture in Church and Community.* Mary Knoll, NY: Orbis Books.
Gilkes examines the significant role of African American women in churches, including how churches work for social justice.

Family Violence Prevention Fund
www.fvpf.org
A nonprofit organization focusing on policy and education about domestic violence. The Web site includes research information, personal testimonies, and national contacts for other resources.

The Center for the Study of American Religion, Princeton University
www.princeton.edu/~nadelman/csar/csar.html
The Center for the Study of American Religion encourages the academic study of religion; the Web site contains information about the center's activities and links to numerous other sites for the study of American religion.

American Religion Links
www.as/wvu.edu/coll03/relst/www/link.htm
Published by West Virginia University, this site includes links to online journals, courses, and other resources pertinent to the study of religion.

CHAPTER THIRTEEN

Education and Health Care

*O*llie Taylor (a pseudonym) is a bright eleven-year-old African American. He is growing up in a two-parent family in Boston. His father works fifty hours a week, but they are still poor. Although he receives considerable encouragement, love, and respect from his family, Ollie Taylor is certain that everything he attempts will fail. He is convinced that he is, in his own words, worthless. In Ollie's case, his feelings about himself were significantly created by the educational system of *tracking*—the grouping or stratifying of students within the education system.

Although tracking is on the downswing in the United States, stories like Ollie Taylor's are still common. His case highlights one problem facing the American education system: Should children be tracked according to their ability, allowing them to learn at their most comfortable pace, or should they be grouped simply by age, perhaps retarding the progress of fast learners and keeping a pace too fast for the slow learners?

There are both positive and negative consequences to early tracking of students (a system discussed in detail later in this chapter), showing that the negatives outweigh the positives. Ollie Taylor's case exemplifies the negative consequences, yet he may also benefit from the positive aspects of getting an education in the United States, even with tracking in place: As an African American, he is six times more likely now than in 1940 to graduate from high school.

His chances of dropping out prior to graduation are, unfortunately, still fairly high (see Map 13.1). They are considerably higher than for a White youngster of his age, but significantly lower than for a Hispanic young man. If he graduates, he will stand a better chance of avoiding the grim path of many urban Black male dropouts and many White youth—a path leading to unemployment and possibly drug abuse, poor health, incarceration, and death at an early age.

Like education, health care in the United States is an institution. And like education, health care as an institution is in crisis. The public wonders: Has the quality of health care in the United States declined over the last two decades? Are doctors and nurses as good as they used to be? Are doctors overpaid? Are hospitals overcharging? Why are costs for medical insurance so high, and why do so many people not have health insurance?

These public issues may seem to be simple matters of personal responsibility or individual rights, but sociologists show that illness in our society is strongly influenced by social factors. How we treat illnesses is highly influenced by race, social class, gender, and age; and the same can be said of how we treat ill people. In different societies, the *same* physical state may be regarded as either sickness or wellness, demonstrating that the definition of illness is at least partly socially constructed. Physical conditions regarded as illness might be treated by prayer or witchcraft, surgery or radiation therapy, depending on the culture or society in question. The definition of pain also varies considerably from culture to culture, so much so that what is experienced as pain in one society may be considered pleasure in another. Witness in our society the following experiences usually thought of as painful, but experienced as pleasurable by the participants in their subculture: swimming in ice-cold water, marathon running, and slam dancing.

■ *Schooling and Society: Theories of Education*

Education in a society is concerned with the systematic transmission of the society's knowledge. This includes teaching formal knowledge such as the "three R's," reading, writing, and arithmetic, as well as morals, values, and ethics. Education prepares the young for entry into society and is thus a form of socialization. Sociologists refer to the more formal, institutionalized aspects of education as *schooling.*

Compulsory education is a relatively new idea. During the nineteenth century, many states did not yet have laws requiring education for everyone. Most jobs in the middle of the nineteenth century demanded no education or literacy whatsoever. Education was considered a luxury, available only to children of the upper classes (Cookson and Persell 1985). Education for slaves was prohibited by law until 1900, long after the Emancipation Proclamation passed in 1863.

When compulsory education was established in 1900, the law passed in all states except a few in the South, where Black Americans were still largely denied formal education of any kind (Higginbotham 1978). In the past, state laws in the South and West have also prohibited education for Hispanics, American Indians, and Chinese immigrants. State laws requiring attendance were generally enforced for White Americans at least through eighth grade. Education all the way through high school lagged considerably. In 1910, *less than 10*

The Functionalist View of Education

All known societies have an education system of some sort. In the United States, as in other industrialized societies, the education system is large and highly formalized. In other societies, such as pastoral societies, it may consist only of parents teaching their children how to till land and gather food. Under these circumstances, the family is both the education system and the kinship institution.

Why does an education institution exist? Functionalist theory in sociology argues that education accomplishes the following consequences, or "functions," for a society:

Socialization is brought about as the cultural heritage is passed on from one generation to the next. This heritage includes a lot more

Ethnic and cultural diversity in the public high school classroom are increasingly common.

© Rick Scott/Index Stock Imagery

percent of White eighteen-year-olds in the United States had graduated from high school. Today, almost 90 percent of those under thirty-five in the United States have received at least a high school diploma, although high school completion for Blacks lags behind that of Whites, and that of Hispanics lags significantly behind that of Blacks. As Figure 13.1 shows, similar trends exist for college graduates.

DEBUNKING
Society's Myths

Myth: To get ahead in society, all you need is an education.

Sociological perspective: Education is necessary, but not sufficient, for getting ahead in society. Success depends significantly on one's class origins; the formal education of one's parent or parents; and one's race, ethnicity, and gender.

FORCES OF SOCIAL CHANGE

Teach for America

Back in 1986, Wendy Kopp was a college senior with an idea, which she wrote up as her senior thesis paper. She wanted to make the world a better place by creating an ethnically diverse corps of dedicated, energetic new teachers who would go out into the poorer communities across the United States and teach children who were at risk of failing.

She was told that the idea would never work; that it was too idealistic and impractical. Even her own senior thesis faculty advisor tried to talk her out of it! But she persisted. Naming her new organization Teach for America, of which she is president, it has now become the most successful and widespread teacher-recruitment effort for needy communities in the history of the country. The heart of the idea was to train young persons who, like herself, were excited about being trained as teachers in poor rural as well as urban communities.

She obtained foundation grants to set up the first teacher training institute. The success of this new venture was overwhelming: Over 2500 applications were received, from which she and the new organization selected 500 recruits to attend the new training institute. By the year 2000 over 5000 newly-trained teachers had completed two years in classrooms in schools all over the United States. Now, at any given time, there are approximately 1000 corps members on the job in the classroom in the United States. As testimony to the ultimate success and practicality of the program, several thousand graduates of the program have continued in the teaching profession, or have become administrators and lawyers in disadvantaged communities. In his 2002 State of the Union Address, President George W. Bush asked Congress to expand the program, but as recently as November of 2003, Teach for America has lost much of its federal funding.

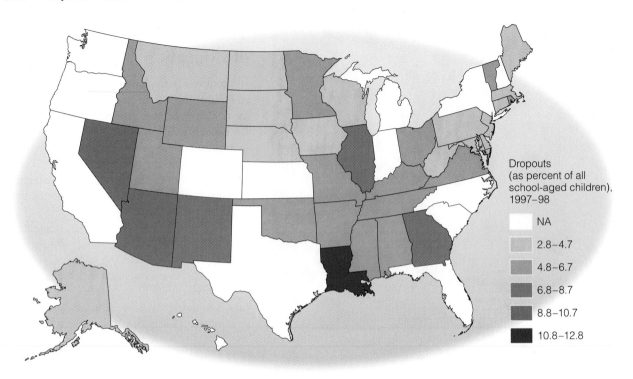

MAP 13.1 Mapping America's Diversity: School Dropout Rates
Notice that states vary quite considerably in their school dropout rates. **Can you locate your home state and its dropout rate? Why are dropout rates higher in some places than others?**

SOURCE: National Center for Educational Statistics. 2003. *Digest of Education Statistics.* Washington, DC: U.S. Department of Education. **nces.ed.gov/quicktables**

than "book knowledge." It includes moral values, ethics, politics, religious beliefs, habits, and norms—in short, culture.

Occupational training is another function of education, especially in an industrialized society such as the United States. In less complex societies, as was the United States prior to the nineteenth century, jobs and training were passed from father to son, or more rarely, from father or mother to daughter. A significant number of occupations and professions today are still passed on from parent to offspring, particularly among the upper classes (a father passing on a law practice to his son), but also among certain highly skilled occupations (plumbers, ironworkers, and electricians), where both training and union memberships may be passed on. Modern industrialized societies need a system that trains people for jobs. Most jobs today require at least a high school education, and many professions require a graduate degree.

Social control, or the regulation of deviant behavior, is also a function of education, although less obvious. Such indirect, subtle consequences emerging from the activities of institutions are called *latent functions.* Increased urbanization and immigration beginning in the late nineteenth century were accompanied by rises in crime, overcrowding, homelessness, and other urban ills. One

perceived benefit of compulsory education was that it kept young people off the streets and out of trouble.

The Conflict View of Education

In contrast with functionalist theory, which emphasizes how education unifies and stabilizes society, conflict theory emphasizes the disintegrative and disruptive aspects of education. Conflict theory focuses on the competition between groups for power, income, and social status, emphasizing the prevailing importance of institutions in the conflict. One intersection of education between group and class competition is embodied in the significant correlations that exist between education and class, race, and gender. The unequal distribution of education allows it to be used to separate groups. The higher the educational attainment of a person, the more likely that person will be middle to upper class, White, and male. Conflict theorists argue that educational level is a mechanism for producing and reproducing inequality.

According to conflict theorists educational level can be a tool for discrimination by using the mechanism of **credentialism**—the insistence upon educational credentials for their own sake, even if the credentials bear little relationship to the intended job (Collins 1979; Marshall

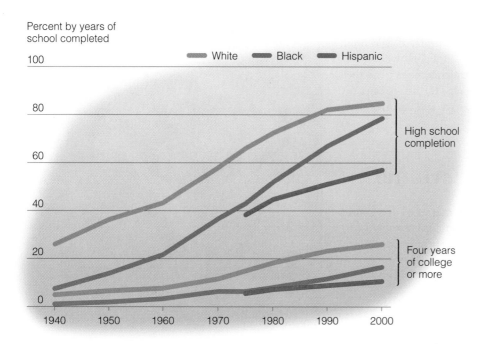

Percent by years of school completed

White   Black   Hispanic

FIGURE 13.1 The Expansion of Education

Source: U.S. Census Bureau. *Statistical Abstract of the United States, 2002.* p. 41.

1997). This device can be used by potential employers to discriminate against minorities, working-class people, or women—that is, those who are often less educated, and least likely to be credentialed because discriminatory practices within the education system limited their opportunities for educational achievement.

Although functionalists argue that jobs are becoming more technical and thus require workers with higher education, conflict theorists argue that the reverse is true—most new opportunities appearing today are in categories such as assembly-line work, jobs that are becoming less complex and less technical and therefore require less traditional education or training. Nonetheless, potential employers will insist on a particular degree for the job even though there should be little expectation that educational level will affect job performance. In this case, education serves as a discriminatory barrier.

The Symbolic Interactionist View of Education

Symbolic interaction focuses on what arises from the operation of the interaction process during the schooling experience. Through interaction between student and teacher, certain expectations arise on the part of both. As a result, the teacher begins to expect or anticipate certain behaviors, good or bad, from students. Through the operation of the *expectancy effect,* the expectations a teacher has for a student can create the behavior in question. Thus

TABLE 13.1 Sociological Theories of Education

	Functionalism	**Conflict Theory**	**Symbolic Interaction**
Education in Society	Fulfills certain societal needs for socialization and training; "sorts" people in society according to their abilities	Reflects other inequities in society, including race, class, and gender inequality, and perpetuates such inequalities by tracking practices	Emerges depending on the character of social interaction between groups in schools
Schools	Inculcate values needed by the society	Are hierarchical institutions reflecting conflict and power relations in society	Are sites where social interaction between groups (such as teachers and students) influences chances for individual and group success
Social Change	Means that schools take on functions that other institutions, such as the family, originally fulfilled	Threatens to put some groups at continuing disadvantage in the quality of education	Can be positive as people develop new perceptions of formerly stereotyped groups

the behavior is actually caused by the expectation, rather than the other way around. For example, if a White teacher expects Latino boys to perform below average on a math test, relative to White students, over time the teacher may act in ways that encourage the Latino boys to get below average test scores. Later we will examine just how the expectancy effect works.

▪ *Does Schooling Matter?*

How much does schooling really matter? Does more schooling actually lead to a better job, more annual income, and greater happiness? Is the effect of education great or small?

Effects of Education on Occupation and Income

One way that sociologists measure a person's social class or socioeconomic status (SES) is to determine the person's amount of schooling, income, and type of occupation (see Chapter 7 on class stratification). Sociologists call these the *indicators* of SES. In the general population there is a strong relationship between formal education and occupation, although the relationship is not perfect. Measuring occupations in terms of social status or prestige, we find that the higher a person's occupational status, the more formal education he or she is likely to have received. Overall, we know that on average, doctors, lawyers, professors, and nuclear physicists spend many more years in school than unskilled laborers, such as garbage collectors and shoe shiners. This relationship is strong enough that we can often, although not always, guess a person's educational attainment just by knowing their occupation. There are indeed instances of semi-skilled laborers, such as taxi drivers, who have Ph.D.s, but they are relatively rare. Also exceedingly rare is the reverse: the self-educated, self-made individual who completed only the fourth grade and is now the CEO of a major corporation. Finally, at least one researcher (Kasarda 1999) argues that there is a serious mismatch between the skills youths learn today and the skills required to enter the job market.

The connection between income (and jobs) and education is not independent of gender. Gender heavily influences the relationship between income and education. Note from Table 13.2 that although the higher one's education, the higher one's (average) income, it is nonetheless true that the average income for women is less than the average income for men at *each* education level. This is because in general, throughout our society, the average woman earns less than a man of the same *or even less* edu-

Japanese students and their parents at this juko, *or "cram" seminar, vow academic success at a meeting in a hotel in Tokyo over the New Year's holiday.*

cation. Men with professional degrees (law, medicine, and so forth) earn a median annual income of $81,606, whereas a woman with that same education earns only $45,999, about 56 percent of what a man earns. A man with no graduate education but a college-only education earns $49,180, more than a woman with a master's degree. And men with some college, but no degree, earn more than women with bachelor's degrees.

Effects of Social Class Background on Education and Social Mobility

Education has traditionally been viewed in the United States as the way out of poverty and low social standing—the main route to upward social mobility. The assumption has been that a person can overcome modest beginnings, starting by staying in school.

Much sociological research has demonstrated that the effect of education on a person's eventual job and income greatly depends on the social class that the person was born into. Among White people of the upper classes, including those who inherited wealth, as well as professionals and high-level managers, social class origin is *more important than education* in determining occupation and income (Blau and Duncan 1967; Jencks 1993; Jencks et al. 1979; Jencks et al. 1972; Bielby 1981; Persell 1990). Class and race work together to "protect" the upper classes from downward social mobility—and to block the lower classes from too much upward mobility. Education is used by the upper classes to avoid downward mobility, by means such as sending their children to elite private secondary schools. A disproportionate number of upper-

TABLE 13.2 Median Income, by Education and Gender In Dollars

Level of schooling	Men (percent of those in category)	Women (percent of those in category)
Less than 9th grade	$14,139 (6.7)	$8,404 (5.9)
9th to 12th grade (no diploma)	18,952 (8.5)	9,995 (8.5)
High school graduate	27,669 (31.6)	15,120 (33.3)
Some college, no degree	33,035 (17.4)	20,181 (17.9)
Associate degree	37,956 (7.4)	23,270 (9.1)
Bachelor's degree	49,180 (18.4)	30,489 (17.3)
Master's degree	59,376 (6.3)	40,246 (6.2)
Professional degree	81,606 (2.1)	45,999 (1.0)
Doctorate degree	71,732 (1.8)	48,885 (.7)

SOURCE: U.S. Census Bureau. 2002. *Money Income in the United States 2000.* Washington, DC: U.S. Department of Commerce.

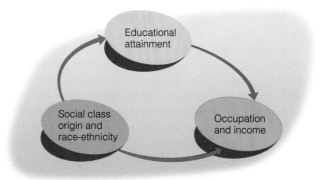

FIGURE 13.2 Relationship of Social Class, Race–Ethnicity, Education, Occupation, and Income

class children attend elite boarding schools and day schools, compared to working-class children who are considerably underrepresented in such schools (Rendon and Hope 1996; Cookson and Persell 1985).

Among middle-class Whites, education considerably improves the chances of getting middle-class jobs; yet access to upper-class positions is limited. Among those of lower-class origins, such as unskilled laborers or the chronically unemployed, chances of getting a good education as well as a prestigious job are poor. In sum, education is affected by social-class origins, and occupation (and income) is heavily influenced by social class and education. Individuals with lower-class origins are less likely to get a college education and thus are less likely to get a prestigious job. These interrelationships are summarized in Figure 13.2.

<hr>

DEBUNKING
Society's Myths

Myth: Education is more important than social class in determining one's job and income.

Sociological perspective: Although education has an effect on the job one gets and the income one earns, overall, social class origin is more important than acquired education in determining one's job and earned income.

<hr>

Education, Social Class, and Mobility Seen Globally

It is sometimes argued that because of our education system, there is more occupational and income mobility in the United States than in other industrialized nations,

particularly England, Germany, and Japan. In general this is true, but not by much. Until a few years ago, students in England were required to take an examination, called the Eleven Plus, at age eleven. A person's score on this examination determined whether he or she was put on a track to prestigious universities such as Oxford or Cambridge or went directly into the labor force from high school. Children of the upper classes stood a *far* better chance of scoring high on this examination than did middle- or working-class children, and the average scores of women and minorities, especially Africans and East Indians, were considerably lower than those of upper-class White males.

A similar situation exists in the United States. Students from lower-class families have lower average scores on exams such as the Scholastic Assessment Test (SAT) and the American College Testing Program (ACT). As shown in Table 13.3, there is a smooth and dramatic increase in average (mean) SAT score as family income is higher, for both SAT verbal as well as math scores. In this sense, one's SAT score is a "proxy" measure of one's social class: *Within a certain range, you can guess one's likely SAT score from knowing only the income and social class of one's parents!* This is ironic, since the multiple-choice SAT was originally designed back in the 1940s in order to combat the pattern of children from wealthy families with an advantage for admission to college.

With lower scores comes a diminished chance of getting into the best colleges or universities. African Americans, Latinos, and American Indians score on the average less than Whites, and women tend to score lower than men on the quantitative (mathematical) sections of the SAT (Table 13.4). Asian Americans as a group have scored higher than Whites in recent years on the quantitative sections of the SAT, but lower on the verbal sections. Women of any ethnic group score less on the quantitative sections than men of the same ethnic group. These patterns indicate that the SAT has an effect in the United States similar to that of the Eleven Plus in England, directing the futures of young people according to the results of widely admin-istered exams.

In Japan, a similar examination given at age twelve determines even more rigidly a child's subsequent edu-cational opportunities. Students who wish to continue their education at a college or university must score high enough to gain admission to prep schools. Especially high scores guarantee admission to prestigious prep schools, which is necessary for later admission to the best universities. Low scorers are virtually shut out from prep school admission and these students become ineligible for a university education. In recent years, many parents have begun to send their children to weekend "cram" seminars called *jukos* to prepare for this examination, adding a grueling additional regimen to the already stiff requirements of the Japanese school system.

▪ *Education and Inequality*

In its original nineteenth-century conception, the educa-tion system was to serve as a leveling force in American society—the road to full equality for all citizens regard-less of race, social-class origin, religion, or gender. Jew and gentile, Black and White, rich and poor, male and female would learn together side by side. Through edu-cation, each student would learn the ways of others and

TABLE 13.3 Average SAT Scores, By Family Income

Family Income	# Students	SAT Verbal Average Scores	SAT Math Average Scores
<$10,000	34,890	421	443
$10,000–$20,000	70,696	442	456
$20,000–$30,000	86,414	468	474
$30,000–$40,000	101,692	487	489
$40,000–$50,000	86,637	501	503
$50,000–$60,000	89,620	509	512
$60,000–$70,000	77,020	516	519
$70,000–$80,000	72,298	522	527
$80,000–$90,000	95,656	534	540
>$100,000	152,191	557	569
No Response	323,451		

SOURCE: College Board, 2001. *College Board Seniors 2001: A Profile of SAT Program Test Takers.* New York: The College Board. Used with permission.

thus come to understand and respect them. Full equality for humankind was to follow.

Education has indeed reduced many inequalities in so-ciety since compulsory education began at the turn of the twentieth century. The percentage of high school gradu-ates has risen among Whites and minorities, both male and female, as have certain types of social mobility. De-

TABLE 13.4 Average SAT Scores, by Ethnicity and Gender

SAT Test Takers Who Described Themselves as:	SAT Verbal Average Scores			SAT Math Average Scores		
	2000 Male	2000 Female	2000 Total	2000 Male	2000 Female	2000 Total
American Indian or Alaskan Native	482	481	482	498	467	481
Asian, Asian American, or Pacific Islander	501	498	499	583	548	565
African American or Black	431	436	434	436	419	426
Hispanic or Latino Background Mexican or Mexican American	458	499	453	480	445	460
Puerto Rican	460	452	456	471	437	451
Latin American, South American, Central American, or other Hispanic or Latino	467	457	461	489	451	467
White	529	526	528	549	514	530
Other	509	506	508	538	497	515
No response	495	495	495	523	493	509

SOURCE: College Board, 2003. *College Board Seniors 2003: A Profile of SAT Program Test Takers.* New York: The College Board.
www.collegeboard.com/about/news_info/ebsenior/yr2003/html/links.html

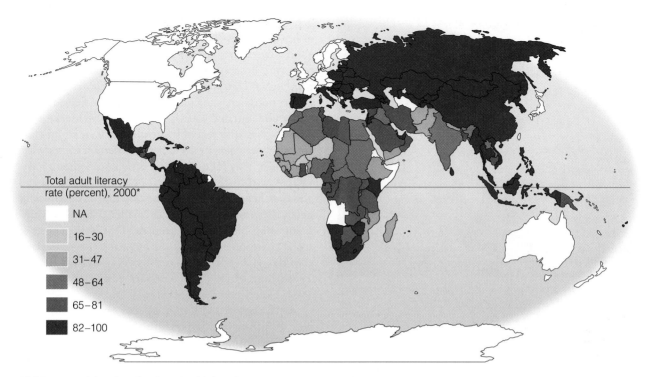

MAP 13.2 Viewing Society in Global Perspective: Literacy Around the World

Literacy rate is an important index. Notice that on some continents (such as Africa), literacy rate varies from country to country. **What social factors would affect this?**

*Percentage of persons aged fifteen and over who can read and write.

SOURCE: From UNICEF, 2003. *State of the World's Children 2003.*
www.unicef.ogr/sowc03/tables/table4.html

spite continuing inequalities in college enrollments comparing African Americans, Hispanics, and Whites, the enrollment of minorities has risen overall. Furthermore, as more minorities and women attend and graduate from two- and four-year colleges, the result has been more employment in mid-level and high-level jobs. Nonetheless, many inequalities still exist in U.S. education.

Cognitive Ability and Its Measurement

Since as long ago as classical Greece, humans have sought to measure a "mental faculty" or "intelligence." It is now called **cognitive ability**—the capacity for abstract thinking. Since early in the twentieth century, educators in our society, from preschools to universities, have attempted to measure intelligence by means of **standardized ability tests,** such as the SAT or IQ tests are intended to measure ability or potential. They are not the same as **achievement tests,** which are intended to measure what has actually been learned, in addition to ability or poten-

tial. Advanced Placement (AP) exams are achievement tests taken before entering college. Students who score high demonstrate that they have already mastered certain material and can skip those courses in college.

The education system in the United States has relied heavily upon the idea that intelligence, or ability, or potential is a single unitary trait. Cognitive ability has been gauged according to the numerical results of the standardized tests. There has been a will to reduce measurements of cognitive ability to a single number, or perhaps two numbers such as language and math scores of SAT tests and IQ tests in the recent past.

Three major criticisms are made of using standardized tests, such as the SAT or ACT, as measures of cognitive ability. First, the tests tend to measure only limited ranges of ability (such as quantitative aptitude or verbal aptitude) while ignoring other cognitive endowments such as creativity, musical ability, or even political skill (Gardner 1999; Sternberg 1988; Lehmann 1999). Second, the tests possess at least some degree of *cultural bias* and *gender bias.* As a result they may perpetuate inequality between different cultural or racial groups, and social

Contrary to the impression given in this photo, girls are frequently underrepresented in scientific and technical classes in school, particularly in upper grades and college.

classes, as well as perpetuate social, economic, and educational inequality between men and women. The tests were designed primarily by middle-class White males, and the "standardization" they strive to achieve mirrors middle-class White male populations. Many studies show that although standardized ability tests are somewhat capable of predicting future school performance for White males, a significant number of studies show less accurate forecasts for the success of minorities, especially Hispanics, African Americans, and American Indians, and they sometimes predict school performance less accurately for women than for men (Jensen 1980; Crouse and Trusheim 1988; Taylor 2002, 1992a, 1981; Epps 2002; Pennock-Roman 1994; Young 1994). In other words, the **predictive validity** of the tests, which is the extent to which the tests accurately predict later college grades, is compromised for minorities and for women.

The third criticism of the SATs is that they do not predict school performance very well, even for White students. For example, SAT scores are only modestly accurate predictors of college grades for White students (Young 1994; Pennock-Roman 1994; Manning and Jackson 1984). This fact is not well known. Grade point average in high school is also only a modestly accurate predictor of success in college—but high school grades are as accurate as the SATs in predicting college grades, which is to say, not very accurate.

Ability and Diversity

As already noted, average scores on IQ tests, and also cognitive ability tests such as the SAT, differ by racial–ethnic group, social class, and gender. Overall, Whites score higher on average than minorities, and in general, the higher a person's social class, the higher his or her test scores. The differences between groups are regarded by experts as primarily environmental in origin, reflecting group differences in years of parental education, social class status, childhood socialization, language, nutrition, and cultural advantages received in the home and during youth. There is no evidence that *between-group* differences by gender, race, or social class are in any way genetically inherited. Certain *within-group* differences may reflect genetic differences among individuals within the *same* racial or ethnic group, social class, or gender. But even the within-group effect of genes is estimated to be much smaller than the within-group effect of social environment. That is, the effects of social environment are greater than the effect of genes, even though genes have some effect (Taylor 2002, 1992a, 1980; Jang et al. 1996; Chipuer et al. 1990; Gould 1981; Goldberger 1979; Kamin 1974).

Both women and minorities have been catching up with White men in SAT math scores during the last few years. The change, coinciding with some social gains on the part of minorities and women over the last decade or so, tends to discredit the traditional belief that women, Blacks, and Latinos have less mathematical ability than White men. This belief has been used in the past to support the argument that women, and minorities, are less fit to perform high-level executive jobs that require number crunching and abstract analytical reasoning. This belief tends to perpetuate both occupational and educational inequality between women and minorities on the one hand, and White males on the other.

The "Cognitive Elite" and The *Bell Curve* Debate

A few years ago, a book titled *The Bell Curve* was published and since then has caused a major stir among educators, lawmakers, teachers, public officials, policymakers, and the general public. In this book, which contains analyses of great masses of data, authors Herrnstein and Murray (1994) argue that not only does the distribution of intelligence in the general population closely approximate a bell-shaped curve (called the *normal distribution*). They also argue there is one basic, fundamental kind of intelligence, not several independent kinds of intelligences, that predict how well an individual will do in school and on the job, thus predicting how successful or not a person will be in society.

Herrnstein and Murray estimate that intelligence is about 70 percent genetically heritable, and only 30 percent determined by environment. Therefore, intelligence is inherited; that is, it is determined primarily by one's genes rather than by one's social and educational environment. How do they arrive at such a figure? They arrived at it by reviewing studies of pairs of biological relatives, then estimating the degree to which any similarity in their intelligence could be due to their biological similarity. To do this, they reviewed data on identical twins who have been separated early in life, and then raised apart. The idea is that because identical twins (as opposed to fraternal twins) are genetic *clones* (exact genetic duplicates), any similarities that remain between them after their separation (such as having the same or similar intelligence) must necessarily be caused by their identical genes rather than by similarities in their social or educational environments. While separated identical twins are approximately 90 percent similar in genetic physical qualities such as height, the authors argue that the similarity in intelligence between separated twins is about 70 percent.

Critics, however, point out that some of the identical twins in the studies cited by Herrnstein and Murray were actually more separated than others. That is, some were not really very separated at all, whereas some were separated for longer periods during their lives, and had fewer similarities in their social and educational environments. When this is taken into account, it is seen that twins who were more separated (attended different schools or were raised in different socioeconomic circumstances) were also less similar in intelligence. In general, *the more separated the twins were, the less similar they were in intelligence.* This shows the effect of their differing social environments over the effect of their identical genes. Some studies show that the similarity in intelligence among truly separated identical twins is only about 50 percent (Chipuer et al. 1990); other studies show the similarity as low as 30 or 40 percent (Taylor 2002, 1998, 1992a, 1980; Kamin 1974; Jencks et al. 1972).

Another point made by *The Bell Curve* authors is that if intelligence is primarily inherited, and if, on average, social classes differ in intelligence, it follows that the lower classes, on average are less endowed with genes for high intelligence than the upper classes. The authors reason that the upper- and upper-middle classes constitute a *genetically based* **cognitive elite** in the United States, those with high IQs, high incomes, and prestigious jobs. They strongly imply, but do not state outright, that any two groups presumed to differ in average intelligence, such as Blacks versus Whites or Latinos versus Whites, and any other minority versus the dominant comparison, may very well differ in genes for intelligence.

The problems with this cognitive-elite argument, largely ignored by the authors, are as follows:

1. Their conclusions tend to ignore the many studies, some discussed earlier, that show intelligence tests and standardized ability tests do not measure intelligence

"You're kidding! You count S.A.T.s?"

of minorities as accurately as that of Whites, or as accurately of women as of men, or individuals of lower socioeconomic status as of individuals with higher status.

2. Their conclusions presume that intelligence is strongly genetically heritable, whereas there is convincing evidence, that even for Whites alone, the relative contribution of environment may be greater than the relative contribution of genes, although intelligence is probably the result of some combination of genes and environment.

3. The authors base a between-group conclusion on a within-group estimate of genetic heritability. Thus they base their conclusions about women versus men, minority versus White, and lower class versus upper class on heritability results attained on White men. The authors ignore all scientific literature detailing why one cannot draw conclusions about between-group genetic differences from within-group results (Fischer et al. 1996; Lewontin 1996/1970; Hauser et al. 1995; Kamin 1995; Gould 1994, 1981; Taylor 1995, 1992a, 1980).

DEBUNKING
Society's Myths

Myth: Intelligence is mostly determined by genetic inheritance.

Sociological perspective: Intelligence is a complex concept not easily measured by one thing and is likely shaped as much by environmental factors as by genetic endowment.

Tracking and Labeling Effects

Over half of America's secondary schools and elementary schools currently use some kind of **tracking** (also called *ability grouping*), which is the separating of students according to some measure of cognitive ability (Taylor et al. 2002; Oakes and Lipton 1996; Maldonado and Willie 1996; Oakes 1985). Tracking has taken place for more than seventy years. Starting as early as first grade, children are divided into high-track, middle-track, and lower-track groups. In high school, the high-track students take college preparatory courses in math and science and read Shakespeare. The middle-track students take courses in business administration and typing. The lower-track students take vocational courses in auto mechanics, metal shop, and cooking.

The original idea behind tracking is that students will get a better education and be better prepared for life after high school if they are grouped early according to cognitive ability. Tracking is supposed to benefit the gifted, the slow learners, and everyone in the middle, but is now severely criticized. Theoretically, students in all tracks learn faster because the curriculum is tailored to their ability level, and the teacher can concentrate on smaller, more homogenous groups.

The opposite argument is given by advocates of *detracking.* The detracking movement is based on the belief that combining students of varying cognitive abilities benefits the students more than tracking, especially by the time students get to junior high and high school. Students of high and low ability can thus learn from each other; the high-ability students are not seen to be "held back" by students with less ability, but are enriched by their presence. Finally, advocates of detracking point out that students in the lower tracks get less teacher attention and simply learn less; and in effect penalized for being in the lower tracks. The idea is mix, don't match.

Which approach is better? Most researchers and educators who have studied tracking agree that not all students should be mixed together in the same classes. The differences between students can be too great, and their needs

TAKING ON SOCIAL ISSUES

Is Ability Tracking Still Around?

In a detailed quantitative analysis, sociological researcher Samuel R. Lucas argues that ability tracking in American high schools is alive and well. It is a system of stratifying students, presumably according to their academic abilities, which was to have been largely phased out twenty to thirty years ago, but has returned in somewhat different forms. It is simply old wine in a new bottle. From the 1940s through the 1970s and early 1980s, most American high schools had roughly three tracks, or ability groupings, based presumably on cognitive ability test scores: the college-bound track, a middle general education track, and a vocational track. Some schools allowed students some input for which track they were to be in, and some did not. It became evident that students were being assigned to tracks more on the basis of their social class and their race–ethnicity than their abilities. Furthermore, women were being unfairly kept from the science tracks or curricula not on the basis of their math or science ability, but because of their gender.

Many schools have argued that they have been phasing out tracking for the last twenty years or more, but a system of stratifying students still remains—in the guise of Advanced Placement programs (tracks), honors tracks, gifted and talented tracks, and other such strata. Yet the disproportionate absence of Blacks and Hispanics from such strata, as well as the relative absence of women from the math and sci-

ence strata, suggests that the older system of tracking in effect continues. Lucas further demonstrates how earlier reliance on the concept of "intelligence" and the use of intelligence quotient (IQ) tests has been replaced with other, yet very similar, forms of standardized testing, such as the Preliminary Scholastic Assessment Test (PSAT), Scholastic Assessment Test (SAT), and American College Test (ACT), and such tests that only serve to rigidify this newer system of academic stratification. He argues that Americans must extricate schools from perpetuating these inequalities, and only frank and forward-looking discussion of such matters as curriculum reform and other issues will accomplish this.

Do you agree that the new tracks such as "gifted and talented," or "honors" tracks, are simply in effect replacements for the older tracks of "college-bound," "business," or "industrial"? How so?

Taking Action

Go to the Taking Action exercise on the companion Web site at **sociology.wadsworth.com/ andersen_taylor/essen3e** to learn more about an organization that addresses this topic.

SOURCE: Lucas, Samuel R. 1999. *Tracking Inequality: Stratification and Mobility in American High Schools.* New York: Teachers College Press.

too dissimilar. Some degree of tracking has always had advocates based on its presumed benefits for all students. This presumption is under attack. One of the most consistent research findings on tracking is that students in the higher tracks receive positive effects, but that the lower-track students suffer negative effects (Lucas 1999; Owens 1998; Rendon and Hope 1996; Cardenas 1996; Perez 1996; Oakes and Lipton 1996; Oakes 1990, 1985; Gamoran 1992; Gamoran and Mare 1989; Braddock 1988).

First of all, students in the lower tracks learn less because they are, quite simply, taught less. They are asked to read less and do less homework. High-track students are taught more; furthermore, they are consistently rewarded by teachers and administrators for their academic abilities. Less is expected of lower-track students, and as a result, their academic performance is lower (Owens 1998; Gamoran and Mare 1989; Braddock 1988). One study found that students assigned to low tracks in the eighth grade performed significantly less well in the tenth grade than students who had the *same* eighth-grade test scores and social class background, but went to untracked schools (Slavin 1993).

Both high- and low-track students are subject to a **labeling effect:** Once a student is assigned to a particular track and is thereby labeled, the label has a tendency to stick, regardless if it is accurate. Once a student is labeled "gifted" or "high ability," teachers, administrators, and other students tend to react in accordance with that label. The student is regarded as smart and high achieving. Students labeled "slow" or "low ability" encounter a negative reaction from the same people, including the expectation of low achievement. Even when a student is transferred from a lower track to a higher track as the result of a recent cognitive ability test, the prior perceptions tend to persist; teachers and students still think of the student as "lower track," and the recently promoted student may also retain the self-perception that developed in response to the lower track assignment.

Who gets assigned to which tracks? Research shows that track assignment is not solely based on the performance in cognitive ability tests. Social class and race are involved. Students with the *same* test scores often get assigned to different tracks because of differences in their social class and race. Few administrators or teachers consciously and deliberately assign students to tracks based on these criteria, but it occurs nevertheless. Researchers have consistently found that when following two students with identical scores on cognitive ability tests, the student of higher social class is more likely than the student of lower social class status to get assigned to the higher track.

Teacher Expectancy Effect

Similar to the labeling effect of tracking is the **teacher expectancy effect,** which is the effect of teacher expectations on a student's actual performance—independent of the student's actual ability. What the teacher expects students to do affects what they will do. The expectations a teacher has for a student's performance can dramatically influence how much the student learns.

Insights into the teacher expectancy effect come from symbolic interactionist theory. In a classic study, Rosenthal and Jacobson (1968) told teachers of several grades in an elementary school that certain children in their class were academic "spurters," who would increase their performance that year. The rest of the students were called "nonspurters." The researchers selected the "spurters" list *completely at random,* unbeknown to the teachers. The distinction had no relation to an ability test the children took early in the school year, although the teachers were told (falsely) that it did. At the end of the school year, it was found that although all students improved somewhat on the achievement test, those labeled spurters made greater gains than those designated nonspurters, especially among first and second graders. This experiment isolates the effect of the label, because it is the only difference that distinguishes the two groups. Variations of this clever and revealing study have been conducted many times over and the results are generally similar.

How are expectations converted into performance? By the powerful mechanism of the **self-fulfilling prophecy,** in which merely applying a label has the effect of justifying the label (Cardenas 1996; Darley and Fazio 1980). Recall the quote from early sociologist W. I. Thomas in Chapter 6: "If men [sic] define situations as real, they are real in their consequences" (Thomas 1928: 572). If a student is defined as a certain type, the student becomes that type. The process unfolds in stages (see Figure 13.3). First, a teacher is told that a student merits a label such as spurter; perhaps the designation originates with administrators or comes from the scoring key of a standardized exam. The teacher's perception of the student is then

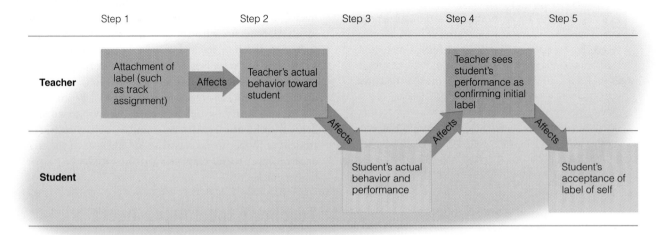

| | Step 1 | | Step 2 | | Step 3 | | Step 4 | | Step 5 |

FIGURE 13.3 The Self-Fulfilling Prophecy

Source: Adapted from Taylor, Shelley E., Letitia Anne Peplau, and David O. Sears, 2003. *Social Psychology*, 11th ed. Upper Saddle River, NJ: Prentice Hall, p. 58.

colored by the label; a student labeled a spurter may be coaxed and praised more often than nonspurters. The student then reacts to the teacher's behavior; students expected to perform well and encouraged to excel actually perform better in class and on exams than other students. Finally, the original prophecy fulfills itself: The teacher observes the behavior of the student, notes the increase in performance, and concludes that the designation spurter is affirmed, because the so-called spurters actually perform better by objective measures than the nonspurters. Further praise and encouragement follows. Teachers unaware of the overall effect will not realize that the label was itself significant in producing the greater performance of the spurters (Lucas 1999; Rendon and Hope 1996; Cardenas 1996; Perez 1996; Hallinan 1994; Gamoran 1972).

Schooling and Gender

Teachers hold different expectations for girls and boys in school, and it comes as no surprise that gender affects teacher expectations and therefore the actual performance of these children. Tracking, particularly in high school, is significantly dependent on gender; for example, a far greater proportion of young men are in the science and math tracks than are young women. Throughout schooling, from preschool through graduate or professional school, women and men are treated differently, with women discriminated against. This consistent and long-term differential treatment has had profound consequences. Girls and boys start out in school roughly equal in skills and confidence, but by the end of high school, women trail men, especially in mathematics and the sciences. What happens in between has been documented in a comprehensive report commis-

sioned by the American Association of University Women (AAUW) that summarizes the results of more than 1000 publications and studies. This extensive research shows the following with regard to schooling and gender (American Association of University Women 1998).

1. In general, teachers pay less attention to girls and women. In elementary school as well as high school, teachers direct more interaction to boys than to girls. As a result, boys tend to talk more in class, and thus teachers tend to interact with them more. The difference is particularly notable in math and science classes.

2. On national tests of reading and writing, girls perform equally to boys. But on advanced mathematics and some science tests, differences emerge. The most dramatic gender differences appear on tests with the highest stakes—the quantitative sections of the Preliminary Scholastic Assessment Tests (PSAT), Scholastic Assessment Tests (SAT), and Advanced Placement (AP) tests. Researchers explain this as the result of several factors, including course-taking patterns and, as we will see below, bias in the tests. With regard to course-taking, young men and women tend to take the same number of math and science courses, but what they take differs substantially. In science, girls are more likely to take biology and chemistry, and boys are more likely to take physics. Girls also tend to end their math studies after a second algebra course; boys are more likely to take trigonometry and calculus, thus giving them a relative advantage on higher-level math skills (American Association of University Women 1998).

3. Some standardized math and science tests still retain gender bias, despite ten years or more of effort to

weed out bias on the part of education specialists and testing organizations such as the Educational Testing Service, manufacturer of the SAT. Bias is especially prevalent in mathematical word problems. Certain mathematics word problems are gender-typed because they employ words and concepts more familiar to men than women (Chipman 1991; American Association of University Women 1998).

4. Standardized tests in math tend to underpredict women's actual grades in mathematics. Women tend to do somewhat better in math courses than their test scores predict.

5. Teachers tend to treat Black women and White women differently by rebuffing Black girls and interacting more with White girls. This is particularly true of Black and White girls during the elementary school years. The trend appears to be independent of the teacher's own race; namely, Black teachers tend to interact more with White girls, just as do White teachers.

6. Textbooks still tend to either ignore women or stereotype them. In this respect, textbooks are gender-role socializers. In elementary school texts, boys are portrayed as building things, being clever, and leading others. Girls tend to be shown performing dull tasks and following the leadership of boys. Even to this day, men are routinely presented as doctors, lawyers, and businesspeople; women as homemakers, librarians, and nurses. There is evidence that such gender typing is decreasing, but the decrease began only recently, and it has not been eliminated.

7. As girls and boys approach adolescence, their self-esteem tends to drop, with the erosion of self-esteem occurring more quickly among girls than boys. The trend is further exacerbated by the discrimination against women in the classroom, gender bias in standardized tests, and stereotyped presentations of women in presumably authoritative textbooks.

Stereotype Threat

As has already been noted, racial and gender stereotypes can affect actual behavior. To what extent can a negative stereotype about *one's self* affect one's *own* behavior and academic performance? As with the self-fulfilling prophecy, to what extent do minorities and women internalize negative stereotypes about themselves that show such effects?

An answer has been provided recently by the research of Claude M. Steele and associates (Steele 1999, 1997, 1996; Steele and Aronson 1995; Steele 1992; Brown and Josephs 1999). They note that two common stereotypes exist in the United States, and other countries as well. First, because on the average Blacks perform less well than Whites on math and verbal ability tests, Blacks must have, or so it is believed, some "inherent" deficiency in math and verbal abilities relative to Whites. Second, because women perform less well than men on math ability tests, women must therefore have some "inherent" deficiency in math ability.

To the extent that Black students in high school or college may believe (internalize) such stereotypes, then they may perform less well on a test if they are told that "this is a genuine test of your true ability," because telling them that would tend to increase their anxiety about the test. The same should apply to women on a math ability test. Either Whites, or males, who are told this should be *less* affected, since these societal stereotypes are not *about* Whites or males.

Results show that this is just what happens. Black college students who are told that the test is a "genuine" test of their true verbal ability perform less well than Whites who are also told the same thing—even though the Whites and Blacks compared start out equal in their average test scores. This is the *stereotype threat effect.* If the groups of Blacks and Whites are told nothing, then they perform about the same on the test. Note that nothing is said to the students specifically about Black and White test performance, only that the test was designed to be a "genuine" test of verbal ability.

Stereotype threat appears to operate in the same way with regard to the presumed female–male difference in math ability test performance. When a group of both men and women are told that a math test given to them is a "genuine" test of their true math ability, the women do worse than the men. If groups of men and women are told nothing, then women and men perform about the same on the test (Lau 2002; Lau and Taylor 2003; Brown and Josephs 1999). This suggests that the long-believed female deficit in math ability may stem at least in part from what they are told before they take the test, and not from "inherent" differences between men and women in math ability.

▪ Health Care in the United States

Like education, the health care system is one of America's major institutions. Generally speaking, the citizens of the United States are quite healthy in relation to the rest of the world. However, there are very great discrepancies among people within the United States in terms of longevity, general health, and access to health care, with the least advantaged part of the curve consisting

The development of new technologies has transformed the delivery of health care. The house call by a physician is now a rarity; many surgical procedures, such as this balloon angioplasty, would have been unimaginable not many years ago.

primarily of minorities, the lower classes, and for a number of ailments, women. But the fact remains that we are a robust nation.

In Colonial times, American physicians received their training in Europe. Their competitors in the healing arts included alchemists, herbalists, ministers, faith healers, and even barbers. Treatments were a combination of folk wisdom, superstition, tried-and-true regimens, and sometimes, dangerous quackery. A simple scratch, once infected, could easily cost a limb or a life. Patients were often "bled" as a cure, which involved the removal of "bad" blood from the patient, sometimes by means of holes poked in the skull. Needless to say, the cure was often worse than the disease.

By the start of the nineteenth century, advances in biology and chemistry ignited a century of explosive growth in medical knowledge. One fruit of the scientific revolution of the mid-1800s was the *germ theory,* the idea that many illnesses were caused by microscopic organisms, or germs. Now considered scientific fact, the claim that something called *germs* caused illness was then hotly debated. Shortly thereafter, germ theory established itself as a foundation of medicine. Doctors were able to show that isolating infected people and sealing infected wells could stop the spread of illness by stopping the spread of germs. Relentless study and research transformed medicine into a science. Coincidentally, the social prestige of medicine greatly increased, contributing mightily to the status of physicians, who had formerly enjoyed more modest social standing. The American Medical Association (AMA) was founded in 1847, after half a century of sweeping away rivals in the healing arts. The AMA successfully campaigned to outlaw or delegit-

imize alternative therapies, and emerged as the most powerful organization in U.S. health care.

In the late 1800s the image of medicine as an upper-class profession took hold. A medical education was expensive, and medical schools drew on White, male, urban populations for their students. Those trained as physicians took their place in the upper social strata. Herbalists and faith healers came more frequently from the rural lower class, and generally remained there. As the ranks of the medical profession swelled with wealthy Whites, African Americans and Hispanics became proportionately more affiliated with older folk practices and midwifery. This overall trend continued through the early part of the twentieth century, and today folk practices continue to have adherents among rural lower-class Whites and rural and urban lower-class Blacks, Hispanics, and Native Americans (Starr 1982).

The U.S. government has for some time sought to have some form of widespread guaranteed health service, at least for certain categories of people, such as veterans, the poor, and the elderly. The **Medicare** program, begun in 1965 under the administration of President Lyndon Johnson, provides medical insurance covering hospital costs for all individuals age sixty-five or older. The Medicare program does not cover physician costs incurred outside the hospital, but other programs do, although the patient must pay a portion of the cost.

Medicaid is a governmental program that provides medical care in the form of health insurance for the poor, welfare recipients, and the disabled. The program is funded through tax revenues. The costs covered per individual vary from state to state, because the state must provide funds to the individual in addition to the funds that are provided by the federal government. The Medicare and Medicaid programs together are as close as the United States has come to the ideal of universal health insurance. More recent attempts to establish universal coverage have not been successful (Weitz 2001; Starr 1995).

Health and Sickness in the United States: A Picture of Diversity

The definitions of *sick* and *well* have varied greatly over time in the United States. For example, from the early 1900s until the mid-1940s, thinness was associated with poverty and hunger. If you were skinny, that meant you were in bad health. From the late 1950s through the present, a positive value has been placed on being thin. Female role models in our society, such as movie stars and fashion models, have firmly established that thin is "in." Millions of young women have tried to copy this look, and one result has been an increased incidence of anorexia nervosa (Weitz 2001; Williams and Collins 1995; Taylor et al. 2003).

Anorexia nervosa (*anorexia* for short) is an eating disorder characterized by compulsive dieting. Victims of this illness starve themselves, sometimes to death, even though sufferers do not typically define themselves as ill, because

Anorexia nervosa is common mostly, but not exclusively, among young women. Those with anorexia falsely believe that they are overweight, although they are exceedingly thin. Many interpret this potentially life-threatening condition as encouraged by a culture that advertises being thin as a beauty ideal for women.

they tend to see themselves as overweight, even though they are dangerously thin. A related malady, *bulimia,* is an eating disorder characterized by alternate binge eating and then purging or induced vomiting to lose weight.

Like many other diseases, anorexia has social as well as biological causes. A majority of people suffering from

---

UNDERSTANDING DIVERSITY

The Americans with Disabilities Act

The Americans with Disabilities Act (ADA), passed by Congress in 1990, prohibits discrimination against disabled persons. In 1999, the U.S. Supreme Court restricted the definition of disability to exclude disabilities that can be corrected with devices such as eyeglasses or with medication. The decision was based on cases in which people had been denied employment because they did not meet a health standard required by the employer, even though, with correction, the standard was met. One case involved two nearsighted women denied jobs as airline pilots because, without glasses, their vision did not meet the airline company's standard of 20/40. With glasses, their vision was 20/20. Another case involved a man whose high blood pressure was above the federal standard for driving trucks. He

was denied a job as a trucker—even though with medication, his pressure was regulated to an acceptable level. The Court's decision denied these people the right to claim discrimination.

The decision raises several interesting sociological questions about disabilities and civil rights. Writing for the majority, Sandra Day O'Connor argued that the law requires people to be assessed based on each individual's condition, not as members of groups affected in a particular way. The disability rights movement would argue that disabled people are a minority group with certain civil rights. The issue being mediated by the courts involves competing definitions of what constitutes a disability. This point intrigues symbolic interactionists who would note the role of socially constructed meanings in legal negotiations. Furthermore, as one

lawyer who drafted the original ADA law has pointed out, according to the original decision, someone may be disabled enough to be excluded from a job, but not disabled enough to claim discrimination. This raises interesting questions about the rights of employers to establish physical and medical standards for certain jobs, even if those standards result in the exclusion from employment for some groups of people. You might ask yourself how you would balance the diverse and competing interests of disabled people, employers, and the courts if it were your responsibility to decide whether the exclusion of some disabled people from a particular job constitutes discrimination. What are the implications of your argument for cases involving race or gender discrimination?

the disease are young, White women, from well-to-do families, most often two-parent families. Many behavioral scientists have noted that generally anorexics have been pressured excessively by their parents to be high achievers. Others have detected a link between anorexia and the socially constructed ideals of beauty in our society, which are fixated on thinness and so-called ideal body types. Images of physical "perfection" are emblazoned across television, magazines, and billboards with slenderness displayed as the ideal of femininity. Researchers note that these social values, which encourage compulsive dieting, are comparable to the foot-binding once practiced in China (recall this from Chapter 1) and other forms of female mutilation found in some foreign cultures (Wolf 1991; M. Levine 1987; Chernin 1991).

Anorexia is least likely to afflict African American women, Latinos, and lesbians. According to one researcher (Thompson 1994), many in these groups overeat, rather than self-starve, thus producing a more familiar disorder: *obesity.* Thompson interprets this behavior as a reaction to oppressive life experiences associated with racism, sexism, and homophobia.

Men have not been exempt from the pressure of such values (Logio 1998). Since the 1940s, and especially from the mid-1970s, one of the most persistent male physical ideals has been the rippling physique of the bodybuilder or weight lifter. Young men have been urged by the media and their peers to "pump iron" for the perfect body. Many athletes, professional and amateur, have been goaded by athletic ambitions to use *anabolic steroids,* powerful hormones that stimulate the growth of muscle. Used widely (despite dire warnings by physicians), steroids not only build muscle as advertised, they can also shrivel the testicles and cause impotence, hair loss, heart arrhythmia, liver damage, strokes, and very possibly some forms of cancer. Lyle Alzado was a huge, fast, incredibly strong football star in the NFL and later a Hollywood actor. As he slowly succumbed to brain cancer in his thirties, Alzado freely admitted to massive abuse of anabolic steroids, which he believed caused his fatal disease.

Race and Health Care

Health and sickness in the United States is influenced by social factors. **Epidemiology** is the study of all the factors—biological, social, economic, and cultural—associated with disease in society. **Social epidemiology** is the study of the effects of social, cultural, temporal, and regional factors in disease and health. Among the more important social factors that affect disease and health in the United States are race–ethnicity, social class, gender, and age. The effects of age on health and life expectancy were discussed in Chapter 3. The effects of race, class, and gender are discussed here.

Among women, African Americans are more likely than Whites to fall victim to diseases such as cancer, heart disease, stroke, and diabetes. Death of the mother during childbirth is three times higher among African American women than among White women, and African American women are three times more likely to die while pregnant (Williams and Collins 1995; Livingston 1994). In the forty-five to sixty-four age group, African American women die at twice the rate of White women. The occurrence of breast cancer is lower among African American women than White women, yet the *mortality rate* (death rate) for breast cancer for African American women is considerably greater than for White women (Weitz 2001; National Cancer Institute 2002). This reflects the fact that White women are more likely to get high-quality care, and get it more rapidly, than African American women. African American women also develop cervical cancer at twice the rate of White women. Hypertension (high blood pressure) afflicts twenty-five percent of all African American women, and only 11 percent of White women. Although differences in culture, diet, and lifestyle account for some of these differences, it is nevertheless clear that African American women and men do not receive medical attention as early as Whites, and when they do eventually get treatment, the stage of their illness is more advanced, and the treatment they receive is not of the same quality (National Cancer Institute 2002).

The mortality rates for Native Americans are one and one-half times greater than the mortality rates for the general population. Among Native Americans under the age of forty-five, the death rate is three times that of Whites. Native American babies are almost twice as likely as White babies to die before they are one year old. Native Americans are in very poor health compared with the general population of the United States (National Cancer Institute 2002; Williams and Collins 1995).

Hispanics, like African Americans, Native Americans, and other minorities, are significantly less healthy than Whites. Hispanics contract tuberculosis at a rate four times that of Whites. Other indicators of health, such as infant mortality, reveal a picture for Hispanics similar to that of African Americans and Native Americans. Hispanics are less likely than Whites to have a regular source of medical care, and when they do, it is likely to be a public health facility or an outpatient clinic. Because of language barriers as well as other cultural differences, Hispanics are less likely than other minority groups to use available health services, such as hospitals, doctors' offices, and clinics (Weitz 2001; Livingston 1994; Vega and Amero 1994; Altman 1991).

One of the most infamous studies to demonstrate, though inadvertently, the connection between race and the treatment of illness in our society is the **Tuskegee**

Syphilis Study (mentioned in Chapter 1). The study was done at the Tuskegee Institute in Macon County, Alabama, a historically Black college. The study begun by the United States Health Service in 1932 as a study of "untreated syphilis in the male Negro" was intended to advance scientific knowledge about syphilis, a sexually transmitted disease (STD) that when left untreated causes blindness, mental deterioration, and death. A group (sample) of about 600 African American males, about 400 of whom were affected with syphilis, were chosen for study, the remainder being used as an uninfected control group. The study continued for forty years (J. Jones 1997).

As many people have become aware of the importance of good health, a major industry has developed to provide assorted health services, such as this exercise class.

During this period, penicillin was discovered as an effective treatment for infectious diseases and was widely available from the early 1950s. Nonetheless, the scientists conducting the study decided not to give penicillin to the African Americans who made up the study sample on the grounds that it would interfere with the study of the physical progress of untreated syphilis. The U.S. government authorized the study to be continued right up through the 1960s and into the early 1970s. By 1972, news of the study began to reach universities and the general public, and the government, through the U.S. Department of Health, Education and Welfare (now the U.S. Department of Health and Human Services), put an end to the project. By then between 30 and 100 of the African American men in the study had died of syphilis, having undergone its horrible physical ravages (J. Jones 1997). In 1997, then President Bill Clinton formally apologized on behalf of the U.S. government to the victims, dead and alive, and to their families—sixty-five years after the start of the study.

The Tuskegee study has become one of the prime examples of ethical violation in medical and behavioral science research. It has also served as an eye into race relations for more than a half-century in the United States. Penicillin was never administered to the infected men for the duration of the study. It seems reasonable to hypothesize that if the individuals in the study had been middle-class Whites instead of poor African Americans, the study would have ended as soon as penicillin, a cure for syphilis, was discovered.

Social Class and Health Care

In the United States, social class has a pronounced effect on health and the availability of health services. This reality is crucial to the current national debate on access to health care and health insurance; the lower the social class status of the person or family, the less access they have to adequate health care. People with higher incomes who are asked to rate their own health tend to rate themselves higher than people with lower incomes. Almost 50 percent of those in the highest income bracket rate their health as excellent, whereas only 25 percent in the lowest income bracket do so. In fact, the effects of social class are nowhere more evident than in the distribution of health and disease, showing up dramatically in the rates of infant mortality, stillbirths, tuberculosis, heart disease, cancer, arthritis, diabetes, and a variety of other illnesses. The reasons lie partly in personal habits that are themselves partly dependent on one's social class. For example, those with lower socioeconomic status smoke more often, and smoking is the major cause of lung cancer and a significant contributor to cardiovascular disease.

Social circumstances also have an effect on health. Poor living conditions, elevated levels of pollution in low-income neighborhoods, and lack of access to health care facilities all contribute to the high rate of disease among lower classes. Another contributing factor is the stress caused by financial troubles. Research has consistently shown correlations between psychological stress and physical illness (Taylor et al. 2003; Worchel et al. 2000; Jackson 1992; Thoits 1991; House 1980). The poor are more subject to psychological stress than the middle and upper classes, and it shows up in their comparatively high level of illness.

With the exception of the elderly, now subsidized by Medicare, low-income people remain largely outside the mainstream of private health care. Nearly 31 million Americans—13 percent of the population—have no health

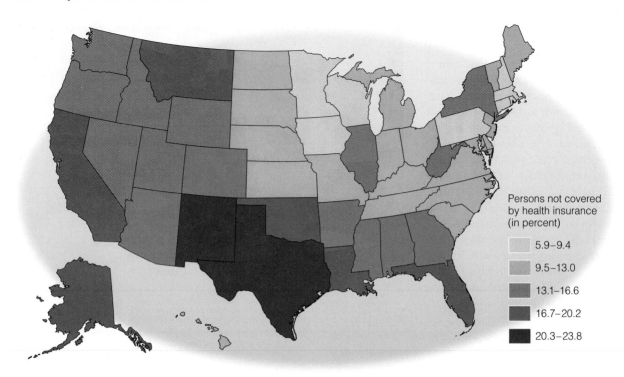

Persons not covered
by health insurance
(in percent)

5.9–9.4

9.5–13.0

13.1–16.6

16.7–20.2

20.3–23.8

MAP 13.3 Mapping America's Diversity: People Not Covered by Health Insurance

The percent of people not covered by health insurance is greatest in states such as California, Texas, Mississippi, Montana, and others. **What is the percent of people not covered by health insurance in your own home state?**

DATA: From the U.S. Census Bureau, *Statistical Abstract of the United States, 2000,* p. 102.

insurance (see Map 13.3). The main sources for medical care for many of them are hospital emergency rooms in the inner cities, often called the "doctor's office of the poor." Even then, emergency room service is lacking. Treatment is given only for specific critical ailments, and rarely is there any follow-up care or comprehensive treatment.

Sociologists have found that during interactions between health care providers and poor patients, the poor, particularly Black and Hispanic poor, are most likely to be *infantilized* and to receive health counseling that is incorrect, incomplete, or delivered in inappropriate language not easily understood by the patient (Weitz 2001; González 1996). The symbolic interaction perspective in sociology has noted the tendency for inadequate care. It has also been attributed to an attitude among health counselors that the poor are charity cases who should be satisfied with whatever they get, because they are probably not paying for their own care (Diaz-Duque 1989).

Gender and Health Care

Although women live longer on average than men, older women are more likely than older men to suffer from stress, obesity, hypertension, and chronic illness. National health statistics show that hypertension is more common among men than women until age fifty-five, when the pattern reverses. This may reflect differences in the social environment experienced by men and women, with women finding their situation to be more stressful as they advance toward old age. Under the age of thirty-five, men are more likely to be overweight than women; after that, women are more likely to be overweight. Women have a higher likelihood of contracting chronic disease than men, although men are more likely to be disabled by disease (Atchley 2000; Williams and Collins 1995; Adler et al. 1993).

The rate of death caused by infectious diseases is higher for men than women and has declined significantly for both since the early 1900s. Researchers cite differences in male and female roles and cultural practices to explain the differences between the genders. In particular, male occupational roles call for more travel and more exposure to other people, the major sources of infection. In addition, men smoke more, and the overall deleterious effect of smoking on health can account for some of the differences in infectious diseases between men and women (National Cancer Institute 2002; Williams and Collins 1995).

Despite what tobacco executives often argue, cigarette smoking is proven to cause cancer and cardiovascular disease, which kill men more frequently than women. Smoking patterns have changed, however, and the proportion of smokers who are women has increased. The most recent research shows a convergence in the smoking rates of men and women, and shows further that more men than women eventually quit smoking. These changes are expected to occur in the future as higher rates of female deaths from diseases are linked to smoking. Reports also show significant increases in smoking among teenagers, with teenage girls leading boys. As a result, we might expect to see future increases in lung cancers and cardiovascular disease among women (National Cancer Institute 2002).

It is typically assumed that the work-oriented, hard-driving lifestyle associated with the traditional role of men tends to produce elevated levels of heart disease and other health problems. In general, this is true. However, the role of women in society is changing, with associated changes in women's health. The health of women and men varies with their social circumstances. People who are "tokens" in the workplace—meaning mainly women and Blacks, especially Black women—suffer more stress in the form of depression and anxiety than nontokens, or women and Blacks who work in places where there is nothing exceptional about their presence (Jackson et al. 1995). Housewives have higher rates of illness than women who work outside the home, indicating that employment can have positive effects on women's health. Moreover, housewives who never worked outside the

DOING SOCIOLOGICAL RESEARCH

Beauty and Health

Beauty is only skin deep, so the saying goes. This implies that beauty is solely a matter of appearance; that is, how we appear to others. Certainly many people spend an enormous amount of time and money trying to appear beautiful. Some such efforts are harmless, but can beauty affect your health? This is the question asked by Jane Sprague Zones in her research on beauty myths and women's health.

Zones identifies the beauty myth as the ideals set for women's appearance in Western culture—ideals that increasingly pressure women to conform to narrow standards. The greatest impact of internalizing such narrow expectations is on women's self-esteem. Focusing too much attention on one's weight, fitness, and physical appearance can lead women to never be satisfied with their bodies and to have nagging self-doubts about their appearance. With models appearing as petite figures, size six or smaller, women may be driven to starve themselves or to take drastic measures to reduce their weight. Thus, not only is internalizing the beauty myth harmful to one's self-esteem and mental health, but it also can be harmful to your physical health.

Likewise, trying to appear eternally youthful may lead you to buy endless products promising to eliminate wrinkles. Or you may dye your hair, chisel your nose, minimize or maximize your breast size through surgery, or use numerous products promising eternal youth. The Consumer Product Safety Commission has noted many consumer-related health problems from the use of some cosmetics. And, the National Cancer Institute has documented a greater risk of cancer of the lymph system among women who use hair coloring. The damage is not only to individuals. Hydrocarbons in hairspray are a primary contributor to pollution in the air and ground, thereby affecting the health of the earth.

Restricted images of beauty not only can harm one's physical and mental health, but also have the consequence of labeling people with visible physical disabilities as unattractive. Likewise, not being able to afford the array of products associated with being beautiful leads people to make invidious class distinctions about who is beautiful and who is not.

Zones concludes that appearance and beauty are powerful forces in women's lives and that both personal and

societal transformation are needed to overcome the deleterious impact of narrow beauty ideals on women's health.

Questions to Consider

1. In your opinion, should even a small part of one's health be sacrificed in order to be "beautiful"?
Keyword: beauty myth

2. In your opinion, to what extent are men affected by beauty standards and by the advertising of male "beauty" products?
Keyword: beauty and gender

3. To what extent are women harmed more than men, healthwise, by society's attention to beauty?
Keyword: anorexia

We have included InfoTrac College Edition keywords at the end of each question to make it easier for you to find more to read on these topics. Go to **www.infotrac-college.com,** an online library, to begin your search.

SOURCE: Zones, Jane Sprague. 1997. "Beauty Myths and Realities and Their Impact on Women's Health." Pp. 249–275 in *Women's Health: Complexities and Differences,* edited by Sheryl B. Ruzek, Virginia L. Olesen, and Adele E. Clarke. Columbus, OH: Ohio State University Press.

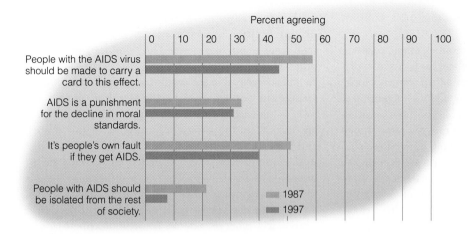

Percent agreeing

FIGURE 13.4 Changing Attitudes About AIDS

DATA: From the Gallup Poll. 2002. *The Gallup Poll.* Princeton, NJ: The Gallup Organization.

home are healthier than those who once worked outside the home but then returned to homemaking. Employed women are more likely than housewives to get well quickly when sick, and they tend to return to their normal activities sooner after illness than do housewives (Andersen 2003).

DEBUNKING
Society's Myths

Myth: Illness is strictly a physical thing.

Sociological perspective: What is defined as illness, even physical illness, is heavily influenced by culture; also, the presence of illness is influenced by social conditions.

AIDS: Illness and Stigma

Given the tendency for people to attribute blame to the victim of illness, a certain amount of stigma will be attached to the person who is sick. Some degree of stigma may become associated with any disease or illness, but attitudes toward people suffering from sexually transmitted diseases, particularly AIDS, represent one of the strongest examples of how stigma operates in our society (see Figure 13.4).

Stigma occurs when an individual is socially devalued because of some malady, illness, misfortune, or similar attribute (see Chapter 6). A stigma is viewed as a relatively permanent characteristic of the stigmatized individual; others expect the negative attribute of the stigmatized person to persist, with no cure in sight (Goffman 1963; Jones et al. 1986; Epstein 1996). In earlier times, the disease of leprosy put a stigma on the victim.

Leprosy was perceived as incurable, and the stigma was permanent. Those with the disease were banished to leper colonies and other far-off places. Today, leprosy continues to carry a negative social stigma, although it is now treatable and victims are no longer cast away as they once were.

THINKING SOCIOLOGICALLY

Regardless of whether you are HIV positive or an AIDS sufferer, it is now true that almost everyone either knows at least one person who is HIV positive or has AIDS. Do you know any such person? Do you know someone else who knows someone who is infected? How do you feel about that person? Do you wonder whether the person was infected through unprotected sex or perhaps some other means such as intravenous drug use? Do you blame the person? What do your observations tell you about *stigma*?

The hospice movement has provided a new form of health care, whereby terminally ill patients, such as this AIDS patient, face death in their homes, instead of the clinical settings of hospitals.

The Sociology of AIDS

Sociologists testified before the Institute of Medicine in 1993, as part of the National Academy of Sciences deliberations about federal policy on AIDS. The focus of this testimony was to review research on the social dimensions of AIDS so that federal policy would not see AIDS simply in medical terms. Here is an excerpt from that testimony, which shows the unique contribution of sociological research to the development of social policy:

Contributions of Sociological Research on AIDS. *Even with limited funding, sociological research has enhanced our knowledge about the social dimensions of AIDS. With our focus on social groups, social processes, and social dynamics, sociologists have made substantial contributions to the AIDS epidemic by applying theory and research on social demography and cultural context, social networks, social norms, case management, social epidemiology, and social change. The following examples show the breadth of this work.*

*   **Social Demographic and Cultural Context.** In the United States, AIDS has hit inner-city minority communities disproportionately hard. These Americans have experienced HIV/AIDS in the context of poverty, poor health, inadequate health care, drug and alcohol abuse, and violence. These contextual problems must be taken into account to reduce infection rates in disadvantaged communities. In addition, social norms affect the age of first intercourse, number of sexual partners, drug use, and homosexual and bisexual sexual practices. For example, based on National Opinion Research Center data, only 0.6% of American adult males reported sex*

with a prostitute in the past year and 80% had 0 or 1 sex partner in the last year. However, in the remaining 20% there are small subgroups of individuals, the bulk unmarried, who have multiple sexual partners and engage in risky behavior. Even drug use varies by race, social group, and class and points to different interventions for different communities.

*   **Social Networks.** Understanding social networks is critical to modeling the spread of AIDS and targeting resources to groups with high risk of infection. Since HIV/AIDS is primarily transmitted as a result of social activities such as sexual relations and the sharing of needles used for drug injections, the unit of analysis ought to be the social networks and relationships in which transmission occurs, not the individuals who have the infection. Networks may be so dense and interconnected, for example, that members interact only with each other as in a well-defined homosexual or drug-injecting community. Or, the network may be diffuse and loosely tied together as with prostitutes and their occasional clients, or young adults that date casually. The identification and characterization of these networks is critical for predicting the spread of infection, focusing and shaping interventions and anchoring them in the communities where people are engaging in risky behaviors. It was precisely this network analysis by sociologists at the CDC in the early 1980s that produced epidemiological mapping of gay men and helped target safe sex education to the most at risk subgroups within that community.*

*   **Social Norms.** Knowledge about safe sex or drug use may*

be overridden by social pressure to engage in risky behavior. Prostitutes, for example, often use condoms with clients but not with their boyfriends. American youth have considerable knowledge about HIV transmission but engage in unprotected sex because of group norms. Drug use, too, typically occurs in groups with strong normative systems of permissible and impermissible behavior. Even medical personnel have been found to ignore health precautions if everyone else on their team does so.

Sociological research examining patterns of IV drug-users and the organization of drug networks illustrates the importance of social norms in prevention, education, and intervention efforts. For example, targeting new IV drug-users is a critical intervention point. Experienced IV drug-users increasingly use precautions to reduce their risk of HIV, but new users do not. The data indicate that IV drug-users reach out to other IV drug-users, and that risk behavior is influenced heavily by group pressure. Drug injectors who took part in organizing other drug injectors *decreased* their injections per month, the sharing of equipment, their use of rented syringes, and their use of shooting galleries and *increased* their use of new needles, bleach, and condoms.

Critical Thinking Exercises

1. Research shows that AIDS tends to follow social network connections. Can you think of examples of such connections (along the lines of social class, race, or others)?

2. Do you know anyone with AIDS? Do you know what kinds of social networks might have been involved?

SOURCE: American Sociological Association, Washington, DC.

In the early 1980s, AIDS appeared. *AIDS (acquired immunodeficiency syndrome)* is the term for a category of disorders that result from a breakdown of the body's immune system. HIV (human immunodeficiency virus), the virus that causes AIDS, was first identified in 1981. Like lepers, people infected with HIV carry a heavy negative stigma and are often regarded with fear and misunderstanding (see Figure 13.4). Patients who are HIV positive but not yet suffering from full-blown AIDS are sometimes so stigmatized that even physicians refuse to see them (Weitz 2001).

The incubation period between infection with HIV and the development of AIDS can stretch longer than ten years; thus, someone can be infected with HIV and yet not have full-blown AIDS. It is not HIV infection itself that causes the death of the individual, but a complex of severe illnesses that thrive in the absence of a working immune system, such as pneumonia, certain cancers, and a number of other illnesses rare enough that their presence is judged to be diagnostic of AIDS.

Since the 1980s, the disease has been spreading rapidly. Over 25 million adults and children worldwide are infected with HIV. In the United States before 1995, AIDS was in higher proportion among Whites than minorities. In 1995, for the first time, the proportion of persons reported with AIDS who are African American was equal to the proportion who are White (40 percent each, among those with AIDS). The AIDS incidence rate per 100,000 among African Americans (93 cases per 100,000 population) was higher than that among Hispanics (46.2 per 100,000), Whites (15.4 per 100,000), Native Americans and Alaskan Natives (12 cases per 100,000), and Asians, for whom it was the lowest (6.2 cases per 100,000 population). These data, collected from medical records, do not include measures of social class such as education, occupation, or income.

The AIDS disease is transmitted through the exchange of bodily fluids, particularly blood and semen. A little more than one-half (51 percent) of all cases of full-blown AIDS are the result of male-to-male sexual contact, 24 percent are caused by intravenous drug use. Women account for 19 percent of AIDS cases. Most women acquire HIV infection through injecting drugs or sexual contact with HIV-infected men. There are no reliable data on AIDS from female-to-female sexual contact.

Health and Sickness Globally

In societies that are largely pastoral or horticultural, the lack of technology severely limits both the development of health care systems and the delivery of health care to the populations of these countries, where poverty also limits access to good health care. As in the United States, elites in third-world countries receive better medical attention than people who are poor and possibly even near starvation.

The global aspect of illness was seen in 2002 with the epidemic outbreak of SARS (Severe Acute Respiratory Syndrome), a potentially fatal viral disease that attacks the lungs and other respiratory organs. Originating in China, where it spread rapidly, cases soon broke out in Western countries such as Canada and the United States. The spread of the disease was rapid across national boundaries. Panicky populations donned face masks for protection, and some individuals even sealed off their houses with plastic duct tape. Quick action by medical science stopped the spread of SARS within a few months, and recently 50 experts from 15 countries are considering distributing a newly developed SARS vaccine (Altman 2003).

Abject poverty in much of the world, particularly in third-world regions and areas of extreme poverty in the United States, cuts life expectancy to far below the seventy-five or eighty years experienced by the wealthy, elite, and middle-class populations in the United States and elsewhere. Life expectancy in the African countries of Niger, Chad, Ethiopia, and Somalia is barely forty-five years of age. It is the same in Afghanistan, Laos, and Cambodia. Serious illness goes hand-in-hand with severe poverty, and lowered life expectancy is the result. This is also the case in many ghettoes and barrios in the United States, although considerably less is written about the conditions. Drinking water contaminated by poor sewage breeds many infectious diseases are fatal. The diseases of tuberculosis and pneumonia, the leading causes of death in the United States nearly a century ago, today kill people in poor areas of the world (Lenski et al. 1998). Health care and poverty are intimately related: Poverty breeds disease, which makes it less likely for people to be able to work, which in turn produces more poverty and more disease and premature death. The absence of health care professionals and facilities only exacerbates this vicious cycle of poverty and disease.

■ *Theoretical Perspectives on Health Care*

A deeper understanding of the nation's health care system and its problems can be achieved by applying the three major theoretical paradigms of sociology: functionalism, conflict theory, and symbolic interaction theory (see Table 13.5).

The Functionalist View

The notion of a **sick role**—a pattern of expectations that society applies to someone who is ill—has been coined by functionalist theory. Functionalism argues that any institu-

TABLE 13.5 Theoretical Perspectives on the Sociology of Health

	Functionalism	Conflict Theory	Symbolic Interaction
Central Point	The health care system has certain functions, both positive and negative	Health care reflects the inequalities in society	Illness is partly socially constructed
Fundamental Problem Uncovered	The health care system produces some negative functions	Excessive bureaucratization of the health care system and privatization lead to excess cost	Patients are patronized and infantilized
Policy Implications	Policy should decrease negative functions of health care system for minority groups, the poor, and women	Policy should improve access to health care for minority racia–ethnic groups, the poor, and women	Doctors, nurses, and other medical personnel should periodically take the sick role of the patient, as an instructional device

tion, group, or organization can be interpreted by looking at its positive and negative functions in society. Positive functions contribute to the harmony and stability of society. The positive functions of the health care system are the prevention and treatment of disease. Ideally, this would mean the delivery of health care to the entire population without regard to race–ethnicity, social class, gender, age, or any other characteristic. At the same time, the health care system is notable for a number of negative functions, those that contribute to disharmony and instability of society.

Prominent problem areas in the U.S. health care system include the following:

■ **Unequal distribution of health care by race–ethnicity, social class, or gender.** Earlier in the chapter we showed that health care is more readily available, and more readily delivered, to White or middle-class individuals in urban and suburban areas than to minorities. The lack of health care delivery to Native American populations is particularly serious. Likewise, men and women receive unequal treatment for certain types of medical conditions, with women more likely than men to receive truncated treatment.

■ **Unequal distribution of health care by region.** Each year, many in the United States die because they live too far away from a doctor, hospital, or emergency room. Doctors and hospitals are concentrated in cities and suburbs; they are much less likely to be situated in isolated rural areas. Rural people in Appalachia and some parts of the South and Midwest may have to travel one hundred miles or more to get to the doctor or emergency room.

■ **Inadequate health education of inner-city and rural parents.** Many inner-city and rural parents do not understand the importance of immunizing their children against smallpox, tuberculosis, and other illnesses, and they are often suspicious of immunization programs. This hesitancy is reinforced by the

depersonalized and inadequate health care ghetto residents often encounter when care is available at all.

The Conflict Theory View

Conflict theory stresses the importance of social structural inequality in society. From the conflict perspective, the inequality inherent in our capitalist society is responsible for the unequal access to medical care. Minorities, the lower classes, and the elderly, particularly elderly women, have less access to the health care system in the United States than Whites, the middle and upper classes, and the middle aged. Restricted access is further exacerbated by the high costs of medical care, stemming from high fees and the abuses of the fee-for-service and third-party-payment systems (explained later in the chapter). The exceptionally high incomes of medical professionals amplify the social chasm between medical practitioners and an increasingly resentful public.

Excessive bureaucratization is another affliction of the health care system that adds to the alienation of patients. The U.S. health care system is burdened by endless forms for both physician and patient, including paperwork to enter individuals into the system, authorize procedures, dispense medicines, monitor progress, and process payments. Long waits for medical attention are normal, even in the emergency room. Prolonged waits have reached alarming proportions in the emergency rooms of many urban hospitals in the United States, and can only deepen the alienation of patients. One study showed that up to 15 percent of emergency room patients give up and leave before receiving care because of long waits—some stretching to an abysmal fifteen hours.

Symbolic Interactionism

Symbolic interactionists hold that illness is partly (although obviously not totally) socially constructed. The definitions of illness and wellness are culturally relative—sickness in

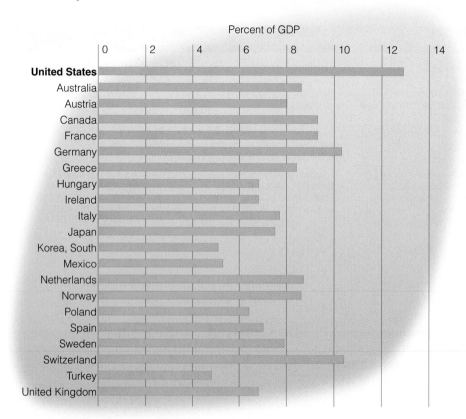

Percent of GDP

FIGURE 13.5
Health Expenditures:
A Comparative
International View

DATA: From the U.S. Census Bureau. *Statistical Abstract of the
United States, 2002.* Data from
the Organization for Economic Cooperation and Development, Paris,
France, OCED Health Data 2001.

one culture may be wellness in another. It is time depen-dent as well. A condition considered optimal in one era (such as being thin) may be defined as sickness at another time in the same culture (at the turn of the twentieth cen-tury in this country, a healthy woman was supposed to be plump). Similarly, the health care system itself has a so-cially constructed aspect. The ways we behave toward the ill, toward doctors, and toward innovative ventures such as HMOs are all social creations.

The symbolic interaction perspective highlights a number of socially constructed problems in the health care system. Medical practitioners frequently subject patients to *infantilization* (treat them like children, even if adult). The patient is assigned a role that depends heavily on the physician and the health care system, much as an infant is dependent on its parents. Doctors and nurses may begin patronizing the patient from the initial greeting, a conde-scending "How are *we* today?" Physicians commonly ad-dress patients by their first names, yet patients virtually always address physicians as "Doctor." Women patients are far more likely than men to be addressed by their first names. Such patronizing and infantilizing of patients is common in emergency rooms, where minority patients are infantilized most often (Weitz 2001; González 1996).

The symbolic interactionist analysis of the health care system allows us to see these problems more clearly. One solution is to give health care professionals training about

such matters in medical school. This is just starting to hap-pen in a few U.S. medical schools. For example, a social issue addressed in some medical school courses on gynecology is how to manage the interaction when a male gynecologist treats his woman patient. Women patients feel uncomfort-able and vulnerable when they lie partially naked on an ex-amination table with their heels in elevated stirrups and their legs apart. Furthermore, strongly fixed social norms say that when a man touches a woman's genitals, it is an act of intimacy. Yet the gynecological examination is supposed to be completely impersonal. Male gynecologists are notori-ous for their failure to appreciate the discomfort of their fe-male patients (Scully 1994; Emerson 1970).

The Health Care Crisis in the United States

Currently, the cost of medical care in the United States is approximately 14 percent of our gross domestic prod-uct, making health care the nation's third leading indus-try. The cost of health care has at times risen at twice the annual rate of inflation. The United States tops the list of all countries in per person expenditures for health care (see Figure 13.5). Despite all that spending, the U.S.

Many emergency waiting rooms in U.S. hospitals contain patients who must wait for long periods of time.

health care system is not the best in the world. Other countries spend considerably less money and deliver a level of health care at least as good. For example, Sweden and France spend roughly one-half as much per capita as the United States, and Great Britain spends a bit more than one-third as much, yet these countries have national health insurance programs that cover virtually their entire populations and deliver a level of care not much different overall from that achieved in the United States.

The battlefronts of the health care crisis extend to the fee-for-service system, the epidemic of malpractice suits, and the struggle for new forms of delivering health services (Starr 1982, 1995; Scarpitti et al. 1997). Here we examine each.

The Fee-for-Service System

Health care must be paid for, and in the United States the structures in place for paying the doctor's bill are in a state of chaos. The central element in the system is the fee-for-service principle. Under this arrangement, the patient is responsible for paying the fees charged by the physician or hospital. Fortunate patients will be adequately insured and able to pass on their health expenses to the insurance company. Many people are not insured, however, especially people with lower incomes. This group must reckon with large bills by drawing on their own limited resources. Overall, thirty-one million people in the United States are without health insurance. Most severely hit are the southern and southwestern states, where people without health insurance reach more than 15 percent of the population (see Map 13.3).

A third source of payment is the government, which is increasingly the ultimate payer of health care expenses.

The greatest contributors to skyrocketing health care costs are the soaring costs of hospital care and the rise in fees for the services of physicians. The services of specialists in particular are hugely expensive. Another culprit is the third-party payment system. With hospitals interested in making a profit, and patients simply passing bills on to insurance providers, there is little pressure to keep down the cost of care. Patients may be treated on an in-patient basis when a hospital stay is not actually necessary, unnecessary treatments may be given, and some diagnostic procedures may be ordered simply because expensive equipment is available that needs to be used to pay for itself.

Malpractice

A rising problem is malpractice insurance, a problem forcing many physicians to abandon some services. Annual insurance premiums (costs) for physicians have risen tenfold in the past decade and range now from about $5000 per year for physicians in family practice to well over $150,000 per year for physicians in specialties such as radiology, anesthesiology, and surgery. The cost of these insurance premiums is simply passed along to consumers (patients) and has contributed to the rise in the overall cost of health care.

The U.S. public has traditionally accorded physicians a high social status and high incomes. The recent increase in malpractice suits suggests that the public is beginning to question the privileged status of doctors. Several specific reasons have been put forward for client revolts against the medical profession. Attorneys claim that the primary cause of the malpractice dilemma is a declining standard of medical care and a rising incidence of medical negligence. Another argument is that, as a result of specialization, doctors now fail to establish old-fashioned rapport with patients, and thus patients are less attached to their physicians and more likely to turn hostile. A third notion is that the high cost of medical care and resentment about the outsized incomes of physicians has generated animosity in patients that is quick to show itself, especially when medical episodes have an unfortunate outcome.

Adding to the crisis is the eagerness with which lawyers take on malpractice suits. About one doctor in five is sued each year; Awards from medical malpractice suits can be in the millions of dollars. This has dramatically increased the malpractice insurance costs for doctors. One unfortunate result of all this is simply that physicians are increasingly leaving the medical field and going into other lines of work (Eisenberg and Siegler 2003).

Artist Gilles Barbier's "Nursing Home" 2002.

Elder care for: Wonder Woman, Superman, Captain America— can you name the rest?

To protect themselves against potential malpractice suits, doctors increasingly practice **defensive medicine** that entails ordering excessively thorough tests, X rays, and so on at the least indication that something might be amiss. This is done partly to ensure that nothing is missed and partly to document that the highest possible level of care was given. Although this extra attentiveness may contribute marginally to favorable medical outcomes, it contributes mightily to the overall cost of health care.

A Response to the Problem: HMOs

Health maintenance organizations (HMOs) are an innovation in health care first begun shortly after the Second World War but becoming widespread only within the last twenty years. The staffs in HMOs can include anywhere from several doctors to several hundred doctors. People who join HMOs are assigned to a physician who administers care and when necessary gives referrals to specialists affiliated with the HMO. The doctors in an HMO earn salaries rather than fees. All services are ultimately paid for by the membership fee paid by subscribers to the HMO. Eliminating both the fee-for-service system and the third-party insurer drives costs down in several ways. Physicians have an incentive to give the most economical levels of care, while presumably retaining their motive to maintain a high standard of care because they want to secure the reputation of the HMO and avoid malpractice suits. The opportunity for fraud, which costs third-party insurers so dearly, is eliminated. Finally, the corporate structure of HMOs presumably offers the economies of scale and economies of organization enjoyed by other profit-oriented corporations, yet often found lacking in the U.S. hospital system.

HMOs are experiencing fast growth as employers and individuals grapple with rising medical costs. In 1986,

there were approximately twenty-six million HMO subscribers in the United States, a number that has risen to more than fifty-five million in 1996. The American Medical Association (AMA) has a history of opposing HMOs on the grounds that they decrease the rights of physicians to determine treatments, and they limit the rights of patients to choose their own doctors or seek out treatments from specialists. The AMA has also argued in a number of forums that HMOs are inclined to pay too much attention to the bottom line and not enough to patient welfare. The problems with HMOs—and health care, more generally—has created a call for major reform in the health care system, but to date there is not a new national plan, even though public concern is high.

Alternative Medicine

As will be seen in Chapter 16, people often form social movements that seek to bring about some kind of change in society. A limited form of social movement is the alternative medicine movement, so named because it attempts some form of limited, focused change in some aspect of society. The New Age movements, which advocate such things as herbal treatments, vegetarianism, and other holistic practices, are examples of alternative movements. The movement away from traditional Western medicine to the use of alternative medicine is a social movement that has sprung up in response to the general health crisis in the United States. Holistic medicine emphasizes the person's entire mental and physical state and the integration of the two, as well as the person's physical and social environment. This is an example of alternative medicine that has developed since the late 1980s. Some forms of alternative medicine have by now become institutionalized, such as chiropracty, and acupuncture.

Practitioners of holistic medicine advocate the treatment of the entire mental and physical person, but they do not necessarily reject the remedies of traditional medicine such as surgery and drugs. They do, however, caution against the use of such measures alone on the grounds that they result in overspecialization and overreliance on drugs. The idea is that the dominance of corporate health organizations, including the pharmaceutical industry, increase health care costs and produce profits for some, but do not fundamentally change the unhealthy lifestyles common in contemporary society.

Holistic practitioners recognize that a variety of illnesses can result from the stresses of one's lifestyle, from work-related stress, or from poverty. The approach of holistic medicine is to decrease the dependency of the patient upon the physician by shifting some of the responsibility of cure from the physician to the patient, such as by advocating health-promoting behaviors involving diet, exercise, and the use of organic foods. As a consequence, holistic medicine takes an active role in combating the environmental origins of health in modern society.

■ Chapter Summary

■ What is the importance of the education institution?

Education is the social institution that is concerned with the formal transmission of society's knowledge. It is therefore part of the socialization process. More money is spent in the United States on education than on any other activity except health care.

■ How does education affect, or not affect, the likelihood of social mobility?

The number of years of formal education for individuals has important, but in many ways modest, effects on their ultimate occupation and income. The effect of education on later occupation is greater than the effect of education on later income. Social class origin affects the extent of educational attainment (the higher the social class origins, the more education is ultimately attained) as well as on occupation and income (higher social class origin likely means a more prestigious occupation and more income).

■ How does the educational system perpetuate inequality, instead of reduce it?

Although the education system in the United States has traditionally been a major means for reducing racial, gender, and class inequalities among people, it is also true that the educational institution has perpetuated these inequalities. Test biases based on culture, language, race, gender, and class have only been slightly reduced in standardized tests. *Tracking* and *labeling* continue to disproportionately affect minorities, women, and the working classes. Students are subject to the *labeling effect,* which affects both teacher expectations and student performance. *Teacher expectancy effects,* the *self-fulfilling prophecy,* and *stereotype threat effect* all work to the detriment of minorities, working-class people, and women.

■ What are the social factors in illness?

The state of health care in the United States is seen by means of *social epidemiology,* the study of the role of social and cultural factors in disease and health. Race–ethnicity, social class, and gender are major factors: Whites live longer than Blacks, and women live longer than men. Black women are more likely than White women to fall victim to cancer, heart

disease, strokes, and diabetes. The mortality rate among Native Americans is one and one-half times that of the general population.

■ How serious are the effects of these social factors?

Hispanics contract tuberculosis at four times the rate for Whites. On other indicators of health, they are similar to Blacks and Native Americans. The lower one's social class status, the greater are one's chances of tuberculosis, heart disease, cancer, and arthritis. The poor are more likely to be depersonalized and treated inadequately by the health care system than those of higher social class status. Men and women tend to be treated differently in the health care system, because there is still a tendency for the male-dominated profession to regard the problems of women as nonmainstream and "special."

■ How has AIDS developed?

A person who is known to be HIV positive, or who has full-blown AIDS, is partly blamed, negatively *stigmatized,* and treated as a social outcast. Although early identified only with gay men, AIDS is increasing among intravenous drug users and among women who are infected from contact with heterosexual men.

■ What is the health care crisis in the United States?

Modern medicine is a highly structured, specialized, high-status profession. High costs, abuses of the fee-for-service system and malpractice suits have resulted in a policy crisis today in the U.S. health care system. The growth of *health maintenance organizations (HMOs)* shows promise for easing the crisis, although programs for large HMOs and national universal health insurance have met with defeat in Congress.

■ Key Terms

achievement test 357
anorexia nervosa 365
cognitive ability 357
cognitive elite 359
credentialism 352
defensive medicine 376
epidemiology 366
health maintenance
   organization (HMO) 376
labeling effect 361
Medicaid 364
Medicare 364
predictive validity 358

self-fulfilling
   prophecy 361
sick role 372
social epidemiology 366
standardized ability
   test 357
stigma 370
teacher expectancy
   effect 361
tracking 359
Tuskegee Syphilis
   Study 366

■ *Researching Society with MicroCase Online*

You can see the results of actual research by using the Wadsworth MicroCase® Online feature available to you. This feature allows you to look at some of the results from national surveys, census data, and some other data sources. You can explore this easy-to-use feature on your own, but try this example. Suppose you wanted to know:

How many people feel that the individual has a right to commit suicide, if they so wish? And suppose you wanted to know: Is their answer dependent upon the amount of their education?

To answer these questions, go to: **sociology.wadsworth .com/andersen_taylor/essen3e**, select MicroCase Online from the left navigator bar, and follow the directions there to analyze the data described below.

Data File: GSS

Task: Cross-Tabulation

Row Variable: SUIC.WISH

Column Variable: I-EDUC

Questions

Once you have your results, answer the following questions.

1. Note that there were 1785 people in this survey. How many said "yes" to whether a person has the right to end his or her own life, if they feel ready to die? What percent of the total is this? Does this surprise you?

2. Does a person's education make a difference as to how they feel about the right to suicide?

Hint: The person's education does make a difference! NOW: Which way does it go? Is it that the more educated the person, the more likely he or she is to favor the right to suicide? OR is it that the less educated the person, the more likely he or she is to favor the right to suicide?

This shows that for the people who were studied, the two things we covered in this chapter are related: their education and their opinion on a matter of health (suicide wish).

■ *The Companion Web Site for Sociology: The Essentials, Third Edition*

sociology.wadsworth.com/andersen_taylor/essen3e

Supplement your review of this chapter by going to the companion Web site to take one of the Tutorial Quizzes, use the flash cards to master key terms, and check out the many other study aids you'll find there. You'll also find special features such as GSS Data and Census 2000 information, data and resources at your fingertips to help you with that special project or do some research on your own.

■ *Suggested Readings and Web Resources*

Fischer, Claude S., Michael Hout, Martin Sanchez Jankowski, Samuel R. Lucas, Ann Swidler, and Kim Voss. 1996. *Inequality by Design: Cracking the Bell Curve Myth.* Princeton, NJ: Princeton University Press.
This is a clearly written and comprehensive critique of Herrnstein and Murray's (1994) The Bell Curve. The authors give attention to definitions and measurements of intelligence, problems with the data in the studies used, race and intelligence, types of inequality in society, and other conceptual and methodological issues important to understanding the public debate about The Bell Curve.

Jencks, Christopher, and Meredith Phillips, eds. 1998. *The Black-White Test Score Gap.* Washington, DC: Brookings Institution Press.
This anthology is a highly readable and well-balanced account of aspects of the Black-White test score gap on the Scholastic Assessment Test (SAT) and other tests. It contains complete discussions of test bias and its different types and forms, the role of socioeconomic background and parenting, teacher expectancy, stereotype threat, and other causes of the test score gap. A number of policy issues are also discussed.

Morgen, Sandra. 2002. *Into Our Own Hands: The Women's Health Movement in the United States, 1969–1990.* Piscataway, NJ: Rutgers University Press.
Morgen chronicles the development of the woman's health movement as it emerged from feminism and challenged the system of medical control—and male authority—over women's bodies. It is a good illustration of how grassroots movements challenge the medical establishment.

Scheff, Thomas. 1984. *Being Mentally Ill: A Sociological Theory,* 2nd ed. New York: Aldine.
This is one of the best explanations and applications of labeling theory as applied to the study of mental illness as a social construction. The work discusses how patients are in effect rewarded for continuing their sickness and punished for trying to get well.

Sjulmana, James L., and William G. Bowen. 2001. *The Game of Life: College Sports and Educational Values.* Princeton, NJ: Princeton University Press.
This book addresses a major issue in education: the influence of college and university athletics on the fundamental

goals of higher education. Based on surveys of athletes, professors, and college administrators, the work presents an impressive study of the issues, pro and con.

American Association of University Women
www.aauw.org
This organization, which promotes equity for woman and education, regularly produces reports about gender and education. Their reports are often the basis for changes in social policy.

Centers for Disease Control and Prevention
www.cdc.gov
A national research center aimed at preventing and controlling disease. Also publishes national data on the health statistics of the population.

National Center for Education Statistics
www.ed.gov/NCES/index.html
This division of the U.S. government collects and publishes reports on the condition of education, including students, faculty and teaching staff, school expenditures, and other useful compilations of data.

Office of Minority Health Resource Center
www.omhrc.gov
An office of the government that provides health information on specific minority populations.

Politics and the Economy

Picture a couple lounging together on a public beach on a national holiday. They imagine themselves married someday, perhaps having children they will send to public school. Does the government have anything to say about the couple's children? They may decide to use birth control until they are ready for children; if so, their choice of birth control methods will be limited to those the government allows. What if they cannot have children? They might consider adopting—if state agencies judge them acceptable as parents.

As you imagined this couple, whom did you picture? Were they the same race? Not so long ago, the law would have forbidden the marriage if it were interracial. Is this a man and a woman or is this a same-sex couple? If they are lesbian or gay, despite being in love and wanting to form a lifelong relationship, in most states they are prevented by law from marrying.

This couple is probably giving no thought to how much their life is influenced by the state at that very moment. Permission to walk on the public beach comes from the state; the day off to celebrate a holiday is sanctioned by the state; the drive to the beach took place in a car registered with the state and inspected by the state, driven by a motorist licensed by the state. The range of things regulated by the state is simply enormous, and yet many are never noticed.

Every day millions of people within this state get up, get dressed, and go to work. Another several million wish they could find work. Many who work wish they earned more or had jobs with better working conditions. Work has an enormous effect on most aspects of your life, including relationships with your family, how much power you have, and what resources are available.

When thinking about work, most people think in terms of what kind of work they might do, how much they can earn, whether their work will be satisfying, and whether their job will give them opportunities for promotion and advancement. Students, for example, may see their education as a way to get work opportunities or promotions, but they may also worry about what work they will find and whether their work will be meaningful, use their talents, and provide a lifetime of rewards. These concerns can be understood in a sociological framework even though people tend to think each is an individual problem. Sociologists study the social forces that shape people's experiences and understand how downsizing, globalization of the economy, corporate restructuring, and technological change affect work.

■ *Defining the State*

The sociological definition of the **state** is the organized system of power and authority in society. The term *state* does not refer to the state in the United States where someone lives. It is an abstract concept that includes the institutions that represent official power in society, such as the government and its legal system (with the courts and the prison system), the police, and the military. Theoretically, the state exists to regulate social order ranging from individual behavior and interpersonal conflicts to international affairs, although it does not always do so fairly or equitably. The guarantee of life, liberty, and the pursuit of happiness promised in the Declaration of Independence, when examined carefully, is not evenly distributed by the state. Less powerful groups in the society may see the state more as an oppressive force than a protector of individual rights. However, they may still turn to the state to rectify injustice. For example, when African Americans sought to end segregation, they sought legal reform through the state, that is, through the courts.

The state has a central role in shaping class, race, and gender relations in society. It determines the rights and privileges of many groups—and defines who is a member in each group. The involvement of the state may include the resolution of management and labor conflicts (such as in airline strikes), congressional legislation determining the benefits of different groups (such as the Americans with Disabilities Act of 1990), or Supreme Court decisions interpreting the U.S. Constitution. The state also provides the basic institutional structure of society by determining through state laws what institutional forms will receive societal support. Laws regulating family relationships also emanate from the state. Thus, families defined as illegitimate by law (or other mechanisms for the state to exert its will, such as tax policy) do not receive the same benefits and rights as families that the state defines as legitimate, even if someone in the family is quite ill.

Sociological analyses of the state focus on several different questions. One important issue is the relationship between the state and inequality in society. State policies can have very different impacts on different groups, as we will see later in this chapter. Another issue explored by sociological theory is the connection between the state and other social institutions—the state and religion, the state and the family, and so on. In this chapter we will examine the connection between the state and the institution of health care.

The Institutions of the State

Numerous institutions make up the state, including the government, the legal system, the police, and the military. The government creates laws and procedures that regulate and guide a society. The military is the branch of government responsible for defending the nation against domestic and foreign conflicts. The court system is designed to punish wrongdoers and adjudicate disputes. Court decisions also determine the guiding principles or laws of human interaction. Law is a fundamental type of formal social control that outlines what is permissible and what is forbidden. The police are responsible for enforcing law in the community and for maintaining public order. The prison system is the institution responsible for punishing those who have broken the law, although as we have already seen in some detail (particularly in Chapter 6), prisons often punish differently depending on a person's race, gender, social class, and other factors.

The State and Social Order

Throughout this book, we have seen that a variety of social processes contribute to order in society, including the learning of cultural norms (that is, socialization), peer pressure, and the social control of deviance. Each plays a part in producing social order, but none so explicitly and unambiguously as the official system of power and authority in society. In making laws, the state clearly decrees what actions are legitimate and which are not. Punishments for illegitimate actions are enforced, and systems for administering punishment are maintained. The state also influences public opinion through its power to regulate the media. In some cases the state circulates **propaganda,** which is disseminated with the intention to justify the state's power. Any group or organization may circulate propaganda. Censorship is another means by which the state can direct public opinion. The movement to censor sexually explicit materials on the Internet is an example of state-based censorship.

The state's role in maintaining public order is also apparent in how it manages dissent. Protest movements perceived by those in power to challenge state authority or threaten the disruption of society may be repressed through state action. Options available to the state range from surveillance through imprisonment all the way to military force. Throughout the late 1950s and 1960s, for example, the FBI conducted illegal surveillance operations targeting Martin Luther King Jr. and other civil rights leaders (Garrow 1981). The FBI also spied illegally on the Beatles and the Grateful Dead.

As the system of institutionalized power and authority in society, the state has the dual role of protecting its citizens and ensuring the preservation of society. Different states work in different ways: Some explicitly protect the status quo and others are more revolutionary or more totalitarian in nature. Even in a democratic state, such as the United States, however, the state typically protects the interests of those with the most power, leaving the least powerful groups in society vulnerable to oppressive state action.

Revolution

A **revolution** is the overthrow of a state or the total transformation of central state institutions. Numerous sociologists as well as other social scientists have studied revolutions and have extensively identified the conditions under which revolutions occur. Revolutions can sometimes break down a state as the result of conflict between the oppressive state and various disenfranchised groups. An array of groups in a society may be dissatisfied with the status quo and organize to replace the established institutions. Dissatisfaction alone is not enough to produce a revolution, however. The structural opportunities must exist, such as through war or an economic crisis, for groups to mobilize people through social movements (see Chapter 16). Groups mobilize to challenge authorities when they are able to garner the resources that enable the challenge to develop (Tilly 1975 1978; Kurzman 1996). Many have noted that the displacement of agriculturally based systems that came with the development of capitalism resulted in state revolutions in western European nations (Skocpol 1979).

People typically think a revolution produces more democratic and open political systems, such as the French Revolution or the American Revolution, but revolutions can also produce a more repressive state, such as the Iranian revolution that brought conservative Shiites to rule. Whether it is a revolution to gain freedom or to gain absolute power, revolution is the total transformation of state institutions.

Global Interdependence and the State

Internationally, there are increasingly strong ties between the state and the global economy. The interdependence of national economies means that political systems are also elaborately entangled—a phenomenon that can be observed daily in the newspaper.

The process of globalization profoundly affects the character of states and their relationships. One example is the World Trade Organization (WTO)—created in 1994 to monitor and resolve trade disputes. Member nations may challenge the decisions made by local and national governments, with the WTO Council in Geneva resolving disagreements. The creation of this organization has produced a system that transcends individual nation–states by formalizing and strengthening the rules that govern many aspects of world trade. This represents the trend, in an increasingly international economy, toward the creation of a single state—at least in the sense of a single governing institution that has the potential for authority over many aspects of people's lives around the world.

▪ *Power and Authority*

The concepts of power and authority are central to sociological analyses of the state. **Power** is the ability of one person or group to exercise influence and control over others. The exercise of power can be seen in relationships ranging from the interaction of two people (husband and wife, police officer and suspect) to a nation threatening or dominating other nations. Sociologists are most interested in how power is structured in society—who has it, how it is used, and how it is built into institutions such as the state. Power can be structured, such as when men as a group have power over women as a group. In the United States, a society that is heavily stratified by race, class, and gender, power is structured into basic social institutions in ways that reflect these inequalities. Sociologists also understand that institutionalized power in society influences the social dynamics within individual and group relationships.

The exercise of power may take the form of persuasion or coercion. For example, a group may be encouraged to act a certain way based on a persuasive argument. A strong political leader may persuade the nation to support a military invasion or a social policy. Or power may be exerted by sheer force. Between persuasion and coercion are many gradations. Generally speaking, groups with the greatest material resources most likely have the advantage in transactions involving power, but this is not always the case. A group may by sheer size be able to exercise power, or groups may use other means, such as armed uprisings or organized social protests, to exert power.

Power can be legitimate—accepted by the members of society as right and just—or it can be illegitimate. **Authority** is power perceived by others as legitimate, and emerges not only from the exercise of power, but from the belief of constituents that the power is legitimate. In the United States, the source of the president's domestic power is not just his status as commander of the armed forces but also the belief by most people that his power is legitimate. The law is also a source of authority in the United States. Those who accept the status quo as a legitimate system of authority perceive the guardians of law to be exercising *legitimate power.* In contrast, *coercive power,* is achieved through force, often against the will of the people being forced. Those people may be only a few dissidents or most of the citizenry of an entire nation. A dictatorship often relies on its ability to exercise coercive power through its control of the military or state police.

Types of Authority

Max Weber (1864–1920), the German classical sociologist, postulated that three types of authority exist in society: traditional, charismatic, and rational–legal (Weber 1978/1921). **Traditional authority** stems from long-established patterns that give certain people or groups legitimate power in society. A monarchy is an example of a traditional system of authority. Within a monarchy, kings and queens rule, not necessarily because of their appeal, or because they have won elections, but because of long-standing traditions within the society.

Charismatic authority is derived from the personal appeal of a leader. Charismatic leaders are often believed to have special gifts, even magical powers, and their presumed personal attributes inspire devotion and obedience. Charismatic leaders often emerge from religious movements, but they come from other realms also. President John F. Kennedy was for many a charismatic leader, admired for the vigorous image he projected of himself and the nation. Arnold Schwarzenegger, a movie star, was elected governor of California partially as the result of his charismatic authority.

Rational–legal authority stems from rules and regulations, typically written down as laws, procedures, or codes of conduct. This is the most common form of authority in the contemporary United States. People obey not because national leaders are charismatic or because of social traditions, but because there is an unquestioned legal system of authority established by formalized rules and regulations. Rulers gain legitimate authority by election or appointment in accordance with society's rules. In systems based on rational–legal authority, the rules are upheld by state agents such as the police, judges, social workers, and other state functionaries to whom power is delegated.

The Growth of Bureaucratic Government

According to Weber, rational–legal authority leads inevitably to the formation of bureaucracies. As we noted in Chapter 5, a **bureaucracy** is a type of formal organization characterized by an authority hierarchy, a clear division of labor, explicit rules, and impersonality. Bureaucratic power comes from the accepted legitimacy of the rules, not personal ties to individuals. The rules may change, but they do so via formal, bureaucratic procedures. People who work within bureaucracies are selected, trained, and

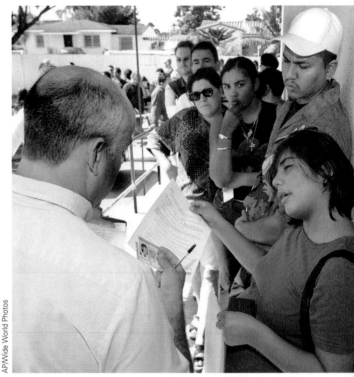

AP/Wide World Photos

Bureaucracies such as the Department of Motor Vehicles are organized according to hierarchical and rule-driven forms of social organization.

TAKING ON SOCIAL ISSUES

Privacy

© Bob Daemmrich/The Image Works

How we communicate and learn raises new concerns about the potential for privacy to be invaded.

Does the government have a right to invade someone's personal privacy? The question has been debated for most of the twentieth century, but only recently have there been social changes toward combating and reducing governmental and other intrusions into personal privacy. The electronic age, itself a major social change, has provided the government with numerous ways and means for accessing private information. Use of the Internet provides us with many examples. Many Internet users have included personal information, even intimate photographs of themselves, on the Internet. In some cases, this involves photographs of a couple engaged in a sex act.

Does the government, either local or federal, have a right to curtail these kinds of activities (such as the sex act on the Internet) on the grounds, say, that it is unfit for children who can access it? Does the government have a right to access your social security number, your course grades, and other highly personal information and then use the information for its own purposes? Does the government have a right to use such nonpublic information "against" you?

Taking Action

Go to the Taking Action exercise on the companion Web site at **sociology.wadsworth.com/ andersen_taylor/essen3e** to learn more about an organization that addresses this topic.

promoted based on how well they apply the rules. Those who establish the rules are unlikely to be the same people who administer them. Bureaucracies are hierarchical, and the bureaucratic leadership may be quite remote. Power in bureaucracies is dispersed downward through the system to those who actually carry out the bureaucratic functions. It is an odd feature of bureaucracy that those with the least power to influence how the rules are formulated—those at the bottom of the hierarchy—are very often the most adamant about strict adherence to the rules.

Is the bureaucratic growth of government in the United States becoming unwieldy? Many would say yes, judging from the sheer size of bureaucratic governmental institutions. Bureaucracy has become the modern system of administration. In principle, bureaucracies are highly efficient modes of organization, but the reality is often very different. Bureaucracies tend to proliferate rules, often causing the organization to become ensnared in its own bureaucratic requirements. For example, government procurement of desktop computers has become so overburdened by bureaucratic government rules for review, comparison, bidding, and approval that by the time the federal government approves a purchase, the approved models may be obsolete.

Within bureaucracies, personal temperament and individual discretion are not supposed to influence the

Observe the national evening news for one week, noting the people featured who have some kind of *authority*. List each of them and note their area of influence. What form of authority would you say each represents: *traditional, charismatic,* or *rational–legal*? How is the kind of authority a person has reflected in his or her position in society (that is, race, class, gender, occupation, education, and so on)?

application of rules. Of course, we know that the face of bureaucracy is not always perfectly stony. As we saw in Chapter 5, bureaucracy has another face. Bureaucratic workers frequently exercise discretion in applying rules and procedures. Some people who encounter bureaucracies know how to "work the system," perhaps by personalizing the interaction and making a willing accomplice of the bureaucrat in dodging bureaucratic stipulations, or perhaps by using knowledge of some rules to evade other rules. People who lack privileged relationships or privileged information are continually at a disadvantage because of their inability to negotiate within the system. Despite the supposed impersonal administration in bureaucracies, people may receive widely varied treatment from bureaucratic workers who may favor some people while discriminating against others based on race, gender, age, or other characteristics.

Our picture of the state so far—bureaucratic, powerful, omnipresent—presents an important question to be

addressed by the sociological imagination: Does the state act in the interests of its different constituencies, or does it merely reflect the needs of a select group positioned at the top of the pyramid of state power? This question has spawned much sociological study and debate and has resulted in several theoretical models of state power.

■ *Theories of Power*

How is power exercised in society? Four theoretical models have been developed by sociologists to answer this question: the *pluralist model*, the *power-elite model*, the *autonomous state model*, and *feminist theories of the state*. Each begins with a different set of assumptions and arrives at different conclusions (see Table 14.1).

The Pluralist Model

The **pluralist model** interprets power in society as derived from the representation of diverse interests of different groups in society. This model assumes that in democratic societies, the system of government works to balance the different interests of groups in society. An **interest group** can be any constituency in society organized to promote its own agenda, including large, nationally based groups such as the American Association of Retired Persons (AARP), the National Gay and Lesbian Task Force, the National Rifle Association (NRA), the National Organization for

TABLE 14.1 Theories of Power in Society

	Pluralism	Power Elite	Autonomous State	Feminist Theory
Interprets . . .				
The State	As representing diverse and multiple groups in society	As representing the interests of a small, but economically dominant, class	As taking on a life of its own, perpetuating its own form and interests	As masculine in its organization and values (that is, based on rational principles and a patriarchal structure)
Political Power	As derived from the activities of interest groups and as broadly diffused throughout the public	As held by the ruling class	As residing in the organizational structure of state institutions	As emerging from the dominance of men over women
Social Conflict	As the competition between diverse groups that mobilize to promote their interests	As stemming from the domination of elites over less powerful groups	As developing between states, as each vies to uphold its own interests	As resulting from the power men have over women
Social Order	As the result of the equilibrium created by multiple groups balancing their interests	As coming from the interlocking directorates created by the linkages among those few people who control institutions	As the result of administrative systems that work to maintain the status quo	As resulting from the patriarchal control that men have over social institutions

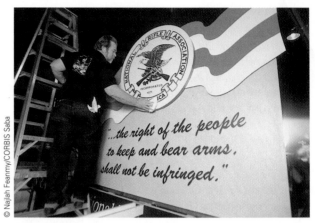

The pluralist model of the state sees diverse interest groups as mobilizing to gain political power.

Women (NOW), and the National Urban League; groups organized around professional and business interests, such as the American Medical Association (AMA), the National Association of Manufacturers, and the Tobacco Institute; or groups that concentrate on one political or social goal, such as Greenpeace and Mothers Against Drunk Driving (MADD). According to the pluralist model, interest groups achieve power and influence through their organized mobilization of concerned people and groups.

The pluralist model has its origins in functionalist theory. This model sees the state as benign and representative of the whole society. No particular group is seen as politically dominant; rather, the pluralist model sees power as broadly diffused across the public. Groups that want to effect a change or express their point of view need only mobilize to do so. The pluralist model also suggests that members of diverse ethnic, racial, and social groups can participate equally in a representative and democratic government assuming that power does not depend on social status or wealth. Various special interest groups compete for government attention and action with equal political opportunity available for any group that organizes to pursue its interests. The pluralist model sees special interest groups as an integral part of the political system even though they are not an official part of government. In the pluralist view, special interest groups make government more responsive to the needs and interests of different people, an especially important function in a highly diverse society (Berberoglu 1990).

The pluralist model helps explain the importance of **political action committees (PACs),** groups of people who organize to support candidates they feel will represent their views. In 1974, Congress passed legislation enabling employees of companies, members of unions, professional groups, and trade associations to support political candidates with money they raise collectively. The number of political action committees has now grown to

almost 4000. PACs have enormous influence on the political process. One measure of their growing influence is the tremendous increase in financial contributions that PACs made to political campaigns over the last two decades—in excess of $220 million in the year 2000 (Federal Election Commission 2001).

The Power Elite Model

The **power elite model** originated in the work of Karl Marx (1818–1883), and developed from the framework of conflict theory. According to Marx, the dominant or ruling class controls all the major institutions in society; the state itself is simply an instrument by which the ruling class exercises its power. The Marxist view of the state emphasizes the power of the upper class over the lower classes, the small group of elites over the rest of the population. The state, according to Marx, is not a representative, rational institution, but an expression of the will of the ruling class (Marx 1972/1845).

Marx's theory was elaborated much later by C. Wright Mills (1956), who popularized the term *power elite.* Mills attacked the pluralist model, arguing that the true power structure consists of people well positioned in three areas: the economy, the government, and the military. These three institutions are considered the bastions of the power elite, although some have argued that Mills overemphasized the role of the military in the power elite (Domhoff 2002). While sharing common beliefs and goals, the power elite shape political agendas and outcomes in the society along the narrow lines of their particular collective interests. This small and influential group at the top of the pyramid of power holds the key positions in the major state institutions, giving them extensive power and control over the rest of society.

The power elite model posits a strong link between government and business, a view supported by the strong hand government takes in directing the economy and by the role of military spending as a principal component of U.S. economic affairs. The power elite model also emphasizes how power overlaps between influential groups. **Interlocking directorates** are organizational linkages created when the same people sit on the board of directors for numerous corporations. People in elite circles may serve on the boards of major companies, universities, and foundations at the same time. People drawn from the same elite group receive most of the major government appointments; thus, the same relatively small group of people tends to the interests of all these organizations and the interests of the government. These interests naturally overlap and reinforce each other.

The power elite model sees the state as part of the structure of domination in society, one in which the state is simply a piece of the whole. Members of the upper class do not need to occupy high office themselves to exert their will, as long as they are in a position to influence people who are in power (Domhoff 2002). The majority of the power elite are White men, which means that the interests and outlooks of White men dominate the national agenda.

The Autonomous State Model

A third view of power developed by sociologists, the **autonomous state model,** interprets the state as its own major constituent. From this perspective, the state develops interests of its own, which it seeks to promote independent of other interests and the public that it allegedly serves. The state does not reflect the needs of the dominant groups, as Marx and power elite theorists would contend. It is an administrative organization with its own needs, such as maintenance of its complex bureaucracies and protection of its special privileges (Evans et al. 1985; Skocpol 1992; Rueschmeyer and Skocpol 1996).

Autonomous state theorists note that states tend to grow over time, including the possible expansion beyond their original boundaries, by military excursions. Another example of expansion is the North American Free Trade Agreement (NAFTA)—in which the United States is expanding its state interests by regulating business not only in the United States, but also in Mexico and Canada.

UNDERSTANDING DIVERSITY

Diversity in the Power Elite

As society has become more diverse, has it made a difference in the makeup of the power elite? Various groups—women, racial–ethnic groups, lesbians, and gays—have vied for more representation in the halls of power, but have their efforts succeeded? If they make it to power, does this change the corporations, military, or government—the major institutions composing the power elite?

Sociologists Richard L. Zweigenhaft and G. William Domhoff examined these questions by analyzing the composition of boards of directors and chief executive officers (CEOs) of the largest banks and corporations in the United States, as well as analyzing Congress, presidential cabinets, and the generals and admirals who form the military elite. In addition, they examined the political party preferences and the political positions of people found among the power elite. Do women and minorities bring new values into power, thereby changing society as they move into powerful positions, or do their values match those of the traditional power elite or become

absorbed by a system more powerful than they are? Zweigenhaft and Domhoff's study looks as well at whether those who do make it into the power elite are within the innermost circles or whether they are marginalized.

They find that women, Jews, gays, lesbians, Black Americans, and Hispanics have become more numerous within the power elite, but only to a small degree. The power elite is still overwhelmingly White, wealthy, Christian, and male. Women and other minorities who make it into the power elite also tend to come from already privileged backgrounds, measured by their social class and education. Among African Americans and Latinos, skin color continues to make a difference, with darker-skinned Blacks and Hispanics less likely to achieve prominence, compared with lighter-skinned people. Furthermore, Zweigenhaft and Domhoff find that the perspectives and values of women and minorities who rise to the top do not differ substantially from their White male counterparts. Some of this is explained by the common class origins of those

in the power elite. The researchers also attribute the managing of one's identity to avoid challenging the system as a sorting factor that perpetuates the dominant worldview and practices of the most powerful.

The authors of this study conclude that "the irony of diversity" is that greater diversity may have strengthened the position of the power elite, because its members appear to be more legitimate through their inclusion of those previously left out. But, by including only those who share the perspectives and values of those already in power, little is actually changed. Clarence Thomas, Sandra Day O'Connor, and Colin Powell may make it seem that women and African Americans have it made, but as long as they support the positions of White male elites, the power elite goes undisturbed.

SOURCE: Zweigenhaft, Richard L., and G. William Domhoff. 1998. *Diversity in the Power Elite: Have Women and Minorities Reached the Top?* New Haven: Yale University Press.

© United Nations

The world's leadership: Where are the women?

The huge government apparatus now in place in the United States is a good illustration of autonomous state theory. The government provides a huge array of social support programs, including Social Security, unemployment benefits, agricultural subsidies, public assistance, and other economic interventions intended to protect citizens from the vagaries of a capitalist market system (Collins 1988). The purpose of these programs is to serve people in need. Autonomous state theory argues that the government has grown into a massive, elaborate bureaucracy, run by bureaucrats more absorbed in their own interests than in meeting the needs of the people. As a consequence, government can become paralyzed in conflicts between revenue-seeking state bureaucrats and those who must fund them. This can lead to revolt against the state, as in the tax revolts appearing sporadically throughout the country (Lo 1990; Collins 1988).

Feminist Theories of the State

Feminist theorists diverge from the preceding theoretical models by seeing men as having the most important power in society. The pluralists see power as widely dispersed through the class system; power elite theorists see political power directly linked to upper-class interests; and autonomous state theorists see the state as relatively independent of class interests.

Some feminist theorists argue that all state institutions reflect men's interests; they see the state as fundamentally patriarchal, its organization embodying the fixed principle that men are more powerful than women. Feminist theories of the state conclude that despite the presence of a few powerful women the state is devoted primarily to men's interests, and moreover, the actions of the state will tend to support gender inequality (Blankenship 1993). One historical example would be laws denying women the right to own property once they married. Such laws protected men's interests at the expense of women.

Evidence that the state "is male" (MacKinnon 1983: 644) is easy to observe by looking at powerful political circles. Despite the recent inclusion of more women in powerful circles, and the presence of some notable women as major national figures, most of the powerful are men. The U.S. Senate is 87 percent men; groups that exercise state power, such as the police and military, are predominantly men. Moreover, these institutions are structured by values and systems that can be described as culturally masculine—that is, based on hierarchical relationships, aggression, and force. Feminist theory begins with the premise that an understanding of power cannot be sound without a strong analysis of gender (Haney 1996).

■ Government: Power and Politics in a Diverse Society

The terms *government* and *state* are often used interchangeably. More precisely, the government is one of several institutions that make up the state. The **government** includes those state institutions that represent the population, making rules that govern the society. The government of the United States is a **democracy;** therefore

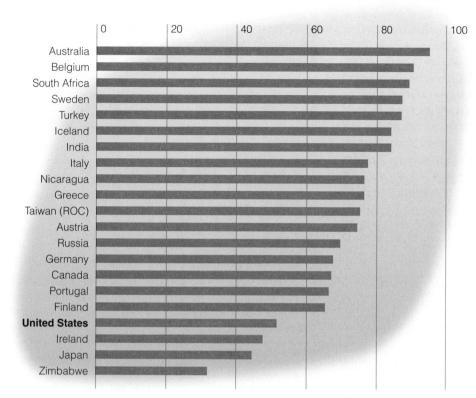

FIGURE 14.1 Voter Participation in Democratic Nations Average Participation, 1945–1989.

SOURCE: Federal Election Commission. 2003. "International Voter Turnout." Washington, DC: Federal Election Commission. **www.fec.gov/votregis/InternatTO.htm**

it is based on the principle of representing all people through the right to vote.

The actual makeup of the government, however, is far from representative of society. Not all people participate equally in the workings of government, either as elected officials or as voters, nor do their interests receive equal attention. Women, the poor and working class, and racial–ethnic minorities are less likely to be represented by government than are White middle- and upper-class men. Sociological research on political power has concentrated on inequality in government affairs and demonstrated large, persistent differences in the political participation and representation of various groups in society.

Diverse Patterns of Political Participation

One would hope that in a democratic society all people would be equally eager to exercise their right to vote and be heard. That is far from the case. Among democratic nations, the United States has one of the lowest voter turnouts (see Figure 14.1). In the 2000 presidential election, the percentage of eligible voters who went to the polls was still only 51 percent of the population. A turnout of 50 percent or less is typical of national elections; voter turnout in congressional and local elections is even lower.

The group most likely to vote is older, better educated, and financially better off than the average citizen. In socio-

logical terms, age, income, and education are the strongest predictors of whether someone will vote. The higher a person's social class, the higher the likelihood that she or he will be a voter. As a result, the upper social classes are far more likely to vote and have their voices heard in the political process. The requirements of voter registration discourage many from voting (Piven and Cloward 1988). Every time you move, you must register again to vote, although the National Voter Registration Act of 1993 provides greater flexibility in how one registers to vote, including "motor voter" procedures (where you register to vote when you apply for a driver's license). To date, however, voter turnout has not significantly increased since implementation of this policy.

There is also significant variation in voting patterns by race. Overall, African Americans are less likely to vote than Whites, a fact reflecting the disproportionate numbers of African Americans in the poor and working classes— groups that typically are less likely to vote than middle- and upper-class people. During the late 1960s, however, controlling for factors such as age, education, and income, African Americans were actually more likely to vote than White Americans, probably because of the heightened sense of the importance of the franchise generated at the time by the civil rights movement and voter registration drives. Beginning in the 1970s, there was a convergence in the likelihood of voting among Blacks and Whites of similar social class, education, and age (Ellison and Gay 1989). During the presidential election of 2000, African American voting turnout was especially high in areas where the

NAACP (National Association for the Advancement of Colored People), labor unions, and the Democratic Party led a barrage of activity to get out the vote (Fletcher 2000).

A subjective factor influencing the voting behavior of African Americans is that they are generally less trusting of the political system than Whites, and are more alienated from politics. Sociological research shows that when Black Americans are approached directly by party representatives, the likelihood they will vote increases substantially—more than it does when Whites are canvassed. In addition, the more that Black Americans and Latinos identify themselves as groups with distinct needs and interests, the more likely they will participate in the political process, reflecting the long-standing sociological finding that a strong sense of ethnic identity is linked to increased political participation (Welch and Sigelman 1993).

Not only do social factors influence the likelihood of voting, they also influence whom people vote for, as Table 14.2 shows. Race is one major social factor that influences voting. African Americans and Latinos, with the exception of Cuban Americans, tend to be markedly Democratic and voted overwhelmingly for Al Gore, the 2000 Democratic presidential candidate; Cuban Americans are disproportionately Republican. One reason both Latinos and African Americans have been more attracted to the Democratic party and its candidates is that Democrats historically have been more committed to government action that promotes social and economic equality. The allegiance of Latino and Black voters to Democratic candidates is also explained in part by socioeconomic factors such as age, gender, income, education, and religion; all these factors, regardless of racial–ethnic identity, are linked to political behavior. Even without controlling for these factors, however, Latinos are more liberal than Anglos. Latinos are generally also more likely than other groups to support government spending (Welch and Sigelman 1993).

Ethnicity of the candidates also influences voting patterns. People tend to vote for those of their own ethnic group. Sociologists have also found that ethnicity can outweigh socioeconomic factors such as occupation, income, and education in predicting voting patterns. White Catholics, for example, have traditionally been aligned with the Democratic Party, although that link has been weakened somewhat by economic changes that have had a strong influence on voting patterns (Legge 1993; R. Smith 1993).

Gender is also a major social factor influencing political attitudes and behavior. **Gender gap** refers to the differences between men and women in political attitudes and behavior. One aspect of the gender gap is that women are more likely than men to identify and vote as Democrats (see Table 14.2), and to have liberal views on a variety of social and political issues. For many decades, men were more likely to vote than women and, when asked, women reported voting

TABLE 14.2 The 2000 Presidential Election: Who Voted How (by Percentage)?			
	George W. Bush (Republican)	Al Gore (Democrat)	Ralph Nader (Green Party)
By gender			
Men	53%	42%	3%
Women	43	54	2
By race			
White	54	42	3
African American	8	90	1
Hispanic	31	67	2
Asian American	42	54	4
By education			
No high school degree	39	59	1
High school graduate	49	48	1
Some college	51	45	3
College graduate	51	45	3
Postgraduate degree	44	52	3
By income			
Less than $15,000	37	57	4
$15,000–$30,000	41	54	3
$30,000–$50,000	48	49	2
$50,000–$75,000	51	46	2
$75,000–$100,000	52	45	2
More than $100,000	54	43	2

SOURCE: Connelly, Marjorie. 2000. "Who Voted: A Portrait of American Politics, 1976–2000." *The New York Times,* November 12, Section 4, p. 4; CNN exit polls, **www.cnn.com**

the same as their husbands and fathers. In recent years, women have been as likely to vote as men, but there are significant differences in their political outlooks (Wilcox et al. 1996; Eliason et al. 1996; Jackson et al. 1996).

Political Power: Who's in Charge?

Although the government in a democracy is supposed to be representative, the class, race, and gender composition of the ruling bodies in this country indicate that this is hardly the case (see Figure 14.2). Most members of Congress are White, well–educated men, from upper middle- or upper-class backgrounds with an Anglo-Saxon Protestant heritage. One-third of the people in Congress are lawyers; another third are businesspeople and bankers. Most other members come from professional occupations; very few senators or representatives were blue-collar workers before coming to Congress (Freedman 1997; Ornstein et al. 1996; Saunders 1990).

Many of the 535 members of Congress are millionaires, and many in Congress have large financial interests in the industries that they regulate. Simply getting into politics requires a substantial investment of money. The average cost of a senate campaign is nearly $4 million; a successful run for the House of Representatives costs nearly $400,000. In 2000, John Corzine, a Wall Street investor and Democrat from New Jersey, spent a record $36 million, closely winning a U.S. Senate seat.

All candidates depend on contributions from individuals and groups to finance their election campaigns. Wealthy families and individuals are among the largest campaign contributors to presidential elections (Allen and Broyles 1991). The largest individual contributors typically have interests in the same industries that fund political action committees. Much of the money given by individuals and PACs goes to incumbents, who in the past had an overwhelming edge in elections, and already sit on the committees where public policy is hammered out. This picture of elites and business interests funneling money to candidates, who return to the same donors

for more money when the next campaign rolls around, has shaken the faith of many Americans in their political system. There is little belief that the political process is a democratic and populist mechanism by which the "little people" can select political leaders to represent them. In fact, national surveys show that only 29 percent of U.S. citizens have a great deal of confidence in Congress, and only 50 percent have some confidence in the Supreme Court (Gallup Organization 2002).

Women and Minorities in Government

Although there have been some gains in the number of women and minorities in government, they are still underrepresented—both at the federal and state level

---

SOCIOLOGY IN PRACTICE

Voting Systems

In a nation as technologically sophisticated as the United States, one would think that counting votes would be a relatively simple and technologically based process. Yet, many were surprised during the 2000 presidential election at just how imperfect voting systems are. In the fall of 2003, a district court in the state of California threatened to postpone an election to recall then-governor Gray Davis, partly on the grounds that voting technologies in certain parts of the state were inadequate.

The first voting machine ever produced was called the Myers Automatic Booth. It was first used in New York in 1892, and 20 percent of voters still use such a mechanical machine, in which they pull a lever to mark your ballot. Mechanical machines are no longer being made. They are being widely replaced with computer "marksense" ballots or other electronic systems, used by 25 percent of voters who mark their choices on a ballot, which is then machine read. The newest electronic machine, used by about 8 percent of voters, is a "direct recording" machine where the

voters mark a ballot by using a touch screen or push-button, similar to an ATM (automatic teller machine). Even this method has been criticized however by computer engineers, on the grounds that should a re-count of the votes be necessary, it would be impossible with this technology. The most widely used form of voting is the now-infamous punchcard ballot, used by about 38 percent of voters. First used in 1964, this method involves punching a hole in a computer card, which is then tabulated by a card-reading machine.

The controversy over the accuracy of voting machines has led people to wonder if a new, nationally based election is needed. While some recommend a direct recording system, perhaps a system that could be used from home via the Web or a telephone, others worry that such a system might further disadvantage voters with less access to home technology. Despite the seeming neutrality of technology, it has many sociological dimensions. Access to technology can be influenced by race and social class, and as we learned in the election of 2000,

machines can be flawed. Who uses them and how they are used are influenced by sociological factors. As the nation debates change in the voting system, sociologists will be observing how factors such as race, gender, age, and social class come into play in voting behavior.

Critical Thinking Exercises

1. Numerous non-profit organizations advocate changes in the voting practices and methods of the U.S. public. Given what you know from sociological research, if you worked for such an organization, what might you recommend to ensure that voting is equally extended to all in this democratic society?

2. What are the factors that encourage or discourage the students in your institution from voting in local, state, and federal elections? What practices would you recommend, based on sociological knowledge, which would lead to higher rates of student participation in elections?

SOURCE: Federal Election Commission. 2000. **www.fec.gov**

FIGURE 14.2 A Representative Government?

SOURCE: U.S. Census Bureau. 2002. *Statistical Abstract of the United States, 2002.* Washington, DC:
U.S. Government Printing Office, p. 247.

(Zweigenhaft and Domhoff 1998). In the Senate of the 108th Congress (convened in 2003), there were fourteen women, no African Americans or Latinos, two Asian Americans, and one Native American (see Figure 14.2). The fourteen women senators are a record high number despite the fact women are 51 percent of the population. The first Native American to be sent to the Senate in more than sixty years was elected in 1992. Currently there are no Black senators, and there have only been two in the recent past, yet 13 percent of the population is Black. Hispanics also make up 13 percent of the population, but have no representation in the Senate, and account for only 5 percent of the House. There is a long way to go before we have a truly representative government, and there is also no guarantee that gains made in one election will be sustained in the next.

Researchers offer several explanations for why women and racial–ethnic minorities continue to be underrepresented in government. Certainly prejudice plays a role. It was not long ago, in the 1960 Kennedy-Nixon election, that Kennedy became the first Catholic president elected. In the 2000 presidential election, Joseph Lieberman was the first Jewish candidate to appear on a major national ticket. Gender and racial prejudice run just as deep in the public mind. Prejudice alone, however, cannot account for the lack of representation. Societal causes

are a major factor in the successful elections of women and people who are better represented in local political office. Women and minority candidates receive a great deal of political support from local groups, but at the national level, they do not fare as well. The power of incumbents, most of whom are White men, is a disadvantage to any new office seeker (Darcy et al. 1994).

The Military

The military arm of the state is among the most powerful and influential social institutions in almost all societies. In the United States, the military is the largest single employer. Approximately 3 million men and women serve in the U.S. military, 1.4 million on active duty, including those in Iraq and Afghanistan, and the rest in the reserves. This does not include the many hundreds of thousands who are employed in industries that support the military, nor does it include civilians who work for the Department of Defense and other military-affiliated agencies (U.S. Census Bureau 2002).

Highly esteemed in the value system of the United States is *militarism,* the pervasive influence of military goals and values throughout the culture. The militaristic bent in our culture is evident in many ways. The toys children play with often inculcate militaristic values.

Military garb falls in and out of fashion. The plots of each summer's biggest blockbuster movies almost always revolve around a burly character hugely gifted in the military arts, often a veteran of the armed forces, who generally stocks up on the latest weaponry. Fighter jets flash over the Super Bowl. Military brass sparkles in parades. Being the strongest nation, militarily, in the world is frequently in the national political rhetoric. Most people in the United States place a lot of confidence in the military.

THE MILITARY AS A SOCIAL INSTITUTION.

Institutions are stable systems of norms and values that fulfill certain functions in society. The military is a social institution whose function is to defend the nation against external (and sometimes internal) threats. A strong military is often considered an essential tool for maintaining peace, although the values that promote preparedness in the armed forces are perilously close to the warlike values that lead to military aggression against others.

The military is one of the most hierarchical social institutions, and its hierarchy is extremely formalized. People who join the military are explicitly labeled with rank, and if promoted, pass through a series of well-defined levels, each with clearly demarcated sets of rights and responsibilities. An explicit line exists between officers and enlisted personnel ("grunts"), and officers have many privileges that others do not. Higher ranks are also entitled to absolute obedience from the ranks below them, with elaborate rituals created to remind both dominants and subordinates of their status. As in other social insti-

tutions, military enlistees are carefully socialized to learn the norms of the culture they have joined. Military socialization places a high premium on conformity and eliminates individuality. All new recruits have their heads shaved, are issued identical uniforms, and are allowed to retain very few of their personal possessions. They must quickly learn new, strictly enforced codes of behavior.

In 1973, the all-male draft for the Army was ended and an all-volunteer force was initiated for enlistment in the U.S. armed services. The idea behind the all-volunteer force was that the Army would be made more professional, because the people who joined would actually be choosing to make the military their career.

RACE AND THE MILITARY.

The greatest change in the military as a social institution is the representation of racial minority groups and women within the armed forces. Picture a U.S. soldier. Whom do you see? At one time you would have almost certainly pictured a young, White male, possibly wearing army green camouflage and carrying a weapon. Today the image of the military is much more diverse. Drawing on the cultural images you have stored in your mind, you are just as likely to picture a young African American man in military blues with a stiffly starched shirt and a neat and trim appearance, or perhaps a woman wearing a flight helmet in the cockpit of a fighter plane.

African Americans have served in the military for almost as long as the U.S. armed forces have been in existence. Except for the Marines, which desegregated in 1942, the armed forces were officially segregated until 1948, when President Harry Truman signed an executive order banning discrimination in the armed services. Although much segregation continued after this order, the desegregation of the armed forces is often credited with promoting more positive interracial relationships and increased awareness among Black Americans of their right to equal opportunities. Until that time the widespread opinion among Whites was that to allow Black and White soldiers to serve side by side would destroy soldiers' morale (Blackwell 1991).

Currently 34 percent of military personnel are racial minorities—20 percent African American, 8 percent Hispanic, and 6 percent other racial minorities (U.S. Department of Defense 2002; Moskos and Butler 1996). For groups with limited opportunities in civilian society, joining the military seems to promise an educational and economic boost. Is this realized? Within the military today there is equal pay for equal rank. African Americans and Latinos, however, are overrepresented in lower-ranking support positions. Often they are excluded from the higher-status, technologically based positions—those most likely to bring advancement and higher earnings both in the military and beyond. Most minorities

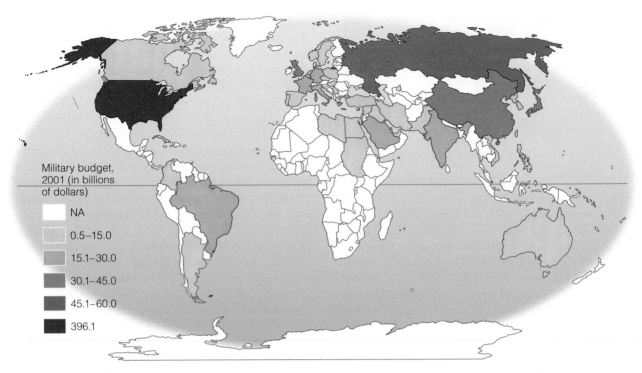

MAP 14.1 Viewing Society in Global Perspective: Military Expenditures per Capita

This map reveals that military expenditures per capita, compared across different countries, are very high in countries such as the United States, Russia, China, and Japan. **What kinds of things does this tell us about these countries, relative to those spending less on military expenditures?**

SOURCE: Data from U.S. Department of Defense and International Institute for Strategic Studies, Center for Defense Information, Washington, DC. Printed in U.S. Census Bureau *Statistical Abstract of the United States, 2002.* p. 860.

remain in positions with little supervisory responsibility. At the highest ranks in the military, there are few African Americans, Latinos, Asian Americans, or Native Americans (U.S. Department of Defense 2002; Moskos 1988; Moskos and Butler 1996).

For both Whites and racial minorities, serving in the military leads to higher earnings relative to someone's nonmilitary peers. The economic payoff is greatest for African Americans and Latinos relative to those of comparable background, education, experience, and ability. The earnings difference between military and civilian groups is substantial. Young Black and Latino men earn $3000 to $5000 more per year in the military than do their civilian peers. For Whites, the difference is less—about $1300 per year (Phillips et al. 1992).

WOMEN IN THE MILITARY. The military academies did not open their enrollment to women until 1976. Since then, the armed services have profoundly changed their admission policies, although the hostile reaction to women who have entered these academies shows how fierce the resistance to including women in

the military can be. Shannon Faulkner, a young woman who won the right to enter the Citadel, an elite military academy, had to embark on a two-and-a-half-year legal struggle to gain admission. Once admitted, she was harassed and ridiculed. When she succumbed to exhaustion during the first week of intense physical training and had to leave, many of the cadets whooped and shouted in glee, leaving many to argue that none of the men had been forced to endure such tribulations. Later, two other women left the Citadel after serious hazing in which, among other things, the women were sprinkled with nail polish remover and their clothes set on fire.

The Supreme Court ruled in 1996 (in *United States* v. *Virginia*) that women cannot be excluded from state-supported military academies such as the Citadel and the Virginia Military Institute (VMI). This was a landmark decision that opened new opportunities for women who want the rigorous physical and academic training that military academies provide (Kimmel 2000).

The marginalization of women in the military has been rationalized by the popular conviction that women should not serve in combat. The traditional belief that men are pro-

*African American soldiers fighting in the Civil War were known
as "Buffalo Soldiers" because their curly hair and brown skin
reminded Native Americans of the buffalo.*

© Corbis

GAYS AND LESBIANS IN THE MILITARY.

According to the "don't ask, don't tell" policy, recruiting officers cannot ask about sexual preference, and individuals in the military who keep their sexual preference a private matter shall not be discriminated against. Those who publicly reveal that they are gay or lesbian can be expelled from the military based on their sexual orientation. In essence, this policy is simply an extension of the already existing military attitude toward gays and lesbians. It does not explicitly permit the military to seek out and discharge service people on the grounds of homosexuality, nor can recruits be screened for the same reason; nevertheless, the policy does not clearly assert the civil rights of gays and lesbians. Gay soldiers and potential recruits have filed several lawsuits against the U.S. military. It remains unclear whether gays and lesbians will ultimately be permitted to live openly as homosexuals while also pursuing careers in the armed services.

Supporters of the ban on gays in the military often use arguments similar to the arguments used before 1948 to defend the racial segregation of fighting units. They claim that the morale of soldiers will drop if forced to serve alongside gay men and women, national security will be threatened, and known homosexuals serving in the military will upset the status quo and destroy the fighting spirit of military units.

The long-standing policy against gays in the military has kept homosexuality in the military hidden, but not nonexistent. Even the military has had to admit that there have always been some gays and lesbians in all branches of the U.S. armed forces. Since their presence clearly did not cause the armed forces to disintegrate, the military has been forced to adapt their argument against gays and lesbians (Enloe 1993). Nonetheless, despite some increased tolerance of gays and lesbians in the military, homophobia is a pervasive part of military culture (Myers 2000; Becker 2000).

tectors and women are dependents has led many to believe that women, especially mothers and wives, should stay on home soil where they can safely carry out their "womanly" duties. Despite these beliefs, women have fought in combat to defend this country. For example, 4100 women served in combat in the Persian Gulf War of 1991; 7.2 percent of the active combat forces in that war were women (Holm 1992; Becraft 1992a). The increased visibility of women soldiers during the Persian Gulf War also shifted public opinion to women serving in combat positions; 55 percent now favor women to serving in combat (Enloe 1993; Cooke and Woollacott 1993). In 1992, the Defense Authorization Act allowed women to fly military aircraft in combat.

The involvement of women in the military has reached an all-time high in recent years. Now, almost 200,000 women are on active duty, with an additional 151,000 in the reserves, not including the Coast Guard and its reserves. The Air Force has the highest proportion of women (18 percent), followed by the Army (15 percent), the Navy (13 percent), and the Marines (6 percent). Minority women are overrepresented in the military, relative to their presence in the general population.

Gender relations in the military extend beyond just women who serve. The experience of military wives, for example, is greatly affected by their husbands' employment as soldiers. Frequent relocation means that military wives are less competitive in the labor market. They have lower labor force participation than their women peers and earn less than their peers at the same educational level (Enloe 1993; Moskos 1992; Payne et al. 1992). Sociologists have found that the presence of a military base depresses wages and employment for all women in the surrounding community (Booth et al. 2000).

■ *Economy and Society*

Politics, then, is part of the political institution of society. We move next to an examination of work and the economy in society. To understand *work,* you first must see it in the context of the broad social institution known as the economy. All societies are organized around an economic base. The **economy** of a society is the system by which goods and services are produced, distributed, and consumed. We first look at the economic significance of

the historic transformation from agriculturally based societies to industrial and, now, postindustrial society.

The Industrial Revolution

In Chapter 4, we discussed the evolution of different
types of societies. One of the most significant of these
changes was, first, the development of agricultural societies and, later, the far-ranging impact of the Industrial
Revolution. Now, the Industrial Revolution is giving
way to the growth of postindustrial societies—a development in the economic system with far-reaching consequences for how society is organized.

The development of agricultural societies followed
after the development of technologies that enabled people to increase the production of food from simple hunting and gathering techniques to more large-scale
production. The invention of the plow, for example, enabled societies to form settlements organized around
farm production in fields instead of the more labor-
intensive methods of gathering small amounts of food.
This transformation meant that societies could settle in
one place and form markets for the sale and distribution
of goods, thereby radically changing how society was organized and how people worked. Agricultural production remains a vast part of the world economy, although
now changed by the processes of industrialization. Prior
to the invention of the silicon chip, industrialization was
probably the most significant historical development affecting the social organization of work.

The Industrial Revolution is usually pinpointed as
beginning in mid-eighteenth–century Europe, soon
thereafter spreading throughout other parts of the world.
The Industrial Revolution led to numerous social
changes since Western economies were organized around
the mass production of goods. The Industrial Revolution
led to the creation of factories, which, as we briefly saw
in Chapter 10, separated work and family by relocating
the place where most people were employed.

We still live in a society that is largely industrial, but
that is quickly giving way to a new kind of social organization: postindustrial society. Whereas industrial societies
are primarily organized around the production of goods,
postindustrial societies (recall from Chapter 4) are organized around the provision of services. Thus, in the United
States, we have moved from being a manufacturing-based
economy to an economy centered on the provision of
services. Service industry is a broad term, meant to encompass a wide range of economic activities now common in the labor market. It includes banking and finance,
retail sales, hotel and restaurant work, and health care; it
also includes parts of the information technology industry—not electronics assembly, but things such as soft-

*The Industrial Revolution transformed labor, moving it from the
household to the factory—or other sites where work was mechanized and oriented to mass production.*

ware design and the exchange of information (through
publishing, video production, and the like).

Comparing Economic Systems

The three major economic systems found in the world
today are *capitalism, socialism,* and *communism.* These are
not totally distinct, that is, many societies have a mix of
these economic systems. **Capitalism** is an economic system based on the principles of market competition, private property, and the pursuit of profit. Within capitalist
societies, stockholders own corporations—or a share of
the corporation's wealth. Under capitalism, owners keep
a surplus of what is generated by the economy; this is
their *profit,* which may be in the form of money, financial
assets, and other commodities.

Socialism is an economic institution characterized
by state ownership and management of the basic industries; that is, the means of production are the property of
the state not of individuals. Modern socialism emerged
from the writings of Karl Marx, who predicted that capitalism would give way to egalitarian, state-dominated
socialism, followed by a transition to stateless, classless
communism.

Many European nations, for example, have strong elements of socialism that mix with the global forces of
capitalism. Sweden supports an extensive array of state-
run social services, such as health care, education, and
social welfare programs, but Swedish industry is capitalist. Other world nations are more strongly socialist although they are not immune from the penetrating
influence of capitalism. The People's Republic of China

was formerly a strongly socialist society that is currently undergoing transformation to a mix of socialist and capitalist principles, including state encouragement of a market-based economy, the introduction of privately owned industries, and increased engagement in the international capitalist economy.

Communism is sometimes described as socialism in its purest form. In pure communism, industry is not the private property of owners. Instead, the state is the sole owner of the systems of production. Communist philosophy argues that capitalism is fundamentally unjust since powerful owners take more from laborers (and society) than they give, and use their power to maintain the inequalities between the worker and owner classes. Communist theorists in the nineteenth-century declared that capitalism would inevitably be overthrown as workers worldwide united against owners and the system that exploited them. Class divisions were supposed to be erased at that time, along with private property and all forms of inequality. History has not borne out these predictions.

■ *The Changing Global Economy*

As we start a new century, one of the most significant developments is the creation of a global economy, which affects work in the United States and worldwide. The concept of the **global economy** acknowledges that all dimensions of the economy now cross national borders, including investment, production, management, markets, labor, information, and technology (Carnoy et al. 1993). Economic events in one nation now can have major reverberations throughout the world. When the economies of Brazil, Japan, China, or Russia are unstable, the effects are felt worldwide.

The global economy links the lives of millions of Americans to the experiences of other people throughout the world. You can see the internationalization of the economy in everyday life: Status symbols like high-priced sneakers are manufactured for just a few cents in China. The Barbie dolls that young girls accumulate are inexpensive by U.S. standards, yet it would require one month's wages for the Indonesian worker who makes the doll to buy it for her child.

In the global economy, the most developed countries control research and management, and assembly-line work is performed in nations with less privileged positions in the global economy (Ward 1990). A single product, such as an automobile, may be assembled from parts made all over the world—the engine assembled in Mex-

ico, tires manufactured in Malaysia, electronic parts constructed in China. The relocation of manufacturing to wherever labor is cheap has led to the emergence of the *global assembly line,* a new international division of labor in which research and development is conducted in the United States, Japan, Germany, and other major world powers, and the assembly of goods is done primarily in underdeveloped and poor nations—mostly by women and children.

Within the United States, the development of a global economy has also created anxieties about foreign workers, particularly among the working class. Because it is easier to blame foreign workers for unemployment in the United States than it is to understand the complex processes that have produced this phenomenon, U.S. workers have been prone to **xenophobia,** the fear and hatred of foreigners. Campaigns to "buy American" reflect this trend, although the concept of buying American is increasingly antiquated in a global economy.

When buying a product from a U.S. company, the likelihood is that the parts, if not the product itself, were built overseas. In a global economy, distinctions between U.S. and foreign businesses blur. Moreover, the label "Made in U.S.A." does not necessarily mean that the product was made by well-paid workers in the United States. In the garment industry, sweatshop workers, many of whom are recent immigrants and primarily women, are likely to have stitched the clothing that bears such a label. Moreover, these workers are likely to be working under exploitative conditions. For example, recent surveys of the garment industry in Los Angeles, where 25 percent of all women's outerwear is made, find that 96 percent of the garment firms are in violation of health and safety regulations for workers, and 61 percent are violating wage regulations (Bonacich and Applebaum 2000; Louie 2001).

The development of a global economy is part of the broad process of **economic restructuring,** which refers to the contemporary transformations in the basic structure of work that are permanently altering the workplace. This process includes the changing composition of the workplace, deindustrialization, and use of enhanced technology. Some changes are *demographic*—that is, resulting from changes in the population. The labor force is becoming more diverse, with women and people of color becoming the majority of those employed. Other changes are driven by *technological developments.* For example, the economy is based less on its earlier manufacturing base and more on service industries—those in which the primary business is not the production of goods, but the delivery of services (banking, health care, provision of food, or the like). All these developments are happening within a global context.

Identify a job you once held (or currently hold) and make a list of all the ways that workers in this segment of the labor market are being affected by the various dimensions of *economic restructuring: Demographic changes, globalization of the economy,* and *technological change.* What does your list tell you about how people's individual work experiences are shaped by social structure?

A More Diverse Workplace

A more diverse workplace is becoming a common result of economic restructuring. In a few years, women and racial minorities are expected to increase to more than one-half of the labor force. Another upcoming change in the labor market will be an increase in the number of older people (those over age fifty-five) as the population bulge of the Baby Boomer generation passes through late middle age (Dohm 2000; Bowman 1999; Fullerton 1999).

These changes in the social organization of work and the economy are creating a more diverse labor force, but much of the growth in the economy is projected to be in service industries where, for the better jobs, education and training are required. People without these skills will not be well positioned for success. Manufacturing industries, where racial minorities have in the past maintained a foothold on employment, are now in decline. New technologies and corporate layoffs have reduced the number of entry-level corporate jobs, which recent college graduates have always used as a starting point for career mobility. Many college graduates are employed in jobs that do not require a college degree. College gradu-

All in the Family: Children of Immigrants and Family Businesses

A common pattern among Asian American immigrants is to establish a small family business, utilizing the labor of family members to establish and run the business. Owning a family business is part of the American dream, thus idealized as promoting entrepreneurial and family values, including the value of hard work, devotion to family, and self-sacrifice. But what kind of life does this produce for the children of immigrant families? This is what sociologist Lisa Park wanted to know in her research on the children of Asian American entrepreneurs.

Park, a child of such entrepreneurs herself, conducted her study by interviewing Korean American and Chinese American high school and college students who grew up in small family businesses. She utilized several qualitative research methods, including in-depth individual interviews, focus group interviews, and participant observation in family stores.

Although many teens hold jobs—often to help support their families, sometimes for their own spending money—Park found that the life of

Asian American teenagers who are sons and daughters of entrepreneurs was difficult. Her research subjects reported wanting to have the freedom to be bored that they associated with White, middle-class teens. They were critical of the popular images of teens in families as only worrying about their hair, their clothes, and their friends.

In contrast to the stereotype of Asian American families as close-knit and conflict-free, Park found that teens in these families report feeling overworked and with little family "quality time." Some of these young people have worked since they were six years old. Often parents set up a small "home away from home" in the family restaurant or business—a small table in the corner where children can read, color, or watch television. But her subjects also reported being burdened and not able to have a normal childhood. They often had to do all the household chores while parents worked, as well as serving customers or helping in other ways.

Park's research shows immigration shapes family structures and effects children's lives. She challenges simplistic

views of the family business as an ideal way of life and helps us understand some of the social forces that are part of the immigrant experience and that shape the life of some Asian American youth.

Questions to Consider

1. Are there businesses in your community run by immigrant families? If so, what evidence of children's involvement in the business do you see and how do you think this influences the children? **Keywords:** immigrant children

2. In addition to immigrant businesses, how are children involved in the work that their parents do? In what ways does this influence the children's identities, values about work, future opportunities? **Keywords:** immigrant labor, immigrant worker

We have included InfoTrac College Edition keywords at the end of each question to make it easier for you to find more to read on these topics. Go to **www.infotrac-college.com,** an online library, to begin your search.

SOURCE: Park, Lisa Sun-Hee. 2002. "A Life of One's Own." *Contexts* 1 (Summer): 56–57.

ates, however, do still have higher earnings than those with less education.

Deindustrialization

Deindustrialization refers to the transition from a predominantly goods-producing economy to one based on the provision of services (Harrison and Bluestone 1982). This does not mean that goods are no longer produced, but that fewer workers in the United States are required to produce goods because machines can do the work people once did and many goods-producing jobs have moved overseas. Different from traditional manufacturing jobs, such as the production of cloth or automobiles, service-based industries provide the delivery of a product or provision of a service.

Deindustrialization is most easily observed by looking at the decline in the number of jobs in the manufacturing sector of the U.S. economy since the Second World War. At the end of the war in 1945, the majority of workers (51 percent) in the United States were employed in manufacturing-based jobs. Now the majority (at least 70 percent) are employed in the *service sector* (U.S. Department of Labor 2002; Wilson 1978). The service sector includes two segments: service delivery (such as food preparation, cleaning, or child care) and information processing (such as banking and finance, computer operation, or clerical work). Service delivery consists of many low-wage, semiskilled, and unskilled jobs and employs many women and people of color.

The human cost of deindustrialization can be severe. When a manufacturing plant shuts down, many people may lose their jobs at the same time, and whole communities can be affected. Among the areas hardest hit by deindustrialization are communities that were heavily dependent on a single industry, such as steel towns or automobile-manufacturing cities like Detroit, Flint, Lansing, Cleveland, and Akron. Some of these communities have rebounded by investing in new, high-tech industries, but this has still left many groups disadvantaged. Groups concentrated in the inner cities at these locations have suffered the most, because they have been the most dependent on manufacturing jobs for economic survival. They are not located in emerging suburban areas to take advantage of new industries. In the early twentieth century, many African Americans migrated from the South to the North in pursuit of manufacturing jobs; Latino groups have more recently flowed into cities for the same reason. Both groups have been hard hit by the declines in urban manufacturing jobs that have characterized the late twentieth century. As a result, there are now extremely high rates of joblessness and dim prospects for economic recovery in these urban communities (Wilson 1996). African American and Latino youth have very high rates of unemployment; in some inner cities, teen unemployment rates exceed 40 percent (U.S. Department of Labor 2002; Wilson 1996).

Technological Change

Coupled with deindustrialization, rapidly changing and developing technologies are bringing major changes in work, including how it is organized, who does it, and how much it pays. One of the most influential technological developments of the twentieth century has been

---

FORCES OF SOCIAL CHANGE

Native American Women and Work

Whether they live on or off the reservations, American Indian men and women live in difficult times, struggling daily against White control, the threat of cultural extinction, and the challenges posed by poverty. . . . Still, American Indians are growing in strength, cultural pride, unity, and militancy.

Native American women's labor force participation [has risen] sharply . . . to 55 percent (in 1990). Those who hold full-time, year-round jobs earn 83 percent as much as White women—but jobs are hard to come by. More than 70 percent of American Indian women hold part-time or part-year jobs—the highest rate for any racial–ethnic group of women—and American Indian women face the highest unemployment rate (13 percent) of the racial–ethnic groups. . . .

Native American women have made substantial progress into the more highly paid, masculine jobs in the lower tier of the primary sector. . . . In the upper tier of the primary labor market, Indian women [have] made real inroads into sales jobs in commodities and finance, and into executive, managerial, and administrative jobs. . . . Many American Indian women have attained primary-sector jobs in the public sector, which [employs] three-fifths of American Indian women. . . .

Despite some gains in the primary sector, over two-thirds of American Indian women were employed in the secondary labor market in 1990, compared to three-fifths of European American women and just under one-third of European American men. . . . Repressive, inaccessible, and inadequate education bears much of the blame for this low occupational status, along with discrimination by employers and fellow employees and the stagnation of the reservation economy.

SOURCE: Amott, Teresa, and Julie Matthaei. 1996. *Race, Gender and Work: A Multicultural Economic History of Women in the United States.* Cambridge, MA: South End Press, pp. 59–61. Used with permission.

© AFP/Corbis

*Automation means that machines can now supply the labor origi-
nally provided by human workers, such as these soccer-playing
robots.*

the invention of the semiconductor. Some have argued
that the computer chip has as much significance for social change as the earlier inventions of the wheel and the
steam engine. Computer technology has made possible
workplace transactions that would have seemed like science fiction just a few years ago. Electronic information
can be transferred around the world in less than a second. Employees can provide work for corporations located on another continent; thus, a woman in Southeast
Asia or the Caribbean can type a book manuscript for a
publishing house in New York. Corporations in the
United States are lured overseas by the extremely low
wages of these workers.

Increasing reliance on the rapid transmission of electronic data has produced *electronic sweatshops,* a term referring to the back offices found in many industries, such
as airlines, insurance firms, mail-order houses, and telephone companies, where workers at computer terminals
process hundreds or thousands of transactions in a day.
Increasingly, workers' performance is monitored by their
computer, thus conjuring images of "Big Brother" invisibly watching. For example, telephone operators are typically given twenty-five seconds to root out a number;
the speed of the transaction is recorded by computer.
Computers can also measure how fast cashiers ring up
groceries and how fast ticket agents book reservations.
Records derived from computer monitoring then become
the basis for job performance evaluation (Kilborn 1990).

Technological innovation in the workplace is a mixed
blessing. **Automation**—the process by which human
labor is replaced by machines—eliminates many repetitive and tiresome tasks, and it makes rapid communica-

tion and access to information possible. But
critics worry that our increasing dependence
on technology also makes workers subservient
to machines. For example, robots now perform
98 percent of the spot-welding on Ford automobiles. Some sophisticated robots are capable
of highly complex tasks, enabling them to
assemble finished products or flip burgers in
fast-food restaurants, replacing the human employees. Robots are expensive to buy, but employers can calculate their advantage given that
"the robot hamburger-flipper would need no
lunch or bathroom breaks, would not take sick
days, and most certainly would neither strike
nor quit" (Rosengarten 2000: 4).

Deskilling is a side effect of automation and
technological progress in which the level of
skill required to perform certain jobs declines
over time. This may result when a job is automated, or
when a more complex job is divided into a sequence of
easily performed units. As work roles become deskilled,
employees are paid less and have less control over their
tasks. Less mental labor is required of workers, and jobs
become routine and boring. Observers of the workplace
note that deskilling contributes to polarization of the
labor force. The best jobs require increasing levels of skill
and technological knowledge; whereas at the bottom of
the occupational hierarchy, people stuck in dead-end positions become alienated from their work (Braverman
1974; Apple 1991).

Along with deskilling has come an increasing reliance on temporary or **contingent workers** who do not
hold regular jobs, but their employment is dependent on
labor demand—contract workers, temporary workers,
on-call workers (those called only when needed), the self-
employed, and day laborers. Women are more likely than
men to be employed in these jobs, and women are concentrated in the least desirable jobs—those with the lowest pay and least likelihood of providing benefits.
Considering race, Whites are more likely to be independent contractors or self-employed, whereas Blacks
and Hispanics are more likely to be found in temporary
and part-time work (Kalleberg et al. 2000; Cook 2000;
Hudson 1999).

▪ *Theoretical Perspectives on Work*

Sociologists have devised a number of theoretical perspectives on the nature of work. These perspectives are
explored in this section.

Defining Work

Most people think of work as an activity for which a person gets paid. This definition is not adequate for a sociological definition of work because it devalues work that people do without pay. Unpaid jobs such as housework, child care, and volunteer activities make up much of the work done in the world. Sociologists define **work** as productive human activity that creates something of value, either goods or services. Work takes many forms. It may be paid or unpaid. It may be performed inside or outside the home. It may involve physical or mental labor, or both.

Under the sociological definition of work, housework, though unpaid, is defined as work, even though it is not included in the official measures of productivity that economists use to indicate the work output of the United States. Influenced by feminist studies, sociologists now recognize that housework and other forms of unpaid labor are an important part of the productivity of a society.

Some sociologists argue that work has been too narrowly defined as referring to only physical and mental labor. Arlie Hochschild (1983) has introduced the concept of emotional labor to address some forms of work that are common in a service-based economy. **Emotional labor** is work specifically intended to produce a desired state of mind in a client, and often involves putting on a false front before clients. Many jobs require some handling of other people's feelings and emotional labor is performed where inducing or suppressing a feeling in the client is one of the primary work tasks. Airline flight attendants perform emotional labor—their job is to please the passenger and, as Hochschild suggests, to make passengers feel as though they are guests in someone's living room.

Some forms of work are more highly valued than others, both in how the work is perceived by society and how it is rewarded. Mental labor is more highly valued than manual labor, and manual labor is more highly valued than emotional labor. In addition, work performed outside the home is typically judged to be more valuable than work performed inside the home. Given stratification of class, race, gender, and age in this society, generally speaking, the work most highly valued is done by White, middle-class, older men. Sociologists debate if this occurs because the most highly valued jobs are reserved for this group, or because this group does these jobs, if the jobs are therefore more highly valued. It is a question of which comes first, but the point is that the prestige attributed to different jobs follows along lines of race, class, gender, and age.

Judgments made about the value of different forms of work have also been turned into judgments about the value of different groups of workers. Men who perform

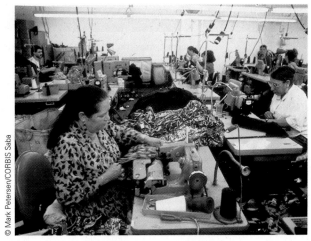

Immigrant women and women of color are the typical employees in sweatshops in the United States, such as this sweatshop in New York City's Chinatown.

manual labor have been devalued as workers, including White men. Women's work (housework and child care), much of which is emotional labor, has also been devalued and been unpaid; when it has been paid, the wages have been extremely low. Work done by many Latinos, Native Americans, African Americans, and Asian Americans has also been some of the most demanding, yet least rewarded, work in society. The labor of the White working class has also been undervalued. In the past, White ethnic groups such as the Irish, Polish, and Italians performed some of the most onerous work; their contributions as workers have also been devalued, because prestige is typically reserved for only the most dominant group in the society.

Some people hold stereotypes about the "undeserving poor"—the belief that the poor have become so because of their own failures and refusal to internalize the values of diligence and hard work. Yet close to half of the poor are working (43 percent), and one-half of these workers are employed full time (Dalaker and Proctor 2000).

The Division of Labor

Recall from Chapter 4 that the **division of labor** is the systematic *interrelatedness* of different tasks that develop in complex societies. When different groups engage in different economic activities, a division of labor is said to exist. In a relatively simple division of labor, one group may be responsible for planting and harvesting crops, whereas another group is responsible for hunting game. As the economic system becomes more complex, the division of labor becomes more elaborate.

In the United States, the division of labor is affected by gender, race, class, and age—the major axes of stratification. The *class division of labor* can be observed by

TABLE 14.3 Theoretical Perspectives on Work

	Functionalism	Conflict Theory	Symbolic Interaction
Defines work	As functional for society because work teaches people the values of society and integrates people within the social order; more "talented" people rank higher	As generating class conflict because of the unequal rewards associated with different jobs	As organizing social bonds between people who interact within work settings
Views work organizations	As functionally integrated with other social institutions	As producing alienation, especially among those who perform repetitive tasks	As interactive systems within which people form relationships and create beliefs that define their relationships to others
Interprets changing work systems	As an adaptation to social change	As based in tensions arising from power differences between different class, race, and gender groups	As the result of the changing meanings of work resulting from changed social conditions
Explains wage inequality	As motivating people to work harder	As reflecting the devaluation of different classes of workers	As producing different perceptions of the value of different occupations

looking at the work done by people with different educational backgrounds, because education is a fairly reliable indicator of class. People with more education tend to work in higher-paid, higher-prestige occupations. Class also leads to perceived distinctions in the value of manual labor versus mental labor. Those presumed to be doing mental labor (management and professional positions) tend to be paid more and have more job prestige than those presumed to be doing manual labor. Class thus produces stereotypes about the working class; manual labor is presumed to be the inverse of mental labor, meaning it is presumed to require no thinking. By extension, workers who do manual labor may be assumed not to be very smart, regardless of their intelligence.

The *gender division of labor* refers to the different work that women and men do in society. In societies with a strong gender division of labor, the belief that some activities are women's work (for example, secretarial work) and other activities men's work (for example, construction) contributes greatly to the propagation of inequality between women and men, especially because cultural expectations usually place more value (both social and economic) on men's work. This helps explain why librarians and social workers are typically paid less than electricians despite the likelihood the women have higher education.

THINKING SOCIOLOGICALLY

Think about the labor market in the region where you live. What racial and ethnic groups have historically worked in various segments of this labor market and how would you now describe the *racial and ethnic division of labor*?

Similarly, the *racial division of labor* is seen in the pattern of workers from different racial groups working, in general, in different jobs. The labor performed by racial minority groups has often been the lowest paid, least prestigious, and most arduous work. The racial division of labor found today is rooted in the past.

Functionalism, Conflict Theory, and Symbolic Interaction

The major theoretical perspectives identified in this book also provide the frameworks for understanding the social structural forces that are transforming work. Each viewpoint—conflict theory, functionalist theory, and symbolic interaction—offers a unique analysis of work and the economic institution of which it is a part (see Table 14.3).

Conflict theorists view the transformations taking place in the workplace as the result of inherent tensions in the social systems, tensions that arise from the power differences between groups vying for social and economic resources. Class conflict is then a major element of the social structure of work, and conflict theorists would look to the class division of labor as the source of unequal rewards that workers receive for work and the unequal way the value of their work is perceived. Conflict theorists analyze the fact that some forms of work are more highly valued than others, both in how the work is perceived by society and how it is rewarded. As noted long ago by social-economic theorist Thorstein Veblen (1931), mental labor has always been more highly valued than manual labor.

Functionalist theorists, in contrast, interpret the work and the economy as a functional necessity for society. Certain tasks must be done to sustain society, and how work is organized reflects the values and other characteristics of a given social order. Functionalists argue that society "sorts" people into occupations with the more able sorted into the more prestigious occupations that pay more because, so the functionalist argues, they are more valuable—more "functional"—for society. When society changes too rapidly, as you could argue is the case with new technological and global developments in the world, then work institutions generate social disorganization—perhaps creating **alienation,** a feeling of powerlessness and separation from society.

Symbolic interaction brings a different perspective to the sociology of work. Less interested in the workings of the whole society, symbolic interaction theorists might study what work means to those who do it and how social interactions in the workplace form social bonds between people. Some classic symbolic interactionist studies have examined how new workers learn their new roles and how workers' identities are shaped by the social interactions in the workplace. Some symbolic interactionist studies also look at creative ways that people deal with routinized jobs, who sometimes develop elaborate and exaggerated displays of routine tasks to bring a human dimension to otherwise dehumanizing work (Leidner 1993).

■ *Characteristics of the Labor Force*

Data on characteristics of the U.S. labor force typically are drawn from official statistics reported by the U.S. Department of Labor. In 2000, the labor force included approximately 141 million people (U.S. Department of Labor 2002). This is 67 percent of the working-age population (those sixteen years old and older)—an increase from 59 percent at the end of the Second World War to 67 percent now. The specific characteristics of those in the labor force have also changed considerably.

Who Works?

Employment varies significantly for different groups in the population. Looking at all groups, Hispanic men are the most likely group to be employed, Hispanic women, the least (see Figure 14.3).

Several trends in who works can be discerned. One of the most dramatic changes in the labor force since the Second World War has been the increase in the number of women employed. Since 1948, the employment of women

has increased from 35 to 60 percent of all women. The calculation is weighted toward White women, because women of color historically have always had a high rate of employment. In fact, the percentage of employed Black and White women has converged in recent years—both are now equally likely to be employed (U.S. Department of Labor 2002). However, Black women are generally employed in lower-paying and less prestigious jobs.

The increase in employment of women with children has also created new demands in the workplace. Some organizations have responded by creating on-site childcare facilities or facilities to care for children who are sick, to allow their parents to come to work. The Family and Medical Leave Act of 1993 has also forced companies to write more progressive policies for medical, maternity, and paternity leave for their employees.

Changes in the employment status of diverse groups reflect the economic restructuring of the workplace, and as conflict theorists would point out, produce strife between groups competing for the jobs that are left. Jobs where White men have predominated are declining, especially in the manufacturing sector, whereas jobs in race- and gender-segregated niches of the labor market are those most likely to increase. The popular belief that women and minorities are taking jobs from White men derives from this fact. Note, however, that women are not taking the jobs where White men have predominated in the past; these jobs simply are not as numerous as before, and growth in the labor market is in areas that have traditionally been considered women's work or other menial jobs where minorities have been likely to be employed. The conflicts that one sees over labor market issues—beliefs that foreign workers are taking U.S. jobs, competition between groups for scarce positions, and debates about the role of immigrant labor in the U.S. economy—are the result of social structural transformations, that is, sociological factors that lie behind statistical patterns.

Unemployment and Joblessness

The U.S. Department of Labor regularly reports data on the **unemployment rate,** the percentage of those not working but officially defined as looking for work. Currently more than six million people are officially unemployed. The official number does not include all people who are jobless. It includes only those who meet the official definition of a job seeker—someone who has actively sought to obtain a job during the previous four weeks and who is registered with the unemployment office. Several categories of job seekers are excluded from the list, including those who earned money at any job during the week prior to the data being collected, even one

Percent of population
age 16+ employed

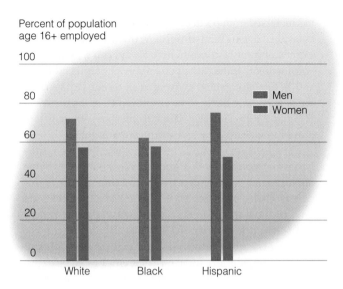

FIGURE 14.3 Employment Patterns by Race and Gender

DATA: From the U.S. Department of Labor. 2002. *Employment and Earnings.* Washington, DC: U.S. Department of Labor, p. 167–169.

day of work with no prospect of more employment. People are excluded who have given up looking for full-time work, because they are discouraged, have settled for part-time work, are ill or disabled, or cannot afford the child care needed to allow them to go to work, among other reasons. Because the number of job-seeking people excluded from the official definition of unemployment can be quite large, the official reported rates of unemployment seriously underestimate the extent of actual joblessness in the United States.

People most likely to be undercounted in unemployment statistics are those for whom unemployment runs the highest—the youngest and oldest workers, women, and members of racial minority groups. These groups are least likely to meet the official criteria of unemployment, because they are most likely to have left jobs that do not qualify them for unemployment insurance. Migrant workers and other transient or mobile populations are also undercounted in the official statistics. People who work only a few hours a week are excluded even though their economic position may differ little from that of someone with no work at all. Workers on strike are also counted as employed, even if they receive no income while they are on strike.

Official unemployment rates also take no notice of **underemployment**—the condition of being employed at a skill level below what would be expected given a person's training, experience, or education. This condition can also include working fewer hours than desired. A laid-off auto-worker flipping hamburgers at a fast-food restaurant is underemployed; so is a person with a law degree who drives a taxi.

The group experiencing the greatest unemployment in the United States at this time is Native Americans. Almost one-half of all Native Americans are unemployed. The greatest barrier to employment is the simple absence of jobs, especially for those Native Americans who live on reservations (about one-quarter of the population). Few jobs are on or near reservations; the few that do exist are often held by Whites. Reservation land is typically cut up so the fertile areas are owned by Whites. Tribal crafts and small-scale farming are usually all that is left to Native Americans. For most jobs, one must leave the community to find work. Lack of appropriate training in schools and job-training programs means that many American Indians are not prepared for the few available jobs (Snipp 1996). Finally, on measures of health, Native Americans fare worse than any other group, making work impossible or difficult for many (National Center for Health Statistics 2002).

Unemployment among African Americans, Puerto Ricans, and Mexican Americans is currently at a level considered to be a major economic depression (between 8 and 10 percent). Contributing to the problem are some of the trends already discussed in this chapter—globalization, economic restructuring, and the move to a service economy—that fall especially hard on minority workers. In addition to more likely being unemployed, African Americans are more likely than Whites to experience the negative effects of job displacement, and the re-employment of African American men after losing a job is significantly lower than the re-employment of White men (U.S. Department of Labor 2002).

Popular explanations often attribute unemployment to the individual failings of workers. Many often claim that unemployed people simply do not try hard enough to find jobs or prefer a welfare check to hard work and a paycheck. This viewpoint reflects the common myth that anyone who works hard enough can succeed. This individualistic perspective traces the cause of unemployment to personal motivation. Rather than blame the victim for joblessness, sociologists examine how changes in the social organization of work contribute to unemployment by looking at structural problems in the economy—rapidly changing technology (which reduces the need for human labor), discriminatory employment practices, deindustrialization, corporate downsizing, and the export of jobs overseas, where cheap labor is abundant.

Some also argue that unemployment for White men is the result of hiring more women and minorities—as if men's unemployment were the result of affirmative action programs. Although on the surface this may seem reasonable because there are a finite number of jobs, the truth is that the employment of women and minorities does not cause White male unemployment, if for no other reason than race and gender segregation. Women are typically not employed in the same jobs as men; race segregation also means that racial minorities are concentrated in certain segments of the labor force.

Popular wisdom holds that the bulk of new immigrants are illegal, poor, and desperate, but the data show otherwise. The contemporary labor force is also being shaped by the employment of recent immigrants (Rumbaut 1996a, 1996b; Pedraza and Rumbaut 1996; Lamphere et al. 1994). In fact, the proportion of professionals and technicians among legal immigrants exceeds the proportion of professionals in the labor force as a whole. Note, however, that this figure is based on formal immigration data that exclude illegal immigrants, most of whom are working class. Still, those who migrate are usually not the most downtrodden in their home country; seldom are the poorest able to migrate. Even illegal immigrants tend to have higher levels of education and occupational skills than the typical workers in their homeland. Among immigrants can be found both the most educated and the least educated segments of the population.

DEBUNKING
Society's Myths

Myth: Because of programs such as affirmative action, women and minorities are taking jobs away from White men.

Sociological perspective: Although women and minorities have made many gains as a result of programs such as affirmative action, women and minority workers still are clustered in occupations that are segregated by race and gender. There is little actual evidence that the progress of these groups has been at the expense of White men.

Diversity in the U.S. Occupational System

From a sociological perspective, jobs are organized into an *occupational system.* This system is the array of jobs that together constitute the labor market. Within the occupational system, people are distributed in patterns that reflect the race, class, and gender organization of society. Jobs vary in their economic rewards, their perceived value and prestige, and the opportunities they hold for advancement, a fact that sociologists explain through a variety of perspectives. Fundamental to sociological analyses of the occupational system is the idea that individual and group experiences at work are the result of social structures, not just individual attributes. There is, for example, a rough

correlation between the desirability of given jobs in the occupational system, and the social status of the group most likely to fill those jobs. This tells us that there is a relationship between work and social inequality. When sociologists study the occupational system, they acknowledge the importance of individual attributes such as motivation, training, and previous work experience in predicting the place of a worker in the occupational system, but they see a greater importance in the societal patterns that structure the experience of workers.

THE DUAL LABOR MARKET. A branch of conflict theory is the **dual labor market theory,** which views the labor market as comprising two major segments: the *primary labor market* and the *secondary labor market,* as we saw in Chapter 10 (see Table 14.4). The primary labor market offers jobs with relatively high wages, benefits, stability, good working conditions, opportunities for promotion, job protection, and due process for workers (meaning workers are treated according to established rules and procedures that are allegedly fairly administered). Blue-collar and service workers in the primary labor market are often unionized, which leads to better wages and job benefits. High-level corporate jobs and unionized occupations fall into this segment of the labor market. The secondary labor market is characterized by low wages, few benefits, high turnover, poor working conditions, little opportunity for advancement, no job protection, and arbitrary treatment of workers. Many service jobs such as waiting tables, nonunionized assembly work, and domestic work are in the secondary labor market. Women and minority workers are the most likely groups to be employed in the secondary labor market. Dual labor market theory traces some of the causes of race and gender inequality to this divided structure within the labor market (U.S. Department of Labor 2002; Reskin and Padavic 1994; King 1992; Bonacich 1972).

OCCUPATIONAL DISTRIBUTION. Occupational distribution describes the pattern by which workers are located in the labor force (see Figure 14.4). Workers are dispersed throughout the occupational system in patterns that vary greatly by race, class, and gender, revealing a certain **occupational segregation** on the basis of such characteristics. Women are most likely to work in technical, sales, and administrative support, primarily because of their heavy concentration in clerical work. This is now true for both White women and women of color. White men are most likely found in managerial and professional jobs, whereas African American and Hispanic men are most likely employed as operators and laborers—among the least well paid and least prestigious in the occupational system (U.S. Department of Labor 2002).

TABLE 14.4 The Segmented Labor Market: Examples of Occupations

Primary Labor Market	Secondary Labor Market	Underground Economy
Upper tier	**Upper tier**	
High status professional specialties (physicians, lawyers, professors, engineers, and so on)	Waitresses, bartenders	Prostitution
	Hairdressers, cosmetologists	Con artists
Business executives	Sales workers, cashiers	Unreported domestic labor
Supervisors	Clerical workers, clerks	Undocumented workers
Farm managers	Machine operators	Sweatshop labor
		Con artists, thieves
		Drug dealers
Lower tier	**Lower tier**	
Lower status professional specialties (teachers, librarians, social workers, actors)	Service work (cooks, maids, janitors, child care)	
Middle managers	Private household workers	
Protective service (police and fire)	Farm labor	
Truck driving	Food counter workers	
Mechanics		
Precision craft, repair, production (electricians, plumbers, welders, construction, and so on)		
Technicians		
Health assessment and training		

ADAPTED FROM: Ammot, Teresa, and Julie Matthaei. 1996. *Race, Gender and Work: A Multicultural History of Women in the United States.* Boston: South End Press, p. 344; U.S. Department of Labor. 2002. *Employment and Earnings.* Washington, DC: U.S. Department of Labor.

When looking at occupational distribution over time, changes are noticeable. One decline has been the number of Black women employed in private domestic work. In 1960, 38 percent of all Black women in the labor force were employed as private domestic workers; by the 1990s, this had declined to less than 2 percent. Over time, there has also been some increase in the number of women employed in working-class jobs traditionally held only by men. Today, women are 9 percent of precision production, craft, and repair workers, compared with 1 percent in 1970 (U.S. Department of Labor 2002). This is a significant increase in the number of women in these jobs, although women are still a small proportion of all such workers. The women most likely to be in such jobs are African American women, low-income mothers, women who previously held lower-rank jobs and disliked their previous job, and women who can work hours other than during the day. From this information, we can conclude that women are attracted to these jobs not just because they prefer them, but because they offer better opportunities (Landry 2000; Padavic 1992).

OCCUPATIONAL PRESTIGE AND EARNINGS.

Occupational prestige is the perceived social value of an occupation in the eyes of the general public (see Chapter 7).

Sociologists have found a strong correlation between occupational prestige and the race and gender of people employed in given jobs. The influence of race on occupational prestige is stronger than that of gender. Thus, African American and Latino men are disproportionately found in jobs that have the lowest occupational prestige scores; White and Asian American men hold the jobs with the highest occupational prestige, followed by White women, Asian American women, African American women, and Latinas. The higher the socioeconomic status of the occupational group, the smaller the proportion of employed African American men (Xu and Leffler 1992; Stearns and Coleman 1990).

Gender also has an effect on occupational prestige. Three patterns are apparent. First, women receive less prestige for the same work as men. Second, the gender composition of the job and its occupational prestige are linked: Jobs that employ mostly women are lower in prestige than those that employ more men. Indeed, jobs often lose their prestige as many women enter a given profession. Likewise, the prestige of jobs increases as more men enter the field. Finally, men and women assign occupational prestige differently; women give occupations where most of the incumbents are women a higher prestige ranking than men do (Bose and Rossi 1983; Tyree and Hicks 1988).

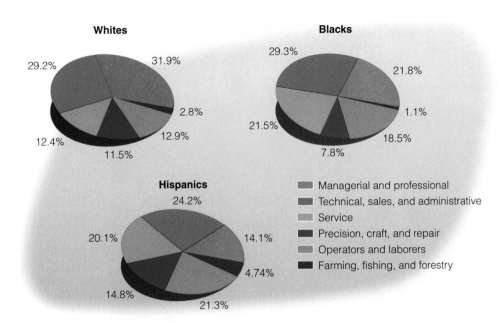

Whites

29.2%   31.9%
2.8%
12.4%   12.9%
11.5%

Blacks

29.3%   21.8%
1.1%
21.5%   18.5%
7.8%

Hispanics

24.2%
20.1%   14.1%
4.74%
14.8%
21.3%

■ Managerial and professional
■ Technical, sales, and administrative
■ Service
■ Precision, craft, and repair
■ Operators and laborers
■ Farming, fishing, and forestry

FIGURE 14.4
Occupational
Distribution of the
Labor Force

DATA: From the U.S. Department of Labor. 2002. *Employment and Earnings.* Washington, DC: U.S. Government Printing Office, p. 175, 182.

An important question for sociologists, as well as for policymakers and individuals, for that matter, is why different groups earn different incomes. Sociologists have extensively documented that earnings from work are highly dependent on race, gender, and class, as shown in Figure 14.5. White men earn the most, with a gap between men's and women's earnings among all groups. African American women and Hispanic men and women earn the least. Occupations in which White men are the numeric majority tend to pay more than occupations in which women and minorities are a majority of the workers. Not all men benefit equally, however, from the earnings hierarchy. CEOs have the highest pay of all—a whopping 150 times (and more) than what workers earn.

Why are there such disparities? Again, we have to turn to theory to put the facts into perspective. According to functionalist theories, workers are paid according to their value—derived from the characteristics they bring to the job: education, experience, training, and motivation to work. As we saw in Chapter 7 when we reviewed functionalist perspectives on inequality, the functionalist theorists see inequality as what motivates people to work. From this point of view, the high wages and other rewards associated with some jobs are the incentive for people to spend long years in training and garnering experience; otherwise, the jobs would go unfilled. To functionalists, then, differential wages are a source of motivation and a means to ensure that the most talented workers fill jobs essential to society and that different wages reflect the differently valued characteristics (education, years experience, training, and so forth) that workers bring to a job.

Conflict theorists radically disagree with the functionalist point of view, arguing that many talented people are thwarted by the systems of inequality they encounter in society. Thus, far from ensuring that the most talented will fill the most important jobs, conflict theorists note that some of the most essential jobs are, in fact, the most devalued and underrewarded—a point also shared by feminist scholars who study women's work, both paid and unpaid. From a conflict perspective, wage inequality is one way that systems of race, class, and gender inequality are maintained.

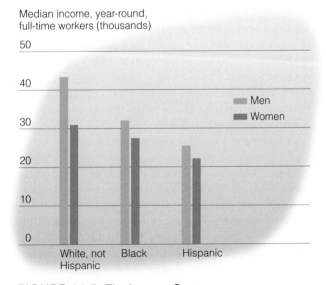

Median income, year-round, full-time workers (thousands)

■ Men
■ Women

White, not Hispanic   Black   Hispanic

FIGURE 14.5 The Income Gap

DATA: From the U.S. Census Bureau. 2003. *Money Income in the United States: 2001.* Washington, DC: U.S. Department of Commerce.
www.census.gov

The Glass Ceiling
Whimsically depicted as an architectural drawing by Norman Andersen, the glass ceiling refers to the structural obstacles still inhibiting upward mobility for women workers. Most employed women remain clustered in low status, low-wage jobs that hold little chance for mobility. Those who make it to the top often report being blocked and frustrated by patterns of exclusion and gender stereotyping.

■ *Power in the Workplace*

Obvious tangible factors that influence the degree of job satisfaction are the employee's level of pay and benefits package. Also very important but less quantifiable is the value accorded to one's job and the opportunity for advancement.

As we saw in Chapter 10, the **glass ceiling** is a popular concept referring to the limits that women and minorities experience in job mobility. Over the last few decades, many barriers to the advancement of women and minorities have been removed, yet as they try to advance, invisible barriers still prevent further advancement. The existence of the glass ceiling is well documented. Although there has been an increase in the number of managers who are women and minorities, most top management jobs are still held by White men, who are far more likely than other groups to control a budget, participate in hiring and promotion, and have subordinates report to them. Women and racial minorities remain clustered at the bottom of managerial hierarchies.

Sexual Harassment

In addition to having less income and authority on the job than men, women workers are also more likely to experience **sexual harassment,** defined as unwanted physical or verbal sexual behavior that occurs in the context of a relationship of unequal power and that is experienced as a threat to the victim's job or educational activities (Martin 1989). Two primary forms of sexual harassment are recognized in the law. *Quid pro quo sexual harassment* forces sexual compliance in exchange for an employment or educational benefit. A professor who suggests to a student that going out on a date or having sex would improve the student's grade is engaging in quid pro quo sexual harassment. The other form of sexual harassment recognized by law is the creation of a *hostile working environment* in which unwanted sexual behaviors are a continuing condition of work. This kind of sexual harassment may not involve outright sexual demands, but includes unwanted behaviors such as touching, teasing, sexual joking, and comments.

Sexual harassment was first made illegal by Title VII of the 1964 Civil Rights Act, which identifies sexual harassment as a form of sex discrimination. In 1986, the

U.S. Supreme Court upheld the principle that sexual harassment violates federal laws against sex discrimination (*Meritor Savings Bank* v. *Vinson*). The law defines sexual harassment as discriminatory because it places workers at a disadvantage on the basis of their sex. By creating a hostile working environment, sexual harassment makes productive work difficult and discourages educational and work advancement.

More recent Supreme Court cases have also upheld that same-sex harassment also falls under this law, as does harassment directed by women against men. Fundamentally, sexual harassment is an abuse of power by which perpetrators use their position to exploit subordinates. The law also makes employers liable for financial damages if they do not have policies appropriate for handling complaints or have not educated employees about their paths of redress.

The true extent of sexual harassment is difficult to estimate because it tends to be underreported. Most studies find that typically neither women nor men are aware of the proper channels for reporting sexual harassment. Women are less likely than men to report sexual harassment primarily because they believe that nothing will be done to stop the behavior (VanRoosmalen and McDaniel 1998; Cortina et al. 1998). Most surveys indicate that as many as one-half of all employed women experience some form of sexual harassment at some time in their working lives. Men are sometimes the victims of sexual harassment, although far less frequently than women; most studies find that less than 3 percent of all sexual harassment cases involve women supervisors harassing male employees. The typical harasser is male, older than his victim, and of the same race and ethnicity. He is also likely to have harassed other women in the past.

Some sociologists have argued that sexual harassment reflects men's resentment of women entering relatively high-paying fields once reserved for men. It is thus a mechanism men use to maintain their dominance in the workplace. Some men say they engage in this activity to show their interest and affection, but others say it is their response to their perception of unfair treatment or that it demonstrates their anger (McKinney 1992). Men are also more likely than women to see sexual harassment as

normal and tolerable. Consequently, they are less likely to think of harassment as doing something wrong (Reilly et al. 1992; Loredo et al. 1995).

Gays and Lesbians in the Workplace

The increased willingness of lesbians and gay men to be open about their sexual identity has resulted in more attention paid to their experience in the workplace. Surveys find that a large majority of the U.S. population (85 percent) endorse the general concept that lesbians and gay men should have equal rights in job opportunities, but when asked about specific occupations, many people think gays should not be hired in some occupations. Thus 78 percent of Americans now say that gays should be hired as doctors, compared with only 44 percent who thought so in the 1970s; 72 percent also think that gays should be employed in the armed forces and be included in the president's cabinet; 63 percent think they should be employed as high school teachers—up from only 36 percent in 1989 (Newport 2001).

There is increasing acceptance of lesbians and gays generally, but negative experiences in the workplace still affect self-esteem, productivity, and economic and social well-being for gay and lesbian workers. Although there are few empirical studies of gay and lesbian work experiences, those that do exist find that gays fear they will suffer adverse career consequences if heterosexual coworkers know they are gay. This leads many to "pass" as heterosexual at work or keep their private lives secret, which puts gay workers at a disadvantage. Shielding themselves from antagonism or rejection may make them appear distant and isolate them from social networks. These behaviors can actually have a negative effect on their performance reviews since fellow workers may find them unfriendly and withdrawn. Research finds that the relationships of gay employees with their coworkers are less stressful when the employees are open about their identity (Schneider 1984). The work organization is also improved for lesbian and gay employees when employee assistance programs encourage open communication, policies are sensitive to lesbian and gay needs, and discriminatory practices can be identified and stopped (Sussal 1994). Nonetheless, one-third of gay employees keep their social life separate from work.

Disability and Work

Not too many years ago, people with disabilities were not thought of as a social group; rather, disability was thought of as an individual frailty or perhaps a stigma. Sociologist Irving Zola was one of the first to suggest that people with

DEBUNKING
Society's Myths

Myth: Sexual harassers are men who are maladjusted and cannot control their sex drive.

Sociological perspective: Sexual harassment is a means of asserting power in the workplace and is most common in settings where women are perceived as intruding in areas where men have been dominant.

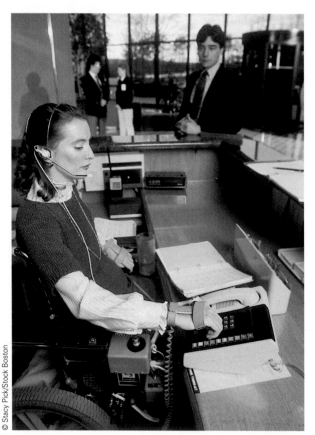

© Stacy Pick/Stock Boston

The Americans with Disabilities Act provides legal protection for disabled workers, giving them rights to reasonable accommodations by employers and access to education and jobs.

disabilities face issues similar to minority groups. Instead of using a medical model that treats disability like a disease and sees individuals as impaired, conceptualizing disabled people as a minority group enabled people to think about the social, economic, and political environment that disabled people face. Instead of seeing disabled people as pitiful victims, this approach emphasizes the group rights of the disabled, illuminating things such as access to employment and education (Zola 1989, 1993).

Now those with disabilities have the same legal protections afforded to other minority groups. Key to these rights is the Americans with Disabilities Act (ADA), adopted by Congress in 1990. Building on the Civil Rights Act of 1964, and earlier rehabilitation law, in particular the Rehabilitation Act of 1973, the Americans with Disabilities Act protects disabled people from discrimination in employment and stipulates that employers and other providers (such as schools and public transportation systems) must provide "reasonable accommodation." Disabled people must be qualified for the jobs or activities for which they seek access, meaning that they must be able to perform the essential requirements of the job or program without accommodation to the disability. For students,

reasonable accommodation includes provision of adaptive technology, exam assistants, and accessible buildings.

The law prohibits employers with fifteen or more employees from discriminating against job applicants who are disabled or current employees who become disabled, including job application, wages and benefits, advancement, and employer-sponsored social activities. The law applies to state and local governments, as well as employers. ADA also legislates that public buses, trains, and light rail systems must be accessible to disabled riders; airlines are excluded from this requirement. The law also requires businesses and public accommodations to be accessible and requires telephone companies to provide services that allow hearing- and speech-impaired people to communicate by telephone.

Not every disabled person is covered by ADA. To be considered disabled, a person must have a condition or the history of a condition that impairs a major life activity. The law specifically excludes the use of illegal drugs as a cause of disability and excludes pregnancy as a disability—which is ironic because pregnancy is treated as a disability by other federal laws for purposes of maternity leave.

What effect does pregnancy have on women's work patterns? The common myths that women who become pregnant drop out of the labor force are simply untrue. Because most women work out of economic necessity, maternity leaves are generally short. Women who work the most hours and women in higher-status jobs are the least likely to leave a job following the birth of a child. Family circumstances are also a strong predictor of whether a woman will return to work following a birth, and how soon. Contrary to what one might expect, mothers with a spouse or another adult in the household return to work more quickly than those without other adults in their household. The greater the proportion of the family income a mother provides, the sooner she returns to work. There are no differences by race in these patterns (Wenk and Garrett 1992).

■ *Chapter Summary*

■ *What is the state?*

The *state* is the organized system of power and authority in society. It comprises different institutions, including the government, the military, the police, the law and the courts, and the prison system. The state is supposed to protect its citizens and preserve society, but it often protects the status quo, sometimes to the disadvantage of less powerful groups in the society.

■ *How do sociologists define power and authority?*

Power is the ability of a person or group to influence another. *Authority* is power perceived to be legitimate. There are three kinds of authority—*traditional author-*

ity, based on long established patterns; *charismatic authority,* based on an individual's personal appeal or charm; and *rational–legal authority,* based on the authority of rules and regulations (such as law).

- **What theories explain how power operates in the state?**

  Sociologists have developed four theories of power. The *pluralist model* sees power as operating through the influence of diverse interest groups in society. The *power elite model* sees power as based on the interconnections between the state, industry, and the military. *Autonomous state theory* sees the state as an entity in itself that operates to protect its own interests. *Feminist theorists* argue that the state is patriarchal, representing primarily men's interests.

- **How well does the government represent the diversity of the U.S. population?**

  An ideal democratic government would reflect and equally represent all members of society. The makeup of the U.S. government does not reflect the diversity of the general population. African Americans, Latinos, Native Americans, Asians, and women are underrepresented within the government. Political participation also varies by a number of social factors, including income, education, race, gender, and age. African Americans and Latinos, however, are overrepresented in the military, in part because of the opportunity the military purports to offer groups otherwise disadvantaged in education and the labor market. There is an increased presence of women in the military.

- **How are societies economically organized?**

  Societies are organized around an economic base. The *economy* is the system on which the production, distribution, and consumption of goods and services are based. *Capitalism* is an economic system based on the pursuit of profit, market competition, and private property. *Socialism* is characterized by state ownership of industry; *communism* is the purest form of socialism.

- **How do sociologists define work?**

  Sociologists define *work* as human activity that produces something of value. Some work is judged to be more valuable than other work. *Emotional labor* is work that is intended to produce a desired state of mind in a client. The *division of labor* is the differentiation of work roles in a social system. In the United States there is a class, gender, and racial division of labor.

- **What are some of the characteristics of the contemporary labor force?**

  In recent years, the employment of women has been increasing, whereas that of men has been decreasing.

Official *unemployment rates* underestimate the actual extent of joblessness. Women and racial minorities are most likely to be unemployed. Recent immigrants also have a unique status in the labor market, often in the lowest paying and least prestigious jobs. The U.S. occupational system is characterized by a *dual labor market.* Jobs in the primary sector of the labor market carry better wages and working conditions, whereas those in the secondary labor market pay less and have fewer job benefits. Women and minorities are disproportionately employed in the secondary labor market. Patterns of occupational distribution also show tremendous segregation by race and gender in the labor market. Race and gender also affect the occupational prestige, as well as the earnings, of given jobs.

- **How does power in the workplace affect women, racial–ethnic groups, and gays and lesbians?**

  Women and minorities often encounter the *glass ceiling*—a term used to describe the limited mobility of women and minority workers in male-dominated organizations. Women, in addition, face *sexual harassment* at work more often than men—defined as the unequal imposition of sexual requirements in the context of a power relationship. Homophobia in the workplace also negatively affects the working experience of gays and lesbians.

▪ Key Terms

alienation 403
authority 383
automation 400
autonomous state
    model 387
bureaucracy 383
capitalism 396
charismatic authority 383
communism 397
contingent worker 400
deindustrialization 399
democracy 388
division of labor 401
dual labor market
    theory 405
economic restructuring 397
economy 395
emotional labor 401
gender gap 390
glass ceiling 408
global economy 397
government 388
interest group 385

interlocking
    directorate 387
occupational
    segregation 405
pluralist model 385
political action committee
    (PAC) 386
postindustrial society 396
power elite model 386
power 383
propaganda 382
rational–legal
    authority 383
revolution 382
sexual harassment 408
socialism 396
state 381
traditional authority 383
underemployment 404
unemployment rate 403
work 401
xenophobia 397

■ *Researching Society with MicroCase Online*

You can see the results of actual research by using the Wadsworth MicroCase® Online feature available to you. This feature allows you to look at some of the results from national surveys, census data, and some other data sources. You can explore this easy-to-use feature on your own but try this example. Suppose you wanted to know the following:

Across all 50 states, is the percent employed in agriculture in the state related to the state's poverty level?

To answer this question, go to **sociology.wadsworth. com/andersontaylor/essen3e**, select Microcase Online from the navigation bar, and follow the directions there to analyze the following data.

Data file: States [this file contains data on all fifty states]

Analysis Task: Scatterplot

Dependent Variable: %POOR — PERCENT BELOW POVERTY LEVEL

Independent Variable: %AGRI.EMP — PERCENT EMPLOYED IN AGRICULTURE

Questions

Once you have your results, answer the following questions:

1. In general, as the percent employed in agriculture, forestry and fisheries in the state increases, would you say the poverty rate increases, decreases, or remains unchanged?

2. These results are based upon the 50 states. (True/False)

3. Among the resources for Chapter 14 on the Companion Web Site for *Sociology: The Essentials,* Third Edition, you will find more information on how to interpret scatterplot graphs. After reading the scatterplot instructions, carefully consider the value of Pearson's r (=0.174). Does the percent of poor in a state appear to be related to the percent of people employed in agriculture, forestry and fisheries? Explain.

■ *The Companion Web Site for* Sociology: The Essentials, *Third Edition*

sociology.wadsworth.com/andersen_taylor/essen3e

Supplement your review of this chapter by going to the companion Web site to take one of the Tutorial Quizzes,
use the flash cards to master key terms, and check out the many other study aids you'll find there. You'll also find special features such as GSS Data and Census 2000 information, data and resources at your fingertips to help you with that special project or do some research on your own.

■ *Suggested Readings and Web Resources*

Amott, Teresa L., and Julie A. Matthaei. 1996. *Race, Gender, and Work: A Multicultural History of Women in the United States,* 2nd ed. Boston: South End Press.
Based on an analysis of the intersections of race, class, and gender in the labor market, this book presents the histories of the work of women of color and White women.

Chang, Grace. 2000. *Disposable Domestics: Immigrant Women Workers in the Global Economy.* Cambridge, MA: South End Press.
Chang argues that immigrant women workers, immigrant domestic workers, and former welfare recipients are used as reserve laborers and pitted against each other by employers seeking cheap labor.

Collins-Lowry, Sharon. 1997. *Black Corporate Executives: The Making and Breaking of a Black Middle Class.* Philadelphia: Temple University Press.
A study of Black executives, this book shows patterns of advancement of this portion of the new Black middle class, while revealing the subtle forms of discrimination that persist in the workplace. Collins shows how much race still matters in employment practices.

Domhoff, G. William. 2002. *Who Rules America?* New York: McGraw-Hill.
This is an updated version of a classic book, detailing the power elite in the United States.

Enloe, Cynthia. 2000. *Maneuvers: The International Politics of Militarizing Women's Lives.* Berkeley: University of California Press.
Enloe examines the effects of militarization of women's lives, both women in the military (including military wives) and women not in the military. This analysis of the military as a gendered institution also shows how pervasive militarization is within society.

Federal Election Commission
http://www.fec.gov
This site includes information on elections, campaign finance, and the various voting systems used in local, state, and federal elections.

National Institute for Occupational Safety and Health
(NIOSH)
http://www.cdc.gov/niosh/homepage.html
*This site contains extensive information on policies and
laws regarding worker safety and health, as well as current information about occupational safety and employment
possibilities in this area.*

U.S. Department of Labor
http://www.dol.gov
*As the federal agency responsible for overseeing issues re-
lated to labor and employment, the U.S. Department of
Labor maintains a site with statistical data on employment, and services such as a job bank in the public employment sector.*

Population, Urbanization, and the Environment

*t*he study of population and environment is a most important topic as we begin the new millennium. A great many issues of central concern to the entire country are driven by population. Population growth and density are responsible for the major policy issues of the day, such as overcrowding in cities, traffic jams, long lines at markets and other stores, environmental pollution, family planning, diminishing resources, and food shortages. Population issues head the federal government's list of problems to be solved, and the U.S. Census Bureau debates with Congress the methods for accurately counting the number of people who constitute the population of the United States. The federal as well as the state governments endlessly debate who should or should not be permitted to immigrate into the United States. Finally, events such as the terrorist attacks on September 11, 2001, presumably by foreign persons residing in the United States, have—rightly or wrongly—resulted in stricter government immigration policies.

The estimated population of the United States is presently more than 280 million. At the current rate of growth, the country will reach almost 300 million by the year 2025. The population has more than doubled since 1946, when it stood at approximately 132 million. In that year, a spike in the number of births began that lasted until 1964—from the end of the Second World War to the beginning of the Vietnam War. The Baby Boom is the name given to that crop of 75 million babies, who are now middle-aged adults constituting nearly one-third of all the people in the United States. The generation that in the tumultuous 1960s warned, "Don't trust anyone over thirty," is now hovering in their forties to late fifties and starting to have grandchildren.

Babies are born every year to about 70 in 1000 American women aged fifteen to forty-five, averaged across all social classes and racial–ethnic groups. Planning for children greatly affects the goals that adults set for themselves. For example, if you want to go directly into a career, you may choose to postpone having a child. Having a career and a child at the same time is a heavy strain—but many people do it nonetheless. College or professional school may cause you to postpone your decision to have a child. That first job or overseas assignment may cause you to put off children yet again. The decision to have or to adopt children is among the most important that you will ever make, affecting not only your own life, but that of your child, the rest of your family, and ultimately, society.

The education and occupation structure of the country has been greatly affected by the decisions of so many people to have children during the previous years. Today, as globalization, economic restructuring, terrorism, and war cause young people to feel insecure about their future, many twenty-something couples are deciding, at least for the present, not to have children. Their decisions will ripple forward in the years to come, as fewer youngsters are enrolled in grade school and then in college two decades down the road. Inevitably, there will follow a decline in the number of middle-aged people to take care of others in their old age.

In this chapter, we examine the nature of human populations. How do births, deaths, and migrations affect society? Who in our society is most likely to die young or die old? How do demographic hazards such as accidental death or exposure to toxic waste differ across racial and ethnic groups? How does the increasingly urban basis of society affecting us? Finally, we will address a question that many people find most chilling of all: Are there too many people on this planet?

■ *Demography and the U.S. Census*

The scientific study of population is called **demography**, which is the study of the current state and changes over time in the size, distribution, and composition of human populations. This field of sociology draws on huge bodies of data generated by a variety of sources. One source is the U.S. Census Bureau. A **census** is a head count of the entire population of a country, usually done at regular intervals. The census conducted every ten years by the U.S. Census Bureau, as required by the U.S. Constitution, attempts not only to enumerate every individual, but also to obtain information such as gender, race, ethnicity, age, education, occupation, and other social factors.

The 2000 U.S. census is estimated to have undercounted a small percentage of the country's population. Among those most likely to have been undercounted by the census are the homeless, immigrants, minorities living in ghetto neighborhoods, and other residents of low social status. The constitutional requirement for a census was included to ensure fair apportionment of representatives in the federal government. Undercounting minorities and the underclass tends to leave these groups underrepresented in government. The estimated undercount for the entire U.S. population overall is only about

FIGURE 15.1 World Population Growth (in Millions)

DATA: From the Population Reference Bureau. 2003. Washington, DC. **www.prb.org.** Reprinted with permission.

2 percent, yet the undercount for African Americans nationally has been estimated to be as high as 20 percent and for Hispanics, as high as 25 percent (NAACP Legal Defense and Education Fund 2003; National Urban League 2002; Harrison 2000).

The U.S. Congress and the U.S. Census Bureau have fiercely debated the following issue: Should people be allowed to select multiracial (or "mixed race") responses on the census questionnaire, which it now does, by allowing someone to check more than one racial–ethnic category from among several, such as African American, Hispanic, non-Hispanic White, Native American, Asian, Eskimo, and Aleut; or, should individuals be limited to checking one category only. The use of the multiracial response option gives individuals an opportunity to define themselves as mixed race. One argument against this option is that it subtracts from the number of people who would have otherwise indicated only one category, especially a racial–ethnic minority category, further undercounting African Americans, Hispanics, and Native Americans. A recent study estimates, however, that only about 2 percent of the persons responding actually indicate a multiracial response (Harrison 2000).

Another body of data used in demography is **vital statistics** that include information about births, marriages, deaths, migrations in and out of the country, and other fundamental quantities related to population. From the census and vital statistics gathered by using a

wide variety of sources, we can create a picture of the U.S. population—who we are, how we are changing, and even who we will be in the future.

▪ Diversity and the Three Basic Demographic Processes

The total number of people in a society at any given moment is determined by only three variables: births, deaths, and migrations. These three variables show different patterns for different racial and ethnic groups, different social strata, and both genders. Births add to the total population, and deaths subtract from it. Migration into a society from outside, called **immigration,** adds to the population, whereas **emigration,** the departure of people from a society (also called "out-migration"), subtracts from the population.

The total population of the world is increasing at a rate of approximately 270,000 people per day, or just less than 200 people per minute. The world's population does not increase in a linear fashion—the line on a graph of population does not rise in a straight line, with the same number of people added each year. Instead, the population grows exponentially, with an upward-accelerating curve, as shown in Figure 15.1. An ever-increasing number of people are added each year. At the present rate of growth, the world's population will double in forty years.

Birthrate

The **crude birthrate** of a population is the number of babies born each year for every 1000 members of the population or, alternatively, the number of births divided by the total population, multiplied by 1000:

$$\text{Crude birthrate (CBR)} = \frac{\text{number of births}}{\text{total population}} \times 1000$$

The crude birthrate for the entire world population is approximately 27.1 births per 1000 people. Various countries and different subgroups within a country can have dramatically different birthrates. For example, the country with the highest birthrate in the world is Niger, with 50.4 births per 1000 people. The lowest birthrate is found in Italy and Belarus, with only 9 births per 1000 people (U.S. Census Bureau 2002).

The crude birthrate reflects what is called the *fertility* of a population, which is live births per number of women in the population. Fertility is different from *fecundity,* which is the potential number of children in a population that could be born (per 1000 women) if every woman reproduced at her maximum biological capacity during the childbearing years. If a majority of women had on the average around twenty or more children, fecundity is what current demographic estimates suggest as a maximum estimate. Fertility rates are lower than fecundity rates because few women in any given population reproduce at anywhere near the theoretical biological maximum.

The overall birthrate for the United States is approximately 16 births per 1000 people, compared with the all-time high rate of 27 births per 1000 people in 1946, the start of the so-called Baby Boom that followed the Second World War. The rate varies according to racial–ethnic group, region, socioeconomic status, religion, and other factors. Overall, we find that for different racial–ethnic groups, the birthrates in the United States are as follows:

Group	Birthrates per Thousand
Whites	14.1
African Americans	17.6
Latinos (Mexican Americans, Puerto Ricans, and other Hispanic groups combined)	24.0
Native Americans	17.1
Asian Americans	17.8

SOURCE: National Vital Statistics Report, Vol. 50, No. 5, Feb 12, 2003.

In general, minority groups tend to have somewhat higher birthrates than White nonminority groups, and lower socioeconomic groups tend to have higher birthrates than those higher on the socioeconomic scale. Native Americans have a birthrate higher than the national average, even though the Native American birthrate has *declined* steadily over the past fifty years.

The effects of birthrates are somewhat cumulative. For example, minorities tend to be overrepresented at the lower end of the socioeconomic scale, compounding the likelihood of a high birthrate. Similarly, religious and cultural differences can make themselves felt. Catholics, for example, have a higher birthrate than non-Catholics of the same socioeconomic status. Hispanic Americans have a high likelihood of being Catholic, another factor that contributes to the higher birthrate among Hispanic Americans. Because minorities tend to have higher birthrates, assuming that present migration rates continue and assuming that death rates do not outstrip the birthrates, in the coming years the United States will have a significantly greater proportion of minorities, thus a relatively lower proportion of Whites.

Given current birthrates, the population of Latinos in the United States will double by the year 2030, and the population of Asian Americans will double by the year 2025. This increase has great implications for local and national policy. Local, state, and federal governments must increasingly take these projected increases into account for future legislation and programs.

Death Rate

The **crude death rate** of a population is the number of deaths each year per 1000 people, or the number of deaths divided by the total population, times 1000:

$$\text{Crude deathrate (CDR)} = \frac{\text{number of deaths}}{\text{total population}} \times 1000$$

The crude death rate can be an important measure of the overall standard of living for a population. In general, the higher the standard of living enjoyed by a country, or a group within the country, the lower the death rate. The death rate of a population also reflects the quality of medicine and health care. Poor medical care, which goes along with a low standard of living, will correlate with a high death rate.

Another measure that can reflect the standard of living in a population is the **infant mortality rate,** which is the number of deaths per year of infants less than one year old for every 1000 live births. In the United States, the overall infant mortality rate is approximately 7 infant deaths for every 1000 live births. The highest infant mortality rates among seventy-seven countries throughout the world are Angola (rate of 200) and Afghanistan, rate of 150 (U.S. Census Bureau 2002).

Infant mortality rates, a measure of the chances of the very survival of members of the population, are important to compare across racial–ethnic groups and across social class strata. They are a good indicator of the overall quality of life, as well as the survival chances for members of that racial or class group. Inadequate health care and health facilities cause higher infant mortality rates. Consequently, the higher infant mortality among minorities and those in lower socioeconomic strata in the United States suggests the lack of adequate health care and adequate access to health facilities. There are also many other causes of higher infant mortality, such as presence of toxic wastes, malnutrition of the mother, inadequate food, and outright starvation.

The **life expectancy** of a population or group is defined as the average number of years a member of the group can expect to live. In the United States, life expectancy has gone from forty years of age in 1900 to over seventy-seven years of age for people born now. Although a life expectancy of seventy-seven years might seem high, the truth is that the United States does not compare very well to other developed nations in either life expectancy or infant mortality. Table 15.1 shows that the United States ranks near the *bottom* among industrialized

TABLE 15.1 Life Expectancy and Infant Mortality (by country, industrialized countries only)

Country	Life Expectancy	Infant Mortality Rate
Japan	80.8	3.9
Australia	79.9	5.0
Canada	79.6	5.0
Italy	79.1	5.8
France	78.9	4.5
Spain	78.9	4.9
Netherlands	78.4	4.4
United Kingdom	77.8	5.5
Germany	77.6	4.7
United States	**77.3**	**6.9**
China	71.6	28.1
Russia	67.3	20.1

SOURCE: U.S. Census Bureau. *Statistical Abstract of the United States, 2002.* Washington, DC: U.S. Bureau of the Census, p. 829.

Jacob Lawrence, "The Migration of the Negro," The Phillips Collection

As shown in this painting by African American artist Jacob Lawrence, in the 1920s from virtually every southern town, African Americans left by the thousands to go north to enter northern industry. This has come to be known as the great Black Migration in America.

nations in life expectancy, behind Japan, the Netherlands, Canada, and several other countries. The picture is similar regarding infant mortality. Interestingly, Russia, with whom the United States was engaged in a long-running, expensive Cold War, also has a low life expectancy and an exceptionally high infant mortality rate.

We saw in Chapter 13 that life expectancy varies with gender, race–ethnicity, and social class. White women live on average five years longer than African American women, and White men on average live seven years longer than African American men. African Americans are twice as likely as Whites of comparable age to die from diseases such as hypertension or the flu, as are Hispanics. Both groups are also considerably more likely than Whites to die of acquired immunodeficiency syndrome (AIDS).

Sadly, racial and ethnic differences are also striking when it comes to infant survival: African American babies are almost *thirty* times more likely to contract AIDS than White babies, and Hispanic babies are twenty-five times more likely. Native Americans are ten times more likely than Whites to get tuberculosis, and nearly seventy times more likely to get dysentery (National Urban League 2002; Jaynes and Williams 1989; Levine 1987). Once again, we see the dramatic effects of gender and race–ethnicity, as well as class, this time on the odds of avoiding the devastation of chronic disease and surviving to a relatively old age. Those odds are lowered considerably in the United States if you are poor and minority.

DEBUNKING
Society's Myths

Myth: High infant mortality and a high death rate for young adults are problems in underdeveloped countries, but not in the United States.

Sociological perspective: Both infant mortality and adult death rates are significantly greater among lower-class than among middle-class persons in the United States, greater among people of color (Latinos, Native Americans, and African Americans) than among Whites of the same social class, and greater among men than women.

Migration

Joining the birthrate and death rate in determining the size of a population is migration of people in and out of the country. Migration affects society in many ways. Israel, since its establishment in 1948, has experienced considerable growth in its population, primarily due to a tremendous migration of Jews from Europe and the United States. These migrants tend to be younger on average than the rest of the Israeli population, therefore their arrival has certain direct consequences, such as increasing the birthrate, which is higher among the young than the older Israelis.

Migration can also occur within the boundaries of a country. In the 1980s, internal migration by African

Americans, Hispanics, Asians, and Pacific Islanders within the borders of the United States has occurred at a rate unmatched since the First World War and the great Black migration from south to north in the United States early in the twentieth century. In that era, Blacks migrated from the South to major industrial urban areas in the North, such as Chicago, New York, Detroit, and Cleveland where jobs were available. The recent pattern of migration for African Americans has been not only from the South, but also from the major northern urban centers to the West, the Southwest, and New England. This migration has carried many African Americans into areas that were previously all White and has frequently been associated with the presence of the migrants at institutions such as military bases or universities (Barringer 1993).

Among Hispanics, migration patterns have traditionally been loosely linked to the agriculture industry. More recently, these patterns are linked to other industries such as meatpacking and textiles, and to industries centered in urban areas (Portes and Rumbaut 2001; Edmondson 2000; Barringer 1993). Although Mexican Americans have traditionally settled in the West and Southwest, recent movement has taken them to Michigan, Washington State, and New England. Farm workers from Mexico have settled near the beet fields of northern Minnesota, tripling the Hispanic population there since 1980. Puerto Rican Americans have migrated northward in increasing numbers to rural, urban, and suburban areas. In New England towns that were once predominantly White, such as Lynn and Lowell, Massachusetts, the Hispanic population has increased 180 percent since 1980 (Rumbaut and Portes 2001; Portes and Rumbaut 2001).

Asians in the last decade have migrated to a variety of destinations within the country. Many Vietnamese joined the fishing industry on Louisiana's Gulf Coast. The Lutheran Church resettled hundreds of Laotians in Wisconsin. In Smyrna, Tennessee, where Nissan has built a truck plant, the Asian population has more than doubled. Finally, Asians, African Americans, and Hispanics have joined Whites in migrating from urban to suburban areas.

■ *Population Characteristics*

The composition of a society's population can reveal a tremendous amount about the society's past, present, and future. The populations of many nations show a striking imbalance in the number of men and women of certain ages, with many men missing. Quite often, the explana-

tion can be found by looking back in time to when those missing were the right age for military service—the demographic vacancy usually coincides with a major war from which many young men failed to return. The demographic data are thus a record of national history. The Second World War was responsible for killing many men, and some women, in the early 1940s—people in their twenties. As a result, this age category in the United States revealed a shortage of people, and considerably fewer men than women, as the entire population of the country aged.

Sociologists put together data about population characteristics to develop pictures of the population in slices or as a whole. Important characteristics of the population are sex ratio, age composition, the age–sex population pyramid, and age cohorts. We examine these main approaches to describing the population in the next section.

Sex Ratio and the Population Pyramid

Two factors that affect the composition of a population are its sex ratio and its age–sex pyramid. The **sex ratio** (also called *gender ratio*) is the number of males per 100 females, or the number of males divided by the number of females, times 100.

$$\text{Sex ratio} = \frac{\text{number of males}}{\text{number of females}} \times 100$$

A sex ratio above 100 indicates there are more males than females in the population; below 100 indicates there are more females than males. The sex ratio could just as easily have been defined as the number of females per 100 males. A ratio of exactly 100 indicates the number of males equals the number of females. In almost all societies, there are more boys born than girls, but because males have a higher infant mortality rate and a higher death rate after infancy, there are usually more females in the overall population. In the United States, approximately 105 males are born for every 100 females, thus giving a sex ratio for live births of 105. After factoring in male mortality, the sex ratio for all ages for the entire country ends up being 94—there are 94 males for every 100 females.

The *age composition* of the U.S. population is presently undergoing major changes. More and more people are entering the sixty-five and older age bracket. This trend is known as the *graying of America,* as described in Chapter 3. The elderly will soon become the largest population category in our society. As our society gets grayer, its older members will have more influence on national policy and a greater say in matters such as health care, housing, and other areas where the elderly traditionally experience age discrimination.

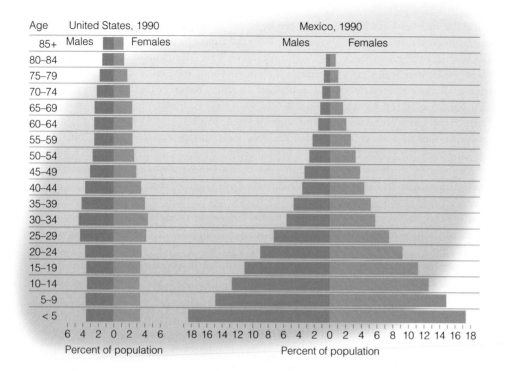

Age   United States, 1990
85+   Males   Females   Males   Females

FIGURE 15.2 A
Comparison of Two
Age–Sex Pyramids

SOURCE: John R. Weeks,
2001. *Population: An Introduction to Concepts and
Issues,* 8th ed. Belmont, CA:
Wadsworth Publishing Co.

Mexico, 1990

Percent of population   Percent of population

Gender and age data are often combined into a graphic format called an **age–sex pyramid** (or age–gender pyramid) that represents the age and gender structure of a society (see Figure 15.2). The left side of the figure shows the age–sex pyramid for the United States. Note that there are slightly more males than females in the younger age ranges (due to the higher birthrate for males), a trend that reverses in the middle-age brackets. At the upper range of the age scale, women outnumber men. The pronounced bulge around the middle of the pyramid represents the Baby Boom generation, people now in their forties and fifties. As these Baby Boomers age, the bulge will rise toward the top of the pyramid, to be replaced underneath by whatever birth trends occur in the coming years. This restructuring of the population pyramid will necessitate restructuring of society's institutions. Marketing will have to be directed more often toward those over age sixty-five; considerably more funds will be needed for their health care; recreational facilities for the elderly will have to be greatly expanded. (Because this bulge is continually moving forward, much like food in a large snake, some demographers have jokingly referred to the Baby Boomers as "the pig in the python.")

The birthrate of a society or group tends to rise and fall in line with the shape of the age–sex pyramid. The right side of Figure 15.2 shows the age–sex pyramid for Mexico. It is quite wide at the bottom and very narrow at the top—exactly pyramidal in shape. This suggests a high birthrate and a death rate that increases rapidly with age. Relatively few males or females survive to fill the elderly age categories. Countries with a high birthrate tend to have a high propor-

tion of women in their childbearing years. A pyramid of this shape is more characteristic of developing nations than the major industrial powers. The birthrate is obviously a statistic of great consequence for the future: Since the children being born will themselves grow up and have children, a high birthrate in the present can be projected to indicate many births a generation further into the future. Within the United States, the population pyramid for African Americans tends to be shaped somewhat like the one on the above Figure 15.2. The same pyramid shape applies to Mexican Americans and Puerto Rican Americans.

THINKING SOCIOLOGICALLY

The *age–sex pyramid* is a graphic representation of the age and gender structure of a society's population. How would the age–sex pyramid for a society look if its men aged eighteen to thirty-five had a greater *crude death rate* than they otherwise would have had because of a major war—such as the one the United States is now in? Draw what the resulting pyramid might look like. What if the women in the society died in the same way by the same war? Now draw the resulting pyramid. What would such dramatic reductions in the numbers of both the women and men in this society mean for the future of the society?

Cohorts

A birth cohort, or more simply, a **cohort**, consists of all the persons born within a given period. A cohort can include all persons born within the same year, decade, or other time period. Over time, cohorts either stay the same in size or get smaller owing to deaths, but can never grow larger. If we have knowledge of the death rates for this population, we can predict quite accurately the size of the cohort as it passes through the stages of life from infancy to old age. This enables us to predict things such as how many people will enter the first grade at age six between the years 2005 and 2010, how many will enroll in college, and how many will arrive at retirement decades down the road. Administrators of social entities such as schools and pension funds can make preparations on the basis of cohort predictions.

To see how dramatically a single cohort can affect a society over time, consider the effect of the cohort born in the United States between 1946 and 1964—the Baby Boom cohort. Many parents of students reading this book are Baby Boomers. The Baby Boom has been one of the most significant demographic events in all of U.S. history, along with the great Black migration from south to north in the late 1880s through the 1920s, the simultaneous massive immigration of Europeans and other groups, and current migration of Hispanic groups (Portes and Rumbaut 2001; Weeks 2001; Kennedy 1989; Ehrlich 1968).

The Baby Boom cohort, now comprising nearly one-third of the entire U.S. population, has had a major impact on the practices, politics, habits, preferences, and culture of our society. Raised in the relatively permissive late 1950s and 1960s, watching the likes of *Howdy Doody* and the *Mickey Mouse Club* on television, they became a large part of the "greed generation" of the 1990s. Dr. Benjamin Spock's book of down-to-earth advice about how to raise healthy children, *Baby and Child Care,* became the greatest bestseller of the twentieth century, with more than 30 billion copies sold. Among its principles was the suggestion that parents should communicate with their children and forego physical punishments when possible. For encouraging this brand of "permissiveness," Dr. Spock has often been blamed at one time or another for nearly every social problem at the time, including the youth rebellions on campuses of the 1960s, protests against the Vietnam War, and experimentation with drugs such as marijuana, LSD, and cocaine.

Once they start to pass age sixty-five beginning in 2010, the Baby Boom cohort will greatly increase the ranks of the elderly. One effect will be an increase in political power for those over age sixty-five. A heavy burden will befall those born between 1965 and 1975, because they will be the main contributors to the Social Security fund just as the fund is required to meet the needs of the giant Boomer population bulge as it comes to rest in its retirement years (Weitz 2001; Persell 1990; Kennedy 1989; Robey 1982).

Theories of Population Growth Locally and Globally

Among the major problems facing modern-day civilization is the specter of uncontrolled population growth. As noted earlier, the world population increases by approximately 270,000 people every day. Some view overpopulation as an epochal catastrophe about to roll over us like a tidal wave. Others dispute whether the problem exists at all, explaining there is no scientific consensus on the *carrying capacity* of the planet. The number of people the planet can support on a sustained basis, and technological advances that have dependably met our needs in the past, can be counted on to do so in the future as the number of mouths to feed continues to grow.

Is the world overpopulated? Is the United States? What can we expect from the future? If the less optimistic scenarios turn out to be accurate, these could be the most important questions facing humankind.

Malthusian Theory

Humans, like animals, can survive and reproduce only when they have access to the means of *subsistence,* meaning the necessities of life, such as food and shelter. Human populations and animal populations are both prone to decline and die off when encountering checks on population growth such as famine, disease, and war. In the face of a daunting environment, humans have managed to thrive, and their population has doubled many times over. The period of doubling gets shorter and shorter.

Thomas R. Malthus, a clergyman born in 1766 in Scotland and educated in England, pondered the realities of life on earth and assembled his observations into a chilling depiction of disastrous population growth called **Malthusian theory,** the idea that a population tends to grow faster than the subsistence needed to sustain it. Malthus propounded his gloomy views in his *First Essay on Population,* published in 1798 (Malthus 1798), and continued to revise and extend his theory until his death in 1834. In sum, Malthus declared that the earth must be near the limits of its ability to support so many humans and that the future must inevitably hold catastrophe and famine.

Malthus noted that populations tend to grow not by *arithmetic increase,* adding the same number of new individuals each year, but by *exponential increase,* in which the number of individuals added each year grows, with the larger population generating an even larger number of births with each passing year. Arithmetic increase would cause a population to double in size at a decelerating rate.

Bubonic plague (called the black death) severely decreased the population of medieval Europe.

Exponential increase, in contrast, causes a population to double ever faster. It took 200 years for the world population to double from one-half billion in 1650 to one billion in 1850. From two billion to four billion took only forty-five years during the twentieth century. The mathematical power of doubling is awesome when applied to population. If we were to start with just one couple and imagine a lineage that doubled itself each generation by having four children, a mere thirty-two generations, roughly 600 years, would result in a population of 8.4 billion. To put Malthus's fears in perspective, in the United States at the time Malthus was writing, the average number of births per couple was seven!

Unchecked doubling of any population must swiftly spawn enough people to carpet the earth many times over. Clearly something prevents populations, human and other, from doubling every generation. Malthus reasoned that two forces were at work to keep population growth in check: (1) the growth in the amount of food produced tends to be only arithmetic and not exponential; and, (2) Malthus surmised that there were three major *positive checks* on population growth—famine, disease, and war. In Malthus's

time, disease could reach apocalyptic scales. The outbreak of bubonic plague in Europe from 1334 to 1354 eliminated one-third of the population; a smallpox epidemic in 1707 wiped out *three-fourths* of the populations of Mexico and the West Indies. Wars took a toll on European men, with deaths in battle causing semipermanent gaps in the population pyramids of European populations. Along with positive checks on population growth, Malthus acknowledged what he called *preventive checks,* such as sexual abstinence, but he knew that sexual abstinence was unlikely to be the behavior change that halted uncontrolled population growth.

Malthusian theory actually predicted rather well the population of many agrarian societies such as Egypt from A.D. 500 through Malthus's own lifetime. However, Malthus failed to foresee three revolutionary developments that derailed his predictions of growth and catastrophe. In agriculture, technological advances have permitted farmers to work larger plots of land and grow more food per acre, resulting in subsistence levels higher than Malthus would have predicted. In medicine, science has fought off diseases that Malthus expected to periodically wipe out entire nations, such as the bubonic plague. Finally, the development and widespread use of contraceptives in many countries have kept the birthrate at a level lower than Malthus would have thought possible.

The technological victories of this century have not completely erased the specter of Malthus. The worldwide AIDS epidemic warns us that nature can still hurl catastrophes our way. Heartrending pictures of swollen, starving babies remind us that famine continues to destroy human populations in some parts of the world just as it has for thousands of years. Overall, Malthus's theory has served as a warning that subsistence and natural resources are limited. The Malthusian doomsday has not yet occurred, but some believe that Malthus's warning was not in error, just premature.

DEBUNKING
Society's Myths

Myth: The average number of children per family in the United States may have decreased a little bit since Malthus's time (around 1800), but not by much.

Sociological perspective: The average number of children has been about 2.1 per family in the United States for the last twenty years or so (which is close to zero population growth level), but the average was seven children per family in Malthus's time! This may have seemed high even for Malthus—which is one reason he became so concerned with the effects of overpopulation.

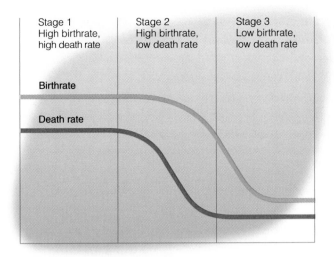

FIGURE 15.3 Demographic Transition Theory

Demographic Transition Theory

An alternative to Malthusian theory is demographic transition theory, developed initially in the early 1940s by Kingsley Davis (Davis 1945) and extended by Ansley Coale (1974, 1986) and others (Weeks 2001). **Demographic transition theory** proposes that countries pass through a consistent sequence of population patterns linked to the degree of development in the society and ending with a situation in which the birthrates and death rates are both relatively low. Overall, the population level is predicted to eventually stabilize, with little subsequent increase or decrease over the long term.

There are three main stages to population change, according to demographic transition theory (see Figure 15.3). Stage 1 is characterized by a high birthrate and high death rate. The United States during its colonial period was in this stage. Women began bearing children at younger ages, and it was not uncommon for a woman to have twelve or thirteen children—a very high birthrate. However, infant mortality was also high, as was the overall death rate owing to primitive medical techniques and unhealthy sanitary conditions.

Stage 2 in the demographic transition is characterized by a high birthrate but a declining death rate. Hence, the overall level of the population increases. The United States entered stage 2 in the second half of the nineteenth century as industrialization took hold in earnest. The norms of the day continued to encourage large families, thereby causing high birthrates, while advances in medicine and public sanitation whittled away at the infant mortality rate and the overall death rate. Life expectancy increased, and the population grew in size.

The characteristics of stage 2 did not apply across all social groups or social classes, however. Minorities at the time (Blacks, and especially Native Americans and Chinese in the Midwest and West) were less likely to benefit from medical advances. The infant mortality and overall mortality rates for Blacks, Native Americans, and Chinese remained high, while their life expectancy remained considerably shorter than life expectancy for the White population. Lack of access to quality medical care was particularly devastating to Native Americans, who had very high death rates for all ages during this period. Demographic transition theory is not completely accurate for different racial–ethnic groups within the same society.

Stage 3 of the demographic transition is characterized by a low birthrate and low death rate. The overall level of the population tends to stabilize in stage 3. Medical advances continue, the general prosperity of the society is reflected in lowered death rates, and cultural changes take place, such as a lowering of the family size. The United States entered this stage prior to the Second World War, and with the notable exception of the Baby Boom, has exhibited stage 3 demographics since then. Again, however, the trend does not apply equally to all groups in U.S. society. Some groups, such as African Americans and Hispanics, continue to have high infant mortality rates and higher death rates owing to the disproportionate impact of disease on these groups, as well as disproportionate lack of access to health resources. Whites in the United States are further along into stage 3 than the rest of U.S. society.

Demographic transition theory has received some criticism primarily because it tends to be based on heavily industrialized countries with a White majority (Coale 1986). In this respect the theory is *ethnocentric* (Weeks 2001). It argues that industrialized countries in the past have gone from high birthrates and death rates to low birthrates and death rates, with the demographic "transition" phase in between. Therefore all countries, and ethnic groups within these countries, should go through these three phases and thus experience a decline in birthrate as well. The theory carried with it the presupposition that nations and ethnic groups of color were considerably less industrialized and were thus at stage 1 with high birthrates and death rates. Yet it is not true that such groups are necessarily nonindustrialized. Thus, such nations and groups can be industrialized yet still be at stage 1.

Nearly forty years after the theory was developed it was discovered that individuals can make their own decisions about how many children to have and when to have them. In other words, people often behave according to their own perception of rational choice, rather than being driven by some theoretical principle over which they are presumed to have no control. This is why **rational choice theory** was used to counter the predictions of demographic transition theory—namely, that humans are capable of making

TABLE 15.2 A Comparison of Demographic Theories

	Malthusian Theory	Demographic Transition Theory	Zero Population Growth (ZPG) Theory
Main Point	A population grows faster than the subsistence (food supply) needed to sustain it	Populations go through predictable stages ("transitions") from high birth and death rates to a stable population with low birth and death rates	Achievement of zero population growth solves the Malthusian problem of unchecked population growth
"Positive" Checks on Population Growth	Famine, disease, and war are likely	Famine, disease, and war are moderately likely	Famine, disease, and war are unlikely
"Preventive" Checks on Population Growth	Sexual abstinence	Sexual abstinence, birth control, and contraceptive methods	Sexual abstinence, birth control, and contraceptive methods
Predictions for the Future	Pessimistic, despite positive and preventive checks, because a population will ultimately outstrip its food supply	Optimistic, given technological and medical advances in a population	Very optimistic; zero population growth has already been achieved in the United States and other countries

cost-benefit analyses of what to do and how many children to have (Weeks 2001).

The "Population Bomb" and Zero Population Growth

In 1968, a modern Malthus appeared in the form of Paul Ehrlich, a biology professor at Stanford University. His book, *The Population Bomb* (Ehrlich 1968), was the first in a series of writings in which Ehrlich argued that many of the dire earlier predictions of Malthus were not far from wrong. The growth in world population, according to Ehrlich, was a time bomb ready to go off in the near future, with dismal consequences. Ehrlich supported his argument with scientific research. This commodity was used rather loosely in the work of Malthus, whose reasoning depended heavily on speculative guesswork about how many people the planet could and should bear. Ehrlich stated that the sheer mathematics of population growth worldwide were sufficient to demonstrate that world population could not possibly continue to expand at its present rates.

Ehrlich pointed out that worldwide population growth has outgrown food production and that massive starvation must inevitably follow. He went beyond Malthusian theory, however, to state that the problem transcended food production and was in fact a problem of the environment. Ehrlich was among the earliest modern thinkers to argue that the quality of the environment, especially the availability of clean air and water, was a critical factor in the growth and health of populations (see Table 15.2).

Many of the dire predictions Ehrlich made back in 1968 have come true. In a later book Ehrlich wrote with his wife, Anne (*The Population Explosion,* 1991), they pointed to a va-

riety of disasters that confirmed the predictions of the 1968 work, and even of Malthus—mass starvation in parts of Africa, starvation in the United States among Black and Hispanic populations, increased homelessness in cities among minorities in particular, acid rain, rampant extinctions of plant and animal species, the irrecoverable destruction of environments such as the rain forests, and global warming.

According to Ehrlich, only limits on population growth can avert disaster. He has advocated the implementation of Malthusian preventive checks by the government by supporting organizations such as Zero Population Growth (ZPG), dedicated to reaching the **population replacement level,** a state in which the combined birthrate and death rate of a population simply sustains the population at a steady level, called the *equilibrium level.* To achieve zero population growth, couples would have to limit themselves to approximately two children per family. By 1980, the United States had indeed reached the replacement level of reproduction with an average of 2.1 children per family, ignoring race–ethnicity and class differences.

Despite these advances, worldwide population growth is still out of control. Population-related maladies such as urban crime, unemployment, and increasing homelessness remain a scourge of worldwide populations, adding an updated twist to the positive checks of the past, such as disease and war, which are still with us. The Ehrlichs deliver a final message: The population bomb must inevitably explode. What remains in doubt is whether we will arrive at that historic moment having made humane preparations, perhaps mitigating the problem with preventive checks, or whether the population crisis will end tragically with a realization of Malthus's vision of people starving worldwide and disease rampaging through a weakened population (Ehrlich and Ehrlich 1991).

THINKING SOCIOLOGICALLY

What is the one major demographic change that would have to take place for a society to achieve *zero population growth* (ZPG)? Can you think of the advantages of ZPG? Any disadvantages? What effect would ZPG likely have on the *demographic transition* process? What is a major sociological barrier that would cause a population to resist adopting a governmental policy of birth control?

■ *Checking Population Growth*

As early as the 1950s, most countries had accepted population growth as a problem that must be addressed. By the 1980s, countries representing 95 percent of the world's population had formulated some policies aimed at stemming population growth; however, no consensus exists on how to control population. For example, many religious and political authorities have argued against the use of birth control. Efforts to encourage the use of contraceptives among rapidly growing populations have therefore had mixed support, whereas other attempts to curb population growth, such as encouraging changes in social habits, generally meet with little success.

Family Planning and Diversity

Many governments, including that of the United States, make contraceptives available to individuals and families. Doing so, however, is not always consistent with the beliefs and cultural practices of all groups in the society. Catholics are taught that it is acceptable to use natural means of birth control (such as the "rhythm method") but are forbidden to use contraceptive devices such as an IUD (intrauterine device), or the "pill." Many Catholics choose to use contraceptives anyway; some studies have shown that the *majority* of Catholics in the

---

SOCIOLOGY IN PRACTICE

The Office of Population Research

The Office of Population Research at Princeton University is the oldest population research center in the country. Founded in 1936, it has trained many persons, from undergraduate degree recipients to doctoral recipients, who have professional positions in the field of demography in the United States, as well as in developing countries. Many of these professionals are concerned with the reduction of population growth, and the Office of Population Research engages in the distribution and training in the use of contraceptives.

The office provides many services in addition to undergraduate and graduate degree programs. Information about reproductive health is provided, as is information on emergency contraception. Research programs housed in the office cover areas such as aging, fertility and fecundity, health and mortality, marriage and the family, demographic methods, migration, and the environment.

A current ongoing project on the environment is housed in Mexico. It

is engaged in a cooperative effort with a grassroots community action organization in Michoacan, Mexico, called ORCA. The purpose of this cooperative effort is to introduce alternative and environmentally positive technologies into the community and then engage in research on their effects. These technologies involve the following:

- Latrines that do not contaminate the groundwater with human wastes
- Stoves (for cooking) and kilns (for pottery) that reduce levels of indoor air pollution through improved ventilation mechanisms
- Elimination of the need for high-priced chemical fertilizers and pesticides
- Introduction of alternative crop rotation strategies

These four projects all form an integrative framework with the existing organizations. They function as a unit. Each project learns from the experiences of the other projects and

thus provides feedback to the benefit of the ecology and inhabitants of the region.

Critical Thinking Exercises

1. What are some ways you can think of to attempt to overcome cultural resistance to contraception and encourage a group or society to adopt some method of contraception? To what extent might it depend upon the type of contraception advocated (for example, an intrauterine device [IUD] versus the pill)?

2. Do you think it is a good idea to try to get any culture to decrease the birthrate by adopting some form of contraception? Do you think such attempts are a threat to the survival of the group or society in question?

SOURCE: Office of Population Research, Princeton University. Web site: **opr.princeton.edu**

A field worker in Bangladesh explains birth control pills and their use to village women.

United States practice forms of birth control forbidden by their church.

Governmental programs that advocate contraception can be successful only if couples themselves choose smaller families over larger ones. This is most likely to occur if the wider culture supports that decision. Creating a new image of the ideal family size is a central concern of those involved in the family planning movement.

Birthrate and family size are known to be related to the overall level of economic development of a country, or even the economic status of certain ethnic groups within a country. As countries in general become more economically developed, their birthrates and average family size generally drop, as predicted by demographic transition theory. Industrialized countries generally prefer smaller families. Developing countries tend to have higher birthrates and give greater cultural value to large families. The same is true of ethnic and racial minorities living in developed nations but not entirely assimilated, such as Hispanics in the United States. Large families are seen as a demonstration of potency, a source of needed labor, and as a preparation for old age when offspring are expected to care for their elders. Before contraceptive devices such as condoms, the IUD, and the pill will be widely adopted, cultural values in favor of undisturbed fertility must be countered (Vanlandingham 1993; Westoff et al. 1990).

A large-scale study has called into question the assumed relationship between economic development and family size in demographic transition theory (Stevens 1994). The study shows that countries in stage 2, such as Bangladesh, which had a declining death rate because of rapid economic and medical developments but re-

tained a high birthrate, have lately become very receptive to birth control programs. As a result, the birthrate and the population level have begun to decline despite the absence of Western-style advanced development. Contraceptive programs have worked in other non-Western countries as well, such as Thailand and Colombia.

Population Policy and Diversity

Findings like those in Bangladesh have an important bearing on population policy elsewhere, including in the United States. Family planning programs offer great potential for achieving large declines in birthrates. In fact, in underdeveloped, overpopulated countries where family planning programs can have the most effect, the demand for resources surpasses the supply. Some cultural resistance is evident from some U.S. racial and ethnic groups to government-sponsored contraceptive programs, including some Hispanic groups and some African American groups. They argue that decreasing the birthrate by means of contraceptive methods is genocidal and threatens the survival of members of these groups. If contraceptive programs are sponsored by the federal government, they are perceived as direct governmental attempts to reduce the number of minority people in the country. To the extent that the government disproportionately promotes the programs in Hispanic or African American communities, and promotes them less aggressively in traditionally White or upper-class areas, the programs are perceived to be racist. As a consequence, individuals are less likely to be convinced to adopt some sort of contraceptive method or device.

At the borderline of policy and social custom are still other cultural barriers against the use of contraceptive methods, including the belief among some young urban men, for instance, that condoms are unmasculine. Still, the popularity of condoms and other means of contraception is increasing, with sterilization (including vasectomies) leading the list, followed by the pill and the condom. Because of controversy over the side effects of the pill, its use has not increased as rapidly as sterilization and the condom. Similarly, the IUD, especially one called the Dalkon Shield, has been criticized for side effects such as fibroid uterine tumors, which may result from prolonged IUD use. Amid numerous lawsuits, its use has been virtually wiped out.

▪ *Urbanization*

The growth and development of cities—centers of human activity with high degrees of population density—is a relatively recent occurrence in the course of human history. Scholars locate the development of the first city around 3500 B.C. (Flanagan 1995). The study of the urban, the rural, and the suburban is the task of *urban sociology,* a subfield of sociology that examines the social structure and cultural aspects of the city compared with rural and suburban centers. These comparisons involve what urban sociologist Gideon Sjøberg (1965) calls the *rural–urban continuum,* those structural and cultural differences that exist as a consequence of differing degrees of urbanization. **Urbanization** is the process by which a community acquires the characteristics of city life and the "urban" end of the rural–urban continuum.

Urbanization as a Lifestyle

Early German sociological theorist Georg Simmel (1905/ 1950) argued that urban living had profound social psychological effects on the individual. Thus he was among the early theorists who argued that social structure could affect the individual. He argued that urban life has a quick pace and is stimulating, but as a consequence of this intense style of life, individuals become insensitive to people and events that surround them. The urban dweller tends to avoid the emotional involvement that, according to Simmel, was more likely found in rural communities. Interaction tends to be characterized as economic rather than social, and close, personal interaction is frowned on and discouraged. Yet urban dwelling can increase the likelihood of other ills: Early theorist Emile Durkheim noted that the suicide rate per 10,000 people was greater in more urbanized areas than in rural areas (Durkheim 1897/1951).

The sociologist Louis Wirth (1938), focusing on Chicago in the 1930s, also argued that the city was a center of distant, cold interpersonal interaction, and as a result the urban dweller experienced alienation, loneliness, and powerlessness. One positive consequence of all this, according to Wirth and Simmel, was the liberating effect that arises from the relative absence of close, restrictive ties and interactions. Thus, city life offered individuals a certain feeling of freedom.

A contrasting view of urban life is offered by Herbert Gans (1962/1982), who studied people in Boston in the late 1950s and concluded that many city residents develop strong loyalties to others and are characterized by a sense of community. Such subgroupings he referred to as the *urban village,* which is characterized by several "modes of adaptation," among them *cosmopolites*—typically students, artists, writers, and musicians, who together form a tightly knit community and choose urban living to be near the city's cultural facilities. A second category are the *ethnic villagers,* people who live in ethnically and racially segregated neighborhoods. Today's urban underclass would encompass what Gans called the *trapped* of late 1950s Boston, individuals unable to escape from the city because of extreme poverty, homelessness, unemployment, and other familiar urban ills.

Race, Class, and the Suburbs

The impact of race and class can clearly be seen in the distinction between city and suburb. Today, only approximately one-fourth of African Americans live in suburban areas. Echoing the earlier *urban villagers* principle of Gans, closely knit communal subgroups form in the suburbs, but the subgroupings tend to form on the basis of class and race, with class according to some (such as DeWitt 1995) being more important than race. In the suburbs, people choose neighbors and friends on the basis of educational and occupational similarity in addition to race.

Pleasant though the suburbs can be, it is also true that people of color, particularly African Americans, often become as segregated there as they do in cities (Feagin and Feagin 1993; Massey and Denton 1993). Racial segregation persists not only in suburban neighborhoods, but in schools as well. Although some may argue that moving to the suburbs and taking up residence is a matter of personal choice, there is ample evidence that residential segregation is maintained by landlords, homeowners, and White realtors who steer people of color to segregated neighborhoods (Feagin and Feagin 1993). The practice of *redlining* by banks, which renders it impossible for a person of color to get a mortgage loan for a specific property, further intensifies residential segregation. Finally, these practices serve only to encourage further segregation in the realm of interpersonal interaction.

The New Suburbanites

The United States ended the twentieth century as it began it—in a great wave of immigration. The 1924 National Origins Quota Law encouraged immigration from northern and western Europe (England, France, Germany, Switzerland, and the Scandinavian countries) but discouraged immigration from eastern and southern Europe (Greece, Italy, Poland, Turkey, and eastern European Jews generally, among others) (see Chapter 9). Despite this openly discriminatory law, millions of eastern Europeans successfully made the journey to Ellis Island and thence the U.S. mainland, only to face prejudice, discrimination, and the accusation that they were taking jobs that would have otherwise gone to the already-present White majority.

At the end of the twentieth century, once again American shores received millions from abroad, and once again prejudice and discrimination were part of the picture, but often in more subtle forms and at times in clearly and fortunately decreased forms. Neighborhoods are now invigorated and culturally enriched by mosques or Buddhist temples; by whole neighborhoods of Vietnamese Catholics,

Koreans, or Asian Indians; or by war refugees from Somalia and Bosnia. The most prominent immigrants in suburban neighborhoods are Hispanic Americans and Asian Americans, the groups that presently make up most of the country's foreign-born population (Edmondson 2000).

One long-term consequence of the current immigration settlement is what at least one demographer (William Frey of the University of Michigan) calls the new *demographic divide.* Because today's immigrants settle in a relatively small number of big cities and their suburbs, mostly located on either the east or west coast, many parts of the United States are still not feeling the effects of these new immigrants. This distinction has a number of consequences. For example, for immigrant groups who are youthful and have a relatively high birthrate, schooling has become a major political issue.

FORCES OF SOCIAL CHANGE

Suburbanization

The growth of suburbs since the Second World War has been so pronounced that, in many ways, it defines the American dream—a house of one's own, good schools, family stability, two cars in the driveway, and green lawns. The process of suburbanization has been profoundly influenced by the growth of the automobile industry after the Second World War and the expansion of state and federal highways. How has suburbanization transformed society, and has the promised dream been realized?

Suburbanization has created massive urban sprawl as most large cities have expanded over formerly rural areas. Once remote areas now are densely populated, placing strains on natural resources and increasing pollution. Witness the political struggles over water in cities of the southwest and southern California or the drying of the Everglades in southern Florida.

The reality of suburbanization may also be quite different from the American dream. Ideals of family togetherness are challenged by the fact that longer commuting times and long distances from work may actually result in the isolation of family members—a development exacerbated by the emphasis on home-centered entertainment and home maintenance.

The suburbs have also contributed to racial segregation, both in housing and schools. As more White, middle-class families move to the suburbs, urban schools suffer from a weakened tax base. "White flight" has then increased the residential segregation of African Americans and, now, Latinos. Moreover, as racial minorities have moved into the suburbs, they tend to live in considerably poorer neighborhoods than is the case for Whites (Logan and Alba 1995). Access to public services reflects this racial disparity.

Such conclusions show the connection between the growth of suburbs and the race and class structure of American society. You might ask yourself how suburbanization has changed the region where you live and how the growth of suburbs might affect the future for diverse groups in your region of the country.

SOURCE: The Urban Institute. 2003. **www.urban.org**

Courtesy Regional History Center, University of Southern California

Suburban sprawl in places like the San Fernando Valley (pictured above in 1930 and the 1990s at right) has transformed not only the natural environment but also social relationships.

© Richard Eller/Aerial Images

But in other areas with a higher proportion of older immigrants, tax cuts for the elderly and Medicare are the major issues.

Although flows of immigrants can change from year to year, most immigrants to the United States recently have been from Mexico, the Philippines, China, and countries of the former Soviet Union. Each group brings its own culture, politics, and differing ages. A consequence of these new suburbanites present across the country is that suburban Whites now often are outnumbered by "minorities" such as African Americans, Asians, and Hispanics. As a result, many Whites now refer to themselves as the "minority majority." One consequence is this "minority majority" may perceive itself to be in competition with the new immigrants for jobs and other resources. In this respect, relations between Whites and the new immigrants may resemble the history of race and ethnic relations of the 1950s and the early 1960s in the United States (Edmondson 2000).

▪ *Ecology and the Environment*

It should be apparent by now that population size has an important social dimension. Social forces can cause changes in the size of the population, and population changes can transform society. Values are acquired from one's culture, including values about what family size is considered ideal, or what degree of crowding in a city is considered tolerable. The values people hold will affect the number of children they want, the place they want to live, and the degree to which they consider population control an urgent problem.

Population density is the total number of people per unit of area, usually per square mile. As population density rises to high levels, as it has in today's cities, the familiar problems of urban living appear, including high rates of crime and homelessness. Interacting with these problems are crises of the physical environment, such as air and water pollution, acid rain, and the growing output of hazardous wastes. Humans sometimes forget that like all other creatures, we are intimately dependent on the physical environment.

Human ecology is the scientific study of the interdependencies that exist between humans and our physical environment. A **human ecosystem** is any system of interdependent parts that involves human beings in interaction with one another and the physical environment. A city is a human ecosystem; so is a rural farmland community. In fact, the entire world is a human ecosystem. Two fundamental and closely related problems confront our present ecosystems: overpopulation and the destruction or exhaustion of natural resources (Weeks 2001; Hawley 1986).

Vanishing Resources

In all ecosystems, whether human, animal, or plant, organisms depend for their survival on one another as well as on the physical environment. Plants use carbon dioxide and give off oxygen, which all animals need to survive. Terrestrial creatures metabolize oxygen and produce carbon dioxide, which is then used by plants, completing a cycle. Humans and other animals require nutrients they can get only by eating plants. When they die, they decompose and provide nutrients to the soil that are taken up by plants, completing another cycle.

The examination of ecosystems has demonstrated two things: the supply of many natural resources is finite, and if one element of an ecosystem is disturbed, the entire system is affected. For much of the history of humankind, the natural resources of the earth were so abundant compared with the amounts used by humans that they may as well have been infinite. No more. Some resources, such as certain fossil fuels, are simply nonrenewable and will be gone soon. Other resources, such as timber or seafood, are renewable as long as we do not plunder the sources of supply so recklessly that they disappear. This is an ecological blunder we have made many times before. Finally, some natural resources are so abundant that they still seem infinite, such as the planet's stock of air and water; but at this stage of our technological development, we are learning that our powers extend to such heights and depths that we can even destroy the near-infinite resources. On the planetary scale, our gaseous wastes are gnawing away at the ozone layer, and our buried chemical wastes are trickling into the water table creating underground pools of poison. One study (Barlow and Clarke 2002) actually notes that pollution has damaged the earth's surface water so badly that the U.S. is mining underground water reserves faster than nature can replenish them. This has led to attempts to privatize water, as in Alltandra Township, South Africa, thereby cutting off water supply to those in this poverty-stricken community who cannot afford it.

One of the best demonstrations of how each part of the ecosystem affects all the other parts was seen in the use of DDT in the United States during the 1940s and 1950s. Dichloro-diphenyl-trichloroethane (DDT) was sprayed on plants by farmers and suburbanites to kill a variety of pests. After just a few years, DDT had seeped through the soil, into the groundwater, on into the seas, then into fish, and finally into birds that ate the fish. Birds that accumulated DDT in their systems appeared healthy enough, but their population plummeted. It was

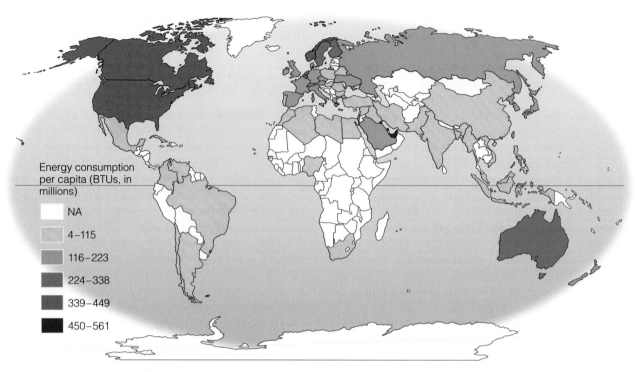

MAP 15.1 Viewing Society in Global Perspective: Energy Consumption Per Capita
Can you name at least three countries that have very high energy consumption per capita? Can you name at least three countries that have the lowest energy consumption per capita?

DATA: From the U.S. Census Bureau, 2002. *Statistical Abstract of the United States, 2002.* Washington, D.C.: U.S. Energy Information Administration, p. 847.

soon discovered that DDT caused a disastrous brittleness in the eggs laid by the birds, decimating succeeding generations. The chemical also found its way into the human food supply, with dangerous consequences such as the contamination of human breast milk in the United States (Carson 1962; Ehrlich and Ehrlich 1991). By the time DDT was identified as a major environmental hazard, tremendous damage had already been done.

If growing population is a problem of the developing world, shrinking resources are a problem of the industrialized world. The United States consumes more than 40 percent of the world's aluminum and coal as well as about 30 percent of its platinum and copper (Ehrlich et al. 1977; Ehrlich and Ehrlich 1991). According to some observers, within forty years we will reach the end of the world's supply of lead, silver, tungsten, and mercury—mainstays of heavy and high-tech manufacturing, including the computer hardware industry.

In the United States alone, real estate development takes over millions of acres of farmland each year. In the western and southwestern United States, the groundwater supply is being depleted at a rapid pace. We are racing through our nonrenewable natural resources and destroying much that should be renewable; however, some activists have begun to claim that the environmental situation, though perilous, is improving (Simon 2001). There is evidence to support this view, but even optimists who wish to show that things are getting better are quick to point out that "better" is not sufficient if the situation is bad enough to begin with (for example, Montagne 1995).

Environmental Pollution

It would be a bitter irony if we managed to avoid exhausting the resources of the planet, only to find that what we had conserved was too degraded by pollution to be useful. The most threatening forms of pollution are the poisoning of the planet's air and water. Air pollution is not only ugly and uncomfortable; it is deadly. The skies of all major cities around the world are stained with pollution hazes, and in cities that rest within geological basins, such as Mexico City and Los Angeles, the concentrations of pollutants can rise so high that pollution-sensitive individuals cannot leave their homes. The occurrence of respiratory cases in the hospitals rises and falls with the passing of weather systems that cause the pollutants to concentrate or disperse.

Water pollution has an especially insidious side to it—most people never see how much is dumped into the world's waterways. Watchers are not present far off shore when the interior walls of vast tankers—acres on acres of fouled surface area—are rinsed with hot seawater and the waste flushed into the ocean. Small factories dump invisibly into canals that feed streams that lead to the sea.

The leading air and water polluters are the United States, Japan, Russia, and Poland. When the reign of secrecy ended in the former Soviet Union, bloodcurdling stories of environmental vandalism emerged. Nuclear-powered ships at the ends of their useful lives were blithely sunk—contaminated reactors, spent fuel, and all—in Antarctic seas. In the farther reaches of the giant Russian territory (which crosses eleven time zones), areas were designated as open dumping sites for toxic wastes and then sealed off. Similarly, a toxic quarantine area exists downwind of the Chernobyl nuclear power plant that blew up in 1986, spewing radioactive poisons over Europe in amounts never accurately determined, but now appearing to be *far in excess* of what was once thought to be the worst case imaginable. For comparison, the Three Mile Island nuclear accident in Pennsylvania in 1979 released 15–20 curies of radioactive iodine-131 into the environment; Chernobyl is now estimated to have released as much as 50 *million* curies of the same dangerous isotope. Incredibly, the Chernobyl nuclear complex was shut down only recently, in November 2000.

A huge portion of the pollutants released into the air come from the exhaust pipes of motor vehicles. The major component of this exhaust is carbon monoxide, a highly toxic substance. Also found in exhaust fumes are nitrogen oxides, the substances that give smog its brownish-yellow tinge. The action of sunlight causes these oxides to combine with hydrocarbons also emitted from exhausts, forming a host of health-threatening substances (see Figure 15.4).

On the industrial side, the Environmental Protection Agency (EPA) has estimated that hazardous and cancer-causing pollutants released into the air by industry are responsible for more than 2000 deaths a year. Electric utility companies and other industries often burn low-grade fossil fuels that emit harmful sulfur dioxide. When mixed with other chemicals normally present in the air, sulfur dioxide turns into sulfuric acid, which gets carried back to earth in droplets of *acid rain*. Acid rain can change the acidity of lakes, soil, and forests so severely they can no longer support life (see Map 15.2).

A daunting international issue has grown around a group of chemicals called chlorofluorocarbons (CFCs),

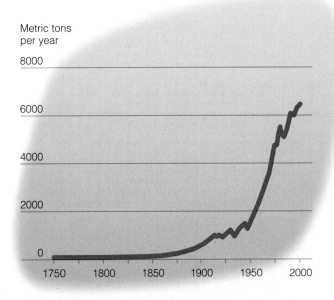

FIGURE 15.4 Worldwide Carbon Dioxide (CO_2) Emissions from Burning Fossil Fuels, 1751–2000 (Metric Tons Per Year)

SOURCE: U.S. Census Bureau, 2002. *Statistical Abstract of the United States, 2002.* Washington, D.C.: U.S. Department of Commerce, p. 831.

used as a coolant in refrigerators, in the manufacture of plastics, and as an aerosol can propellant. CFCs released into the air find their way to the ozone layer in the upper atmosphere, where they eliminate the highly reactive ozone. The ozone layer is a shield that blocks dangerous ultraviolet light, and as this shield is destroyed, more ultraviolet light gets through, causing an increase in sunburn, skin cancer, and other illnesses. In 1987, a treaty named the Montreal Protocol on Substances that Deplete the Ozone Layer called for drastic reduction in the use of CFCs, but the alternatives are expensive, and developing nations are being called on to forgo refrigeration.

Related to the problem of ozone depletion is the **greenhouse effect**. As the sun's energy pours onto the earth, some is reflected from the earth's surface to the earth's atmosphere. Of the reflected energy, a portion is captured by carbon dioxide in the earth's atmosphere, while the rest radiates into space. If the amount of solar energy trapped by carbon dioxide rises, the temperature increases, producing global warming. Rather small changes in the average temperature of the earth can have dramatic consequences. A few degrees of difference can cause greater melting in the arctic regions, which raises the level of the sea, affecting water, land, and weather systems worldwide. The exact effects are unpredictable.

In the face of warning about water pollution, many people take comfort in the vastness of the ocean—three-quarters of the earth's surface is covered with water.

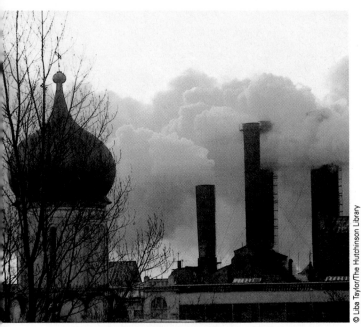

This power plant in Moscow, Russia, spews pollution into the environment, a problem affecting nearly all major industrial cities throughout the world.

However, only a tiny portion of the planet's water is usable by humans. Nearly all the water on earth is seawater—too salty to drink. Of the freshwater on earth, most is locked in the polar ice caps. Of the remainder, most is inaccessible groundwater. All that is left and available to us is the trickle of the planet's river systems and its lakes, and this fragile supply we are polluting. Since about 1955, it has been clear that water is not the infinite resource we once thought it to be (Rice 1986). The nation's rivers and lakes have long been dumping grounds for heavy industry. Yet these same industries—paper, steel, automobile, and chemical—depend on clean water for their production processes, during which they take water from the rivers and lakes and return it heated and polluted. The difference in temperature can alter aquatic habitats and kill aquatic life, earning this change the name of **thermal pollution**. The chemical pollutants that industries discharge into rivers, lakes, and the oceans include solid wastes, sewage, nondegradable by-products, synthetic materials, toxic chemicals, and radioactive substances. Add the polluting effects of sewage systems of towns and large cities, detergents, oil spills, pesticide runoff, and runoff from mines, and the enormity of the problem is clear.

The EPA estimates that 63 percent of rural Americans may be drinking water contaminated by agricultural runoff and the improper disposal of toxic substances in landfills. Thousands of rural water wells have been abandoned due to contamination. Households served by mu-

nicipal water systems are also endangered; fully 20 percent of the country's public water systems do not meet the minimum toxicity standards set by the government (Weeks 2001; Shaberoff 1988).

Federal and state statutes now prohibit industry from polluting the nation's water, but the pollution continues. Why? The answer is economic, political, and sociological. Industries that contribute to a vigorous economy have traditionally met little interference from the government. Public awareness and outrage can force the government to crack down on major polluters. Nevertheless, the federal government often chooses a look-the-other-way attitude. This problem was addressed in 1993 by the inauguration of then Vice President Albert Gore's GLOBE project (Global Organization for a Better Environment). Administered by the Congressional Institute for the Future, GLOBE is an international organization that is attempting to stop all forms of pollution, particularly water pollution, through a combined effort by several major polluters, including the United States and Japan. Despite such national and international efforts, federal or local legal actions against major polluters often result in a relatively painless fine for the corporation that continues to pollute as appeals and further proceedings for new violations wind their way slowly through the cumbersome regulatory and judicial systems.

Many argue that of all environmental problems facing the United States today, the most urgent is the dumping of hazardous wastes, if only for the sheer noxiousness of the materials being dumped. It is estimated that since 1970, the production of toxic wastes increased five-fold (Weeks 2001). This dramatic increase in the amount and variety of hazardous waste production is traceable to new

TAKING ON SOCIAL ISSUES

Environmental Racism

Environmental racism has become a cause for concern among people worried about the impact of pollution and waste on the nation's already most disadvantaged groups. What sociological factors influence environmental racism, and what groups have developed to promote social action and social policy on this issue? Are there such organizations in your community or state, and what communities in your region are most vulnerable to environmental hazards?

Taking Action

Go to the Taking Action exercise on the companion Web site at **sociology.wadsworth.com/ andersen_taylor/essen3e** to learn more about an organization that addresses this topic.

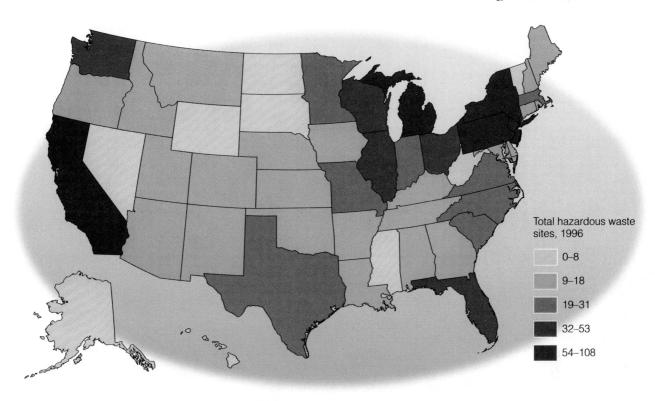

MAP 15.2 Total Hazardous Waste Sites by State
The total number of waste sites in a state varies greatly from state to state. **Pick out your home state on this map. What is the approximate number of hazardous waste sites in it?**

DATA: From the U.S. Environmental Protection Agency. 1994. *Supplementary Materials: National Priorities List.* Washington, D.C.

and profitable industrial technologies. The public creates great demand for products that inevitably produce hazardous wastes—insecticides and other useful poisons; products requiring mercury or lead (both acutely toxic when released into the environment); a variety of dyes, pigments, and paints; and an endless list of specialty plastics whose manufacture produces dangerous byproducts.

Environmental Racism and Classism

Adding to the social problem of toxic wastes is the fact that wastes are dumped with disproportionate frequency in areas that have high concentrations of minorities, particularly American Indians, Hispanics, and African Americans, as well as people of lower socioeconomic status (Pellow 2003; Holmes 2000; Boer et al. 1997; Pollock and Vittas 1995; Bullard 1994a, 1994b; Williams 1987). One study determined that it was "virtually impossible" that dumps were being placed so often in minority and lower socioeconomic status (SES) communities by chance alone (Bullard 1994a, 1994b). The same study found that communities with the

greatest number of toxic dumps had the highest concentration of non-White residents. Such communities also tended to fall below the national average economically and educationally. **Environmental racism** consists of the dumping of toxic wastes with disproportionate frequency at or very near areas with high concentrations of minorities.

DEBUNKING
Society's Myths

Myth: Environmental pollution is in fact more common in or near economically poor areas, but race has nothing to do with it.

Sociological perspective: Even when comparing areas of the same low economic status but different racial compositions, the areas with a greater percent of minorities are on average closer to polluted areas than those with a lower percentage of minorities.

One study of households throughout Florida found that Native American, Hispanic, and particularly African American populations reside disproportionately

Visual concept by Norman Andersen

Environmental racism refers to the pattern whereby people living in predominantly minority communities are more likely exposed to toxic dumping and other forms of pollution. Nuclear waste and testing in the American Southwest, for example, have been located in areas predominantly inhabited by Native Americans. In other areas, African Americans and Latinos are exposed to the effects of industrial waste.

closer to toxic sources than do Whites. This pattern is *not* explainable by social class differences alone. That is, when communities of the same socioeconomic characteristics but different racial–ethnic compositions are compared, Native Americans, Hispanics, and African Americans of a given socioeconomic level live still closer to toxic dumps than do Whites of the *same* socioeconomic level (Holmes 2000; Pollock and Vitas 1995).

The studies found that a greater proportion of ethnic minority households are closer to toxic sites (TRIs, or toxic release inventories) even when considering households of comparable low-income status. The authors note the amount of exposure to the harmful effects of pollution is directly related to physical distance from a toxic facility and that an *environmental inequity* exists among ethnic groups, with African Americans, Hispanics, and Native

Americans bearing a greater share of the burden of exposure to the harmful effects of environmental pollution.

In a similar study of Los Angeles, Boer and associates (1997) found that lower social class areas were significantly nearer to toxic waste dumps, as were areas that were predominantly Latino or African American. Generally, they found that communities most affected by toxic waste dumps were working-class communities of people of color located near industrial areas.

One of the largest commercial hazardous waste landfills in the nation is located in Emelle, Alabama, where Blacks comprise nearly 80 percent of the population. In Scotlandville, Louisiana, the site of the fourth largest toxic landfill in the country, Blacks comprise 93 percent of the population. In Kettleman City, California, the site of the fifth largest toxic landfill, more than 78 percent of

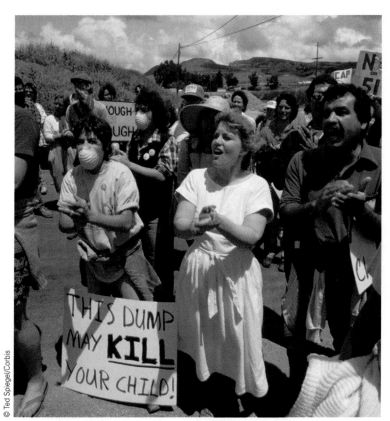

These townspeople are protesting a toxic waste site located next to an Hispanic neighborhood.

From the 1950s through the 1970s, the Navajo population of Shiprock, New Mexico, was exposed to waste from uranium mining and dumping that was 90 to 100 times more radioactive than the level permissible by law. Kerr-McGee, the corporation responsible, was forced out of the area in the early 1970s. When it left, it simply abandoned the site, leaving 70 acres of radioactive mine tailings (the residue from the separation of ores). An even worse situation developed during the same time in Laguna, New Mexico, involving the Pueblo Indians. Anaconda Copper, a subsidiary of the Atlantic-Richfield Corporation, virtually wrecked the traditional Pueblo economy by recruiting the community's youth for hazardous jobs even as it contaminated their environment with the wastes from uranium mining. A high rate of cancer deaths in these communities serves as testimony to the horrible consequences of carelessly discarding toxic wastes (Churchill 1992).

Feminism and the Environment

Women and men do not regard environmental issues equally. In general, women tend to be more concerned with issues of environmental risk, and this has important policy implications. Lack of attention on the part of local and federal governments to environmental issues can be interpreted as lack of attention to policy that differentially affects women. In this respect, it is a feminist issue.

In one recent study (Bord and O'Connor 1997), women and men were both asked a set of detailed questions pertaining to their perceptions of risk to themselves from environmental hazards. Women consistently showed more concern than men for environmental issues and perceived themselves to be at considerably more risk from environmental hazards than did men. For example, women were more likely than men to believe that abandoned waste sites cause cancer, and produce miscarriages and other health problems. They were also more likely than men to feel that waste sites posed dangers to trees, fish, and other wildlife. Women were also more likely than men to perceive dangers in global warming; they were more likely to predict, as a result, coastal flooding from polar ice meltdown; loss of forests; increased killing off of certain animal species; increases in hurricanes and tornadoes; and increased air and water pollution.

The issue is not, for example, whether global warming will definitely result in such calamities, because there is

the residents are Hispanic. In many cases, the siting of the landfills was linked to the economic interests of both residents and corporations. Companies with profit in mind negotiated favorable deals with the residents of these communities to permit the dumping of wastes, often misrepresented as nontoxic, in exchange for jobs and other economic incentives, which were often slow in coming (Bullard 1994b).

THINKING SOCIOLOGICALLY

The *human ecosystem* can be adversely affected by environmental hazards such as toxic wastes. Have you ever witnessed the effects on a population of a major environmental hazard disaster such as Love Canal or Three Mile Island? Did you grow up in or near such an area, or know someone who did? From your observations, are toxic waste dumps more likely to be in or near areas that are working class or heavily occupied by people of color, as shown by research? Quickly survey a few women you know, and then a few men, and find out how concerned they are about environmental issues. Do the women on average show more concern—as shown by past research?

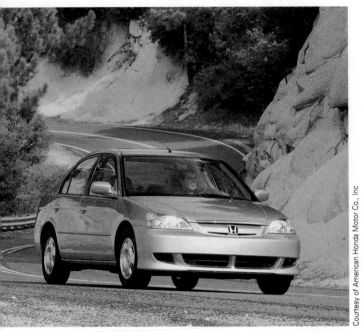

Honda recently released this "hybrid" (gas and electric) pollution-reducing automobile.

Courtesy of American Honda Motor Co., Inc

room for debate on the issue. The issue is that women feel more vulnerable than men to the risks posed by such environmental problems (Bord and O'Connor 1997; Blocker and Eckberg 1997), and as a consequence, women are more concerned that policymakers act to reduce these risks.

Environmental Policy

Environmental policy of the U.S. government over the last thirty years or so has been affected, to greater or lesser degrees, by what has come to be called the environmental movement, a social movement (see Chapter 16) consisting of various loosely organized groups such as the Earth Day Group, NIMBY ("Not in my backyard"), the Sierra Club, and other similar organizations. Biologist Rachel Carson's seminal book *The Silent Spring* (1962) served as a significant impetus to the environmental movement. The book was a scathing indictment concerning the pesticide chemical DDT and its far-reaching polluting effects from toxic runoff, including the severe reduction of many bird populations and the contamination of human breast milk. The Earth Day mobilization in 1970, now noted every year, received tremendous support from the U.S. public (nearly 70 percent according to one survey; Dunlop and Mertig 1992).

The infamous Love Canal debacle is often cited as one of the historical spurs to the environmental movement. During the 1980s, in an area of upstate New York near Niagara Falls called Love Canal, new homes were discov-

ered to have been built on land previously used as large toxic waste dumps and landfills. The pollution was so severe that many of the homeowners discovered a dark, gray chemical ooze issuing from their backyard lawns (Levine 1982). The homeowners abandoned their properties, which remain unoccupied and unsellable to this day.

In the past three decades, federal and local agencies have made concerted efforts to bring the problems of environmental pollution under control, although in most cases environmental pollution is seen by these agencies as affecting women and men equally. The main lines of attack have been stiffer antipollution laws and the encouragement of alternative technologies.

Antipollution laws have been resisted by industry because the laws require expensive adaptations of manufacturing processes. They have also been resisted by unions that fear the added expense to industry would cost jobs. Despite these points of opposition, many antipollution laws have been passed since the late 1960s and have won great public support. However in the early 1980s, President Ronald Reagan's administration relaxed antipollution standards based on the claim that they were too costly for industry, and these relaxed policies were continued under the administration of President George H. W. Bush. Questions still persist involving the balance of interests of big business and environmental protection.

The development of new technologies in the last twenty years has played a major role in the reduction of certain kinds of pollution. Since the early 1970s, emissions controls for automobile exhaust have been widely installed. Electric cars are once again enjoying a vogue, as is the search for alternative fuels to replace gasoline, such as methanol, or methane from the fermentation of human and animal waste products.

■ *Globalization: Population and Environment in the Twenty-First Century*

The U.S. Census Bureau predicts that the world's population will increase from the 6 billion it is now to 7.9 billion by the year 2020. Even more upsetting is the United Nation's revised predictions concerning stabilization of the world's population. A few years ago, the United Nations Division on Population estimated that the world population would stabilize at around 9 billion. That estimate has been revised to 10 billion, with a high estimate of as much as 14 billion.

Sociologists predict that the United States will continue to experience increasing suburban development, with accompanying increases in heavy industry, and thus additional pollution. The rate at which people are leaving the centers of today's cities will slow somewhat. A major concern that today's sociologists have for the future is the effect that a changing planet will have on our lifestyle; and the reverse—the effect our lifestyle will have on the planet (Weitz 2001; Brown et al. 2000; Logan and Molotch 1987; Palen 1992). For the first time in our history, our lifestyle may threaten our existence. Perhaps, as philosopher Matthew Arnold has said, humankind "carries with it the seeds of [its] own destruction."

One analyst, admittedly combining speculation with only a dash of science fiction, foresees a depressing outcome to our abuse of the environment:

> The year—2035. In an effort to hold back the rising seawater, massive dikes have been built around New Orleans, New York, and Miami. Phoenix is baking in its third week of temperatures of 155 degrees. Decades of drought have laid waste to the once fertile Midwest farm belt. Hurricanes batter the Gulf Coast and forest fires continue to blacken thousands of acres across the country. (Rifkin 1989)

Ecological concern has stimulated such developments in the field of **ecological demography,** which combines the studies of demography and ecology (Namboodiri 1988). This field would monitor experimentation with alternative fuels, fertilizers, and pesticides; efforts at the recycling of toxic wastes; and protection for the ozone layer. It would also observe the use and success of alternative technologies, such as solar, wind, and geothermal power. The development of such alternative technologies offers some hope for deflecting Rifken's dire predictions.

As the twenty-first century dawns, earth seems to be shrinking, giving ecology a worldwide, or global, dimension. **Ecological globalization** is now upon us—the worldwide dispersion of problems and issues involving the relationships between humans and the physical and social global environment. Goods, money, people, ideas, and pollution are traveling around the world on an unprecedented scale. With the upward soaring of international trade in fish and timber comes the internationalization of environmental issues. Environmental problems are escalating on the international politics agenda, at times occupying the attention of diplomats as much as the issues of arms control and war. Fears arising from the introduction of *genetically modified organisms* (GMOs) permeate the governments of many nations. Many of these governments are ill-suited for managing environmental problems that transcend their borders, whether via air, water, or international commerce. Yet global environmental governance is still in its infancy, and nations and economies are realizing that international coordination in ecological globalization has become necessary for any significant likelihood of global human survival.

■ *Chapter Summary*

■ *What is demography?*

Demography is the study of population, a field that focuses on three fundamental processes, all of which determine the level of population at a given moment: births, deaths, and migrations. We noted that the United States ranks very low in *life expectancy,* and high in *infant mortality,* relative to other Western countries.

■ *How is diversity relevant?*

Diversity is of great significance since both *infant mortality* and *life expectancy* are not equal across all races, social classes, or for men and women. Women have a greater life expectancy than men in virtually all countries and at all social class levels. However, the lower one's social class, the lower one's life expectancy, regardless of gender, and the greater the infant mortality. Minority group individuals, especially African Americans, Hispanics, and American Indians, all have lower life expectancies and higher infant mortality, than Whites.

■ *What about current migration patterns?*

Current migration patterns show that in addition to movement from city to suburb, not only by Whites but by people of color as well, including the "new suburbanite" populations from other countries and cultures, large portions of populations, such as the underclass, remain stuck in central cities. The study of a *cohort,* the Baby Boomers, showed how a demographic cohort can both use and produce cultural change.

■ *What is the* Malthusian problem, *and why is it important?*

Malthusian theory, still relevant today, warns us about the dangers of exponential population growth along with only arithmetic increases in food and natural resources. To avoid the so-called Malthusian positive checks of famine and war, population control can be, and is being, instituted by programs for family planning and birth control. The level of zero population growth and replacement-level birthrates can be achieved and already has been accomplished in many parts of the United States. Whether methods of contraception advocated by the government are adopted, either in the United States or in other countries, depends largely on the culture of the group in question. Some Latino groups and some African Americans consider advocacy of contraception for people of color, without equally rigorous contraception advocacy for middle-class Whites, to border on genocide.

- *What are the current problems pertaining to urbanization, human ecology, and the environment?*

  Any society is a *human ecosystem* with interacting and interdependent forces, consisting of human populations, natural resources, and the state of the environment. Depletion of one natural resource affects many other things in the ecosystem. The dumping of toxic wastes is a very major problem in our society, especially when toxic dumps are found more frequently, as they are, in or very near African American, Hispanic, and Native American communities. Such practices constitute what some researchers call *environmental racism*. Surveys have shown that environmental risks are of more concern to women than to men. As a consequence, environmental policy has more impact on women than on men. *Ecological globalization* shows that environmental issues are now international in scope and interconnected among countries around the globe.

■ *Key Terms*

<table>
<tr><td>age–sex pyramid 420</td><td>human ecology 429</td></tr>
<tr><td>census 415</td><td>human ecosystem 429</td></tr>
<tr><td>cohort 420</td><td>immigration 416</td></tr>
<tr><td>crude birthrate 416</td><td>infant mortality rate 417</td></tr>
<tr><td>crude death rate 417</td><td>life expectancy 417</td></tr>
<tr><td>demographic transition
    theory 423</td><td>Malthusian theory 421</td></tr>
<tr><td>demography 415</td><td>population density 429</td></tr>
<tr><td>ecological demography 437</td><td>population replacement
    level 424</td></tr>
<tr><td>ecological globalization 437</td><td>sex ratio 419</td></tr>
<tr><td>emigration 416</td><td>thermal pollution 432</td></tr>
<tr><td>environmental racism 433</td><td>urbanization 427</td></tr>
<tr><td>greenhouse effect 431</td><td>vital statistics 416</td></tr>
</table>

■ *Researching Society with MicroCase Online*

You can see the results of actual research by using the Wadsworth MicroCase® Online feature available to you. This feature allows you to look at some of the results from national surveys, census data, and other data sources. You

can explore this easy-to-use feature on your own, but try this example. Suppose you wanted to know the following:

Which states in the United States are the most dense in population, in terms of persons per square mile? Which states are the least dense? Which are somewhere in the middle?

To answer this question, go to **sociology.wadsworth .com/andersen_taylor/essen3e**, select MicroCase Online from the left navigation bar, and follow the directions there to analyze the data described below:

Data file: States—The 50 United States

Task: Mapping

Variable: Density—Population Per Square Mile

Questions

Once you have your results, answer the following questions:

1. Which states are the most dense? Which states are the least dense?

2. Which states have a moderate amount of density?

3. Locate your home state on the map. What is the approximate density of your home state?

4. To what extent do you think many modern environmental problems, such as pollution, are related to population density? Are the more densely populated states those with more pollution?

■ *The Companion Web Site for Sociology: The Essentials, Third Edition*

sociology.wadsworth.com/andersen_taylor/essen3e

Supplement your review of this chapter by going to the companion Web site to take one of the Tutorial Quizzes, use the flash cards to master key terms, and check out the many other study aids you'll find there. You'll also find special features such as GSS Data and Census 2000 information, data, and resources at your fingertips to help you with that special project or do some research on your own.

■ *Suggested Readings and Web Resources*

Brown, Lester R. 2000. *State of the World: A Worldwatch Institute Report on Progress Toward a Sustainable Society*. New York: W. W. Norton and Co.

This is a collection of articles discussing environmental issues and risks globally.

Bullard, Robert. 1994. *Dumping in Dixie: Race, Class, and Environmental Quality.* Boulder, CO: Westview Press. *Bullard's book is a readable and glaringly clear account of how race as well as class is connected with toxic waste disposal. It is a major source of hard evidence of environmental racism and classism.*

Carson, Rachel. 1962. *The Silent Spring.* New York: Knopf. *This book is the classic on how pollution from DDT affected the environment, birds, other animals, and humans. The book represents a major phase in the environmental movement.*

Gaard, Greta, ed. 1993. *Ecofeminism: Women, Animals, Nature.* Philadelphia: Temple University Press. *Gaard looks at the central role of feminism versus sexist ideologies in the environmental movement and explores connections among oppressions of humans by gender, race, and class.*

Pellow, David. 2002. *Garbage Wars: The Struggle for Environmental Justice in Chicago.* Cambridge, MA: MIT Press. *This book establishes a theoretical framework for understanding the issue of environmental justice.*

Environmental Protection Agency
www.epa.gov/
The EPA is the government agency responsible for monitoring the environment and developing public policy to protect it.

Population Reference Bureau
www.prb.org
This is an organization that provides timely information on a variety of population topics in the United States.

World Resources Institute
www.wri.org/
This international organization is dedicated to protecting the earth's environment.

CHAPTER SIXTEEN

Social Change and Social Movements

Social norms about dress and human activity are sometimes made evident through historical contrast.

technological innovation can transform an entire society. Consider the following: A gigabyte of information can travel from China to the United States in less time than it takes you to read this paragraph. At the same time, someone can send a fax in the opposite direction while also sipping coffee grown in Colombia, roasted in Seattle, distributed across the nation, and delivered via express mail. Was this imaginable fifty years ago? Even thirty years ago? Not really. What will the next thirty to fifty years bring?

We are quick to think of change as progress, but sometimes people in a changing society wonder if the things gained from progress are not overbalanced by the things lost. The Alaskan pipeline and related innovations have brought considerable wealth to the communities of northern Alaska, and many Eskimo entrepreneurs have prospered from the changes. Others have fared less well. Some researchers have attributed increases in suicide and alcohol-related deaths to changes that simply came too rapidly in the social structure and culture of the Eskimos (Klausner and Foulks 1982; Simons 1989).

Social movements often produce major social change in a society. Fads and fashions often serve as a basis for relatively permanent social change. For example, blue jeans have been around since the late 1800s and show no signs of becoming less popular. Skateboarding, begun in the early 1960s, has endured for nearly fifty years. Other social movements have resulted in deeper and more far-reaching cultural and structural changes in society, such as the civil rights movement, the social movement to protect the environment, or the animal rights movement—examples of true social movements. Finally, changes in society resulting from the September 11, 2001, terrorist attacks are sure to be significant.

What is social change? What causes it? What has the power to launch deep changes in society in norms, habits, practices, beliefs, gender roles, racial and ethnic relations, and class distinctions? This chapter examines the causes and consequences of societies in change.

■ *What Is Social Change?*

Social change is the alteration of social interactions, institutions, stratification systems, and elements of culture over time. Societies are in a constant state of flux. Some changes are rapid, such as those brought about by desktop computers in little more than ten years. Other changes are more gradual, such as the increasing urbanization that characterizes the contemporary world. Sometimes people adapt quickly to change, in response to the development of electronic communication. Other times people resist change or are slow to adapt to new possibilities. Despite decades of effort to promote contraceptive methods, in some developing nations are only the most sluggish gains (Goldman et al. 1989). The speed of social change varies from society to society and from time to time within the same society. As societies become more complex, the pace of change increases. In U.S. society, this truism can be seen by comparing the rate of change during the 1990s with the same rate during the 1950s (Lenski et al. 1998). Most people would agree that the United States during the 1950s was far more predictable and staid than today as the twenty-first century gets underway.

Microchanges are subtle alterations in the day-to-day interactions between people. A fad "catching on" is an example of a microchange. Take the popularity of bungee jumping. Although not as widespread as some previous fads, this highly dangerous recreation is one of a group of "extreme sports" that have become popular across the country. Bungee jumping has caused quite a few serious injuries and deaths, but has also provided thrilling footage for soft-drink commercials. This may account for why a large number of youths have suddenly developed a taste for putting themselves in bone-smashing danger. Although the overall change in the structure of society caused by fads is quite small, some minor effects may persist. Skateboarding has had several rises and falls as a fad, starting in the early 1960s, and in that time has never completely faded from the repertoire of youthful recreations—an example of how a microchange can persist.

Macrochanges are gradual transformations that occur on a broad scale and affect many aspects of society. In the process of *modernization,* societies absorb the changes that come with new times and shed old ways. One frequently noted trend accompanying modernization is that societies develop greater differentiation in social rank, divisions of labor, and so on. The effects of the fast food industry and its impact on social structure exemplify a macrochange (see the discussion of McDonaldization in Chapter 5). In the United States, the rise of the computer through all its generations from vacuum tube to microchip has dramatically changed society, another example of a macrochange. Not many years ago, who would have imagined that you could "surf the Web" to the extent possible today? As recently as 1990, few people had heard of the Internet, much less used it (Friedman 1999). Now it is a daily presence in the lives of millions. Although this macrochange to a digital culture was swift, some macrochanges can take generations. Whatever time they require, macrochanges represent deep and pervasive changes in social structure and culture.

Large or small, fast or slow, social change generally has in common the following characteristics:

1. **Social change is uneven.** The various parts of a society do not all change at the same rate; some parts lag behind others. This is the principle of *culture lag,* a term coined by sociological theorist William F. Ogburn (1922) and first described in Chapter 2. Recall that culture lag refers to the delay between when social conditions change and when cultural adjustments are made. Often the first change is a development in material culture (such as a technological change in computer hardware), which is followed by a change in nonmaterial culture (meaning the habits and mores of the culture). The symptoms of culture lag can be seen in the uneven dissemination of computer power. Some organizations and bureaucracies adopt state-of-the-art hardware and software more quickly than others, leaping ahead of their colleagues and competitors. Even within single organizations, change occurs unequally, with older employees tending to adapt to new technology more slowly than younger employees.

2. **The onset and consequences of social change are often unforeseen.** The inventors of the atomic bomb in the early 1940s could not predict the vast changes in the character of international relations, including a Cold War that lasted until the demise of the Soviet Union in the early 1990s. Television pioneers, who envisioned a mode of mass communication more compelling than radio, could not predict television would become such a dominant force in determining the interests and habits of youth and the activities and structure of the family. Culture lag is present in both examples: A change in material culture (invention of the atomic bomb, invention of television) precedes later changes in nonmaterial culture (international relations, youth culture, and family structure).

3. **Social change often creates conflict.** Change often triggers conflicts along racial–ethnic lines, social class lines, and gender lines. Terrorism—both in the United States and abroad—focuses attention on the deep conflicts that exist worldwide in political, ethnic, and religious division. These conflicts not only produce international tension, they often drive the world events that generate social change.

4. **The direction of social change is not random.** Change has "direction" relative to a society's history. A populace may want to make a good society better, or it may rebel against a status quo regarded as unendurable. Whether change is wanted or resisted, when it occurs, it takes place within a specific social and cultural context.

Social change cannot erase the past. As a society moves toward the future, it carries along its past, its traditions, its institutions (Lenski et al. 1998; McCord 1991; McCord and McCord 1986). A generally satisfied populace that strives to make a good society better obviously wishes to preserve its past, but even when a society is in revolt against a status quo that is intolerable, the social change that occurs must be understood in the context of the past as much as the future.

▪ *Theories of Social Change*

As we have seen, social change may occur for different reasons. It may occur quickly or slowly, may be planned or unplanned, and may represent microchange or macrochange.

Different theories of social change emphasize different aspects of the change process. The three main lines of contention in social change theory are functionalist theories, conflict theories, and cyclical theories (see Table 16.1). Later in this chapter we consider three additional global theories: modernization theory, world systems theory, and dependency theory. We will consider each individually.

Functionalist and Evolutionary Theories

Recall from previous chapters that functionalist theory builds on the postulate that all societies, past and present, possess basic elements and institutions that perform

FORCES OF SOCIAL CHANGE

A Nation Changed?

Following the terrorist attacks on the United States on September 11, 2001, many people wondered if U.S. society was changed forever. Perhaps it was. The spontaneous creation of shrines, the efforts of relief workers, and the organization of candlelight vigils and other memorials demonstrate a major principle of collective behavior: Even under tragic conditions, human beings form meaningful relationships with each other.

However, the bonds of solidarity that emerged among many Americans after September 11th also reveal a less

© Carolina Salguero/Sipa Press

noble sociological process: The creation of in-group solidarity also produces antagonism toward out-groups, as evidenced by the ethnic profiling of Arab Americans and, in some cases, hate crimes directed against those thought to be Arab Americans. Such acts also show how prejudice can lead people to falsely generalize to all people in a minority group.

Many other sociological processes became visible as a result of these attacks. In our increasingly technologically reliant society, the media play a key role in shaping public opinion and transmitting information. Years from now, few people will forget the televised images of planes crashing into two treasured national symbols. And the use of cell phones, particularly the last minute calls from victims, will haunt many memories. The surge of patriotic displays also constructed a sense of national identity that may not have been felt so keenly before. For years to come sociologists will be analyzing many facets of this tragedy, including its long-term impact on civil rights and the response of social institutions (such as the military, transportation systems, the economy) to such a disaster.

Current generations will now likely always remember what they were doing when they first learned of the attacks. The power of this memory reminds us of an important sociological point that C. Wright Mills made years ago: People's individual lives are shaped by the social forces of history.

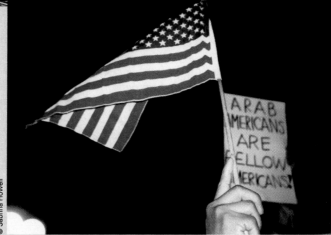

© Sabrina Howell

certain functions permitting a society to survive and persist. A *function* is a consequence of a social element that contributes to the continuance of a society. For example, an institution is society such as the family has a function to provide the society with sufficient population to assure its continuance.

The early theorists Herbert Spencer (1882) and Emile Durkheim (1964/1895) both argued that as societies move through history, they become more complex. Spencer argued that societies moved from "homogeneity to heterogeneity." Durkheim similarly argued that societies moved from a state of *mechanical solidarity,* a cohesiveness based on the similarity among its members, to *organic solidarity* (also called *contractual solidarity*), a cohesiveness based on difference—a division of labor that exists among its members joins them together, because each depends on the others to perform specialized tasks (see Chapter 4). Through the creation of specialized roles, structures, and institutions, societies thus move from a condition of relative undifferentiation to higher social differentiation.

According to functional theorists, societies that are structurally simple and homogeneous, such as foraging or pastoral societies where all members engage in similar tasks, move to societies more structurally complex and heterogeneous, such as agricultural, industrial, and postindustrial societies, where great social differentiation exists in the division of labor among people who perform many specialized tasks. The consequence (or function) of increased differentiation and division of labor is a higher degree of stability and cohesiveness in the society, brought about by mutual dependence (Parsons 1951a, 1966).

Evolutionary theories of social change are a branch of functionalist theory. One variety, called **unidimensional evolutionary theory,** argued that societies follow a single evolutionary path from simple, undifferentiated societies to more complex and highly differentiated societies. The more differentiated societies are then perceived as more "civilized." Early theorists such as Lewis Morgan (1877) labeled the distinctions between societies as "primitive" and "civilized," an antiquated notion that has been severely criticized; there is no reason to suppose that an undifferentiated society is necessarily more "primitive" than a more differentiated one. Furthermore, these earlier theories offered no firm definitions for the terms *primitive* or *civilized.* Nevertheless, the notion that some societies are primitive continues to persist today.

Unidimensional theories of social change fell out of favor because social change occurs in several dimensions and affects a variety of institutions and cultural elements. Meeting the need for a theory that better matches what is actually observed, **multidimensional evolutionary theory** (also called *neoevolutionary* theory) argues that the structural, institutional, and cultural development of a society can simultaneously follow many evolutionary paths, with the different paths all emerging from the circumstances of the society in question.

One formulation of multidimensional evolutionary theory is that of Lenski and his associates (Lenski et al. 1998). Lenski gives a central role to technology, arguing that technological advances are significantly (though not wholly) responsible for other changes, such as alterations in religious preference, the nature of law, the form of government, and relations between races and genders. Although the role of technology is presented as central, other relationships among institutions continue to be important. For example, advances in computer hardware and software can produce changes in the legal system by creating a need for new laws to deal with computer crimes—such as child pornography on the Internet.

In support of the overall argument that social change is in fact evolutionary—cumulative and not easily reversible—Lenski and his associates point out that many agricultural societies have transformed into industrial societies throughout history, but few have made the reverse trip from industrial to agricultural—although certain countercultural groups have tried, such as hippie communes of the 1960s and 1970s. Lenski also argues that social advances can be reversed. For example, a cataclysm such as an earthquake or flood can humble a technologically advanced society. Following a natural disaster, especially in the developing world, city dwellers may find themselves foraging for food if the elaborate infrastructure supporting urban life is destroyed. The September 11, 2001, terrorist attack that destroyed the twin towers of the World Trade Center in New York City has already resulted in major economic and social changes—dramatically increased airport security, and changes in U.S. immigration policy.

Unlike the early theories of Spencer, Durkheim, and Parsons, newer functionalist theories emphasize the role of racial–ethnic, social class, and gender differences in the process of social change (Lenski et al. 1998; Alexander and Colomy 1990; McCord 1991; McCord and McCord 1986). The same early theories made the implicit assumption that European and American societies, predominantly White, were more evolved or advanced. Societies largely comprising people of color were usually assumed to be less evolved and more primitive. This bias was often projected onto analyses *within* a society. For example, in the United States, Native American and Latino cultures were often seen as less advanced, and therefore less intelligent. The new functionalists, as well as social and behavioral researchers, reject the "primitive" versus "civilized" dichotomy and its implicit commentary on racial groups.

TABLE 16.1 Theories of Social Change					
General Theories			**Global Theories**		
Functionalist/ Evolutionary Theory	**Conflict Theory**	**Cyclical Theory**	**Modernization Theory**	**World Systems Theory**	**Dependency Theory**
How do societies change? Societies change from simple to complex and from an undifferentiated to a highly differentiated division of labor	Conflict is inherent in social relations, and society changes from a class-based to a classless society	Societies develop in cycles from idealistic culture to sensate culture	Societies become more homogenized as the result of technological change	Unequal political and economic relationships between nations result in some ("core nations") becoming more advanced than others ("peripheral nations")	The most successful nations control the development of less powerful nations, which become dependent on them
Primary cause of social change Technology	Economic conflict between social classes	Necessity for growth	Technology and global development	Growth of international capitalism	Economic inequality in the global economy

Conflict Theories

Karl Marx, the founder of conflict theory (Marx 1967/1867), was influenced by the early functionalist and evolutionary theories of Herbert Spencer. Marx agreed that societies change and social change has direction, the central principle in Spencer's social evolutionary theory, but Marx placed greater emphasis on the role of economics. He argued that societies could indeed "advance" and that advancement was to be measured by the movement from a class society to a society with no class structure. Marx believed that, along the way, class conflict was inevitable.

As noted earlier in this book, the central notion of conflict theory is that conflict is inherently built into social relations (Dahrendorf 1959). For Marx, social conflict, particularly between the two major social classes—working class versus upper class, proletariat versus bourgeoisie—was not only inherent in social relations but was indeed the driving force behind all social change. Marx believed

that the most important causes of social change were the tensions between social groups, especially those defined along social class lines. Different classes have different access to power, with the relatively lower class carrying less power. Although the groups Marx originally referred to were indeed social classes, subsequent interpretations include conflict between any socially distinct groups that receive unequal privileges and opportunities (G. Marx 1967; Rodney 1974). However, be aware that the distinction between class and other social variables is necessarily murky. For example, conflict between Whites and minorities is at least partly (but not wholly) class conflict, because minorities are disproportionately represented among the less well-off classes.

Racial and ethnic conflict in the United States involves far more than class differences alone: Many *cultural* differences exist between Whites and Native Americans, Latinos, Blacks, and Asians. Furthermore, cultural differences exist *within* broadly defined ethnic groups as well. We have pointed out earlier in this book that there are broad differences in norms and heritage among Chinese Americans, Japanese Americans, Vietnamese Americans, and so on—all often grouped rather coarsely as Asian Americans. The central idea of conflict theory is the notion that social groups will have competing interests regardless of how they are defined. Conflict is an inherent part of the social scene in any society.

A central theme in Marx's writing is that revolution and dramatic social change would come about when class conflict inevitably led to a decisive social rupture. Marx predicted that the capitalist class would progressively eliminate or absorb competitors and relentlessly pursue profits while squeezing the wages of the working class, thereby crushing dissent. Among the working classes discontent was supposed to blossom into a recognition that the common enemy of the worker was the capitalist class. The workers would then join in revolution, overthrow the system of capitalism, eliminate privately owned property, and establish a new economic system that would exist for the good of all.

Although the worldwide revolution predicted by Marx has never occurred, his highly refined analyses of class-related conflict have advanced our understanding of social change, and his work continues to be of interest. However, Marx seems to overemphasize the role of economics in the network of social tensions he observed, while ignoring the importance of other relevant factors related to class. Sociologist Theda Skocpol (1979) has noted that in France, Russia, and China—countries where major revolutions have occurred—serious internal conflicts between social classes were combined with major international crises that the elite social classes proved unable to resolve before they were overthrown. The French Revolution, begun in 1789, erupted during a period when the newly arisen capitalist class was asserting itself worldwide against the old monarchies; and while France was bankrupt from the many wars of the seventeenth and eighteenth century, the country intervened in the American Revolution. The Russian Revolution occurred while Russia was flattened from its disastrous defeat in the First World War, and the communist revolution in China occurred as the world was still putting out the flames of the Second World War. In each case, internal social change was linked to relations between entire societies as well as relations among social classes within each society.

The collapse of the Soviet Union (now Russia) offers some support for Skocpol's hypothesis. Years of international trade sanctions and rejection of its currency by foreign traders had eroded the economic foundations of the Soviet Union, and headlong military competition with the United States helped drive the Soviet Union into bankruptcy. Although economic considerations were paramount in the fall of the Soviet Union, the relationships *between* societies, and not just among classes within a society, were crucial in undoing the former superpower. Nevertheless, conflicts among Russians along religious, social class, ethnic, and regional lines also contributed to the social and cultural disintegration of the Soviet state.

Ethnic, racial, religious, and tribal differences join social class differences as major causes of conflict within and between countries. Cases in point include recent bouts of so-called *ethnic cleansing,* which is vicious battles between ethnic groups in which one group attempts to annihilate the other. The Serbians in the early 1990s attempted this on the Muslims in Bosnia, and then in the late 1990s attempted this on the Albanians in Kosovo. The Taliban's systematic slaughter of many of Afghanistan's minorities provides another example of ethnic cleansing among groups living in the same society.

Cyclical Theories

Cyclical theories of social change invoke patterns of social structure and culture that are believed to recur at regular intervals. Cyclical theories build on the idea that societies have a life cycle, like seasonal plants, or at least a life span, like humans. Arnold J. Toynbee, a social historian and a principal theorist of cyclical social change, argues that societies are born, mature, decay, and sometimes die (Toynbee and Caplan 1972). For at least part of his life, Toynbee believed that Western society was fated to self-destruct as energetic social builders were replaced by entrenched elite minorities who ruled by force and society would wither under the sterile regimes. Some believe that societies become more decrepit, only to be replaced by more youthful societies. This belief is typified in Oswald Spengler's famous work, *The Decline of the West* (1932), which held that western European culture was already deeply in decline, following a path Spengler believed was observable in all cultures.

Sociological theorists Pitrim Sorokin (1941) and, more recently, Theodore Caplow (1991), have argued that societies proceed through three phases or cycles. In the first phase, the *idealistic culture,* the society wrestles with the tension between the ideal and the practical. An example would be the situation captured in Gunnar Myrdal's classic work, *An American Dilemma* (1944), in which our nation declared a belief in equality for all, despite intractable racial, class, and gender stratification.

The second phase, *ideational culture,* emphasizes faith and new forms of spirituality as a phase in social change. The current New Age spirituality movement stresses nontraditional techniques of meditation and the use of crystals and body massage oils in a journey toward self-fulfillment and spiritual peace (Wuthnow 1994).

The third phase is *sensate culture,* which stresses practical approaches to reality, and involves the hedonistic and the sensual ("sex, drugs, and rock and roll"). Sorokin may have foreseen the hedonistic elements of popular culture in the 1960s and 1970s as indicative of sensate culture. According to the theory, when a society tires of the sensate, the cyclical process begins again with the society seeking refuge in idealistic culture. The emphasis beginning in the late 1980s and continuing now for a return to "family values," meaning older and more traditional values, is an example of a return to idealistic culture, presumably as a response to a perceived sensate culture.

Global Theories of Social Change

Globalization is the increased interconnectedness and interdependence of numerous societies around the world. No longer can the nations of the world be viewed as separate and independent societies. The irresistible current trend has been for societies to develop deep dependencies on each other, with interlocking economies and social customs. In Europe, this trend proceeded as far as developing a common currency, the *euro,* for all nations participating in the newly constructed common economy.

If the world is becoming increasingly interconnected, does this mean we are moving toward a single, homogeneous culture—the culture that futurist Marshall McLuhan once called the "global village" (Griswold 1994)? Are cities such as New York, London, and Tokyo, becoming *world cities*—cities that connect entire societies, as some (Sassen 1991) have argued? In such formulations, electronic communications, computers, and other developments would erase the geographic distances between cultures and eventually the cultural differences. However, greater interconnectedness among societies may *magnify* the cultural differences between interacting groups by emphasizing their incompatibilities.

In fact, both processes take place. As societies become more interconnected, cultural diffusion between them creates common ground, while cultural differences may become more important as the relationships among nations becomes more intimate. The different perspectives on globalization are represented by three main theories that we will review: modernization theory, world systems theory, and dependency theory, which are included in Table 16.1.

Modernization Theory

Strongly influenced by functionalist theories of social change, **modernization theory** states that global development is a worldwide process including nearly all societies affected by technological change. As a result, societies are more homogeneous in terms of differentiation and complexity. Modernization theory traces the beginnings of globalization to technological advances in western Europe and the United States that propelled them ahead of the less developed nations of the world, which were left to adopt the new technologies years later. Homogenization resulted, with developing nations being shaped in the mold of the Western nations that had modernized first.

Recent proponents of modernization theory, such as William McCord and Arline McCord, reject the assumption that only western European countries and the United

States have led the technological globalization (McCord 1991; McCord and McCord 1986). The McCords argue that non-Western societies, most notably Japan, have also been leaders in modernization. As a result, Japanese culture has profoundly influenced other countries and cultures with its emphasis on the importance of small friendship groups in the workplace and a traditional work ethic. According to the McCords, Japan and other technological leaders, such as Taiwan and South Korea, have added to the impetus of global economic growth.

World Systems Theory

Formulated by theorist Immanuel Wallerstein (1989, 1979, 1974), **world systems theory** argues that all nations are members of a worldwide system of unequal political and economic relationships that benefit the developed and technologically advanced countries at the expense of the less technologically advanced and less developed. (See also Chapter 8 on global stratification.)

Wallerstein divides the world system into two camps. *Core nations,* such as the United States, England, and Japan, produce goods and services both for their own consumption and for export. The core nations import raw materials and cheap labor from the *noncore nations* (or *peripheral nations*), of Africa, Latin America, South America, and parts of Asia. These nations occupy lower positions in the global economy, thus showing a stratification of the global economy. Certain populations in the noncore nations suffer as a result. Children are used as low-paid laborers in parts of Malaysia, Singapore, and Latin America, for the manufacturing of shirts, soccer balls, and blankets. By manufacturing these goods, the noncore nations end up contributing to the wealth of the core nations.

DEBUNKING
Society's Myths

Myth: Different countries, especially smaller ones, exist largely to themselves, and what they do economically or socially has little effect on other countries in the world.

Sociological perspective: Countries are part of a worldwide network of interdependencies. World systems theory notes that this interdependence tends to benefit the developed and technologically advanced countries at the expense of the less technologically advanced and less developed.

Dependency Theory

Closely allied with Wallerstein's world systems theory is **dependency theory**, which maintains that highly industrialized nations tend to imprison developing nations in dependent relationships rather than spurring the upward mobility of developing nations with transfers of technology and business acumen (Rodney 1981, 1974; Reich 1991). Dependency theory sees the highly industrialized core nations as transferring only those narrow capabilities that it serves them to deliver. Once these unequal relationships are forged, core nations seek to preserve the status quo because they benefit from the cheap raw materials and cheap labor from the noncore nations. In this sense the core nations actively *prevent* upward mobility within the developing noncore nations. In the meantime, the developing nations remain dependent on the core nations for markets and support in maintaining what industry they have acquired, while they experience minimal social development, limited economic growth, and increased income stratification among their own population. Rodney (1981) has argued that this pattern of dependency is to blame for the exceptional underdevelopment of a number of African countries.

Borrowing dependency is a form of a dependent relationship. Former Secretary of Labor Robert Reich (1991) has noted that core nations have been willing to lend money to noncore nations, but often at high interest rates that put severe economic strain on these nations, sometimes requiring interventions such as wage and price freezes in the developing societies to maintain solvency. The hardship produced falls disproportionately on the lower social classes; the upper classes are less affected, and occasionally they benefit extravagantly.

As economist Reich (1991) and sociologists McCord and McCord (1986; also McCord 1991) have noted, the network of dependency is complicated by the fact that in today's global economic system, it is often difficult to determine just who owns what. For example, in the early 1990s, General Motors in the United States owned almost half of the stock of Isuzu in Japan. Japanese companies own a large number of American enterprises in the automotive and entertainment business. Such takeovers can also spawn humorous incidents. In the early 1990s, a construction company in California turned down a low bid from a Japanese company (Haimatsu) to spite them for a previous deal and accepted a higher bid from John Deere, the tractor maker. As it turned out, Haimatsu was a U.S.-owned company, and John Deere was Japanese owned!

▪ *Modernization*

As societies grow and change, in a general sense they become more modern. As already noted, sociologists use the term *modernization* in a specific sense: **Modernization** is a process of social and cultural change initiated by industrialization and followed by increased social differentiation and division of labor. Societies can, of course, experience social change without industrialization. Modernization is

a specific type of social change that industrialization tends to bring about. The change toward an industrialized society can have positive consequences such as improved transportation and a higher gross national product; or negative consequences such as pollution, elevated stress, and increases in certain job discrimination.

Modernization has three general characteristics (Berger et al. 1974). First, *modernization is typified by the decline of small, traditional communities.* The individuals in foraging or agrarian societies live in small-scale settlements with their extended families and neighbors. The primary group is prominent in social interaction. Industrialization causes an overall decline in the importance of primary group interactions and an increase in the importance of secondary groups, such as colleagues at work. Second, *with increasing modernization, a society becomes more bureaucratized;* interactions come to be shaped by formal organizations. Traditional ties of kinship and neighborhood feeling decrease; members of the society tend to experience feelings of uncertainty and powerlessness. Third, *there is a decline in the importance of religious institutions,* and with the mechanization of daily life, people begin to feel that they have lost control of their own lives; people may respond by building new religious groups and communities (Wuthnow 1994).

From Community to Society

The German sociologist Ferdinand Tönnies, who died in 1936, formulated a theory of modernization that still applies to today's societies (Tönnies 1963/1887). Tönnies viewed the process of modernization as a progressive loss of **gemeinschaft** (German for "community"), a state characterized by a sense of common feeling, strong personal ties, and sturdy primary group memberships, along with a sense of personal loyalty to one another. Tönnies argued the Industrial Revolution that emphasized efficiency and task-oriented behavior, destroyed the sense of community and personal ties associated with an earlier rural life. At the crux of this was a society organized on the basis of self-interest, which caused the condition of **gesellschaft** (German for "society"), a kind of social organization characterized by a

---

THINKING SOCIOLOGICALLY

Did you grow up in what was primarily a rural community (*gemeinschaft*), or in what was primarily an urban or suburban environment (*gesellschaft*)? Do you remember how your community or neighborhood changed over time? What were some of those changes—in population, in ethnic composition, in the nature of interpersonal relationships? Would you say that your community encouraged *inner-directedness*, *other-directedness*, or *tradition-directedness*?

These Amish women in Lancaster County, Pennsylvania, illustrate gemeinschaft *("community") social organization as they work on a quilt.*

These subway riders illustrate the impersonality of gesellschaft *("society") as they ride to work.*

high division of labor, less prominence of personal ties, the lack of a sense of community among the members of society, and the absence of a feeling of belonging—maladies often associated with modern urban life.

According to Tönnies, the United States was characterized by gemeinschaft through the year 1900. Life was mainly rural, characterized by families that had lived for generations in villages, and one's work was closely tied to the family. In terms of gender roles, patriarchy was prominent, and most women centered their lives on the home, with very few women holding jobs outside the home, at least among the White middle class. At the time, there were no radios, no televisions, and few telephones. As a result, family members depended on each other for entertainment, information, and support. Despite the relative intimacy of the gemeinschaft, social interaction tended to remain within racial–ethnic and social class boundaries. Mass transportation was not yet developed, and people tended to base their lives in their own town. These characteristics of the United States at the turn of the century are preserved today in the communities of the Amish people in parts of Pennsylvania and Ohio. The Amish are a classic example of a present-day gemeinschaft.

The United States since the 1940s has become a gesellschaft with social interaction less intimate and less emotional, although certain primary groups such as the family and the friendship group still permit strong emotional ties. However, Tönnies noted that the role of the family is considerably less prominent in a gesellschaft than in a gemeinschaft. Patriarchy is less prominent, yet more public, and more women are employed outside the home. In the large cities that characterize the gesellschaft, people live among strangers and pass people on the street that are unfamiliar. In a gemeinschaft, most of the people one encounters one has seen before. The level of interpersonal trust is considerably less in a gesellschaft. Social interaction tends to be even more confined within ethnic, racial, and social class groups. To find personal contact and to satisfy the need for intimate interaction, individuals often join small church groups, training groups, or personal awareness groups (Wuthnow 1994).

Mass Society and Bureaucracy

According to sociologists Rolf Dahrendorf (1959) and Peter Berger and his associates (1974), modernization has produced what they call a *mass society,* one in which industrialization and bureaucracy reach exceedingly high levels. In the mass society, the change from gemeinschaft to gesellschaft is accelerated, and the breakup of primary, family, and kinship ties is particularly pronounced. The government and its functions expand to the extent that much of someone's personal life falls under government management, including tasks previously performed by family. Care for the elderly, for example, may be placed in the hands of unfamiliar, faceless bureaucrats who run elder-care facilities and administer financial benefits for the aged.

Dahrendorf, Berger, and other mass society theorists argue that not only have we moved from gemeinschaft to gesellschaft, with all the attendant negatives described by Tönnies, but that bureaucracies have obtained virtually complete control of an individual's life. As people moved from town to city during the twentieth century, divisions of labor became more pronounced, and social differentiation increased in the workplace, education, government, and other institutions. It became more common to identify people by personal attributes such as their job ("He's John, a lawyer") or their gender ("She's Ms. Blackburn, a woman judge"), rather than by their kinship ("She's a Smith") or their hometown ("He's from Mantua, Ohio"), which is more commonly done in the gemeinschaft. The importance of newspapers, television, magazines, radio, and movies took on more prominent roles in society. People became more mobile geographically, and less dependent on neighbors and kin. All these changes worked together to increase the feeling that most people in someone's immediate environment are strangers.

The rise of large government is a major part of the overall increased bureaucratization of social life. In the preindustrial societies of both the United States and Europe, government may have been only a clergyman, a nobleman, a justice of the peace, or a sheriff. Industrialization allowed government to expand at the national, state, and community levels, therefore becoming more complex and bureaucratized. Government demonstrates an eagerness to involve itself in many aspects of life formerly left to community standards or private resolution—regulating working conditions, setting wages and salaries, establishing standards for products and medicines, health care, and the care of the poor, as well as all sorts of intimate behaviors. Most political and social power today resides in such large bureaucracies, thus leaving individuals a diminishing degree of control over their lives.

Social Inequality, Powerlessness, and the Individual

Another product of modernization, along with mass society, is pronounced social stratification, according to theorists such as Karl Marx (1967/1867) and Jurgen Habermas (1970). In their view, the personal feelings of powerlessness that accompany modernization are due to social inequalities related to race, ethnicity, class, and gender stratification. Marx argued that inequalities are the inevitable product of the capitalist system. Habermas argued that inequalities are the cause of social conflict.

The social structural conditions that arise from modernization, such as increased social stratification, are by the individuals. Building a stable personal identity is difficult in a highly modernized society that presents the individual with complex and conflicting choices about how to live. Many individuals flounder among lifestyles while searching for personal stability and a sense of self.

According to Habermas, individuals in highly modernized environments are more likely than their less modernized peers to experiment with new religions, social movements, and lifestyles in search of a fit with their conception of their own "true self." These individual responses to social structural conditions reveal how the social structure can affect personality.

Social theorist David Riesman (1970, 1950) argued that there are three main orientations of personality that can be traced to social structural conditions:

- **other-directedness,** wherein the behavior of the individual is guided by the observed behavior of others and is characterized by rigid conformity and attempts to "keep up with the Joneses"

- **inner-directedness,** wherein the individual is guided by internal principles and morals and is relatively impervious to the superficialities of other people

- **tradition-directedness,** or strong conformity to long-standing and time-honored norms, practices, and styles of life

According to Riesman, modernization tends to produce other-directedness, whereas less modernized gemeinschafts, such as horticultural or agricultural societies, tend to produce tradition-directedness. The inner-directed individuals, because they are guided by internal rather than external forces, are less likely to sway with the presence or absence of modernization.

If modernization tends to produce other-directedness, then anyone who happens to be inner-directed or tradition-directed in a highly modernized and rapidly changing society, such as the United States, is most likely seen as deviant. The other-directed person, in contrast to the inner-directed or tradition-directed person, is highly flexible, capable of rapid personal change, and more open to the influences of group pressures, changing styles, and shifting interests. These qualities can leave the other-directed individual in the highly modernized society stranded and searching for his or her "true self."

The poignant question "Who am I?" can give rise to feelings of individual powerlessness. The influential social theorist Herbert Marcuse (1964) has argued that modernized society fails to meet the basic needs of people, among them the need for a fulfilling identity. In this respect, modern society and its attendant technological advances are not stable and rational, as is often argued, but unstable and irrational. The technological advances of modern society do not increase the feeling of having control over one's life, but instead reduce that control and lead to feelings of powerlessness.

This powerlessness leads to the *alienation* of the individual from society—the individual experiences feelings of separation from the group or society. This alienation is most likely to affect people traditionally denied access to power, such as racial minorities, women, and the working class. This alienation from the highly modernized, technological society is, in Marcuse's view, one of the most pressing problems of civilization today. Marcuse argues that despite the popular view that technology is supposed to yield efficient solutions to the world's problems, it may be more accurate to say that technology is a primary cause of many problems in modern society.

■ *The Causes of Social Change*

The causes of social change are many and varied, but fall into several broad areas, including cultural diffusion, inequality, changes in population, war, technological innovation, and the mobilization of people through collective behavior and social movements. We examine each of these topics in the following sections.

Cultural Diffusion

Cultural diffusion (as noted in Chapter 2) is the transmission of cultural elements from one society or cultural group to another. Cultural diffusion can occur by trade, migration, mass communications media, and social interaction. Anthropologist Ralph Linton (1937) long ago alerted us to the fact that much of what many people regard as "American" originally came from other lands— cloth (developed in Asia), clocks (invented in Europe), coins (developed in Turkey), and much more.

Expressions and cultural elements found in the English-speaking United States have been harvested from all over the world. Barbecued ribs, originally eaten by Black slaves in the South after the ribs were discarded by White slaveowners who preferred meatier parts of the pig, are now a delicacy enjoyed throughout the United States by virtually all ethnic and racial groups. One theorist, Robert Ferris Thompson (1993), points out that an exceptionally large range of elements in material and nonmaterial culture that originated in Africa have diffused throughout virtually all groups and subcultures in the United States, including aspects of language, dance, art, dress, decorative styles, and even forms of greeting. These examples illustrate cultural diffusion not only from one place to another (such as from West Africa to the United States), but also diffusion across time from a community in the past to many diverse ethnic groups in the present.

The Kaipo people of Brazil wear colorful formal dress. Technology from outside this society (TV, guns) presently threatens the persistence of such cultural practices. Recently the Kaipo have mobilized to oppose outside intervention such as oil drilling.

© "Disappearing World," Granada TV/The Hutchinson Library

Similarly, the immigration of Latino groups into the United States over time has dramatically altered U.S. culture by introducing new food, music, language, slang, and many other cultural elements (Muller and Espenshade 1985). By a similar token, popular culture in the United States has diffused into many other countries and cultures: Witness the adoption of American clothing styles, rock, rap, and Big Macs in countries such as Japan, Germany, Russia, and China. In grocery shops worldwide, from the rain forests of Brazil to the ice floes of Norway, can be found the Coca-Cola logo.

At one time, it was thought that slavery killed off most of the institutions and cultural elements that the slaves brought to the Americas (Herskovits 1941). Extensive research over the past three decades now demonstrates that elements of culture carried from Africa by Black slaves continue to survive among African Americans and, thanks to cultural diffusion, among many other groups as well. A *step show* is an energetic, highly rhythmic, group choreography performed as a special event by predominantly Black fraternities and sororities. Researchers have traced these displays to traditional West African and central African group dances (Thompson 1993; Gates 1988, 1992). The step show has recently been noticed by non-Black students at universities and colleges all over the country, with a few White groups, fraternal, sororal, and otherwise, taking up "steppin'."

Many religious practices among African Americans are also traceable to Africa. As noted by religious historian Albert J. Raboteau (1978), the religious singing

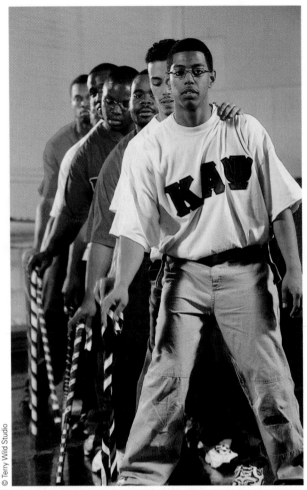

© Terry Wild Studio

Here members of a predominantly African American fraternity, Kappa Alpha Psi (KAΨ) put on a step show, a highly rhythmic and energetic dance form with roots in slave society as well as in West Africa.

styles of the slaves, influenced by their African heritage, had four attributes: polyrhythms, syncopation, glissandos (slides) from one musical note to another, and repetition. African lineage is clearly detectable in jazz, rock, rhythm and blues, and rap music, diffusing far beyond the African American community today.

Inequality and Change

Inequalities between people on the basis of class, ethnicity, gender, or other social structural characteristics can be a powerful spur toward social change. Social movements may blossom into full-blown revolution if the underlying tension is great enough. An example of the mechanism of change can be seen when inequalities between the middle class and the urban underclass produce governmental initiatives, such as increased ed-

ucation for the poor, which are designed to reduce this inequality.

Culture itself can sometimes contribute to the persistence of social inequality and thus becomes a source of discontent among the individuals in the society. Inequalities within the education system often have a cultural basis. For example, a poor child in the United States, who adopts a language useful in the ghetto, is at a disadvantage in the classroom where standard English is used. Culturally specific linguistic systems such as urban Black English, called Ebonics (Dillard 1972; DiAcosta 1998), are generally not adopted by schools. As a result, this may serve to strengthen the inequalities between the poor and the privileged—unless the child is bicultural and can speak both standard English and Ebonics, which many African Americans can do.

Compounding the problem, a Hispanic or Black child may be criticized by his or her peers for "acting White" if the child studies hard (Fordham 1996). A female student may shrink from studying mathematics because she has received the cultural message that to be adept at mathematics is not feminine (Lau and Taylor 2003; Lau 2002; Shih et al. 1999; Sadker and Sadker 1994). The perpetuation of the inequalities of class, race, and gender can stoke the desire for social change on the part of the disadvantaged groups.

Population and Change

Changes in the population, that is, demographic change (see Chapter 15), can greatly influence the nature of interpersonal relations in society. Limitations placed on the population by the natural environment can shape social relations. In Japan, a small country with a large population, crowding is a fact of life that affects how people interact with one another. In Japanese cities, bus drivers negotiate streets that U.S. bus drivers would consider far too narrow for even a small bus. Japanese subways are packed so tightly that white-gloved "pushers" must squeeze commuters bodily into subway cars. Riders on the subway are so tightly packed that their entire bodies are in constant contact, a situation in the United States that would be considered taboo, because close physical contact has sexual overtones. In Japan, the contact is not considered sexual (although there are a few exceptions), nor is it considered a violation of the other's personal space, as it would be in the United States. This is one example of how population density can affect the nature of interpersonal relations among people.

Immigration has profound effects on the overall ethnic and racial composition of the United States. Each year roughly 750,000 immigrants take up permanent residence in the United States (Edmondson 2000; Es-

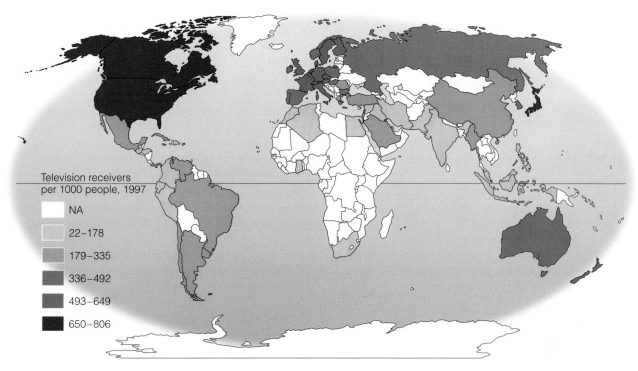

MAP 16.1 Viewing Society in Global Perspective: Transmitting World Affairs (television receivers per 1000 people)
Can you identify two countries with the most TVs? Two with the least? What does this map tell us about the relationship between the industrialization of a country and the number of TVs in it?

SOURCE: U.S. Census Bureau. 2002. *Statistical Abstract of the United States, 2000.* Washington, D.C.: U.S. Government Printing Office, p. 836.

Population density can affect social interaction and cultural norms, as illustrated here in Japan, where a subway worker (a "pusher") causes close physical contact among subway riders.

penshade 1995; U.S. Census Bureau 2002). Approximately one-half are from Mexico or Latin America, and about one-fourth are from Asia. The United States is presently about 11 percent Hispanic; by the year 2025, that figure will be about 18 percent. Currently approximately 4 percent of the U.S. population is of Asian ancestry. By the year 2025, that figure will be approximately 7 percent. By the year 2050, it is expected that Hispanics will be 25 percent of the population and Asians will be 9 percent. These population shifts will cause major changes in society's institutions. The structure of the economy will change, as will the ethnic mix in education, the ethnic complexion of jobs, and the strong influence of Hispanic culture, including styles of dance, language, and other behaviors.

Age, Gender, and Social Change

As demographic variables, age and gender are influenced by and exert influences upon social change in society. The age structure of a society can create social changes, and the changes that occur can affect age groups in different ways.

Current generations—whether young, middle-aged, or old—will be profoundly influenced by the *graying of America,* a phrase referring to the fact that the proportion of old people in the population is increasing dramatically. Consider the following:

- By the year 2015, 27 percent of the population will be age 55 and older (U.S. Census Bureau 2002).

- The proportion of the population classified as the "oldest old," those over the age of 85, will continue to increase.

- Women will continue to outnumber men, among the old as well as among the oldest old.

How well we adapt to the graying of America may partially be the result of how carefully we can analyze the potential effects of population changes. The *contract between generations* is the expectation that the first genera-

tion (say, your grandparents' generation) will grow up and raise the second generation (your parents' generation) who, in turn, produce a third generation (your generation). The expectation has been that parents care for children who in turn care for their children; the children and then grandchildren take care of their parents or grandparents once they are too old to care for themselves.

Another problem relating to the age and gender structure of the future population involves the condition of the Social Security program. Currently, Social Security is one of the older and most successful national social program. Can it continue? Established in 1935 under the Social Security Act, the Old Age, Survivors' and Disability Insurance Commission created the Social Security system. Without significant changes in Social Security policy, most agree that there will not be enough workers to support the number of retirees as soon as the year 2020 (Kingson and Quadagno 1995).

SOCIOLOGY IN PRACTICE

Disaster Studies and Social Change

Dr. Lee Clarke, a sociologist and author, is one founder of a relatively new field: disaster studies. The field of disaster studies investigates the ways in which people manage and organize themselves around earthquakes, fires, floods, and terrorist attacks. Dr. Clarke has found contrary to widespread belief, people do not panic when they are hit with a disaster of great magnitude. Instead, they react in an organized and careful manner that shows adherence to existing norms. He notes that people are guided by norms and societal rules, and those norms do not disappear simply because we are terrified, or because our environment is falling apart around us. By examining past disasters, such as earthquakes, plane crashes, and the World Trade center terrorist attacks, Dr. Clarke makes policy recommendations to the American Association for the Advancement of Science, and to the federal government.

Interestingly, Dr. Clarke thinks that in the history of society, a disaster is a *normal event.* Disasters happen with some degree of regularity throughout history. He argues that

defining a disaster as normal reveals that most people actually know how to cope with it in an organized manner. Studying what people do as a result of a disaster can teach us things that can relieve suffering. That in turn can result in helpful policy recommendations.

It is a myth that in a disaster, the police and firefighters are the first responders. They are indeed responders, but they are not the first. The first responder is likely to be a schoolteacher whose class is being stalked by a sniper, or an executive whose high-rise office building is on fire on a lower floor. As an illustration, Dr. Clarke notes that school officials reacted in a highly organized way in the fall of 2002 during the Montgomery County, MD and Washington, D.C. sniper shootings.

Finally, Dr. Clarke argues that we need to get more serious about disasters and make plans that increase the ways in which our lives are patterned. This means, for example, that we need to plan even for highly unlikely events, such as what scientists call "near-earth events," like an immi-

nent asteroid collision with earth. He notes that if our country can spend tens of billions of dollars deposing dictators in other countries, then we can spend a few million dollars thinking about what to do in the event of an asteroid hit.

Critical Thinking Exercises

1. Interview some of your friends and family, and ask them that as best they can tell, what would they do in the first minutes if they were directly threatened with a sniper shooting? An earthquake? Is there evidence in their answers that they would be reacting in a highly organized manner, as Dr. Clarke would predict?

2. Have you yourself, or a close friend or family member, ever been in a major disaster? What did you, or they, do? Do you think that Dr. Clarke's finding and predictions concerning nonpanic and organized reactions are for the most part accurate?

SOURCE: Dreifus, Claudia. 2003. "Living One Disaster After Another, and Then Sharing the Experience." *The New York Times,* May 20.

War, Terrorism, and Social Change

War and severe political conflict result in large and far-reaching changes for both the conquering society, or a region within a society (as in civil war), and for the conquered. The conquerors can impose their will on the conquered and restructure many of their institutions, or the conquerors can exercise only minimal changes.

The U.S. victory over Japan and Germany in the Second World War resulted in societal changes in each country. The war transformed the United States into a mass-production economy affected family structure (father absence increasing and women not previously employed joining the labor force) and education (men of college age went off to war in large numbers). Many in the armed forces who returned from the war were educated under a scholarship plan called the GI Bill.

The war also transformed Germany in countless ways, given the vast physical destruction brought on by U.S. bombs and the worldwide attention brought to anti-Semitism and the Nazi Holocaust. The cultural and structural changes in Japan were extensive, as well. The decimation of the Jewish population in Germany, and other nations throughout Europe, resulted in the massive migration of Jews to the United States. More recently, the Vietnam War also resulted in many social changes, including the migration of Vietnamese to the United States.

As we noted in Chapter 6, terrorism is a type of crime—the use of force or violence to coerce a government or population in the furtherance of political or social objectives. Threats of bioterrorism have resulted in recent microchanges in the United States where some families wrapped their houses in plastic and duct tape. As we have already noted in Chapter 6, Osama Bin Laden had a role in the international opium trade. His al Qaeda organization was headquartered in Afghanistan, the world's largest grower of opium-producing poppies. The profits from this trade may well have financed the September 11th terrorist attacks in the United States. Terrorism has global significance, and social changes resulting from terrorism occur not only in that society, but in other societies as well.

Technological Innovation and the Cyberspace Revolution

Technological innovations can be strong catalysts of social change. The historical movement from agrarian societies to industrialized societies has been tightly linked to the emergence of technological innovations and inventions. Inventions often come about because they answer a need in the society that promises great rewards. The waterwheel promised agrarian societies greater power to raise crops despite dry weather, while also saving large amounts of time

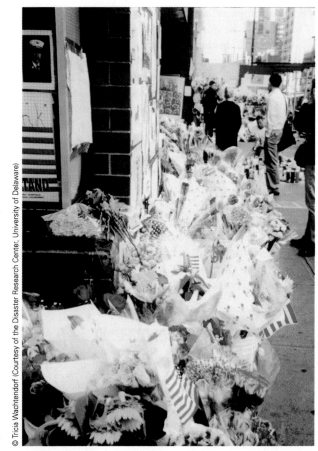

Collective behavior is spontaneous, as when people created memorials to those lost on 9/11/01.

and labor. It is possible to trace a timeline from the use of the waterwheel to the use of the large hydroelectric dams that power industrialized societies, and along the way find evidence of how each major advance changed society.

In today's world, the most obvious technological change transforming society is the rise of the digital computer, and the subsequent development of desktop computing since the 1980s. The invention and development of the Internet and the resulting communication is now called *cyberspace,* which includes the use of computers for communication between persons and communication between persons and computers. Unique in its vastness and lack of a required central location, the Internet has very rapidly become so much a part of human communication and social reality that it pervades and has transformed literally every social institution—educational, economic, political, familial, and religious.

The cyberspace revolution began with vacuum tube mainframe computers in the 1950s and early 1960s, followed by the transistorized computer of the mid-1960s and the integrated circuit computers of the late 1960s and 1970s, and was accelerated by the advent of the PC (personal computer) and the invention of the microchip. What can now be stored in a microchip memory the size of a wristwatch, in the late 1960s would have required a transistorized computer the size of a small auditorium.

Few institutional structures have not been transformed by the cyberspace revolution. Most transactions that are part of everyday life—such as cooking and banking have been changed by the permeation of computers into everyday life. Even interpersonal relationships are being affected by the cyberspace revolution. Computer users can now develop a new self, a new identity with the use of the Internet. One person can communicate with another on the Internet via email and chat rooms with the protection of anonymity. As one user has noted, "You are what you pretend to be" (recall the discussion of this in Chapter 4). Thus the revolution in cyberspace has not only transformed society's institutions, but has also begun to transform the nature of "the self" and how we define ourselves.

The path by which technology is introduced into society often reflects the predominant cultural values in that society. Some cultural values may prevent a technological innovation from changing a society. For example, anthropologists have noted that new technologies introduced into an agrarian society very often meet with resistance even though the new technology might greatly benefit the society. The Yanomami, an agrarian society existing deep in the rain forests of South America, live without electricity, automobiles, guns, and other items of material culture associated with industrialized societies. The Yanomami place great positive cultural value on their way of hunting and engaging in war (Cohen and Eames 1985). The recent introduction of steel into Yanomami culture, however, may have introduced major social changes and changed them into a more warlike society (Tierney 2000), as noted in the "Understanding Diversity" box below.

UNDERSTANDING DIVERSITY

The Yanomami: Fierce People or Fierce Anthropologist?

The Yanomami Indians (singular: Yanomamo) of Venezuela and Brazil have generally been regarded by anthropologists, sociologists, and social scientists as among the most remote and isolated societies on earth. When first encountered by an anthropologist named Napoleon A. Chagnon in 1964, the Indians slept on bark hammocks arranged in a circle around a communal roundhouse. They subsisted mainly on vegetation such as plantains and possessed no steel tools for farming or other activities. They engaged in a ritual form of symbolic combat involving chest pounding and duels with long wooden poles, but little evidence exists that at the time they engaged in brutal warfare either within or between tribes or between different towns. By 1968, however, when Chagnon published his book titled Yanomamo: The Fierce People (Chagnon, 1968), the society had, according to Chagnon, become considerably more warlike.

Over the years, the Yanomami were beset by journalists, filmmakers, logging companies, and anthropologists. Questions have arisen concerning the extent to which such forces have introduced social and cultural change into what had previously been a relatively untouched and undisturbed society. A recent and controversial book by Patrick Tierney titled Darkness in El Dorado: How Scientists and Journalists Devastated the Amazon charges that for a period of more than thirty years, anthropologist Chagnon was among those who not only studied Yanomami society but who in addition brought social and cultural change to it. Tierney argues that before Chagnon's arrival, the Yanomami engaged primarily in ritual combat, but that Chagnon introduced them to steel in the form of machetes and other metal tools in exchange for cooperating with him in obtaining oral histories and other verbal interaction from them. Tierney tells of occasions when Chagnon appeared before them in war paint and brandishing a shotgun—acts geared to encourage warfare among the villages. During this period the Yanomami did engage in fierce combat leading in many cases to injury and death of other Yanomami.

Chagnon attributed these warlike practices among the men to competition for women, but Tierney attributes this fierceness to Chagnon's own warlike displays and his introduction of steel weapons to the society. The men were not so much competing for the attention of women, but instead for the attention of anthropologist Chagnon and his gifts.

Tierney's book has not gone without criticism. Several anthropologists (such as Professor Irving Devore of Harvard University) have argued that Tierney has greatly exaggerated Chagnon's role in bringing social change in the form of warlike behavior to the Yanomami and that, as Chagnon argued, war behavior had already been an important part of Yanomami society prior to Chagnon's arrival (Roosevelt, 2000). This controversy is a heated one and raises important questions about the sources of social change in other societies.

SOURCE: Tierney, Patrick. 2000. Darkness in El Dorado: How Scientists and Journalists Devastated the Amazon. New York: W. W. Norton and Co.; Roosevelt, Margot. 2000. "Yanomami: What Have We Done To Them?" Time (October 2), pp. 77–78.

Mobilizing People for Change

Social change does not develop in the abstract. Change comes from the actions of human beings. Collective behavior and social movements are ways that people organize to promote, or in some cases, to resist change. *Collective behavior* occurs when normal conventions cease to guide people's behavior, and people establish new patterns of interaction and social structure. It is often associated with fads, crazes, and fashions that can initiate social change and may produce more sustained efforts at change, such as in the development of social movements.

Social movements are organized and persistent forms of collective behavior. The purpose of a social movement is often to initiate or vigorously resist social change. Examples abound: the civil rights movement, the women's movement, the environmental movement, and the militia movement, just to name a few. So significant are the changes that result from collective behavior and social movements that we examine them in detail now.

■ *Collective Behavior and Social Movements*

Social change is propelled by the actions of people who engage in collective behavior and social movements. As we have seen, **collective behavior** occurs when the usual conventions to guide behavior are suspended and people establish new norms of behavior in response to an emerg-

ing situation (Turner and Killian 1988: 3). Although collective behavior may emerge spontaneously, it can be predicted. Some of the phenomena defined as collective behavior are whimsical and fun, such as fads and fashions and certain crowds. Other collective behaviors can be terrifying, as in panics or riots. Whether whimsical or awesome, collective behavior is innovative, sometimes revolutionary, and it is this feature that links collective behavior to social change.

Social movements are led by groups that act with some continuity and organization to promote or resist change in society (Turner and Killian 1988: 246). Social movements tend to persist over time more than other forms of collective behavior. Evidence of social movements can be seen throughout society, in movements to protect the environment, promote racial justice, defend the rights of diverse groups (including animal rights), attack the government (such as militia groups), or advocate particular beliefs (such as the Christian Coalition).

DEBUNKING
Society's Myths

Myth: Rebellious social movements such as the Black power movement or the gay rights movements are simply people blowing off steam. They do not result in long-lasting changes in society.

Sociological perspective: Social movements are one of several major causes of long-lasting social change, resulting in enduring structural and cultural changes in society.

TAKING ON SOCIAL ISSUES

Bringing in Social Change

Social change can be purposely created in a society, or in a specific group or culture within society. As suggested in several earlier chapters, this change may occur, for example, by introducing a type of contraceptive device or a new technology, such as electronic computers or cell phones. What specific changes do you think cell phones, for example, have had on things like family relationships, people's use of time, and so forth?

Taking Action

Go to the Taking Action exercise on the companion Web site at **sociology.wadsworth.com /andersen_taylor/essen3e** to learn more about an organization that addresses this topic.

Characteristics of Collective Behavior

Collective behavior always represents the actions of groups of people, not individuals. The action of a lone gunman who opens fire in a post office or a high school cafeteria is not collective behavior because it is one person acting alone. However, groups that gather at the scene of the incident to observe the emergency response are engaged in collective behavior.

Collective behavior involves new or emergent relationships in groups that arise in unusual or unexpected circumstances. The behavior of people who commute to work together is not considered collective behavior because commuting is an ordinary part of their everyday life. But when a community is struck by a natural disaster, such as a flood, earthquake, or hurricane, suddenly nothing can be taken for granted—not food, water, transportation, electricity, nor shelter. Collective behavior emerges to meet the new needs that people in the community face. Following a hurricane, people may form

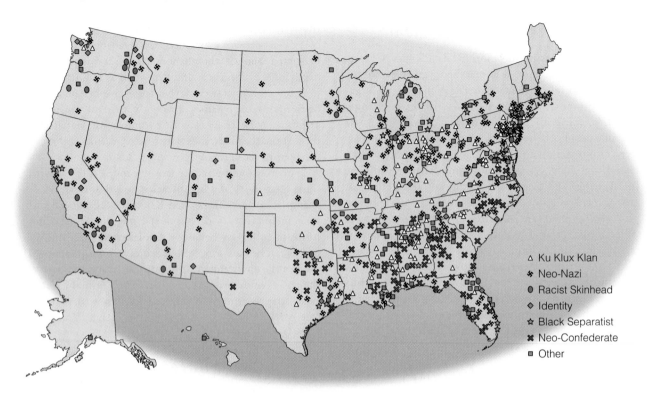

MAP 16.2 Mapping America's Diversity: Hate Groups in the United States
What parts of the country have the heaviest concentration of hate groups? What hate groups concentrate in your own home state?

SOURCE: **www.Splcenter.org** [2003]

neighborhood work groups to clear debris, or they may organize teams to stack sandbags in the threat of a flood. Following the collapse of the World Trade Center, there were numerous reports of people helping each other to the exits, as well as heroic efforts of firefighters and other rescue workers who quickly organized—even at risk of death—to save as many people as they could.

Collective behavior captures the more novel, dynamic, and changing elements of society to a greater degree than other forms of social action. An example is fads that introduce something new into everyday social life. Collective behavior may mark the beginnings of more organized social behavior and often precedes the establishment of formal social movements. People who spontaneously organize to protest something may develop structured ways of sustaining their protest. The environmental justice movement, includes a wide array of Native American, African American, Latino, and other communities that have organized to protest the dumping and pollution that imperil their neighborhoods (Pellow 2003; Bullard 1994a).

During episodes of collective behavior, which is patterned and not the irrational, overly emotional behavior of crazed individuals, people may follow new guidelines of social behavior, but they do follow guidelines. Even episodes

of panic, which appear to be asocial and disorganized, follow a relatively orderly pattern. Episodes of collective behavior often exhibit the more emotional side of life. For example, people may communicate extensively through *rumors*. Lacking communication channels or distrusting the ones available, people use rumors to help define an otherwise ambiguous situation (Turner et al. 1986). Rumors are transmitted by people who are piecing together information about a story whose facts are partly obscured. Rumoring is most common when there is inadequate information to interpret a problematic situation or event (Dahlhamer and Nigg 1993; Shibutani 1966).

DEBUNKING
Society's Myths

Myth: In the face of disasters and other unexpected events, people do not behave under the normal social influences.

Sociological perspective: When faced with unexpected events, people develop norms to guide their behavior, often drawing on previous social behavior and knowledge to guide new interactions.

Social movements such as the disability rights movement can raise public awareness and result in new forms of social behavior.

The Organization of Social Movements

Social movements are both spontaneous and structured, although within movements, tension typically exists between spontaneity and structure (Freeman 1983a). Unlike everyday organizations they thrive on spontaneity and often must swiftly develop new strategies and tactics in the quest for change. During the civil rights movement, students improvised the technique of sit-ins, which quickly spread because they succeeded in gaining attention for the activists' concerns. Social movements differ from other forms of collective behavior, however, by containing routine elements of organization and lasting for longer periods.

There are three broad types of social movements: personal transformation movements, political or social change movements, and reactionary movements. **Personal transformation movements** aim to change the individual. Rather than pursuing social change, participants adopt a new identity—one they use to redefine their life, both in its current and former state. They focus on the development of new meaning within individual lives (Klapp 1972). The contemporary New Age movement defines mainstream life as stressful and overly rational and promotes relaxation and spiritualism as an emotional release and route to expanded perceptions. New Age music, crystals, massage therapy, and meditation are intended to restore the New Age person to a state of unstressed wholeness. Like many other social movements, New Ageism is supported by an array of dues-charging organizations and commercial products, from tapes and crystals to sessions

with the spirits of the dead, retreats in yoga ashrams, and guided tours of Native American holy sites. Religious and cult movements are also personal transformation movements. The recent rise in evangelical religious movements can be explained in part by the need people have to give clear meaning to their lives in a complex and sometimes perplexing society.

Social change movements aim to change some aspect of society, such as the environmental movement, the gay and lesbian movement, the civil rights movement, the animal rights movement, and the religious right movement. All seek social change, although in distinct and sometimes oppositional ways. Some movements want radical change in existing social institutions; others want a retreat to a former way of life or even a move to an imagined past (or future) that does not exist. Social movements use a variety of tactics, strategies, and organizational forms to achieve their goals. The civil rights movement, starting in the early 1950s, used collective action during sit-ins and organizational activity to overturn statutes that supported the "separate but equal" principle of segregation. These efforts culminated in the U.S. Supreme Court decision *Brown v. Board of Education* of Topeka, Kansas, which declared the "separate but equal" doctrine unconstitutional (Morris 1999).

Social change movements may be either reformist or radical (Turner and Killian 1988). **Reform movements** seek change through legal or other mainstream political means, typically working *within* existing institutions. **Radical movements** seek broader-based fundamental change in the basic institutions of society. Instead of working within society's institutions, radical social movements tend to work outside of society's institutions. Although most movements are primarily reformist or radical, within a given movement both factions may exist. In the environmental movement, for example, the Sierra Club is a classic reform movement that lobbies within the existing political system to promote legislation protecting the environment. Greenpeace, in contrast, is a more radical group that sometimes uses dramatic tactics to disrupt activities the group finds objectionable, such as the killing of whales.

Reactionary movements are organized to resist change or to reinstate an earlier social order that participants perceive to be better, and they are reacting against contemporary changes in society. The Aryan Nation, a White supremacist coalition, is a reactionary movement that wants to suppress Jews and minorities and institute a "racially pure" decentralized state (Ferber 1998). The militia movement is also a reactionary movement, seeking to resist government authority and reinstate the perceived lost power of White people. Reactionary movements represent an organized backlash against social values and societal changes that participants find deeply objectionable. Rather than adjust to the future, they may instead hark back to some mythical past that their movement ideology defines as ideal.

THINKING SOCIOLOGICALLY

Identify a *social movement* in your community or school that you find interesting. By talking to the movement leaders and participants, and if possible, by examining any written material from the movement, how would you describe this movement in sociological terms? Is it *reform*, *radical*, or *reactionary*? How have the available resources helped or hindered the movement's development? What tactics does the movement use to achieve its goals? How is it connected to other social movements?

Origins of Social Movements

Social movements do not typically develop out of thin air. For a movement to begin, there must be *a preexisting communication network* (Freeman 1983a). The importance of a preexisting communication network is well illustrated by the beginning of the civil rights movement, which most people date to December 1, 1955, the day Rosa Parks was arrested in Montgomery, Alabama, for refusing to give up her seat on a municipal bus to a White man. Although she is typically understood as simply too tired to give up her seat that day, Rosa Parks had been an active member of the movement against segregation in Montgomery. Parks was secretary of the local NAACP chapter that had already been organizing to boycott the Montgomery buses. She was the one chosen to be the plaintiff in a test case against the bus company because she was soft-spoken, middle aged, and a model citizen. NAACP leaders believed her to make a credible and sympathetic plaintiff in

DOING SOCIOLOGICAL RESEARCH

White Man Falling

How can some groups hate and fear Jewish and African American people so much they would organize a social movement to promote this hate? This is what the sociologist Abby Ferber wanted to know when she began the difficult project of studying White supremacist movements. Ferber did her research by analyzing the newsletters and other publications of numerous White supremacist organizations. Reflecting on the difficulty of doing so as a White, educated, Jewish American woman, she says, "Reading white-supremacist literature is a profoundly disturbing experience, and even more difficult if you are one of those targeted for elimination" (Ferber 1999:6).

She found that the development of such movements stems from White groups wanting to maintain clear boundaries around what they perceive as "whiteness." Emphasizing "racial purity," these groups perceive interracial relationships, especially interracial sexuality, as the ultimate threat to White power relations.

White supremacist movements have a long history, which includes the eugenics movement and the Nazi movement in Germany. Now the White supremacist movement includes numerous organizations and branches, some of which are affiliated with far right Christian organizations. The major organizations are the Ku Klux Klan, neo-Nazis, the militia movement, and the Christian Identity Movement—an organization that also links other groups such as Posse Comitatus and Aryan Nations. Some of these organizations are paramilitary organizations; that is, they are heavily armed and believe in war as the way to win their cause.

White supremacist groups have proliferated in recent years, although they are still estimated as a very small percentage of the population. Groups within this movement have a shared ideology. Ferber concludes that we have to understand White supremacy by understanding how those in the mainstream culture define racial and gender dichotomies. By challenging the constructed meaning of race and gender as opposite categories we can debunk the systems of power that are built around such conceptions and, thereby, challenge the grounds on which White supremacist movements are created.

Questions to Consider

1. What racial–ethnic groups (in addition to Asian Americans) have developed a common identity even though there are national, ethnic, or other cultural differences among them? What events have produced this common identity?
Keywords: anti-feminism, white backlash

2. Using one of the groups in the first question as an example, identify any *social movement* that has influenced the formation of a common identity among them. How would you describe this movement in sociological terms?
Keywords: militia movement, neo-Nazism, white supremacist movements

SOURCE: Ferber, Abby. 1998. *White Man Falling: Race, Gender, and White Supremacy.* Lanham, MD: Rowman and Littlefield; Ferber, Abby. 1999. "What White Supremacists Taught a Jewish Scholar About Identity." *The Chronicle of Higher Education* (May 7): B6–B7.

what they had long hoped would be a significant legal challenge to segregation in public transportation.

When Rosa Parks refused to give up her seat, the movement stood ready to mobilize. News of her arrest spread quickly via networks of friends, kin, church, and school organizations. A small group, the Women's Political Council, had previously discussed plans to announce a boycott of the bus system. The arrest of Rosa Parks presented an opportunity for implementation. One member of the Women's Political Council, Jo Ann Gibson Robinson, called a friend who had access to the mimeograph machine at Alabama State College. In the middle of the night, Robinson and two of her students duplicated 52,500 leaflets calling for the boycott and to be distributed among Black neighborhoods (Robinson 1987).

Movements are fueled by the news media, which bring public attention to the movement's cause. With the extraordinarily widespread availability of television and now the Internet, cellular phones, and standard radio transmissions, news of movements around the world spreads quickly. The Internet in particular has become increasingly important for the mobilization of social movements. Communication via the Internet was an important organizing tactic for the diverse groups that participated in the Seattle demonstrations against the World Trade Organization in 1999 and the more recent anti-war demonstrations. The Internet has also been a tool of White supremacist groups for recruiting new members and promoting their views. This is particularly effective because of the appeal of the Internet to young people and the anonymity it can provide.

Celebrities can also advance the cause of social movements by bringing visibility to the movement, although sociologists have found that celebrities typically involve themselves in less controversial movements that already have widespread popular support. The entry of celebrities into social movements can unintentionally hurt a movement's development, because celebrities tend to depoliticize it (Meyer and Gamson 1995). Their endorsement and presence, nonetheless, brings visibility to a movement.

Another cause for a movement to begin must be *a perceived sense of injustice among the potential participants.* The environmental justice movement has emerged largely from grassroots organizations formed in communities where residents have organized to clean up a toxic waste site, close a polluting industry, or protect children from a perceived threat to their health and safety.

A final condition needed to get a movement started is *the ability of groups to mobilize.* **Mobilization** is the process by which social movements and their leaders secure people and resources for the movement. Grievances exist all the time in society, but a movement cannot be started (or continue) if people are not mobilized. For ex-

© Mystic Seaport, Rosenfeld Collection, Mystic, CT

The suffragettes of the early twentieth century, advocating the rights of women to vote, were some of the earliest feminists in the United States.

ample, a person might think he or she has been wronged by a company and might communicate this grievance to networks of friends and associates. Those people might even share the same grievance, but until they are able to mobilize on behalf of their collective sense of a need for change, there will be no social movement.

As movements develop, they quickly establish an organizational structure. The shape of the movement's organization may range from formal bureaucratic structures to decentralized, interpersonal, and egalitarian arrangements. Many movements combine both. Examples of large bureaucracies are the National Organization for Women, the National Association for the Advancement of Colored People (NAACP), Amnesty International, Greenpeace, the Jewish Defense League, and the National Rifle Association. As social movements become institutionalized, they are most likely to take on bureaucratic form. Bureaucratically organized movements affirm Max Weber's prediction that social movements gradually rationalize their structures to efficiently meet the needs of members and the goals of the organization.

Theories of Social Movements

Sociologists have developed several theories to explain the development of social movements, including resource mobilization theory, political process theory, and new social movements theory.

Resource mobilization theory is an explanation of the development of social movements that focuses on how

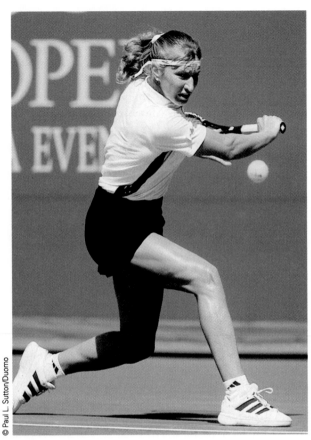

Social change is sometimes apparent by contrasting the social norms of different historical periods.

movements gain momentum by successfully garnering resources, competing with other movements, and mobilizing the resources available to them (Marx and McAdam 1994; McCarthy and Zald 1973). Money, communication technology, special technical or legal knowledge, and people with organizational and leadership skills are all examples of resources that can be put to use in organizing a social movement (Zald and McCarthy 1975). Interpersonal contacts are one of the most important resources a group can mobilize because the contacts provide a continuous supply of new recruits, as well as money, knowledge, skills, and other assistance (Snow et al. 1986). Sometimes social movement organizations acquire the resources of other organizations. Aldon Morris, an African American sociologist, has used resource mobilization theory to explain the development of the civil rights movement. That nationwide movement relied heavily on Black churches and colleges for resources such as money, leadership, meeting space, and administrative support (Morris 1984). In other words, it mobilized existing resources on behalf of its own cause.

Resource mobilization theory, among other things, notes how movements are connected to each other. The gay and lesbian movement has used many strategies used

by the violence against women movement in developing its own campaign to halt hate crimes against gay men and lesbian women (Jenness 1995). This movement has been able to employ some of the same "collective action frames"—a term sociologists use to talk about how movements organize thinking about the issues they address (Gamson 1992; Snow and Benford 1988).

Political process theory posits that movements achieve success by exploiting a combination of internal factors, such as the ability of organizations to mobilize resources, and external factors, such as changes occurring in the society (McAdam 1982). Some structural conditions provide opportunities for collective action. A war, pressure from international parties, demographic shifts, or an economic crisis may create the possibility for those who challenge the social order to mobilize a movement (McAdam 1999). Political process theory explicitly acknowledges the effects that larger social and political processes have on the mobilization of social movements. Large-scale changes such as industrialization, urbanization, or ending repression may provide opportunities for the mobilization of social movements not present previously. Charles Tilly argued that as capitalism developed after popular uprisings in seventeenth-century France, markets emerged in cities for grain from the countryside. To meet the needs of the new markets, grain had to be stored and transported. Rural peasants, angry that their food supply was being transported away, saw the opportunity for collective action and attacked and sabotaged storage and transportation facilities (Tilly 1986).

Political process theory also stresses the vulnerability of the political system to social protest. For example, several groups in Watsonville, California, used the Loma Prieta earthquake in 1989 as an opportunity to protest. Organized Latino groups demanded better low-income housing in that community for approximately a decade (Simile 1995). Among Mexican farm laborers in the valley, there was already a long tradition of labor organizing, including a cannery workers' strike in 1986 (Bardacke 1988; Amott and Matthaei 1996). After the 1989 earthquake, these groups mobilized around the issues of temporary and permanent housing, and the way that aid had been distributed to Latinos. In other words, groups already organized for protest on other issues were ready to squeeze an opportunity out of disaster.

Resource mobilization theory and political process theory are social structural as opposed to individual-level explanations. Other explanations of social movements are more cultural in focus (see Table 16.2). People will not organize within social movements unless they develop a shared definition of the situation that gives meaning to their action, in other words, a culture. Sociologists use the concept of framing to explain this process. **Frames** are specific schemes of interpretation that allow people to perceive, identify, and label events within their lives that can become the basis for collective action (Snow et al. 1986; Snow and Benford 1988; Goffman 1974). The framing process emphasizes that social movements do not emerge unless people have a shared understanding of the causes of a perceived injustice or a shared definition of their opposition. As an example, framing can help you understand the emergence of Ralph Nader and the Green Party. Here the frame is a shared understanding of corporate domination as the major source of political grievance, providing the lens through which people have been mobilized to join this movement.

Frames can also help us to understand how movements change or break down. During the civil rights movement, participants shared a frame, or definition of the situation, that Jim Crow laws were the main obstacle to Black social progress. When this singular frame broke down as more radical forms of protest emerged in the late 1960s and as laws were passed to eliminate old forms of segregation, the movement subsided.

Cultural and social structural explanations of social movements come together in what is called **new social movement theory** that conceptually links culture, ideology, and identity to explain how new identities are

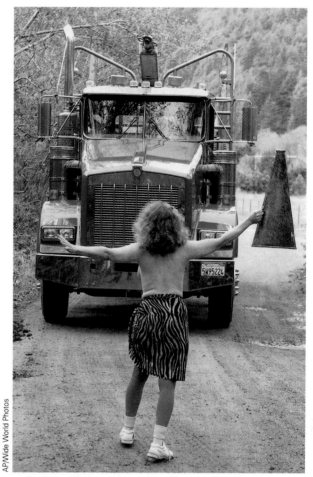

Dramatic tactics are often used by social movements to bring attention to their causes. Here, La Tigresa protests the logging of redwood forests, calling attention to the environmental movement.

forged within social movements. Whereas resource mobilization theory emphasizes the rational basis for social movement organization, new social movement theorists are especially interested in how identity is socially constructed through participation in social movements (Gamson 1995; Larana et al. 1994; Calhoun 1994). This new development in social movement theory links structural explanations with cultural and social-psychological theories, investigating how social movements provide foundations for people to construct new identities (Gamson 1992; Gamson 1995; Morris and Mueller 1992).

Each theoretical viewpoint is helpful in explaining different aspects of how movements organize and how, in some cases, they fail. One team of sociologists has examined the demise of the American Indian Movement (AIM)—a specific organization that was prominent in the Native American liberation movement from about 1968 to 1990. These sociologists argue that AIM ultimately failed to reach its goal of building a pantribal sense of identity among American Indians because they were unable to mobilize resources

TABLE 16.2 Sociological Theories of Social Movements

	Resource Mobilization Theory	Political Process Theory	New Social Movement Theory
How do social movements start?	People garner resources and organize movements by utilizing such things as money, knowledge, skills	Movements exploit social structural opportunities, such as economic crises and wars	New forms of identity are created as people participate in social movements
What does the theory emphasize?	Linkages among groups within a movement	Vulnerability of political system to social protest	Interconnection between social structural and cultural perspectives

in the face of strong government repression. AIM was a threat to both government and corporate interests because of its focus on reclaiming energy resources on lands Native Americans argued were rightfully theirs. The authors conclude that resource mobilization theory, political process theory, and new social movement theory each explain different dimensions of this movement (Stotik et al. 1994). This is a good illustration of how sociological theory can be used to explain the contemporary social movement activity.

▪ *Diversity, Globalization, and Social Change*

As we have noted previously, the term *globalization* refers to the increased interconnectedness and interdependence of different societies around the world. No longer can

the nations of the world be viewed as separate and independent societies. The irresistible trend has been for societies to develop deep dependencies on each other, with interlocking economies and social customs.

Issues of race, class, and gender—in other words, diversity issues—have played a major role in social change, both as causes of change and as social institutions directly affected by change. Tensions and aspirations arising from diversity can produce major changes within the structure and culture of a society. Social change can also affect the relations *between* societies. In this respect, globalization has had dramatic effects on the entire world, and on the question of diversity within as well as between societies.

The most welcome and long-lasting effect of diversity in the global arena is the erosion of the tendency to regard the technology of developing nations as more primitive than the technologies of the dominant Western countries. Although it is certainly true that the technological base in

A SOCIOLOGICAL EYE ON THE MEDIA

The Media as a Source of Social Change

We have all no doubt wondered whether or not the major media of our age (TV, magazines, newspapers, and Internet) not only report significant social events, but whether these media themselves actually become a cause of social change. Does the way in which something gets reported cause significant social, institutional, structural, and psychological changes in a society? Are any resulting changes only *microchanges,* or do *macrochanges* caused by the media sometimes occur?

Media treatment of certain subjects no doubt results in certain kinds of social changes. The TV series special *Roots,* about a Black American slave family's historical beginnings in Africa, a program aired in the mid-1970s, is still talked about and has resulted in long-term changes in how people of all races now study and trace their own family histories. The assassination of President John F. Kennedy over forty years ago on November 22, 1963, was dramatically presented on television on that day and for years after. Probably as a result of

the vividness of the event as displayed in the media, Americans became more aware of their own vulnerabilities and became convinced of the frailties in the security systems that surround even the highest office in the land. Finally, the media image of the two aircraft striking the World Trade Center towers on September 11, 2001, has become firmly ingrained in the memories of virtually the entire U.S. population, causing many to think of our society as irrevocably changed in numerous ways yet to be documented and researched.

many developing nations is far behind that of Western countries, it is now fully recognized that some technologies of the future are being developed overseas. In Singapore and Taiwan, state-of-the-art computer products are prototyped in dust-free clean rooms. Japan was among the pioneers of low-volume, high-efficiency, high-quality steel making. The growing army of software writers in India has become a resource drawn on by the entire world. The distinction between "civilized nation" and "primitive nation" has lost what little meaning it ever had.

Globalization and diversity also mean that, as social movements develop in one part of the world, they are rapidly communicated to other parts of the world. What would the United States be like had the civil rights movement not been inspired by Mohandas Gandhi's liberation movement in India? How would contemporary politics be different had the African National Congress and other movements for the liberation of Black South Africans not dismantled apartheid? Would the world be so conscious of human rights issues in China had they not witnessed the killing of students demonstrating in Tiananmen Square in 1989? Likewise, the civil rights movement in the United States has not only transformed U.S. society, but has since inspired similar movements throughout the world. And the women's movement is now a global movement, although the particular issues for women vary from place to place. Finally, the terrorist attacks on the United States on September 11, 2001, have already been felt in virtually every corner of the globe.

In the future, it is likely that there will be further worldwide reach of movements that originate in a particular country. Modern communication systems, transformed by the increasingly penetrating influence of the Internet, will bring social movements in distant parts of the world closer to home. And as the world becomes increasingly interdependent—through its economies, the environment, and the ease of international travel and communication—social movements in one part of the world are likely to have a broad influence on other parts.

Diversity as a cause of change is exemplified by the effects of immigration into a country and the resultant changes in society. The influx of Latinos into the United States has in a relatively short time resulted in profound cultural changes throughout the nation. From east to west, new tastes can be seen in eating habits, music, language, literature, and many other venues. The changes in the United States brought about by African Americans, beginning as long ago as the slavery era, have been documented throughout this book.

The effects of diversity upon cultural lag are of particular interest. New cultural elements (language, music, technology) introduced to a nation by its racial and ethnic minorities are often adopted by the dominant culture of that nation. The adoption may occur quickly, or even instantly, as when White youths adopt African American dance steps or dress. At other times, it can take decades or longer for particular cultural transfers to take hold. The length of cultural lag may depend upon a number of factors, such as the "foreignness" of the minority culture, the degree to which the minority culture has already been assimilated, the ongoing state of relations between the minority and the dominant group, and a variety of other variables that can be as trivial as the vagaries of fashion or as deep-rooted as historical ethnic animosities.

■ *Chapter Summary*

■ *What is social change and what are its types?*

Social change is that process by which social interaction, the social stratification system, and entire institutions in a society change over time. Social change can take place quickly or it can take longer, sometimes involving *microchanges* (such as a fad that "catches on"), and at other times, *macrochanges* (such as a technological innovation).

■ *How do sociologists explain social change?*

Functionalist theories and *evolutionary theories* predict that societies move or evolve from the structurally simple to the structurally complex. *Unidimensional evolutionary theory* predicts that societies evolve along a path from simpler socially undifferentiated societies to more complex highly differentiated ones. *Multidimensional evolutionary theory* predicts that societies follow not one but several different paths in the process of social change. *Conflict theories* predict that social conflict is an inherent part of any social structure and that conflict between social class strata or racial–ethnic groups can bring about social change. *Cyclical theories,* such as those of Arnold J. Toynbee and Pitrim Sorokin, predict that certain patterns of social structure and culture recur in a society at different times. *Modernization theory* states that global development among societies is a worldwide process not confined to any one society. *World systems theory,* formulated by Immanuel Wallerstein, predicts that societies are members of a worldwide system of inequality that benefits the more technologically developed societies (core nations) at the expense of the less technologically developed countries (noncore or peripheral nations). *Dependency theory* notes that industrialized core nations tend to keep noncore nations economically dependent, and this retards the economic development and upward mobility of the noncore nations.

- **What is modernization and what are its aspects?**

  Modernization is a complex set of processes initiated by industrialization. It results from the decline of small, traditional communities (*gemeinschafts*) and the change to generally larger, more differentiated and impersonal societies (*gesellschafts*). With modernization goes increased bureaucratization of a society. Modernization tends to produce other-directedness, where one person's behavior is strongly guided by the perceived behavior of others; it also tends to produce individual feelings of powerlessness and an increased search for individual identity and one's "true self."

- **What are the causes of social change?**

  Sources of social change include cultural diffusion, social inequalities, demographic changes, age-gender structure, war, terrorism, technological innovation, collective behavior, and social movements.

- **What are collective behavior and social movements?**

  Social movements are organized social groups that have some continuity and promote or resist social change. Social movements start when there is a preexisting communication network, a collective sense of grievance, a precipitating factor initiating the movement, and mobilization of a group of people. *Resource mobilization theory* suggests that social movements develop when people can compete for and gain resources needed for mobilization. *Political process theory* suggests that large-scale social changes, such as industrialization or urbanization, provide the conditions that spawn social movements. *New social movement theory* adds that social movements are places where people construct their identities.

- **What effects do globalization and diversity have on social change?**

  Globalization is the increased economic, political, and social interconnectedness among different societies in the world. Different forms of diversity, such as immigration, and the organizational activities of African Americans, have promoted long-term social change.

■ Key Terms

■ *Researching Society with MicroCase Online*

You can see the results of actual research by using the Wadsworth MicroCase® Online feature available to you. This feature allows you to look at some of the results from national surveys, census data, and some other data sources. You can explore this easy-to-use feature on your own, but try this example. Suppose you wanted to know some social facts, such as:

Has the public's view on legalizing marijuana changed over time, say from about 1970 to 2000?

To answer this question, go to **sociology.wadsworth.com/andersen_taylor/essen3e**, select MicroCase Online from the left navigation bar, and follow the directions there to analyze the following data.

Data File: U.S. Trends 1970–2000

Analysis Task: Historical Trends

Select Variable: Variable 1: GRASS?—%SAYING MARIJUANA SHOULD BE LEGAL

Questions

Now click on "Continue" to get the results, and answer the following questions:

1. In this time period, the percent of the public that favored legalizing marijuana ("grass") increased two times; when was this?

2. In this time period, there was a long decline in the percent of the public that favored legalizing marijuana. What period was this?

3. Do you think these changes reflect major social changes (*macrochanges*) in our society? How so?

■ *The Companion Web Site for* Sociology: The Essentials, *Third Edition*

sociology.wadsworth.com/andersen_taylor/essen3e

Supplement your review of this chapter by going to the companion Web site to take one of the Tutorial Quizzes, use the flash cards to master key terms, and check out the many other study aids you'll find there. You'll also find special features such as GSS Data and Census 2000 information, data and resources at your fingertips to help you with that special project or do some research on your own.

■ *Suggested Readings and Web Resources*

D'Emilio, John. 1998. *Sexual Politics, Sexual Communities: The Making of a Homosexual Minority in the United States, 1940–1970.* Chicago: The University of Chicago Press.
D'Emilio analyzes the growth of the gay and lesbian rights movement, showing how the movement broke down the invisibility of gays and lesbians and brought to the public eye a new analysis of gay identity as socially constructed.

Ferber, Abby. 1998. *White Man Falling: Race, Gender, and White Supremacy.* Lanham, MD: Rowman and Littlefield.
Ferber analyzes the way perceptions of race and gender identity shape the development of White supremacist movements. Her book includes analysis of these movement ideologies and how they are connected to assumptions about race, gender, and sexuality.

Freeman, Jo. 1999. *Waves of Protest: Social Movements Since the Sixties.* Lanham, MD: Rowman and Littlefield.
This anthology analyzes the sociological and political structure of contemporary social movements, looking especially at how movements mobilize, how they are organized, how they use strategies and tactics, how they change consciousness, and how they decline.

Morris, Aldon. 1984. *The Origins of the Civil Rights Movement.* New York: Free Press.
This now classic study shows that the civil rights social movement, as a source of social change in America, was not a unique event but an outgrowth of long-standing struggles of the African American community over the years.

Scott, Catherine V. 1995. *Gender and Development: Rethinking Modernization and Dependency Theory.* Boulder, CO: Lynne Rienner Publishers.
Scott demonstrates that prevailing theories about development, dependency, capitalism, and socialism are anchored in social constructions of gender differences. She critically evaluates modernization theory and dependency theory, plus other theories of social change.

Tierney, Patrick. 2000. *Darkness in El Dorado: How Scientists and Journalists Devastated the Amazon.* New York: W. W. Norton and Co.
Tierney shows how anthropologists and others brought unintended social and cultural change to the Yanomamo tribespeople of the Amazon region in South America. The changes include instruments of war and general social unrest. The book is a major treatise on how scientists studying social change can themselves become the agents (causes) of social change.

Progress of Nations
www.unicef.org/
A report from UNICEF detailing various aspects of worldwide social change.

The World Factbook
www.odci.gov/cia/publications.nsolo/factbook /global.httm#W
A collection of data prepared by the CIA that provides detail on various countries around the world.

Glossary

absolute poverty: the situation in which individuals live on less than $365 a year, or $1.00 a day

achieved status: a status attained by effort

achievement test: test intended to measure what is actually learned rather than potential

adult socialization: the process of learning new roles and expectations in adult life

affirmative action: programs in education and job hiring that recruit minorities over a wide range, but do not use rigid quotas, or, that use admissions slots (quotas) for minorities in education and set aside contracts in the economy

age cohort: an aggregate group of people born during the same time period

age discrimination: different and unequal treatment of people based solely on their age

age prejudice: a negative attitude about an age group that is generalized to all people in that group

age stereotype: preconceived judgments about what different age groups are like

age stratification: the hierarchical ranking of age groups in society

ageism: the institutionalized practice of age prejudice and discrimination

age–sex (or age–gender) pyramid; also population pyramid: a graphic representation of the age and gender structure of a society

alienation: the feeling of powerlessness and separation from one's group or society

altruistic suicide: the type of suicide that can occur when there is excessive regulation of individuals by social forces

anomic suicide: the type of suicide occurring when there are disintegrating forces in the society that make individuals feel lost or alone

anomie: the condition existing when social regulations (norms) in a society break down

anorexia nervosa: a condition characterized by compulsive dieting resulting in self-starvation

anticipatory socialization: the process of learning the expectations associated with a role one expects to enter in the future

antimiscegenation laws: legal policies preventing marriage between members of different racial groups

anti-Semitism: the belief or behavior that defines Jewish people as inferior and that targets them for stereotyping, mistreatment, and acts of hatred

applied sociology: the use of sociological research and theory in solving real human problems

ascribed status: a status determined at birth

assimilation: process by which a minority becomes socially, economically, and culturally absorbed within the dominant society

attribution error: error made in attributing the causes for someone's behavior to their membership in a particular group, such as a racial group

attribution theory: the principle that dispositional attributions are made about others (what the other is "really like") under certain conditions, such as out-group membership

authoritarian personality: a personality characterized by a tendency to rigidly categorize people, and to submit to authority, rigidly conform, and be intolerant of ambiguity

authority: power that is perceived by others as legitimate

automation: the process by which human labor is replaced by machines

autonomous state model: a theoretical model of the state that interprets the state as developing interests of its own, independent of other interests

beliefs: shared ideas held collectively by people within a given culture

bilateral kinship: a kinship system where descent is traced through the father and the mother

biological determinism: explanations that attribute complex social phenomena to physical characteristics

bioterrorism: a form of terrorism involving the dispersion of chemical or biological substances intended to cause widespread disease and death

bureaucracy: a type of formal organization characterized by an authority hierarchy, a clear division of labor, explicit rules, and impersonality

capitalism: an economic system based on the principles of market competition, private property, and the pursuit of profit

caste system: a system of stratification (characterized by low social mobility) in which one's place in the stratification system is determined by birth

census: a count of the entire population of a country

charisma: a quality attributed to individuals believed by their followers to have special powers

charismatic authority: authority derived from the personal appeal of a leader

church: a formal organization that sees itself and is seen by society as a primary and legitimate religious institution.

class: see social class

class consciousness: the awareness that a class structure exists and the feeling of shared identification with others in one's class with whom one perceives common life chances

cognitive ability: the capacity for abstract thinking

cognitive elite: the idea that there is a presumably genetically based elite class in the United States containing those with high IQs, high incomes, and prestigious jobs

cohort (birth cohort): see age cohort

collective behavior: behavior that occurs when the usual conventions are suspended and people collectively establish new norms of behavior in response to an emerging situation

collective consciousness: the body of beliefs that are common to a community or society and that give people a sense of belonging

coming out: the process of defining oneself as gay or lesbian

commodity chain: the network of production and labor processes by which a product becomes a finished commodity. By following the commodity chain, it is evident which countries gain profits and which ones are being exploited

communism: an economic system where the state is the sole owner of the systems of production

comparable worth: the principle of paying women and men equivalent wages for jobs involving similar levels of skill

compulsory heterosexuality: the idea that heterosexual identity is not a choice, but is created by institutions that treat heterosexuality as the only legitimate form of sexual identity

conflict theory: a theoretical perspective that emphasizes the role of power and coercion in producing social order

contact theory: the theory that prejudice will be reduced through social interaction with those of different race or ethnicity but of equal status

content analysis: the analysis of meanings in cultural artifacts like books, songs, and other forms of cultural communication

contingent worker: those who do not hold regular jobs, but whose employment is dependent upon demand

controlled experiment: a method of collecting data that can determine whether something actually causes something else

core countries (core nations): within world systems theory, those nations that are more technologically advanced

correlation: a statistical technique that analyzes patterns of association between pairs of sociological variables

counterculture: subculture created as a reaction against the values of the dominant culture

credentialism: the insistence upon educational credentials only for their own sake

crime: one form of deviance; specifically, behavior that violates criminal laws

criminology: the study of crime from a scientific perspective

crude birthrate: the number of babies born each year for every 1000 members of the population

crude death rate: the number of deaths each year per 1000 members of the population

cult: a religious group devoted to a specific cause or charismatic leader

cultural capital: (also known as *social capital*) cultural resources that are socially designated as being worthy (such as knowledge of elite culture) and that give advantages to groups possessing such capital

cultural diffusion: the transmission of cultural elements from one society or cultural group to another

cultural hegemony: the pervasive and excessive influence of one culture throughout society

cultural pluralism: pattern whereby groups maintain their distinctive culture and history

cultural relativism: the idea that something can be understood and judged only in relationship to the cultural context in which it appears

culture: the complex system of meaning and behavior that defines the way of life for a given group or society

culture lag: the delay in cultural adjustments to changing social conditions

culture of poverty: the argument that poverty is a way of life and, like other cultures, is passed on from generation to generation

culture shock: the feeling of disorientation that can come when one encounters a new or rapidly changed cultural situation

cyberspace interaction: interaction occurring when two or more persons share a virtual reality experience via communication and interaction with each other

cyberterrorism: the use of the computer to commit one or more terrorist acts

cyclical theory: the idea that societies go through a "life cycle," as for example from idealistic through hedonistic culture and back to idealistic

data: the systematic information that sociologists use to investigate research questions

data analysis: the process by which sociologists organize collected data to discover what patterns and uniformities are revealed

debunking: the process of looking behind the facades of everyday life

defensive medicine: practiced by physicians who order extra tests on a patient in an effort to fend off a lawsuit by the patient

deindividuation: the feeling that one's self has merged with a group

deindustrialization: the transition from a predominantly goods-producing economy to one based on the provision of services

democracy: system of government based on the principle of representing all people through the right to vote

demographic transition theory: the theory that societies pass through phases based on economic development, which affects the birth and death rates

demography: the scientific study of population

dependency theory: the global theory maintaining that industrialized nations hold less industrialized nations in a dependency, thus exploitative, relationship that benefits the industrialized nations at the expense of the less industrialized ones

dependent variable: the variable that is a presumed effect

deviance: behavior that is recognized as violating expected rules and norms

deviant career: the sequence of movements people make through a particular system of deviance

deviant community: groups that are organized around particular forms of social deviance

deviant identity: the definition a person has of himself or herself as a deviant

differential association theory: theory that interprets deviance as behavior one learns through interaction with others

discrimination: overt negative and unequal treatment of the members of some social group or stratum solely because of their membership in that group or stratum

disengagement theory: theory predicting that as people age, they gradually withdraw from participation in society and are simultaneously relieved of responsibilities

diversity: the variety of group experiences that result from the social structure of society

division of labor: the systematic interrelation of different tasks that develops in complex societies

domestic colonialism: the view that a minority in a society is forced to be a colonized group within the dominant society

dominant culture: the culture of the most powerful group in society

dominant group: the group that assigns a racial or ethnic group to subordinate status in society

dual labor market theory: the idea that women and men have different earnings because they tend to work in different segments of the labor market

dyad: a group consisting of two people

ecological demography: a field that combines the studies of demography and human ecology

ecological globalization: the worldwide dispersion of problems involving relationships between humans and the physical environment

economic restructuring: contemporary transformations in the basic structure of work that are permanently altering the workplace, including the changing composition of the workplace, deindustrialization, the use of enhanced technology, and the development of a global economy

economy: the system on which the production, distribution, and consumption of goods and services is based

educational attainment: the total years of formal education

ego: the part of the self representing reason and common sense

egoistic suicide: the type of suicide that occurs when people feel totally detached from society

elite deviance: the wrongdoing of wealthy and powerful individuals and organizations

emigration (vs. immigration): migration of people from one society to another (also called out-migration)

emotional labor: work that is explicitly intended to produce a desired state of mind in a client

empirical: refers to something that is based on careful and systematic observation

endogamy: the practice of selecting mates from within one's group

Enlightenment: the period in eighteenth and nineteenth century Europe characterized by faith in the ability of human reason to solve society's problems

environmental racism: the dumping of toxic wastes with disproportionate frequency at or very near areas with high concentrations of minorities

epidemiology: the study of all factors—biological, social, economic, and cultural—that are associated with disease and health

estate system: a system of stratification in which the ownership of property and the exercise of power is monopolized by an elite or noble class, which has total control over societal resources

ethnic group: a social category of people who share a common culture, such as a common language or dialect, a common religion, and common norms, practices, and customs

ethnocentrism: the belief that one's in-group is superior to all out-groups

ethnomethodology: a technique for studying human interaction by deliberately disrupting social norms and observing how individuals attempt to restore normalcy

eugenics: a social movement in the early twentieth century that sought to apply scientific principles of genetic selection to "improve" the offspring of the human race

evaluation research: research assessing the effect of policies and programs

evolutionary theory: the idea that societies go through stages of advancement, as from structurally undifferentiated to more complex and structually differentiated

exchange theory: theory arguing that behavior is determined by the rewards or punishments people receive as they interact with others

exogamy: the practice of selecting mates from outside one's group

expressive needs: needs for intimacy, companionship, and emotional support

extended families: the whole network of parents, children, and other relatives who form a family unit and often reside together

extreme poverty: the situation in which people live on less than $275 a year, or 75 cents a day

false consciousness: the thought resulting from subordinate classes internalizing the view of the dominant class

family: a primary group of people—usually related by ancestry, marriage, or adoption—who form a cooperative economic unit to care for any offspring (and each other) and who are committed to maintaining the group over time

Family and Medical Leave Act (FMLA): federal law requiring employers of a certain size to grant leave to employees for purposes of family care

feminism: a way of thinking and acting that advocates a more just society for women

feminist theory: analyses of women and men in society intended to improve women's lives

feminization of poverty: the process whereby a growing proportion of the poor are women and children

first-world countries: industrialized nations based on a market economy and with democratically elected governments

folkways: the general standards of behavior adhered to by a group

formal organization: a large secondary group organized to accomplish a complex task or set of tasks

forms of racism: types of racism such as traditional, aversive, laissez-faire, color-blind, and institutional

frames: specific schemes of interpretation that allow people to perceive, identify, and label events within their lives that can become the basis for collective action

functionalism: a theoretical perspective that interprets each part of society in terms of how it contributes to the stability of the whole society

game stage: the stage in childhood when children become capable of taking a multitude of roles at the same time

gemeinschaft: German for *community,* a state characterized by a sense of common feeling among the members of a society, including strong personal ties, sturdy primary group memberships, and a sense of personal loyalty to one another; associated with rural life

gender: socially learned expectations and behaviors associated with members of each sex

gender apartheid: the extreme segregation and exclusion of women from public life

gender development index: a measure of women's well-being in different nations, calculated based on gender inequalities in life expectancy, educational attainment, and income

gender gap: gender differences in behavior, such as voting behavior

gender identity: one's definition of self as a woman or man

gender segregation: the distribution of men and women in different jobs in the labor force

gender socialization: the process by which men and women learn the expectations associated with their sex

gender stratification: the hierarchical distribution of social and economic resources according to gender

gendered institution: the idea that whole institutions are patterned by gender

generalization: the ability to make claims that a finding represents something greater than the specific observations on which the finding is based

generalized other: the abstract composite of social roles and social expectations

gesellschaft: German for *society,* a form of social organization characterized by a high division of labor, less prominence of personal ties, the lack of a sense of community among the members, and the absence of a feeling of belonging; associated with urban life

glass ceiling: popular concept referring to the limits that women and minorities experience in job mobility

global culture: the diffusion of a single culture throughout the world

global economy: term used to refer to the fact that all dimensions of the economy now cross national borders

global stratification: the systematic inequalities between and among different groups within nations that result from the differences in wealth, power, and prestige of different societies relative to their position in the international economy

globalization: increased economic, political, and social interconnectedness and interdependence among societies in the world

government: those state institutions that represent the population and make rules that govern the society

greenhouse effect: a rise in the earth's surface temperature caused by heat trapped by excess carbon dioxide in the atmosphere

group: a collection of individuals who interact and communicate, share goals and norms, and who have a subjective awareness as "we"

group size effect: the effect upon the person of groups of varying sizes

groupthink: the tendency for group members to reach a consensus at all costs

hate crime: assaults and other malicious acts (including crimes against property) motivated by various forms of bias, including that based on race, religion, sexual-orientation, ethnic and national origin, or disability

health maintenance organization (HMO): a cooperative of doctors and other medical personnel who provide medical services in exchange for a set membership fee

hermaphroditism: a condition produced when irregularities in chromosome formation or fetal differentiation produces persons with mixed sex characteristics

heterosexism: the institutionalization of heterosexuality as the only socially legitimate sexual orientation

HMO: see Health Maintenance Organization

homophobia: the fear and hatred of homosexuality

human capital theory: a theory that explains differences in wages as the result of differences in the individual characteristics of the workers

human ecology: the study of the interdependence between humans and their physical environment

human ecosystem: any system of interdependent parts that involves human beings in interaction with one another and with the physical environment

human poverty index: a multidimensional measure of poverty meant to indicate the degree of deprivation in four dimensions: life expectancy, education, economic well-being and social inclusion

hypothesis: a statement about what one expects to find in research

id: the part of the personality that includes various impulses and drives, including sexual passions and desires, biological urges, and human instincts

identity: how one defines oneself

ideology: a belief system that tries to explain and justify the status quo

imitation stage: the stage in childhood when children copy the behavior of those around them

immigration (vs. emigration): the migration of people into a society from outside (also called in-migration)

impression management: a process by which people control how others perceive them

income: the amount of money brought into a household from various sources during a given year (wages, investment income, dividends, etc.)

independent variable: a variable which is the presumed cause of a particular result

index crimes: the FBI's tallying of violent crimes of murder, manslaughter, rape, robbery, and aggravated assault, plus property crimes

indicator: something that points to or reflects an abstract concept

infant mortality rate: the number of deaths per year of infants less than one year old, for every thousand live births

inner-directedness: a condition wherein the individual's behavior is guided by internal principles and morals

institutional racism: racism involving notions of racial or ethnic inferiority that have become ingrained into society's institutions

instrumental needs: emotionally neutral, task-oriented (goal-oriented) needs

interest group: a constituency in society organized to promote its own agenda

interlocking directorate: organizational linkages created when the same people sit on the boards of directors of a number of different corporations

issues: problems that affect large numbers of people and have their origins in the institutional arrangements and history of a society

kinship system: the pattern of relationships that define people's family relationships to one another

labeling effect: the effect of track (role) assignment as distinct from the effect of cognitive ability

labeling theory: a theory that interprets the responses of others as most significant in understanding deviant behavior

labor force participation rate: the percentage of those in a given category who are employed

language: a set of symbols and rules that, when put together in a meaningful way, provides a complex communication system

law: the written set of guidelines that define what is right and wrong in society

liberal feminism: a feminist theoretical perspective asserting that the origin of women's inequality is in traditions of the past that pose barriers to women's advancement

life chances: the opportunities that people have in common by virtue of belonging to a particular class

life course: the connection between people's personal attributes, the roles they occupy, the life events they experience, and the social and historical context of these events

life expectancy: the average number of years individuals and the group can expect to live

looking glass self: the idea that people's conception of self arises through reflection about their relationship to others

macroanalysis: analysis of the smallest, most immediately visible parts of social life, such as people interacting

macrochange: gradual transformations in a society that occur on a broad scale and affect many aspects of a society making cost-benefit analysis in deciding, for example, how many children to have

Malthusian theory: after T.R. Malthus, the principle that a population tends to grow faster than the subsistence (food) level needed to sustain it

mass media: channels of communication that are available to very wide segments of the population

master status: some characteristic of a person that overrides all other features of the person's identity

matriarchal religion: a religion based on the centrality of a female goddess or goddesses

matriarchy: a society or group in which women have power over men

matrilineal kinship: kinship systems in which family lineage (or ancestry) is traced through the mother

mean: the sum of a set of values divided by the number of cases from which the values are obtained; an average

mechanical solidarity: unity based on similarity, not difference, of roles

median: the midpoint in a series of values that are arranged in numerical order

median income: the midpoint of all household incomes

Medicaid: a governmental assistance program that provides health care assistance for the poor, including the elderly

medicalization of deviance: explanations of deviant behavior that interpret deviance as the result of individual pathology or sickness

Medicare: a governmental assistance program established in the 1960s to provide health services for older Americans

microanalysis: analysis of the whole of society, how it is organized and how it changes

microchange: subtle alterations in the day-to-day interaction between people, such as a fad "catching on"

minority group: any distinct group in society that shares common group characteristics and is forced to occupy low status in society because of prejudice and discrimination

mobilization: the process by which social movements and their leaders secure people and resources for their movement

modernization: a process of social and cultural change that is initiated by industrialization

and followed by increased social differentiation and division of labor

modernization theory: a view of globalization in which global development is a worldwide process affecting nearly all societies that have been touched by technological change

monogamy: the marriage practice of a sexually exclusive marriage with one spouse at a time

monotheism: the worship of a single god

mores: strict norms that control moral and ethical behavior

multidimensional evolutionary theory: a theory predicting that over time societies follow not one but several evolutionary paths

multinational corporations: companies that draw a large share of their profits from overseas investments and that conduct business across national borders

multiracial feminism: form of feminist theory noting the exclusion of women of color from other forms of theory and centering its analysis in the experiences of all women

neocolonialism: a form of control of the poor countries by the rich countries, but without direct political or military involvement

new international division of labor: the organization of production so that a product is made in several countries

new social movement theory: a theory about social movements linking culture, ideology, and identity conceptually to explain how new identities are forged within social movements

newly industrializing countries (NICs): countries that have shown rapid growth and have emerged as developed countries

norms: the specific cultural expectations for how to act in a given situation

nuclear family: family in which a married couple resides together with their children

object relations theory: a psychoanalytic theory of socialization positing that social relationships children experience early in life determine the development of their personality

occupational prestige: the subjective evaluation people give to jobs as better or worse than others

occupational segregation: a pattern in which different groups of workers are separated into different occupations

organic metaphor: refers to the similarity early sociologists saw between society and other organic systems

organic (contractual) solidarity: unity based on role differentiation, not similarity

other-directedness: a condition wherein the individual's behavior is guided by the behavior of others

out-group homogeneity effect: the tendency for an in-group member to perceive members of any out-group as similar or identical to each other

paralinguistic communication: meaning in communication that is conveyed by pitch loudness, rhythm, emphasis, and frequency

participant observation: a method whereby the sociologist becomes both a participant in

the group being studied and a scientific observer of the group

patriarchy: a society or group where men have power over women

patriarchal religion: religion in which the beliefs and practices of the religion are based on male power and authority

patrilineal kinship: a kinship system that traces descent through the father

peers: those of similar status

peripheral countries: poor countries, largely agricultural, having little power or influence in the world system

personal transformation movements: social movements that aim to change the individual

play stage: the stage in childhood when children begin to take on the roles of significant people in their environment

pluralist model: a theoretical model of power in society as coming from the representation of diverse interests of different groups in society

political action committees (PACs): groups of people who organize to support candidates they feel will represent their views

political process theory: explanation of social movements positing that movements achieve success by exploiting a combination of internal organizational factors as well as external changes in society

polygamy: a marriage practice in which either men or women can have multiple marriage partners

polytheism: the worship of more than one deity

popular culture: the beliefs, practices, and objects that are part of everyday traditions

population: a relatively large collection of people (or other unit) that a researcher studies and about which generalizations are made

population density: the number of people per square mile

population replacement level: a situation in which the birthrate and death rate of a population sustains the population at a steady level

positivism: a system of thought that regards scientific observation to be the highest form of knowledge

postindustrial society: a society organized primarily around the provision of services

postmodernism: a theoretical perspective based in the idea that communication in all its forms is reality, such that understanding society requires studying all forms of communication, including cultural ideas, language, texts, and self-conceptions

poverty line: the figure established by the government to indicate the amount of money needed to support the basic needs of a household

power: a person or group's ability to exercise influence and control over others

power elite model: a theoretical model of power positing a strong link between government and business

predictive validity: the extent to which a test accurately predicts later college grades, or some other criterion such as likelihood of graduating

preindustrial society: one that directly uses, modifies, and/or tills the land as a major means of survival

prejudice: the negative evaluation of a social group, and individuals within that group, based upon conceptions about that social group that are held despite facts that contradict it

prestige: the value with which different groups or people are judged

primary group: a group characterized by intimate, face-to-face interaction and relatively long-lasting relationships

probability: the likelihood that a specific behavior or event will occur

profane: that which is of the everyday, secular world and is specifically not religious

propaganda: information disseminated by a group or organization (such as the state) intended to justify its own power

Protestant ethic: belief that hard work and self-denial lead to salvation

proxemic communication: meaning conveyed by the amount of space between interacting individuals

psychoanalytic theory: a theory of socialization positing that the unconscious mind shapes human behavior

qualitative research: research that is somewhat less structured than quantitative research, but that allows more interpretation and nuance in what people say and do

quantitative research: research that uses numerical analysis

race: a social category, or social construction, that we treat as distinct on the basis of certain characteristics, some biological, that have been assigned social importance in the society

racial formation: process by which groups come to be defined as a "race" through social institutions such as the law and the schools

racial profiling: the use of race alone as the criterion for deciding whether to stop and detain someone on suspicion of their having committed a crime

racialization: a process whereby some social category, such as a social class or nationality, is assigned what are perceived to be race characteristics

racism: the perception and treatment of a racial or ethnic group, or member of that group, as intellectually, socially, and culturally inferior to one's own group

radical feminism: feminist theoretical perspective that interprets patriarchy as the primary cause of women's oppression

radical movements: social movements that seek fundamental change in the structure of society

random sample: a sample that gives everyone in the population an equal chance of being selected

rate: parts per some number (e.g., per 10,000; per 100,000)

rational choice theory: theory positing that choices human beings make are guided by logical reason

rational–legal authority: authority stemming from rules and regulations, typically written down as laws, procedures, or codes of conduct

reactionary movements: social movements organized to resist change or to reinstate an earlier social order that participants perceive to be better

reference group: any group (to which one may or may not belong) used by the individual as a standard for evaluating her or his attitudes, values, and behaviors

reflection hypothesis: the idea that the mass media reflect the values of the general population

reform movements: social movements that seek change through legal or other mainstream political means, by working within existing institutions

relative poverty: a definition of poverty that is set in comparison to a set standard

reliability: the likelihood that a particular measure would produce the same results if the measure were repeated

religion: an institutionalized system of symbols, beliefs, values, and practices by which a group of people interprets and responds to what they feel is sacred and that provides answers to questions of ultimate meaning

religiosity: the intensity and consistency of practice of a person's (or group's) faith

replication study: research that is repeated exactly, but on a different group of people at a different point in time

residential segregation: the spatial separation of racial and ethnic groups in different residential areas

resocialization: the process by which existing social roles are radically altered or replaced

resource mobilization theory: theory of how social movements develop that focuses on how movements gain momentum by successfully garnering organizational resources

revolution: the overthrow of a state or the total transformation of central state institutions

risky shift (also polarization shift): the tendency for group members, after discussion and interaction, to engage in riskier behavior than they would while alone

rite of passage: ceremony or ritual that symbolizes the passage of an individual from one role to another

ritual: symbolic activities that express a group's spiritual convictions

role: the expected behavior associated with a given status in society

role conflict: two or more roles associated with contradictory expectations

role modeling: imitation of the behavior of an admired other

role set: all roles occupied by a person at a given time

role strain: conflicting expectations within the same role

sacred: that which is set apart from ordinary activity, seen as holy, and protected by special rites and rituals

salience principle: categorizing people on the basis of what initially appears prominent about them

sample: any subset of units from a population that a researcher studies

Sapir–Whorf hypothesis: a theory that language determines other aspects of culture since language provides the categories through which social reality is defined and perceived

scapegoat theory: argument that dominant group aggression is directed toward a minority as a substitute for frustration with some other problem

scientific method: the steps in a research process, including observation, hypothesis testing, analysis of data, and generalization

secondary group: a group that is relatively large in number and not as intimate or long in duration as a primary group

second-world countries: socialist countries with state-managed economies and typically without a democratically elected government

sect: groups that have broken off from an established church

secular: the ordinary beliefs of daily life that are specifically not religious

segregation: the spatial and social separation of racial and ethnic groups

self-fulfilling prophecy: the process by which merely applying a label changes behavior and thus tends to justify the label

semiperipheral countries: semi-industrialized countries that represent a kind of middle class within the world system

sex: used to refer to biological identity as male or female

sex ratio (gender ratio): the number of males per 100 females

sexism: an ideology that defines women as different from and inferior to men

sexual harassment: unwanted physical or verbal sexual behavior that occurs in the context of a relationship of unequal power and that is experienced as a threat to the victim's job or educational activities

sexual orientation: the manner in which individuals experience sexual arousal and pleasure

sexual politics: the link feminists argue exists between sexuality and power and between sexuality and race, class, and gender oppression

sexual revolution: the widespread changes in men's and women's roles and a greater public acceptance of sexuality as a normal part of social development

sexual scripts: the ideas taught to us about what is appropriate sexual behavior for a person of our gender

sick role: a pattern of expectations of behaviors defined in society as appropriate for one who is ill

significant others: those with whom we have a close affiliation

social capital: see *cultural capital*

social change: the alteration of social interaction, social institutions, stratification systems, and elements of culture over time

social change movements: movements that aim to change some aspect of society

social class: the social structural hierarchical position groups hold relative to the economic, social, political, and cultural resources of society

social construction perspective: a theoretical perspective that explains sexual identity (or any other identity) as created and learned within a cultural, social, and historical context

social control: the process by which groups and individuals within those groups are brought into conformity with dominant social exceptions

social control agents: those who regulate and administer the response to deviance, such as the police, or mental health workers

social control theory: theory that explains deviance as the result of the weakening of social bonds

social Darwinism: the idea that society evolves to allow the survival of the fittest

social differentiation: the process by which different statuses in any group, organization, or society develop

social epidemiology: the study of the effects of social and cultural factors upon disease and health

social facts: social patterns that are external to individuals

social institution: an established and organized system of social behavior with a recognized purpose

social interaction: behavior between two or more people that is given meaning

social learning theory: a theory of socialization positing that the formation of identity is a learned response to social stimuli

social mobility: a person's movement over time from one class to another

social movements: a group that acts with some continuity and organization to promote or resist change in society

social network: a set of links between individuals or other social units such as groups or organizations

social organization: the order established in social groups

social sanctions: mechanisms of social control that enforce norms

social stratification: a relatively fixed hierarchical arrangement in society by which groups have different access to resources, power, and perceived social worth; a system of structured social inequality

social structure: the patterns of social relationships and social institutions that comprise society

socialism: an economic institution characterized by state ownership and management of the basic industries

socialist feminism: a feminist theoretical perspective that interprets the origins of women's oppression as lying in the system of capitalism

socialization: the process through which people learn the expectations of society

socialization agents: those who pass on social expectations

society: a system of social interaction that includes both culture and social organization

socioeconomic status (SES): a measure of class standing, typically indicated by income, occupational prestige, and educational attainment

sociological imagination: the ability to see the societal patterns that influence individual and group life

sociology: the study of human behavior in society

standardized ability test: tests given to large populations and scored with respect to population averages

state: the organized system of power and authority in society

status: an established position in a social structure that carries with it a degree of prestige

status attainment: the process by which people end up in a given position in the stratification system

status inconsistency: exists when the different statuses occupied by the individual bring with them significantly different amounts of prestige

status set: the complete set of statuses occupied by a person at a given time

stereotype: an oversimplified set of beliefs about the members of a social group or social stratum that is used to categorize individuals of that group

stereotype interchangeability: the principle that negative stereotypes are interchangeable from one racial group (or gender or social class) to another

stigma: an attribute that is socially devalued and discredited

structural strain theory: a theory that interprets deviance as originating in the tensions that exist in society between cultural goals and the means people have to achieve those goals

subculture: the culture of groups whose values and norms of behavior are somewhat different from those of the dominant culture

superego: the dimension of the self representing the standards of society

symbolic interaction theory: a theoretical perspective claiming that people act toward things because of the meaning things have for them

symbols: things or behavior to which people give meaning

taking the role of the other: the process of imagining oneself from the point of view of another

teacher expectancy effect: the effect of the teacher's expectations on the student's actual performance, independent of the student's ability

terrorism: the unlawful use of force or violence against persons or property to intimidate or coerce a government or population in furtherance of political or social objectives

thermal pollution: the heating up of the earth's rivers and lakes as a result of the chemical discharges of heavy industry

third-world countries: countries that are poor, underdeveloped, largely rural, and with high levels of poverty; typically governments in such countries are autocratic dictatorships and wealth is concentrated in the hands of a small elite

total institution: an organization cut off from the rest of society in which individuals who reside there are subject to strict social control

totem: an object or living thing that a religious group regards with special awe and reverence

tracking: grouping, or stratifying, students in school on the basis of ability test scores

traditional authority: authority stemming from long-established patterns that give certain people or groups legitimate power in society

tradition-directedness: conformity to long-standing and time-honored norms and practices

transnational family: families where one parent (or both) live and work in one country while their children remain in their countries of origin

triad: a group consisting of three people

triadic segregation: the tendency for a triad to separate into a dyad and an isolate

troubles: privately felt problems that come from events or feelings in one individual's life

Tuskegee Syphilis Study: an unethical study of about 400 syphilis-infected African American men who went untreated for the disease for 40 years, from 1932 to 1972, even though a cure (penicillin) was discovered in the early 1950s

underemployment: the condition of being employed at a skill level below what would be expected given a person's training, experience, or education

unemployment rate: the percentage of those not working, but officially defined as looking for work

unidimensional evolutionary theory: a theory that predicts that societies over time follow a single path from simple and structurally undifferentiated to more complex and structurally differentiated

urban underclass: a grouping of people, largely minority and poor, who live at the absolute bottom of the socioeconomic ladder in urban areas

urbanization: the process by which a community acquires the characteristics of city life

validity: the degree to which an indicator accurately measures or reflects a concept

values: the abstract standards in a society or group that define ideal principles

variable: something that can have more than one value or score

verstehen: the process of understanding social behavior from the point of view of those engaged in it

vital statistics: information about births, deaths, marriages, and migration

wealth: the monetary value of what someone actually owns, calculated by adding all financial assets (stocks, bonds, property, insurance, value of investments, etc.) and subtracting debts; also called net worth

work: productive human activity that produces something of value, either goods or services

world cities: cities that are closely linked through the system of international commerce

world systems theory: theory that capitalism is a single world economy and that there is a worldwide system of unequal political and economic relationships that benefit the technologically advanced countries at the expense of the less technologically advanced

xenophobia: the fear and hatred of foreigners

References

Aberle, David F., Albert K. Cohen, A. Kingsley Davis, Marion J. Levy, Jr., and Francis X. Sutton. 1950. "The Functional Prerequisites of a Society." *Ethics* 60 (January): 100–111.

Acker, Joan. 1992. "Gendered Institutions: From Sex Roles to Gendered Institutions." *Contemporary Sociology* 21 (September): 565–569.

Acker, Joan, Sandra Morgen, and Lisa Gonzales. 2002. "Welfare Restructuring, Work & Poverty: Policy from Oregon." Working Paper, Eugene, OR: Center for the Study of Women in Society.

Adams, Rebecca. 1995. "The Sociology of Jerry Garcia." *Garcia: Reflections* 1: 16–18.

Adler, N. E., T. Booyce, M. A. Chesney, S. Falkman, and S. L. Syme. 1993. "Socioeconomic Inequalities in Health: No Easy Solution." *Journal of the American Medical Association* 269: 3140–3145.

Adler, Patricia, and Peter Adler. 1998. *Peer Power: Preadolescent Culture and Identity.* New Brunswick, NJ: Rutgers University Press.

Adorno, T. W., Else Frenkel-Brunswik, D. J. Levinson, and R. N. Sanford. 1950. *The Authoritarian Personality.* New York: Harper & Row.

AFL-CIO. 2002. "Executive Pay Watch." Web site: www.afl-cio.org

Alan Guttmacher Institute. 1994. *Sex and America's Teenagers.* New York: Alan Guttmacher Institute.

Alan Guttmacher Institute. 1999a. "Facts in Brief: Contraceptive Use." New York: Alan Guttmacher Institute. http://www. agi-usa.org

Alan Guttmacher Institute. 1999b. "Facts in Brief: Teen Sex and Pregnancy." New York: Alan Guttmacher Institute. http://www.agi-usa.org

Alan Guttmacher Institute. 2002. *Teenagers' Sexual and Reproductive Health.* New York: Alan Guttmacher Institute. Web site: www.agi-usa.org

Alan Guttmacher Institute. 2003. "Trends in Abortion in the United States." New York: Alan Guttmacher Institute. Web site: www.agi-usa.org

Alba, Richard. 1990. *Ethnic Identity: The Transformation of Ethnicity in the Lives of Americans of European Ancestry.* New Haven, CT: Yale University Press.

Alba, Richard, and Gwen Moore. 1982. "Ethnicity in the American Elite." *American Sociological Review* 47 (June): 373–383.

Albas, Daniel, and Cheryl Albas. 1988. "Aces and Bombers: The Post-Exam Impression Management Strategies of Students." *Symbolic Interaction* 11: 289–302.

Albelda, Randy, and Chris Tilly. 1996. "It's a Family Affair: Women, Poverty, and Welfare." Pp. 79–86 in *For Crying Out Loud: Women's Poverty in the United States,* edited by Diane Dujon and Ann Withorn. Boston: South End Press.

Albelda, Randy, and Ann Withorn. 2002. *Lost Ground: Welfare Reform, Poverty and Beyond.* Boston: South End Press.

Albrow, Martin, John Eade, Neil Washbourne, and Jorg Durrschmidt. 1994. "The Impact of Globalization on Sociological Concepts: Community, Culture, and Milieu." *Innovation* 7: 371–389.

Aldag, Ramon J,. and Sally R. Fuller. 1993. "Beyond Fiasco: A Reappraisal of the Groupthink Phenomenon and a New Model of Group Decision Processes." *Psychological Bulletin* 113: 533–552.

Alden, Helena L. 2001. "Gender Role Ideology and Homophobia." Paper presented at the Annual Meetings of the Southern Sociological Society.

Alexander, Jeffrey C., and Paul Colomy (eds.). 1990. *Differentiation Theory and Social Change: Comparative and Historical Perspectives.* New York: Columbia University Press.

Allen, Michael Patrick, and Philip Broyles. 1991. "Campaign Finance Reforms and the Presidential Campaign Contributions of Wealthy Capitalist Families." *Social Science Quarterly* 72 (December): 738–750.

Allen, Paula Gunn. 1986. *The Sacred Hoop: Recovering the Feminine in American Indian Traditions.* Boston: Beacon Press.

Allison, Anne. 1994. *Nightwork: Sexuality, Pleasure, and Corporate Masculinity in a Tokyo Hostess Club.* Chicago: University of Chicago Press.

Allport, Gordon W. 1954. *The Nature of Prejudice.* Reading, MA: Addison-Wesley.

Altemeyer, Bob. 1988. *Enemies of Freedom: Understanding Right-Wing Authoritarianism.* San Francisco: Jossey-Bass.

Altman, Dennis. 2001. *Global Sex.* Chicago: University of Chicago Press.

Altman, Laurence K. 1991. "Many Hispanic Americans Reported in Ill Health and Lacking Insurance." *The New York Times* (January 9): A16.

Altman, Lawrence K. "Progress Reported in SARS Vaccine Effort." *New York Times,* Nov. 9, 2003, p. 13.

American Association of University Women. 1992. *How Schools Shortchange Girls.* Washington, DC: American Association of University Women.

American Association of University Women. 1998. *Gender Gaps: Where Schools Still Fail Our Children.* Washington, DC: American Association of University Women.

American Medical Association. 2003. "Women Physicians by Speciality—2001." Web site: www.ama-assn.org/ama/pub/article/171-198.html

Amott, Teresa L., and Julie A. Matthaei, 1996. *Race, Gender, and Work: A Multicultural History of Women in the United States,* 2nd ed. Boston: South End Press.

Andersen, Margaret L. 2000. *Thinking About Women: Sociological Perspectives on Sex and Gender,* 5th ed. Boston: Allyn and Bacon.

Andersen, Margaret L. 2003. *Thinking About Women: Sociological Perspectives on Sex and Gender.* 6th ed. Boston: Allyn and Bacon.

Andersen, Margaret L., and Patricia Hill Collins (eds.). 2001. *Race, Class, and Gender: An Anthology,* 4th ed. Belmont, CA: Wadsworth.

Andersen, Margaret L., and Patricia Hill Collins. 2004. *Race, Class, and Gender: An Anthology,* 5th ed. Belmont, CA: Wadsworth.

Anderson, Elijah. 1976. *A Place on the Corner.* Chicago: University of Chicago Press.

Anderson, Elijah. 1990. *Streetwise: Race, Class, and Change in an Urban Community.* Chicago: University of Chicago Press.

Anderson, Kristin J., and Campbell Leaper. 1998. "Meta-Analyses of Gender Effects of Conversational Interruption: Who, What, When, Where, and How." *Sex Roles* 39 (August): 225–252.

Andreasse, Arthur. 1997. "Evaluating the 1995 Industry Employment Projections." *Monthly Labor Review* 120 (September): 9–31.

Angotti, Joseph. 1997. "Content Analysis of Local News Programs in Eight U.S. Television Markets." Miami: University of Miami Center for the Advancement of Modern Media.

Ansari, Maboud. 1991. "Iranians in America: Continuity and Change." Pp. 119–142 in *Rethinking Today's Minorities,* edited by Vincent N. Parillo. New York: Greenwood Press.

Apple, Michael W. 1991. "The New Technology: Is It Part of the Solution or Part of the Problem in Education?" *Computers in the Schools* 8 (April–October): 59–81.

Argyle, Michael. 1975. *Bodily Communication.* London: Methuen.

Argyris, Chris. 1990. *Overcoming Organizational Defenses: Facilitating Organizational Learning.* Boston: Allyn and Bacon.

Armas, Genaro C. 2003. "Asian American Divorce Rate Up." *San Francisco Chronicle:* A4.

Asch, Solomon. 1951. "Effects of Group Pressure upon the Modification and Distortion of Judgments." In *Groups, Leadership, and Men,* edited by H. Guetzkow. Pittsburgh: Carnegie Press.

Asch, Solomon. 1955. "Opinions and Social Pressure." *Scientific American* 19 (July): 31–35.

Atchley, Robert C. 2000. *Social Forces and Aging,* 9th ed. Belmont, CA: Wadsworth.

Atkin, Ruth, and Adrienne Rich. 2001. "J.A.P.:-Slapping: The Politics of Scapegoating." Pp. 201–204 in *Race, Class and Gender: An Anthology,* edited by Margaret L. Andersen and Patricia Hill Collins. Belmont, CA: Wadsworth Publishing.

Avakame, Edem F., James J. Fyfe, and Candace McCoy. 1999. "'Did You Call the Police? What Did They Do?' An Empirical Assessment of Black's Theory of Mobilization of Law." *Justice Quarterly* 16 (December): 765–792.

Babbie, Earl. 2001. *The Practice of Social Research,* 9th ed. Belmont, CA: Wadsworth.

Babbie, Earl. 2003. *The Practice of Social Research,* 10th ed. Belmont, CA: Wadsworth.

Baca Zinn, Maxine. 1995. "Chicano Men and Masculinity." Pp. 33–41 in *Men's Lives,* 3rd ed., edited by Michael S. Kimmel and Michael A. Messner. Boston: Allyn and Bacon.

Baca Zinn, Maxine, and D. Stanley Eitzen. 2002. *Diversity in Families.* Boston: Allyn and Bacon.

Baca Zinn, Maxine, and Bonnie Thornton Dill. 1996. "Theorizing Difference from Multiracial Feminism." *Feminist Studies* 22 (Summer): 321–331.

Baca Zinn, Maxine, Pierrette Hondagneu-Sotelo, and Michael A. Messner (eds.). 2000. *Gender Through the Prism of Difference,* 2nd ed. Boston, MA: Allyn and Bacon.

Baker, Douglas D., and David E. Terpstra. 1986. "Locus of Control and Self-Esteem versus Demographic Factors as Predictors of Attitudes Toward Women." *Basic and Applied Social Psychology* 7 (June): 163–172.

Banks, W. Curtis. 1976. "White Preference in Blacks: A Paradigm in Search of a Phenomenon." *Psychological Bulletin* 83: 1179–1186.

Barber, Benjamin R. 1995. *Jihad vs. McWorld: How Globalism and Tribalism Are Reshaping the World.* New York: Random House.

Barber, Jennifer S., and William G. Axinn. 1998. "Gender Role Attitudes and Marriage among Young Women." *Sociological Quarterly* 39 (Winter): 11–31.

Bardacke, Frank. 1988. "Watsonville: A Mexican Community on Strike." Pp. 149–182 in *Reshaping the US Left: Popular Struggles in the 1980s,* edited by Mike Davis and Michael Sprinker. London: Verso.

Barlow, Maude and Tony Clarke. 2002. "Who owns Water?" *The Nation* (Sept. 2/9): 11–14.

Barringer, Felicity. 1993. "Minorities on the Move." *The New York Times* (June 6): Section 4, p. 4.

Basow, Susan A. 1992. *Gender: Stereotypes and Roles,* 3rd ed. Pacific Grove, CA: Brooks/Cole.

Basow, Susan A., and Kelly Johnson. 2000. "Predictors of Homophobia in Female College Students." *Sex Roles* 42 (March): 391–404.

Bates, Eric. 1998. "Private Prisons." *The Nation* (January 5): 11–17.

Baumeister, Roy F. 1998. "The Self." Pp.680–740 in *The Handbook of Social Psychology,* vol. 1, edited by D. T. Gilbert,

S. F. Fiske, and G. Lindzey. New York: McGraw Hill.

Bean, Frank D., and Marta Tienda. 1987. *The Hispanic Population of the United States.* New York: Russell Sage Foundation.

Becker, Elizabeth. 2000. "Harassment in the Military Is Said To Rise." *The New York Times* (March 10): 14.

Becker, Howard S. 1963. *Outsiders: Studies in the Sociology of Deviance.* New York: Free Press.

Becker, Penny Edgell, and Heather Hofmeister. 2001. "Work, Family, and Religious Involvement for Men and Women." *Journal for the Scientific Study of Religion* 40 (December): 707–722.

Becraft, Carolyn H. 1992a. Pp. 8–17 in *Women in the Military,* edited by E. A. Blacksmith. New York: H. W. Wilson.

Beggs, John J. 1995. "The Institutional Environment: Race and Gender Inequality in the U.S. Labor Market." *American Sociological Review* 60 (August): 612–633.

Belknap, Joanne. 2001. *The Invisible Woman.* Belmont, CA: Wadsworth.

Belknap, Joanne, Bonnie S. Fisher, and Francis T. Cullen. 1999. "The Development of a Comprehensive Measure of the Sexual Victimization of College Women." *Violence Against Women* 5 (February): 185–214.

Bell, Daniel. 1973. *The Coming Crisis of Postindustrial Society.* New York: Basic Books.

Bellah, Robert (ed.). 1973. *Emile Durkheim on Morality and Society: Selected Writings.* Chicago: University of Chicago Press.

Belli, M. M. 1954. *Modern Trials.* Indianapolis: Bobbs-Merrill (Supplement, 1966).

Benedict, Ruth. 1934. *Patterns of Culture.* Boston: Houghton Mifflin.

Benin, Mary Holland, and Linda B. Robinson. 1997. "Marital Happiness Across the Family Life Cycle: A Longitudinal Analysis." Paper presented at the American Sociological Association, August.

Ben-Yehuda, Nachman. 1986. "The European Witchcraze of the Fourteenth–Seventeenth Centuries: A Sociologist's Perspective." *American Journal of Sociology* 86: 1–31.

Berberoglu, Berch. 1990. *Political Sociology: A Comparative/Historical Approach.* New York: General Hall.

Berger, Joseph, and Morris Zelditch, Jr. (eds.). 1985. *Status, Rewards, and Influence.* San Francisco: Jossey-Bass.

Berger, Peter L. 1963. *Invitation to Sociology: A Humanistic Perspective.* Garden City, NY: Doubleday Anchor.

Berger, Peter L., and Thomas Luckmann. 1967. *The Social Construction of Reality: A Treatise in the Sociology of Knowledge.* Garden City, NY: Anchor Books.

Berger, Peter L., Brigitte Berger, and Hansfried Kellner. 1974. *The Homeless Mind: Modernization and Consciousness.* New York: Vintage Books.

Berheide, Catherine W. 1992. "Women Still 'Stuck' in Low-Level Jobs." *Women in Public Services: A Bulletin for the Center for Women in Government* 3 (Fall). Albany, NY: Center for Women in Government, The State University of New York.

Berkman, Lisa F., Thomas Glass, Ian Brissette, and Teresa E. Seeman. 2000. "From Social Integration to Health: Durkheim in the New Millenium." *Social Science and Medicine* 51 (September): 843–857.

Bernstein, Nina. 2002. "Side Effect of Welfare Law: The No-Parent Family." *The New York Times,* July 29: A1.

Berscheid, Ellen, and Harry R. Reis. 1998. "Attraction and Class Relationships." Pp. 193–281 in *The Handbook of Social Psychology,* 4th ed., edited by Daniel T. Gilbert, Susan T. Fiske, and Gardner Lindzey. New York: Oxford University Press and McGraw-Hill.

Best, Joel. 1999. *Random Violence: How We Talk About New Crimes and New Victims.* Berkeley: University of California Press.

Best, Joel. 2001. *Damned Lies and Statistics: Untangling Numbers from the Media, Politicians, and Activists.* Berkeley: University of California Press.

Bezilla, Robert. 1990. *Religion in America 1990: Approaching the Year 2000.* Princeton, NJ: Princeton Religious Research Center.

Binns, Allison. 2003. *White Gold, Weed, and Blow: The Drug Trades of Afghanistan, Columbia, and Mexico in Comparative Historical Perspective.* Senior Thesis, Princeton University, Princeton, NJ.

Blackwell, James. 1991. *The Black Community: Diversity and Unity,* 3rd ed. New York: HarperCollins.

Blake, C. Fred. 1994. "Footbinding in Neo-Confucian China and the Appropriation of Female Labor." *Signs* 19 (Spring): 676–712.

Blalock, Hubert M., Jr. 1982. *Race and Ethnic Relations.* Englewood Cliffs, NJ: Prentice Hall.

Blalock, Hubert M., Jr. 1991. *Understanding Social Inequality.* Newbury Park, CA: Sage.

Blankenship, Kim. 1993. "Bringing Gender and Race In: U.S. Employment Discrimination Policy." *Gender & Society* 7 (June): 204–226.

Blaskovitch, J. 1973. "Blackjack and the Risky Shift." *Sociometry* 36 (March): 42ff.

Blassingame, John. 1973. *The Slave Community: Plantation Life in the Antebellum South.* New York: Oxford University Press.

Blau, Peter M. 1986. *Exchange and Power in Social Life,* revised ed. New Brunswick, NJ: Transaction.

Blau, Peter M., and Marshall W. Meyer. 1987. *Bureaucracy in Modern Society,* 3rd ed. New York: Random House.

Blau, Peter M., and Otis Dudley Duncan. 1967. *The American Occupational Structure.* New York: Wiley.

Blau, Peter M., and W. Richard Scott. 1974. *On the Nature of Organizations.* New York: Wiley.

Blauner, Robert. 1969. "Internal Colonialism and Ghetto Revolt." *Social Problems* 16 (Spring): 393–408.

Blauner, Robert. 1972. *Racial Oppression in America.* New York: Harper & Row.

Blee, Kathleen M., and Ann R. Tickamyer. 1995. "Racial Differences in Men's Attitudes about Women's Gender Roles." *Journal of Marriage and the Family* 57 (February): 21–30.

Blinde, Elaine M., and Diane E. Taub. 1992a. "Homophobia and Women's Sport: The Disempowerment of Athletes." *Sociological Focus* 25 (May): 151–166.

Blinde, Elaine M., Diane E. Taub, and Lingling Han. 1993. "Sport Participation and Women's Personal Empowerment: Experiences of the College Athlete." *Journal of Sport and Social Issues* 17 (April): 47–60.

Blinde, Elaine M., Diane E. Taub, and Lingling Han. 1994. "Sport as a Site for Women's Group and Social Empowerment: Perspectives from the College Athlete." *Sociology of Sport Journal* 11 (March): 51–59.

Block, Alan. 1991. *Perspectives on Organizing Crime.* The Netherlands: Kluwer.

Block, Alan, and Frank R. Scarpitti. 1993. *Poisoning for Profit: The Mafia and Toxic Waste in America.* New York: Morrow.

Blum, Linda. 1991. *Between Feminism and Labor: The Significance of the Comparable Worth Movement.* Berkeley: University of California Press.

Blumer, Herbert, 1969. *Studies in Symbolic Interaction.* Englewood Cliffs, NJ: Prentice Hall.

Bobo, Lawrence, and James R. Kluegel. 1991. "Modern American Prejudice: Stereotypes, Social Distance, and Perceptions of Discrimination Toward Blacks, Hispanics, and Asians." Paper presented before the American Sociological Association, Cincinnati, Ohio.

Bobo, L., J. R. Kluegel, and R. A. Smith. 1997. "Laissez-Faire Racism: The Crystallization of a 'Kinder, Gentler' Anti-Black Ideology." Pp. 93–120 in S. A. Tuch and J. K. Martin, eds., *Racial Attitudes in the 1990s: Continuity and Change.* Greenwook, CT: Praeger.

Bobo, L., and R. A. Smith. 1998. "From Jim Crow Racism and Laissez-Faire Racism: An Essay on the Transformation or Racial Attitudes in America." Pp. 182–220 in W. Katkin, N. Landsmand, and A. Tyree, eds., *Beyond Pluralism: Essays on the Conception of Groups and Group Identities in America.* Urbana, IL: University of Illinois Press.

Bobo, Lawrence D. 1999. "Prejudice as Group Position: Microfoundations of a Sociological Approach to Racism and Race Relations." *Journal of Social Issues* 55 (3): 445–492.

Boer, J. Tom, Manuel Pastor, Jr., James L. Sadd, and Lori D. Snyder. 1997. "Is There Environmental Racism? The Demographics of Hazardous Waste in Los Angeles County." *Social Science Quarterly* 78 (December): 793–810.

Boeringer, Scott B. 1999. "Associations of Rape Supportive Attitudes with Fraternal and Athletic Participation." *Violence against Women* 5 (January): 81–90.

Boggs, Vernon W. 1992. *Salsiology: Afro-Cuban Music and the Evolution of Salsa in New York City.* Westport, CT: Greenwood Press.

Bonacich, Edna. 1972. "A Theory of Ethnic Antagonism: The Split Labor Market." *American Sociological Review* 37 (October): 547–559.

Bonacich, Edna, and Richard P. Applebaum. 2000. *Behind the Label: Inequality in the Los Angeles Apparel Industry.* Berkeley: University of California Press.

Bonilla-Silva, Eduardo.1997. "Rethinking Racism: Toward a Structural Interpretation." *American Sociological Review* 62 (June): 465–480.

Bonilla-Silva, Eduardo. 2001. *White Supremacy and Racism in the Post-Civil Rights Era.* Boulder, CO: Lynne Rienner.

Bontemps, Arna (ed.). 1972. *The Harlem Renaissance Remembered.* New York: Dodd, Mead.

Booth, Bradford, William W. Falk, David R. Segal, and Mady Wechsler Segal. 2000. "The Impact of Military Presence in Local Labor Markets and the Employment of Women." *Gender & Society* 14 (April): 318–332.

Bord, Richard J., and Robert E. O'Connor. 1997. "The Gender Gap in Environmental Attitudes: The Case of Perceived Vulnerability to Risk." *Social Science Quarterly* 78 (December): 831–840.

Bose, Christine E., and Peter H. Rossi. 1983. "Gender and Jobs: Prestige Standings of Occupations as Affected by Gender." *American Sociological Review* 48 (June): 316–330.

Bourdieu, Pierre. 1984. *Distinction: A Social Critique of the Judgement of Taste,* translated by Richard Nice. Cambridge, MA: Harvard University Press.

Bowditch, Christine. 1993. "Getting Rid of Troublemakers: High School Disciplinary Procedures and the Production of Dropouts." *Social Problems* 40 (November): 493–510.

Bowles, Samuel, and Herbert Gintis. 1976. *Schooling in Capitalist America.* New York: Basic Books.

Bowman, Charles. 1999. "BLS Projections to 2008: A Summary." *Monthly Labor Review* 122: 3–4.

Braddock, Jomills H. 1988. *National Education Longitudinal Study of 1988.* Washington, DC: U.S. Department of Education, National Center for Educational Statistics.

Brake, Mike. 1985. *Comparative Youth Culture: The Sociology of Youth Subcultures in America, Britain, and Canada.* Boston: Routledge & Kegan Paul.

Branch, Taylor. 1988. *Parting the Waters: America in the King Years, 1954–1963.* New York: Simon & Schuster.

Braverman, Harry. 1974. *Labor and Monopoly Capital.* New York: Monthly Review Press.

Brehm, S. S., R. S. Miller, D. Perlman, and S. M. Campbell. 2002. *Intimate Relationships.* 3rd ed. Boston: McGraw-Hill.

Brener, Nancy D., Thomas R. Simon, Etienne G. Krug, and Richard Lowry. 1999. "Recent Trends in Violence-Related Behaviors among High School Students in the United States." *JAMA* 282 (August 4): 440–446.

Bridges, George, and Robert Crutchfield. 1988. "Law, Social Standing and Racial Disparities in Imprisonment." *Social Forces* 66 (June): 699–724.

Brines, Julie, and Kara Joyner. 1999. "The Ties That Bind: Principles of Cohesion in Cohabitation and Marriage." *American-Sociological Review* 64 (June): 333–355.

Britt, Chester L. 1994. "Crime and Unemployment among Youths in the United States, 1958–1990: A Time Series Analysis." *American Journal of Economics and Sociology* 53 (January): 99–109.

Brooks, Clem. 2002. "Religious Influence and the Politics of Family Decline Concern: Trends, Sources, and U.S. Political Behavior." *American Sociological Review* 67 (April): 191–211.

Brooks-Gunn, Jeanne, Wen-Jui Han, and Jane Waldfogel. 2002. "Maternal Employment and Child Cognitive Outcomes in the First Three Years of Life: The NICHD Study of Early Child Care." *Child Development* 73 (July–August): 1052–1072.

Brown, Clare. 2000. "'Judge Me All You Want': Cigarette Smoking and the Stigmatization of Smoking." Paper presented at the Annual Meetings of the Society for the Study of Social Problems.

Brown, Cynthia. 1993. "The Vanished Native Americans." *The Nation* 257 (October 11): 384–389.

Brown, Elaine. 1992. *A Taste of Power: A Black Woman's Story.* Pantheon: New York.

Brown, Lester R., Christopher Flavin, and Hilary French. 2000. *State of the World 2000: World-Watch Institute Report on Progress Toward A Sustainable Society.* New York: W. W. Norton and Co.

Brown, Roger. 1986. *Social Psychology,* 2nd ed. New York: Free Press.

Brown, Ryan P., and Robert A. Josephs. 1999. "A Burden of Proof: Stereotype Relevance and Gender Differences in Math Performance." *Journal of Personality and Social Psychology* 76 (No. 2): 246–257.

Browne, Irene, ed. 1999. *Latinas and African American Women at Work: Race, Gender, and Economic Inequality.* New York: Russell Sage Foundation.

Bryant, Susan Leslie, and Lillian M. Range. 1995. "Suicidality in College Women Who Were Sexually and Physically Abused and Physically Punished by Parents." *Violence and Victims* 10 (Fall): 195–201.

Budig, Michelle J. 2002. "Male Advantage and the Gender Composition of Jobs: Who Rides the Glass Escalator?" *Social Problems* 49 (May): 257–277.

Bullard, Robert D. 1994a. *Dumping in Dixie: Race, Class, and Environmental Quality.* Boulder, CO: Westview.

Bullard, Robert D. 1994b. *Unequal Protection: Environmental Justice and Communities of Color.* San Francisco: Sierra Club Books.

Burgess, Samuel H. 2001. "Gender Role Ideology and Anti-Gay Opinion in the United States." Paper presented at the Annual Meetings of the Southern Sociological Association.

Burris, Val. 2000. "The Myth of Old Money Liberalism: The Politics of the *Forbes 400* Richest Americans." *Social Problems* 47 (Summer): 360–378.

Burt, Cyril. 1966. "The Genetic Determination of Differences in Intelligence: A Study of Monozygotic Twins Reared Together and Apart." *British Journal of Psychology* 57: 137–153.

Butsch, Richard. 1992. "Class and Gender in Four Decades of Television Situation Comedy: Plus ça Change . . ." *Critical Studies in Mass Communication* 9: 387–399.

Buunk, Bram and Ralph B. Hupka. 1987. "Cross-Cultural Differences in the Elicitation of Sexual Jealousy." *Journal of Sex Research* 23 (February): 12–22.

Calhoun, Craig. 1994. *Social Theory and the Politics of Identity.* Cambridge, MA: Blackwell.

Cameron, Deborah. 1998. "Gender, Language, and Discourse: A Review Essay." *Signs* 23 (Summer): 945–974.

Campbell, Anne. 1987. "Self-Definition by Rejection: The Case of Gang Girls." *Social Problems* 34 (December): 451–466.

Campbell, S. 1972. "The Multiple Function of the Criminal Defense *voir dire* in Texas." *American Journal of Criminal Law* 1: 255–282.

Campenni, C. Estelle. 1999. "Gender Stereotyping of Children's Toys: A Comparison of Parents and Nonparents." *Sex Roles* 40 (January): 121–138.

Cantor, Joanne. 2000. "Media Violence." *Journal of Adolescent Health* 27 (August): 30–34.

Caplow, Theodore. 1991. *American Social Trends.* New York: Harcourt Brace Jovanovich.

Cardenas, Jose A. 1996. "Ending the Crisis in the K–12 System." Pp. 51–70 in *Educating a New Majority: Transforming America's Educational System for Diversity,* edited by Laura I. Rendon and Richard O. Hope. San Francisco: Jossey-Bass.

Carmichael, Stokely, and Charles V. Hamilton. 1967. *Black Power: The Politics of Liberation in America.* New York: Vintage.

Carnoy, Martin, Manuel Castells, Stephen S. Cohen, and Fernando Henrique Cardoso. 1993. *The New Global Economy in the Information Age.* University Park, PA: The Pennsylvania State University Press.

Carr, C. Lynn. 1998. "Tomboy Resistance and Conformity: Agency in Social Psychological Gender Theory." *Gender & Society* 12 (October): 528–553.

Carroll, J.B., 1956. *Language, Thought, and Reality: Selected Writings of Benjamin Lee Whorf.* Cambridge, MA: M.I.T. Press.

Carson, Rachel. 1962. *The Silent Spring.* New York: Knopf.

Carter, Timothy S. 1999. "Ascent of the Corporate Model in Environmental-Organized Crime." *Crime, Law and Social Change* 21: 1–30.

Cashmore, Ellis. 1991. "Black Cops Inc." Pp. 87–108 in *Out of Order: Policing Black People,* edited by Ellis Cashmore and Eugene McLaughlin. New York: Routledge.

Cassen, Robert. 1994. "Population and Development: Old Debates, New Conclusions." *U.S.–Third World Policy Perspectives* 19: 282.

Cassidy, J., and P. R. Shaver, eds. 1999. *Handbook of Attachment: Theory, Research, and Critical Applications.* New York: Guilford.

Cassidy, Linda, and Rose Marie Hurrell. 1995. "The Influence of Victim's Attire on Adolescents' Judgments of Date Rape." *Adolescence* 30 (Summer): 319–323.

Cassidy, Margaret L., and Bruce O. Warren. 1997. "Family Employment Status and Gender Role Attitudes: A Comparison of Women and Men College Graduates." *Gender & Society* 10 (June): 312–329.

Catanzarite, Lisa, and Vilma Ortiz. 1996. "Family Matters, Work Matters? Poverty among Women of Color and White Women." Pp. 121–140 in *For Crying Out Loud: Women's Poverty in the United States,* edited by Diane Dujon and Ann Withorn. Boston: South End Press.

Cavalier, Elizabeth. 2003. "'I Wear Dresses, I Wear Muscles': Media Images of Women Soccer Players." Paper presented at the Annual Meetings of the Southern Sociological Society, New Orleans.

Centeno, Miguel A. and Eszter Hargittai. 2003. "Defining A Global Geography." *The American Behavioral Scientist* 44 (no. 10).

Centers, Richard. 1949. *The Psychology of Social Classes.* Princeton, NJ: Princeton University Press.

Chafetz, Janet. 1984. *Sex and Advantage.* Totowa, NJ: Rowman and Allanheld.

Chambliss, William J., and Howard F. Taylor. 1989. *Bias in the New Jersey Courts.* Trenton, NJ: Administrative Office of the Courts.

Chang, Jung. 1991. *Wild Swans: Three Daughters of China.* New York: Simon & Schuster.

Chen, Elsa, Y. F. 1991. "Conflict Between Korean Greengrocers and Black Americans." Unpublished senior thesis, Princeton University.

Chernin, Kim. 1991. *The Obsession.* New York: Harper Colophon.

Chesney-Lind, Meda. 1992. "Women's Prisons: Putting the Brakes on the Building Binge." *Corrections Today* 54 (August): 30–34.

Chia, Rosina C., Jamie L. Moore, Ka Nei Lam, C. J. Chuang, and B. S. Cheng. 1994. "Cultural Differences in Gender Role Attitudes between Chinese and American Students." *Sex Roles* 31 (July): 23–30.

Chipman, Susan. 1991. "Word Problems: Where Bias Creeps In." Unpublished Research Report, Office of Naval Research, Arlington, VA.

Chipuer, H. M., M. J. Rovine, and R. Plomin. 1990. "LISREL Modeling: Genetic and Environmental Influences on IQ Revisited." *Intelligence* 14: 11–29.

Chiricos, Ted, Sarah Eschholz, and Marc Gertz. 1997. "Crime, News and Fear of Crime: Toward an Identification of Audience Effects." *Social Problems* 44 (August): 342–357.

Chodorow, Nancy. 1978. *The Reproduction of Mothering: Psychoanalysis and the Study of Gender.* Berkeley: University of California Press.

Chodorow, Nancy. 1994. *Femininities, Masculinities, Sexualities: Freud and Beyond.* Lexington: University of Kentucky Press.

Chon, Jordan. 2001. Personal comment, University of Delaware, Spring.

Chow, Esther Ngan-Ling, Doris Wilkinson, and Maxine Baca Zinn (eds.) 1996. *Race, Class, & Gender: Common Bonds, Different Voices.* Thousand Oaks, CA: Sage.

Churchill, Ward. 1992. *Struggle for the Land.* Toronto: Between the Lines.

Cialdini, R. B. 1993. *Influence: Science and Practice,* 3rd ed. New York: Harper Collins.

Cicourel, Aaron V. 1968. *The Social Organization of Juvenile Justice.* New York: John Wiley and Sons.

Clark, Kenneth B., and Mamie P. Clark. 1947. "Racial Identification and Preference in Negro Children." Pp. 602–611 in *Readings in Social Psychology,* edited by T. M. Newcomb and E. L. Hartley. New York: Holt.

Clawson, Dan, and Naomi Gerstl. 2002. "Caring for Our Young: Child Care in Europe and the United States." *Contexts* 1 (Fall–Winter): 28–35.

Clifford, N. M., and Elaine Walster. 1973. "Research Note: The Effects of Physical Attractiveness on Teacher Expectations." *Sociology of Education* 46: 248–258.

Coale, Ansley. 1974. "The History of the Human Population." *Scientific American* 231 (3): 40–51.

Coale, Ansley. 1986. "Population Trends and Economic Development." Pp. 96–104 in *World Population and the U.S. Population Policy: The Choice Ahead,* edited by J. Menken. New York: W.W. Norton.

Cohen, Bernard P., and Xueguang Zhou. 1991. "Status Processes in Enduring Work Groups." *American Sociological Review* 56 (April): 179–188.

Cohen, Eugene N., and Edwin Eames. 1985. *Cultural Anthropology.* Boston: Little, Brown.

Cohen, Philip N. 1999. "Racial–Ethnic and Gender Differences in Returns to Cohabitation and Marriage: Evidence from the Current Population Survey." Paper presented at Annual Meeting of the Population Association of America. Available at: **www.census.gov**

Collins, Patricia Hill. 1987. "The Meaning of Motherhood in Black Culture and Black Mother–Daughter Relationships." *Signs* 4 (Fall): 3–10.

Collins, Patricia Hill. 1990. *Black Feminist Theory: Knowledge, Consciousness and the Politics of Empowerment.* Cambridge, MA: Unwin Hyman.

Collins, Patricia Hill. 1998. *Fighting Words: Black Women and the Search for Justice.* Minneapolis, MN: University of Minnesota Press.

Collins, Patricia Hill, Lionel A. Maldonado, Dana Y. Takagi, Barrie Thorne, Lynn Weber, and Howard Winant. 1995. "On West and Fenstermaker's 'Doing Difference.'" *Gender & Society* 9 (August): 491–505.

Collins, Randall. 1979. *The Credential Society.* New York: Academic Press.

Collins, Randall. 1988. *Theoretical Sociology.* San Diego: Harcourt Brace Jovanovich.

Collins, Randall. 1994. *Four Sociological Traditions.* New York: Oxford.

Collins, Randall, and Michael Makowsky. 1972. *The Discovery of Society.* New York: Random House.

Collins, Sharon M. 1983. "The Making of the Black Middle Class." *Social Problems* 30 (April): 369–382.

Collins, Sharon M. 1989. "The Marginalization of Black Executives." *Social Problems* 36: 317–331.

Collins-Lowry, Sharon M. 1997. *Black Corporate Executives: The Making and Breaking of a Black Middle Class.* Philadelphia: Temple University Press.

Coltrane, Scott, and Melinda Messineo. 2000. "The Perpetuation of Subtle Prejudice: Race and Gender Imagery in 1990s Television Advertising." *Sex Roles* 42 (March): 363–389.

Conley, Dalton. 1999. *Being Black, Living in the Red: Race, Wealth, and Social Policy in America.* Berkeley: University of California Press.

Connell, R. W. 1992. "A Very Straight Gay: Masculinity, Homosexual Experience, and the Dynamics of Gender." *American Sociological Review* 57 (December): 735–751.

Conrad, Peter, and Joseph W. Schneider. 1992. *Deviance and Medicalization: From Badness to Sickness,* expanded edition. Philadelphia: Temple University Press.

Cook, Christopher D. 2000. "Temps Demand a New Deal." *The Nation* (March 27): 13–19.

Cook, Karen S., Karen A. Hegtvedt, and Toshio Yamagishi. 1988. "Structural Inequality, Legitimation, and Reactions to Inequality in Exchange Networks." Pp. 291–308 in *Status Generalization: New Theory and Research,* edited by M. Webster, Jr., and M. Foschi. Stanford, CA: Stanford University Press.

Cook, S. W. 1988. "The 1954 Social Science Statement and School Desegregation: A Reply to Gerard." Pp. 237–256 in *Eliminating Racism: Profiles in Controversy,* edited by D. A. Taylor. New York: Plenum.

Cooke, Miriam, and Angela Woollacott (eds.). 1993. *Gendering War Talk.* Princeton, NJ: Princeton University Press.

Cookson, Peter W., Jr., and Caroline Hodges Persell. 1985. *Preparing for Power: America's Elite Boarding Schools.* New York: Basic Books.

Cooley, Charles Horton. 1902. *Human Nature and Social Order.* New York: Scribner's.

Cooley, Charles Horton. 1967 [1909]. *Social Organization.* New York: Schocken Books.

Cooper, Alvin, and Coralie R. Scherer. 1999. "Sexuality on the Internet: From Sexual Exploration to Pathological Expression." *Professional Psychology Research and Practice* 30. World Wide Web siste: **http://www.sex-centre.com/Internetsex_Folder/MSNBC_Study_pp.htm**

Coren, Stanley, and P. L. Hewitt. 1999. "Sex Differences in Elderly Suicide Rates: Some Predictive Factors." *Aging and Mental Health* 3 (May): 112–118.

Cortese, Anthony J. 1999. *Provocateur: Images of Women and Minorities in Advertising.* Lanham, MD: Rowman and Littlefield.

Cortina, Lilia M., Suzanna Swan, Louise F. Fitzgerald, and Craig Walo. 1998. "Sexual Harassment and Assault: Chilling the Climate for Women in Academia." *Psychology of Women Quarterly* 22 (September): 419–441.

Coser, Lewis. 1977. *Masters of Sociological Thought.* New York: Harcourt Brace Jovanovich.

Crandall, C. S., S. D'Anello, N. Sakalli, E. Lazarus, G. Wieczorkowska, and N. T. Feather. 2001. An Attribution-Value Model of Prejudice: Anti-Fat Attitudes in Six Nations." *Personality and Social Psychology Bulletin* 27: 30–37.

Crane, Diana (ed.). 1994. *The Sociology of Culture: Emerging Theoretical Perspectives.* Cambridge, England: Blackwell.

Crawford, Mary. 1995. *Talking Difference: On Gender and Language.* Thousand Oaks: Sage.

Crowley, Sue M. "Men's Self-Perceived Adequacy as the Family Breadwinner: Implications for Their Psychological, Marital, and Family Well-Being." *Journal of Family and Economic Issues* 19 (Spring): 7–23.

Csikszentmihalyi, Mihaly, and Barbara Schneider. 2000. *Becoming Adult: How Teenagers Prepare for the World of Work.* New York: Basic Books.

Currie, Dawn. 1997. "Decoding Femininity: Advertisements and Their Teenage Readers." *Gender & Society* 11 (August): 453–477.

Curtiss, Susan. 1977. *Genie: A Psycholinguistic Study of a Modern-Day "Wild Child."* New York: Academic Press.

D'Alessio, Stewart J., and Lisa Stolzenberg. 2003. "Race and the Probability of Arrest." *Social Forces* 81 (June): 1381–1397.

D'Emilio, John. 1998. *Sexual Politics, Sexual Communities: The Making of a Homosexual Minority in the United States, 1940–1970,* rev. edition. Chicago: University of Chicago Press.

Dahlhamer, James, and Joanne M. Nigg. 1993. "An Empirical Investigation of Rumoring: Anticipating Disaster under Conditions of Uncertainty." Paper presented at the Annual Meetings of the Southern Sociological Society, Chattanooga, TN, April.

Dahrendorf, Rolf. 1959. *Class and Class Conflict in Industrial Society.* Stanford, CA: Stanford University Press.

Dalaker, Joseph, and Bernadette D. Proctor. 2000. *Poverty in the United States 1999.* Washington, DC: U.S. Government Printing Office.

Darcy, R., Susan Welch, and Janet Clark. 1994. *Women, Elections, and Representation.* Lincoln, NE: University of Nebraska Press.

Darley, John M., and R. H. Fazio. 1980. "Expectancy Confirmation Processes Arising in the Social Interaction Sequence." *American Psychologist* 35: 867–881.

Davies-Netzley, Sally Ann. 1998. "Women above the Glass Ceiling: Perceptions on Corporate Mobility and Strategies for Success." *Gender & Society* 12 (June): 339–355.

Davis, Angela. 1981. *Women, Race, and Class.* New York: Random House.

Davis, James A., and Tom Smith. 1984. *General Social Survey Cumulative File, 1972–1982.* Ann Arbor, MI: Inter-University Consortium for Political and Social Research.

Davis, Kingsley. 1945. "The World Demographic Transition." *Annals of the American Academy of Political and Social Sciences* 237: 1–11.

Davis, Kingsley, and Wilbert E. Moore. 1945. "Some Principles of Stratification." *American Sociological Review* 10 (April): 242–247.

Deegan, Mary Jo. 1988. "W. E. B. Du Bois and the Women of Hull-House, 1895–1899." *The American Sociologist* 19 (Winter): 301–311.

Deegan, Mary Jo. 1990. *Jane Addams and the Men of the Chicago School, 1892–1918.* New Brunswick, NJ: Transaction Books.

DeFleur, Lois. 1975. "Biasing Influences on Drug Arrest Records: Implications for Deviance Research." *American Sociological Review* 40 (March): 88–103.

Dellinger, Kristen, and Christine L. Williams. 1997. "Makeup at Work: Negotiating Appearance Rules in the Workplace." *Gender & Society* 11 (April): 151–177.

D'Emilio, John. 1998. *Sexual Politics, Sexual Communities: The Making of a Homosexual Minority in the United States, 1940–1970,* rev. edition. Chicago: University of Chicago Press.

Demeny, Paul. 1991. "Tradeoffs between Human Numbers and Material Standards of Living." Pp. 408–421 in *Resources, Environment, and Population: Present Knowledge, Future Options,* edited by Kingsley Davis and Michail S. Bernstam. New York: Population Council.

Demo, David H., and Alan C. Acock. 1988. "The Impact of Divorce on Children." *Journal of Marriage and the Family* 50 (August): 619–648.

DeNavas-Walt, Carmen, and Robert W. Cleveland. 2002. *Money Income in the United States 2002.* Washington, DC: U.S. Census Bureau.

DeVault, Marjorie. 1991. *Feeding the Family: The Social Organization of Caring as Gendered Work.* Chicago: University of Chicago Press.

DeWitt, Karen. 1995. "Blacks Prone to Job Dismissal in Organizations." *The New York Times* (April 20): A19.

DiAcosta, Diego. 1998. "A Sociolinguistic Study of Two Baptist Churches." Senior thesis, Princeton Universtiy.

Diaz-Duque, Ozzie F. 1989. "Communication Barriers in Medical Settings: Hispanics in the United States." *International Journal of the Sociology of Language* 79: 93–102.

Dillard, J.L. 1972. *Black English: Its Historical Usage in the United States.* New York: Random House.

DiMaggio, Paul, and Francie Ostrower. 1990. "Participation in the Arts by Black and White Americans." *Social Forces* 68 (March): 753–778.

DiMaggio, Paul J., and Walter W. Powell. 1991. "Introduction." Pp. 1–38 in *The New Institutionalism in Organizational Analysis,* edited by W. W. Powell and P. J. DiMaggio. Chicago: University of Chicago Press.

Diner, Hasia. 1996. "Erin's Children in America: Three Centuries of Irish Immigration to the United States." Pp. 161–171 in *Origins and Destinies: Immigration, Race, and Ethnicity in America,* edited by Silvia Pedraza and Rubén Rumbaut. Belmont, CA: Wadsworth.

Dines, Gail, and Jean M. Humez (eds.). 1995. *Gender, Race and Class in Media: A Text-Reader.* Thousand Oaks, CA: Sage.

Dion, K. K. 1972. "Physical Attractiveness and Evaluating Children's Transgressions." *Journal of Personality and Social Psychology* 24: 285–290.

Dixit, Avinash K. and Susan Sneath. 1997. *Games of Strategy.* New York: W. W. Norton.

Dohm, Arlene. 2000. "Gauging the Labor Force Effects of Retiring Baby-Boomers." *Monthly Labor Review* 123 (July): 17–28.

Domhoff, William. 2002. *Who Rules America?* New York: McGraw-Hill.

Dominguez, Silvia, and Celeste Watkins. 2003. "Creating Networks for Survival and Mobility: Social Capital Among African-American and Latin-American Low-Income Mothers." *Social Problems* 50 (no. 1): 111–135.

Donnerstein, Edward, Daniel Linz, and Steven Penrod. 1987. *The Question of Pornography: Research Findings and Policy Implications.* New York: Free Press.

Douglass, Jack D. 1967. *The Social Meanings of Suicide.* Princeton, NJ: Princeton University Press.

Dovidio, J. F. and S. L. Gaertner (eds.). 1986. *Prejudice, Discrimination, and Racism.* New York: Academic Press.

Dowd, James J., and Laura A. Dowd. 2003. "The Center Holds: From Subcultures to Social Worlds." *Teaching Sociology* 31 (January): 20–37.

Doyal, I. 1990. "Hazards of Hearth and Home." *Women's Studies International Forum* 13: 501–517.

Du Bois, W. E. B. 1901. "The Freedmen's Bureau." *Atlantic Monthly* 86: 354–365.

Due, Linnea. 1995. *Joining the Tribe: Growing Up Gay & Lesbian in the '90s.* New York: Doubleday.

Dugger, Karen. 1988. "Social Location and Gender-Role Attitudes: A Comparison of Black and White Women." *Gender & Society* 2 (December): 425–448.

Duneier, Mitchell. 1999. *Sidewalk.* New York: Farrar, Strauss and Giroux.

Dunlop, Riley E., and Angela G. Mertig. 1992. *American Environmentalism: The U.S. Environmental Movement, 1970–1990.* Philadelphia: Taylor and Francis.

Durkheim, Emile. 1897/1951. *Suicide.* Glencoe, IL: Free Press.

Durkheim, Emile. 1912 [1947]. *Elementary Forms of Religious Life.* Glencoe, IL: Free Press.

Durkheim, Emile. 1938 [1950]. *The Rules of Sociological Method.* Glencoe, IL: Free Press.

Durkheim, Emile. 1964 [1895]. *The Division of Labor in Society.* New York: Free Press.

Dworkin, Shari L., and Michael A. Messner. 1999. "Just Do . . . What?" Pp. 341–361 in Myra Marx Ferree, Judith Lorber, and Beth B. Hess (eds.), *Revisioning Gender.* Thousand Oaks, CA: Sage.

Eagly, A. H., R. D. Ashmore, M. G. Makhijani, and L. C. Longo. 1989. "What Is Beautiful Is Good, But: A Meta-Analysis." *Psychological Bulletin* 110: 109–128.

Eckberg, Douglass Lee. 1992. "Social Influences on Belief in Creationism." *Sociological Spectrum* 12 (April–June): 145–165.

Edin, Kathryn. 1991. "Surviving the Welfare System: How AFDC Recipients Make Ends Meet in Chicago." *Social Problems* 38 (November): 462–472.

Edin, Kathryn. 2000. "What Do Low-Income Single Mothers Say About Marriage?" *Social Problems* 47 (February): 112–133.

Edin, Kathryn, and Laura Lein. 1997. *Making Ends Meet: How Single Mothers Survive Welfare and Low-Wage Work.* New York: Russell Sage Foundation.

Edmondson, Brad. 2000. "Immigration Nation." *Preservation* (January/February): 31–38.

Ehrlich, Paul. 1968. *The Population Bomb.* New York: Ballantine Books.

Ehrlich, P. 1990. *The Population Explosion.* New York: Ballantine Books.

Ehrlich, Paul R., and Anne H. Ehrlich. 1991. *The Population Explosion.* New York: Touchstone/Simon & Schuster.

Ehrlich, Paul R. Anne H. Ehrlich, and John P. Holdren. 1977. *Ecoscience: Population, Resources, Environment.* San Franciso: Freeman.

Eichenwald, Kurt. 1996. "The Two Faces of Texaco." *The New York Times,* (November 10): Section 3: 1ff.

Eichenwald, Kurt. 2002. "Two Ex-Officials at WorldCom Are Charged in Huge Fraud." *The New York Times* (August 2): A1 and A11.

Eisenberg, Daniel, and Maggie Sieger. 2003. "The Doctor Won't See You Now: The Soaring Cost of Malpractice." *Time* (June): 46–60.

Eitzen, D. Stanley, and Maxine Baca Zinn. 2000. *In Conflict and Order: Understanding Society,* 9th ed. Boston: Allyn and Bacon.

Eitzen, D. Stanley, and Maxine Baca Zinn. 2004. *In Conflict and Order,* 10th ed. Boston: Allyn and Bacon.

Ekman, Paul. 1982. *Emotion in the Human Face,* 2nd ed. Cambridge, MA: Cambridge University Press.

Ekman, Paul, and W. V. Friesen. 1974. "Detecting Deception from the Body or Face." *Journal of Personality and Social Psychology* 29: 288–298.

Ekman, Paul, W. V. Friesen, and M. O'Sullivan. 1988. "Smiles When Lying." *Journal of Personality and Social Psychology* 54: 414–420.

Eliason, Michele J., and Salome Raheim. 1996. "Categorical Measurement of Attitudes About Lesbian, Gay, and Bisexual People." *Journal of Gay and Lesbian Social Services* 4: 51–65.

Elizabeth, Vivienne. 2000. "Cohabitation, Marriage, and the Unruly Consequences of Difference." *Gender & Society* 14 (February): 87–110.

Eller, T. J. 1996. *Who Stays Poor? Who Doesn't?* Current Population Reports: Dynamics of Economic Well-Being: Poverty, 1992–1993. Washington, DC: U.S. Department of Commerce, Economics and Statistics Administration, June.

Elliott, Marta. 2001. "Gender Differences in the Causes of Depression." *Women and Health* 22: 163–177.

Ellison, Christopher G., and David A. Gay. 1989. "Black Political Participation Revisited: A Test of Compensatory, Ethnic Community, and Public Arena Models." *Social Science Quarterly* 70 (March): 101–119.

Ellison, Christopher G., and John P. Bartkowski. 2002. "Conservative Protestantism and the Division of Household Labor among Married Couples." *Journal of Family Issues* 23 (November): 950–985.

Emerson, Joan P. 1970. "Behaviors in Private Places: Sustaining Definitions of Reality in Gynecological Examinations." Pp. 74–97 in *Recent Sociology,* vol. 2, edited by H. P. Dreitzel. New York: Collier.

England, Paula, Barbara Stanek Kilbourne, George Farkas, and Thomas Dou. 1988. "Explaining Occupational Sex Segregation and Wages: Findings from a Model with Fixed Effects." *American Sociological Review* 53 (August): 544–558.

Enloe, Cynthia. 1989. *Bananas, Beaches, and Bases: Making Feminist Sense of International Politics.* Berkeley: University of California Press.

Enloe, Cynthia. 1993. *The Morning After: Sexual Politics at the End of the Cold War.* Berkeley: University of California Press.

Epps, Edgar T. 2002. "Race, Class and Educational Opportunity: Trends in the Sociology of Education." In *2001 Race Odyssey: African Americans and Sociology,* edited by Bruce R. Hare. Syracuse, NY: Syracuse University Press.

Epstein, Steven. 1996. *Impure Science: AIDS, Activism, and the Politics of Knowledge.* Berkeley: University of California Press.

Erikson, Eric. 1980. *Identity and the Life Cycle.* New York: W.W. Norton.

Erikson, Kai. 1966. *Wayward Puritans: A Study in the Sociology of Deviance.* New York: Wiley.

Erikson, Robert. 1985. "Are American Rates of Social Mobility Exceptionally High? New Evidence on an Old Issue." *European Sociological Review* 1 (May): 1–22.

Ermann, M. David, and Richard J. Lundman. 1992. *Corporate and Governmental Deviance.* New York: Oxford University Press.

Esbensen-Finn, Aage, Elizabeth Piper Deschenes, and Thomas L. Winfree, Jr. 1999. "Differences between Gang Girls and Gang Boys: Results from a Multisite Survey." *Youth and Society* 31 (September): 27–53.

Eschholz, Sarah, Jana Bufkin, and Jenny Long. 2002. "Symbolic Reality Bites: Women and Racial/Ethnic Minorities in Modern Film." *Sociological Spectrum* 22 (July–August): 299–334.

Espenshade, Thomas J. 1995. "Unauthorized Immigration to the United States." *Annual Review of Sociology* 21: 195–216.

Essed, Philomena. 1991. *Understanding Everyday Racism.* Newbury Park, CA: Sage.

Etzioni, Amatai. 1975. *A Comparative Analysis of Complex Organization: On Power, Involvement, and Their Correlates,* revised ed. New York: Free Press.

Etzioni, Amatai, John Wilson, Bob Edwards, and Michael W. Foley. 2001. "A Symposium on Robert D. Putnam's *Bowling Alone: The Collapse and Revival of American Community.*" *Contemporary Sociology* 30 (May): 223–230.

Evans, Lorraine, and Kimberly Davies. 2000. "No Sissy Boys Here: A Content Analysis of the Representation of Masculinity in Elementary School Reading Textbooks." *Sex Roles* 42 (February): 255–270.

Evans, Peter B., Dietrich Ruesschemeyer, and Theda Skocpol. 1985. *Bringing the State Back In.* Cambridge, MA: Cambridge University Press.

Farber, Naomi. 1990. "The Significance of Race and Class in Marital Decisions Among Unmarried Adolescent Mothers." *Social Problems* 37 (February): 51–63.

Farley, Reynolds, and Walter R. Allen. 1987. *The Color Line and the Quality of Life in America.* New York: Russell Sage Foundation.

Fattah, Ezzat A., 1994. "The Interchangeable Roles of Victim and Victimizer." *HEUNI Papers* 3: 1–26.

Fausto-Sterling, Anne. 1992. *Myths of Gender: Biological Theories About Women and Men.* New York: Basic Books.

Fausto-Sterling, Anne. 2000. *Sexing the Body: Gender Politics and the Construction of Sexuality.* New York: Basic Books.

Feagin, Joe R. 1991. "The Continuing Significance of Race: Antiblack Discrimination in Public Places." *American Sociological Review* 56 (February): 101–116.

Feagin, Joe R. 2000. *Racist America: Roots, Future Realities, and Racial Reparations.* New York: Routledge.

Feagin, Joe R., and Clairece B. Feagin. 1993. *Racial and Ethnic Relations,* 4th ed. Englewood Cliffs, NJ: Prentice Hall.

Feagin, Joe R., and Hernán Vera. 1995. *White Racism.* New York: Routledge.

Federal Bureau of Investigation. 2000. *Uniform Crime Reports.* Washington, DC: U.S. Department of Justice.

Federal Bureau of Investigation. 2002. *Uniform Crime Reports.* Washington, DC: U.S. Department of Justice.

Federal Election Commission. 2001. "PAC Financial Activity through December 31, 2000." Web page: www.fec.gov

Fein, Melvyn L. 1988. "Resocialization: A Neglected Paradigm." *Clinical Sociology.* 6: 88–100.

Ferber, Abby. 1998. *White Man Falling: Race, Gender, and White Supremacy.* Lanham, MD: Rowman and Littlefield.

Ferber, Abby. 1999. "What White Supremacists Taught a Jewish Scholar about Identity." *The Chronicle of Higher Education* (May 7): 86–87.

Fernald, Anne, and Hiromi Morikawa. 1993. "Common Themes and Cultural Variations in Japanese and American Mothers' Speech to Infants." *Child Development* 64 (June): 637–656.

Fernandes-y-Freitas, Rosa L. 1996. "The Minitel and the Internet: New Houses for Our Old Phantoms." *Societies* 51 (February): 49–57.

Festinger, Leon, Stanley Schachter, and Kurt Back. 1950. *Social Pressures in Informal Groups: A Study of Human Factors in Housing.* Stanford, CA: Stanford University Press.

Fields, Jason. 2003. *Children's Living Arrangements and Characteristics, Detailed Tables, Current Population Report P20–547.* Washington, DC: U.S. Census Bureau. Web site: www.census.gov

Fine, Michelle, and Lois Weis. 1998. *The Unknown City: The Lives of Poor and Working-Class Young Adults.* Boston: Beacon Press.

Finer, Lawrence B., and Stanley K. Henshaw. 2003. "Abortion Incidence and Services in the United States in 2000." *Perspectives on Sexual and Reproductive Health* 35: 6–15.

Fischer, Claude. 1981. *To Dwell among Friends: Personal Networks in Town and City.* Chicago: University of Chicago Press.

Fischer, Claude S., Michael Hout, Mártin Sánchez Jankowski, Samuel R. Lucas, Ann Swidler, and Kim Voss. 1996. *Inequality by Design: Cracking the Bell Curve Myth.* Princeton, NJ: Princeton University Press.

Fisher, Bonnie S., Francis T. Cullen, and Michael G. Turner. 2001. *Sexual Victimization of College Women.* Washington, DC: Bureau of Justice Statistics.

Flanagan, William G. 1995. *Urban Sociology: Images and Structure.* Boston: Allyn and Bacon.

Fleisher, Mark. 2000. *Dead End Kids: Gang Girls and the Boys They Know.* Madison, WI: University of Wisconsin Press.

Fletcher, Michael. 2000. "In The Targeted States, a Striking Turnout of Black Voters." *The Washington Post* (November 17): A29.

Flowers, M.L. 1977. "A Laboratory Test of Some Implications of Janis' Groupthink Hypothesis." *Journal of Personality and Social Psychology* 35 (December): 888–896.

Folbre, Nancy. 2001. *The Invisible Heart: Economics and Family Values.* New York: New Press.

Fordham, Signithia. 1996. *Blacked Out: Dilemmas of Race, Identity, and Success at A. I. High.* Chicago: University of Chicago Press.

Fouts, Gregory, and Kimberley Burggraf. 1999. "Television Situation Comedies: Female Body Images and Verbal Reinforcements." *Sex Roles* 40 (March): 473–481.

Frankenberg, Erica, Chungmei Lee, and Gary Orfield. 2003. "A Multiracial Society with Segregated Schools: Are We Losing the Dream?" Civil Rights Project Harvard University. Web site: www.civilrightsproject.harvard.edu

Frazier, E. Franklin. 1957. *The Black Bourgeoisie.* New York: Collier Books.

Freedman, Allan. 1997. "Lawyers Take a Back Seat in the 105th Congress." *Congressional Quarterly* 55 (January 4): 27–30.

Freedman, Estelle B., and John D'Emilio. 1988. *Intimate Matters: A History of Sexuality in America.* New York: Harper & Row.

Freeman, Jo. 1983a. "A Model for Analyzing the Strategic Options of Social Movement Organizations." Pp. 193–210 in *Social Movements of the Sixties and Seventies,* edited by Jo Freeman. New York: Longman.

Freud, Sigmund. 1901 [1965]. *The Psychopathology of Everyday Life,* translated by Alan Tyson and edited by James Strachey. New York: W.W. Norton.

Freud, Sigmund. 1923 [1960]. *The Ego and the Id,* translated by Joan Riviere. New York: W.W. Norton.

Freud, Sigmund. 1930 [1961]. *Civilization and Its Discontents,* translated by James Strachey. New York: W.W. Norton,

Fried, Amy. 1994. "'It's Hard to Change What We Want to Change': Rape Crisis Centers as

Organizations." *Gender & Society* 4 (December): 562–583.

Friedman, Thomas L. 1999. *The Lexus and the Olive Tree.* New York: Farrar, Strauss, and Giraux.

Fryberg, Stephanie. 2003. "Really: You Don't Look Like an American Indian: Social Representations and Social Group Identities." Ph.D. Dissertation, Department of Psychology, Stanford University.

Frye, Marilyn. 1983. *The Politics of Reality.* Trumansburg, NY: The Crossing Press.

Fukuda, Mari. 1994. "Nonverbal Communication within Japanese and American Corporations." Unpublished manuscript, Princeton University.

Fullerton, Howard F. 1999. "Labor Force Projections to 2008: Steady Growth and Changing." *Monthly Labor Review* 122: 19–32.

Gagné, Patricia, and Richard Tewksbury. 1998. "Conformity Pressures and Gender Resistance among Transgendered Individuals." *Social Problems* 45 (February): 81–101.

Gallup and Simmons. 2000. "6 in 10 American Read Bible at Least Occasionally." *The Gallup Poll.* Princeton, NJ: The Gallup Organization. Web site: www.gallup.com

Gallup Organization. 2000b. "Tobacco and Smoking." *The Gallup Poll.* Princeton, NJ: The Gallup Organization. World Wide Web site: http://www.gallup.com

Gallup Organization. 2002. "Confidence in Institutions." June. Princeton, NJ: Gallup Organization. Web Site: www.gallup.com

Gallup Organization. 2003. "Homosexual Relations." Princeton, NJ: The Gallup Organization.

Gallup, George, Jr. 2001. "Americans More Religious Now Than Ten Years Ago, but Less So Than in 1950s and 1960s." *The Gallup Poll.* Princeton, NJ: The Gallup Organization.

Gamoran, Adam. 1992. "The Variable Effects of High School Tracking." *American Sociological Review* 57: 812–828.

Gamoran, Adam, and Robert D. Mare, 1989. "Secondary School Tracking and Educational Inequality: Compensation, Reinforcement, or Neutrality?" *American Journal of Sociology* 94: 1146–1183.

Gamson, Joshua. 1995. "Featured Essay." *Contemporary Sociology* 24 (May): 294–298.

Gamson, Joshua. 1998. *Freaks Talk Back: Tabloid Talk Shows and Sexual Nonconformity.* Chicago: University of Chicago Press.

Gamson, William A. 1992. "The Social Psychology of Collective Action." Pp. 53–76 in *Frontiers in Social Movement Theory,* edited by Aldon D. Morris and Carol McClurg Mueller. New Haven, CT: Yale University Press.

Gamson, William, and Andre Modigliani. 1974. *Conceptions of Social Life: A Text-Reader for Social Psychology.* Boston: Little, Brown.

Gans, Herbert. 1979. *Deciding What's News: A Study of the CBS Evening News, NBC Nightly News, Newsweek and Time.* New York: Pantheon.

Gans, Herbert. 1982 [1962]. *The Urban Villagers: Group and Class in the Life of Italian Americans.* New York: Free Press.

Gans, Herbert J. 1999. *Popular Culture and High Culture: An Analysis and Evaluation of Taste.* New York: Basic Books.

Gardner, Gary, and Brian Halweil. 2000. "Feeding the Underfed and Overfed." Pp. 59–78 in *State of the World 2000.* New York: W.W. Norton.

Gardner, Howard. 1999 [1993]. *Frames of Mind: The Theory of Multiple Intelligences.* New York: Basic Books.

Garfinkel, Harold. 1967. *Studies in Ethnomethodology.* Englewood Cliffs, NJ: Prentice Hall.

Garrow, David J. 1981. *The FBI and Martin Luther King.* New York: Norton.

Garst, J., and G. V. Bodenhausen. 1997. "Advertising's Effects on Men's Gender Role Attitudes." *Sex Roles* 36 (May): 551–572.

Gates, Henry Louis, Jr. 1988. *The Signifying Monkey: A Theory of African-American Literary Criticism.* New York: Oxford University Press.

Gates, Henry Louis, Jr. 1992. "Integrating the American Mind." Pp. 105–120 in *Loose Canons: Notes on the Culture Wars,* edited by Henry Louis Gates, Jr. New York: Oxford University Press.

General Social Survey. 1998. Ann Arbor, MI: University of Michigan. Web site: **www.icpsr. umich.edu:8080/GSS/homepage.htm**

Genovese, Eugene. 1972. *Roll, Jordan, Roll: The World the Slaves Made.* New York: Pantheon.

Gerami, Shahin, and Melodye Lehnerer. 2001. "Women's Agency and Houshold Diplomacy: Negotiating Fundamentalism." *Gender & Society* 15 (August): 556–573.

Gerson, Kathleen. 1993. *No Man's Land: Men's Changing Commitments to Family and Work.* New York: Basic Books.

Gerth, Hans, and C. Wright Mills (eds.). 1946. *From Max Weber: Essays in Sociology.* New York: Oxford University Press.

Giannarelli, Linda, and James Barsimantov. 2000. *Child Care Expenses of America's Families.* Washington, DC: Urban Institute.

Giddings, Paula. 1988. *In Search of Sisterhood: Delta Sigma Theta and the Challenge of the Black Sorority Movement.* New York: Quill.

Gilbert, Daniel R., Susan T. Fiske, and Gardner Lindzey (eds.). 1998. *The Handbook of Social Psychology,* 4th ed. New York: Oxford University and McGraw-Hill.

Gilbert, D. T. and P. S. Malone. 1995. "The Correspondence Bias." *Psychological Bulletin* 117: 21–38.

Gilkes, Cheryl Townsend. 2000. *"If It Wasn't For the Women..." Black Women's Experience and Womanist Culture in Church and Community.* Maryknoll, NY: Orbis Books.

Gilligan, Carol. 1982. *In a Different Voice: Psychological Theory and Women's Development.* Cambridge, MA: Harvard University Press.

Gitlin, Todd. 2001. *Media Unlimited: How the Torrent of Images and Sounds Overwhelms Our Lives.* New York: Metropolitan Books.

Glass Ceiling Commission. 1995. *Good for Business: Making Full Use of the Nation's Human Capital.* Washington, DC: U.S. Government Printing Office.

Glazer, Nathan. 1970. *Beyond the Melting Pot: The Negroes, Puerto Ricans, Jews, Italians, and Irish of New York City.* Cambridge, MA: MIT Press.

Glenn, Evelyn Nakano. 1986. *Issei, Nisei, War Bride: Three Generations of Japanese American Women in Domestic Service.* Philadelphia: Temple University Press.

Glenn, Evelyn Nakano. 2002. *Unequal Freedom: How Race and Gender Shaped American Citizenship and Labor.* Cambridge: Harvard University Press.

Gluckman, Amy, and Betsy Reed (eds.). 1997. *Homo Economics: Capitalism, Community, and Lesbian and Gay Life.* New York: Routledge.

Goffman, Erving. 1959. *The Presentation of Self in Everyday Life.* Garden City, NY: Doubleday.

Goffman, Erving. 1961. *Asylums: Essays on the Social Situation of Mental Patients and Other Inmates.* Garden City, NY: Anchor.

Goffman, Erving. 1963. *Stigma: Notes on the Management of Spoiled Identity.* Englewood Cliffs, NJ: Prentice Hall.

Goffman, Erving. 1974. *Frame Analysis.* Cambridge, MA: Harvard University Press.

Goldberger, Arthur S. 1979. "Heritability." *Econometrica* 46: 327–347.

Goldman, Noreen, Yorenzo Moreno, and Charles F. Westoff. 1989. *Peru Experimental Study: An Evaluation of Fertility and Child Health Information.* Princeton, NJ: Office of Population Research.

Goldshmidt, Orly Turgeman, and Leonard Weller. 2000. "'Talking Emotions': Gender Differences in a Variety of Conversational Contexts." *Symbolic Interaction* 23: 117–134.

Goldstein, A.P. 1994. *The Ecology of Aggression.* New York: Plenum.

González, Tina Esther. 1996. *Social Control of Medical Professionals, Cultural Notions of Pain, and Doctors as Social Scientists.* Unpublished junior thesis, Princeton University.

Gordon, Linda. 1977. *Woman's Body/Woman's Right.* New York: Penguin.

Gordon, Margaret T., and Stephanie Riger. 1989. *The Female Fear.* New York: Free Press.

Gorman, Thomas J. 2000. "Cross-Class Perceptions of Social Class." *Sociological Spectrum* 20 (January–March): 93–120.

Gossett, Jennifer L. and Sarah Byrne. 2002. "'Click Here': A Content Analysis of Internet Rape Sites." *Gender & Society* 16 (October): 689–709.

Gottfredson, Michael R., and Travis Hirschi. 1990. *A General Theory of Crime.* Palo Alto, CA: Stanford University Press.

Gottfredson, Michael R., and Travis Hirschi. 1995. "National Crime Control Policies." *Society* 32 (January/February): 30–36.

Gould, Stephen Jay. 1981. *The Mismeasure of Man.* New York: W.W. Norton.

Gould, Stephen Jay. 1994. "Curveball." *The New Yorker* 70 (November 28): 139–149.

Gould, Stephen Jay. 1999. "The Human Difference." *The New York Times* (July 2).

Graefe, Deborah Roempke, and Daniel T. Lichtor. 1999. "Life Course Transitions of American Children: Parental Cohabitation, Marriage, and Single Motherhood." *Demography* 36 (May): 205–217.

Graham, Lawrence Otis. 1999. *Our Kind of People: Inside America's Black Upper Class.* New York: Harper Collins.

Gramsci, Antonio. 1971. *Selections from the Prison Notebooks of Antonio Gramsci,* edited by Quintin Hoare and Geoffrey Nowell. London: Lawrence and Wishart.

Granovetter, Mark. 1973. "The Strength of Weak Ties." *American Journal of Sociology* 78 (May): 1360–1380.

Granovetter, Mark. 1974. *Getting a Job: A Study of Contacts and Careers.* Cambridge, MA: Harvard University Press.

Granovetter, Mark S. 1995. "Afterward 1994: Reconsiderations and a New Agenda." Pp. 139-182 in Mark S. Granovetter, *Getting A Job,* 2nd ed. Chicago: University of Chicago Press.

Grant, Don Sherman, II, and Ramiro Martinez, Jr. 1997. "Crime and the Restructuring of the U.S. Economy: A Reconsideration of the Class Linkages." *Social Forces* 75 (March): 769–799.

Green, Gary Paul, Leam M. Tigges, and Daniel Diaz. 1999. "Racial and Ethnic Differences in Job Search Strategies in Atlanta, Boston, and Los Angeles." *Social Science Quarterly* 80 (June): 263–290.

Greenfeld, Lawrence A., and Tracy L. Snell. 1999. *Women Offenders.* Washington, DC: U.S. Bureau of Justice Statistics.

Greenhouse, Linda. 1996a. "Gay Rights Laws Can't Be Banned, High Court Rules." *The New York Times* (May 21): A1ff.

Greenhouse, Steven. 2000b. "Poll of Working Women Finds Them Stressed." *The New York Times,* April 3.

Grindstaff, Laura. 2002. *The Money Shot: Trash Class, and the Making of TV Talk Shows.* Chicago: University of Chicago Press.

Griswold, Wendy. 1994. *Cultures and Societies in a Changing World.* Thousand Oaks, CA: Pine Forge Press.

Gross, E. F., A. Juvonen, and S. L. Gable. 2002. "Internet Use and Well-Being in Adolescense." *Journal of Social Issues* 58 (1): 75–90.

Guinther, J. 1988. *The Jury in America.* New York: Facts on File Publications.

Habermas, Jürgen. 1970. *Toward a Rational Society: Student Protest, Science, and Politics.* Boston, MA: Beacon Press.

Hadaway, C. Kirk, and Penny Long Marler. 1993. "All in the Family: Religious Mobility in America." *Review of Religious Research* 35 (December): 97–116.

Hagan, John. 1993. "The Social Embeddedness of Crime and Unemployment." *Criminology* 31 (November): 465–491.

Hall, Edward T. 1966. *The Hidden Dimension.* New York: Doubleday.

Hall, Edward T., and Mildred Hall. 1987. *Hidden Differences: Doing Business with the Japanese.* New York: Anchor Press/Doubleday.

Hall, Elaine J. 1993. "Waitering/Waitressing: Engendering in the Work of Table Servers." *Gender & Society* 7 (September): 329–346.

Hallinan, Maureen T. 1994. "Tracking: From Theory to Practice." *Sociology of Education* 67: 79–84.

Hamer, Jennifer. 2001. *What It Means to Be Daddy.* New York: Columbia University Press.

Handlin, Oscar. 1951. *The Uprooted.* Boston: Little, Brown.

Haney, Lynne. 1996. "Homeboys, Babies, Men in Suits: The State and the Reproduction of Male Dominance." *American Sociological Review* 61 (October): 759–778.

Hans, Valerie, and Ramiro Martinez. 1994. "Intersections of Race, Ethnicity, and the Law." *Law and Human Behavior* 18 (June): 211–221.

Harding, Sandra G. 1998. *Is Science Multicultural? Postcolonialisms, Feminisms, and Epistemologies.* Bloomington: Indiana University Press.

Harris, Allen C. 1994. "Ethnicity as a Determinant of Sex-Role Identity: A Replication Study of Item Selection for the Bem Sex-Role Inventory." *Sex Roles* 31 (August): 241–273.

Harris, Ian, José B. Torres, and Dale Allender. 1994. "The Responses of African American Men to Dominant Norms of Masculinity within the United States." *Sex Roles* 31 (December): 703–720.

Harris, Marvin. 1974. *Cows, Pigs, Wars, and Witches: The Riddles of Culture.* New York: Vintage.

Harrison, Bennett, and Harry Bluestone. 1982. *The Deindustrialization of America: Plant Closings, Community Abandonment, and the Dismantling of Basic Industry.* New York: Basic Books.

Harrison, Roderick. 2000. "Inadequacies of Multiple Response Race Data in the Federal Statistical System." Manuscript. Washington, DC: Joint Center for Political and Economic Studies and Howard University, Department of Sociology.

Harry, Joseph. 1979. "The Marital 'Liaisons' of Gay Men." *The Family Coordinator* 28 (October): 622–629.

Hastie, Reid, Steven D. Penrod, and Nancy Pennington. 1983. *Inside the Jury.* Cambridge, MA: Harvard University Press.

Hastorf, Albert, and Hadley Cantril. 1954. "They Saw a Game: A Case Study." *Journal of Abnormal and Social Psychology* 40 (2): 129–134.

Hatfield, Elaine S., and S. Sprecher. 1986. *Mirror, Mirror: The Importance of Looks in Everyday Life.* Albany: State University of New York Press.

Hauan, Susan M., Nancy S. Landale, and Kevin T. Leicht. 2000. "Poverty and Work Effort among Urban Latino Men." *Work and Occupations* 27 (May): 188–222.

Hauser, Robert M., Howard F. Taylor, and Troy Duster. 1995. "The Bell Curve." *Contemporary Sociology* 24 (March): 149–161.

Hawley, Amos H. 1986. *Human Ecology: A Theoretical Essay.* Chicago: University of Chicago Press.

Healey, Joseph H. 1995. *Race, Ethnicity, Gender, and Class: The Sociology of Group Conflict and Change.* Thousand Oaks, CA: Pine Forge Press.

Hearnshaw, Leslie. 1979. *Cyril Burt: Psychologist.* Ithaca, NY: Cornell University Press.

Heider, Fritz. 1958. *The Psychology of Interpersonal Relations.* New York: Wiley.

Heimer, Karen. 1997. "Socioeconomic Status, Subcultural Definitions and Violent Delinquency." *Social Forces* 75 (March): 799–833.

Hendy, Helen M., Cheryl Gustitus, and Jamie Leitzel-Schwalm. 2001. "Social Cognitive Predictors of Body Images in Preschool Children." *Sex Roles* 44 (May): 557–569.

Henslin, James M. 1993. "Doing the Unthinkable." Pp. 253–262 in *Down to Earth Sociology,* 7th ed., edited by James M. Henslin. New York: Free Press.

Herrnstein, Richard J., and Charles Murray. 1994. *The Bell Curve: Intelligence and Class Structure in American Life.* New York: Free Press.

Herskovits, Melville J. 1941. *The Myth of the Negro Past.* New York: Harper and Brothers.

Higginbotham, A. Leon. 1978. *In the Matter of Color: Race and the American Legal Process.* New York: Oxford University Press.

Higginbotham, Elizabeth. 2001. *Too Much to Ask: Black Women in the Era of Integration.* Chapel Hill, NC: University of North Carolina Press.

Higginbotham, Elizabeth, and Lynn Weber. 1992. "Moving Up with Kin and Community: Upward Social Mobility for Black and White Women." *Gender & Society* 6 (September): 416–440.

Higher Education Research Institute. 2002. *American Freshman Survey.* Los Angeles, CA: University of California.

Hill, C.T., Z. Rubin, and L.A. Peplau. 1976. "Breakups Before Marriage: The End of 103 Affairs." *Journal of Social Issues* 32: 147–168.

Hill, Lori Diane. 2001. *Conceptualizing Educational Attainment Opportunities of Urban Youth: The Effects of School Capacity, Community Context and Social Capital.* Ph. D. Dissertation, University of Chicago.

Hill, Shirley. 1994. "Motherhood and the Obfuscation of Medical Knowledge: The Case of Sickle Cell Disease." *Gender & Society* 8 (March): 29–47.

Hirschi, Travis. 1969. *Causes of Delinquency.* Berkeley: University of California Press.

Hirschman, Charles. 1994. "Why Fertility Changes." *Annual Review of Sociology* 20: 203–223.

Hochschild, Arlie [Russell]. 1997. *The Time Bind: When Work Becomes Home and Home Becomes Work.* New York: Metropolitan Books.

Hochschild, Arlie Russell, with Anne Machung. 1989. *The Second Shift: Working Parents and the Revolution at Home.* New York: Viking.

Hochschild, Arlie. 1983. *The Managed Heart: Commercialization of Human Feelings.* Berkeley: University of California Press.

Hodge, Robert W., and Donald J. Treiman. 1968. "Class Identification in the United States." *American Journal of Sociology* 75: 535–547.

Hodson, Randy. 1996. "Dignity in the Workplace under Participative Management." *American Sociological Review* 61 (October): 719–738.

Hofstadter, Richard. 1944. *Social Darwinism in American Thought.* Philadelphia: University of Pennsylvania Press.

Hollingshead, August B., and Frederick C. Redlich. 1958. *Social Class and Mental Illness: A Community Study.* New York: Wiley.

Holm, Maj. Gen. Jeanne. 1992. *Women in the Military.* Novato, CA: Presidio Press.

Holmes, David, ed. 1997. *Virtual Politics: Identity and Community in Cyberspace.* Thousand Oaks, CA: Sage.

Holmes, Schuyler. 2000. "Environmental Racism and Classism in Toxic Waste Dumping in Cleveland, Ohio." Junior thesis. Princeton University, Princeton, NJ.

Homans, George. 1961. *Social Behavior: Its Elementary Forms.* New York: Harcourt Brace Jovanovich.

Homans, George. 1974. *Social Behavior: Its Elementary Forms,* revised ed. New York: Harcourt Brace Jovanovich.

Hondagneu-Sotelo, Pierrette. 1994. *Gendered Transitions: The Mexican Experience of Immigration.* Berkeley: University of California Press.

Hondagneu-Sotelo, Pierrette. 2001. *Doméstica: Immigrant Workers Cleaning and Caring in the Shadows of Affluence.* Berkeley: University of California Press.

Hondagneu-Sotelo, Pierrette, and Ernestine Avila. 1997. "'I'm Here, but I'm There': The Meanings of Latina Transnational Motherhood." *Gender & Society* 11 (October): 548–571.

Hong, Laurence K. 1978. "Risky Shift and Cautious Shift: Some Direct Evidence on the Culture-Value Theory." *Social Psychology* 41 (December): 342–346.

Hornung, Carlton A. 1977. "Social Status, Status Inconsistency and Psychological Stress," *American Sociological Review* 42 (August): 623–638.

Horowitz, Ruth. 1995. *Teen Mothers: Citizens or Dependents?* Chicago: University of Chicago Press.

Horton, Hayward Derrick, Beverlyn Lundy Allen, Cedric Herring, and Melvin E. Thomas. 2000. "Lost in the Storm: The Sociology of the Black Working Class, 1850 to 1990." *American Sociological Review* 65 (February): 128–137.

Horton, Jacqueline A., ed. 1995. *The Women's Health Data Book,* 2nd ed. Washington, DC: Jacobs Institute of Women's Health.

House, James S. 1980. *Occupational Stress and the Mental and Physical Health of Factory Workers.* Ann Arbor, MI: Survey Research Center.

Hout, Michael. 1988. "More Universalism, Less Structural Mobility: The American Occupational Structure in the 1980s." *American Journal of Sociology* 93 (May): 1358–1400.

Hoyt, Wendy, and Lori R. Kogan. 2001. "Satisfaction with Body Image and Peer Relationships for Males and Females in a College Environment." *Sex Roles* 45 (August): 199–215.

Hudson, Ken. 1999. "No Shortage of 'Nonstandard' Jobs." *Briefing Paper.* Washington, DC: Economic Policy Institute, December.

Hughes, Langston. 1967. *The Big Sea.* New York: Knopf.

Humphries, Drew. 1999. *Crack Mothers: Pregnancy, Drugs, and the Media.* Columbus, OH: Ohio State University Press.

Hunt, Matthew O. 1996. "The Individual, Society, or Both? A Comparison of Black, Latino, and White Beliefs About the Causes of Poverty." *Social Forces* 75 (September): 293–322.

Hunter, Andrea, and James Davis. 1992. "Constructing Gender: An Exploration of Afro-American Men's Conceptualization of Manhood." *Gender & Society* 6 (September): 464–479.

Hunter, Andrea, and Sherrill L. Sellers. 1998. "Feminist Attitudes among African American Women and Men." *Gender & Society* 12 (February): 81–99.

Hurlbert, Jeanne S., Valerie A. Hanes, and John J. Beggs. 2000. "Core Networks and Tie Activation: What Kinds of Routine Networks Allocate Resources in Nonroutine Situations?" *American Sociological Review* 65 (August): 598–618.

Hyde, J. S. 1984. "Children's Understanding of Sexist Language." *Developmental Psychology* 20: 697–706.

Ignatiev, Noel. 1995. *How the Irish Became White.* New York: Routledge.

Inciardi, James A. 2001. *The War on Drugs: The Continuing Saga of the Mysteries and Miseries of Intoxication, Addiction, Crime, and Public Policy,* 3rd ed. Boston: Allyn and Bacon.

International Labour Organization. 2002. *Every Child Counts: Estimates on Child Labour.* Web site: **www.ilo.org.**

Irwin, Katherine. 2001. "Legitimating the First Tattoo: Moral Passage through Informal Interaction." *Symbolic Interaction* 24 (March): 49–73.

Jackman, Mary. 1983. *Class Awareness in the United States.* Berkeley: University of California Press.

Jackson, Elton F., and Richard F. Curtis. 1968. "Conceptualization and Measurement in the Study of Social Stratification." Pp. 112–149 in *Methodology in Social Research,* edited by H. M. Blalock, Jr., and A. B. Blalock. New York: McGraw-Hill.

Jackson, Linda A., Ruth E. Fleury, and Donna M. Lewandowski. 1996. "Feminism: Definitions, Support, and Correlates of Support Among Male and Female College Students." *Sex Roles* 34 (May): 687–693.

Jackson, Pamela B., Peggy A. Thoits, and Howard F. Taylor. 1994. "The Effects of Tokenism on America's Black Elite." Paper read before the American Sociological Association. Los Angeles, August.

Jackson, Pamela B., Peggy A. Thoits, and Howard F. Taylor. 1995. "Composition of the Workplace and Psychological Well-Being: The Effects of Tokenism on America's Black Elite." *Social Forces* 74 (December): 543–557.

Jackson, Pamela Braboy. 2000. "Stress and Coping among Black Elites in Organizational Settings." Manuscript.

Jackson, Pamela Brayboy. 1992. "Specifying the Buffering Hypothesis: Support, Strain, and Depression." *Social Psychology Quarterly* 55: 363–378.

Jacobs, Jerry A., and Ronnie J. Steinberg. 1990. "Compensating Differentials and the Male–Female Wage Gap: Evidence from the New York State Comparable Worth Study." *Social Forces* 69 (December): 430–469.

Janis, Irving L. 1982. *Groupthink: Psychological Studies of Policy Decisions and Fiascos,* 2nd ed. Boston: Houghton Mifflin.

Janus, Samuel S., and Cynthia L. Janus. 1993. *The Janus Report on Sexual Behavior.* New York: Wiley.

Jaynes, Gerald D., and Robin M. Williams, Jr. 1989. *A Common Destiny: Blacks and American Society.* Washington, DC: National Academy Press.

Jencks, Christopher. 1993. *Rethinking Social Policy: Race, Poverty, and the Underclass.* New York: Harper Collins.

Jencks, Christopher, Marshall Smith, Henry Ackland, Mary Jo Bane, David Cohen, Herbert Gintis, Barbara Heyns, and Stephan Michelson. 1972. *Inequality: A Reassessment of the Effect of Family and Schooling in America.* New York: Basic Books.

Jencks, Christopher, Susan Bartlett, Mary Corcoran, James Crouse, David Eaglesfield, Gregory Jackson, Kent McClelland, Peter Mueser, Michael Olneck, Joseph Schwartz, Sherry Ward, and Jill Williams. 1979. *Who Gets Ahead? The Determinants of Economic Success in America.* New York: Basic Books.

Jenness, Valerie. 1995. "Social Movement Growth, Domain Expansion, and Framing Processes: The Gay/Lesbian Movement and Violence Against Gays and Lesbians as a Social Problem." *Social Problems* 42 (February): 145–170.

Jenness, Valerie, and Kendall Broad. 1994. "Antiviolence Activism and the (In)Visibility of Gender in the Gay/Lesbian and Women's Movements." *Gender & Society* 8 (September): 402–423.

Jennings, M. K., and R. G. Niemi. 1974. *The Political Character of Adolescence.* Princeton, NJ: Princeton University Press.

Jensen, Arthur R. 1980. *Bias in Mental Testing.* New York: Free Press.

Johnson, Kim K. P. 1995. "Attributions About Date Rape: Impact of Clothing, Sex, Money Spent, Date Type, and Perceived Similarity." *Family and Consumer Sciences Research Journal* 23 (March): 292–310.

Johnson, Norris R., James G. Stember, and Deborah Hunter. 1977. "Crowd Behavior as Risky Shift: A Laboratory Experiment." *Sociometry* 40 (2): 183–187.

Johnston, David Cay. 2000. "Corporations' Taxes are Falling Even as Individual Burden Rises." *The New York Times* (February 20): A1ff.

Johnstone, Ronald L. 1992. *Religion in Society: A Sociology of Religion,* 4th ed. Englewood Cliffs, NJ: Prentice Hall.

Jones, Diane Carlson. 2001. "Social Comparison and Body Image: Attractiveness Comparison to Models and Peers among Adolescent Girls and Boys." *Sex Roles* 45 (November): 645–664.

Jones, Edward E., Amerigo Farina, Albert H. Hastorf, Hazel Markus, Dale T. Miller, and Robert A. Scott. 1986. *Social Stigma: The Psychology of Marked Relationships.* New York: W. H. Freeman and Co.

Jones, Edward E., and Keith E. Davis. 1965. "From Acts to Dispositions: The Attribution Process in Person Perception." Pp. 219–266 in *Advances in Experimental Social Psychology,* edited by Leonard Berkowitz. New York: Academic Press.

Jones, James M. 1997. *Prejudice and Racism,* 2nd ed. New York: McGraw-Hill.

Jones, Steven G. 1997. *Virtual Culture: Identity and Communication in Cybersociety.* Thousand Oaks, CA: Sage.

Jordon, Winthrop D. 1968. *White Over Black: American Attitudes Toward the Negro 1550–1812.* Chapel Hill: University of North Carolina Press.

Jordan, Winthrop D. 1969. *The White Man's Burden: Historical Origins of Racism in the United States.* New York: Oxford University Press.

Joseph, Janice. 1997. "Fear of Crime among Black Elderly." *Journal of Black Studies* 27 (May): 698–717.

Jucha, Robert. 2002. *Terrorism.* Belmont, CA: Wadsworth.

Kadushin, Charles. 1974. *The American Intellectual Elite.* Boston: Little, Brown.

Kall, Denise. 2002. *Smoking Gun or Organizational Haze?* The Tobacco Companies' Response to Cancer Research. Unpublished senior thesis, University of Delaware.

Kalleberg, Arne L., Barbara F. Reskin, and Ken Hudson. 2000. "Bad Jobs in America: Standard and Nonstandard Employment Relations and Job Quality in the United States." *American Sociological Review* 65 (April): 256–278.

Kalof, Linda. 1999. "The Effects of Gender and Music Video Imagery on Sexual Attitudes." *Journal of Social Psychology* 139 (June): 378–385.

Kamin, Leon J. 1974. *The Science and Politics of IQ.* Potomac, MD: Erlbaum.

Kamin, Leon J. 1995. "Behind the Curve." *Scientific American* 272 (February): 99–103.

Kanter, Rosabeth Moss. 1977. *Men and Women of the Corporation.* New York: Basic Books.

Kaplan, Elaine Bell. 1996. *Not Our Kind of Girl: Unraveling the Myths of Black Teenage Motherhood.* Berkeley: University of California Press.

Kasarda, Jack. 1999. "Industrial Restructuring and the Changing Location of Jobs." In *State of the Union: America in the 1990s: Economic Trends,* edited by Reynolds Farley. New York: Russell Sage Foundation.

Katz, I., J. Wackenhut, and R. G. Hass. 1986. "Racial Ambivalence, Value Duality, and Behavior." Pp. 35-60 in *Prejudice, Discrimination, and Racism,* edited by J. F. Dovidio and S. L. Gaertner. New York: Academic Press.

Kaufman, Gayle. 1999. "The Portrayal of Men's Family Roles in Television Commercials." *Sex Roles* 41 (September): 439–458.

Keil, Thomas J., and Gennaro F. Vito. 1995. "Factors Influencing the Use of 'Truth in Sentencing' Law in Kentucky Murder Cases: A Research Note." *American Journal of Criminal Justice* 20 (Fall): 105–111.

Kelley, J. R., J. W. Jackson, and S. L. Huston-Comeaux. 1999. "The Effects of Time Pressure and Task Differences on Influence Models and Accuracy in Decision-Making Groups." *Personality and Social Psychology Bulletin* 23: 10–22.

Kendall, Lori. 2002. "'Oh No! I'm a Nerd!': Hegemonic Masculinity on an Online Forum." *Gender & Society* 14 (April): 256–274.

Kennedy, Robert E. 1989. *Life Choices: Applying Sociology,* 2nd ed. New York: Holt, Rinehart and Winston.

Kerr, N. L. 1992. "Issue Importance and Group Decision Making." Pp. 68–88 in *Group Process and Productivity,* edited by S. Worchel, W. Wood, and J. A. Simpson. Newbury Park, CA: Sage.

Kessler, Suzanne J. 1990. "The Medical Construction of Gender: Case Management of Intersexed Infants." *Signs* 16 (Autumn): 3–26.

Kilborn, Peter T., and Lynette Clemetson. 2002. "Gains of 90s Did Not Lift All, Census Shows." *The New York Times,* June 5: A1.

Kilborn, Peter. 1990. "Workers Using Computers Find a Supervisor Inside." *The New York Times* (December 23): A1ff.

Kim, Elaine H. 1993. "Home is Where the *Han* is: A Korean American Perspective on the Los Angeles Upheavals." Pp. 215–235 in *Reading Rodney King/Reading Urban Uprising,* edited by Robert Gooding-Williams. New York: Routledge.

Kimmel, Michael. 2000. "Saving the Males: The Sociological Implications of Virginia Military Institute and the Citadel." *Gender & Society* 14 (August): 494–516.

Kimmel, Michael S. 2001. "Masculinity as Homophobia: Fear, Shame, and Silence in the Construction of Gender Identity." Pp. 266–287 in *The Masculinities Reader,* edited by Stephen M. Whitehead and Frank J. Barrett. Cambridge: Polity.

Kimmel, Michael S., and Michael A. Messner. 2000. *Men's Lives,* 5th ed. Boston: Allyn and Bacon.

King, Mary C. 1992. "Occupational Segregation by Race and Sex, 1940–1988." *Monthly Labor Review* 11: 30–36.

Kingson, Eric R., and Jill Quadagno. 1995. "Social Security: Marketing Radical Reform." *Generations* 19 (Fall): 43–49.

Kirby, Douglas. 1997. "No Easy Answers: Research Findings on Programs to Reduce Teen Pregnancy." Washington, DC: National Campaign to Prevent Teen Pregnancy. Web site: **www.teenpregnancy.org**

Kitano, Harry. 1976. *Japanese Americans: The Evolution of a Subculture,* 2nd ed. New York: Prentice Hall.

Kitsuse, John I. 1980. "Coming Out All Over: Deviants and the Politics of Social Problems." *Social Problems* 28 (October): 1–13.

Kitsuse, John I., and Aaron V. Cicourel. 1963. "A Note on the Uses of Official Statistics." *Social Problems* 11 (Fall): 131–139.

Klausner, Samuel Z., and Edward F. Foulks. 1982. *Eskimo Capitalists: Oil, Alcohol, and Politics.* Totowa, NJ: Allanheld.

Kleinfeld, Judith S. 2002. "The Small World Problem." *Society* 39:61-66.

Klinger, Lori J., James A. Hamilton, and Peggy J. Cantrell. 2001."Children's Perceptions of Aggression and Gender-Specific Content in Toy Commercials." *Social Behavior and Personality* 29: 11–20.

Kluegel, J. R., and Lawrence Bobo. 1993. "Dimensions of Whites' Beliefs About the Black–White Socioeconomic Gap." Pp. 127–147 in *Race and Politics in American Society,* edited by P. Sniderman, P. Tetlock, and E. Carmines. Stanford, CA: Stanford University Press.

Kluegel, James R., and Eliot R. Smith. 1986. *Beliefs About Inequality.* New York: Aldine de Gruyter.

Kniss, Fred. 2003. "Church and State." *Contexts* 2 (Spring) 62–63.

Knoke, David. 1992. *Political Networks: The Structural Perspective.* New York: Cambridge University Press.

Kochen, M. (ed.). 1989. *The Small World.* Norwood, NJ: Ablex Press.

Kocieniewski, David, and Robert Hanley. 2000. "Racial Profiling Was Routine, New Jersey Says." *The New York Times* (November 28): 1.

Kohlberg, Lawrence. 1969. "'Stage and Sequence': The Cognitive-Developmental Approach to Socialization." Pp. 347–480 in *Handbook of Socialization and Research,* edited by D.A. Goslin. Chicago: Rand McNally.

Kovel, Johnathan. 1970. *White Racism: A Psychohistory.* New York: Pantheon.

Krasnodemski, Memory. 1996. "Justified Suffering: Attribution Theory Applied to Perceptions of the Poor in America." Unpublished senior thesis, Princeton University, Princeton, NJ.

Kraut, R., S. Kiesler, B. Boneva, J. Cummings, V. Helgeson, and A. Crawford. 2002. "Internet Paradox Revisited." *Journal of Social Issues* 58 (1): 49–74.

Kray, Susan. 1993. "Orientalization of an 'Almost White' Woman: The Interlocking Effects of Race, Class, Gender and Ethnicity in American Mass Media." *Critical Studies in Mass Communication* 10 (December): 349–366.

Kristof, Nicholas. 1996. "Aging World, New Wrinkles." *The New York Times* (September 22): Section 4: 1ff.

Kuhn, Harold W. and Sylvia Nasar. 2002. *The Essential John Nash.* Princeton: Princeton University Press.

Kulis, Stephen, Flavio Francisco Marsiglia, and Michael L. Hecht. 2002. "Gender Labels and Gender Identity as Predictors of Drug Use among Ethnically Diverse Middle School Students." *Youth and Society* 33 (March): 442–475.

Kurz, Demi. 1989. "Social Science Perspectives on Wife Abuse: Current Debates and Future Directions." *Gender & Society* 3 (December): 489–505.

Kurzman, Charles. 1996. "Structural Opportunity and Perceived Opportunity in Social Movement Theory: The Iranian Revolution of 1979." *American Sociological Review* 61 (February): 153–170.

Ladner, Joyce A. 1986. "Teenage Pregnancy: Implications for Black Americans." Pp. 65–84 in *The State of Black America 1986,* edited by James D. Williams. New York: National Urban League.

Ladner, Joyce A. 1995 [1971]. *Tomorrow's Tomorrow the Black Woman,* rev. ed. Garden City, NY: Doubleday.

LaFlamme, Darquise, Andree Pomerrleau, and Gerard Malcuit. 2002. "A Comparison of Fathers' and Mothers' Involvement in Childcare and Stimulation Behaviors during Free-Play with Their Infants at 9 and 15 Months." *Sex Roles* 11–12 (December): 507–518.

Lamanna, Mary Ann, and Agnes Riedman. 2003. *Marriage and Families: Making Choices in a Diverse Society.* Belmont, CA: Wadsworth

Lamb, Michael. 1998. "Cybersex: Research Notes on the Characteristics of the Visitors to Online Chat Rooms." *Deviant Behavior* 19 (April–June): 121–135.

Lamont, Michèle. 1992. *Money, Morals, and Manners: The Culture of the French and the American Upper-Middle Class.* Chicago: University of Chicago Press.

Lamont, Michèle. 2000. "Meaning-Making in Cultural Sociology: Broadening Our Agenda." *Contemporary Sociology* 29 (July): 602–607.

Lamphere, Louise, Alex Stepick, and Guillermo Grenier (eds.). 1994. *Newcomers in the Workplace: Immigrants and the Restructuring of the U.S. Economy.* Philadelphia: Temple University Press.

Landry, Bart. 2000. *Black Working Wives: Pioneers of the Americana Family Revolution.* Berkeley: University of California Press.

Langhinrichsen-Rohling, Jennifer. Peter Lewinsohn, Paul Rohde, John Seeley, Candice M. Monson, Kathryn A. Meyer, and Richard Langford. 1998. "Gender Differences in the Suicide-Related Behaviors of Adolescents and Young Adults." *Sex Roles* 39 (December): 839–854.

Langlois, J. H., L. Kalakanis, A. J. Rubenstein, A. Larson, M. Hallam, and M. Smoot. 2000. "Maxims or Myths of Beauty? A Meta-Analytic and Theoretical Review." *Psychological Bulletin* 126: 390–423.

Larana, Enrique, Hank Johnston, and Joseph R. Gusfield (eds.). 1994. *New Social Movements: From Ideology to Identity.* Philadelphia: Temple University Press.

Lau, Bonnie. 2002. *Stereotype Threat: Minority Education, Intelligence Theory, Affirmative Action, and an Empirical Study of Women in the Quantitative Domain.* Princeton, NJ: Princeton University Senior Thesis.

Lau, Bonnie, and Howard F. Taylor. 2003. "Ethnic and Gender Stereotype Threat Among Asian Women in Quantitative Test Performance." Manuscript, Department of Sociology, Princeton University.

Laumann, Edward O., John H. Gagnon, Robert T. Michael, and Stuart Michaels. 1994. *The Social Organization of Sexuality: Sexual Practices in the United States.* Chicago: University of Chicago Press.

Lavelle, Louis. 2001. "Executive Pay." *Business Week,* April 16. Web site: **www.businessweek.com**

Lederman, Douglas. 1992. "Men Outnumber Women and Get Most of the Money in Big-Time Sports Programs." *The Chronicle of Higher Education* 38 (April): A1ff.

Lee, Matthew T., and M. David Ermann. 1999. "Pinto 'Madness' as a Flawed Landmark Narrative: An Organizational and Network Analysis." *Social Problems* 46 (February): 30–47.

Lee, Sharon M. 1993. "Racial Classification in the U.S. Census: 1890–1990." *Ethnic and Racial Studies* 16(1): 75–94.

Lee, Sharon M. 1994. "Poverty and the U.S. Asian Population." *Social Science Quarterly* 75 (September): 541–559.

Lee, Stacey J. 1996. *Unraveling the "Model Minority" Stereotype: Listening to Asian American Youth.* New York: Teacher's College Press.

Legge, Jerome S. Jr., 1993. "The Persistence of Ethnic Voting: African Americans and Jews in the 1989 New York Mayoral Campaign." *Contemporary Jewry* 14: 133–146.

Lehmann, Nicholas. 1999. *The Big Test: The Secret History of the American Meritocracy.* New York: Farrar, Straus, and Giroux.

Leidner, Robin. 1993. *Fast Food, Fast Talk: Service Work and the Routinization of Everyday Life.* Berkeley: University of California Press.

Lemert, Edwin M. 1972. *Human Deviance, Social Problems, and Social Control.* Englewood Cliffs, NJ: Prentice Hall.

Lempert, Lora Bex, and Marjorie DeVault. 2000. "Guest Editors' Introduction: Special Issue on Emergence and Reconfigured Forms of Family Life." *Gender & Society* 14 (February): 6–10.

Lenski, Gerhard, Jean Lenski, and Patrick Nolan. 1998. *Human Societies: An Introduction to Macro-Sociology,* 8th ed. New York: McGraw Hill.

Lenski, Gerhard, Jean Lenski, and Patrick Nolan. 2001. *Human Societies: An Introduction to Macro-Sociology.* 9th ed. New York: McGraw Hill.

Lersch, Kim-Michelle, and Joe R. Feagin. 1996. "Violent Police–Citizen Encounters: An Analysis of Major Newspaper Accounts." *Critical Sociology* 22: 29–49.

Lever, Janet. 1978. "Sex Differences in the Complexity of Children's Play and Games." *American Sociological Review* 43 (August): 471–483.

Levine, Adeline. 1982. *Love Canal: Science, Politics, and People.* Lexington, MA: Lexington Books.

Levine, Art. 1987. "The Uneven Odds." *U.S. News and World Report* (August 17): 31–33.

Levine, Felice J., and Katherine J. Rosich. 1996. *Social Causes of Violence: Crafting a Science Agenda.* Washington, DC: American Sociological Association.

Levine, John M., and Richard L. Moreland. 1998. "Small Groups." Pp. 415–469 in *The Handbook of Social Psychology,* 4th ed., edited by Daniel T. Gilbert, Susan T. Fiske, and Gardner Lindzey. New York: Oxford University and McGraw-Hill.

Levine, Lawrence. 1984. "William Shakespeare and the American People: A Study in Cultural Transformation." *American Historical Review* 89 (1): 34–66.

Levy, Marion J. 1949. *The Structure of Society.* Princeton, NJ: Princeton University Press.

Lewin, Tamar. 2002. "Study Links Working Mothers to Slower Learning." *The New York Times.* July 17: A14.

Lewis, Dan A., Amy Bush Stevens, and Kristen Shook Slack. 2002. *Illinois Families Study, Welfare Reform in Illinois: Is the Moderate Approach Working?* Evanston, IL: Institute for Poverty Research, Northwestern University.

Lewis, Oscar. 1960. *Five Families: Mexican Case Studies in the Culture of Poverty.* New York: Basic Books.

Lewis, Oscar. 1966. "The Culture of Poverty." *Scientific American* 215 (October): 19–25.

Lewontin, Richard. 1996. *Human Diversity.* New York: W. H. Freeman.

Lewontin, Richard C. 1996 [1970]. "Race and Intelligence." *Bulletin of the Atomic Scientists* 26: 2–8.

Lieberson, Stanley. 1980. *A Piece of the Pie: Black and White Immigrants Since 1880.* Berkeley: University of California Press.

Light, Ivan, Rebecca Kim, and Connie Hum. 1998. "Globalization, Vacancy Chains, or Migration Networks? Immigrant Employment and Income in Greater Los Angeles, 1970-1990." Paper presented at the International Sociological Association.

Lin, Carolyn A. 1998. "Uses of Sex Appeal in Prime-Time Television Commercials." *Sex Roles* 38 (March): 461–475.

Lin, Nan. 1989. "The Small World Technique as a Theory Construction Tool." Pp. 231–238 in *The Small World,* edited by M. Kochen. Norwood, NJ: Ablex Press.

Linton, Ralph. 1937. *The Study of Man.* New York: Appleton-Century.

Livingston, I. L. 1994. *Handbook of Black American Health: The Mosaic of Conditions, Issues and Prospects.* Westport, CT: Greenwood.

Lo, Clarence. 1990. *Small Property Versus Big Government: Social Origins of the Property Tax Revolt.* Berkeley: University of California Press.

Locklear, Erin M. 1999. *Where Race and Politics Collide: The Federal Acknowledgement Process and Its Effects on Lumsee and Pequot Indians.* Unpublished senior thesis, Princeton University.

Logan, John, and Harvey L. Molotch. 1987. *Urban Fortunes: The Political Economy of Place.* Berkeley: University of California Press.

Logio-Rau, Kim. 1998. "Here's Looking at You, Kid: Race, Gender and Health Behaviors among Adolescents." Unpublished doctoral dissertation, University of Delaware.

Longman, Jere. 1996. "Left Alone in His Frigid House, DuPont Heir Is Seized by Police." *The New York Times* (January 29): A1.

Lopata, Helene Z., and Barrie Thorne. 1978. "On the Term 'Sex Roles.'" *Signs* 3 (Spring): 718–721.

Lorber, Judith. 1994. *Paradoxes of Gender.* New Haven, CT: Yale University Press.

Loredo, Carren, Anne Reid, and Kay Deaux. 1995. "Judgments and Definitions of Sexual Harassment by High School Students." *Sex Roles* 32 (January): 29–45.

Lorenz, Konrad. 1966. *On Aggression.* New York: Harcourt.

Louie, Miriam Ching Yoon. 2001. *Sweatshop Warriors: Immigrant Women Workers Take on the Global Factory.* Cambridge, MA: South End Press.

Lovejoy, M. 2001. "Disturbances in the Social Body: Differences in Body Image and Eating Problems among African American and White Women." *Gender & Society* 15, Part 2: 239–261.

Lucal, Betsy. 1994. "Class Stratification in Introductory Textbooks: Relational or Distributional Models?" *Teaching Sociology* 22 (April): 139–150.

Lucas, Samuel R. 1999. *Tracking Inequality: Stratification and Mobility in American High Schools.* New York: Teacher's College Press.

Luckenbill, David F. 1986. "Deviant Career Mobility: The Case of Male Prostitutes." *Social Problems* 33 (April): 283–296.

Luker, Kristin. 1975. *Taking Chances.* Berkeley, CA: University of California Press.

Luker, Kristin. 1984. *Abortion and the Politics of Motherhood.* Berkeley, CA: University of California Press.

Luker, Kristin. 1996. *Dubious Conceptions: The Politics of Teenage Pregnancy.* Cambridge, MA: Harvard University Press.

Lupton, Deborah. 2002. "Road Rage: Drivers' Understandings and Experiences." *Journal of Sociology* 36 (September): 275–290.

Lyons, Linda. 2002. "Teen Attitudes Contradict Sex-Crazed Stereotype." *Gallup Poll.* January 29. www.gallup.com

Lyons, Linda. 2003. "U.S. Next Down the Aisle Toward Gay Marriage?" Princeton, N.J.: The Gallup Poll. www.gallup.com

Machel, Graca. 1996. *Impact of Armed Conflict on Children.* New York: UNICEF/United Nations.

MacKay, N. J., and K. Covell. 1997. "The Impact of Women in Advertisements on Attitudes Toward Women." *Sex Roles* 36 (May): 573–583.

MacKinnon, Catherine. 1983. "Feminism, Marxism, Method, and the State: An Agenda for Theory." *Signs* 7 (Spring): 635–658.

MacKinnon, Neil J., and Tom Langford. 1994. "The Meaning of Occupational Prestige Scores: A Social Psychological Analysis and Interpretation." *Sociological Quarterly* 35 (May): 215–145.

Mackintosh, N. J. 1995. *Cyril Burt: Fraud or Framed?* Oxford: Oxford University Press.

MacLeod, Jay. 1995. *Ain't No Makin' It: Aspirations and Attainment in a Low-Income Neighborhood.* Boulder, CO: Westview Press.

Madriz, Esther. 1997. *Nothing Bad Happens to Good Girls: Fear of Crime in Women's Lives.* Berkeley: University of California Press.

Maguire, Kathleen, Ann L. Pastore, and Timothy Flanagan. 1993. *Sourcebook of Criminal Justice Statistics.* Washington, DC: U.S. Department of Justice.

Malcomson, Scott L. 2000. *The American Misadventure of Race.* New York: Farrar, Strauss, and Giroux.

Maldonado, Lionel, A. 1997. "Mexicans in the American System: A Common Destiny." In *Ethnicity in the United States: An Institutional Approach,* edited by William Velez. Bayside, NY: General Hall.

Maldonado, Lionel A., and Charles V. Willie. 1996. "Developing a 'Pipeline' Recruitment

Program for Minority Faculty." Pp. 330–371 in *Educating a New Majority: Transforming America's Educational System for Diversity,* edited by Laura I. Rendon and Richard O. Hope. San Francisco: Jossey-Bass.

Malthus, Thomas Robert. 1798 [1926]. *First Essay on Population 1798.* London: Macmillan.

Manning, Wendy, Monica Longmore, and Peggy Giordano. 2000. "The Relationship Context of Contraceptive Use at First Intercourse." *Family Planning Perspectives* 32 (May/June): 104–110.

Manning, Winton H., and Rex Jackson. 1984. "College Entrance Examinations: Objective Selection or Gatekeeping for the Economically Privileged." Edited by Cecil R. Reynolds and Robert T. Brown. *Perspectives on Bias in Mental Testing* New York: Plenum.

Marciniak, Liz-Marie. 1998. "Adolescent Attitudes Toward Victim Precipitation of Rape." *Violence and Victims* 12 (Fall): 287–300.

Marcuse, Herbert. 1964. *One-Dimensional Man.* Boston: Beacon Press.

Margolin, Leslie. 1992. "Deviance on Record: Techniques for Labeling Child Abusers in Official Documents." *Social Problems* 39 (February): 58–70.

Marks, Carole. 1989. *Farewell, We're Good and Gone: The Great Black Migration.* Bloomington: Indiana University Press.

Marks, Carole. 1991. "The Urban Underclass." *Annual Review of Sociology* 11 (1985): 445–466.

Marks, Carole, and Deana Edkins. 1999. *The Power of Pride: Stylemakers and Rulebreakers of the Harlem Renaissance.* New York: Crown.

Marquis, Christopher. 2003. "Total of Unmarried Couples Surged in 2000 Census." *The New York Times* (March 13): A32.

Marshall, Susan. 1997. *Splintered Sisterhood: Gender & Class in the Campaign against Woman Suffrage.* Madison, WI: University of Wisconsin Press.

Martin, Patricia Yancey, and Robert A. Hummer. 1989. "Fraternities and Rape on Campus." *Gender & Society* 3 (December): 457–473.

Martin, Susan Ehrlich. 1989. "Sexual Harassment: The Link between Gender Stratification, Sexuality, and Women's Economic Status." Pp. 57–75 in *Women: A Feminist Perspective,* 4th ed., edited by Jo Freeman. Mountain View, CA: Mayfield.

Martinez, Ramiro. 1996. "Latinos and Lethal Violence: The Impact of Poverty and Inequality." *Social Problems* 43 (May): 131–146.

Martinez, Ramiro. 2002. *Latino Homicide: Immigration, Violence and Community.* New York: Routledge.

Marx, Anthony. 1997. *Making Race and Nation: A Comparison of the United States, South Africa, and Brazil.* New York: Cambridge University Press.

Marx, Gary T. 1967. "Religion: Opiate or Inspiration of Civil Rights Militancy among Negroes." *American Sociological Review* 32 (February): 64–72.

Marx, Gary T., and Douglas McAdam. 1994. *Collective Behavior and Social Movements: Process and Structure.* Englewood Cliffs, NJ: Prentice Hall.

Marx, Karl. 1967 [1867]. *Capital.* Edited by F. Engels. New York: International Publishers.

Marx, Karl. 1972 [1845]. "The German Ideology." Pp. 110–164 in *The Marx-Engels Reader,* edited by Robert C. Tucker. New York: W.W. Norton.

Massey, Douglas S. 1993. "Latino Poverty Research: An Agenda for the 1990s." *Social Science Research Council Newsletter* 47 (March): 7–11.

Massey, Douglas S., and Nancy A. Denton. 1993. *American Apartheid: Segregation and the Making of the Underclass.* Cambridge, MA: Harvard University Press.

Mast, Marianne Schmid. 2001. "Gender Differences and Similarities in Dominance Hierarchies in Same-Gender Groups Based on Speaking Time." *Sex Roles* 44 (May): 537–556.

Mathews, Linda. 1996. "More Than Identity Rests on a New Racial Category." *The New York Times* (July 6): 1–7.

Mauer, Marc. 1999. *Race to Incarcerate.* New York: The New Press.

McAdam, Doug. 1982. *Political Process and the Development of Black Insurgency.* Chicago: University of Chicago Press.

McAdam, Doug. 1999. *Political Process and the Development of Black Insurgency. 1930–1970,* 2nd ed. Chicago: University of Chicago Press.

McCall, Leslie. 2001. *Complex Inequality: Gender, Class, and Race in the New Economy.* New York: Routledge.

McCarthy, John, and Mayer Zald. 1973. *The Trend of Social Movements in America: Professionalism and Resource Mobilization.* Morristown, NJ: General Learning Press.

McCauley, C. 1989. "The Nature of Social Influence in Groupthink: Compliance and Internalization." *Journal of Personality and Social Psychology* 57 (August): 250–260.

McClelland, Susan. 2003. "A Grim Toll on the Innocent." *Maclean's* (May 12): 20.

McCord, William. 1991. "The Asian Renaissance." *Society* 28 (September–October): 50–61.

McCord, William, and Arline McCord. 1986. *Paths to Progress: Bread and Freedom in Developing Societies.* New York: W.W. Norton.

McCrate, Elaine, and Joan Smith. 1998. "When Work Doesn't Work: The Failure of Current Welfare Reform." *Gender & Society* 12 (February): 61–81.

McGuire, Gail M., and Barbara F. Reskin. 1993. "Authority Hierarchies at Work: The Impacts of Race and Sex." *Gender & Society* 7 (December): 487–506.

McKenna, K. Y. A., A. S. Green, and M. E. J. Gleason. 2002. "Relationship Formation on the Internet: What's the Big Attraction?" *Journal of Social Issues* 58 (1): 9–32.

McKinney, Kathleen. 1992. "Contrapower Sexual Harassment: The Offender's Viewpoint." *Free Inquiry in Creative Sociology* 20 (May): 3–10.

McLane, Daisann. 1995. "The Cuban-American Princess." *The New York Times Magazine* (February 26): 42.

McLoyd, Vonnie C., Ana Mari Cauce, David Takeuchi, and Leon Wilson. 2000. "Marital Processes and Parental Socialization in Families of Color: A Decade Review of Research." *Journal of Marriage and the Family* 62 (November): 1070–1093.

Mead, George Herbert. 1934. *Mind, Self, and Society.* Chicago: University of Chicago Press.

Meng, Susan. 2001. "Pet Sanctuary." *Forbes* (October 8): 236.

Meredith, Martin. 2003. *Elephant Destiny: Biography of an Endangered Species in Africa.* New York: HarperCollins.

Mernissi, Fataima. 1987. *Beyond the Veil: Male-Female Dynamics in Modern Muslim Society.* Bloomington, IN: Indiana University Press.

Merton, Robert K. 1957. *Social Theory and Social Structure.* New York: Free Press.

Merton, Robert K. 1968. "Social Structure and Anomie." *American Sociological Review* 3: 672–682.

Merton, Robert, and Alice K. Rossi. 1950. "Contributions to the Theory of Reference Group Behavior." Pp. 279–334 in *Continuities in Social Research Studies, Scope and Method of "The American Soldier* edited by Robert K. Merton and Paul F. Lazarsfeld. New York: Free Press.

Messerschmidt, James W. 1997. *Crime as Structured Action: Gender, Race, Class and Crime in the Making.* Thousand Oaks, CA: Sage.

Messner, Michael A. 1992. *Power at Play: Sports and the Problem of Masculinity.* Boston: Beacon Press.

Messner, Michael A. 2002. *Taking the Field: Women, Men, and Sports.* Minneapolis: University of Minnesota Press.

Metz, Michael A., B. R. Rosser-Simon, and Nancy Strapko. 1994. "Differences in Conflict-Resolution Styles Among Heterosexual, Gay, and Lesbian Couples." *Journal of Sex Research* 31: 293–308.

Meyer, David S., and Joshua Gamson. 1995. "The Challenge of Cultural Elites: Celebrities and Social Movements." *Sociological Inquiry* 65 (Spring): 181–206.

Michael, Robert T., John H. Gagnon, Edward O. Laumann, and Gina Kolata. 1994. *Sex in America: A Definitive Survey.* Boston: Little, Brown and Company.

Michel, Robert T., Heidi I. Hartmann, and Brigid O'Farrell (eds.). 1989. *Pay Equity: Empirical Inquiries.* Washington, DC: National Academy Press.

Mickelson, Roslyn Arlin, ed. 2000. *Children on the Streets of the Americas: Globalization, Homelessness, and Education in the United States, Brazil, and Cuba.* New York: Routledge.

Milgram, Stanley. 1974. *Obedience to Authority: An Experimental View.* New York: Harper & Row.

Milkie, Melissa A. 1999. "Social Comparisons, Reflected Appraisals, and Mass Media: The Impact of Pervasive Beauty Images on Black and White Girls' Self-Concepts." *Social Psychology Quarterly* 62 (June): 190–210.

Miller, Eleanor. 1986. *Street Women.* Philadelphia: Temple University Press.

Miller, Eleanor. 1991. "Jeffrey Dahmer, Racism, Homophobia, and Feminism." *SWS Network News* 8 (December): 2.

Mills, C. Wright. 1956. *The Power Elite.* New York: Oxford University Press.

Mills, C. Wright. 1959. *The Sociological Imagination.* New York: Oxford University Press.

Min, Pyong G. 1990. "Problems of Korean Immigrant Entrepreneurs." *International Migration Review* 24 (Fall): 436–455.

Mink, Gwendolyn. 1999. *Whose Welfare?* Ithaca, NY: Cornell University Press.

Mintz, Beth, and Michael Schwartz. 1985. *The Power Structure of American Business.* Chicago: University of Chicago Press.

Mirandé, Alfredo. 1985. *The Chicano Experience.* Notre Dame, IN: Notre Dame University Press.

Mishel, Lawrence, Jared Bernstein, and Heather Boushey. 2003. *The State of Working America 2002–03.* Washington, DC: Economic Policy Institute.

Mizruchi, Mark S. 1992. *The Structure of Corporate Political Action: Interfirm Relations and Their Consequences.* Cambridge, MA: Harvard University Press.

Mizutami, Osamu. 1990. *Situational Japanese.* Tokyo: The Japan Times.

Moen, Phyllis, Jungmeen E. Kim, and Heather Hofmeister. 2001. "Couples' Work/Retirement Transitions, Gender, and Marital Quality." *Social Psychology Quarterly* 64 (March): 55–71.

Moller, Lora C., Shelley Hymel, and Kenneth H. Rubin. 1992. "Sex Typing in Play and Popularity in Middle Childhood." *Sex Roles* 26 (April): 331–353.

Money, John. 1985. "Gender: History, Theory and Usage of the Term in Sexology and Its Relationship to Nature/Nurture." *Journal of Sex and Marital Therapy* 11 (Summer): 71–79.

Montada, L., and M. Lerner Jr. (eds.). 1998. *Responses to Victimization and Beliefs in a Just World.* New York: Plenum.

Montagne, Peter. 1995. "Review of Julian L. Simon, ed., *The State of Humanity.*" Cambridge, MA: Blackwell.

Montgomery, James D. 1992. "Job Search and Network Composition: Implications of the Strength of Work Ties Hypothesis." *American Sociological Review* 57 (October): 586–596.

Moore, Gwen. 1979. "The Structure of a National Elite Network." *American Sociological Review* 44 (October): 673–692.

Moore, Joan. 1976. *Hispanics in the United States.* Englewood Cliffs, NJ: Prentice Hall.

Moore, Joan W., and John M. Hagedorn. 1996. "What Happens to Girls in Gangs?" Pp. 205–218 in *Gangs in America,* edited by C. Ronald Huff. Thousand Oaks, CA: Sage.

Moore, Robert B. 1992. "Racist Stereotyping in the English Language." Pp. 317–328 in *Race, Class, and Gender: An Anthology,* 2nd ed., edited by Margaret L. Andersen and Patricia Hill Collins. Belmont, CA: Wadsworth.

Moore, Valerie A. 2001. "'Doing' Racialized and Gendered Age to Organize Peer Relations: Observing Kids in Summer Camp." *Gender & Society* 15 (December): 835–858.

Moreland, Richard L., and Scott R. Beach. 1992. "Exposure Effects in the Classroom: The Development of Affinity among Students." *Journal of Experimental Social Psychology* 28: 255–276.

Morgan, Lewis H. 1877. *Ancient Society, or Researches in the Lines of Human Progress, from Savagery Through Barbarism to Civilization.* Cambridge: Harvard University Press.

Morris, Aldon. 1984. *The Origins of the Civil Rights Movement: Black Communities Organizing for Change.* New York: Free Press.

Morris, Aldon D. 1999. "A Retrospective on the Civil Rights Movement: Political and Intellectual Landmarks." *Annual Review of Sociology* 25: 517–539.

Morris, Aldon, and Carol McClurg Mueller (eds.). 1992. *Frontiers in Social Movement Theory.* New Haven, CT: Yale University Press.

Moskos, Charles. 1988. *Soldiers and Sociology.* Alexandria, VA: U.S. Army Research Institute for the Social and Behavioral Sciences.

Moskos, Charles. 1992. "Right Behind You, Scarlett!" Pp. 40–54 in *Women in the Military,* edited by E. A. Blacksmith. New York: H. W. Wilson.

Moskos, Charles C., and John Sibley Butler. 1996. *All That We Can Be: Black Leadership and Racial Integration the Army Way.* New York: Basic Books.

Moynihan, Daniel P. 1965. *The Negro Family: The Case for National Action.* Washington, DC: Office of Policy Planning and Research, U.S. Department of Labor.

Muller, Thomas, and Thomas J. Espenshade. 1985. *The Fourth Wave: California's Newest Immigrants.* Washington, DC: The Urban Institute Press.

Mumola, Christopher J., and Allen J. Beck. 1997. *Prisoners in 1996.* Washington, DC: U.S. Department of Justice.

Myers, Steven Lee. 2000. "Survey of Troops Finds Antigay Bias Common in Service." *The New York Times* (March 24): 1.

Myers, Walter D. 1998. *Amistad Affair.* New York: NAL/Dutton.

Myerson, Allen R. 1998. "Rating the Bigshots: Gates vs. Rockefeller." *The New York Times* (May 24): 4.

Myrdal, Gunner. 1944. *An American Dilemma: The Negro Problem and Modern Democracy.* 2 Vols. New York: Harper and Row.

NAACP Legal Defense and Education Fund. 2003. *Annual Report.* Washington DC: NAACP Legal Defense Fund.

Nack, Adina. 2000. "Damaged Goods: Women Managing the Stigma of AIDS." *Deviant Behavior* 21: 95–121.

Nagel, Joane. 1996. *American Indian Ethnic Renewal: Red Power and the Resurgence of Identity and Culture.* New York: Oxford University Press.

Nagel, Joane. 2003. *Race, Ethnicity, and Sexuality: Intimate Intersections, Forbidden Frontiers.* New York: Oxford University Press.

Namboodiri, Krishnan. 1988. "Ecological Demography: Its Place in Sociology." *American Sociological Review* 53 (August): 619–633.

Nanda, Serena. 1998. *Neither Man Nor Woman: The Hijras of India.* Belmont, CA: Wadsworth Publishing Co.

Nardi, Peter M., and Beth Schneider. 1997. *Social Perspectives on Lesbian and Gay Studies.* New York: Routledge.

Nash, John F. 1951. "Non-Cooperative Games." *Annals of Mathematics* 54: 286–295.

Nathanson, Constance A. 1999. "Social Movements as Catalysts for Policy Change: The Case of Smoking and Guns." *Journal of Health Politics, Policy, and Law* 24 (June): 421–488.

National Cancer Institute. 2000. *Cancer among Blacks and Other Minorities: Statistical Profiles.* Washington, DC: U.S. Department of Health and Human Services, Public Health Service, National Institutes of Health.

National Cancer Institute. 2002. *Cancer Among Blacks and Other Minorities: Statistical Profiles.* Washington, DC: U. S. Department of Health and Human Services, National Institutes of Health.

National Center for Health Statistics. 2001. *Health United States 2001.* Washington, DC: Department of Health and Human Services.

National Center for Health Statistics. 2002. *Health United States 2002.* Hyattsville, MD: U.S. Department of Health and Human Services.

National Center for Health Statistics. 2002. *National Vital Statistics Report* 50 (No. 6, March 21).

National Coalition for the Homeless. 2002. *Facts about Homelessness.* Washington, DC: National Coalition for the Homeless. Web site: **www.nationalhomeless.org**

National Collegiate Athletic Association. 2002. *NCAA Year-by-Year Sports Participation (1982–2001).* Indianapolis, IN: NCAA. Web site: **www.ncaa.org**

National Opinion Research Center. 2002. *General Social Survey.* Web site: **www.norc. uchicago.edu**

National Television Violence Study. 1997. *National Television Violence Study.* Thousand Oaks, CA: Sage Publications.

National Urban League. 2002. *The State of Black America.* New York: National Urban League.

Nee, Victor. 1973. *Longtime Californ': A Documentary Study of an American Chinatown.* New York: Pantheon Books.

Neppl, Tricia K., and Ann D. Murray. 1997. "Social Dominance and Play Patterns among Preschoolers: Gender Comparisons." *Sex Roles* 36 (March): 381–394.

Newman, Katherine S. 1988. *Falling from Grace: The Experience of Downward Mobility in the American Middle Class.* New York: Free Press.

Newman, Katherine S. 1993. *Declining Fortunes: The Withering of the American Dream.* New York: Basic Books.

Newman, Katherine. 1999. *No Shame in My Game: The Working Poor in the Inner City.* New York: Russell Sage Foundation/Vintage.

Newport, Frank. 2000. "Women's Most Pressing Concerns Today are Money, Family, Health, and Stress." *The Gallup Poll Monthly* (March): 40–41.

Newport, Frank. 2001. "American Attitudes Toward Homosexuality Continue to Be More Tolerant." *The Gallup Poll* (June 4): Princeton, NJ: Gallup Organization.

Newport, Frank. 2003. "Six Out of 10 Americans Say Homosexual Relations Should Be Recognized As Legal." *The Gallup Poll.*

Princeton, NJ: The Gallup Organization. Web site: www.gallup.com

Nisbet, Paul A. 1997. "Suicide Opportunity as a Function of Effective Network Size." Paper presented at the Annual Meetings of the American Sociological Association.

Nock, Steven L. 1998. "The Consequences of Premarital Fatherhood." *American Sociological Review* 6 (April): 250–263.

Oakes, Jeannie. 1985. *Keeping Track: How Schools Structure Inequality.* New Haven: Yale University Press.

Oakes, Jeannie. 1990. "Multiplying Inequalities: The Effects of Race, Social Class and Tracking on Opportunities to Learn Mathematics and Science." RAND for National Science Foundation.

Oakes, Jeannie, and Martin Lipton. 1996. "Developing Alternatives to Tracking and Grading." Pp. 168–200 in *Educating A New Majority: Transforming America's Educational System for Diversity,* edited by Laura I. Rendon and Richard O. Hope. San Francisco: Jossey-Bass.

Ogburn, William F. 1922. *Social Change with Respect to Cultural and Original Nature.* New York: B. W. Huebsch.

Oliver, Melvin, and Thomas M. Shapiro. 1995. *Black Wealth/White Wealth: A New Perspective on Racial Inequality.* New York: Routledge.

Ollivier, Michele. 2000. "'Too Much Money off Other People's Backs': Status in Late Modern Societies." *Canadian Journal of Sociology* 25 (Fall): 441–470.

Omi, Michael, and Howard Winant. 1994. *Racial Formation in the United States,* 2nd ed. New York: Routledge.

O'Neil, John. 2002. "Parent Smoking and Teenage Sex." *The New York Times,* September 3: F7.

Ono, Hiroshi, and Madeline Zavodny. 2003. "Gender and the Internet." *Social Science Quarterly* 84 (March).

Ornstein, Norman J., Thomas E. Mann, and Michael J. Malbin. 1996. *Vital Statistics on Congress, 1995–1996.* Washington, DC: Congressional Quarterly, Inc.

Ortiz, Vilma, and Rosemary Santana Cooney. 1984. "Sex Role Attitudes and Labor Force Participation among Young Hispanic Females and Non-Hispanic White Females." *Social Science Quarterly* 6 (June): 392–400.

Ouchi, William. 1981. *Theory Z: How American Business Can Meet the Japanese Challenge.* Reading, MA: Addison-Wesley.

Owens, Sarah E. 1998. "The Effects of Race, Gender, Their Interactions, and Selected School Variables upon Educational Aspirations and Achievements." Senior thesis, Princeton University, Department of Sociology.

Padavic, Irene. 1992. "White Collar Values and Women's Interest in Blue-Collar Jobs." *Gender & Society* 6 (June): 215–230.

Padavic, Irene, and Barbara Reskin. 2002. *Women and Men at Work,* 2nd ed. Thousand Oaks: Sage.

Page, Charles H. 1946. "Bureaucracy's Other Face." *Social Forces* 25 (October): 89–94.

Palen, John J. 1992. *The Urban World.* New York: McGraw-Hill.

Palmore, Erdman, and Daisaku Maeda. 1985. *The Honorable Elders Revisited: A Revised Cross-Cultural Analysis of Aging in Japan.* Durham, NC: Duke University Press.

Park, Robert E., and Ernest W. Burgess. 1921. *Introduction to the Science of Society.* Chicago: University of Chicago Press.

Parreñas, Rhacel Salazar. 2001. *Servants of Globalization: Women, Migration, and Domestic Work.* Stanford, CA: Stanford University Press.

Parsons, Talcott (ed.). 1947. *Max Weber: The Theory of Social and Economic Organization.* New York: Free Press.

Parsons, Talcott. 1951a. *The Social System.* Glencoe, IL: Free Press.

Parsons, Talcott. 1951b. *Toward a General Theory of Action.* Cambridge, MA: Harvard University Press.

Parsons, Talcott. 1966. *Societies: Evolutionary and Comparative Perspectives.* Englewood Cliffs, NJ: Prentice Hall.

Paternoster, Raymond et al. 2003. "An Empirical Analysis of Maryland's Death Sentencing System with Respect to the Influence of Race and Legal Jurisdiction." **http://www. urhome.umd.edu/newsdesk**

Pattillo-McCoy, Mary. 1999. *Black Picket Fences: Privilege and Peril among the Black Middle Class.* Chicago: University of Chicago Press.

Payne, Deborah M., John T. Warner, and Roger D. Little. 1992. "Tied Migration and Returns to Human Capital: The Case of Military Wives." *Social Science Quarterly* 73 (June): 324–339.

Pedraza, Silvia. 1996a. "Cuba's Refugees: Manifold Migrations." Pp. 263–279 in *Origins and Destinies: Immigration, Race, and Ethnicity in America,* edited by Silvia Pedraza and Rubén Rumbaut. Belmont, CA: Wadsworth.

Pedraza, Sylvia, and Rubén G. Rumbaut. (eds.). 1996. *Origins and Destinies: Immigration, Race, and Ethnicity in America.* Belmont, CA: Wadsworth.

Pellow, David N., 2003. *Garbage Wars: The Struggle for Environmental Justice in Chicago.* Cambridge, MA: The MIT Press.

Pennock-Roman, Maria. 1994. "College Major and Gender Differences in the Prediction of College Grades." College Board Research Report No. 94–2, ETS Research Reports No. 94–24.

Peralta, Robert L. 2002. *Getting Trashed in College: Doing Alcohol, Doing Gender, Doing Violence,* Ph. D. Dissertation, University of Delaware.

Perez, Denise N. 1996. *A Case for Derailment: Tracking in the American Public School System as an Obstacle to the Improvement of Minority Education.* Senior thesis, Princeton University, Department of Sociology.

Perrow, Charles. 1986. *Complex Organization: A Critical Essay,* 3rd ed. New York: Random House.

Perrow, Charles. 1994. "The Limit of Safety: The Enhancement of a Theory of Accidents." *Journal of Contingencies and Crisis Management* 22: 212–220.

Persell, Caroline Hodges. 1990. *Understanding Society: An Introduction to Sociology.* New York: Harper & Row.

Peters, Debra K., and Lillian M. Range.1995. "Childhood Sexual Abuse and Current Suicidality in College Women and Men." *Child Abuse and Neglect* 19 (March): 335–341.

Petersen, Trond, Ishak Saporta, and Mark-David L. Seidel. 2000. "Offering A Job: Meritocracy and Social Networks." *American Journal of Sociology* 106 (November): 763–816.

Peterson, Richard R. 1996a. "A Re-Evaluation of the Economic Consequences of Divorce." *American Sociological Review* 61 (June): 528–536.

Peterson, Richard R. 1996b. "A Re-Evaluation of the Economic Consequences of Divorce: Reply to Weitzman." *American Sociological Review* 61 (June): 539–540.

Pettigrew, Thomas F. 1992. "The Ultimate Attribution Error: Extending Allport's Cognitive Analysis of Prejudice." Pp. 401–419 in *Readings About the Social Animal,* edited by Elliott Aronson. New York: Freeman.

Phillips, Robert L., Paul J. Andrisani, Thomas N. Daymont, and Curtis L. Gilroy. 1992. "The Economic Returns to Military Service: Race-Ethnic Differences." *Social Science Quarterly* 73 (June): 340–359.

Piaget, Jean. 1926. *The Language and Thought of the Child.* New York: Harcourt.

Piven, Frances Fox, and Richard A. Cloward. 1988. *Why Americans Don't Vote.* New York: Pantheon.

Polce-Lynch, Mary, Barbara J. Myers, Wendy Kliewer, and Christopher Kilmartin. 2001. "Adolescent Self-Esteem and Gender: Exploring Relations to Sexual Harassment, Body Image, Media Influence, and Emotional Expression." *Journal of Youth and Adolescence* 30 (April): 225–244.

Pollock, Philip H., and M. Elliot Vittas. 1995. "Who Bears the Burdens of Environmental Pollution: Race, Ethnicity, and Environmental Equity in Florida." *Social Science Quarterly* 76 (June): 294–310.

Popenoe, David. 2001. "Today's Dads: A New Breed?" *The New York Times,* June 19, 2001: A22.

Popkin, Susan. 1990. "Welfare: Views from the Bottom." *Social Problems* 37 (February): 64–79.

Portes, Alejandro, and Rubén G. Rumbaut. 1996. *Immigrant America: A Portrait,* 2nd ed. Berkeley: University of California Press.

Portes, Alejandro, and Rubén G. Rumbaut. 2001. *Legacies: The Story of the Immigrant Second Generation.* Berkeley: University of California Press.

Powell-Hopson, Darlene, and Derek S. Hopson. 1988. "Implications of Doll Color Preferences Among Black Preschool Children and White Preschool Children." *The Journal of Black Psychology* 14 (February): 57–63.

Press, Andrea. 2002. "The Paradox of Talk." *Contexts* 1 (Fall/Winter): 69–70.

Press, Eyal. 1996. "Barbie's Betrayal." *The Nation* (December 30): 11–16.

Press, Julie E., and Eleanor Townsley. 1998. "Wives and Husbands' Reporting: Gender, Class, and Social Desirability." *Gender & Society* 12 (April): 188–218.

Proctor, Bernadette D., and Joseph Dalaker. 2002. *Poverty in the United States: 2001.* Washington, DC: U.S. Census Bureau.

Pruitt, D. G. 1971. "Choice Shifts in Group Discussion." *Journal of Personality and Social Psychology* 20 (December): 339–360.

Prus, Robert, and C. R. D. Sharper. 1991. *Road Hustler.* New York: Kauffman and Greenberg Publishers.

Punch, Maurice. 1996. *Dirty Business: Exploring Corporate Misconduct; Analysis and Cases.* Thousand Oaks, CA: Sage.

Putnam, Robert D. 2000. *Bowling Alone: The Collapse and Revival of American Community.* New York: Simon and Schuster.

Raaj, Tarja, and Christine L. Rackliff. 1998. "Preschoolers' Awareness of Social Expectations of Gender: Relationships to Toy Choices." *Sex Roles* 38 (May): 685–700.

Raboteau, Albert J. 1978. *Slave Religion: The "Invisible Institution" in the Antebellum South.* New York: Oxford University Press.

Rampersad, Arnold. 1986. *The Life of Langston Hughes: Vol. I: 1902–1941. I, Too, Sing America.* New York: Oxford University Press.

Rampersad, Arnold. 1988. *The Life of Langston Hughes: Vol. II: 1941–1967. I Dream A World.* New York: Oxford University Press.

Read, Piers Paul. 1974. *Alive: The Story of the Andes Survivors.* Philadelphia: Lippincott.

Reeves, B., and M. M. Miller. 1978. "A Multidimensional Measure of Children's Identification with Television Characters." *Journal of Broadcasting* 22 (Winter): 71–86.

Reich, Robert. 1991. *The Work of Nations: Preparing Ourselves for 21st Century Capitalism.* New York: Knopf.

Reilly, Mary Ellen, Bernice Lott, Donna Caldwell, and Luisa DeLuca. 1992. "Tolerance for Sexual Harassment Related to Self-Reported Sexual Victimization." *Gender & Society* 6 (March): 122–138.

Reiman, Jeffrey. 2002. *The Rich Get Richer and the Poor Get Prison,* 7th edition. Boston: Allyn and Bacon.

Reingold, Jennifer. 2000. "Executive Pay." *Business Week,* April 17. Web site: **www. businessweek.com**

Rendon, Laura I., and Richard O. Hope (eds.). 1996. *Educating a New Majority: Transforming America's Educational System for Diversity.* San Francisco: Jossey-Bass.

Reskin, Barbara. 1988. "Bringing the Men Back In: Sex Differentiation and the Devaluation of Women's Work." *Gender & Society* 2 (March): 58–81.

Reskin, Barbara F., and Irene Padavic. 1994. *Women and Men at Work.* Thousand Oaks, CA: Pine Forge.

Reynolds, Ariel Catherine. 2003. "Religiosity as a Predictor of Attitudes toward Homosexuality." Paper presented at the Annual Meetings of the Southern Sociological Society, New Orleans.

Rice, Berkeley. 1986. "Water Shocks of the '80s." *Across the Board* (March): 17.

Rich, Adrienne. 1980. "Compulsory Heterosexuality and Lesbian Existence." *Signs* 5 (Summer): 631–660.

Rieff, David. 1993. "A Global Culture?" *World Policy Journal* 10 (Winter): 73–81.

Riesman, David. 1970[1950]. *The Lonely Crowd: A Study of the Changing American Character.* New Haven, CT: Yale University Press.

Rifkin, Jeremy. 1989. *Entropy: Into the Greenhouse World,* rev. ed. New York: Bantam Books.

Rifkin, Jeremy. 1998. "The Biotech Century: Human Life as Intellectual Property." *The Nation* 266 (April): 11–89.

Risman, Barbara, and Pepper Schwartz. 2002. "After the Sexual Revolution: Gender Politics in Teen Dating." *Contexts* 1 (Spring): 16–24.

Ritzer, George. 2000. *The McDonaldization of Society: An Investigation into the Changing Character of Contemporary Social Life,* 3rd ed. Thousand Oaks, CA: Pine Forge Press.

Robbins, Thomas. 1988. *Cults, Converts, and Charisma: The Sociology of New Religious Movements.* Beverly Hills, CA: Sage.

Roberts, Dorothy. 1997. *Killing the Black Body: Race, Reproduction and the Meaning of Liberty.* New York: Vintage Books.

Robertson, Tatsha, and Garrance Burke. 2001. "Fighting Terror: Concerned Family;" "Shock, Worry for Family of U.S. Man Captured with Taliban." *The Boston Globe,* December 4: A1.

Robey, Bryant. 1982. "A Guide to the Baby Boom." *American Demographics* 4 (September): 16–21.

Robinson, Jo Ann Gibson. 1987. *The Montgomery Bus Boycott and the Women Who Started It.* Knoxville: The University of Tennessee Press.

Rodgers, Joan R. 1995. "An Empirical Study of Intergenerational Transmission of Poverty in the United States." *Social Science Quarterly* 76 (March): 178–194.

Rodney, Walter. 1974. *How Europe Underdeveloped Africa.* Washington, DC: Howard University Press.

Rodney, Walter. 1981. *How Europe Underdeveloped Africa,* revised edition. Washington, DC: Howard University Press.

Rodriquez, Nestor P. 1999. "Globalization, Autonomy, and Transnational Migration: Impacts on U.S. Intergroup Relations." *Research in Politics and Society* 6: 65-84.

Roethlisberger, Fritz J., and William J. Dickson. 1939. *Management and the Worker.* Cambridge, MA: Harvard Univesity Press.

Rollins, Judith. 1985. *Between Women: Domestics and Their Employers.* Philadelphia: Temple University Press.

Romain, Suzanne. 1999. *Communicating Gender.* Mahwah, NJ: Erlbaum.

Roof, Wade Clark. 1999. *Spiritual Marketplace.* Princeton, NJ: Princeton University Press.

Root, Maria. P. P. 2001. *Love's Revolution: Interracial Marriage.* Philadelphia: Temple University Press.

Roper Organization. 1990. *Virginia Slims American Women's Opinion Poll.* Storrs, CT: Roper Organization.

Roper Organization. 1995. *The 1995 Virginia Slims Opinion Poll: A 25–Year Perspective of Women's Lives.* Storrs, CT: Roper Organization.

Rose, Stephen J. 2000. *Social Stratification in the United States.* New York: The New Press.

Rosenau, Pauline Marie. 1992. *Post-Modernism and the Social Sciences: Insights, Inroads, and Intrusions.* Princeton, NJ: Princeton University Press.

Rosengarten, Danielle. 2000. "Modern Times." *Dollars & Sense* (September): 4.

Rosenhan, David L. 1973. "On Being Sane in Insane Places." *Science* 179 (January 19): 250–258.

Rosenthal, Robert, and Lenore Jacobson. 1968. *Pygmalian in the Classroom: Teacher Expectations and Pupils' Intellectual Development.* New York: Holt, Rinehart and Winston.

Rostow, W.W. 1978. *The World Economy: History and Prospect.* Austin: University of Texas Press.

Rubenzahl, Samuel-A., and Kevin J. Corcoran. 1998. "The Prevalence and Characteristics of Male Perpetrators of Acquaintance Rape." *Violence Against Women* 4 (December): 713–725.

Rubin, Gayle. 1975. "The Traffic in Women." Pp. 157–211 in *Toward an Anthropology of Women,* edited by Rayna Reiter. New York: Monthly Review Press.

Rubin, Z., F. J. Provenzano, and C. T. Hull. 1974. "The Eye of the Beholder: Parents' Views on Sex of Newborns." *American Journal of Orthopsychiatry* 44: 512–519.

Rueschmeyer, Dietrich, and Theda Skocpol. 1996. *States, Social Knowledge, and the Origins of Modern Social Policies.* Princeton, NJ: Princeton University Press.

Rumbaut, Rubén G. 1996a. "Origins and Destinies: Immigration, Race, and Ethnicity in Contemporary America." Pp. 21–42 in *Origins and Destinies: Immigration, Race, and Ethnicity in America,* edited by Sylvia Pedraza and Rubén G. Rumbaut. Belmont, CA: Wadsworth.

Rumbaut, Rubén. 1996b. "Prologue." Pp. xvi–xix in *Origins and Destinies: Immigration, Race, and Ethnicity in America,* edited by Silvia Pedraza and Rubén Rumbaut. Belmont, CA: Wadsworth.

Rumbaut, Rubén G., and Alejandro Portes (eds.). 2001. *Ethnicities: Children of Immigrants in America.* Berkeley, CA: University of California Press.

Rupp, Leila J., and Verta Taylor. 2003. *Drag Queens at the 801 Cabaret.* Chicago: University of Chicago Press.

Rust, Paula C. 1993. "'Coming Out' in the Age of Social Constructionism: Sexual Identity Formation among Lesbian and Bisexual Women." *Gender & Society* 7 (March): 50–77.

Rust, Paula. 1995. *Bisexuality and the Challenge to Lesbian Politics.* New York: New York University Press.

Ryan, William. 1971. *Blaming the Victim.* New York: Pantheon.

Rymer, Russ. 1993. *Genie: A Scientific Study.* New York: HarperCollins.

Saad, Lydia. 2002. "There's No Place Like Home to Spend an Evening, Say Most Americans" *The Gallup Poll.* Princeton, NJ: Gallup Organization. Web site: **www.gallup.com**

Sadker, Myra, and David Sadker. 1994. *Failing at Fairness: How America's Schools Cheat Girls.* New York: Scribner's.

Saks, M. J., and M. W. Marti. 1997. "A Meta-Analysis of the Effects of Jury Size." *Law and Human Behavior* 21: 451–467.

Sanchez, Laura, Wendy D. Manning, and Pamela J. Smock. 1998. "Sex-Specialized or Collaborative Mate Selection? Union Transitions among Cohabitors." *Social Science Research* 27 (September): 280–304.

Sanchez, Lisa Gonzalez. 1999. "Reclaiming Salsa." *Cultural Studies* 13 (April): 237–250.

Sanday, Peggy. 2002. *Women at the Center: Life in a Modern Matriarchy.* Ithaca, NY: Cornell University Press.

Sanders, Bernie, and Marcy Kaptur. 1997. "Just Do It, Nike." *The Nation* (December 8): 6.

Sanders, Clifford. 1999. *Understanding Dogs: Living and Working with Canine Companions.* Philadelphia: Temple University Press.

Sandnabba, N. Kenneth, and Christian Ahlberg. 1999. "Parents' Attitudes and Expectations About Children's Cross-Gender Behavior." *Sex Roles* 40 (February): 249–263.

Sapir, Edward. 1921. *Language: An Introduction to the Study of Speech.* New York: Harcourt Brace.

Sassen, Saskia. 1991. *The Global City: New York, London, Tokyo.* Princeton, NJ: Princeton University Press.

Saunders, Laura. 1990. "America's Richest Congressmen." *Forbes* 145 (February 19): 44–45.

Scarpitti, Frank R., Margaret L. Andersen, and Laura O'Toole. 1997. *Social Problems,* 3rd ed. New York: Addison Wesley Longman.

Schacht, Steven P. 1996. "Misogyny on and off the 'Pitch': The Gendered World of Male Rugby Players." *Gender & Society* 10 (October): 550–565.

Scheff, Thomas J. 1966. *Being Mentally Ill: A Sociological Theory.* Chicago: Aldine.

Scheff, Thomas. 1984. *Being Mentally Ill: A Sociological Theory,* 2nd ed. New York: Aldine.

Schlosser, Eric. 2001. *Fast Food Nation: The Dark Side of the All-American Meal.* New York: Perennial.

Schmitt, Eric. 2001. "Segregation Growing among U.S. Children." *The New York Times* (May 6): 28.

Schmitt, Frederika E., and Patricia Yancey Martin. 1999. "Unobtrusive Mobilization by an Institutionalized Rape Crisis Center: 'It Comes From the Victims.'" *Gender & Society* 13: 364–384.

Schneider, Barbara, and David Stevenson. 1999. *The Ambitious Generation: Motivated but Directionless.* New Haven: Yale University Press.

Schneider, Beth. 1984. "Peril and Promise: Lesbians' Workplace Participation." Pp. 211–230 in *Women Identified Women,* edited by Trudy Darty and Sandee Potter. Mountain View, CA: Mayfield.

Schumann, Howard, Charlotte Steeh, Lawrence Bobo, and Maria Krysan. 1997. *Racial Attitudes in America: Trends and Interpretations.* Cambridge, MA: Harvard University Press.

Schur, Edwin M. 1984. *Labeling Women Deviant.* New York: Random House.

Schwartz, John, and Matthew L. Wald. 2003. "NASA's Failings Go Far Beyond Foam Hitting Shuttle, Panel Says." *The New York Times* (June 7): 1 and 12.

Schwartz, Pepper, and Virginia Rutter. 1998. *The Gender of Sexuality.* Thousand Oaks, CA: Sage.

Scott, Tracy Lee. 2000. "What's God Got to Do with It? Protestantism, Gender, and the Meaning of Work in the U.S." Dissertation Abstracts International, A: The Humanities and Social Sciences, April.

Scully, Diana. 1990. *Understanding Sexual Violence: A Study of Convicted Rapists.* Boston: Unwin Hyman.

Scully, Diana. 1994. *Men Who Control Women's Health: The Miseducation of Obstetrician-Gynecologists.* New York: Teacher's College Press.

Sedlak, Andrea J., and Diane D. Broadhurst. 1996. *Executive Summary of the Third National Incidence Study of Child Abuse and Neglect.* Washington, DC: National Clearinghouse on Child Abuse and Neglect. Web site: **www. com**

Segal, Mady W. 1974. "Alphabet and Attraction: An Unobtrusive Measure of the Effect of Propinquity in a Field Setting." *Journal of Personality and Social Psychology* 30: 654–657.

Seidman, Steven. 1994. "Symposium: Queer Theory/Sociology: A Dialogue." *Sociological Theory* 12 (July): 178–187.

Sen, Amartya. 2000. "Population and Gender Equity." *The Nation* (July 24-31): 16–18.

Sen, Amartya. 2002. "How to Judge Globalism." *The American Prospect,* Special Supplement (Winter): A2–A6.

Serbin, L. A., P. Zelkowitz, A. Doyle, D. Gold, and B. Wheaton. 1990. "The Socialization of Sex-Differentiated Skills and Academic Performance: A Mediational Model." *Sex Roles* 23: 613–628.

Shaberoff, Philip. 1988. "Water Supplies in Ground Held Generally Safe." *The New York Times* (October 8): 1, 6.

Shapiro, Laura. 1997. "Book Review: 'The Time Bind.'" *Newsweek* 129 (April 28): 6.

Sharp, Susan F., Toni L. Terling-Watt, Leslie A. Atkins, Jay Trace Gilliam, and Anna Sanders. 2000. "Purging Behavior in a Sample of College Females: A Research Note on General Strain Theory and Female Deviance." *Deviant Behavior* 22: 171–188.

Shea, Martha. 1995. "Dynamics of Economic Well-Being: Poverty, 1990 to 1992." U.S. Bureau of the Census, Current Population Reports, Series P 70–42. Washington, DC: U.S. Government Printing Office.

Sherkat, Darren E. 2002. "Sexuality and Religious Commitment in the United States: An Empirical Examination." *Journal for the Scientific Study of Religion* 41 (June): 313–323.

Shibutani, Tomatsu. 1961. *Society and Personality: An Interactionist Approach to Social Psychology.* Englewood Cliffs, NJ: Prentice Hall.

Shibutani, Tomatsu. 1966. *Improvised News.* Indianapolis: Bobbs-Merrill.

Shih, Margaret, Todd L. Pittinsky, and Nalini Ambady. 1999. "Stereotype Susceptibility: Identiy Salience and Shifts in Quantitative Performance." *Psychological Science* 10 (January): 80–83.

Siegel, Judith M. 2002. "Body Image Change and Adolescent Depressive Symptoms." *Journal of Adolescent Research* 17 (January): 27–41.

Sigall, H., and N. Ostrove. 1975. "Beautiful but Dangerous: Effects of Offender Attractiveness and Nature of Crime on Judicial Judgment." *Journal of Personality and Social Psychology* 31: 410–414.

Sigelman, Lee, and Paul J. Wahlbeck. 1999. "Gender Proportionality in Intercollegiate Athletics: The Mathematics of Title IX Compliance." *Social Science Quarterly* 80 (September): 518–538.

Signorielli, Nancy. 1989. "Television and Conceptions About Sex Roles: Maintaining Conventionality and the Status Quo." *Sex Roles* 21: 341–360.

Signorielli, Nancy. 1991. *A Sourcebook on Children and Television.* New York: Greenwood Press.

Signorielli, Nancy, and Aaron Bacue. 1999. "Recognition and Respect: A Content Analysis of Prime-Time Television Characters across Three Decades." *Sex Roles* 40 (April): 527–544.

Signorielli, Nancy, Douglas McLeod, and Elaine Healy. 1994. "Gender Stereotypes in MTV Commercials: The Beat Goes On." *Journal of Broadcasting and Electronic Media* 38 (Winter): 91–101.

Silverthorne, Zebulon A. and Vernon L Quinsey. 2000. "Sexual Partner Age Preferences of Homosexual and Heterosexual Men and Women." *Archives of Sexual Behavior* 29 (No. 1): 67–76.

Simile, Catherine. 1995. *Disaster Settings and Mobilization for Contentious Collective Action: Case Studies of Hurricane Hugo and the Loma Prieta Earthquake.* Unpublished dissertation, University of Delaware.

Simmel, Georg. 1902. "The Number of Members as Determining the Sociological Form of the Group." *The American Journal of Sociology* 8 (July): 1–46.

Simmel, Georg. 1950 [1905]. *The Sociology of George Simmel,* edited by Kurt H. Wolff. New York: Free Press.

Simon, David R. 2001. *Elite Deviance,* 7th ed. Boston: Allyn and Bacon.

Simons, Marlise. 1989. "The Amazon's Savvy Indians." *The New York Times Magazine* (February): 36ff.

Simpson, George Eaton, and J. Milton Yinger. 1985. *Racial and Cultural Minorities: An Analysis of Prejudice and Discrimination,* 5th ed. New York: Plenum.

Sirvananadan, A. 1995. "La trahision des clercs. (Racism)." *New Statesman and Society* 8: 20–22.

Sjøberg, Gideon. 1965. *The Preindustrial City: Past and Present.* New York: Free Press.

Skocpol, Theda. 1979. *States and Social Revolutions: A Comparative Analyses of France, Russia, and China.* New York: Cambridge University Press.

Skocpol, Theda. 1992. *Protecting Soldiers and Mothers: The Origins of Social Policy in the United States.* Cambridge, MA: Belknap Press.

Slavin, Robert E. 1993. "Ability Grouping in the Middle Grades: Achievement Effects and Alternatives." *The Elementary School Journal* 93 (No. 5): 535–552.

Slevin, Kathleen F., and C. Ray Wingrove. 1998. *From Stumbling Blocks to Stepping Stones: The Life Experiences of Fifty Professional African American Women.* New York: New York University Press.

Smelser, Neil J. 1992a. "Culture: Coherent or Incoherent." Pp. 3–28 in *Theory of Culture,* edited by R. Münch and N. J. Smelser. Berkeley: University of California Press.

Smelser, Neil J. 1992b. "The Rational Choice Perspective: A Theoretical Assessment." *Rationality and Society* 4: 381–410.

Smith, A. Wade. 1989. "Educational Attainment as a Determinant of Social Class Among Black Americans." *Journal of Negro Education* 58 (Summer): 416–429.

Smith, Barbara. 1983. "Homophobia: Why Bring It Up?" *Interracial Books for Children Bulletin* 14: 112–113.

Smith, Christian, and Robert D. Woodberry. 2001. "Sociology of Religion." Pp. 100–113 in *The Blackwell Companion to Sociology,* edited by Judith Blau. Malden, MA: Blackwell Publishers.

Smith, Heather. 1999. "The Promotion of Women and Men." Unpublished doctoral dissertation, University of Delaware.

Smith, M. Dwayne, Joel A. Devine, and Joseph F. Sheley. 1992. "Crime and Unemployment: Effects Across Age and Race Categories." *Sociological Perspectives* 35 (Winter): 551–572.

Smith, Richard B., and Robert A. Brown. 1997. "The Impact of Social Support on Gay Male Couples." *Journal of Homosexuality* 33: 39–61.

Smith, Robert B. 1993. "Social Structure and Voting Choice: Hypotheses, Findings, and Interpretations." Paper presented at the Annual Meeting of the American Sociological Association, August, Miami.

Smith, Tom W. 1992. "Changing Racial Labels: From 'Colored' to 'Negro' to 'Black' to 'African American.'" *Public Opinion Quarterly* 56: 496–512.

Smith, Tom W. 1999. "The Religious Right and Anti-Semitism." *Review of Religious Research* 40 (March): 244–258.

Smolen, Rick, and Jennifer Erwitt. 1996. *24 Hours in Cyberspace.* New York: Macmillan.

Snipp, C. Matthew. 1989. *American Indians: The First of This Land.* New York: Russell Sage Foundation.

Snipp, C. Matthew. 1996. "The First Americans: American Indians." Pp. 390–404 in *Origins and Destinies: Immigration, Race, and Ethnicity in America,* edited by Sylvia Pedraza and Rubén G. Rumbaut. Belmont, CA: Wadsworth.

Snow, David A., and Robert D. Benford. 1988. "Ideology, Frame Resonance, and Participant Mobilization." *International Social Movements Research* 1: 197–217.

Snow, David A., Susan G. Baker, Leon Anderson, and Michael Martin. 1986. "The Myth of Pervasive Mental Illness among the Homeless." *Social Problems* 33 (June): 407–423.

Sorokin, Pitrim. 1941. *The Crisis of Our Age.* New York: Dutton.

Sowell, Thomas. 1983. *The Economics and Politics of Race: An International Perspective.* New York: Morrow.

Spangler, Eve, Marsha A. Gordon, and Ronald Pipkin. 1978. "Token Women: An Empirical Test of Kanter's Hypothesis." *American Journal of Sociology* 84: 160–170.

Speed, A., and S.W. Gangestad. 1997. "Romantic Popularity and Mate Preferences: A Peer-Nomination Study." *Personality and Social Psychology Bulletin* 23: 928–936.

Spencer, Herbert. 1882. *The Study of Sociology.* London: Routledge.

Spitzer, Steven. 1975. "Toward a Marxian Theory of Deviance." *Social Problems* 22: 638–651.

Sprock, June, and Carol Y. Yoder. 1997. "Women and Depression: An Update on the Report of the APA Task Force." *Sex Roles* 36 (March): 269–303.

Stacey, Judith, and Timothy J. Bibliarz. 2001. "(How) Does the Sexual Orientation of Parents Matter?" *American Sociological Review* 66 (April): 159–183.

Starr, Paul. 1982. *The Social Transformation of American Medicine.* New York: Basic Books.

Starr, Paul. 1995. "What Happened to Health Care Reform?" *The American Prospect* (Winter, No. 20): 20–31.

Stearns, Linda Brewster, and Charlotte Wilkinson Coleman. 1990. "Industrial and Labor Market Structures and Black Male Employment in the Manufacturing Sector." *Social Science Quarterly* 71 (June): 285–298.

Steele, Claude M. 1992. "Race and the Schooling of Black Americans." *The Atlantic Monthly* 269 (April): 68–78.

Steele, Claude M. 1996. "A Burden of Suspicion: How Stereotypes Shape the Intellectual Identities and Performance of Women and African-Americans." Paper read before the Princeton Conference on Higher Education, February, Princeton, New Jersey.

Steele, Claude M. 1997. "A Threat in the Air: How Stereotypes Shape Intellectual Identity and Performance." *American Psychologist* 52 (June): 613–629.

Steele, Claude M. 1999. "Thin Ice: Stereotype Threat and Black College Students." *The Atlantic Monthly* (August): 44–54.

Steele, Claude M., and Joshua Aronson. 1995. "Stereotype Vulnerability and African American Intellectual Performance." Pp. 409–421 in *Readings About the Social Animal,* 7th ed, edited by Elliot Aronson. New York: W. H. Freeman.

Steffensmeier, Darrell, Jeffery Ulmer, and John Kramer. 1998. "The Interaction of Race, Gender, and Age in Criminal Sentencing: The Punishment Cost of Being Young, Black and Male." *Criminology* 36 (November): 763–797.

Steffensmeier, Darrell, and Stephen Demuth. 2000. "Ethnicity and Sentencing Outcomes in U.S. Federal Courts: Who Is Punished More Harshly?" *American Sociological Review* 65 (October): 705–729.

Stein, Arlene, and Ken Plummer. 1994. "'I Can't Even Think Straight': Queer Theory and the Missing Sexual Revolution in Sociology." *Sociological Theory* 12 (July): 178–187.

Steinberg, Ronnie. 1992. "Gendered Instructions: Cultural Lag and Gender Bias in the Hay System of Job Evaluation." *Work and Occupations* 19 (November): 387–424.

Stern, Kenneth S. 1996. *A Force upon the Plain.* New York: Simon and Schuster.

Stern, M. and K. H. Karraker. 1989. "Sex Stereotyping of Infants: A Review of Gender Labeling Studies." *Sex Roles* 20 (May): 501–522.

Sternberg, Robert J. 1988. *The Triarchic Mind: A New Theory of Human Intelligence.* New York: Penguin.

Stevens, Ann Huff. 1994. "The Dynamics of Poverty Spells: Updating Bane and Ellwood." *The American Economic Review* 84 (May): 34–37.

Stewart, Susan D. 2001. "Contemporary American Stepparenthood: Integrating Cohabiting and Nonresident Stepparents." *Population Research and Policy* 20 (August): 345–364.

Stockard, Jean, and Miriam M. Johnson. 1992. *Sex and Gender in Society,* 2nd ed. Englewood Cliffs, NJ: Prentice Hall.

Stoller, Eleanor Palo, and Rose Campbell Gibson. 2000. *Worlds of Difference: Inequality in the Aging Experience.* Thousand Oaks, CA: Pine Forge Press.

Stombler, Mindy, and Irene Padavic. 1997. "Sister Acts: Resisting Men's Domination in Black and White Fraternity Little Sister Programs." *Social Problems* 44 (May): 257–275.

Stoner, J.A.F. 1961. *A Comparison of Individual and Group Decisions Involving Risk.* Unpublished master's thesis, Massachusetts Institute of Technology (MIT).

Stotik, Jeffrey, Thomas E. Shriver, and Sherry Cable. 1994. "Social Control and Movement Outcome: The Case of AIM." *Sociological Focus* 27 (February): 53–66.

Stover, R. G., and C. A. Hope. 1993. *Marriage, Family and Intimate Relationships.* New York: Harcourt Brace Jovanovich.

Strate, Lance, Ron L. Jacobson, and Stephanie Gibson, eds. 2003. *Communication and Cyberspace.* Cresskill, NJ: Hampton Press.

Sudnow, David N. 1967. *Passing On: The Social Organization of Dying.* Englewood Cliffs, NJ: Prentice Hall.

Suggs, Welch. 2002. "Title IX at 30." *The Chronicle of Higher Education.* June 21: A38–42.

Suitor, Jill J. 1988. "Husbands' Educational Attainment and Support for Wives' Return to School." *Gender & Society* 2 (December): 482–495.

Sullivan, Teresa A., Elizabeth Warren, and Jay Lawrence Westbrook. 2000. *The Fragile Middle Class: Americans in Debt.* New Haven: Yale University Press.

Sumner, William Graham. 1906. *Folkways.* Boston: Ginn.

Sussal, Carol M. 1994. "Empowering Gays and Lesbians in the Workplace." *Journal of Gay and Lesbian Social Services* 1: 89–103.

Sutherland, Edwin H. 1940. "White Collar Criminality." *American Sociological Review* 5 (February): 1–12.

Sutherland, Edwin H., and Donald R. Cressey. 1978. *Criminology,* 10th ed. New York: Lippincott.

Swidler, Ann. 1986. "Culture in Action: Symbols and Strategies." *American Sociological Review* 51: 273–286.

Switzer, J.Y. 1990. "The Impact of Generic Word Choices: An Empirical Investigation of Age- and Sex-Related Differences." *Sex Roles* 22: 69–82.

Szasz, Thomas S. 1974. *The Myth of Mental Illness.* New York: Harper & Row.

Takaki, Ronald. 1989. *Strangers from a Different Shore: A History of Asian Americans.* New York: Penguin.

Tannen, Deborah. 1990. *You Just Don't Understand: Women and Men in Conversation.* New York: William Morrow.

Taylor, Howard F. 1973. "Linear Models of Consistency: Some Extensions of Blalock's Strategy." *American Journal of Sociology* 78 (March): 1192–1215.

Taylor, Howard F. 1980. *The IQ Game: A Methodological Inquiry into the Heredity—Environment Controversy.* New Brunswick, NJ: Rutgers University Press.

Taylor, Howard F. 1981. "Biases in *Bias in Mental Testing.*" *Contemporary Sociology* 10:172–174.

Taylor, Howard F. 1992a. "Intelligence." Pp. 941–949 in *Encyclopedia of Sociology,* edited by E. F. Borgatta and M. L. Borgatta. New York: Macmillan.

Taylor, Howard F. 1992b. "The Structure of a National Black Leadership Network: Preliminary Findings." Unpublished manuscript, Princeton University.

Taylor, Howard F. 1995. "Symposium on 'The Bell Curve'." *Contemporary Sociology* 24 (March): 153–158.

Taylor, Howard F. 2002. "Deconstructing the Bell Curve: Racism, Classism, and Intelligence Measurement in America. "*In 2001 Race Odyssey.": African Americans and Sociology,* edited by Bruce R. Hare. Syracuse, NY: Syracuse University Press.

Taylor, Howard F., and Carlton A. Hornung. 1979. "On A General Model for Social and Cognitive Consistency." *Sociological Methods and Research* 7 (February): 259–287.

Taylor, Shelley E., Letitia Ann Peplau, and David O. Sears. 1997. *Social Psychology,* 9th ed. Englewood Cliffs: Prentice Hall.

Taylor, Shelley E., Letitia Anne Peplau, and David O. Sears. 2000. *Social Psychology,* 10th ed. Upper Saddle River, NJ: Prentice Hall.

Taylor, Shelley E., Letitia Anne Peplau, and David O. Sears. 2003. *Social Psychology,* 11th ed. Upper Saddle River, NJ: Prentice Hall.

Taylor, Verta, and Leila J. Rupp. 1993. "Women's Culture and Lesbian Feminist Activism: A Reconsideration of Cultural Feminism." *Signs* 19 (Autumn): 32–61.

Taylor, Verta, and Nicole C. Raeburn. 1995. "Identity Politics as High-Risk Activism: Career Consequences of Lesbian, Gay and Bisexual Sociologists." *Social Problems* 42 (May): 252–274.

Teaster, Pamela B. 2000. "A Response to the Abuse of Vulnerable Adults: The 200 Survey of State Adult Protective Services." Washington, DC: National Center on Elder Abuse. Web site: **www.elderabusecenter.org**

Tepper, Clary A., and Kimberly Wright Cassidy. 1999. "Gender Differences in Emotional Language in Children's Picture Books." *Sex Roles* 40 (February): 265–280.

Tewksbury, Richard. 1994. "Gender Construction and the Female Impersonator: The Process of Transforming 'He' to 'She.'" *Deviant Behavior* 15: 27–43.

Thakkar, Reena R., Peter M. Gutierrez, Carly L. Kuczen, and Thomas R. McCanne. 2000. "History of Physical and/or Sexual Abuse and Current Suicidality in College Women. *Child Abuse and Neglect* 24 (October): 1345–1354.

Thibaut, John W., and Harold H. Kelley. 1959. *The Social Psychology of Groups.* New York: Wiley.

Thibodeau, R. 1989. "From Racism to Tokenism: The Changing Face of Blacks in New Yorker Cartoons." *Public Opinion Quarterly* 53: 482–494.

Thoits, Peggy A. 1991. "On Merging Identity Theory and Stress Research." *Social Psychology Quarterly* 54: 101–112.

Thomas, W. I. 1918 [1919/1958]. *The Polish Peasant in Europe and America.* New York: Dover.

Thomas, William I. 1931. *The Unadjusted Girl.* Boston: Little, Brown.

Thomas, William I. 1966 [1931]. "The Relation of Research to the Social Process." Pp. 289–305 in *W. I. Thomas on Social Organization and Social Personality,* edited by Morris Janowitz. Chicago: University of Chicago Press.

Thomas, William I. with Dorothy Swaine Thomas. 1928. *The Child in America.* New York: Knopf.

Thompson, Becky. 1994. *A Hunger So Wide and So Deep: American Women Speak Out on Eating Problems.* Minneapolis: University of Minnesota Press.

Thompson, Robert Ferris. 1993. *Flash of the Spirit.* NY: Random House.

Thompson, William E., and Joseph V. Hickey. 1994. *Society in Focus.* New York: Harper-Collins.

Thorne, Barrie. 1993. *Gender Play: Girls and Boys in School.* New Brunswick, NJ: Rutgers University Press.

Thorne, Barrie, and Zella Luria. 1986. "Sexuality and Gender in Children's Daily Worlds." *Social Problems* 33 (February): 176–190.

Thornton, Russell. 2001. "Trends among American Indians in the United States." Pp. 135–169 in *America Becoming: Racial Trends and Their Consequences, Volume I,* edited

by Neil J. Smelser, William Julius Wilson, and Faith Mitchell. Washington, DC: National Academy Press.

Tichenor, Veronica Jaris. 1999. "Status and Income as Gendered Resources: The Case of Marital Power." *Journal of Marriage and the Family* 61(August): 638–650.

Tiefer, Leonore. 1978. "The Kiss." *Human Nature* (July): 28–37.

Tienda, Marta, and Haya Stier. 1996. "Generating Labor Market Inequality: Employment Opportunities and the Accumulation of Disadvantage." *Social Problems* 43 (May): 147–165.

Tierney, Patrick. 2000. *Darkness in El Dorado: How Scientists and Journalists Devastated the Amazon.* New York: W.W. Norton.

Tilly, Charles. 1975. *The Formation of National States in Europe.* Princeton, NJ: Princeton University Press.

Tilly, Charles. 1986. *The Contentious French.* Cambridge, MA: Harvard University Press.

Tilly, Louise, and Joan Scott. 1978. *Women, Work, and Family.* New York: Holt, Rinehart, and Winston.

Tjaden, Patricia, and Nancy Thoennes. 2000. *Extent, Nature, and Consequences of Intimate Partner Violence.* Washington, DC: National Institute of Justice and the Centers for Disease Control and Prevention.

Tönnies, Ferdinand. 1963 [1887]. *Community and Society (Gemeinschaft and Gesellschaft).* New York: Harper & Row.

Toobin, Jeffrey. 1996. "The Marcia Clark Verdict." *The New Yorker* (September 9): 58–71.

Toynbee, Arnold J., and Jane Caplan. 1972. *A Study of History.* New York: Oxford University Press.

Travers, Jeffrey, and Stanley Milgram. 1969. "An Experimental Study of the Small World Problem." *Sociometry* 32: 425–443.

Treiman, Donald J. 2001. "Occupations, Stratification and Mobility." Pp. 297–313 in *The Blackwell Companion to Sociology,* edited by Judith R. Blau. Malden, MA: Blackwell.

Trent, Katherine, and Sharon L. Harlan. 1990. "Household Structure Among Teenage Mothers in the United States." *Social Science Quarterly* 71 (September): 439–457.

Tuan, Yi-Fu. 1984. *Dominance and Affection: The Making of Pets.* New Haven, CT: Yale University Press.

Tuchman, Gaye. 1979. "Women's Depiction by the Mass Media." *Signs* 4 (Spring): 528–542.

Tumin, Melvin M. 1953. "Some Principles of Stratification." *American Sociological Review* 18 (August): 387–393.

Turkle, Sherry. 1995. *Life on the Screen: Identity in the Age of the Internet.* New York: Simon & Schuster.

Turner, Jonathan. 1974. *The Structure of Sociological Theory.* Homewood, IL: Dorsey Press.

Turner, Ralph, Joanne M. Nigg, and Denise Paz. 1986. *Waiting for Disaster: Earthquake Watch in California.* Berkeley: University of California Press.

Turner, Ralph, and Lewis Killian. 1988. *Collective Behavior,* 3rd ed. Englewood Cliffs, NJ: Prentice Hall.

Turner, Terence. 1969. "Tchikrin: A Central Brazilian Tribe and Its Symbolic Language of Body Adornment." *Natural History* 78 (October): 50–59.

Tyree, Andrea, and R. Hicks. 1988. "Sex and the Second Moment of Occupational Basic Distributions." *Social Forces* 66 (June): 1028–1037.

U.S. Bureau of Justice Statistics. 2000. *Sourcebook of Criminal Justice Statistics 2000.* Washington, DC: U.S. Department of Justice.

U.S. Bureau of Justice Statistics. 2002. "Prisons." U.S. Bureau of Justice Statistics Web site: http://www.ojp.usdoj.gov/bjs/

U.S. Bureau of Justice Statistics. 2002. *Sourcebook on Criminal Justice Statistics.* Washington, DC: U.S. Government Printing Office.

U.S. Bureau of Labor Statistics. 2003. "Pilot Survey on the Incidence of Child Care Resource and Referral Services in June 2000." Washington, DC: U.S. Department of Labor.

U.S. Census Bureau. 1999. *Statistical Abstract of the United States 1999.* Washington, DC: U.S. Government Printing Office.

U.S. Census Bureau. 2001. *Statistical Abstract of the United States 2001.* Washington, DC: U.S. Government Printing Office.

U.S. Census Bureau. 2002. *Statistical Abstract of the United States 2002.* Washington, DC: U.S. Government Printing Office.

U.S. Conference of Mayors. 2001. *A Status Report on Hunger and Homelessness in America's Cities: 2001.* Washington, DC: U.S. Conference of Mayors.

U.S. Department of Defense. 2002. Population Representation in the Military Services, Fiscal Year 2000. Washington, DC: U.S. Department of Defense. Web site: www.defenselink.mil

U.S. Department of Education and U.S. Department of Justice. 2000 (May). *1999 Annual Report on School Safety Report.* Washington, DC: U.S. Department of Education, U.S. Department of Justice.

U.S. Department of Labor. 2002. *Employment and Earnings.* Washington, DC: U.S. Department of Labor.

U.S. Department of Labor. 2003. *Employment and Earnings.* Washington, DC: U.S. Department of Labor.

Uleman, J. S., L. S. Newman, and G. B. Moskowitz. 1996. "People as Flexible Interpreters: Evidence and Issues From Spontaneous Trait Inference." Pp. 211–279 in *Advances in Experimental Social Psychology,* vol. 28, edited by Mark Zanna. Boston: Academic Press.

Ullman, Sarah E., George Karabatsos, and Mary P. Koss. 1999."Alcohol and Sexual Assault in a National Sample of College Women." *Journal of Interpersonal Violence* 14 (June): 603-625.

UNICEF. 2000. *Domestic Violence against Women and Girls.* New York: United Nations.

United Nations. 2000a. *Human Development Report.* New York: United Nations.

United Nations. 2000b. *The World's Women, 2000: Trends and Statistics.* New York: United Nations.

United Nations Commission on the Status of Women. 1996. *Report of the World Conference of the United Nations Decade for Women.* Copenhagen: United Nations.

Urban Institute, The. 2000. *A New Look at Homelessness in America.* Washington, DC: The Urban Institute. Web site: www.urban.org

Uvin, Peter. 1998. *Aiding Violence.* West Hartford, CT: Kumarian Press.

Vail, D. Angus. 1999. "Tattoos Are Like Potato Chips...You Can't Have Just One: The Process of Becoming and Being a Collector." *Deviant Behavior* 20: 253–273.

Van Ausdale, Debra, and Joe R. Feagin. 1996. "The Use of Racial and Ethnic Concepts by Very Young Children." *American Sociological Review* 61 (October): 779–793.

Vanlandingham, Mark. 1993. *Two Perspectives on Risky Sexual Practices among Northern Thai Males: The Health Belief Model and the Theory of Reasoned Action.* Unpublished doctoral dissertation, Princeton University.

Vanneman, Reeve, and Lynn Weber Cannon. 1987. *The American Perception of Class.* Philadelphia: Temple University Press.

VanRoosmalen, Erica, and Susan A. McDaniel. 1998. "Sexual Harassment in Academia: A Hazard to Women's Health." *Women and Health* 28: 33–54.

Varelas, Nicole, and Linda A. Foley. 1998. "Blacks' and Whites' Perceptions of Interracial and Intraracial Date Rape." *Journal of Social Psychology* 138 (June): 392–400.

Varney, Wendy. 2002. "Of Men and Machines: Images of Masculinity in Boys' Toys." *Feminist Studies* 28 (Spring): 153–174.

Vaughan, Diane. 1996. *The Challenger Launch Decision: Risky Technology, Culture, and Deviance at NASA.* Chicago: The University of Chicago Press.

Veblen, Thorstein. 1899 [1953]. *The Theory of the Leisure Class: An Economic Study of Institutions.* New York: The New American Library.

Vega, William A., and H. Amero. 1994. "Latino Outlook: Good Health, Uncertain Prognosis." *Annual Review of Public Health* 15: 39–67.

VonNeumann, John, and Oskar Morgenstern. 1944. *The Theory of Games and Economic Behavior.* Princeton: Princeton University Press.

Voss, Laurie Scarborough. 1997. "Teasing, Disputing, and Playing: Cross-Gender Interactions and Space Utilization among First and Third Graders." *Gender & Society* 11 (April): 238–256.

Wadham, Nick. 2003. "'Griefers' Form Harassing Mob in Sims Game." Associated Press, July 5.

Waldfogel, Jane, Wen-Jui Han, and Jeanne Brooks-Gunn. 2002. "The Effects of Early Maternal Employment in Child Cognitive Development." *Demography* 39: 369–392.

Walker-Barnes, Chanequa J., and Craig A. Mason. 2001. "Perceptions of Risk Factors for Female Gang Involvement among African American and Hispanic Women." *Youth and Society* 32 (March): 303–336.

Wallerstein, Immanuel. 1974. *The Modern World System: Capitalist Agriculture and the Origins of the European World Economy in the Sixteenth Century.* New York: Academic Press.

Wallerstein, Immanuel. 1979. *The Capitalist World-Economy.* New York: Cambridge University Press.

Wallerstein, Immanuel. 1989. *The Modern World System III: The Second Era of Great Expansion of the Capitalist World-Economy, 1730–1840.* New York: Academic Press.

Wallerstein, Immanuel M. 1980. *The Modern World-System II.* New York: Academic Press.

Walsh, Anthony. 1994. "Homosexual and Heterosexual Child Molestation: Case Characteristics and Sentencing Differentials." *International Journal of Offender Therapy and Comparative Criminology* 38: 339–353.

Walster, Elaine, V. Aronson, D. Abrahams, and L. Rottman. 1966. "The Importance of Physical Attractiveness in Dating Behavior." *Journal of Personality and Social Psychology* 4: 508–516.

Walters, Suzanna Danuta. 1999. "Sex, Text, and Context: (In) Between Feminism and Cultural Studies." Pp. 222–260 in *Revisioning Gender,* edited by Myra Marx Ferree, Judith Lorber, and Beth B. Hess. Thousand Oaks, CA: Sage.

Walters, Vivienne. 1993. "Stress, Anxiety, and Depression: Women's Accounts of Their Health Problems." *Social Science and Medicine* 36 (February): 393–402.

Ward, Kathryn. 1990. *Women Workers and Global Restructuring.* Ithaca, NY: ILR Press.

Wasserman, Stanley, and Katherine Faust (eds.). 1994. *Social Network Analysis: Methods and Applications.* New York, MA: Cambridge University Press.

Waters, Mary C. 1990. *Ethnic Options: Choosing Identities in America.* Berkeley: University of California Press.

Watkins, Susan. 1987. "The Fertility Transition: Europe and the Third World Compared." *Sociological Forum* 2 (Fall): 645–673.

Watt, Toni Terling, and Susan F. Sharp. 2001. "Gender Differences in Strains Associated with Suicidal Behavior among Adolescents." *Journal of Youth and Adolescence* 30 (June): 333–348.

Watts, Duncan J. 1999. "Networks, Dynamics, and the Small-World Phenomenon." *American Journal of Sociology* 105 (September): 493–527.

Watts, Duncan J. and Stephen H. Strogatz. 1998. "Collective Dynamics of 'Small World' Networks." *Nature* 393: 440–442. Web site: www.sentencing project.org

Weber, Max. 1925 [1947]. *The Theory of Social and Economic Organization.* New York: Free Press.

Weber, Max. 1958 [1904]. *The Protestant Ethic and the Spirit of Capitalism.* New York: Scribner's.

Weber, Max. 1962 [1913]. *Basic Concepts in Sociology.* New York: Greenwood.

Weber, Max. 1978 [1921]. *Economy and Society: An Outline of Interpretive Sociology,* edited by

Guenther Roth and Claus Wittich. Berkeley: University of California Press.

Webster, Murray, Jr., and Stuart J. Hysom. 1998. "Creating Status Characteristics." *American Sociological Review* 63 (June): 351–378.

Weeks, John R. 2001. *Population: An Introduction to Concepts and Issues,* 8th ed. Belmont, CA: Wadsworth.

Weinrath, Michael, and John Gartrell. 1996. "Victimization and Fear of Crime." *Violence and Victims* 11 (Fall): 187–197.

Weisburd, David, Stanton Wheeler, Elin Waring, and Nancy Bode. 1991. *Crimes of the Middle Class: White Collar Defenders in the Courts.* New Haven, CT: Yale University Press.

Weitz, Rose. 2001. *The Sociology of Health, Illness, and Health Care: A Critical Approach.* Belmont, CA: Wadsworth.

Weitzman, Lenore J. 1985. *The Divorce Revolution: The Unexpected Consequences for Women and Children in America.* New York: Free Press.

Weitzman, Lenore J. 1996. "A Re-Evaluation of the Economic Consequences of Divorce: Reply to Peterson." *American Sociological Review* 61 (June): 537–538.

Welch, Susan, and Lee Sigelman. 1993. "The Politics of Hispanic Americans: Insights from the National Surveys, 1980–1988." *Social Science Quarterly* 74 (March) 76–94.

Wenk, Deeann, and Patricia Garrett. 1992. "Having a Baby: Some Predictions of Maternal Employment Around Childbirth." *Gender & Society* 6 (March): 49–65.

West, Candace, and Don Zimmerman. 1987. "Doing Gender." *Gender & Society* 1 (June): 125–151.

West, Candace, and Sarah Fenstermaker. 1995. "Doing Difference." *Gender & Society* 9 (February): 8–37.

West, Cornel. 1993. *Race Matters.* Boston: Beacon Press.

Westoff, Charles F., Noreen Goldman, and Lorenzo Moreno. 1990. *Dominican Republic Experimental Study: An Evaluation of Fertility and Child Health Information.* Princeton, NJ: Office of Population Research.

Wharton, Amy S., and Deborah K. Thorne. 1997. "When Mothers Matter: The Effects of Social Class and Family Arrangements on African American and White Women's Perceived Relations with Their Mothers." *Gender & Society* 11 (October): 656–681.

White, Deborah Gray. 1985. *Ar'n't I a Woman?: Female Slaves in the Plantation South.* New York: W. W. Norton and Co.

White, Paul. 1998. "The Settlement Patterns of Developed World Migrants in London." *Urban Studies* 35 (October): 1725–1744.

Whiten, A., J. Goodall, W. C. McGrew, T. Nishida, V. Reynolds, Y. Sugiyama, C. E. G. Tutin, R. W. Wrangham, and C. Boesch. 1999. "Cultures in Chimpanzees." *Nature* 399 (June 17): 682–684.

Whorf, Benjamin. 1956. *Language, Thought, and Reality: Selected Writings.* Cambridge, MA: Technology Press of Massachusetts Institute of Technology.

Whyte, William F. 1943. *Street Corner Society.* Chicago: University of Chicago Press.

Wilder, Esther I., and Toni Terling Watt. 2002. "Risky Parental Behavior and Adolescent Sexual Activity at First Coitus," *The Milbank Quarterly* 80 (September): 481–524.

Wilkie, Jane. 1993. "Changes in U.S. Men's Attitudes Toward the Family Provider Role, 1972 to 1989." *Gender & Society* 7 (June): 261–279.

Williams, Christine L. 1989. *Gender Differences at Work: Women and Men in Nontraditional Occupations.* Berkeley: University of California Press.

Williams, Christine L. 1992. "The Glass Escalator: Hidden Advantages for Men in the 'Female' Professions." *Social Problems* 39 (August): 253–267.

Williams, Christine L. 1995. *Still a Man's World: Men Who Do Women's Work.* Berkeley: University of California Press.

Williams, David R., and Chiquita Collins, 1995. "U.S. Socioeconomic and Racial Differences in Health: Patterns and Explanations." *Annual Review of Sociology* 21: 349–386.

Williams, Lena. 1987. "Race Bias Found in Location of Toxic Dumps." *The New York Times* (April): A20.

Willie, Charles V. 1979. *The Caste and Class Controversy.* Bayside, NY: General Hall.

Willis, Paul. 1977. *Learning to Labor: How Working Class Kids Get Working Class Jobs.* New York: Columbia University Press.

Wilson, Barbara J., Stacy L. Smith, W. James Potter, Dale Kunkel, Daniel Linz, Carolyn M. Colvin, and Edward Donnerstein. 2002. "Violence in Children's Television Programming: Assessing the Risks." *Journal of Communication* 52 (March): 5–35.

Wilson, James Q., and Richard J. Herrnstein. 1985. *Crime and Human Nature.* New York: Simon and Schuster.

Wilson, John F. 1978. *Religion in American Society: The Effective Presence.* Englewood Cliffs, NJ: Prentice Hall.

Wilson, John. 1994. "Returning to the Fold." *Journal for the Scientific Study of Religion* 33 (June): 148–161.

Wilson, William Julius. 1978. *The Declining Significance of Race: Blacks and Changing American Institutions.* Chicago: University of Chicago Press.

Wilson, William Julius. 1987. *The Truly Disadvantaged: The Inner City, the Underclass and Public Policy.* Chicago: University of Chicago Press.

Wilson, William Julius. 1996. *When Work Disappears: The World of the New Urban Poor.* New York: Knopf.

Winnick, Louis. 1990. "America's 'Model Minority.'" *Commentary* 90 (August): 222–229.

Wirth, Louis. 1938. "Urbanism as a Way of Life." *American Journal of Sociology* 40: 1–24.

Wolcott, Harry F. 1996. "Peripheral Participation and the Kwakiutl Potlatch." *Anthropology and Education Quarterly* 27 (December): 467–492.

Wolf, Naomi. 1991. *The Beauty Myth: How Images of Beauty Are Used Against Women.* New York: William Morrow and Co.

Woo, Deborah. 1998. "The Gap Between Striving and Achieving." Pp. 247–256 in *Race, Class, and Gender: An Anthology,* 3rd ed., edited by Margaret L. Andersen and Patricia Hill Collins. Belmont, CA: Wadsworth.

Wood, Julia T. 1994. *Gendered Lives: Communication, Gender and Culture.* Belmont, CA: Wadsworth.

Wood, Richard L. 2002. *Faith in Action: Religion, Race, and Democratic Organizing in America.* Chicago: University of Chicago Press.

Wootton, Barbara H. 1997. "Gender Differences in Occupational Employment." *Monthly Labor Review* 170 (April): 15–24.

Worchel, Stephen, Joel Cooper, George R. Goethals, and James L. Olsen. 2000. *Social Psychology.* Belmont, CA: Wadsworth.

Workman, Jane E., and Elizabeth W. Freeburg. 1999. "An Examination of Date Rape, Victim Dress, and Perceiver Variables within the Context of Attribution Theory." *Sex Roles* 41 (August): 261–277.

World Bank. 2002. *World Bank Atlas.* Washington, DC: The World Bank.

World Health Organization. 2002. Web site: **www.who.org**

Wright, Erik Olin. 1979. *Class Structure and Income Determination.* New York: Academic Press.

Wright, Erik Olin. 1985. *Classes.* London: Verso.

Wright, Laurence. 1994. "One Drop of Blood." *The New Yorker* 70 (July 25): 46–55.

Wrong, Dennis. 1961. "The Oversocialized Conception of Man in Modern Sociology." *American Sociological Review* 26 (April): 183–192.

Wuthnow, Robert (ed.). 1994. *I Come Away Stronger: How Small Groups Are Shaping American Religion.* Grand Rapids, MI: Eerdmans.

Wuthnow, Robert, and Marsha Witten. 1988. "New Directions in the Study of Culture." *Annual Review of Sociology* 14: 49–67.

Wuthnow, Robert. 1988. *After Heaven: Spirituality in America Since the 1950s.* Berkeley: University of California Press.

Wysocki, Diane Kholos. 1998. "Let Your Fingers Do the Talking: Sex on an Adult Chat-Line." *Sexualities* 1 (November): 425–452.

Xu, Wu, and Ann Leffler. 1992. "Gender and Race Effects on Occupational Prestige, Segregation, and Earnings." *Gender & Society* 6 (September): 376–392.

Xuewen, Sheng, Norman Stockman, and Norman Bonney. 1992. "The Dual Burden: East and West (Women's Working Lives in China, Japan, and Great Britain)." *International Sociology* 7 (June): 209–223.

Yeats, Dale E. 1991. "Self-Managed Work Teams: Innovation in Progress." *Business and Economic Quarterly* (Fall): 2–6.

Yoder, Janice. 1991. "Rethinking Tokenism: Looking Beyond Numbers." *Gender & Society* 5 (June): 178–192.

Young, J. W. 1994. "Differential Prediction of College Grades by Gender and by Ethnicity: A Replication Study." *Educational and Psychological Measurement* 54: 1022–1029.

Zajonc, Robert B. 1968. "Attitudinal Effects of Mere Exposure." *Journal of Personality and Social Psychology.* Monograph Supplement, Part 2: 1–29.

Zald, Mayer, and John McCarthy. 1975. "Organizational Intellectuals and the Criticism of Society." *Social Service Research* 49: 344–362.

Zelizer, Viviana. 1985. *Pricing the Priceless Child: The Changing Social Value of Children.* Princeton, NJ: Princeton University Press.

Zhou, Min, and Carl L. Bankston. 2000. "Immigrant and Native Minority Groups, School Performance, and the Problem of Self-Esteem." Paper presented at the Southern Sociological Society, New Orleans, April.

Zimbardo, Phillip G., Ebbe B. Ebbesen, and Christina Maslach. 1977. *Influencing Attitudes and Changing Behavior.* Reading, MA: Addison-Wesley.

Zimmerman, Don H. 1992. "They Were All Doing Gender, But They Weren't All Passing." *Gender & Society* 6 (2): 191–198.

Zola, Irving Kenneth. 1989. "Toward the Necessary Universalizing of a Disability Policy." *Milbank Quarterly* 67 (Supplement 2): 401–428.

Zola, Irving Kenneth. 1993. "Self, Identity and the Naming Question: Reflections on the Language of Disability." *Social Science and Medicine* 36 (January): 167–173.

Zuberi, Tukufu. 2001. *Thicker Than Blood: How Racial Statistics Lie.* Minneapolis: University of Minneapolis Press.

Zuckerman, Phil. 2002. "The Sociology of Religion of W. E. B. Du Bois." *Sociology of Religion* 63: 239–253.

Zweigenhaft, Richard L., and G. William Domhoff. 1998. *Diversity in the Power Elite: Have Women and Minorities Reached the Top?* New Haven, CT: Yale University Press.

Zwerling, Craig, and Hilary Silver. 1992. "Race and Job Dismissals in a Federal Bureaucracy." *American Sociological Review* 57 (October): 651–660.

Photo Credits

Author Index

Subject Index